THE VAMPIRE ALMANAC

THE COMPLETE HISTORY

About the Author

J. Gordon Melton, an internationally known author, lecturer, and scholar, is the Distinguished Professor of American Religious History at the Institute for Studies of Religion at Baylor University. Dr. Melton is best known for his work on new religious movements, and he is considered America's senior scholar in the field of new, minority, and unconventional religions, having studied them for more than 50 years. Simultaneously, he has emerged as a leading scholar of vampire and Dracula studies and previously served a tenure as the American president of the Transylvanian Society of Dracula, an international association of vampire and Dracula scholars. He has authored multiple books in the field, two of which received the Lord Ruthven Award as the best nonfiction book in vampire studies. He currently resides in Waco, Texas, with his wife, Suzie.

THE VAMPIRE ALMANAC

THE COMPLETE HISTORY

J. GORDON MELTON, PH.D.

VISIBLE
INK
PRESS

DETROIT

THE VAMPIRE AMLANAC

Visible Ink Press®
43311 Joy Rd., #414
Canton, MI 48187-2075

Visible Ink Press is a registered trademark of Visible Ink Press LLC.

Most Visible Ink Press books are available at special quantity discounts when purchased in bulk by corporations, organizations, or groups. Customized printings, special imprints, messages, and excerpts can be produced to meet your needs. For more information, contact Special Markets Director, Visible Ink Press, www.visibleinkpress.com, or 734-667-3211.

Managing Editor: Kevin S. Hile
Cover Design: Mary Claire Krzewinski
Page Design: Cinelli Design
Typesetting: Marco Divita
Proofreaders: Larry Baker and Shoshana Hurwitz
Indexer: Shoshana Hurwitz

Cover images: Shutterstock.

Paperback ISBN: 978-1-57859-719-2
Hardcover ISBN: 978-1-57859-763-5
eBook ISBN: 978-1-57859-754-3

Cataloging-in-Publication data is on file at the Library of Congress.

Printed in the United States of America.

10 9 8 7 6 5 4 3 2 1

DEDICATION

To Margaret Mannatt

ALSO FROM VISIBLE INK PRESS

Real Encounters, Different Dimensions, and Otherworldly Beings
By Brad Steiger with Sherry Hansen Steiger
ISBN: 978-1-57859-455-9

Real Ghosts, Restless Spirits, and Haunted Places, 2nd edition
By Brad Steiger
ISBN: 978-1-57859-401-6

Real Miracles, Divine Intervention, and Feats of Incredible Survival
By Brad Steiger and Sherry Hansen Steiger
ISBN: 978-1-57859-214-2

Real Monsters, Gruesome Critters, and Beasts from the Darkside
By Brad Steiger and Sherry Hansen Steiger
ISBN: 978-1-57859-220-3

Real Vampires, Night Stalkers, and Creatures from the Darkside
By Brad Steiger
ISBN: 978-1-57859-255-5

Real Visitors, Voices from Beyond, and Parallel Dimensions
By Brad Steiger and Sherry Hansen Steiger
ISBN: 978-1-57859-541-9

Real Zombies, the Living Dead, and Creatures of the Apocalypse
By Brad Steiger
ISBN: 978-1-57859-296-8

The Sci-Fi Movie Guide: The Universe of Film from Alien to Zardoz
By Chris Barsanti
ISBN: 978-1-57859-503-7

Secret History: Conspiracies from Ancient Aliens to the New World Order
By Nick Redfern
ISBN: 978-1-57859-479-5

Secret Societies: The Complete Guide to Histories, Rites, and Rituals
By Nick Redfern
ISBN: 978-1-57859-483-2

The Spirit Book: The Encyclopedia of Clairvoyance, Channeling, and Spirit Communication
By Raymond Buckland
ISBN: 978-1-57859-172-5 (ebook)

Supernatural Gods: Spiritual Mysteries, Psychic Experiences, and Scientific Truths
By Jim Willis
ISBN: 978-1-57859-660-7

The UFO Dossier: 100 Years of Government Secrets, Conspiracies, and Cover-Ups
By Kevin D. Randle
ISBN: 978-1-57859-564-8

Unexplained! Strange Sightings, Incredible Occurrences, and Puzzling Physical Phenomena, 3rd edition
By Jerome Clark
ISBN: 978-1-57859-344-6

The Vampire Book: The Encyclopedia of the Undead, 3rd edition
By J. Gordon Melton
ISBN: 978-1-57859-281-4

The Werewolf Book: The Encyclopedia of Shape-Shifting Beings, 2nd edition
By Brad Steiger
ISBN: 978-1-57859-367-5

The Zombie Book: The Encyclopedia of the Living Dead
By Brad Steiger and Nick Redfern
ISBN: 978-1-57859-504-4

"Real Nightmares" E-Books by Brad Steiger

Book 1: *True and Truly Scary Unexplained Phenomenon*

Book 2: *The Unexplained Phenomena and Tales of the Unknown*

Book 3: *Things That Go Bump in the Night*

Book 4: *Things That Prowl and Growl in the Night*

Book 5: *Fiends That Want Your Blood*

Book 6: *Unexpected Visitors and Unwanted Guests*

Book 7: *Dark and Deadly Demons*

Book 8: *Phantoms, Apparitions, and Ghosts*

Book 9: *Alien Strangers and Foreign Worlds*

Book 10: *Ghastly and Grisly Spooks*

Book 11: *Secret Schemes and Conspiring Cabals*

Book 12: *Freaks, Fiends, and Evil Spirits*

Photo Sources

20th Century Fox: pp. 402, 408, 506.
20th Television: p. 534.
ABC Television: p. 378.
Accolade, Inc.: p. 570.
Act1 (Wikicommons): p. 350.
Chris Allen / *Bray Film Studios: p. 418.*
Alte Nationalgalerie, Berlin: p. 324 (left).
American International Pictures: p. 319.
Anime International Company: p. 16.
A. Aruninta: p. 369.
Asahi Sonorama and Asahi Shimbun Publications: p. 353.
Associazione Amici di Piero Chiara: p. 202.
Bahooka (Wikicommons): p. 531.
H. M. Bec: p. 136.
Michelle Belanger: p. 548.
Georges Biard: p. 381.
Bibliothèque Nationale de France: p. 266.
Bin im Garten (Wikicommons): p. 160.
Nicholas Brendon: p. 499.
British Broadcasting Corporation: pp. 230, 390.
British Museum: p. 305.
Dwight Burdette: p. 346.
Niccolò Caranti: p. 567.
Carnival Films: p. 233.
Cartoon Network: p. 286.
Cassell's Universal Portrait Gallery: p. 239.
CINAR Corporation/Alphanim: p. 289.
Columbia Pictures: pp. 281, 575.
Concorde Pictures: p. 320.
Creativ Studios: p. 237.
Culeshope (Wikicommons): p. 179.
Dan Curtis Productions: pp. 298, 509, 511, 513, 525.
Daughters of Darkness: p. 84.
DC Comics: pp. 546, 555.
Antonio De Lorenzo: p. 174.
Gore De Vol: p. 520.
DiscipulusMundi (Wikicommons): p. 102.
Disney–ABC Domestic Television: p. 540.

Doubleday & McClure: p. 221.
Dynamite Entertainment: p. 607 (bottom).
Seb Eko (Wikicommons): p. 178.
Filmation: p. 473.
First Vampire in China: p. 124.
FORTEPAN: p. 385.
Fox Film Corp.: p. 593.
Fuzheado (Wikicommons): p. 343.
Gallica Digital Library: p. 88.
Gaumont Film Company: p. 185.
Samantha George: p. 95.
Gheungsberg (Wikicommons): p. 194.
M. Gillespie: p. 573.
Goethe National Museum: p. 147.
Gonzo K.K.: p. 131.
Hammer Film Productions: pp. 50, 382, 411.
Hanna-Barbera Pty. Ltd.: p. 474.
The Haunted Castle: p. 130.
Hearst's International: p. 282.
Here! Network: p. 80.
Orval Hixon: p. 405.
Hodgehouse: p. 464.
JaSunni (Wikicommons): p. 522.
Heide Kraut: p. 526.
Kunsthistorisches Museum Wien, Gemäldegalerie: p. 58.
George Lester: p. 71.
Library of Congress: p. 324 (right).
Alan Light: p. 205.
Alex Lozupone: p. 107.
Jenniely LY (Wikicommons): p. 365.
Macwhiz (Wikicommons): p. 355.
Madman2001 (Wikicommons): p. 114.
Erling Mandelmann: p. 414.
Marvel Comics: pp. 559, 579, 591.
Lvov Maximov: p. 163.
Jim McCullars: p. 518.
J. Gordon Melton (courtesy of): pp. 19, 54, 59, 61, 62, 76, 85, 87, 94, 96, 101, 104, 217, 244, 295, 296, 334, 339, 347, 370, 372, 377, 379,

383, 389, 404, 415, 419, 421, 427, 442, 445, 467, 476, 477, 523, 536, 538, 550, 552, 572, 576, 577, 590, 606.

Metro-Goldwyn-Mayer: p. 426.

Metropolitan Museum of Art, New York City: p. 279.

Larry D. Moore: p. 356.

Musée Carnavalet: p. 265.

Museum of Fine Arts, Houston: p. 262.

Mutant Enemy Productions: p. 6 (left and right).

Nac1959 (Wikicommons): p. 337.

Nationaal Archief, The Hague: p. 607 (top).

National Portrait Gallery, London: pp. 273, 291, 308.

New Line Cinema: p. 563.

New York Times: p. 224.

Nimrod (Wikicommons): p. 335.

Luigi Novi: p. 558.

OmahaStar (Wikicommons): p. 344.

Ottre (Wikicommons): p. 331.

Palace of Versailles: pp. 184 (top), 199.

Panyd (Wikicommons): p. 53.

Paramount Pictures: p. 440.

Michael Pereckas: p. 348.

Pinguino K (Wikicommons): p. 360.

Power Productions: p. 112.

Prana Film: pp. 195, 400.

Producers Releasing Company: p. 387.

Angela Radulescu: p. 271.

Sara Reyes: p. 300.

Rlarrett (Wikicommons): p. 608.

Patricia Rogers: p. 312.

Xavier Romero-Frias: p. 133.

Melissa Rosenberg and Lev L. Spiro: p. 465.

Screen Gems: p. 434.

Sebb (Wikicommons): p. 206.

Georges Seguin: p. 342.

Showtime Networks: p. 533.

Shutterstock: pp. 2, 5, 8, 10, 13, 17, 21, 23, 32, 33, 37, 38, 44, 46, 66, 73, 78, 82, 121, 122, 123, 127, 129, 142, 149, 152, 154, 158, 159, 168, 175, 188, 215, 225, 242, 245, 247, 249, 354, 435, 451, 458, 459, 460, 486, 491, 493, 495, 498, 500, 501, 502, 508, 566, 582, 583, 602.

Walter William Skeat: p. 132.

Gage Skidmore: pp. 351, 557.

Sony Pictures: p. 424.

Sony Pictures Television: p. 528.

SpA Cinematografica: p. 201.

Catriona Sparks: p. 359.

Teddyfan (Wikicommons): p. 196.

Thames Television: p. 562.

Elizabeth Thor: p. 155.

Touchpaper Television: p. 484.

Touchstone Television: p. 479.

Universal Cable Productions: p. 485.

Universal-International: p. 437.

Universal Pictures: pp. 228, 235, 391, 395.

Universal Television: pp. 475, 530.

Manohara Upadhya: p. 125.

U.S. National Park Service: p. 254.

Valiant Pictures: p. 318.

Vereingte Star-Film GmbH: p. 439.

Vertigo/DC Comics: p. 586.

Danie Ware: p. 294.

Warner Bros.: pp. 412, 448, 449, 456, 480, 535.

Window & Grove: p. 259.

Work Projects Administration Federal Art Project, California: p. 257.

Wikipedia: p. 119.

Marv Wolfman: p. 612.

Joe Zattere: p. 200.

Public domain: pp. 15, 25, 27, 40, 41, 47, 49, 57, 68, 69, 93, 113, 118, 139, 143, 145, 165 (top and bottom), 171, 183, 184 (bottom), 190, 192, 219, 267, 275, 278, 293, 301, 302, 316, 322, 326, 410, 430, 444.

Table of Contents

Dracula in the Cinema ... 375

Other Cinematic Vampires ... 403

INTRODUCTION

Having spent much of the last three decades trying to get a comprehensive, overall picture of the growing presence of a seemingly fictional entity, the vampire, in human consciousness and culture, I have been somewhat surprised at what began as simply an entertaining leisure-time pursuit in my younger years grew to become a compelling intellectual concern worthy of claiming so many of my waking hours. That concern led to my compiling *The Vampire Book: The Encyclopedia of the Undead*, the most recent edition of which appeared a decade ago. This *Vampire Almanac* continues the desire to understand the overarching significance of the image of the vampire, the myth(s) to which it has become attached, the permeation of popular culture by that myth, and the community of people who have made that myth an important element in their lives (the vampire community).

While continuing the concern for an overview of the vampire world, *The Vampire Almanac* differs significantly from the editions of *The Vampire Book*. First, it arranges the presentation of material around the big questions in the vampire world, beginning with defining the basics about vampires, reviewing the vampire's origin in history and folklore, and then addressing vampire scholarship; the book moves on to the important realms of its presence among us in literature, the dramatic stage, the cinema, television, and the additional segments of the popular culture. This new format has forced new decisions upon me to focus upon the most important aspects of the vampire community. Third, *The Vampire Almanac* has a very contemporary, twenty-first-century emphasis, an emphasis that feels strange to someone who considers himself a historian. The vampire community has, however, passed through a distinct growth trajectory over the last two decades that has been marked by the continued permeation of the vampire into the popular consciousness, the development of blockbuster vampire movies and best-selling novels—even series of novels—and the emergence of a new generation of scholarly voices who have chosen to focus on Dracula and the vampire as a serious academic endeavor.

The Vampire Almanac has assumed a decided bias toward the present moment and has assumed some basic observations about its central concern. 1) The publication of *Dracula* was a notable cultural event in the English-speaking literary world. Although seen as a just another novel when published, it has joined the relatively short list of books that have remained in print since its publication and continue to be reprinted in new editions to the present. As of 2020, it has emerged as the single piece of fictional writing that has most frequently been brought to the screen (more than 40 times). 2) The vampire has shown itself to be a useful metaphor to describe unbalanced elements in human relationships, from the ability of dictatorial states to suck the life out of large groups of people, to the ability of charismatic leaders to suck the life from followers, to the ability of unscrupulous individuals to suck the life from family and friends. 3) The usefulness of the vampire to both entertain and inform our daily life is manifest in the thousands of vampire novels and feature movies, dozens of which appear annually in spite of the conclusion of many critics that the subject has been exhausted. Novelists and screenwriters continue to find new and innovative ways to approach what some have dismissed as a worn-out topic.

With these several working hypotheses, I am happy to offer *The Vampire Almanac* as a handy guide to those seeking to explore the vampire world and those seeking to understand how and why it has provoked such enthusiasm from its fans. It is my hope that readers can come to appreciate their friends and acquaintances who just can't wait for the next big novel and who re-arrange their lives to see the next adventure of their favorite bloodsucker.

But first we have an important task: defining exactly what we are talking about under the rubric of "vampire." Fortunately, from my previous work *The Vampire Book* in the early 1990s, I wrote a brief article on what a vampire is, which I have reprinted below. Those who are already familiar with the different kinds of vampire can skip these next pages.

What's a Vampire?

The common dictionary definition for "vampire" serves as a starting point for inquiry. A vampire is a reanimated corpse that rises from the grave to suck the blood of living people and thus retain a semblance of life. That description certainly fits Dracula, the most famous vampire, but it is only a starting point and quickly proves inadequate in approaching the realm of vampire folklore.

By no means do all vampires conform to this definition. For example, while the subject of vampires almost always leads to a discussion of death, all vampires are not resuscitated corpses. Numerous vampires are disembodied demonic spirits. In this vein are the numerous vampires and vampire-like demons of Indian mythology and the *lamiai* of Greece. Vampires can also appear as the disembodied spirit of a dead person that retains a substantial existence; like many reported ghosts, these vampires can be mistaken for a fully embodied, living corpse. Likewise, in the modern secular literary context, vampires sometimes emerge as a different species of intelligent life (possibly from outer space or the product of genetic mutation) or to otherwise normal human beings who have an unusual habit (such as blood-drinking) or an odd power (such as the ability to drain people emotionally). Vampire animals, from the traditional bat to the delightful children's characters Bunnicula and Count Duckula, are by no means absent from the literature. These vampires exist in several forms, although by far the majority of them are the risen dead.

As commonly understood, the characteristics shared by all vampire entities is their need for blood, which they take from living human beings and animals. A multitude of creatures from the world's mythology have been labeled vampires in the popular literature simply because periodic bloodsucking was among their many attributes. When the entire spectrum of vampires is considered, however, that seemingly common definition falls by the wayside, or, at the very least, must be considerably supplemented. Some vampires do not take blood—rather, they steal what is considered the life force from their victims. A person attacked by a traditional vampire suffers the loss of blood, which causes a variety of symptoms: fatigue, loss of color in the face, listlessness, depleted motivation, and weakness. For example, left unchecked, tuberculosis is a wasting disease that is similar to the traditional description of the results of a vampire's attack.

Nineteenth-century romantic authors and occultists suggested that real vampirism involved the loss of psychic energy to the vampire, and they wrote of vampiric relationships that had little to do with the exchange of blood. Dracula himself quoted the Bible in noting that "the blood is the life." Thus, it is not necessarily the blood itself that the vampire seeks but the psychic energy or "life force" believed to be carried by it. The metaphor of psychic vampirism can easily be extended to cover various relationships in which one party steals essential life elements from the other, such as when rulers sap the strength of the people they dominate.

On the other extreme, some modern "vampires" are simply blood drinkers. They do not attack and drain their victims but obtain blood in a variety of legal manners (such as locating a willing donor or a source at a blood bank). In such cases, the consumption of the blood has little to do with any more-or-less ongoing relationship to the source of the blood. It, like food, is merely consumed. Often, modern vampires even report getting a psychological or sexual high from drinking blood.

Once it is settled that the word "vampire" covers a wide variety of creatures, a second problem arises. As a whole, the vampires themselves are unavailable for direct examination. With a few minor exceptions, the subject matter of this volume is not vampires *per se*, but human belief about vampires and vampirism. That being the case, some methodology was needed for considering human belief in entities that objectively do not exist, and, indeed, for understanding my own fascination with a fictional archetype. Not a new problem, the vast literature on vampirism favors one or two basic approaches. The first offers explanations within a social context. That is to say, the existence of vampires provides people with an explanation for otherwise inexplicable events (which in the modern West we tend to explain in scientific terms). The second approach is psychological and explains the vampire as existing in the inner psychic landscape of the individual. The two approaches are not necessarily exclusive of each other.

The worldwide distribution of creatures that can properly be termed "vampires" or have vampire-like characteristics suggests an approach that allows some semblance of order to emerge from the chaos of data. I begin with the obvious. The vampire-like creatures around the world function quite differently in their distinct cultures and environments. Thus, the *camazotz* of Central America shares several characteristics with the vampire of Eastern Europe, but each plays a distinct role in its own culture's mythology and is encountered in different situations. While a host of statues and pictures of the *camazotz* survived in Central America, no Eastern European peasant would think of creating such a memorial to the vampire. In each culture, the "vampire" takes on unique characteristics because each must be considered in its indigenous context.

Despite these cultural differences, there are common vampire types that seem to bridge cultural boundaries. For example, among the older of the Greek vampire creatures is the *lamiai*, which seems to have arisen in response to the variety of problems surrounding childbirth. The *lamiai* attacked babies and young children. It was a way to explain—and cope with—the deaths of newly or recently born infants that you could then attribute to vampires. This is similar to the function of the Indonesian *langsuyar* and the Jewish Lilith.

In like measure, vastly different cultures possessed vampire myths concerning primarily attacks on young women. Such vampires, which appeared repeatedly in the folklore of Eastern Europe, served a vital role in the process of social control. The stories of these young, handsome, male vampires warned maidens in their early post-pubescent years not to stray from the counsel of their elders and priests and to avoid glamorous visiting strangers who would only lead them to disaster.

Another large group of vampires grew out of encounters with death, especially the sudden, unexpected death of a loved one due to suicide, accident, or an unknown illness. People dying unexpectedly left relatives and friends behind with unfinished agendas with the deceased. Strong emotional ties and uncorrected wrongs felt by the recently deceased caused them to leave their resting place and attack family members, lovers, and neighbors against whom they might have had a grievance. If unable to reach a human target, they turned to the victim's food supply (i.e., livestock). Stories of attacks by those recently deceased adult vampires on their relatives and neighbors or their livestock directly underlie the emergence of the modern literary and cinematic vampire.

Leaving folktales behind, the literary vampire of the nineteenth century transformed the ethnic vampire into a cosmopolitan citizen of the modern imagination. The literary vampire interacted in new ways with human society. While the early literary vampires pictured by Goethe, Coleridge, Shelly, Polidori, Byron, and Nodier were basically parasites, possessing few traits to endear them to the people they encountered, nevertheless they performed a vital function by assisting the personification of the darker side possessed by human beings. The romantic poets of the nineteenth century assigned themselves the task, among others, of exploring the dark side of the human consciousness.

In the movement to the stage and screen, the vampire was further transformed. The demonic vampire gained some degree of human feelings, and even as a villain, possessed some admirable traits that brought the likes of Bela Lugosi a large and loyal following. Lugosi brought before the public an erotic vampire that embodied the release of the sexual urges that were so suppressed by Victorian society. In the original stage and screen presentations of *Dracula*, the vampire's bite substituted for the sexual activity that could not be more directly portrayed. This inherent sexuality of the vampire's attack upon its victims became more literally portrayed in the 1960s, on the one hand through new adult-oriented, pornographic vampire movies and on the other in a series of novels and movies that centered upon a sensual, seductive vampire. Frank Langella's *Dracula* (1979) and Gary Oldman's *Bram Stoker's Dracula* (1992) were outstanding examples of this latter type of seductive vampire.

The vampire's amazing adaptability accounts for much of its popularity. It served numerous vital functions for different people during previous centuries. For enthusiasts, today's vampire symbolizes important elements of their lives that they feel are being otherwise suppressed by the culture. The most obvious role thrust upon the contemporary vampire has been that of cultural rebel, a symbolic leader advocating outrageous alternative patterns of living in a culture demanding conformity. An extreme example of this new vampire is the vegetarian vampire, such as Bunnicula and Count Duckula, who introduces the vampire to children and who has emerged as an effective tool in teaching children tolerance of other children who are noticeably different.

A psychological approach to the vampire supplements an understanding of its social function. Twentieth-century psychotherapy discovered that modern post-Dracula vampires and vampiric relationships actively distorted their patients' lives. Out of the experiences reported to them, particularly the classic nightmare, many psychologists called attention to the role of specific, common, human, psychological events in the creation and continual reinforcement of vampire beliefs. Psychologist Margaret Shanahan has noted the role of the vampire as a symbol of the widespread experience of inner emptiness she and her colleagues find in their clients. Such inner emptiness leads to a longing for emotional nutrients. Such longing can lead some to become food or inspire envy of those perceived to possess an abundance of nutrients (rich in the life force) and create an accompanying desire to steal that energy. In its most extreme form, such fixation can lead to various forms of blood consumption and even homicidal acts.

The various psychological approaches also explain some popular social pathologies, especially the common practice of scapegoating. Groups can be assigned characteristics of a vampire and treated accordingly with rhetoric that condemns them to the realms outside of social communion. If not checked, such rhetoric can lead to modern forms of staking and decapitation. Throughout the twentieth century, various groups have been singled out and labeled as "vampires." Women became "vamps," and bosses became bloodsuckers. Self-declared victims have branded a wide variety of social groups, rightly or wrongly, as their vampire oppressors.

These two approaches to the vampire seem to account for most of the phenomena of vampirism that I have encountered. Further, they suggest that the vampire (or its structural equivalent) was a universal figure in human culture, which emerged independently at many points in different societies. There is little evidence to suggest that the vampire emerged in one time and place and then diffused around the world from a primal source, a notable exception being the migration of the West African vampire to the Caribbean during the slave era.

The development of the literary vampire since its introduction into the Romantic culture of early nineteenth-century Europe, the many variations the character has shown in its myriad appearances in world cultures, and the multiple and varied fruitful approaches taken by modern scholars to address the vampire phenomenon have shown the need for some overview of the vampire and its most popular exemplar, Dracula. The continuing publication and release of vampire novels and movies in the 21st century certainly supplies the rationale for this *Vampire Almanac*. It makes me hopeful that it will remain a useful tool for my fellow researchers and academic colleagues for years to come.

J. Gordon Melton
Baylor University
September 2020

THE VAMPIRE WAY

In stark contrast to the other monsters that inhabited our literature in the last centuries, the vampire was distinct in its ability to live among us. It blended into human society disguised as one of us, maybe a little odd, but certainly within the bounds of normal variation in humankind. Dracula moved through London with little problem until targeted by a group seeking to confirm his vampiric nature. The vampire's enemies must first accept the fact that vampires exist, learn the characteristics of the vampire life, and then search out and identify the particular vampires in their midst.

Origins of the Vampire

How did vampires originate? If vampires did (or do) exist, where did they come from? The answers to these questions have varied widely, as the vampire has appeared in the folklore of different countries, and various fiction writers have speculated on the nature of vampirism.

The Folkloric Vampire: The vampire figure in folklore emerged as an answer to otherwise unsolvable problems within culture. The vampire was seen as the cause of certain unexplainable evils, accounted for the appearance of some extraordinary occurrences within society, and was often cited as the end product of immoral behavior. The earliest vampires seem to have originated as an explanation of problems in childbirth. For example, the *langsuyar*—the primary vampire figure of Malaysia—was a beautiful, young woman who had given birth

to a stillborn child. Upon hearing of her child's fate, she clapped her hands and flew away into the trees. Henceforth, she attacked children and sucked their blood. A similar tale was told of the *lamiai*, the original vampire of Greece. Just as tales of vampires were inspired by childbirth problems, they also originated from unusual circumstances surrounding births. Children who were different at birth were considered to be vampire candidates. For example, among the Kashubian people of Poland, children born with a membrane cap on their heads or with two teeth were likely to become vampires unless dealt with properly while growing up.

Similarly, some vampire stories originated from problems surrounding the death of a loved one. In Eastern Europe, vampires were individuals who returned from the grave to attack their

The vampire has taken many forms over the centuries, emerging in medieval folklore and morphing slowly into a hip, modern, goth form in TV and film.

spouses, their immediate families, and possibly other acquaintances in the village. Symptoms of a vampiric attack included nightmares, apparitions of the dead, and the death of family members by a wasting disease (such as tuberculosis). Some of the symptoms point to the vampire as a product of the grieving process, especially the continued ties of the living to the dead, often taking the form of unfinished emotional business. Thus, vampires were seen as originating from the failure of the family (in a time before the existence of funeral parlors) to perform the funeral and burial rites with exacting precision. A common event that allegedly led to the creation of a vampire was allowing an animal such as a cat to jump over the body of a dead person prior to burial.

Vampirism was also caused by unexpected and sudden, violent deaths either from accidents or suicides. Victims of suicides were also part of a larger class of vampires that existed as a result of the immoral behavior of the person who became a vampire. The vampire served as an instrument of social control for the moral leaders of the community. Thus, people who stepped outside of the moral and religious boundaries of the community not only jeopardized their souls but might become vampires. A potential vampire committed evil acts, among them suicide, and anyone guilty of great evil, especially of an antisocial nature, was thought likely to become a vampire after death.

In some Christian countries, notably Russia and Greece, heresy could also lead to vampirism. The heretic was one type of person who died in a state of excommunication from the church. Excommunication could be pronounced for a number of unforgiven sins from actions directly attacking the church to more common immoralities such as adultery or murder. Heresy was also associated in some cultures with witchcraft, defined as consorting with Satan and/or the working of malevolent, antisocial magic. Witches who practiced their craft in their earthly lives might become vampires after their deaths.

Vampire Contamination: After the first vampire was created, a community of vampires might soon follow. When a particular vampire figure, such as the original *lamiai*, took its place in the mythology of a people as a lesser deity or demon, they sometimes multiplied into a set of similar beings. Thus, Greek mythology posed the existence of numerous *lamiai*, a class of demonic entities. They were assumed to exist as part of the larger supernatural environment and, as such, the question of their origin was never raised. Also, such demonic entities did not create new vampires by attacking people. Their victims might suffer either physical harm or death as the result of the vampire's assault, but they did not become vampires. Things were quite different in Eastern Europe. There, vampires were former members of the community. Vampires could draw other members of the community into their vampiric existence by contaminating former family and neighbors, usually by biting them. In the famous case of Arnold Paole, the vampiric state was passed by meat from cows that had been bitten by Paole.

The Literary Vampire: In the nineteenth century, the vampire figure was wrenched from its rural social context in Eastern Europe and brought into the relatively secularized culture of Western European cities. It was introduced into the Romantic imagination of writers cut off from the mythological context in which the

vampire originated. Those writers had to re-create a new context from the few bits of knowledge they possessed. In examining the few vampire cases at their disposal, most prominently the Arnold Paole case, they learned that vampires were created by people being bitten by other vampires.

The imaginary vampire of nineteenth-century Romanticism was an isolated individual. Unlike the Eastern European vampire, the literary vampire did not exist in a village culture as a symbol that warned residents of the dangerous and devilish life outside the boundaries of approved village life. The imaginary vampire was a victim of irresistible supernatural attack.

> In the nineteenth century, the vampire figure was wrenched from its rural social context in Eastern Europe and brought into the relatively secularized culture of Western European cities.

Against their wills, they were overwhelmed by the vampiric state and, much like drug addicts, forced to live lives built around their bloodlust. The majority of beliefs associated with the origins of vampires were irrelevant to the creators of the literary vampire, although on occasion, one element might be picked up to give a novel twist to a vampire tale.

Underlying much of the modern vampire lore was the belief that vampires attacked humans and, through that attack, drew victims into their world. Again, like drug addicts might share an addiction and turn others into addicts, so the vampire infected nonvampires with their condition. Writers have generally suggested that vampires primarily, if not exclusively, created new vampires by their bites. The radical simplification of the vampire myth can be seen in *Dracula* (1897), especially in its treatment on the stage and screen. Bram Stoker did not deal directly with the problem of Dracula's origin as a vampire. In Dr. Abraham Van Helsing's famous speech in chapter 18, where he described in some detail the nature of the vampire, he suggested that Dracula became a vampire because he "had dealings with the Evil One."

More importantly, however, was his ability to transform people into vampires. Dracula's bite was a necessary part of that transmission but, of itself, not sufficient. Jonathan Harker was bitten a number of times by the three vampire women but did not become a vampire. On the other hand, following multiple bites from Dracula, Lucy Westenra did turn into a vampire, and Mina Murray was in the process of being transformed into a vampire when the men interrupted Dracula. In the key scene in chapter 21, Dracula, having previously drunk Mina's blood, forced her to drink his. Thus, in *Dracula*, new vampires originated not from the bite of the vampire but by an exchange of blood.

Bram Stoker had little material to draw upon in considering this question of the vampire's origin. The question was avoided by John Polidori in his original vampire story. *Varney the Vampyre*, the subject of the 1840s novel, became a vampire as punishment for accidentally killing his son, but the actual manner of transformation was not revealed. Sheridan Le Fanu was familiar with the folkloric tradition and suggested suicide as the cause of new vampires but saw the death of a person previously bitten by a vampire as the basic means of spreading vampirism. His antiheroine, Carmilla, was the product of a vampire's bite.

In the rewriting of *Dracula* for screen and stage, the scene from the book during which Mina consumed Dracula's blood was deleted. It was considered too risqué, but without it, some other means had to be found to transmit the vampiric state, thus came the suggestion that merely the vampire's bite transmitted the condition—the common assumption in most vampire novels and movies. At times, vampires required multiple bites or the bite had to take enough blood to cause the death of the victim. While most vampire books and movies have

not dealt with the question of vampire origins apart from the passing of the vampiric condition through the bite of a preexisting vampire, occasionally, writers have attempted to create a vampire myth that covers the ancient origin of the original vampire(s).

Among the more intriguing of recent origin stories was that told by Anne Rice in the third of her *The Vampire Chronicles* series, *The Queen of the Damned*. Akasha and her husband Enkil ruled as queen and king of ancient Egypt. In the midst of their reign, Akasha had two witches, Maharet and Mekare, brought to her court. They allowed her to see the world of spirits, but then, one of the spirits, Amel, attacked her. Akasha turned on the two witches and, in her rage, ordered them raped publicly and then banished. However, both Akasha and Enkil were intrigued by the spirit world and began to explore it on their own. Meanwhile, an uprising occurred, and the rulers were seriously wounded. Akasha's soul escaped from her body temporarily only to encounter the spirit Amel, who joined himself to her. Her soul re-entered her body and brought Amel with it. Fused with her brain and heart, the presence of Amel turned her into a vampire. She, in turn, passed the vampiric condition to Enkil and to their steward Khayman by the more traditional bite. All other vampires in the book, who originated from a vampire's bite, have a lineage that can ultimately be traced to these three first vampires.

The Vampire Bat: In chapter 12 of *Dracula*, Bram Stoker suggested, but did not develop, the idea that vampire bats might ultimately be the cause of vampirism. Quincey P. Morris delivered a brief oration on his encounter with vampire bats in South America. Although vampire bats made numerous appearances in vampire lore—primarily as humans temporarily transformed into animal form—

> Bram Stoker had little material to draw upon in considering this question of the vampire's origin. The question was avoided by John Polidori in his original vampire story.

Although a popular creature in vampire fiction, the vampire bat is very real indeed. Interestingly, they are native to Central and South America, not Transylvania or anywhere else in Europe.

few writers developed the idea of vampirism originating with vampire bats.

Most prominent among the few stories in which vampirism originated with a bat was *Dark Shadows*. The *Dark Shadows* storyline took Barnabas Collins back to 1795 and his origin as a vampire. Spurning the witch Angélique's love for him, Barnabas wound up in a fight with her and shot her. Wounded and near death, she cursed Barnabas, and a bat attacked him. He died from the bite and arose from the grave as a vampire. Subsequently, Barnabas created other vampires in the common manner: by biting them and draining their blood to the point of death.

The Science Fiction Vampire: A final option concerning the origin of vampires was derived from science fiction. As early as 1942 in his short story "Asylum," A. E. van Vogt suggested that vampires were an alien race who originated in outer space. The most successful of the comic book vampires, Vampirella, was a space alien. She originated on the planet Drakulon and came to earth to escape her dying planet. Ultimately, in the *Vampirella* storyline, even Dracula was revealed to be an alien.

Science fiction also suggested a second origin for the vampire: disease. Not incompatible with either vampire bats or outer space aliens, disease (either in the form of germs or altered blood chemistry) provided a nonsupernatural explanation of the vampire's existence—an opinion demanded by many secularized readers or theater-goers. Disease explained the vampire's strange behavior from its nocturnal existence to its "allergy" to garlic to its bloodlust. This idea was explored most prominently in Richard Matheson's *I Am Legend*. In the end, however, the science fiction space vampire was like its supernatural cousin. Whatever its origin, the vampire was the bearer—at least potentially—of its condition to anyone it attacked, and the vampire's bite was the most common way to spread vampirism.

Most recently, the idea of vampirism being a disease was integral to the storyline of *The Strain*, three novels by Guillermo del Toro and Chuck Hogan made into a four-season television series. The books pictured the coming of the vampires to America, unleashing a plague that brought an epidemiologist to the fore as the hero who must take the lead in the fight against the master and his minions, who are spreading the strain of disease.

Appearance of the Vampire

Any discussion of the appearance of the vampire must take into account the several vampire types. The contemporary vampires of the 1980s and 1990s have shown a distinct

In the TV series Buffy the Vampire Slayer, *vampires could appear normal and attractive one moment, terrifying and evil the next.*

trend toward a normal appearance that allows them to completely fit in with human society and move about undetected. Such modern vampires have almost no distinguishing characteristics, with the exception of fangs (extended canine teeth), which may be retractable and show only when the vampire is feeding. As such, the contemporary vampire harks back to the vampire characters of the pre-Dracula literary vampires. Little in the appearance of Geraldine, Lord Ruthven, Varney the Vampyre, or Carmilla distinguished them from their contemporaries (though Varney had prominent fangs).

In the last generation, vampire novelists have occasionally sought some way to make the vampire's appearance distinctive while keeping them capable of blending into society. Anne Rice describes the vampire's skin as pale and reflective, though possibly the most notable alteration is a set of fingernails that look like they were made of glass. Stephenie Meyer, in her *Twilight* series, posits vampires who have a heightened, even supernatural, beauty. While Rice's vampires are beautiful, because of the tendency of older vampires to turn humans whom

they find attractive and with whom they have fallen in love, Meyer suggests that becoming a vampire enhances the level of beauty in the person who is turned. Their skin becomes flawless and takes on a texture and feel resembling marble. If exposed to sunlight, it will sparkle.

In the television series *Buffy the Vampire Slayer* and its spin-off *Angel*, the vampires usually appeared just as they had in real life. Only when aroused, angry, or about to feed do they take on a distinctive appearance. As was the case in the 1990s television series *Forever Knight*, the vampires in *Buffy* for a brief time change dramatically and horrifically. They are said to put on their "game face." The eyes change color, the face distorts, and the fangs come out of hiding. They are obviously something different.

In spite of the changes introduced by *Forever Knight, Buffy the Vampire Slayer*, and the writings of Anne Rice and Stephenie Meyer, the contemporary vampire is still largely based on the dominant figure of Dracula as developed for the stage by dramatist Hamilton Deane and especially as portrayed by Bela Lugosi. Deane must be credited with the domestication of Dracula and making him an acceptable attendee at the evening activities of Victorian British society. Deane's Dracula donned evening clothes and an opera cape with a high collar.

Bela Lugosi in the movie *Dracula* (1931) confirmed Deane's image of the vampire in popular culture and added to it. He gave Dracula an Eastern European accent and a swept-back, slicked-down hairdo with a prominent widow's peak. In *Horror of Dracula* (1958), Christopher Lee added the final prominent feature to Dracula's appearance: the fangs. Prior to Lee, the vampire had no fangs, at least no visible ones. Lee, the first prominent vampire in Technicolor, also gave Dracula a set

In the overwhelming number of twenty-first-century vampire novels, movies, and television shows, the vampires appear as normal human beings, at least at first sight.

of red eyes, which, to a lesser extent, has become a standard (though by no means unanimous) aspect of the vampire's appearance, especially in motion pictures. Since Lee, the image of the vampire in popular culture has been set. The fangs, the cape, and, to a lesser extent, the evening clothes, the red eyes, and the widow's peak now quickly convey the idea that a person is a vampire. The use of these definitive signs of a vampire's appearance is most evident on greeting cards and the artwork on the cover of vampire novels and comic books.

This modern image of the vampire, with the exception of the extended canine teeth, varies considerably from both that of Dracula as presented in the original novel of Bram Stoker and the vampire of folklore. The latter, at least in its Eastern European incarnation, was a corpse but notable for several uncorpselike characteristics. Its body might be bloated and extended so that the skin was tight like a drum. It would have extended fingernails that had grown since its burial. It would be dressed in burial clothes. It would stink of death. The ends of its appendages might show signs of having been eaten away. In appearance, the folkloric vampire was horrible not so much because it was monstrous but because of its disgusting, semidecayed nature.

Between the folklore vampire and the contemporary vampire of popular culture lies the Dracula of Bram Stoker's novel. He was described in some detail in the second chapter of the book: he was dressed in black clothes; his hair was profuse and his eyebrows massive and bushy; he had a heavy moustache; his skin was pale; he had hair in the palm of his hand and long, extended fingernails. Most noticeable were the brilliant, extended canines that protruded over his lower lips when the mouth was closed. His eyes were blue, though they flashed red when he was angry or upset. He was of mature years, though he got younger as the novel proceeded. John Carradine's stage productions of *Dracula* in the 1950s were probably closest to Dracula as he appeared in the novel.

In the overwhelming number of twenty-first-century vampire novels, movies, and television shows, the vampires appear as normal human beings, at least at first sight. They may be beautiful or not; they may be of any gender, race, or age; and they might inhabit any social or economic status—until they get ready to feed. Then, the fangs will appear and a more or less radical alteration in appearance occurs. This change was integral to the vampires in the *Buffy the Vampire Slayer* TV series. One of the more elaborate changes was integral to the plot of Robert Rodriguez's movie trilogy *From Dusk till Dawn* and its subsequent TV series, in which the vampires mixed nightly with the clientele in their entertainment establishments only to take on a vicious, snakelike appearance when about to feed. Similar, if less elaborate, changes have become almost universal in vampire settings.

The major exception relative to the humanlike appearance of the vampire is Count Orlock, the name given to Dracula in the 1922 movie *Nosferatu*. Director F. W. Murnau, in attempting to disguise his appropriation of *Dracula* without paying royalties to Bram Stoker's widow, created a version of the vampire that emphasized his rodentlike appearance. He was completely bald, with skin devoid of color and the face taking on a deathly pallor. His fingers were extended, as were the fingernails, and his fangs were close together in the front of his teeth. This ratlike appearance would be adopted by only a small minority of vampires over the succeeding century but would appear in a notable set of vampire movies, including the remake of *Nosferatu* in 1979, the two versions of Stephen King's several *Salem's Lot* movies, the Master in the first season of *Buffy the Vampire Slayer* (1997), the vampire character Charles Manx in Joe Hill's novel *NOS4A2*, Petyr in the movie *What We Do in the Shadows* (2014), and the Master and his fellow *strigoi* in the television series *The Strain* (2014–2017). It had also been one of the distinct appearances of Dracula in *Bram Stoker's Dracula* (1992).

Characteristics of the Vampire

Throughout history, vampires have been known by their defining characteristics. Vampires were understood to be dead humans who returned from the grave and attacked and sucked the blood of the living as a means of sustaining themselves. The idea of the vampire came to the attention of both the scholarly community and the public in the West because of reports of the manifestation of such creatures in Eastern Europe in the seventeenth and eighteenth centuries. The vampire was seen as a prominent character in the folklore of people from Greece and Turkey in the south to Germany and Russia in the north. The descriptions of vampires in these countries set the image of vampires for the debates about their existence in the eighteenth century. The descriptions of the vampire from Greece and among the southern Slavs became the basis of the development of the literary vampire of the nineteenth century. Bram Stoker, the author of *Dracula* (1897), drew heavily upon earlier vampire stories and the accounts of vampires in Transylvania and Romania. By the end of the nineteenth century and through the twentieth century, using a definition of the vampire drawn from European folklore and mythology, ethnographers and anthropologists began to recognize the existence of analogous beings in the folklore and mythology of other cultures around the world. While these entities from Asian, African, and other cultures rarely conformed entirely to the Eastern European vampire, they shared enough characteristics that they could

Vampires in modern-day tales are often portrayed as average Joes who could be like any of your neighbors, except for the fangs and their need to drink blood.

rightly be termed vampires or, at least, vampire-like entities.

The Modern Vampire: The vampire has become an easily recognizable character in Western popular culture. As defined by recent novels and motion pictures and as pictured in comic books and on greeting cards, vampires have several key attributes. Vampires are like "normal" human beings in most respects and are thus able to live more or less comfortably in modern society. They are different, however, in that they possess a pair of fangs, tend to dress in formal wear with an opera cape, have a pale complexion, sleep in coffins, are associated with bats, and only come out at night. Their fangs are used to bite people on the neck and suck blood, the substance from which they are nourished. Fangs have become the single most recognizable feature of a male or female vampire, immediately identifying the vampire character to an audience and signaling immediate danger to the prospective victim.

In addition, vampires are basically creatures of the night, and during the day, they enter a comalike vampire sleep. They have red eyes and are cold to the touch. They may not be able to enter a room until invited. In addition, vampires possess some unusual "supernatural" attributes. They have great strength, they can fly (or at least levitate), they possess a level of hypnotic power (thus forcing the compliance of victims or causing a forgetfulness of the vampire's presence), they have acute night vision, and they can undergo a transformation into a variety of animals (usually a bat or possibly a wolf). Vampires avoid garlic, sunlight, sacred symbols such as the cross (the crucifix) and holy water, and they may need to sleep on their native soil. They may be killed by a wooden stake thrust in their heart or by fire. While the stereotype has been challenged in recent decades, a disproportionate number of vampires were drawn from European nobility. They were suave and cultured and readily welcomed into almost any social context. The most recognizable vampire is, of course, Dracula. He was preceded by Lord Ruthven and Countess Carmilla Karnstein. More recently, Barnabas Collins, of an aristocratic American family, and Lestat de Lioncourt, born of the French lesser nobility, have reinforced popular images of the vampire.

Folkloric Vampires: The vampire was not always so described. Folkloric vampires appeared in numerous forms as demonic creatures. The Malaysian *penanggalan*, for example, was pictured as a severed head with entrails dangling down. The Indian goddess Kali had a hideous form and was often shown dancing on corpses with fangs protruding from her bloodied lips. However, most commonly, the vampire appeared as the corpse of a person recently deceased. Vampires could be recognized by their dress in burial clothes and could be identified by someone who had known them in life and who understood that they were deceased and should not be walking around the town. As often as not, the vampire would never be seen, but its presence would be detected by the effects of its action, usually the wasting away and dying of people from unknown causes or the unusual and unexpected deaths of livestock.

Vampires, if seen, generally appeared to the people closest to them in their former lives. In some cases, especially among the Romani people and southern Slavs, they would return to engage in sexual relations with a former spouse or lover; in most other cases, they would launch a personal attack on family members, friends, or local livestock. Often, the vampire would assume a new existence, something that approached normal life. In Malaysia, for example, the *langsuyar* assumed the role of a wife and could bear and raise children. She would usually

> Vampires, if seen, generally appeared to the people closest to them in their former lives.

be detected by some chance event during the course of her life. In Eastern Europe, primarily male vampires were reported to have ventured far from home, where they were not known, and continued their life as before their death, even to the point of marrying and fathering children.

The vampire of folklore had some supernatural attributes above and beyond the mobility one generally does not expect of the dead. It could change form and appear as a host of different animals from a wolf to a moth. Interestingly, the bat was rarely reported as a vampiric form. Some people reported vampires with flying ability, especially in Oriental cultures, but flying or levitation was not prominent among Eastern European vampires.

The original vampires, those described in the folklore and mythology of the world's people, exist as an evil entity within a complex understanding of the world by a particular ethnic group. Thus, they would assume characteristics drawn from that group's culture and fitting that group's particular fears/needs. Given the variety of vampire-like creatures, both demons and revenants reported from cultures around the world, almost any characteristic reported of a vampire would be true of one or more such entities.

The Literary Vampire: At the beginning of the nineteenth century, the vampire became the focus of a set of writers, primarily in France and the United Kingdom. In their hands, the folkloric vampire, almost exclusively in its Eastern and Southern European form, was transformed into a gothic villain. While retaining many of the characteristics from the reports of vampires that had filtered into Western Europe in the previous century, writers were quite selective in their choice of acceptable attributes. In the process of creating a literary character, they also added attributes that had no correlation in the folklore literature. Lord Ruthven, the character of the original vampire story written by John Polidori, was of noble birth.

Crucifix

The crucifix, a major symbol of the Christian faith, is a Latin cross with a figure of Jesus on it. A crucifix is often attached to one end of the rosary, the string of prayer beads popular in the expression of piety among some Christians. The cross represents Jesus as he was executed on the original Good Friday. The crucifix is used primarily in the Roman Catholic Church, the several branches of the Eastern Orthodox Church, and other church bodies that follow a similar liturgical style of Christianity. In general, Protestant and free churches do not utilize the crucifix. They prefer a plain cross, sometimes thought of as an empty cross, without the corpus, a symbol of the resurrected Christ.

In the first chapter of the novel *Dracula* (1897), a woman in Bistritz, Transylvania, took

The Christian symbol of the crucifix is now accepted in popular culture as a tool to ward off vampires.

a rosary from her neck and gave it to Jonathan Harker upon hearing that he was going to visit Count Dracula. Harker, a member of the protestantized Church of England, had been taught that such an object was a product of idolatrous thinking. However, he put it around his neck and left it there. A short time after his arrival at Castle Dracula, Dracula made a grab for Harker's throat. Harker reported, "I drew away, and his hand touched the string of beads which held the crucifix. It made an instant change in him, for the fury passed so quickly that I could hardly believe that it was ever there." Having yet to figure out what Dracula was, he wondered about the meaning of the crucifix.

The crucifix played an important role in several other scenes in the novel. One appeared again in the hands of a man aboard the *Demeter*, the ship that brought Dracula to England. He was found tied to the ship's wheel with the crucifix in his hands, the beads wrapped around an arm and a wheel spoke. Later, after Lucy Westenra died and while she was experiencing life as a vampire herself, vampire hunter Abraham Van Helsing locked her in her tomb for a night with a crucifix and garlic, described as things she would not like. In Van Helsing's famous speech in chapter 18, he described the crucifix as one of the things that, like garlic, so afflicted the vampire that the creature had no power. So, when the men burst into the bedroom where Dracula was sharing blood with Mina Murray (by then Mina Harker), they advanced upon him with their crucifixes raised in front of them. Dracula retreated.

Through the tale *Dracula*, then, the crucifix entered vampire lore as a powerful tool against vampires, especially when confronting one directly. It was not mentioned in historic vampire stories, though many priests who participated in the dispatching of a vampire no doubt wore the crucifix. The emergence of the crucifix came directly from Bram Stoker's combining some popular ideas about the magical use of sacred objects by Roman Catholics and the medieval tradition that identified vampirism with Satanism (through Emily Gerard, Stoker developed the notion that Dracula became a vampire due to his having intercourse with Satan). In addition, a significant amount of Roman Catholic piety focused around the crucifix, and among church members it could easily take on not just sacred but magical qualities. It was not just a symbol of the sacred but also the bearer of the sacred.

If, then, the vampire was of the realm of Satan, it would withdraw from a crucifix. For Stoker, the presence of the crucifix caused the vampire to lose its supernatural strength. Thus, in the case of Harker, Dracula lost his fury; Lucy could not escape her tomb; and when the men burst into Mina's bedroom, the weakened Dracula, faced with overwhelming odds, departed quickly. In the wake of *Dracula*, the crucifix became a standard element of vampire plays, movies, and novels through the twentieth century. A second sacred object with similar effects as the crucifix, the eucharistic wafer, largely dropped out of the picture. However, the crucifix acquired one of the properties Stoker assigned to the wafer. It burned vampire flesh and left a mark on those tainted with the vampire's bite. Thus, the crucifix not only caused the vampire to lose strength but actually did it harm. If a potential victim wore a crucifix, the vampire must find some method of removing it either through hypnotic suggestion or with the help of a human cohort.

In the wake of *Dracula*, the crucifix became a standard element of vampire plays, movies, and novels through the twentieth century.

While the crucifix was a standard item in the vampire hunter's kit, it was not omnipresent in vampire books and movies. The relation to the holy was among the first elements of the tradition to be challenged as the vampire myth developed. Writers who were not Roman Catholic or even Christian found no meaning in the crucifix and the eucharistic elements and simply dropped them from consideration. However, others, most prominently Chelsea Quinn Yarbro and Anne Rice, chose to acknowledge the sacred world but essentially deny its power, specifically mentioning the immunity of their vampires to holy objects. Yarbro's vampire, Saint Germain, existed prior to Christianity and never converted to its beliefs. Rice, writing in Catholic New Orleans, created her vampire, Lestat de Lioncourt, as a child of Roman Catholics in France, and at various points in *Interview*

The vampires of the *Twilight* saga are affected by neither crosses nor holy water.

with the Vampire and *The Vampire Lestat*, Roman Catholic supernaturalism was specifically cast aside. Lestat was described, for example, as already being an atheist when he was transformed into a vampire. Nevertheless, he called upon those bits of Christianity he remembered in an attempt to keep the vampire Magnus from him. His efforts were useless. Then, accompanying the bites that made Lestat a vampire, Magnus pronounced the words of consecration from the Mass: "This is my Body, This is my Blood." Like Yarbro, Rice replaced Christianity in her writings with a new, pre-Christian myth that began in ancient Egypt with the original vampire couple, Akasha and Enkil.

The challenge to the effectiveness of the crucifix in vampire novels symbolizes a larger challenge to the role of the supernatural in modern life. It includes a protest against the authority of any particular religion and its claims of truth in a religiously pluralistic world. While the lessening of the role of the supernatural in the novels of Rice and Yarbro has its supporters, the crucifix remains a popular protective object for fictional characters. Consideration of their reaction to sacred objects likely will continue to be a conscious element in the development of new vampire characters in the future.

In *Buffy the Vampire Slayer*, the cross remains an object that can affect vampires negatively, but it obviously does not have the power it has manifested in the past. Possibly the most telling episode relative to the cross was in season four. In "Who Are You," a group of vampires take over a church on a Sunday morning. Standing before the assembled congregation, their leader makes a short speech noting his previous fear of entering such a building and enjoying his discovery that no negative effects occurred. As he speaks, a crucifix is displayed prominently in the window above the altar behind the vampire. He closes his speech by noting that the Lord seems to be absent; at least no visible effects of his presence are apparent. He mockingly informs the congregation that he had come to the church primarily because he had heard that the Lord would be present.

Similarly, in the *Twilight* series, the cross is no longer a factor. Author Stephenie Meyer is a member of the Church of Jesus Christ of Latter-day Saints, a Christian church that does not particularly favor the display of crosses. The vampires of *Twilight* are affected by neither crosses nor holy water.

Destroying the Vampire

Almost everywhere, vampires have been seen as evil, monstrous creatures. Once a vampire was confirmed to be wandering in a neighborhood, people hastened to locate and destroy it. In the most famous vampire novel, *Dracula*, the lengthy process of destroying Dracula consumes half of the novel.

Dracula's death was presaged by the killing of Lucy Westenra, whom Dracula had turned into a vampire. Confronted in her crypt, the men who knew her in life put a stake through her heart, decapitated her, and filled her mouth with garlic. Later, in his speech to the men assembled to kill Dracula (chapter 18), Dr. Abraham Van Helsing informed them of the means of destroying vampires:

> ... The branch of the wild rose on his coffin keep him so that he move not from it; a sacred bullet fired into the coffin kill him so that he be true dead, and as for the stake through him, we know already of its peace; or the cut off head that giveth rest. We have seen it with our eyes.

In the end, however, the men deviated from the formula. Dracula was killed with a Bowie knife plunged into his heart by Quincey P. Morris; Jonathan Harker then carried out the decapitation. His body then crumpled to dust as everyone watched. Among the sources he used for his novel, Bram Stoker referred to Emily Gerard, whose *The Land beyond the Forest* was a major source of information on vampires. Concerning the killing of vampires, she had observed in her travels that the vampire ...

> ... will continue to suck the blood of other innocent persons till the spirit has been exorcised by opening the grave of the suspected person, and either driving a stake through the corpse, or else firing a pistol-shot into the coffin. To walk smoking round the grave on each anniversary of the death is also supposed to be effective in confining the vampire. In very obstinate cases of vampirism it is recommended to cut off the head, and replace it in the coffin with the mouth filled with garlic, or to extract the heart and burn it, stewing the ashes over the grave.

Placing a thorny rose stem upon the dead before burial is thought to prevent a vampire from rising from their grave.

She noted further that it was a common practice to lay a thorny branch of the wild rose across the body at the time of burial to prevent a suspected vampire from leaving its coffin.

Folklore Traditions: In his treatment of the methods of destroying the vampire, Stoker reached back into the folklore of Eastern Europe to develop his own myth. While traditions concerning vampires varied widely on some issues, when it came to killing them, a consensus occurred across cultures from Greece and the southern Slavic lands to Poland and Russia. In Eastern Europe, vampire activity would be traced to the graveyard and to a particular body, usually that of a recently deceased person, as the suspected vampire. The body would then be disinterred, examined for signs of vampiric activity (lifelike appearance, blood around the mouth), and a determination made that the person was indeed the vampire. Once the designation was made, a tendency occurred to treat the corpse at two levels. First, steps would be taken to stop its vampiric activity by specific actions against the body. Among the least intrusive would be the firing of a bullet into the coffin.

In Eastern Orthodox countries, the local priest might repeat the services for the dead, which in effect would again dispatch the soul on its journey to the realm of the dead. If the coffin was opened, the suspected vampire's clothing might be nailed to the sides of the coffin (away from the mouth area). Commonly, however, the body would be mutilated in one of several ways. It could be staked (with different cultures using materials that varied from an iron stake to a hat pin or local wood). In most cultures, the stake did not have to go through the heart and usually was put through the stomach area. In these cases, it was assumed that the stake would hold the body in the ground. At times, the body would be turned face downward and then staked. If the stake did not work, the corpse would only dig itself deeper into the earth. Occasionally, the body might have been staked with a nail or pin even before it was buried; in that instance, a subsequent opening of the grave would be followed immediately by more drastic activity.

> Once the vampire became an object of fiction, its death frequently became the point of the story. Such was not the case in the beginning.

Along with staking, decapitation was common. Among the Kashubian Poles, the severed head might be placed between the legs. If mutilating the body with a stake and decapitating it did not work, the last resort was to burn the body. Few reports have occurred of vampire activity continuing after cremation. It was, of course, this mutilation and cremation of long-dead persons that moved the authorities to suppress belief in vampires in the eighteenth century. Through the early part of that century, the ruling powers not only were receiving accounts of vampire activity but also had to deal with complaints of families against hysterical townspeople who were mutilating the corpses of loved ones.

Thus, the authorities, primarily Roman Catholic Austrians, were forced to take action against antivampire attacks on the graveyards.

While edicts against mutilating bodies did not end belief in vampires (which persists to this day in some areas), they did slow the reports of vampires and spread skepticism.

The Fictional Vampire: Once the vampire became an object of fiction, its death frequently became the point of the story. Such was not the case in the beginning. Both Samuel Taylor Coleridge and John Polidori, who respectively wrote the first vampire poem and short story in English, left their vampires free to attack the next victim. Polidori did allow his vampire to be killed in quite normal ways by the bandits who attacked Lord Ruthven and his traveling companion, but he could always be revived by the light of the full moon. Varney the Vampyre, after what seemed like endless adventures, finally committed suicide by jumping into a volcano. Thus, the current conventions concerning the death of vampires have to be traced to the story of "Carmilla." Drawing from the folkloric traditions, author Sheridan Le Fanu suggested that the vampire should be decapitated, staked, and then burned, and such was the fate of Carmilla. As noted previously, Stoker's characters saw the staking of the corpse as adequate and, thus, did not advocate its burning.

The development of staking as a conventional means of destroying the vampire led to two important reinterpretations of the vampire myth. First, by emphasizing that the stake had to be driven into the heart rather than the stomach or back, a change in the myth occurred. The vampire no longer was pinned to the ground. The stake now attacked the heart, the organ that pumped the blood, and "the blood is the life." Second, the vampire, being seen as in some way immortal, could be brought back to life by pulling the stake from the chest.

Crucial to the development of the vampire myth was the movie *Nosferatu, Eine Sym-*

phonie des Grauens. Director Friedrich Wilhelm Murnau, in altering the storyline of *Dracula*, created the idea that the vampire could be killed if a beautiful woman held his attention until dawn. The vampire could not return to his resting place and would be killed by the sunlight. The vampire's death in the dawn's light was one of the most memorable scenes in the movie. This perspective on the vampire was an addition to the myth. Previously, while the vampire preferred the night, it was not limited to it. Its powers were enhanced during the evening, but Lord Ruthven, Varney, and Dracula all made daytime appearances. Folkloric vampires were nocturnal creatures, but the daylight merely protected the living from them.

While folklore offered no hint that daylight killed vampires, however, once suggested, the negative effects of sunlight became a common element in twentieth-century vampire stories. In the movie *Mark of the Vampire*, Bela

Considered a master of German Expressionist theater, director F. W. Murnau is most often remembered for Nosferatu *(1922)*.

Lugosi's character disintegrated in the presence of sunlight. The effects of sunlight were used effectively in *Horror of Dracula*, which climaxed as Abraham Van Helsing ripped the draperies from the wall of Castle Dracula and caught the vampire in the dawn's early light. Frank Langella's *Dracula* (1979) was impaled on a ship's hook and hoisted high into the sunlight. Lesser bits of sunlight would do significant damage but not be fatal. In one episode of the television series *Forever Knight*, for example, a boy innocently opened a window, and the little beam of light falling on vampire Nick Knight's eyes temporarily blinded him. The clan of vampires in the movie *Near Dark*, while able to be active in daylight, received severe burns each time the sunlight penetrated their barriers of drapes and tin foil.

Modern Vampires: As the myth has been restructured in the twentieth century, vampires face three fatal dangers: a stake in the heart, sunshine, or fire. Usually, being revived by removal of the stake or by a magical ritual is also a possibility and/or by adding blood to the ashes of someone who had died after being burned in the sun or by fire.

In the face of these assumptions, several prominent contemporary vampire writers have attempted to reinterpret the vampire tale. Chelsea Quinn Yarbro, for example, wrote a series of novels concerning the vampire Saint Germain. Saint Germain was affected by the sun but not fatally. However, a condition termed "true death" was possible: the vampire would die if his spine was severed or if he was consumed in fire. Stakes could hurt, but unless they cut the spine, he would recover.

Anne Rice thoroughly and systematically demythologized the vampire myth. Her vampires were not affected by many of the traditional forces or objects (especially holy objects) that have plagued other vampires and reduced their powers. Though her vampires were nearly immortal, they could be killed by sunlight or fire and the subsequent scattering of the ashes.

However, some vampires (those older and closer to Akasha in lineage) were somewhat immune to sunlight. Rice's vampires also faced a threat over which they had little or no control and of which most were unaware. In Rice's world, vampires were created by the merger of a spirit that moved into Akasha, the first vampire. All vampires remained in some way tied to Akasha; hence, whatever happened to her was passed on to them. Were she to be killed and the spirit driven out, all vampires would cease to be.

In the post-Rice era, playing with the vampire myth has become common. One popular variation has been to provide a motivation for the vampire hero/villain to become a daywalker, someone who is immune to the effects of sunlight. His ability to maneuver in daylight makes the vampires hunted by the Marvel Comics hero and half vampire Blade envious of him. Blade is, of course, a variation on the *dhampir*, a character in Slavic vampire lore who

Undercover as a high school student, Miyu is a vampire and daywalker who, in a way similar to Buffy, works to send demons back to their dark world in the Japanese manga series Vampire Princess Miyu.

is the product of a human mother and vampire father, a hybrid child with the power to discern, hunt, and destroy vampires regardless of the time of day. A *dhampir* is the also the hero in Rebecca York's 2007 novel *Daywalker*. In 1999, Marvel villainess Baroness Blood, the spouse of Baron Blood, discovers a means to become a daywalker using the Holy Grail and almost succeeds. At about the same time, daywalkers began to appear in Japanese anime/manga. In the popular children's series *Tsukuyomi: Moon Phase*, the evil Count Kinkell is able to bend light around himself so it will not consume him. Daywalking vampires also appear in various anime/manga series such as *Vampire Princess Miyu*, *Negima!*, and *Hellsing*.

In season four of the TV series *Buffy the Vampire Slayer*, Buffy is briefly able to realize her desire of a life with the vampire Angel when she gains possession of the Gem of Amarra and passes it on to him. A vampire wearing the ring can experience the sunlight unharmed. In the end, however, Angel smashes the ring and continues his business of slaying various denizens of the night. In the *Twilight* series of popular novels, the vampires are able to move about in daylight but have moved to the rainy world of Forks, Washington, to escape the harmful effects of direct sunlight (which Edward Cullen used in his suicide attempt in volume two, *New Moon* [2006]).

The idea of vampires walking in sunlight has been at least discussed in a number of twenty-first-century vampire movies and television shows. As the *True Blood* series progresses, it is disclosed that the primary human protagonist, Sookie Stackhouse, is highly sought by vampires because of her special blood, its quality enabling the vampire who drinks it to walk in the daylight. In the movie *Dracula Untold* (2014), Vlad III Dracula walks during the day but only when the sky is overcast, as direct sunlight will burn his skin. In the highly acclaimed movie *Byzantium* (2012), vampires can freely walk in daylight, but they remain largely nocturnal simply as a means of social concealment.

Dust

Stoker's Dracula, a vampire could turn into dust and back into human form; in later iterations, vampires turn to dust when exposed to sunlight.

and then slowly took on a recognizable shape, the three phantomlike images.

Dracula made his first and only appearance in this form during his attacks upon Lucy Westenra. The wolf Beserker had broken some of the glass from the window in her room. Then, suddenly, the room seemed to fill with "a whole myriad of little specks" blowing in the window and forming themselves into a "pillar of dust" inside the room. She passed out and, upon regaining consciousness, noticed that the air again was full of these dusty specks. While a notable element in the novel *Dracula*, this vampiric ability was not of importance to the twentieth-century conception of the vampire.

Similar to his ability to transform himself into animals or a mist, as described in the 1897 novel in which he initially appears, Dracula could also transform into a cloud of dust. Dr. Abraham Van Helsing made reference to the comings and goings of the three women in Castle Dracula. While Jonathan Harker looked on, they transformed themselves into a dust form while standing in the moonlight. In his second encounter with the women, Harker saw the moonlight quiver as the dust danced around

The vampire transforming into dust is, of course, separate from the vampire turning into a pile of dust when killed. This later concept appeared at the end of *Dracula* and was used, for example, in the Hammer Films adaptation of the novel *Horror of Dracula* in which Dracula burns in the light of the sun. In its sequel, the dust (or ash) is reanimated by dripping fresh blood on it. That process would be used in several movies as a means of reviving a deceased vampire. In the *Buffy the Vampire Slayer* television series, as vampires are killed, they are said to be "dusted," a reference to their immediate disintegration into a pile of ash/dust after being staked or beheaded.

Fangs

Early in Bram Stoker's *Dracula* (1897), at the time of his first encounter with Dracula, Jonathan Harker sketched his impressions. Besides Dracula's other prominent physical features, he noted that the vampire's mouth "was fixed and rather cruel-looking, with peculiarly sharp white teeth; these protruded over the lips …" (chapter

2). Later in that same chapter, he reinforced his initial description by referring to Dracula's "protuberant teeth" and, as they conversed, he could not take his eyes from the smiling count, for "as his lips ran back over his gums, the long, sharp, canine teeth showed out strangely." Thus, Stoker wedded what has become one of the most identifiable features of the modern vampire to its most popular representative figure.

Like Dracula, the three women in the castle, more recently referred to as the vampire brides, also possessed the extended canines. As one of the women approached him, Harker noted not only her bad breath but felt the hard dents of the sharp teeth on his skin. He could see the moonlight illuminate the teeth of the other two women. Stoker reinforced the importance of the teeth in identifying the vampire during Dracula's attacks on Lucy Westenra. As her strange illness progressed, the knowledgeable Dr. Abraham Van Helsing called attention to "the little punctures on her throat and the ragged exhausted appearance of their edges" (chapter 10). As the end approached, he noted the transformation overtaking her, signaled by her teeth: her canine teeth looked longer and sharper than the rest. After her death, they had grown even longer and sharper. Dracula was not the first vampire to have fangs. In describing the first attack on Flora Bannerworth by Varney the Vampyre, author James Malcolm Rymer (writing in the 1840s, a full half century before *Dracula*) noted, "With a plunge he seizes her neck in his fang-like teeth—a gush of blood, and a hideous sucking noise follows." In examining Flora later, her mother brought a light close by so that "all saw on the side of Flora's neck a small puncture wound; or, rather two, for there was one a little distance from the other." Laura, the victim of Carmilla, in Sheridan Le Fanu's 1872 tale, had a somewhat different experience. She remembered being attacked as a child and feeling two needles plunging into her chest, but upon examination, no wounds were visible. Later in the story, Carmilla and Laura were speaking to a wandering peddler, who noted that Carmilla had the "sharpest tooth—long thin, pointed, like an owl, like a needle." He offered to cut it off and file it to a dull point so that it would no longer

be "the tooth of a fish." Later, in a dream, Laura again had the experience of two needles piercing the skin of her neck. The doctor found a little blue spot at that place on her neck. The daughter of General Spielsdorf reported an experience similar to Laura's—a pair of needles piercing her throat. It was finally concluded that both had been attacked by a vampire, who would have—as was well known—two long, thin, and sharp teeth that would leave a distinguishing puncture wound on its victim.

While both Varney and Dracula possessed extended canine teeth, as Martin V. Riccardo has noted, this trait was not yet a permanent feature. When Dracula was brought to the screen in 1922's *Nosferatu, Eine Symphonie des Grauens*, Graf Orlock, the Dracula figure, had two ratlike teeth protruding from the front of his mouth rather than the extended canines mentioned by Stoker. Then, when Bela Lugosi turned Dracula into a household word through his performance in the 1931 film, he did so without any fangs. Nor did he ever have protruding teeth in any of his subsequent performances. Dracula was also portrayed by Lon Chaney Jr. (*Son of Dracula*, 1943) and John Carradine (*House of Frankenstein*, 1944 and *House of Dracula*, 1945), but neither actor sported fangs. The fangs had appeared twice before Lee in the 1952 Turkish version of *Dracula*, which did not receive broad distribution, and a 1957 Roger Corman film *Blood of Dracula*, with a female, wolflike vampire. Only in 1958, in the Hammer Films bloodfest *Horror of Dracula*, did Christopher Lee turn to the camera and show audiences his extended canines. He would repeat this act in subsequent films, and after him, many others would do likewise. Thus, while Lugosi (following Hamilton Deane's lead) established the image of the vampire dressed in an evening suit and cape, it was Lee who fixed the image of the fanged vampire in popular culture. Since Lee's portrayal, most (though by no means all) cine-

> While both Varney and Dracula possessed extended canine teeth, as Martin V. Riccardo has noted, this trait was not yet a permanent feature.

matic vampires have shown the required teeth, as did Barnabas Collins in the *Dark Shadows* television series late in the 1960s.

Once established, fangs became an artistic convention to call attention to the presence of vampires. Fangs commonly appeared in advertising for monster movies and on the cover art of vampire novels, quickly identifying those titles not possessing an obvious vampiric name. They were used in a like manner on comic book covers, Dracula dolls, and Halloween greeting cards. A relatively new feature introduced into vampire films and novels in the late twentieth century has been retractable vampire teeth. Vampires would thus appear normal when interacting with humans and show their fangs only when angry, aroused, or about to feed.

Retractable teeth seem to have derived from the favorable reaction to the transformation into a werewolf shown in the Oscar-winning *An American Werewolf in London*. Such

Grace Jones (center) with two of her vampire girlfriends in the 1986 movie Vamp.

a dramatic transformation from a normal appearance into a monsterlike figure was graphically portrayed by Grace Jones and her fellow vampires in *Vamp* (1986) and would be followed in a number of movies where close-up shots of a vampire's mouth would show the fangs moving into place for a bite. It became a standard element in many episodes of *Buffy the Vampire Slayer* and *Angel*. The appearance of the extended canine teeth accompanied other changes in facial expressions and signaled the emergence of the darker, predatory side of the vampire's personality. More recently, in the television series *From Dusk till Dawn*, the vampires transformed into snakes and, as they transformed for feeding, their viperlike fangs suddenly snapped into place, protruding outwardly for the coming bite.

The conventional canine fangs created a problem for the cinematic vampire. Lee's canine teeth appeared to be used more for ripping flesh than for neatly puncturing the skin and jugular vein. The two holes would be so far apart that the vampire would find it difficult to suck from both holes at the same time. Therefore, it has been common to picture the two holes as being much closer together than the distance between the canine teeth would suggest. This discrepancy, overlooked by most fans, has given feminist interpreters of vampires an opening to find something positive in the male-dominated myth. Penelope Shuttle and Peter Redgrove, for example, suggested that the wounds were not those of a carnivore but of a viper, a snake. They suggested that the film directors, without consciously knowing what they were doing, were harking back to an ancient myth that associated the beginning of menstruation with a snake's bite. After being bitten by the snake, the girl became a woman and began menstruating; after being bitten by the vampire, the women tended to become more active and sexual. While the vampire myth has been associated with the particular anxieties of teenage males, possibly it also has something subtle to communicate directly to young females. *Twilight* author Stephenie Meyer decided to drop the fangs altogether and replaced them with strong, piercing teeth suitable for tearing the flesh rather than puncturing it. They work on the wild animals that are the major food of her vampires.

Garlic

Like the crucifix, vampires are believed to have an intense aversion to garlic, and thus, people have used garlic to keep vampires away. Introduced into the literary realm in Bram Stoker's novel, garlic became central to the developing vampire myth throughout the twentieth century. Garlic was the first treatment Dr. Abraham Van Helsing applied in the case of Lucy Westenra. Van Helsing had a box of garlic flowers sent from the Netherlands and decorated Lucy's room with them. He hung them around Lucy's neck and told her that the little flower contained much virtue. The garlic worked until Lucy's mother, not knowing the flowers' purpose, tore the smelly floral garb from her neck.

In the southern Slavic countries and neighboring Romania, garlic was integrated into the vampire myth. It was used in both the detection of and prevention of attacks by vampires.

Garlic was a crucial element in killing the vampire. After driving a stake through the vampire's body and removing its head, garlic was placed in the mouth. In fact, this was how Van Helsing finally treated Lucy's body. This treatment was effective, however, only for recently created vampires because the older ones (for example, Dracula and the three women in Castle Dracula) disintegrated into dust once a stake was thrust into their bodies. Stoker got the idea of using garlic following decapitation of the vampire from Emily Gerard's study of Transylvanian vampires, *The Land beyond the Forest*. Her book suggested that it was the method employed in Romania in very obstinate cases of vampirism (i.e., those that had not been cleared up by methods that did not require any mutilation of the body).

Garlic, a member of the lily family, has been used since ancient times as both an herb and a medicine. It developed a reputation as a powerful healing agent, and it was rumored that it possessed some magical powers as a protection agent against the plague and various supernatural evils. In southern Slavic regions, it became known as a potent agent against demonic forces, witches, and sorcerers. The Christian St. Andrew was said to be the donor of garlic to humanity.

In the southern Slavic countries and neighboring Romania, garlic was integrated into the vampire myth. It was used in both the detection of and prevention of attacks by vampires. Vampires living incognito in the community could be spotted by their reluctance to eat garlic. In the 1970s, Harry Senn was advised by his Romanian informants that the distribution of garlic during a church service and observation of those who refused to eat their portion was an acceptable manner of detecting a vampire hidden in the community.

Vampires were especially active in these regions around St. Andrew's Eve and St. George's Eve. On those days, windows and other openings in the house were anointed with garlic to keep the vampires away. Cattle might also be given a garlic rubdown. In some communities, garlic was mixed with food and fed to cattle before every important holiday. If a recently deceased person was suspected of vampirism, garlic might be stuffed in the deceased's mouth or placed in the coffin. If detection and the need to destroy a vampire required exhumation of its body, the vampire might face decapitation and garlic might be placed in the mouth or within the coffin.

Garlic was also prominent in Eastern Europe and was served as the most universal protective device used against vampires and vampiric entities. It appeared in the folklore of Mexico, South America, and China. Throughout the twentieth century, garlic became one of the most well-known objects associated with vampires. Not a particularly religious symbol, garlic survived while the crucifix slowly disappeared from the list of antivampire weapons. On occasion, as in the book and film *The Lost Boys*, the effectiveness of garlic was denied, but through the 1990s, it continued to appear as a viable vampire detection and/or prevention substance.

While continuing as an item in the vampire hunter's arsenal, it has been less used in the twenty-first century and has gradually been discarded under the weight of denials of its efficacy. It was used by Buffy and her friends on the TV show *Buffy the Vampire Slayer* but infrequently. It is ineffective for the vampires in the book series *Twilight*. Garlic repels the vampires in Charlaine Harris's novels and the resulting TV series *True Blood*, but it is more of a nuisance than harmful and is not even mentioned in Laura Smith's *The Vampire Diaries*.

Mirrors

The now popular idea that vampires cast no reflection in a mirror (and often have an intense aversion to them) seems to have first been

Another first for Dracula *was introducing the idea that vampires have no reflections because they lack a soul. This trope has become a permanent part of the vampire mythos.*

put forward in Bram Stoker's novel *Dracula*. Soon after his arrival at Castle Dracula, Jonathan Harker observed that the building was devoid of mirrors. When Dracula silently came into Harker's room while he was shaving, Harker noticed that Dracula, who was standing behind him, did not appear in the shaving mirror as he should have. Dracula complained that mirrors were objects of human vanity and, seizing the shaving mirror, he broke it.

When the novel was brought to the stage and the episode in Castle Dracula deleted, the incident of the mirror was transformed into a confrontation between Dracula and Dr. Abraham Van Helsing. The mirror incident does not seem to have any precedent in either vampire folklore or the earlier vampire short stories and dramas, although Stoker seemed to have been aware of folklore about mirrors. Mirrors were seen as somehow revealing a person's spiritual double, the soul. In seeing themselves revealed in a mirror, individuals found confirmation that a soul was present and, hence, life went on. They also found in the reflection a new source of anxiety, as the mirror could be used to affect the soul negatively.

The notion that the image in the mirror was somehow the soul was the source of the idea that breaking a mirror brought seven years' bad luck. Breaking the mirror also damaged the soul.

Thus, one could speculate that the vampire had no soul, so nothing to reflect in the mirror. The mirror forced the vampire to confront the nature of his/her existence as the undead, neither living nor dead. On occasion, in both vampire fiction and the cinema, the idea of nonreflection in mirrors has been extended to film; that is, the vampire would not appear in photographs if developed.

In her popular reinterpretation of the vampire myth, Anne Rice dropped Stoker's mirror convention. She argued in part that although vampires have certain "supernatural" attributes, they existed in the same physical universe as mortals and generally had to con-form to the same physical laws, including those of optics. Hence, in *Interview with the Vampire* and *The Vampire Lestat*, Louis and Lestat de Lioncourt, respectively, saw themselves in a mirror and experienced a moment of self-revelation about their new vampire image. (Of course, Rice's vampires did not follow all physical laws since they had the ability to fly.)

Through the 1990s and into the new century, vampire writers and movies have moved back and forth on the problem of mirrors and the related problem of capturing the image of the vampire on film, television, or with the new digital cameras. Some—for example, the vampires of Stephenie Meyer's *Twilight* and the *Vampire Huntress* series books of L. A. Banks—can see and be seen in mirrors. Meanwhile, most still cannot, including those of television series such as *Buffy the Vampire Slayer* and *Being Human* and the popular books of Charlaine Harris and Laurell K. Hamilton.

Protection against Vampires

Coinciding with the emergence of the belief in vampires was the designation of methods of, if not destroying them, at least protecting oneself from them. Vampires were continually being produced by reoccurring conditions, and some means of self-protection had to be found that operated while the current vampire was being sought for, designated, and eventually destroyed.

In the West, vampire characters initially appeared as threats to infants and to mothers at the time of birth, and the best protection available was the use of magic. The earliest barriers known to have been used against vampire attacks were magical words and acts, which survived in the more recent use of prayer and Bible quotes. In the first century, Ovid left an account of an ancient ritual to protect a child, which included touching the door where the infant resided with a branch of a plant, sprinkling the entrance of the house with water, and killing a pig that was offered to the *strix* (vampire) as alternative food. The words spoken during this ritual included:

> Birds of the night (i.e., the *strix*), spare the entrails of the boy. For a small victim (the pig) falls. Take heart for heart, I pray, entrails for entrails. This life we give you in place of a better one.

After the pronunciation of the formula, the house was further secured with thorn branches at the window. This ancient account of warding off the attack of a vampire mentions one of the several most common items that served to protect people from vampires: the thorn. The hawthorn, in part because of its association with the story of Jesus's death, was the most common across Southern Europe, but other thorns were used as magical barriers against both vampires and witches. Both the obvious problems that the wild thorn bush had presented to humans and its many values when properly utilized suggested the extension of its role into the supernatural realm and, in fact, it was reported as an antiwitch and antivampire shield not only in Europe but in Asia and the Americas.

Possibly even more than thorns, the pungent herb garlic, which was utilized as both a medicine and a food flavoring, was also a protective device used to ward off witches and vampires. Garlic was found in all parts of the world, particularly in the warmer climates, and everywhere found its way onto the list of antivampire items. Garlic's inherent value as a medicine,

Another weapon in the arsenal to fight vampires is holy water like what is used to perform baptisms.

coupled with its strong, offensive smell, suggest its power to drive away the forces of evil.

The other ubiquitous protective device against vampires was seeds. All around the world, people scattered seeds between themselves and the suspected vampire as a barrier. Vampires were thought to be fascinated with counting seeds, be they mustard, millet, grass, linen, carrot, poppy, or rice.

The seeds might be scattered in the coffin, over the grave, on the path between the gravesite and the village, or around a home that the vampire might enter. The vampire would either have to count the seeds slowly, one per year, or be caught in a situation of having to collect and count enough seeds that it could not finish its task before dawn.

In Europe, especially since medieval times, objects sacred to Christianity, most commonly the crucifix, the eucharistic wafer, and holy water, have been cited as effective protective devices. Vampires were identified with the realm of the devil, and Satan and his minions could not exist in the presence of the holy. Mere priests, also being sinners, were not considered completely holy, whereas the cross and eucharistic host were symbolic of the very presence of God. In Latin American countries, sacred pendants were attached to a child's bedclothes. In Eastern Orthodox countries, an icon (such as a holy picture) had the same sacred value as a crucifix.

Around the world, several other sacred objects have been noted but were not prominent in non-Christian societies. Here, the vampire, indeed the whole realm of evil, was not seen in such polarized categories as it was in the Christian world. (In an early episode of *Buffy the Vampire Slayer*, Buffy's friend Willow [whose parents were Jewish] wonders if and how she could make use of the cross against vampires, a question raised previously in several movies such as *Love at First Bite* [1979]). The idea expresses the problem of affirming particularly the sacred in a more pluralistic religious setting.) The use of holy objects that banished the unholy also led to a consideration of various purifying agents. The most universal was fire. Fire, while destructive, cleansed. It was a major agent in destroying the vampire but could also be used to drive the vampire away. From accounts around the world, numerous items have been used to ward off vampiric evil. Some are purely defensive, forming a barrier between the vampire and its potential victim.

Others create an aura or atmosphere that the vampire would avoid. A few were more offensive and would actually harm the vampire. Typical of the defensive protective devices would be the many things that could be placed in a bedroom to ward off a vampire. Shoes turned around, a mirror placed by the door, and a broom put behind a door all served in one or more cultures as vampire barriers.

Items with illumination or smell, such as candles or garlic, were usually the best to create a protective atmosphere. However, metal—typically pieces of iron, placed under or near a baby's crib—was thought to keep vampires away in many diverse cultures. Iron, when used as a structural feature, could form a strong physical barrier, for it was a substance that vampires avoid. To a lesser extent, silver was used in a similar manner. Needles, knives, and scissors were also placed near the bed to be used against the vampire in the advent of an attack.

Protection against the Modern Vampire: With the secularization of the vampire myth in the late twentieth century, most of the prophylactic attributes of traditional protective items were lost. Recent vampires have been affected little by holy objects, thorns, or seeds. Garlic alone remained an almost universal item that vampires were believed to avoid, but only a minority of contemporary Westerners used garlic with any regularity. Modern novels left victims with few protections from the onslaught of a vampire. Even fire, also still universally avoided by vampires, rarely occurred in modern society in a form useful to stave off a vampire's effort to reach its victim. Modern vampires generally have extra strength but can be overcome by a group of people.

In recent novels and films, victims have had little to protect them should a vampire single them out. The only forces holding the vampire in check were a possible moral commitment not to kill or rational consideration, to be discrete, that kept a vampire from leaving a trail of blood-drained bodies to be found by authorities who would then discern the vampire's existence.

Some help survives. Taoist magical formulas written on paper and stuck to the forehead of a Chinese vampire have been a standard feature of Hong Kong movies. In the British television series *Being Human*, the Jewish werewolf found that the Star of David he wore around his neck kept the evil vampires at bay. The cross still works occasionally but is less and less effective all the time.

> Iron, when used as a structural feature, could form a strong physical barrier, for it was a substance that vampires avoid.

Psychic Vampirism

Among the most popular theories to explain the persistency and universality of vampire myths, the concept of psychic vampirism traces the belief in the vampire to various occult, psychic, or paranormal phenomena. Such explanations have their origin in folktales that identified the vampiric entity as a ghostly figure rather than a resuscitated body—or even further back to ancient times and the earliest vampire-like figures who were described as evil gods or demons, such as the *lamiai* of Greece. Such entities were closely related to the medieval incubus/succubus.

Psychic explanations of vampirism emerged in the nineteenth century simultaneously with the rise of psychical research, a scientific discipline that assigned itself the task of investigating experiences formerly assigned to the realm of the occult or supernatural. It attempted to discern which experiences were illusional, which had fairly mundane psychological explanations, and which were truly paranormal or psychic. Psychical research borrowed many terms from Spiritualism and occultism as a part of its early working language. While vampirism was not the most popular topic for discussion among spiritualists and occultists, it appeared occasionally and seemed to need an explanation from the perspective of the occult worldview.

Astral Vampirism: Among ritual magicians and theosophists, vampirism was explained as due to the astral body. It was their understanding that each person had not only a physical body but a second body, usually invisible, which was often seen separating from the physical body at the moment of death. This astral body accounted for such phenomena as ghosts and out-of-body experiences. Henry Steel Olcott, the first president of the Theosophical Society, speculated that occasionally when a person was buried, the person was not really dead but in a catatonic or trancelike state yet still barely alive. Citing the experience of yogis who could slow their breathing to an indiscernible rate and survive without air for many weeks, Olcott surmised that a person could survive for long periods in the grave. In the meantime, the person would send his or her astral double to suck the blood or life force from the living and, thus,

Henry Steel Olcott, founding president of the Theosophical Society, believed that sometimes people were buried who were close to death but not completely dead.

gain nourishment. This explanation, to Olcott, seemed to explain why a body that had been buried for weeks or months would be dug up and appear as if it had recently gorged itself on blood. It was his belief that the blood or life force swallowed by the astral form passed immediately to the organs of the physical body lying in the tomb, and then, the astral body quickly returned to that corpse.

Olcott also commented on the practice of burning the corpse of a suspected vampire. He argued that vampirism, and the possibility of premature burial and vampirism, made cremation the preferable means of disposing of the physical remains of the deceased. Cremation severed the link between the astral and physical body and prevented the possibility of vampirism. Olcott's original observations, including his preference for cremation, were later expanded on by other prominent theosophical writers such as Charles W. Leadbeater, Arthur E. Powell, and Franz Hartmann.

Hartmann traced the astral vampirism theory back to the alchemist Paracelsus (1493–

1541) through Olcott and his mentor, H. P. Blavatsky, but seemed to have developed the theosophical position directly from the work of pioneer psychical researcher Z. J. Piérart. Hartmann, who related several vampire stories in the pages of the *Occult Review*, developed his own variation of astral vampirism in his theory of an "astral tumour." He saw the vampire as a force field of subhuman intelligence that acted out of instinct rather than any rational thought. He differed from Olcott by suggesting that the vampire was malignant, but since it lacked any intelligence, it was not morally evil.

> Vampirism was not due to a living agent but to a disassociated portion of the human that remains intact and capable of some degree of human consciousness after death.

Two modern versions of the astral vampirism hypothesis have been articulated. In the 1960s, parapsychologist D. Scott Rogo formulated a theory based upon broad reading in both vampire and psychic literature and attention to some of the more exotic psychic occurrences. He posed the definition of a vampire as "a certain kind of haunting which results in an abnormal loss of vitality through no recognized channel." Vampirism was not due to a living agent but to a disassociated portion of the human that remains intact and capable of some degree of human consciousness after death. This remnant eventually dissipated, but that disintegration was postponed by its ability to take life from the living. Martin V. Riccardo, founder of the Vampire Studies network, suggested that astral vampirism may account for many of the reports of vampirism. He focused, however, upon the activity of individuals who sent their astral bodies to attack their sleeping neighbors. Riccardo cited a detailed case reported by occultist Dion Fortune (1890–1946), author of a volume on the prevention of various negative occult experiences, *Psychic Self-Defense*. Fortune discovered that some of her neighbors shared a nightmare attack attributed to the same person. Fortune confronted the person, who admitted to having magical powers and to harming others.

Vampiric Entities: Among the "I AM" Ascended Masters groups that have grown out of the original work of Guy Ballard (1878–1939), a somewhat different emphasis on the vampire theme has been evident. These groups posited the idea that over the centuries, humankind created a large number of what were termed "mass entities." Through calling up negative realities, thinking about them, and feeling violently about them, they called these mass entities into existence. Every time a person gave attention to one of these mass entities, it drew strength from that individual and became more powerful in altering the course of humanity. The legion of mass entities went under names like war, pestilence, and fear.

These mass entities acted like vampires and, as one of the Masters speaking to the members of the Bridge to Freedom asserted, it was the task of those related to the Ascended Masters and their cause to dissolve the "vampire activity of the mass humanly created entities." The work of dissolution was accomplished through decreeing, the particular process of prayer utilized by the "I AM"-related groups.

The Church Universal and Triumphant organization, under the leadership of Ascended Masters Messenger Elizabeth Clare Prophet (1939–2009), identified a number of disincarnate mass entities, including drug and tobacco entities, insanity entities, sex entities, and entities aligned against the church. One set of entities was termed Halloween entities, which included the horror entity named Dracula (female) or Draculus (male). The church has given its members a ritual of exorcism of these entities.

Magnetic Vampirism: The most common form of psychic vampirism, however, did not involve an astral body. Magnetic vampirism was the sapping of life force by one person from another. The idea of magnetic vampirism was based on the commonly reported experience of a loss of vitality caused by simply being in the presence of certain people. Hartmann referred to psychic sponges: people who unconsciously vampirized every sensitive person with whom they came into contact. He believed such a person was possessed by a vampiric entity who continually drained both the energy of its possessed host and all of his or her acquaintances. Scott Rogo, author of the article "In-depth Analysis of the Vampire Legend," cited the case of clairvoyant Mollie Flancher who, because of some unrelated condition, was kept under careful observation for many years.

It was noted that any animals that she attempted to keep as pets soon died, and those close to her speculated that she had sapped them of their psychic energy.

Anton LaVey (1930–1997), founder of the Church of Satan, taught church members about psychic vampirism and how to avoid it as a key element in the church's ego development program.

Psychic vampirism made a significant comeback in the 1990s. A new movement of real vampires, the sanguinarians, became visible and were identified by their consumption of blood.

Mary "Mollie" Flancher was known as the "Brooklyn Enigma." She could last up to seven weeks without eating. Diagnosed with dyspepsia, modern doctors later theorized she may have suffered from anorexia.

As the new phase of the real vampire movement developed, however, it became evident that the great majority did not drink blood or had abandoned the practice for a number of reasons, including the transmission of blood diseases. At this point, voices favoring psychic vampirism came to the fore, and longtime Ohio vampire Michelle Belanger emerged as their primary spokesperson. The real vampires enjoyed their highest profile in the first decade of the new century and, while continuing to exist as a community, subsequently faded from public view.

Suicide

Suicide was one of the acts universally associated with vampirism. In cultures as varied as in Russia, Romania, West Africa, and China, suicide was considered an individual's pathway into vampirism. In the West in Jewish, Christian, and Muslim cultures, suicide has traditionally been considered a sin. In most other cultures, suicide was frowned upon in an equivalent manner. Japan has generally been considered somewhat unique in its designation of a form of suicide called *hari-kari* as a means of reversing the dishonor that initially led to the suicide.

Suicide was among the more serious antisocial actions a person could commit that caused vampirism. In Eastern Europe, additional actions that could predict a person eventually becoming a vampire included being a quarrelsome person, a drunkard, or a person associated with heresy or sorcery/witchcraft. Each society had activities considered a threat to the community's well-being that branded a person as different. While these varied considerably from culture to culture, suicide was among the most ubiquitous in its condemnation.

Suicide signaled the existence of extreme unresolved tension in the social fabric of a community. It was viewed as evidence of the family's and the community's inability to socialize an individual as well as a statement by the individual of complete disregard for the community's existence and its prescribed rituals. The community, in turn, showed its disapproval in its treatment of the suicide's corpse. In the West, it was often denied Christian burial and its soul considered outside of the realm of salvation (the subject having committed mortal sin without the benefit of confession and forgiveness prior to death). Those who committed suicide were buried at a crossroads or at a distance from the village. The corpse might even be thrown in a river to be carried away by the current.

Those who committed suicide died leaving unfinished emotional business with relatives and close acquaintances. They left people with unresolved grief, which became a factor, sometimes unspoken, in the survivors' personalities for the rest of their lives. Their corpses often returned to the living in dreams and as apparitions. They

> Those who committed suicide died leaving unfinished emotional business with relatives and close acquaintances…. Their corpses often returned to the living in dreams and as apparitions.

were the subjects of nightmares, and families and friends occasionally felt under attack from their presence. The deceased became a vampire, and actions had to be taken to break the connection that allowed the dead to disturb the living. The various actions taken against a corpse could be viewed as a means of emotional release for the survivors. The break in the connection was first attempted with harmless actions of protection but, if ineffective, those efforts moved to a more serious level with mutilation (with a stake) or complete destruction (by fire) of the corpse.

Novelists and screenwriters have utilized suicide in their consideration of the problems faced by vampires who have found themselves bored with their long life, displaced in time, or concluded that their vampire state is immoral.

Immediately after becoming a vampire, for example, Lestat de Lioncourt (the continuing character in Anne Rice's vampire novels) had to witness the suicide (by fire) of the vampire who had made him. Eventually, Armand, the leader of the Parisian community, eventually committed suicide by basking in the sunlight. Placing oneself in the open as the dawn approaches is the suicide method of choice for vampires, as recently exemplified by Boya (in the 1996 movie *Blood and Donuts*) and Countess Maria Viroslav in Kathryn Reines's *The Kiss* (1996). Toward the end of *Memnoch the Devil*, the fifth of *The Vampire Chronicles* of Anne Rice, Armand walks into the sunlight out of his intense religious feelings after seeing Veronica's veil that Lestat had returned with after his adventure in heaven and hell.

Both the Chevalier Futaine (the vampire in Henry Kuttner's 1937 pulp short story "I, the Vampire") and Batman (in the alternative-universe Batman story *Batman: Bloodstorm*) committed suicide by leaving their sleeping place open for someone they knew would come in to kill them. Possibly the most ingenious suicide device was created for Yaksha, the original vampire in Christopher Pike's *The Last Vampire* series. Yaksha had made a deal to redeem himself by killing all of the vampires and then himself. He saved his former lover for last. She rigged a set of explosives in a room that would kill both of them but then cleverly concealed a shield that would protect her at the crucial moment. Yaksha was killed, but she survived.

In the second season of *True Blood* (the television series drawing on the novels of Charlaine Harris), Godric, the sheriff of Dallas, committed suicide by standing in the open on top of a building to greet the morning sun as Sookie Stackhouse watched.

❧ *Vision* ❧

According to Abraham Van Helsing, the voice of authority on vampires in *Dracula* (1897), the vampire can see in the dark. Although this is not mentioned in the folk literature, it was a logical conclusion because vampires were nocturnal creatures who moved about freely in the darkness of the evening hours. Some of the vampire's attributes were derived from its association with the bat. Bats, for instance, have a radar system that make them extremely well-adapted night creatures. Dracula was pictured as regularly leaving his castle each evening to feed and return with food for his vampire brides. He also used his acute sight in his attacks on Lucy Westenra and Mina Murray. Modern vampire writers have cited night vision as one of the positive characteristics of the vampiric existence, frequently mentioned as allowing vampires to feel natural and at home in the nocturnal world. Night vision counterbalanced the blinding effect of direct sunlight.

HISTORY

Approaching the Vampire

We begin our exploration of the vampire world with a look back at history. A significant moment in the emergence of the vampire into popular consciousness occurred in 1972 when two university professors at Boston College, Raymond T. McNally and Radu R. Florescu, picked up and expanded upon an idea earlier proposed by several European colleagues who suggested that the fictional Count Dracula of Bram Stoker's novel was somewhat based on a heretofore obscure Romanian ruler, Vlad Tepes (Vlad the Impaler), sometimes called Dracula (a title designating him the son of Vlad Dracul, or Vlad the Dragon). They turned the idea into a book, *In Search of Dracula* (1972), which found both a popular audience but also gave a group of scholars otherwise interested in things vampiric something to talk about at their academic gatherings. While historians could judge the adequacy of their treatment of Vlad, gothic scholars had much to discuss relative to Stoker's actual awareness of Vlad among the many sources he used. While much of McNally's and Florescu's thinking has been discarded, the debate they unleashed provided much fodder for colleagues to chew.

In Search of Dracula also had an immediate effect on popular culture. Within a few years, a new screen version of *Dracula* integrated material about Vlad into the screenplay, finding in Vlad's life motivation for the action of Dracula coming to England and focusing on the particular women whose blood he chose to drain. Shortly after Dan Curtis's production of *Dracula* (starring Jack Palance in the title role) drew a record-breaking audience to its television premiere, the first *Dracula*-based novel to integrate Vlad's life into its presentation of the Transylvanian count was penned by Gail Kimberly as *Dracula Began* (1976).

Quite apart from the accuracy of the McNally–Florescu thesis concerning Vlad, he was, over the decades after their book, identified as Dracula, and in his many appearances in books and movies, Count Dracula's given name was popularly thought to be Vlad. Their work also set up a search for other historical characters who could also be thought of as vampires, beginning with Countess Elizabeth Báthory (1560–1614), the Slovak noblewoman accused of being a serial killer who bathed in the blood of her victims. In the wake of Vlad and Báthory, others would be identified and included in a more or less subtle argument for the reality of vampires. Below, we shall explore some of the more prominent people branded as vampires over the centuries.

❦ *Real Vampires* ❦

The vampire has generally been thought of as a peculiar kind of revenant, a dead person who had returned to life and continued a form of existence through drinking the blood of the living. Hence, the vampire was considered to be "undead," having completed earthly life but still being tied to that life and not yet welcomed by the realm of the dead. The vampire is distinguished from the ghost, a disembodied spirit, in that the vampire was embodied in an animated material existence. It was distinguished from the ghoul in that the ghoul had no intelligent control, being guided solely by its hunger as it feasted off the bodies of its victims rather than just supping on their blood. Consuming blood was the most characteristic activity of vampires, so the term "vampire" has also been used to describe

Vampires in modern fiction are increasingly portrayed as sexy, alluring, and, let's face it, cool.

many mythological creatures and a variety of animals who drink blood, not to mention living persons who engage in similar activities. Finally, the term has been used to describe people (and spirits) who engage in psychic vampirism, the process of draining the life force or energy (rather than the blood) of other people.

The Eighteenth-century Vampire Controversy: In the eighteenth century, Western scholars for the first time considered the question of the existence of vampires as something more than just another element of the vast supernatural world of rural folk culture. The controversy was set off by a series of incidents of vampire hysteria that occurred in East Prussia in 1721 and in the lands of the Austro-Hungarian Empire from 1725 through 1732. These cases culminated in the famous events surrounding Arnold Paole, a retired Austrian soldier who had settled in Serbia and was accused of being the source of an outbreak of vampirism in his community. Several of these cases became the object of formal government investigations and reports, and a hastily prepared volume on Paole sold widely around Europe.

The publication of the Paole book led to no fewer than a dozen treatises and four dissertations, and the controversy over him lasted for a generation. It eventually involved some of the most intellectual voices of Europe, including Diderot and Voltaire. The question of the existence of vampires was argued on legal, theological, and scientific grounds. The question became more than academic in that villagers, affected by a belief that vampires were active in their community, opened graves and mutilated or destroyed any bodies showing characteristics believed to indicate blood-consuming activity. Although some members of the scholarly community attempted to defend the existence of vampires, the majority concluded that evidence suggested they did not exist. The latter cited a host of natural phenomena that accounted for vampire reports, such as premature burial and rabies (which causes an insatiable thirst in anyone infected). They also attributed the reports to theological polemics in areas where a Roman Catholic Austrian government had been imposed on an Eastern Orthodox population.

The most careful defense of vampires came from French biblical scholar Dom Augustin Calmet (1672–1757) in his 1746 *Dissertations sur les Apparitions des Anges des Démons et des Esprits, et sur les revenants, et Vampires de Hingrie, de Boheme, de Moravie, et de Silésie.* The publication of Calmet's treatise, given his reputation as a scholar, initiated a second stage of the academic controversy, which was largely settled by the end of the 1830s. Even the Vatican ignored Calmet, its opinion that vampires did not exist having been set by the conclusions of Archbishop Giuseppe Davanzati, published just two years before Calmet's book. A decade after Calmet's book appeared—and in the midst of the controversy it sparked—a new wave of vampire hysteria occurred in Silesia. Austrian Empress Maria Theresa sent her personal physician to investigate the incident. In his report, Dr. Gerhard van Swieten ridiculed the practice of exhuming and executing purported vampires as "posthumous magic." As a result, in 1755 and 1756, Maria Theresa forbade church and village authorities from taking any action in cases of reported vampires. Only officials of the central government could respond to such cases. The actions of the Austrian empress squelched what was left of any remaining public debate.

Real Vampires in the Nineteenth Century: From the middle of the seventeenth century until the second half of the nineteenth century, no serious attempt to prove the existence of vampires, at least in their folkloric form, was made. An attempt to defend the folkloric vampire was launched in the mid-1800s by the spiritualist community. Spokespersons who emerged during the first generation of spiritualism in Europe, where the tales of vampires were most prevalent, offered a new rationale for vampires: psychic vampirism. In the 1860s, Z. J. Piérart suggested that the phenomena described in the folkloric reports of vampires could be attributed to the astral bodies of either the living or dead, which fed off the life energy of the living. The astral body, however elusive, provided an agent for transmitting vitality to the dead and accounted for bodies that, though lying buried for some weeks or months, did not decay and, when uncovered, manifested numerous signs of a continuing life. Piérart's suggestion, which had precursors in previous occult writers, was picked up by spir-

German theosophist and astrologer Franz Hartmann was one of the founders of the occult organization Ordo Templi Orientis.

itualist and theosophical exponents, and accounts of "true vampires" began to appear in occult journals.

Typical of these reports was one of the many published by theosophist Franz Hartmann in the 1890s. The story concerned an alcoholic who had been rejected by a woman with whom he was in love. Dejected, he committed suicide by shooting himself. Soon afterward, the woman began to complain of vampiric attacks from a specter in the form of the recently dead suitor. She could not see him but was aware of his presence. Doctors diagnosed her as a hysteric but could do little to relieve her symptoms. She finally submitted herself to an exorcism conducted by a person who accepted her explanation of vampirism. After the exorcism, the attacks ceased. Today, various psychological theories, shorn of any need to posit the existence of vampires, could account for all of the woman's symptoms, and steps to deal with her unresolved guilt over the suitor's suicide could be pursued. However, these were as yet unavailable to the medical world, and the spiritualist perspective gained its share of support.

Increasing reports of vampirism, including accounts of the living vampirizing their acquaintances, at times seemingly without any conscious awareness of what they were doing, led to the discarding of the more supernatural spiritualist explanations of vampirism, in which astral bodies attacked the living. Such theories, although maintained in some occult movements, were for the most part replaced with references to "psychic sponges," people who were themselves low on psychic energy, manifested by frequent periods of fatigue but who, in the presence of high-energy people, had the ability to take energy from them. Many people seemed to know such psychic sponges, individuals who regain their vitality in the company of others even as their companions experience a distinct loss of energy and interest in immediate activities. Although

the notion of psychic sponges was a popular one, at least in different metaphysical and psychic-oriented groups, it is extremely difficult to document and has produced only a minuscule amount of literature.

Vampirism as Blood Fetish: While the more benign incidents of psychic vampirism were being reported, accounts of vampire crime began to appear. In the 1920s, two cases of serial killers with vampiric tendencies shocked the people of Europe. In 1924, they read of Fritz Haarmann of Hanover, Germany, who killed no fewer than 24 young men. He earned the appellation "vampire" killer by biting the necks of those he murdered and drinking some of their blood. Five years later, Peter Kürten of Düsseldorf went on a killing spree, later confessing that he received a sexual thrill and release while watching blood spurt from his victims.

Rare accounts of serial killers with some form of blood fetish were also reported. One of the more gruesome ones concerned a series of murders of prostitutes in Stockholm, Sweden, in the period from 1982 to 1987. During this period, at least seven prostitutes disappeared from the streets, and their bodies were later discovered surgically dismembered and drained of blood. Eventually arrested and tried in the case were two physicians, Teet Haerm and Thomas Allgren.

Haerm's arrest shocked many. He was the senior police medical examiner and one of the leading forensic pathologists in the world. His articles had appeared in several professional publications, including *The Lancet*, a prominent British medical journal. He had even been called in to examine the remains of several of the women he was later accused of murdering. Allgren, Haerm's best friend, was a dermatologist. In the end, Allgren confessed and gave testimony at Haerm's trial. According to Allgren, Haerm had an intense desire to brutalize and kill prostitutes. To justify the satiation of that desire, the two had started on a righteous crusade to rid Stockholm of streetwalkers. However, Allgren also discovered that Haerm had a lust for blood and gore and that after the killings, he drained and drank the blood of his victims. Eventually, Allgren was turned in by his daughter, who claimed that he had sexually molested her. In the process of talking about her experience, she also described in some detail a murder of one of the prostitutes she had witnessed. The testimonies of Allgren and his daughter were heard at a 1988 trial in which the latter testified that bloodlust led Haerm into the field of pathology, but he eventually found the work on bodies less than satisfying. Then, he began his killing spree.

> Allgren also discovered that Haerm had a lust for blood and gore and that after the killings, he drained and drank the blood of his victims.

Both Haerm and Allgren were convicted in a 1988 trial and sentenced to life imprisonment. However, their convictions were overturned and, in a retrial, they were found not guilty, even though the judge wrote in his decision that reasonable evidence existed that they were guilty. Both defendants were freed.

Another more recent case of a "vampire" killer concerned Richard Chase of Sacramento, California. The documented nefarious deeds committed by Chase began in December 1977 with the shooting of Ambrose Griffin. A month later, on January 23, 1978, Chase shot Theresa Wallin, after which he mutilated her body with a knife. In that process, he collected her blood in a cup and consumed it. A week after the Wallin attack, he killed four people at Evelyn Miroth's home, including Miroth, whom he mutilated and whose blood he also drank. Miroth's baby nephew, who was visiting her, was taken home by Chase, who killed him, drank his blood, and tossed his body in the garbage. According to Chase, he believed that he suffered from a form of blood poisoning and needed blood to relieve his condition. He had in the past hunted animals (beginning with small animals such as rabbits and cats and moving on to cows). He killed the animals and drank their blood, and his messiness led to several prior encounters with the authorities. After such an encounter in 1977, he made a decision to start killing people. A year earlier, he had spent time in a mental facility. While there, he had manifested a mania over blood, and his fellow patients had begun to call him Dracula. Arrested soon after the Miroth murder, he was convicted of the six killings. He died in prison, where he committed suicide in 1980 at the age of 31.

The examples of Haarmann, Kürten, and Haerm are only tangential to what traditionally has been thought of as vampirism. They are serial killers with, among other problems, a blood fetish. The blood was not the object of their quest, and the drinking of blood was just one of the more gruesome (and somewhat superficial) practices in which they engaged. Chase was somewhat different and more closely approached true vampirism. Although he was not seeking blood to prolong his life, he sought regular ingestions of blood to counteract the effects of poison he believed he was receiving. In the end, however, his vampiric activity also fell into the serial killing mode, the bloodlust being somewhat peripheral to the killings.

Some Real Vampires Emerge: In the 1960s, as a result of the Hammer Films Dracula movies and the *Dark Shadows* television series, public interest in vampires increased noticeably, and the first of the present-day vampire fan clubs and interest groups was founded. By the early 1970s, the Count Dracula Fan Club (now the Vampire Empire), the Vampire Information Exchange, and the Vampire Studies Society (now Vampire Studies) had formed in the United States; the Vampire Research Society and the Dracula Society soon followed in England. As these groups emerged, the leaders began to encounter people who claimed to be vampires. In the beginning, devoted as they were to the literary vampire (and not really believing that such things as vampires existed), leaders of the vampire interest groups largely discounted such stories. Among those who did take the reports seriously were psychical researcher Scott Rogo; Rev. Sean Manchester, founder of the Vampire Research Society in London; and Stephen Kaplan, founder of the Vampire Research Center in New York.

> As these groups emerged, the leaders began to encounter people who claimed to be vampires.

Rogo, Manchester, and Kaplan each began their research from a point of prior interest with psychic phenomena. In the late 1960s, Rogo tried to interest the American Society for Psychical Research in vampirism but was unable to budge the group from its more central concerns. Most parapsychologists thought that their field was already far enough out on the fringe. Forced to choose, Rogo soon suppressed his interest in vampirism and, in the 1970s and 1980s, made his own contribution as a writer, attempting to bring psychical research into the mainstream of the scientific community. Sean Manchester's Vampire Research Society grew out of his previous leadership role in an occult investigations bureau. The society investigates all aspects of "supernatural vampire phenomena," a task that has led to a variety of research projects, including the famous Highgate and Kirklees vampire projects.

Stephen Kaplan founded the Vampire Research Center in 1972. His first interview of alleged vampires was with a couple who introduced him to the nocturnal world of vampires, their alternative sexual practices (in this case, sadomasochism), and the existence of donors, people who (for a price) allow vampires to drink their blood. From his early encounters, Kaplan began to develop a working definition of vampires. They were people who met three criteria: they need regular quantities of blood, they believe that the blood will pro-

long their life and help them remain youthful, and they often find the blood and its consumption to be sexually arousing. Over the years, Kaplan had the opportunity to meet and correspond with other vampires and was able to fill out his picture of them. They do not drink great quantities of blood—only a few ounces a day—but they need that blood daily and will go to extreme measures to receive it. Denied it, they become irritable, depressed, fatigued, and somewhat aggressive. They tend to be nocturnal in their habits, and many profess to be extremely sensitive to light. Otherwise, they appear normal and dress in such a way as not to call attention to themselves. To obtain blood, vampires often engage in various forms of sadomasochistic behavior that lead to some bloodletting. They often exchange sexual favors for blood. Some join groups that engage in ritual blood-drinking. If unable to obtain a willing donor, they will, according to their own testimony, occasionally attack a victim but, as a rule, will not kill for blood.

The vampires Kaplan studied were neither psychic nor supernatural beings. They were, apart from their blood-drinking activities, somewhat normal human beings. Some professed to be far older than their youthful appearance suggested, but their true age was rarely verifiable. Above and beyond the relatively small number of vampires Kaplan encountered (fewer than 100 in two decades), he discovered hundreds of people he described as vampire-like individuals. These people seek to imitate vampires in various ways to gain some of the positive qualities associated with vampiric existence from immortality to the ability to dominate others, sexually and otherwise.

As early as the 1970s, he was able to locate people who had adopted the vampire persona by wearing black clothes or altering their teeth. They drank blood but, not liking the

Some modern-day vampires will trade sexual favors for blood or partake in sadomasochistic games to the point that someone bleeds and they can feast on those fluids.

which he decided to focus. Not only did he face tremendous ridicule, but fear of the legal and medical authorities and an intolerant public caused many of the subjects of his study to back away from any situations that might threaten their anonymity, classify them as lawbreakers, or question their mental competence. No real comprehensive and systematic study of vampires has been possible, and knowledge of them still relies on anecdotes related by their few spokespersons. Most importantly, no medical data of the kind that could provide any evidence of physical traits shared by people who claim to be vampires is available.

Real Vampires in the 1990s: In the decade after Kaplan published his research in the volume *Vampires Are* (1984), a gothic subculture emerged across America. The gothic life was centered on eerie, atmospheric, gothic rock music, and nightclubs and theaters regularly provided a stage for gothic bands to perform. Individual "goths" emulated the nocturnal vampiric life, and many assumed a vampiric persona complete with dark clothes, pale makeup, and artificial fangs. They also advocated lifestyles based on androgyny, which was so central to the character Lestat de Lioncourt, the popular vampire star of the novels of Anne Rice. Almost all forms of sexual expression among consenting adults, from sadomasochism to blood fetishism, were welcomed. Thus, the gothic subculture created a space in which self-designated vampires can move somewhat freely and mingle without anyone questioning their nonconventional habits.

taste, they put it in a fruit juice cocktail. Many of the people attracted to vampirism find themselves drawn by the eroticism of the vampires' lives. Vampirism, especially in its literary and cinematic expressions, is inherently sexual. The vampire's bite has often been compared to sexual intercourse and blood likened to semen. Worldwide over the centuries, blood acquired both a sexual and religious connotation, but the dominant Western Christian religion retained the religious meaning without the sexual element. In the activities of many nonconventional persuasions, such as the contemporary sex magic practiced by the followers of Aleister Crowley, the sexual and religious elements of blood have been reunited. A few have united sex and blood-drinking in more sinister forms.

In the process of his research, Kaplan discovered just how difficult the area was on

At the same time, the voices of "non-goths" who profess to be vampires also continued to be heard. Carol Page, in a far less systematic way than Kaplan, wrote of her experiences with contemporary blood-drinkers in *Bloodlust: Conversations with Real Vampires* (1991). Page, who interviewed numerous "vampires," reached many of the same conclusions as Kaplan:

Some people in the Goth subculture also profess to be vampires.

The blood they drink has no effect on them physiologically. It does not keep them young and they do not physically need it, although some vampires believe they do. It doesn't make them high, except psychologically, or give them nutrition, since human blood passes through the digestive system without being absorbed. They do not have superhuman strength. They cannot turn into bats and wolves. Some sleep in coffins during the day and dress in black capes or indulge in other affectations inspired by fictional vampires. (p. 15)

Page and Kaplan, as well as other sources, have made the point that vampires—that is, blood-drinkers—existed and described their world in some detail. Furthermore, they suggested that these vampires lived a camouflaged life in the midst of more conventional society and that, except within the cordial atmosphere of the gothic world or the nocturnal world of their own kind, they rarely dropped their conforming persona or allowed the nature of their life to be known by any people they do not fully trust. However, enough of them exist, some of whom with relatively open and accessible lives, that serious researchers would have little difficulty in making contact with them.

Through the 1990s into the new century, the world of "real" vampires has continued to evolve. Many first met while engaged in the role-playing game *Vampire: The Masquerade.* At the beginning of the new century, an initial group of people who drank small quantities of blood, called "sanguinarians," emerged. They were distinguished by a variety of claims about the need of and benefit derived from the periodic consumption of at least a few drops of blood. They were being serviced by a slightly larger group of people who volunteered to donate their blood, usually retrieved by making small wounds on their bodies.

To the sanguinarians was soon added a larger and increasingly vocal group of energy vampires, or psychic vampires, who claimed to have a regular need to drain the energy of others, without which they would suffer a variety of conditions marked by extreme fatigue. In spite of the ethical questions raised by their taking energy from unsuspecting donors, the energy vampires violated no laws, and no ready method of verifying their claims has been available. Such vampires soon emerged as the much larger segment of the vampire community. While many associated themselves with the esoteric community, which at least admitted the existence of energy exchange, many were living incognito lives in society, holding jobs, raising families, and even worshipping in mainstream churches.

> A code, called the Black Veil, was created from the rule used within *Vampire: The Masquerade.*

Most of the early organizations of vampires based their organization on models derived in part from *Vampire: The Masquerade*, which was notable for its attempt to imagine a clandestine vampire community operating incognito within the larger mundane human world. These early organizations went under names like house, clan, and coven. Beginning in the 1990s, a New York–based organization, the Sanguinarium, served as a focal point of a loose association of local vampire groups.

As the vampire community became more public, some called for a code of ethics to guide it. A code, called the Black Veil, was created from the rule used within *Vampire: The Masquerade*. Its first draft, published by Father Sebastiaan of the Ordo Strigoi Vii, was further

reworked by Michelle Belanger, one of the most public of the energy vampires. In the meantime, the internet facilitated people who self-identified as vampires to communicate while keeping the degree of anonymity most desired and felt they required. Their community became most visible in New York City, annually on Halloween in New Orleans where large gatherings were held, and through the Atlanta Vampire Alliance (AVA) in Georgia. The AVA, originally founded to promote unity among Atlanta's vampire community, has, as a result of it sending out a lengthy questionnaire to the more visible real vampires around the world, resulted in its becoming an international nexus for self-identified vampires. Close to 1,000 people responded to the survey between 2006 and 2009.

The vampire community now exists as what Professor Joseph Laycock describes as an identity community, a very loosely organized community created by the self-identity as a vampire of its constituents. Worldwide, it consists of numbers counted in the thousands, the several thousand known to the AVA being its most visible core. At one end of the spectrum of real vampires are formally organized groups such as the Temple of the Vampire, the Order of the Vampyre, and the House Kheperu. Other vampires gather for periodic gatherings such as the annual Endless Night Vampire Ball in New Orleans or show up at designated times in late-night rock clubs. Most, however, exist as individuals known as vampires only to themselves and a few intimate friends.

In the new century, two attempts have been made to organize gatherings for vampires at which the more serious issues facing the emerging community can be discussed and steps to improve the image of the community can be developed. The first of these organizations, Voices of the Vampire Community, founded in 2005, has attempted to bring together representative leaders of the community. The other, the Twilight Gatherings, founded in 2007, has included both vampires and outsiders seriously interested in the vampire existence.

🦇 *Christianity and Vampires* 🦇

Belief in vampires preceded the introduction of Christianity into Southern and Eastern Europe. It seems to have originated independently as a response to unexplained phenomena

The lamia *is a mythical creature often described as a half-snake/half-woman seductress with vampire-like qualities, as depicted in* The Knight and the Seductress *(1890) by painter Isobel Lilian Gloag.*

common to most cultures. Ancient Greek writings tell of the *lamiai*, the *mormolykiai*, and other vampire-like creatures. Independent accounts of vampires emerged and spread among the Slavic people and were passed to their non-Slavic neighbors. Possibly, the Romani brought some belief in vampires from India that contributed to the development of the myth. As Christianity spread through the lands of the Mediterranean Basin and then northward across Europe, it encountered these vampire beliefs that had already arisen among the many Pagan peoples. However, vampirism was never high on the Christian agenda and was thus rarely mentioned. Its continued presence was indicated by occasional documents, such as an eleventh-century law promulgated by Charlemagne as emperor of the new Holy Roman Empire. The law condemned anyone who promoted a belief in the witch/vampire (specifically in its form as a *strix*) and anyone who, on account of that belief, caused a person thought to be a vampire to be attacked and killed.

By the end of the first Christian millennium, the Christian Church was still organizationally united and in agreement upon the basic Christian affirmation (as contained in the Nicene Creed) but had already begun to differentiate itself into its primarily Greek (Eastern Orthodox) and Latin (Roman Catholic) branches. The church formally broke in the year 1054 with each side excommunicating the other.

In the second Christian millennium, the two churches completed their conquests through the remaining parts of Europe, especially Eastern Europe. Meanwhile, quite apart from the major doctrinal issues that had separated them in the eleventh century, the theology in the two churches began to develop numerous lesser differences. These would become important especially in those areas where the boundaries of the two churches met and wars brought people of one church under the control of political leaders of the other. Such a situation arose, for example, in the twelfth century, when the predominantly Roman Catholic Hungarians conquered Transylvania, then populated by Romanians, the majority of whom were Eastern Orthodox. Slavic but Roman Catholic Poland was bounded on the east by Orthodox Russian states. In the Balkans, Roman Catholic Croatia existed beside predominantly Eastern Orthodox Serbia.

One divergence between the two churches frequently noted in the vampire literature was their different understanding of the incorruptibility of dead bodies. In the East, if the soft tissue of a body did not decay quickly once placed in the ground, it was generally considered a sign of evil. The fact that the body refused to disintegrate meant that the earth would, for some reason, not receive it. An incorrupt body became a candidate for vampirism. In the West, quite the opposite was true. The body of a dead saint often did not experience corruption like that of an ordinary body. Not only did it not decay, but it frequently emitted a pleasant odor. It did not stink of putrefaction. These differing understandings of incorruptibility explain in large part the demise of belief in vampires in the Catholic West and the parallel survival of belief in Eastern Orthodox lands, even though the Greek Church officially tried to suppress the belief.

Vampires and Satan: Admittedly, vampires were not a priority issue on the agenda of Christian theologians and thinkers of either church. However, by 1645, when Leo Allatius (1586–1669) wrote the first book to treat the subject of vampires systematically, it was obvious that much thought, especially at the parish level, had been devoted to the subject. The

Greek scholar Leo Allatius wrote an early definitive book on the vampire in 1645.

vampire had been part of the efforts of the church to eliminate Paganism by treating it as a false religion. The deities of the Pagans were considered unreal, nonexistent. In like measure, the demons of Pagan lore were unreal.

Through the thirteenth and fourteenth centuries, as the Inquisition became a force in the Roman Catholic Church, a noticeable change took place in theological perspectives. A shift occurred in viewing Paganism (or witchcraft). It was no longer considered merely a product of the unenlightened imagination; it was the work of Satan. Witchcraft was transformed in the popular mind into Satanism. The change of opinion on Satanism also provided an opening for a reconsideration of, for example, the incubus/succubus and the vampire as also somehow the work of the devil. By the time Allatius wrote his treatise on the vampire, this changing climate had overtaken the church. Allatius was Greek, but he was also a Roman Catholic rather than an Eastern Orthodox believer. He possessed a broad knowledge of both churches. In his *De Graecorum hodie quorundam opinationibus*, the vampire toward which he primarily turned his attention was the *vrykolakas*, the Greek vampire.

Allatius noted that among the Eastern Orthodox Greeks a noncanon, that is, an ordinance of uncertain authorship and date, was operative in the sixteenth century. It defined a *vrykolakas* as a dead man who remained whole and incorrupt and did not follow the normal pattern of disintegration, which usually occurred very quickly in the time before embalming. Occasionally, such a *vrykolakas* was found, and it was believed to be the work of the devil. When a person discovered a *vrykolakas*, the local priest was to be summoned. The priest chanted an invocation to the Mother of God and again repeated the services of the dead. The earlier noncanon, however, originated in the period when the church was attacking the belief in vampires as superstition and was designed to reverse some centuries-old beliefs about vampires. It ascribed incidents involving *vrykolakas* to someone seeing a dead person, usually at night, frequently in dreams. Such dreams were the work of the devil. The devil had not caused the dead to rise and attack its victims but deluded the individual with a false dream.

Allatius himself promoted the belief that was gaining dominance in the West through the sixteenth century: vampires were real and were themselves the work of the devil. Just as the Inquisition in the previous century had championed the idea that witchcraft was real and that witches actually communed with the devil, so, too, vampires were actually walking around the towns and villages of Europe. They were not the dead returned; they were bodies reanimated by the devil and his minions. Allatius even quoted the witchfinder's bible, *The Malleus Maleficarum* (*The Hammer of Witches*),

> Vampirism became another form of Satanism and the vampire the instrument of the devil. Also, his victims were tainted by evil.

which noted the three conditions necessary for witchcraft to exist: the devil, a witch, and the permission of God. In like measure, Allatius asserted that for vampires to exist, all that was needed was the devil, a dead body, and the permission of God.

The tying of vampirism to the devil by Allatius and his colleagues brought Satan into the vampire equation. Vampirism became another form of Satanism and the vampire the instrument of the devil. Also, his victims were tainted by evil. Like the demons, vampires were alienated from the things of God. They could not exist in the realms of the sacred and would flee from the effective symbols of the true God, such as the crucifix, or from holy things, such as holy water and the eucharistic wafer, which both Eastern Orthodox and Roman Catholics believed to be the very body of Christ. In like measure, the offices of the church through the priest were an effective means of stopping the vampire. In the Eastern Orthodox Church, the people always invited the priest to participate in their antivampire efforts. In its attempt to counter the superstitious beliefs in vampires, the Eastern Orthodox Church ordered its priests not to participate in such activities, even threatening excommunication.

The Eighteenth-century Vampire Debates: In the seventeenth century, reports, not just of vampires but of vampire epidemics, began to filter out of Eastern Europe, especially Prussia and Poland. These incidents involved cases in which bodies were exhumed and mutilated. The mutilation of the bodies of people buried as Christians and presumably awaiting the resurrection was of utmost and serious concern to Christian intellectuals and church leaders in Western Europe. The majority of these reports came from Roman Catholic–dominated lands, the most important from the area of Serbia which had been taken over by Austria in the wake of a fading Ottoman Empire. The cases of Peter Plogojowitz and Arnold Paole launched a heated debate in the German (both Lutheran and Catholic) universities. In the midst of this debate, Cardinal Schtrattembach, the Roman Catholic bishop of Olmütz, Germany, turned to Rome for some advice on how to handle the vampire reports. The pope, in turn, called upon the learned archbishop of Trani, Italy, Giuseppe Davanzati, who spent five years studying the problem before writing his *Dissertazione sopra i vampiri*, finally published in 1744.

Davanzati was swayed by the more skeptical arguments that had emerged as the consensus in the German debates. He advised the pope that the vampire reports were originating in human fantasies. While these fantasies might possibly be of diabolical origin, pastoral attention should be directed to the person reporting the vampire.

> Even members of the Benedictine Order, of which he was a member, chided him for giving credence to what amounted to nothing more than childrens horror stories.

The bodies of the suspected vampires should be left undisturbed. The church followed Davanzati's wisdom.

Meanwhile, as Davanzati was pursuing his research, so was Dom Augustin Calmet. Calmet, known throughout France as a Bible scholar, published his *Dissertations sur les Apparitions des Anges des Démons et des Esprits, et sur les revenants, et Vampires de Hingrie, de Boheme, de Moravie, et de Silési* (*Treatise on the Apparitions of Spirits and on Vampires or Revenants*) two years after Davanzati. Calmet played devil's advocate to his fellow churchmen. He described in some detail the reports of the Eastern European vampires and called upon theologians and his scholarly colleagues to give them some serious study. He explored various possibilities concerning the accounts and left open the medieval position that the bodies of suspected vampires were animated by the devil and/or evil spirits. His colleagues in the church

did not receive his report favorably. Even members of the Benedictine Order, of which he was a member, chided him for giving credence to what amounted to nothing more than children's horror stories. In the third edition of his book, he finally did away with the devilish option and concluded that vampires did not exist. However, by this time, his earlier editions had spread far and wide and had become the basis for translations. Few noted the final position he had reached. Though his colleagues dismissed him, he found broad popular support, and his book went through several printings in France and was translated and published in Germany and England.

The sign of the future came in 1755 and 1756 when in two actions, Empress Maria Theresa took the authority of handling the vampire cases out of the hands of parish priests and local authorities and placed them in the hands of Austrian government officials. The clear intent of the law was to stop the disturbance of the graves. In the decades following Maria Theresa's action, the spokespersons of what would become known as the Enlightenment would take over the final stages of the debate and essentially end it with their consensus opinion that vampires were unreal. After a generation in which the likes of Diderot and Voltaire expressed their opinion of vampires, scholars have not found it necessary to refute a belief in the vampire. Calmet became an intellectual relic, though he provided a number of interesting stories from which a popular literary vampire could be created.

Dracula and the Church: Interestingly enough, the first vampire stories—from Johann Wolfgang von Goethe's "The Bride of Corinth" to Sheridan Le Fanu's "Carmilla"—were largely secular works. Religious artifacts and religious characters were almost completely absent. At the end of "Carmilla," as Laura's father began his quest to locate and destroy Carmilla, he suggested to Laura that they call upon the local priest. The priest performed certain solemn, but unnamed, rituals that allowed the troubled Laura to sleep in peace. However, he did not accompany the men to finally kill Carmilla, though two medical men were present to oversee the act. It was left to Bram Stoker and his novel *Dracula* (1897) to reintroduce Christianity into the vampire's life. In the very first chapter, as Jonathan Harker made his way to Castle Dracula, a woman took off a rosary, with an attached crucifix, and gave it to him. In spite of his anti-Roman Catholic background, Harker put the rosary around his neck and wore it. Later, an enraged Dracula lunged for Harker's neck but quickly withdrew when he touched the rosary. Abraham Van Helsing, the pious vampire hunter from Holland, explained that the crucifix was one of several sacred objects whose presence deprived the vampire of its power.

Besides the crucifix, Van Helsing used the eucharistic wafer, the bread consecrated as the body of Christ in the church's communion service (in this case, the Roman Catholic mass).

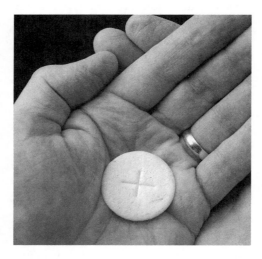

You probably know about using garlic or a crucifix to protect yourself from vampires, but according to Stoker you might also use a eucharist wafer just as well.

He placed the wafers around the openings of the tomb of Lucy Westenra and sanitized (destroyed the effectiveness of) the boxes of native soil Dracula had brought from his homeland. Most importantly, the wafer burned its imprint into the forehead of the tainted Mina Murray after her encounter with Dracula.

In subsequent productions of *Dracula*, the eucharistic wafer largely dropped from the picture. It was used on occasion to sanitize the earth, but only in *Bram Stoker's Dracula* (1992) did the scene of Mina's being branded by the wafer become a part of a dramatic presentation. Instead, it was the crucifix that became the religious symbol most frequently used to cause the vampire to lose its strength or to harm the vampire.

The Vampire and the Church Since Stoker: Through the twentieth century, the crucifix became a standard part of the vampire hunter's kit. Frequently, he would flash it just in time to save himself. On many occasions, heroines were saved from a vampire about to pounce upon them by a shining cross hanging around their neck. At the same time, especially since midcentury, the vampire novel began to show signs of secularization. Some vampires came from outer space or arose as victims of a disease. Such vampires, lacking any negative supernatural origins, were unaffected by the holy objects.

As the century progressed, vampire writers challenged the role of Christianity in the culture. Some expressed their doubts as to its claims to exclusive truth concerning God and the world. Writer Anne Rice, for example, became a skeptic of Roman Catholicism, in which she was raised, very early in her life. Her vampires, reflecting her nonbelief, were unaffected by Christian symbols. They walked in churches with impunity and handled crucifixes with no negative reaction. In like measure, Chelsea Quinn Yarbro's hero, Saint Germain, and other good-guy vampires were not Satanic; quite the opposite, they were moral agents. The vampires in Yarbro's books had no negative reaction to Christian objects or places.

Vampires in science fiction were raised in an alien culture that had never heard of Christianity. They were among the first group of vampires that had no reaction to Christian sacred symbols. The vampires of *The Hunger* by Whitley Strieber and those in Elaine Bergstrom's novels were unaffected by the cross because they were aliens. Bergstrom's vampires, the Austra family, made their living working in cathedrals repairing stained glass. Other writers affected by the religiously pluralistic culture in the West questioned the value of Christian symbols for people raised in or adhering to another faith. For example, they asked if Jewish symbols served as protection from Jewish vampires. In Roman Polanski's *The Fearless Vampire Killers; or, Pardon Me But Your Teeth Are in My Neck*

(1967), one of the more humorous moments came from a Jewish vampire attacking a young girl who tried to protect herself with a cross.

The relation to the sacred in general and Christianity in particular will continue to be a problem for vampire novelists, especially those working in the Christian West. The vampire is a supernatural gothic entity whose popular myth dictated its aversion for the crucifix. The literary vampire derives its popularity from the participation of its readers in a world of fantasy and supernatural power. At the same time, an increasing number of novelists do not have a Christian heritage and thus possess no understanding or appreciation of any power derived from Christian symbols. For the foreseeable future, new vampire fiction will be written out of the pull and tug between these traditional and contemporary perspectives.

🦇 *Vampires through the Centuries* 🦇

Alnwick Castle, the Vampire of

Among the famous case reports of real vampires were those of William of Newburgh, who, in the twelfth century, collected a variety of accounts of vampires in England. One incident that occurred in his lifetime concerned a man who served the Lord of Alnwick Castle. The man, who was himself known for his wicked ways, was further plagued by an unfaithful wife. Having hidden on the roof above his bed to see her actions for himself, he fell to the ground and died the next day.

Following his burial, the man was seen wandering through the town. People became afraid of encountering him and locked themselves in their houses after dark each day. During this time, an epidemic of an unnamed disease broke out, and a number of people died. The sickness was blamed on the "vampire." Finally, on Palm Sunday, the local priest assembled a group of the more devout residents and some of the leading citizens, who proceeded to the cemetery. They uncovered the body, which appeared gorged with blood and gushed forth when it was struck with a spade. Deciding that the body had fed off the blood of its many victims, the residents dragged it out of town and burned it. Soon thereafter, the epidemic ended, and the town returned to normal.

Báthory, Elizabeth (1560–1614)

Elizabeth Báthory, a Slovak countess who lived a generation after Vlad the Impaler, was reputed to have tortured and murdered numerous young women and, in the twentieth century, has been pulled from obscurity to become known as one of the "true" vampires in history. Contemporary scholars have cast doubt on the story told about her, suggesting that she was a

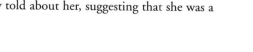

Alnwick Castle in Northumberland, England, is the seat of the 12th Duke of Northumberland. Today, it is a popular tourist attraction, welcoming about 800,000 visitors a year.

victim of political intrigue and the account of her murders as largely fabricated.

Elizabeth was born in 1560, the daughter of George and Anna Báthory. Though frequently cited as Hungarian due in large part to the shifting borders of the Hungarian Empire, she actually lived most of her life in what is now the Slovak Republic. Her adult life was spent largely at Castle Cachtice near the town of Vishine, northeast of present-day Bratislava, where Austria, Hungary, and the Slovak Republic come together. (The castle was mistakenly cited by Raymond T. McNally as being in Transylvania.) Elizabeth grew up in an era when much of Hungary had been overrun by the Turkish forces of the Ottoman Empire and was a battleground between Turkish and Austrian (Hapsburg) armies. The area was also split by religious differences. Her family sided with the new wave of Protestantism that had attempted to reform traditional Roman Catholicism. She was raised on the Báthory family estate at Ecsed in Transylvania.

As a child, she was subject to seizures accompanied by intense rage and uncontrollable behavior. In 1571, her cousin Stephen became the prince of Transylvania and, later in the decade, additionally assumed the throne of Poland. He was one of the most effective rulers of his day, though his plans for uniting Europe against the Turks were somewhat foiled by having to turn his attention toward fighting Russia, whose czar, Ivan the Terrible, desired Stephen's territory.

In 1574, Elizabeth became pregnant as a result of a brief affair with a peasant man. When her condition became evident, she was sequestered until the baby arrived because she was engaged to marry Count Ferenc Nadasdy. The marriage took place in May 1575. Count Nadasdy was a soldier and frequently away from home for long periods. Meanwhile, Elizabeth assumed the duties of managing the affairs at Castle Sarvar, the Nadasdy family estate. It was here that her reputed career of evil is said to have begun with the disciplining of

Elizabeth Báthory is infamously honored in Guinness World Records *as the most murderous woman in history. It is estimated she killed as many as 650—mostly women and girls—and mutilated them horribly.*

the large household staff, particularly the young girls.

According to the story that would be repeated many times, Elizabeth's level of cruelty was noteworthy even in light of the relatively high level of cruel and arbitrary behavior directed by those in power toward those who were servants. It was said that she went out of her way to find excuses to inflict punishments and delighted in the torture and death of her victims far beyond what her contemporaries could accept. She would stick pins in various sensitive body parts, such as under the fingernails. In the winter, she would execute victims by having them stripped, led out into the snow, and doused with water until they were frozen.

Elizabeth's husband was also accused of joining in on some of the sadistic behavior and

actually teaching his wife some new varieties of punishment. For example, he is credited with showing her a summertime version of her freezing exercise: he had a woman stripped, covered with honey, and then left outside to be bitten by numerous insects. Following his death in 1604, Elizabeth moved to Vienna and also began to spend time at her estate at Beckov and at a manor house at Cachtice, both located in the present-day Slovak Republic. These were the scenes of the most famous and vicious acts associated with Elizabeth.

In these years, Elizabeth's main confidant was a woman named Anna Darvulia, about whom little is known. When Darvulia's health failed in 1609, Elizabeth turned to Erzsi Majorova, the widow of a local tenant farmer. Majorova is credited with Elizabeth's eventual downfall by encouraging her to include a few women of noble birth among her victims. Because she was having trouble procuring more young servant girls as rumors of her activities spread through the countryside, Elizabeth followed Majorova's advice. At some point in 1609, Elizabeth was accused of killing a young noblewoman and attempting to cover it by claiming her death to be a suicide.

As early as the summer of 1610, an initial inquiry had begun into Elizabeth's affairs. Underlying the inquiry, quite apart from the steadily increasing number of victims, were political concerns. The crown hoped to confiscate Elizabeth's large landholdings and escape payment of an extensive loan received from her husband. With these things in mind, Elizabeth was arrested on December 29, 1610.

Elizabeth was placed on trial a few days later. It was conducted by Count Thurzo as an agent of the king. As noted, the trial (rightly characterized as a show trial by Elizabeth's biographer, Raymond T. McNally) was initiated to not only obtain a conviction but to also confiscate her lands. A week after the first trial, a second trial was convened on January 7, 1611.

At this trial, a register found in Elizabeth's living quarters was introduced as evidence. It noted the names of 650 victims, all recorded in her handwriting.

The trials included testimonies of both those who witnessed deaths and some who had survived. The latter recounted how they had been pierced, pinched, beaten, and burned, and they identified Elizabeth as their torturer. In the end, the court received evidence of recovered skeletons and cadaver parts, the reports of the witnesses, and a letter from the Hungarian king Matthias II (r. 1608–1619) indicating that he knew of at least 300 victims. They convicted the countess and her coconspirators of only 80 counts of murder, still a hefty number. Her accomplices were sentenced to be executed, the manner determined by their roles in the tortures. Elizabeth was sentenced to life imprisonment in solitary confinement. She was placed in a room in her castle at Cachtice without windows or doors and only a small opening for food and a few slits for air. There she remained for the next three years until her death on August 21, 1614. She was buried in the Báthory land at Ecsed.

> The crown hoped to confiscate Elizabeths large landholdings and escape payment of an extensive loan received from her husband.

At least two basic questions have arisen out of Elizabeth's trial and conviction. The first regards the actual extent of the crimes of which she was accused. She claimed innocence on all counts, a view largely supported by Laszlo Nagy. Writing in the early 1980s, he suggested that she was the victim of a pro-Hapsburg, anti-Protestant conspiracy. However, Nagy is in the minority. Most researchers over the years have suggested that she killed at least 50 to 60 victims, with some accepting the higher numbers of 300, 600, or 650. Contemporary forensic psychologist Katherine Ramsland concluded, "Even disregarding tales gained through torture, the evidence from the many missing girls, testimony from damaged survivors, and the discovery of human remains all serve to underscore the charge of extreme torture and serial murder."

Elizabeth as Vampire: Above and beyond Elizabeth's reputation as a sadistic killer with at least 80 victims, she has also been accused of being both a werewolf and a vampire. During her trials, testimony was presented that on occasion, she bit the flesh of the girls while torturing them. These accusations became the basis of her connection with werewolfism. The connection between Elizabeth and vampirism is somewhat more tenuous. Of course, it was a popular belief in Slavic lands that people who were werewolves in life became vampires in death, but that was not the accusation leveled at Elizabeth. Rather, she was accused of draining the blood of her victims and bathing in it to retain her youthful beauty: she was, by all accounts, a most attractive woman.

No testimony to this activity was offered at her trial, and, in fact, no contemporary testimony proves that she engaged in such a practice. Following her death, the records of the trials were sealed because the revelations of her activities were quite scandalous for the Hungarian ruling community. King Matthias forbade the mention of her name in polite society. It was not until 100 years later that a Jesuit priest, Laszlo Turoczy, located copies of some of the original trial documents and gathered stories circulating among the people of Cachtice, the site of Elizabeth's castle. Turoczy included an account of her life in a book he wrote on Hungarian history. His book initially suggested the possibility that she bathed in blood. Published in the 1720s, it appeared during the wave of vampirism in Eastern Europe that excited the interest of the continent. Later writers would pick up and embellish the story. Two stories illustrate the legends that had gathered around Elizabeth in the absence of the court records of

An 1895 painting by Csók István shows Elizabeth Báthory presiding over a display of depravity and pain in her castle.

her life and the attempts to remove any mention of her from Hungarian history:

It was said that one day, the aging countess was having her hair combed by a young servant girl. The girl accidentally pulled her hair, and Elizabeth turned and slapped the servant. Blood was drawn, and some of it spurted onto Elizabeth's hands. As she rubbed it on her hands, they seemed to take on the girl's youthful appearance. It was from this incident that Elizabeth developed her reputation for desiring the blood of young virgins.

The second story involves Elizabeth's behavior after her husband's death, when it was said that she associated herself with younger men. On one occasion, when she was with one of those men, she saw an old woman. She remarked, "What would you do if you had to kiss that old hag?" He responded with expected words of distaste. The old woman, however, on hearing the exchange, accused Elizabeth of excessive vanity and noted that such an aged appearance was inescapable, even for the countess. Several historians have tied the death of Elizabeth's husband and this story into the hypothesized concern with her own aging and, thus, the bathing in blood.

Elizabeth has not been accused of being a traditional blood-drinking or bloodsucking vampire, though her attempts to take and use the blood to make herself more youthful would certainly qualify her as at least a metaphorical vampire. Previously a little-known historical figure, she was rediscovered, and the worst stories about her spread with the sharp rise in interest in vampires during the 1970s; since that time, she has regularly been tied to vampirism in popular culture.

Noticeable interest in Elizabeth was evident in the publication of a series of books in

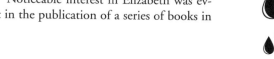

the early 1970s beginning with Valentine Penrose's *Erzsebet Báthory, La Comtesse Sanglante*, a 1962 French volume whose English translation, *The Bloody Countess*, was published in 1970. Elizabeth was also mentioned in later books: Donald Glut's *True Vampires of History* (1971) and Gabriel Ronay's *The Truth about Dracula* (1972). Penrose's book inspired the first of the Elizabeth films; the movie, in turn, inspired a novel based on its screenplay, *Countess Dracula* by Michael Parry. The celebration of the mythical countess in the 1970s motivated Dracula scholar Raymond McNally (1931–2002) to produce by far the most authoritative book on Elizabeth through the late twentieth century, *Dracula Was a Woman: In Search of the Blood Countess of Transylvania*, which appeared in 1984. Based on a new search through the original court documents and a broad understanding of Eastern European history and folklore, McNally thoroughly demythologized the legend and explained many of the problems that had baffled previous researchers.

Elizabeth on Film: The first movie inspired by the stories connecting Elizabeth to vampires was the now largely forgotten *I Vampiri* (released in the United States as *The Devil's Commandment*), notable today because of the work of future director Mario Bava as the film's cameraman. A decade later, as part of its vampire cycle, Hammer Films released what is possibly the best of the several movies based on Elizabeth's life, *Countess Dracula* (1971). Ingrid Pitt starred in the title role. The film was built around the mythical bloodbaths and portrayed her as going increasingly crazy as she continued her murderous career. *Daughters of Darkness* (1971), one of the most artistic of all vampire films, brought the countess into the twentieth century in a tale with strong lesbian overtones. In the movie, Elizabeth and her companion, Ilona, check into an almost empty hotel, where they meet a newlywed couple. When it is revealed that the husband has a violent streak, the stage is set for Elizabeth and Ilona to move in and "help" the new bride. A series of vampiric

Actress Ingrid Pitt portrayed Báthory in the 1970 Hammer film, Countess Dracula.

encounters ensues, and in the end, the wife (the newest vampire) emerges as the only survivor. Jesús Franco's 1973 erotic film *Báthory, Las avaleuses* is remembered more for its challenge to censorship standards of the day and appeared in a variety of cuts under almost a dozen different names, such as *The Bare Breasted Countess, Female Vampire, Jacula, La comtesse noire,* and *The Loves of Irina.*

Elizabeth (or a character modeled on her) also appeared in *Legend of Blood Castle* (1972), *Curse of the Devil* (1973), *Immoral Tales* (1974), and *Mama Dracula* (1979), all films of lesser note. In 1981, a full-length animated version of Elizabeth's story was released in Czechoslovakia. Additional films featuring the countess include *Thirst* (1979), *The Mysterious Death of Nina Chereau* (1987), *Vampire Ecstasy* (1999), *Mistress of Seduction* (2000), *Metamorphosis* (2004), *Tomb of the Werewolf* (2004), *Night Fangs* (2005), *Stay Alive* (2006), *Demon's Claw* (2006), and *Blood Countess* (2008). They were joined by Don Glut's film trilogy in which a contemporary Elizabeth (now assuming the title Countess Dracula as the widow of the infamous Transylvanian count) goes in search of a formula that will allow her to walk in the daylight without harm: *The Erotic Rites of Countess Dracula* (2003), *Countess Dracula's Orgy of Blood* (2004), and *Blood Scarab* (2008).

The most recent efforts to bring the countess to the screen have been *Báthory: Countess of Blood* (2008); *The Countess* (2009); the comedic *Chastity Bites* (2013); *Elizabeth Báthory* (2014); and *The Blood Queen* (2015). She has, of course, made a variety of appearances in various television shows as a guest villain.

Elizabeth and Dracula: Bram Stoker, the author of *Dracula* (1897), possibly read about Elizabeth in *The Book of Werewolves* by Sabine Baring-Gould (1865), where the first lengthy, English-language account of Elizabeth's life appeared. In his book on Elizabeth, Raymond McNally suggests that the description of Elizabeth might have influenced Stoker to shift the site of his novel from Austria (Styria), where he initially seemed to have set it, to Transylvania. In like measure, McNally noted that Dracula became younger and younger as the novel proceeded, an obvious allusion to the stories of Elizabeth bathing in blood to retain her youth. He made a strong case that the legends about her "played a major role in the creation of the character of Count Dracula in the midst of Bram Stoker." In her survey of problems in Dracula research, however, Elizabeth Miller calls McNally's suggestion into question. She argues that the real connection between Elizabeth and Dracula do not go back to Baring-Gould or Stoker but rather are of more recent origin, namely Donald Glut's *True Vampires of History* (1971) and Gabriel Ronay's *The Dracula Myth* (1972). Miller bases her case primarily her study of Stoker's notes for *Dracula*, in which Elizabeth is not mentioned anywhere. More recently, in the annotated edition of the notes, she added that "there is no proof that her story

influenced the creation of Dracula" (Eighteen-Bisang & Miller 2008).

Croglin Grange, the Vampire of

Among frequently cited incidents involving "real" vampirism, the story of the Vampire of Croglin Grange, an old house located in Cumberland, England, has proved very intriguing. An account of the vampire originally appeared in *The Story of My Life* by August Hare, written in the last years of the 1890s. According to Hare, the various episodes occurred around 1875 to 1876. Owned at the time by a family named Fisher, the house was rented to a woman and her two brothers: Amelia, Edward, and Michael Cranswell. During one summer, the district experienced a hot spell, so when the three retired for the night, the woman slept near the window. She shut the window but did not close the shutters. Unable to go to sleep, she spotted something approaching that eventually reached the window and began to scratch and then pick at it, removing a pane. A creature then reached in and unlocked the window. The terrified woman, frozen in fear, waited as a brown face with flaming eyes came to her, grabbed her, and bit her throat.

She screamed, and when her brothers rushed to her rescue, the creature hurriedly left. One brother tended to his sister and the other pursued the creature, which disappeared over a wall by a nearby church. The doctor who later treated the woman suggested a change of scenery, and the brothers took her to Switzerland for an extended visit. The three eventually returned to Croglin Grange. The following spring, the creature appeared again. One brother chased it, shot it in the leg, and traced it to a vault in the local cemetery. The next day, accompanied by some townspeople,

> The terrified woman, frozen in fear, waited as a brown face with flaming eyes came to her, grabbed her, and bit her throat.

the brothers entered the vault, which was in complete disarray except for one coffin. When they opened the coffin, they found a body with a fresh gunshot wound in the leg. A bullet was extracted, and they burned the corpse.

In 1924, Charles G. Harper, basing his assertions on a visit to the area, challenged the Hare book. Harper could find no place named Croglin Grange. Though he found two other buildings, Croglin High Hall and Croglin Low Hall, neither fit the description of Croglin Grange. He found no church, the closest one being over a mile away, and no vault corresponding to the description of the one opened by the brothers and their neighbors. Harper's own account was challenged at a later date, when F. Clive-Ross visited the area. In interviews with the local residents, he determined that Croglin Low Hall was the house referred to in Hare's story and that a chapel had existed near it for many years, its foundation stones still visible into the 1930s. Clive-Ross seemed to have answered all of Harper's objections.

The Croglin Grange story continued when, in 1968, psychic researcher Scott Rogo offered a new challenge. He noted the likeness of the story of the Vampire at Croglin Grange to the first chapter of *Varney the Vampyre*, the popular vampire story originally published in 1847. The accounts, both of which were published in 1929 by Montague Summers, are very similar, and it is likely that one is based on the other, according to Rogo. He suggested that the entire Croglin Grange story could be dismissed as a simple hoax.

A final footnote to the controversy: Clive-Ross later discussed the case again with residents of the area and was told that a significant mistake was found in Hare's original account: The story took place not in the 1870s but in the 1680s, almost two centuries earlier. While this fact would definitely place the events prior to the publication of *Varney*

the Vampyre, it also pushes the story far enough into the past as to turn it into an unverifiable legend.

The Highgate Vampire

One of the more interesting interludes in vampire history concerns events that took place at a cemetery in the Highgate section of London in the years 1967–1983. The cemetery, officially called the Cemetery of St. James, was consecrated by the bishop of London in 1839, four days before Queen Victoria's 20th birthday. It gained some association through its slightly disguised use by Bram Stoker as the burial place of Lucy Westenra after her death (as a result of Dracula's attacks). The modern story of vampires at Highgate began with reports of a phantomlike entity seen in the cemetery in the evenings. While rumors of a ghost circulated, occultist and head of the Vampire Research Society Sean Manchester received the account of schoolgirl Elizabeth Wojdyla and her friend, who claimed to have seen some graves open and the dead rise from them. Wojdyla also reported having nightmares in which something evil tried to come into her bedroom. Over several years, Manchester collected similar accounts of unusual sightings associated with the cemetery. In 1969, Wojdyla's nightmares returned, except now, the malevolent figure actually came into her room. She had developed the symptoms of pernicious anemia, and on her neck were two small wounds suggestive of a classic vampire's bite. Manchester and Wojdyla's boyfriend treated her as a victim of vampirism and filled her room with garlic, crucifixes, and holy water. She soon improved. Meanwhile, various people continued to add new reports of seeing a ghostly being in the cemetery.

Because they were of a common sort, no one probably would have heard of the Highgate reports had not signs been found

Highgate Cemetery on the north end of London is actually quite lush and beautiful. It is a national historic site as well as a nature preserve.

that the cemetery and a nearby park were being used for rituals that involved the killing of animals. Some of the dead animals had been drained of blood, and the local newspaper asked in its headline, "Does a Wampyr Walk in Highgate?" Manchester then reported that he had been contacted by another woman who had the same symptoms as Wojdyla. The young woman, followed while sleepwalking, led Manchester to a cluster of burial vaults in the cemetery. Manchester told the press that he believed a genuine vampire existed at Highgate and should be dealt with accordingly. The newspaper story and a subsequent feature spot on the independent Thames TV led to the cemetery becoming a gathering point of the curious. A group of amateur filmmakers used it as the site for a film, *Vampires by Night*. On Friday, March 13, 1970, before an assembled crowd of on-

lookers, Manchester and two cohorts entered the vault, where three empty coffins were found. They lined the coffins with garlic, and in each, they placed a cross. The vaults were sprinkled with salt (used for exorcisms) and holy water.

Events turned nasty in August, when the body of a young woman was found at the cemetery. It appeared that someone had treated the corpse as a vampire and had decapitated and tried to burn it. An enraged citizenry demanded that the authorities protect the bodies of loved ones from abuse. Before the month was out, the police arrested two men who claimed to be vampire hunters. The men were a factor in the souring relationship between Manchester and the police, but while the police were distracted by the amateur vampire hunters, Manchester had quietly entered another vault and discovered what he believed was a real vampire. Rather than mutilating the body (a crime in England), he read an exorcism and sealed the vault with cement permeated with pieces of garlic.

In the summer of 1970, David Farrant, another amateur vampire hunter, entered the field. He claimed to have seen the vampire and went hunting for it with a stake and crucifix but was arrested. He later became a convert to a form of Satanism. He was later convicted on two charges of breaking into tombs at Highgate. In 1978, he denounced the vampire as a hoax he had created by himself in 1970. Manchester quickly responded, noting that the reports originated prior to Farrant's involvement and that he was not privy to the incidents that had made the Highgate Vampire so newsworthy.

Meanwhile, in 1977, Manchester began an investigation of a mansion near Highgate Cemetery that had a reputation of being haunted. On several occasions, Manchester and his associates entered the house. In the basement, they found a coffin, which they dragged into the backyard. Opening the casket, Manchester saw the same vampire he had seen seven years before in Highgate Cemetery. This time, he conducted an exorcism by staking the body, which disintegrated into a slimy, foul-smelling substance, and burned the coffin. He had destroyed the Highgate Vampire. Soon after this incident, the mansion was demolished, and an apartment house was erected in its place.

The consequences from the Highgate Vampire did not end with its death, however. In 1980, reports of dead animals found drained of blood began to appear in Finchley. Manchester believed that a vampire created by the bite of the Highgate Vampire was the cause. He contacted many of the people he had met in 1970 and eventually targeted a woman he called Lusia as the culprit. He discovered that Lusia had died and was buried in the Great Northern London Cemetery, and he had dreams in which she came to him. One autumn evening in 1982, Manchester entered the cemetery. There, he encountered a large, spiderlike creature about the size of a cat. He drove a stake through it. As dawn approached, it metamorphosed into Lusia; she had only now truly died. He returned her remains to the grave, thus ending the case of the Highgate Vampire. Manchester wrote an account of his perspective in *The Highgate Vampire* (1985; revised 1991), which he expanded in *The Vampire Hunter's Handbook* (1997); the Vampire Research Society offers a cassette tape concerning the incident. Meanwhile, David Farrant founded the Highgate Vampire Society (http://www.davidfarrant.org) and continues to present his side of the story in a series of booklets and through the website.

A memorial of Karl Marx stands in the Eastern Cemetery of Highgate, London.

Paole (Paul), Arnold

Arnold Paole (or Paul) was the subject of one of the most famous eighteenth-century vampire cases. In the late seventeenth century and into the eighteenth century, a spate of attacks in Central Europe were attributed to vampires. These cases in general, and the Paole case in particular, were one of the causes of a revival of interest in vampires in England and France in the early nineteenth century.

Paole's birthdate is unknown, but it seems he was born in the early 1700s in Medvegia, north of Belgrade, in an area of Serbia that was at that time part of the Austrian Empire. He later served in the army in what was "Turkish Serbia" and then returned home in the spring of 1727. Paole purchased several acres of land and settled down to farming. Soon afterward, he became engaged to a young woman from a neighboring farm. Although he was considered a good-natured and honest person, some of the townspeople noted that he sometimes tended to be gloomy.

Paole told his fiancée that his problem stemmed from his war days. While he was in service in Turkish Serbia, he said, he had been visited and attacked by a vampire. According to Paole, he killed the vampire after following it to its grave, ate some of the dirt from the vampire's tomb, and bathed his wounds in the blood of the vampire to cleanse himself of the effects of the attack. However, he was fearful of having been tainted by the attack. A week later, Paole died as the result of a fatal accident. He was buried immediately.

However, three weeks after his burial, people reported that Paole had appeared around town. After four people who made reports died, the community panicked. Community leaders felt it was best to disinter the body to determine if Paole was a vampire. So, 40 days after Paole was buried, the grave was opened. Two military surgeons were present. The lid was removed from the coffin, and the witnesses found a body that appeared as if it had just recently died. What was apparently new skin was evident under a layer of dead skin, and the nails had continued to grow. They pierced the body, and blood flowed out of the corpse. It was determined by those present that Paole was indeed a vampire. To destroy the vampire, they drove a stake into his body, and he was heard to utter a loud groan. His head was severed, and his body was burned. Although the case could have ended there, it did not. The four other people who had died were treated the same way in case they were also vampires.

Three years later, in 1731, in the same area, some 17 people died of the symptoms of vampirism in a matter of three months. No action was taken until one victim, a young girl, claimed that a man named Milo, who had recently died, had attacked her in the middle of the night. Word of this second wave of vampirism reached Vienna, and the Austrian emperor ordered an inquiry to be conducted by Regimental Field Surgeon Johannes Fluckinger. Subsequently, Fluckinger traveled to Medvegia to gather accounts of what had occurred. When Milo's body was disinterred, it had the same characteristics as that of Arnold Paole. Milo's body was then staked and burned. An inquiry into the reason that the vampirism that had been eradicated in 1727 had returned led to the determination that Paole had vampirized several cows that the recently dead had fed on. Under Fluckinger's orders, the townspeople dug up the bodies of all who had died in recent months. It was found that, of the 40 bodies that were disinterred, 17 were in the same preserved state. They were all staked and burned.

Fluckinger wrote a full report of his activities and presented it to the emperor early in

> They pierced the body, and blood flowed out of the corpse. It was determined by those present that Paole was indeed a vampire.

1732. His report was soon published and became a best seller. As early as March 1732, accounts of Paole and the Medvegia vampires were circulated in the periodicals of France and England. Because the case was so well documented and became the focus of many studies and reflections about vampires, Arnold Paole became the most famous "vampire" of the era. It is also noteworthy that the Paole case was instrumental in shaping the conclusions reached by both Dom Augustin Calmet and Giuseppe Davanzati, two Roman Catholic scholars who prepared books on vampirism in the middle of the century.

Plogojowitz, Peter

One of the more famous historical vampires, Peter Plogojowitz (also spelled Petar Blagojevi c lived in Kisolova, a small village in Austrian-occupied Serbia, an area officially incorporated into the province of Hungary. The town of Kisolova was not far from Medvegia, the home of Arnold Paole, another famous "vampire," whose case occurred at the same time.

Plogojowitz died in September 1728 at the age of 62, but three days later in the middle of the night, he returned to his home and asked his son for food, then left. Two evenings later, he reappeared and again asked for food. When the son refused, he was found dead the next day. At roughly the same time, several villagers became ill with exhaustion, diagnosed with an excessive loss of blood. They claimed that they had been visited by Plogojowitz in a dream and that he bit them on the neck and sucked their blood. All in all, nine persons mysteriously died of this strange illness during the following week.

When the chief magistrate sent a report of the deaths to the commander of the Imperial forces, the commander responded with a visit to the village. He demanded that the graves of all the recently dead be opened. Astonishingly, they found that the body of Plogojowitz looked less like a corpse and more like a man in a trance, breathing very gently. His eyes were open, his flesh was plump, and his complexion was ruddy. His hair and nails appeared to have grown since his burial, and fresh skin was found just below his scarf. Most importantly, his mouth was smeared with fresh blood.

> Astonishingly, they found that the body of Plogojowitz looked less like a corpse and more like a man in a trance, breathing very gently.

The commander quickly concluded that Plogojowitz was a vampire. The executioner who came to Kisolova with the commander drove a stake through his body. When he did, blood gushed from the wound and from the orifices of the body. The body was then burned. None of the other bodies manifested signs of vampirism, but to protect them and the other villagers, garlic and whitethorn were placed in their graves, and their bodies were returned to the ground.

The story was reported by the Marquis d'Argens in his *Lettres Juives*, which was quickly translated into an English version in 1729. Even though his story was not as well known as the incidents that began with Arnold Paole, the Plogojowitz case was a major element in the European vampire controversy of the 1730s.

Vlad Dracul (1390?–1447)

Vlad Dracul was the father of Vlad the Impaler (1431–1476), the person who has been identified as the historical Dracula. He was the illegitimate son of Prince Mircea, the ruler of Wallachia, that area of present-day Romania south of the Carpathian Mountains. His mother might have been Princess Mara of the Tomaj family of Hungary. He possibly spent a period of his youth at the court of Sigismund I of Luxembourg, the king of Hungary, as a token of faithfulness of Mircea's alliance with Sigismund. Thus, Vlad might have grown up in Buda and in locations in Germany. He married and had a son, also named Mircea. In 1430, Vlad appeared in Transylvania as an official in charge of securing the Transylvanian border with Wallachia. He resided in Sighisoara, where toward the end of the year, his second son, Vlad (later called Vlad Tepes or Vlad the Impaler), was born. Shortly after the child's birth, it became known that Sigismund had selected Vlad as his candidate to rule Wallachia. Vlad was invited to Nüremberg to be invested by the Order of the Dragon (Sigismund had founded the order in 1418), which among its several key goals was an agreement to oppose Islam. Though he now bore the title of prince of Wallachia, he was unable to secure his throne. He eventually created a powerful alliance by marrying Eupraxia, the sister of the ruler of Moldavia, as a second wife. Then, in 1436, he was finally able to secure the Wallachian throne, and in the winter of 1436–1437, he moved to Tirgoviste, the Wallachian capital. During the years of his rule, he had three additional children: Radu, a second son also named Vlad (commonly referred to as Vlad the Monk), and another son named Mircea.

In 1437, following the death of Sigismund, the insecure Vlad Dracul signed an alliance with the Turks. Adhering to his agreement, in March 1442, he allowed Mezid Bey to pass through Wallachia and attack Transylvania. However, the Hungarians defeated the Turkish army and subsequently pursued Mezid Bey back through Wallachia. In the process, the Hungarians drove Vlad Dracul from the throne. He sought refuge among the Turks, with whose help he regained the throne the following year. To secure the new relationship, Vlad Dracul left two sons, Vlad and Radu, in Turkish hands. Then in 1444, Hungary moved against the Turks. Vlad Dracul, attempting to keep his pledge to the sultan but also aware of his obligations to the Christian community, sent a small contingent to assist the Hungarian forces. The Christian alliance met with a resounding defeat, which Vlad Dracul and his son Mircea blamed on John Hunyadi, the governor of Hungary. In 1447, Hunyadi led a war against Vlad Dracul. The decisive battle was fought near Tirgoviste, and as a result, Vlad was killed and Mircea captured by the Romanian boyars (the ruling elite) and tortured and killed. The year after Vlad Dracul's death, his son Vlad Dracula ("son of Dracul") attempted to assume his throne. He was unable to do so until 1456. Soon after becoming the prince of Wallachia, he avenged the death of his father and brother.

Also known as Vlad II and Vlad the Dragon, because he was a member of the chilvaric Order of the Dragon, Vlad Dracul ruled over Wallachia from 1436 to 1447.

Vlad the Impaler (1431–1476)

Vlad the Impaler, an obscure historical figure who during his life had little to nothing

Vlad III was the second son of Vlad Dracul and ruled Wallachia (in what is now Romania). He was called Vlad the Impaler because of his penchant for impaling his conquered enemies on pikes for public display.

to do with vampires, was lifted from obscurity and forever identified with vampire lore when Bram Stoker named the title character of his novel *Dracula* (1897) after him. The origin of the name Dracula was highlighted by two scholars, Raymond McNally and Radu Florescu, in their 1972 book *In Search of Dracula*, which ignited modern Dracula and vampire studies, set off a heated debate on the role of Vlad in the creation of *Dracula*, and injected Vlad the Impaler into popular culture.

In chapter 18 of *Dracula*, Stoker indicated his knowledge of Vlad through the words of Dr. Abraham Van Helsing:

> He (Dracula) must, indeed, have been that Voivode Dracula who won his name against the Turk, over the great rivers on the very frontier of Turkey-land. If that be so, then was he no common

man; for in that time, and for centuries after, he was spoken of as the cleverest and most cunning, as well as the bravest of the sons of the "land beyond the forest." That mighty brain and that iron resolution went with him to the grave, and are even now arrayed against us. The Draculas were, says Arminius, a great and noble race, though now and again were scions who were held by their coevals to have had dealings with the Evil One. They learned his secrets in the Scholomance, amongst the mountains over Lake Hermanstadt, where the devil claims the tenth scholar as his due. In the records are such words as "Stregoica"—witch; "ordog" and "pokol"—Satan and hell; and in one manuscript this very Dracula is spoken of as "wampyr," which we all understand too well.

Here, Stoker combined possible references to (1) the historical Vlad, (2) a folklore tradition that saw vampirism as rooted in Satan's actions, and (3) the modern term "vampire."

Recent interest in *Dracula* produced among a few researchers a desire to know more about the historical figure behind the fictional character. The important breakthrough came in 1972 with the publication of *In Search of Dracula*, the initial findings of historians Raymond T. McNally and Radu Florescu, who gathered the basic contemporary documents concerning the Romanian prince Vlad and visited Vlad's former territory to investigate his career. The following year, the even more definitive *Dracula: A Biography of Vlad the Impaler, 1431–1476*, also by McNally and Florescu, appeared. Even though earlier material had mentioned the connection between Vlad and Dracula, these books made the career of this obscure Romanian ruler, who actually exercised authority for only a relatively short period of time, an integral part of the modern Dracula myth.

The name Dracula was applied to Vlad during his lifetime. It was derived from "dracul," a Romanian word that can be interpreted variously as "devil" or "dragon." Vlad's father had joined the Order of the Dragon, a Christian brotherhood dedicated to fighting the Turks, in 1431, shortly after Vlad's birth. The oath of the order required, among other things, wearing the order's insignia at all times. The name Dracula means "son of Dracul" or "son of the dragon/devil." The actual birth date of Vlad, later called Vlad the Impaler, is unknown, but it was probably late in the year 1430. He was born in Schassburg (aka Sighisoara), a town in Transylvania.

Sighisoara was the birthplace of Vlad the Impaler, the historical Dracula. Sighisoara is a small town in south-central Transylvania. A former Roman town, it was settled by the Germans in 1150 C.E. Burned down by the Tartars in 1241, it emerged in the fifteenth century as one of the strongest fortified centers of Hungarian rule. In 1430, Vlad Dracul was sent there as commander of the guard, and Vlad the Impaler was born (probably in 1430 or 1431) in the home in which Vlad Dracul resided. The family lived in the house until 1436, when Vlad Dracul became the prince of Wallachia and moved to Tirgoviste. That home survived the vicissitudes of time, and in 1976, it was designated a part of the Romanian national heritage. The restoration that followed uncovered frescoes decorating the walls—one of which is believed to picture Dracula.

Soon after his birth, in February 1431, his father, also named Vlad (Vlad Dracul), traveled to Nüremberg, Germany, where he was invested with the insignia of the Order of the Dragon. The accompanying oath dedicated the family to the fight against the Turks, who had begun an attack upon Europe that would eventually carry them to the very gates of Vienna.

Vlad was a claimant to the throne of Wallachia, which was part of contemporary Romania south of the Transylvanian Alps. He was able to wrest the throne from his half-brother in 1436.

Two years later, Vlad Dracul entered an alliance with the Turks that called for sending two sons, Mircea and Vlad, with the sultan on a raid into Transylvania. Doubting Vlad Dracul's loyalty, the sultan had him brought before him and imprisoned. Dracul nevertheless reaffirmed his loyalty and had Vlad (Dracul had two sons named Vlad, born to different mothers) and Radu, his younger sons, remain with the sultan to guarantee their pact. They were placed under house arrest at Egrigoz. The period of imprisonment deeply affected Vlad. On one hand, he took the opportunity of his confinement to learn the Turkish language and customs, but his treatment ingrained the cynicism so evident in his approach to life and infused in him a Machiavellian attitude toward political

This bust of Vlad the Impaler is by an unknown artist. It is maintained at the Vienna Historical Museum in Austria.

matters. His early experiences also seem to have set within his personality the desire to seek revenge from anyone who wronged him.

In December 1447, his father was murdered and his older brother burned alive under the orders of Hungarian governor John Hunyadi (aka Ioande Hunedoara) with the assistance of the boyars, the ruling elite families of Wallachia. The death of Mircea made Vlad the successor, but with Hunyadi's backing, Vladislav II, a member of another branch of the family, assumed the Wallachian throne. Vlad tried to claim the throne in 1448, but his reign lasted only a couple of months before he was forced to flee to the neighboring kingdom of Moldavia. In 1451, while he was at Suceava, the Moldavian capital, the ruler was assassinated. For whatever reasons, Vlad then went to Transylvania and placed himself at the mercy of Hunyadi, the very person who had ordered his father's assassination. The alliance between Hunyadi and Vlad may have been made possible by Vladislav II's adoption of a pro-Turkish policy, which alienated Hunyadi. Vlad fought beside Hunyadi, who in the end acknowledged Vlad's claim to the Wallachian throne. Hunyadi died of the plague at Belgrade on August 11, 1456. Immediately after that event, Vlad left Transylvania for Wallachia. He defeated Vladislav II and on August 20 caught up with the fleeing prince and killed him. Vlad then began the six-year reign during which his reputation was established. In September, he took both a formal oath to Hungarian king Ladislaus V and, a few days later, an oath of vassalage to the Turkish sultan.

Early in his reign, probably in the spring of 1459, Vlad committed his first major act of revenge. On Easter Sunday, after a day of feasting, he arrested the boyar families, whom he held responsible for the death of his father and brother. The older ones he simply impaled out-side the palace and city walls. He forced the rest to march from the capital city of Tirgoviste to the town of Poenari, where over the summer, in the most humiliating of circumstances, they were forced to build his new outpost overlooking the Arges River. This chateau would later be identified as Castle Dracula. Vlad's actions in destroying the power of the boyars was part of his policy of creating a modern, centralized state in what is today Romania. He turned over the estates and positions of the deceased boyars to people who owed their loyalty only to him.

> Vlads brutal manner of terrorizing his enemies and the seemingly arbitrary manner in which he had people punished earned him the nickname "Tepes" or "the Impaler"....

Vlad's brutal manner of terrorizing his enemies and the seemingly arbitrary manner in which he had people punished earned him the nickname "Tepes" or "the Impaler," the common appellation by which he is known today. He not only used the stake against the boyars, whom he was trying to bring into subservience, he also terrorized the churches, both the Eastern Orthodox and the Roman Catholic, each of which had strength in his territory. He paid particular attention to the Roman Catholic monastic centers, which he saw as points of unwelcome foreign influence. His "Romania for the Romanians" policies also led to actions against foreign merchants, especially the Germans, whom he saw as preventing the development of Romanian industry. Vlad the Impaler used his position to enforce his personal moral code of honesty and sexual morality, and various stories have survived of his killing people who offended his sense of moral value. He also would, on occasion, retaliate against an entire village because of the actions of one resident.

Vlad also used terrorist tactics against his foreign enemies. When he thought that merchants (mostly of German origin) from Transylvania had ignored his trade laws, he led raids across the border in 1457 and again in 1459 and 1460 and used impalement to impose his

Vlad Tepes built this palace in Bucharest, the city in Romania that he also constructed and heavily fortified in the mid-fifteenth century.

will. During the latter incursion, he looted the Church of Saint Bartholemew, burned a section of Brasov, and impaled numerous people. That raid was later pictured in anti-Dracula prints showing him dining among the impaled bodies. During his reign, Vlad moved to the village of Bucharest and built it into an important fortified city with strong outer walls. Seeing the mountains as protective bulwarks, Vlad built his castle in the foothills of the Transylvanian Alps. Later, feeling more secure and wishing to take control of the potentially wealthy plains to the south, he built up Bucharest.

Vlad was denounced by his contemporaries, and those in the next several generations who wrote about him published numerous tales of his cruelty. He was noted for the number of victims, conservatively set at 40,000, in his brief, six-year reign. He thus became responsible for the largest number of deaths by a single ruler until modern times. Ivan the Terrible (1530–1584), with whom he has been frequently compared, put fewer than 10,000 to death. Furthermore, Vlad the Impaler ruled over fewer than half a million people. Above and beyond the number who died as a result of his policies, as McNally and Florescu noted, Vlad refined the use of methods of torture and death to a degree that shocked his contemporaries. He not only impaled people in various ways but also often executed his victims in a manner related to the crime for which they were being punished.

The beginning of the end of his brief reign can be traced to the last months of 1461. For reasons not altogether clear, Vlad launched a campaign to drive the Turks from the Danube River Valley south and east of Bucharest. In spite of his early successes, when the Turks finally mounted a response, Vlad found himself without allies and was forced to retreat in the face of overwhelming numbers. The Turkish assault was slowed on two occasions. First, on June 17, several hours after sunset, Dracula attacked the Turkish camp in an attempt to capture the sultan. Unfortunately, he was directed to the wrong tent, and while many Turks were slain in the attack, the sultan got away. Unable to follow up on his momentary victory, Vlad was soon on the retreat again. When the sultan reached the capital city of Târgoviște, he found that Dracula had impaled several people outside the town, a fact that impressed the sultan and gave him pause to consider his course of action. He decided to return to Adrianople (now Edirne) and left the next phase of the battle to Vlad's younger brother Radu, now the Turkish favorite for the Wallachian throne. Radu, at the head of a Turkish army and joined by Vlad's Romanian detractors, pursued him to his castle on the Arges River. At "Castle Dracula," he was faced with overwhelming odds, his army having melted away. He chose to survive by escaping through a secret tunnel and then over the Carpathians into Transylvania. His wife (or mistress), according to local legend, committed suicide before the Turks overran the castle. In Transylvania, he presented himself to the new king of Hungary, Matthias Corvinus, who arrested him. At this time, the first publications of stories of Vlad's cruelties were circulating through Europe.

Vlad was imprisoned at the Hungarian capital at Visegrád, although it seems he lived under somewhat comfortable conditions after 1466. By 1475, events had shifted to the point that he emerged as the best candidate to retake the Wallachian throne. In the summer of 1475, he was again recognized as the prince of Wallachia. Soon thereafter, he moved with an army to fight in Serbia, and upon his return, he took up the battle against the Turks with the king of Moldavia. He was never secure on his throne. Many Wallachians allied themselves with the Turks against him. His end came at the hand of an assassin at some point toward the end of December 1476 or early January 1477. The actual location of Vlad's burial site is unknown, but a likely spot is the church at the Snagov Monastery, an isolated rural monastery built on an island, though modern excavations there have found little. A tomb near the altar thought by many to be Vlad's resting place was empty when opened in the early 1930s. A second tomb near the door, however, contained a body richly garbed and buried with a crown.

Knowledge of the historical Dracula has had a marked influence on both Dracula movies and fiction. Two of the more important Dracula movies, *Dracula* (1974), starring Jack Palance, and *Bram Stoker's Dracula*, the 1992 production directed by Francis Ford Coppola, attempted to integrate the historical research on Vlad the Impaler into the story and used it as a rationale to make Dracula's actions more comprehensible.

Several movies have been made about Vlad from semidocumentaries to historical drama. Christopher Lee portrayed Vlad in the 1974 Swedish documentary *Vem var Dracula?*, released in the English-speaking world as *In Search of Dracula*, not to be confused with two more re-

Chindia Tower (Turnul Chiniei) was built by Vlad the Impaler, known as Dracula, in Târgoviște, România.

cent American productions: *In Search of Dracula* with Jonathan Ross (1996) and *In Search of History: The Real Dracula* (2000). They have been joined by *The Impaler: A Biographical/Historical Look at the Life of Vlad the Impaler, Widely Known as Dracula* (2002); *Vlad the Impaler: The True Story of Dracula* (2002); *Dracula: The True Story* (2007); and *Vlad the Impaler* (2020).

Even as Vlad's fame has risen, Dracula scholars have begun to downplay the role of Vlad in informing Stoker while writing his novel. It appears that he knew little more than that Vlad existed and his name/title, which was put on the novel after it was completed. Scholars were especially scornful of the 2000 biographical drama *Dark Prince: The True Story of Dracula* (2000) not so much for the acting but for the script's departure from the facts of Vlad's life. The 2003 film simply titled *Vlad* was, of course, intended as nothing more than a fictional tale that included the historical Vlad as a character.

STUDYING THE VAMPIRE

Scholarly Perspectives on the Vampire

Scholarly attention to the vampire originated early in the eighteenth century, when German scholars spent a decade considering the relevance of stories of vampire attacks that had sprung up in various locations around the continent. They essentially arrived at a negative conclusion, a conclusion given reappraisal by French biblical scholar Dom Augustin Calmet (1672–1757), who gave serious consideration to the existence of vampires before, in the end, he also arrived at an essentially skeptical conclusion. In the meantime, a variety of European intellectuals from Voltaire to Karl Marx dismissed any direct reference to real vampires by directing attention from mythical beings to power and exploitive groups in society; the vampire was transformed into a metaphor for autocratic rulers, dictatorial governments, owners of corporations, and anyone in entrenched authority who would exploit a segment of the population under its control.

Vampires began to make a comeback in the later nineteenth century as psychology

began to emerge as a separate academic and professional discipline. Psychologists found a place for a vampire disease and launched a search for natural explanations of vampire stories under the general assumption that the stories were real, but the observed phenomenon popularly attributed to vampirism was, in fact, due to heretofore-unacknowledged natural causes, be it psychological conditions, ill-defined disease, or psychoactive drugs.

Psychological perspectives would dominate academic discussions of vampires until the 1970s. By this time, vampires—and Dracula in particular—had become a topic of discourse in the popular culture, and the novel *Dracula* also gained a following among literary scholars. Then, in 1972, several books by scholars—*In Search of Dracula* by Raymond T. McNally and Radu Florescu and *A Dream of Dracula* by Leonard Wolf—called attention to new directions for Dracula and his vampire minions, each with an academic payoff. Scholars responded, and a new subfield of Dracula and vampire studies was born and has remained in a growth perspective ever since.

Dracula and vampire studies had an immediate natural home in English departments, especially in gothic studies, but quickly found academics in history, film and television studies, and popular culture to lead the way in creating a multidisciplinary approach that united a broad spectrum of scholars around some basic questions on the social, psychological, and actual reality of vampires and their effect on society and the individual.

Explanations of Vampirism

When reports of vampirism filtered into Western and Central Europe from the east in the eighteenth century, along with accounts of otherwise credible western witnesses offering support to the vampire hypothesis, scholars and church leaders attempted to find some explanation. Some simply dismissed the reports as stories of primitive superstitions. Many, however, otherwise unable to fit vampires into their worldview, took the reports seriously. They began to propound various alternative explanations to account for what people had observed, especially the phenomena reported in the case of Arnold Paole. Actual reports of vampirism, rather than the general folklore concerning vampires, usually began with people dying from a lingering disease. After some of these people died, neighbors dug up the corpses and observed a variety of unusual conditions, all signs of continuing life. The bodies had not decayed. The skin had a ruddy complexion, and the hair and fingernails had continued to grow. Fresh flesh had appeared as the outer layer of skin had peeled off. Blood was present around the mouth and in the body when it was cut or punctured. A sexual erection might be present on the bodies of males. If staked, the body reacted as if in pain. Occasionally, when a stake was thrust into the body, the corpse was heard to cry out. In northern Europe, reports of chewed-off appendages suggested to observers that vampires fed on themselves before leaving the grave to feed on others.

By far, the most popular explanation of vampire reports was premature burial. Many people in the eighteenth and nineteenth centuries knew of catalepsy, a disease in which the person affected took on many of the symptoms of death; on occasion, such people were removed by the undertaker and even buried before they reawakened. Herbert Mayo presented an extensive argument for this thesis in his volume *On the Truths Contained in Popular Superstitions* (1851). In 1896, theosophist Franz Hartmann wrote a book based on widespread accounts of accidental interments. Premature burial remained a popular explanation of vampirism into the twentieth century, and Mon-

One way to become a vampire, it was believed centuries ago, is to be buried alive. Accidentally burying someone did happen on occasion back in the eighteenth and nineteenth centuries.

tague Summers, in his famous treatise on vampirism, felt the need to devote a number of pages to a discussion of it before making his own case for the reality of the vampire in *The Vampire: His Kith and Kin* (1928). He also admitted that cases of premature burial "may have helped to reinforce the tradition of the vampire and the phenomenon of vampirism." As recently as 1972, Anthony Masters also argued for the plausibility of premature burials to account for vampire beliefs.

Others suggested that anomalous incidents of preservation of the body from its normal rate of decay accounted for the state of the exhumed bodies. Perhaps, something in the soil or an unusual lack of air or moisture slowed the decay. Possibly, the shriek heard when the corpse was staked was the escape of trapped air. Similarly, others suggested that what was being observed was simply the natural decay of the body. Most people were unaware of continued changes in the body after death, such as the loss of rigidity. As debate over the reasons for the vampire epidemics continued, other explanations were offered. For example, one set of literature suggested that some form of disease accounted for the vampire symptoms. High on the list was the plague—sometimes known as black death. An epidemic of the plague occurred simultaneously with a vampire outbreak in East Prussia in 1710. The spread of plague germs could account for the spread of vampire symptoms. In the twentieth century, rabies was offered as a specific explanation of vampirism. People with rabies would bite others, manifest animal-like behavior, and possess an unquenchable thirst. Outbreaks of rabies also occurred in Hungary, Saxony, and East Prussia in the eighteenth century. In nineteenth-century New England, families suffering from tuberculosis used vampirism as an explanation after experiencing multiple deaths and treated the bodies of the deceased accordingly. Most recently, in the 1960s, the disease porphyria has been suggested as an explanation of vampire reports. A prominent characteristic of porphyria is an extreme sensitivity to light.

Social explanations were also offered for the spread of vampirism. For example, some noticed that vampire reports came from areas in which the Roman Catholic Church and the Eastern Orthodox churches were in contention for the faith of the people. Others saw the reports as a reaction to national defeat, especially in those areas taken over by Austria in the seventeenth and eighteenth centuries. Pope Benedict XIV, who ruled in the mid-eighteenth century, believed that his own priests were the problem. They supported and spread the accounts of vampirism to get superstitious people to pay them to do exorcisms and additional masses.

> Pope Benedict XIV ... believed that his own priests were the problem. They supported and spread the accounts of vampirism to get superstitious people to pay them to do exorcisms and additional masses.

The most satisfying explanation of the vampire reports to date has come from cultural historian Paul Barber, who in the 1980s conducted a thorough survey of the original reports. Barber also had the benefit of modern medical knowledge concerning the process of the decay of human bodies. He analyzed the arguments against the previously cited explanations; none really explained the broad range of phenomena reported in the vampire stories. Vampires were reported whether the factors cited were present or not. Barber has built a comprehensive case that the various accounts of vampires fairly accurately report what actually was observed. The eighteenth-century observers saw bodies in different states of decay from a perspective of limited understanding of the normal processes of decomposition. They tended to offer both natural and supernatural explanations of the unexpected things that they saw. Barber was able to account for the overwhelming majority of the reported attributes of the bodies observed by the eighteenth-century vampire hunters. The hunters had dug up bodies within a few months of their original burial. Some were bodies of people who had died during the winter and had been kept in cold storage (which significantly inhibited decomposition) for burial after the spring thaw. He also accounted for such odd phenomena (to modern researchers) as the appendages seen sticking out of graves (usually of bodies buried without coffins) and appendages that appeared to have been eaten by the corpse, both of which probably derive from the activity of various animal predators on bodies buried in shallow graves without a coffin.

Conclusion: A consideration of the strengths and limitations of many explanations of vampires suggests that the belief in vampirism is a very old and possibly cultural

response to an event that happens in all cultures: the untimely death of a loved one as a result of childbirth, accident, or suicide, followed by an intense experience of interacting with the recently dead person. Given that belief, a variety of events, such as the irregular rate of decay of the soft flesh of corpses, could be cited as visible "proof" that vampires exist or as factors that on occasion correlate to their presence. Since "unnatural" deaths still occur and people still have intense experiences with the dead (now usually thought of as encounters with ghosts or apparitions), those people who also believe in vampires can point to those experiences as in some manner substantiating their belief. Thus, these experiences indicate the presence of vampires. Hence, we know that vampires exist because of these experiences.

Vampire Crime

The great majority of people labeled as "real" vampires in the last two centuries manifested symptoms of what psychologists call hematomania, a blood fetish. (Sexual pleasure and other psychological needs of persons with this condition are met by the regular consumption of human blood, occasionally in conjunction with the eating of human flesh.) Presumably, most of those who regularly drank blood located legal means of obtaining it, usually from a willing donor. Some, however, turned to crime, and a few joined the list of the West's most notorious serial killers. The modern stream of vampiric crime related to hematomania had its precedent in the career of Countess Elizabeth Báthory (1560–1614), who allegedly killed more than 600 people for their blood.

The Marquis de Sade and Gilles de Rais are frequently listed among the modern vampiric criminals, but the list of crimes attributed to them never included drinking the blood they might have shed. A distinction exists between

The French revolutionary and politician the Marquis de Sade was infamous for his erotic writings featuring his libertine sexual practices. His often sadistic and bloody, erotic practices lent credence to the idea he was a vampire.

those who draw pleasure from killing people or from the drawing of blood and those vampiric types who derive pleasure from its consumption. Likewise, a distinction exists between people who drink blood for the overpowering pleasure it brings and those who occasionally sip blood (usually of an animal) as part of a religious ritual and believe they draw some supernatural power from the otherwise repulsive act.

Several vampiric killers emerged in the nineteenth century. The earliest reported case was that of a man named Sorgel, a German who killed a man in the forest and drank his blood in an attempt to cure himself of epilepsy. His actions led to his arrest and confinement in an asylum. That same year, Antoine Léger killed a 12-year-old girl, drank her blood, and ate her heart. After his execution, Sorgel's brain was examined by pathologists.

A more famous incident involved Sergeant François Bertrand (1824–1849), who was arrested in 1849 in Paris for opening the graves of the dead and eating flesh from the corpses. While termed a vampire by some, he engaged in much more ghoul-like behavior and went on to become the model of one of the more successful novels about werewolves, including *The Werewolf of Paris*. A generation later, in 1886, Henri Blot was arrested for a similar crime. He was caught because he fell into a sleeplike, hypnotic trance after completing his work. He was apprehended quickly; he had violated only two bodies.

The United States has been home to one vampire killer, seaman James Brown. In 1967, Brown was discovered aboard his ship, a fishing boat on its way to Labrador, sucking the blood from the body of a crewman he had murdered. He had already killed and drained another sailor. He was arrested and returned to Boston. Brown was sentenced to life in prison, where he killed at least two more people and drank their blood. Following the second killing, he was sent to the National Asylum in Washington, D.C., where he remained confined in a padded cell until he died.

Fritz Haarmann (1879–1924) is another famous vampiric killer. By the time of his arrest and execution in 1924 in Germany, he had killed and cannibalized more than 20 people. However, in the last several years, he also began to bite and suck the blood of his victims. Contemporary with Haarmann was Peter Kürten (1883–1931), also from Germany. Kürten killed first as a nine-year-old boy. He killed again in 1913. Then, in 1929, he began a series of ghoulish crimes in which he stabbed and then mutilated his victims. At the height of his crime spree in August of that year, he killed nine people, mostly young women. His initial excitement at killing someone gave way to a fixation on blood. He began to drink the blood

Known variously as the Wolfman, the Butcher of Hanover, and the Vampire of Hanover, serial murderer Fritz Haarmann mutilated, sexually molested, and dismembered two dozen boys and girls in Germany between 1918 and 1924.

of his victims, continuing even after the blood he consumed made him sick. In one case, he bit and drank from the wound. Finally arrested in 1930, he was executed the following year.

Through the twentieth century, a number of reports of vampire-like criminals have surfaced. A few, such as John George Haigh (1910–1949) and Richard Chase (1950–1980), became famous. Others received no more than passing notice. In the 1940s, Haigh operated out of a home in London. There, he killed his victims, drained their blood, and then disposed of the bodies in a vat of sulfuric acid. Richard Chase began his crime spree in Sacramento, California, in December 1977, when he shot and killed a man. The following month, he killed again, and this time, he drank his victim's blood. He continued this practice in a string of killings in January until his arrest at the end of the month. It turned out that as early as 1974, he had killed a cat and drunk its blood. In the following years, he killed a number of animals and drank their blood in the hope that it would improve his physical health. After his arrest, he moved through a complex legal process, including scrutiny of his sanity. Tried and convicted of multiple murders, he was sentenced to death but cheated the executioner by committing suicide.

The most famous case of vampire-related crime in recent years has been that of Roderick Justin "Rod" Ferrell (1980–) and the small "Vampire Clan" he led. Ferrell claimed to be Vesago, a 500-year-old vampire. The product of a teenage marriage that quickly fell apart, his mother abandoned him during his teen years. Shortly thereafter, he began to adopt his vampire persona. He was known to spend time in cemeteries through the evening hours. While he became delinquent with schoolwork and attendance, he became active in the role-playing game *Vampire: The Masquerade*, through which he came to know a wide range of people interested in vampirism.

In the spring of 1996, Ferrell reconnected by telephone with an old girlfriend, Heather Wendorf, who apparently told Rod that her parents were hurting her and that she wanted him to come get her, but he would have to kill them to do so. In November 1996, Ferrell and several companions went to Florida, met up with Wendorf, killed her parents, and fled the state. They would later be arrested in Louisiana. He was convicted of murder and sentenced to death in 1998, but his sentence was later reduced to life imprisonment without parole.

Beginning in the 1990s, the media developed an interest in "vampire"-related crime and regularly gave wide coverage to any cases that in any way related to vampiric activity. The advent of the internet facilitated the wide dissemination of the accounts of such crimes and related court action. While most vampire crimes concern serial killers who in some manner include blood drinking in their crimes, it would also include any crimes in which the killer was motivated by the blood of the victim, any crime committed by someone involved in the vampire subculture, and any crime directed against people who developed a vampire persona. A reminder that many folk beliefs about vampires survive around the world occurred in 2007 in Guyana, when three people were arrested for killing a woman who had wandered into the town of Bare Root. Shortly after she appeared, a resident saw a child with a red mark on her chest, an indication of an "Old Higue," a traditional vampire in the East African-based vampire beliefs of the country. Vampires, there, are women who may shed their skin and fly around drinking the blood of small children and infants. The woman was called out as a possible vampire, and several techniques were applied to identify her. In the end, she was stabbed and left to die. The woman turned out to be a person suffering from a mental

> The most famous case of vampire-related crime in recent years has been that of Roderick Justin "Rod" Ferrell (1980–) and the small "Vampire Clan" he led.

disorder, incapable of rationally responding to the people who initially encountered her. Several vampire-related crimes are reported annually worldwide.

Political/Economic Vampires

The description of a vampire as a creature who attacks people and saps their life's blood easily lends itself to various metaphorical extensions. Some of the most popular have been in the political realm, in which governments and other powerful social structures have been seen as vampires sucking the life out of people over whom they rule or have some control. This political and economic usage of vampires and vampirism has frequently been obscured by the dominance of psychological interpretations of vampirism, which directed attention to the personal psychological forces operating in vampire accounts. However, the political element inherent in vampirism has also been recognized almost from the entrance of the word "vampire" into Western Europe.

Shortly after the introduction of the word "vampire" in an English publication in 1732 (an account of the investigation of Arnold Paole in Serbia), *The Gentleman's Magazine* of May 1732 carried a satirical article treating the Paole story as a metaphor of appalling social conditions. A decade later, a more serious utilization of the vampire as a political metaphor occurred in *Some Queries and Observations Upon the Revolution in 1688* (written in 1688 but published in 1741), which noted:

> Our Merchants indeed, bring money into their country, but it is said, there is another Set of Men amongst us who have as great an Address in sending out again to foreign Countries without any returns for it, which defeats the Industry of the Merchant. These are the Vampires of the Publick, and Riflers of the Kingdom.

A few years later, in 1764, Voltaire, in his *Philosophical Dictionary*, writing in response to the many vampires reported to exist in Eastern Europe, sarcastically responded:

> We never heard a word of vampires in London, nor even Paris. I confess that in both these cities there are stock-jobbers, brokers, and men of business, who sucked the blood of the people in broad daylight; but they were not dead, though corrupted. These true suckers lived not in cemeteries, but in very agreeable palaces.

Communism and the Vampire: The most famous use of the vampire image in political

German philosopher Friedrich Engels (pictured) referred to those holding property as "vampires," an image Karl Marx comandeered.

rhetoric came in the nineteenth century in the writings of Karl Marx. Marx borrowed the image from his colleague Friedrich Engels, who had made a passing reference to the "vampire property-holding" class in *The Condition of the Working Class in England*. Marx commandeered the image and turned it into an integral element of his condemnation of the bourgeoisie (middle class). The bourgeoisie supported the capitalist system—the very system that had it in its grip.

Thus, Marx could speak of British industry as vampire-like, living by sucking blood, or the French middle class as stealing the life of the peasant. In France, the system had "become a vampire that sucks out the peasant's blood and brains and throws them to the alchemist's cauldron of capital." As Chris Baldick noted, for Marx, the essential vampiric relationship was between capital and labor. Capital sucks the life out of living labor and changes it into things of value, such as commodities. He contrasted living labor (the working class) with dead labor (raw products and machinery). Living labor was sentenced to be ruled by the "dead" products of its past work.

These products did not serve living labor, but living labor served the products it had created. Its service provided the means to obtain the products (which made up the wealth of the middle and upper class). Very early in *Capital*, Marx stated, "Capital is dead labour which, vampire-like, lives only by sucking living labour, and lives the more, the more labour it sucks."

Dracula and Xenophobia: More recent commentary on the novel *Dracula*, especially that of Stephen D. Arata, emphasized the social commentary that Bram Stoker more or less consciously embedded in his novel. *Dracula*, like other British novels of the period, expressed the fear that had developed as the British Empire declined: as the civilized world declined, Great Britain and, by extension, Western Europe and North America were under the threat of reverse colonization from the earth's "primitive" outposts. Stoker was well known for placing his gothic setting at a distant place rather than pushing his storyline into the distant past. In the persona of Dracula, he brought the wild unknown of the imagined East, of Transylvania, to contemporary London.

Arata convincingly argued that Stoker held Transylvania as a fresh and appropriate symbol of the strife believed to be inherent in the interaction of the races of Eastern Europe and the Middle East. Dracula was not like Lord Ruthven or Carmilla, merely another decadent member of displaced royalty. He was a warrior in a land that pitted warriors against each other as a matter of course. His intentions were always domination and conquest. The coming of vampirism could bring the racial heterogeneity (and the racial strife inherent within it) to Great Britain. After figuring out what Dracula was and what he intended by his purchase of property in London, Jonathan Harker lamented his role in introducing Dracula to the city's teeming millions. He would conquer the land and foul the blood of the British race; the threat to the body was also a threat to the body politic.

The central problem for Stoker was a form of Victorian racism and the threatened pollution that the savage races, represented by the figure of Dracula, brought. After Dracula bit Mina Murray, she became "unclean." The boxes of foreign earth he brought to England had to be "sanitized." The untouchable Dracula was also sexually virile, capable of making any number of offspring, while British men, by contrast, were unproductive. Unlike the moth-

> Arata convincingly argued that Stoker held Transylvania as a fresh and appropriate symbol of the strife believed to be inherent in the interaction of the races of Eastern Europe and the Middle East.

ers, the fathers of the major characters were not mentioned, the only exception being Arthur Holmwood's father, who died over the course of the novel. Only at the end, after Dracula was killed, did Harker symbolize the father of a new generation with a pure racial heritage.

The Contemporary Vampire: Throughout the twentieth century and into the twenty-first, the vampire has become a stock image utilized internationally by political cartoonists and commentators to describe the objects of their hostile political commentary. In recent decades, war, fascism, and even the country of Ghana have been labeled as vampiric entities. One recent vivid example of such usage of the vampire metaphor appeared in the wake of the fall of Communism in Russia and Eastern Europe at the end of the 1980s and the proclamation by then U.S. president George H. W. Bush of a "New World Order."

This term had previously entered the language through its use by a wide variety of political utopians from which it had acquired a spectrum of controversial connotations and sparked a host of negative comments. The most virulent of the opposition, claiming that a New World Order amounts to the arrival of a world government, organized the Police Against the New World Order and launched Operation Vampire Killer 2000. Its program consisted of a step-by-step plan to inform police, the military, and other law-enforcement units about the New World Order and, thus, prevent their cooperation with it.

Sexuality and the Vampire

Essential to understanding the appeal of the vampire is its sexual nature. While it frequently has been pointed out that traditional vampires cannot engage in "normal" sexual activity, the vampire is not necessarily asexual. As twentieth-century scholars turned their attention to the vampire both in folklore and literature, underlying sexual themes quickly became evident. The sexual nature of vampirism formed an underlying theme in *Dracula*, but it was disguised in such a way that it was hidden from the literary censors of the day, the consciousness of the public, and probably from the awareness (as many critics argued) of author Bram Stoker himself. Carol Fry, for example, suggested that vampirism was, in fact, a form of "surrogate sexual intercourse."

Sexuality in *Dracula*: The sexual nature of vampirism is first seen in *Dracula* during Jonathan Harker's encounter with the three vampire brides residing in Castle Dracula. Harker confronted them as extremely appealing sex objects who embody an element of danger. Harker noted, "I felt in my heart a wicked, burning desire that they would kiss me with their red lips" (chapter 3). Stoker went on to describe the three as sensual predators and their vampire's

The horror of vampirism has long been laced with overt or implied sexuality and sexual imagery. The sexual aspect of vampirism has only become more prevalent in modern films and novels.

bite as a kiss. One of the women anticipated the object of their desire: "He is young and strong; there are kisses for us all." As they approached, Harker waited in delightful anticipation.

Attention in the novel then switched to the two "good" women, Lucy Westenra and Mina Murray. Lucy, as the subject of the attention of three men, reveled in their obvious desire of her before she chose Arthur Holmwood, the future Lord Godalming, as her betrothed. Mina, on the contrary, was in love with Jonathan and pined in loneliness while he was lost in the wilds of Transylvania. While preparing for her wedding, however, Lucy was distracted by the presence of Dracula. While on a seaside vacation in Whitby, Lucy began sleepwalking. One evening, Lucy was discovered by Mina in her nightclothes across the river. As Mina approached, she could see a figure bending over Lucy. Dracula left as Mina approached, but she found Lucy with her lips parted and breathing heavily. Thus began Lucy's slow transformation from a virtuous and proper, if somewhat frivolous, young lady into what Judith Weissman termed a "sexual monster." By day, she was faint and listless, but by night, she took on a most unladylike voluptuousness.

Shortly before her death, she asked Arthur to kiss her, and when he leaned toward her, she attempted to bite him. Stoker's understanding, however unconscious, of the sexual nature of the vampiric attack became most clear in the blood transfusions that were given to Lucy in the attempt to save her life. Arthur, who never was able to consummate his love for Lucy, suggested that in the sharing of blood, he had, in the eyes of God, married her. The older and wiser Abraham Van Helsing rejected the idea, given the sexual connotation for himself and the others who also gave her blood, but by this time, the women's sexual interest in Dracula was firmly established and led directly to the most sexual scene in the book.

Having given Lucy her peace (and, by implication, returned her virtue) in the act of staking and decapitating her, the men called together by Van Helsing to rid the world of Dracula were slow to awaken to his real target: Mina. When they finally became aware of this, they rushed to Mina's bedroom. There, they found Dracula sitting on her bed, forcing her to drink from a cut on his chest. Dracula turned angrily to those who had interrupted him. "His eyes flamed red with devilish passion...." Once Dracula was driven away and Mina came to her senses, she realized that she had been violated. She declared herself unclean and vowed that she would "kiss" her husband no more.

The Sexual Vampire of Folklore: While little evidence exists that Stoker was intimately aware of Eastern European vampire lore, he could have found considerable evidence of the vampire's sexual nature, particularly in the folklore of the Romani and their neighbors, the southern Slavs. For example, corpses dug up as suspected vampires occasionally were reported to have an erection. The Romani thought of the vampire as a sexual entity. The male vampire was believed to have such an intense sexual drive that his sexual need alone was sufficient to bring him back from the grave. His first act usually was a return to his widow, with whom he engaged in sexual intercourse. Nightly visits could ensue and continue over a period of time, with the wife becoming exhausted and emaciated. In more than a few cases, the widow was known to become pregnant and bear a child by her vampire husband. The resulting child, called a *dhampir*, was a highly valued personage deemed to have unusual powers to diagnose vampirism and to destroy vampires attacking the community.

In some cases, the vampire would return to a woman with whom he had been in love but with whom he had never consummated that love. The woman would then be invited to return with him to the grave, where they could share their love through eternity. The idea of the dead returning to claim a living lover was a popular topic in European folklore. By far, the most famous literary piece illustrating the theme was Gottfried August Bürger's ballad "Lenora," known in English by Sir Walter Scott's translation.

The folklore of Russia also described the vampire as a sexual being. Among the ways in which it made itself known was to appear in a village as a handsome, young stranger. Circulating among the young people in the evening, the vampire lured unsuspecting women to their doom. Russian admonitions for young people to listen to their elders and stay close to home are reminiscent of the ancient story from Greece that tells of Apollonius, who saved one of his students from the allure of the *lamiai*, whom he was about to marry.

The *langsuyar* of Malaysia was also a sexual being. A female vampire, she was often pictured as a desirable, young woman who could marry and bear children. *Langsuyars* were believed to be able to live somewhat normally in a village for many years, revealed only by their inadvertent involvement in an activity that disclosed their identity.

The Modern Literary Vampire: While overt sexual activity was not present in *Dracula*, sexual themes were manifest in the vampire literature of the previous century. The original vampire poem written by Goethe, "The Bride of Corinth," drew upon the story from ancient Greece concerning a young woman who had died a virgin. She returned from the dead to her parents' home to have sexual experiences with a young man staying temporarily in the guest room. The strong sexual relationship at the heart of Samuel Taylor Coleridge's "Christabel" was expanded in "Carmilla," the popular vampire story by Sheridan Le Fanu.

In the story, Carmilla Karnstein moved into the castle home of Laura, her proposed victim. She did not immediately attack Laura but proceeded to build a relationship more befitting a lover. Laura experienced the same positive and negative feelings that Harker had felt toward the three women in Castle Dracula. As she put it:

> Now the truth is, I felt unaccountably toward the beautiful stranger. I did feel, as she said, "drawn towards her," but there was also something of repulsion. In this ambiguous feeling, however, the sense of attraction immensely prevailed. She interested and won me; she was so beautiful and so indescribably engaging.

Carmilla went about her assault upon Laura while inducing her to be cooperative. She would draw Laura to her with pretty words and embrace and gently press her lips to Laura's cheek. She would take Laura's hand while at the same time locking her gaze on her eyes and breathing with such passion that it embarrassed the naïve Laura. So attracted was Laura to Carmilla that only slowly did she come to the realization that her lovely friend was a vampire.

The Sensuous Vampire Onstage and On-screen: Carol Fry, author of the article "Fictional Conventions and Sexuality in Dracula," has properly pointed out that Dracula was, in part, a stereotypical character of popular nineteenth-century literature, the rake. The rake appeared in stories to torment and distress the pure women of proper society. The rake was, to some extent, the male counterpart of the vamp; however, the consequences of falling victim to a seductive male were far more serious for a woman than they were for a man who was victimized by a seductive woman. The man who loved and left

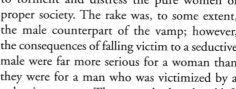

The idea of the dead returning to claim a living lover was a popular topic in European folklore.

Gloria Holden (seen here with Otto Kruger) starred in the 1936 flick Dracula's Daughter.

was thought to have left behind a tainted woman. Just as a state of "moral depravity" contaminated the fallen woman, so, too, vampirism infected the one bitten.

The vampire's victim became like him and preyed on others. The fallen woman might become a vamp, professional or not, who in turn led men to engage in her immoral ways.

Once brought to the stage, Dracula's rakish nature was heightened. No longer hovering in the background as in the novel, he was invited into the living rooms of his intended victims. In this seemingly safe setting, he went about his nefarious business, though what he actually did had to be construed from the dialogue of those who would kill him. Only after the play was brought to the screen, and the public reacted to Bela Lugosi, did some under-

standing of the romantic appeal of this supposed monster become evident to a widespread audience. However, not until the 1950s would the vampire, in the persona of Christopher Lee, be given a set of fangs and allowed to bite his victims on-screen.

Interestingly, the obvious sexuality of the vampire was first portrayed on-screen by a female vampire. In retrospect, the scene in *Dracula's Daughter* (1936) in which the female vampire seduced the young model was far more charged with sexuality than any played by Lugosi. A quarter of a century later, Roger Vadim brought an overtly sensual vampire to the screen in his version of "Carmilla," *Blood and Roses* (1960). In 1968, French director Jean Rollin produced the first in a series of semipornographic features, *Le Viol du Vampire* (released in English as *The Rape of the Vampire*). The story centered around two women who believed that they were cursed by a vampire to follow his bloodsucking life. The sexuality of "Carmilla" was even more graphically pictured in *The Vampire Lovers*, Hammer Films's 1970 production in which the unclad Carmilla and Laura romped freely around their bedroom.

From these and similar early softcore productions, two quite different sets of vampire films developed. On one hand, some pornographic vampire films featured nudity and sex. Among the earliest was *Dracula (The Dirty Old Man)* (1969), in which Count Alucard kidnapped naked virgins to fulfill his sexual and vampiric needs. Spanish director Jesús Franco produced *La Comtesse aux Seins Nus* (1973) (released on video in the United States as *Erotikill*), in which Countess Irina Karnstein (a character derived from "Carmilla") killed her victims in an act of fellatio. (These scenes were cut from the American version.) The trend toward pornographic vampire movies culminated in 1979 with *Dracula Sucks* (also released as *Lust at First Bite*), a remake of *Dracula* that closely followed the 1931 movie. It starred Jamie Gillis as Dracula. The more interesting 1980s adult vampire movies include *Dracula Exotica* (1981), also starring Gillis; *Gayracula* (1983), a homosexual film; *Sexandroide* (1987); *Out for Blood* (1990); *Princess of the Night* (1990); and *Wanda Does Transylvania* (1990).

Most of these were shot in both hardcore and softcore versions. Until the 1990s, pornographic vampire movies were relatively few in number and poorly distributed. With the arrival of the internet and the burgeoning of the adult film industry through the 1990s and into the new century, the number of vampire-themed adult movies of the most explicit nature also increased. By the end of the first decade of the new century, more than 100 had been made, including an adaptation of *Dracula* by Mario Salieri and a half dozen building off the popularity of the television show *Buffy the Vampire Slayer*.

The Vampire in Love: Of far more importance in redefining the contemporary vampire were the novels and films that transformed the evil monster of previous generations into a romantic lover. The new vampire hero owed much to Chelsea Quinn Yarbro's Saint Germain. In a series of novels beginning with *Hotel Transylvania* (1978), Saint Germain emerged not as a monster but as a man of moral worth, extraordinary intellect, and captivating sensuality. He even occasionally fell in love. He was unable to have ordinary sexual relations because he could not have an erection. However, his bite conveyed an intense experience of sexual bliss that women found to be a more-than-adequate alternative.

At the time Yarbro was finishing *Hotel Transylvania*, a new stage production, *Dracula: The Vampire Play in Three Acts*, had become a hit on Broadway. The play was the first dramatic production of *Dracula* to reintroduce the scene in which Dracula forced Mina to drink from his blood.

The scene, a rapelike experience in the novel, had been transformed into one of seduction. In 1979, the larger populace was introduced to this more sensual Dracula when Frank Langella recreated his stage role for the motion picture screen. He presented Dracula as not only a suave, foreign nobleman but as a debonair, attractive male who drew his victims to him by the sheer power of his sexual presence. The scenes in which Lucy, over the objections of her elders, rushed to Carfax to join her lover and drink his blood completed a transformation of Dracula from mere monster into a hero who lived up to the movie's billing: "Throughout history he has filled the hearts of men with terror, and the hearts of women with desire." Langella's *Dracula* directly informed the 1992 production of *Bram Stoker's Dracula* under the writing and direction of Francis Ford Coppola.

Coppola not only brought the vampire into proper society but turned him into a hand-

Director and writer Francis Ford Coppola greatly added to the image of the vampire as a handsome, sexy seducer in the 1992 film Bram Stoker's Dracula.

some, young man who, with his money and foreign elegance, was able to seduce the betrothed Mina from her wimpish fiancé. He returned the final blood-drinking scene to her bedroom, revealed Dracula at his most human, and made their lovemaking the sensual climax of the movie's love story subplot, which Coppola had added to explain Dracula's otherwise irrational acts against the British family he had assaulted. The transformation of the vampire into a hero lover was a primary element in the overall permeation of the vampire myth into the culture of late twentieth-century America (which included the emergence of the vampire in humor and the vampire as a moral example). As such, the contemporary vampire has had to deal with a variety of sexual patterns.

Television detective Nick Knight developed an ongoing relationship with a researcher who was trying to cure him. Mara McCuniff, the centuries-old vampire of Traci Briery's *The Vampire Memoirs*, was overtaken by her sexual urges for three days each month at the time of the full moon. In *Domination*, Michael Ce-

cilone placed his vampires in the world of sadomasochism. Lori Herter's romance novels elevated the vampire as the object of female fantasies.

The response to the conscious development of the vampire as a sexual being has almost guaranteed future exploration in fictional works. *Prisoners of the Night*, a periodical of vampire fiction that appeared annually for several years in the 1990s, focused on sexuality in several issues. Editor Mary Ann B. McKinnon added an impetus to exploring the theme in her fanzine *Good Guys Wear Fangs*, which covers good-guy vampires, most of them romantic heroes.

Sexual tension was a constant element in the highly successful *Buffy the Vampire Slayer* television series, which featured high school and young-adult characters discovering their sexuality and major characters developing relationships with vampires (both good guys and bad boys), werewolves, and demons. Meanwhile, both Anne Rice and Laurell K. Hamilton were accused of upping the sexual content in their later vampire novels as a device to keep their readership despite lagging storylines.

The entrance of the vampire into romance literature, with romance novels now claiming half of the paperback book market, has made the sexually attractive male vampire (both the good guys and the bad-boy vampire) a prominent character in popular fiction. The overwhelming number of plots place a desirable female human into a partially forbidden relationship with a handsome vampire. Human–vampire romances came into their own in the 1990s with the writings of Lori Herter, Maggie Shayne, Linda Lael Miller, and Amanda Ashley, who set the stage for the explosion of vampire paranormal romances in the new century. Possibly the most successful of the new romance writers is Charlaine Harris, whose vampire stories center on Sookie Stackhouse, a waitress who finds true love after rescuing a vampire from some people out to steal his blood and subsequently become desirable to other vampires.

Through the first decade of the new century, romance novels became increasingly explicit in their sexual content. The more extreme examples (avoided by the major romance houses) were described as the female equivalent of the most explicit male adult literature.

From adult romance novels, the love theme found its way into young-adult novels, an early example being Lisa Jane Smith's *The Vampire Diaries* series in the 1990s. The romance theme in young-adult novels reached a new height a decade later in *Twilight* and its sequels (2005–2020) from Stephenie Meyer.

Meyer's heroine, a high school girl, finds her true love in a handsome vampire, though not without being challenged by her attraction to a werewolf. Bella Swan and her vampire love object, Edward Cullen, must make a range of decisions about limiting the expression of their sexual attraction to each other before their marriage (which does not occur until the fourth volume of the series).

> The entrance of the vampire into romance literature, with romance novels now claiming half of the paperback book market, has made the sexually attractive male vampire … a prominent character in popular fiction.

Such sexualizing and romanticizing of the vampire, while departing from the common image of the vampire as mere monster, has not been foreign to the creature itself.

From the beginning, a seductive sexuality has existed as an element of the literary vampire, comingling with that of the monstrous, and goes far to explain the vampire's appeal relative to its monstrous cousins.

Homosexuality and the Vampire

The vampire, especially in its literary and cinematic form, mixed elements of horror and sexuality. To many, it became a symbol of the release of the powerful emotional energies believed to be bottled up by restrictions on sexual behavior common to many societies. Homosexual behavior had always been suppressed during the centuries of Christian dominance of the West and, thus, it could be expected that in the heightened sensuality associated with vampirism, some homosexual elements might be present—and such has been the case. Literary critics have long noted a homosexual aspect among the very first pieces of vampire literature.

Samuel Taylor Coleridge's "Christabel," the first vampire poem in English, portended a theme that would reappear in vampire literature: lesbian vampire relationships. The poem centers upon the vampiric relationship of Christabel and Geraldine, the vampire. It became the inspiration for "Carmilla," the 1872 short story by Sheridan Le Fanu, in which the sexual element was even more pronounced. As other female vampires appeared in succeeding decades, primarily in short stories, the lesbian element often hovered in the background.

However, while a recurring lesbian presence existed in vampire literature, the same could not be said of male homosexuality. The male vampires of the nineteenth century—from Lord Ruthven to Varney the Vampyre to Dracula—invariably sank their teeth into female victims. This strict male heterosexuality was emphasized in *Dracula* (1897), the first major work to include male vampire victims. Jonathan Harker was not touched by Dracula but remained behind as a feast for his vampire brides when Dracula departed for London. Nor did Dracula view any of Lucy Westenra's suitors as additional sources of blood; he turned, rather, to Mina Murray. His several confrontations with men were only in terms of physical combat. In the movies, one could also note the absence of male vampires attacking male victims. When the plot called for such men-on-men attacks, they were always mediated by modern medicine in the form of needles and transfusions (as in *The Return of Dr. X* and *Blood of the Vampire*) or by way of an animal (as in *The Devil Bat*). Not until the sexual revolution of the 1960s did a male homosexual vampire appear. The first gay vampire movie, a pornographic production, was *Does Dracula Really Suck?* (also released as *Dracula Sucks* and as *Dracula and the Boys*). In the 1970s, several additional titles with gay vampires appeared: *Sons of Satan* (1973), *The Tenderness of Wolves* (1973), and an Italian film, *Il Cavaliere Costante Nicosia Demoniaco Ovvero Dracula in Brianza* (1975). Of these, only *The Tenderness of Wolves* was released to the general public. The movie was devoted to the case of Fritz Haarmann, a homosexual serial killer who murdered a number of young boys and drank their blood. Two additional gay vampire movies also appeared in the filmographies: *Gayracula* (1983) and the undated *Love Bites* (c. 1993). A small selection of X-rated movies with a vampire theme exists, such as *The Vampire of Budapest* (1995).

In 2007, the first gay-oriented vampire television series, *The Lair*, aired on Here!, a gay television network. Developed from the successful series *Dante's Cove*, *The Lair* was built around a nightclub that gave its name to the series. The club is home to a group of vampires that includes Colin (Dylan Vox), who manages the club, and Damian (Peter Stickles), the group's leader. Action centers on the vulnerability of the club from law enforcement and

An investigative journalist discovers why dead bodies are turning up at a gay club in the Here! network TV series The Lair.

the press discovering the dangers to those who wander in, unsuspecting of the club's true nature. The first season (six episodes) aired in 2007, season two (13 episodes) in 2008, and the third season in 2009. The first two seasons were released on DVD.

In literature, gay and lesbian vampires have made relatively few appearances. The first writer to become known for his gay vampire writings was Jeffrey N. McMahan. His initial book, *Somewhere in the Night*, a Lambda Literary Award winner, was a collection of short horror stories that included several vampire tales, in one of which he introduced the character of Andrew. A gay vampire, Andrew would later become the subject of a novel, *Vampires Anonymous*, in which a modern-day vampire hunter and a vampire recovery group work to cure individuals of vampirism. Andrew and the vampire community, however, see no need to be cured.

The most significant expression of a vampiric gay relationship came not from a gay writer but in several novels by Anne Rice. Her first novel, *Interview with the Vampire*, featured the intense relationship between Louis and Lestat de Lioncourt, the homosexual connotations of which were not missed by reviewers. Rice was not attempting to highlight sexual orientation issues so much as gender issues—specifically, androgyny. However, this idea of male androgyny has frequently masked a more central concern for homosexuality or bisexuality. Lestat was pictured as one who easily bonded with males and frequently cried. Yet, when he briefly switched bodies with mortal Raglan James, he raped a woman. In several of Rice's novels, male vampires could not have "normal" intercourse, their sex organs being dysfunctional. She suggested, however, that the experience of biting and sucking blood was a far superior form of sex; the mutual sharing of blood by two vampires was an act analogous to intercourse. The Rice novels have been a source for the modern gothic rock movement, whose fans value the androgynous ideal and have opened their circles to homosexuality and other sexual expressions, such as transvestism and sadomasochism.

> In the wake of Rice's popularity in the gay/lesbian community, a host of novels and short-story collections have appeared specifically geared for a lesbian and gay audience.

In the wake of Rice's popularity in the gay/lesbian community, a host of novels and short-story collections have appeared specifically geared for a lesbian and gay audience. Emerging in the first decade of the twenty-first century as a gay vampire writer is Michael Schiefelbein. Schiefelbein uses his years of training for the priesthood and his ultimate rejection of the Roman Catholic Church as the emotional hook into the continuing stories of Victor Decimus, a Roman officer who served in Palestine at the time of Jesus. When Jesus rejected him, he became a vampire and now spends his time corrupting devout, young men (mostly in monastic settings), thereby undermining the church that grew from Jesus's life. The adventures began with *Vampire Vow* (2001) and have continued in *Vampire Thrall* (2003), *Vampire Transgression* (2006), and *Vampire Maker* (2009).

Lesbian readers found their vampire interests best expressed by African American writer Jewelle Gomez, whose *Gilda Stories* (1991) has been recognized from beyond the lesbian and gay communities. It traces the story of a lesbian vampire who began life as a slave in Mississippi in the 1850s. She ran away from serfdom, and each chapter allows the reader to see her maturation and development once she is introduced to a vampiric existence. While the short story has become the most prominent focus of lesbian vampires, additional novels include *Virago* (1990) and *Bloodsong* (1997) by Karen Marie Christa Minns, *Shadows after Dark* (1992) by Ouida Crozier, *Scarlet Thirst* (2002) by Crin Claxton, and *Soapsuds* (2005) by Finola Hughes and Digby Diehl.

Gays and lesbians interested in vampires founded two organizations in the early 1990s (though neither survived for many years). Bite Me in the Coffin Not in the Closet Fan Club was a vampire fan organization for gay and lesbian people who had an interest in vampires and vampirism. Founder Jeff Flaster of Middletown, New York, also edited the club's monthly fanzine, which published short fiction for and about gay and lesbian vampires, contact information for members, and other items of interest. Also operating for a few years in the early 1990s was the Secret Room, a Texas-based organization for gay/lesbian/bisexual fans of the *Dark Shadows* television series. Lesbian and gay interest in vampires is currently (2020) given focus online at the *Queer Vampires* website, http://www.queerhorror.com/Qvamp.

Lesbian Vampires

The incidents of lesbian vampiric relationships, which appeared first in the literary vampire tradition in the nineteenth century and more recently in the cinema, further illustrate the essential sexual nature of the vampire's relationship with its victim. The lesbian vampire can also be seen as a special case of both the homosexual vampire and women as vampires. The earliest vampires were probably female, such as the Malaysian *langsuyar* and the Greek *lamiai*.

The historical reference for the lesbian vampire is Elizabeth Báthory, the so-called blood countess who lived in the seventeenth century and whose story Bram Stoker used to develop the character of Dracula. The story of Báthory suggested several unique ideas about

The concept of lesbian vampires goes back to Malaysian and Greek mythology and also the unholy deeds of Elizabeth Báthory.

vampires not connected to the historical Dracula, Vlad the Impaler. As Radu Florescu and Raymond T. McNally have noted, in the Stoker novel, Dracula was seen as a Hungarian (not a Romanian), he drank blood, he grew younger as he drank blood, and he existed in an erotic atmosphere. Although none of these attributes could be derived from the story of Vlad, they all were descriptive of Elizabeth Báthory. She was related to Hungarian royalty, and she killed hundreds of young girls, whose blood she drained. Several who survived her torture sessions testified that she bathed in human blood to retain and restore her youth.

Although few have considered Báthory a lesbian, her victims were almost exclusively young women. She was assisted in her crimes by her aunt Klara, who has been described as a lesbian who liked to dress in male clothing and "play men's games." As the vampire became the subject of modern literature and the vampiric relationship became a means of illustrating erotic situations, the attraction of females to those of their own gender frequently appeared. On occasion, this relationship was reciprocal, but more often than not, it was a form of rape in which the vampire, generally a woman possessed of some social status or power, attacked or seduced a woman of no status, such as a student or a maid.

From "*Christabel*" to "Carmilla": At the beginning of the English-language literary vampire tradition, lesbianism arose in Samuel Taylor Coleridge's poem "Christabel" (1816). Among the first poems about vampires, "Christabel" featured an "attack" upon the title character by Geraldine, the vampiric figure. Geraldine first appeared in the woods near the castle of Christabel's father and told a story of having been brought there by kidnappers. Christabel invited Geraldine to take shelter in the castle. They shared a bottle of wine. Then, at Geraldine's suggestion, Christabel undressed and got into bed. Geraldine joined her guest.

Whatever passed between them, more implied than stated, the morning found Geraldine refreshed and restored, "fairer yet! and yet more fair!" Christabel arose with a perplexity of mind and a deep sense of having sinned and went immediately to prayer. Christabel, nevertheless, took Geraldine to her father. Unfortunately, Geraldine beguiled the naïve Sir Leoline, who ultimately dismissed his daughter and left with the vampire.

Later, in the nineteenth century, the most famous vampire story with lesbian overtones was penned by Irish writer Sheridan Le Fanu. "Carmilla," which was, next to *Dracula*, the vampire story most often brought to the screen, concerned Millarca Karnstein (also known by two other names made by scrambling the letters of her name: Carmilla and Mircalla), who attacked young women to suck their blood. "Carmilla" can be seen, in part, as an attempt to rewrite "Christabel" in prose form. Early in the story, the vampire was stranded near a castle and invited inside by the unsuspecting residents. Once accepted, she targeted nineteen-year-old Laura, the daughter of the retired Austrian official who had purchased the castle some years before. Carmilla began to "seduce" her hostess.

At one point, Laura recalled, "She used to place her pretty arms around my neck, draw me to her, and laying her cheek to mine, murmur with her lips near my ear.... And when she had spoken such a rhapsody, she would press me more closely in her trembling embrace, and her lips in soft kisses glow upon my cheek." Laura would try to pull away but found herself without energy. She later described the strange nature of their relationship as simultaneously one of adoration and abhorrence. Later, Car-

milla was tracked down and killed before she could kill Laura, but it was not before she had killed the daughter of a neighbor, General Spielsdorf.

Lesbian Vampires in the Movies: With vampirism as a metaphor for sexual behavior, a variety of sexual actions could be pictured on the screen in vampire movies. At a time when explicit lesbian behavior was banned from the movies, vampirism offered a means for women to relate to each other. Contemporary lesbian writers such as Bonnie Zimmerman and Pam Keesey have traced the first lesbian vampire to *Dracula's Daughter*, a 1936 Universal Pictures production. Countess Zaleska (Gloria Holden) satiates her lust by drinking the blood of a series of beautiful models.

It was more than two decades later before another female vampire attacking female victims appeared on the screen. In 1957, *Blood of Dracula* (released in England as *Blood Is My Heritage*) pictured a teenage vampire (Sandra Harrison) attacking her classmates at an all-girls boarding school. That same year, the first of a series of movies based loosely upon the life of Countess Elizabeth Báthory appeared. In *Lust of the Vampire* (aka *I, Vampiri*), a doctor periodically stole the blood of women to give to the countess in order to preserve her youthful appearance. Mario Bava filmed this early Italian entry in the vampire/horror field.

By far, the most acclaimed of the several movies inspired by the Báthory legend is *Daughters of Darkness* (1971), in which a young couple met the still-lively and beautiful Countess Báthory in a contemporary Belgian hotel. They were seduced and attacked by Báthory and her female traveling companion. The husband turned out to be a sadist, and the wife and Báthory combined forces to kill him. Although *Daughters of Darkness* was the most crit-

> "Carmilla," which was, next to *Dracula*, the vampire story most often brought to the screen, concerned Millarca Karnstein ..., who attacked young women to suck their blood.

Originally released as Les lèvres roughes (Red Lips) *in 1971,* Daughters of Darkness *features Delphine Seyrig as Countess Báthory, who seduces the young Ilona (Andrea Rau).*

ically acclaimed of the Báthory films, the blood countess's most memorable appearance was that portrayed by Ingrid Pitt in Hammer Films's *Countess Dracula* (1971). The film was produced at a time when Hammer Films was allowing more nudity and explicitly sexual situations to invade its movies.

"Carmilla" inspired a host of films, possibly the best one being the first, Roger Vadim's *Blood and Roses* (1960), made to showcase his then-wife, Annette Stroyberg. The story also underlies Hammer Films's *The Karnstein Trilogy: The Vampire Lovers* (1970), *Lust for a Vampire* (1971), and *Twins of Evil* (1971). Such movies can be considered lesbian movies only by the most liberal of standards. They starred glamorous female stars, and their male direction and screenplays suggested something more closely approaching a male fantasy of lesbianism. Also, the movies of Jean Rollin frequently included lesbian characters pictured in much the same manner as pornographic movies that picture women engaged in sex scenes shot entirely for a male audience.

More closely portraying a lesbian relationship in a manner acceptable to lesbians was *Vampyres* (1974), which concerned the murder of a lesbian couple by a homophobic man. The two return from the dead as a lesbian vampire couple and work together attacking male victims. *The Hunger*, basically the story of an alien vampire and her human, male lovers, has found an appreciative lesbian audience for the scene in which the vampire (Catherine Deneuve) seduced the doctor (Susan Sarandon), whom she contacted in hope of finding a cure for her lovers' swift aging. Two other lesbian vampire movies, *Mark of Lilith* (1986) and *Because the Dawn* (1988), both explore the possibility of using the vampire image in a positive way for women.

Recent Additions: The growth and the growth of visibility of the lesbian subculture in the 1980s led to the production of significant

David Bowie (right) and Ann Magnuson in The Hunger.

new literature consciously written by lesbians for lesbians. Several volumes stand out. Pam Keesey has assembled two collections of lesbian vampire short fiction in *Daughters of Darkness* (1993) and *Dark Angels* (1995). The earlier volume included a chapter from the single piece of African American lesbian vampire fiction, Jewelle Gomez's *The Gilda Stories* (1991). Gilda was a vampire who was born into slavery and learned to survive over the decades in a world dominated by white males. *Virago*, Karen Marie Christa Minns's first vampire novel, explored the relationship of a lesbian couple attacked by a vampire college teacher.

In contrast to the many male gay vampire books and anthologies that have appeared in recent years, only a relatively few lesbian vampire novels have been published in the new century, such as Crin Claxton's *Scarlet Thirst* (2002)

and Finola Hughes and Digby Diehl's *Soapsuds* (2005), and, more recently, *The Midnight Hunt* (2010), the first of the popular *Midnight Hunters* series by L. L. Raand, and *Hunger for You* by Jenny Frame (2018), leaving the short story as the most prominent place for new lesbian vampire literature. Prominent collections of lesbian vampire stories include *Women of Bite: Lesbian Vampire Erotica*, edited by Cecilia Tan (2010), and *Girls Who Bite*, edited by Deliah Devlin (2011).

At the same time, few lesbian vampire relations have been pictured on film apart from the made-for-males female-on-female sex scenes in some adult movies. Possibly the most notable lesbian-themed vampire movie since the beginning of the new century is *Eternal* (2004), starring Caroline Neron as a modern-day Elizabeth Báthory. The most prominent vampire-related lesbian character on television was Willow Rosenberg, the witch- and vampire-fighting companion on *Buffy the Vampire Slayer*, who emerged as a lesbian halfway through the series.

More recently, she was joined by Tara Thornton, a gay character on *True Blood* (2008–2014), who was turned into a vampire as the series proceeded.

 The Scholars

Artenie, Cristina (1971–)

Canadian Dracula scholar Cristina Artenie emerged at the end of the second decade of the twenty-first century as a leading voice among a small cadre of academics calling for a reappraisal of Dracula studies based on both fresh theoretical approaches and new information pertinent to the understanding of *Dracula*, the novel by Bram Stoker. Artenie obtained her Ph.D. degree from Laval University (2015) with a dissertation on the annotated editions of *Dracula*. She subsequently published *Dracula: A Study of Editorial Practices* (2016), in which she challenged misinformation about Romania and Transylvania perpetuated in the various annotated editions of *Dracula* through the twentieth century.

She also issued *Dracula Invades England* (2015), in which, with the help of Romanian sources, she challenged misconceptions about Stoker's intentions and about Vlad Tepes. Among her most important contributions has been a new annotated edition (coedited with Dragos Moraru) of Stoker's classic text, *Dracula: The Postcolonial Edition* (2016), the first edition that uses Romanian sources, goes beyond Stoker's notes for the novel to the full versions of the texts that he read, and critically offers a postcolonial analysis of the novel in light of Romania's status in the 1890s as a periphery of Britain's informal empire.

She advocates a postcolonial turn in

Dracula studies, which would involve both taking into account Britain's relations with Eastern and Central Europe in the nineteenth century and the long experience of Romanian anthropologists studying supernatural beliefs. Such a turn would finally accept that no actual vampire beliefs exist in Romanian folklore and that Bram Stoker was more deeply invested in the study of Romania and Transylvania than he is usually given credit for.

A prolific scholar, she is also the editor of *Gothic and Racism* (2015) and *My Own Land's Sins: An Anthology of Victorian Poetry* (2015) and the coeditor of *Monsters and Monstrosity: 21st-Century Film and Television* (2017) and *Specialists: Passions and Careers* (2017).

Artenie currently serves as the editor-in-chief of Universitas Press in Montreal.

Bacon, Simon

British scholar Simon Bacon is an independent researcher/scholar currently (2020) residing in Poznan, Poland. He emerged in 2011 when he organized the conference Vampires: Myth of the Past and the Future, held at the University of London, and afterward edited the postconference publication (foreword by Sir Christopher Frayling). He also served a tenure as editor of the academic journal *Monsters and the Monstrous*.

> Through the remainder of the decade, Bacon has authored numerous articles on vampires, monstrosity, science fiction, and media studies and has written/edited several books....

Through the remainder of the decade, Bacon has authored numerous articles on vampires, monstrosity, science fiction, and media studies and has written/edited several books, including *Undead Memory: Vampires and Human Memory in Popular Culture* (2014); *Seductive Concepts: Perspectives on Sins, Vices and Virtues* (2014); *Little Horrors: Interdisciplinary Perspectives on Anomalous Children and the Construction of Monstrosity* (2016); with Katarzyna Bronk, *Growing Up with Vampires: Essays on the Undead in Children's Media* (2018); *Horror: A Companion* (2019); and *Dracula as Absolute Other: The Troubling and Distracting Specter of Stoker's Vampire on Screen* (2019). His most recent publication was *Eco-Vampires: The Undead and the Environment* (2020). Two of Bacon's books, *Undead Memory* and *Growing Up with Vampires*, were coedited with his wife, Katarzyna Bronk-Bacon, an assistant professor of English at Adam Mickiewicz University in Poznan, Poland.

Much of his work has focused on an exploration of the nature of the vampire as a symbol of the Other and the spectrum of ways the Other manifests in human society.

A professor of liberal arts at the Savannah College of Art and Design in Atlanta, Georgia, John Edgar Browning researches and lectures on vampires in film, literature, and culture.

Culture Before 9/11." Browning is currently a professor of liberal arts at the Savannah College of Art and Design (SCAD) in Atlanta.

Browning, John Edgar (1980–)

Through the first decades of the twenty-first century, John Edgar Browning (1980–) emerged as a scholar of note on horror and monsters in general and Dracula and vampires in particular. His academic career began with his earning a B.A. from Florida State University and a M.A. at the University of Central Oklahoma. He pursued doctoral studies at Louisiana State University, which were completed in American Studies at the State University of New York at Buffalo. In completing his dissertation, he spent five years in the field conducting ethnographic observations of people who self-identify as vampires, the results of which were included in his doctoral dissertation, "Redeeming the Un-Dead in American Media and

Browning initially came to the attention of his scholarly colleagues in Dracula and vampire studies while still in graduate school at the end of the first decade of the new century as the coeditor (with Caroline Joan Picart) of *Draculas, Vampires, and Other Undead Forms: Essays on Gender, Race, and Culture* (2009), a collection of essays. He followed over the next three years with a set of edited books: *Bram Stoker's Dracula: The Critical Feast, An Annotated Reference of Early Interviews and Reactions, 1897–1913* (2011); *The Forgotten Writings of Bram Stoker* (2012); and a new critical edition of Montague Summers's *The Vampire: His Kith and Kin* (2011), which he followed with Summers's *The Vampire in Europe: A Critical Edition* (2014). Meanwhile, he again teamed with Caroline Joan Picart in the preparation of a book-length source book, *Dracula in Visual Media: Film, Television, Comic Book and Electronic Game Appearances, 1921–2010* (2010), which earned him and Picart the Lord Ruthven Award.

Since completing his doctorate, Browning has remained productive with work as an editor on, for example, *The Fantastic in Holocaust Literature and Film: Critical Perspectives* (2014) and the projected *New Queer Horror Film and Television* (2021), and with a spectrum of papers published in various books and journals. He is currently preparing a new annotated edition of *Dracula* for W. W. Norton, scheduled to appear at the end of 2021.

Calmet, Dom Augustin (1672–1757)

Dom Augustin Calmet, a French Benedictine monk, biblical scholar, and the most famous vampirologist of the early eighteenth century, was born on February 26, 1672, at Mesnil-la-Horgne, Lorraine, France. He studied at the Benedictine monastery at Breuil and entered the order in 1688. He was ordained to the priesthood in 1696. He taught philosophy and theology at the Abbey at Moyen-Moutier and in the early years of his career worked on a massive, twenty-three-volume commentary of the Bible, which appeared between 1707 and 1716. His biblical writings established him as one of the church's leading scholars, and he spent many years trying to popularize the work of biblical exegesis in the church. He was offered a bishopric by Pope Benedict XIII, but Calmet turned it down. However, in spite of his learned accomplishments, Calmet is most remembered today for his single 1746 work on vampires, *Dissertations sur les Apparitions des Anges des Démons et des Esprits, et sur les revenants, et Vampires de Hingrie, de Boheme, de Moravie, et de Silésie.*

Like the work of his Italian colleague, Giuseppe Davanzati, Calmet's study of vam-

pirism was started by the waves of vampire reports from Germany and Eastern Europe. Vampirism, for all practical purposes, did not exist in France and was largely unknown to the scholarly community there until the early eighteenth century. Calmet was impressed with the detail and corroborative testimonies of incidents of vampirism coming out of Eastern Europe and believed that it was unreasonable to simply dismiss them. In addition, as a theologian, he recognized that the existence and actions of such bloodsucking revenants could have an important bearing on various theological conclusions concerning the nature of the afterlife. Calmet felt it necessary to establish the veracity of such reports and to understand the phenomena in light of the church's view of the world. Calmet finished his work a short time after the Sorbonne roundly condemned the reports and especially the desecration of the bodies of the people believed to be vampires.

Calmet defined vampires as people who had been dead and buried and then returned

Dom Augustin Calmet, an admired philosopher and abbot who served twice as abbot general under Pope Benedict XIII, was a highly regarded vampirologist.

from their graves to disturb the living by sucking their blood and even causing death. The only remedy for vampirism was to dig up the body of the reported vampire and either sever its head and drive a stake through its chest or burn the body. Using that definition, Calmet collected as many accounts of vampirism as possible from official reports, newspapers, eyewitness reports, travelogues, and critical pieces from his learned colleagues. The majority of space in his published volume was taken up with the anthology of all his collected data.

Calmet then offered his reflections upon the reports. He condemned the hysteria that had followed several of the reported incidents of vampirism and seconded the Sorbonne's condemnation of the mutilation of exhumed bodies. He also considered all of the explanations that had been offered for the phenomena, including regional folklore, normal but little-known body changes after death, and premature burial. He focused a critical eye upon the reports and pointed out problems and internal inconsistencies.

In the end, however, Calmet was unable to conclude that the reports supported the various natural explanations that had been offered, though he was unwilling to propose an alternative. He left the whole matter open but seemed to favor the existence of vampires by noting that "it seems impossible not to subscribe to the belief which prevails in these countries that these apparitions do actually come forth from the graves and that they are able to produce the terrible effects which are so widely and so positively attributed to them." He thus touched off the heated debate, which was to ensue in the 1750s. As contemporary scholar Massimo Introvigne has noted, in his first edition, Calmet had posed five possible explanations of the stories he had considered. Three he dismissed, leaving him with the possibility

that vampires were the result of the devil's activity or mere superstition. While leaning toward superstition, he did not reach a firm conclusion. However, in his third and last edition, he did conclude that such creatures as vampires could return from the grave.

Calmet's book became a best seller. It went through two French editions in 1746 and 1749, then the third edition in 1751 appeared under a new title, *Traité sur les Apparitions des esprits et su les vampires ou les revenans de hongrie, de moravie, etc.* It appeared in a German edition in 1752 and an English edition in 1759 (reprinted in 1850 as *The Phantom World*). Relying primarily on the first edition, Calmet was immediately attacked by colleagues for taking the vampire stories seriously. While he tried to apply the criticism, he only lightly questioned the legitimacy of the reports of vampiric manifestations. In 1751, he did question the reports in reaching his more skeptical conclusion.

> In ... 1755 and 1756, Maria Theresa issued laws to stop the spread of the vampire hysteria, including removing the matter of dealing with such reports from the hands of the clergy....

As the controversy swelled following the publication of his book, a skeptical Empress Maria Theresa stepped in. A new outbreak of vampirism had been reported in Silesia. She dispatched her personal physician to examine the case. He wrote a report denouncing the incident as supernatural quackery and condemned the mutilation of the bodies. In response, in 1755 and 1756, Maria Theresa issued laws to stop the spread of the vampire hysteria, including removing the matter of dealing with such reports from the hands of the clergy and placing it instead under civil authority. Maria Theresa's edicts came just before Calmet's death on October 25, 1757.

In the generation after his death, Calmet was treated harshly by French intellectuals both inside and outside the church. Later in the century, Diderot condemned him. Possibly the final word on Calmet came from Voltaire, who sarcastically ridiculed him in his *Philosophical Dictionary*. Though Calmet was favorably cited by Montague Summers, who used him as a major source for his study of vampires, his importance lies in his reprinting and preserving some of the now obscure texts of the vampire wave of eighteenth-century Europe.

Carter, Margaret Louise (1948–)

Margaret Louise Carter, bibliographer, author, and editor, was born in Norfolk, Virginia. She developed an interest in vampires after reading *Dracula* (1897) at the age of 13. In 1970, while in college, she compiled an anthology of vampire stories, *Curse of the Undead*. That same year, she wrote the preface to a reprint of *Varney the Vampyre*, edited by D. P. Varma. Two years later, she edited a second collection of short stories, *Demon Lovers and Strange Seductions*.

In 1975, she began the work that has, to date, brought her the greatest degree of fame in the vampire world. *Shadow of a Shade: A Survey of Vampirism in Literature*, which won the Dracula Society award in 1976, was the first of four books on vampire and gothic horror bibliography and literary fiction. It was followed by *Specter or Delusion? The Supernatural in Gothic Fiction* (1987), *Dracula: The Vampire and the Critics* (1988), and her monumental *The Vampire in Literature: A Critical Bibliography* (1989), which included a comprehensive listing of English-language vampire fiction. Each item in the bibliography was annotated with a set of codes indicating the nature of the vampire and/or vampirism to be found in the work. It appeared amid an unprecedented growth in interest in the literary vampire. Through the 1990s and into the new century, Carter annually issued a supplement that cited all of the year's new fiction as well as any past items she missed in the original bibliography. In recent years, the annual supplements have been issued in electronic form on her website. In this work, she has placed future writers on vampires in her debt.

More recently, she has contributed to nonfiction writing with her study of *Different Blood: The Vampire as Alien*, in which she explores the continuing relevance of the vampire as Other against the popular sympathetic vampire one often finds in romantic fiction.

Carter is also a writer of vampire fiction. Her first vampire short story, "A Call in the Blood," appeared in 1987. She continued as a productive author into the new century, with her titles including *Sealed in Blood* (2003), *Child of Twilight* (2003), *Crimson Dreams* (2004), *Vampire Heat* (2017), and *Passion in the Blood* (2019). For over a decade, she edited *The Vampire's Crypt*, a journal featuring vampire-oriented short fiction (1991–2002).

Carter has been an active participant and officer in the Lord Ruthven Assembly. She continues to promote young authors through her website, *Carter's Crypt* (http://www.margaretlcarter.com).

Crişan, Marius-Mircea (1977–)

Marius-Mircea Crişan, an associate professor at West University of Timişoara, Romania, has emerged in the second decade of the twenty-first century as one of the leading voices in a new generation of Dracula scholars. Crişan received his Ph.D. in 2008 at the University of Turin with a thesis on the image of Transylvania in Bram Stoker's *Dracula* and in the novelist's sources on Transylvania. Through the next decade, he began to develop a new international dialogue on Dracula with special concern for its of Transylvanian locations and the resultant connection to modern Hungary and Romania. Transylvania was taken from Hungary after World War I and became part of Romania.

Crisan has hosted several conferences at West University of Timişoara on various topics in Dracula and vampire studies beginning with a 2013 conference on Dracula and the image of Romania in British and American literature. At about the same time, he completed his first books: *The Birth of the Dracula Myth: Bram Stoker and Transylvania* (2013) and *The Impact of a Myth: Dracula and the Fictional Representation of the Romania Space* (2013). In 2015 and 2016, Crisan organized a workshop called "Where's the Place of Dracula: (De)Constructing Stereotypes in the Study of the Mythical Space in Literature and the Arts" as an event included within the International Conference of Beliefs and Behaviours in Education and Culture, held at West University of Timişoara, Romania, in June 2015 and June 2016. The discussion focused upon Dracula, its various representations in literature, film, visual arts, etc., and the accompanying images of Transylvania in the Western imagination. On the heels of the conference, he assembled a broad set of articles from an international set of Dracula scholars for his book *Dracula: An International Perspective* (2017).

From 2017 to 2019, Crisan was the scientific chair of the Helion International Conference's Frontiers of the Possible: Borders and Openings in Speculative Fiction and, in 2019, edited, together with Cornel Secu, the special issue of *Biblioteca Nova Bulletin* on the theory, critique, and history of science fiction literature. This special issue has studies translated into Romanian on topics of contemporary interest,

such as the connection between vampires, aliens, and zombies.

Dalby, Richard (1949–2017)

Richard Dalby, independent scholar, bookseller, bibliographer, and fiction editor, emerged through his career as one of the most knowledgeable experts on Bram Stoker, *Dracula*, and the literary vampire. He was born in London and educated at Haberdashers' Aske's Boys' School, one of the top independent boys' schools in the United Kingdom. He was diagnosed with diabetes at the age of 16 and did not attend college. As a young adult, he began to work in bookstores and eventually founded his own used bookstore, which he operated out of his home in Scarborough, Yorkshire. Simultaneously, he began to build his own personal library of horror and fantasy fiction.

> While informally becoming known for his extensive knowledge of *Dracula* and related vampire literature, he [Dalby] gained some fame with the public for editing ghost stories.

While informally becoming known for his extensive knowledge of *Dracula* and related vampire literature, he gained some fame with the public for editing ghost stories. Editions included *Ghost for Christmas* (1988), *Phantastic Book of Ghost Stories* (1990), and *The Mammoth Book of Victorian and Edwardian Ghost Stories* (1995).

Dalby also became known for his particular interest in Bram Stoker. He owned a copy of *Dracula* with Stoker's personal annotations in it. He also published a major bibliographical work, *Bram Stoker: A Bibliography of First Editions* (1983). He maintained contact via the mail with a broad spectrum of *Dracula* scholars whom he assisted with their research.

Dalby drew on his knowledge of the literature to bring out two early anthologies of *Dracula*- and vampire-related short fiction:

Dracula's Brood (1987) and *Vampire Stories* (1992) and more recently collaborated with Robert Eighteen-Bisang on *Vintage Vampire Stories* (2011) and with Brian J. Frost on *Dracula's Brethren* (2017).

Amid his many contributions to vampire studies, Dalby may be best remembered for publishing a translation of Stoker's preface to what he assumed was an early (1901) Icelandic edition of *Dracula*. The discovery called scholars' attention to an early adaptation of *Dracula* in a language little understood outside of Scandinavia. The text was recently revealed to be an adaptation, not a translation, of *Dracula*.

> Eighteen-Bisang's chief interests were the vampire myth in literature and popular culture and bibliographic research.

Following his death, Dalby's personal library was offered for sale, a process that continues as this almanac goes to press.

Eighteen-Bisang, Robert (1947–2020)

Independent Canadian scholar Robert Eighteen-Bisang, who was possibly best known as the owner of the world's largest collection of rare vampire books, was born in Brantford, Ontario. He attended the University of British Columbia. After receiving his bachelor's degree in sociology in 1976, he worked in advertising and marketing.

Eighteen-Bisang began collecting books on Dracula and vampires in the 1970s. With the help of rare-book dealers Lloyd W. Currey and Peter Howard in America and George Locke in London, he discovered hundreds of rare vampire books before other collectors were aware that they existed. He also purchased much of the vampire collections assembled by Forrest J. Ackerman in Hollywood and Marlene Woods in Longview, Texas.

Eighteen-Bisang's chief interests were the vampire myth in literature and popular culture and bibliographic research. Over the years, he shared his expertise with numerous scholars, collectors, and fans. He wrote articles for and acted as an advisor to dozens of books on Dracula and vampires, including several annotated editions of *Dracula*. His expertise led to invitations to lecture across North America and in the United Kingdom. In 1997, he was one of the guests of honor at Dracula '97 in Los Angeles.

Bram Stoker's Notes for Dracula: A Facsimile Edition (2008), which he and Elizabeth Miller coedited, has been acknowledged as a core text for understanding Dracula and vampires. It received glowing reviews and won the Lord Ruthven Award as the best nonfiction vampire book of 2008. In 2018, after reading *Bram Stoker's Notes for Dracula*, Philip Spedding discovered that Bram Stoker had been a member of the London Library from 1890 to 1897 and did much of his research for *Dracula* there. In February 2019, Creation Theatre Company staged an avant-garde adaptation of *Dracula* in the library. An expanded edition of the notes, retitled *Drafts of Dracula*, appeared in 2019.

Eighteen-Bisang founded Transylvania Press, Inc., which, among its notable publications, issued the first reprint of Bram Stoker's 1901 abridged edition of *Dracula*. In addition, he is also credited with the discovery of Hutchinson's colonial edition of *Dracula*; demonstrating that parts of *Dracula* are based on the Jack the Ripper murders of 1888; and proving that one of Sherlock Holmes's cases, "The Adventure of the Illustrious Client," is a rationalized adaptation of *Dracula*. The Canadian journal *University Affairs* cited him as one of the leading independent Dracula scholars in Canada.

Eighteen-Bisang passed away in 2020. He was, at the time, working with Dacre Stoker on compiling a new annotated edition of *Dracula*, the first to be authorized by Bram Stoker's estate.

Florescu, Radu R. (1925–2014)

Radu R. Florescu was an Eastern European historian who, along with his colleague Raymond T. McNally, was one of the most prominent scholars calling attention to Vlad the Impaler, the historical Dracula, and his relationship to the vampire legend. One of his ancestors, Vintila Florescu, was Vlad's contemporary but was a supporter of Vlad's brother, Radu the Handsome, who took the Wallachian throne in 1462 at the end of Vlad's reign. Florescu seemed destined for an obscure life as a specialist in Eastern European politics and culture. His first book was *The Struggle Against Russia in the Romanian Principalities* (1962). However, in the early 1970s, he teamed with his Boston College colleague Raymond T. McNally as the author

An emeritus professor of history at Boston College, the late Radu Florescu was an expert on Romania and a former advisor to Edward Kennedy on Eastern Europe and the Balkans.

of *In Search of Dracula* (1972), a popular book on the vampire myth. Their book drew upon the historical data concerning Vlad the Impaler, the fifteenth-century Romanian prince who had been associated with the vampire legend by Bram Stoker. Some years previously, McNally had become interested in tracking down any real history behind Stoker's novel. His search led him to Vlad the Impaler; after McNally joined the faculty at Boston College, Florescu discovered that the two shared a mutual interest. In the late 1960s, they formed a team with Romanian historians Constantin Giurescu and Matei Cazacu to perform research on Dracula and vampire folklore. It was found that in Romania, vampire folklore was not tied to Dracula (until very recently). Stoker possibly learned of Vlad from Arminius Vámbéry, a Romanian scholar he met in the 1890s in London.

In Search of Dracula was designed as a miniature encyclopedic survey of aspects of the Dracula legend. Some reviewers, noting the lack of footnotes concerning the historical Dracula, suggested that Florescu and McNally had made up the details of his life. Those reviews led to their next work, a complete biography of Vlad titled *Dracula: A Biography of Vlad the Impaler, 1431–1476*, published in 1973. This study not only spurred further work on the fifteenth-century prince by Romanian historians but also altered the treatment of Dracula in the movies. Among several such movies, two versions of *Dracula*—the 1974 version with Jack Palance and the 1992 version by Francis Ford Coppola—emphasized the relationship between Bram Stoker's *Dracula* and the historical Romanian prince. A number of recent novels, such as the several books written by Peter Tremayne and Dan Simmons's *Children of the Night*, also built their plot on the connection. In 1974, a Swedish documentary about Vlad with actor Christopher Lee took Florescu's and McNally's first book as its title.

Florescu continued his productive collaboration with McNally. In 1979 (coinciding with the release of the new version of *Dracula* [1979] with Frank Langella), they completed an edited version of *Dracula* under the title *The Essential "Dracula": A Completely Illustrated and Annotated Edition of Bram Stoker's Classic Novel.* This edition was noteworthy for its extensive use of notes that Stoker made while writing the novel. More recently, Florescu and McNally issued a comprehensive presentation of Vlad's life in its context in the broad sweep of fifteenth-century history, *Dracula, Prince of Many Faces: His Life and Times* (1989). The fall of the Ceauşescu government in Romania has allowed increased contact and collaborative activity between Romanian scholars and their Western counterparts. In 1991, building on an idea first proposed in the 1970s by Florescu and McNally, Kurt W. Treptow brought together Romanian, British, and American scholars to create an anthology of contemporary research on Dracula. Florescu contributed a paper to this work called "Vlad II Dracula and Vlad III Dracula's Military Campaigns in Bulgaria, 1443–1462." Florescu was one of the speakers at Dracula '97: A Centennial Celebration in Los Angeles and received an award from the Transylvanian Society of Dracula for his contributions to Dracula scholarship.

Among his last projects, Florescu combined his interest in Romanian history with an exploration of his own family's contribution in *General Ioan Emanoil Florescu: Organizer of the Romanian Army* (2007).

Garza, Thomas J. (1958–)

Thomas Jesús Garza is the University Distinguished Teaching Associate Professor in the Department of Slavic and Eurasian Studies, Director of the Texas Language Center, and the Director of the Arabic Flagship Program at the University of Texas at Austin. He is also Affiliated Faculty in the Program in Comparative Literature, the Center for Mexican-American Studies, and Middle Eastern Studies. A native

An associate professor at the University of Texas, Austin, Thomas J. Garza is the author of the important study Slavic Blood: The Vampire in Russian and East European Cultures.

Texan, Dr. Garza received his doctorate from Harvard University (1987). He initially came to the University of Texas in 1990 and, during his lengthy tenure, has distinguished himself as an instructor and won a spectrum of awards for undergraduate and graduate teaching; in 2003, he was inducted into the University Academy of Distinguished Teachers.

His research has led into a variety of studies in Russian and Eastern European countries. In the midst of these studies, he became interested in Slavic folklore in general and Slavic vampire lore in particular. His major contribution to the field has been a massive compilation of writings on the Slavic vampire, published in 2009 as *The Vampire in Slavic Cultures* (recently revised and expanded as *Slavic Blood: The Vampire in Russian and East European Cul-*

tures). His articles on the subject include "From Russia with Blood: Imagining the Vampire in Contemporary Russian Culture" in *The Universal Vampire: Origins and Evolution of a Legend*, Barbara Brodman and James Doan, eds. (2013) and "The Slavic Vampire in Texas: Problems and Methods of Vampire Studies" [in Russian] in *Bibliotechnoe delo* (2014). He also served as a subject expert in the History Channel's dramatized documentary *Vampire Secrets* (2006) for the DVD release of the film *30 Days of Night* (2007) and for the HBO series *True Blood* (2008–2014).

George, Samantha

Samantha George is a senior lecturer in literature at the Social Sciences, Arts & Humanities Research Institute at the University of Hertfordshire. She had previously completed a Ph.D. at the University of York in 2004. She taught at Sheffield University prior to her moving to Hertfordshire in 2007. Her initial research on eighteenth-century literature and science would lead to her first major scholarly book, *Botany, Sexuality and Women's Writing* (2007).

A lecturer at the University of Hertfordshire, Samantha George is the organizer of Open Graves, Open Minds: Vampires and the Undead in Modern Culture.

Shortly after moving to Hertfordshire, she organized a major research project on gothic literature called Open Graves, Open Minds: Vampires and the Undead in Modern Culture (OGOM). In 2010, the project held its first major event, the OGOM conference. Widely covered in the press, the conference gave George a high profile among vampire researchers and enthusiasts. In 2012, a symposium to mark the centenary of Bram Stoker's death was held, in the wake of which she joined with colleague William Hughes to issue an initial major work product from the project called *Open Graves, Open Minds: Representations of Vampires and the Undead from the Enlightenment to the Present Day* (2013). George also edited a special issue on vampires for *Gothic Studies* in May 2013.

Further expansion of the Open Graves, Open Minds project provided the context for a focus on werewolves through the last half of the second decade of the new century. This focus led to two conferences and a resultant volume, also coedited with Hughes, called *In the Company of Wolves: Werewolves, Wolves, and Children* (2019).

The OGOM project continues as an active program at Hertfordshire. Among its recent activities has been a two-day Polidori Vampire Symposium (2019) held in commemoration of the publication of "The Vampyre" (1819), whose character Lord Ruthven dominated the presentation of the vampire in nineteenth-century literature. One may keep up with the project at its website: http://www.opengravesopenminds.com.

Hughes, William F. (1964–)

British professor William Hughes has, since the late 1990s, emerged as a prominent scholar of gothic studies with a particular specialized knowledge of Bram Stoker's *Dracula*. He attended the Liverpool Collegiate School and the University of East Anglia and also earned a postgraduate certificate in education from Christ Church, Canterbury. In the mid-1990s, he joined the faculty of the Bath Spa University, England, where he served for a quarter of a century before moving (2019) to Macau (China) to become the professor of literature in English at the University of Macau.

Hughes began his serious study of Stoker while at the University of East Anglia. Over the years, he would come to see *Dracula* as both a gothic masterpiece and as a fictional work speaking to a spectrum of issues that had come alive in the 1890s, including gender, the new secular technologies, attacks on religious faith and race, and the decline of the state of the British empire. He also gained an appreciation of the many additional writings, especially the novels, authored by Stoker, most of which go largely unnoticed by contemporary students of *Dracula*.

Hughes's work on *Dracula* first manifested outside of his university classes in 1997 with his *Bram Stoker: A Bibliography* (1997), a work produced in part for the *Dracula* centennial. The next year, he joined with Andrew Smith to

British academic William Hughes is noted not only as a scholar of Stoker's Dracula, *but also for his many Gothic studies.*

produce *Bram Stoker: History, Psychoanalysis, and the Gothic*, noting along the way the dominant role that psychology played in interpretations of *Dracula*. Then, through the next decade, he produced the majority of his scholarly output on Stoker and *Dracula* beginning with an annotated edition of Stoker's *The Lady of the Shroud* (2000). His major works included *Beyond Dracula: Bram Stoker's Fiction and Its Cultural Context* (2000); a critical annotated edition of *Dracula* (with Diane Mason); and *Bram Stoker's Dracula: A Reader's Guide* (2009).

Meanwhile, in 1999, Hughes became the editor of the newly founded *Gothic Studies*, the journal of the International Gothic Studies Association, a post he held for the next 20 years (until his move to Macau). While remaining at his editorial post, in 2009, he was also elected chair of the association, serving for four years. He also edited several collections of scholarly articles, *Queering the Gothic* (2009).

In the second decade of the twenty-first century, Hughes continued his prolific output with *The Victorian Gothic: An Edinburgh Companion* (2012, coedited with Andrew Smith); *Ecogothic* (2013); the two-volume *The Encyclopedia of the Gothic* (2013, coedited with David Punter and Andrew Smith); and *Gothic Britain: Dark Places in the Provinces and Margins of the British Isles* (2019, coedited with Ruth Heholt).

Also, during this decade, Hughes joined in the project led by colleague Samantha George at the University of Hertfordshire to organize the Open Graves, Open Minds: Vampires and the Undead in Modern Culture conference. A follow-up Open Graves, Open Minds symposium was held in 2012, occasioned by the 100th anniversary of Bram Stoker's death. One product of this effort was the volume coedited by Hughes and George, *Open Graves, Open Minds: Representations of Vampires and the Undead from the Enlightenment to the Present Day* (2013). More recently, the project led to a second volume, also edited by George and Hughes, called *In the Company of Wolves: Werewolves, Wolves, and Children* (2019).

Hughes is a Fellow of the Royal Historical Society, the Society of Antiquaries of Scotland, and the Higher Education Academy.

McNally, Raymond T. (1931–2003)

Raymond T. McNally, a leading historian and scholar on vampires in folklore and fiction and expert on Vlad the Impaler—the historical Dracula—was born on May 15, 1931, in Cleveland, Ohio, the son of Marie Kinkoff and Michael Joseph McNally. After completing his education, McNally took a position as instructor at John Carroll University in his hometown. He moved on to Boston College in Chestnut Hill, Massachusetts, in 1958. In 1961, he was named an American Exchange Scholar to the USSR and spent the year at the University of Leningrad. From 1964 to 1974, he also served as director of Boston College's Slavic and East European Center. He was appointed full professor in 1970.

After joining the faculty at Boston College, he met Radu R. Florescu, a Romanian historian with whom he shared an interest in Dracula and vampire lore.

They formed a team to do research on the historical Dracula, a fifteenth-century ruler named Vlad the Impaler, and his relationship to the novel by Bram Stoker. In 1967, McNally was one of a party of men who discovered and explored the authentic Castle Dracula. His continued collaboration with Florescu proved fruitful, its first product being *In Search of Dracula* (1972), one of the early nonfiction works on *Dracula* and the first to offer details about the obscure Vlad the Impaler. It became a popular best seller. The following year, they completed a more scholarly biography, *Dracula: A Biography of Vlad the Impaler, 1431–1476*. These books have become two of the most influential works for people interested in vampires. Christopher Lee, the actor most identified at the time with the dramatic role of Dracula, starred in a documentary film based on the two books, *In Search of Dracula* (1974), made by a Swedish film company. Later books and movies have incorporated data from the two volumes as part of the Dracula storyline.

McNally followed the success of the two volumes with an anthology of vampire writings (both fiction and nonfiction), *A Clutch of Vampires: These Being among the Best from History and Literature* (1974). Through the 1970s, he continued to work with Florescu, and in 1979, they completed a new edition of Stoker's novel, *The Essential Dracula: A Completely Illustrated and Annotated Edition of Bram Stoker's Classic Novel.* Meanwhile, McNally had also become fascinated with Elizabeth Báthory, the other historical personage who stood behind the Dracula myth. Báthory, a Czechoslovakian countess, was (like Vlad) not a vampire, but she did kill many young girls, and it was said that she would bathe in their blood, a practice she thought would preserve her youth. *Dracula Was a Woman: In Search of the Blood Countess of Transylvania* appeared in 1983. Two decades of work on the historical Dracula led to the publication of *Dracula, Prince of Many Faces: His Life and Times* (1989), a comprehensive attempt to put the life story of Vlad the Impaler into the broad context of fifteenth-century European history.

In the early 1970s, while researching and writing their first books, McNally and Florescu had suggested some collaborative work between British, Romanian, and American scholars interested in Vlad and Dracula. The fall of the Romanian dictatorship in 1990 has allowed

> In 1967, McNally was one of a party of men who discovered and explored the authentic Castle Dracula.

such an endeavor to proceed. The first product was an edited volume, *Dracula: Essays on the Life and Times of Vlad Tepes*, to which McNally contributed an essay, "An Historical Appraisal of the Image of Vlad Tepes in Contemporary Romanian Folklore." McNally continued as a leading figure in the field through the 1990s. A new addition of his landmark volume coauthored with Radu Florescu, *In Search of Dracula*, was released in 1994. He was a presenter at both the World Dracula Conference in Romania in 1995 and at Dracula '97: A Centennial Celebration in Los Angeles, at which the Transylvanian Society of Dracula gave him an award for his historical scholarship. He was an active member of the Lord Ruthven Assembly and was named one of its honorary presidents. In 1997, he completed a new annotated version of *Dracula* on CD, *Dracula: Truth and Terror*.

In the last decade of his life, McNally received the accolades of his colleagues for his work in putting the study of Dracula on the academic agenda, while at the same time, a growing critique of his early work suggested that he had significantly overstated the case for identifying Count Dracula with Prince Vlad Dracula as well as overemphasizing the role of Elizabeth Báthory on Bram Stoker and the writing of *Dracula*. Most recently, Dracula scholars Robert Eighteen-Bisang and Elizabeth Miller praised McNally for his role in making Stoker's notes on Dracula, long hidden away in the Rosenbach Museum and Library in Philadelphia, known to the world of Dracula scholars; at the same time, they criticized him for his role in spreading the false impression that Vlad was the model for Count Dracula.

During his many years at Boston College, McNally founded and headed the school's Russian and East European Center (1964). In 1995, he joined with his colleague Donald Carlisle in founding the Balkan Studies Institute, also based at Boston College.

Miller, Elizabeth (1939–)

Elizabeth Miller, who emerged in the 1990s as one of the most widely hailed Dracula scholars, was born in St. John's, Newfoundland. She taught in the English department at Memorial University of Newfoundland for over 30 years. In 1991, she received the university's President's Award for Distinguished Teaching. Upon her retirement, the university named her professor emeritus.

With Nicolae Paduraru, Miller co-organized the first World Dracula Congress, held in Romania in 1995, and, along with Jeanne Youngson and J. Gordon Melton, Dracula '97: A Centennial Celebration. She founded the Canadian chapter of the Transylvanian Society of Dracula and, at the 1995 World Dracula Conference, held in Romania, she was made a baroness of the House of Dracula.

> In the 1990s and through the first decade of the new century, Miller became one of the most productive scholars in Dracula and vampire studies.

In the 1990s and through the first decade of the new century, Miller became one of the most productive scholars in Dracula and vampire studies. She published seven books, including *Reflections on Dracula* (1997), *Dracula: Sense and Nonsense* (2000, 2006), *A Dracula Handbook* (2004), and *Bram Stoker's Notes for Dracula: A Facsimile Edition* (with Robert Eighteen-Bisang, 2008). She edited the *Journal of Dracula Studies*. *Dracula: Sense and Nonsense* became a watershed volume in Dracula studies by compiling information from two decades of scholarly research and providing a new plateau from which further scholarly discourse could proceed. *Bram Stoker's Notes for Dracula: A Facsimile Edition* (with an expanded edition in 2019 as *Drafts of Dracula*) received the Lord Ruthven Award as the best nonfiction title in vampire studies of 2009.

Prior to her retiring in the second decade of the new century, Miller lectured widely at a variety of venues across North America and Europe. From Vancouver to Bucharest, she was interviewed for many television documentaries, including ones for the National Geographic channel, the Discovery Channel, PBS, BBC, and ABC's *20/20*. Her expertise was frequently sought for articles on the subject and she was widely quoted in, among others, *The New York Times, U.S. News & World Report, The Chicago Tribune,* and *The Wall Street Journal.*

Miller maintains two authoritative and expansive Dracula websites as well as a blog. She currently resides in Toronto.

Nevárez, Lisa

Lisa Nevárez, an associate professor of English at Siena College in Loudonville, New York, emerged in the second decade of the twenty-first century as one of the new voices in vampire studies. She previously attended the University of San Francisco (B.A.) and Vanderbilt University (M.A., Ph.D.) and joined the faculty at Siena in 2002.

Her interest in the literary vampire is informed by an equally strong pursuit of Latinx studies. She serves as cochair of the Vampire Studies group within the Popular Culture Association, where she has presented on such works as Marta Acosta's *Casa Dracula* trilogy, the vampire novels of Justin Cronin, and the *Twilight* series. Her major contribution, to date, has emerged from her interest in research and teaching relative to vampires, the gothic, and horror fiction. She assembled a collection of essays published as *The Vampire Goes to College: Essays on Teaching with the Undead* (2014) that highlights a spectrum of pedagogical tools, methods, and approaches for incorporating the figure of the vampire into the learning environment of the college classroom, the vampire providing a rich context for discussion of exploring questions surrounding death and immortality, social alienation, love and passion, gender, monstrosity, and Otherness. Other publications include essays on Lindqvist's *Let the Right One In* and King's *Salem's Lot,* on Latina vampires in selected graphic novels, and on the *Twilight* series. Her current projects include an essay on Kostova's *The Historian* and Sanvoisin's *The Ink Drinker/Le Buveur d'Encre* and an essay on teaching Stoker's *Dracula.*

She continues to focus on diversity and gender in vampire studies scholarship.

Ramsland, Katherine (1953–)

Katherine Ramsland, a psychologist who specialized in forensic psychology, emerged in the 1990s as a major interpreter of Anne Rice's writings. Born in Ann Arbor, Michigan, Ramsland attended Northern Arizona University, where she received her bachelor's degree in 1978; Duquesne University, where she received her master's degree in forensic psychology in 1979; and Rutgers University, where she received her Ph.D. in philosophy in 1984. Following her graduation, she began teaching in the philosophy department at Rutgers and wrote her first book on the Danish existentialist philosopher Søren Kierkegaard entitled *Engaging the Immediate: Applying Kierkegaard's Indirect Communication to Psychotherapy* (1988).

In 1997, Ramsland's interest in vampires led to her becoming editor of a short-lived periodical, *The Vampyre Magazine*....

In the 1980s, she became acquainted with Anne Rice and saw in her a subject worthy of her time and scholarly interpretation. Even though Ramsland had been working in a genre field, she was able to reach a mass audience. Over several years, she produced *Prism of the Night*, which became the first in a series of books on Rice that have ranged from *The Anne Rice Trivia Book* to the collection of scholarly papers assembled for *The Anne Rice Reader*. In the process of her writings and scholarship, Ramsland gained an in-depth familiarity with Rice's vampire books and had become privy to many considerations that underlay the novels. She brought all that she had learned together in the massive volume *The Vampire Companion: The Official Guide to Anne Rice's The Vampire Chronicles* (1993). She also prepared a similar volume on Rice's *Lives of the Mayfair Witches* novels.

In 1997, Ramsland's interest in vampires led to her becoming editor of a short-lived periodical, *The Vampyre Magazine*, published by Sabertooth, Inc. She had, by this time, become intrigued by the phenomenon of real vampires, which led to the very successful volume *Piercing the Darkness* (1998), which highlighted her adventures into the darker side of the community. In the new century, an interest in crime appeared that led to a number of books. The two interests merged in her book *The Science of Vampires* (2002) and a lengthy article, "The Vampire Killers," for the TruTV Crime Library.

Ramsland currently teaches forensic psychology at DeSales University in Center Valley, Pennsylvania. In the new century, she has authored multiple texts on serial killers, the psychology of the criminal mind, and forensics. She has most recently returned to the vampire world with her book *The Vampire Trap: When Pop Culture Inspires Murder* (2018).

Senf, Carol

Carol Senf, a professor at the School of Literature, Media, and Communication at the Georgia Institute of Technology, emerged in the 1990s as one of the major scholars of Dracula and vampire studies. Her work in the field began in her graduate studies years and her concentration on Victorian studies at the State University of New York at Buffalo. She completed her Ph.D. in 1979 with her dissertation, "Daughters of Lilith: An Analysis of the Vampire Motif in Nineteenth-Century English Literature."

In 1981, she joined the faculty at Georgia Tech and launched a steady stream of publications in gothic and Victorian studies in general and Dracula and vampire studies in particular. She capped the 1980s with her important text *The Vampire in Nineteenth-Century English Literature*, issued in 1988. Focusing more closely on Dracula in the 1990s, she produced two significant works as the editor of *Critical Response to Bram Stoker* (1993) and the author of *Dracula: Between Tradition and Modernism* (1998), for which she received the Lord Ruthven Award for the best nonfiction vampire work of the year.

> She [Senf] capped the 1980s with her important text *The Vampire in Nineteenth-Century English Literature*, issued in 1988.

Senf has continued a prodigious output in the new century, highlighted by *Science and Social Science in Bram Stoker's Fiction* (2002), an annotated edition of Bram Stoker's *Lady Athlyne* (2007), an annotated edition of *Stoker's Mystery of the Sea* (2007), and her study of Stoker as a gothic writer, *Bram Stoker* (2010), a contribution to the *Gothic Authors: Critical Revisions* series from the University of Wales Press. In addition, she has authored a number of noteworthy papers in the field.

In 2012, Senf was invited to deliver the keynote address at the Bram Stoker Centenary Conference, held at Trinity College in Dublin. She continues as a leading voice in Dracula studies.

Skal, David J. (1952–)

David J. Skal, an American writer and film historian, is best known for his series of books on the gothic/horror tradition in film and literature. Skal attended Ohio University in Athens, Ohio, where he earned his bachelor's degree in general studies in 1974. His scholarship on the horror genre was brought to public attention by his 1990 study of Dracula's appearances in various media, *Hollywood Gothic*, touted as the most detailed published work of Dracula's movement from the 1897 novel to the stage and screen. The book includes the full story of the campaign by Bram Stoker's widow, Florence, to destroy all prints of the German silent film *Nosferatu* (1922), which infringed her copyright, as well as the first in-depth account of Universal Pictures's Spanish-language version of *Dracula*, for which Skal located a crucial missing reel in Havana, thus making possible the film's complete restoration.

Skal followed his initial success with a series of additional books, including *The Monster Show: A Cultural History of Horror* (1993), *Dark Carnival* (1995), a biography of Tod Browning coauthored with Elias Savada, and *V Is for Vampire* (1996), which established Skal as one of the leading cultural historians in his field. As the Dracula centennial approached, he worked to complete his contributions (along with those of Nina Auerbach) to the Norton Critical Edition of *Dracula* and worked on *Dracula '97: A Centennial Celebration*, held in Los Angeles in 1997. For television, he scripted the A&E *Biography* documentary on the life of Bela Lugosi.

In the new century, he continued his contributions to Dracula and vampire studies with *Vampires: Encounters with the Undead* (2006), a collection of vampire stories from the nineteenth and twentieth centuries, and *Romancing the Vampire: Collectors Vault* (2009). Most recently, he wrote a major biography of Stoker, *Something in the Blood: The Untold Story of Bram Stoker, The Man Who Wrote Dracula* (2016).

Stokes, Dax (1978–)

Dax Stokes, an academic librarian located in northern Texas, is the force behind *The Vampire Historian*, a podcast that came online in 2015 to cover vampires in folklore, history, literature, television, and film. Stokes's own research centers on the origins of vampire lore and legend in Eastern Europe, especially in Christianity and the vampire in popular culture. Paralleling the podcast is a similarly named blog, which may be accessed at https://thevampirehistorian.com. The podcast and blog won the Lord Ruthven Award for Best Vampire Media in 2017.

As the podcast emerged, Stokes organized two vampire studies symposia, which brought scholars and the interested public to his campus: the There Are Such Things! Vampire Studies Symposium 2015 and the World Dracula Day 2017 Symposium. Stokes has emerged as a popular lecturer on Dracula and vampire studies in the Dallas–Fort Worth Metroplex and

Dax Stokes is a librarian and creator of the podcast The Vampire Historian.

throughout northern Texas. *The Vampire Historian* has built and maintains a network of vampire researchers worldwide and makes available an archive of the ever-growing number of podcasts.

Summers, Montague (1880–1948)

Alphonsus Joseph-Mary Augustus Montague Summers was the author of a number of important books on the supernatural, including several classic studies on vampires. Very early in his life, he began reading many of the more obscure writings by English fiction writers, including those of the gothic genre.

In 1899, Summers entered Trinity College and pursued a course toward the Anglican ministry. He went on to Lichfield Theological College, where he received his bachelor's degree

An expert on seventeenth-century English drama, Montague Summers wrote about werewolves, witches, and vampires.

(1905) and master's degree (1906). He was ordained as a deacon in 1908 and assigned to a parish in a Bristol suburb.

While there, he was charged and tried for pederasty (i.e., sex between a man and a male minor) but was found not guilty. As a consequence of the trial, however, he left the Church of England and became a Roman Catholic. At some point—whether before or after he left the Church of England was not altogether clear—he was ordained to the priesthood. He was briefly assigned to a parish in London, but in 1911, he moved from the parish into the teaching school.

During his teaching years, Summers gathered an outstanding collection of books in various languages (many of which he learned) on occultism and the supernatural from magic and witchcraft to vampires and werewolves. He also became an enthusiastic fan of Restoration drama and was one of the founders of The Phoenix, a society established to revive Restoration plays, many of a somewhat risqué nature. After 15 years as an instructor in various schools, Summers moved to Oxford and began the period of scholarly writings that was to make him a memorable author of works on the occult and related fields. His first important work, *The History of Witchcraft and Demonology*, appeared the year he retired from teaching. Largely because of his choice of topics, his books sold well, and Summers was able to make a living from his writings.

The first years of his Oxford period focused on his study of vampirism. In 1928, Summers finished his broad survey, *The Vampire: His Kith and Kin*, in which he traced the presence of vampires and vampire-like creatures in the folklore around the world from ancient times to the present. He also surveyed the rise of the literary and dramatic vampire. Summers's broad mastery of the mythological, folkloric, anthropological, and historical material on the vampire (a mastery rarely equaled) has been obscured by his own Catholic supernaturalism. On several occasions, he expressed his opinion of the evil reality of the vampire, an opinion very much out of step with his secular colleagues.

The following year, Summers published his equally valuable *The Vampire in Europe*, which focused on various vampire accounts in Europe (especially Eastern Europe), where the legend found its most complete development. Summers combined his reading of the diverse literature with personal observations formulated from visits to some of the more important centers where vampire belief had survived. Summers completed two volumes of a country-by-country report on vampire lore. While they were superseded by a number of studies of particular areas, the volumes remain standard sources for vampire studies. The continuing importance of Summers's work was underscored by the publication of a critical edition of *The Vampire: His Kith and Kin* (edited by John Edgar Browning) in 2011 and a like edition of *The Vampire in Europe* in 2014.

In the 1930s, Summers continued his prodigious output and successively published *The Werewolf* (1933), a companion volume to his vampire studies; *The Restoration Theatre* (1934); *A Popular History of Witchcraft* (1937); and *The Gothic Quest: A History of the Gothic Novel* (1938), an enthusiastic history of gothic fiction. In the 1940s, he added *Witchcraft and Black Magic* (1946). His last book, *The Physical Phenomena of Mysticism*, was published posthumously in 1950.

In the last 20 years of his life, Summers also edited numerous volumes. He released new editions of some of the most important texts on witchcraft and several anthologies of ghost stories. Toward the end of his life, he produced an autobiographical volume, *The Galantry Show*, which was eventually published in 1980. Beginning in 1956, many of Summers's works, including the two vampire books, were reprinted in American editions.

Summers remains an enigma. A defender of a traditional supernatural Catholic faith, he was the target of numerous rumors concerning homosexuality and his seeming fascination with those very subjects, which he on one hand condemned and on the other spent so much time mastering.

Wynne, Catherine

Dr. Catherine Wynne, a reader in English at the University of Hull with a specialization in nineteenth- and early twentieth-century literature and visual culture, emerged in recent decades as a leading scholar on Bram Stoker and Dracula. She attended University College in Dublin, where she earned her M.A. in modern English and American literature and was later awarded her doctorate from the University of Oxford. She joined the faculty at the University of Hull in 2000, and her first major scholarly contribution, *The Colonial Conan Doyle: British Imperialism, Irish Nationalism and the Gothic*, appeared in 2002.

Wynne turned to the study of mesmerism in the late nineteenth century, which led to her 2006 study *Victorian Literary Mesmerism*. This early exploration of occult rituals on the stage led to interest in Bram Stoker's place in the theater, beginning with his role as critic, later as Henry Irving's business manager, and finally with the way the theater impacted his literary career. This attention to Stoker, Dracula, and the stage resulted in a set of books for which Wynne is best known, beginning with her editing two volumes of Bram Stoker's theatrical writings, *Bram Stoker and the Stage: Reviews, Reminiscences, Essays and Fiction* (2012). She subsequently authored *Bram Stoker, Drac-*

ula and the Victorian Gothic Stage (2013) and edited *Stoker and the Gothic: Formations to Transformations* (2015), a collection of essays on Stoker.

In the midst of this marathon of writing/editing, in April 2012, Wynne organized the Bram Stoker Centenary Conference, sessions of which met at the University of Hull and at Sneaton Castle in Whitby. With the support of the British Academy, the conference became the largest international conference to date on Bram Stoker, with some 90 delegates, including special guests Dacre Stoker, Jenne Stoker, and Robin MacCaw from the Bram Stoker Estate. Wynne subsequently organized the first-ever Bram Stoker Birthday Lecture and Symposium on November 8, 2012, in Hull, with the inaugural lecture by Professor Sir Christopher Frayling, followed by the second Bram Stoker Birthday Lecture and Symposium in Whitby on November 8, 2013.

Most recently, Wynne produced the introductory material for a collection of the *Bram Stoker Horror Stories* (2018).

Scholarly Organizations

Bram Stoker Estate

Early in the twenty-first century, Dacre Stoker, the great-grandnephew of Bram Stoker, began to gain an awareness of his illustrious ancestor. Dacre had grown up in Ontario, attended St. Lawrence University, from which he graduated in 1981, and took a teaching position at Aiken Preparatory School in South Carolina. A new level of interest in Bram Stoker was greatly increased in 2003 after meeting screenwriter Ian Holt and their decision to collaborate on a sequel to *Dracula*. The resultant novel, *Dracula the Un-Dead*, appeared in 2009 to critical and popular acclaim. Writing the novel, which included much necessary research on *Dracula*, also produced a new sensitivity to the unique contributions that the Stoker family could offer.

Thus, in 2010, as a response to the continuing worldwide fascination with Bram Stoker, his major character, Count Dracula, and his novel, Dacre Stoker, his wife, Jenne Stoker, and Bram's great-grandson, Robin Guy MacCaw, formally established the Bram Stoker Estate, with a goal of assuming a public role to ensure that their ancestor's intellectual property rights are preserved and protected. That mission includes providing historically accurate information about Bram Stoker and his life and to collaborate with individuals and entities of like purpose. When possible, the estate grants permissions for the use of images and documents in academic research and publications and licenses Bram Stoker trademarks commercially.

The great-grandnephew of Bram Stoker, Dacre Stoker wrote a sequel to Dracula *in an effort to regain control over creative rights of the original vampire tale.*

Among the estate's first projects was a collaboration between Dacre Stoker and Elizabeth Miller to publish *The Lost Journal of Bram Stoker: The Dublin Years* (2012). Then, in November of that year, the Stokers and MacCaw were guests at the Bram Stoker Birthday Lecture and Symposium, organized at the University of Hull (United Kingdom) by Stoker scholar Catherine Wynne.

In the decade since the organization of the estate, Dacre Stoker has emerged as its major spokesperson; made numerous appearances on its behalf; brought out a new edition of *Dracula*; produced *Dracul*, a prequel to *Dracula*, with J. D. Barker; and contributed a foreword to *Drafts of Dracula*, Bram Stoker's notes for *Dracula* that were compiled and edited by Robert Eighteen-Bisang and Elizabeth Miller.

The Bram Stoker Estate can be contacted through the website http://www.bramstoker-estate.com.

Children of the Night

In 2016 at the World Dracula Conference held in Dublin, Ireland, representatives of the Transylvanian Society of Dracula, based in Romania, announced that the Romanian branch of the society was disbanding and collapsing into the remaining North American chapter, based at Kutztown University in Pennsylvania. That action left the U.S.–Canadian TSD chapter as the only remaining active remnant of the organization. In the wake of that announcement and the vacuum it created, independent scholar Hans de Roos and film specialist Dr. Magdalena Grabias, who had organized the Dublin conference, proposed the creation of a new international series of Dracula conferences and the formation of a new initiative group, Children of the Night, to facilitate the same. The first such conference was held in Brasov, Romania, in October 2018.

Hans de Roos, an artist and art historian, was among those whose attention was caught by Richard Dalby's 1986 discovery of a brief text reputedly written by Bram Stoker as an introduction for an Icelandic edition of *Dracula*, published in 1901 as *Makt Myrkranna* (*Powers of Darkness*). Copies have survived in only a few European, mostly Icelandic, libraries. Working with a copy of the original preface, de Roos was initially led to a heretofore-unknown, serialized newspaper version of *Makt Myrkranna* in an Icelandic newspaper. He would also discover an early serialization of *Dracula* in a Hungarian newspaper. He subsequently made an initial translation of *Makt Myrkranna* using Google Translate, which, upon a cursory reading, suggested that the Icelandic text was more than a simple translation of *Dracula* but, rather, a distinct adaptation of the text. This discovery led de Roos to create a more formal translation project that would produce a formal English translation, published in 2017. In recognition of his effort, in 2018, the Lord Ruthven Assembly presented a special Lord Ruthven Award to de Roos for his translation work on *Makt Myrkranna*.

Meanwhile, Children of the Night understands itself to be a nonprofit academic initiative that hopes to carry on its work by attracting the support of a global contingent of Dracula and vampire studies experts. Conferences are projected to be held biannually, beginning with the 2018 conference. The organization maintains a website at https://dracongress.jimdofree.com.

Lord Ruthven Assembly

The Lord Ruthven Assembly (LRA) was founded in 1988 as a scholarly organization dedicated to the serious pursuit of scholarship on and research of the vampire/revenant figure in a variety of disciplines. Most of its members are active participants in the International Association for the Fantastic in the Arts (IAFA), which has recognized the assembly as a special-interest group within its organization (and is the only organization officially affiliated with the IAFA). The assembly holds its meetings during the annual conference of the IAFA, held in central Florida, with multiple sessions of academic papers being offered.

The LRA originated out of the desire of the "vampire people" who attended the IAFA's annual conference to get together to discuss common interests. Spearheading the formation of the assembly was Lloyd Worley of the University of Northern Colorado, who became the founding president. Other original officers include Veronica Hollinger, Allienne R. Becker, and Lillian Heldreth. The decision was made to name the assembly after author John Polidori's Lord Ruthven, the first vampire in English prose fiction.

> The LRA originated out of the desire of the "vampire people" who attended the IAFA's annual conference to get together to discuss common interests.

The LRA annually presents several Lord Ruthven Awards. The first, an award for the best work of fiction, was presented in 1989. An award for the best nonfiction work was added in 1994. It has since added an award for media and popular culture and periodically offers special awards for unique accomplishments.

The Lord Ruthven Assembly may be contacted through its Facebook page, https://www.facebook.com/pg/lordruthvenassembly/about/?ref=page_internal.

Popular Culture Association, Vampire Studies

The Popular Culture Association, a scholarly organization focusing on the study of popular culture, has been open to papers on Dracula and vampire studies from its beginning, but a continuing substantive interest in the area in the new century led to the formation of the

Vampire Studies group within the association in 2007. Initially called the Vampire in Literature, Culture, and Film group, it took its more inclusive present name in 2018. The group issues an annual call for papers to be presented at the regular meetings of the association and has generated a close-knit cohort of repeat presenters while experiencing growth with a steady influx of new "blood." In its short history, the group has become noteworthy for its nurturing of a new generation of vampire studies scholars, such as Amanda Hobson, Cait Coker, and James Saubrey.

As of 2020, the group was led by U. Melissa Anyiwo and Lisa Nevárez. It may be contacted at pcavampires@gmail.com and maintains a website at https://pcaaca.org/area/vampire-studies.

Slayage

Slayage refers to an academic journal, a website, and a community of scholars originally assembled for the study of and dialogue around the television series *Buffy the Vampire Slayer* and its spin-off show *Angel*, though increasingly, it has refocused its attention to include the ever-increasing body of work produced by Joss Whedon, termed the Whedonverse. *Slayage: The Online International Journal of Buffy Studies* emerged in stages in 2001 and transformed in 2009 into *Slayage: The Journal of the Whedon Studies Association* and then in 2015 into *Slayage: The Journal of Whedon Studies*. The journal is now found online at https://www.whedonstudies.ev/slayage-the-international-journal-of-buffy.html

Slayage was the brainchild of two English professors, David Lavery (1940–2016) of Middle Tennessee State University and Rhonda V. Wilcox of Gordon College (Barnesville, Georgia). As they gathered essays

English professors David Lavery (pictured) along with Rhonda Wilcox founded Slayage *dedicated to the study of* Buffy the Vampire Slayer.

Georgia (2006), Henderson State University in Arkadelphia, Arkansas (2008), Flagler College (2010), the University of British Columbia (2012), California State University (2014), Kingston University, United Kingdom (2016), and the University of North Alabama (2018). Late in 2008, the Whedon Studies Association was formed as a legal nonprofit educational organization devoted to the study of Whedon and his associates.

Slayage ties together an interdisciplinary network of scholars united initially by their mutual appreciation of the *Buffy the Vampire Slayer* series, which has faded only slightly by the demise of the series and its offshoot, *Angel*. Scholarly commentary, initially centered in television and movie studies and English literature, has reached out to include perspectives from sociology, anthropology, philosophy, and religious studies. The end result was that by 2009, almost half of all the scholarly articles ever written on vampires, and a significant percentage of the scholarly books, have been devoted to the work product of Joss Whedon. Through the second decade of the twenty-first century, the association's work has extended to facilitate discussion around the "wider oeuvre of Joss Whedon and those who have collaborated with him. That is, we encourage investigation into the ways the Whedon influence, themes, and aesthetic have formed and informed the TV, film, and pop-cultural landscape."

for a book, *Fighting the Forces: What's at Stake in Buffy the Vampire Slayer*, they discovered that two additional books on *Buffy* were already being prepared and subsequently realized that their interest in the popular television show was shared by an unusually large number of their scholarly colleagues—even more than had been manifested around other pop culture phenomena such as *Star Trek* or *The X-Files*. Using the online journal of *Xena* studies as a model, they created the quarterly journal for *Buffy* studies, which continues to the present.

Further interest in studies on *Buffy* was manifested in an international conference held at East Anglia University in Norwich, England, in the fall of 2002, attended by scholars from more than 20 countries. Thus, beginning in 2004, Slayage began sponsoring biannual conferences, the first of which brought some 400 scholars to Nashville, Tennessee. Subsequent conferences were held at Gordon College in

Besides the *Slayage* journal, the association also publishes *Watcher Journal: The Undergraduate Journal of Whedon Studies*. Slayage also supports the work of Alysa Hornick, who oversees the ongoing site *Whedonology: An Academic Whedon Studies Bibliography* Hornick has emerged (along with Don MacNaughton and J. Gordon Melton) as the primary Whedon (and *Buffy*) bibliographer (https://www.whedonstudies.tv/whedonology-an-academic-whedonstudies-bibliography.html). Slayage also annually presents the Mr. Pointy Awards (named for the stake inherited by Buffy from her sister

Slayer, Kendra, in the series) (https://www.whe
donstudies.tv/mr-pointy-awards.html).

Transylvanian Society of Dracula

The Transylvanian Society of Dracula
(TSD), a cultural historical organization, was
founded in the early 1990s by a group of leading Romanian historians, ethnographers, folklorists, tourist experts, writers, and artists as
well as non-Romanian experts in the field of
Dracula and vampire studies. Its goal was the
interpretation of Romanian history and folklore, especially as it relates to the fifteenth-century ruler Vlad the Im-
paler (the historical
Dracula) and Roma-
nian folklore concern-
ing vampires. The
group also attempted to
identify dracularian traces of the myth in the
folklore of other countries around the world.
The founding president of the society was Nicolae Paduraru (1932–2009), who for many years
had been an official with the Romanian Ministry of Tourism. He also was the general administrator of Count Dracula Treasures, Ltd.

The society initially organized tours of
various sites in southern Romania associated
with Vlad the Impaler and those in Transylvania
(in the northern area of Romania) associated
with the novel *Dracula* (1897). Some 300
people attended the World Dracula Congress
sponsored by the Society in Romania in 1995,
an event that marked its worldwide expansion.
The American and Canadian chapters were
founded during that week, headed by Drs. J.
Gordon Melton and Elizabeth Miller, respectively. Dr. Massimo Introvigne, who attended
the congress, subsequently formed an Italian
chapter. At its height soon after the turn of the
century, Japan and various European countries
also had chapters.

> The group also attempted to identify
> dracularian traces of the myth in
> the folklore of other countries
> around the world.

In 1997, the American and Canadian
chapters, along with the Count Dracula Fan
Club (now the Vampire Empire), sponsored
Dracula '97: A Centennial Celebration, the international *Dracula* commemorative event held
August 14–17, 1997, in Los Angeles. Delegates
from some 20 countries, including a delegation
from Romania, attended, and more than 90
scholarly papers were presented on Dracula and
vampire studies.

The various chapters sponsored different
events, among which the several Romanian
chapters organized a symposium in Transylvania
each May on the anniversary of Jonathan
Harker's arrival at Castle Dracula. The international society spon-
sored the second World
Dracula Congress, Drac-
ula 2000, held at Poiana
Brasov, Transylvania, the
site of Vlad the Im-
paler's attack upon the German Transylvanian
community during his reign of Wallachia in the
fifteenth century. The theme of the congress
was "Redefining the Diabolic from the Perspective of Contemporary Society." Through the
initial decades of the twenty-first century, the
society sponsored conferences in Romania at
least annually, and promoted tours of Dracula
sites each October around Halloween through
the Company of Mysterious Journeys. It offered
a variety of Dracula-related products through
Count Dracula Treasures, Ltd.

Outside of Romania, the most active chapter has been the Canadian chapter, headed by
Dracula scholar Elizabeth Miller. Miller founded
the *Journal of Dracula Studies*, which in 2009
was transferred from Canada to be henceforth
edited by Anne DeLong and Curt Herr, both
professors at Kurtztown University in Pennsylvania. Then, in 2016, with the American chapter
having become defunct, DeLong and Herr
formed a new North American chapter of the
TSD, which assumed responsibility for future
issues of the journal (now appearing annually).

Over the years, the TSD had sponsored the periodic World Dracula Conference. In 2016, at the World Dracula Conference in Dublin, it was announced that the Transylvanian Society of Dracula in Romania was being closed and that the Dublin conference would be its last event. A new organization, Children of the Night, was being founded to pick up TSD's work relative to the organization of international conferences. That action left the North American chapter as the only active remnant of the TSD.

The North American chapter of the TSD may now be contacted through its website at https://www.kutztown.edu/academics/colleges-and-departments/liberal-arts-and-sciences/departments/english/journal-of-dracula-studies.html.

VAMPIRES AROUND THE WORLD

Vampires! They're Everywhere!

In the nineteenth century, Western anthropologists began to explore the world's cultures in a somewhat systematic way, their work introducing an international readership to the diversity of belief and practice found around the world. As researchers and writers began to focus on the vampire in the last half of the twentieth century, they began to sample the anthropological literature and, to their initial surprise, found vampire-like beings in cultures on every continent from China to Mexico, from West Africa to India. As the number of such vampire-like entities grew, some began to jump far beyond what the data actually documented and suggested that every culture had a vampire.

What we have come to think of as vampires do exist in many cultures throughout the world, but many of the world's peoples have shown no knowledge of such an entity. The entities we have found also vary considerably from the Eastern European vampire that has served as the basis of the popular fictional character in contemporary Western popular culture. Some vampires from folk cultures are revenant, some living beings (often also identified as witches), and some purely supernatural creatures, gods, impish lesser beings, or demons. They are tied together by their ability to suck the blood or life force from their victims.

Below, we take a world tour to visit various peoples and cultures, where we will briefly introduce various vampire and vampire-like characters. It should be noted that among the places where the vampire traditionally was most often absent were Western Europe and North America, where with only a few exceptions, the vampire was introduced in the eighteenth century.

ᕯ *The Americas* ᕯ

African American Vampires

Vampire beliefs have not been prominent among African Americans, though a few have been reported. These few were seemingly derived from the mythologies of Africa, which believed in both vampires and witches who acted like vampires and were brought to the United States either directly or by way of Haiti or the other French islands in the Caribbean. Folklorists working among African Americans in the southern United States in the late-nineteenth and early twentieth centuries found accounts of vampires. Some were more traditional bloodsuckers. One account from Tennessee told of an old woman whose health seemed to constantly improve, while the children's health declined because she sucked their blood while they slept: "De chillun dies, an' she keeps on a-livin'." The most definable vampire figure reported among African Americans was the *fifollet* or the *feu-follet*, known to the residents of Louisiana. The *fifollet*, the traditional will-o'-the-wisp (a light seen at night over the swamp areas) derived from the French incubus/succubus figure, was the soul of a dead person that had been sent back to Earth by God to do penance but instead attacked people. Most of the attacks were mere mischief, but on occasion, the *fifollet* became a vampire that sucked the blood from people, especially children. Some believed that the *fifollet* was the soul of a child who had died before baptism.

Modern African American Vampires: Vampires have made only infrequent appearances in African American folklore and, similarly, African Americans have been largely absent from vampire movies and novels through the twentieth century. The few Black vampire movies emerged in the era of blaxploitation movies in the early and mid-1970s. Only one African American vampire character, Prince Mamuwalde (better known as Blacula), attained any fame beyond the fans of vampire movies.

The prince, portrayed by Shakespearean actor William Marshall, appeared in two movies, *Blacula* (1972) and *Scream Blacula Scream* (1973). Released the same year as *Blacula* was *Alabama's Ghost* (1972), a blaxploitation movie in which a vampire rock group battles a ghost.

Another lesser-known African American vampire movie is the 1973 *Ganja and Hess* (released in video under a variety of names, including *Blood Couple*, *Double Possession*, *Black Evil*, and *Black Vampire*). Like *Blacula*, the movie was set in New York. It concerned Dr. Hess Green (played by Duane Jones), who becomes a vampire after being stabbed with an ancient African dagger by his assistant. While largely ignored by American horror fans, the movie received some notice by internationals and was honored as a Critics Choice film at the 1973 Cannes Film Festival. More recently, director Spike Lee remade *Ganja and Hess*, his work being released as *Da Sweet Blood of Jesus* (2014).

The vampire never became a prominent role for black actors, however, and with a few

William Marshall plays the title role in 1973's Scream Blacula Scream, *the sequel to* Blacula *(1972).*

notable instances—Teresa Graves in *Old Dracula* (also known as *Vampira*) and Grace Jones in *Vamp*—few appeared in leading roles.

Meanwhile, in the 1970s, Marv Wolfman, who created the very successful vampire comic series *The Tomb of Dracula*, included the African American Blade the Vampire Slayer among the major characters. Through several attempts to revive the series, Blade emerged as the single most popular of Wolfman's characters and eventually, in the mid-1990s, got his own Marvel comic book series. As Blade emerged to prominence, the character was altered to more closely conform to the superhero for which Marvel was best known and his half-vampire nature emphasized. Beginning in 1997, this new Blade became the subject of three very successful movies starring Wesley Snipes. In the wake of Blade's success, as the DVD market and independent movie industry expanded, a set of new African American vampire movies, most going straight to DVD, appeared. These latter include *Cryptz* (2002), *Vegas Vampires* (2004), *Vampiyaz* (2004), *Vampz* (2004), *Vampire Assassin* (2005), *Bloodz vs. Wolvez* (2006), and *Dead Heist* (2007).

Like the new set of vampire movies, some vampire novels were included among the growing number of books written especially for an African American audience. Only a few of these, most notably Jewelle Gomez's *The Gilda Stories* (1991), gained a larger audience. Of course, earlier, science fiction pioneer Octavia Butler wrote the important *Patternmaster* series, which featured some energy vampires. In the first, *Patternmaster* (1974), Doro, an African, survived over the centuries by transferring his consciousness from one body to another and feeding on each new victim's mental energy in the process. The storyline was continued in *Mind of My Mind* (1977), *Clay's Ark* (1984), and *Survivor* (1979), though this final novel would later be disowned by the author.

Then in 2003, Leslie E. Banks, writing under her pseudonym L. A. Banks, issued *Minion*, the first of what became her *Vampire Huntress* books. Amid the success of *Buffy the Vampire Slayer*, Banks's series was constructed around a young, African American vampire hunter named Damali. It found an audience among readers of romance novels, and by 2010, Banks, with a dozen titles on the shelves, had emerged as the most successful African American writer of vampire fiction to date. In subsequent years, no one has appeared to overtake her lead.

Mexico

Accounts of vampires in Mexico can be traced as far back as the ancient Maya, whose territory centered on what is now Guatemala but also reached north into the Yucatán Peninsula and the southern part of present-day Mexico.

This was the territory of the vampire bats, which were incorporated into the mythol-

The oldest surviving manuscript of the Popol Vuh *is this 1701 text by Francisco Ximénez. It is a sacred narrative of the Maya, which includes a tale of the Camazotz cave god.*

ogy of the Maya. Camazotz, the fierce cave god of the Maya underworld, is best known from his appearance in the *Popol Vuh*, a foundational sacred narrative of the K'iche' people, one of the Maya peoples, and from his representations in Maya art.

In the *Popol Vuh*, two brothers entered the underworld to avenge the death of their father. To accomplish their task, they had to pass through a number of obstacles, one of which was the Bat House. They were first attacked by a horde of bats and then by Camazotz himself. Camazotz was pictured as a man-bat with a sharp nose and large teeth and claws. At one point, one of the brothers stuck his head out of their hiding place, and Camazotz quickly decapitated him. The head was then used as the ball in a game. The decapitated brother obtained a substitute head, and the brothers eventually played the game and won.

Camazotz, with his sharp nose and large teeth and claws, was a popularly feared figure among the Maya, and numerous representations appeared in Maya art. Camazotz served two diverse purposes. He was integral to the basic agricultural myth built around the cycle of growing maize. In his descent, he brought death to the maize grain at the time it was buried in the earth, a necessary step leading to its rebirth in the harvest. He was also a feared, bloodthirsty god of the caves. People avoided places believed to be his dwelling place.

The Aztecs: From the elaborate mythology of the Aztecs, whose territory was north of the Maya lands, came several vampire-like deities. Among those cited as vampiric was the lord of the underworld, the region of the dead; however, he appeared to have been more a devourer of the souls of the dead than a vampiric figure. Nevertheless, a set of vampire-like figures was evident in the goddesses related to the "earth lady," Tlalteuctli, the personification of the rock and soil upon which humans lived. Tlalteuctli was also a terror-producing figure.

Never pictured as a woman, she was shown as a huge toad with blood covering her jaws. Several of the female figures that surrounded the earth lady shared a common hideousness and thirst for blood: Coatlicue, "serpent skirt"; Cihuacoatl, "snake woman"; Itzpapalotl, "obsidian knife butterfly"; and the *cihuateteo*. These goddesses were also known as the *cihuapipiltin*, or princesses.

Coatlicue was described as black, dirty, disheveled, and ugly. A statue of her survived and has been placed in the National Museum in Mexico City. It has a skirt of snakes and a necklace of hands and hearts with a skull-shaped pendant. The head is missing, and in its stead

A 14th-century statue of the Aztec fertility goddess Cihuacoatl is maintained at the Museo Nacional Antropologia in Madrid, Spain.

is a stream of gushing blood that becomes two rattlesnake heads.

Cihuacoatl was the ancient goddess of Culhuacan, but after the fifteenth century, her worship was centered in Xochimilco. Her appearance was terrifying: stringy hair, her mouth open to receive victims, and two knives gracing her forehead. However, she had the ability to change herself into a beautiful, young woman who, like vampire demons in many lands, enticed young men to their doom. They had sexual relations with her only to wither away and die afterward. Cihuacoatl survived into this century both as the Virgin of Guadalupe in Roman Catholic lore and as La Llorona, the Weeping Woman, in popular folklore. As such, she could be heard at night weeping for her dead children. Cihuacoatl represented the hunger of the gods for human victims, and state prisoners were regularly sacrificed to satisfy her need for blood. Itzpapalotl, not as specifically vampiric as the other two, was a personification of the ritual sacrificial knife.

The *cihuateteo* were the most vampiric of all the Aztec deities. They originated from women who died in childbirth. They had once been mortal, had struggled with the child, and had succeeded in holding it until both died in the struggle. Thus, they attained the status of warrior. As demonic figures, the *cihuateteo* very much resembled such other vampiric figures as the *lamiai* of ancient Greece or the *langsuyar* of Malaysia. The *cihuateteo* wandered the night and attacked children, leaving them paralyzed or otherwise diseased. They held counsel with other *cihuateteo* at local crossroads. Food offerings were placed at crossroads in structures dedicated to the *cihuateteo* so that they would gorge themselves and not attack the children; also, if the vampiric beings remained at the crossroads until morning, they would be killed by the sunlight. In recent years, the *cihuateteo* have been described as having white faces and chalk-covered arms and hands. They wear the costume of Tlazolteotl, the goddess of all sorcery, lust, and evil.

The *Tlahuelpuchi*: The Aztec culture was largely destroyed by the European invasion and the religious conquest of the land by Roman Catholicism. The goddesses continued somewhat, however, transformed in the popular imagination into witches that survived under different names. They were called *bruja* (feminine) or *brujo* (masculine) by the Spanish and *tlahuelpuchi*, the bloodsucking witch, by the descendants of the Aztecs.

The *tlahuelpuchi* was a person (most often a woman) believed to possess the power to transform itself into one of several animals and, in that form, attack and suck the blood of infants or, on rare occasions, children and adults. The *tlahuelpuchi* drew elements from both the ancient Aztec goddesses and the witches of Spain, who had the power to transform themselves into animals and liked to suck the blood of infants. The most common animal into which the witches transformed themselves was a turkey, but animals as varied as fleas, cats, dogs, and buzzards were reported. Such witches lived incognito in their communities, and witches became objects of fear, especially among couples with infants.

> The *tlahuelpuchi* was born a witch and had no control over her condition, which remained with her for life.

The *tlahuelpuchi* was born a witch and had no control over her condition, which remained with her for life. Since the condition was a chance occurrence of birth, the witch could not pass her condition to another. It was impossible to tell if a person was a witch until she reached puberty. The power of transformation arrived with the first menses. At that time, the young witch also developed an insatiable thirst for human blood. The fact that a person was a witch would soon become known to relatives, of course, but out of shame and fear, they would seek to conceal the fact. A witch would kill anyone who revealed her identity but would otherwise not attack kinspeople. The *tlahuelpuchi* had to have blood at least once a month and some as much as four times a month.

On the last Saturday of every month, the *tlahuelpuchi* entered the kitchen of her dwelling and performed a magical rite. She lit a fire made of special substances and then transformed into an animal, usually a dog.

> As recently as 1954, the state of Tlaxcala passed a law requiring that infants reportedly killed by witchcraft had to be referred to medical authorities.

Her lower legs and feet were left behind in the form of a cross. Upon her return from feeding, she retransformed into a human and reattached her appendages. The witch could, on occasion, be known by the limp developed from her regular transformations. Occasionally, the witch might attack children, adults, or the livestock of a person they had quarreled with.

The *tlahuelpuchi* also had hypnotic power over individuals and could cause them to kill themselves primarily by having them walk to a high place and jump to their death. They might also attack livestock of people they wished to harm. Thus, particular kinds of evil that affected people were routinely attributed to the witches in their midst.

Protection from witches was most ensured by use of the ubiquitous garlic. Wrapped in a tortilla, cloves of garlic might be placed in the clothes of an infant. In the absence of garlic, an onion might be substituted.

Additionally, a bright metal was considered effective, and parents sometimes placed a machete or a box of pins under their infant's crib. Pins or other metal objects might be fashioned into a cross. Parents also used clear water, mirrors, or holy medals. Infant deaths were attributable to parents having relaxed their vigilance in protecting their child.

On occasion, people reported seeing a witch in animal form. It was spotted and distinguished from other animals by the phosphorous illumination it emitted. Often, an attempt to kill it would follow either by stoning or clubbing (to avoid direct physical contact), but more often than not, the witch escaped by changing form. On vary rare occasions, a woman in the community was called out as a *tlahuelpuchi*. If the accusation was accepted by a group of people, that person would be attacked in her home and clubbed and/or stoned to death. Afterward, the sense organs, including the fingers, were removed, and the body, unburied, was disposed of in a deserted spot.

Belief in the *tlahuelpuchi* has continued to the present day in rural Mexico. As recently as 1954, the state of Tlaxcala passed a law requiring that infants reportedly killed by witchcraft had to be referred to medical authorities. Researchers Hugo G. Nutini and John M. Roberts, working in the same state in the 1960s, had no trouble gathering numerous tales of witchcraft.

Also see "Mexican and Latin American Films," p. 426.

South America

South America has not been an area rich in vampire lore; however, the fact that vampire bats are native to the continent suggests that some recognition of vampirism would have appeared in the continent's folklore—and such is the case.

The *Asema*: Among the South American vampires, for example, was the *asema* of Suriname. The *asema* was very much like the *loogaroo* of Haiti and the *sukuyan* of Trinidad—all three were derived from the vampire/witch of West Africa. The *asema* took the form of an old man or woman who lived a normal community life during the daylight hours but a quite different secret existence after dark. At night, it had the ability to transform into a vampire.

It did so by taking off its skin and becoming a ball of blue light. In that form, it is said that the *asema* flew through the air, entered houses in the village, and sucked the blood of its victims. If it liked the blood, it would continue taking it until the person died. Also, as with the *loogaroo*, garlic was the best protection against the *asema*. Herbs might be taken to turn the blood bitter so the *asema* would not like it, a practice noted in both Haiti and Africa. Further protection came from scattering rice or sesame seeds outside the door.

The seeds would be mixed with the nails of a ground owl. The *asema* had to pick up the seeds before entering, but because of the nails, it would continually drop them. If it remained at its task until dawn, the sunlight killed it.

Those who were suspected of being an *asema* were placed under surveyance. Their identity could be determined by watching them take off their skin. The skin was then treated with salt or pepper so that it shrank, and the vampire could not get back into it.

The *Lobisomen*: From Brazil, accounts of the *lobisomen* described it as a small, stumpy, hunchbacked, monkey-like being. It had a yellow face, bloodless lips, black teeth, a bushy beard, and plush-covered feet. It attacked females and caused them to become nymphomaniacs. It would become vulnerable when drunk on blood, thus making it easier to catch. It could then be crucified on a tree. The *lobisomen* was not a vampire, however, but rather the Portuguese form of a werewolf. It was

> From Brazil, accounts of the *lobisomen* described it as a small, stumpy, hunchbacked, monkey-like being.

created through witchcraft or from parents who were improperly cohabiting (incest). Its werewolflike nature appeared around the time of puberty when it left home and, for the first time, assumed the form of one of several animals. From that time on, usually on Tuesdays and Thursdays, it assumed an animal form. In its human form, it could be identified by a yellowish tinge to its skin and blisters on its hands from running in the woods. The werewolf condition could only be stopped if the *lobisomen* was cut with steel. Care had to be taken not to touch the werewolf's blood, however, because it was fatal. The fact of its transformation into different animals tied the werewolf to the *bruxa*, the Portuguese witch, who was the more vampire-like entity in Portuguese mythology.

Also see the Vampire Movies in Mexico and Latin America entry.

United States

European settlers who came to America brought their belief in vampires with them, though most English colonists arrived before the vampire became part of the popular culture of Great Britain. Certainly, Polish settlers from the northern Kashab area of Poland brought and kept alive vampire beliefs in their Canadian settlements. Amid the vast mythology of the many Native American tribes, few vampires have been reported, and even passing references to American Indians are rare in vampire literature. Similarly, few reports have emerged from the African American community, though remnants of African vampire mythologies have appeared in the South.

Vampirism in New England: While reports of vampires in the United States have been infrequent, stories have been scattered throughout the nineteenth century of what ap-

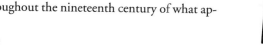

pear, at least on a cursory examination, to document a belief in vampires and action taken against them by settlers in a rather confined area in New England. The first such incident reportedly occurred during the American Revolution. A man named Stukeley, who had 14 children, began to experience the death of his brood one by one. After six had died, one of the deceased, his daughter Sarah, began to appear in dreams to his wife. The bodies were exhumed, and all but that of Sarah had decomposed. Her body was remarkably well preserved. From each body, they cut out the heart, which they burned before reburying the bodies. The first account of this story was not published until 1888, a century after it supposedly occurred, however, and no contemporary accounts of this story exist.

A similar early case was reported in 1854, much closer to the time of its occurrence. It concerned the Ray family of Jewett City, Connecticut, which consisted of a father, mother, and five children. Between 1845 and 1854, the father and two sons died of consumption, and a third son had taken ill. (Throughout the nineteenth century, consumption—i.e., tuberculosis—was a deadly disease with no known cause or cure. It thus became the subject of much occult speculation.) The family, believing that their deceased relatives were the cause of the problem, exhumed the bodies and burned them. How prevalent this belief was is not known, but a community of belief certainly existed that passed from generation to generation. Henry David Thoreau recorded in his journal on September 16, 1859, "I have just read of a family in Vermont who, several of its members having died of consumption, just burned the lungs, heart, and liver of the last deceased in order to prevent any more from having it." Another story was published in a Vermont paper in 1890. It concerned the Corwin family, who lived in Woodstock, Vermont. Six months after one of the Corwins had died of consumption, a brother took sick. The family disinterred the body of the first brother and burned the heart.

Unfortunately, no contemporary account of this incident exists, only a newspaper story published 60 years after the reported occurrence.

Among the widely retold accounts was that of the family of Mary E. Brown of Exeter, Rhode Island. Mary died of tuberculosis in December 1883. Six months later, her oldest daughter also died. In 1888, her son Edwin and his sister Mercy contracted the disease. Mercy died in January 1892. Edwin, though ill, clung to life. Two months later, the family, deciding that a vampire was involved, exhumed the bodies of all their dead relatives. The mother and oldest daughter were mere skeletons, but Mercy's body appeared to be healthy and full of blood, and the body was turned sideways in the coffin. They concluded that Mercy was a vampire, and therefore, her heart was cut out and burned before the body was reburied. The ashes were dissolved in medicine and given to Edwin. It did not help, however, and he died

The American transcendental philosopher Henry David Thoreau once recorded how a Vermont family burned the heart, liver, and lungs of their deceased as a way of stopping the spread of consumption and vampirism.

soon afterward. Mercy's body remains buried in the cemetery behind the Chestnut Hill Baptist Church in Exeter, and some local residents still think of her as the town's vampire.

George R. Stetson, the first scholar to examine the stories, noted, "In New England the vampire superstition is unknown by its proper name. It is there believed that consumption is not a physical but a spiritual disease, obsession, or visitation; that as long as the body of a dead consumptive relative has blood in its heart it is proof that an occult influence steals from it for death and is at work draining the blood of the living into the heart of the dead and causing its rapid decline." John L. Vellutini, editor of the *Journal of Vampirology*, did a thorough re-examination of the accounts and made pertinent observations on these cases. Like Stetson, he found that the term "vampirism" was not used in the earlier accounts to describe the actions against the corpses. The subject of vampirism was seemingly added into the accounts by later writers, especially journalists and local historians. Thus, by the time of the Mercy Brown case in 1892, vampirism was being used as a label to describe such incidents.

Psychic Vampirism in New England: As early as 1871, pioneer anthropologist Sir Edward Burnett Tylor, in his work *Primitive Culture*, proposed a definition of vampirism, possibly with the New England cases in mind. Tylor wrote, "Vampires are not mere creations of groundless fancy, but causes conceived in spiritual form to account for specific facts of wasting disease." In this interpretation, vampirism occurred when "the soul of a dead man goes out from its buried corpse and sucks the blood of living men. The victim becomes thin, languid, bloodless, and, falling into rapid decline, dies." He further noted, "The corpse thus supplied by its returning soul with blood, is imagined to remain unnaturally fresh and supple and ruddy." Tylor's definition of vampirism was close to what had become known as psychic vampirism. It was almost identical to the defi-

Sir Edward Burnett Tylor, the founder of cultural anthropology, explained in his Primitive Culture *that the belief in vampires might have arisen to explain wasting diseases.*

nition proposed by the French psychical researcher Z. J. Piérart in the 1860s that was popular in occult circles for the rest of the 1800s. It differed radically from the idea of the Eastern European vampire, which was believed to be a revived corpse that attacked living people from whom it sucked the blood.

The belief, discovered by Stetson, underlying the practice of removing and burning the heart of a deceased tubercular patient could properly be described as a form of psychic vampirism. Vellutini also observed that no belief in vampires (that is, the resuscitated corpse of Eastern European vampire lore) was ever present in the belief system of New England.

The practice of attacking the corpses of dead tubercular patients disappeared in the early twentieth century due, no doubt, to the discovery of the cause and then the cure of tuberculosis. Periodically, accounts of the New England cases were rediscovered and published. In 1993, for example, Paul S. Sledzik of the National Museum of Health and Medicine reported on his examination of a cemetery near Griswold, Connecticut, of corpses that showed signs of tuberculosis, which had been mutilated in the nineteenth century. Finally, in 2001, folklorist Michael E. Bell completed two decades of study of the New England cases in his most thorough survey, *Food for the Dead.*

Asia and Oceana

Australia

Vampires do not play a large part in the folklore of Australia. However, in Aboriginal cultures existed the *yara-ma-yha-who*, a vampire-like being. It was described as a little red man, approximately four feet tall, with an exceptionally large head and mouth. It had no teeth and simply swallowed its food whole. Its most distinguishing features, however, were its hands and feet. The tips of the fingers and toes were shaped like the suckers of an octopus.

The *yara-ma-yha-who* lived in the tops of wild fig trees. It did not hunt for food but waited until unsuspecting victims sought shelter in the tree and then dropped on them. The story of the *yara-ma-yha-who* was told to young children who might wander from the tribe, and naughty children were warned that it might come and take them away.

> When a person camped under a fig tree, a *yara-ma-yha-who* might jump down and place its hands and feet on the body. It would then drain the blood from the victim....

When a person camped under a fig tree, a *yara-ma-yha-who* might jump down and place its hands and feet on the body. It would then drain the blood from the victim to the point that the person was left weak and helpless but rarely enough, at least initially, to cause the victim to die. The creature would later return and consume its meal. It then drank water and took a nap. When it awoke, the undigested portion of its meal would be regurgitated. According to the story, the person regurgitated was still alive, and children were advised to offer no resistance should it be their misfortune to meet a *yara-ma-yha-who.* Their chances of survival were better if they let the creature swallow them.

People might be captured on several occasions. Each time, they would grow a little shorter until they were the same size as the *yara-ma-yha-who.* Their skin would first become very smooth and then they would begin to grow hair all over their body. Gradually, they were changed into one of the mythical, little, furry creatures of the forest.

Australian Pop Culture: Quite separate from Aboriginal folklore, the British settlers brought the vampire to Australia in the later nineteenth century. Among the first reprints of *Dracula* (occurring almost simultaneously with the first edition) was the colonial edition released by Hutchinson that circulated outside England in what were then colonies, including Australia. As Australia developed its own distinctive popular culture, the vampire was present in, for example, the 1950s novellas of Michael Waugh and the 1970s vampire comic books of Gerald R. Carr. Outside the country, most note has been taken of several Australian vampire movies, which would include *Barry MacKenzie Holds His Own* (1974), *Thirst* (1979), *Outback Vampires* (1987), *Pandemonium* (1988), *Bloodlust* (1992), *Island of the Vampire Birds* (1999), *Bloodspit* (2002), *Reign in Darkness* (2002), and *Daybreakers* (2009).

China

When Western scholars began to gather the folklore of China in the nineteenth century, they very quickly encountered tales of the *chiang-shih* (also spelled *kiang shi*), the Chinese vampire, generally translated into English as "bloodsucking ghost." Belief in vampires partially derived from a Chinese belief in two souls. Each person had a superior or rational soul and an inferior or irrational soul. The former had the form of the body and, upon separation, could appear as its exact double. The superior soul could leave the sleeping body and wander about the countryside. For a short period, it could possess the body of another and speak through it. If accidents befell the wandering soul, it would have negative repercussions on the body. On occasion, the superior soul appeared in an animal form.

The inferior soul, called the *p'ai* or *p'o*, was the soul that inhabited the body of a fetus during pregnancy and often lingered in the body of a deceased person, leading to its unnatural preservation. When the *p'ai* left, the

Two women dress up as chiang-shih *in a Halloween celebration in China.*

body disintegrated. The *p'ai*, if strong, preserved and inhabited the body for a long period and could use the body for its own ends. The body animated by the *p'ai* was called a *chiang-shih*, or vampire. The *chiang-shih* appeared normal and was not recognized as a vampire until some action gave it away. However, at other times, it took on a hideous aspect and assumed a green, phosphorescent glow. In this form, the *chiang-shih* developed serrated teeth and long talons.

The Origin and Destruction of the *Chiang-shih*. The *chiang-shih* seems to have originated as a means of explaining problems associated with death. The *chiang-shih* arose following a violent death due to suicide, hanging, drowning, or smothering. It could also appear in a person who had died suddenly or as a result of improper burial procedures. The dead were thought to become angry and restless if their burial was postponed for a long time after their death. Also, animals, especially cats, were kept away from the unburied corpse to prevent them from jumping over it, lest they become vampires themselves.

The *chiang-shih* lacked some of the powers of the Slavic vampire. It could not, for example, dematerialize; hence, it was unable to rise from the grave, being inhibited both by coffins and the soil. Thus, their transformation had to take place prior to burial, an added incentive to a quick burial of the dead. The Chinese vampires were nocturnal creatures and limited in their activity to the night hours. The *chiang-shih* had trouble crossing running water. They were very strong and vicious. Reports detailed their attacks upon living people, where they ripped off the head or limbs of their victims. This homicidal viciousness was their most often reported trait. They usually had to surprise their victims because they had no particular powers to lure or entice them. Besides their homicidal nature, the *chiang-shih* might also demonstrate a strong sexual drive that led it to attack and rape women. Over a period of time, the vampires gained strength and began to transform to a mobile state. They would forsake the coffin habitat, master the art of flying, and develop a covering of long, white hair. They might also change into wolves.

In general, the vampire began its existence as an unburied corpse. However, on occasion, reports of unburied body segments appeared, especially the head, being reanimated and having an existence as a vampire. Also, reports have survived of the ever-present Chinese dragon appearing as a vampire.

People knew of several means of protection from a vampire. Garlic, an almost universal medicinal herb, kept vampires away. Salt was believed to have a corrosive effect on the vampire's skin. Vampires were offended by loud noises, and thunder would occasionally kill one. Brooms were handy weapons with which a brave soul could literally sweep the vampire back to its resting spot. Iron filings, rice, and red peas created barriers to the entry of the vampire and would often be placed around a

Garlic is a well-known defense against the vampire, but did you know that salt, rice, and red peas could also work? Not to mention brooms, loud noises, and iron filings!

vacant coffin to keep a vampire from taking it as a resting place.

If the vampire reached its transformative stage as the flying, hairy creature, only thunder or a bullet could bring it down. In the end, the ultimate solution was cremation, the purifying fire being something of a universal tool of humankind.

The *Chiang-shih* in Literature: The *chiang-shih* was the subject of numerous stories and folktales. In the seventeenth century, the vampire became the subject for one of China's most famous short story writers, Pu Songling (1640–1715), author of the 16-volume *Liao Choi*. His story "The Resuscitated Corpse," for example, concerned four merchants who stopped at an inn. They were housed for the night in the barn, where, as it happened, the body of the innkeeper's daughter-in-law lay awaiting burial. One of the four could not sleep and stayed up reading. The corpse, now bearing fangs, approached the three sleeping men and bit each one. The other man watched frozen in fright. He finally came to his senses and, grabbing his clothes, fled, with the vampire hot on his trail. As she caught up to him, he stood under a willow tree. She charged with great speed and ferocity, but at the last second, the man dodged, and she hit the tree with full force, her long fingernails embedded in the tree. The man fainted from fright and exhaustion. The next day, the innkeeper's staff found the three dead merchants and the body of his daughter-in-law lying in her place but covered with blood. She was as fresh as the day she died, as she still had her *p'ai*, her inferior soul. The innkeeper confessed that she had died six months earlier, but he was waiting for an astrologically auspicious day for her burial. (A vague possibility exists that Pu Songling was influenced by European sources via Russia, as the vampire is a relative latecomer in Chinese ghostly tales. A variety of his stories have been translated into English, and a complete edition translated into German was made by Gottfried Rösel and published in five large volumes between 1987 and 1992.)

Ullambana, the Festival of Hungry Ghosts, is celebrated on August 15, a day when the gates of hell open up and ghosts who have been forgotten by their living descendants wander the earth.

Hungry Ghosts: The modern idea of the vampire in Chinese culture is also tied to the notion of the hungry ghost. This concept has roots in both Buddhism and Taoism, which posit that neglect of one's ancestors can lead to the emergence of hungry ghosts. The Buddhist Avatamsaka or Flower Garland Sutra, for example, suggests that evil deeds can cause a soul to be born in one of six possible realms. Serious evil deeds such as killing, stealing, or sexual misconduct will cause a soul to be born as a hungry ghost, while desire, greed, and ignorance effect such rebirth, as they are motives for people to perform evil deeds. Many legends speak of a greedy woman who refused to share food becoming a hungry ghost in the next life.

Each summer, the Chinese celebrate Ullambana, the Festival of Hungry Ghosts, on the fifteenth day of the seventh month in the Chinese lunar calendar (usually in August). The fifteenth day of a lunar month is the full moon. The Chinese believe that during the seventh month, the gates of hell are opened up and hungry ghosts are free to roam the earth seeking food and making mischief. These ghosts are the forgotten people whose living descendants no longer offer homage. They have long, thin necks and large, empty bellies. At this time, people will burn specially printed currency, popularly called "hell money," which the ghosts can spend in hell to make more comfortable lives for themselves.

People will acknowledge the wandering ghosts at this time to prevent them from making mischief and/or bringing bad luck. This acknowledgment will take the form of a ritual activity during Ullambana in which food is offered to the ghosts.

Modern Vampires in China: The Chinese vampire was given a new lease on life by the post–World War II development of the film industry in Hong Kong and, to a lesser extent, in Taiwan. Actually, at least three vampire movies were made in Hong Kong in the 1930s prior to World War II: *Midnight Vampire, The Three-Thousand-Year-Old Vampire*, and *Vampires of the Haunted Mansion*. Several more would appear in the 1950s, such as *Vengeance of the Vampire* (1959); however, the late twentieth-century explosion of vampire movies really begins with two Hong Kong–based firms, Catay-Keris and the Shaw Brothers, which began making vampire films in Malaysia using Malaysian themes in the 1950s but were rather late in developing Chinese vampire movies. Among the first Chinese vampire movies was *Xi Xuefu* (*Vampire Woman*), produced by Zhong Lian in 1962. Like many first ventures into vampirism, it was ultimately a case of mistaken attribution. The story concerned a woman who, after she was found sucking the blood out of her baby, was accused of vampirism and was executed by burning. Later, it was discovered that the baby had been poisoned, and she was only trying to save it.

The vampire theme in Chinese movies was really launched a decade later with the first of the vampire martial arts movies, *Vampire Kung-fu* (1972). Then, two years later, a combined Shaw Brothers–Hammer Films production, variously titled *The Legend of the Seven Golden Vampires* and *The Seven Brothers Meet Dracula*, became one of the great disasters in horror film history. *The Legend of the Seven Golden Vampires*, directed by Roy Ward Baker and starring Peter Cushing, transferred the Dracula story to China, where Abraham Van Helsing was called to protect a village from a band of vampires who had learned martial arts skills. The film was so bad that its American distributor refused to handle it.

In the 1980s, Hong Kong filmmakers rediscovered the vampire horror genre. Among

the best-known movies was the *Mr. Vampire* comedy series that was started in 1985 by Golden Harvest and Paragon Films. Drawing on several aspects of Chinese folklore, the films featured what have come to be known as the hopping vampires—loose-robed vampires that hopped to move around—a character developed from a character in Chinese mythology, the bloodsucking ghost. The first film was so popular it spawned four sequels, a television series in Japan, and a rival production, *Kung-fu Vampire Buster* (1985). A second very successful movie was *Haunted Cop Shop* (1984), concerning vampires who took over a meat-packing plant and were opposed by a Monster Police Squad. A sequel appeared in 1986. Other notable Hong Kong films included *Pao Dan Fei Che* (*The Trail*, 1983), *Curse of the Wicked Wife* (1984), *Blue Lamp in a Winter Night* (1985), *Dragon against Vampire* (1985), *The Close Encounter of the Vampire* (1985), *Love Me Vampire* (1986), *Vampire's Breakfast* (1986), *Hello Dracula* (1986), *Vampires Live Again* (1987), *Toothless Vampires* (1987), *Vampires Strike Back* (1988), *Spooky Family* (1989), *Crazy Safari* (1990), *First*

Some offerings from Asia can be quite odd, such as First Vampire in China, *a 1990 movie from Hong Kong in which an ancient king is killed by wizards, dressed in armor made of gold and jade, and then transformed into a vampire.*

Vampire in China (1990), *Spooky Family II* (1991), and *Robo Vampire* (1993). As might be perceived by the titles, many of these movies were comedies, a few unintentionally so. Taiwanese films of the same era included *The Vampire Shows His Teeth I, II,* and *III* (1984–1986), *New Mr. Vampire* (1985), *Elusive Song of the Vampire* (1987), and *Spirit vs. Zombie* (1989).

With the hopping or jumping vampires, a different mythology about dealing with vampires evolved. They could be subdued with magical talismans, usually wielded by a Taoist priest, who became a staple character in vampire cinema. Holding one's breath would temporarily stop them. Eating sticky rice was an antidote to a vampire bite. By creating a separate vampire myth, the Chinese movies have built a new popular image of the vampire in the Orient as much as the Dracula movies created one in the West.

Interest in the vampire continued in Hong Kong through the 1980s but appeared to decline significantly through the 1990s, especially after the Chinese takeover of Hong Kong in 1997. Only a very few vampire movies have appeared in the new century: *Vampire Combat* (2001), *Tsui Hark's Vampire Hunters* (2002), *My Honey Moon with a Vampire* (2003), *The Twins Effect* (2003), *The Twins Effect II* (2004), *Shaolin vs. Evil Dead* (2004), *Shaolin vs. Evil Dead: Ultimate Power* (2006), and *Dating a Vampire* (2006). Through the twentieth century, however, over 100 vampire movies were made in Hong Kong.

India

Among the vast number of deities and supernatural entities found in India's religious world were a number that possessed vampiric characteristics and were noted in the vampire literature. They merge into a wide variety of demonic entities that more closely resemble ghosts, ghouls, living witches, and sorcerers. The Indian vampire and vampiric entities ap-

peared in ancient Indian texts, and some have speculated that India was one place where belief in vampires originated and from there spread to surrounding lands. It was certainly evident that the Romani people brought a form of vampire belief from India with them when they migrated westward.

In ancient Hinduism (the dominant religion of India), creation was portrayed as beginning with the formation of a golden egg (cosmic intelligence). Visible creation resulted from the division of the egg into the heavens, the earth, and the 21 regions of the cosmos. These 21 regions of the cosmos were roughly divided into three zones, one of which was the Tala, or subterranean, region, the abode of the chthonian entities, including ogres, spectres, and demons.

A supernatural creature from Hindu and, later, Buddhist mythology, the rakshasha *were described as maneaters with fangs and a monstrous appearance.*

The most well known of the vampiric beings from the Tala were the *rakshasas* (feminine, *rakshasis*), generally described as ogres and demons who lived in cemeteries and disturbed the affairs of people by disrupting rituals and interrupting devotions. The slaying of infants was among their most loathsome actions. The *rakshasas* came in a variety of forms, some male and some female, some more humanoid and some half animal. Hanuman, the deity that appeared in the form of a monkey, was reported to have observed *rakshasas* in every imaginable shape when he entered the city of Lanka as an envoy of Rama. They were characters in many Indian epics, such as the *Mahabharata* and the *Ramayana* (which contains the Hanuman episode), and many of the deities and mythical heroes gained their reputation by slaying them. The *rakshasas* were cited as vampires because of some of their characteristics. For example, they were nocturnal wanderers of the night. They had a fearsome appearance with elongated fangs. Texts described them as *asra-pa* or *asrk-pa* (literally: "drinkers of blood"). Like the Greek *lamiai*, they sought pregnant female victims and were known to attack infants. The natural enemy of the *rakshasas* was Agni, the dispeller of darkness and officiator at sacrificial rituals, and people called on Agni to destroy or ward off demons.

Closely associated with the *rakshasas* were the *yatu-dhana* (or *hatu-dhana*), sorcerers who devoured the remains left by the *rakshasas*. On occasion, the term *yatu-dhana* was used interchangeably with *rakshasas*. Also frequently mentioned with the *rakshasas* but even lower on the scale of beings were the *pisachas* (literally: "eaters of raw flesh"), also described as hideous in appearance, repellant, and bloodthirsty. The texts described them as flesh-eating ghouls and the source of malignant disease. In the *Puranas*, a set of Hindu writings, the *pisachas* were described as the products of the anger of the deity Brahma.

After creating gods, demons (*asuras*), ancestors, and humankind, Brahma became afflicted with hunger, and they began to eat his body, for they were *rakshasas* and *yaksas*. When Brahma saw them, he was displeased, and his hair fell out and became serpents. When he saw the serpents, he was angry, and the creatures born of his anger were the fierce, flesh-eating *pisachas*. Thus, Brahma created cruel creatures and gentle creatures, *dharma* and *adharma*, truth and falsehood.

Also possessing some vampiric characteristics were the *bhutas*, the souls of the dead, specifically those who had died an untimely death, had been insane, or had been born deformed. They wandered the night and appeared as dark shadows, flickering lights, or misty apparitions. On occasion, they would enter a corpse and lead it in its ghoulish state to devour living persons. The *brahmaparusha* was a similar entity known in northern India.

Bhutas lived around cremation grounds, old ruins and other abandoned locations, and deserts. They might undergo a transformation into either owls or bats. The owl had a special place in Indian mythology. It was considered unlucky to hear the owl's hoot, possibly fatal if heard in a burial ground. Owl flesh could be used in black magic rituals. *Bhutas* were the ever-present evil spirits and were considered dangerous for a wide variety of reasons. They ate filthy food and were always thirsty. They liked milk and would attack babies who had just fed. They could enter the body through various orifices and possess a person. While the *bhutas* might act in a vampirish way on occasion, they generally were seen as simply malevolent beings.

The Indian demonlike figures possibly closest to the Western vampire were the *vetalas* or *betails*, spirits that inhabited and animated the bodies of the dead. A *betail* was the central character in the *Vetala-Pachisi*, a classic piece of Indian literature comparable to Chaucer's *Canterbury Tales* or the *Arabian Nights*. Originally translated and published in English in the mid-nineteenth century, a new translation of 11 of what he deemed were the most interesting of the stories was made by Sir Richard F. Burton and published in 1870 under the title *Vikram and the Vampire*. The *Vetala-Pachisi* described the encounter of King Vikram with a *betail*, who told him a series of tales. Vikram, like King Arthur, was an actual person who lived in the first century C.E. and became a magnet for many tales and fables. In the book, a yogi cajoled Vikram to spend an evening with him in the cemetery. He then asked Vikram to bring him a body he would find some four miles to the south at another burial ground. The body, the yogi told him, would be hanging on a mimosa tree. The body turned out to be a *betail*. Vikram encountered great difficulty in getting the vampire to accompany him back to the yogi but finally succeeded through his persistence. To entertain them on the return trip, the *betail* told a series of stories that formed the body of the book.

When they reached the cemetery with the yogi, the king found him invoking Kali. He was surrounded by the host of demons from Indian lore, including the *rakshasas*, the *bhutas* (who had assumed various beastly shapes), and the *betails*. The yogi led them to the shrine of the goddess Kali. There, Vikram killed the yogi, who was about to kill him. As a boon, the gods granted him fame.

A survey of Indian vampiric entities would be incomplete without further mention of the goddess Kali, often associated with Siva as a consort. She was a dark goddess, usually pictured as having black skin. She had a terrible and frightening appearance, wearing parts of the human body as ornaments. Her favorite places were the battlefield, where she became drunk on the blood of her victims, and the bu-

Kali is the Hindu goddess of power and death. A consort of the god Siva, she is a warrior being who would get drunk drinking the blood of her victims.

rial/cremation ground. In *Vikram and the Vampire*, Kali appeared in the shrine located at the cemetery and, as Vikram entered, he saw her:

> There stood Smashana-Kali, the goddess, in her most horrible form. She was a naked and a very black woman, with half-severed head, partly cut and partly painted, resting on her shoulder; and her tongue lolled out from her wide yawning mouth; her eyes were red like those of a drunkard; and her eyebrows were of the same colour; her thick coarse hair hung like a mantle to her knees.

Burton comments on this passage:

> Not being able to find victims, this pleasant deity, to satisfy her thirst for the curious juice, cut her own throat that the blood might spout up into her mouth.

Other Vampiric Entities: Throughout India, among the various ethnic/linguistic groups were a multitude of ghosts, demons, and evil spirits who lived in or near cemeteries and cremation locations and bore some resemblance to the vampires of Europe. Many fooled others by assuming the form of a living person. They reverted to a horrible, demonic appearance just before attacking their victims. For example, in Gujarat were the *churels*, women who died an unnatural death (in western India, the *churels* were also known as a *jakhin, jakhai, mukai, nagulai,* and *alvantin*). If such a woman had been treated badly by her family, she would return to harass them and dry up the blood of the male family members. Such a woman could become a *dakini*, an associate of the goddess Kali and partaker in her vampirish and ghoulish activities. If a young man was tempted by a *churel* and ate of the food she offered, she would keep him with her until dawn and return him to his village as a gray-haired, old man. The *churel* had one noticeable feature that gave her away: her feet were turned backward, so her heel was in the front and her toes in the back.

Women at the time of childbirth and their infants were given great attention by family and friends. A woman who died in childbirth was likely to become a ghost. To prevent that from occurring, the family would bury rather than cremate the body. They would then fix four nails in the ground at the corners of the burial spot and plant red flowers on top of the grave. A woman who died in childbirth was also buried in a special place (the exact spot differing in various sections of India). For example, the corpse could be carried outside the house by way of a side door and buried within the shadow of the house by the noontime sun. It was believed that by not using the front door, the *churel* would be unable to find her way home. Some used iron nails in the house's threshold and sprinkled millet seeds on

the road to the burying ground. As in Eastern Europe, the *churel* must count the seeds, a task that kept her busy until daybreak. In Punjab, a woman who died in childbirth would have nails driven through her hands and feet, red pepper placed in her eyes, and a chain wrapped around her feet. Others broke the legs above the ankles and turned the feet around backward, bound the big toes together, or simply bound the feet with iron rings.

> The *chedipe* was pictured as riding a tiger through the night. Unclothed, she entered the home of a sleeping man and sucked his blood out of his toe.

Among the most interesting vampires was the *chedipe* (literally, "prostitute"), a type of sorceress in the Godavari area. The *chedipe* was pictured as riding a tiger through the night. Unclothed, she entered the home of a sleeping man and sucked his blood out of his toe. Using a form of hypnotism, she put the others in the household into a trancelike sleep so that they were unaware of her presence. In the morning, the man would awaken but feel drained of energy and somewhat intoxicated. If he did not seek treatment for his condition, the *chedipe* would return. On occasion, the *chedipe* would attack men in the jungle in the form of a tiger with a human leg.

Devendra P. Varma has made a case that the vampire deities of the ancient Hindus are the source of vampire beliefs in Europe. He asserted that such beliefs were carried by the Arab caravans over the Great Silk Route from the Indus Valley into the Mediterranean Basin. They probably arrived in Greece around the first century C.E. This theory, while entirely possible, has yet to be developed in the depth necessary to place it beside alternative theories that project multiple origins of vampiric myth in different cultures to meet a set of fairly universal needs.

Japan

The varied creatures of Japanese folklore did not include a classical, bloodsucking vampire. Possibly the most vampire-like of the numerous mythological beings was the *kappa*. Described as fabulous creatures of the waters—rivers, ponds, lakes, and the sea—the *kappas* penetrated the Japanese culture and now appear in fiction, cartoons, toys, and art. The *kappa* was first widely written about in the eighteenth century. It was described as an unattractive, humanlike child with greenish-yellow skin, webbed fingers and toes, and looked somewhat like a monkey with a long nose and round eyes. It had a shell similar to a tortoise and smelled fishy. It had a concave head that held water. If the water in its head spilled, the *kappa* would lose its strength. The *kappas* operated from the edge of the water in which they lived. Many stories related attempts by *kappas* to grab horses and cows, drag them into the water, and suck their blood through their anuses (the main trait that has earned *kappas* some recognition as vampires). However, they have been known to leave the water to steal melons and cucumbers, rape women, and attack people for their livers. People would propitiate the *kappas* by writing the names of their family members on a cucumber and throwing it into the river where the *kappas* lived.

A statue of a kappa *on display in Thailand appears almost whimsical.*

The *kappas* were viewed as part of the rural landscape. They were not attacked by humans, but on occasion, *kappas* attempted to strike deals with them. Such a relationship was illustrated in the story of "The *Kappa* of Fukiura." The *kappa* near Fukiura was a troublesome creature until one day, it lost an arm trying to attack a horse. A farmer retrieved the arm, and that night, the *kappa* approached the farmer to ask for its return. Rebuffed at first, the *kappa* finally convinced the farmer to return the arm by promising that it would never again hurt any of the villagers. From that time forward, as reported by the villagers, the *kappa* would warn them by saying, "Don't let the children go out to the beach, for the guest is coming." The guest was another *kappa* not bound by the *kappa* of Fukiura's agreement.

Another popular story of the *kappas* told of one who lived at Koda Pond. A man left his horse tied by the pond. A *kappa* tried to pull the horse into the pond, but the horse bolted and ran home. The *kappa* spilled its water, lost its strength, and was carried to the stable. The man later found his horse along with the *kappa*. Caught in a weakened condition, the *kappa* bargained with the man, "If you prepare a feast in your home, I will certainly lend you necessary bowls." From that time on, whenever the man got ready to hold a feast, the *kappa* would bring bowls. After the feast, the bowls would be set out, and the *kappa* would retrieve them.

Apart from the *kappa*, the Japanese had another interesting folktale. "The Vampire Cat of Nabeshima" told the story of Prince Nabeshima and his beautiful concubine, Otoyo. One night, a large vampire cat broke into Otoyo's room and killed her in the traditional manner. It disposed of her body and assumed her form. As Otoyo, the cat began to sap the life out of the prince each night while the guards, strangely, fell asleep. Finally, one young guard was able to stay awake and saw the vampire in the form of the young girl. As the guard stood by, the girl was unable to approach the prince,

In the Japanese film Hiroku kaibyô-den *("The Haunted Castle"; 1969), a woman seeks revenge on a warlord by drawing upon supernatural powers. It doesn't end well for her.*

who then slowly recovered. Finally, it was deduced that the girl was a malevolent spirit who had targeted the prince. The young man, with several guards, went to the girl's apartment. The vampire escaped, however, and removed itself to the hill country. From there, reports of its work were soon received. The prince organized a great hunt, and the vampire was finally killed. The story has been made into a play, *The Vampire Cat* (1918), and a movie, *Hiroku kaibyô-den* (1969).

Contemporary Japanese Vampires: The Japanese, while lacking an extensive vampire lore, have in the last generation absorbed the European vampire myth and contributed to it primarily through the film industry. Their contemporary vampire is called a *kyuketsuki*. As early as 1956, a film with a vampire theme, *Kyuketsuki Ga*, was released. It concerned a series of murders in which all the victims had fang marks on their necks, but in the end, the killer turned out not to be a vampire. Some years later, the director of *Kyuketsuki Ga* worked on another film, *Onna Kyuketsuki* (1959), which told of a real vampire who kidnapped the wife of an atomic scientist. Among Japan's 1960s vampire movies was *Kuroneko* (1968), which built upon the vampire cat legend. A

woman and her daughter were raped and murdered by a group of samurai. They returned from the grave as vampires who could transform themselves into black cats and attack their murderers. In *Yokai Daisenso*, a provincial governor was possessed by a bloodsucking Babylonian demon, an early signal of the coming absorption of Western elements into the Japanese movies.

Hammer Films's vampire movies inspired the 1970 *Chi i Suu Ningyo* (*The Night of the Vampire*) and the 1971 *Chi o Suu Me* (released in the West as *Lake of Dracula*), both directed by Michio Yamamoto. Dracula made his first appearance in Japan in the 1970s. In *Kyuketsuki Dorakyura Kobe ni Arawaru: Akuma wa Onna wo Utsukushiku Suru* (*Vampire Dracula Comes to Kobe: Evil Makes a Woman Beautiful*) (1979), Dracula discovered that a reincarnation of the woman he loved lived in Kobe, Japan. In 1980, *Dracula*, a full-length, animated movie based on the Marvel Comics characters in the very successful *The Tomb of Dracula*, was the first of a number of excellent cartoon vampire features out of Japan. It was followed by *Vampire Hunter D* (1985) and *Vampire Princess Miyu* (1988), some of the most watched of the Japanese features in the West. In *The Legend of the Eight Samurai* (1984), director Kinji Fukasaku offered a Japanese version of the Elizabeth Báthory story in which an evil princess bathes in blood to keep her youth. The vampire theme was carried into the 1990s with such movies as *Tale of a Vampire*, directed by Shimako Sato and based upon the Edgar Allan Poe poem "Annabel Lee."

By the end of the 1990s, manga, the Japanese comic books, and anime, the animated version of comic art, had found an audience, and amid the hundreds of titles making their way to the West were a representative number of vampire titles. The more successful manga had originated as anime or were made into anime. Through the first decade of the twenty-first century, a number of vampire-oriented television series for children and youth appeared, most animated, including *Descendants of Darkness* (2000), *Hellsing* (2001), *Vampiyan Kids* (2001–2002), *Lunar Legend Tsukihime* (2003), *Vampire Host* (*The Vampire Gigolo*) (2004), *Tsukuyomi: Moon Phase* (2004–2005), *Karin* (2005), *Trinity Blood* (2005), *Blood+* (2005–2006), *Negima!?* (2006–2007), *Black Blood Brothers* (2006–2008), *Rosario + Vampire* (2008), *Higanjima* (2013), and *Tokyo Vampire Hotel* (2017). Translated and transferred to DVDs, these television

Vampires have flapped into quite a few Japanese anime films and TV, including the miniseries Hellsing *(2001), in which vampires team up to save England from a Nazi major who commands a vampire army of his own.*

shows were later released in the West, along with their related comic books.

After *Vampire Hunter D* appeared, it became recognized as one of the finest vampire films of all time, and both writer Hideyuki Kikuchi and artist Yoshitaka Amano were recognized for their talents. Kikuchi went on to write a series of *Vampire Hunter D* novels, and Amano illustrated the movie's sequel, *Vampire Hunter D: Bloodlust* (2000), and the covers of the novels. Subsequently, Digital Manga Publishing and Hideyuki Kikuchi collaborated on a project to adapt and publish all of the *Vampire Hunter D* novels in a manga format.

Java (Indonesia)

The Javanese shared much of their mythology with Malaysia and the rest of Indonesia. Included in that mythology was the belief in the *pontianak*. The *pontianak* was a bansheelike creature that flew through the night in the form of a bird. It could be heard wailing in the evening breeze as it sat in the forest trees. It was described variously as a woman who died a virgin (de Wit) or a woman who died giving birth (Kennedy). In both cases, it appeared as beautiful, young women and attacked men whom it emasculated. De Wit noted that the *pontianak* appeared fairer than any love goddess. Such creatures would embrace a man but immediately withdraw after a single kiss. In the process, they revealed the hole in their backs, which had been covered by the long tresses of hair. The man had to grab the hair and pull out a single strand or he would be vampirized by the woman. If he failed, he would soon die; if he succeeded, he would live a long and happy life.

The *pontianak* also attacked babies and sucked their blood out of jealousy over the happiness of the mother. Infants who were stillborn or died soon after birth of an unknown cause would be thought of as victims of a *pontianak*.

Malaysia

Western observers who began to look at the magical/religious world of Malaysians in the nineteenth century discovered belief in several vampire-like beings somewhat analogous to the *lamiai* of the mythology of Greece. These beliefs have survived to this day in spite of the overlay of Hindu and Islamic thought that has come to dominate the religious life of the peninsula. Vampires still inhabit the very lively world of the average Malaysian.

The langsuyar *of Malaysian tales is a revenant woman, who is easily identified by long fingernails and a green robe.*

The Vampire in Malaysian Folklore: Two Malaysian beings are closely related to the Greek *lamiai*: the *langsuyar* and the *pontianak*. The former was described as a bansheelike, flying demon. The original *langsuyar* was a woman of extreme beauty who bore a stillborn baby. When told of the condition of the child, she recoiled from the shock. Suddenly, she clapped her hands and flew away into a nearby tree. She was seen from time to time and identified by her green robe, long fingernails (considered a mark of beauty in Malaysian society), and ankle-length, black hair. The hair concealed an opening in her neck through which she sucked the blood of children. The first *langsuyar* then gave way to groups of similar beings. Later *langsuyars* were seen as flesh eaters with a particular fondness for fish (a staple of the Malaysian diet).

If a woman died either in childbirth or in the 40 days immediately following (during which time she was considered unclean), it was believed she might become a *langsuyar*. To prevent that from occurring, her family placed glass beads in her mouth (which stopped any bansheelike shrieks). To prevent her from flying, they would place eggs under her arms and a needle in the palm of each hand. However, it was also possible to tame a *langsuyar* by capturing it, cutting off its hair and nails, and stuffing them into the hole in the neck. In that case, the *langsuyar* became domesticated and could live in human society somewhat normally. Reports have been collected claiming that such *langsuyars* came into villages, married, and bore children.

However, their new life ended usually at a village party when they began to dance. Suddenly, they would revert to their more spiritlike form and fly off to the jungle, leaving their husband and child behind.

The origin of the *pontianak* was directly linked to that of the *langsuyar*: it was the creature's stillborn child. It was believed to take the form of a night owl. To prevent a deceased baby from becoming a *pontianak*, it was treated somewhat like its mother: with beads, eggs, and needles. As with the *langsuyar*, specific words were to be spoken when "laying" a possible *pontianak*. Walter William Skeat, an early authority on Malaysian mythology, noted some confusion between the *langsuyar* and the *pontianak*. Both could appear as a night owl, both were addressed in invocations as if they were the same, and both mother and child were treated alike to prevent them from becoming a vampire after their deaths. This confusion has been somewhat cleared up by noting that in parts of Malaysia and throughout much of Indonesia in places such as Java, what Skeat described as the *langsuyar*, the female vampire, was called a *pontianak*.

Meanwhile, the *penanggalan* was a third vampire-like creature in Malaysian folklore. According to tradition, it originated with a woman in the midst of performing *dudok bertapa*, a penance ceremony. She was sitting in a large, wooden vat used for holding the vinegar derived from the sap of the palm tree. In the midst of her ceremony, a man found her and asked her what she was doing. Startled, she moved to leave, doing so with such force that her head separated from her body and, with the entrails of her stomach trailing behind, she flew off into a nearby tree. That severed head with the dangling stomach attached below it became an evil spirit. It appears on the rooftops of the homes where children are being born. It whines a high-pitched sound and tries to get to the child to suck its blood.

Writing in the early 1800s, P. J. Begbie described the *penanggalan* as an evil spirit that possessed a woman and turned her into a sorcerer. When it wished to travel, it would detach its head and, with its entrails trailing behind, fly off in pursuit of food in the form of the blood of both the living and dead. He also told the story of a man with two wives, one of dark skin and one of light skin. He was told that they were both *penanggalans*. The man did not believe it, so to test them, he watched one night

and saw them leave to feed. He then switched their bodies. When they returned, they attached their heads to the wrong bodies. When the king was presented with this irrefutable proof of their evil nature, both were executed.

An alternate version of the story stated that the *penanggalan* originated from a woman who had been using magic arts and finally learned how to fly. At that time, her head and neck were separated from her body and, with her intestines dangling, she took up her abode in a tree. From there, she flew from house to house to suck the blood of not only babies but also mothers giving birth. To protect the birthing site, the leaves of the jeruju (a kind of thistle) were hung around the house and thorns stuck in any blood that was spilled. As might be expected, blood and other juices dripped from the dangling intestines, and should such drippings fall on anyone, they would immediately fall ill.

The penanggalan *is a creature that could separate its head, heart, and entrails from its body in order to fly in pursuit of victims.*

Two other blood-drinking entities, the *polong* and the *pelesit*, were closely related in Malaysian lore. The former appeared in the form of a very small, female creature (about one inch in height) and the latter as a house cricket. The *polong* operated somewhat like a witch's familiar in traditional Western mythology. It could be attracted by gathering the blood of a murder victim in a bottle, over which a seven-day (some say 14-day) ritual

> It [the *eng banka*] attacked humans who cut the plant in which it resided by biting them and sucking their blood.

was performed. Then, one waited for the sound of young birds chirping, a sign that the *polong* had taken up residence in the bottle. The *polong* was fed by cutting a finger, inserting it into the bottle, and allowing the *polong* to suck the blood. (In the West, the witch's familiar was said to suckle from a hidden protuberance on the witch's body—a witch's teat). In return for a daily supply of blood, the *polong* was available to do a variety of tasks, including attacking one's enemies. If one was attacked by a *polong*, which was signaled by various kinds of wild ravings, wise men were called in to exorcise it and attempt to discover who sent it to torment the victim. Deaths were occasionally attributed to the attack of a *polong* who remained unexorcised.

The *pelesit* generally accompanied the *polong* in its travels and arrived before it. If the *polong* was sent to attack someone, the *pelesit* would first attempt to enter the body of the victim and, in a sense, prepare the way for the *polong*. Walter William Skeat reported a rather gruesome method of creating a *pelesit*. The potential owner dug up a recently deceased infant. The infant's corpse was carried to an ant hill. After a while, the child would cry out and, at that moment, its tongue would have to be bitten off. The tongue was then dipped in specially prepared coconut oil and buried for three nights.

After the third night, the tongue turned into a *pelesit*. The Chewong were among the many peoples in the very diverse population of Malaysia. They possessed their own mythology, which included the existence of many spirits, collectively called the *bas*. Various kinds of *bas* existed, some of which attacked humans under certain circumstances. The usual food of the *bas* was a *ruwai*, roughly translated as "soul or life" or "vitality." Their preferred prey was the wild pig, and the *bas* set invisible traps to snare the pig's *ruwai*. Sometimes, a human *ruwai* was caught in the trap, and in such a case, the *bas* would eat the human spirit/soul. The *bas* might also encounter a human *ruwai* when it was traveling about during a person's dreams. The *bas* usually did not attack humans or approach human places of habitation. They knew fire as a sign of human presence, and a person in the woods who encountered a *bas* could build a fire to make the *bas* depart.

On rare occasions, the *bas* were thought to attack humans. They attacked in different ways, although most sought only the *ruwai*. For example, the *eng banka*, the ghost of a dead dog that inhabited swamp areas, would steal a *ruwai*. If it was not recovered, the victim died within a few days; someone who suddenly became ill and died a few days later was seen as the victim of an *eng banka*. The *maneden*, which lived in the wild pandanus plant, differed quite a bit from the *eng banka*. It attacked humans who cut the plant in which it resided by biting them and sucking their blood. It attached itself to the elbow of men or the breast nipples of women. To stop the attack, the person had to give the *bas* a substitute, such as the oily nut from the hodj nut tree. Thus, the attack of the *eng banka* was a variety of psychic vampirism and that of the *maneden* a more literal vampiric attack.

The Modern Malaysian Vampire: It was not until after World War II that the film industry (always under strict British control) began to develop in Malaysia. Shaw Brothers, a firm based in Hong Kong, established Malay Film Productions in 1947. It was soon joined by Catay-Keris Productions. In their drive to compete with Western films, which dominated the market, the Malaysians sought particularly Malaysian themes and locales for their films. The Malaysian vampire thus entered the film world, one of the first such films being *Pontianak* in 1956. In this film, Maria Menado played a hunchbacked, young woman made beautiful by magic. After her husband was bitten by a snake and she sucked his blood to get the poison out, she was turned into a vampire, the *pontianak*. The vampire movies drew on the broad use of the term *pontianak* throughout Indonesia and always pictured the vampire as a young and beautiful woman. The stories told in the movies were made plausible to viewers by the numerous reports from Malaysians who claimed to actually know a vampire who was living a more or less normal life as a wife and mother. In the late 1950s and 1960s, Catay-Keris eventually produced a series of six movies featuring a *pontianak*. The original Catay-Keris film has been lost and no known copies exist, but several of the others, such as *Pontianak Gua Musang* (1964) and a later movie, also called simply *Pontianak* (1975), have been released in the video CD format still popular as the twenty-first century began in southeast Asia. After the Shaw Brothers closed their Malaysian operation in the 1960s, few horror movies were made in Malaysia. The film industry largely disappeared in the mid-1970s.

When Malaysian films began to be made again in the 1990s, a series of restrictions had been placed on the books primarily to guide Muslim censors in reviewing Hollywood movies. Among the characters banned from the screen were vampires and monsters, who could only appear in dream sequences. The first attempt to make a horror movie within the stated guidelines was the popular *Pontianak Sundal Malam* (2001). Its success opened the door both to more vampire movies and a loosening of the restrictions. As the

> When Malaysian films began to be made again in the 1990s, a series of restrictions had been placed on the books primarily to guide Muslim censors in reviewing Hollywood movies.

industry revived, a new series of *pontianak* films have appeared, such as *Pontianak Harum Sundal Malam* (2004) and its sequel, *Pontianak Menjerit* (2005), *Kuntilanak* (2006), *Pontianak Sesat Dalam Kampung* (2016), and *Dendam Pontianak* (2019).

Philippines

The modern Philippines is a country composed of numerous peoples whose belief systems survive, some in a rather secularized form, in spite of several centuries of Islamic and Christian missions and the development of a host of modern indigenous religions. The tribes of the Philippine Islands had an elaborate mythology, which included demonic beings, dragons, were-animals, giants, ghouls, and vampires. The Capiz section of the island of Panay was especially associated with the vampire, where many were believed to reside.

Of the vampire-like creatures, the *aswang* was by far the most well known throughout the islands. The term *aswang* was used to describe a set of different creatures that were analogous to vampires, werewolves, ghouls, and witches and, in the folklore, literature could be found under any one of those headings.

The flying *aswang*, or the bloodsucker, usually appeared as a beautiful maiden who engaged in vampiric activities at night, always returning home to resume her normal life before dawn. Some women have an ointment that they rub on their bodies prior to their nocturnal activities. The ointment was the source of their supernatural abilities. In its vampiric state, the *aswang* became a large bird that flew through the sky, crying out *kakak* or *kikak*. It would land on the roof of a prospective victim's house and let down a long tongue with a sharp point. The point was used to prick the jugular vein, and the blood was sucked up through the hollow tongue's tubular structure. Children were told stories of the possibility of being attacked by an *aswang*. Once filled with blood, the *aswang* resembled a pregnant woman. Upon returning home, she fed her children, who suckled at her breast. The *aswang's* supernatural powers ceased either with its washing off the ointment or the coming of dawn.

The *aswang* was a common bugaboo parents used to keep children in line. A large percentage of Filipinos grew up with at least some belief in its existence. The strength of this belief was documented quite vividly in the 1950s when it was used against a group of insurgents (the Huks or Hukbalahaps) during the presidency of Ramon Magsaysay (1907–1957), a Philippine leader strongly supported by the American government. American advisors to Magsaysay convinced him to create a psychological warfare unit to counter the efforts of Huk leaders to win people away from their support of the central government. Among the efforts of this unit, noted in General E. G. Lansdale's account, was an attempt to convince a Huk unit to abandon a position in fear of an *aswang's* attack.

An aswang *is any type of shapeshifting creature from Filipino mythology, including vampires, witches, werebeasts, and ghouls.*

The operation began with a rumor planted in a community threatened by a Huk attack. People were told that a vampire had moved into the area. The Huks were barricaded at the top of a nearby hill. They soon became aware of the rumor that was spreading through the area. Several days later, the psychological warfare unit was able to capture a Huk soldier and kill him by draining his blood. They made two puncture wounds on his neck and left him on the road near the hill, where he would be found. When he was found, the Huks believed their dead comrade to be a victim of the *aswang*. The next day, all of the Huk troops left.

Building on Lansdale's account, Norine Dresser noted that in the late 1980s, she found that the story of the *aswang* and the Huks and other tales of the *aswang* were still very much alive in the Filipino immigrant community in California. They told her the old stories of the vampire creatures, and she discovered that several of her informants still believed in the *aswang*. They also reflected on the long-range effect of the 1950s incident that many local people, not just the Huks, attributed to a vampire. Once the Huks left, people began to wonder who the *aswang's* next victims would be. Some started wearing garlic necklaces. Some left the area, and their abandoned land was taken over by the government and used in its land redistribution programs.

Despite the fear caused by the incident, everyone recognized its effectiveness in destroying the Huks' support among the people.

One tale told by the Isneg people related the origin of the vampire, which they called a *danag*. According to the story, several people were in the fields planting their crops when a woman cut her finger. Another woman sucked the wound and thereby discovered that she liked the taste of blood. She went on sucking until she had taken all of the blood. The story concluded by noting that the bloodsucking replaced farming.

The Tagalog people spoke of a vampire called the *mandurugo*, about which they told the story of "The Girl with Many Loves." The young woman was described as one of the most beautiful women ever to live in the land. She married at the age of 16. Her husband, a husky youth, withered away in less than a year. After his death, she married again, with the same result. She married a third time and then a fourth. The fourth husband, having been warned, feigned sleep one night holding a knife in his hand. Soon after midnight, he felt a presence over him and then a prick on his neck. He stuck the knife into the creature on top of him. He heard a screech and the flapping of wings. The next day, his bride was found dead some distance from the house with a knife wound in her chest.

As the Philippine film industry developed after World War II, the vampire became a subject of its attention. Given the large Roman Catholic influence on the islands, however, the films tended to relate more to the European vampire than the *aswang* or associated Philippine vampire characters. Beginning in the 1960s, a number of inexpensive B movies were made in the Philippines by American companies, including some of the most forgettable in the horror and vampire genres. Due to a variety of copyright, trademark, and trade agreement obstacles, many of the Philippine movies have never been released in the United States.

> Beginning in the 1960s, a number of inexpensive B movies were made in the Philippines by American companies, including some of the most forgettable in the horror and vampire genres.

Since the 1960s, Philippine vampire films have been rare but include *Aswang* (1992), *Corazon: Ang Unang Aswang* (2012), and *Maria Labo* (2015). The *aswang* also makes sporadic appearances in the popular *Shake, Rattle & Roll* horror film series, most notably in *Shake, Rattle & Roll 2* (1990), *Shake, Rattle & Roll 2k5* (2005), and *Shake, Rattle & Roll 8* (2006).

Central and Eastern Europe

Bulgaria

Bulgaria is one of the oldest areas of Slavic settlement. It is located south of Romania and sandwiched between the Black Sea and Macedonia. In the seventh century C.E., the Bulgar tribes arrived in the area of modern Bulgaria and established a military aristocracy over the Slavic tribes of the region. The Bulgars were only a small percentage of the population, and they eventually adopted the Slavic language.

Christianity arrived with force among the Bulgarians in the ninth century when Pope Nicholas I (r. 858–867) claimed jurisdiction over the lands of the former Roman province of Illyricum. He sent missionaries into Bulgaria and brought it under Roman hegemony. The Bulgarian ruler, Boris-Michael, was baptized in 865, and the country officially accepted Christianity. The pope sent two bishops but would not send an archbishop or appoint a patriarch, causing Boris to switch his allegiance to the Eastern Orthodox Church based in Constantinople. A Slavic liturgy was introduced to the church and has remained its rite to the present.

Among the many side effects of Byzantine influence in Bulgaria was the growth of a new rival religious group, the Bogomils. The Bogomils grew directly out of an older group, the Paulicians, whose roots went back to the dualistic Maniceans. The Paulicians had been moved into Bulgaria from Asia Minor to prevent their alignment with the Muslim Arabs. The Bogomils believed that the world had been created by the rejected son of God, Satanael. While the earthly bodies of humans were created by Satanael, the soul came from God. Their beliefs were seen by the church as a rebirth of the old Gnostic heresy. Jan L. Perkowski has argued at length that it was from the conflict of Bogomil ideas, surviving Paganism, and emerging Christianity that the mature idea of the Slavic vampire developed and evolved. However, his argument was not entirely convincing in that vampires developed in quite similar ways in countries without any Bogomilism.

> Most commonly, the Bulgarian vampire was associated with problems of death and burial, and the emergence of vampires was embedded in the very elaborate myth and ritual surrounding death.

When the Christian Church split in 1054, the Bulgarians adhered to the Eastern Orthodox Church of Constantinople. The Bulgarians attained their status as an autonomous Eastern Orthodox Church at the end of the twelfth century but were subsequently overrun by the Ottomans (followers of Islam) in 1396. They remained under Ottoman rule for almost 500 years, until 1878, when Turkish control was limited by the Congress of Berlin, but they did not regain complete independence until 1908.

The Bulgarian Vampire: The Bulgarian words for the vampire, a variety of the Slavic vampire, derived from the original Slavic word *opyrb/opirb*. Its modern form appears variously as *vipir, vepir,* or *vapir* or, even more commonly, as *vampir,* a borrowing from Russian. The modern idea of the vampire in Bulgaria evolved over several centuries. Most commonly, the Bulgarian vampire was associated with problems of death and burial, and the emergence of vampires was embedded in the very elaborate myth and ritual surrounding death. At the heart of the myth was a belief that the spirits of the dead went on a journey immediately after death. Guided by their guardian angel, they

traveled to all of the places they had visited during their earthly life. At the completion of their journey, which occurred in the 40 days after their death, the spirit then journeyed to the next life. However, if the burial routine was done improperly, the dead might find their passage to the next world blocked. Generally, in Bulgaria, the family was responsible for preparing the body for burial. The family could err or become negligent in their preparation in a number of ways. Also, the body had to be guarded against a dog or cat jumping over it or a shadow falling on it prior to burial. The body had to be properly washed. Even with proper burial, a person who died a violent death might return as a vampire.

As in other Slavic countries, certain people were likely candidates to become vampires, such as those who died while under excommunication from the church. Drunkards, thieves, murderers, and witches were also to be watched. Bulgaria was a source of tales of vampires who had returned to life, taken up residence in a town where they were not known, and lived for many years as if alive. They even married and fathered children. Such people were detected after many years because of some unusual event that occurred. Apart from their nightly journeys in search of blood, the vampire would appear normal, even eating a normal diet.

Among the Gagauz people—Bulgarians who speak their own language, Gagauzi—the vampire was called *obur*, possibly a borrowing from the Turkish word for "glutton." As with other vampires among the southern Slavs, the *obur* was noted as a gluttonous blood drinker. As part of the efforts to get rid of it, it would be enticed by the offerings of rich food or excrement. The *obur* was also loud, capable of creating noises like firecrackers, and could move objects like a poltergeist.

Scottish social anthropologist and folklorist James Frazer studied mythologies and religions across cultures. So many cultures have vampires in their folklore, and Frazer noted that the Bulgarian ustrel *is one of them.*

Social anthropologist and folklorist James Frazer noted the existence of a particular Bulgarian vampire, the *ustrel*. The *ustrel* was described as the spirit of a child who had been born on a Saturday but died before receiving a baptism. On the ninth day after its burial, a *ustrel* was believed to work its way out of its grave and attack cattle or sheep by draining their blood. After feasting all night, it returned to its grave before dawn. After some ten days of feeding, the *ustrel* was believed to be strong enough that it did not need to return to its grave. It found a place to rest during the day either between the horns of a calf or ram or between the hind legs of a milch cow. It was able to pick out a large herd and begin to work its way through it, the fattest animals first. The animals it attacked—as many as five a night—would die the same night. If a dead animal was cut open, the signs of the wound that the vampire made would be evident.

As might be suspected, the unexplained death of cows and sheep was the primary sign that a vampire was present in the community. If a *ustrel* was believed to be present, the owner of the herd could hire a *vampirdzhija*, or vampire hunter, a special person who had the ability to see vampires, so that all doubt as to its presence was put aside. Once it was detected, the village would go through a particular ritual known throughout Europe as the lighting of a needfire. Beginning on a Saturday morning, all the fires in the village were put out. The cattle and sheep were gathered in an open space. They were then marched to a nearby crossroads, where two bonfires had been constructed. The bonfires were lit by a new fire created by rubbing sticks together. The herds were guided between the fires. Those who performed this ritual believed that the vampire dropped from the animal on whose body it had made its home and remained at the crossroads, where wolves devoured it. Before the bonfires burned out, someone took the flame into the village and used it to rekindle all the household fires.

Other vampires, those that originated from the corpse of an improperly buried person or a person who died a violent death, were handled with the traditional stake. Reports also came from Bulgaria of a unique method of dealing with the vampire: bottling. This practice required a specialist, the *djadadjii*, who had mastered the art. The *djadadjii's* major asset was an icon, a holy picture of Jesus, Mary, or one of the Christian saints. The vampire hunter took his icon and waited where the suspected vampire was likely to appear. Once he saw the vampire, he chased it, icon in hand. The vampire was driven toward a bottle that had been stuffed with its favorite food. Once the vampire entered the bottle, it was corked and then thrown into the fire.

The folklore of the vampire has suffered in recent decades. The government manifested great hostility toward all beliefs it considered superstitious, which included both vampires

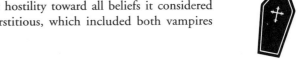

and the church. As the church was suppressed, so was the unity of village life that provided a place for tales of vampires to exist.

Czech Republic and Slovak Republic

The first historical state in what is now the territory occupied by the Czech Republic and the Slovak Republic was founded by tribes that settled in the mountainous region north of present-day Austria and Hungary. The state founded in the seventh century would, two centuries later, be united with the Great Moravian Empire, which in 836 C.E. invited Cyril and Methodius, the Christian missionaries, into their land. While among the Czechs and Slovaks, the pair preached and taught the people in their native Slavic language. However, Roman Catholicism, not Eastern Orthodoxy, dominated church life, and Latin, not Old Church Slavic, became the language of worship. The Moravian Empire disintegrated early in the tenth century, and the Slovak Republic became part of Hungary. After a period under German control, the Czech state reemerged as the Czech (Bohemian) Kingdom. Like Poland, both the Czechs and the Slovaks became Roman Catholic.

The Bohemian Kingdom survived through the Middle Ages but gradually, through the sixteenth century, came under Austrian hegemony and, in the next century, was incorporated into the Hapsburg Empire. At the end of the eighteenth century, a revival of Czech culture nurtured a revival of Czech nationalism. Finally, in 1918, at the end of World War I, Czechoslovakia was created as an independent state. That country survived through most of the twentieth century, though 1,000 years of separate political existence had driven a considerable wedge between the Czechs and the

Slovaks. After World War II, Communist rule replaced the democratic government that had been put in place in 1918. The Communist system was renounced in 1989, and shortly thereafter, Bohemia and Moravia parted with the Slovak Republic. On January 1, 1993, two separate and independent countries, the Czech Republic and the Slovak Republic, emerged.

The Vampire in the Czech Republic and the Slovak Republic: The Czech and Slovak vampire—called an *uppyr* and, to a lesser extent, *nelapsi* in both Czech and Slovak—was a variety of Slavic vampire. The *uppyr* was believed to have two hearts and, hence, two souls. The presence of the second soul would be indicated by a corpse's flexibility, open eyes, two curls in the hair, and a ruddy complexion. Among the earliest anecdotes concerning Czech vampires were two fourteenth-century stories recounted by E. P. Evans in his volume on the *Criminal Prosecution and Capital Punishment of Animals* (1906), as mentioned in Dudley Wright's survey. The first concerned a revenant that terrorized the town of Cadan. The people he attacked seemed destined to become a vampire like him. They retaliated, attacking his corpse and driving a stake through it. That remedy proved ineffective, and they finally burned him. In 1345 in Lewin, a woman believed to be a witch died. She returned in various beastly forms and attacked villagers. When uncovered in her grave, it was reported that she had swallowed her facecloth; when the cloth was pulled out of the grave, it was stained with blood. She also was staked, which again proved ineffective. She used the stake as a weapon while walking around town. She was finally destroyed by fire.

Writing in 1863, Henry More recorded events that occurred in the late 1500s to Johannes Cuntius (or Kunz), a merchant who troubled his family and neighbors following his

> The Czech and Slovak vampire—called an *uppyr* and, to a lesser extent, *nelapsi* in both Czech and Slovak—was a variety of Slavic vampire.

violent death. Cuntius lived in the town of Pentsch (present-day Horni Benesov). His son lived in Jagerdorf (present-day Krnov) in a part of Moravia dominated by Lutheran Protestants. Dom Augustin Calmet included reports of vampires from Bohemia and Moravia in his famous 1746 treatise. He noted that in 1706, a treatise on vampires, *Magia Posthuma* by Charles Ferdinand de Schertz, was published in Olmutz (Moravia). *Magia Posthuma* related a number of incidents of vampires that made their first appearance as troublesome spirits that would attack their former neighbors and the village livestock. Some of the reports were of classic nightmare attacks accompanied with pain, a feeling of being suffocated, and squeezing around the neck area. Those so attacked would grow pale and fatigued. Other stories centered on poltergeist effects featuring objects being thrown around the house and possessions of the dead person mysteriously moving. One of the earliest and more spectacular cases concerns a man of the Bohemian village of Blow (Blau) in the fourteenth century. As a vampire, he called upon his neighbors, and whomever he visited died within eight days. The villagers finally dug up the man's body and drove a stake through it. The man, however, laughed at the people and thanked them for giving him a stick to fend off the dogs. That night, he took the stick out of his body and began again to appear before people. After several more deaths occurred, his body was burned. Only then did the visitations end. Schertz, a lawyer, was most concerned with the activity of villagers who would take the law into their hands and mutilate and burn bodies. He argued that in cases of severe disturbances, a legal process should be followed before any bodies were desecrated. Included in the process was the examination of the body of any suspected vampire by physicians and theologians. Destruction of the vampire, by burning, should be carried out as an official act by the public executioner.

Montague Summers was most impressed by the evidence of vampirism detailed by Count de Cadreras, who early in the 1720s was commissioned by the Austrian emperor to look into events at Haidam, a town near the Hungarian border. The count investigated a number of cases of people who had been dead for many years (in one case 30 years and another 16 years) and reportedly returned to attack their relatives.

Upon exhumation, each still showed the classic signs of delayed decomposition, including the flow of "fresh" blood when cut. With the count's consent, each was beheaded (or nails driven into the skull) and then burned. The extensive papers reporting these incidents to the emperor survived as well as a lengthy narrative given by the count to an official at the University of Fribourg.

> The count investigated a number of cases of people who had been dead for many years (in one case 30 years and another 16 years) and reportedly returned to attack their relatives.

It is unlikely that the town of "Haidam" will ever be identified. No place by that name has been recorded. It has been suggested most convincingly that the term derived from the word *haidamak*, a Ukrainian term meaning "outlaw" or "freebooter." *Haidamak*, derived from the Slavic word *heyduck*, referred to a class of dispossessed who had organized themselves into loose, itinerant bands to live off the land. Eventually, the Austrian Hapsburg rulers employed them as guardians along their most distant frontiers. This Haidam probably referred to the land of a *haidamak* rather than a specific town by that name.

As recently as the mid-twentieth century, folklorist Ján Mjartan reported that the belief in vampires was still alive in the Slovak Republic. The vampire was thought to be able to suck the blood of its victims (humans and cattle) and often suffocated them. The vampire also was believed capable of killing with a mere glance (evil eye), thus devastating whole villages. Preventing the rise of a suspected vampire was accomplished by placing various objects in the coffin (coins,

The concept of the "evil eye" (being able to curse someone with a potent glare) is omnipresent in many world cultures. These nazar from Turkey are ornaments designed to protect against the evil eye.

Christian symbols, various herbs, the dead person's belongings), putting poppyseeds or millet seeds in the body orifices, and nailing the clothes and hair to the coffin. Finally, the head or heart could be stabbed with an iron wedge, an oak stake, a hat pin, or some thorn, such as the hawthorn. The body was carried headfirst to the grave, around which poppyseeds or millet seeds were scattered. The seeds also were dropped on the path homeward and, once home, various rituals, such as washing one's hands and holding them over the stove, were followed. The family of the deceased repeated these measures if they proved ineffective the first time.

Contemporary Vampire Lore: As with other Slavic countries, the belief in vampires receded to rural areas of the Czech Republic and the Slovak Republic through the twentieth century. It made a brief appearance in the midst of the Czech cultural revival of the nineteenth century in a famous short story, "The Vampire" by Jan Neruda (1834–1891). In recent decades, Josef Nesvadba, a Czech psychiatrist, has emerged as an impressive writer of horror fiction. A collection of his stories in English was

published in 1982 as *Vampires Ltd.* In the twenty-first century, Czechs and Slovaks have rediscovered Elizabeth Báthory, one of the superstars of the vampire world, though they are caught in the middle of promoting her for the sake of tourism while having their most famous citizen vilified as a monster. A few have arisen to seriously look at the defense of Báthory as a victim of Catholic anti-Protestantism, published in the 1980s by Laszlo Nagy. However, as books on Báthory continue to appear, the legend generally wins over history. A variety of publications on Báthory have appeared in the Czech Republic and the Slovak Republic since the fall of the Berlin Wall, as have several movies (*Demons Claw*, 2006; *Báthory: Countess of Blood*, 2008; and *Blood Countess*, 2008).

Greece

Greece is one of the oldest sources for the contemporary vampire legend. Ancient Greek writings record the existence of three vampire-like creatures: the *lamiai*, the *empusai*, and the *mormolykiai*. Also known in Greece was the *strige*, a vampire witch. *Strige* was derived from the Latin word *strix*, which originally referred to the screech owl and later to a night-flying demon that attacked and killed infants by sucking their blood. The *lamiai* was named after Lamia, who was said to have been a Libyan queen. She was the daughter of Belus and Libya and, as the story was told, was loved by Zeus, the king of the Greek gods. Hera, Zeus's wife, became jealous and took out her resentment by robbing Lamia of all her children, who had been fathered by Zeus. Unable to strike at Hera, Lamia retired to a cave from where she took out her anger by killing the offspring of human mothers, usually by sucking the blood out of the children. Her actions led to her transformation into a hideous beast. (The story of the *mormolykiai* is very similar—they are named after a woman named Mormo, who cannibalized her own children.) Later, Lamia became identified with a class of beings modeled after her, described as coarse-looking women with deformed, serpentlike lower bodies. Their feet were not identical; instead, one was brass and the other was shaped like that of an animal, commonly a goat, donkey, or ox. The *lamiai* were known primarily as demonic beings who sucked the blood from young children; however, they had the power to transform themselves into beautiful, young maidens in order to attract and seduce young men. Philostratus included a lengthy account of the *lamiai* in this transformation in chapter 25 of the fourth book of his *Life of Apollonius*. One of Apollonius's students, Menippus, was attracted to a beautiful, rich woman whom he had first encountered as an apparition. In a dreamlike state, he was told when and where he would find her. The young man fell in love and contemplated marriage. When he related his story to Apollonius, the latter informed his young student that he was being hunted by a serpent. Upon meeting the woman, he told Menippus, "And that you may realize the truth of what I say, this fine bride is one of the vampires (*empusai*), that is to say of those beings whom many regard as *lamiai* and hobgoblins (*mormolykiai*). These beings fall in love, and they are devoted to the delights of Aphrodite, but especially in the flesh of human beings, and they decoy with such delights those whom they mean to devour in their feats." In spite of protestations by Menippus, Apollonius confronted the *lamiai* with the facts. One by one, the elements of her environment disappeared. She finally admitted her plans and her habit of feeding "upon young and beautiful bodies because their blood is pure and strong." Philostratus called this account the "best-known story of Apollonius." Apuleius, in the very first chapter of the *The Golden Ass*, recounted the story of an encounter with a *lamiai* who caught up with her fleeing lover and killed him by first thrusting her sword into his neck, taking all of his blood, and then cutting out his heart.

The people soon lost their fear of the *lamiai* and, even in ancient times, they had simply become a tool for parents to frighten

In Greek mythology, Lamia was one of Zeus's lovers and bore him several children. When Zeus's wife, Hera, killed Lamias children in a rage, Lamia's took out her anger by drinking the blood of humans.

their children. However, when a child dies suddenly from an unknown cause, a saying still popular in Greece suggests that the child had been strangled by the *lamiai*. The *lamiai* were rediscovered in literature in the fifteenth century when Angelo Poliziano of Florence published a poem, "Lamia" (1492). In 1819, British poet John Keats authored a poem with the same name. Since the time of Keats, the *lamiai* have appeared in numerous poems, paintings, sculptures, and musical pieces. For example, August Enna authored an opera called *Lamia*, which was first performed in Antwerp, Belgium, in 1899. Poems on the same theme were written by Edward MacDowell (1888), Arthur Symons (1920), Frederick Zeck (1926), Robert

Graves (1964), and Peter Davidson (1977). Among recent novels featuring the *lamiai* were the four books of J. N. Williamson—*Death Coach* (1981), *Death School* (1981), *Death Angel* (1982), and *Death Doctor* (1982)—featuring the character of Lamia Zacharias. Also in the 1980s, Tim Powers's novel *The Stress of Her Regard* (1989), set in early nineteenth-century England, featured a *lamia* interacting with Keats, Lord Byron, John Polidori, Mary Godwin, and Percy Shelley.

The *Vrykolakas*: Although the *lamiai*, *empusai*, and *mormolykiai* were known for drinking blood, they were not vampires in the same sense as those of Eastern Europe. They were spirit beings rather than revivified corpses (revenants). The ancient Greeks, however, did have a class of revenants, *vrykolakas*, which would develop into true vampires. The term was derived from the older Slavic compound term *vblk'b dlaka*, which originally meant "wolf-pelt wearer." The term developed among the southern Slavs, from whom it probably passed to the Greeks.

The best description of revenants in ancient Greek literature appears in a story told by Phlegon, a freed man who lived in the time of the Roman emperor Hadrian. It seems that some six months after her death, Philinnon, the daughter of Demostratus and Charito, had been observed entering the room of Machates, a young man staying in the parents' guest chamber. A servant told the couple about seeing their daughter, but when they peeped into the guest chamber, they could not ascertain who Machates was entertaining. The next morning, Charito told Machates about her daughter's death. He admitted that Philinnon was the name of the girl in his room. He then produced the ring she had given him and a breast band she had left behind. The parents recognized both as possessions of their late daughter. When the girl returned that evening, the parents

stepped into the room to see their daughter. She reproached them for interrupting her visits with Machates and said she had been granted three nights with him.

However, because of their meddling, she would now die again. Sure enough, Philinnon again became a corpse. At this point, Phlegon entered the picture as a witness. As town official, he was called upon to keep order as word of Philinnon's return spread through the community that night. He led an examination of her burial vault, finding the gifts she had taken away from her first visit to Machates—but no body. The townspeople turned to a local wise man, who advised that the body be burned and appropriate purification rituals and propitiatory rites to the deities be observed.

> The ancient Greek ... did have a class of revenants, *vrykolakas*, which would develop into true vampires.

This basic story of the returned dead contains some unique aspects of the later Greek *vrykolakas* account. Once discovered, the body was, for example, characteristically burned rather than decapitated or staked through the heart. The ancient revenant was not yet a vampire or even an object of much fear. The revenant often returned to complete unfinished business with a spouse, family member, or someone close to him or her in life. On this early account of a brief visit by a revenant, more elaborate accounts would build. In later centuries, stories would be told of much lengthier visits and of *vrykolakas* who resumed life in the family.

Occasionally, a report would emerge of a revenant who went to a location where he was unknown and then remarried and fathered children. One of the oldest reports of the *vrykolakas* was written by the French botanist Joseph Pitton de Tournefort. While on the island of Mykonos in 1700, he heard of a man who had recently died yet had been reported walking about town generally making a nuisance of himself. After various noninvasive remedies failed, on the ninth day after his burial, the body was disinterred, and the heart removed and burned. The troubles did not stop. The townspeople tried sticking swords into the grave since it was a common belief that sharp objects prevented vampires from rising. At one point, an Albanian visitor to the island suggested that the problem was the sticking of "Christian" swords in the top of the grave since the cross shape of the sword would prevent the devil who was animating the corpse from leaving. He suggested using Turkish swords. It did not help. In the end, on January 1, 1701, the corpse was consumed in a fire.

Greece produced the first modern writer on vampires, Leone Allacci (commonly known as Leo Allatius). In 1645, he authored *De Graecorum hodie quorundam opinationibus*, a volume on the beliefs of the Greek people, in which he discussed the *vrykolakas* at great length. Early in the twentieth century, John Cuthbert Lawson spent considerable time investigating the *vry-*

While on the Greek island of Mykonos, French botanist Joseph Pitton de Tournefort recorded how villagers were harassed by a dead man who refused to stay buried.

kolakas in Greek folklore. He noted its development in three stages, beginning with that of pre-Christian times, represented by Phlegon's account. In that account, the return was by divine consent for a specific purpose. Lawson also found, in the ancient Greek texts, an underlying belief in revenant status as a punishment for human failure. In the likes of Euripides and Aeschylus, Lawson noted instances when people were cursed with an incorruptible body, meaning that in death, the individual would be denied communion with those on the other side of the grave. Thus, the ancient Greek writers entertained a concept of the "undead." Lawson noted three circumstances that would predispose an individual to become a *vrykolakas*. The first was the curse of a parent or someone who an individual had failed, such as that placed by Oedipus against his undutiful son. Oedipus called upon Tartarus (the place of the dead) to refuse to receive the son and drive him forth from his place of final rest. Second, one might become undead because of an evil or dishonorable act, most notably against one's family, such as the murder of a kinsman or adultery with a sister- or brother-in-law. Third, the dead might join the undead by dying violently or not being buried. The popular belief in *vrykolakas* was taken into the doctrinal perspective of the Greek Eastern Orthodox Church as it became the dominant force in Greek religious life in the first millennium C.E. The church developed a teaching both about the dead, whose bodies remain uncorrupted, and about true revenants, those who are resuscitated and return to life. Concerning the former, the church taught that a curse could in fact prevent the natural decay of the body, which at the same time became a barrier to the progress of the soul. However, the curses pronounced by parents and others took second place to the "curse" pronounced by the church in its act of excommunication (which effectively denied the victim the saving sacraments of the church). Stories of the accursed dead whose bodies did not decay gradually became the basis of a belief that excommunication produced physical results. Reports of changes in the bodies of excommunicated individuals who later had their excommunication lifted joined the popular hagiography of the church.

When it came to the *vrykolakas*, the church seemed plainly embarrassed but had to deal with what many thought, even in ancient times, to be illusionary. Multiple church documents spoke of the devil stirring up the imagination of people who believed that a dead person had come to visit. In the face of persisting accounts, however, the church developed an explanation, claiming that the devil inhabited the body of the dead and caused it to move. However, such occurrences tended to be tied to the activities of mediums in a manner reminiscent of the biblical story of the woman at Endor (1 Samuel 28).

> Multiple church documents spoke of the devil stirring up the imagination of people who believed that a dead person had come to visit.

Thus, as the church came to dominate Greek religious life, it proposed that the dead might become *vrykolakas* if they died in an excommunicated state, if they were buried without the proper church rites, or if they died a violent death. To these, it added two other causes: stillborn children or those who were born on one of the great church festivals. These causes expanded the earlier Greek notions of those who died under a familial curse or in great sin. The Christianization of the Slavic and Balkan peoples effectively began toward the end of the first Christian millennium and made impressive gains in the tenth through twelfth centuries. As the Eastern Orthodox Church gained dominance in Russia, Romania, Hungary, and among the southern Slavs, beliefs from those countries flowed back into Greece and began to alter still further the understanding of the revenant, transforming it into a true vampire. The significant concept was that of the werewolf. It was from the Slavs that the word *vrykolakas*, derived from an Old Slavic term for "wolf-pelt," was adopted as the Greek designation for a resuscitated corpse.

Some Slavic people believed that werewolves became vampires after they died. Lawson argued that the Slavic term came into Greece to describe the werewolf (a term he still found in use in a few places at the beginning of the twentieth century) but gradually came to designate the revenant or vampire. The Greeks also absorbed a Slavic view of the possible vicious nature of vampires. The ancient Greek revenant was essentially benign and returned primarily to complete some unfinished family business. On occasion, it committed an act of vengeance, but it was always one that most would consider logical. It did not enact chaotic violence.

Gradually, the view that vampires were characteristically vicious came to dominate Greek thought about the *vrykolakas*. The vampire's vicious nature was focused on its bloodthirstiness and wanton nature. The Slavic vampire also characteristically returned to work its violence upon those closest to it. A popular form of cursing one's enemy was to say, "May the earth not receive you" or "May the earth spew you forth." In effect, one was suggesting that the accursed person return as a vampire and wreak havoc on his or her nearest and dearest.

The *Callicantzaros*. One other type of vampire existed in Greece. The *callicantzaros* was a peculiar kind of vampire that was discussed at some length by Leo Allatius in his 1645 treatise *De Graecorum hodie quorundam opinationibus*. The *callicantzaros* was related to the extraordinary sanctity ascribed to the Christian holy days at Christmastime. Children born during the period after Christmas ending with the Epiphany or Twelfth Night (the evening when the Three Wise Men are supposed to have arrived at Bethlehem to present their gifts to the baby Jesus) are considered unlucky. They were described as feast-blasted and believed to be destined to become vampires after their death.

The *callicantzaros* was also distinct among vampires in that its activities were limited to Christmas Day and the week or 12 days afterward. During the rest of the year, it traveled in some vague netherworld. It was distinguished by its manic behavior and extended fingernails. It would seize people with its talons and tear them to pieces. Reports on the *callicantzaros* vary widely as to its appearance, possibly related to the state of maturity of the person deemed to be a future vampire. The *callicantzaros* had an effect upon everyday life, as any person born during the forbidden period was viewed with some degree of hostility. Parents would fear that these children would act out vampiric fantasies as they grew up and would harm their brothers and sisters.

The Modern Literary Vampire: These legends propagated the Greek idea of the vampire, which was still alive at the time British, French, and German writers began to explore

the vampire theme in poems, stories, and stage productions. As vampire literature developed, the early authors established an association between Greece and the vampire. Goethe, for example, set his 1797 poem "The Bride of Corinth" in Greece. John Keats drew upon ancient Greek sources for his poem "Lamia" (1819), and John Polidori placed much of the action for "The Vampyre" (1819) in Greece.

In the nineteenth and twentieth centuries, numerous observers discovered that belief in the *vrykolakas* was still alive in rural Greece. In 1835, William Martin Leake's *Travels in North Greece* contained several accounts of the disposal of bodies believed to be *vrykolakas*. Lawson's study, previously noted, recounted many anecdotes he had retrieved in his fieldwork, and as recently as the 1960s, G. F. Abbott, Richard Blum, Eva Blum, and their staff had no problem collecting reports of Greeks who had encountered *vrykolakas*. Though mentioned by Lawson, Abbott and the Blums both reported multiple stories that suggested people became *vrykolakas* because animals, such as cats, jumped over their bodies between the time of death and burial. Abbott recounted a story of the body of a suspected *vrykolakas* being scalded with boiling water rather than burned.

Greece stands as one of the oldest and most important centers for vampire lore. Its idea of the vampire, having passed through a complicated process of development, remains strong today and continues as a resource for understanding the impact of the vampire myth. In addition, Greece also has contributed significantly to the emerging image of the modern fictional vampire.

One of Germany's most famous literary figures, Johann Wolfgang von Goethe, also wrote about the vampire in his poem "The Bride of Corinth."

Hungary

Hungary, Bela Lugosi's native country, has a special place in the history of vampires. Vampire historian Montague Summers opened his discussion of the vampire in Hungary by

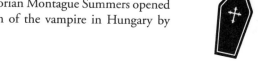

observing, "Hungary, it may not untruly be said, shares with Greece and the Slovak Republic the reputation of being that particular region of the world which is most terribly infested by the Vampire and where he is seen at his ugliest and worst." Bram Stoker's *Dracula* (1897) opened with Jonathan Harker's trip through Hungary. Harker saw Budapest as the place that marked his leaving the (civilized) West and entering the East. He proceeded through Hungary into northeast Transylvania, then a part of Hungary dominated by the Szekelys, a Hungarian people known for their fighting ability. (Dracula was identified as a Szekely.) In the face of Stoker and Summers and before Dom Augustin Calmet, Hungarian scholars have argued that the identification of Hungary and vampires was a serious mistake of Western scholars ignorant of Hungarian history. To reach some perspective on this controversy, a brief look at Hungarian history is necessary.

The Emergence of Hungary: The history of modern Hungary began in the late ninth century, when the Magyar people occupied the Carpathian Basin. They had moved into the area from the region around the Volga and Kama rivers. They spoke a Finnish–Ugrian language, not Slavic. Their conquest of the land was assisted by Christian allies and, in the tenth century, the Christianization of the Magyars began in earnest. In 1000 C.E., Pope Sylvester crowned István, the first Hungarian king. Later in that century, when the Christians split into Roman Catholic and Eastern Orthodox branches, the Hungarians adhered to the Roman church.

István's descendants moved into Transylvania gradually but had incorporated the area into Hungary by the end of the thirteenth century. The Hungarian rulers established a system by which only Hungarians controlled the land.

> Hungarian scholars have argued that the identification of Hungary and vampires was a serious mistake of Western scholars ignorant of Hungarian history.

A Magyar tribe, the Szekleys were given control of the mountain land in the northeast in return for their serving as a buffer between Hungary and any potential enemies to the east. The Romanian people of Transylvania were at the bottom of the social ladder. Above them were the Germans, who were invited into cities in southern Transylvania. In return for their skills in building the economy, the Germans were given special privileges. By the fourteenth century, many Romanians had left Transylvania for Wallachia, south of the Carpathians, where they created the core of what would become the modern state of Romania. Following the death of the last of István's descendants to wear the crown of Hungary, it was ruled by foreign kings invited into the country by the nobles. The height of prosperity for the nation came in the late fifteenth century when Matthias Corvinus (1458–1490), a Romanian ethnic and contemporary of Wallachian prince Vlad the Impaler, ruled. He built his summer capital at Visegrád, one of the most palatial centers in Eastern Europe.

Hungarian independence ended essentially at the Battle of Mohács in 1526, which sealed the Turkish conquest of the land. During the years of Turkish conquest, while Islam was not imposed, Roman Catholic worship was forbidden. The Reformed Church was allowed, however, and remains a relatively strong body to the present. Transylvania existed as a land with an atmosphere of relative religious freedom, and both Calvinist Protestantism and Unitarianism made significant inroads. Unitarianism made significant gains at the end of the sixteenth century following the death of Roman Catholic Cardinal Báthory at the Battle of Selimbar (1599). The Szekelys were excommunicated and as a group turned to Unitarianism.

The Turks dominated the area until 1686, when they were defeated at the Battle of

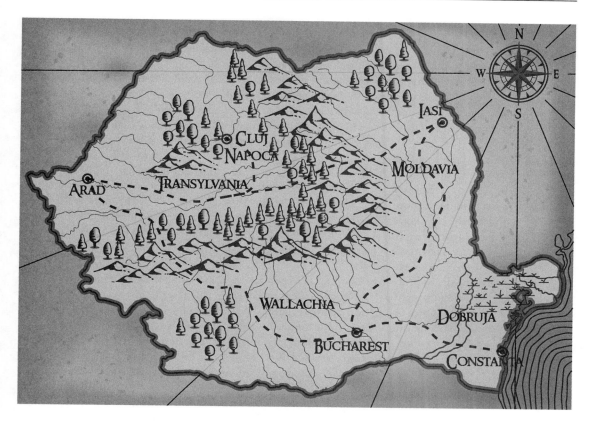

Transylvania, as shown on this map, inhabits the west-central geography of the modern state of Romania in south-eastern Europe.

Buda. Hungary was absorbed into the Hapsburg Empire, and Roman Catholicism was revived. The Austrian armies would soon push farther south into Serbia, parts of which were absorbed into the Hungarian province.

The eighteenth century was characterized by the lengthy rulerships of Karoly III (1711–1740) and Maria Theresa (1740–1780). Hungarian efforts for independence, signaled by the short-lived revolution in 1848, led to the creation in 1867 of Austria-Hungary. Austria-Hungary survived for a half century but then entered World War I on Germany's side. In 1919, Austria-Hungary was split into two nations, and the large segments of Hungary inhabited by non-Hungarian ethnic minorities were given to Romania, Serbia, and Czechoslovakia. Most

importantly, Transylvania was transferred to Romania, a matter of continued tension between the two countries to the present. Hungary was left a smaller but ethnically homogeneous land almost entirely composed of people of Hungarian ethnicity but with a small but measurable number of Romani people. Beginning in 1920, Hungary was ruled by Miklós Horthy (1868–1957), a dictator who brought Hungary into an alliance with Hitler and Germany as World War II began. After the war, in 1948, the country was taken over and ruled by Communists until the changes of the 1990s led to the creation of a democratic state.

The Vampire Epidemics: Following the Austrian conquest of Hungary and regions south, reports of vampires began to filter into

Western Europe. The most significant of these concerned events during the period between 1725 and 1732, their importance due in large measure to the extensive investigations of the reported incidents carried on by Austrian officials. The cases of Peter Plogojowitz and Arnold Paole spurred lengthy debates in German universities. Different versions of the incidents identified the locations of the vampire epidemics as Hungary rather than (more properly) a Serbian province of the Austrian province of Hungary. The debate was summarized in two important treatises, the first of which, *Dissertazione sopra i vampiri* by Archbishop Giuseppe Davanzati, assumed a skeptical attitude. The second, Dom Augustin Calmet's *Dissertations sur les Apparitions des Anges des Démons et des Esprits, et sur les revenants, et Vampires de Hingrie, de Boheme, de Moravie, et de Silésie*, took a much more nuanced, accepting attitude.

Calmet's work was soon translated and published in German (1752) and English (1759) and spread the image of Eastern Europe as the home of the vampire. While Calmet featured vampire cases in Silesia (Poland), Bohemia, and Moravia (Czechoslovakia), the "Hungarian" cases of Paole and Plogojowitz were the most spectacular and best documented. The image of Hungary as a land of vampires was reinforced by Stoker and Summers and later by both Raymond T. McNally and Leonard Wolf, who suggested that the Hungarian word *vampir* was the source of the English word "vampire." That theory has more recently been countered by Katerina Wilson, who argued that the first appearance of the word *vampir* in print in Hungarian postdates the first published use of the term in most Western languages by more than a century (actually by some 50 years). The question remains open, however, in that it is highly possible that someone (for example, a German-speaking person in Hungary in the early eigh-

> While Calmet featured vampire cases in Silesia (Poland), Bohemia, and Moravia (Czechoslovakia), the "Hungarian" cases of Paole and Plogojowitz were the most spectacular and best documented.

teenth century) might have picked up the term in conversation and transmitted it to the West.

Meanwhile, Hungarian scholars confronted the issue. As early as 1854, Roman Catholic bishop and scholar Arnold Ipolyi assembled the first broad description of the beliefs of pre-Christian Hungary. In the course of his treatise, he emphasized that Hungarians did not believe in vampires. That observation was also made by other scholars, whose Hungarian articles and treatises were destined never to be translated into Western languages. In current times, the case was again presented by Tekla Dömötör, whose book *Hungarian Folk Beliefs* was translated and published in English in 1982. He asserted, "There is no place in Hungarian folk beliefs for the vampire who rises forth from dead bodies and sucks the blood of the living." The conclusions of the Hungarian scholars have been reinforced by the modern observations of Western researchers, who have had to concede that few reports of vampires originated in Hungary. Most also assert, however, that in Hungarians' interaction with the Romani and their Slavic neighbors, such beliefs likely did drift into the rural regions.

Vampire-like Creatures in Hungary: Having denied the existence of the vampire in Hungarian folk culture, the Hungarian scholars from Ipolyi to Dömötör also detailed belief in a vampire-like being, the *lidérc*. The *lidérc* was an incubus/succubus figure that took on a number of shapes. It could appear as a woman or a man, an animal, or a shining light. Interestingly, the *lidérc* did not have the power of transformation but rather was believed to exist in all its shapes at once. Through its magical powers, it caused the human observer to see one form or another. As an incubus/succubus, it attacked victims and killed them by exhaustion. It loved them to death. Defensive measures against the *lidérc* included the placing of garters on the bedroom doorknob and the use of the ubiquitous garlic. Hungarians also noted a belief in the *nora*, an invisible being described by those to whom he appeared as small, humanoid, bald, and running on all fours. He was said to jump on his victims and suck on their breasts. Victims included the same type of person who in Slavic cultures was destined for vampirism, namely the immoral and irreverent. As a result of the *nora*, the breast area swelled. The antidote was to smear garlic on the breasts.

Romani People

In the opening chapters of Bram Stoker's novel *Dracula*, Jonathan Harker discovered that he was a prisoner in Castle Dracula, but he was given hope by the appearance of a band of Romani people (formerly known as gypsies):

> A band of Szgany have come to the castle and are encamped in the courtyard. These Szgany are gypsies; I have notes of them in my book. They are peculiar to this part of the world, though allied to the ordinary gypsies all the world over. There are thousands of them in Hungary and Transylvania who are almost outside all law. They attach themselves as a rule to some great noble or boyar and call themselves by his name. They are fearless and without religion, save superstition, and they talk only their own varieties of the many tongues.

He soon discovered that the Romani were allied to the count. The letters he attempted to have the Romani mail for him were returned to Dracula. The Romani were overseeing the preparation of the boxes of native soil that Dracula took to England. The Romani then reappeared at the end of the novel, accompanying the fleeing Dracula on his return to his castle.

In the end, they stepped aside and allowed their vampire master to be killed by Abraham Van Helsing and his cohorts.

The Emergence of the Romani People: Since the fourteenth century, the Romani have formed a distinct ethnic minority group in the Balkan countries. Within the next two centuries, they were found across all of Europe. While they received their name from an early hypothesis that placed their origin in Egypt, recent genetic studies have confirmed that they originated in India and were related to similar nomadic tribes that survive to this day in northern India. At some point, around 1000 C.E., some of these tribes wandered westward. A large group settled for a period in Turkey and incorporated many words from that country into their distinctive Romani language. Crossing the Bosporous, the Romani found their way to Serbia and traveled as far north as Bohemia through the fourteenth century. They were noted as being in Crete as early as 1322. In the fifteenth century, a short time before the emergence of Vlad Dracul and Vlad the Impaler as rulers in Wallachia, they moved into what are now Romania and Hungary. The Romani fanned out across Europe throughout the next century. They were in Russia and Poland, eventually making their way to France and Great Britain.

In Romania and Hungary, the Romani were often enslaved and persecuted. Their nomadic, nonliterary culture left them vulnerable to accusations of wrongdoing, and they became known not only as traveling entertainers but as thieves, con artists, and stealers of infants; despised minority groups in Europe faced the latter charge quite often. As the Nazis came to power, they initiated an extermination program targeting the Romani in what became a "final solution" to what they had defined as "the gypsy problem."

The Romani and the Supernatural: The Romani developed a sophisticated and complicated supernatural religious worldview, made

The Romani people—also known as Gypsies—are an ethnic group originally from northern India who settled in eastern Europe. They have been associated with tales of vampires and of Dracula stories for many years.

more difficult to describe by the diversity of the variant bands of Romani people in various countries and the reluctance of the Romani to talk to outsiders about their most sacred beliefs. Only the most diligent and persistent effort by a small band of scholars yielded a picture of the Romani worldview and its variations from country to country. Romani theology affirmed the existence of *o Del* (literally, "the God"), who appeared one day on Earth ("Earth" being the eternally present, uncreated world). Besides *o Del*, the principle of Good, was *o Bengh*, or Evil; *o Del* and *o Bengh* competed in the creation of humanity.

O Bengh formed two statuettes out of earth, and *o Del* breathed life into them. Because no written text existed, the account differed from tribe to tribe. The expanded world of the Romani was alive with the forces of Good and Evil contending with each other through-

out nature. The wise Romani learned to read the signs and omens to make the forces work for them and prevent evil forces from doing them harm.

The Romani maintained a living relationship with the dead (some have called it a cult of the dead), to whom they had a great loyalty. They regularly left offerings of food, especially milk, so the dead would protect living family members. E. B. Trigg, in *Gypsy Demons & Divinities: The Magical and Supernatural Practices of the Gypsies*, described this practice as a form of worshipping vampire gods, which he compared to the activity of Indian worshippers toward the vampire figures of their mythology.

What happened to the dead? Among the Romani of the Balkans existed a belief that the soul entered a world very much like this one except for the absence of death. Bosnian Romani, heavily influenced by Islam, believed in a literal paradise, a land of milk and honey. Others, however, believed that the soul hovered around the grave and resided in the corpse. As such, the soul might grow restless, and the corpse might develop a desire to return to this world. To keep the dead content, funeral rites were elaborate, and families made annual visits to the gravesites. Within this larger world was ample room for the living dead, or vampires. This belief was found among the Romani across Europe but was especially pronounced, as might be expected, in Hungary, Romania, and the Slavic lands.

The *bhutas* wandered around at night, and among its attributes was the ability to animate dead bodies, which in turn attacked the living in ghoulish fashion.

Questions have been posed as to the origins of Romani vampire beliefs. In India, the Romani land of origin, there were a variety of acknowledged vampire creatures. For example, the *bhutas*, found in western India, was believed to be the soul of a man who died in an untimely fashion (such as an accident or suicide). The *bhutas* wandered around at night, and among its attributes was the ability to animate dead bodies, which in turn attacked the living in ghoulish fashion. In northern India, from whence the Romani probably started their journey to the West, the *brahmaparusha* was a vampire-like creature who was pictured with a head encircled by intestines and a skull filled with blood from which it drank. The Romani also had a belief in Sara, the Black Virgin, a figure derived from the bloodthirsty goddess Kali. Thus, the Romani may have brought a belief in vampires, or at least a disposition to believe in them, to the Balkan Peninsula. Once in the area, however, they obviously interacted with the native populations and developed a belief in what became a variety of the Slavic vampire.

The Romani vampire was called a *mulo* (or *mullo*; plural *mulé*), literally "one who is dead." The Romani people viewed death essentially as unnatural, hence any death was an affront and viewed as being caused by evil forces attacking the individual. Thus, any individual—but especially anyone who died an untimely death (by suicide or an accident)—might become a vampire and search out the person or persons who caused the death. Given the clannish nature of Romani life, these people were most likely those close to the deceased. Prime candidates would be relatives who did not destroy the belongings of the deceased (according to Romani custom) but kept them for themselves. The vampire also might have a grudge against anyone who did not properly observe the elaborate burial and funeral rites.

The vampire usually appeared quite normal but often could be detected by some sign in its physical body. For example, the creature might have a finger missing or have animal-like appendages. Easier to detect was the vampire that took on a horrific appearance and could only be viewed under special conditions. Vampires might be seen at any time of day or night, though some believed them to be strictly nocturnal creatures. Others thought that vampires could appear precisely at noon, when they would cast no shadow. The Slavic and German Romani believed that vampires had no bones in their bodies, a belief based upon the observation that a vampire's bones are often left behind in the grave.

The Romani believed that vampires engaged in various forms of malicious activity upon their return from the dead. They attacked relatives and attempted to suck their blood. They destroyed property and became a general nuisance by throwing things around and making noises in the night. Male vampires were known to have a strong sexual appetite and returned from the dead to have sexual relations with a wife, girlfriend, or other women. Female vampires were thought to be able to return from the dead and assume a normal life, even to the point of marrying, but would exhaust her husband with her endless sexual demands. The Romani thought that animals and, on occasion, even plants became vampires. Dead snakes, horses, chickens, dogs, cats, and sheep were reported as returning as vampires, especially in Bosnia. In Slavic lands, it was thought that if an animal such as a cat jumped over a corpse prior to burial, the corpse would become a vampire. The Romani believed that the animal might become a vampire at the time of its death. Plants such as pumpkin or watermelon could, if kept in the house too long, begin to stir, make noises, and show a trace of blood; they would then cause trouble, in a limited way, for both people and cattle. In the most extreme cases, family tools might become vampires. The wooden knot for a yoke or the wooden rods for binding sheaves of wheat became vampires if left undone for more than three years.

It was believed that action could be taken to prevent a dead person from returning as a vampire. As a first step, the victim of a vampire

The Romani even have stories of animals and vegetables coming back to life. A pumpkin could, in fact, begin to bleed and start to move on its own like an undead squash!

called upon a *dhampir*, the son of a vampire. The Romani believed that intercourse between a vampire and his widow might produce a male offspring. This child would develop unusual powers for detecting vampires, and a *dhampir* might actually hire out his services in the case of vampire attacks. Some believed that the *dhampir* had a jellylike body (because some thought that vampires had no bones) and hence would have a shorter life span. Many Romani people thought that iron had special powers to keep away evil. To ward off vampires, at the time of burial, a steel needle was driven into the heart of the corpse, and bits of steel were placed in the mouth, over the ears and nose, and between the fingers. The heel of the shoe could be removed and hawthorn placed in the sock, or a hawthorn stake could be driven through the leg. If a vampire was loose in a village, one might find protection in different charms, such as a necklace with an iron nail. A ring of thorn could be set around one's living quarters. The Christian Romani used a crucifix. The Slavic Romani prized the presence of a set of twins, one male and one female, who were born on a Saturday and willing to wear their underclothes inside out. Such people could scare off vampires immediately, it was believed.

The gravesite might be the focus of a suspected vampire. The Romani have been known to drive stakes of ash or hawthorn into a grave or pour boiling water over it. In more problematic cases, coffins were opened, and the corpse was examined to see if it had shifted in the coffin or had not properly decomposed. In the case of a body thought to be a vampire, the Romani followed the practices of their neighbors: having the prayers for the dead recited; staking it in either the stomach, heart, or head; or resorting to decapitation and/or, in extreme cases, cremation.

The need to destroy the vampire was slight among some of the Romani, who believed its life span was only 40 days. However, some granted it a longer life and sought specific means to kill it. An iron needle in the stomach often would be enough. In Eastern Orthodox countries, such as Romania, holy water would be thrown on the vampire. If these less intrusive means did not work, the Romani might resort to more conventional weapons. If captured, a vampire might be nailed to a piece of wood. If one was available, a *dhampir* might be called upon to carry out the destruction. Black dogs and wolves were known to attack vampires, and some of the Romanian Romani believed that white wolves stayed around the gravesites to attack vampires; otherwise, the world would be overrun with the dead.

Numerous reports on the *mulo* have been collected and show significant variance among geographically separated Romani groups. Some have speculated that their vampire beliefs originated in India, from whence the Romani originated. India had a rich vampiric lore.

The legends have also developed variations over the centuries as the Romani dispersed around Europe and North America and interacted with various local cultures. Thus, while the belief in vampires has survived among the Romani, like all supernatural beliefs, it has shown signs of disappearing. In particular, the strength of this belief has been affected by secular schooling, modern burial practices, and governments hostile to actions taken in response to vampires, such as the mutilation of bodies.

Romania

No contemporary country is as identified with vampires as much as Romania. A land of rich folklore concerning vampires, its reputation was really established by Bram Stoker, whose novel *Dracula* (1897) began and ended in Transylvania. Though at the time, Transylvania was a part of Hungary, it has, since the end of World War I, been a part of Romania. Recent scholarship has confirmed that the title of Stoker's novel was a reference to Vlad the Impaler, a fif-

teenth-century prince of Wallachia, a section of modern Romania that lies south of the Carpathian Mountains.

Stoker derived much of his knowledge of Transylvania, where he located Castle Dracula, from Emily Gerard's *The Land Beyond the Forest* (1888). Gerard was a Scottish woman who had married a Polish officer serving in the Austrian army. As a brigade commander, he was stationed in Transylvania in the 1880s. The couple resided in Sibiu and Brasov. In describing the several supernatural entities encountered in her research on practices surrounding death, she wrote:

> More decidedly evil is the *nosferatu*, or vampire, in which every Romanian peasant believes as firmly as he does in heaven or hell. There are two sorts of vampires, living and dead. The living vampire is

OLD TOWN GATE AT HERMANSTADT (ELIZABETH THOR).

The frontispiece, illustrated by Elizabeth Thor, for the Emily Gerard book The Land beyond the Forest. *The 1888 work served as a resource on Transylvania for Stoker's novel.*

generally the illegitimate offspring of two illegitimate persons; but even a flawless pedigree will not insure anyone against the intrusion of a vampire into the family vault, since every person killed by a *nosferatu* becomes likewise a vampire after death, and will continue to suck the blood of other innocent persons till the spirit has been exorcised by opening the grave of the suspected person, and either driving a stake through the corpse, or else firing a pistol-shot into the coffin. To walk smoking around the grave on each anniversary of the death is also supposed to be effective in confining the vampire. In very obstinate cases of vampirism it is recommended to cut off the head, and replace it in the coffin with the mouth filled with garlic, or to extract the heart and burn it, strewing its ashes over the grave. (p. 185)

Romanian concepts concerning the vampire are strongly related to folk beliefs of the Slavic vampire in general, though the Romanians, in spite of being largely surrounded by Slavic peoples, are not themselves Slavic. Romanians locate their origins in ancient Dacia, a Roman province that emerged in Transylvania and the surrounding territories after Emperor Trajan captured the land in the second century C.E. He also brought in thousands of colonists in the sparsely settled area. As the colonists and the indigenous people intermarried, a new ethnic community was born. This new community spoke a form of Latin—the basis for modern Romanian. Their subsequent history, especially over the next century, is a matter of great controversy between Romanians and

their neighbors, a controversy difficult to resolve due to the paucity of archaeological evidence.

Following the abandonment of the territory at the end of the third century, Transylvania became the target of various invaders, including the early Slavic tribes. In the seventh century, it was absorbed into the Bulgar Empire. Though some Romanians had become Christians as early as the fourth century, the systematic conversion of the land began in the ninth century, soon after the conversion of the Bulgarians under the brothers Cyril and Methodius. The Romanian church eventually aligned itself to Eastern Orthodoxy under Bulgarian Episcopal authority.

At the end of the tenth century, the Magyars (present-day Hungarians) included Transylvania in their expanding kingdom. The Hungarians were Roman Catholics, and they imposed their faith in the newly conquered land. They also encouraged immigration by, among others, the Szekleys, a branch of Magyars, and Germans. In the thirteenth century, seizing upon a moment of weakened Hungarian authority in Transylvania, a number of Romanian Transylvanians migrated eastward and southward over the Carpathian Mountains and found the kingdoms of Moldavia and Wallachia. An Eastern Orthodox bishop was established a century later in Wallachia. From

> No sooner had Wallachia and Moldavia been established than a new force arose in the area. The Ottoman Empire expanded into the Balkans and began the steady march across the peninsula....

that time to the present day, Transylvania would be an item of contention between Hungary and Wallachia (which grew into the present-day Romania). Ecclesiastically, both Roman Catholics and the Eastern Orthodox would compete for the faith of the people.

No sooner had Wallachia and Moldavia been established than a new force arose in the area. The Ottoman Empire expanded into the Balkans and began the steady march across the peninsula that would carry it to the very gates of Vienna in the early sixteenth century. In the fourteenth century, Hungary and the Turks vied for hegemony in Wallachia, thus providing a context for a prince of Wallachia by the name of Vlad to travel to the court of the emperor Sigismund, where he would join the Order of the Dragon and pledge to defend Christian lands against the invading Muslims. The Wallachian prince would become known as Vlad Dracul (1390?–1447). He, in turn, would be succeeded by his son, Vlad the Impaler (1431–1476), known as Dracula.

Vlad the Impaler is remembered today in Romania as a great patriot and a key person in the development of the Romanian nation. After Vlad's death, Wallachia fell increasingly under Turkish hegemony, and Moldavia soon followed suit. Through the 1530s, the Turkish army moved through Transylvania to conquer the Hungarian capital in 1541. The remainder of the Hungarian land fell under the control of the Austrian Hapsburg Empire. The incorporation of the Romanian kingdoms into the Turkish empire allowed a degree of religious freedom, and Protestantism made inroads, particularly in Transylvania. Contemporary scholars have emphasized that none of the vampire legends from Romania or the surrounding countries portrays Vlad the Impaler as a vampire. In the German and some Slavic manuscripts, Vlad's cruelty and his identification as Dracula and the devil were emphasized; however, Dracula as a vampire was a modern literary creation.

In the seventeenth century, the Hapsburgs began to drive the Ottomans from Europe and, by the end of the century, assumed dominance of Transylvania and began to impose a Roman Catholic establishment. Transylvania remained a semi-autonomous region until 1863, when it was formally unified with Hungary. For over a century, Moldavia survived amid Russians, Greeks, and Turks, each fighting for control until a united Romania came into existence in 1861. Through a series of annexations at the beginning and end of World War I, including that of Transylvania in 1920, Romania, in roughly its present size, came into existence. The Romanian majority exists side by side with a significant Hungarian minority in Transylvania, and the Romanian Eastern Orthodox Church competes with both a strong Roman Catholic and persistent Protestant presence.

The Vampire in Romania: The Romanian vampire, in spite of the distinct ethnic origin of the Romanians, appears to be a variation of the Slavic vampire. However, like the vampire in various Slavic lands, the vampire in Romania has acquired some distinguishing elements. That distinctiveness begins with the major term used to label vampires, as found by Harry Senn in his fieldwork in the 1970s. *Strigoi* (female, *strigoaica*) is closely related to the Romanian word *striga* (a witch), which in turn was derived from the Latin word *strix*, the word for a screech owl that was extended to refer to a demon that attacked children at night. A second term, *moroi* (female, *moroaica*), also spelled *murony* in older sources, seems to be the common term in Wallachia, as *strigoi* is in Transylvania. The Romanians also distinguish between the *strigoi vii* (plural, *strigoi*), or live vampire, and the *strigoi mort* (plural, *strigoi morti*), or dead vampire. The *strigoi vii* are witches who are destined to become vampires after death and can send out their souls and/or bodies at night to cavort with the *strigoi mort*.

> The Romanian vampire, in spite of the distinct ethnic origin of the Romanians, appears to be a variation of the Slavic vampire.

The live vampires tend to merge in thought with the *striga* (witches), who have the power to send their spirits and bodies to meet at night with other witches. The dead vampires are, of course, the reanimated bodies of the dead who return to life to disturb and suck the blood of their family, livestock, and—if unchecked—their neighbors. The *strigoi mort* was a variation of the Slavic vampire, although the Romanians were not Slavs and used a Latin word to designate their vampire. The *strigoi* was discovered by an unusual occurrence either at their birth or death, and a living *strigoi* was a person who was born with either a caul or a little tail. A *strigoi vii* may become a *strigoi mort*, as well as other people who died irregularly by suicide or an accident. Romanians also use the term *vircolac*, but this is almost exclusively to describe the old, mythological, wolflike creature who devoured the sun and moon.

The closely related terms *pricolici* or *tricolici* were also wolves. *Vircolac* is a variation of the Greek *vrykolakas* or the Serbo-Croatian *vukodlak*. Agnes Murgoci, who worked in Romania in the 1920s, found that they still connected the term with its prevampiric, mythological meaning of a creature who devours the sun and moon. At times, when the moon appears reddish, it was believed to be the blood of the *vircolac* flowing over the moon's face. More definitive work was pursued by Harry Senn in

The Romanian mythology of striga (witches) is often conflated with tales of vampires. Both striga and vampires are associated with the reanimation of the dead.

Transylvania in the 1970s. He found that popular use of the *vircolac* distinguished it from the *strigoi*. The term *vircolac* described a person who periodically changed into one of several animals, usually a pig, dog, or wolf. As such, it was much closer to the popular concept of werewolves than vampires. *Nosferatu* is an archaic, Old Slavic term apparently derived from the word *nosufuratu*, from the Greek word *nosophoros*, meaning "plague carrier."

From the religious context, the word passed into popular usage. It has been variously and mistakenly cited as a Romanian word meaning either "undead" (Wolf) or the devil (Senn). Through the twentieth century, it seems to have dropped from use in Romania. Stoker's use of the term derived from Gerard. It was used by Friedrich Wilhelm Murnau in his attempt to disguise his movie, *Nosferatu, Eine Symphonie des Grauens*, from *Dracula*. He tied the story to the great plague that hit Bremen, Germany, in 1838.

In Romania, the vampire was believed to come into existence first and foremost as the product of an irregular birth, and any number of conditions have been reported that could predispose a person to become a vampire. Children born out of wedlock, born with a caul, or who died before their baptism could become vampires. Pregnant women who did not eat salt or who have allowed themselves to be gazed upon by a vampire could bear a vampiric child. The seventh child of the same sex in one family was likely to have a tail and become a vampire. Though children with an irregular birth were the prime candidates of vampirism, anyone could become a vampire if bitten by one. Other potential vampires included people who led wicked lives (including men who swore falsely), witches (who had relations with the devil), a corpse over whom a cat had jumped, or a person who had committed suicide.

The presence of vampires was usually first noticed when several unexpected deaths

Celebrants have a merry time at a St. George's Day festival in Ollerton, Nottinghamshire, England. In addition to honoring the saint, the day is also when witches and vampires supposedly meet and plan evil doings for the year.

in a family and/or of livestock followed the death of either a family member or of someone suspected of being a vampire. The vampire might, on occasion, appear to the family, and female vampires were known to return to their children. The home of a suspected vampire often was disturbed by its activity, either in throwing things around (poltergeist) or getting into the food supplies. The vampire would first attack the family and its livestock and then move on to others in the village. If not destroyed, it might move on to more distant villages and even other countries, where it could reassume a normal role in society. Vampires were especially active on the eve of St. George's Day (either April 23 or May 5), the day witches and vampires gathered at the edge of the villages to plan their nefarious activities for the next year. Villagers would take special precautions to ward off the influences of supernatural beings

on that evening. Stoker's character Jonathan Harker made the last leg of his journey and finally arrived at Castle Dracula on St. George's Eve. Vampires and witches were also active on St. Andrew's Day. St. Andrew was the patron of wolves and the donor of garlic. In many areas of Romania, vampires were believed to become most active on St. Andrew's Eve, continued to be active through the winter, and ceased their period of activity at Epiphany (in January), Easter, or St. George's Day.

St. George's Day was and is celebrated throughout much of Europe on April 23, hence St. George's Eve would be the evening of April 22. St. Andrew's Day is November 11, and the eve immediately precedes it. Romania, which was on the old Julian calendar, was 12 days behind the modern Gregorian calendar. Thus, in Stoker's day, St. George's Day would have been celebrated

This 800-year-old skeleton was found buried near Sofia, Bulgaria, with a metal rod through its chest, clear evidence for the centuries-old fear of vampires in Europe.

in Romania on what was the evening of May 4 in Western Europe. Likewise, St. Andrew's Eve would have been the evening of November 23–24. The lag time between the Julian and Gregorian calendars increases by one day every century.

The grave of a suspected vampire would be examined for telltale signs. Often, a small hole would be found in the ground near the tombstone, a hole by which the vampire could enter and leave the coffin. If someone was suspected of being a vampire, the grave was opened. Those opening the coffin would expect to find the corpse red in the face. Often, the face would be turned downward with fresh blood on it or, on occasion, cornmeal. One foot might have retracted into a corner of the coffin. Senn reported that a vampire in the community could be detected by distributing garlic at church and watching to see who did not eat it.

It was the common practice of Romanians to open the graves of the deceased three

years after the death of a child, four or five years after the death of a young person, and seven years after an adult's death. Normally, only a skeleton would be found, which would be washed and returned to the grave. If, however, the body had not decayed, it was treated as if it were a vampire.

A wide variety of precautions could be taken to prevent a person either from becoming a vampire or doing any damage if they did become one. A caul might be removed from the face of a newborn and quickly destroyed before it was eaten. Careful and exacting preparation of the body of the recently dead also prevented their becoming a vampire. The thorny branch of the wild rose might be placed in the tomb. Garlic was also very useful in driving away vampires. On St. Andrew's Eve and St. George's Eve, the windows (and other openings of the house) were anointed with garlic, and the cows would be given a garlic rubdown. Once the vampire was in the tomb, distaffs might be driven into the ground above the grave, upon which the vampire would impale itself if it were to rise.

On the anniversary of the death of a suspected vampire, the family walked around the grave. Once a vampire began an attack on the community and its identity was discerned, the vampire had to be destroyed. Emily Gerard, author of *The Land Beyond the Forest*, found the emergence of a relatively new tradition in nineteenth-century reports in which a vampire might be killed by firing a bullet into the coffin. The preferred method, however, was to drive a stake into the body, followed by decapitation and the placing of garlic in the mouth prior to reburial. This method was adopted by Stoker in *Dracula* as a means of destroying the vampiric nature that had taken over Lucy Westenra's body. In Romania, the staking could be done with various materials, including iron or wood, and the stake was driven into either the heart or the navel. Instead of decapitation, the body could also be turned face downward and reversed in the coffin. Millet seeds might be placed in the coffin to delay the vampire, who must first go through a lengthy process of eating the millet before rising from the grave. An even more thorough process might be followed in the case of a vampire resistant to other preventive measures. The body might be taken from the grave to the woods and dismembered. First, the heart and liver were removed, then piece by piece, the body was burned. The ashes could then be mixed with water and given to afflicted family members as a curative for the vampire's attack.

Vampire Folktales: The Romanian vampire has also become the subject of a number of folktales. Folklorists have noticed that many relate to the cases of couples in which one has recently died. Frequently reprinted was the story "The Girl and the Vampire" (which also exists in a Russian variant), in which the boy committed suicide following his failure to gain the marriage blessing of his girlfriend's parents. As a result of his manner of death, he became a vampire and began to visit the girl at night. The girl spoke with a wise elder woman in the village, who instructed her to attach a thread to his shirt. She then traced the thread, which led to the graveyard and disappeared into the grave of her late boyfriend.

The vampire continued to visit the girl, and they continued their sexual liaison, until her parents died. She refused the vampire's request for her to tell what she had seen the night she followed him to the graveyard, and the girl soon also died. She was buried according to the wise woman's instruction. A flower grew from her grave, which was seen by the son of the emperor. He ordered it dug up and brought to his castle. There, in the evening, it turned into a maiden. Eventually, she and the emperor's son were wed. Some time later, she accompanied her husband to church and had an encounter with the vampire. He followed her into church, where she hid behind an icon, which then fell on the vampire and destroyed him. The story served as a discouragement to out-of-wedlock sexual relations while at the same time reaffirming the wisdom of older people and upholding the church as a bastion against evil. Similar values were affirmed in other stories.

It was once the case, according to one folktale, that "vampires were as common as leaves of grass, or berries in a pail." They have, however, in the decades since World War II, become rarer and more confined to rural areas. In the mid-1970s, Harry Senn had little trouble locating vampire accounts in a variety of Romanian locations. Admittedly, however, the vampire suffered during recent decades from both the spread of public education and the hostility of the government to any tales of the supernatural. The importance of vampires in the overall folk belief of Romanians was also

> It was once the case, according to one folktale, that "vampires were as common as leaves of grass, or berries in a pail."

demonstrated in a recent study of a Wallachian immigrant community in Scandinavia.

The *strigoi mort*, the Romanian vampire, conformed in large part to the popular image of the vampire. It was a revenant of the deceased. It had powers to product poltergeistlike phenomena, especially the bringing to life of common household objects. It was seen as capricious, mischievous, and very debilitating. However, the vampire's attack was rarely seen as fatal. Also, it rarely involved the literal biting and draining of blood from its victim (the crux of the distortion of the vampire's image in films in the eyes of Romanian folklorists). The *strigoi* usually drained the vital energy of a victim by a process of psychic vampirism. The description of the *strigoi's* attack, described in vivid, metaphorical language, was often taken in a literal sense by non-Slavic interpreters, who then misunderstood the nature of the Slavic vampire.

Of contemporary note, Mircea Eliade, the outstanding Romanian scholar of world religion, was fascinated with vampires, and among his first books was a vampire novel, *Dominisoara Christina* (*Miss Christina*). This obscure work was rediscovered years later by Eliade fans in France and Italy and republished in both countries.

In the 1990s, Romania became the focus of vampire tourism, and several tour companies emerged to support vampire-related visits, especially in October. A new Dracula hotel in the Borgo Pass was created to serve Dracula-thirsty visitors. Attempting to provide a more nuanced appropriation of Romania's vampire-related culture was the now defunct Transylvanian Society of Dracula, which annually sponsored a scholarly seminar on a folklore-related subject. The country has also tried to promote itself as the site for movies, the most notable ones being the half dozen *Subspecies* vampire movies produced by Full Moon in the 1990s. In the new century, vampire flicks shot in Romania include martial arts master Steven Seagal's single vampire movie

Against the Dark (2009), the Indian homage to Bram Stoker *Dracula 2012 3D* (2013), and the British film *Crucible of the Vampire* (2019).

Russia

The former Soviet Union, including Russia, Siberia, Ukraine, and Byelorussia (Belarus), has been one of the homelands of the Slavic vampire. The first mention of the word *vampir* in a Slavic document was in a Russian one, *The Book of Prophecy*, written in 1047 C.E. for Vladimir Jaroslav, Prince of Novgorod, in northwest Russia. The text was written in what is generally thought of as proto-Russian, a form of the language that had evolved from the older, common Slavic language but had not yet become the distinctive Russian language of the modern era. The text gave a priest the unsavory label *Upir Lichy*, literally "wicked vampire" or "extortionate vampire," an unscrupulous prelate. The term—if not the concept—was most likely introduced from the southern Slavs, possibly the Bulgarians. The Russians of Kiev had adopted Eastern Orthodox Christianity in 988 C.E. and had drawn heavily on Bulgaria for Christian leadership.

Those areas of Russia under Prince Vladimir, centered around the city of Kiev (Ukraine), accepted Christianity in 988, at which time Vladimir declared war on indigenous Paganism. Christianity then spread from Kiev northward and westward. For several centuries, Christianity existed side by side with existing tribal faiths but became an integral part of the amalgamation of the tribal cultures into unified states. The invasion of the Mongols in the 1240s, including their destruction of Kiev and their decade of rule, led to a shift of power to Novgorod under Alexander Nevsky (1221–1263). In the fourteenth century, power began to shift to the princedom of Muskovy and the chief Christian cleric established himself in Moscow, though still titled as the metropolitan of "Kiev and all Rus." Westernmost Russia, including Ukraine and Byelorussia, came under the expanded Lithuanian empire. Thus, modern Russia emerged by pushing back the Mongols in the East and the Lithuanians (and Poles) in the West. While the state fought back foreign territorial rivals, Eastern Orthodox Christianity was in the very process of driving out the pre-Christian religions. That process was accompanied by the rise of new heretical religious movements, some being amalgamations of Christian and Pagan practices. With the emergence of a strong central state in Moscow in the fourteenth century, the state periodically moved against dissident movements. Surviving through this entire period into modern times were people who practiced (or who were believed to practice) magic. They were known as witches and sorcerers.

During the long reign of Vasili II (r. 1425–1462) in the mid-fifteenth century, vast

Vasili II (Vasili Vasiliyevich of Novgorod, also of Moscow) ruled during a violent civil war in Russia. He made his son Ivan III the Great his coruler after he was blinded by the enemy.

changes occurred in Russia, including an expansion of its territory. In 1448, following the breakup of the Roman Catholic and Eastern Orthodox union to combat Islam and just five years before the fall of Constantinople, the bishop in Moscow declared his autonomous status. A period of expansion, both secular and ecclesiastical, followed. The Russian church assumed many of the prerogatives formerly held by Constantinople, and early in the sixteenth century, the concept of Moscow as the "third Rome," the new center of Christian faith, arose. Under Ivan III the Great (r. 1547–1584), territorial expansion reached new heights with the incorporation of Finland and Russian movement to the east across the Urals. Thus, the stage was set for the expansion into the Volga River Valley under Ivan the Terrible and the incorporation of Siberia and lands all the way to the Pacific Ocean in the seventeenth century. During the several centuries of Romanov rule, Russia continued westward into the Baltic states, Byelorussia, and Ukraine, though its most impressive conquests were southward to the Caspian Sea and the Persian border. By the time of the Russian Revolution in 1917, the country had assumed the proportions it maintains in the early twenty-first century.

The Russian Revolution (1917) brought the Union of Soviet Socialist Republics (USSR) into existence. The USSR collapsed in December 1991 and was superseded by the Commonwealth of Independent States (CIS), after which a number of the former Soviet states (such as Lithuania and Estonia) did not align with the CIS and chose to reestablish themselves as independent countries. This essay deals primarily with two lands of the CIS—Russia and Byelorussia—and a third nation that was briefly a part of the CIS, but subsequently withdrew, Ukraine.

The Russian Vampire: In modern Russia, the most common term for a vampire is *uppyr*, a term probably borrowed from the Ukrainian word *upyr*. In Russia, the idea of the vampire became closely associated with that of the witch or sorcerer, which in turn had been tied to the concept of heresy. Heresy is defined as the deviation on matters considered essential to Orthodox faith, in this case, Eastern Orthodox Christianity. This idea can be viewed as an extension of the Eastern Orthodox belief that a body would not decay normally if death occurred when the individual was outside the communion of the church. The person could be in an excommunicated state due either to immoral behavior or heresy. Thus, a heretic (i.e., *eretik* or, in related dialects and languages, *eretnik, eretica, eretnica,* or *erestun*) might become a vampire after death. In Russian thought, the relationship between heresy and the existence of vampires was simply strengthened to the point of identifying one with the other.

The person who was a heretic in this life might become a vampire after death. The most likely heretic to turn into a vampire was the practitioner of magic under a variety of names: *kudesnik, porcelnik, koldun,* or *snaxar*. The method of transformation into a vampire varied widely.

An *eretik* was also associated with sorcery, a practice that also led to one's becoming a vampire. Over the years and across the very large territory comprising Russia, the *eretik* assumed a number of additional connotations. At times, it referred to members of the many sectarian groups that drew people from the true faith. It also referred to witches who had sold their soul to the devil. The vampire *eretik* possessed an evil eye that could draw a person caught in the vampire's gaze into the grave. Dmitrij Zelenin has traced the emergence of the *eretik* vampire from the fight conducted by the Eastern Orthodox against the medieval religious sectarians. Sectarians were designated *inovercy* (i.e., persons who adhere to a different faith). Upon death, the *inovercy* were associated with the *zaloznye pokojniki,* or unclean dead, and thus were not buried in cemeteries. They had died without confession and thus were seen as dying in sin. Since they did not believe in the true God, it was possible that they had served the devil and, hence, were considered sorcerers.

Eretiks generally were destroyed by the use of an aspen stake driven into the back or by fire. In the Olonecian region, accounts suggested that any person, including a pious Christian, could become a vampire if a sorcerer entered and took over the body at the moment of death. The peasant would appear to have recovered but, in fact, had become an *erestuny* (vampire), who would begin to feed on members of the family. People in the nearby village would start to die mysteriously. In the Elatomsk district of east-central Russia were even reports of the *ereticy*—women who sold their soul to the devil. After their death, these women roamed the earth in an attempt to turn people from the true faith. They might be found near graveyards, as they slept at night in the graves of the impious. They could be identified by their appearance at the local bathhouse, where they made an unseemly noise.

> The most likely heretic to turn into a vampire was the practitioner of magic under a variety of names: *kudesnik, porcelnik, koldun,* or *snaxar.*

Vampire Folktales: The vampire has been the subject of many Russian folk stories collected in the nineteenth and early twentieth centuries beginning with the work of Alexander Afanasyev in the 1860s. As was common with many folktales, they served to promote community values and encouraged specific kinds of behavior. The tale "Death at the Wedding," for example, related the adventure of a soldier proud of his service to God and the emperor. When he returned to his hometown on a visit, he encountered a sorcerer/vampire. Unknowingly, the soldier took the vampire to a wedding, where the vampire began to drain the blood of the newlyweds. Horrified, the soldier nevertheless engaged the sorcerer in conversation until he discovered the secret of stopping him. First, he

Russian ethnographer and Slavist Alexander Afanasyev collected over 600 Russian folk and fairy tales, including a number of vampire stories and legends.

The Vampire in Russian Literature: In the nineteenth century, the vampire entered the world of Russian literature seemingly through the popularity of the German Romantic stories of E. T. A. Hoffmann and the writings of Goethe. In the 1840s, Alexey K. Tolstoy (1817–1875) combined the vampire of popular Russian folklore with the literary vampire that had emerged in Germany and France. His two stories, "Upyr" and "The Family of the Vourdalak," became classics of both the horror genre and Russian literature. The latter was brought to the movie screen by Italian producer Mario Bava as part of his horror anthology *Black Sabbath*. More recently, "The Family of the Vourdalak, the Vampire" has become the subject of a Russian-made movie released in the United States as *Father, Santa Claus Has Died* (1992).

At least two other Russian vampire stories have been translated and given worldwide distribution, "Vij" (or "Viv") by Nikolai Gogol

stole some of the blood the vampire had collected into two vials and poured the blood back into the wounds the vampire had made on the couple's bodies. He next led the villagers out to the cemetery, where they dug up the vampire's body and burned it. The soldier was generously rewarded for his actions and his display of courage in service to God and the emperor.

The dispatch of the Russian vampire followed traditional means known throughout Slavic countries. The body of a suspected vampire was first disinterred. Often, a stake (aspen was a preferred wood) was driven through the heart. Sometimes, the body would be burned (Afanesyev's account mentioned that aspen wood was used in the cremation of the vampire). In the account from the Olonecian region, the corpse was whipped before the stake was driven through the heart.

Alexey Tolstoy, who remains among the most important Russian playwrights, poets, and novelists of all time, penned a vampire novella called The Family of the Vourdalak, the Vampire.

and "Phantoms" by Ivan Turgenev. The former became the basis of two movies, *La Maschera del Demonio* (released in the United States as *Black Sunday*), also directed by Mario Bava, and a 1990 remake with the same name by Mario's son Lamberto Bava. A Russian film based on "Vij" was filmed in 1967. What was possibly the first vampire film, *The Secret of House No. 5*, was made in Russia in 1912. An unauthorized version of *Dracula* (1920), the first screen adaptation of the Bram Stoker novel, was reportedly filmed in Russia two years before *Nosferatu, Eine Symphonie des Grauens*, the more famous film by Friedrich Wilhelm Murnau, though no copy has emerged to confirm the rumor. However, the vampire has not been a consistent topic for movies in Russia over the years.

Russia was finally heard from again in 1998, when Sergei Lukyanenko released the first of his series of supernatural novels, *Night Watch*, which portrayed a very different Moscow than that seen by the tourist. The hero, Anton Gorodetsky, is an agent for the Night Watch, an unusual "police" force that protects humanity from a spectrum of supernatural creatures, both good and bad, including vampires, werewolves, incubi/succubi, and witches. *Night Watch* was quickly followed by *Day Watch*, *Twilight Watch*, and *The Last Watch*. The first two novels were made into movies and found a ready audience across Europe and North America.

Slavic Lands

While vampires and vampire-like creatures appeared in the mythology of many of the world's peoples, nowhere were they more prevalent than among the Slavs of Eastern and Central Europe. Because of their belief in vampires, the Slavs experienced several panic-stricken "vampire" outbreaks in the late seventeenth and early eighteenth centuries, which resulted in the opening and desecration of numerous graves. This belief system brought the vampire to the attention of the West and led directly to the development of the contemporary vampire myth.

The Slavic people include most Eastern Europeans, from Russia to Bulgaria and from Serbia to the Czech Republic and Poland. Pouring into the region between the Danube River and Adriatic Sea, the people known collectively as the southern Slavs created several countries— Serbia, Croatia, Bosnia and Herzegovina, and Macedonia. In the midst of the Slavic lands are two non-Slavic countries, Romania and Hungary, though each has shared much of its language and lore with its Slavic neighbors. The Romani have been a persistent minority throughout the Slavic lands, though much of the Romani community was decimated by the Nazi Holocaust.

The exact origin of the Slavs is a matter of continuing historical debate, but most scholars agree that they came from river valleys north of the Black Sea and were closely associated with the Iranians, with whom they shared a religious perspective that gave a central place to a sun deity. At some point prior to the eighth century C.E., the Slavs, made up of numerous tribes, migrated north and west into the lands they now inhabit. Once settled in their new homes, they began to unite into national groups.

The most important event to give direction to the Slavs was the introduction of Christianity. Initial penetration of the church into Slavic lands began as soon as the Slavs occupied the lands formerly in the hands of the Byzantine Empire. However, systematic conversion attempts emerged as an outcome of the extensive reforms instituted during the long reign of Charlemagne (768–814). Charlemagne saw to the development of missions among the Moravians and Croatians and had a bishop placed at Salzburg to further the Christianization of the Slavs. Most Slavs, however, recognize the work of the brothers Cyril (827–869) and Methodius (825–885) as the real beginning of Slavic Christianity. The brothers developed a Slavic alphabet capable of expressing all of the sounds in the Slavic language in its various dialects.

They borrowed letters from Greek, Hebrew, and Armenian and created a new literary language that included Greek loan-words and new Slavic words that expressed some of the subtleties of Greek. This new literary language, most closely resembling Old Bulgarian, became Old Church Slavic and influenced the various new national languages (from Bulgarian and Serbian to Polish and Russian) that were beginning to emerge from the older common language of the Slavic tribes. Cyril and Methodius translated the Bible and Greek liturgy into Old Church Slavic. Out of their missions grew the several national Eastern Orthodox communions, autonomous churches affiliated with the Ecumenical Patriarch in Constantinople (now Istanbul), the spiritual (though not administrative) head of Eastern Orthodoxy.

Through the ninth and tenth centuries, the Eastern Orthodox Church and the Western Roman Church engaged in a fight over policy and administrative matters that was to lead to their break and mutual excommunication of each other in 1054 C.E. That break had immense significance for the Slavic people, as the Bulgarians, Russians, and Serbians adhered to the Eastern Church, while the Poles, Czechs, and Croatians gave their loyalties to the Roman Church. This split bore directly on the development of vampire lore, as the two churches disagreed over their understanding of the noncorruption of the body of a dead person. In the West, the non-corruption of the body of some saintly people was seen as an additional sign of their holiness, while in the East, the incorruptibility of the body was viewed as a sign of God's disfavor resting upon the dead person and, hence, the likelihood of the individual's becoming a vampire. Paradoxically, the church, especially in

Russia, also knows and values the idea of the incorruptibility of the bodies of saints. Dom Augustin Calmet and others discuss the differences (e.g., the smell: saints don't stink).

Origin of the Slavic Vampire: Jan L. Perkowski, who pursued the most thorough study of Slavic vampirism, concluded that it originated in the Balkans. Beginning around the ninth century, speculation on vampires evolved as a result of the confrontation between pre-Christian Paganism and Christianity. Bogomilism, a dualistic religion with roots in Iran that emerged in Macedonia in the tenth century, added yet another element to the developing concept. Eventually, Christianity won over the other religions, and Pagan and Bogomil ideas, including the belief in vampires, survived as elements of popular demonology. (Perkowski's reconstruction has been challenged by others, who have found that it lacks evidence.) As the concept of the vampire evolved in Slavic mythology, several terms emerged to designate it.

(Note: The discussion of terminology quickly brings even the most accomplished scholar into an area of possible confusion simply because of the dynamic nature of language in which words are constantly shifting in meaning or connotation. A major disagreement has occurred among authorities over the primacy of older Slavic origins or Turkish origins. Perkowski favors a Slavic origin, and his approach has been accepted as a framework for this discussion.)

> Beginning around the ninth century, speculation on vampires evolved as a result of the confrontation between pre-Christian Paganism and Christianity.

The most widely used term was one or the other of many variants of the original Slavic term that lay behind our modern word "vampire," which seems to have evolved from the common form *obyri* or *obiri*. Each language group has a cognate form of the older root word: *upirina* (Serbian and Croatian), *upirbi* (Ukrainian), *up'r* (Byelorussian, Czech, Slovak), *upi-r* (Polish), *wupji* (Kashubian), *lampir* (Bosnian), and *vampir* (Bulgarian, also *vbpir*, *vepir*, or *vapir*). A wide range of opinion exists on the origin of the root term *opyrb*, which is an unsolvable problem because most of the history of the early Slavic tribes has been lost.

The second popular term, especially among the Greeks and southern Slavs, is *vry-kolakas* (which, like vampire, possessed a number of forms in the different Slavic languages). This term seems to have derived from the older Serbian compound word *vblkb* plus *dlaka*, meaning "one who wore wolf pelts." Perkowski argues that the term designated someone who wore a wolfskin in a ritual situation. By the thirteenth century, when the word first appeared in a written text, the earlier meaning had been dropped and *vlbkodlaci* referred to a mythological monster who chased the clouds and ate the sun and moon (causing eclipses). Still later, by the sixteenth century, it had come to refer to vampires and, as such, had passed into both Greek and Romanian culture. The older southern Slavic term appears today as *vrykolakas* (Greek), *vircolac* (Romanian), *vbkolak* (Macedonian, Bulgarian), and *vukodlak* (Serbo-Croatian, sometimes shortened to *kudlak*). Because of the root meaning of the term, *vukodlak* has become part of the discussion of the relation of werewolves and the vampire.

Three other words have assumed some importance in the literature as designations of the vampire. *Strigoi* (female: *strigoaica*) is the popular Romanian word for "witch." Harry Senn, author of *Were-Wolf and Vampire in Romania*, found a variant, *strigoi mort* ("dead witch"), as a common term for a vampire. *Strigoi* is derived from the Latin word *strix* ("screech owl"), which had also come to refer to a night demon that attacked children. Russians commonly replaced *up'r*, their older Slavic term for a vampire, with *eretik* ("heretic"), a Greek ecclesiastical word for "one who has departed from the true faith." *Vjesci* (alternate spellings

vjeszczi and *vjeszcey*) is a term employed by the Kashubs of northern Poland.

The Slavic Vampire: The vampire found its place within the worldview of the people of Eastern and Central Europe. It was associated with death and was an entity to be avoided. However, it was not the all-pervasive symbol of evil it would come to be in nineteenth-century Western European literature. Within the prescientific world of village life, the role of the vampire was to explain various forms of unpredicted and undeserved evil that befell people.

The Slavic vampire differed considerably from the popular image of the creature that evolved in twentieth-century novels and movies. First, it generally appeared without any prior

Vampires of the Slavic tradition didn't become undead beings in the conventional sense. They didn't have to be attacked by a vampire; instead, they could emerge as a result of a tragic death or improper birth or burial.

contact with another vampire. The vampire was the product of an irregularity in community life, most commonly a problem with the process of either death and burial or of birth. People who met a violent death, which cut them off from the normal completion of their lives, could become vampires. Thus, people who committed suicide or died as the result of an accident might become vampires. Most Slavic cultures had a precise set of ritualized activities to be followed after someone's death and even for some days following the interment of the body. Deviation from that procedure could result in the deceased becoming a vampire. In a community where the church was integral to social life and deviation from the church a matter of serious concern, to die in a state of excommunication was seen as a cause of vampirism.

Vampirism also could result from problems associated with birth. For example, most Slavic communities had certain days of the year when intercourse was frowned upon. Children conceived by parents who had violated such taboos could become vampires. Bulgarians believed that an infant who died before it was baptized could become a *ustrel*, a vampire that would attack and drink the blood of cows and sheep. Among the Kashubs, a child born with teeth or with a membrane cap (a caul) on its head could become a vampire after its death.

Thus, Slavic society offered many reasons why vampires could appear. Of course, part of the horror felt toward vampires was the possibility of its passing on its condition to others. The vampire tended to attack its family, neighbors, friends, and people with whom it had unfinished business. Those attacked assumed the possibility of also becoming a vampire. The belief that a number of community members might become vampires contemporaneously brought on waves of vampire hysteria experienced in Slavic communities.

In the cases where a deceased person was suspected of becoming a vampire, a wide variety of preburial actions were reportedly taken as precautions. Among the most widespread was the placing of various materials into the coffin that were believed to inhibit a vampire's activity. Religious objects, such as a crucifix, were the most common. Such plants as the mountain ash were believed to stop the vampire from leaving its grave.

Since vampires had a fascination with counting, seeds (millet or poppyseed) were spilled in the grave, on top of the grave, and on the road from the graveyard. The vampire slowly counted the seeds before it assumed the privilege of engaging in any vampiric activity. On occasion, in more extreme cases, the body might be pierced with thorns or a stake, different groups having preferences for wood (hawthorn, aspen, or oak) or iron.

Believing that vampires would first attack and eat their burial garments, every effort was made to keep the clothes away from the corpse's mouth. A wooden block might be placed under the chin, or the clothes might be nailed to the side of the coffin.

While many possible causes existed for the creation of a vampire, the existence of one became apparent through the negative effects of its activities. Most commonly, the unexplained death of sheep and cattle (a community's food supply) was attributed to vampires. Strange experiences of the kind usually studied by parapsychologists also suggested the presence of vampires. Included in the stories of vampires were accounts of poltergeist activity, the visitation of an incubus/succubus, or the appearance of the specter of a recently deceased person to a relative or friend. The sudden illness or death of a person, especially a relative or friend, soon

> While many possible causes existed for the creation of a vampire, the existence of one became apparent through the negative effects of its activities.

after the death of an individual suggested that the person had become a vampire. Vampires also were associated with epidemics.

Once the suggestion that a community was under attack by a vampire was taken seriously by several residents, the discovery and designation of the vampire proceeded. The most likely candidate was a person who had recently died, especially in the previous 40 days (which was derived from the 40 days between Jesus's death and ascension). The body of the suspected vampire might then be exhumed and examined for characteristic signs. The body of a vampire was believed to appear lifelike and show signs of continued growth and change. It would possess pliable joints, and blood would ooze from its mouth or other body openings. It might have swelled up like a drum filled with blood. Its hair may have continued to grow, and new fingernails may have appeared.

When the supposed vampire was located, it had to be destroyed. Destroying the vampire usually involved action against the corpse; most commonly, the body was staked using a variety of wood or metal materials. The stake was driven into the head, heart, or stomach. In some instances, decapitation might occur. The Kashub people placed the severed head between the feet of the corpse before reburial. In the most extreme cases, the body was destroyed by burning. These actions were accompanied, where the services of a priest could be obtained, by such ritual activity as the re-

> Governments hostile to any form of supernaturalism have had a marked influence on the loss of belief in vampires, effectively eradicating most such beliefs....

peating of the funeral service, the sprinkling of holy water, or even an exorcism.

While the belief in vampires was quite widespread, especially in rural Eastern Europe, the cases of a community detecting a vampire and taking action against the corpse of the suspect were relatively rare. This was true especially after the widely reported incidents of vampires in the eighteenth century and the subsequent institution of legal penalties, both secular and ecclesiastical, against people who desecrated the bodies of the dead. However, besides the reports of contemporary vampires, a large body of vampire folktales set in the indefinite past circulated in Slavic lands. Like Aesop's fables, these stories functioned as moral tales to teach behavioral norms to members of the community. Among the more famous was one titled simply "The Vampire," originally collected by A. N. Afanasyev in Russia in the nineteenth century. It told of a young girl, Marusia, who became infatuated with a handsome, young man who ventured into her town. He was rich, personable, and mannered, but he was also a vampire. Even after she discovered his nature, she did not act, and as a result, several members of her family died. She finally learned what to do from her grandmother. The story offered the listener a number of guidelines. For example, it taught that wisdom was to be sought from one's elders and that young people should beware of attractive strangers, as they might be the source of evil. Other stories offered similar advice.

The Slavic Vampire Today: Folklorists such as Harry Senn have had little difficulty collecting vampire stories, both folktales and accounts of the apparent actual vampires, among Slavic populations throughout the twentieth century, though increasingly, they have had to travel to the more isolated, rural communities to find such accounts. Governments hostile to any form of supernaturalism have had a marked influence on the loss of belief in vampires, effectively eradicating most such beliefs in the urban areas and among more educated persons. Also assisting in the decline of belief has been the rise of the modern undertaker, who has assumed the burial functions previously done by the family of the deceased. The removal of the burial ceremony from the people has caused a cer-

The Battle of Kosovo in 1389 was a turning point in the history of the Balkans, as the Ottoman defeated Serbian forces after fierce fighting and immense losses on both sides (art by Adam Stefanović).

tain distancing from the experience of death, which has contributed to the decline of many beliefs about human interaction with the dead.

Southern Slavic Lands

The region consisting of what was formerly Yugoslavia and Albania now comprises eight countries of diverse religious, ethnic, and linguistic backgrounds. Although very diverse in some respects, these eight nations share a common folk heritage that becomes quite evident upon examination of the reports of vampires and vampire beliefs in the area. Thus, it became fitting to treat vampires and vampirism in these lands as a whole phenomenon.

Background: Albania traced its history to ancient Illyria, a Roman province that reached from present-day Albania north and east across Croatia to Romania. Beginning in the fourth century C.E., it was successfully in-

vaded and occupied by Goths, Bulgars, Slavs, and Normans.

Albanians, much like Romanians, asserted their Roman ties. In the twelfth century, Albania was conquered by the Ottoman Turks and remained in the empire until after World War I. As a legacy, the retreating Ottoman rulers left a population that had primarily been converted to Islam. Albania gained a measure of independence following World War I but was occupied by Italy during World War II. After the war, it became an independent nation. Under dictator Enver Hoxha (r. 1941–1985), it was an independent Communist nation with a repressive government that was officially atheist and hostile to religion. Following Hoxha's death, the country regained some degree of freedom.

Today, the majority of ethnic Albanians live outside the boundaries of their homeland. A small but important Albanian community exists in the United States, and many live in Italy. The largest number of Albanians outside of Albania live in Serbia and constitute more than 90 percent of the relatively new country of Kosovo.

Yugoslavia was created in 1918, following World War I, as a centralized state uniting the former independent countries of Serbia, Bosnia and Herzegovina, Croatia, and Montenegro. To these countries, a part of Macedonia, previously a part of the Ottoman Empire, and Slovenia, a part of the Austrian (Hapsburg) Empire, were added to the new country. Slavic tribes had first moved into the Balkan Peninsula in the sixth century and, by the eighth century, had established themselves as the dominant influence in the area. Some unity was brought by the expansive Bulgar Empire at the beginning of the tenth century, which controlled most of present-day Serbia, Macedonia, and Bosnia and Herzegovina.

Christianity moved into the Balkans in strength through the ninth century. Following the division of the Christian movement in 1054 C.E., Serbia, Montenegro, and Macedonia became largely Eastern Orthodox, while Croatia and Slovenia were Roman Catholic. Bosnia and Herzegovina was split between the two groups of Christians with a significant Muslim minority. The Bosnian Muslims derive largely from the surviving remnants of the Bogomils, who had persisted to the time of the Turkish conquest and chose Islam over both Eastern Orthodoxy and Catholicism.

In 1389, the Turks defeated the combined Slavic forces at the Battle of Kosovo, following which the Ottoman Empire established itself across the southern Balkans. Only Slovenia, controlled by the Germanic (and, after the thirteenth century, Austrian) Kingdom remained free of Ottoman control. During the years of Muslim control, proselytization occurred most strongly in Bosnia and Croatia. At the end of the seventeenth century, the Hapsburgs pushed further south across Croatia to the Sava River, which flowed into the Danube River at Belgrade. This territory was formally ceded to Austria in 1699. Through the next two centuries, the line between the Ottoman Empire and the Hapsburg Empire continued to fluctuate. Serbians began to assert their political independence, which was formally granted in 1878.

Following World War II, strongman Josef Broz Tito (r. 1953–1980) ruled Yugoslavia until his death in 1980. A decade of weakened central control led to the breakup of the country at the end of the 1980s. Six separate countries emerged in the early 1990s, plus one more in the first decade of the new century.

The Southern Slavic Vampire: The southern Slavic vampire was a variation of the vampire of the Slavs, and the beliefs and practices related to it were influenced by those of their neighbors in every direction. The lands of the former Yugoslavia have been cited as the most likely land of origin of the Slavic vampire. Jan L. Perkowski has suggested that the peculiar shape assumed by the vampire originated through a combination of Pagan and Bogomil beliefs (religious ideas dominant in the region at the end of the tenth century) that were pushed aside by the conquest of Christianity, though he has found little support for his hypothesis. In any case, through the centuries, Christian leaders attempted to destroy belief in vampires but were often forced to accommodate them as they remained strong among the people. Islam proved quite accommodating to belief in vampires.

> Perkowski … traced the origin of the modern word "vampire" to an Old Slavic form *obyrbi* or *obirbi*.

Perkowski also traced the origin of the modern word "vampire" to an Old Slavic form *obyrbi* or *obirbi*. Among the various Slavic groups and their neighbors, different forms of the word evolved. Dominant in the region in the modern era was *upirina*, a Serbo-Croatian word. The word *vampir*, with the addition of an "m" sound, was also present, and in Bosnia, *lampir* was used. Also present was *vukodlak* (Croatian) or *vurvulak* (Albanian), words similar to the Greek designation of the vampire, *vrykolakas*. *Vukodlak* was often shortened to *kudlak*. In the late nineteenth century, in Istria near the Italian border, a *kudlak* was believed to be attached to each clan. It was considered an evil being that attacked people at night. It was opposed by another entity, the *krsnik*, which often interrupted a *kudlak's* attack and fought it.

In addition to the more ubiquitous words, the term *tenatz* has been found in Montenegro. This was used interchangeably with *lampir*, the local variation on *vampir*. It was believed to be the body of a deceased person that had been taken over by evil spirits. The *tenatz* wandered at night and sucked the blood of the sleeping. They transformed themselves into mice to re-enter their burial place. A primary means of detecting a vampire in Montenegro was to take a black horse to the cemetery.

The horse would be repelled by the grave of the vampire and refuse to walk across it. Once detected, the body would be disinterred and if, upon further determination, the vampire hunters decided it was a vampire, the corpse would be impaled with a stake and burned.

In Croatia, one also might find *kosac*, *prikosac*, *tenjac*, and *lupi manari* as terms for a vampire. Albanian names for a vampire included *kukuthi* or *lugat*. The *strigon* (Slovenian) and *shtriga* (Albanian, Macedonian) are bloodsucking witches related to the Romanian *strigoi*. Another bloodsucking witch related to the *strigoi* was the *vjeshtitza* (also spelled *veshtitza*). During her fieldwork in Montenegro early in this century, M. Edith Durham discovered that people no longer believed that *vjeshtitza* existed but retained a rich lore about them.

Vjeshtitza were older women who were hostile to men, other women, and all children. Possessed by an evil spirit, the sleeping witch's soul wandered at night and inhabited either a moth or a fly. Using the flying animal, the witch entered into the homes of neighbors and sucked the blood of victims. The victim, over a period of time, grew pale, developed a fever, and died. The witches were especially powerful during the first week of March, and protective measures would be taken against them. The protective ceremony, performed the first day of March each year, included stirring the ashes in the family hearth with two horns, which were then stuck into the ash heap. Garlic was also a common protective substance.

The vampire was a revenant, a body that returned from the grave with some semblance of life. Some believed that it was a body inhabited by an evil spirit. A person was believed to become a vampire in several ways, but a sudden, unexpected, and/or violent accidental death; a wasting sickness; or suicide were seen as primary causes. M. Edith Durham, for example, recorded the story in Bosnia of an epidemic of vampirism associated with a typhus epidemic. Vampirism was also associated, in a day prior to professional undertakers, with the need to follow a prescribed process of preparation of the body of a deceased person and its subsequent burial. Irregularities in the process could cause a person to turn into a vampire. In particular, it had to be watched so that animals, especially cats, did not jump over the body prior to burial. In Macedonia, if a cat did jump over the body, the corpse would then be pierced with two needles. Vampirism was also assumed to be contagious: an attack by a vampire would lead to vampirism.

The *shtriga* and *vjeshtitza* were bloodsucking witches. Although not revenants, the witches were members of the community believed to be living incognito. They were difficult to identify, although a sure sign was a young girl's hair turning white. *Shtriga* attacked in the

The word shtriga, *meaning witch, comes from the Latin* strix, *for owl, because owls are nocturnal, flying hunters.*

night, usually in the form of an animal such as a moth, fly, or bee. In fact, the word *shtriga* was derived from the Latin word *strix*, a screaming owl, that referred to a flying demon that attacked in the night. The Albanian *shtriga* could be detected by placing a cross made with pig bones on the church door when it was crowded with people. The witch was unable to leave the church and would be seen running around the church trying to find a safe exit. A Slovenian variation of the *shtriga* had similar attributes.

The *shtrega* traveled at night and, often in the form of an animal, attacked people and sucked their blood. If a *shtrega* was sighted, it could be followed and positively identified be-

cause it had to stop and vomit up the blood it had sucked. The vomited blood could then be used to make an amulet to protect one from witchcraft and vampirism.

Slovenian historian Baron Jan Vajkart Valvasor (1641–1693) recounted the killing of a *strigon* in Istria (western Slovenia). A person who was the suspected vampire had recently died and was seen by several people walking around the town. His suspected vampirism was reported by his wife after he returned home and had sexual relations with her. The *strigon* was killed by a stake made of hawthorn driven into its stomach while a priest read an exorcism. The corpse was then decapitated. All the while, the corpse reacted as if it were alive—it recoiled as the stake was driven in, cried while the exorcism was pronounced, and screamed out as its head was severed. After the decapitation, it bled profusely.

Vampires attacked people it had strong emotional attachments to—both positive (family and friends) and negative (those with whom it had quarreled in life)—and sucked their blood. A sure sign of a vampire was an outbreak of various kinds of contagious illnesses. People who became sick and died from what were then unknown causes were often considered victims of vampiric activity. The vampire could also attack the village livestock in a similar manner.

The southern Slavic vampire was, like that among the Romani, capable of having sex with a spouse or lover. Durham related the story of a girl in Montenegro who was forced to marry the man chosen by her parents rather than her true love. Her beloved left the country and, in his despair, died. He returned from the grave as a vampire and visited the girl, who eventually became pregnant by him. In appearance, the child closely resembled the deceased man.

The villagers were frustrated because the man had died abroad and, thus, they could not destroy him. Bodies of males uncovered in the search for a vampire would often have an erect sex organ.

The existence of a vampire could be detected by a variety of means. In Montenegro, for example, a black horse (in Albania, a white horse was used) would be led to a local cemetery; the horse would be repelled by a vampire's grave. The horse usually had to be ridden by a boy who had not yet experienced puberty or a virginal girl. In Croatia, reports were made of strange animal sounds coming from the grave of someone later determined to be a vampire. The body was then disinterred. The discovery of a body turned facedown or bloated to the point that the skin was stretched like a drum indicated that the correct body had been uncovered. If only bones remained in the grave, it was not considered a vampire. The Serbians and Bosnians shared the belief with the Romani in the *dhampir*, the son of a vampire. The offspring of a vampire was considered to have the power to both see and destroy his father and other vampires. In Macedonia was the belief in the power of people born on Saturday. Such Sabbatarians, as they were termed, were thought to have a great influence over vampires, including the power to lure them into traps where they could be destroyed. On Saturdays, the Sabbatarians could see and kill vampires.

For average people, protection from vampires was secured by barricading their homes with thorn bushes (an old remedy for witches). Once discovered, the vampire could be rendered harmless or destroyed by the traditional means of fixing the body to the ground with a stake and/or decapitation. In the most severe cases, the body might be dismembered or burned. In general, a priest was asked to be present to repeat the funeral prayers over the person who was perceived to be dying a second time. (As part of an attempt to stop the mutilation of dead bodies, the churches in Serbia and Montenegro threatened any priest who cooperated in such activity with excommunication.)

In both Montenegro and Albania, it was believed that a vampire could be stopped by hamstringing the corpse. G. F. Abbott reported observing the destruction of a vampire by scalding it with boiling water and driving a long nail into its navel. The body was returned to the ground and the grave covered with millet seeds so if the vampire was not destroyed, it would waste its time counting the millet until dawn. In Croatia, it was believed that a stake driven into the ground over the grave prevented the vampire from rising. In Serbia, a whitethorn or hawthorn stake or other sharp objects might be stuck into the ground over a vampire or a sickle placed over the neck of the corpse when it was reburied.

It was common among the southern Slavs (as it was among the Greeks) to dig up bodies some years after their burial to cleanse the bones and rebury them in a permanent location. It was important that the soft tissue be completely

In Croatia it is believed that driving a stake into the soil above a grave kept a vampire from emerging from its burial spot.

decomposed by that time; delays in decomposition were cause for concern and could lead to suggestions of vampirism.

The Vampire Epidemics, 1727–1732: The beliefs and practices of the southern Slavs concerning vampires were brought to the attention of Western Europe primarily through two spectacular cases that were publicized due to official inquiries into the cases by Austrian authorities. Both cases occurred in a region of Serbia north of Belgrade that had been taken over by Austria from the Ottoman Empire at the end of the seventeenth century and, subsequently, incorporated into the Hungarian province. One incident began with the sudden death of Peter Plogojowitz. He was seen by his family several nights after his death. Shortly thereafter, Plogojowitz appeared to several people in their dreams. In one week, nine people died of no known cause. When the local army commander arrived to investigate, Plogojowitz's body was taken from the grave. It was found to be as fresh as it had been when buried. The eyes were open, and the complexion was ruddy. His mouth was smeared with fresh blood. Fresh skin appeared just below an old layer of dead skin he appeared to be shedding, and his hair and nails had grown. It was concluded that he was a vampire. Plogojowitz's body was staked and burned.

More famous than the Plogojowitz incident was the case of Arnold Paole. Paole lived in the village of Medvegia (spelled in numerous ways in different sources), Serbia, north of Paracin. He told his neighbors that while he had been serving in the army in Turkey, he had been bitten by a vampire. A week later, he died. Several weeks after his death, people began to report seeing him, and four such people died. On the 40th day after his burial, the grave was opened, and he was found in a lifelike condition. When his body was cut, he bled freely. When staked, it was later reported that he groaned aloud. He and the four people he reportedly vampirized were decapitated and their bodies burned.

The Arnold Paole case should have ended with his funeral pyre. However, in 1731, some 17 people in the village died of an unknown cause. Vampirism was suggested. Word of the unusual occurrences reached all the way to Vienna, and the emperor ordered an official inquiry. Following the arrival of Johannes Fluckinger in Medvegia, the body of a new suspected vampire was disinterred. He was also found to be in a healthy state. After some further investigation, it was discovered that Paole had vampirized several cows. Those who ate the meat from the cows were infected with a vampiric condition. The bodies of the recently dead were then disinterred, and all were staked and burned.

Fluckinger returned to Vienna and presented the emperor with a complete report. In 1732, the report and several journalistic versions of it became best sellers throughout Europe. The two cases became the basis of a heated debate in German universities, and after a decade of arguing, the participants concluded that vampires did not exist. However, the debate spurred the interest of Dom Augustin Calmet, a French biblical scholar who, in 1746, completed a most important treatise on the subject, published in England as *The Phantom World*.

The fame of Plogojowitz and Paole should have focused attention on Serbia and the southern Slavic countries. Instead, from mere geographical ignorance, many involved in the debate placed the occurrences in Hungary, and thus, Hungary—which has the least vampire mythology of all the Eastern European countries—became known for vampirism. As a result, scrutiny of vampire beliefs was directed away from Serbia and its southern Slavic neighbors. The misdirection given to vampire phenomena by Calmet was reinforced by the writings of Montague Summers and a number of writers on vampires who essentially copied him.

The vampire has had a long and interesting history in what is now the independent country of Slovenia. Largely Roman Catholic in background, the country existed for many centuries as an Austrian province; however, south of the Drava River, especially in rural areas, Slovenes resisted Germanization and retained their own language and folklore. One of the earliest books to deal with vampires was Count Valvasor's *Die Ehre des Herzogthums Krain* (1689), which told the story of Grando, a peasant of the district of Kranj. A quiet man in life, in death, Grando began to attack his neighbors and his body was ordered exhumed. His body was found with a ruddy complexion, and he appeared to have a smile on his face. A priest called upon the vampire to look to his savior Jesus Christ, at which the body took on a sad expression, and tears were flowing down his cheek. The body was then decapitated and reburied. A more general account of vampires in the region was given in the famous 1734 travelogue *The Travels of Three English Gentlemen, from Venice to Hamburg, Being the Grand Tour of Germany, in the Year 1734, Etc.*

> The fame of Plogojowitz and Paole should have focused attention on Serbia and the southern Slavic countries. Instead, from mere geographical ignorance, many involved in the debate placed the occurrences in Hungary....

Modern Vampires among the Southern Slavs: Vampire beliefs have continued into the twentieth century in spite of several generations of hostile governments that denounced both religion and superstitions. Folklorists have had no trouble locating vampire stories. The depth and persistence of vampire belief was vividly illustrated in a most unexpected manner early in 1993 in the midst of the most violent era experienced directly by Serbia following the breakup of the former Yugoslavia. In that year, a man made a number of appearances on Serbia's state-controlled television station at the height of the country's conflict. He, in all seriousness, argued that at the moment when final destruction threatened the Serbian nation, a fleet of vampires would arise from the cemeteries to defeat Serbia's enemies.

In preparation for this event, he advised viewers to keep a supply of garlic on hand lest the vampires attack them by mistake.

Middle East and Africa

Africa

The peoples of Africa have not been known, in spite of their elaborate mythology, to hold a prominent belief in vampires. Montague Summers, in his 1920 survey of vampirism around the world, could find only two examples: the *asasabonsam* and the *obayifo*. Since Summers, very little work has been done to explore vampirism in African beliefs.

The *obayifo*, unknown to Summers, was actually the Ashanti name for a West African vampire that reappeared under similar names in the mythology of most of the neighboring tribes.

For example, among the Dahomeans, the vampire was known as the *asiman*. The *obayifo* was a witch living incognito in the community. The process of becoming a witch was an acquired trait; no genetic link existed. Hence, it was impossible to tell who might be a witch. Secretly, the witch was able to leave its body and travel at night as a glowing ball of light. The witches attacked people—especially children—and sucked their blood. They also had the ability to suck the juice from fruits and vegetables.

The *asasabonsam* was a vampire-like monster species found in the folklore of the Ashanti people of Ghana in western Africa. In

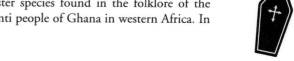

the brief description provided by R. Sutherland Rattray, the *asasabonsam* was humanoid in appearance and had a set of iron teeth. It lived deep in the forest and was rarely encountered. It sat on treetops and allowed its legs to dangle downward, using its hook-shaped feet to capture unwary passersby.

Working among the tribes of the Niger River's delta area, Arthur Glyn Leonard found a belief that witches left their homes at night to hold meetings with demons and to plot the death of neighbors. Death was accomplished by "gradually sucking the blood of the victim through some supernatural and invisible means, the effects of which on the victim is imperceptible to others." Among the Ibo, it was believed that the bloodsucking process was done so skillfully that the victim felt the pain but was unable to perceive the physical cause of it, even though it would eventually prove fatal. Leonard believed that actually, witchcraft was a very sophisticated system of poisoning (as was a certain amount of sorcery in medieval Europe).

P. Amaury Talbot, working among the tribes in Nigeria, found witchcraft a pervasive influence and that the most terrible power attributed to witches was the "sucking out the heart" of the victims without them knowing what was happening to them. The witch could sit on the roof at night and, by magical powers, accomplish the sucking. A person dying of tuberculosis was often thought to be the victim of such witchcraft.

Among the Yakö people of Nigeria, Daryll Forde discovered that disembodied witches were believed to attack people while they slept at night. They could suck their blood, and ulcers were believed to be a sign of their attack. They could also operate like an incubus/succubus and suffocate people by lying on top of them.

The question of witchcraft was evoked by anyone who suffered a hurtful condition, and anyone accused was severely dealt with by

The Yakö people of Nigeria had to leave their homeland in the seventeenth century after losing a war that arose over a misunderstanding about burial ceremonies.

various trials by ordeal. Generally, women who were barren or postmenopausal were primary subjects for accusations. It was not uncommon to sentence a convicted witch to death by fire.

Melville Herskovits and his wife, Frances Herskovits, were able to trace a witch/vampire, whose existence was acknowledged by most West African tribes, to similar vampire figures found in the Caribbean, the *loogaroo* of Haiti, the *asema* of Suriname, and the *sukuyan* of Trinidad. These three vampires are virtually identical, though found in colonies of the French, Dutch, and English. The vampire beliefs seem to be an obvious example of a common view carried from Africa by the slaves, which then persisted through the decades of slavery into the present.

Following up on the work of the anthropologists, John L. Vellutini, editor of the *Journal of Vampirology*, took up the challenge of exploring the whole question of vampirism in Africa. The results of his discoveries were summarized in two lengthy articles. Like researchers before him, Vellutini found scarce literal vampirism in Africa. However, he argued that beneath the surface of African beliefs about witchcraft, much material analogous to the Eastern European or Slavic vampire could be found. Witches were seen as powerful figures in African culture with numerous powers, including the ability to transform into a variety of animal shapes. Using their powers, they indulged themselves in acts of cannibalism, necrophagy (i.e., feeding on corpses), and vampirism. These actions usually constituted acts of psychic vampirism rather than physical malevolence. For example, Thomas Winterbottom, working in Sierra Leone in the 1960s, noted:

> A person killed by witchcraft is supposed to die from the effects of a poison secretly administered or infused into his system by the witch; or the latter is supposed to assume the shape of some animal, as a cat, or a rat, which, during the night, sucks the blood from a small and imperceptible wound, by which a lingering illness and death are produced.

With similar results, the *obayifo*, an Ashanti witch, sucked the blood of children as it flew about in its spirit body at night. Among the Ga people, M. J. Field found that witches gathered around a baisea, a type of pot, which contained the blood of their victims, though anyone looking into it would see only water. In fact, the liquid was believed to hold the vitality they had taken from their victims.

When a person was accused of witchcraft, he or she was put through an ordeal to determine guilt and, if found guilty, executed. The methods adopted by some tribes bore a strange resemblance to the methods applied to suspected vampires in Eastern Europe. For example, one tribe began the execution by pulling the tongue out and pinning it to the chin with a thorn (thus preventing any final curses to be given to the executioners). The witch was then killed by being impaled on a sharpened stake. On occasion, the head was severed from the body, and the body was burnt or left in the woods for predators.

Even more closely tied to the practices of European witchcraft were the efforts taken to ascertain if a deceased person was a witch. The corpse of the accused witch would be taken from the ground and examined for signs of blood in the burial plot, incorruption, and abnormal swelling of the corpse. The grave of a true witch would be found to have a hole in the dirt that led from the body to the surface that the witch could use to exit the ground in the form of a bat, rat, or other small animal. It was believed that the witch could continue to operate after his/her death and that the body would remain as it was at the time of death. By destroying the body, the spirit was unable to continue its witchcraft activity.

Witches also had the power to raise the dead and capture a departed spirit, which they turned into a ghost capable of annoying the kinsmen of the departed person. Widespread belief also existed throughout West Africa in the *isithfuntela* (known by different names

A traditional Ashanti funeral ceremony is performed here in 2020. As with many world cultures, the Ashanti also had practices for ensuring that the deceased was not a witch.

among different peoples), the disinterred body of a person enslaved by a witch to do the witch's bidding. The witch reportedly cuts out the tongue and drives a peg into the brain of the creature so that it becomes zombielike. The *isithfuntela* similarly attacked people by hypnotizing them and then driving a nail into their heads.

Vellutini concluded that Africans shared the belief with Europeans in the existence of a class of persons who could defy death and exert a malignant influence from the grave. Like the European vampires, African vampires were often people who died in defiance of the community mores or from suicide. Unlike the literary vampire, the African vampires were simply common people like the vampires of Eastern Europe.

Vellutini speculated that African beliefs in witches and witchcraft might have spread to the rest of the world, although anthropologists and ethnologists did not encounter these beliefs firsthand until the nineteenth century. While certainly possible, further research and comparison with evidence for alternative theories, such as that proposed by Devendra P. Varma for the Asian origin of vampire beliefs, must be completed before a consensus can be reached.

Armenia

Armenia is an ancient land situated between Turkey and Russia. It was the first land to make Christianity its state religion. The Armenian church is similar to the Eastern Orthodox churches but did not follow the development of Eastern Orthodox theology through the fifth to seventh centuries. Late in the nineteenth century, Armenia was the location of a number of massacres by occupying Turkish soldiers. Throughout most of the twentieth century, it was a part of the Soviet Union until that country broke up in the early 1990s.

Little has been written about vampirism in Armenia. Its place in vampire history is due

to an account in an 1854 text by Baron August von Haxthausen that was mentioned by Montague Summers. Von Haxthausen visited Mount Ararat in the Caucasians. According to local legend, a vampire, Dakhanavar, protected the valleys in the area from intruders. He attacked travelers in the night and sucked the blood from people's feet. He was outwitted by two men who heard of the vampire's habits and slept with their feet under the other's head. The vampire, frustrated by encountering a creature that seemed to have two heads and no feet, ran away and was never heard of again.

Babylon and Assyria

In the nineteenth century, the writings of ancient Mesopotamia (the lands between the Tigris and Euphrates River valleys, i.e., present-day Iraq) were discovered and translated. They indicated the development of an elaborate mythology and a universe inhabited by a legion of deities of greater and lesser rank. From this vast pantheon, the closest equivalent of the true vampire in ancient Mesopotamian mythology were the seven evil spirits described in a poem quoted by R. Campbell Thompson that begins with the line, "Seven are they! Seven are they!":

> Spirits that minish heaven and
> earth.
> That minish the land.
> Spirits that minish the land.
> Of giant strength,
> Of giant strength and giant tread.
> Demons (like) raging bulls, great
> ghosts,
> Ghosts that break through all
> houses,
> Demons that have no shame.
> Seven are they!
> Knowing no care, they grind the
> land like corn;
> Knowing no mercy, they rage
> against mankind.
> They spill their blood like rain,

Devouring their flesh (and) sucking their veins.

…

They are demons full of violence,
ceaselessly devouring blood.

Montague Summers suggested that vampires had a prominent place in Mesopotamian
mythology beyond that suggested by belief in
the seven spirits. In particular, he spoke of the
ekimmu, the spirit of an unburied person. He
based his case on an exploration of the literature
concerning the Netherworld, the Abode of the
Dead. The Netherworld was portrayed as a
somewhat gloomy place. However, an individual's life there could be considerably improved
if, at the end of their earthly existence, they received a proper, if simple, burial that included
the affectionate care of the corpse. At the end
of tablet 12 of the famous Gilgamesh (or Gilgamish) Epic was an accounting of the various
degrees of comfort of the dead. It closed with
several couplets concerning the state of the person who died alone and unburied, which
Summers quoted as:

The man whose corpse lieth in
the desert—
Thou and I have often seen such
an one—
His spirit resteth not in the earth;
The spirit hath none to care for
it—
Thou and I have often seen such
an one—
The dregs of the vessel, the leav-
ings of the feast,
And that which is cast into the
street are his food.

The key line in this passage was "His
spirit resteth not in the earth," which Summers
took to mean that the spirits of those who died
alone (i.e., the *ekimmu*) could not even enter
the Netherworld and thus were condemned to
roam the earth. He then connected this passage
with other passages concerning the exorcism of

ghosts and quoted at length various texts that
enumerated the various ghosts that had been
seen. However, the ghosts were of a wide variety,
as one text stated:

The evil spirit, the evil demon,
the evil ghost, the evil devil,
From the earth have come forth;
From the underworld into the
land of the living they have
come forth;
In heaven they are unknown
On earth they are not understood
They neither stand nor sit,
Not eat nor drink.

It appeared that Summers confused the
issue of revenants and the return of the dead
who could become vampires with ghosts of
the deceased who might simply haunt the
land. The ghosts were plainly noncorporeal:
they neither ate nor drank, whereas the dead
in the underworld had a form of corporeal
existence and enjoyed some meager pleasures.
The source of this misunderstanding was an
inadequate translation of the last parts of the
Gilgamish Epic. The line "The spirit resteth
not in the earth" was originally translated in
such a way as to leave open the possibility of
the dead wandering in the world of human
habitation. However, more recent translations
and a survey of the context of the last couplets of the Gilgamish Epic made it clear that
the dead who died in the desert uncared for
(the *ekimmu*) roamed restlessly not on the
earth but through the Netherworld. David
Ferry's translation, for example, rendered the
passage thusly:

And he whose corpse was
thrown away unburied?
He wanders without rest through
the world down there
The One who goes to the Netherworld without leaving behind anyone to mourn for
him?

Garbage is what he eats in the
  Netherworld.
No dog would eat the food he
  has to eat.

Thus, while the idea of vampires did exist in Mesopotamia, it was not as prominent as Summers would indicate. Summers should not be overly chastised for his error, however, because even eminent scholar E. A. Wallis Budge made a similar mistake in his brief comments on tablet 12 in 1920:

The last lines of the tablet seem to say that the spirit of the unburied man reposeth both in the earth, and that the spirit of the friendless man wandereth about the street eating the remains of food which are cast out of the cooking pots.

However, neither Budge nor R. Campbell Thompson, whom Summers quoted from directly, made the error of pushing these several texts in the direction of a vampirish interpretation.

Western and Northern Europe

France

French records supply only a limited number of texts for vampire researchers. Among them are folklore stories of Melusine, a creature reminiscent of the classical *lamiai* figure. Melusine reportedly was the daughter of King Elinas and his fairy wife. Angry at her father, she and her sisters turned their magic against their parents. For her actions, her mother turned her into a serpent from the waist down. Melusine would remain this way until she found a man who would marry her on the condition that he would never see her on Saturdays (when her serpentlike body reappeared). She found such a person in Raymond of Poitoi and, once married, she used her magic to help him build a kingdom. The problem emerged when their children arrived—each was deformed. The situation came to a head when one of the children burned an abbey and killed 100 people. In his anger, Raymond revealed that he knew Melusine's secret. She reacted by accepting the curse upon her and realizing that she was condemned to fly through the air in pain until the day of judgment. Until the castle fell, she would

appear before the death of each of Raymond's heirs to voice her lament. She thus became the banshee—the wailing spirit of the House of Lusignan. Even after the castle fell to the French crown, people reported that Melusine appeared before the death of a French king. She was not a vampire but did show the direction in which at least one of the older vampires evolved.

When the idea of the vampire was introduced into France at the end of the seventeenth century, it was an unfamiliar topic. The subject seemed to have been raised initially in 1693 when a Polish priest asked the faculty at the Sorbonne to counsel him on how he should deal with corpses that had been identified as vampires. That same year, newspaper reports of vampires in Poland appeared in a French periodical, *Mercure Galant*. A generation later, the *Lettres Juives* (*Jewish Letters*), published in 1737, included the account of several of the famous Serbian (mistakenly reported as Hungarian) vampire cases. However, the issue of vampirism was not raised for the French public until the 1746 publication of Dom Augustin Calmet's *Dissertations sur les Apparitions*

> When the idea of the vampire was introduced into France at the end of the seventeenth century, it was an unfamiliar topic.

Julius Hübner's 1844 painting Die schöne Melusine *depicts the discovery of Melusine's secret that she is half serpent.*

des Anges des Démons et des Esprits, et sur les revenants, et Vampires de Hingrie, de Boheme, de Moravie, et de Silésie. This treatise by the French Bible scholar reopened a debate that had previously been carried out in the German universities. That debate had reached a negative assessment concerning the existence of vampires, and Calmet called for what he thought of as both a more biblical and a more scientific view. He built his argument from the accounts of vampires in Eastern Europe and called for further study. While largely rejected by his scholarly colleagues, Calmet's book was a popular success, reprinted in 1747 and 1748, and translated into several foreign languages.

Calmet brought the debate into the Parisian salons, where his volume soon found a number of detractors. Voltaire reacted sarcastically and spoke of businessmen as the real bloodsuckers. Diderot followed a similar line

in his salon of 1767. Only Jean-Jacques Rousseau supported Calmet's line of reasoning and his rational approach to the evidence.

French Vampires: No survey of French vampires would be complete without mention of the several historical figures who have been cited as actual vampires. Leading the list was Gilles de Rais (1404–1440). A hero of France, de Rais was a brilliant general who fought with Joan of Arc but was also a man known to have few equals as a sadistic murderer. He tortured and killed a number of young boys (and a few girls), receiving intense sexual gratification in the process. He also practiced a form of Satanism. It was only with great difficulty that he was brought to trial. Upon conviction, he was strangled, and his body burned.

Somewhat different was the Viscount de Moriéve, a French nobleman who, by strange

A famed knight and companion of Joan of Arc, Gilles de Rais was accused of experimenting with the occult and, worse, killing children as part of his Satanic practices.

fortune, kept his estates through the period of the French Revolution. Following the revolution, he took out his animosity against the common people by executing many of his employees one by one. Eventually, he was assassinated. Soon after his burial, a number of young children died unexpectedly. According to reports, they all had vampire marks on them. These accounts continued for some 72 years. Finally, his grandson decided to investigate the charges that his grandfather was a vampire. In the presence of local authorities, he had the vault opened. While other corpses had undergone the expected decomposition, the viscount's corpse was still fresh and free of decay. The face was flushed, and the heart and chest contained blood. New nails had grown, and the skin was soft.

The body was removed from its resting place, and a whitethorn was driven into the heart. As blood gushed forth, the corpse made a groaning sound. The remains were then burned. No more reports of unusual deaths of children occurred from that day forward. J. A. Middleton, who originally wrote of de Moriéve, discovered that he had been born in Persia, married an Indian, and later moved to France as a naturalized citizen. She believed that he had brought his vampirism with him from the East.

While the de Moriéve case carried many of the elements of traditional European vampirism, that of François Bertrand did not. In the 1840s, Bertrand, a sergeant in the French Army, desecrated a number of graves in Paris before being caught in 1849. After opening graves, he would mutilate bodies in a ghoul-like fashion. His story became the basis of a famous novel, *Werewolf of Paris* (1933) by Guy Endore.

François Bertrand was convicted of robbing graves and eating corpses in 1841, but he only served a year in prison. He lived out the rest of his life quietly in Le Havre, France (illustration from Détective *magazine, c. 1880).*

A rather fanciful scene from the 1915 serial Les Vampires *about a reporter who unveils a secret society of criminals calling themselves vampires.*

The Literary Vampire: France's real contribution to vampire lore came in its nurturing of the literary vampire. Soon after its publication, copies of "The Vampyre" (1819), written by John Polidori but initially published under Lord Byron's name, arrived in Paris. It was hailed as a great product of Byron and inspired several of the literary elite, most notably Jean Charles Nodier (1780–1844), who wrote *Le Vampire*, a drama based on Polidori's story and featuring his vampire star Lord Ruthven. *Le Vampire* led to other Parisian vampire plays, several of them farces, and was translated into English for performance in London.

Through Nodier, the vampire was introduced into French Romantic literature. The Romantic exploration of the inner self, often with the assistance of mind-altering drugs, soon encountered the negative aspect of the human psyche. The vampire emerged as a symbol of the dark side of human nature, and most of the French Romantics utilized it at one point or another. Théophile Gautier (1811–1872) authored a vampire story, "La Morte Amoureuse" (published in English as "The Beautiful Vampire" and "Clarimonde"), in 1836 and a poem titled "Les Taches Jaunes" ("The Yellow Bruises"). Poet Charles Baudelaire (1821–1867) wrote several vampire poems, including "The Vampire" and "Metamorphoses of the Vampire," both published in 1857. Alexandre Dumas (1802–1870) brought to an end this generation of Romantic interest in the vampire with his short story "The History of the Pale Woman" and his dramatic version of *Le Vampire* (1851). During this era, Alexey Tolstoy (1817–1875), the first Russian writer of vampire stories, pub-

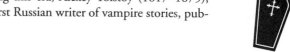

lished his novellas "Upir" and "The Family of the Vourdalak" in French, and they were first circulated and read in the salons of Paris.

Since the mid-nineteenth century, the vampire has appeared only occasionally in French novels. Paul Féval wrote two vampire novels, *Le Vampire* (1867, English translation as *The Vampire Countess*, 2003) and *La Ville Vampire* (1875, English translation as *Vampire City*, 2003). Later novelists included Gustave Lerouge, *La Guerre des Vampires* (1909); Jean Mistler, *Le Vampire* (1944); Maurice Limat, *Moi, Vampire* (1966); Claude Klotz, *Paris Vampire* (1974); and Christine Renard, *La Mante au Fil des Jours* (1977).

In the last generation, the French have picked up on the contemporary vampire craze, and while French authors have not utilized the vampire to anything like the extent of English-speaking countries, a number of French vampire novels have appeared, and their number has been supplemented by the many novels originally written in English, including those by Stephen King and Anne Rice, that have been translated and published in France. Among the authors producing multiple titles are Jeanne Faivre d'Ardier, Claude Klotz, and Michel Pagel. In addition, a steady supply of texts aimed at children and teenagers built around the vampire theme continue to appear. Most of the *Buffy the Vampire Slayer* and *Angel* novels were also translated into French.

The Cinematic Vampire: France produced two of the earliest vampire films. *Le Vampire* (1914) was a silent film in which a man attempted to get a vampire bat to kill his wife. *Les Vampires* (1915) was a ten-part serial built around a secret society of supercriminals. It starred Eugene Ayme as Le Grand Vampire (a criminal master, not a real vampire) and Juliet Musidora as Irma Vep

(an anagram of the word "vampire"). After these early silent movies, it would be 30 years before the next vampire films were produced. Immediately after World War II, Jean Painleve directed a documentary on *Le Vampire*. It was followed by a short feature that appeared in 1947 as *Les Vampires*. Over the next 20 years, additional vampire movies were produced in France, most now forgotten. Rising above the crowd was *Et Mourir de Plaisir* (*Blood and Roses*), produced by Roger Vadim and starring his wife, Annette Vadim, as Carmilla in this remake of the Sheridan Le Fanu tale.

The French movies have become known for continually pushing the amount of overt nudity and sex on the screen. *Et Mourir de Plaisir* paved the way for the work of Jean Rollin, the French director who has most frequently utilized the vampire theme. His first feature-length vampire film, *Le Viol du Vampire* (*The Rape of the Vampire*), inaugurated a series of increasingly explicit films that have become among the most notable of all vampire motion pictures. *Le Viol du Vampire* was followed by *La Nue Vampire* (*The Nude Vampire*, 1969), *Le Frisson des Vampires* (*Sex and the Vampires*, 1970), and *Le Cult de Vampire* (*The Vampire Cult*, 1971). Through the 1970s, he produced *Requiem pour un Vampire* (1972), *Levres se Sang* (1975), and *Fascination* (1979). After his 1982 feature *La Morte-Vivante*, it would be a number of years before he again approached the vampire, but finally, he returned to the theme in the well-received *Les Deux orphelines vampires* (1997).

Rollin created an era of French vampire movies, but after he moved on to other subjects,

> Rollin created an era of French vampire movies, but after he moved on to other subjects, few French producers have picked up on the theme.

few French producers have picked up on the theme. Through the late 1980s to the present, less than a dozen French vampire movies have been released. The French vampire films include *Sexandroide* (1987), which combined sex, science fiction, and vampires; *Baby Blood* (1990); *Un Vampire au Paradis* (1992); *Trouble Every Day* (2001); *Dracula's Fiancée* (2002); *Blood Mallory* (2002); *Perfume* (2007); and *Les Dents de la nuit* (2008).

Popular Culture: As in North America and the United Kingdom, the vampire has entered the popular culture of France, most notably in comic books. In the 1970s, vampire stories began to appear in such horror comics as *La Maison du Mystère* and *La Manoir des Fantomes*. Among the early independent vampire issues was a 12-part serialization of *Jacula: Fête à la Morgue*, the translation of a 1969 Italian adult comic. As French comic books developed into some of the best examples of comic book art, vampires periodically appeared, though they were by no means as popular as in the United States. Among the outstanding issues were Philippe Druillet's *Nosferatu* (1989) (also translated into English) and *Le Fils de Dracuella* by J. Ribera (1991) and its sequels.

Among the most noteworthy of French vampire comic books are the two series by Joann Sfar featuring as main characters the *Grand Vampire* (six volumes, 2001–2005) and the *Petit Vampire* (six volumes, 1999–2004). The latter series became the basis of a 52-episode animated television series in 2004.

Contemporary French scholars and writers have joined in efforts to educate the public on vampires and vampirism. This interest can be traced to the early 1960s with the publication of two books, Tony Faivre's *Les Vampires* (now an extremely rare volume) and the very popular *Le Vampire* by Ornella Volta, which has been translated into English and Spanish. These initial efforts were followed by such volumes as Roland Villeneuve's *Loups-garous et Vampires* (1963), François R. Dumas's *A la Recherche des Vampires* (1976), Robert Ambelain's *La Vampirisme*

> The broad spectrum of French scholarship on vampires had been showcased in several anthologies of articles, the most notable being *Les Vampires* (1993)....

(1977), Jean-Paul Bourre's *Le cult du vampire aujourd'hui* (1978), Roger Delorme's *Les Vampires Humains* (1979), and Jean-Paul Bourre's *Dracula et les Vampires* (1981). The first wave of French scholarship on the vampire was capped by Jean Marigny's *Le Vampire dans la Littérature anglo-saxonne* (1985). Jacques Finné included an extensive list of additional French vampire titles in his 1986 bibliography. In the 1990s, partially in response to the 1997 *Dracula* centennial, French scholars expanded their work and produced a number of notable studies. The decade was launched by the likes of Jean Markale's *l'Enigme des vampires* (1991), which was followed by an additional discussion of the vampire phenomena as a whole in *La chair et le sang: vampires et vampirisme* (1997) by Elisabeth Campios and Richard D. Nolane. The discussion of Count Dracula, his significance, and the ties to Prince Vlad the Impaler were carried forward by Denis Buican's *Les Metamorphoses de Dracula* (1993); Matei Cazacu's *L'Histoire du Prince Dracula* (1996); and Jean Marigny's *Dracula: figures mythiques* (1997). More recent studies include Sabine Jarrot's *La Vampire dans la Littérature du XIX and XX siecle* (2000) and Estelle Valls de Gomis's *Le Vampire: enquête autour d'un mythe* (2005).

The broad spectrum of French scholarship on vampires had been showcased in several anthologies of articles, the most notable being *Les Vampires* (1993), papers from a colloquy held at Cerisy, which includes both an introduction and papers by France's two most notable vampire scholars, Jean Marigny and Antoine Faivre, and a bibliographical article on eighteenth-century studies of vampires. Other collections appeared as *Les Vampires* (1995), edited by Jean-Marie Beurq and Bruno Lapeyre, and *Dracula: de la mort a la vie* (1997), compiled by Charles Grivel. Many vampire novels have appeared in the French language, both translations of the more numerous English-language novels, and original novels by French-speaking novelists. Also, in anticipation of the centennial, two fine collections of vampire fiction appeared: the first, compiled by Francis Lacassin and entitled *Vampires analogie* (1995), includes many of the prominent nineteenth-century writings; the second, compiled by Jean Marigny and entitled *Vampires et les Seins* (1997), is a more extensive contemporary collection.

In 2005, Jacques Sirgent, a vampire enthusiast, opened the Musées des Vampires (Vampire Museum) in a Paris suburb. The Irish ambassador to France graced the opening with an appearance. The museum is open by appointment, and those who wish to take a guided tour or attend a movie screening are invited to contact the museum directly.

Germany

As among the Slavic peoples of Eastern Europe, vampires and vampire-like figures have a long history in Germany, and the first literary and completely fictional presentations of vampires in literature (poems and novels) are in the German language (though vampires in folklore are much older). By the tenth century, Slavic expansion had reached into what is today the eastern part of Germany. Slavs and Germanic people have mixed together through to the modern era. Thus, vampire figures in the region are difficult to distinguish from those of their neighbors, such as the Kushubian people of northern Poland.

A well-known early vampire-like figure is the *Nachzehrer*. The term is not connected with the German word for night but rather stands for "he who devours after (his death)." He is also called *Gierrach* or *Gierhals* ("having a ravenous throat"), *Dodelecker*, or even *Totenküsser*, and he is often mentioned in German folklore from the sixteenth to the eighteenth century, though certainly known earlier. Recent

researchers have shown that he was not just known in parts of Germany in contact with Slavic people but also in western parts, such as the Eifel. More rarely, a dead person is called *Blutsauger* (with dialect variants) or "bloodsucker" (a term also used in popular speech to describe disagreeable people). A special figure is the *Neuntöter* or "killer of nine," who as a child is born already with his teeth or even two rows of teeth, then usually dies quickly and may catch or grasp others after his death so they die also.

Like the Slavic vampire, the *Nachzehrer* was a revenant (a recently deceased person who returned from the grave to attack the living, usually family and village acquaintances). Also like the Slavic vampire, he may have originated from unusual death circumstances. A person who died suddenly from suicide or an accident may in this sense become a *Nachzehrer*. Similar to the *vjesci* of Poland, a child born with a caul (an amniotic membrane that covers the face of

One of several ways that gave birth, so to speak, to vampires was when someone committed suicide. But deadly accidents might also cause someone to turn into a Nachzehrer.

some babies) might become a *Nachzehrer*, especially if the caul was red. This figure was also associated with epidemic sickness. When a group of people died from the same disease, survivors often identified the first to die as the cause of the others' deaths. In the tomb, *Nachzehrer* (singular and plural of the word are identical) were known for their habit of chewing on their own extremities and clothes or shroud (a belief likely derived from the finding of bodies that had been subject to predator damage or whose gums had quickly disappeared due to decomposition). The activity of the *Nachzehrer* in the grave continued until he ceased consuming his body and clothes. As a rule, he does not leave his grave, but in a magical way, he destroys the life of family members who die immediately after him (thus "he who devours after his death").

He is never called a vampire in German texts, a word that became popular only with the Slavic vampire exhumations of the 1730s, though he can be found lying in pools of blood. Many ideas connected with the *Nachzehrer* occur only in a small number of texts, but quite often, he can be identified from the sucking, chewing, and gnawing noises that come from his grave. In the eighteenth century, this belief was generally regarded as superstition and became a subject for scholarly inquiry and naturalist explanations. To prevent the *Nachzehrer* from destroying living people, various preventive measures were proposed. Some people placed a clump of earth under his chin; others placed a coin or stone in his mouth; still others tied a handkerchief tightly around his neck. As a more drastic measure, some people cut off the potential *Nachzehrer's* head, drove a spike into his mouth to pin the head to the ground, or fixed the tongue in place.

In the nineteenth- and even twentieth-century cases of *Nachzehrer* belief, a comparison with vampires became possible. By this time, the word and Slavic vampire ideas had become common knowledge. Alfons Schweiggert investigated some *Blutsauger* (bloodsucker) ideas

of Bavaria in the 1980s. He found that *Blutsaugers* were believed to become undead because they were not baptized (Bavaria is a mostly Roman Catholic part of Germany), were involved in witchcraft, lived an immoral life, or committed suicide. They might also have become vampires from eating the meat of an animal killed by a wolf. During the burial process, an animal jumping over the grave might have caused a person to return as a vampire. In like measure, Bavarians reported that a nun stepping over a grave could have the same effect. Their appearance is described as pale in color, somewhat resembling a zombie. If such a *Blutsauger* were loosed upon a community, residents were told to stay inside at night, to smear their doors and windows with garlic, and to place hawthorn around their houses. If members of the community owned a black dog, an extra set of eyes could be painted upon the animal, causing the vampire to flee. To effectively kill the vampire, a stake through the heart and garlic in the mouth were recommended. Such beliefs are considered the German equivalents of vampire stories, but it is extremely improbable that anything in them is independent of the Slavic vampire tales or even goes back to pre-nineteenth-century times.

Exhumations of dead people suspected of vampire-like influences on the living happened a number of times as recently as the nineteenth century in Germany, as in West Prussia 1870–1873 (cases of G. Gehrke and Franz von Poblocki and a few less well-documented ones; the last exhumation was in 1913 in the Kreis Putzig, West Prussia). Of course, both state and ecclesiastical authorities tried to forbid these clandestine exhumations but without success. Cholera epidemics were sometimes interpreted as influenced by vampires, as in 1855 in Danzig, but it is not quite clear how serious these interpretations were.

The Great Vampire Debate: The beliefs and practices in Germany and Eastern Europe concerning vampire-like figures and vampiric

An engraving from the 1734 book Tractat von dem Kauen und Schmatzen der Todten in Gräbern, *which addresses necrophilia in graveyards.*

happenings became the subject of several books written as early as the seventeenth century (although none used the term "vampire" in its text). Notable treatises included *De Masticatione Mortuorum* (1679) by Philip Rohr, which discussed the eating habits of the *Nachzehrer*, and Christian Frederic Garmann's *De Miraculis Mortuorum* (1670). In the early eighteenth century, a flood of reports of Eastern European vampires began to filter into Germany, where they prompted a massive debate in the universities. Although Germany did not escape the vampire hysteria (epidemics were reported in East Prussia in 1710, 1721, and 1750), the vampire issue seems to have been initially raised by the widespread newspaper reports of vampire investigations in Serbia in 1725 and especially the 1731–1732 investigation of the Arnold Paole case. A popularized version of the Arnold

Paole case was a best seller at the 1732 Leipzig book fair. Helping to initiate the debate were theologian Michael Ranft's *Tractat von dem Kauen und Schmatzen der Todten in Gräbern* (1734; a German translation appeared 2006) and John Christian Stock's *Dissertio de Cadauveribus Sanguisugis* (1732). The *Philosophicae et Christianae Cogitationes de Vampiris* (*Philosophical and Christian Thoughts on Vampires*) by Johann Christian (not Christofer) Harenberg (1739) is still mentioned in Sheridan Le Fanu's "Carmilla," who knew this and similar items through the English translation of Dom Augustin Calmet's great work on vampires, translated into English by Henry Christmas (1850). The debate in German scholarly circles centered on various nonsupernatural (or at least nonvampiric) explanations of the phenomena reported by the vampire investigators, especially in the Paole case. Ranft led the attack on the existence of vampires by suggesting that although the dead can influence the living, they could never assume the form of resuscitated corpses. Others assumed that the changes in the corpses (offered as proof of vampirism) could have resulted from perfectly natural alterations due to premature burial, plague or rabies, unnaturally well-preserved corpses, or the natural growth of hair and nails after death.

The debate resulted in the relegation of the vampire to the realm of superstition and left scholars with only a single relevant question concerning the vampire: "What causes people to believe in such an unreal entity as the vampire?" The primary dissenting voice, which emerged as the German debate was coming to an end, belonged to the French biblical scholar Dom Augustin Calmet. He dissented from his German colleagues simply by leaving the question of the vampire's existence open. Calmet implied the possibility of vampires by suggesting that the very thing that would establish their existence was still lacking solid proof. Although he did not develop any real argument in favor of vampires, Calmet took the reports very seriously and suggested that vampires were a subject suitable for further consideration by his colleagues. Interestingly enough, while most of the works of his German contemporaries were soon confined to the shelves of a few university libraries, Calmet's work was translated into various languages and reprinted as late as the 1850s (and in English as recently as 1993). Recent research on vampires of the 1720s and 1730s has concentrated on the forensic and medical aspects but also on the role of the vampire as a successor to the witch as a scapegoat. In the 1730s, belief in witchcraft had almost disappeared in Germany and Austria, and the vampire stories took over some of its imaginative functions for the public.

The Literary Vampire: Germany and Austria also gave birth to the modern literary vampire. In all probability, the first modern piece of vampire literature was a short poem, "Der Vampir" by Heinrich August Ossenfelder (1748). Not strictly a poem about vampires but much more influential in the development of vampire literature in both Germany and England was "Lenora" (1774) by Gottfried August Bürger, a ballad about a revenant who returned to claim his love and take her to his grave as his bride. This very well-known poem was translated into English by Sir Walter Scott as "William and Helen" (1797); in the eighteenth century, four other translations appeared, such as those by William Taylor (1765–1836) and Rev. J. Beresford, and also the first parody, "Miss Kitty: A Parody, on Lenora." Bram Stoker quotes it in his story "Dracula's Guest" (published posthumously 1914). Even more influential to the popularity of the vampire theme was Johann Wolfgang von Goethe's poem "Die Braut von Korinth" ("The Bride of Corinth"), originally published in 1797. Goethe emerged as the leading literary figure on the continent, and his attention to the vampire theme legitimized it for others.

What may have been the first vampire novel in any language was written by Ignaz Fer-

dinand Arnold (1774–1812; he also wrote as Theodor Ferdinand Kajetan Arnold). In his time, Arnold was a well-known and quite successful musician and writer. He wrote popular novels on crime, conspiracies, conjurers, secret societies, ghosts, and other sensationalist subjects. Although never taken as serious literature, his three-volume novel published in 1801, entitled *Der Vampir* (also known as *Der Vampyr*), was noticed in some contemporary catalogues and biographies, even though no copy is known to be in existence. Such books were not bought by libraries in the early nineteenth century. *Der Vampir* was probably the first vampire novel ever published, and the vampire is certainly meant in a literal, not a metaphorical, sense, as can be concluded from the sensationalist supernaturalism of Arnold's other books. Germany also produced the first monograph on vampires not in folklore but in literature: Stefan Hock, *Die Vampirsagen und ihre Verwertung in der deutschen Literatur* (1900; reprinted in 2006); by the time this monograph was written, Hock was not able to find a copy of Arnold's book. Other German vampire novels were written almost as early, for example *Der Vampyr oder die blutige Hochzeit mit der schönen Kroatin; Eine sonderbare Geschichte vom böhmischen Wiesenpater* (1812) or Theodor Hildebrand(t), *Der Vampyr oder die Todtenbraut. Ein Roman nach neugriechischen Volkssagen* (1828). A tale by Ernst Theodor Amadeus Hoffmann (1776–1822) is also sometimes mentioned in this context. This story—often called "Aurelia" (1820), though originally without title and part of a larger composition and published in English under a variety of names—is in fact about ghouls and even has a model in the *Arabian Nights* (Night 351, "Story of *Sîdîî Nu'mân*").

Some argument has occurred about another early German vampire story that may have been the first short piece of vampire fiction. An English version of a story called "Wake Not the Dead" was published in 1823 and be-

> Germany and Austria also gave birth to the modern literary vampire.

came attributed to the famous German writer Johann Ludwig Tieck, but the story is in fact by Ernst Raupach. It was originally entitled "Laszt die Todten ruhen" ("Let the Dead Rest"), and a play was also written using the same title. The tale is notable for featuring a female vampire, Brunhilda, who was brought back to life by Walter, a powerful nobleman. Walter was in love but awoke one evening to find his wife draining his blood. The German version has more clear-cut allusions to the Elizabeth Báthory tradition. Another later vampire tale is Edwin Bauer's "Der Baron Vampyr, ein Kulturbild aus der Gegenwart" (1892).

The first extensive German treatment of vampires in Eastern European folklore in the nineteenth century was written by Georg Con-

rad Horst, *Zauber-Bibliothek*, Vol. 1 (1821), who stated that even the word "vampire" had become little known by then. This certainly changed with the successful Romantic opera *Der Vampyr* (1828) by Heinrich Marschner (1795–1861), with a libretto by Wilhelm August Wohlbrick, based vaguely on Polidori's "The Vampyre" and more particularly on the play *Der Vampir oder die Totenbraut* (1821), written by Heinrich Ludwig Ritter. The opera is still occasionally performed. It is also discussed in Karl Rosenkranz's very influential *Ästhetik des Häszlichen* (1853) together with Goethe's and Lord Byron's (i.e., Polidori's) vampiric texts. Another theoretical and ethnological text of some impact (perhaps even on Stoker via Arminius Vámbéry or other channels) is Wilhelm Mannhardt's *Über Vampirismus* (1859).

The flow of vampire novels and tales in Germany since then never abated. Ferenz Köröshazy (pseudonym of Seligmann Kohn) wrote *Die Vampyrbraut oder die Wirkungen des bösen Blickes. Aus dem Ungarischen* (1849). Perhaps the most interesting of these nineteenth-century German vampire novels is by Hans Wachenhusen (1822–1898) entitled *Der Vampyr, Novelle aus Bulgarien* (1878), where the vampire is an evil former Eastern Orthodox priest in pursuit of a young woman until she is rescued by an English officer. The real strength of the novel, however, is its careful description of the multicultural society in the late Ottoman Empire, which Wachenhusen knew well from travels (and about which he had published many books). The Romani are also mentioned a number of times and have a similar role to those in Stoker's *Dracula*. Indeed, the atmosphere of the novel in some parts is comparable to *Dracula*, though Stoker's is a much more complex tale. In 1860 in the publication *Odds and Ends*, an anonymous short story, "The Mysterious Stranger," appeared, which was translated from German. The story tells of a certain Azzo von Klatka, a nobleman living in the Carpathian Mountains. He attacked the daughter of a neighbor, an Austrian nobleman.

Heinrich Marschner's successful 1828 opera, Der Vampyr, *was based on a play by Heinrich Ritter that, in turn, was based on the story by John Polidori.*

She began to weaken and had wounds on her neck. Meanwhile, von Klatka grew visibly younger. In the end, the victim was forced to drive nails into the vampire's head to kill him.

Elements of this tale may have echoes in *Dracula*; both stories open with a person traveling into the strange territory of the Carpathian Mountains and being impressed by the picturesque scenery. In "The Mysterious Stranger," the traveling knight and his family were startled by the appearance of wolves, but the "stranger" calmed and commanded them (as did Dracula). The stranger is found to live entirely on liquids and appears only in the daytime. Eventually, he is discovered sleeping in an open coffin in a ruined chapel below the castle. One character in the story, Woislaw, an older man who was quite knowledgeable about vampires, may also have inspired Stoker's vampire-hunting character Abraham Van Helsing.

"Psychic vampirism" is somewhat rare in German novels, though the theosophists often wrote about it, influencing Franz Hartmann's article "Seelenbräute und Vampirismus" (1895), which was later published as a stand-alone monograph. Ladislaus Stanislaus Reymont's "Der Vampir, Roman" (1914, from the Polish "Wampir") is a story about a weak-willed protagonist who falls victim to a demonic, strong-willed woman in London. More important is another tale of psychic vampirism, Georg von der Gabelentz's "Das Rätsel Choriander" (1929). The erotic side of vampirism is most clearly expressed in Toni Schwabe's story "Der Vampir" (1921).

The German version of the first homosexual vampire novel by German author George Sylvester Viereck, *Das Haus des Vampyrs* (1909), was originally published in English (*The House of the Vampire*, 1907). It was translated into German by the author himself. An unpublished German drama by Viereck also exists called *Der Vampyr, Schauspiel in 3 Akten* (1905?). Another stylistically elegant vampire story is Leonhard Stein's *Der Vampyr* (1918), where the female vampire can be read as a metaphor of the psychic side of social decline.

> Elements of this tale may have echoes in *Dracula*; both stories open with a person traveling into the strange territory of the Carpathian Mountains and being impressed by the picturesque scenery.

Almost nothing from the classic German vampire literature has been translated into English. In these golden years of the German phantasmic tale (1900–1930), vampires even became a subject of children's literature: Friedrich Meister's *Der Vampyr, eine Seegeschichte* (1910). As is to be expected, many novels about vampires are more popular reading than high literature, just as in many other languages. For example, Paul Pitt, whose real name is Paul Oskar Ernst Erttmann, wrote *Der Mitternachtsvampir, John Kling's Erinnerungen Bd. 15* (1931), and L. Hackenbroich's *Ein Vampyr. Kriminalroman* (1908) is a nonsupernatural crime story.

Stoker's *Dracula* first came out in German in 1908, translated by Heinz Widtmann. By then, vampires were firmly established in the German supernatural tale. In 1912, a psychoanalytical analysis of vampire tales appeared, written by Ernest Jones, a follower of Sigmund Freud, entitled *Der Alptraum in seiner Beziehung zu gewissen Formen des mittealterlichen Aberglaubens*.

The undisputed masterpiece of German vampire tales is Karl Hanns Strobl's *Das Grabmal auf dem Père Lachaise* (1913), a short novelette comparable in complexity to "Carmilla." A young scholar is financed by Countess Anna Feodorowna Wassilska (a character reminiscent of Elizabeth Báthory) if he is willing to live for a year after her death in her tomb, where he is sometimes visited by his fiancée. There, he soon encounters strange phenomena. Fed by

Winner of the 2004 Nobel Prize in Literature, Austrian author Elfriede Jelinek is the author of Die Kinder der Toten *("Children of the Dead").*

meals devilishly well prepared by a Tatar servant of the countess, he quickly finds he cannot leave the tomb and becomes convinced that he is to be the victim of a vampire, but things are more complicated. This subtle tale can be read as a study in personality deterioration and allows both for a supernatural and a non-supernatural reading.

During the Nazi era, fantastic literature virtually disappeared in Germany, but in the 1970s, it was revived, most of it quite stereotypical. However, some items deserve mention. For example, Barbara Neuwirth, a successful Austrian writer, edited an anthology of vampire stories written by German and Austrian female writers, some of them with a feminist approach (*Blasz sei mein Gesicht*, 1988). The Austrian writer Elfriede Jelinek (1946–; Nobel laureate, 2004) is certainly the most important living writer deeply interested in the vampire motif, which she has used many times (*Die Kinder der Toten*, 1995), and, of course, many supernatural and fantasy writers in present-day Germany have written vampire tales, sometimes long cycles of novels, as with Wolfgang Hohlbein (1953–) or, more rarely, cycles of

rather sophisticated short stories, as with Christian von Aster (1973–). Jörg Weigand's *Isabella oder eine ganz besondere Liebe* (1993) uses the vampire theme for a complex story of Eastern and Western Germany (which became reunited in 1990). Hans Carl Artmann (1921–2000) wrote many satiric pieces, such as "Dracula, Dracula" (1966). Especially noticeable has been original juvenile literature on vampires, and among children's authors, Angela Sommer-Bodenburg (1948–) has emerged as an international favorite. Her series of children's novels starring "the little vampire" Rüdiger, who befriends the human child Anton, started in 1979 and has been translated into over 30 languages and sold many millions of copies.

As in most western countries, vampires are a beloved part of public imagination. A vampire museum existed for some years in the Gieszen era but at present is not open to the public. Germany has shared the international vampire fashions from *Buffy the Vampire Slayer* to *Twilight*, but in the late twentieth century and early twenty-first century, Germany has produced extensive and substantial scholarship on vampires in folklore, mythology, literature, and the arts, none of which has been translated into English so far.

The Cinematic Vampire: Germany re-emerged as an important locale for the developing vampire myth in the early twentieth century. In 1922, Prana Film released *Nosferatu, eine Symphonie des Grauens*, directed by Friedrich Wilhelm Murnau. *Nosferatu* was a greatly disguised but recognizable movie adaptation of *Dracula*. It was screened only once before Bram Stoker's widow, Florence, charged Prana Film with literary theft. Meanwhile, as she pursued the case, the financial instability of Prana Film forced it into a receivership. After three years of litigation, Stoker finally won the case, and all copies of the film were ordered to be destroyed. In recent years, *Nosferatu* has been hailed as one of the great films of German expressionism and the silent era. However, it could

Nosferatu is revealed in this scene from the 1922 German silent film that was an obvious adaptation of Stoker's novel.

be argued that it had only a minimal role in the development of the modern vampire. The few copies that survived were hidden and not seen by audiences until the 1960s. By then, Florence Stoker was dead and both the Bela Lugosi and Christopher Lee versions of *Dracula* were already finished.

Although *Nosferatu* remains the most famous German vampire film, Germany has given the public other important cinematic treatments of the subject. The German vampire emerged in the 1960s in a series of forgettable films, including (as released in English) *Cave of the Living Dead* (1964), *Blood Suckers* (1966), and *The Blood Demon* (1967) with Christopher Lee. The 1964 movie *The Vampire of Düsseldorf* told the story of Peter Kürten, a true-life serial murderer who drank the blood of his victims. It was followed in the 1970s by *The Tenderness of Wolves* (1973), which treated the

vampiric/ghoulish murders of Fritz Haarmann, who had murdered some 25 boys and consumed their blood.

In the 1970s, Germany was the location for two of the most unique and thoughtful vampire films. *Jonathan* (1970) used vampirism as a parable for the rise of fascism. *Martin* (1976) explored the life of a young, sophisticated vampire who moved from biting to using a razor blade and syringe. Through the last generation, German vampire movies include *The Werewolf vs. the Vampire Woman* (1970), *Mosquito the Rapist* (1973), *The Vampire Happening* (1978), *A Lovely Monster* (1991), *Night of the Vampire Hunter* (2000), *We Are the Night* (2010), and *Therapy for a Vampire* (2014).

The Twentieth-century Literary Vampire: In the last two decades, Germany provided a fruitful environment for the vampire novel.

The country has been an ever-present element of horror literature, and numerous vampire short stories appeared in Germany's several horror fiction magazines. For three decades, a host of contemporary popular fiction writers have mined the vampire cave of legend. They were led by Jason Dark (the pen name for Helmut Rellergerd), who wrote more than 300 popular novels, including some 20 featuring Dracula and other vampires. His vampire books were published in a series of horror pulps by Bastei-Lübbe Verlag at Bergisch Gladbach. Frederic Collins, who had also written several vampire novels, was the editor of the series. Among the writers who also developed multiple vampire novels for Bastei-Lübbe were Brian Elliot, Robert Lamont, Frank de Lorca, A. F. Morland, Mike Shadow, and Earl Warren. Many of these names, of course, are pseudonyms; some are house names used by different writers.

Zauberkreis-Verlag and Pabelhaus, both pulp publishers located in Rastatt, also released a set of vampire titles in a horror series. Among the more popular writers for Zauberkreis-Verlag

Author Helmut Rellergerd, writing under the pseudonym Jason Dark, has written about 20 popular novels featuring Dracula or other vampires.

were Maik Caroon, Roger Damon, Marcos Mongo, Dan Schocker, John Spider, and W. J. Tobien. Pabelhaus writers included James R. Buchette, Neal Davenport, Frank Sky, and Hugh Walker. The majority of German vampire novels continue to be published by these three publishing companies.

Ireland

Ireland, like its neighbor the United Kingdom, does not have a rich vampire lore in spite of a mythology that contains numerous stories of preternatural beings and contact between the living and the dead in the form of ghosts and revenants. Montague Summers spoke of an Irish vampire, the *dearg-dul*, but supplied little information about it. Irish folklorists found no mention of it in the folklore they compiled. The most famous vampire tale was that of "The Blood-Drawing Ghost," collected and published by Jeremiah Curtin in 1882. It told the story of a young woman named Kate. She was one of three women whom a man from County Cork was thinking of marrying.

To test the women, he placed his cane at the entrance of the tomb of a recently deceased person and then challenged them to fetch it. Only Kate accepted the challenge. Upon arriving at the tomb, she encountered the dead man, who forced her to take him into town. There, he drew blood from three young men who subsequently died. He mixed the blood with oatmeal he had forced Kate to prepare. While he devoured his meal, Kate secretly hid her portion. Unaware that she had not eaten her oatmeal, the "vampire" confided in her that the blood—oatmeal mixture would have brought the men back to life. As they were returning to his tomb, the "vampire" told Kate of a fortune in gold to be found in a nearby field.

The next day, the three young men were found. Kate then struck a bargain with their parents. She offered to bring them back to life if she could marry the oldest one and if the land where she knew the gold was located could be deeded to her. Deed in hand, she took the oatmeal she had hidden and put some in the mouth of each man. They all quickly recovered from the vampire's attack. With her future husband, she dug up the gold, and the wealthy couple lived a long life and passed their wealth to their children.

Dudley Wright, in *Vampires and Vampirism*, mentioned a female vampire who lured people to her by her beauty. She supposedly resided in the graveyard at Waterford near Strongbow's Tower. Summers conducted one of his rare personal investigations only to discover that no Strongbow's Tower existed near Waterford. He suggested that Wright made a mistaken reference to another structure, Reginald's Tower, but upon checking with authorities on Irish lore, he was told that no vampire legends were known about Reginald's Tower. As a final explanation, Summers suggested that Wright's story was a confused version of a story told of the Anglo-Saxon conquest of Waterford, after which a frog (not native to Ireland) was found and interred in Reginald's Tower.

In 1925, R. S. Breene reported another Irish story concerning a priest who died and was properly buried. Upon their return trip from the graveside, mourners from the funeral parlor met a priest on the road and were upset to discover that it was the man they had just buried. He differed only in that he had pale skin; wide-open, glittering eyes; and prominent, long, white teeth.

They went immediately to the farmhouse of the priest's mother. They found her lying on the floor. It seemed that shortly before the funeral party arrived, she had heard a knock at the door. Looking outside, she saw her son. She made note of the pale complexion and the prominent teeth. Fear overcame her and, rather than letting him in, she fainted.

The Literary Vampire: Ireland gave birth to two of the most famous vampire authors, Sheridan Le Fanu (1814–1873), who wrote the novella "Carmilla" and Bram Stoker, the author of *Dracula*. Le Fanu drew on his Irish homeland for his early stories, but both men had moved to England by the time they wrote their most famous vampire stories, which they set in continental Europe.

The vampire rarely appeared in Irish literature. One appearance that attained a relative level of fame occurred in James Joyce's *Ulysses* (1922), which used vampire imagery. The vampire first appeared early in the novel when Stephen, the main character, spoke of the moon kissing the ocean: "He the moon comes, pale vampire, through storm her eyes, has bat sails bloodying the sea, mouth to her mouth." He makes later reference to the "… potency of vampires mouth to mouth." Joyce injected the vampire into his very complex ruminations on divinity, creativity, and sexuality. In another reference, Stephen spoke of the vampire man's involvement with chic women. Finally, Stephen identified God as the "black panther vampire." Joyce seemed to be settling on an image of the creative Father god as a vampire who preyed upon his victims—virgin women. The insertion of the virgin assisted Joyce in making the point that creation was also inherently a destructive process. In any case, the several brief references to the vampire supplied Joyce's literary critics with the substance for a lively debate.

Through the last decades of the twentieth century, the tradition of Irish vampire lore was celebrated in the work of the Bram Stoker Society and the Bram Stoker Club. Following the death of the society's cofounder, Les Shepard (1917–2004), his daughter donated his large Dracula-related collection to the Dublin City Council, which continues to organize a variety of events to remember Bram Stoker's presence in the city. The society promoted the status of Bram Stoker's writings, especially *Dracula*, while calling attention to Irish gothic literature in general. For many years, it sponsored an annual school on Dracula and related topics each summer.

Italy

In Italy, the vampire phenomenon took on a modern identity when a "vampiric plague" hit Serbia and other lands in Eastern Europe in the seventeenth century. Italians contributed to the animated international debate that began on the nature of this phenomenon, which ultimately contributed to and inspired nineteenth-century vampire literature. Within the debate, various positions reflective of different theological and ideological positions were articulated throughout the centuries.

As the vampiric plague was beginning, a Franciscan from Pavia, Ludovico Maria Sinistrari (1622–1701), included vampirism in a study of demonic phenomena, *De Daemonialitate, et Incubis, et Succubis,* and offered a theological interpretation of them. Far from the contemporary rationalism of the Enlightenment that emerged in the following century, he thought of vampires as creatures that had not originated from Adam (i.e., humanity). While they had a rational soul equal to humans, their corporeal dimension was of a completely different, perfect nature. He thus enforced the idea that vampires were creatures that parallel human beings rather than being opposite chthonius, underground beings. (The oddness of Sinistrari's views may be because his study was a hoax. It was reportedly written in the nineteenth century by Isidore Lisieux, which would account for the fact that the study was not mentioned by Italian authors through the 1700s.)

Credit for initiating the modern view of vampirism is usually given to J. H. Zedler, whose *Grosses volständige Universal-Lexicon aller*

> **Far from the contemporary rationalism of the Enlightenment that emerged in the following century, he [Sinistrari] thought of vampires as creatures that had not originated from Adam (i.e., humanity).**

Wissenschaften und Künste (1745) saw vampirism as a superstition used to explain what were, in reality, certain diseases. However, two years earlier, in his 1743 *Dissertazione sopra i vampiri,* Cardinal Giuseppe Davanzati, noticing that the belief in vampires mostly occurred in rural and less populated areas of the world, labeled vampirism as simply the "fruit of imagination," arguing that such a belief was not found in the metropolitan milieus of Western Europe.

Davanzati's work was looked upon with favor by Pope Benedict XIV, who, when he was still Prospero Lambertini (1675–1758), wrote what remained for many years the standard Roman Catholic sourcebook on miracles and the supernatural, *De servorum Dei beatifications et Beatorum canonizations* (Rome, 1934). As pope, he reprimanded some Polish bishops who were making their belief in vampires too public. While the first edition of his book did not deal with vampires, the second edition added two pages punctuating his negative conclusions on the subject.

Nevertheless, reports of vampirism became a more widespread phenomenon in the mid-eighteenth century throughout the central and eastern parts of Europe. Accounts that were documented in *Traité sur les apparitions et sur les vampires ou le revenans d'Hongire, de Moravie* (1749), by French Benedictine scholar Dom Augustin Calmet, became a source of inspiration for vampire novels throughout the following centuries. Gerhard van Swieten's *Remarques sur les vampirisme* (1755) suggested that vampirism was a superstition generated out of ignorance. The opinion recanted Calmet's tales and represented the triumph of the scientific rationalism that predominated in the culture of the late eighteenth century.

The Literary Vampire: In the early nineteenth century, the first literary works on vam-

Before he became pope, Benedict XIV penned De servorum Dei beatifications et Beatorum canonizations, *which was used as a resource on the supernatural and miracles.*

pires and vampirism began to appear, mostly in Northern Europe. Reportedly, a vampire-oriented literary tradition also began in early nineteenth-century Italy with the opera *Il Vampiro* by A. De Gasperini (first presented in Turin in 1801); however, a copy of the opera has never been found in Italian libraries, and some are doubtful that it ever existed.

Romanticism, a popular literary movement that reflected on inner human experience, itself enforced a mythic image of the vampire with its emphasis on the symbology of blood, the night, melancholy, and the "erotic tenderness for corpses." Mostly in the northern part of Europe from superstitious popular belief, vampirism was introduced to the literate metropolitan milieu through the literary works of Novalis, Goethe, and John Keats. In 1819, John Polidori created Lord Ruthven, the protagonist in his short story "The Vampyre" (translated into Italian as "Il Vampiro" in the twentieth century). Vampires especially began to appear in French and Russian literature in the works

of Charles Nodier, Charles Baudelaire, Alexandre Dumas, Alexey Tolstoy, and Nikolai Gogol.

The first "romance" to be published in Italy, *Il Vampiro,* written by Franco Mistrali, appeared in 1869. Mistrali's story, which takes place in Monaco in 1862, was centered on blood and incestuous lovers. It presented the vampire in a literary, decadent, and aristocratic manner that was influenced by the contemporary literature of Keats, Goethe, Polidori, and Lord Byron. The historical folkloric connotations of vampirism, as documented at the time of the vampiric plague, became the subject of *Vampiro,* a novel written in 1908 by Enrico Boni. It was perhaps the only work that illustrated the popular universe of superstition and fears of the rural culture.

A naturalist approach to the phenomenon was found in the work of Luigi Capuana, *Un Vampiro* (1904; 2nd ed., 1907). The author aimed at an objective description of facts that could be explained scientifically (vampirism as a hallucination), although some skepticism remained at the end of the novel. In 1907, the same year as the second edition of Capuana's *Un Vampiro,* Daniele Oberto Marrama published *Il Dottore nero* (translation: *The Black Doctor*).

Significant works on vampires in the following decades included Nino Savarese's *I ridestati del cimitero* (translation: *The Reawakened of the Cemetery,* 1932); Tommaso Landolfi's *Il racconto del lupo mannaro* (translation: *The Tale of the Werewolf,* 1939); *Racconto d'autunno* (translation: *Fall Tale,* 1947); Bacchelli's *Ultimo licantropo* (translation: *The Last Lycanthrope,* 1947); and Guadalberto Titta's *Il cane nero* (translation: *The Black Dog,* 1964). As can be discerned from the titles, vampires and werewolves were closely associated in the writings of Italian authors.

In the wake of the successful Italian movies *I Vampiri* in 1957 by Riccardo Freda, *Tempi duri per i Vampiri* (*Uncle Was a Vampire*)

in 1959 by Stefano Steno, and Mario Bava's movies in the 1960s, a new wave of commercial vampire horror literature emerged in the form of series, such as *I Romanzi del Terrore*, *KKK Classici dell'orrore*, and *I Racconti di Dracula* (translation: *Dracula's Stories*). The most renowned author of a series was Gaetano Sorrentino (aka Max Dave). In contrast with the commercial literature of those years, a more sophisticated image of vampires appeared in the novels of the authors of these last decades, such as the grotesque and comic vampire (with a benign social criticism) in *Il mio amico Draculone* (translation: *My Friend Draculone*) by Luigi Pellizzetti in 1970 and Italo Calvino's vampire in *Il Castello dei destini incrociati* (translation: *The Castle of Crossed Destinies*). Several works featured an "existential trickster" representing the ambiguity of life in contrast to death. Also published in the same period was Giovanni Fontana's *Tarocco Meccanico* (translation: *Mecanic Tarot*), where the vampire was used as a literary image in the game of oxymora and metaphors that constitute the author's *romanzo sonoro* ("sound romance").

By this time, the traditional stereotype of the vampire had been replaced by sophisticated, metaphorical images that expressed undefinable images. A new connotation of this archetype, in a total break with the tradition, was developed in *Anemia* by Alberto Abruzzese (1984). Here, the protagonist was a highly placed officer of the Communist Party who, in his everyday life, gradually discovered, through a series of initiationlike psychological fears and physical changes, his real identity as a vampire. He had to accept his metamorphosis to maintain the balance needed to stand the rhythm of his ordinary life. The play seems to be a commentary on the difficulty of the old Italian Communist Party in adapting to the changes that transformed it into the post-Communist Democrat Party of the Left.

Another original approach to the vampire theme can be found in the novels of Furio Jesi

(1941–1980). He presented a playful vampire in a short story for children, "La casa incantata" ("The Enchanted House"), published posthumously in 1982, but his major contribution was *L'ultima notte* (*The Last Night*). An expert in mythology and anthropology, Jesi described vampires as mythological archetypes symbolizing life, drawing on pre-Christian and Oriental traditions (Mesopotamia, ancient Mexico, Greece, Tibet, and India). Dracula himself was used as a symbol of fertility and the endless flow of planetary existence, while the mission of these vampires was to reconquer the earth and human species that were heading toward ecological destruction.

Finally, vampires themselves revealed their identity in Gianfranco Manfredi's collection *Ultimi vampiri* (*The Last Vampires*, 1987). In the several novels of the series, *I figli del fiume* (*The Children of the River*), *La guarigione* (*Recovery*), *Il metodo vago* (*The Vague Method*), and *Il pipistrello di Versailles* (*Versailles Bat*), the

Also a songwriter, composer, and cartoonist, the Italian screenwriter Gianfranco Manfredi wrote several vampire novels of note.

Hercules (Reg Park, right) and his friend Theseus (George Ardisson) must journey to Hell to find the magical Stone of Forgetfulness that can free his love, Daianara, in 1961's Hercules in the Haunted World, *directed by Stefano Steno.*

surviving "last vampires" described their historical experience throughout the centuries living side by side with humans, coping with their tricks, and, finally, being defeated by them. Here, some of the major events that radically changed the course of human history (such as the Lutheran Reformation and the Spanish Inquisition—a consequence of the vampiric plague—Versailles and Waterloo) were explained from the perspective of the vampires.

Vampire Poetry: It was within two avant-garde artistic movements, Scapigliatura and Futurism, in the late nineteenth and early twentieth century respectively, that an Italian vampire poetry genre developed. The central topic in this poetry was the vamp, the seductive and fatal vampire woman, caught in her erotic and most aggressive dimension.

These images were heavily inherited by late Romanticism and French poetry, in particular the poems of Baudelaire ("Les Métamorphoses du Vampire," "Le Vampire," "La Fontaine de Sang"). Within the Scapigliatura movement, the most popular poets to write of vampires were Nicola Maciarello, Arrigo Boito (1842–1918), Amilcare Ponchielli, Ugo Tarchetti, Achille Torelli (1841–1922), and Olindo Guerrini. The most influential Futurist poet was Filippo Tommaso Marinetti (1876–1944).

In the decades following the 1920s, with the exhaustion of the Futurist movement, Italian poetry drew little inspiration from vampirism. Midcentury, authors such as Aldo Palazzeschi and Dino Campana only vaguely alluded to vampires in their work. Since the 1970s, however, the *lamiai,* a Greek vampire entity, appeared in Giovanni Fontana's "Le Lamie del labirinto" (translation: "The Labyrinth Lamias"). In the tradition of the "sound romance," Tarocco Meccanico developed the image of the vampire as a metaphorical, artistic, and poetic function.

The Cinematic Vampire: At the same time that Stefano Steno's vampire comedy *Tempi duri per i Vampiri* was released in 1959, Riccardo Freda's *I Vampiri* (*The Devil's Commandment*) (1957) and *Caltiki, il mostro immortale* (*Caltiki, the Immortal Monster*) (1959) also appeared, which brought fame to the movie's special photography cameraman Mario Bava. Bava went from being a mere cameraman to directing more than 20 movies distinguished by his use of haunting Baroque imagery. Bava's most important and representative works included *La Maschera del Demonio* (aka *The Mask of Satan, Black Sunday,* and *Revenge of the Vampire*), 1961; *Ercole al centro della terra* (aka *Hercules in the Haunted World*), also in 1961, where he mastered color special effects; *La Frusta e il corpo* (*The Whip and the Body*), 1963; *I tre volti della paura* (*Black Sabbath*), also in 1963; a series of three short stories; "Sei donne per l'assassino" ("Blood and Black Lace"), 1964; and "Terrore nello spazio" ("Planet of the Vampires"), 1965.

Bava's influence spread internationally and was evident in such movies as Giorgio Ferroni's *La notte dei diavoli* (1971), Ray Danton's *Hannah, Queen of the Vampires,* Paolo Solvay's *Il plenilunio delle vergini,* and the later features from Hammer Films. Some Italian vampire actors should also be mentioned because of the successful roles they played. Many of Bava's movies starred Barbara Steele, who became the horror vamp of Italian movies. In 1963, she played in *La danza macabra* (directed by Antonio Margheriti); in 1965, she was in Mario Caiano's *Gli amanti d'oltretomba* (*The Faceless Monster*) and appeared in Michael Reeves's *La Sorella di Satana* (*Revenge of the Blood Beast*). A specialized Italian vampire was Walter Brandi, who played in Piero Regnoli's *L'ultima preda del vampiro* (*The Playgirls and the Vampire*), 1960; Renato Polselli's *L'Amante del vampiro* (*The Vampire and the Ballerina*); and Roberto Mauri's *La Strage dei Vampiri* (*Slaughter of the Vampires*), 1962. Finally, Giacomo Gentiomo's *Maciste contro il vampiro* (*Goliath and the Vampires*), 1961, should be mentioned because its style also manifests traces of Bava's influence. (Bava's son was also responsible for *Fantaghirò,* a fantasy series whose star character was a young girl in a fantasy medieval world who hunts witches, ogres, and occasionally, like Buffy the Vampire Slayer, tracks down vampire-like creatures. *Fantaghirò* ran for five seasons on Italian television (1991–1995) and was syndicated in several countries (not including the United States).

The Contemporary Scene: After a heyday in the 1960s, the Italian cinematic vampire fell into disfavor and has since made only infrequent appearances. Movies include *Fracchia contro Dracula* (1985), *Anemia* (1986, an adaptation of the Abruzzese novel whose showings were limited to several experimental theaters), *Vampire a Venezia* (1988), and the 1990 remake of *La Maschera del Demonio.* Throughout the 1980s, the Italian literary vampire merged with the Western European and North American vampire. Many novels originally written and published in English have now been translated and published in Italy. Italians have also continued to write about vampires both in popular

Founding director of the literary magazine Poesia, *Italian author Patrizia Valduga is also notable for her 1991 novel,* Woman of Pain.

works and more serious fiction. Among the most prominent of the new Italian authors to contribute to the tradition is Patrizia Valduga, notable for the originality of her work. In 1991, she authored *Donna di dolori* (translation: *Woman of Pain*), in which the vampires appeared to remind the reader of the horrors of the twentieth century.

Scholarship on vampires has blossomed in the 1990s. Among prominent studies published in this decade are Marinella Lorinza's *Nel dedalo del drago* (1993); Vito Teti's *La Melanconia del Vampiro: mito, storia, immaginario* (1994); Carla Corradi Musi's *Vampiri europei e vampiri dell'area sciamanica* (1995); Mario Barzaghi's *Il vampiro o il sentimento della modernita* (1996); Massimo Centini's *Dracula un Mito Immortale* (1997); and Massimo Introvigne's *La Stripe di Dracul: Indagine sul vampirirismo dall'antiochita al nostri giorni* (1997).

In 1995, Introvigne, a religious studies scholar, founded the Italian chapter of the Transylvanian Society of Dracula, the historical and cultural association of people interested in vampire lore and Dracula studies. Introvigne has a significant collection of vampire books, and the society cooperated with television producer Riccardo Mazzoni in his staging of Dracula 1998, the Italian celebration of the Dracula centennial. Centered on a museum display in Milan in the spring, the program included a number of invited guests and several commemorative publications, including a substantial survey of the Italian vampire and a new edition of artist Guido Crepax's *Conde Dracula*, one of the finest graphic-art versions of the novel.

Many Italians were introduced to vampires through comic books in which vampires began to appear in the 1960s, and vampire stories were soon standard fare in the horror anthologies. While Italian publishers translated and republished many American comics (*Vampirella, Morbius, Rune,* etc.), Italians were the most prolific among European nations in generating their own characters and stories. Among early independent vampire titles was *Jacula*, an adult vampire comic featuring a female vampire, reminiscent of the bad-girl vampires of the 1990s. *Jacula* went on to become the single longest-lasting vampire series ever published, running for 327 issues over a 14-year period (1969–1982). In the wake of *Jacula's* success, several imitations were issued, including the almost equally successful *Zora*, which ran for 235 issues (1973–1985).

Through the years, Italian comics gave Dracula (both Count Dracula and Vlad the Impaler) ample treatment. Other aristocratic Eastern European vampires included Bela Rakosi, who invaded the American West in the 1970s series *Zagor*. Zagor, though having no experience with vampires, figured out their weaknesses and dispatched Rakosi on two different occasions. Vampires frequently appear as guest villains in several Italian adventure comics with a horror slant. Even toward the end of the twentieth century and into the next, vampire comics have remained as popular as ever.

Scandinavia

Geographically, Scandinavia consists of three countries of Northern Europe: Norway, Sweden, and Finland. Historically and culturally, it also generally includes Denmark and Iceland. Linguistically, each of these country's languages includes strong elements of Old Norse, the common language of the Scandinavian Vikings. The vampire, though present, was not a prominent element in Viking folklore and did not become one in subsequent Scandinavian folk traditions.

Rosalie H. Wax, author of *Magic, Fate and History: The Changing Ethos of the Vikings*, pointed out that in the old Scandinavian literature, matter was conceived as substantial, and semitransparent ghostly figures were nonexistent. A tradition of ghosts did exist, however, some friendly and some harmful. The latter had greater interaction with the world, more like revenants than ghosts. At times, revenants behaved, at least superficially, like a vampire or a ghoul and usually were treated in ways reminiscent of the vampires of Eastern Europe: by a stake and decapitation. They also have been reported as vampires in some of the popular surveys of vampires around the world.

In the *Eyrbyggia Saga* of Iceland, for example, Thorolf, an early settler of the island, reappeared after his burial. Cattle that went near his tomb became mad and died. His hauntings at home caused his wife's death. His wanderings were stopped for a while by the removal of his body to a new location, but he returned and, finally, his new tomb was opened and his body burned and ashes scattered. The *Grettis Saga* reported the decapitation of Karr, another Icelander, whose head was laid at his thigh, and of Glam, who was both decapitated and burned. Glam was a strong man who hated his former employer, killing his cattle and driving off members of his household. Glam finally was beaten in a fight with a visiting hero, Grettir. Ancient Danish records told of Mithothin, a juggler who had earned the wrath of Odin. He fled to Finland but was killed by the Finns. However, in death, he operated from the barrow where his body was laid. Deaths of people near his barrow and sicknesses that spread through the populace were attributed to his taking revenge. To stop his bloody deeds, the people beheaded and staked him.

More central to Scandinavian belief was a *mara*, the nightmare. A *mara* was seen as a beautiful woman but was in fact a troll. She came to people as they slept and lay upon their breast so that they could neither draw a breath nor move a limb. She would attempt to put her finger in the victim's mouth and count their teeth. If she was given time to do her

counting, the victim usually died. According to some sources, a *mara* was an unknown person in love with its victim. She also was known to attack the horses and ride one all night so that it would be found in its stable the next morning all sweaty. Steps could be taken against the nightmare spirit, including the spreading of seeds around the house, turning shoes the wrong way at the side of the bed, and placing a scythe on the front of the bed.

A knife or sharp instrument was the most effective means of killing or driving away the *mara*. It has been suggested that a vampire appears in the *Kalevala*, the ancient saga of Finland. Over the threshold of the Abode of the Dead in the saga stood Surma, the personification of violent death. Surma was ready to seize any imprudent person who wandered too near to him and to devour the victim with his notable set of teeth. Surma was a horrible figure but does not appear to have been a vampire.

Modern Scandinavia: The tradition of the substantial dead returning to interact with the living has continued into the twentieth century. It includes stories of the return of dead lovers (à la Bürger's "Lenora") and the gathering of the dead in church buildings to hold their own worship services. More to the point, traditions existed of the dead returning because they had committed suicide, because they were overly greedy, or because they wanted to revenge themselves on the living.

Children who were murdered or who died before baptism also returned. An evil woman of Ris, Denmark, walked around after her death. Following a very old tradition, a wooden stake was stuck into the earth above her grave and thrust through her body, thus pinning her to the ground. In order to prevent the dead from arising, people would throw soil in the grave or place needles in the soles of the

> More central to Scandinavian belief was a *mara*, the nightmare. A *mara* was seen as a beautiful woman but was in fact a troll.

feet. More recently, a tradition emerged of shooting the corpse with a bullet made of silver. The treatment of revenants in Scandinavia points to the common ways of dealing with nonvampiric revenants and its continuity with similar practices carried out against the vampire in Eastern Europe.

One popular story, "Gronnskjegg" ("The Vampire" or, in a better translation, "The Ghoul"), has been collected across Norway. In the story, a young girl married an unknown man with a green beard. On returning home, she discovered that her new husband had eaten corpses from the local church graveyard. Later, he appeared to her in the form of different relatives and questioned her. When he appeared in the form of her mother, she told all that she knew of him, and he killed her.

The late sci-fi author Ray Bradbury penned a vampire short story that was later adapted as the Spanish short film Parque de Juegos (1963).

Spain

Spain, geographically separated from the Eastern European home of the Slavic vampire, has been largely devoid of vampire reports in its folklore tradition, although a strong presence of witchcraft has existed. Like the witch in ancient Rome, medieval Italy (*strega*), and Portugal (*bruxa*), the witch in medieval Spain was believed to have the power to transform into various animal forms, to steal infants, and to vampirize children. Vampirism of children, for example, figured prominently in a lengthy trial at Logrono in the fall of 1610. A century earlier, one of the leading Roman Catholic spokespersons on witchcraft, Fray Martin Castenega, cited vampirism as one of the evil actions in which witches engaged. Spain did not participate significantly in either the vampire debates of the eighteenth century or the development of the literary vampire of the nineteenth century. However, in the post–World War II world of the cinematic vampire, Spain has played a strong role.

The Cinematic Vampire: The vampire in Spanish films emerged at the end of the

1960s just as the Italian and Mexican vampire movies were at their peak. The first Spanish vampire film seems to have been *Parque de Juegos* (*Park of Games*), a 1963 production based on a Ray Bradbury story. It stood alone until 1968, when *La Marca del Hombe Lobo* (*The Mark of the Wolfman*) and *Malenka la Vampira* (a joint Spanish–Italian production released in English as *Fangs of the Living Dead*) appeared.

Fangs of the Living Dead introduced director Amando de Ossorio who, through the 1970s, became one of the most prolific instigators of vampire films. He successively directed *La Noche del Terror Ciego* (*Tombs of the Blind Dead*, 1971), *El Ataque de los Muertos sin Ojos* (*Return of the Evil Dead*, 1973), *La Noche de los Brujos* (*Night of the Sorcerers*, 1973), *El Buque Maldito* (*Horror of the Zombies*, 1974), and *La Noche de las Saviotas* (*Night of the Seagulls*, 1975). He is most remembered for introducing the blind vampires in *La Noche del Terror Ciego*, which centered upon the Knights Templars, a religious order whose members were blinded and murdered in the thirteenth century. They returned in two of Ossorio's other films to attack people they located with their acute hearing.

In 1970, Leon Klimovsky, an experienced Spanish director, joined veteran werewolf star Paul Naschy to produce his first vampire movie, *La Noche de Walpurgis* (*The Werewolf vs. the Vampire Woman*). In this fifth in a series of werewolf movies for Naschy, his character, Count Waldemar Daninsky, attacked the vampire witch Countess Waldessa. Klimovsky then made *La Orgia Nocturna de los Vampiros* (*The Vampire's Night Orgy*, 1973), *La Saga de las Draculas* (*The Dracula Saga*, 1973), and *El Extrano Amor de los Vampiros* (*Strange Love of the Vampires*, 1974). Naschy first encountered a vampire in *Dracula vs. Frankenstein* (1971), one of the earlier Daninsky films. He would later slip out of his werewolf role to play Dracula in *Le Gran Amor del Conde Dracula* (*Dracula's Great Love*, 1972). In 2004, American director Don Glut coaxed Naschy out of retirement to make his first appearance in an American movie, *Countess Dracula's Orgy of Blood*.

By far, the most renowned of Spain's vampire filmmakers was Jesús Franco, Spain's equivalent of Italy's Mario Bava. In his first vampire film, Franco cajoled Hammer Films star Christopher Lee to Spain to do a remake of *Dracula*. Lee was intrigued by the opportunity to play a more faithful Dracula than he had been allowed to perform in England. The result was the film *El Conde Dracula* (1970), which had a script (and a characterization of Dracula) that followed the book more closely than either the Universal Pictures or Hammer Films productions. No one realized at the time, given the movie's slow and ponderous pace, that this would be remembered as Franco's best vampire movie.

That same year, Franco also made *Vampyros Lesbos die erbin des Dracula*, his version of the Elizabeth Báthory story, which was more typical of the adult erotic vampire movies that Franco was famous for making. The German

Famous for his B- and exploitation films, Spanish filmmaker Jesús Franco completed over 170 films from the 1960s until his death in 2013.

version, released in 1971, included heightened levels of sex and violence, both of which were toned down for the Spanish- and English-language versions. He followed in 1972 with *La Fille de Dracula* (*Dracula's Daughter*), another adult erotic movie that began with the death of Dracula and followed the adventures of his female offspring. Also that year, he filmed *Dracula contra Frankenstein*, which continued his vampire series while launching a three-film Frankenstein series. In the initial film, Dr. Frankenstein revived Dracula to create a vampire horde as part of a plan to take over the world.

In 1973, Franco moved on to make his version of the "Carmilla" story, *La Comtesse aux Seins Nus*, an X-rated story of Countess Irina Karnstein, a voiceless descendant of Carmilla who attacked men and killed them through fellatio. The heightened element of sexuality was the only thing of value in this film, and much of the sexual content was deleted in various ways for the different markets. Only the nudity remained in the American video version, finally released as *Erotikill*. Following these six movies, Franco seemed to have exhausted the vampire theme, at least for him. He turned to other topics and continued to release movies annually. However, these six films—the one notable effort with Lee and the five erotic films—were enough to establish him in the vampire cinema hall of fame and provide Spanish vampire films with a distinctive image.

After an intense period of releasing vampire movies, Spanish filmmakers, like their colleagues in neighboring countries, reacted to the pressure from American movies and largely abandoned the vampire (and horror) theme. Only one vampire film, *Tiempos duros para Dracula* (1976), was made in the last half of the decade. Naschy, who had continued his werewolf series, revived the vampire twice in the 1980s. *El Returno del Hombre Lobo* (released in English as *The Craving*), the ninth Wolfman movie, pitted Daninsky against Elizabeth Báthory and her cohorts. Then in 1982, Naschy made a children's movie, *Buenas Noches, Senor Monstruo*, which included Dracula and other famous monsters. Of the several vampire movies made in Spain since the beginning of the 1990s, two feature films, *Killer Barbys* (1996) and its sequel *Killer Barbys vs. Dracula* (2002), have received the most widespread distribution. Both were directed by Jesús Franco (1930–2013). Since Franco's passing from the scene, no one has arisen to fill the vacuum.

United Kingdom

The United Kingdom includes the countries of England, Scotland, Wales, and Northern Ireland. None of the four lands has a reputation for being a prominent home to real vampires or even vampire folklore, but they have been significant contributors to the development of the literary vampire. England's vampire heritage is largely confined to reports contained in two volumes, both written at the end of the twelfth century, which describe vampiric creatures. Among several accounts in Walter Map's *De Nagis Curialium* (c. 1190 C.E.), for example, was the story of a knight and his wife. She gave birth to a son, but on the morning following his birth, the baby was found dead with his throat cut. The same fate awaited both a second and a third child in spite of extra precautions. When a fourth child was born, the entire house was called to stay up to keep the child safe. A stranger in the house also kept watch. As the evening progressed, the stranger noticed all of the household falling asleep. He watched as a matronly woman came to the cradle and bent over it. Before she could hurt the baby, he seized the woman (who appeared to be a wealthy matron of the town). The real woman of the town was summoned, and it was seen that the person captured at the cradle had assumed the matron's form. The captured woman was declared a demon, escaped from the men's grip, and flew away with a loud screech.

William of Newburgh finished his *Chronicles* in 1196. In his fifth book, among the stories he recounted was one "of the extraordinary happening when a dead man wandered abroad out of his grave." Some years previously, in Buckinghamshire, a husband appeared in his wife's bedroom the day after his burial. After he returned a second night, she reported his visits to her neighbors. On the third evening, several people stayed with her, and when he appeared, they drove him away. He then turned to visiting his brothers and, upon being repelled, he disturbed the animals. The town was terrified by his sudden appearances at various hours of the day and night. They consulted the local clergy, who referred the matter to the bishop of London. The bishop first considered burning the body but, after further thought, advised exhumation of the corpse and the placement of a "chartula of episcopal absolution" on the body. It was further advised that the corpse should then be returned to the grave. The villagers followed his instructions. The body was found in the same condition it had been in on the day of burial. However, from that day forward, it never disturbed anyone again. William of Newburgh was also the source of the more famous cases of the vampires of Melrose Abbey and Alnwick Castle.

Both the stories of Map and William of Newburgh (quoted at length in the works of both Montague Summers and Donald Glut) contain many elements of the classical vampire tales of Eastern Europe, but each is missing an essential element—any reference to blood drinking. However, they are similar enough to illustrate the manner in which the vampire tales fit into the larger category of contact with revenants and the manner in which people from widely separated parts of Europe followed a similar set of actions in dealing with the problem.

> Both the stories of Map and William of Newburgh (quoted at length in the works of both Montague Summers and Donald Glut) contain many elements of the classical vampire tales of Eastern Europe....

In Scotland, several additional traditional vampiric figures could be found. The *baobban sith*, for example, were known to appear as ravens or crows but more often as young maidens dressed in green dresses that hid their deer's hooves. Katheryn Briggs related one of the more famous *baobban sith* stories (first published by C. M. Robertson) concerning its encounter with four unfortunate men. The four hunters were camping for the evening. They entertained themselves with dancing and singing. As they danced, they were joined by four maidens seemingly attracted by their music. One of the men sang as the other men danced. The singer noticed that each of his comrades had blood on their necks and shirts. Frightened, he ran into the woods, with one of the women running behind him. He finally found shelter among the horses where, for some reason, the woman did not come. The following morning, he found his hunting mates dead and drained of blood.

The redcap was a malignant spirit who haunted abandoned castles and other places where violence had occurred. If one slept in a spot haunted by the redcap, it would attempt

to dip its cap in human blood. Not as sinister as some, it could be driven off with a word from the Bible or a cross.

During the centuries of the modern era, these beliefs seemed to have largely died out. If such beliefs, which appeared to be widespread in the twelfth century, survived into the modern era, one would expect to see references to them, for instance, in the records of the many proceedings against witches, but none exist. Also, in the seventeenth century, the initial reports of vampires from Eastern Europe were received as if they were describing a new and entirely continental phenomenon. In the years since news of the Slavic vampire became known in England, two significant cases of vampire infestation became known. The first, the Vampire of Croglin Grange, was initially reported in the 1890s, while the more recent case was of the Highgate Vampire at the famous Highgate Cemetery in London in the 1960s and 1970s.

The Modern Vampire: The term "vampire" appears to have been introduced to the English in 1741. It appeared in a footnote in an obscure book titled *Observations on the Revolution* in 1688, which, though written in 1688, was not published until 60 years later. Interestingly, the term "vampire" did not refer to a bloodsucking entity in the book but was used metaphorically in a political sense, with no explanation, as if the term was fairly well known. The author said:

> Our Merchants, indeed, bring money into their country, but it is said, there is another Set of Men amongst us who have as great an Address in sending out again to foreign Countries without any Returns for it, which defeats the In-

dustry of the Merchant. These are the Vampires of the Publick, and Riflers of the Kingdom.

Actually, some years earlier in 1679, a book entitled *State of the Greek and Armenian Churches* by Paul Ricaut (or Rycaut) described:

> ... a pretended demon, said to delight in sucking human blood, and to animate the bodies of dead persons, which when dug up, are said to be found florid and full of blood.

A more important reference to vampires, which not only used the term but described an encounter with them in some depth, appeared in the 1810 publication *The Travels of Three English Gentlemen, from Venice to Hamburg, Being the Grand Tour of Germany, in the Year 1734, Etc.* The author, the earl of Oxford, offered the first serious explanation of the vampire phenomenon in English. At the time it was written, Germany was in the midst of the great vampire debates that followed on the heels of the vampire epidemics reported throughout the Hungarian Empire. Though written in 1734, *The Travels of Three English Gentlemen* remained unpublished for many decades. Meanwhile, Dom Augustin Calmet's 1746 treatise on apparitions, demons, and vampires was translated and published in an English edition in 1759. Both Calmet's and the earl of Oxford's books informed the development of the literary vampire in England.

The English Literary Vampire: England's main contribution to contemporary vampire lore was derived not so much from its folklore tradition as from its nurturing of vampire literature in the nineteenth century. While the origins of the literary vampire must be sought in Germany, British poets were quick to discover the theme. Samuel Taylor Coleridge, Robert Southey, and John Stagg were among the writers who were influenced by such popular translations as Gottfried August Bürger's "Lenora" by Sir Walter Scott.

Then in 1819, John Polidori, out of his love–hate relationship with Lord Byron, launched the vampire legend with his initial short story "The Vampyre." Polidori's story of an aristocratic vampire who preyed upon the women of Europe was loosely based upon a story fragment originally written by Lord Byron in 1816, although Polidori's story took the fragment in a distinctly new direction. More important than Byron's plot contribution to Polidori's story was its original publication under Byron's name. Because of the name attached, it was hailed as a great work by German and French Romantic writers, was quickly translated into various languages, and became the basis of a generation of dramatic productions in Paris and a German vampire opera.

> Then in 1819, John Polidori, out of his love–hate relationship with Lord Byron, launched the vampire legend with his initial short story "The Vampyre."

In 1820, it was brought to the London stage by James Robinson Planché. Through the nineteenth century, some of the most famous and influential vampire stories were written. Drawing on ideas introduced by Polidori, James Malcolm Rymer wrote *Varney the Vampyre*, one of the most successful penny dreadfuls (a novel published chapter by chapter as a weekly serial publication). This highly successful story, which ran to 220 chapters, rivaled Polidori's effort through the rest of the century. *Varney the Vampyre* was followed by a number of pieces of short fiction. Compiled into a single volume, they would constitute a relatively large body of vampire literature and would include William Gilbert's "The Last Lords of Gardonal" (1867); Sheridan Le Fanu's highly influential "Carmilla" (1872); Philip Robinson's two stories, "The Man-Eating Tree" (1881) and "The Last of the Vampires"

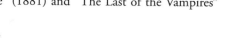

(1892); Anne Crawford's "A Mystery of the Campagna" (1887); H. G. Wells's "The Flowering of the Strange Orchid" (1894); and Mary Elizabeth Braddon's "Good Lady Ducayne" (1896). All of these stories stand behind the single most famous and influential piece of vampire literature of all time: Bram Stoker's *Dracula*, published in London in 1897.

More than any other single work, *Dracula* created the modern image of the vampire and brought the idea to the atten-

These Hammer Films productions made international stars of Christopher Lee, who joined Bela Lugosi and John Carradine as memorable Draculas, and Peter Cushing as Dracula's ever-present nemesis, Abraham Van Helsing.

tion of the English-speaking public around the world. The character Dracula became synonymous with the vampire in many ways, and one could think of contemporary vampires as primarily variations of Stoker's character. It initiated the concept of the vampire as a somewhat tamed monster capable of the incognito penetration of human society. Inspired by Stoker, a century of fiction writers would develop numerous concepts of the vampire in ways Stoker only hinted at. Dracula now stands beside Sherlock Holmes as the single most popular character in English literature and the one most frequently brought to the screen. Dracula was brought to the stage in 1924 by Hamilton Deane.

Deane's play enjoyed great success during his lifetime but has rarely been revived in recent years. More importantly, Deane's play was extensively revised by John L. Balderston for presentation on the American stage in 1927. Balderston's revision, published by an American drama publishing house, has been frequently produced over the years. It was the basis of the three Universal Pictures productions: *Dracula* (1931), with Bela Lugosi; the Spanish version, also filmed in 1931; and the 1979 version, starring Frank Langella. The Langella version resulted from a major Broadway revival of the Balderston play in 1977.

England was also home to Hammer Films, which for 20 years (beginning around the mid-1950s) produced a host of horror films in general and vampire films in particular that defined an entire era of horror motion picture production. The distinctive Hammer Films vampire productions, beginning with *The Curse of Frankenstein* (1957) and *Horror of Dracula* (1958), were notable for their technicolor presentations and the introduction of a fanged vampire who bit his victims on-screen. These Hammer Films productions made international stars of Christopher Lee, who joined Bela Lugosi and John Carradine as memorable Draculas, and Peter Cushing as Dracula's ever-present nemesis, Abraham Van Helsing. They inspired a new wave of vampire films in Europe and America, and with the demise of Hammer Films in the mid-1970s, British leadership in the production of vampire movies passed to the United States.

The Contemporary English Vampire: The United Kingdom has been an integral factor in the current revival of interest in vampires. It is now home to a number of vampire interest groups. The Dracula Society, formed in 1973, is among the oldest, and the Whitby Dracula Society, which puts on a variety of celebrative events at Whitby (where Dracula first landed in England), is the most active. Other organizations that focused vampire fandom in the late twentieth century included the Vampyre Society and the Vampire Guild, which published the journal *Crimson*. The more distinct Vampire Research Society, headed by Sean Manchester, looks with disdain on the vampire as an evil creature.

British authors have also contributed their share of novels to the new vampire literature, among the more significant being Brian Lumley, Barbara Hambly, Tanith Lee, Peter Tremayne, Steve Jones, and Kim Newman. The

United Kingdom was also the home of the
emergence of gothic music promoted by the
Gothic Society.

DRACULA

From Rural Transylvania to Ruler of the World's Vampires

Without doubt, the story of vampires in the modern world begins with and continues to focus upon the novel *Dracula*, written by Bram Stoker and published in 1897 as the nineteenth century drew to an end. While the vampire originated as a character in the world's folklore, the vampire with which we currently deal is a creation of the vivid imagination of a set of nineteenth-century poets and novelists, most notably Stoker. As important as the vampire of folklore is, including the folklore that directly informed Stoker about vampires, it was the character he created that entered into the public consciousness and became the reference point for the popular attention that the vampire currently receives.

It is to the novel that we now turn our attention. Stoker worked on it for years, laying out plot options, positing and discarding characters, expanding his sources, and finally settling on his presentation as if he was assembling a set of documents, a relatively unique means of telling his complex story at the time. Below, we will come to know the major character who would give his name to the novel, introduce the major characters with whom Dracula interacts (several of which have become famous for their association with Count Dracula), and highlight the prominent settings that Stoker chose for the novel's action: his adopted hometown (London), his favorite vacation spot (Whitby), and the land largely unknown to his readers (Transylvania).

Dracula the Legend

Dracula, the title character in Bram Stoker's 1897 novel, set the image of the vampire into the popular culture of the twentieth century. Stoker took the rather vague and contradictory picture of the vampire that had emerged from the nineteenth-century literature and earlier times and developed a fascinating, satisfying, and powerful character whose vampiric life assumed mythical status in the world of literature, the cinema, and the arts.

The Emergence of Dracula: Dracula appeared in print in the very first chapter of Stoker's novel. The reader, however, did not learn until later in the text that the driver who met Jonathan Harker at Borgo Pass and took him to Castle Dracula was none other than Dracula himself. Harker's diary did note that the driver possessed great strength, a "grip of steel." The second chapter opened with Harker entering the castle after his long journey and finally meeting Dracula. He later recorded his impressions in his diary, writing that Dracula was "a tall man, clean shaven save for a long white moustache, and clad in black from head to foot, without a single speck of colour about him anywhere." (It will be noted that this description varies greatly from the common image of Dracula in formal evening dress, an image fostered by Bela Lugosi in the American play and the *Dracula* [1931] movie.) In excellent English but with a strange intonation, he spoke one of his most famous lines, "Welcome to my house! Enter freely and of your own will!" After Harker stepped inside, Dracula moved to shake hands. Harker noted that his host had "a strength which made me wince, an effect which was not lessened by the fact that it seemed as cold as ice—more like the hand of a dead than a living man." Over supper, Harker had a chance to study Dracula with some leisure and was able to develop a more complete description:

> His face was a strong—a very strong—aquiline with high bridge of the thin nose and peculiarly arched nostrils; with lofty domed forehead, and hair growing scantily round the temples, but profusely elsewhere. His eyebrows were very massive, almost meeting over the nose, and with bushy hair that seemed to curl in its own profusion. The mouth, so far as I could see it under the heavy moustache, was fixed and rather cruel looking, with peculiarly sharp white teeth; these protruded over the lips, whose remarkable ruddiness showed astonishing vitality in a man of his years. For the rest, his ears were pale and the tops extremely pointed; the chin was broad and strong, and the cheeks firm though thin. The general effect was one of extraordinary pallor.
>
> Hitherto I had noticed the backs of his hands as they lay on his knees in the firelight, and they had seemed rather white and fine; but seeing them now close to me, I could not but notice that they were rather coarse—broad, with squat fingers. Strange to say, there were hairs at the centre of the palm. The nails were long and fine, and cut to a sharp point. As the Count leaned over me and his hands touched me, I could not repress a shudder. It may have been that his breath was rank, but a horrible feeling of nausea came over me, which, do what I would, I could not conceal. The Count, evidently noticing it, drew back; and with a grim sort of smile, which showed more than he had yet done his protuberant teeth, set himself down again on his own side of the fireplace. We were both silent for a while; and as I looked towards the window I saw the first dim streak of the coming dawn. There seemed a strange stillness over everything....

Harker's first encounter with Dracula included what would become basic elements of the vampire's image. He had unusual strength. He had a set of fangs (extended canine teeth). His skin was very pale, and his body was cold to the touch. He had a noticeable case of bad breath. Among the elements that were soon forgotten were the hairy palms of his hands and sharp fingernails. Only in the 1970s did the need for the sharp fingernails return, as movie directors added the scene from the book in which Dracula used his nails to cut his skin so the heroine, Mina Murray, could drink his blood. An encounter between Dracula and Harker the next day began with Harker noticing the lack of mirrors in the castle. Again, Dracula's long teeth were evident, but more importantly, Harker noted:

> … I had hung my shaving glass by the window, and was just beginning to shave.… This time there could be no error, for the man was close to me, and I could see him over my shoulder. But there was no reflection of him in the mirror!… but at that instant I saw that the cut had bled a little, and the blood was trickling over my chin. I laid

Keanu Reeves is one of numerous actors who have played the role of Jonathan Harker in television and film adaptations of Bram Stoker's Dracula.

down the razor, turning as I did so half-round to look for some sticking plaster. When the Count saw my face, his eyes blazed with a sort of demonic fury, and he suddenly made a grab at my throat. I drew away, and his hand touched the string of beads which held the crucifix. It made an instant change in him, for the fury passed so quickly that I could hardly believe that it was ever there.

Slowly, Dracula's unusual nature became a matter of grave concern, not just a series of foreign eccentricities. Harker dutifully noted that "I have yet to see the Count eat or drink.…" And in light of the bizarre situation in which he had been entrapped, he wondered, "How was it that all the people at Bistritz and on the coach had some terrible fear for me? What meant the giving of the crucifix, of the garlic, of the wild rose, of the mountain ash? Bless that good, good woman who hung the crucifix round my neck.…" The next day, Harker began to gain some perspective on Dracula. He asked him about Transylvania's history, and Dracula responded with a spirited discourse. Dracula resided in the mountainous borderland of Transylvania, an area that, centuries earlier, had been turned over to the Szekelys, tribes known for their fierceness and effectiveness in warfare. Their role was to protect Hungarian territory from invasion. Dracula spoke as a boyar, a feudal lord and member of Hungarian royalty: "We Szekelys have a right to be proud, for in our veins flows the blood of many brave races who fought as the lion fights, for Lordship." In chapter 3, during his encounter with the three women who lived in the castle, Harker noted other revealing facts about Dracula. While his cheeks were red with rage, his eyes were blue, but as his rage grew, his eyes also became red with the flames of hell behind them.

The Fictional Dracula and the Historical Dracula: In chapter 3, Dracula also spoke the line that first suggested a tie between him and Vlad the Impaler, the original historical Dracula:

> ... who was it but one of my own race who as Voivode crossed the Danube and beat the Turk on his own ground! This was a Dracula indeed. Who was it that his own unworthy brother, when he had fallen, sold his people to the Turk and brought the shame of slavery on them! Was it not this Dracula, indeed, who inspired that other of his race who in a later age again and again brought his forces over the great river into Turkeyland; who, when he was beaten back, came again, and again, and again, though he had come alone from the bloody field where his troops had been slaughtered, since he knew that he alone could ultimately triumph....

Later, in chapter 18, Abraham Van Helsing would elaborate on Dracula as Vlad the Impaler, though Vlad was never mentioned by name. Stoker, it seems, constructed his leading character, at least to some small extent, from the historical Dracula. That Dracula was a prince not of Transylvania but of the neighboring kingdom of Wallachia. Stoker turned the Wallachian prince into a Transylvanian count. The real Dracula's exploits largely occurred south of the Carpathian Mountains, which divided Wallachia and Transylvania, and he only infrequently ventured into Transylvanian lands. The real Dracula was a Romanian, not a Szekely, though given the location chosen by Stoker for Castle Dracula, he was correct to think of his main character as a Szekely. Stoker drew the reader's attention, however, not to the fifteenth-century Dracula and the account of his earthly exploits but to someone who was meeting daily with Jonathan Harker and to the way in which each encounter with Dracula's

increasingly weird behavior shattered Harker's conventional understanding of the world. The most mind-boggling event occurred as Harker peered out the window of his room and observed Dracula outside on the castle wall:

> ... I saw the whole man slowly emerge from the window and begin to crawl down the castle wall over that dreadful abyss, face down, with his cloak spreading out around him like great wings....

As he focused on the count's strange behavior, he put the fragments of his observations together:

> ... I have not yet seen the Count in the daylight. Can it be that he sleeps when others wake, that he may be awake whilst they sleep!

Finally, he made a definitive observation that completed the picture of Dracula as a vampire. In chapter 4, he discovered Dracula in his daytime sleep:

> There, in one of the great boxes, of which there were fifty in all, on a pile of newly dug earth, lay the Count! He was either dead or asleep, but I could not say which— for the eyes were open and stony, but without the glassiness of death—and the cheeks had the warmth of life through all their pallor, and the lips were as red as ever. But there was no sign of movement, no pulse, no breath, no beating of the heart. I bent over him, and tried to find any sign of life, but in vain.

> ... There lay the Count, but looking as if his youth had been half-renewed, for the white hair and moustache were changed to dark iron-

Jack Straw's Castle in London is, as you can see, a real place. In Stoker's novel, it is one of the places where Van Helsing dines.

grey; the cheeks were fuller, and the white skin seemed ruby-red underneath; the mouth was redder than ever, for on the lips were gouts of fresh blood, which trickled from the corners of the mouth and ran over the chin and neck. Even the deep, burning eyes seemed set amongst swollen flesh, for the lids and pouches underneath were bloated. It seemed as if the whole awful creature were simply gorged with blood; he lay like a filthy leech, exhausted in his repletion.

Dracula in England: At the end of the fourth chapter, the storyline of Dracula reverted to England, where the count was en route. Dracula's intention was to move to London and reestablish himself, though to what end was not yet revealed. Leaving Harker to his fate in the castle and carrying with him fifty boxes of his native soil, Dracula traveled to the Black Sea. There, he secretly boarded the *Demeter*, the ship that would take him to his new home.

Aboard the *Demeter*, he quietly came out of his box each night and fed on the sailors. One by one, the men grew weak, and as the journey continued, they died. Finally, off the shore of Whitby, a town in northern England, a sudden storm called forth by Dracula blew the ship aground. Dracula transformed himself into a wolf and left the derelict ship. The storyline then shifted to two women, Lucy Westenra and Mina Murray, and the men in their lives. Dracula made only fleeting appearances through the rest of the novel. Instead, he hovered as a vague menace, constantly disturbing the natural course of Lucy and Mina's lives and requiring a cadre of men to search out and destroy him.

Dracula attacked Lucy first. He lured her out of her apartment to a seat on the opposite side of the river, where a suicide had been memorialized. He proceeded to bite her on the neck and drink her blood. He next appeared outside her room in the form of another animal, a bat. Meanwhile, having retrieved his boxes of earth from the *Demeter*, he had them shipped into London, where the novel's action now moved. Dracula distributed the boxes from his main home at his Carfax estate to other locations around the city.

Dracula renewed his attacks upon Lucy, who received a transfusion from her doctor, John Seward, after each attack. The men who assisted her, however, failed to realize that they were merely postponing her ordeal and her ultimate death and transformation into a vampire. Lucy's death and Van Helsing's demonstration of her vampiric powers welded the men into a unit to fight Dracula. Van Helsing was first able to obtain their assistance in killing Lucy with a stake, garlic, and decapitation. He then trained the men as vampire hunters. In this process, in chapter 18, Van Helsing described Dracula and all his powers and weaknesses. A vampire commands the dead and the animals, especially the "meaner things": rats, bats, owls, and foxes. He can disappear at will, reappear in many forms (especially a wolf, a bat, and as a mist), and alter the weather. Slightly changing the folk tradition, Van Helsing noted that Dracula preyed not upon the ones he loved best but upon the ones we loved best. Dracula cast no shadow, he did not reflect in mirrors, he could see in the dark, and he could not enter anywhere without first being invited.

Dracula had grown strong through his long years of existence. However, his strength was strictly limited during the day. For example, while he could move around during the day, he could transform himself only at the moment of sunrise, high noon, and sunset. He could pass over running tide only at high or low tide. Dracula was somewhat vulnerable. His power was taken away by garlic, various sacred objects (the crucifix, the eucharistic wafer), and the wild rose. He could be destroyed by being attacked in his coffin with a bullet fired into the body, a stake through his body (not necessarily the heart), and decapitation. Van Helsing's (i.e.,

Stoker's) understanding of Dracula was derived primarily from the folklore of vampires in Transylvania/Romania as described by Emily Gerard in her popular travel book *The Land beyond the Forest* (1885).

Soon after the session where Van Helsing trained the vampire hunters, Dracula attacked and killed R. N. Renfield, the madman who had been trying to become Dracula's faithful servant. Then, Dracula renewed his attack on Mina that had begun earlier in the book. The men broke into her bedroom and found her drinking Dracula's blood, presumedly the crucial step in becoming a vampire. Those who were merely drained of blood by a vampire simply died. After driving Dracula away, Van Helsing and the men organized by him counterattacked first by sanitizing Dracula's boxes of native soil. All but one of the 50 were found, and in each, a piece of the eucharist was placed. While the men were at work, in the daylight hours, Dracula suddenly appeared in his home in Piccadilly but fled after a brief confrontation.

With only one box of the refreshing earth left, Dracula returned to his homeland. While he traveled by boat, Van Helsing, Mina, and the men took the train. The final chase led to Dracula's castle. Arriving first, Van Helsing sanitized the castle, including Dracula's tomb. Soon thereafter, Dracula appeared, with the other men in hot pursuit. Just as sunset approached and Dracula's powers were restored, Jonathan Harker and Quincey P. Morris killed him by simultaneously decapitating him (Harker) and plunging a Bowie knife into his heart (Morris). The centuries-old Dracula crumbled to dust.

Dracula in Films, Drama, and Books: *Dracula* was well received by the reading public, and both filmmakers and dramatists soon saw its potential. Not long after the book appeared, Stoker moved to assert his rights to any dra-

> Lucy's death and Van Helsing's demonstration of her vampiric powers welded the men into a unit to fight Dracula.

Florence Stoker (née Balcombe) became the literary executor of her husbands estate after his death.

matic productions by staging a single public dramatic performance of *Dracula* in London. Then, after Friedrich Wilhelm Murnau filmed *Nosferatu*, a slightly disguised version of *Dracula*, Florence Stoker asserted her ownership of the dramatic and film rights to her late husband's novel. The initial dramatic rights were sold to Hamilton Deane in 1924 and the American rights to Horace Liveright three years later. The film rights to *Dracula* were sold in 1930 to Universal Pictures, which in the 1950s passed them to Hammer Films. Both the stage and film versions of *Dracula* radically altered the character's image. Deane dropped attributes of Dracula that would prevent his acceptance by middle-class British society. Thus, Dracula lost his bad breath, hairy palms, and odd dress. He donned a tuxedo and an opera cape and moved into the Harkers' living room. The Universal Pictures movie had an even more influential role in reshaping the image. Bela Lugosi's portrayal in the American stage play was succeeded by others, but in the movie, he reached millions who never saw the stage play, and what they saw was his suave, aristocratic, European manner and pronounced Hungarian accent. He reinforced that image in subsequent films. For many, the Stoker character and Bela Lugosi's representation of him merged to create the public image of Dracula. In future portrayals of Dracula, as frequently as not, the actors who played Dracula offered their interpretation of the Lugosi/Dracula persona rather than the character presented in Stoker's novel.

Stoker's novel was reprinted frequently in the following decades. Doubleday brought out the first American edition in 1899. After it entered the public domain, many reprints were published along with condensed versions and adaptations for juvenile audiences. As early as 1972, a version for children, abridged by Nora Kramer, was published by Scholastic Book Services.

At the same time, authors initiated efforts to create new interpretations of this highly intriguing literary figure. Prior to 1960, Dracula seems to have appeared in only one novel, in the 1928 *Kasigli Voyvode* (*The Impaling Vampire*) by Turkish writer Ali Riga Seifi. He was the subject of several short stories, such as Ralph Milne Fraley's "Another Dracula," which appeared in the September and October 1930 issues of *Weird Tales*. In 1960, two new Dracula novels, Otto Frederick's *Count Dracula's Canadian Affair* and Dean Owen's *The Brides of Dracula*, were the first of more than 100 Dracula novels that would be published over the next three decades. Memorable among these are the several series of Dracula novels by Robert Lory (nine action stories), Fred Saberhagen (seven novels), and Peter Tremayne (three novels).

Following the success of the Hammer Films Dracula movies, the vampire movie in general, and the Dracula vampire movie in particular, made a marked comeback. Over 100 movies have featured Dracula, and many others star vampires who are only thinly veiled imitations. The first movie that attempted to bring the *Dracula* novel to the screen may have been a silent film made in Russia (1920), although after a generation of searching, no copy or further evidence of the movie's existence has been uncovered. Following *Nosferatu* and the Bela Lugosi film, other versions have included *Dracula* (Spanish, 1931), *Horror of Dracula* (1958), *El Conde Dracula* (1970), *Dracula*

(1979), and *Bram Stoker's Dracula* (1992). The novel *Dracula* has become the single literary work that has most frequently been brought to the screen, and Dracula has become the fictional character who has made the most appearances on the screen, with the possible exception of Sherlock Holmes.

Beyond the cinema, Dracula made his first appearance on television in the 1960s through Bela Lugosi (who made a brief appearance as Dracula on the popular television series *You Asked for It*) and John Carradine, who appeared in an NBC production of the play. Other television specials that attempted to dramatize the novel featured Denholm Elliott (1971), Jack Palance (1974), and Louis Jourdan (1977). A comic contemporary, Grandpa Count Dracula (portrayed by Al Lewis), was a regular character in the 1964–1966 series *The Munsters*. During the 1990–1991 season, a more serious and sinister count appeared briefly in his own *Dracula: The Series*.

As early as 1953, Dracula was featured in comic books in *Eerie's* (Avon) adaptation of the novel. He made several additional appearances before vampires were banished in 1954 under the conditions of the Comics Code. During the period of banishment, Dell brought out one issue of a *Dracula* comic, but Dracula mostly was limited to guest shots in humorous comics such as *The Adventures of Jerry Lewis* (July–August 1964), *The Adventures of Bob Hope* (October–November 1965), and *Herbie* (September 1966). Dracula did appear in several European and South American comic books, but it was not until the 1970s that he made his comeback in one of the most successful comics of the decade, *The Tomb of Dracula*. In this version, Marvel Comics brought Dracula into the contemporary world in conflict with the descendants of his antagonists in the Stoker

novel. He soon got a second Marvel series, *Dracula Lives!*, and made numerous appearances in different Marvel comics as a guest villain. In the 1990s, Dracula was the subject of two comic books from Topps. These grew out of the noteworthy effort to bring *Dracula* to the screen in Francis Ford Coppola's *Bram Stoker's Dracula*.

Dracula's image (as portrayed by Lugosi) has been a favorite in merchandising from candy labels to ads selling various products. Each October before Halloween, his face graces greeting cards, posters, buttons, party favors, and miscellaneous paraphernalia. Many Dracula statues, dolls, and action figures in almost every medium, from artistic to cute, have been produced.

> Following the success of the Hammer Films Dracula movies, the vampire movie in general, and the *Dracula* vampire movie in particular, made a marked comeback.

Dracula also has been celebrated in music. As early as 1957, "Dinner with Drac" (Cameo, 1957) appeared on a hit record by John Zacherle. A 1950s humor album, *Dracula's Greatest Hits*, had parodies of popular hit tunes that had been transformed into songs about Dracula. Dracula made a number of musical appearances through the 1960s and 1970s, primarily in comic situations, but in 1979, what would become known as the gothic subculture emerged. That musical community was launched by the rock band Bauhaus, whose first hit was an eerie piece titled "Bela Lugosi's Dead." The gothic world found the vampire an apt symbol of the dark world they were creating, and Bela Lugosi's Dracula served as a starting point for their funeral dress. Vlad, former leader of the gothic band Dark Theater, was a Lugosi/Dracula fan who not only adopted aspects of Lugosi's persona into his own but also created a shrine to Lugosi in the living room of his home.

Dracula's permeation into culture during the last generation led to the formation of clubs and organizations that celebrated and promoted him. These include the Count Dracula

Fan Club (now the Vampire Empire), the Count Dracula Society, the Dracula Society, and the Bram Stoker Society. As the centennial of the publication of Bram Stoker's *Dracula* approached, Dracula had become one of the most recognizable images in all of popular culture. His popularity provided the base from which other popular vampire figures, such as Barnabas Collins and Lestat de Lioncourt, could evolve.

Dracula, the Novel

After years of working out his characters and plot, Bram Stoker was able to see the publication of his new novel *Dracula*. It was released on May 16, 1897, by Archibald Constable and Company in London. Simultaneously, another London publishing house, Hutchinson & Company, released what is generally referred to as the colonial edition, specifically produced for circulation in India, Australia, Canada, and the other British colonies around the world. Also, in May 1897, Stoker submitted the script for a play based upon his novel to the Lord Chamberlain's office. The text was made up of printed extracts cut and pasted from one of the novel's galley proofs, with handwritten additions by Stoker connecting the printed clippings. The play was given the title *Dracula; or, The Un-Dead*, which combined the two titles originally considered for the novel.

The single performance of the hastily composed drama was held on the morning of May 18, 1897, at the Lyceum Theatre in London, where Stoker was employed, and was presented by a cadre of the Lyceum's actors. Having submitted the play to the Lord Chamberlain, Stoker made sure that he (and, by extension, his estate) retained copyright not just to the novel but also to the characters and the plot of his novel should they ever be used on the stage (and, again by extension, the cinema, though that was not in anyone's mind in 1897).

Constable passed the publishing rights of *Dracula* to North America, and it was serialized in a variety of newspapers before the new firm of Doubleday & McClure issued the first

American edition in 1899. Doubleday & McClure had been created the same year that *Dracula* was initially published, the brainchild of Frank Nelson Doubleday and Samuel McClure. The American edition had several textual changes, and the paragraphs were somewhat rearranged. One of the changes, for example, occurs in the very first line of any given printing. The Constable text reads:

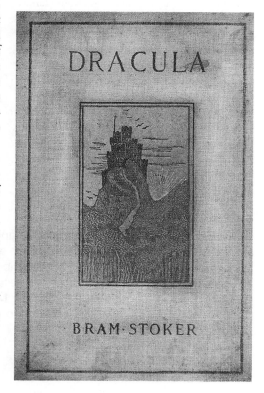

The first American edition of Dracula *was published in 1899.*

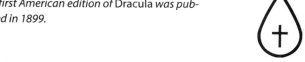

3 May. Bistritz. - Left Munich at 8.35 p.m. on 1st May…

The Doubleday text reads:

3 May. Bistritz. - Left Munich at 8:35 P.M., on 1st May…

Possibly the most important variation occurs in chapter 4 near the end of Harker's diary entry for June 29, in which he describes a conversation overheard between the count and the three women who also resided in his castle. In the British edition, Dracula says, "Wait. Have patience. Tomorrow night, tomorrow night, is yours!" while the American edition reads, "Wait! Have patience! Tonight is mine. Tomorrow night is yours!" The origin and meaning of this change are obscure, but the American edition implies that Dracula will directly take blood from Harker, the only hint of Dracula feeding on a male. This slight alteration in the text would later become a significant issue in understanding the text.

Thus, as *Dracula* moved around the world as the nineteenth century came to a close, four versions of the text existed—the original manuscript, the Constable (and Hutchinson) edition, the hastily prepared drama, and the Doubleday edition—their differences becoming important as *Dracula* took its place among noteworthy English literature in the late twentieth century. Within a few years, in the early twentieth century, two additional versions of the text would emerge. In 1901, Stoker edited the text and created an abridged version of *Dracula* that was published in a paperback edition. Then, in 1912, William Rider & Son obtained the British rights to *Dracula*. Rider reset the text and corrected some of the errors (typos) that existed in the Constable edition. Subsequently in England and through the former British colonies,

the Rider text became the dominant text for new editions and reprints.

Once released on the world, *Dracula* began to find an audience in non-English-speaking countries. Even before the American edition was printed, a Hungarian translation was prepared and printed in Budapest in 1898. It would be followed by an Icelandic edition (1901), to which Stoker contributed a brief preface, and then Russian (1902) and German (1908) editions. These four would be the only ones to appear before Stoker's passing in 1912, but after a pause through the years of World War I, new translations were made into Czech (1919), French (1920), Italian (1922), Slovak (1922), Turkish (1928), and Dutch (1928). In the 1930s, translations appeared in Irish (Gaelic) (1933) and Spanish (1935). Only after World War II did editions appear in additional European languages (Swedish, Finnish, Estonian, Romanian, Ukrainian) and the Asian languages (Japanese, Chinese, Korean).

Dracula Studies: While critical observations of the Dracula character can be traced to the initial reviews of the novel in 1897, Dracula and vampire studies were essentially given a new beginning in 1972 with the publication of *In Search of Dracula* by historians Raymond T. McNally and Radu Florescu, picking up an idea that had been around for a half century that suggested that an obscure Romanian ruler, Vlad Tepes (aka Vlad Dracula), was the inspiration for Stoker's character Count Dracula. While previously suggested, the two historians directed their focus on the idea and

> Dracula and vampire studies were essentially given a new beginning in 1972 with the publication of *In Search of Dracula* by historians Raymond T. McNally and Radu Florescu….

transformed it into the basic thesis of their book. Their book is now credited with significantly stimulating the study of *Dracula* in particular and of the vampire in general through the last decades of the twentieth century. The emergence of an expanded and interdisciplinary cadre of *Dracula* scholars led to a broad critique of the main thesis of *In Search of Dracula* as the twentieth century drew to a close, even as the high level of interest in *Dracula* fed the broader realm of vampire studies.

As the twenty-first century began, a certain malaise crept into *Dracula* studies, with some feeling that the field may have been exhausted. However, several unexpected developments injected new energy into the scholarly community. First, in 2002, what had been thought lost, the typescript of *Dracula* that Stoker presented to the original publisher, surfaced and was for auction. It was purchased by a private collector and is now available to scholars, at least on a limited basis, for perusal. Among the immediate effects of its availability was the laying to rest any remaining doubts that the Stoker short story "Dracula's Guest" was originally a chapter of *Dracula* that was removed shortly before publication.

Second, in 2008, the notes assembled by Bram Stoker while researching and writing *Dracula,* with extensive comments by Robert Eighteen-Bisang and Elizabeth Miller, were published and made available to the larger community of *Dracula* scholars. It is to be noted that the discovery of the notes' survival, and their location in the Rosenbach Museum and Library in Philadelphia, had been an important occurrence in the writing of *In Search of Dracula* several decades earlier, but henceforth, they would be immediately available for all to reference as they studied the novel's text.

Third, through the last decades of the twentieth century, researchers had searched unsuccessfully for rumored copies of a serialized form of *Dracula* in one or more American newspapers. As an initiative to digitize American newspapers gained traction, in the middle of the second decade of the new century, copies of the long-sought serialization of *Dracula* began to appear, the first being discovered by David Skal as a text serialized in the *Charlotte*

Daily Observer and then in the *Buffalo Courier.* Additional serializations have subsequently appeared, and even more are expected as more newspapers are digitized.

Fourth, in 1986, *Dracula* researcher Richard Dalby had obtained and published a translation of what was believed to be Stoker's preface to the Icelandic edition of *Dracula* (published under the title *Makt Myrkranna* (*Powers of Darkness).* That event was newsworthy at the time, as it linked the production of *Dracula* to Stoker rumination on the Jack the Ripper case. Then, in 2016, Hans Corneel de Roos, an independent *Dracula* scholar, published the results of his effort to have *Makt Myrkranna,* written in a language spoken by very few English speakers, into English. The translation was startling in that it revealed *Makt Myrkranna* to be anything but a simple translation of *Dracula.* It turned out to be a rather free adaptation of Stoker's novel, with new characters added and a significantly altered plot. Work on the Icelandic edition also revealed the existence of a heretofore-lost Swedish edition (*Mörkrets makter*), initially serialized in a Stockholm newspaper, upon which the Icelandic edition appears to have been based. In the process of his research, de Roos also discovered an early serialization of *Dracula* in Hungarian that had appeared in a Budapest newspaper.

Meanwhile, the publication of the Icelandic *Powers of Darkness* (2016) was quickly followed by the production of an English translation of the Turkish version of *Dracula* (1928) and its publication in 2017 as *Dracula in Istanbul.* Like the Icelandic version, the Turkish *Dracula* also proved to be a free adaptation of Stoker's novel, with characters renamed and the plot adjusted.

These recent events in *Dracula* studies have injected new life into the field while simultaneously drawing in a new generation of scholars with new, even radical, perspectives on the text into *Dracula* studies. Not only have *Dracula* studies become an international endeavor, but a new generation of scholars are expected to bring fresh theoretical perspectives to the academic encounters.

Stoker, Abraham "Bram" (1847–1912)

Bram Stoker was the author of *Dracula*, the key work in the development of the modern literary myth of the vampire. He was born in Dublin, Ireland, and, at the age of 16, he entered Trinity College at the University of Dublin. Stoker joined the Philosophical Society, where he authored his first essay, "Sensationalism in Fiction and Society." He later became president of the Philosophical Society and an auditor of the Historical Society. He graduated with a bachelor's degree and honors in science (1870) and, as his father before him, went to work as a civil servant at Dublin Castle. He continued as a part-time student at the University of Dublin and eventually earned his master's degree (1875).

Bram Stoker is pictured here in 1906, the year his The Personal Reminiscences of Henry Irving *was published.*

Stoker's favorable impression of British actor Henry Irving (1838–1905), who appeared locally with a traveling drama company, led him to offer his services to the *Dublin Evening Mail* as a drama critic without pay. As his reviews began to appear in various papers, he was welcomed into Dublin social circles and soon met the Wildes, the parents of Oscar Wilde. In 1873, he was offered the editorship of a new newspaper, the *Irish Echo* (later renamed the *Halfpenny Press*), part time and without pay. The paper did not succeed, and early in 1874, he resigned. From that point on, Stoker found his major entertainment in the theater. He also began to write his first pieces of fiction, short stories, and serials, which were published in the local newspapers. His first bit of horror writing, "The Chain of Destiny," appeared as a serial in the *Shamrock* in 1875.

In 1878, Henry Irving took over the management of the Lyceum and invited Stoker to London as the theater manager, and the Irving–Stoker partnership was to last until Irving's death in 1905. During these first years in London, Stoker found the time to author his first book of fiction, a collection of children's stories, *Under the Sunset*, published in 1882.

Toward the end of the 1880s, amid his duties at the Lyceum, he increased his writing efforts. The result was his first novel, appearing first as a serial in *The People* in 1889, and was published in book form the following year.

The story of *The Snake's Pass* centered on the legendary Shleenanaher, an opening to the sea in the mountain of Knockcalltecrore in western Ireland.

In 1890, Stoker began work on what was to become the watershed piece in the development of the literary vampire. Meanwhile, he wrote several short stories and two short novels. The novels, *The Watter's Mou* and *The Shoulder of Shasta*, are largely forgotten today. However, his short stories, especially "The

A dramatic reading of Dracula *was first staged at London's Lyceum Theatre, which is still open and running plays and other performances today.*

Squaw," have survived and are still read by horror enthusiasts.

Stoker's decision to write *Dracula* seems to have been occasioned by a nightmare, in which he experienced a vampire rising from a tomb. He had read Sheridan Le Fanu's "Carmilla," first published in 1872, several years before and had rounded out his knowledge with numerous discussions on the supernatural. To these, he added his own research and modeled his main character on a fifteenth-century Transylvanian nobleman. He also decided, probably suggested by Wilkie Collins's *The Moonstone*, to tell the story through the eyes of several different characters. In the end, the story was told through a variety of documents from diaries to letters to newspaper clippings.

Published in 1897, little suggested that Stoker considered *Dracula* as more than a good

horror story. He received mixed reviews. Some loved it as a powerful piece of gloomy fascination. Others denounced it for its excessive strangeness and complained of its crudity. A very few recognized its importance and compared it to *Frankenstein*. None realized that Stoker had risen to a literary height to which he would never return—but then again, very few authors even approached the peak Stoker had attained.

At about the time of the publication of *Dracula*, Stoker organized a four-hour dramatic reading of its text. This odd event was presented complete with announcements that the dramatic version, *Dracula; or, The Un-Dead*, would be presented at the Lyceum. The event was designed purely to protect the plot and dialogue from literary theft, a protection that would turn out to be quite important. He had members of the Lyceum company join him in the performance, which was the only dramatic presentation of *Dracula* during his lifetime.

The year after *Dracula* was published, Stoker's career took a downward turn. A fire swept through the Lyceum, destroying most of its costumes, props, and equipment. Irving's health, already failing, began to worsen. The theater was turned over to a syndicate and, in 1902, closed for good. Irving died in 1905. Stoker turned to writing and produced a series of novels: *Miss Betty* (1898), *The Mystery of the Sea* (1902), *The Jewel of the Seven Stars* (1903), *The Man* (1905), and *The Lady of the Shroud* (1909). Of these, *The Lady of the Shroud* was possibly the most successful. It reached a twentieth printing by 1934. *The Jewel of the Seven Stars* would later become the inspiration for two motion pictures: *Blood of the Mummy's Tomb* (1971) and *The Awakening* (1980). Of his later writings, Stoker put his most strenuous efforts into his two-volume tribute to his late boss, *The Personal Reminiscences of Henry Irving* (1906). His last books were the nonfiction *Famous Impostors* (1910), which included some interesting sketches of inherently interesting people, and *The Lair of the White Worm* (1911). *The Lair of the White Worm* enjoyed some success over the years and was reprinted in popular, inexpensive paperback editions in 1925, 1945, 1961, and most recently in 1989 in conjunction with a British motion picture adaptation directed by Ken Russell in 1992.

Only with great difficulty did Stoker write his last books. In 1905, his health took a decidedly downward turn. That year, he had a stroke and soon developed Bright's disease, which affects the kidneys. His condition steadily deteriorated until his death at his home on April 12, 1912. Stoker's biographer, Daniel Farson, a great nephew, first suggested that Stoker had died of tertiary syphilis. His conclusions were

strongly refuted by Dracula scholar Leslie Shepard but have recently been reaffirmed by writers Peter Haining and Peter Tremayne.

Possibly the most important of his post-*Dracula* literary products, a collection of short stories entitled *Dracula's Guest, and Other Weird Stories* (1914), was published by his widow shortly after his death. She claimed that "Dracula's Guest" was actually a chapter deleted from *Dracula* by the publishers, who felt that the original manuscript was too long, a view that has been verified by recent Dracula scholars.

Stoker was not a wealthy man when he died, and his wife, Florence, was often hard-pressed for money. She inherited Stoker's copyrights and had periodic income from book sales. Then in 1921, Friedrich Wilhelm Murnau decided to make a film version of *Dracula*. He adapted it freely by, among other things, changing its setting to Germany and altering the names of several characters. For example, Dracula became Graf Orlock. Although he gave Stoker and the book due credit, Murnau neglected to obtain copyright permission. Florence Stoker sued and finally won. The German court ordered all copies of the film destroyed (although, fortunately, one copy survived). In the meantime, playwright Hamilton Deane obtained permission to adapt the novel to the stage. The play opened in June 1924 in Derby and, after many performances around England and Scotland, finally opened in London in 1927.

Through Deane, Florence Stoker lived to see the success of *Dracula* first onstage and then in the 1931 filming of a highly revised version of Deane's play, starring Bela Lugosi. After her death in 1937, *Dracula* went on to become the single literary piece most frequently adapted for the motion picture screen (over 40 times) and its lead character the single literary figure

> Florence Stoker lived to see the success of *Dracula* first onstage and then in the 1931 filming of a highly revised version of Deane's play, starring Bela Lugosi.

most portrayed on the screen other than possibly Sherlock Holmes. The most recent Hollywood film adaptation, *Bram Stoker's Dracula,* directed by Francis Ford Coppola, appeared in 1992. In 1987, the Horror Writers of America instituted a set of annual awards for writings in their field, which they named after Bram Stoker.

🦇 *Draculas Friends and Enemies* 🦇 *(the Major Characters)*

Brides, Vampire

Dracula's vampire brides are a reference to the haremlike arrangement that appeared to exist between the male vampire Dracula and the group of young, female vampires pictured in Bram Stoker's novel *Dracula.* In the opening chapters, the title character lived in his remote castle home with three young women. They were described by a number of names, including "young women," "weird sisters," and "ghostly women." At the end of the novel, Abraham Van Helsing entered Castle Dracula to kill the women, whom he simply called "sisters." The idea of calling them "brides" possibly derived from the incident in the novel when, following the death of Lucy Westenra, Lucy's fiancé, Arthur Holmwood, suggested that the sharing of blood created a husband–wife relationship between himself and his now dead wife-to-be. However, the idea also received its substance from various movies that pictured a male vampire in a continuing relationship with several female vampires.

Commonly in vampire novels and movies, vampires attack a person of the opposite sex. Most vampires were male, and most of their victims, with whom they developed a close relationship, were women. This relationship has often been developed, by implication if not actual reference, in a manner similar to the popular image of the Middle Eastern harem. Frequently, the women were clothed in frilly bedclothes while the man was in formal dress. This image of vampire brides was present in the two *Count Yorga* films and in John Carradine's *The Vampire Hookers* (1979).

The idea of vampire brides emphasized the sexual nature of the vampire's relationship to his victims. The vampire attacked (raped) his victims and then tied them to him in a slavelike relationship, in which love played little or no part. In *Dracula,* the three women accused him of never having loved and of loving no one in the present.

As part of the 1990s wave of interest in all things related to *Dracula,* it seemed inevitable that the stories of the brides would be explored by novelists. The first was Elaine Bergstrom in her *Dracula* sequel, *Mina,* and at the end of the 1990s, Chelsea Quinn Yarbro published two volumes of a projected trilogy telling their story. In his alternate history novels (*Anno Dracula, The Bloody Red Baron,* and *Judgment of Tears*) in which Dracula takes over England, Kim Newman turns Dracula into a polygamist who not only has Queen Elizabeth as a spouse/prisoner but a half dozen others: some real historical figures (such as Barbara of Celje, c. 1395–1441) and some female characters from other fictional works (Sadie Thompson, Princess Asa).

In the movies, especially the various adaptations of *Dracula,* the brides have been minor characters, though they are involved in a famous attack/seduction scene with Jonathan Harker (Keanu Reeves) in Francis Ford Coppola's *Bram Stoker's Dracula.* They have their most expansive

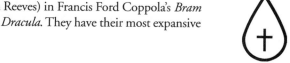

The brides of Dracula assume a horrific version as they prepare to attack villagers in a scene from 2004's Van Helsing.

participation in *Van Helsing*, where Marishka (Josie Maran), Aleera (Elena Anaya), and Verona (Silvia Colloca) assume a place in the battles between the movie's title character and Dracula.

Harker, Jonathan

Jonathan Harker is one of the half dozen major characters in the novel *Dracula*, and as the novel opens, he is in the midst of a journey from London to Transylvania, having just passed through Budapest. As he entered the mysterious East, he arrived in Bistritz, Transylvania (then Hungary, now Romania), the last large town before reaching his goal: Castle Dracula. Upon his arrival at the Golden Krone Hotel, a note from Count Dracula awaited him. The letter instructed him to proceed to the Borgo Pass, where a carriage from the castle would pick him up. When people learned of his destination to the castle, they were frightened and concerned for his welfare, and one lady gave him a rosary with a crucifix to wear. He was taken to Borgo Pass and then transported to Castle Dracula, where Dracula invited

him in. Harker ignored the unusual appearance and manner of the count as he ate that evening. The next afternoon as he explored the castle, he noticed the lack of mirrors. He and Dracula spoke of England and worked to complete Dracula's purchase of Carfax, a house in the London suburb of Purfleet.

The next day, the visit to Castle Dracula took on a strange and even sinister quality. As Harker shaved, Dracula suddenly appeared behind him. Dracula knocked the mirror aside but not before Harker noticed that no image of Dracula standing behind him was reflected in the mirror. He also noticed that Dracula recoiled from the crucifix. Harker began to catalog the strange occurrences day by day and concluded that for some reason he was being held prisoner. He tried to act as if the visit was normal, but then, he was ordered to write a series of letters telling his employer that he was extending his visit.

Harker became convinced of Dracula's supernatural nature as he watched him crawl down the outside wall of the castle. He subsequently encountered the other residents of the castle, the vampire brides, three women who were about to attack him only to be thwarted at the last moment by Dracula's sudden appearance. As he pondered his condition and strategized ways to flee, he noticed that a band of Romani people had arrived. He escaped from his room and roamed through the castle. He found the count lying in a box of earth and considered killing him, but he did not. A second time, he approached Dracula, immobile in his vampire sleep, but again, he found himself unable to complete the kill. Dracula escaped and left Harker behind in the castle.

Somehow, Harker finally escaped and made his way to Budapest, where he became a patient at the Hospital of St. Joseph and St. Mary. The sisters who ran the hospital informed his fiancée, Mina Murray, of his arrival. Mina left England, in spite of the declining health of her friend, Lucy Westenra, to go to Budapest, where she and Harker were married.

Upon their return to England, they were informed of Lucy's death, and Harker met Dr. Abraham Van Helsing, who had been called in as a consultant in her case. By adding the journal of his experiences in Castle Dracula to the data on Lucy's death, a picture of what was occurring began to emerge. Also, he had spotted Dracula walking around London. Once Harker recovered his health and his sense of sanity, he and Mina worked together to compile and correlate information on Dracula's activities. Harker then traveled into London to locate and track the movement of the boxes of earth Dracula had brought with him from the castle. Harker attended the meeting at which Van Helsing organized an informal committee, and he was the first to answer Van Helsing's call for a commitment to destroy Dracula. Harker joined in the search for the boxes of earth, unaware

that Mina was at that very moment under attack. He had believed her fatigue to be caused by stress. Several days later, he was at home with Mina when Dracula arrived. Dracula put Harker to sleep while he proceeded to exchange blood with Mina, a process interrupted by the timely arrival of the other men. They succeeded in driving Dracula away.

Harker accompanied Van Helsing on the final chase back to Castle Dracula. He traveled the last leg of the journey on horseback, along with associate Arthur Holmwood, and arrived with the others just as the box containing Dracula's body was deposited in front of the castle. With Quincey P. Morris, he approached the box and used a large knife to slit Dracula's throat. At the same moment, Morris plunged his Bowie knife into Dracula's heart. In the fracas that concluded with Dracula's death, Morris was killed. Harker and Mina went on to live happily ever after and named their first child after Morris. Seven years after killing Dracula, the couple returned to Transylvania, where many of the memories of their life converged.

It has been suggested that the character of Jonathan Harker was based upon Joseph Harker, a young artist who worked at the Lyceum Theatre, where Bram Stoker was employed. Harker worked with a team of designers that created the stage setting for the theater's production of *Macbeth*. Stoker had known Harker's father, a character actor who had been kind to Stoker in his earlier years. When the job was completed, Stoker returned the favors shown him by helping Harker establish himself independently as an artist.

As *Dracula* was brought to the stage and screen, Harker's role in the story frequently suffered, though not as much as the character of Quincey P. Morris, who was cut out completely

> **It has been suggested that the character of Jonathan Harker was based upon Joseph Harker, a young artist who worked at the Lyceum Theatre, where Bram Stoker was employed.**

in order to simplify the complex plot for dramatic presentation. In the stage versions, Harker's important opening trip to Transylvania was deleted. When that segment of the novel was returned to the script in the movie version of *Dracula* (1931) with Bela Lugosi, R. N. Renfield—not Harker—made the trip to Castle Dracula. In *Horror of Dracula* (1958) with Christopher Lee, Harker arrived at Castle Dracula not as a naïve real estate dealer but as a secret agent in league with Van Helsing. However, he was attacked and killed early in the course of the events before Van Helsing could appear to assist him. Only in Francis Ford Coppola's *Bram Stoker's Dracula* did Harker (played by Keanu Reeves) have the central role he played in the novel from the opening chapter to the final death of Dracula at his hand.

Actor Dan Stevens portrayed Arthur Holmwood in the 2006 British version of Dracula.

Holmwood, Arthur

The Honorable Arthur Holmwood, one of the leading characters in Bram Stoker's novel, *Dracula* (1897), was first mentioned in chapter 5 as Lucy Westenra's true love, and soon afterward, he asked Lucy to marry him. He was also closely related to two other characters, Dr. John Seward and Quincey P. Morris, with whom he had traveled to various parts of the world. Holmwood did not participate in much of the early action of the novel because his father's illness had called him from Lucy's side. Later in the novel, following his father's death, he became the new Lord Godalming.

Holmwood shows up in Whitby following Lucy's first encounter with Dracula. He called Seward to examine her and provides her with one of the transfusions needed to keep her alive. He also joined in the futile watch before Dracula's last attack. Just before her death, as she was turning into a vampire, Lucy tried to attack him, but he was saved by Abraham Van Helsing, who had been called in as a consultant by Seward. Holmwood was hesitant in responding to Van Helsing's call to treat Lucy

as a vampire, but he finally joined Van Helsing, Seward, and Morris in trapping and killing her. With Van Helsing at his side, he drove the stake into her body and assisted in removing her head and filling her mouth with garlic.

Becoming an integral part of the team to search out and destroy Dracula, Holmwood entered Carfax to sanitize Dracula's home base of the vampire's influence. He also went into south and west London with Morris to seek out Dracula's other resting places. He traveled with Mina Murray and the team to Transylvania and was present in the final confrontation near the castle when both Dracula and Morris were killed. In the movement of the novel to the stage and screen, Holmwood has received quite varied treatment. He, like Morris, was dropped from the stage play as a superfluous character. And, as might be expected, he did not appear with Bela Lugosi in *Dracula* (1931), which was based on the play. However, he came to the center in *Horror of Dracula* (1958) as the husband of Mina and brother of Lucy. In that movie, the Holmwood household became the target of Dracula's attack in England. He was also present in Francis Ford Coppola's *Bram*

Stoker's Dracula, where his part (portrayed by Cary Elwes) most closely approximated his role in the novel.

Morris, Quincey P.

Quincey P. Morris was one of the leading characters in *Dracula*, the 1897 novel by Bram Stoker. Prior to the time of action covered by the novel, he had been a friend of both Arthur Holmwood and John Seward, the three having been together in Korea and he and Holmwood having traveled together in South America and the South Seas. Morris was the only American character in the novel, first appearing in chapter 5 (along with Seward and Holmwood) as a suitor of Lucy Westenra. His desires for Lucy led to concern for her declining health and then commitment to the conspiracy to destroy Dracula. He was first described in a letter from Lucy to her friend Mina Murray:

> … He is such a nice fellow, an American from Texas, and he looks so young and so fresh, that it seems almost impossible that he has been so many places and has had such adventures…. Mr. Morris doesn't always speak slang—that is to say he never does so to strangers or before them, for he is really well educated and has exquisite manners—but he found out that it amused me to hear him talk American slang, and whenever I was present, and there was no one to be shocked, he said such funny things.

He proposed to Lucy, but she was already engaged to Arthur Holmwood. She kissed him, and he offered his friendship and departed. He reappeared later (chapter 12) at Holmwood's request to check on Lucy's failing health (she had been bitten by Dracula). He arrived just in time to donate his blood. In the subsequent discussion of Lucy's condition, Morris, from his experience in South America, was able to introduce the idea of a vampire bat. Of course, his story of a big bat that could bring down a cow was not factual; the several species of vampire bats are small, and no one bat can drink enough to do more harm than mildly irritate a cow. Put in the mouth of Morris, however, the speech served an important literary purpose, with Stoker tying the bat and the vampire together in his plot. Abraham Van Helsing later reinforces Morris's statements.

> In the subsequent discussion of Lucy's condition, Morris, from his experience in South America, was able to introduce the idea of a vampire bat.

Morris assumed the task of patrolling the outside of the house to stop any "bat" from reaching Lucy. Once Lucy died and it was determined that she had been transformed into a vampire, Van Helsing recruited Morris to join a group of men who set out to drive the prescribed stake through her heart. He was present for the driving of the stake but stepped outside as Van Helsing and Holmwood cut off her head and stuffed the mouth with garlic. After this event, he became an integral part of the effort to kill Dracula. He joined the group as they entered Carfax to sanitize the earth upon which Dracula slept. The four men then split into two groups, with Holmwood and Morris going to find Dracula's other hideaways in London.

Morris rejoined the other group as it prepared to track Dracula back to his castle in Transylvania. Morris arrived on horseback as everyone converged on the entrance to the castle. Dracula was carried in, resting in a box of his native soil, as the evening was fast approaching. When Dracula awakened, Morris and Jonathan Harker killed him. Morris plunged his Bowie knife into Dracula's heart as Harker decapitated him. Unfortunately, in the fight to reach Dracula's box, Morris was wounded, and a few minutes later, he died. His last words to Mina were, "I am only too happy to have been of service!" Mina and Jonathan named their son after him.

As Dracula's story made its way from the novel to the stage to the screen, the character of Morris suffered greatly. As the novel was condensed, the Morris character was the first to be dropped. Hamilton Deane deleted him as a Texan from the British play and gave his name to a female character, ostensively to create a part for a member of his theater company. However, Morris remained absent from the American play and from the several Dracula movies, beginning with the Bela Lugosi version in 1931. He reappeared in *El Conde Dracula* (1970), Jesús Franco's Spanish version, but as a British nobleman replacing Arthur Holmwood, who did not appear. In the 1977 *Count Dracula*, Morris was also Lucy's fiancé but as a staff person at the American embassy in London. Not until Francis Ford Coppola's 1992 feature, *Bram Stoker's Dracula*, did Morris's character, as he appeared in the book, finally make an appearance. He also appeared in *Dracula: Pages from a Virgin's Diary*, the ballet version of *Dracula* directed by Guy Maddin (2002).

In recognition of his being slighted in the stage and screen productions, one group of Dracula enthusiasts formed the Quincy P. Morris Dracula Society. In addition, Mina Murray and Jonathan Harker's son, Quincey (named for Morris) was a leading character in Marvel Comics's *The Tomb of Dracula* in the 1970s.

With the burgeoning of vampire literature in the 1990s, it was inevitable that Morris would make additional appearances. Among the more notable are Norman Partridge's short story "Do Not Hasten to Bid Me Adieu," which appeared in the 1994 *Love in Vein* collection assembled by Poppy Z. Brite, and P. N. Elrod's novel *Quincey Morris, Vampire.* Justin Gustainis launched a mystery series (five volumes, 2008–2015) featuring a descendant of Morris, also named Quincey.

Murray (Harker), Mina

Mina (short for Wilhelmina) Murray, one of the leading characters in Bram Stoker's *Dracula*, made her first appearance in the book through correspondence with her longtime friend Lucy Westenra. As with Lucy, Stoker said very little about Mina's physical appearance, but she was obviously an attractive, young woman in her twenties.

She was engaged to Jonathan Harker, who at the beginning of the novel had traveled to Transylvania to arrange for the sale of some property to Count Dracula. While she was awaiting his return, she joined Lucy in Whitby, a resort town in northern England, for a vacation together. The visit went well until Lucy began to sleepwalk. One night in the middle of the night, Mina found Lucy sleepwalking on the East Cliff and thought she saw someone with her. Taking Lucy home, she noticed that her friend had two small prick marks on her neck. Mina began to worry about Lucy and also about Jonathan, who had yet to return from Transylvania nor written her to explain his delay.

Finally, a letter concerning Harker arrived. He was in the Hospital of St. Joseph and St. Mary in Budapest recovering from his experiences in Castle Dracula. Mina dropped everything and went to Budapest, where she married Jonathan without further delay. She and Jonathan returned to England, where they learned of Lucy's death.

Abraham Van Helsing, who had been brought into Lucy's case as a consultant while Mina was in Hungary, immediately engaged Mina in his search for information concerning the vampire that caused Lucy's death. Mina was interested in how Lucy's death and Jonathan's condition were related. She volunteered to transcribe Dr. John Seward's diary concerning the events leading to Lucy's death. She was present when Van Helsing organized the men to destroy

Jemma Redgrave (right) plays Mina to Katie McGrath's Lucy in the short-lived series Dracula (2013–2014), *created by producer Cole Haddon.*

Dracula. To Jonathan's relief, having completed the transcription work, Mina initially agreed to "hold back" and let the men do the work of actually killing Dracula.

However, Mina began to have the same symptoms as Lucy before her death. She grew pale and complained of fatigue. During her major encounter with Dracula, mist floated through the cracks in the door and filled her room. The mist formed a whirling cloud. Mina saw the two red eyes and white face she had seen while with Lucy. Meanwhile, as Mina's fatigue increased, the men went about the work of discovering the locations of Dracula's resting places.

The men finally realized that Dracula was attacking Mina and hurried to her room. Dracula had entered some moments earlier and, while Jonathan slept, told Mina that she was to become "flesh of my flesh; blood of my blood; kin of my kin; my bountiful wine-press

for a while; and shall be later on my companion and my helper." He then opened a wound in his chest with his sharp fingernails and forced Mina to drink the blood. He pushed her aside and turned his attention to the men as they rushed into the room; they held him at bay with a eucharistic wafer and a crucifix. Dracula turned into mist and escaped. Mina had the marks of his teeth on her neck, and her own teeth had become more prominent, a sign that she was in the process of becoming a vampire. Van Helsing, wishing to protect her, touched her forehead with the wafer. Unexpectedly, it burned its impression into her forehead as if it was a branding iron.

Left behind while the men destroyed Dracula's resting places in London, Mina suggested that Van Helsing hypnotize her. In her hypnotic state, she revealed that Dracula had left England on a ship. Mina traveled with the men as they chased him to Castle Dracula for a final confrontation.

When the last encounter with Dracula began, Mina was en route to the castle with Van Helsing. When they arrived, Van Helsing drew a protective circle around Mina, at the edge of which he placed pieces of the eucharistic host.

> Only in the American version of the play by John L. Balderston did Mina disappear and have her character combined with that of Lucy.

Among the entities who tried, unsuccessfully, to invade the circle were the three vampire brides who lived in the castle. During the daylight hours, Mina remained in the circle while Van Helsing went into the castle to kill the three vampires, sanitize Dracula's tomb, and make the castle inhospitable to any "undead." The next day, Mina and Van Helsing made their way some distance from (but still in view of) the castle to a spot safe from wolves, and again, Van Helsing drew a circle. From their protected cover, they saw Dracula approach. He rested in his box, being transported by a band of Romani people. Following close behind were the men in hot pursuit. In front of the castle, Dracula was finally killed. The impression of the eucharistic wafer on Mina's forehead subsequently disappeared, and she and Jonathan returned to England.

Mina on Film and Stage: As the primary female character in *Dracula*, Mina generally had a prominent part in both stage and screen versions of the book. Only in the American version of the play by John L. Balderston did Mina disappear and have her character combined with that of Lucy. In the Frank Langella movie version, *Dracula* (1979), her role was reversed with that of Lucy. Winona Ryder played Mina in *Bram Stoker's Dracula*, the movie that most closely approximated Stoker's original story. Ryder's portrayal deviated from the book most clearly in the movie's subplot about her romantic interest in the youthful-appearing Dracula.

Mina was one of the most appealing of Stoker's characters and almost always appears in the cinema remakes of the novel, though occasionally conflated with Lucy Westenra. She also appears in a variety of stories claiming to be sequels to *Dracula* or later adventures of the count. Alan Moore included her in his graphic novel, *The League of Extraordinary Gentlemen*, and she was depicted as a vampire in the cinematic adaptation (2003). Fred Saberhagen sends Dracula to assist a distressed descendant of Mina in *An Old Friend of the Family* (1987).

Mina was the main subject of several books: Elaine Bergstrom's *Mina* (1994) and *Bound by Blood* (1998) and Dotie Bellamy's *The Letters of Mina Harker* (1998), among others. She was a significant character in Freda Warrington's *Dracula the Undead* (1997), Victor Kelleher's *Into the Dark* (1999), Kimberley Zagoren's *Mina's Journal* (2002), and the sequel to *Dracula* by Dacre Stoker and Ian Holt, *Dracula; or, The Un-Dead* (2009). She has most recently been featured in a 2017 trilogy by L. D. Goffigan (*The Beast of London, Fortress of Blood,* and *Realm of Night*), in Jack Wallen's *Dracula Theory* (2019), and in *Life beyond Dracula* by V. A. Wolfe (2020).

Renfield, R. N.

R. N. Renfield was one of the major characters in Bram Stoker's novel *Dracula* (1897). At the beginning of the novel, Renfield had been confined to the lunatic asylum managed by Dr. John Seward. Apart from demonstrating a set of unusual symptoms, no history of or specific reason for his confinement was given. When first described, Seward praised Renfield for his love of animals; however, he revised his opinion somewhat after Renfield ate them in order to absorb their life forces. Seward then coined a new term to describe him: "zoophagous," or life-eating.

Renfield's symptoms took a radical turn just at the time Dracula moved from Whitby, where he had arrived in England, to London. Renfield announced to his attendant, "I don't want to talk to you: you don't count now; the Master is at hand." Seward initially interpreted his words as the sign of a religious mania. The next day, he made the first of several attempts to escape and headed toward Carfax, where Dracula had deposited his boxes of earth. Captured, he was returned to the asylum but escaped again several days later.

Seward's attention was diverted from Renfield for several weeks as he treated Lucy Westenra. However, one evening, Renfield escaped and broke into the doctor's study. He attacked Seward with a knife and then dropped to the floor to lick up the drops of blood that had fallen from the cut. Again, he is forgotten for several weeks, during which time Lucy died, and it was determined that she was a vampire. He inserts himself into the story when he called Seward to come to his cell. He spoke sanely to Seward and the men who accompanied him— Dr. Abraham Van Helsing, Quincey P. Morris, and Arthur Holmwood. Later that day, Seward and Renfield had a long conversation, and Seward determined that Dracula had been with him. The following day, it was found that Renfield had been attacked in his cell. Seward and Van Helsing attended him, and Renfield described Dracula's attack. He mentioned Mina Murray's (now Harker's) name as he lay dying. From his words, Van Helsing determined that Mina was under attack, and the men left Renfield to die alone as they attempt to save her. They broke into her bedroom just in time as she and Dracula were sharing each other's blood.

The character of Renfield, the mad man—one of the most vivid and interesting characters in the novel—has been given quite varied treatment in the several stage and screen adaptations, though most often, he was used to promote atmosphere or as comic relief. Dwight Frye was especially remembered for his

Character actor Dwight Frye was an accomplished actor, as he proved in a number of films from the 1920s and 1930s, brilliantly getting his creepiness on in this scene from 1931's Dracula.

frantic portrayal of Renfield in Universal Pictures's *Dracula* (1931).

The presence of Renfield, however, vividly portrayed the intense evil represented by the vampire. Supernatural explanations vie, even in the modern secular world, with scientific "psychological" explanations that have no need to appeal to either the sacred or preternatural. In the end, even Dr. Seward agreed that the psychological explanations were inadequate, and he joined Van Helsing on the crusade to destroy the vampire.

Renfield has become the subject of several works designed as comments on and sequels of *Dracula*. Kyle Garrett (pseudonym of Gary Reed) led the way in 1994 with a three-issue comic book series about Renfield that told the story of Dracula from Renfield's perspective. Both Tim Lucas in *The Book of Renfield* (2005) and Barbara Hambly in *Renfield: Slave of Dracula* (2006) have imagined a more sympathetic Renfield as the victim of Dracula, who did what he could to fend off the overpowering vampire.

Seward, John

Dr. John Seward, one of the leading characters in Bram Stoker's *Dracula*, appeared early in the story as a suitor of Lucy Westenra. In a letter to her friend Mina Murray (chapter 5), Lucy described Seward:

> He is a doctor and really clever. Just fancy! He is only nine and twenty, and he has an immense lunatic asylum all under his own care. Mr. Holmwood introduced him to me, and he called here to see us, and often comes now. I think he is one of the most resolute men I ever saw, and yet the most calm. He seems absolutely imperturbable. I can fancy what a wonderful power he must have over his patients.

Previously, Seward had been a friend of Arthur Holmwood and Quincey P. Morris, with whom he had traveled in the Orient. At the asylum, he was giving a significant amount of attention to his patient R. N. Renfield, who displayed some unusual symptoms. Renfield wanted to consume various animals in an attempt to take in their lives. Seward called this unique form of madness "zoophagous," or life-eating. After Dracula headed for England, Renfield began to react to his movements. Seward dutifully recorded the changes in Renfield's behavior but had no understanding of their cause.

While attracted to Lucy, Seward was shut out of her life by her choice of Holmwood (Lord Godalming) but was called back into the plot as Lucy's health failed. Unable to find any cause of her illness, he called in his mentor, Abraham Van Helsing of Amsterdam, to consult on the case. Initially, Van Helsing was stumped, but he immediately recognized that Lucy needed blood. Seward participated in giving her a transfusion, and while Van Helsing traveled back and forth to Holland, Seward watched over Lucy's progress and recorded her decline.

After Lucy's death, he became one in the team under Van Helsing who sought out and destroyed Dracula and was present when Lucy's body was staked. Seward eventually understood the relationship between Renfield and Dracula and began the process of deciphering his actions. He introduced Van Helsing to Renfield and was present when Renfield connected Dracula to Mina. In fact, he was with the other men who rushed to her bedroom to save her from the vampire's attack.

He then went to Dracula's base at Carfax and his house in Piccadilly to destroy the boxes of Transylvanian earth. Once it was discovered that Dracula had escaped England and fled to Transylvania, Seward joined the rush to Castle Dracula. In the final push to get to the castle, the team split up, and Seward traveled by horse with Morris. He arrived immediately after Dracula's Romani allies had deposited the box of earth containing Dracula's body before the castle doors. Rifle in hand, he held the Romani back while Morris and Jonathan Harker killed the vampire.

In the later dramatic and cinematic productions of *Dracula*, unlike the other characters, Seward almost always appeared. In the drama by Hamilton Deane and John L. Balderston, he became the father of (rather than the suitor of) Lucy Westenra, an alteration also evident in the several movies based upon the play. Possibly the most interesting twist on Seward's character came in Fred Saberhagen's novels *The Dracula Tape* (1975) and especially *The Holmes–Dracula File* (1978), in which Seward emerged as one of the villains. That idea was seconded by Kim Newman, who transformed Seward into Jack the Ripper in his novel *Anno Dracula* (1992).

Seward eventually understood the relationship between Renfield and Dracula and began the process of deciphering his actions.

More recently, Dr. Seward showed up in the gothic television series *Penny Dreadful* (2014–2016), where she (portrayed by Patti LuPone) is an alienist (a precursor term for psychiatrist).

Van Helsing, Abraham

A major character in Bram Stoker's *Dracula* (1897), whose name has become synonymous with the role of the vampire hunter/slayer, Van Helsing was the wise elder scholar who brought enlightenment to the confusing and threatening situation that the other characters, all in their twenties, had become enmeshed. Van Helsing, who lived in Amsterdam, was originally called to England by Dr. John Seward, who described him as an "old friend and master" and an expert in obscure diseases. Van Helsing was a philosopher, metaphysician, and advanced scientist.

Van Helsing's first task was to examine the ailing Lucy Westenra. He found nothing wrong except a loss of blood and noted that she was not suffering from anemia. He then

Actor Mark Topping is the latest successor in the string of actors playing Dracula nemesis Van Helsing. This time, it is in the 2021 adaptation Bram Stoker's Van Helsing, *directed by Steve Lawson.*

returned to Amsterdam. In less than a week, with Lucy's condition taking a decided turn for the worse, Van Helsing returned. He prescribed an immediate transfusion. He eventually noticed the two marks on Lucy's neck, which led him to return to Amsterdam to consult his books. Upon his arrival back in England a few days later, Lucy again received a transfusion. Actually, by this time, Van Helsing had figured out the cause of Lucy's problem, but he delayed his divulging it at the moment. He merely took steps to block the vampire's access by surrounding Lucy with garlic. She improved, and Van Helsing departed for Amsterdam.

Lucy lost her garlic several days later, and Dracula again attacked her in her bedroom. Following this attack, a third transfusion could not save her. Quincey P. Morris raised the possibility of vampires. After Lucy's death, Van Helsing convinced the men, especially Lucy's fiancé, Arthur Holmwood, to treat Lucy's corpse as a vampire. He had them observe her movements after she was placed in her crypt to ensure that she did not join the undead. While Holmwood pounded a stake into Lucy, Van Helsing read a prayer for the dead from a prayer book, after which he and Seward decapitated the corpse and filled the mouth with garlic. Van Helsing then turned to the task of learning all he could about Dracula, with the goal of first discovering his hiding places and eventually destroying him. In a meeting with the other principal characters, he received their commitment to join the fight under his leadership. At this gathering, he finally laid out, in a most systematic fashion, the theory of vampires (which had been only partially revealed earlier), emphasizing their many powers and the manner by which they may be killed.

Meanwhile, Mina Murray (by this time married to Jonathan Harker) was showing signs of having been attacked by Dracula. She was pale and fatigued, but Van Helsing and the others were slow to recognize what was occurring. Then, while talking to the madman R. N. Renfield,

Van Helsing realized that Mina was under attack and immediately led Seward, Holmwood, and Morris to the Harker house, where they found Mina drinking from Dracula's chest. Van Helsing drove him off with a crucifix and a eucharistic wafer (consecrated wafers are believed by Roman Catholic Christians to be the very body of Christ). To protect Mina, he held the wafer to her forehead only to have it burn its imprint there much like a branding iron.

Mina, who had stepped aside so the men could engage Dracula, now became an active participant in the fight. She invited Van Helsing to hypnotize her and thus tap into her psychic tie to Dracula. In this manner, Van Helsing, who had led in the destruction of Dracula's boxes of dirt (which he needed to survive), discovered that the vampire had left England to return to Transylvania. He accompanied Mina and the men on a chase to catch Dracula. During the last leg of the journey, the group split into three pairs. Van Helsing traveled with Mina, and they were the first to arrive at Castle Dracula. He drew a circle around her with the eucharistic wafers and then went into the castle. He killed the three vampire brides who resided there, sanitized Dracula's crypt, and finished by treating the castle's entrances so that no vampire could use them.

Returning to Mina, Van Helsing moved her some distance from the castle entrance to protect them from the wolves while awaiting the others to converge for the final confrontation. Once all arrived, Van Helsing held a rifle on the Romani people who had assisted Dracula as Morris and Harker approached the box in which the vampire rested and killed him.

As *Dracula* was brought to the stage and screen, Van Helsing assumed a key role, the plot often being simplified to a personal battle

between Dracula and Van Helsing as the representatives of evil and good, respectively. Interestingly, Hamilton Deane, who wrote the original *Dracula* play for his theater company, chose to assume the role of Van Helsing rather than Dracula. However, Peter Cushing, who played the part in several Hammer Films motion pictures (pitted against Christopher Lee as Dracula), has been identified with the role of Van Helsing more than any other actor. He not only played Van Helsing at various times but, on occasion, also portrayed several of his twentieth-century descendants continuing his fight against vampiric evil.

In both the movies and comic books, descendants of Van Helsing have flourished. Cushing played Van Helsing's grandson in Hammer Films's *Dracula A.D. 1972.* Other descendants were portrayed by Richard Benjamin in *Love at First Bite* (1979) and by Bruce Campbell in *Sundown: The Vampire in Retreat* (1989). Marv Wolfman of Marvel Comics invented Rachel Van Helsing, a granddaughter who continued his search-and-destroy mission against Dracula in the pages of *The Tomb of Dracula* through the 1970s. Conrad and Adam Van Helsing emerged in the pages of *Vampirella* as vampire hunters. More recently, Hugh Jackman portrayed Gabriel Van Helsing in the appropriately named *Van Helsing* (2004). Jackman was also the voice of Van Helsing for the cartoon spin-off prequel of the movie, *Van Helsing: The London Assignment* (2004).

Among the more intriguing of recent portrayals of a Von Helsing character has been in the Japanese manga/anime series *Hellsing*, which follows the modern activities of the Hellsing Organization in its attempts to counter the vampires and other supernatural creatures active in contemporary England. Writer/artist Kouta Hirano saw the modern organization as derived from the Royal Order of Protestant

Knights, originally led by Abraham von Helsing and now led by Sir Integra Fairbrook Wingates Hellsing, Abraham's daughter, who is assisted by several capable assistants, including the original Count Dracula, who swore allegiance to the Hellsing family after Abraham defeated him in the 1890s. In the 1990s, vampires were on the rise in England, and the Hellsing Organization was called to action after discovering that it made a common cause with a remnant of the Nazis. Originally begun as a print (manga) series in the 1990s, *Hellsing* was adapted in a very successful anime series that aired in Japan beginning in 2001 and was released in the West later in the decade.

Several people have been suggested as possible models for the Van Helsing character, including author (Abraham) Stoker himself. Some have suggested Arminius Vámbéry, mentioned in chapter 18 as a friend of Van Hel-

A friend of Stoker's who may have been a model for the Van Helsing character, Arminius Vámbéry (1832–1913) was a Hungarian Turkologist and professor at the Royal University of Pest.

sing's. Vámbéry was a real person who at one time was a professor at the University of Budapest and the probable source of Stoker's initial knowledge of Vlad the Impaler, a historical model for Count Dracula. In *The Essential Dracula* (1979), editors Raymond T. McNally and Radu Florescu suggest Max Muller, a famous Orientalist at the University of Oxford, as a possibility. They also suggest that Dr. Martin Hasselius, the fictional narrator in Sheridan Le Fanu's *In a Glass Darkly*, might also have helped inspire Van Helsing.

Westenra, Lucy

Lucy Westenra, one of the major characters in Bram Stoker's *Dracula*, made her initial appearance in the fifth chapter, where her correspondence with her longtime friend Mina Murray was recorded.

While never described physically in any detail, she obviously was an attractive, young woman in her twenties, the object of the affection of three men: Arthur Holmwood, to whom she became engaged; Dr. John Seward; and Quincey P. Morris. In the meantime, she lived with her mother. As the novel begins, she is in Whitby, a resort town in the north of England, about to be joined on vacation by her friend Mina.

On July 24, Lucy met Mina at the Whitby station, and they retired to the home at the Crescent, where they would stay for the next several weeks. On July 26, Mina noted that Lucy had begun walking in her sleep. On August 8, a sudden storm hit Whitby and the *Demeter*, the ship on which Dracula came to England, wrecked onshore. On August 11 at 3:00 A.M., Mina discovered that Lucy had left her bed, and she went in search of her. Lucy was on the East Cliff in their favorite seat. As Mina made her way to Lucy, she saw "something, long and black, bending over her." When she called out, the something looked up, and Mina saw Dracula's white face and red eyes. After she helped

Lucy home, she saw two tiny marks on Lucy's neck. Over the next few days, Lucy grew more and more tired, and the wounds on her neck did not heal. At this juncture, Lucy seemed to get better and Mina, having finally heard from her true love, Jonathan Harker, on August 19, left for Budapest to join him.

Lucy returned to London, where Holmwood joined her, and they set plans to marry on September 28. However, her condition worsened, and Holmwood called Seward in to examine her. Unable to figure out what was wrong, he called Abraham Van Helsing as a consultant, as Van Helsing knew of obscure diseases. Lucy seemed to improve, but then, she turned pale and lost all of her strength. Van Helsing prescribed a blood transfusion. As they were about to perform the procedure, Lucy's fiancé, Holmwood, arrived, and the blood was taken from him. Later, a second transfusion was taken from Seward, after which, without giving his reason, Van Helsing surrounded Lucy with garlic.

Dracula returned to attack Lucy on September 17. The attack followed the removal of the garlic that Van Helsing had ordered to be put around her neck.

Morris was next in line to supply the blood needed to preserve Lucy's life, but by this time, it was already too late; she was turning into a vampire. She died and was laid to rest in the family crypt. Van Helsing immediately wanted to treat the body as a vampire. Holmwood (who by this time had inherited his father's title as Lord Godalming) opposed any mutilation of the body. Though they had not married, he saw Lucy as his wife. In his opinion, the transfusion had served to marry them; they were married in the sight of God.

> While never described physically in any detail, she obviously was an attractive, young woman in her twenties, the object of the affection of three men....

While the men rested, reports surfaced of missing children who, upon being found, told of being with a "boofer lady." Van Helsing persuaded the men to institute a watch at Lucy's tomb. They viewed her empty coffin and finally saw her walking around. In the end, they cornered her in her coffin.

Holmwood assumed his responsibility and drove the stake through her chest. At this point, it was noted that the harsh, fiendish expression, which had characterized Lucy's appearance at the time of her death, departed, and a face of sweetness and purity returned. Van Helsing cut off her head and filled her mouth with garlic. The men then turned their attention to killing Dracula.

When Dracula was brought to the stage and screen, the character of Lucy was handled quite differently. She disappeared completely from *Nosferatu, Eine Symphonie des Grauens* (1922) and Hamilton Deane's *Dracula* play. She returned in John Balderston's revision of Deane's play for the American stage, though now she was Lucy Seward, Dr. Seward's daughter. Both she and Mina returned in the 1931 films in both the English and Spanish versions. In 1958's *Horror of Dracula*, Lucy was transformed into Holmwood's sister and the fiancée of Jonathan Harker. She was given strong parts in the Jack Palance version of *Dracula* (1974) and became central to Frank Langella's *Dracula* (1979). She was returned to a role more closely approaching the one in the novel in Francis Ford Coppola's *Bram Stoker's Dracula* (1992).

In literature, her character has made few appearances. Apparently, authors have felt that since Lucy was killed off fairly definitively in *Dracula*, she has no real place in the vampire literature of the last century.

🦇 *Dracula's Habitats* 🦇

Castle Dracula

The first section of Bram Stoker's novel *Dracula* (1897) concerns Jonathan Harker's trip to Castle Dracula and his adventures after he arrives. In the last generation, as it was discovered that Stoker's character of Dracula was based, in part, upon a real person, Vlad the Impaler, the question was posed, "Could Castle Dracula be a real place?" The search for Dracula's castle began and quickly emerged around two thrusts: the pursuit for the castle that was the home for Vlad the Impaler and the determination of the castle that Bram Stoker actually used as a model for the castle described in his novel.

As described in the novel, the castle was near Borgo Pass. It was reached from Pasul Ti-huts, a point near the summit of the crossing on a road leading south along a mountainous road into the high mountains, where the castle was reputedly located. Harker's journey from the pass to the castle was at night, and he reached it by horse-drawn coach with enough of the evening left to have dinner and his first visit with Dracula before dawn. Upon his arrival, he noticed a large courtyard. He was dropped in front of an old, large door, placed at an opening in a stone wall. Even in the dim light of the evening, the wall showed signs of age and weathering. In the light of day, he discovered that the castle sat on a great rock overlooking the surrounding forest, which was sliced by several river gorges.

The castle was built so as to be nearly impregnable to attack. The large windows were placed above the level where arrows and other projectiles (at least those of premodern warfare) could reach. To the west was a large valley and a mountain range.

Entering the castle, he saw a large, winding staircase and a long corridor. At the end of the corridor, he entered a room where supper awaited him. The rooms in which Harker was to spend most of his time joined an octagonal room that stood between the room in which he ate and his bedroom. His bedroom overlooked the court where he had originally stepped off the coach. The door to the room opposite his bedroom was locked, but another door opened to the library, which was full of materials from England.

He explored one forbidden wing of the castle in the southwest corner at a lower level. Here, he found comfortable furniture, but it lay covered in the dust of abandonment. The windows were filled with diamond-shaped panes of colored glass. Here, he would have his encounter with the three vampire brides who resided at the castle with Dracula.

Harker climbed out a window on the south wall to make his way to the window on the east side of the castle, below his bedroom, into which he had seen Dracula go. In the first room he entered, he found a pile of gold, also covered with dust. He followed a staircase downward to a tunnel and, meandering through the tunnel, he came upon the chapel that had been used as a burial place. Here, he discovered the boxes of native soil ready to be sent to England, in one of which Dracula lay in his sleeplike state. The three women slept in the chapel. One large tomb, not noticed by Harker but later sanitized by Abraham Van Helsing, was labeled with the single word DRACULA.

The Search for Castle Dracula: Beginning in the 1970s with the observation that

> Given the accuracy of Stoker's novel in describing many aspects of the Transylvanian landscape, the first place to look for a real Castle Dracula would seem to be near Borgo Pass.

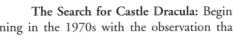

Now known as Tihuça Pass in northern Romania, the bucolic Borgo Pass is the region Dracula called home in the Stoker novel.

the title character in Stoker's novel was possibly based on a real person, Vlad the Impaler, a ruler in what today is Romania, people suspected that a real Castle Dracula possibly existed, too. Given the accuracy of Stoker's novel in describing many aspects of the Transylvanian landscape, the first place to look for a real Castle Dracula would seem to be near Borgo Pass. In fact, two different castles were found near both Bistritz (also spelled Bistrita) and the Borgo Pass road. The first was built in the thirteenth century some five kilometers north of the city at Dealu Cetatii. It fell into disuse and was in a dilapidated state by the early fifteenth century, at which time the townspeople took the stones and reused them in refortifying Bistritz proper.

Castle Bistrita was built in the 1440s by John Hunyadi (c. 1406–1456), a contemporary of Vlad the Impaler. Hunyadi was the "governor" of Hungary, whose territory covered much of Transylvania. The two, whose lands adjoined each other, were in frequent competition and, on occasion, were allied. Hunyadi died in the siege of Belgrade, though the Christian forces won the battle and turned back the Turkish attempt to take the city. While it may be that Vlad the Impaler resided at Castle Bistrita for a brief period during the last years of Hunyadi's life, it could in no sense be called Castle Dracula. Today, no remains of Castle Bistrita exist. It was destroyed at the end of the fifteenth century by the largely German population of the area in an act of defiance against their former Hungarian rulers.

Hunyadi had a second and more important castle, located at Hundoara, some 100 miles southwest of Borgo Pass. This impressive, thirteenth-century structure still exists and has been restored and opened to the public. Vlad Dracul was believed to have visited this castle on at least one occasion during his early years. In 1452, while loosely allied with Hunyadi, Dracula was greeted somewhat as a friend. A decade later, however, he returned as a prisoner of Hunyadi's son Matthias Corvinus and began 12 years of imprisonment at Pest and Visegrád. Despite Vlad's presence at the castle at Hundoara, it was not Castle Dracula.

Dracula was actually the prince (ruler) of Wallachia. His territory was south of Transylvania immediately on the other side of the Carpathian Mountains. In the mountains, overlooking the Dambovita River near the town of Campulung and protecting Bran Pass (the road through the Bucegi Mountains), is Castle Bran. It was originally built in the thirteenth century by the knights of the Teutonic Order. In the fourteenth century, the Teutonic Order having been expelled, the castle was taken over by the German merchants of Brasov, who used it as their defense post and customs station. Brasov was located in the Transalpine area, which included the Carpathian Mountains and the area immediately to the north and south of the mountains. Though the Transalpine area was officially part of Hungarian territory, the Prince of Wallachia served as military overseer of the area in return for certain Transylvania duchies. Most of the time, neither Hungary nor Wallachia actually controlled the castle, which was in the hands of the very independent German merchants.

Castle Bran has often been touted, especially by Romanian tourist authorities, as the real Castle Dracula. During its years under the control of the German leadership in Brasov, it is possible that Vlad Dracula visited it on occasion in the early 1450s. He was officially the voivode of the Transalpine area. Historians Radu Florescu and Raymond T. McNally noted that it possessed the atmosphere that Stoker was attempting to evoke in his descriptions of Castle Dracula. "The analogies between Stoker's mythical Castle Dracula and the real Castle Bran are simply too close to be coincidental." It had an inner courtyard and a secret, underground passageway. A steep, winding staircase could take a resident to a secret escape route deep inside the mountain. Though Florescu and McNally may have somewhat overstated their case, Dracula may have drawn, in part, from his knowledge of Castle Bran when he built his own mountain retreat.

The Real Castle Dracula: The only castle that might be considered the actual Castle Dracula (remembering that no castle other than the one in Stoker's imagination ever had that name) was the castle built and inhabited by Vlad the Impaler during his years as Prince of Wallachia. This castle overlooks the Arges River near the town of Poenari, in the foothills of the Transylvanian Alps. It is located approximately 20 miles north of Curtea de Arges, the original capital of Wallachia, and was for many years the center of the Romanian Orthodox Church. When Vlad assumed the throne in 1456, two fortresses existed, located about a mile from each other on opposite sides of the river. Castle Poenari, the castle on the left side of the river, seems to have been built on the site of an even older fortress on the Arges River when this land was the center of the country called Dacia. Abandoned, it was rebuilt in the thirteenth century by Romanians attempting to block the incursions by Hungarian and/or Teutonic soldiers from the north. In 1455, it was in disrepair from recent battles with various invading armies, but it was still habitable.

On the right side of the river was the Castle of the Arges. It was built a century before Vlad's time, although some historians have argued that even earlier, it was a Teutonic outpost tied to the castle at Fagaras, just across the mountains to the north. McNally and Florescu argued that it was not Teutonic but built by the early Wallachian rulers and modeled on Byzantine patterns.

At the end of the fourteenth century, Tartars invaded the area. The remnant of the Wallachian forces (and many of the country's

Poenari Castle in Romania was once the home of Vlad the Impaler.

elite) eventually took refuge in the Castle of the Arges. The Tartars lay seize to the castle and, finding almost no opposition, soon captured it. However, its inhabitants escaped through the secret passageway under the castle. As a consolation prize, the Tartars largely destroyed the castle.

Of the two castles that Dracula/Vlad found, the Castle of the Arges was in the more strategic position, possibly the major reason for his choice to rebuild it instead of settling at Poenari. It was located on a precipice overlooking the Arges River at the point where the valley of the Arges narrows and the foothills of the Carpathians turn into mountains.

The rebuilding process has become one of the more famous stories of Vlad and one of the earlier incidents confirming his nickname, "the impaler." He had discovered that the boyars, the elite families of Wallachia, had been responsible for the death of his father and the torture and murder of his older brother. He decided to gain his revenge and get his castle built at the same time. During the Easter celebration following his taking up residence in the capital at Tirgoviste, he arrested all of the boyars (men, women, and children). Still dressed in their finest Easter clothes, they were forced to march to Poenari and rebuild the castle. The material from Poenari was carried across the river to construct the new residence overlooking the Arges. The boyars were

Though often identified in tourist literature as Castle Dracula, the castle at Bran was never visited by Vlad the Impaler nor known to Bram Stoker's character, Count Dracula.

forced to work until the clothes fell off their backs … and then had to continue naked.

Vlad's castle was quite small when compared to either Castle Bran or Hundoara. It was only some 100 by 120 feet in size. It rested on a precipice that looked out over the Arges River. To the north were the mountains dividing Transylvania and Wallachia, and to the south was a commanding view of the countryside. It had three towers and walls thick enough to resist Turkish cannon fire. It seems to have been made to house about 200 people. According to legend, a secret staircase led into the mountain to a tunnel that, in turn, led to a grotto that opened on the bank of the river below the castle, though no evidence of a secret passage has yet been uncovered.

The Turks attacked and captured the castle in 1462. Vlad escaped north through the mountains, but his castle was severely damaged by the invaders. It was used by some of his successors as a mountain retreat. However, it was gradually abandoned and left to the ravages of time and weather. Built originally as a defensive post, in later centuries, it was too far outside the main commercial routes that dominated the life of the region.

As late as 1912, the towers of the castle still stood. However, on January 13, 1913, an earthquake hit the area. It toppled the main tower into the river. A second earthquake in 1940 further damaged the castle. Then, in the 1970s, the Romanian government, responding to increased tourist interest in locations associated with Dracula, carried out a partial reconstruction and built a walkway up the mountainside to the castle's entrance. Today, the mountain upon which Castle Dracula rests can be reached by car, about an hour's drive north of the city of Pitesti. The walk up the mountain to the entrance takes approximately 45 minutes.

The Problem of Castle Dracula: The search for Castle Dracula highlighted the problem of reconciling Stoker's fictional *Dracula* with historical reality, a problem created by readers' excursions into Stoker's fictional world and made possible by Stoker's attempts to create as realistic a setting as possible. His book was set in Transylvania. Vlad the Impaler was a prince of Wallachia. While born in Transylvania, he resided all of his adult life in Wallachia except for a period of imprisonment in Hungary. The geography of the novel and of Vlad's life are impossible to reconcile, a fact clearly demonstrated in Francis Ford Coppola's movie *Bram Stoker's Dracula* and its almost comical attempts to place Dracula at the Castle of the Arges and near Borgo Pass at the same time.

No actual structure was ever called Castle Dracula, only a small castle built by Vlad the Impaler. Though Vlad the Impaler's small castle had its place of importance in Romanian history, it was not known by Stoker and did not serve as a model for his Castle Dracula. It is probable that no castle in Eastern Europe served as the model for Castle Dracula, and the search must be directed closer to home. Thus, some suggested that a castle at Cruden Bay, Scotland, where Stoker stayed while writing *Dracula*, was the model. However, from Stoker's manuscripts, it is now known that the section of the novel in which the castle was introduced and described was written before he traveled to Cruden Bay. Also, that opening section of the book remained essentially unchanged through the time Stoker finished his novel for publication. It would appear that Stoker's castle was a matter of pure imagination, a castle constructed from images of the romantic castles of European fairy tales and folklore.

> No actual structure was ever called Castle Dracula, only a small castle built by Vlad the Impaler.

London, Dracula's Nineteenth-Century

London, the capital of what is today known as the United Kingdom (England, Scotland, Wales, and Northern Ireland), was one of three major sites of action in Bram Stoker's *Dracula* (1897). Some of the sites mentioned by Stoker were entirely fictitious locations, but many were quite real, although a few have disappeared or changed names since the novel appeared in 1897, and some were slightly disguised by Stoker.

The action in the novel began with Jonathan Harker traveling to Transylvania to make arrangements for Dracula's move to England. The focus of their negotiations was an estate in a town outside of London called Purfleet. Purfleet is a real place located on the north bank of the Thames River, downstream from London. Semi-industrialized and almost a suburb today, in the 1890s, it was a quiet, rural Essex village some 10 miles beyond the fringe of London's East End. Carfax, the estate in Purfleet, had about 20 acres and was surrounded by a stone wall. On the land was an old house, dating to medieval times, and a nearby chapel. Stoker, through his character Harker, suggested that the name Carfax was a derivative of *quartre face*, referring to its four walls being aligned with the cardinal points of the compass. From his reading of *The Oxford Dictionary of Etymology*, Leonard Wolf has suggested that the name derived from the Anglo-Norman term *carfuks*, the significance being that it was a place where four roads met. Wolf further noted, quite correctly, that suicides were buried at crossroads and that people who committed suicide were often thought to return as vampires.

Dracula traveled to England by ship along with the native soil so necessary for his survival. He landed at Whitby, in the far north, and from there, he had the dirt shipped to his estate. It

While there have been many updates inside, the exterior of King's Cross Station looks much like it did in the nineteenth century setting of Stoker's Dracula.

arrived from Whitby via rail into King's Cross Station, a very real location, the southern terminus of the Great Northern Railway (which connected London with points north, including Whitby). From there, they were then taken to Carfax by Messrs. Carter, Paterson & Co., a real cartage firm that was founded in 1860 and continued to operate in London during Stoker's time. It was a prosperous firm, with its headquarters on Gorwell Road in London. In Stoker's day, Purfleet was connected to central London by the London, Tilbury, and Southend Railway, which had its terminus at Fenchurch Street. The characters in *Dracula* could thus travel from Purfleet to central London in about 30 minutes.

Once in England, Dracula began an attack upon Lucy Westenra, his first victim, while she was still in Whitby, the town where Dracula

initially arrived. However, the action soon moved to London. The Westenra fictional home, Hillingham, was a large mansion, reflecting a relatively wealthy family. The kitchen was in back, several bedrooms were on the second floor, and maids' rooms presumably occupied the third floor. It was probably located in the Haverstock Hills neighborhood on the slopes leading to Hampstead, not too far from the Zoological Gardens. When Dr. Abraham Van Helsing arrived on the scene, he stayed at several of the city's finer hotels, including the Great Eastern Hotel on Liverpool Street and the Berkeley at Berkeley Street and Piccadilly.

In one of Dracula's earliest actions, he helped the wolf Berserker escape from the Zoological Gardens. The Zoological Gardens were located in the northeast corner of Regent's Park,

one of London's largest parks. The wolves' cage was on the edge of the zoo near the lions' house. Berserker had only a short distance to travel to reach the Westenra home. The Harker residence was located outside of London, in Exeter. His law office was in Devonshire. At one point, they came into London to attend the funeral of Harker's former employee, Mr. Hawkins. Before returning to their home, they strolled from Hyde Park to Piccadilly, where the novel's action periodically returned, and stopped in front of Guillano's, one of the most fashionable court jewelers in London. (Later, its premises were replaced by one of the shops given extended frontage of the Park Lane Hotel.) Here, they saw Dracula, appearing much younger than when Harker last saw him in the castle in Transylvania.

In the meantime, Lucy had died and was buried at what Stoker described as "a lordly death-house in a lonely churchyard away from teeming London; where the air is fresh and the sun rises over Hampstead Hill." He spoke of the churchyard (or cemetery) at Kingstead. No Hampstead Hill or Kingstead existed in real life, and it was not clear which site Stoker had in mind as Lucy's resting place. Raymond T. McNally and Radu Florescu have suggested that he, in fact, was referring to Highgate Hill and the relatively well-known Highgate Cemetery, which fits the basic description of Lucy's resting place (one with impressive burial mausoleums and away from London). The cemetery was the only such structure near Jack Straw's Castle, a still-existing inn located on Hampstead Heath, where Dr. Van Helsing and the other men dined before going to Lucy's grave to put the stake in her heart. Once inside the cemetery, they found their way to Lucy's resting place. Evidence suggested that it was actually in the Old Ground or Western Cemetery, probably in a somewhat secluded location near the middle of the cemetery. Afterward, they found their way to a still-

> The cemetery was the only such structure near Jack Straw's Castle, a still-existing inn located on Hampstead Heath....

existing pub, the Spaniards Inn, and there, they caught a cab back into London.

Following the settling of Lucy's situation and the organization of Mina and the men into a covenanted group to destroy Dracula, Dr. John Seward's house near Purfleet increasingly became the center of the group's campaign to defeat Dracula. Seward lived at his private asylum, which was actually located next door to Carfax. Their efforts would take them back to London, as Dracula had distributed his boxes of dirt around the city. Of the original 50 boxes, six were carried to the East End, to 197 Chicksand Street, Mile End New Town. This detached portion of Mile End was entirely surrounded by Spitalfields, just off Brick Lane in the heart of Jack the Ripper territory. Three of Ripper's murders were committed just a few blocks away. (Stoker began writing *Dracula* just a year or so after the panic over the Ripper murders, and in the preface he wrote for the 1898 Icelandic edition of *Dracula*, he made reference to them.) Part of Chicksand Street still exists today.

Another six of the boxes were dropped south of the Thames on Jamaica Lane, a fictitious location. While no Jamaica Lane exists, a Jamaica Road, the main artery in Bermondsey, a warehouse district of London just east of Walworth, exists on the south side of the river. Nine boxes were delivered to a house in London's fashionable West End on a street called Piccadilly, a residence located near the end of the street farthest away from Piccadilly Circus, the popular shopping area where a number of streets converge and which today is a theater/nightclub spot. As early as 1973, the building at 138–139 Piccadilly was suggested as the location of Dracula's residence in an article by Art Ronnie in the *Los Angeles Herald Examiner*. Interestingly, this building has been the London headquarters of Universal Pictures. In the 1890s, the building existed as two separate houses. Bernard Davies,

Situated at the terminus of the River Esk as it empties into the sea in northern Yorkshire, the town of Whitby was familiar to Stoker, explaining why he set much of his novel's action there.

cofounder and chairman of the Dracula Society, has suggested that 138 Piccadilly possessed the correct architectural and stylistic details as described in the novel, including a bow window, an iron-railed balcony, and a backyard. Dracula finally left London and England from the docks along the Thames aboard the *Czarina Catherine*, a fictitious ship.

Whitby

Whitby, a small town in northern England, was the setting for a major segment of Bram Stoker's novel *Dracula*. Whitby is located in Yorkshire at the mouth of the River Esk, where it empties into the North Sea. Stoker provided a fairly accurate description of the town as background to the story. Dominating the town on the east side of the river was St. Mary's (Anglican) Church and the ruins of Whitby Abbey. The abbey dates to the seventh century. It was destroyed in the ninth century, rebuilt, and later abandoned.

As chapter 5 began, Lucy Westenra met her friend Mina Murray at the train station, and together, they went to what has been identified as Number Four Crescent Terrace, where Mina joined the Westenra family in the rooms they had taken for a summer vacation. Stoker selected Whitby as a site for the events in his novel because he knew the town from his own visits in the years from 1885 to 1890. During their first days in town, Lucy and Mina visited the local tourist spots: Mulgrave Woods, Robin Hood's Bay, Rig Mill, Runswick, and Staithes.

Meanwhile, Dracula was aboard the *Demeter*, which was speeding north from Gibraltar toward the British coast. Two weeks later, the *Demeter* was spotted off Whitby shortly before a storm hit. The ship was beached on the sand near Tate Hill Pier, one of two piers at Whitby, and Dracula (in the form of a dog) was seen leaving the ship. Onboard the wreck, the boxes of earth that Dracula traveled with were discovered. Dracula stayed in Whitby for a week and a half and attacked Lucy twice.

The first attack came several days after the wreck. Mina discovered that Lucy (who had a record of sleepwalking) had disappeared. Standing on the West Cliff, Mina looked across the river to where she could see St. Mary's Church and the ruins of Whitby Abbey. She saw a figure in white (Lucy) seated at what was called the "suicide's seat," under which was a stone noting the death of George Canon, who had committed suicide on that spot. Mina then ran to the bridge that connected the two parts of town on either side of the river.

From where Mina stood to the spot Lucy was located is almost a mile and required her to walk down the cliff face on one side of the river and walk up the cliff face on the other side. As she reached the top of the steps near Whitby Abbey, she saw someone with Lucy, but he disappeared in a moment of darkness as a cloud briefly blocked the moonlight.

Several days later, Mina saw Lucy lean out of the window of her room. Beside her on the windowsill was "something that looked like a good-sized bird," which turned out to be Dracula in the form of a bat. By the time Mina reached Lucy's room, Dracula had completed drinking Lucy's blood, and Mina helped her to bed. Shortly after this second attack, Dracula, his boxes of earth, and the action of the novel moved to London.

Today, modern tourists can visit all of the sights mentioned by Stoker in the novel, including the apartment on the Crescent where Lucy and Mina were supposed to have stayed. The late Bernard Davies (1924–2010), cofounder of the Dracula Society, prepared a walking-tour guidebook, while local vampire enthusiasts organized to meet the needs of Dracula-oriented visitors. In the 1990s, the main event has been the Whitby Goth Weekend, a biannual gathering for goths, first held in 1994, continued until 1997, and has been a biannual event since. The Whitby Goth Weekend (http://www.whitby gothweekend.co.uk) occurs in April and at the end of October over Halloween weekend.

THE VAMPIRE ONSTAGE

Introducing the Dramatic Vampire

Internationally, interest in the vampire began with a piece of short fiction, "The Vampyre" by a still-largely unknown writer, John William Polidori. In fact, Polidori was such a nonentity in the literary world of the early nineteenth century that when his story was originally published (in 1819) in the *New Monthly Magazine*, it was presented as by Lord Byron, one of the generation's superstars. Another literary star of the day, Goethe, pronounced it Byron's masterpiece. Then, when Polidori's novella was published as a monograph, it was initially issued as a story "related by Lord Byron to Dr. Polidori." Only after the story was passed off as the product of Byron, thus gaining a wide readership, did an issue of his work finally appear under its true author's name.

"The Vampyre" would begin the process of the vampire's permeation of popular culture with its presence on the stage. French playwright Charles Nodier would rush a dramatic adaptation of Polidori's work to his Parisian theater,

and several other dramatic presentations (including some comedies) would quickly follow. An English version would follow as the vampire made its way to London. Through the nineteenth century, vampires would become a "go-to" character for playwrights when short of an idea or short of cash.

Prior to the emergence of the cinema early in the twentieth century, the stage would become second only to literature as a means of satiating a growing public thirst for their favorite bloodsucker. It would be the stage plays of *Dracula* that would call the attention of moviemakers to the potential of Stoker's character for the silver screen, and while the live stage has become a second to the cinema through the twentieth century, Dracula and his vampire cousins have continually been called upon to entertain audiences from Broadway to local high schools.

Soon after the 1819 publication of John Polidori's *The Vampyre*, the vampire was brought to the stage in France. There, Polidori's dark tale caught the interest of a group of French Romantics who were attracted to the story because they thought it had been written by Lord Byron. Before the year was out, it had been translated and published in Paris as *Le Vampire, nouvelle traduite de l'anglais de Lord Byron.* However, for many of these early explorers of the subconscious, the vampire became a fitting symbol of the darker, nightmarish side of the inner reality they were discovering. An expanded sequel to the story appeared early in 1820 as *Lord Ruthwen ou les vampires,* authored by Cyprien Bérard. Bérard's colleague Charles Nodier was the first to adapt "The Vampyre" for the stage. He merely had to alter the ending of Polidori's story to assure his audience that the forces of good were still in control. In the end, these forces triumphed over the lead antihero, Lord Ruthven, who in Nodier's version was killed.

Nodier's three-act play, *Le Vampire, mélodrame en trois actes,* opened on June 13, 1820, at the Théâtre de la Porte Saint-Martin in Paris. It was an immediate and somewhat unexpected success and inspired several imitations. It was translated into English by J. R. Planché and opened in London as *The Vampire; or, The Bride of the Isles.* Later in the decade, it would inspire a vampire opera, *Der Vampyr* by German musician Heinrich August Marschner. Two days after Nodier's play premiered, a second vampire play, a farce also called *Le Vampire,* opened at the Vaudeville in Paris. This comedic version of Polidori's tale was set in Hungary and featured a young suitor mistakenly believed to be a vampire. A short time later, a second comedy, *Les trois Vampires, ou le chair de la lune,* opened at the Varieties. It centered on a young man who imagined that vampires were after him as a result of his reading vampire and ghost stories. In 1820, no fewer than four vampire plays, all comedies, opened in Paris under the titles *En-*

core un Vampire; Les Etrennes d'un Vampire; Cadet Buteux, vampire; and *Le Vampire, mélodrame en trois actes.*

The vampire seemed to have run its course with Parisian audiences after a year or two, but in 1822, a new play, *Polichinel Vampire,* premiered at the Circus Maurice. The following year, a revival of Nodier's play again attracted a crowd at the Porte Saint-Martin. Among those who attended was the young Alexandre Dumas, who was just beginning his literary career. He later would recall his traumatic evening at Nodier's play, where he was seated next to the author, by composing his own stage version of *Le Vampire.* The 1851 production of that play closed out the Parisian phase of Dumas's life.

> Nodier's three-act play, *Le Vampire, mélodrame en trois actes* … was an immediate and somewhat unexpected success and inspired several imitations.

Over the next few years, writers periodically would fall back on the vampire theme, which always attracted an audience hungry for the supernatural. In England, for example, records have survived of St. John Dorset's *The Vampire: A Tragedy in Three Acts* (1831); Dion Boucicault's *The Vampire* (1852, generally revived under the title *The Phantom*); George Blink's *The Vampire Bride* (1834); and Robert Reece's *The Vampire* (1872).

Théâtre du Grand Guignol: At the end of the nineteenth century, a theatrical innovation in Paris had an immense effect upon the image of the vampire. Max Maurey opened the Théâtre du Grand Guignol in 1899. The drama offered at the theater followed the old themes of dark Romanticism but treated them in a fresh manner. It attracted numerous working-class people, who seemed fascinated with the presentation of gruesome situations and ultrarealistic stage effects, however horrific. The theater developed its own vampire drama called, fittingly, *Le Vampire.* Grand Guignol, slightly tempered by stricter censorship laws, opened in London in 1908. The English version emphasized the gothic element in its stage productions. Most importantly, Grand Guignol flourished in both England and France, producing original drama as well as utilizing established horror stories such as *Dracula* and Edgar Allan Poe's tales.

Through the first half of the twentieth century, the theater influenced individual motion pictures, but after World War II, it became important in the creation of the Hammer Films horror classics, beginning with *The Curse of Frankenstein* (1957) and *Horror of Dracula* (1958).

Dracula **Dramatized:** The entire thrust of vampire drama would change following the publication of *Dracula* by Bram Stoker in 1897. In the twentieth century, the overwhelming majority of new vampire plays and dramatic productions would be based on *Dracula*, and the character of Lord Ruthven, who dominated the stage in the nineteenth century, would all but disappear. The dramatizing of *Dracula* was initiated immediately after the publication of the book, Stoker himself taking the lead with the intention of protecting the rights to his literary property. Using the cast of the Lyceum Theatre, where he worked, he presented *Dracula; or, The Un-Dead* as a five-act, 47-scene play. Ellen Terry (1847–1928), the cast's star, portrayed Mina Murray. Even Stoker described the hastily prepared production "Dreadful!" Its opening night was also its last performance. The intricacies of the plot served as an obstacle to playwrights who might have wanted to bring the story to the stage. However, in the years after World War I, an old friend of the Stoker family, Hamilton Deane, then the head of his own dramatic company, began to think seriously about a *Dracula* play. He asked a number of acquaintances to give it a try but was always turned down. Finally, in 1923 during a period of illness, he accepted the challenge himself. Four weeks later, he had a finished script. He overcame the book's problem by deleting the opening and closing chapters in Transylvania and Whitby, setting all the action in three scenes in London and bringing Dracula onstage in London to interact with his archenemy Abraham Van Helsing. Deane, not at ease in London and fearing the ridicule of the London critics, opened the play in rural Derby, England, in June 1924. It was a success, and the public's demands soon made it the company's most frequently performed play. Finally, on February 14, 1927, Deane opened his play in London. The public loved his work, and while most critics panned it, others gave it very high marks. It played at the Little Theatre on the West End and, after several months, moved to large facilities at the Duke of York's Theatre. It ran for 391 performances. Deane then took it back to the countryside, where it ran successfully through the 1930s. At one point, he had three companies touring with the play.

> In the twentieth century, the ... character of Lord Ruthven, who dominated the stage in the nineteenth century, would all but disappear.

Soon after *Dracula* opened in London, Horace Liveright purchased the American rights for the play from Florence Stoker, Bram Stoker's widow. To assist with the delicate negotiations, Liveright had engaged the services of John L. Balderston, an American playwright and journalist then living in London. Balderston continued in Liveright's employ to do extensive rewriting of Deane's play for the American audience. Balderston also streamlined the plot, eliminating several characters and significantly changing the ones who remained. Dr. John Seward, the youthful suitor of Lucy Westenra in the original story, became the central character in the revised plot as Lucy's father. Mina Murray, the leading woman in the novel, was eliminated and her role collapsed into that of Lucy, who also became the love object of Jona-

The first Broadway production of Dracula *premiered at the Fulton Theater in Manhattan, New York, in 1927.*

than Harker. The Balderston version of *Dracula* opened on Broadway on October 5, 1927, following a brief tryout at the Shubert Theater in New Haven, Connecticut. Bela Lugosi assumed the title role.

The play was an immediate success and played for 33 weeks and 241 performances. Liveright had hesitated in developing a touring company to take it around the country, but Deane (who retained a small financial stake in the American enterprise) threatened to write a play based on a vampire other than Dracula and bring it to the United States. Balderston convinced Liveright of the need to send a company on the road. Lugosi

joined the West Coast cast that played Los Angeles and San Francisco. The success on the West Coast convinced Liveright to create a second company to tour the East Coast and the Midwest.

The original Deane version of the play significantly affected the image of Dracula and the appearance of the vampire in general. Deane domesticated Stoker's *Dracula* by dressing him in formal evening wear and ridding him of his extreme halitosis. The formal opera cloak, the cape with the high collar, would be clearly identified with the vampire character. Balderston's rewrite of Deane's play, however, was the more influential dramatic version of the novel. It introduced Bela Lugosi, later typecast as Dracula, to the part.

Balderston's version served as the basis of the 1931 Universal Pictures *Dracula* movie and the 1979 remake with Frank Langella. Published by Samuel French, the Balderston play became the version to which producers turned when they decided to revive *Dracula* on the stage.

> Deane domesticated Stoker's Dracula by dressing him in formal evening wear and ridding him of his extreme halitosis.

The most notable revival, of course, was the 1977 stage version starring Langella, which inspired Universal Pictures's remake.

***Dracula* Clones, Variations, and Parodies:** For a generation after the success of the Balderston play, dramatists did little with the vampire theme, although in England, a satire of Deane's play appeared briefly in the 1930s and a musical version surfaced in the 1950s. While a few variations on the *Dracula* theme were written in the 1960s, generally, whenever a vampire play was sought, the Balderston play was revived yet again. The situation did not change until 1970, when suddenly, four new vampire plays were published: Bruce Ronald's *Dracula, Baby;* Leon Katz's *Dracula: Sabbat;* Sheldon Allman's *I'm Sorry the Bridge Is Out, You'll Have to Spend the Night;* and a more obscure *Johnny Appleseed and Dracula.* Since that time, almost 50 vampire plays have been published. They vary from one-act plays for high school productions to more serious dramas designed for the Broadway stage. Only a few, such as *The Passion of Dracula* (1977), *Dracula Tyrannus* (1982), and *Vampire Lesbians of Sodom* (1984), have risen above the crowd to receive some national attention. *The Passion of Dracula* opened for a successful run at the Cherry Lane Theatre in New York City on September 30, 1977, just three weeks before the award-winning revival of the Balderston play with Frank Langella opened at the Martin Beck Theatre on October 20. It was a variant of the *Dracula* story, with Christopher Bernau as Count Drac-

ula and Michael Burg as his archenemy, Abraham Van Helsing. On August 23, 1978, it began a successful run in London.

Ron Magid's *Dracula Tyrannus: The Tragical History of Vlad the Impaler* was the first play to use all of the newly available material on the historical Dracula, Vlad the Impaler, the fifteenth-century Romanian ruler. It built on the ruler's rivalry for the throne with his cousin, Dan. *Vampire Lesbians of Sodom,* whose three acts take the audience on a romp through history from ancient Sodom to Hollywood in the 1920s and modern Las Vegas, is based more upon the vamp, the female seductress, than the classical vampire.

Among the lesser-known plays, made available in large part for amateur productions, were several written by Stephen Hotchner and Tim Kelly. In 1975, Hotchner wrote three one-act *Dracula* plays: *Death at the Crossroads, Escape for Dracula's Castle,* and *The Possession of Lucy Wenstrom.* These were adapted for use at high schools, colleges, and community festivals from a full-length *Dracula* play Hotchner published in 1978 that combined the three one-act plays. In the 1970s, Kelly also produced a number of Dracula-based plays, including musical variations such as *Seven Wives for Dracula* (1973) and *Young Dracula; or, The Singing Bat* (1975). Hotchner and Kelly's primary publisher, Pioneer Drama Service, based in Denver, Colorado, specialized in plays for amateur productions. The Dramatic Publishing company of Chicago also published a number of Dracula-based dramas, including the first one, *I Was a Teen-Age Dracula* by Gene Donovan (1958). These productions characteristically used a lighter treatment of the vampire/Dracula theme and were targeted to younger audiences or people attending less serious entertainment events.

Of the vampire plays written since 1965, the overwhelming majority have been variations on the *Dracula* story or, at the very least, have used the word "Dracula" in the title. "Carmilla" comes in a distant second, with three plays based on Sheridan Le Fanu's story. During this period, the number of vampire plays has steadily increased and, given the heightened interest in vampires at the beginning of the 1990s, it is likely that new plays will continue to be written.

Vampire Theater: The gothic movement that developed in the United States in the late 1970s has had a noticeable influence upon vampire drama. The movement itself was very dramatic, built as it was around bands who used theatrical effects as an integral part of their performances. Possibly the principal examples were those choreographed by Vlad, the Chicago rock musician who headed the band Dark Theater.

In 1992, Tony Sokol created La Commedia del Sangria as a dramatic company that performs "vampire theater," which included a strong element of audience interaction. The company's very metaphysical production examines questions of the vampiric condition (limited immortality) and the existence of God. Some of the actors begin the performance portraying audience members and then enter the stage as an apparent interruption. The production received a warm response from people in the vampire subculture, who attended to cheer on the vampires each time they bit someone.

Balderston, John Lloyd *(1889–1954)*

John L. Balderston was the playwright of the American version of *Dracula: The Vampire Play in Three Acts*. He was born on October 22, 1889, in Philadelphia, the son of Mary Alsop and Lloyd Balderston. He attended Columbia University and began a career in journalism in 1911 as the New York correspondent of the *Philadelphia Record*. In 1915, he moved to England and worked as editor for *The Outlook*; from 1923 to 1931, he was the chief London correspondent of the *New York World*.

Balderston authored his first play, *The Genius of the Marne*, in 1919. He followed it with *Morality Play for the Leisured Class* (1920), *Tongo* (1924), and *Berkeley Square* (1926). Balderston was still in England in 1927 when producer Horace Liveright attempted to purchase the American dramatic rights to *Dracula* from Bram Stoker's widow. Florence Stoker did not like Liveright, who turned to Balderston to assist him in the negotiations. Balderston had be-

come known to Liveright after his play *Berkeley Square*, a ghost story, became a hit both in London and New York. Balderston secured the rights from Mrs. Stoker, and Liveright then hired him to modernize the stage version of *Dracula* by Hamilton Deane that had been playing in England.

Balderston's version of the play was very different from earlier ones. His major changes included combining the characters of Lucy Westenra and Mina Murray into a single character, Lucy Seward, who became the daughter of the now mature John Seward. Originally, Seward had been Lucy's young suitor. Lucy's other suitors, Quincey P. Morris and Arthur Holmwood, completely disappeared from the play.

Published by Samuel French, Balderston's version has become the most influential of the several dramatic versions of the novel. It opened on Broadway on October 5, 1927, and, after 241 performances, went on the road to Los

A 1938 poster of the Hamiton Deane/John Balderston stage adaptation of Dracula, *originally written in 1927.*

Angeles and San Francisco. It spawned both a Midwestern and East Coast touring company. It has subsequently been the version most frequently used when the play has been revived through the years. Its most important revival began in 1977, when it opened for a new run on Broadway. Balderston's version also became the basis of two film versions of *Dracula*: the 1931 version with Bela Lugosi and the 1979 version with Frank Langella. Langella, it should be noted, also starred in the 1977 stage revival.

Balderston went on to work on two more plays: *Red Planet* (1932, with J. E. Hoare) and *Frankenstein* (1932, with Peggy Webling). He also translated the Hungarian play *Farewell Performance* (1935) into English. He retired to Beverly Hills, California, where he died on March 8, 1954.

Balderston's papers are on deposit at the Billy Rose Theatre Division of the New York Public Library for the Performing Arts.

🦇 *Deane, Hamilton (1880–1958)* 🦇

Hamilton Deane, the playwright and director who initially brought *Dracula* to the stage, was born near Dublin. His family owned an estate adjacent to that of Bram Stoker's father, and his mother had been acquainted with Bram Stoker in her youth. Deane entered the theater as a young man, first appearing in 1899 with the Henry Irving Vacation Company (Stoker worked for Henry Irving in London

for many years). Even before he formed his own troupe in the early 1920s, Deane had been thinking about bringing *Dracula* to the stage. Unable to find a scriptwriter to take on the project, he wrote it himself in a four-week period of inactivity while he was suffering from a severe cold. He also contacted Florence Stoker, Bram's widow, and negotiated a deal for the dramatic rights.

In order to more easily stage the detailed story, he dropped the book's beginning and ending sections that occurred in Transylvania. He transformed Quincey P. Morris into a female to accommodate the gender makeup of his company at the time. He also recast the more sinister Dracula of the novel into a representative of cultured continental royalty capable of fitting into British society. Deane was the first to dress Dracula in evening clothes and a cape (an opera cloak).

> People were known to memorize entire scenes and to become so involved in the play that they shouted out lines before the actors could deliver them.

Deane submitted his play for government approval in 1924. The license was issued on August 5, but censors insisted that one scene be altered. The death of Dracula at the hands of the men had to be changed so that the hammering of the stake was not actually shown. Instead, the men were to gather around the coffin in such a manner as to block the action from the audience.

When the play opened in Derby, England, Deane assumed the role of Abraham Van Helsing, Dracula's archenemy. Fearing that London critics would pan his play, Deane stayed away for three years, but he finally risked an opening there on February 14, 1927, at the Little Theatre. Though the reviews were largely unfavorable, the audiences filled the house each night. By the end of the summer, he had moved the production to the larger Duke of York's Theatre. Following up on a casual remark by a reporter, Deane pulled off an almost legendary publicity stunt. He hired a nurse to be present at each performance to assist any viewers who reacted badly to the play by fainting or taking ill.

Deane's desire to return to the countryside led to a brief break between himself, Florence Stoker, and one of his backers, Harry War-

burton. The split led to Warburton's commissioning, with Stoker's approval, a second version of the play (which opened in September 1927), but it proved unsuccessful and soon closed. Deane kept the London company running, but at one point, he had three different groups performing the play at various locations in the countryside.

People were known to memorize entire scenes and to become so involved in the play that they shouted out lines before the actors could deliver them. In 1927, Horace Liveright bought the American dramatic rights from Florence Stoker and hired newspaperman John L. Balderston to edit it for the New York stage. Balderston's editing constituted a full rewriting, though Deane's name has been retained on the publication and on the various revisions of the Balderston version. The Universal Pictures movie with Bela Lugosi merely increased the demand in England for Deane to keep his production of the play alive.

In 1939, Deane played the role of Dracula for the first time. Later that year, he brought his troupe to the Lyceum Theatre, where Stoker had worked when he wrote the play and where he had staged a one-time-only reading of his work in order to establish his dramatic rights. After a brief run of *Dracula* and then of *Hamlet*, the Lyceum closed its doors permanently. During one performance at the Lyceum, Lugosi, who was in the audience, rushed onstage at the close of the play to embrace Deane.

Deane's last performance as Dracula was in 1941 at St. Helen's, Lancastershire. After his death late in 1958, his version of the play largely fell into disuse, with most revivalists preferring the Balderston rewrite.

🦇 *Dracula; or, The Un-Dead:* 🦇 *A Play in Prologue and Five Acts (1897)*

The initial dramatic presentation of *Dracula* occurred on May 18, 1897, at 10:15 A.M. at the Lyceum Theatre in London. This singular performance was staged by author Bram Stoker to secure himself the performance copyright from the many writers who were constantly searching for inspirations for new dramatic works for the London stage. Since the Lyceum was fully booked for its regular season's performances, a weekday morning was virtually all the space available. In fact, the performance was not intended as a profit-making performance attracting a large audience but merely the

Dame Alice Ellen Terry (known as Ellen Terry) was a renowned actress from the mid-1800s through the 1920s. She played the role of Mina in the stage adaptation of Dracula.

minimal fulfillment of a legal regulation. It is assumed that the audience was composed of a few of the theater staff and some invited friends.

The text for what amounted to a dramatic reading was hastily prepared by Stoker using proof copies of the novel's text. He adapted the text for the stage and made changes he knew would be demanded by Lord Chamberlain, who was charged with the power of censorship over such public performances. It is likely that his final text was treated liberally, as he made it known that no real public performances were to be staged. Only a single copy of the manuscript, now located in the British Museum, survived.

While Stoker's mentor, Henry Irving, and his star actress, Ellen Terry, declined to participate in the dramatic reading, Terry's daughter, Edith Cragg, assumed the role of Mina Murray. The program lists a Mr. Jones, probably T. Arthur Jones, as portraying Dracula. Other leading parts were taken by Herbert Passmore (Jonathan Harker), Ken Rivington (Dr. John Seward), and Tom Reynolds (Abraham Van Helsing). Some disagree as to whether Kate Gurney or Ida Yeolande played Lucy Westenra, as two variations of the playbill exist. The performance lasted for more than four hours.

For those who have tried to comment on the evolving perception of its title character, the manuscript of *Dracula; or, The Un-Dead* has been one of the most obscure texts of *Dracula*. However, in the mid-1990s, Sylvia Starshine copied the manuscript located in the British Museum and reproduced an edited and annotated edition (1997). On the 100th anniversary of the initial performance, a second reading was performed at the Spaniards Inn, one of the locations in the novel that is an actual site in London. The cast included Mitch Davies, Maureen Evans, Suzanne Barbieri, Jo Fletcher, Caroline Jones, Eric Arthur, Gerald Hill, Jason Brooks, and Sylvia Starshine.

🦇 *Dracula: The Vampire Play* 🦇 *in Three Acts (1924)*

The first vampire story by John Polidori, published in 1819, immediately inspired a number of stage adaptations in Paris and London. No such wave of enthusiasm followed *Dracula*'s publication in 1897. However, shortly after his novel was published, author Bram Stoker did assemble the members of the Lyceum Theatre company and worked with them for a dramatic presentation of the book. That one-time event was held merely to establish Stoker's ownership of the book's plot and dialogue.

The story of *Dracula*'s initial appearance onstage began two years later when Hamilton Deane, having quit his job as a London bank clerk, made his stage debut with the Henry Irving Vacation Company. There, he met Bram Stoker and initially read *Dracula*. He saw its dramatic potential at once and concluded that someone should write a stage play based upon it. However, Deane had a career to concentrate on, and over the following years, he spent his time becoming first a well-known actor and then the head of his own theater company. In 1918, Deane ended a lengthy stay on the New York stage and returned to England; in his suitcase was a copy of *Dracula*. As he moved through the British theatrical world, he approached numerous authors to write the *Dracula* play. He even went so far as to outline the acts and scenes. Most writers gave up in the face of the numerous characters and complicated subplots. Finally, during a period of sickness in 1923, Deane took the suggestion of one of his actresses and started to write the play himself. He became immersed in the new drama and finished it in four weeks. He ob-

tained permission from Stoker's widow to use the material. The play debuted in Derby in June 1924.

This production became immensely important in the development of the modern image of the vampire. In the original novel, the title character was dressed completely in black. He was an aristocrat of arrogant manners and had very bad breath. In contrast, Deane gave Dracula a somewhat sanitized presence. Dracula was dressed in formal evening wear, complete with an opera cloak that would further identify him with the bat. A cape had been mentioned by Stoker, most dramatically when it spread out as Dracula was crawling on the outside wall of Castle Dracula. While Dracula rarely appeared in London, he entered the play ready to match wits with the other characters, especially Abraham Van Helsing, rather than simply hovering as a presence backstage.

Deane, in his negotiations with Florence Stoker, seemed to have consciously moved away from the image of the film *Nosferatu, Eine Symphonie des Grauens,* in which Dracula was portrayed as a monster of truly odd appearance, not a character that could interact with polite society. To reduce the storyline to manageable proportions, Deane cut out the first section of the book, which took place in Transylvania, and allowed the play to open in London in the Hempstead home of Jonathan Harker. The play then followed the storyline of the book, except that Dracula was killed at Carfax, his British home, instead of being tracked to the continent. For the original performances, the government licensing agent insisted that Dracula's death not be shown; hence, the cast gathered around the coffin and blocked the audience's view of the staking.

Deane also wrote what became a noteworthy addendum to the play. After the final act, as members of the audience were preparing to leave, he appeared onstage, still in his Van Helsing persona. He addressed them briefly, apologizing beforehand if the play were to cause nightmares, but then, tongue-in-cheek, warning that such things as vampires might exist. Deane assumed the role of Van Helsing; his future wife, Dora Mary Patrick, played Mina. Edmund Blake became the first actor to play Dracula. He was soon followed by Raymond Huntley. The character of Quincey Morris, the Texan who courted Lucy, became a woman, ostensibly to create an additional part for a female member of the Deane Theatre Company. Deane's company traveled for three years around England and Scotland. So popular was the play that it began to push aside other plays in the company's repertoire.

In 1927, Deane decided to risk the play in London. It opened on February 14 at the Little Theatre on the West End. As he had expected, the press reviews were quite hostile. Almost everything about the play was criticized, and Deane thought that it would have a very short run. Instead, the public overrode the critics, and *Dracula* sold out night after night. Over the summer, the production moved to the larger Duke of York's Theatre. Deane turned an off-the-cuff comment by a newspaperman into one of the more famous publicity stunts in theatrical history. He had the Queen Alexandra Hospital send over a nurse who could attend to anyone who fainted from fright during the course of the play. At the end of one performance, a reported 39 members of the audience took advantage of her presence.

> After the final act, [Dean] addressed them briefly, apologizing beforehand if the play were to cause nightmares, but then, tongue-in-cheek, warning that such things as vampires might exist.

A problem developed when Deane decided to take his company back on the road. Wanting to continue the London success, Florence Stoker commissioned a second *Dracula* play. A much inferior drama, it had only a brief run, by which time she had completed an agreement with Deane. About the same time, she accepted an offer from New York producer Horace Liveright to stage a version of Deane's play on Broadway. Liveright engaged John L. Balderston to do a complete rewrite.

The Balderston version was even further removed from the book. Lucy Westenra and Mina Murray were collapsed into a single character, Lucy Seward, who became the daughter of Dr. John Seward. Seward, one of Lucy's youthful suitors in the novel, became a middle-aged father of a grown daughter. Lucy's other two suitors, Quincey P. Morris and Arthur Holmwood (Lord Godalming), completely disappeared. The Balderston play opened in the library of Seward's sanatorium. Huntley, originally offered the Dracula role, declined. The part was given to a little-known actor who could not understand English, Bela Lugosi. Bernard H. Jukes came from England to play R. N. Renfield. The Balderston production was tried out in New Haven, Connecticut, and then opened formally at the Fulton Theater in New York City on October 5, 1927. The play ran for 241 performances. It reopened in Los Angeles and San Francisco with Lugosi and Jukes joining the West Coast cast. Touring companies were established for the Midwest and the East Coast. The success of the American play led directly to the purchase of its rights by Universal Pictures and its translation to the motion picture screen. The Balderston version of *Dracula* was published by Samuel French in 1933 and has remained in print to the present.

Meanwhile, Hamilton Deane continued to produce the play in England, the movie version having given it new life. In 1939, he presented it in the Lyceum Theatre in London, the very theater where Bram Stoker had worked when he was writing *Dracula*. These last performances at the Lyceum were made more memorable one evening when Lugosi attended and came onstage to embrace Deane at the play's conclusion. Following *Dracula*'s run and a brief run of *Hamlet*, the theater closed forever. Deane continued the play in London for two more years.

Dracula was produced by different companies on a number of occasions through the years, but it experienced a major revival in 1977, opening on Broadway on October 20, 50 years after its debut. Frank Langella assumed the title role. Equally heralded were the scenery and costumes by Edward Gorey. (Gorey had designed the scenery for the summer theater production of the Nantucket Stage Company on Nantucket Island, Massachusetts.) The new production received two Tony Awards, one for best production of a revival and one for best costume design. It then served as a basis for the 1979 film starring Langella and directed by John Badham. Since its publication by Samuel French, the Deane–Balderston play has been popular for local drama groups and is annually produced by both amateur and semiprofessional theaters around the country.

Dumas, Alexandre (1802–1870)

Alexandre Dumas (Davy de la Pailleterie), a prominent French novelist and playwright

Best known for his novels The Three Musketeers *and* The Count of Monte Cristo, *French author Alexander Dumas also composed a version of the Dracula tale,* Le Vampire.

best remembered for his novels *The Three Musketeers* and *The Count of Monte Cristo*, was born on July 24, 1802, in Villers-Cotterets, France, the son of Thomas Alexandre Dumas Davy de la Pailleterie, a general in Napoleon's army, and Marie Louise Elisabeth Labouret. His father's mother was an African slave. Dumas's father died in prison when his son was four. Dumas showed few outstanding qualities as he was growing up. He had beautiful handwriting and was a good conversationalist but proved to be a dullard in arithmetic and only average in his other schoolwork.

However, he had a vivid imagination, which led him into the theater. Dumas turned to the theater at the age of 18 after seeing a performance of *Hamlet*. He organized his own drama company, for which he wrote material, directed the plays, and often performed. Fired by ambition, he moved to Paris early in 1823, ready to take the city by storm. Interestingly enough, his career was to begin and end with a vampire.

Shortly after Dumas's arrival in Paris, Charles Nodier's play *Le Vampire* opened for its second run at the Porte-Sainte-Martin theater. As Dumas was about to sit down for the performance, someone made a comment about his head of bushy, red hair. Insulted, he challenged the man to a duel and left the theater. By the time he got to the street, however, he thought better of his actions and, after purchasing a second ticket, returned to the theater through another door. He was seated in the orchestra section next to a well-dressed gentleman, and they conversed until the play began. While Dumas enjoyed the play, the gentleman next to him obviously did not and let his displeasure show. Following the second act, the man stood up and announced he could stand no more. Then, during the third act, the performance was interrupted by some shrill whistles. The gentleman, whom Dumas later learned was none other than Charles Nodier, was ushered from the theater. The evening was to prove a significant one, and Dumas devoted three chapters of his *Memoirs* to a description of his reactions to the play.

Dumas spent the next few years reading, writing poetry, and working hard at his job. In 1827, he finished a play, *Christine*, but he had no connections to present it to a producer. Someone suggested that he try to reach Baron Taylor of the Comédie-Française. Taylor was a good friend of Nodier, and even though Dumas had not seen Nodier since the night at *Le Vampire*, he risked sending a letter to the author. He reminded Nodier of the evening and asked for an introduction to Taylor. Nodier arranged an appointment, and Dumas was able to sell Taylor on the play. His literary career was launched. Instead of making the revisions requested by Taylor, however, he wrote a second play, *Henri III et Sa Cour*, which opened on February 10, 1829. With a new job as the librarian of the Duc d'Orleans, he was finally able to mingle with the artistic and intellectual community of Paris.

He spent his spare time with a variety of mistresses. Dumas was one of the most successful playwrights in Paris for the rest of the decade. His career was interrupted in 1830 by the emergence of Louis Philippe, who did not like Dumas's republican political views.

Dumas took the occasion to absent himself from Paris. Several unsuccessful plays in a row occasioned the writing of the first volume of *The Three Musketeers* in 1844. It was soon followed by *The Count of Monte Cristo* and a series of very successful adventure novels. The dramatization of *The Three Musketeers* was also well received, and Dumas was again financially successful. He built a large estate, the Château de Monte Cristo. In 1847, the Théâtre Historique was constructed to show his plays.

However, this all came to an end with the French Revolution of 1848. The theater was closed during the Revolution, and attendance lagged in the aftermath. His debts mounted. Then, on December 2, 1851, Louis Napoleon, the president of France, dismissed the Assembly and launched his coup d'état. Dumas had been desperately trying to recoup his fortunes, but his new plays all failed. Finally, in a last attempt, he turned to the vampire theme he had encountered when he arrived in Paris. On December 30, less than a month after the coup, his version of *Le Vampire* opened at the Ambigu-Comique.

At about the same time, he also authored a vampire-themed short story, "The Pale Lady" (1848). It was to be his last play for the city he had so loved. Early in 1852, he left for Belgium to get away from his creditors and a government that, once again, did not appreciate his politics. Once in Belgium, he began work on his *Memoirs* and wrote several other books reflecting on his career and travels. He died at the home of his son in

> Dumas ... is important in the development of the modern vampire myth as the last of a generation of great French writers to explore the theme.

Puys, France, on December 5, 1870. Dumas holds a prominent place in nineteenth-century French literature for his fast-paced action novels and the vivid imagination he brought to his writing. He also is important in the development of the modern vampire myth as the last of a generation of great French writers to explore the theme.

Kelly, Tim (1937–1998)

Tim Kelly, known for the large number of plays he wrote over his career, including the many vampire and Dracula plays he authored, was born in Saugus, Massachusetts, and attended Emerson College (B.A.) and Yale University (M.A.). His first stage play, *Widow's Walk*, was published in the 1960s. He aimed most of his plays for the amateur stage, and they proved immensely popular for presentations by high school and college casts.

Kelly's first vampire-oriented play appears to have been *Lady Dracula*, a one-act play published in 1973. He would follow up with a full three-act play, *Dracula, "The Vampire Play,"* which would open in London at the Queen's Theatre on August 23, 1978. Over the next few years, he would write and publish over a dozen plays focusing on horror themes that featured a vampire. Among these would be *Young Dracula; or, The Singing Bat* (1975); *Lady Dracula* (1980); *The Dracula Kidds: The House on Blood Pudding Lane* (1986); and *Renfield of the Flies and Spiders, or, Tell Dracula to Bug Off* (1993). Another early play, *Seven Wives for Dracula* (1973), would be adapted as a musical with lyrics added by Larry Nestor and reissued as *Seven Brides for Dracula* (1983).

Over his career, Kelly won a number of awards and, in 1995, was elected a member of the College of Fellows of the American Theatre. He died suddenly from a brain hemorrhage in 1998.

Nodier, Charles (1780–1844)

Jean Charles Nodier, a dramatist who introduced the vampire theme to the French stage, was born on April 29, 1780, in Basancon, France. As a young man, he began his writing career and became politically involved. In 1818, Nodier settled in Paris, where he remained for the rest of his life. That same year, *Jean Shogar*, his first novel, was published. In Paris, he became associated with several authors who were exploring what, in the post-Freudian world, would be known as the subconscious. His literary works began to explore the world of dreams and included some attention to the nightmare. The larger movement would become known as the Romantic movement and was seen as a distinct reaction to the limitations of the rationalism typified by Voltaire and his colleagues of the previous generation.

Nodier had just settled into his life in Paris when, in April 1819, John Polidori's short story "The Vampyre" appeared in the *New Monthly Magazine*. The story attracted considerable attention, in part because of its initial attribution to Lord Byron. Nodier was asked to write a review of it. He saw in the tale the expression of a widespread need in his generation to relieve its boredom through the experience of the outrageous and fantastic. The review was the first manifestation of a love–hate relationship with the vampire. Although Nodier seemed fascinated with it, he also saw a need, as an up-and-coming

French Romanticist author Charles Nodier was well known for his gothic and vampire tales, including his adaptation of the Polidori stage play The Vampyre.

leader in Parisian literary and intellectual circles, to show a certain disdain. He did recognize its importance and termed the legend of the vampire "the most important of all our superstitions." In an 1819 article, he called his readers' attention to the stories of people who confessed to being vampires and doing horrible things during their sleeping hours.

In 1820, his colleague Cyprien Bérard's two-volume sequel to "The Vampyre," *Lord Ruthven ou Les Vampires*, was published anonymously but included an introductory article by Nodier. Many then assumed that Nodier had written both Lord Ruthven tales. After some investigation, Bérard's authorship was discovered. Meanwhile, Nodier was at work on his own vampire production, a stage melodrama called *Le Vampire* (Pierre François Carmouche and Achille de Jouffroy collaborated on the piece). In *Le Vampire*, Nodier presented his own interpretation of Lord Ruthven, the lead character in Polidori's tale.

Ruthven was introduced as the hero who had saved the life of Sir Aubrey. Aubrey believed him dead, but when Ruthven arrived on the scene to marry Malvina, Aubrey's sister, he was welcomed. Meanwhile, Ruthven was shot while attending the wedding feast of Lovette and Edgar after Edgar had been angered at Ruthven's attempts to seduce his wife-to-be. Again, Aubrey thought Ruthven was dying and swore not to tell Malvina about his actions. As Aubrey was about to tell Malvina about her fiancé's death, Ruthven suddenly appeared and reminded Aubrey of his oath. Aubrey was momentarily lost in the conflict between his duty and his oath, and Ruthven moved on to the church with his prospective bride, Malvina. Ruthven was foiled only in the last moment when Aubrey came to his senses and interrupted the service.

Le Vampire opened on June 13, 1820, at the Théâtre de la Porte Saint-Martin. Despite mixed reviews, some by his political detractors, Nodier's drama was an immediate success. The text of the play was soon published and also found a popular audience. In the wake of the immense audience reaction, two other vampire plays soon opened at competing theaters, as did several comical and satirical plays lampooning it. *Le Vampire* had a long and successful run; in 1823, it was revived for a second lengthy run with the same stars, Monsieur Philippe and Madame Dorval. Alexandre Dumas attended the revival. He included a lengthy account of the performance in his memoirs, and the play would later inspire his own vampire drama in the 1850s. Nodier returned to the subjects of nightmares and vampires in his opium-inspired 1821 story, *Smarra; ou, Les Demons de la Nuit*. Opium, he believed, provided a gate to another world: the realm of dreams and nightmares. *Smarra* told the story of Lorenzo, who experienced an encounter with a vampire. However, the vampire was not Lord Ruthven, the almost human creature who mingled in society and delighted in destroying others, but more of a spiritlike creature of the dream world.

Famed author Victor Hugo was a critic of Nodier's Le Vampire.

Among Nodier's Paris acquaintances in the early 1820s was the youthful Victor Hugo, who published his first novel, a gothic horror story titled *Hans de'Islande*, in 1823. *Hans de'Islande* (*Hans of Iceland*) featured a central character who consumed the blood of his victims but did so by gathering and then drinking the blood in a skull as an act of revenge. Although Nodier tried to validate the horror fantasy realm as a reasonable one for a neophyte writer to explore, Hugo explicitly denounced *Le Vampire* in a review of the play's opening. Nodier had the opportunity to review *Hans de'Islande* and gave it a sympathetic review, calling attention to Hugo's latent talent.

In 1824, in recognition of his work (especially that devoted to the vampire theme), Nodier was appointed curator of the Bibliothèque de l'Arsenal, one of Paris's outstanding libraries. He later founded a salon where the literary world gathered and he authored a number of works, the best being his many short stories that explored the fantasy world of dreams, both good and bad. A 13-volume collected work was published during the years 1832–1841. In 1833, he was elected to the French Academy. He died on January 27, 1844. Throughout the nineteenth century, many writers were inspired by Nodier's fantastic tales, and he eventually found a new audience in the French surrealists. Recently, *Le Vampire* and Nodier's other dramatic works were reprinted in the *Textes Littéraires Français* series.

ᕦ *Planché, James Robinson* ᕤ *(1706–1880)*

James Robinson Planché, a popular British nineteenth-century dramatist, produced his first successful burlesque at the age of 22. That production launched a career that, while centering on the writing and translating of various dramas (most of a comedic nature), found him working in many varied capacities. Thus, for many of the plays on which he worked, he was the producer, manager, and/or costume designer. In addition, he occasionally wrote libretti for operas and songs for vaudeville.

Planché became involved in the world of vampires in 1820 in response to their popularity on the French stage following Jean Charles Nodier's production of *Le Vampire*. He adapted Nodier's play for the London stage. His resulting product, *The Vampire; or, The Bride of the Isles*, opened at the Lyceum Theater on August 9, 1820. Because the theater had a ready collection of Scottish clothing, Planché set the action in Scotland (one land not readily associated with vampires). The play was most remembered, however, for the trap door through which

Prolific author James Robinson Planché penned tales in genres ranging from comedy farce and melodrama to opera and extravaganzas. He also adapted Nodier's play as a vampire tale set in Scotland.

the vampire, Lord Ruthven (played by Thomas Potter Cooke), could disappear. It became known in the theater as the "vampire trap." The many-faceted Planché had a lifelong interest in heraldry, and many consider his *The History of British Costumes* (1834) his most permanent contribution. His writing was a strong influence on W. S. Gilbert (of the team Gilbert and Sullivan).

THE LITERARY VAMPIRE

From Minor Poetic Concern to Fictional Hero and Heroine

The emergence of the modern vampire we love (and love to hate) really begins as poets and novelists discover the vampire at the beginning of the nineteenth century and their readers let their enjoyment of reading about their favorite bloodsucker known, primarily by purchasing poem books and novels at their local bookstore. To the present day, writers, with a passing mention of those editors who assemble those all-important short fiction collections, create the vampire's presence on the popular culture (without taking anything from the vampire on the stage, cinema, and television).

The literary vampire really originates among the Romantic poets at the beginning of the nineteenth century. It is carried by novelists and short-story writers through the century and has come to be dominated by the novelists of recent decades. In this chapter, we introduce the more prominent of the thousands of writers, primarily those writing in the English language, who have satiated our desires for a vampire or two to inhabit our own imaginative world.

Note: The present generation of vampire writers are covered in chapter 13.

Banks, L. A. (1959–2011)

L. A. Banks, a pen name for Leslie Esdaile-Banks, was the writer of the popular *Vampire Huntress* series of romance novels, the first volume of which appeared in 2003. She emerged through the first decade of the twenty-first century as one of the most successful and prominent African American authors. Banks was a graduate of the University of Pennsylvania and subsequently received her master's degree from Temple University. A product of Philadelphia, she has made it her home as an adult.

Banks introduced her main character, Damali Richards, a strong female slayer—termed a Neteru, a balance-swaying force of light—in *Minion*. In her normal persona, Richards is a spoken-word performer who works with a band. The band's musicians—Marlene, Shabazz, Big Mike, Rider, Jose, J. L., and Dan—live together and hunt vampires after their gigs.

In *Minion*, local gang members have come under attack, and those who fell victim have been found mutilated to a point beyond recognition. The perpetrator is discovered to be Fallon Nuit, a power vampire, who is the ongoing villain in the series. Enter Richards and her cohorts and her former lover, Carlos Rivera, who is now a youthful vampire growing stronger night by night and who will push the plot forward as he runs between Richards and Nuit.

> Banks introduced her main character, Damali Richards, a strong female slayer—termed a Neteru, a balance-swaying force of light—in *Minion*.

As the story develops, Banks introduces a spectrum of variations on the vampire myth. The vampires believe, for instance, that if they could impregnate Richards as she enters into adulthood (i.e., her 21st birthday), the child would be a daywalker, a vampire freed from its nocturnal limitations with the power to create further daywalkers. When vampires feed, they hide the bite marks to conceal their presence

from humans. Vampires emanate from the sixth level of hell. They are ruled by a Vampire Council, with one council level vampire master for each of the five inhabited continents. It is from this powerful realm that all evil comes; thus, a huntress is needed to balance the situation for the embattled human race.

Beginning with an idea from *Buffy the Vampire Slayer*, in Banks's world, a vampire huntress is born every millennium, surrounded by a group of associates who protect her backside and a vampire lover in search of his soul, but Banks set the idea in a hip-hop urban African American setting and developed it with her own unique slant. The huntress, for example, is special, in part, because she is born to live through the change of the millennium and, as such, she has a different alignment of the planets in her horoscope. As she grows, her powers slowly emerge. She will develop her full powers on her 21st birthday but begins vampire hunting before that time. Eventually, the biblical origins of Banks's books become important as the events of the biblical apocalypse begin to unfold.

Banks was not limited to writing her vampire series, which included more than a dozen titles, but produced 25 additional novels in a variety of genres written under several pen names. Her prolific career was cut short by her untimely death in 2011.

❧ *Beloved by Toni Morrison* ❧

African American author Toni Morrison's (1931–2019) novel *Beloved*, hailed as one of the great twentieth-century works of American fiction, is also a notable gothic adventure tale. It focuses upon Sethe, a black woman, who in the 1870s resides in Cincinnati, Ohio. In the

1850s, she had been a slave in Kentucky but fled across the Ohio River to freedom with her daughters to escape existence under an extremely abusive owner. She is initially caught by her owner and, in the process, tried to kill her children to prevent their being enslaved

Toni Morrison might not be the first author whose name comes to mind when you think of vampires, but her famous novel Beloved *features a psychic vampire.*

however; she manifests as what some have seen as a succubus or as a psychic or emotional vampire. She sucks the energy, soul, and spirit out of Sethe.

Beloved's haunting and vampiric activity is temporarily calmed after Paul, a former slave from the same plantation where Sethe had lived, arrives. He and Sethe begin a relationship. Then, a young woman who calls herself Beloved arrives, and Sethe comes to believe that she might be her deceased daughter newly incarnated. When the young woman reveals to Paul that Sethe has killed her young daughter, he abandons her. Sethe now must confront her previous actions as she works out her relationship to the young woman, whom she has come to know as Beloved.

Beloved is actually based on the true story of one Margaret Garner, who had escaped slavery with her husband, Robert, and their children. They sought freedom in Ohio, and she had, when recaptured by their owner, killed her young daughter in order to prevent her from growing up in slavery.

While not her first novel, *Beloved* gave Morrison a new level of fame and appreciation by her contemporaries. *Beloved* won the Pulitzer Prize, and Morrison subsequently won the Nobel Prize for Literature (1993).

again. She succeeds in killing only her two-year-old daughter, but her actions convince her owner that she was crazy, and he decided not to attempt to take her back to Kentucky. Sethe decided to bury her daughter and marked her grave with the single word "Beloved," the word giving its name to the novel.

Years later, in 1973, Sethe lives with her now teenage daughter, Denver, in a house haunted by the angry ghost Beloved, the child Sethe had killed. Beloved is not just a ghost,

🦇 *Bunnicula* 🦇

This vampire, a favorite of children, does not wear a tuxedo and cape, and his hair does not sweep back in a widow's peak. He also does not need to shape-shift into an animal form because he already is a rabbit. He does not partake of blood but rather enjoys a series of adventures, all chronicled by James Howe.

According to the premiere story in 1979, Bunnicula made his first appearance in a theater

during a Dracula movie. He was found by Pete and Toby Monroe, who made him their pet, and named him after the movie. He joined the Monroes' other two pets, Chester the cat and Harold the dog.

One evening soon after his arrival, Bunnicula awoke from his daytime sleep and, during the night, headed for the kitchen. Chester spotted him raiding the refrigerator. He left behind the white husk of a tomato, from which he had sucked the life (color) and juice. While Mrs. Monroe was baffled, Chester, who spent his spare time reading books, became the first to figure out that the new houseguest was a vampire. Even though he does not suck blood, Bunnicula attacks objects such as carrots and tomatoes and sucks the juice out of them, leaving only a husk behind. He sleeps all day and has two fangs, just like Count Orlock.

> Even though he does not suck blood, Bunnicula attacks objects such as carrots and tomatoes and sucks the juice out of them, leaving only a husk behind.

Chester also knew how to deal with the situation. He placed garlic on the floor in such a way as to keep the rabbit out of the kitchen. It was Harold who recognized that Chester was starving Bunnicula and doing so for no reason. Harold believed the rabbit was not doing anyone any harm, and Chester should not act in a hostile manner toward him. While convincing Chester of the righteousness of his argument, he smuggled the thirsty Bunnicula into the kitchen. Eventually, Chester, Harold, and Bunnicula would become friends and share a number of adventures.

The original *Bunnicula* book was coauthored by James Howe and his wife, Deborah, but unfortunately, she died of cancer in 1978 before it was published. Through the 1980s, Bunnicula became a well-recognized character in English-language children's literature, completely accepted by teachers and parents alike in spite of the vampire element. In the wake of the original book's success, James Howe turned out a host of additional stories and a variety of activity books that provided additional entertainment and education for Bunnicula's youthful fans. Additionally, the earlier books remained in print in new editions into the new century, a 40th-anniversary edition of the original book being released in 2019.

A generation after his initial appearance, Bunnicula got a new shot at life when Warner Brothers and the Cartoon Network teamed up to produce a new television series featuring Bunnicula. The storyline was somewhat altered, with Bunnicula now being the pet of one Mina Monroe, who lives in New Orleans. Using a key left to her by her deceased aunt, she unlocks a basement door that frees Bunnicula, a bunny formerly the pet of Dracula. The rabbit quickly displays his unique attributes—he attacks vegetables and fruit to gain his life and strength, he stays away from sunlight, he sleeps in a coffin, and he flies around with batlike wings. As the series has progressed, Bunnicula regularly joins Mina's other pets, Chester and Harold, in a series of esoteric adventures. *Bunnicula* premiered in 2016 and continues as this almanac goes to press.

Also see the *Bunnicula* TV series, p. 507.

Byron, Lord George Gordon (1788–1824)

Lord George Gordon Byron, purported author of the first modern vampire story in English, was born in 1788 in London, the son of Catherine Gordon and John Byron. After his father spent the fortune brought to the marriage by Catherine, she took Byron to Aberdeen, Scotland, in 1790, where he had a relatively poor but somewhat normal childhood, disturbed only by a lame foot. His father died in 1791. Due to the untimely death of a cousin

The poet Lord Byron talks about vampires in his 1813 verse "The Giaour."

in 1794, he became the family heir, and when his great-uncle died in 1798, he became Lord Byron. Soon thereafter, he and his mother moved to the family estate in Nottinghamshire. In 1801, he entered Harrow School, and four years later, he went on to Trinity College at the University of Cambridge.

While at Cambridge, Byron privately published his first poetry collection, *Fugitive Pieces* (1806). The next year, a second collection was published as *Hours of Idleness* (1807). He received his master's degree in 1808 and the following year took his seat in the House of Lords. He spent much of 1809 and 1810 traveling and writing Cantos I and II of *Childe Harolde*. Its publication in 1812 brought him immediate fame. He also began his brief liaison with Lady Caroline Lamb.

The following year, he broke off the relationship with Lamb and began his affair with his half sister Augusta Leigh. At about the same time, he was also initially exploring the subject of vampirism in his poem "The Giaour," completed and published in 1813. In the midst of the battles described in the poem, the Muslim antagonist speaks a lengthy curse against the title character, the *giaour* (an infidel, one outside the faith). Upon death, the infidel's spirit would surely be punished. However, the Muslim declared that more was to come:

> But first, on earth as Vampire sent,
> Thy corpse shall from its tomb be
>   rent:
> Then ghastly haunt thy native place,
> And suck the blood of all thy race;
> There from thy daughter, sister,
>   wife,
> At midnight drain the stream of
>   life;
> Yet loathe the banquet which per-
>   force
> Must feed thy livid living corpse.
> Thy victims are they yet expire
> Shall know the demon for their
>   sire,
> As cursing thee, thou cursing them,
> Thy flowers are withered on the
>   stem.

In "The Giaour," Byron demonstrated his familiarity with the Greek *vrykolakas*, a corpse that was animated by a devilish spirit and returned to its own family to make them its first victims. While the Greek vampire in "The Giaour" would be the only overt mention of the vampire in Byron's vast literary output, it merely set the stage for the more famous "vampiric" incident in Byron's life. Meanwhile, in January 1814, Byron married Annabelle Milbanke. Their daughter was born in December. Early in 1816, the couple separated after she and British society became aware of Byron's various sexual encounters. When both turned on him, he decided to leave the country (for good, as it turned out).

In the spring of 1816, Byron left for the continent. Accompanying him was a young physician/writer, John Polidori, who, among other services, supplied Byron with a spectrum of mood-altering and hallucinogenic drugs. By the end of May, they had arrived in Geneva and, early in June, rented the Villa Diodati, overlooking the Lake of Geneva. Joining him were Percy Shelley, Mary Godwin, and Godwin's stepsister, Claire Clairmont, another of Byron's mistresses. On June 15, bad weather having forced them inside, Byron suggested that each person write

Polidori kept notes on Byron's story, which Byron had jotted down in his notebook.

and share a ghost story with the small group. Two evenings later, the stories began. The most serious product of this adventure was, of course, *Frankenstein*, Godwin's story that was later expanded into a full novel under her married name, Mary Shelley.

Byron's meager contribution to the ghostly evening was soon abandoned and never developed. It concerned two friends who, like himself and Polidori, left England to travel on the continent, in the story's case, to Greece. While there, one of the friends died, but before his death, he obtained from the other a promise to keep secret the matter of his death. The second man returned to England only to discover that his former companion had beaten him back home and had begun an affair with the second man's sister. Polidori kept notes on Byron's story, which Byron had jotted down in his notebook. (Two novels, both later made into movies, *Gothic*, directed by Ken Russell, and *Haunted Summer*, offered an account of Byron and his associates during these weeks in Switzerland.) Byron and Polidori parted company several months later. Polidori left for England, and Byron continued his writing and the Romantic adventures that were to fill his remaining years. The ghost story seemed a matter of no consequence. Then, in May 1819, he saw an item concerning a tale, "The Vampyre," supposedly written by him and published in the *New Monthly Magazine* in England. He immediately wrote a letter denying his authorship and asking for a retraction. As the story unfolded, Byron

discovered that Polidori had written a short story utilizing his notes on the tale told by Byron in 1816 in Switzerland. Polidori's story was the first piece of prose fiction to treat a literal vampire, and the publisher of the *New Monthly Magazine* took it upon himself, based upon Polidori's account of the story's origin, to put Byron's name on it. In the light of a not unexpected response, he quickly published it in a separate booklet over Byron's name and had it translated into French and German. Both Polidori and Byron made attempts to correct the error, and before the year was out, Byron had the "Fragment of a Story" published as part of his attempt to distance himself from the finished story. The problem he encountered in denying his authorship was amply demonstrated in 1830 by the inclusion of "The Vampyre" in the French edition of his collected works. Byron must have been further irritated by Polidori's choice of a name for the vampire character in the story, Lord Ruthven, the same name given to the Byron figure in Lady Caroline Lamb's fictionalized account of their liaison, *Glenarvon* (1816).

Once the Polidori incident was behind him, Byron never returned to the vampire in any of his writings. Twentieth-century critics, however, have seen vampirism as a prominent metaphor in the Romantic treatment of human relations, especially destructive ones. Vampires are characters who suck the life force from those they love, and the Romantic authors of the early nineteenth century, such as Byron, utilized psychic vampirism despite never labeling such characters as vampires.

For example, critic James B. Twitchell saw the psychic vampire theme as an integral aspect of Byron's dramatic poem "Manfred," the first acts of which were written in the summer of 1816 at the Villa Diodati. Illustrative of this "vampirism" was a scene in the first act, in which the person who had just stopped Manfred from suicide offered him a glass of wine. Manfred refused, comparing the wine to blood—both his blood and that of his half sister, with whom he'd had an affair. Here, Twitchell saw a return to the Greek vampires, who first drank/attacked the blood/life of those closest to them. Manfred was an early manifestation of *l'homme fatal*, the man who acts upon those around him as if he were a vampire.

During a severe illness in April 1824, Byron underwent a series of bleedings that, ironically, probably caused his death. He died on April 19, 1824. His body was returned to England for burial. In the mid-1990s, novelist Tom Holland issued *The Vampyre: Being the True Pilgrimage of George Gordon, Sixth Lord Byron*, an entertaining book based on the premise that Byron did not die but lives on as a vampire.

 Carmilla

Carmilla is the title character in the vampire novelette by British writer Sheridan Le Fanu. "Carmilla" was originally published as a short story in a story collection entitled *In a Glass Darkly* in 1872. The story took

An illustration by Michael Fitzgerald for the story "Carmilla," a novella originally published serially in the literary magazine The Dark Blue *from 1871 to 1872.*

place in rural Styria, where Laura, the heroine and narrator, lived. Her father, a retired Austrian civil servant, had been able to purchase an abandoned castle cheaply. Carmilla first appeared in the opening scene of the story as she entered the six-year-old Laura's bed. Laura fell asleep in her arms but suddenly awakened with a sensation of two needles entering her breast. She cried out, and the person Laura described only as "the lady" slipped out of bed onto the floor and disappeared, possibly under the bed. Her nurse and the housekeeper came into the room in response to her cries but found no one, and no marks were found on her chest.

Carmilla reappeared when Laura was 19 years old. The carriage in which Carmilla was traveling had a wreck in sight of the castle. Carmilla's mother, seemingly in a hurry to reach her destination, left Carmilla at the castle to recover from the accident. When Laura finally met their new guest, she immediately recognized Carmilla as the same person who had visited her 12 years previous and, thus, the vampire was loosed again to prey on Laura. Gradually, her identity was uncovered. She began to visit Laura in the form of a cat and a female phantom. Laura also noticed that she looked exactly like the 1698 portrait of Countess Mircalla Karnstein. Through her mother, Laura was a descendant of the Karnsteins.

At this point, an old friend of the family, General Spielsdorf, arrived at the castle, where he relates the account of his own daughter's death. She had been wasting away; her condition had no known natural causes. A physician deduced that she was the victim of a vampire. The skeptical general waited, hidden in his daughter's room, and actually caught the vampire, a young woman he knew by the name of Millarca, in the act. He tried to kill her with his sword, but she easily escaped.

In horror stories, in general, authors have been able to treat sexual themes in ways that would not have been available to them otherwise.

As he finished his account, Carmilla entered. He recognized her as Millarca, but she escaped them before they could deal with her. They all then tracked her to the Karnstein castle some three miles away, where they found her resting in her grave. Her body was lifelike, and a faint heartbeat was detected. The casket floated in fresh blood. They drove a stake through her heart, in reaction to which, Carmilla let out a "piercing shriek." They finished their gruesome task by severing her head, burning the body, and scattering the ashes.

One can see in Le Fanu's tale, which would later be read by Bram Stoker, the progress of the developing vampire myth to that point. People became vampires after committing suicide or following their death if they had been bitten by a vampire during their life. The latter was the cause in Carmilla's case. Le Fanu understood the vampire to be a dead person returned, not a demonic spirit. The returned vampire had a tendency to attack family and loved ones—in this case, a descendant—and was somewhat geographically confined to the area near their grave. While somewhat pale in complexion, the vampire was quite capable of fitting into society without undue notice. The vampire had two needlelike teeth (fangs), but these were not visible at most times. Bites generally occurred on the neck or chest.

Carmilla had nocturnal habits but was not totally confined to the darkness. She had superhuman strength and was able to undergo a transformation into various shapes, especially those of animals. Her favorite shape was that of a cat rather than either a wolf or a bat. She slept in a coffin, which she could leave without disturbing any dirt covering the grave.

As would be true in *Dracula* (1897), the mere bite of the vampire neither turned victims into vampires nor killed them. The vampire fed off the victim over a period of time while the victim slowly withered away. The victim thus fulfilled both the vampire's daily need for blood and its fascination for a particular person whom it chose as its victim.

As many have noted in discussing Carmilla, her fascination with Laura and the general's daughter, an attachment "resembling the passion of love," has more than passing lesbian overtones. In horror stories, in general, authors have been able to treat sexual themes in ways that would not have been available to them otherwise. Early in the story, for example, Carmilla began her attack upon Laura by placing her "pretty arms" around her neck and with her cheek touching Laura's lips, speaking soft, seductive words. While earlier writers had written about the vampire-like *lamiai* and other female vampires who attacked their male lovers, "Carmilla" introduced the female revenant vampire to gothic literature.

One unique element of vampire lore in "Carmilla" that was not used by later writers was Le Fanu's suggestion that the vampire was limited to choosing a name that was anagrammatically related to its real name. Both Carmilla and Millarca were derived from Mircalla.

"Carmilla" would directly influence Stoker's presentation of the vampire, especially his treatment of the female vampires who attack Jonathan Harker early in *Dracula*. The influence of "Carmilla" was even more visible in "Dracula's Guest," the deleted chapter of *Dracula* that was later published as a short story.

Through the twentieth century, "Carmilla" has had a vital existence on the motion picture screen. The story served loosely as inspiration for *Vampyr*, Carl Theodor Dreyer's 1932 classic, though "Dracula's Guest" provided the basis for Universal Pictures's first post-*Dracula* movie with a female vampire, *Dracula's Daughter* (1936). However, with the expanded exploration of the vampire theme in the movies after World War II, "Carmilla" would be rediscovered. The first movie based directly on "Carmilla" was the 1960 French *Et Mourir de Plaisir* (also called *Blood and Roses*), directed by Roger Vadim and starring his wife, Annette Vadim. It was followed in 1964 by *La maldición de los Karnstein* (also known as *Terror in the Crypt*).

Then, at the beginning of the 1970s in the wake of its other successful vampire movies, Hammer Films would turn to Carmilla and her family for three movies: *Lust for a Vampire* (1971), *The Vampire Lovers* (1970)—possibly the most faithful attempt to tell the Le Fanu story—and *Twins of Evil* (1971). The Hammer Films movies inspired other attempts to bring "Carmilla" to the screen, the first being three Spanish productions. *La Hija de Dracula* (*The Daughter of Dracula*) was released in 1972. *La Comtesse aux Seins Nux* (1973) was released under a variety of titles, including a highly edited version in 1981, *Erotikill*. *La Novia Ensangretada* (1974) was released in the United States as *Till Death Do Us Part* and *The Blood-Spattered Bride*. Through the last decades of the twentieth century, "Carmilla"-inspired movies included *The Evil of Dracula* (1975), *Valerie* (1991), and *Vampires vs. Zombies*, also released as *Carmilla the Lesbian Vampire* (2004). Carmilla has continued to inspire filmmakers in the new century and has most recently appeared in *The Carmilla Movie* (2017) and *Carmilla* (2020). Television adaptations were made in England in 1966, in Spain in 1987, and in the United States as part of a short-lived series, *Nightmare Classics*, in 1989.

"Carmilla" was brought to the world of comic books in 1968 by Warren Publishing Company's *Creepy* issue #19, one of the comic magazines that operated outside of the Comics Code, which forbade the picturing of vampires in comic books. In the 1970s, Malibu Comics released a six-part adult version of "Carmilla". In 1972, the story was included on a record album, *Carmilla: A Vampire Tale*, released under the Vanguard label by the Etc. Company.

Coleridge, Samuel Taylor *(1773–1834)*

Samuel Taylor Coleridge, a Romantic poet and the first to introduce the vampire theme to British poetry, was born in Ottery St. Mary, the son of a minister in the Church of England. His father died when Coleridge was nine, and he was sent to Christ's Hospital, London, as a charity pupil. In 1790, he entered Jesus College, Cambridge. He left college briefly in 1793 but returned the following year. There, he met fellow poet Robert Southey, who would become his lifelong friend. Through Southey, he met Sara Fricker, his future wife, and got his first contract to prepare a book of poetry.

In 1797, Coleridge met William Wordsworth, who was credited with bringing Coleridge's poetic genius to the public's attention. The initial result of this friendship was "The

One of the famous Romantic movement poets of England, Samuel Taylor Coleridge penned a poem about vampirism called "Christabel," written in two parts in 1797 and 1800.

Rime of the Ancient Mariner," published in the celebrated *Lyrical Ballads*, which Wordsworth put together. Coleridge wrote almost all of his famous poems during the next five years of his close association with Wordsworth.

Among the poems Coleridge worked on during this creative period was "Christabel." Though never mentioning vampires directly, it is now generally conceded that vampirism was the intended theme of "Christabel," the substantive case having been made by Arthur H. Nethercot in the 1930s. Nethercot argued that the essential vampiric nature of the Lady Geraldine, who was "rescued" after being left in the woods by her kidnappers, was demonstrated by examining her characteristics. First, throughout the poem, Christabel was portrayed as being a potential victim who needed to be shielded from the forces of evil. Geraldine, however, was pictured as a richly clad woman, first seen bath-

ing in the moonlight (the element that revived vampires in nineteenth-century vampire tales). Second, as Geraldine approached the door of the castle of Christabel's father, she fainted. After Christabel assisted her across the threshold, she was quickly revived. Vampires had to be formally invited into a home the first time they entered. Third, Geraldine then walked by the dog, who let out an uncharacteristically angry moan. It was commonly believed that vampires had negative effects upon animals. Coleridge dwelt upon the evening encounter of the two women. Christabel showed Geraldine to a place of rest. She opened a bottle of wine, which they shared. At Geraldine's suggestion, Christabel undressed, after which Geraldine partially disrobed, revealing her breast and half of her side. What did Christabel see? In lines later deleted from the published version, Coleridge noted that Geraldine's appearance was "lean and old and foul of hue." Christabel entered a trancelike state:

> Yet Geraldine nor speaks nor stirs;
> Ah! what a stricken look was hers!
> Deep from within she seems half-
>   way
> To lift some weight with sick assay,
> And eyes the maid and seeks
>   delay;
> Then suddenly, as one defied,
> Collects herself in scorn and pride,
> And lay down at the Maidens
>   side!

In a scene with obvious lesbian overtones, the two women lay together for an hour and, again, the animals were affected:

> O Geraldine! one hour was thine
> Thoust had thy will! By tairn and
>   rill,
> The night-birds all that hour
>   were still.
> But now they are jubilant anew,
> From cliff and tower, tu-whoo!
>   tu-whoo!

The next morning, Geraldine awoke refreshed, and her lean, old, and foul body was rejuvenated: "That (so it seemed) her girded vests/Grew tight beneath her heaving breasts." Christabel, on the other hand, awoke with a sense of guilt and immediately went to prayer. She then led Geraldine to the audience with her father, the lord of the castle. Geraldine immediately attached herself to the Lord Leoline while Christabel had a momentary flashback of Geraldine's body when she first disrobed. She attempted to have her father send Geraldine away, but he was already enraptured and, in the end, turned from his daughter and departed with Geraldine at his side.

"Christabel" was composed in two parts, the first being written and published in 1798.

A second part was finished around 1800. "Christabel" thus preceded Southey's "Thalaba the Destroyer," the first English-language poem to actually mention the vampire in its text. Also, the imagery of "Christabel" is an obvious and important source of Sheridan Le Fanu's story "Carmilla." After 1802, Coleridge wrote little and drew his income primarily from lecturing and writing critical articles. Most of his life, he was addicted to drugs, having been hooked on opium in an attempt to deal with chronic pain and later consuming vast quantities of laudanum. He received some recognition of his literary work in 1824, when he was named a royal associate of the Royal Society of Literature. He died on July 25, 1834, at the age of 61.

 # *Gautier, Théophile (1811–1872)*

Pierre Jules Théophile Gautier, a French Romantic author, was born in southern France, the son of Antoinette Adélaide Cocard and Jean Pierre Gautier. As a child, he read *Robinson Crusoe* and, at school, he associated with Gérard de Nerval (who later translated *Faust* into French).

As a young man, he was affected by E. T. A. Hoffmann's tales and Goethe's "The Bride of Corinth." Gautier also became associated with the circle of writers around Victor Hugo. Throughout the early 1830s, he frequented a variety of literary gatherings, including one that assembled at the Hotel Pimodan, which was famous for its indulgence in opium.

A change in family fortune in the 1830s forced Gautier into journalism as a means of supporting himself; he worked at it, somewhat unhappily, for the rest of his life. He turned out thousands of reviews as a literary, theater, and art critic. Gautier's long hours of work earned

French critic, author, and journalist Théophile Gautier was held in high regard by the literary society of his day, influencing such writers as Ezra Pound, Gustave Flaubert, and T. S. Eliot.

little more than a modest living and few honors during his lifetime. Apart from newspaper work, he wrote many Romantic stories, although his role in the larger Romantic movement was overshadowed by that of Victor Hugo. His own exploration of the psyche, in part stimulated by the use of opium, gained greater acknowledgment in the years since his death, when Gautier's place among France's outstanding nineteenth-century writers was acknowledged.

Like many other French Romantic writers, Gautier found great inspiration in the vampire myth. His earliest and most famous vampire story, "La Morte Amoureuse" (literally, "the dead woman in love"), appeared in 1836. An English translation appeared in *The World of Théophile Gautier's Travel Accounts* in 1907 and was published separately in 1927 as "The Beautiful Vampire." The story used what was to become a recurring theme in Gautier's fiction. It told of a woman who returned from the dead to vampirize the male subject of the story. In "The Beautiful Vampire," the dead woman, Clarimonde, made herself so attractive to her male lover, the priest Romuald, that he chose to bleed to death rather than lose her attention.

The theme would reappear, for example, in *Aria Marcella*, which was directly inspired by Goethe's "The Bride of Corinth," in which Gautier declared, "No one is truly dead until they are no longer loved." The 1863 novel *The Mummy's Foot* was set among archaeologists in Egypt. In it, a mummy, which retained the elasticity of living flesh and had "enamel eyes shining with the moist glow of life," was compared to a vampire lying in its tomb dead … yet alive.

Another vampiric story, "Spirite" (1866), used recently popularized spiritualism as the setting. The story told of a man who experienced both the symbolic and actual death of his love. She first became a nun (and thus died to the world) and then physically died. When the woman took her vows, she gave herself to her love and vowed to be his beyond the grave. Contact was made in a seánce, and she ultimately lured the man to his death.

In the last years of his life, Gautier lived in a Paris suburb, where he died from a heart condition in 1872. Through the twentieth century, most of his Romantic tales were translated into English.

Good-Guy Vampires

Margaret L. Carter, a scholar of vampire literature, has defined good-guy vampires as vampires who act morally when dealing with mortals and, as a whole, conform their moral perspective to a human ethical perspective. In order to obtain blood without killing or "raping" their victims, they will attempt to acquire it from animals, blood banks, or willing human donors. A few, like Vampirella and Blade, use synthetic blood substitutes. Carter also maintains that the good-guy vampires retain personality and freedom of choice and are not so consumed with bloodlust that ethical decisions become impossible. Good-guy vampires tend

to emerge in one of two situations: either they are basically good people who discover themselves trapped in the evil condition—vampirism—and are forced to continually fight against it, or vampirism is pictured as an ethically neutral state, in which vampires can make ethical decisions on how to find their needed sustenance: blood.

In the 1960s, good-guy vampires Vampirella and Barnabas Collins appeared in popular culture, while literary examples of that time include the Dracula of science fiction writer Fred Saberhagen and Saint Germain, the hero

Geraint Wyn Davies starred as Nick Knight, a good-guy vampire who works as a detective in the 1990s television series Forever Knight.

in vampires in the 1990s. When in 1992 Mary Ann B. McKinnon announced her intention of starting a fanzine dedicated to good-guy vampires, she received encouraging responses. For several years, she turned out substantial issues annually. *Good Guys Wear Fangs* featured original short stories and poetry in which the vampire is a hero.

The good-guy vampire found its real home in both romantic fiction and teenage fiction. Good-guy vampires emerged as the heroes for novelists Amanda Ashley, Christine Feehan, and Charlaine Harris, whose books were adapted for the HBO television series *True Blood*. Good-guy detectives include Jack Fleming in P. N. Elrod's many books and Henry Fitzroy in the novels of Tanya Huff. Simultaneously, in the early episodes of *Buffy the Vampire Slayer*, a good-guy vampire, Angel, would be introduced as a romantic love interest of the Slayer. In the teen book series *Twilight*, a family of good-guy vampires, the Cullens, take center stage, along with narrator Bella Swan, as the main protagonists. Good-guy vampires have shown up on many television shows, notably the vampires of *Vampire High*, Nick St. John of *Moonlight*, the two rival vampires in Laura Smith's *The Vampire Diaries*, Bill Compton and his vampire friends of *True Blood*, and a number of anime series from Japanese television. Many of the television vampires were aimed at a youthful audience, and many were developed from and/or spawned teenage vampire novels.

vampire of the novels of Chelsea Quinn Yarbro. Throughout the 1980s, good-guy vampires multiplied in literature and media but most notably reappeared in the 1990s in the persona of Nick Knight, the vampire lead of the television series *Forever Knight*. Carter has rightfully pointed out that the good-guy vampire is a feature of modern vampire lore that separates it radically from nineteenth-century vampire literature. It is worth noting, however, that the idea of a morally responsible vampire was not really common in twentieth-century literature until after the 1950s. Good-guy vampires have been an essential part of the revival of interest

Holmes, Sherlock

Dracula and Sherlock Holmes vie with each other for the title of the most popular fictional character in the English-speaking world. *Dracula* (1897) is the single novel most frequently made into a movie, while Sherlock Holmes, the subject of 56 short stories and four novels, is the character most frequently brought to the screen (with Dracula being a close second). Both have been the subject of many additional books and stories by authors who use one or the other as their central figure.

The Sussex Vampire: Sherlock Holmes had only one brush with a "vampire." The short story "The Adventure of the Sussex Vampire" appeared in the January 1924 issue of *The*

An illustration by W. T. Benda for the Sir Arthur Conan Doyle story "The Sussex Vampire," published in the 1924 edition of Hearst's International.

Strand Magazine just six months before the dramatic version of *Dracula*, written by Hamilton Deane, opened in rural England. The story began with an inquiry concerning vampires, to which Holmes made what has become one of his more famous lines: "Rubbish, Watson, rubbish! What have we to do with walking corpses who can only be held in their grave by stakes driven through their hearts? It's pure lunacy." Watson reminded him that vampirism might take the form of a living person sucking the blood of someone younger in order to retain his or her youth (a probable reference to the case of Elizabeth Báthory). Their client, Robert Ferguson, related an incident in which his wife was found apparently biting the neck of their infant son and immediately afterward was seen with blood on her mouth. To Holmes, the idea

of a vampire, even the more human one described by Watson, was absurd. "Such things do not happen in criminal practice in England"; but, Holmes asked rhetorically, "could not a bleeding wound be sucked for other than vampiric reasons?" Holmes simply thought of the alternative, that the mother was, in fact, sucking poison from a wound the child had received from his older, jealous stepbrother.

While *Dracula* was enjoying success on the stage throughout the country, "The Adventure of the Sussex Vampire" received its first dramatization in a 1929–1930 British radio series, *The Adventures of Sherlock Holmes*, prepared for broadcast by Edith Meiser. Her version would be the one most frequently used when other adaptations were made, such as the first American radio dramatization in 1936 and the Basil Rathbone/Nigel Bruce portrayals in 1939–1940 and 1941–1942. The first television adaptations occurred in the fall of 1964 for the BBC. Most recently, the story has become the subject of two movies: *Sherlock Holmes in Caracas* (Venezuela, 1992) and *Sherlock Holmes: The Last Vampire* (United Kingdom, 1992), the latter being a made-for-television movie in the Jeremy Brett/Edward Hardwicke series of Sherlock Holmes stories.

Holmes Meets Dracula: Over the decades, several attempts have been made to link Sherlock Holmes to the *Dracula* story. For instance, Sherlockians have entertained themselves with a debate that Dr. Abraham Van Helsing was, in fact, Sherlock Holmes in disguise. Purists, however, have rejected such a notion. Since both Sherlock Holmes and Dracula were pictured by their creators, Arthur Conan Doyle and Bram Stoker, as contemporaries in the Victorian world of the late nineteenth century, it was inevitable that, in view of the revived interest in each in the late twentieth century, someone would suggest their interaction. A hint of what was to come appeared in 1976, when Nicholas Meyer added Bram Stoker as a character in *The West End Horror*, a new Sherlock Holmes story. Two years later, two different authors picked up on the suggestion.

Loren D. Estleman, writing as Holmes's chronicler Dr. John H. Watson, authored *Sherlock Holmes vs. Dracula: The Adventures of the Sanguinary Count.* What would happen if Holmes were called in to solve the case of the *Demeter*, the ship that brought Dracula to London but then was found mysteriously wrecked at Whitby with all its crew dead? Then, while working on the case, Holmes's interest was drawn to the accounts of the "Bloofer Lady," Lucy Westenra turned vampire, who was preying on the local children of Hampstead Heath.

The great detective followed his clues as he became involved in the events of the original novel and was led to his own confrontation with Dracula.

> The great detective followed his clues as he became involved in the events of the original novel and was led to his own confrontation with Dracula.

Estleman closely followed the characterizations of the creators of Holmes and Dracula: Holmes was good; Dracula was the epitome of evil. Not so for Fred Saberhagen. In his series of novels, Saberhagen saw Dracula as a misunderstood and maligned figure, the victim of the ignorant and malicious Dr. John Seward. In the second of his series of novels, *The Holmes–Dracula Files*, Saberhagen brought the two characters together but had to accommodate the plot to fit the reversal already made in *The Dracula Tape* (1975). The story revolved around a plot to destroy London during Queen Victoria's Diamond Jubilee celebration. The story was complicated by Dracula's being hit on the head, resulting in a case of amnesia. He could not remember who he was, not even his vampiric nature. To add a little color, he and Holmes were the spitting image of each other; even Holmes's companion, Dr. Watson, had trouble telling them apart. Could they, however, pool their resources to defeat the evil Dr. Seward?

After the double-barreled blast from Estleman and Saberhagen, it wasn't until the 1980s that Dracula and Holmes would again be brought together. They had a brief encounter in *Dracula's Diary* (1982), in which Dracula made a scenic tour of Victorian characters. Then in the early stages of the vampire's return to comic books in 1987, Dracula was pitted against several of his Victorian contemporaries from Jack the Ripper to Sherlock Holmes. On the centennial of "A Study in Scarlet," the first Holmes story, Martin Powell published *Scarlet in Gaslight*, a four-issue series that began with Holmes's traditional nemesis, Professor Moriarty, traveling to Transylvania to make common cause with Dracula. Holmes had been drawn into the count's domain, however, by the mother of Lucy

Westenra, who had begun to show mysterious symptoms of fatigue and blood loss. Holmes was sharp enough to trace Dracula to Lucy's bedroom in Whitby. In the end, however, he was unable to prevent her death.

Meanwhile, Moriarty had developed a plot to release a plague of vampires on London, though his alliance with Dracula had fallen apart. Eventually, Dracula and Holmes united to stop the professor. Dracula only wanted to have the now vampiric Lucy at his side. He was thwarted when she was killed (the true death) in the final encounters in London. The main characters survived to meet one last time at the famous falls in Switzerland, where Holmes faked his own death and, with relish, Dracula killed Moriarty. In *The Dracula Caper* (1988, the eighth in the *Time Wars* series by Simon Hawke), Holmes does not appear, but Doyle teams with Bram Stoker to save the world from Dracula. Another recent encounter between Holmes and Dracula found but a small audience of Holmes enthusiasts. Published in a limited edition, it quickly sold out. In *The Tangled Skein* (1995), author David Stuart Davies picked up the plot of *The Hound of the Baskervilles*, one of the most famous Holmes stories. Stapleton, the villain of the earlier story, returns to continue his evil but was soon surpassed by a series of bloody murders that served to bring Dr. Van Helsing into Holmes's territory. The two were forced to unite their efforts to deal with both Stapleton and Dracula.

> The possible encounter of Sherlock Holmes and a vampire has just been too tantalizing to leave alone; several authors have picked up the challenge....

The possible encounter of Sherlock Holmes and a vampire has just been too tantalizing to leave alone; several authors have picked up the challenge of keeping Holmes true to Doyle's character while sending him off to pit his mind against the irrational. Val Andrews's *Sherlock Holmes and the Longacre Vampire* (2001) begins with a series of unusual murders occasioned by, or at least associated with, the opening of *Dracula* in Henry Irving's theater (which, of course, never occurred). Holmes must move in to discover what lies behind the seemingly vampire-caused deaths. In Stephen Seitz's *Sherlock Holmes and the Plague of Dracula* (2006), Mina Murray engages Holmes's services to locate Jonathan Harker, her future husband, who has disappeared during his trip to Transylvania. Holmes must go east to encounter Dracula and bring his client's lost love back home. More recently, Holmes and Dracula have had one of their rare meetings in "Red Sunset" (2013) by Bob Madisen and in "Sherlock Holmes and Count Dracula: The Adventure of the Solitary Grave" (2017) by Christian Klaver, both short stories.

🦇 *Juvenile amd* 🦇 *Young Adult Literature*

Vampire fiction was exclusively an adult literature until the appearance of horror comic books in the 1940s. In the wake of the controversy over the hypothesized harmful content of comic books in the 1950s (which had the effect of banishing the vampire from their pages for two decades), no support existed for expanding the scope of juvenile literature in general by the inclusion of vampire stories. This condition would change radically in the 1970s.

The ban on vampires in comic books began to be lifted in the late 1960s with the appearance of *Dark Shadows* and *Vampirella*

and was done away with completely in 1971. That same year, the first novel written specifically for young people that included a vampire theme was published. *Danger on Vampire Trail* was No. 50 in the very popular *Hardy Boys* series of mystery books. The youthful detectives were tracking some credit card thieves, who they traced to a remote location called Vampire Trail. The site recently had been renamed following reported attacks by bats and, on an exploration of the trail, the Hardys found a dead vampire bat seemingly far away from his natural habitat. However, in the end, they found no vampires, and the bat turned out to have been imported from Central America simply to scare locals away from the crooks' hideout.

The 1970s: The real introduction of the juvenile audience to the subject came in 1973 with the publication of Nancy Garden's nonfiction *Vampires*. Based on two books by Montague Summers and the research of Radu Florescu and Raymond T. McNally, Garden presented a broad survey of vampire lore, the literary and cinematic vampire, and the reputed real Dracula, Vlad the Impaler. The obvious popularity of the vampire in this decade prompted two similar nonfiction vampire books by Thomas Aylesworth and Margaret and Eve Ronan. That same year, the first juvenile vampire novel, Vic Crume's *The Mystery in Dracula's Castle*, a novelization of the Walt Disney movie *The Mystery in Dracula's Castle*, concerned 12-year-old amateur movie producer–director Alfie Booth, who had decided to spend his summer making a Dracula movie. In the process, Alfie and his brother ran into several jewelry thieves, whose eventual detection and capture supplied the real drama of the movie. Thus, it was not until the last half of the decade that the initial real bloodsucking vampires made their appearances.

Among books aimed at a high school audience, evil vampires bared their teeth in Steven

Otfinoski's *Village of Vampires* (1978). The novel's hero, Dr. John Lawrence, his daughter Sandy, and assistant Paul Ross had journeyed to the village of Taaxacola, Mexico, where cows had begun to die of a strange malady. Several years before, Lawrence had been in the village to administer a serum to the cattle, which had been under attack from vampire bats. Upon his return, however, he discovered that the entire village now had been turned into vampires. It became the Lawrence party's task to kill them in the traditional manner (a stake through the heart). In the end, the men had to rescue Sandy, as she also was about to be made into a vampire. In Kin Platt's *Dracula Go Home!*, a 1979 comic novel, Larry Carter, a high schooler working at his aunt's hotel during summer vacation, checked a Mr. A. L. R. Claud from Belgrade into a room. The man was pale and wore a black suit with a large hat. He asked for Room 13. Larry was sure that Mr. Claud was a vampire and set out to find the proof. In the end, he was found not to be a vampire but a jewel thief who had returned to town to recover stolen merchandise.

For the younger audience still in elementary school, a more benign vampire strolled across the pages of a host of books. For example, in 1979, Deborah Howe and her husband, James Howe, introduced possibly the most lovable vampire of all time, the vegetarian vampire rabbit Bunnicula. Bunnicula, who was given his name after having been found in the theater during a Dracula movie, was the pet of Pete and Toby Monroe. The rabbit became the third animal pet in a home that already included Harold the dog and Chester the cat. Bunnicula was a strange rabbit; he slept all day and, instead of two bunny teeth in front, he had two fangs.

It was Chester who first spotted the rabbit leaving his cage at night to raid the refrigerator. The next morning, the Monroes discovered a white tomato from which all the juice and color

> The real introduction of the juvenile audience to the subject came in 1973 with the publication of Nancy Garden's nonfiction *Vampires*.

(and life) had been sucked. It was the knowledgeable Chester, who spent all of his spare time reading books, who was the first to determine that Bunnicula was a vampire. Having made his discovery, Chester proceeded to block Bunnicula's path to the kitchen with a garlic barrier. Bunnicula almost starved until Harold, concluding that Bunnicula was causing no harm, intervened and smuggled him into the kitchen.

Bunnicula proved as popular as he was lovable, and his story was made into a movie for children's television. Through the 1980s, he returned in a series of stories, beginning with the 1983 volume *The Celery Stalks at Midnight*. For the youngest audience, a vampire literature developed out of the popular television show *Sesame Street*, one of the most heralded products of PBS. The show specialized in the socialization of preschool children and the teaching of basic knowledge, such as the alphabet and numbers. Soon after the show began, the teaching of numbers became the special domain of Count von Count, a puppet version of a Bela Lugosi-like vampire, complete with a widow's peak and fangs. Through the 1970s, Count made such tapes as *The Count Counts* (1975) and was the subject of several books, including *The Counting Book* (1971), *The Count's Poem* (1976), *The Day the Count Stopped Counting* (1977), and *The Count's Number Parade* (1977).

The 1980s: The 1980s saw the development of a full range of vampire literature for all ages. Literature for the youngest children was launched with the continuing volumes featuring Count von Count of *Sesame Street*. He began the decade with *The Count's Counting Book* (1980). When the book's cover was opened, Count and his castle popped up to say, "Aha! Another wonderful day to count on." He then counted various things in his atmospheric neighborhood. In 1981, he followed with *The Count Counts a Party* and other items through the decade. For elementary school-aged people, several popular vampire series joined the *Bunnicula* titles. In 1982, for example, the first vol-

The story of a veggie-sucking, befanged bunny named Bunnicula was turned into a cartoon television series on Cartoon Network.

ume of Ann Jungman's series, featuring Vlad the Drac, another vegetarian vampire, appeared.

That same year in Germany, Angela Sommer-Bodenburg published the first of her four books featuring the young vampire Rudolph Sackville-Bagg, Rudolph's vampire sister Anna, and their human friend Tony Noodleman. These were promptly translated into English and published in the United States as *My Friend the Vampire*, *The Vampire Moves In*, *The Vampire on the Farm*, and *The Vampire Takes a Trip*. Typical of children's literature, the vampire was a somewhat sympathetic character, at worst a mischievous boy, with the primary elements of horror hovering in the background. *The Vampire Moves In*, for instance, revolved around Rudolph's move into the family storage bin in the basement of the apartment building where Tony's family lived. He had been kicked out of his own family vault because of his fraternizing with humans. The plot centered on the problems created by the vampire's presence, not the least of which was the terrible smell that began to radiate from the vampire's coffin and the presence of the undead.

A third series that began later in the decade by author Mel Gilden featured the "fifth-grade monsters." In the opening volume, *M Is for Monster*, Danny Keegan began a new school year as a fifth grader. His major problem was bully Stevie Brickwald. However, upon his arrival at school, he discovered four new classmates. One possessed a huge mane of hair and slightly pointed ears. His name was Howie Wolfner. A brother and sister team by the name of Elsie and Frankie Stein each had metal bolts coming out of the sides of their necks. The fourth new classmate was the short, fanged kid with slicked-back hair, a black suit, a white bow tie, and a satin-lined cape. His name was C. D. Bitesky, whose family came from Transylvania. C. D. carried a Thermos bottle, from which he frequently sipped a red liquid that he termed the "fluid of life," and he had a pet bat named Spike.

After an initial hesitancy, Danny became friends with these different but nonetheless special people and, within a few years, their adventures would fill 15 volumes, with no end in sight. C. D. was especially featured in Volume 10, *How to be a Vampire in One Easy Lesson* (1990), in which the persistent Stevie Brickwald tried to make friends with the "monsters" and asked C. D. to make him into a vampire. C. D. first invited him to his home, where his parents started to teach Stevie Romanian history. The impatient Stevie learned that he must meet the Count, C. D.'s patriarchal uncle, who lived in the basement of the local theater, appropriately named Carfax Palace. When Stevie appeared at school the next day dressed in a crumpled tuxedo following his private session with the Count, he announced that he was a "freelance vampire first class." Stevie wished to use his newfound "will" to keep him from having to go to school, but his teacher and the principal were finally able to persuade him that he was not a vampire.

The final vampire series aimed at elementary school-aged people to appear in the 1980s was written by Ann Hodgman. Her first volume, *There's a Batwing in My Lunchbox*, was published by Avon in 1988. The young people's vampire, while borrowing from the more traditional character of horror fiction, to some extent had his (and it has almost exclusively been a male) fangs pulled. He was a good person—definitely not the sinister figure of the adult novels or the movies.

Absent from the youthful vampire book was any hint of horror, any factor that might lead to the young reader having nightmares. He was never pictured as biting anyone, though oblique references existed, and, of course, no harm resulted from a vegetarian like Bunnicula biting a plant. Placed within the context of the young person's world, the vampire was either a lovable pet, a comic figure, or, more likely, a somewhat out-of-the-ordinary classmate who can become, in spite of his differences, a close friend.

As the number of titles for elementary school children expanded, so did the number aimed at high schoolers. Typical of these was *The Initiation* by Robert Brunn (1982). The story concerned Adam Maxwell, a student at Blair Prep School. Adam had a problem: he was a misfit. He was totally unappreciative of the elitism and snobbery so evident among both his classmates and the students of nearby Abbott, a girls' school similar to Blair. Both were founded by a Transylvanian couple, Isadore and Bella Esterhaus. Adam soon met his counterpart at Abbott, Loren Winters. Four days after his arrival to the school, Adam found a body in one of the school lockers. Loren had witnessed one of her classmates leaving campus with a man, who was reported dead the next day.

Together, Adam and Loren attempted to figure out the situation they were in. The focus

> The young people's vampire, while borrowing from the more traditional character of horror fiction, to some extent had his … fangs pulled. He was a good person.…

of their search led to an initiation ceremony that occurred during the biweekly mixers promoted by the two schools. Selected students were invited to the basement to be inducted into "a serious organization." Blindfolded and paired with an initiator of the opposite sex, they were attacked in the dark, and all that could be heard was a "wet slurping noise." In the 1970s, the vampire had received some recognition from the new respect given to classic horror and gothic fiction within the academic community—a respect reflected in the addition of such stories to elementary and high school curricula. By the 1980s, Bram Stoker's *Dracula* (1897) was recognized as a classic piece of horror literature, and condensed versions of *Dracula*, designed for a juvenile audience, began to appear.

In the early 1970s, a black-and-white comic version of *Dracula* (1973) became the first juvenile adaptation of the story, and a version for children was published in 1976 as *Paint Me the Story of Dracula*. Then, at the beginning of the next decade, Delacorte Press released Alice and Joel Schick's color comic book version of *Dracula*. Several years later, Stephanie Spinner and illustrator Jim Spence prepared a condensed version, often reprinted, for elementary schoolers. In addition, a juvenile version of John Polidori's original vampire story, "The Vampyre," appeared in England in 1986.

The 1990s: Through the 1980s, the production rate of new vampire-oriented juvenile literature had steadily increased. That increase did not stop in the early 1990s. In the 1980s, some 50 titles were published. In the three years from 1990 to 1992, over 35 titles appeared. Series begun in the 1980s by Mel Gilden, Ann Hodgman, and James Howe continued, and a new series for high schoolers, *The Vampire Diaries* by L. J. Smith, explored the triangle of vampire brothers Damon and Stefan

and high school girl Elena, whom they both desired and who was continually being forced to choose between them. For the youngest vampire fans, a pop-up version of *Dracula* was published by Gallery Books in 1990. Preschoolers could start their learning process with Alan Benjamin's board book *Let's Count, Dracula* (1991).

In the 1980s, two vampire stories were included in the very popular *Choose Your Own Adventure* series. A third such vampire volume, *Vampire Invaders* by Edward Packard, appeared as No. 118 in the series in 1991. Additionally, several general juvenile horror series added a vampire novel. Carl (pseudonym for Richard) Laymon's *Nightmare Lake*, for example, appeared as No. 11 in Dell's *Twilight* series. Burt Elliot, and his sister, Sammi, while on an island vacation, discovered a skeleton, after which their dog removed a stick protruding from its ribcage. The children reported their discovery to the police, but upon their return to the island, the skeleton had disappeared. The mystery increased when two bodies were found in a canoe. One had a bloody wound on his neck and, as was later determined, had died from loss of blood. The other person awoke in a state of near hysteria and complained of an attack by a bat. The emergence of vampire believers and skeptics set the stage for the final revelation of the true vampire in their midst.

Among the more outstanding of the new novels was Annette Curtis Klause's *The Silver Kiss*, which centered upon the experience of Zoë, a young girl with a fatally ill mother and an emotionally distant father, who tried to protect her from the reality of death. Her loneliness opened her to a relationship with Simon, a vampire. Simon had grown up in Cromwellian England. A business acquaintance of his father introduced vampirism to the family and chose

> In the early 1970s, a black-and-white comic version of *Dracula* (1973) became the first juvenile adaptation of the story, and a version for children was published in 1976 as *Paint Me the Story of Dracula*.

The 1999 animated TV series Mona the Vampire *is based on the Hiawyn Oram and Sonia Hollyman books about a girl who imagines she is a vampire fighting monsters invading her hometown.*

Simon's older brother Christopher as his first victim. Christopher disappeared for many years but, at one point, returned to attack his brother Simon, now a young man, and transform him into a vampire. He also learned that Christopher had killed their mother. Simon was determined to hunt down and kill his brother. That drive had brought him to America in the 1930s. Meanwhile, between her seemingly immortal friend, who was ready for a final encounter with his brother, and her dying mother, Zoë overcame her father's protecting her from the reality of death and arrived at some understanding of its role in life.

Of a lighter nature was *Great Uncle Dracula* by Jayne Harvey, a modern-day parable for children who feel they just do not fit in. It was the story of Emily Normal, a third grader who moved with her father and brother from Plainville to Transylvania, U.S.A., to live with her uncle. Soon after she arrived for her first day at school, she realized that Transylvania was a creepy place: all the girls dressed in black and

claimed to be witches; the class pets were tarantulas; her teacher's name was Ms. Vampira; and the principal was named Frank N. Stein. Emily just did not fit in. She had always done well as a speller, but the "spell"-ing bee did not concern "spelling" words but rather doing magic "spells." She soon made some friends, however, and, after a short time, she found herself at a party. However, the party turned into a disaster when Emily fell on the birthday cake while playing pin the tail on the rat. Emily finally got her chance to shine: in the grossest-face contest. Angry at being called names since her arrival at school, she won the contest by the face she made just as she shouted out, "I am not a weirdo." She was awarded the prize for making the grossest face anyone in Transylvania could ever remember.

Through the 1990s and the first decades of the new century, vampire storybooks for children and novels for youth have continued to proliferate. For the youngest, a series called *Mona the Vampire* by Hiawyn Oram and Sonia Hollyman would later inspire an animated television program. Young readers could also get into the *Monster Manor* series by Paul Martin and Manu Boisteau or the *My Sister the Vampire* series by Sienna Mercer. Slightly older readers could find the *Vampirates* series by Justin Somper, the *Vampire Plagues* series by Sebastian Rooke, and the *Vampire Beach* series by Alex Duvall.

Richie Tankersley Cusack's *Buffy the Vampire Slayer* (1992), the novelization of the movie, heralded the series of *Buffy* novels that would begin to appear after the television show began, which were originally pitched at a high school audience but found a much broader appeal. Continuing to appear into the second decade of the new century, eventually, more than 100 *Buffy* novels, some completely new stories and some novelizations of episode screenplays, were published.

Buffy the Vampire Slayer identified a youth market for vampire novels, and a number of authors responded to it. As the new century began, several series written for a junior high school and high school readership shared the spotlight with *Buffy* in the juvenile vampire market. Leading off the decade was Amelia Atwater-Rhodes, whose *In the Forests of the Night* (1999) was the first of a half dozen books built around vampires and associated creatures.

Among the most successful of the new vampire authors was Darren O'Shaughnessy, who wrote the *Cirque Du Freak* series under the pen name Darren Shan. His dozen novels traced the adventures of a young Darren Shan who, as he grew up, had to adjust to life as a half vampire.

High school vampire fans could assuage their thirst with the *House of Night* series by mother–daughter team P. C. and Kristin Cast, the *Vampire Kisses* series by Ellen Schreiber, *The Vampire Academy* series by Richelle Mead, the *Bloodline* series by Katy Cary, the *Lords of Darkness* series by L. G. Burbank, or the *Morganville Vampires* series by Rachel Caine.

> By far, the most successful post-*Buffy* vampire books were the *Twilight* series by Stephenie Meyer....

By far, the most successful post-*Buffy* vampire books were the *Twilight* series by Stephenie Meyer, which trace the story of a high school girl, Bella Swan, who by her own definition was clumsy and lacked self-assurance in the extreme. She meets the love of her life, a vampire classmate, Edward Cullen. *Twilight* was made into the largest-grossing vampire movie of all time and was followed by its equally successful sequel, *The Twilight Saga: New Moon.* After some years away from the series, Meyer returned to the *Twilight* world with *Midnight Sun* (2020), a revisiting of the original story of Bella and Edward but this time from Edward's perspective.

Keats, John (1795–1821)

John Keats, a British Romantic poet, was born in London, the son of Frances Jennings and Thomas Keats. His father, a livery stable keeper, was killed in 1804 after a fall from a horse. His mother remarried, but it proved an unhappy union, and she soon separated. She died in 1810 from tuberculosis. It was as his mother's condition worsened that Keats, never the scholarly type, began to read widely. He

especially liked the Greek myths. After his mother's death, he was apprenticed to a surgeon and, in 1814, moved to London to study at the joint school of St Thomas' Hospital and Guy's Hospital. He passed his examination in 1816 and began a career as a surgeon.

During his years in school in London, poetry came to dominate his leisure time. He was still in his teens when he wrote his first poems and, in 1815, he produced "On First Looking into Chapman's Homer," still hailed as one of the finest sonnets in the English language. At about this time, he met Leigh Hunt, also a poet, who introduced Keats into various literary circles. Keats's volume of verse was published in 1817. While the book did not do well, he decided to halt his surgical career to seek a quiet existence pursuing his poetry. Through the rest of the year, he produced "Endymion," "Ode to Psyche," "Ode to a Nightingale," and one of his most enduring efforts, "Ode on a Grecian Urn." Through 1819, he worked on "Otho the Great," "Hyperion," "The Eve of Saint Agnes," and "Lamia."

With "Lamia," he picked up the vampire theme, which was then becoming popular in Western literature. Interestingly enough, he began working on the poem soon after the publication of John Polidori's "The Vampyre" (the first piece of vampire fiction in English) in the *New Monthly Magazine*. At this time, Keats was under some financial strain, and his love affair with Fanny Brawne was having its ups and downs. He also had developed a full-blown case of tuberculosis, a wasting disease that occasioned the periodic spitting up of blood.

Keats's "Lamia" derived from the ancient account of the *lamiai*, the Greek vampire-like demons described by Philostratus in his *Life of Apollonius*. The story told of a *lamia* attempting to seduce a young man of Corinth. As he was about to marry the *lamia*, who would have turned on him and killed him, the wise Apollonius intervened. He unmasked her for what she was, and as he pointed out the illusionary environment she had created, its beauty faded away. She, of course, then departed. As Keats did not read Greek and no English translation of the *Life of Apollonius* had been published, he had to rely upon Richard Francis Burton's version of the story in his *Anatomy of Melancholy*.

Crucial to Burton's retelling was his deletion of a crucial sentence in Philostratus's text:

"… she admitted she was a vampire and was fattening up Menippus (Lucius) with pleasure before devouring his body, for it was her habit to feed upon young and beautiful bodies because their blood was pure and strong." Burton presented a somewhat sanitized *lamia*, but Keats metaphorically pulled her fangs even farther. To best understand "Lamia," one must view the story, as James B. Twitchell and other critics have done, as Keats's having adopted the vampire theme as a metaphor of human relations seen as the interchange of life-giving energies. In the process, Philostratus's story is changed considerably. According to Keats, in her thirst for love, the *lamia* dropped her traditional serpentlike form and moved into Lucius's human world. Lucius responded by becoming vampiric and attempting to gain some of the *lamia*'s former powers. Thus, Keats pictured the *lamia* using powers of psychic vampirism, drawing on Lucius's love as her metaphorical life blood. In return, Lucius also became a vampire, willing to drain all the blood from the *lamia* in order to gain new powers. Keats noted that Lucius had "drunk her beauty up." At this juncture, Apollonius appeared. He recognized the *lamia*

The famous Romantic poet John Keats included a vampire theme in his tragic verse "Lamia" (1820).

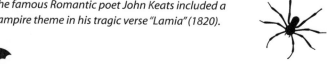

and, over Lucius's protests, drove her away. Without her, Lucius soon died.

Some critics of Keats's poetry have suggested that an even more unambiguous vampire existed in his poetry. In "La Belle Dame sans *Merci*," also composed in 1819, a knight met a lady with whom he became entranced. She fed him exotic foods and told him she loved him. He visited her underground home, where her mood changed to one of sadness. As the knight slept, he saw pale warriors and was told that he was soon to join them. After his awakening, while "palely loitering," he encountered the narrator of the poem. There, the poem ended.

As early as 1948, critic Edwin R. Clapp suggested that the unnamed female, the title character in "La Belle Dame sans Merci," was best understood as a vampire. Clapp, for example, noted the likeness of the victim of Polidori's vampire ("There was no color upon her cheek, not even upon her lip.") with images developed by Keats ("pale were the lips I saw/Pale were the lips I kiss'd ..."). Critic James B. Twitchell, picking up on Clapp, suggested that Keats had joined Samuel Taylor Coleridge in expanding upon the *lamia* myth and liberating it from the past. The *lamia* became a very real character, and the encounter of the male with the female, who had no pity, became a somewhat universal experience. More detailed analysis of the poem easily led to Freudian interpretations such as the one suggested by Ernest Jones, which tied the vampire–*lamia* myth to the initiation of adolescent males into the mysteries of sexuality.

Twitchell suggested that the *lamia* theme subtly reappeared in much of Keats's poetry, though "Lamia" and "La Belle Dame sans Merci" were its best examples. Keats, of course, went on to write many more poems, but in 1820, his health took a decidedly downward turn. He died on February 23, 1821, in Rome.

 Le Fanu, Sheridan (1814–1873)

Joseph Thomas Sheridan Le Fanu, poet and author of short stories in the horror genre, was born on August 28, 1814, in Dublin, Ireland. His father was chaplain of the Royal Hiberian Military School, and Le Fanu was born on its premises. His great-uncle was the heralded Irish dramatist Richard Brinsley Sheridan. At age 14, the young Sheridan composed a long Irish poem, which launched his literary career.

Le Fanu's formal literary career began in 1838, when "The Ghost and the Bone-Setter" was published in the *Dublin University Magazine*. Over the next 15 years, he wrote 23 stories and two novels. Most of these were set in Ireland and focused on aspects of the Irish character. With few exceptions, they have generally been judged as mediocre, in part due to Le Fanu's inability to relate to the Irish masses, whom he tended to stereotype because of the religious disagreements that separated him from them. However, he did begin his venture into supernatural horror, and in one of his stories, "Strange Event in the Life of Schalken the Painter," he touched on themes later developed in his most famous work, "Carmilla."

In 1861, Le Fanu purchased the *Dublin University Magazine*, which he edited for the next eight years. In the early 1860s, Le Fanu wrote four novels. He continued to write novels for the rest of his life, but they never gained a popular audience. It was his short stories that brought him public attention, and the year 1866 proved to be a watershed year: seven of his short stories appeared in Charles Dickens's

Besides Stoker, the other important Irish author who wrote about vampires and other gothic tales was Sheridan Le Fanu, who wrote "Carmilla".

All the Year Round, among the most prestigious periodicals in England. Le Fanu began a period of production of some masterful short literary pieces. At this time, he was becoming increasingly pessimistic about life in general and the course of Irish politics in particular. He seems to have drawn on the negative aspects of his own life in order to write some of the great supernatural horror tales of the period.

Critics agree that the stories published in his collection *In a Glass Darkly* (1872) are his best stories, though they would disagree on which one is actually the best. However, the one that has attained the highest level of fame, even after long neglect of Le Fanu's work, is "Carmilla." "Carmilla," only the third vampire story in English, is still one of the best. It told the story of Laura, the daughter of an Austrian civil servant named Karnstein, who was attacked by a female vampire variously named Carmilla, Mircalla, and Millarca. The story traced Laura's early childhood encounter with Carmilla, an

experience almost forgotten until the vampire reappeared when Laura was in her late teens. In the end, the victims and their families tracked Carmilla to her resting place and destroyed her. First published in several parts in *Dark Blue* magazine (December 1871 to March 1872), "Carmilla" provided a major building block of the modern vampire myth. It was read by Bram Stoker, a later resident of Dublin and, like Le Fanu, a graduate of Trinity College.

After his death in Dublin on February 7, 1873, Le Fanu's reputation drifted into almost a century of obscurity, although he had as fans such writers as Henry James and Dorothy Sayers. A major reason for his neglect by the literary elite seems to be the subject of his writing. For many decades, the great majority of literary critics held supernatural horror fiction in disdain and, thus, neglected its more able writers. As gothic fiction came into its own in the last half of the twentieth century, critical reappraisal of the genre quickly followed. The new era of appreciation of Le Fanu really began in 1964, when E. F. Bleiler completed an edited edition of the *Best Ghost Stories of J. S. Le Fanu*, published by Dover. Then in 1977, under the editorship of Devendra P. Varma, Arno Press released the 52-volume *Collected Works of Joseph Sheridan Le Fanu*.

It is among vampire fans, however, that Le Fanu is most remembered. Next to *Dracula* (1897), "Carmilla" has become the single vampire story most frequently brought to the screen and, like *Dracula*, it has inspired other stories of its leading vampire characters. Among the film versions of "Carmilla" are *Blood and Roses* (1960), *Blood and Black Lace* (1964), and *The Vampire Lovers* (1970).

One of its best adaptations is a made-for-television version entitled *Carmilla*, which was presented in 1989 on Showtime's *Nightmare Classics* series. Additional versions, all entitled simply *Carmilla* and more or less true to the original story, were made in 1999, 2000, and 2009. It has often been said that *Vampyr*, the classic vampire movie directed by Carl Theodor Dreyer, was based on "Carmilla" but, except for being a story about a female vampire, it bears little resemblance to "Carmilla." Le Fanu wrote a second, lesser-known story at least suggestive of vampirism, "The Room in the Dragon Volant," which was made into a movie, *The Inn of the Flying Dragon* (originally *Ondskans Vardshus*), in 1981.

Lee, Tanith (1947–2015)

Tanith Lee, a British writer of dark fantasy, began writing children's books, and in 1975, her first novel for adults, *The Birthgrave*, appeared. Born and educated in London, after secondary school, Lee studied art and held various jobs before becoming a writer. Her best work takes themes from horror, fantasy, and science fiction and integrates a feminist vision and a dark twist, which provides the vehicle for exploring some of the larger issues to which Lee speaks (the nature of morality, the individual's sense of control of their life, etc.). She attained some degree of fame for her retelling of children's stories with an adult twist in her *Red as Blood, or Tales from the Sisters Grimmer* (1983).

Vampiric themes began to appear quite early in her writings, such as *Kill the Dead* (1980) and, especially, *Sabella, or The Blood Stone* (1980), which begins with Sabella Quay, an 11-year-old resident of Mars, finding a plum-sized stone with a ring at one end, which she later began to wear all the time. When she was 14, she had her first sexual encounter and then killed the boy. Out of the experience, she came to understand that she really was not human. Though not of the undead, she lived a nocturnal existence because her blood was vulnerable to the rays of the sun. She finally learned not to kill the men with whom she had sex and took blood primarily from the deer in the nearby countryside. Along the way, her Aunt Cassi had figured out that Sabella was a vampire and left her niece a jeweled crucifix. However, Sabella settled into a nice existence with her lover, Jace, from whom she took blood and whom she allowed to dominate her, realizing that the victim had to be stronger than the oppressor or else he dies.

Possibly, Lee's most important vampire fiction is the *Blood Opera* series: *Dark Dance* (1992), *Personal Darkness* (1993), and *Darkness, I* (1994), which reveal the life of the Scarabae. The story begins as Rachaela Day, a seemingly normal and unexceptional woman, is called to her family home, where she meets her ageless relative and is seduced by the handsome Adamus (whom her mother had told her to avoid). She soon learns that she is part of a plan to

The late, prolific, sci-fi and fantasy author Tanith Lee earned numerous awards, including the Bram Stoker Award for Lifetime Achievement.

perpetuate the family. The three volumes follow Rachaela and her daughter Ruth's efforts to cope with their heritage.

Lee won numerous awards for her writings, including the World Fantasy Convention Award on two occasions. Additional vampire writings include *The Beautiful Biting Machine* (1984), a chapbook, and *The Blood of Roses* (1990). While repeatedly drawn to the vampire theme, she did not return to it in the last two decades of her life.

Matheson, Richard (1926–2013)

Richard Matheson, a screenwriter and science fiction/horror novelist, was born in Allendale, New Jersey. His first publications were science fiction stories, although it has been noted that at least a hint of horror had been part of his writing from the beginning. His first sale was a short story, "Born of Man and Woman" (1950), which then became the title of his first book (1954), a collection of his stories. His first vampire short story, "Drink My Red Blood," appeared in 1951 and has been frequently reprinted. It was three years later that he completed the novel that has been hailed as one of the classics of the vampire genre, *I Am Legend* (1954).

I Am Legend recounted the problem caused by a new bacterium that created an isotonic solution in human blood, from which it lived. It slowly turned humans into vampires. As the story developed, Robert Neville, who was immune to the bacteria, survived as the only untainted human. Most of the action took place at Neville's fortified home. He was opposed by his former neighbor, Ben Cortland, who led the vampire hordes in their search for fresh blood. As the bacteria invaded the body, they caused the canine teeth to elongate and turned the skin a pale gray-white color. The bacteria were killed by the light of the sun and by garlic and, thus, those infected adopted the habits of traditional vampires. Cortland was nearly unkillable. He survived bullets, knife wounds, and other normally fatal traumas. The bacteria im-

mediately sealed wounds. However, if a person was staked, the stake kept the wound open, and the bacteria died. At the end of the story, humans developed a vaccine that killed the germ.

Matheson occasionally returned to the vampire theme in his stories, including "The Funeral" (1955) and "No Such Thing as a Vampire" (1959), and he went on in his lengthy career to write several horror screenplays. His 1956 novel *The Incredible Shrinking Man* was made into a movie in 1957. He adapted several

Vincent Price sees all of humanity either dead or turned into zombies in 1964's The Last Man on Earth.

of Edgar Allan Poe's stories for the screen for producer Roger Corman. His novel *Bid Time Return* (1975) won the Howard Award as the best fantasy novel of the year.

I Am Legend has been adapted to the screen three times but without the use of Matheson's own screenplay. First, an Italian production, released in America as *The Last Man on Earth* (1964), starred Vincent Price. Then, *I Am Legend* served as the basis for the 1971 American production *The Omega Man*, starring Charlton Heston; however, in this latter production, the vampire theme was largely eliminated. The vampire theme was somewhat revived in the third attempt to bring *I Am Legend* to the screen (2007), starring Will Smith.

In 1968, Matheson's "No Such Thing as a Vampire" was brought to the television screen as an episode of the BBC's *Late Night Horror* show. Then in 1972, Matheson began a period of creative work with producer/director Dan Curtis. His first effort was a screenplay for the made-for-television movie *The Night Stalker*. Matheson's story of a vampire-hunting reporter became the most-watched made-for-television movie up to that time. On the heels of that success, he wrote the screenplay for Curtis's new production of *Dracula* (1974), starring Jack Palance in the title role. Then in 1975 and 1977, Matheson's short stories became the basis for two additional made-for-television movies, *Trilogy of Terror* and *Dead of Night*. The latter, directed by Curtis as the pilot for a never-produced series, brought "No Such Thing as a Vampire" to the screen again as one of three stories.

After a search for a cure for cancer unintentionally wipes out humanity and leaves some survivors as nocturnal mutants, Dr. Robert Neville (Will Smith) searches for a cure in I Am Legend *(2007). It is another adaptation of the 1954 Richard Matheson novel that also inspired* The Omega Man *and* The Last Man on Earth.

In 1989, the Horror Writers of America gave Matheson the first of two Bram Stoker Awards for the best volume of collected fiction for his *Richard Matheson: Collected Stories*. The following year, they presented him with the award for lifetime achievement. In 2006, Gauntlet Press, a publishing house specializing in editions for collectors, released a collection of Matheson's vampire writing under the title *Bloodlines*.

Paranormal Romance 🦇
Literature

According to the Romance Writers of America organization, the romance novel is defined by the prominence of two elements: a central love story, in which two individuals fall in love and struggle to make the relationship work, and a storyline ultimately brought to an emotionally satisfying and optimistic (that is, happy) ending, meaning that their relationship is rewarded with emotional justice and unconditional love. The story requires a strong female character who is searching, however consciously, for an ideal romantic love and whose feelings about the men she encounters are in the foreground as the novel proceeds. The male figure may approach any of a spectrum of ideals and is often pictured as larger than life relative to strength, courage, will, handsomeness, recklessness, ability to bear suffering, knowledge of women, and/or mystery.

Romance novels are usually written by women for a female audience, though a few men (usually writing under a female pen name) have proven successful masters of the genre. The primary storyline is usually the female character's account of events and, in many cases, is written in the first person.

The romance genre is often traced to the eighteenth century and the novel *Pamela, or Virtue Rewarded* (1740) by Samuel Richardson, one of the earliest popular novels to have a storyline written from the woman's point of view. Romantic writing was further popularized in the nineteenth century, Jane Austen being a noteworthy exemplar. Such novels both accepted the social roles into which women were pushed while providing an element of escape in romantic adventures. The genre blossomed in the twentieth century with British writers such as Barbara Cartland (1901–2000), who wrote over 700 novels, and Georgette Heyer (1902–1974), who invented the regency romance. Their careers blossomed in the 1930s and continued until shortly before their deaths.

> The romance genre is often traced to the eighteenth century and the novel *Pamela, or Virtue Rewarded* (1740) by Samuel Richardson, one of the earliest popular novels to have a storyline written from the woman's point of view.

The British company Mills and Boon was the first publisher specializing in romance titles, and Harlequin Enterprises, a Canadian publisher, emerged as their North American equivalent. Both companies initially specialized in historical romances, historical settings providing some rationale for the perpetuation of what many post–World War II readers began to see as outmoded emphases on traditional sexual mores. The success of the new romance novels with a modern setting, pioneered by Avon in the 1970s, led to the growth of the field in the 1980s and 1990s. By the beginning of the twenty-first century, romance novels accounted for about half of all the new paperback book sales in North America—much to the disdain of both writers and publishers in other fields. The most important romance publishing imprints include Avon, Dorchester, Kensington/Zebra, Dell, Berkley, Love Spell, and, of course, Harlequin (and its imprints, Mira and Silhouette).

The vampire theme in romance writing emerged in the 1970s with the burgeoning of gothic romance. This new wave of vampire novels appears to have been occasioned by the success of the television show *Dark Shadows* and the accompanying singular phenomenon of Daniel Ross, who wrote numerous romance novels under the pseudonym Marilyn Ross. He began to produce original stories (all quickly written) using the characters and settings of the popular television show late in 1966. The first six (1966–1968) featured Victoria Winters, but with the addition of the vampire Barnabas Collins, by the end of 1968, the stories moved to him and the women in his life. Ross would go on to author more than 20 additional *Dark Shadows* novels over the next three years.

In the wake of the popularity of *Dark Shadows*, writers of gothic romances found that

Actor Jonathan Frid played the vampire Barnabas Collins in the seminal horror TV series Dark Shadows, *which originally ran from 1966 to 1971.*

dropping vampires into their novels was relatively easy. In the three years from 1969 to 1971, more than a dozen romance novels appeared, including titles by Dorothea Nile (a pen name of Michael Avallone), Barbara Michaels, Virginia Coffman, Elna Stone, and Florence Stevenson. Ross would even contribute one non-*Dark Shadows* novel under another of his pseudonyms, Clarissa Ross, while Stevenson would go on to write additional vampire romance novels into the 1980s.

Through the 1980s, vampires would show up sporadically in the occasional romance novel but would not again enjoy anything like the presence it had manifested in the early 1970s until the mid-1990s. By this time, the romance genre had expanded to the point that numerous subdivisions had emerged, among them the paranormal romance. Paranormal romance was envisioned as encompassing a variety of phenomena: ghosts, witches, werewolves, time travelers, and vampires. Most importantly, Anne Rice, whose novels were seen by many as

approaching the romance genre, was enjoying great success, and Laurell K. Hamilton was beginning her emergence into prominence.

Heralding the new wave of vampire romance novels was Lori Herter, who issued four vampire romance novels in the early 1990s, and Maggie Shayne, who issued her first vampire romance in 1993. Then in 1994–1995, following the release of the movie version of Rice's *Interview with the Vampire*, more than a dozen vampire-related romance novels suddenly appeared. Maggie Shayne (aka Margaret Benson) was already producing a vampire romance series and would now be joined by Linda Lael Miller and Amanda Ashley (aka Madeline Baker). Miller's *For All Eternity* and Ashley's *Embrace the Night* launched two new vampire series. While a number of popular romance writers would attempt a single vampire novel, Miller and Ashley began to redefine the field, suggesting that vampire romances could become more than just another occasional option for paranormal romances.

By the end of the 1990s, however, some editors at the different houses specializing in romance novels diverged significantly in their view of the vampire. While many felt that the vampire was a passing fad and that its time had come and gone, a growing number, taking note of continuing high sales figures and the popularity of *Buffy the Vampire Slayer*, persisted in accepting them and even solicited new vampire novels. In 1999, two new and very successful vampire series were initiated by Christine Feehan and Shannon Drake (aka Heather Graham Pozzessere).

Through the early years of the new century, publishers, one by one, recognized that vampires had carved out a secure niche in the expanding romance field. At the same time, writers who were unable to find a publisher took their novels to publish-on-demand (POD) printers and issued their books in both electronic and trade paperback formats. A few writers who initially demonstrated their ability with POD houses such as Ellora's Cave were able to jump to one of the larger romance publishing houses. By the end of the decade, more than 50 writers, almost all women, had written and published multiple vampire titles. A few, like Charlaine Harris, became superstars, but a number found fame among existing fans for their writing of vampire novels: Nina Bangs, MaryJanice Davidson, Sherrilyn Kenyon, Katie MacAleister, Lynsay Sands, Susan Sizemore, Kerrelyn Sparks, Susan Squires, and J. R. Ward.

At the same time, several romance writers had been able to adapt their vampire novels toward a high school and even junior high school audience. The field had been opened by *Buffy the Vampire Slayer* and its many spin-off novels (at one point, 18 were being published annually). The novels of Stephenie Meyer, P. C. and Kristin Cast, and Ellen Schreiber opened the vampire realm to young women, a space previously inhabited almost exclusively by young males. In the wake of the success of Stephenie Meyer's *Twilight* series, an early young adult romance series, *The Vampire Diaries* series, written by Lisa Jane Smith and originally published in the 1990s, was reprinted and adapted into a hit television show.

> By the end of the decade, more than 50 writers, almost all women, had written and published multiple vampire titles.

The romance field is served by the Romance Writers of America (RWA), its primary professional organization, and the *Romantic Times (RT)*, its primary trade magazine. Amid a variety of romance awards given annually by various organizations, those offered by the RWA and the *RT* are the most coveted. The Romance Writers of America has, since 1982, given annual awards (known since 1990 as the Rita Awards) for excellence in the field. Authors of vampire romances were recognized only recently by the Ritas, which have been awarded to Maggie Shayne (2005), Kresley Cole (2007), and J. R. Ward (2008). In 2007, Linda Lael Miller won the RWA's Nora Roberts Lifetime Achievement Award.

The *RT* began issuing awards in 1987, the first for the years 1986–1987. Initially issued to authors for a body of work, the *RT* added a second award for best books in 1995. The first writer known primarily for her vampire-oriented titles to be honored was Heather Graham (Pozzessere), who received awards in 1988–1989, 1991–1992, and 2000. In the mid-1990s, Fantasy was added as a category, and Maggie Shayne (1995, 1998, and 2000) and Linda Lael Miller (1997) received awards. Madeline Baker (aka Amanda Ashley) and Christine Feehan received awards in 1999 and 2003.

In 2004, the Paranormal Romance category was first recognized with three separate awards. Among the early recipients were Kelley Armstrong (2004), who has written primarily about werewolves (but ones who live in a world also inhabited by vampires), and

Fantasy author Kelley Armstrong is known for her books set in worlds inhabited by werewolves as well as vampires.

Susan Sizemore (2005). For the first time, in 2006, Vampire Paranormal Romance was recognized as a separate category, the first award for career achievement going to J. R. Ward. That same year, the number of categories was significantly increased in recognition of both the growth of the field and the emergence of new subgenres, and both Charlaine Harris and Linda Lael Miller were also recognized in other categories.

In 2007, the number of categories would be radically cut back, and the vampire and paranormal categories collapsed into a single Paranormal award, received by Angela Knight largely for her werewolf/vampire crossover novels. The same award would go to the writing team of C. T. Adams and Cathy Clamp, who wrote both a vampire and a werewolf series. Heather Graham and Keri Arthur also received awards in other categories.

When the *RT* began its awards for best books in 1995, fantasy was an established cat-

egory, and the first award went to Susan Krinard for her vampire book, *Prince of Dreams*. Maggie Shayne would receive the award in 1997. In 2000, an award for Best Vampire Paranormal Romance was added, and Christine Feehan won the first and the second in 2001. In 2002, the award went to Sherrilyn Kenyon, though Feehan also won for Best Historical Paranormal Fantasy. In 2003, the vampire award went to Susan Sizemore, with additional Paranormal awards going to Kelley Armstrong and Thea Devine.

In 2004, the Best Vampire Novel award went to MaryJanice Davidson, with additional awards going to Kim Harrison and Angela Knight. Sherrilyn Kenyon walked away with the Best Vampire Novel award in 2005, with additional recognition of a vampire title going to C. T. Adams and Cathy Clamp. J. R. Ward had the best vampire title in 2006, with additional vampire titles by Angela Knight also receiving an award. Ward again won the vampire award in 2007; additional vampire books also receiving awards included books by P. C. and Kristin Cast, Kim Harrison, and Jeaniene Frost. Michele Bardsley won her first award for her vampire novel in 2008, with Paranormal awards going to MaryJanice Davidson, Sherrilyn Kenyon, and Jeanne C. Stein. In 2007, the *RT* had given its first award to the best book in the *Silhouette Nocturne* series. In 2008, that award went to Anne Rice for her new vampire title.

Through the second decade of the twenty-first century, the Romance Writers of America gave its Paranormal Romance Best Novel award to multiple vampire novels. Kresley Cole won twice for *Kiss of a Demon King* (2020) and *Shadow's Claim* (2013) and J. R. Ward for *Dearest Ivie* (2019), the last being granted just prior to the RWA discontinuing its awards altogether. Meanwhile, other vampire novels were recognized in other categories, including *The Problem with Forever* by Jennifer L. Armentrout as the best young-adult romance novel in 2017.

Poetry, Vampires in

It is not surprising that writers found poetry to be a natural vehicle of expression for the vampire theme. Poetry speaks with some facility to the intense passions and dark concerns that have been suppressed by conventional society. It relates the central human needs of love and community (family) commonly celebrated by society with other key concerns of death and sexuality. The latter concerns, while just as important to human life, are often neglected and the emotions attached to them denied, while discussion of them has been pushed to the fringe of social discourse.

The vampire, especially after its unreality was established by Enlightenment science, became an ideal vehicle for writers to express their own complex feelings and to make visible their personally frightening experiences. The dead-yet-alive vampire, blending into the shadows of society, obsessed with blood (and other body fluids), embodies the darker but no less real side of human existence. Given any of the commonly accepted positive human virtues/emotions, the literary vampire immediately juxtaposed in his or her person both the lights and shadows of the author's life.

The Vampire in Germany: The emergence of the modern literary vampire began with the exploration of the vampiric theme in the poetry of Germany. More than a generation prior to John Polidori's famous 1819 novella "The Vampyre," poets were reacting to the intense debate on the subject of vampirism that was taking place in the German universities in the mid-eighteenth century. Possibly the first such poem was "Der Vampir," written by Heinrich August Ossenfelder:

> My dear young maiden clingeth
> Unbending, fast and firm
> To all the long-held teaching
> Of a mother ever true;
> As in vampires unmortal

> Folk on the Theyse's portal
> Heyduck-like do believe.
> But my Christian thou dost dally,
> And wilt my loving parry
> Till I myself avenging
> To a vampires health a-drinking
> Him toast in pale tockay.
> And as softly thou art sleeping
> To thee shall I come creeping
> And thy life's blood drain away.
> And so shalt thou be trembling
> For thus shall I be kissing
> And death's threshold thoult be
>   crossing
> With fear, in my cold arms.
> And last shall I thee question
> Compared to such instruction
> What are a mother's charms?

Many similar poems show up in the collections of other poets. More important than any of these specifically vampire poems,

Lenora and her love, William, as depicted by illustrator Johann David Schubert, c. 1800.

however, was Gottfried August Bürger's "Lenora" (also translated as "Lenore," "Leonore," or "Ellenore"). "Lenora" told the story of William, a young man who died but came back to claim his bride. Arriving in the middle of the night, he called his unsuspecting Lenora to travel with him to their bridal bower. She responded:

> "Say on, where is our bridal hall?
> Where, how the nuptial bower?
> Far, far from here! Still, cool, and
>   small,
> Where storms do never lower.
> Hast room for me.
> For me and thee.
> Come up and dress and mount
>   with me!
> The wedding guests are waiting
> No more of this debating!"

After a ride across the country at breakneck speed, William spoke again:

> "In somber gloom we near the
>   tomb
> With song and wailing tearful!
> Come, open stands the bridal
>   room,
> Though all around look fearful.
> Come sexton, quick! Come with
>   the choir,
> Our bridal song with reed and
>   lyre!
> Come, priest, and say the blessing,
>
> Nor wait for our confessing."

The couple rode into the graveyard:

> "High reared the steed and wildly
>   neighed;
> Fire from his nostrils started.
> And lo! from underneath the maid
> The earth to 'dmit them parted.

While not a vampire poem, "Lenora" does play upon the themes of love and death,

German poet Gottfried August Bürger, author of what is considered the first vampire poem, "Lenora."

which are so essential to the vampire's life. Denounced by the literary critics, it nevertheless found a popular following. In the 1790s, it was translated into English by William Taylor of Norwich and, for several years, circulated around Norwich as a favored topic for poetry reading/discussion groups, which were at the time a widespread entertainment event. Sir Walter Scott heard of "Lenora" from the discussions of Taylor's as-yet-unpublished poem and went about securing a copy of the original German text. Upon reading it, he, too, became enthusiastic and chose to make his own translation of the ballad the initial publication of his lengthy literary career. Published the same year as Taylor's translation, it became by far the more popular version. The importance of "Lenora" was further demonstrated by the fact that at least three additional translations were made in 1796 alone and others in subsequent years.

In Germany, "Lenora" inspired what has been traditionally called the first vampire poem, "The Bride of Corinth" ("Die Braut von Korinth"), published in 1797 by Johann Wolfgang von Goethe. In most later commentaries on the vampire in literature, Goethe was said to have based his poem on the account from ancient Greece of the encounter of the philosopher Apollonius with a *lamiai*. However, it is, in fact, a retelling of another story: that of Philinnon as related by Phlegon. Goethe's version told of a young man who had traveled to Athens to claim his bride, the daughter of his father's comrade.

Shown into a guest room after his travels by the woman of the house, he was surprised by the arrival of a beautiful, young woman at his door. He noted her paleness but, nevertheless, invited her in. She wanted a lock of his hair. He offered her wine, but she would not drink until midnight, at which time she assumed a new vitality. As dawn approached, the mother heard the activity of the two lovers and burst into the room. The girl turned out to be the recently deceased daughter of the family. She had returned from her grave to find that her love had denied her. Before she left, she told the young man that he would soon join her in death and asked her mother to see that their bodies were burned. She had been given an ineffective Christian burial and was now roaming the land without the peace of death.

The Vampire in England: "Lenora" and "The Bride of Corinth" became standard reading for the emerging Romantic movement and the poets who were exploring their inner consciousness. Both Shelley and Lord Byron were enthusiastic about it, and "Lenora" directly influenced Samuel Taylor Coleridge and Robert Southey, who shared the honors for producing the first vampire poems in English. Geraldine, the vampiric figure in Coleridge's 1801 poem "Christabel," was never identified as a vampire but did, as Arthur H. Nethercot effectively argued, have many of its characteristics. The first hint that something was wrong with Ger-

aldine was revealed as Christabel assisted Geraldine, who had appeared outside the castle walls, into her castle home:

> The lady Geraldine sank, belike
>   through pain,
> And Christabel with might and
>   main
> Lifted her up, a weary weight,
> Over the threshold of the gate:
> Then the lady rose again,
> And moved, as she were not in
>   pain.

Coleridge seemed to be making reference to the vampire's inability to enter a home without first being invited, now a standard aspect of vampire lore. Then, Christabel's father's dog gave an uncharacteristic "angry" moan as Geraldine passed; vampires have a strange effect on animals. As Christabel showed her guest to a place of rest, Geraldine noted that the midnight hour was hers.

> Coleridge seemed to be making reference to the vampire's inability to enter a home without first being invited, now a standard aspect of vampire lore.

The two women lay together, and Christabel took Geraldine in her arms.

During Geraldine's hour, Christabel entered a trancelike state while all the night birds quieted their chirping. The following morning, Christabel awoke refreshed as one who had "drunken deep of all the blessedness of sleep!"

While Coleridge must be credited with writing the first English-language vampire poem, Southey was the first to introduce a traditional vampire as a character in one of his poems. In the poem "Thalaba the Destroyer," the hero, Thalaba, had a brief encounter with a vampire, his recently deceased bride, Oneiza, who had died on their wedding day. He was forced to kill her anew by thrusting a lance through her. Southey based his addition of the vampire character to his poem upon reading accounts of the Eastern European vampires—the same ones that had, a half century earlier, caused the debate over vampires in Germany.

Once introduced into British poetry, the vampire made a number of appearances throughout the early nineteenth century. Possibly the first poem dedicated to the vampire was John Stagg's "The Vampyre," published in his 1810 collection *The Minstrel of the North*. Like Southey, Stagg derived the material for his poem from reading the Eastern European vampire reports. It related a vampire's attack on Herman, the young husband of Gertrude. Herman was under attack from his recently deceased friend Sigismund:

> From the drear mansions of the
>   tomb,
> From the low regions of the
>   dead,
> The ghost of Sigismund doth
>   roam,
> And dreadful haunts me in my
>   bed!
> There vested in infernal guise,
> By means to me not understood,
> Close to my side the goblin lies,
> And drinks away my vital blood!

As he predicted, Herman died that night, and a frightened Gertrude saw Sigismund at their house. The next day, Sigismund's tomb was opened, and his body was found "still warm as life, and undecay'd." The townspeople drove a stake through the bodies of both Sigismund and Herman.

Stagg was followed by Lord Byron's "The Gaiour," the story of an "infidel," a term for non-Muslims in Islamic lands. As an infidel, the story's hero was cursed by a Muslim to become a vampire and roam the earth, sucking the blood of those closest to him. John Keats's

"Lamia" (1819) drew inspiration from the ancient account of Apollonius and the *lamiai*, though the translation he used lacked the key original reference to the vampire. In Keats's poem, the *lamiai* established a vampiric relationship, a form of psychic vampirism, with Lucius, her human love.

Keats also drew on the vampiric relationship in several other poems, such as "La Belle Dame sans Merci." After Keats, however, the vampire appeared only rarely in English literature. Henry Thomas Liddell, a youthful James Clark Maxwell, and Arthur Symons were among the authors who made the few British contributions to the genre between the Romantics and the 1897 effort of poet laureate Rudyard Kipling. Kipling's brief "The Vampire" was a lament to the "rag and a bone and a hank of hair," that is, the "woman who did not care" for the man who worshipped her. Kipling's poem was inspired by a painting of a beautiful woman looking down on the man who had died out of love unreturned. It was memorable as a defiant statement about the vamp, the nonsupernatural femme fatale, the subject of numerous silent movies, epitomized by the characters portrayed by actress Theda Bara.

The French Poetic Vampire: In France, the vampire emerged after the 1819 novella by Polidori. It found its most expansive expression in drama, with the production of no fewer than five French vampire plays within two years. In the nineteenth century, however, the short story was the primary vehicle for the vampire's French apparitions. Few poets made reference to the vampire. Among these was Théophile Gautier, more notable for his vampire stories but who, in 1844, also wrote "Les Taches Jaunes." A man who had lost his love sat alone and noted:

> But there are yellow bruises on
>   my body

And violet stains;
Though no white vampire come
    with lips blood-crimsoned
To suck my veins!
Then, he asked:
Oh, fondest of my loves, from
    that far heaven
Where thou must be,
Hast thou returned to pay the
    debt of kisses
Thou owest me?

A decade later, when Charles Baudelaire began his probings of the human experience, he dedicated his poems, including his vampire poems, to Gautier.

Baudelaire succeeded in outraging even French society in the mid-nineteenth century. His poems "The Vampire" and "Les Métamorphoses du Vampire," which appeared in the 1857 collection *Les Fluers du Mal*, earned him a trial for obscenity. In the latter, for example, he described the morning-after relationship of a man and woman. The man lamented:

Also noted for being an early translator of Poe, poet Charles Baudelaire came under fire for obscenity after publishing two poems about vampirism.

When out of all my bones she
    had sucked the marrow
And as I turned to her, in the act
    to harrow
My senses in one kiss, to end her
    chatter,
I saw the gourd that was filled
    with foul matter!

The New Wave of Vampire Poetry: In the twentieth century, the vampire made an increasing number of appearances. Notable among the poems early in the century was the Irish writer James Joyce's brief vampire poem, which was embedded in *Ulysses*:

On swift sail flaming
From storm and south
He comes, pale vampire
Mouth to my mouth.

In this brief poem, Joyce draws on the flying Dutchman legend as treated in Richard Wagner's opera, to which Joyce added mention of the vampire, an image that he uses in several places in *Ulysses*. Wagner, in turn, had been inspired by *Der Vampyr*, the opera by Heinrich August Marschner. Joyce's fellow countryman, magician and poet William Butler Yeats, also penned a brief vampire verse titled "Oil and Blood":

In tombs of gold and lapis lazuli
Bodies of holy men and women
    exude
Miraculous oil, odour of violet.
But under heavy loads of tram-
    pled clay
Lie bodies of the vampires full of
    blood:
Their shrouds are bloody and
    their lips are wet.

In the twentieth century, American poets appropriated the vampire and, as the century progressed, they seemed to have become the largest community of poets to make use of it.

Among the first was Conrad Aiken. He initially composed a poem, "La Belle Morte," inspired by Gautier's "La Morte Amoureuse," but his "The Vampire" (published in 1914) was a delightful piece of light verse:

> She rose among us where we lay.
> She wept, we put our work away
> She chilled our laughter, stilled
>   our play;
> And spread a silence there.
> And darkness shot across the sky,
> And once, and twice, we heard
>   her cry;
> And saw her lift white hands on
>   high
> And toss her troubled hair.

Aiken described the beautiful vampire, who had affected all (at least all of the males) who saw her, like this:

> "Her eyes have feasted on the
>   dead,
> And small and shapely is her
>   head,
> And dark and small her mouth,"
>   they said,
> "And beautiful to kiss;
> Her mouth is sinister and red
> As blood in moonlight is."

During the pulp era, as the horror short story in general, and the vampire short story in particular, found a new audience, the number of vampire poems showed a marked increase, but it was nothing to compare to the flood of vampire poems that have appeared since World War II. In recent generations, with the development of a noticeable vampire subculture and the rise of vampire fanzines, a flurry of poetic efforts have responded to a community that lives for the vampire and finds its inspiration in the shadowy side of life. More than half of all the vampire poems ever written have been published

More than half of all the vampire poems ever written have been published since 1970.

since 1970. They have been regularly featured in various vampire magazines from such purely literary magazines as Margaret Louise Carter's *The Vampire's Crypt* to the more general periodicals, such as *Realm of the Vampire, Bloodlines, Fresh Blood, Onyx, Shadowdance,* and *Nefarious.*

Contemporary vampire poems, like poetry in general, tend to be short and revel in images and the feelings of the poet. They stand in sharp contrast to the epic storytelling verse of the nineteenth century. Also, contemporary poets celebrate the vampire and the dark images of life in the evening, whereas nineteenth-century poets tended to operate in the sunlight and point the finger of moral judgment—or, at the very least, the righteous indignation of a wronged lover—at the vampires who inhabited their imaginations. Common to both the newer and older poetry is the use of the vampire as a metaphor to highlight the different levels of power assumed as lovers come together and the willingness of the more dominant partner to take from the other and leave them empty. Some of the distinct flavor of the poetry of this generation, as well as the continuing common theme, was vividly illustrated in a poem by Ryan Spingola that appeared in *Nefarious* (1993):

> I was never what you wanted
> but my blood will serve your pur-
>   pose
> quench your hunger for a short
>   time
> use me, I give you my life and
>   soul
> they mean nothing to me now
> you always had my soul
> Since that day long ago
> now you don't want it
> my blood is all you want
> you'll take it and leave me
> lying on the cold floor to die
> alone and drained
> of my very life

The vampire revival of the 1990s provided space for poetry on vampires, whose rich imagery supplies poets with endless quantities of inspiration.

Serving as an early venue for the new vampire-oriented poets was Preternatural Press, located in Silver Spring, Maryland, which published a number of volumes through the mid-1990s and, beginning in 1990, issued an annual periodical, *Rouge et Noir: Les poemes des Vampires*. *Rouge et Noir* was succeeded by *Dreams of Decadence: Vampire Poetry and Fiction*, a literary magazine that appeared in 1995, which soon picked up national distribution and continued to appear into the new century. Along with the more serious efforts at poetry represented by *Rouge et Noir* and *Dreams of Decadence*, poetry served as a vehicle for humor, nowhere more vividly demonstrated than in the three massive, self-published volumes by Vlad Tepid, aka Count Flapula.

In the new century, poetry, like many things vampiric, shifted to the internet. Few indeed were publications such as Maria Alexander and Christina Kiplinger Johns's *Biting Midnight: A Feast of Darksome Verse* (2002). Instead, online, vampire poetry has found a home, and a number of sites and many works are featured on the poetry pages of the Vampire Legacy Society, the Realms of Darkness, and the Vampire Forum. Several more or less ephemeral poetry groups have operated under the name Undead Poets Society. While yet to make the impact of fiction writers, vampire poets have kept their art very much alive.

Vampire fans are indebted to the Count Dracula Fan Club (now the Vampire Empire) and compiler Steven Moore for the publication *The Vampire Verse: An Anthology*. It is a comprehensive collection of vampire-oriented poems up to the modern era, with a sampling of contemporary verse. It also has an extensive bibliography of additional contemporary vampire poems.

Germany and Austria also have a significant tradition of vampire poems, some quite serious and some parodies and even limericks. A collection of such texts is found in Simone Frieling's *Von Fledermäusen und Vampiren. Geschichten und Gedichte* (2003).

Polidori, John (1795–1821)

John Polidori was the author of "The Vampyre," the first modern vampire story. As a teenager, he attended Edinburgh University, from which he received his medical degree at the age of 19. He wrote his thesis in 1815 on the nightmare. Even as his age put obstacles in his way to opening a medical practice, he had ambitions to become a writer. He was delighted to be invited to be the traveling companion of Lord Byron, who was leaving England for a tour of continental Europe in the spring of 1816. In Geneva, they were joined by Claire Clairmont, Mary Godwin, and Percy Shelley.

Several days later, occasioned in part by bad weather that limited their movements, Byron suggested that each person begin a "ghost" story. He primed the pump somewhat by reading some tales from *Fantasmagoriana* to the small group. One evening, each began a story, but Mary Godwin was the only one who took the project seriously. Her story eventually grew into the novel *Frankenstein*. Polidori began a story about a skull-headed lady who was punished for peeking through a keyhole but, like the rest, soon lost interest in developing it very far.

Polidori kept a journal of his experiences in Europe, including some detailed notes on the evening of the storytelling and, most importantly, a synopsis of Byron's story. It con-

John Polidori's story "The Vampyre" was based on a story fragment by Lord Byron and featured some now common tropes, such as the aristocratic vampire who preyed on attractive women.

cerned two friends traveling in Greece, where one of them died. Before his death, however, he extracted an oath from the other that he reveal nothing about the conditions leading to his death. Upon his return to England, he discovered his dead friend very much alive and having an affair with his sister.

Byron saw no future in his story, so he abandoned it. Polidori, however, after severing his relationship with his employer, took Byron's summer tale and developed the meager plot into a short story of his own. "The Vampyre" was published in the April 1819 issue of *New Monthly Magazine*. He took at least a light swing at Byron in his choice of the name of the vampire, Lord Ruthven, the name chosen by Byron's former lover, Caroline Lamb, to lampoon Byron in her novel, *Glenarvon*. In addition, through no fault of Polidori, the story was published under Lord Byron's name, which caused it to receive far more immediate attention than it otherwise would have gotten.

Goethe pronounced it Byron's best work, and it was quickly translated into French and

hailed as a new Byron masterpiece. The May issue of *New Monthly Magazine* included Polidori's explanation of the circumstances surrounding the writing of "The Vampyre," and Byron wrote a letter to *Gallignani's Magazine* in Paris, but by then, it was too late. *New Monthly Magazine's* owner continued his insistence that he had published an original Byron story and emphasized the assertion by publishing it separately as a stand-alone book, also under Byron's name.

One can only speculate what might have happened had the story been published under Polidori's name and without the controversy with Byron. With Byron's unwanted assistance, the story launched the first wave of interest in the vampire in Western Europe and went on to become, with the exception of *Dracula*, the most influential vampire tale of all time. The

THE

V A M P Y R E;

𝕬 𝕿ale.

LONDON:

PRINTED FOR SHERWOOD, NEELY, AND JONES,

PATERNOSTER-ROW.

1819.

[Entered at Stationers' Hall, March 27, 1819.]

After Stoker's Dracula, *John Polidori's* The Vampyre: A Tale, *published in 1819, is often considered the most important fiction work in the genre.*

young Parisian Romantics immediately saw its potential. Cyprien Bérard wrote a lengthy sequel detailing further adventures of its vampire character, *Lord Ruthwen ou les Vampires* (1820). Charles Nodier, who wrote the preface to the French translation of "The Vampyre," turned the plot into a three-act play. The play launched a theatrical fad that saw five Paris playhouses offering vampire productions by the end of the year. Lord Ruthven periodically reappeared onstage over the next 30 years, his last ventures being recounted by Alexandre Dumas in 1852.

Unfortunately, Polidori did not live to see the far-reaching results of his story. His life took a negative turn and, in 1821, he committed suicide. He was 26 years old.

Ruthven, Lord

Eight decades before anyone had heard of Dracula, the vampire Lord Ruthven was created by John Polidori and introduced to the world in the first vampire short story, "The Vampyre," which was published in 1819. Within a few years, Lord Ruthven would appear on both the Paris and London stage and inspire a generation of literary activity. "The Vampyre," derived from a story fragment written by Lord Byron, was developed by Polidori after his hostile break with Byron, who served as the model for the leading character. The story concerned Aubrey, a wealthy young man who became friends with Lord Ruthven, a mysterious stranger who entered London society. Ruthven was pale in complexion and somewhat cold in demeanor, but he was a favorite of the women. He freely loaned money to people to use at the gaming tables, but those who accepted his money generally lost it and were led further into debt and eventual degradation.

As Polidori had accompanied Byron on a continental journey, so, too, in the story, Aubrey traveled to Rome with Ruthven, where he became upset at Ruthven's attempts to seduce the young daughter of an acquaintance. Unable to stop his course of action, Aubrey left Ruthven and went on to Greece without him. In Greece, he found himself attracted to Ianthe, the daughter of the innkeeper. It was she who introduced him (and the reader) to the legend of the vampire. While Aubrey lost himself in his new relationship and the visiting of the local sights, Ruthven arrived. A short time later, Ianthe was attacked and killed by a vampire. Aubrey, recovering from his loss and not yet connecting Ruthven with his newly acquired knowledge of the vampire, rejoined him to travel around Greece. As they journeyed across the country, they were attacked by bandits. Ruthven was killed in the attack, but before he died, he made Aubrey swear to conceal the manner of his death and of any crimes he might have committed for the period of a year and a day. The bandits carried Ruthven's body to a nearby site, where it would be exposed to the moon's light. Aubrey returned to London and, along the way, began to realize that Ruthven destroyed all upon whom he showered his favors, especially the women who became his lovers. Soon, the seemingly deceased Ruthven reappeared in London and reminded Aubrey of his promise of silence. Aubrey had a nervous breakdown and, while he was recovering, Ruthven ingratiated himself with the sister. They were engaged to be married, and Aubrey, because of his oath, felt unable to prevent the occurrence. The marriage took place on the day the oath ran out, but it was not in time to prevent Ruth-

> Polidori developed his character Lord Ruthven from elements of European folklore that circulated across Europe after the vampire epidemics of the previous century.

ven from killing the sister and disappearing to work his evil elsewhere.

Polidori developed his character Lord Ruthven from elements of European folklore that circulated across Europe after the vampire epidemics of the previous century. In his introduction, Polidori refers specifically to the Arnold Paole vampire scare and the survey of vampirism written by Dom Augustin Calmet. While the vampire had been the subject of some German and British poems, Polidori, as noted by Carol Senf, took the crude entity of European folklore and transformed it into a complex and interesting character, the first vampire in English fiction. No longer was the vampire simply a mindless, demonic force unleashed on humankind but rather a real person—albeit a resurrected one—capable of moving unnoticed in human society and picking and choosing victims. He was not an impersonal evil entity but rather a moral degenerate dominated by evil motives and a subject about whom negative moral judgments were proper.

Because "The Vampyre" originally appeared under Byron's name, it attracted much more attention than it might have otherwise. In France, before the matter of its authorship was cleared up, it was widely reviewed and greatly affected many of the new generation of Romantic writers. Playwright Charles Nodier was asked to review it and wrote the preface to the French edition. His friend Cyprien Bérard wrote a lengthy, two-volume sequel to the story, *Lord Ruthwen ou les Vampires*, which appeared early in 1820. Because it was published anonymously, many ascribed it to Nodier; however, Nodier wrote his own version of the Ruthven story in *Le Vampire*, the first vampire drama, which opened in Paris in the summer of 1820. In Nodier's tale, Ruthven finally was forced to face the fatal consequences of his evil life. Within two months, James R. Planché adapted *Le Vampire* and brought Lord Ruthven to the London stage in *The Vampire, or, The Bride of the Isles*. Meanwhile, back in Paris, Lord Ruthven appeared in four other vampire plays—two serious melodrama, two comedic—before the year was out. He made his debut in Germany in 1828 in an opera, *Der Vampyr*, by Heinrich August Marschner.

Before he left Paris and retired to Belgium, Lord Ruthven made his last appearance on the Parisian stage in 1851 in Alexandre Dumas's final work. After Dumas's play, Lord Ruthven went into retirement as a character to be succeeded by Varney the Vampyre, Carmilla, and Dracula. He would not be rediscovered until the mid-twentieth century. Ruthven served as the initial inspiration for a movie, *The Vampire's Ghost* (1945), produced by Republic Pictures. However, by the time the script was developed, the storyline barely resembled the original, and its leading character had only the vaguest likeness to Lord Ruthven. Lord Ruthven also made a brief appearance when *Vampire Tales*, the Marvel comic book, adapted "The Vampyre" for its first issue in 1973.

The most recent revival of Lord Ruthven, a new version of Marschner's opera, appeared on BBC television in 1992. In *Der Vampyr—A Soap Opera*, Ruthven was now a modern Londoner, and his name had been changed to Ripley the Vampyr.

🦇 *Rymer, James Malcolm* 🦇 *(1804–1884)*

James Malcolm Rymer, the author of *Varney the Vampyre*, was born in Scotland. He emerged out of obscurity in 1842 as the editor of the quite respectable *Queen's Magazine*. Prior to that time, he had been a civil engineer, surveyor, and mechanical draftsman. As he became a successful writer, he dropped these prior occupations. In 1842, he authored an article for *Queen's Magazine* in which he made disparaging remarks about popular fiction written for the working masses. However, the next year, *Queen's Magazine* failed, and he became the editor of *Lloyd's Penny Weekly Miscellany*. Cheap, popular fiction, the so-called "penny dreadful," had emerged in England in the 1830s. The penny dreadfuls were of two basic kinds: magazines that cost a penny and specialized in serialized, popular novels and novels published in sections that sold for a penny each.

Originally ostensibly for adults, by the 1850s, the market was directed primarily at children. As Rymer wrote under a variety of pseudonyms, it is not known when he first began to write popular fiction, but in 1841, he authored a very popular novel, *The Black Monk*. His most popular pseudonyms were Malcolm J. Errym and Malcolm J. Merry. The most popular book written largely by Rymer was *Varney the Vampyre; or, The Feast of Blood*. It appeared in the mid-1840s and, in the end, ran to 220 chapters and 868 pages. The chapters were then collected in a single volume (1847) and continued to sell for the next 15 years. The idea for *Varney* seems to have been an 1840 reprinting of John Polidori's "The Vampyre" by the Romancist and Novelist's Library in a penny dreadful format. *Varney* included most of Polidori's distinctive opinions about vampires.

Since *Varney* was issued anonymously, for many years, the identity of its author was unclear. Montague Summers believed it to be Thomas P. Prest, author of *Sweeney Todd*, the best known of the penny dreadfuls. However, in 1963, Louis James, who had inherited several of Rymer's own scrapbooks, found conclusive evidence of Rymer's authorship of the majority of the work. It was common for different writers to work on various sections of long-running serials such as *Varney*, and other writers might have been employed to write new chapters. (That fact might account for its often uneven style and contradictory statements about the lead character.) Rymer continued to write for *Lloyd* until 1853, when he was employed by another popular penny dreadful publisher, John Dicks. From 1858 to 1864, he wrote for *Reynolds' Miscellany*, and in 1866, he wrote for the *London Miscellany*.

Saberhagen, Fred (1930–2007)

Frederick Thomas Saberhagen, known primarily as a writer of science fiction, was also the author of a notable series of novels expanding upon the *Dracula* theme. Saberhagen originally began to build his career as a freelance writer in 1962 and saw his first novel, *The Golden People*, published by Ace Books in 1964. It was followed by *The Water of Thought* (1965) and a number of short stories. In 1967, Saberhagen took a job as an assistant editor with *Encyclopedia Britannica*, a position he held for six years before returning to full-time writing.

In 1967, *Beserker*, a set of short stories and the first book in what was to become the *Beserker* series, began to establish Saberhagen as a leading science fiction writer. The "berserkers" are self-programming and self-replicating robotic spacecraft engineered to kill anything that still lives by their creators, a race long since dead. The appearance of these mechanical, demonic forces drives the divided remaining intelligent life forms to unite against them. In the process, the berserkers become a stimulus to increased progress,

Noted sci-fi/fantasy author Fred Saberhagen penned a series of 10 novels in his "Dracula" series.

norance of blood types, was killing her with his transfusions. In the end, her only hope was to be turned into a vampire. His involvement with Lucy led to his falling in love with Mina Murray, who was, at that point, married to Harker. His love for Mina would drive the plot in later volumes of the series.

The Dracula Tape received mixed reviews, especially among Saberhagen's science fiction fans, but it gained an enthusiastic audience among vampire/Dracula fans. It initiated what has become a new approach to the vampire myth. By treating Dracula sympathetically, Saberhagen enlarged the myth in such a way that it could speak to the contemporary need for individuals to develop an understanding of others who are very different. It also opened the possibility of making the vampire a hero, not just an antihero.

which probably would have not have been made otherwise.

Saberhagen's work is characterized by the blend of science, in which he shows a solid grounding, with mythic and legendary materials. Integrating the two provides him a base for metaphysical speculation. The *Beserker* series, for example, became the vehicle for a lengthy treatment of the role of evil in human life.

In the mid-1970s, Saberhagen stepped out of his science fiction world to publish the first of ten novels with the *Dracula* theme. These novels started with the counterintuitive hypothesis that Dracula was, in fact, the hero in the events that took place in Bram Stoker's novel. In the first volume in the series, *The Dracula Tape* (1975), Dracula recounts the events from Stoker's novel into a tape recorder. He takes the reader step by step through the main events, explaining, for example, how he (that is, Dracula) tried not to vampirize Jonathan Harker but to protect him. He justified his actions regarding Lucy Westenra as a reaction to Abraham Van Helsing who, in his ig-

Dracula as a hero allowed a broad, new expanse into which he could be introduced. Saberhagen first developed an obvious theme, the possible encounter of Dracula with his contemporary Sherlock Holmes. In *The Holmes–Dracula File*, the two joined forces to prevent the introduction of plague-bearing rats into London during Queen Victoria's Diamond Jubilee celebrations. Continuing the attack upon the heroes of Stoker's *Dracula*, Saberhagen introduced John Seward (the character from the original novel) into *The Holmes–Dracula File* as the villain behind the dastardly plot.

Dracula's feelings for Mina Murray, who made a brief appearance in the Holmes story to reaffirm her love for Dracula, served as the basis for the third volume, *An Old Friend of the Family* (1979). Dracula had developed a means by which Mina and her descendants could contact him should circumstances demand it. An extreme situation would arise in the late 1970s in Chicago, Saberhagen's hometown.

Summoned by Judy Southerland, Dracula, using the pseudonym of Dr. Emile Corday, arrived to find that the incidents experienced by Mina's descendants merely masked a plot directed against him by Morgan, a redheaded vampiress who resented Dracula's influence on the vampire community. After defeating Morgan, Dracula settled in the United States.

In the fourth novel, *Thorn* (1980), Dracula changed his name to Jonathan Thorn and became involved in a conspiracy to steal a painting that turned out to be a portrait of Helen Hundayi. She was, according to the story, Dracula's first wife. In *Dominion* (1982), Dracula, now known as Talisman, encountered Nimue, the Lady of the Lake, who was attempting to bring the master magician, Falerin, to the fore as the supreme ruler. Dracula had an ally in Ambrosius (known to the world as Merlin), whose magical power was needed to finally defeat Nimue.

The sixth of Saberhagen's *Dracula* novels appeared in 1990. *A Matter of Taste* returned Dracula, now known as Matthew Maule, to Chicago, where he had settled as the Southerland family's uncle Matthew. The story concerned an attempt by Dracula's vampire enemies to kill him. Very early on, Dracula was poisoned and lay near death in his bed. The Southerlands protected him against his foes until he could recover and defeat them decisively. This novel also had Dracula recounting the story of his origins—an inventive tale of Prince Dracula becoming a vampire. In *A Question of Time* (1992), Dracula joined forces with detective Joe Keogh to fight Edgar Tyrell, a menacing vampire who seemed to be able to affect time itself. Saberhagen continued his *Dracula* series through the mid-1990s with *Séance for a Vampire* (1994) and *A Sharpness in the Neck* (1996)

and into the new century with *A Coldness in the Blood* (2002).

Saberhagen's *Dracula* series appeared on the heels of Daniel Ross's *Dark Shadows* novels but took Ross's sympathetic treatment of the vampire one step further. *The Dracula Tape* was followed by Anne Rice's *Interview with the Vampire*, which also had the vampire telling his story into a tape recorder. Saberhagen's Dracula character differed strongly, however, from both the *Dark Shadows* and Anne Rice vampires. Unlike Barnabas Collins, Dracula had no problem with his vampire state, no anguish about his uncontrollable drive, and no wish to change. Unlike Rice's Louis and Lestat de Lioncourt, Saberhagen's Dracula manifested little ambiguity in his situation. Dracula was a hero whose moral situation was rather clear: he had found the means to handle most of the questions that would be raised about his preying upon the human race.

While producing the *Dracula* novels, Saberhagen continued to publish science fiction novels at a steady pace and, in the 1970s, he also began to write fantasy novels, most prominently the *Swords* and *Lost Swords* series. He edited anthologies on chess, *Pawn to Infinity* (1982), and archaeology, *A Spadeful of Spacetime* (1981), as well.

Saberhagen's *Dracula* novels brought him to the attention of Francis Ford Coppola, and he was chosen, along with coauthor James V. Hart, to write the novelization of Coppola's screenplay for *Bram Stoker's Dracula*. He was the literary guest of honor at Dracula '97: A Centennial Celebration, at which he was honored by the Transylvanian Society of Dracula for his *Dracula* series.

Saint Germain

Saint Germain, the central figure in a series of novels by Chelsea Quinn Yarbro, is a 4,000-year-old vampire. Yarbro developed Saint

Germain from a historical personage, the Count de Saint Germain, a mysterious individual and reputed alchemist who lived in eighteenth-century France. He moved in cultured circles of his day, composed music, and was fluent in several languages. The count was a prince from Transylvania whose real name was Francis Ragoczy according to most sources. His money came from international trade, possibly centering on jewels. The few accounts of his life suggested that he was of medium height, wore black and white, rarely ate in public (even at his own parties), claimed extraordinary powers (including being an age of several thousand years), and encouraged an aura of mystery about the details of his life. In the historical Saint Germain, Yarbro found someone who closely fit her evolving image of what a vampire should be. She made Saint Germain her central character by merely using facts about him in a vampire mythical context.

At the same time, Yarbro was consciously reworking the Dracula myth as it had developed through the twentieth century. She approached the vampire logically and saw many problems in the tradition. First, she removed the overlay of medieval Christianity, which left very little "evil" in the vampire's character. In his bite, he shared a moment of sexual bliss and had the power to grant a degree of immortality. Second, she decided that the vampire would need to be quite intelligent to survive in what was a hostile environment and would find creative and entertaining ways to spend centuries of time.

Yarbro also found the essence of vampirism to be the act of taking blood, the intimacy of contact, and the "life" that came from it rather than the nourishment of the blood's ingredients. Thus, the bite became a sexual act.

Yarbro introduced Saint Germain in *Hotel Transylvania* (1978), a novel set in eighteenth-century France. This historical romance revolves around the relationship of Saint Germain and a young woman, Madelaine de Mon-

talia. Some years earlier, Madelaine's father had promised her to a group of Satanists with whom he had become involved. As she and Saint Germain were falling in love, the coven of devil worshippers began to put pressure on her father to live up to his bargain and turn her over to them for their own cultic purposes.

Hotel Transylvania slowly revealed facts about Saint Germain, though an alert reader might guess what was coming when, early in the first chapter, he repeated Dracula's famous line, "I do not drink wine." Saint Germain was a vampire but a vampire of a different breed. In conversations with Madelaine, Saint Germain slowly revealed his nature. He was many centuries old. As a vampire, he needed only small quantities of blood to survive and would normally take only a wineglass full. Contrary to popular opinion, he was not affected by sacred objects, such as the crucifix. He could walk freely on consecrated ground. He was negatively affected by running water and sunlight but drew strength from his native soil. He had constructed shoes with hollow heels and soles, into which he put the earth, which countered the effect of running water and allowed him to walk around in daylight. Among his few superhuman abilities was his strength, which he amply demonstrated in his final confrontation with the coven of Satanists.

Saint Germain possessed very human emotions, though time had taught him to stay above most affairs of humans. He had developed his own set of morals, especially concerning attacks on individuals for his blood supply.

Periodically, however, he had fallen in love, as he did with Madelaine in *Hotel Transylvania*. His love affairs revealed his quite different sexuality: while he could participate in most sexual activity, he could not have an erection. The bite, however, was a more than adequ-

> **Yarbro also found the essence of vampirism to be the act of taking blood, the intimacy of contact, and the "life" that came from it rather than the nourishment of the blood's ingredients.**

ate substitute for him and his sexual partner. Sexual relations were limited in that they could not occur between two vampires. Thus, if an affair between a vampire and human progressed to the point that the human became a vampire, the affair would necessarily end. They could, and often did, remain friends, but the affair was not part of their immortal existence.

The centuries-old saga of Saint Germain has been laid out in the subsequent novels, the second of which, *The Palace* (1979), was set in fifteenth-century Florence and the third, *Blood Games*, in Rome under Nero. In each of these, Saint Germain confronted life-and-death experiences that forced discussion of the possibility of the "true death." Vampires could be killed by the severing of the spine (such as when the head is cut off) and by being consumed in fire.

The Palace also introduced Saint Germain's former lover and present-day colleague, Atta Olivia Clemens, and the account of her origin was spelled out in *Blood Games*. She had been forced into a marriage with an influential Roman official who had ambitions to become emperor. He was also somewhat of a pervert and forced her to have relations with many men while he watched. Then, she met Saint Germain, and he arranged for her to escape her husband's power and become a vampire. He created a new vampire by drinking too much blood from someone or allowing them to drink of his blood.

While the origin of Saint Germain was never fully revealed, Yarbro did construct a history for him. He was born 4,000 years ago in what is today Transylvania, of Proto-Etruscan stock. His people had a vampiric priesthood and, as he was born in the winter (the dark of the year in agricultural societies), he was initiated into the priesthood. Some details of this priesthood were provided in *Path of the Eclipse*. The protector god of his people was a vampire, and the priests also were vampires. Saint Germain had been initiated, but before he could assume his position, he was captured and taken into slavery. He served very successfully in the army of his captors, for which he was rewarded with execution. Saint Germain, however, survived because his executioners did not know they had to either decapitate him or burn his body.

More recent volumes have brought Saint Germain into the twentieth century in Nazi Germany (*Tempting Fate*, 1982) and in various other modern situations (*The Saint-Germain Chronicles*, 1983). In the meantime, Atta Olivia Clemens has continued her career quite apart from Saint Germain, though they occasionally make contact through correspondence. During the time of the emperor Justinian, she moved from Rome to Constantinople and, before her return to Rome in 1214 C.E., had lived for a time in Tyre (in the Holy Land). She left Rome for France in the seventeenth century where, following an adventure with the famous Musketeer d'Artagnan, she has drifted in obscurity.

By the beginning of the new century, Yarbro had produced a dozen Saint Germain volumes, including a collection of short stories. She continued to produce new volumes over the next decade and a half, the latter volumes showing no diminution in quality. In addition to these works, she has written an additional three Olivia and two Madelaine volumes. Yarbro's novels have been consistently characterized by well-thought-out plots and set in thoroughly researched historical settings.

> By the beginning of the new century, Yarbro had produced a dozen Saint Germain volumes, including a collection of short stories.

The final volume of the series, *Sustenance* (2014), has Saint Germain in post–World War II Paris, where he is assisting some Americans who have run afoul of the anti-Communist witch hunt being conducted by the House Un-American Activities Committee in the United States in the 1950s.

Yarbro received the Grand Master Award at the World Horror Convention in 2003 and the Bram Stoker Lifetime Achievement Award at the meeting of the Horror Writers Association in 2009. She was a guest of honor at the World Science Fiction Convention in 2017.

🦇 *Science Fiction, Vampires in* 🦇

As the vampire myth developed and went through a rationalizing/secularizing process, various authors have posed alternative, nonsupernatural theories for the origin of vampires from disease to altered blood chemistry. Eventually, at the height of interest in flying saucers in the 1950s, it was inevitable that the idea of vampires as space aliens would be posed. However, such an idea had a number of precursors. In 1894, for example, H. G. Wells, in his story "The Flowering of the Strange Orchid," had explored the possibility of a space alien taking over a human body in order to live off the life energies of others. This theme was picked up in the pulp magazines in such stories as Sewell Wright's "Vampires of Space" and C. L. Moore's "Black Thirst." A truly bloodthirsty space alien seems to have first appeared in 1942 in A. E. van Vogt's story "Asylum." Van Vogt's villains were a pair of aliens who arrived on Earth in a spaceship. They lived for thousands of years by preying on the life forms of different planets. On Earth, they encountered reporter William Dreegh, who eventually was able to stifle their invasion.

By the mid-1950s, interest in flying saucers was on the rise, and science fiction had begun to blossom. Richard Matheson, who had written both horror and science fiction for many years, was the first to explore the traditional vampire theme in popular science fiction. In *I Am Legend*, Matheson, who had authored several vampire stories, created an end-of-the-world situation in which the hero, Robert Neville, was the only human left. The others had either been killed or turned into vampires. During battle with the vampires, Neville had to figure out which parts of the old vampire myth were accurate and, hence, which weapons would work against them. *I Am Legend* has been made into a movie three times—*The Last Man on Earth* (1964), *The Omega Man* (1971), and *I Am Legend* (2007)—and, in each, the vampirism was played down, as was the meaning of the title of Matheson's original work.

After Matheson, the mixture of science fiction and vampires occurred occasionally, mostly in short stories. Among the several

It should not surprise you that H. G. Wells, one of the most famous authors of speculative fiction of all time, once wrote a story about aliens that sustain themselves on the energies of human life.

novels on this theme, the more notable included Colin Wilson's *The Space Vampires* (1976); Tanith Lee's *Sabella, or The Blood Stone* (1980); Brian Aldiss's *Dracula Unbound* (1991); and Robert Frezza's *McLennon's Syndrome*. Two *Star Trek* novels with a vampire theme have been published, but neither appears to have been made into an episode of the popular television show. However, the major presence of space alien vampires would be felt in the movies.

The Space Alien Vampire in the Movies: By 1953, Universal Pictures had a waning interest in the classic monsters it had made famous in the 1930s. Their last scenes were played out in *Abbott and Costello Meet Dr. Jekyll and Mr. Hyde*, in which Dracula made a cameo appearance. However, a variety of companies were exploiting the classic monsters—including the vampire—within the context of science fiction motion pictures; these were the hot, new items on the agenda, especially for companies specializing in B movies. The questions they posed their youthful audiences included: What if vampires are real and are space aliens? What if Earth is being invaded by space aliens who came to drain either our blood, our life force, or both? How should we react to a space alien vampire? The first science fiction movie to explore these questions was the 1951 production from RKO Radio Pictures *The Thing from Another World* (remade in 1982 as *The Thing*). It starred James Arness as an alien creature (actually an eight-foot vegetable) who needed blood to reproduce. *The Thing* was discovered in the Arctic snow by a research team, and the military eventually had to be brought in to stop the threat. Six years later, Roger Corman produced and directed *Not of This Earth* (remade in 1988), which saw a humanoid from the dying planet Davanna settle in a small town to search out the viability of human blood as a replacement for that of their own race.

Not of This Earth was soon followed by United Artists's *It! The Terror from Beyond Space* (1958). *It!* began with Colonel Carruthers, the sole survivor of a space expedition to Mars, being arrested by the commander of his rescue ship, who suspected him of cannibalizing his crew in order to survive. On the way home, with Carruthers in lockup, members of the crew were mysteriously murdered by It. The commander finally realized his error and was able to isolate the vampiric alien in a cargo chamber. All the survivors donned space suits and the oxygen was let out of the ship, thus killing the creature. *It! The Terror from Beyond Space* became the direct inspiration for the 1979 classic space horror movie *Alien* (which deleted the original's vampire theme).

The last of the 1950s space alien vampire movies would become by far the most famous and financially successful. *Plan 9 from Outer Space* (1959) began with an old man, played by Bela Lugosi, leaving the grave of his recently deceased wife, Vampire Girl, played by television horror movie hostess Vampira. A ray flashed down from outer space, reviving Vampire Girl, who then attacked the attendants who were about to bury her body. Subsequently, she killed the police inspector, who had arrived to examine the bodies of the gravediggers. The scene then changed to an invasion of flying saucers over Los Angeles. Eros and Tanna, who led the invasion, announced Plan 9, their intention to revive all of the dead on Earth and use them as their instrument to take over the planet. The forces of good organized to counter the invasion and, in the end, the space people were repulsed.

Plan 9 from Outer Space became famous after being placed at or near the top of several lists of the world's worst movies. The product of director Edward D. Wood Jr. (1924–1978), famous for his quick production of cheap movies, the film was "unintentionally" hilarious for its errors of production. In the graveyard scene, for example, cardboard tombstones swayed when accidentally touched, a cement floor was visible under the cemetery grass, and a mattress (to cushion a fall) could be seen.

So hysterically bad it's good, 1959's Plan 9 from Outer Space, *directed by Ed Wood, was one of Bela Lugosi's last films. In the story, Lugosi's wife, played by Vampira (pictured here), is brought to life by space aliens.*

Plan 9 also became notable, as it was Bela Lugosi's last film. Wood seems to have integrated some brief footage of Lugosi that originally had been shot for another movie. The brief segments of actual Lugosi scenes were each shown several times. Lugosi died before *Plan 9* could be finished, and a body double stood in for him. In the later parts of the movie, this stand-in wore Lugosi's cape and walked before the camera in a sinister fashion, with his arm raised over his face.

It! and *Plan 9*, the flying saucer movies, would be followed by a set of feature films thematically tied together by the early space explorations. In *First Man into Space* (1959), for example, an astronaut's body was taken over by a space creature. Upon his return to Earth, the vampiric creature needed blood and began killing to get it. He broke into a blood bank but finally was cornered in a decompression tank and killed.

The space alien vampire theme continued through the 1960s, beginning with Mario Bava's *Planet of the Vampires* (originally titled *Terrore nello Spazio*). The story concerned a spaceship that was commanded by Captain Mark Markary (played by Barry Sullivan) and forced to land on the planet Aura. Here, Markary discovered another ship, whose crewmembers were dead. The dead rose, their bodies inhabited by disembodied residents of Aura, who had turned them into vampires and attacked Markary's crew. Once Markary discovered what was oc-

In 1966's Queen of Blood, *an alien ship crashes on Mars. One passenger, a woman, is rescued by the Earth crew, but she turns out to have a thirst for their blood.*

curring, he and two of his crewmembers escaped. Then, he realized that the two crewmembers already had been vampirized and would invade a defenseless Earth. The movie ended before he decided what course of action he should follow.

Planet of the Vampires was followed the next year by one of the better space vampire movies, *Queen of Blood*, with a rather impressive cast of John Saxon, Basil Rathbone, and a youthful Dennis Hopper. The story was constructed from a Russian film, the footage of which had been purchased by Roger Corman. The star was a beautiful woman called the Queen of Mars, who had been invited back to Earth by members of a U.S. spaceship. On the return trip, however, the captain discovered that she was a vampire and was killing off the crewmembers one by one. Her weakness proved to be a hemophiliac condition and, after being cut during a struggle with a crewmember, she bled to death.

In the mid-1970s, occult author Colin Wilson tried his hand at the vampire theme in his novel *The Space Vampires* (1976), a volume originally marketed as a science fiction novel. The novel also fit within the theme of psychic vampirism, as the creatures drained their victims' "life force" rather than their blood (as the carrier of life energy). In the year 2080, a spacecraft encountered another mysterious craft, housing several bodies in lifelike condition that were alive and turned out to be vampires.

In the early 1980s, Tobe Hooper saw the possibilities of Wilson's novel for the screen and began an adaptation that was released in the United States as *Lifeforce* in 1985. It changed the setting to 1986 to coincide with the return of Halley's Comet. In the movie, the action was centered around the relationship between Commander Carlson, who found the space vampires, and the single female vampire. Hooper also added a typical vampire feature: having the vampire be killed by a stake through her energy center (a feature absent from the novel).

Science Fiction Vampires in Comic Books: The several space vampires who appeared on the movie screen in the 1960s were eclipsed by the most famous one of all, Vampirella. She appeared originally not in a movie but as a comic book character created by Forrest J. Ackerman and James Warren, the owner of Warren Publishing Company. Ackerman would go on to become the original writer for *Vampirella*, the most successful vampire comic book of all time. Vampirella was distinguished by being the first space vampire who was the heroine of the story rather than the villain. She hailed from the dying planet Drakulon and came to Earth, where blood was readily available. She tried not to kill to obtain blood and was remorseful when she had to take a life to survive.

The Vampirella character was partially inspired by the title character from another Mario Bava movie, *Barbarella*. She was a young, sexy, scantily clad female.

As the plot was developed through the 1970s, even Dracula was discovered to be a former resident of Drakulon, who had left for Earth many centuries ago.

Vampirella became one of the most successful comic books of the 1970s and, in the 1990s, enjoyed a new wave of success in the hands of Harris Comics. In the new century, Dynamite Entertainment picked up the rights to *Vampirella* and, in 2019, led the celebration of *Vampirella*'s 50th anniversary imprint as a comic book.

Contemporaneously with Colin Wilson's novel, a science fiction story with a vampire theme came briefly to the world of comic books in a short-lived series, *Planet of the Vampires*. The story concerned space explorers who had returned to Earth after a long stay on Mars. They found the people divided into two fac-

tions following a devastating nuclear war: one faction was centered in the former New York City; the other was in the countryside. The city people had taken cover under a dome. It protected them somewhat, but they lacked immunity to diseases that had developed as a result of the war. The outsiders, on the other hand, had developed a natural resistance. The city dwellers captured outsiders, from whom they drained blood to be used for a serum. The vampires were the machines created by the city dwellers to forcefully take the blood of any outsiders who could be caught.

Planet of the Vampires, published by Atlas Comics, lasted only three issues. Its demise left *Vampirella* as the only comic book with a space vampire theme. Once *Vampirella* was discontinued, space vampires largely disappeared, except for *Lifeforce*. With the new wave of vampire comics in the 1990s, the space alien vampire was revived, primarily in the adaptation of movies to comic book format. In 1990, *Plan 9 from Outer Space* was adapted in a single issue from Malibu Comics. The following year, *I Am Legend* (which had previously been made into a movie twice, in 1964 and 1971) appeared in three issues, and a sequel to *Plan 9 from Outer*

Talisa Soto starred in the 1996 movie adaptation of Vampirella.

Space lasted for three issues, though the vampire element had been deleted from the storyline.

The original series of *Vampirella* ran for 112 issues but was discontinued when Warren Publishing Company went bankrupt in 1983. Rights were acquired by Harris Comics, which revived *Vampirella* in 1991 (with reprints of the 1970s stories), and a series with new stories began in 1992. *Vampirella* was the only space vampire among the new wave of comic book vampires in the early 1990s. Vampirella has continued to appear through the second decade of the new century, and all of its various incarnations have been reprinted for a new generation of fans.

The Twenty-first Century: Amid the vampire boom of the 1990s that continues through the first decade of the new century, the lack of science fiction vampires has been noticeable. Among the few that have been published, glimpses of the future (*Ultraviolet, Vampire Hunter D: Bloodlust*) have been more apparent than flights to outer space (*Dracula 2000, Bloodsuckers*) or mad scientific experiments (*Blade II*). The same could be said of comic books where, in the futuristic *Frey*, Joss Whedon introduced a vampire Slayer far into the future. Of course, the movie version of *The League of Extraordinary Gentlemen* draws on an old science fiction theme, Captain Nemo's famous submarine, which is juxtaposed with a vampire. One can always look to anime for horror–science fiction crossovers, and recent examples would include *Vampire Wars, Trinity Blood,* and *Blood: The Last Vampire.*

One science fiction theme that has become popular has to do with the development of a blood substitute that allows vampires to rejoin human society. With the substitute, they no longer have to kill humans to survive, nor do they have to rely on animal blood. This theme

> One science fiction theme that has become popular has to do with the development of a blood substitute that allows vampires to rejoin human society.

begins with Vampirella, who discovers such a substitute soon after her arrival from outer space. In *Sundown: The Vampire in Retreat* (1989), the reformed vampires of the town of Purgatory drink an ill-colored blood substitute as part of the program of pacifism toward humans. Batman became a vampire in the graphic novel series by Doug Moench, and in *Batman: Bloodstorm* (1994), he tried to deal with his bloodlust through the use of a blood substitute.

A blood substitute was central to the *Southern Vampire Mysteries*, a set of vampire novels by Charlaine Harris. Following the development of a synthetic blood product, which is marketed as "Tru Blood," vampires go public and make their presence known to humankind. Once their existence is revealed, they must struggle for equal rights, even as antivampire organizations emerge to oppose them and as an internal argument developed over having to give up human blood for its less-than-perfect substitute. *True Blood* ran for seven seasons on HBO (2008–2014).

In *Vampire Science* (1997), Jonathan Blum and Kate Orman send the fabled time lord Doctor Who up against vampires who are engaging in genetic engineering to find a new source of blood. In the Canadian movies *Karmina* (1996) and *Karmina 2* (2000), the vampires of Montreal have invented a potion that allowed them to exist among humans as one of them but also allowed them to revert rather quickly to their vampiric state. In the movie trilogy featuring the half vampire Blade the Vampire Slayer, the title character also consumes a blood substitute. In *The Breed* (2001), the blood substitute allows the futuristic vampires to avoid falling victim to the bloodlust that turns them into irrational killers, a problem preventing their integration into human society, while in *Daybreakers* (2009), a plague has turned most humans into vampires, and a blood substitute is the only way to prevent starvation. In Brian Meehl's young adult novel *Suck It Up* (2008), the main character, Morning McCobb, dines on a blood substitute made from soy called "Blood Lite."

Possibly, the most successful science fiction vampire series in the wake of *True Blood* was *The Strain*, which began as three novels by Guillermo del Toro and Chuck Hogan, *The Strain* (2009), *The Fall* (2010), and *The Night Eternal* (2011). In the novels, a vampire disease is introduced into New York City, which quickly reaches epidemic proportions and calls for a medical response complicated by the "supernatural" vampire role in directing the spread of the viral strain. The disease calls into action Dr. Ephraim Goodweather, who leads the Canary Project, a rapid-response team of the Centers for Disease Control and Prevention (CDC). As he comes to understand the vampire's role in the spread of the disease, he must continually adapt his tactics to overcome it. As a television series, it ran for four seasons (2014–2017) on FX.

Southey, Robert (1774–1843)

Robert Southey was a British poet and writer who was among the first to introduce the vampire theme into English literature. While attending the University of Oxford, he met Samuel Taylor Coleridge, who became a lifelong friend, mentor, and supporter. Toward the end of the 1790s, Southey's health failed, and he moved to Portugal to recuperate. While there, he completed his first major work, a long poem titled "Thalaba the Destroyer."

"Thalaba" was to be the first of a series of epic poems drawing upon the mythologies of different cultures and portraying the fight of good over evil. In the midst of the story, Thalaba comes face to face with the vampire.

Southey was inspired to write "Thalaba" by the *Arabian Tales*, in which mention is made of Domdaniel, a training school for evil magicians. In Southey's story, set in Arabia, the title character lived in exile with his mother. His father and kinspeople had been slain by evil magicians. The magicians resided in a cavern, where they kept his father's sword, which was to be the instrument of their destruction. Thalaba's life turned into a quest to find the cavern, retrieve the sword, and avenge his father.

In pursuit of his quest (in Book VII of the poem), Thalaba sought shelter from the rain in the chamber of the tombs and, there, had his brief encounter with a vampire. The vampire was none other than his bride Oneiza, who had recently died on their wedding day. Oneiza's body had been reanimated by an in-

One of the Romantic Lake Poets, Robert Southey penned a poem that builds on the myth of how someone who dies on their wedding day might become a vampire.

vading, demonic force. Her cheeks were livid, her lips were blue, and her eyes possessed a terrible brightness. Thalaba grasped a lance, and:

> … through the vampire corpse
> He thrust his lance; it fell,
> And howling with the wound,
> Its fiendish tenant fled.

Immediately afterward, Oneiza's spirit appeared and urged Thalaba to continue his great quest. In evoking the vampire, Southey demonstrated his awareness of the vampire tales from continental Europe. He mentioned the outbreaks of vampirism on the continent early in the eighteenth century in his notes, especially the case of Arnold Paole in Serbia and more recent cases in Greece. In relating the case of the vampire Oneiza, Southey assumed the Greek notion that a vampire was a corpse inhabited by an evil spirit. Equally important for Southey were the translations of the German poem "Lenora," which had been published in English by William Taylor in 1796 and adapted into a more popular form by Sir Walter Scott later that same year.

Even before finishing "Thalaba," Southey wrote a ballad titled "The Old Woman of Berkeley." The title character was a witch who possessed the characteristics of a *lamiai*, the ancient Greek, vampire-like creature who preyed upon infants. As she herself was made to say:

> From sleeping babes I have
> sucked the breath,
> And breaking by charms the
> sleep of death,
> I have call'd the dead from their
> graves.

Thus, Southey vied with Coleridge for the distinction of having introduced the vampire into English literature. Coleridge's poem "Christabel" was published before "Thalaba," and while most agree that "Christabel" was a vampire poem, Coleridge never identified it as such. After Southey introduced the vampire to the English-speaking public, he did not linger over the vampire myth or further develop gothic themes. He did, however, go on to become one of England's finer writers, the author of numerous poems and prose works of history and biography. In general, his prose writing received better reviews than his poetry, although he was credited with expanding the number of metrical patterns available to poets who came after him.

Tolstoy, Alexey Konstantinovitch (1817–1875)

Alexey Konstantinovitch Tolstoy, the nineteenth-century, Russian writer who introduced the vampire into Russian literature, was born in St. Petersburg, Russia. Tolstoy was educated at home and, at the age of 16, entered government service at the Moscow Archives of the Ministry of Foreign Affairs. While in Moscow, he was able to study at Moscow State University, where he absorbed German idealistic philosophy. He received his diploma from the university in 1835.

At the beginning of his literary career, influenced by E. T. A. Hoffmann's tales, Tolstoy wrote several fantasy/horror stories, the first of which was "Upyr" ("The Vampire"). "Upyr" was the story of a young couple, Runevsky and Dasha. The story opened in nineteenth-century Moscow with a group at a ball. Runevsky conversed with a pale young man, Rybarenko, on the subject of vampires. He predicted that if Dasha went to visit her grandmother, she would die. Eventually, after a series of adventures and

A German author of the Romantic period known for his fantasy and horror tales, E.T.A. Hoffmann was the author of "Upyr," a vampire tale set in Russia.

Famous for such classics as War and Peace *and* Anna Karenina, *the Nobel Prize–winning Leo Tolstoy also wrote ghost and vampire stories.*

some visionary experiences, Runevsky learned the truth. The problem in Dasha's family stemmed from previous generations to an unfaithful wife who killed her husband. As he was dying, he pronounced a curse of madness and vampirism upon her and their heirs. She eventually went insane and committed suicide. Dasha's grandmother inherited the curse. As a vampire, she had already killed Dasha's mother and was prepared to kill Dasha. In the end, he became a believer in the supernatural, although Dasha dismissed everything that happened and believed in a more naturalistic explanation.

Tolstoy first read the story at one of the local salons and then, after passing a censor, had it published under the pseudonym Krasnorogsky in 1841. It was followed by a second supernatural tale, "The Reunion after Three-Hundred Years," a ghost story. Tolstoy returned to the vampiric theme in his third story, "The Family of the Vourdalak." (The *vukodlak* was the vampire of the southern Slavs.) Written in French, it began with the Congress of Vienna

in 1815, where the Marquis d'Urfé entertained some aristocratic friends with his story. While traveling through Serbia, d'Urfé stopped for the night. The family he stayed with was upset, as the father had left to fight the Turks. Before he left, d'Urfé told the family to beware if the father returned in less than ten days; it was a sign that he had become a *vukodlak* and should be impaled with an aspen stake. Almost ten days passed before the father returned. The older son was about to kill him but was overruled by the family, although the father refused to eat or drink and otherwise behaved strangely. The father then attacked the family, including the daughter to whom d'Urfé had been attracted. D'Urfé continued on his journey but returned to the village some months later. He was told that the entire family had become vampires. He sought out the young girl but soon discovered that, in fact, she was now a vampire. He barely escaped from the family.

After writing "The Family of the Vourdalak," which was not published during his lifetime, Tolstoy wrote a fourth supernatural story, "Amena." These four stories formed a prologue to his formal literary career that was really thought to have begun when he started writing poetry in the late 1840s. The high point of his career as a poet came in the late 1850s, the period after his service in the Crimean War (1855–1856). In 1861, he resigned from the Imperial Court and devoted the rest of his life to his writing. Tolstoy has been hard to classify, as his works do not readily fit into any of the major schools of nineteenth-century Russian writing. A loner, he rarely participated in the literary circles of his time and, after leaving the court, settled on his estate in Ukraine. Tolstoy approved of some westernization but did not like the more radical activists. He did inject the vampire theme into Russian writing, a theme that would later be picked up by Nikolai Gogol and Ivan Turgenev. In 1960, Italian director Mario Bava brought "The Family of the Vourdalak" to the screen as one of three Russian stories in his *La Maschera del Demonio* (released in the United States as *Black Sunday*). Boris Karloff, who narrated the breaks between the stories, also played the father, who had become a *vukodlak*. English editions of Tolstoy's stories were initially published in 1969.

Varney the Vampyre; or, The Feast of Blood

One of the most famous vampires in literature is Sir Francis Varney, the title character in *Varney the Vampyre; or, The Feast of Blood*, a nineteenth-century British novel written by James Malcolm Rymer. The story originally appeared in 109 weekly installments in the mid-1840s. The entire manuscript was then collected and printed as a single volume of over 800 pages. It was the first vampire novel in English and the first vampire fiction since the original short story by John Polidori and the stage dramas that his story inspired. The story thus served as an important transitional piece between the original written accounts of vampires in the early nineteenth century and the writing of Sheridan Le Fanu and Bram Stoker.

Through the twentieth century, *Varney* had a checkered career. Copies of Rymer's poorly written novel were seldom saved, so it became a rare book. Although different authors made reference to it, few had seen a copy and fewer still had taken the time to work their way through it. The book was published anonymously, and it was only in the 1970s that its true authorship was established. It was unavailable for many decades, but two reprints were published in 1970 and 1972. It found a new audience among vampire enthusiasts and has remained in print through the first decades of the new century.

The story of *Varney* opened with his attack upon the young Flora Bannerworth. Having entered her bedroom, he sank his fangs into her neck and began to suck the gushing blood. The first half of the book followed his increasingly complex relationship with the Bannerworth family and their close friends and associates. Varney possessed white skin (as if bloodless), long, fanglike teeth, long fingernails, and shining, metallic eyes. Immediately after feasting, his skin took on a reddish hue.

Varney's initial attack had left two puncture marks in Flora's neck. Interrupted by members of the family during his repast, Varney was shot but nevertheless escaped. Henry Bannerworth quickly concluded that Flora had been attacked by a "vampyre." From a book he had read in Norway, he noted that vampires attempted to drink blood in order

*The 1845 cover page to the English edition of
James Rymer's* Varney the Vampire.

to revive their bodies. In addition, they tended to do their feeding on evenings just prior to a full moon so that, should they meet with any physical problem, they could revive themselves by basking in the rays of the full moon. It was in this manner that Varney had revived from the gunshot wounds he had received. (The importance given to moonlight throughout the novel shows Rymer's reliance on John Polidori's "The Vampyre.")

While bits and pieces of Varney's history were recounted throughout the novel, the reader had to wait until the end to get the full story. Varney's name before he had become a vampire was Mortimer. He originally had been a supporter of the British Crown and was living in London at the time of the beheading of Charles I and the proclamation of the Commonwealth under Oliver Cromwell in 1649. During this

period, he assisted members of the royalty in escaping to Holland, for which he was handsomely rewarded. In a moment of passion, Mortimer struck his son, accidentally killing him. The next thing he remembered was a flash of light and being struck to the earth with great force. When he recovered consciousness, he was lying on the ground next to a recently opened grave. A voice told him that for his deed, thenceforth, he would be cursed among men and known as Varney the Vampyre. Varney later discovered that he was shot by Cromwell's men and that two years had passed since he lost consciousness. In the meantime, Cromwell had been deposed and the crown restored. His former house was burned, but the money he had buried under the floor was still there. With it, he made a new beginning. He slowly learned the rules of his new nature.

Like Lord Ruthven, the vampire in Polidori's tale, Varney had great strength, he could walk around freely in the sunlight, and he needed blood only occasionally (not nightly). He could be wounded and even killed but would be revived simply by bathing in the moonlight. First pictured as something entirely evil, Varney later took on a more complex nature and showed himself to be an individual of feelings and honor. So appealing were his virtues that the Bannerworths, once they develop some understanding of his condition and his relationship with one of their ancestors, eventually became his protectors from a mob that set out to destroy him.

Rymer was also familiar with the Eastern European vampire cases, probably through Dom Augustin Calmet, who had been published in an English edition in the 1700s. For several chapters beginning with chapter 44, Varney's story turned on the action of a mob. An unnamed individual, who had traveled on the continent, informed the people that the sign of the presence of a vampire was the sudden, mysterious deaths of people who seem to have wasted away. He warned them that such people would also return as vampires. Armed with this information, the mob, unable to locate Varney, moved on to the local graveyard and attacked the body of one Miles, who had recently died. Their eagerness to kill a vampire was thwarted when Miles's coffin was found to be empty. After completing his interaction with the Bannerworths, Varney moved on to a series of increasingly brief encounters with various people in what became a very repetitive storyline. He would try to establish himself in a new social setting, then attempt to bite someone, be discovered and hunted, and have to escape. Varney was singularly inept at attacking people (almost always a young woman) and was continually caught by people responding to the cries of his victims.

Varney was condemned by modern critics as poorly written and somewhat chaotic.

Varney was condemned by modern critics as poorly written and somewhat chaotic. It was not written as fine literature or even as a novel, however. It was written in weekly installments over a two-year period, probably by several different authors, in such a way as to keep the readers entertained and coming back for the next installment. It accomplished that rather limited goal in spectacular fashion, becoming one of the most successful of the penny weeklies of the mid-nineteenth century.

Wolf, Leonard (1923–2019)

Leonard Wolf, writer and college professor, was born on March 1, 1923, in Vulcan, Romania, the son of Rose Engel and Joseph Ludovic. The family name was changed when they migrated to the United States in 1930. He attended Ohio State University (1941–1943) and then transferred to the University of California at Berkeley, from which he received his bachelor's degree in 1945 and his master's in 1950. While at Berkeley, he published his first book, *Hamadryad Hunted* (1945), a book of poems. In 1954, he completed his doctorate at the University of Iowa. That fall, he joined the faculty at St. Mary's College. He later taught at San Francisco State University for two years and then moved to New York as a professor of English at Columbia University, where he remained until his retirement.

Amid Wolf's varied interests, his Romanian heritage asserted itself in the late 1960s when he created and taught a course on Dracula at Columbia. His experiences with students and his own research in vampire literature and films through the early 1970s led to his writing *A Dream of Dracula: In Search of the Living Dead* (1972), an impressionistic exploration of the various ways that the Dracula myth had invaded his life. The flavor of the book was aptly illustrated, for example, in his discussion of his attempt to reconcile what he saw as three very different Romanias: the dreamlike one of his childhood memories, the one he traveled through as an adult in preparation for writing his book, and the one of Stoker's gothic imagination. *A Dream of Dracula* appeared at a time when nonfiction books on Dracula were rare, and it found a large audience among a new generation of vampire fans, who had been flocking to the vampire movies being produced at that time. Wolf made a second significant contribution in 1974 with *The Annotated Dracula*, a copy of the text of Bram Stoker's 1897 novel with extensive notes.

The annotations provided a useful reference to the many actual locations (with handy maps) and historical facts that Stoker mentioned and offered a variety of information about the folklore to which he referred. Wolf also created a calendar of events in the story, which he believed probably occurred in 1887. (Subsequent research of both historical facts mentioned in the novel and Stoker's own notes has revealed the actual date of the novel to be 1893.) After writing his Dracula books, Wolf continued work in the horror field. He wrote a book called *Monsters* (1974), which included a picture of Christopher Lee on the cover and a chapter on Dracula. He compiled an anthology of horror stories, *Wolf's Complete Book of Terror* (1979), and wrote a biographical volume, *Bluebeard: The Life and Crimes of Gilles de Rais* (1980). Gilles de Rais, while not a vampire, has often been covered in vampire books because of the bloody nature of his crimes. In 1984, Wolf completed a play, *The Dracula School for Vampires*, which premiered in San Francisco. Wolf's interest in vampires continued, and in 1991, he penned an introductory reflection on Bela Lugosi's *Dracula* (1931) on

the occasion of the 60th anniversary of its release, along with a vampire filmography for an anthology of vampire stories, *The Ultimate Dracula*.

As the centennial of *Dracula* approached in 1997, Wolf prepared a new edition of *The Annotated Dracula*, released as *The Essential Dracula*, edited a volume of short fiction, and wrote a new volume reflecting his mature opinions on *Dracula* specifically and vampirism in general. He also organized the Dracula Centennial: The Esthetics of Fear, a symposium conference at New York University that featured the likes of Joyce Carol Oates, Stephen King, and Stephen Jay Gould. Wolf's reflections on *Dracula* culminated in his last major works devoted to the vampire theme: *Dracula: The Connoisseur's Guide* and an edited volume, *Blood Thirst: 100 Years of Vampire Fiction*, both released in 1997.

MODERN AUTHORS OF THE VAMPIRE WORLD

The foundation of the vampire's continued popularity in the modern Western world remains that the writers of hundreds of novels tell many stories about how we mere humans can interact with the bloodsuckers in our lives. These stories range from the bearers of social apocalypse to the handsome and beautiful creatures who enter our life briefly but literally take our breath away. Through the first two decades of the new century, several dozen writers have emerged as the authors of choice, whose reworking of the image of Dracula and his cohorts keeps our understanding of the vampire's place in the larger culture ever fresh and up to date. Month by month, if not week by week, these writers remind us of the ever-malleable appearance of the vampire, always ready to present itself in such a way that we can locate the one we want and need.

Each of the writers highlighted below has written multiple titles and, almost from their first publication, proved themselves to be wordsmiths, quickly finding a devoted fan base that awaited their next book.

Adrian, Lara (1966–)

Lara Adrian (a pseudonym of Tina St. John), the author of the *Midnight Breed* paranormal romance series, is from an old New England family that traces its lineage back to William Bradford and the *Mayflower* and even further back to the royal court in England. Though she grew up in Michigan, she now resides in New England. She began writing in the 1990s and had her first novel published as Tina St. John in 1999. Adrian developed an early attraction to vampires, which would lead her into making them the subject of her initial book, *Kiss of Midnight* (2007), from which became a new and most successful series. Adrian introduces a world in which several unique paranormal types exist. Vampires, i.e., the Breed, are the most important. They exist secretly on Earth beside the human race, and within their number is a select group, the Order, that are dedicated to protecting humans from the unbridled bloodlust of the other subgroup, the renegade rogue vampires.

Humans and vampires are of different races, but among the humans are a select group, the Breedmates, humans with a DNA that is compatible with that of the vampires. Vampires are aliens who derive from eight original vampires (all males), who crash-landed on Earth in prehistoric times but were able to perpetuate themselves by locating female partners from among the Breedmates within the human community. The existence of Breedmates presents the opportunity for romance.

In her initial novel, Gabrielle is a Breedmate who unexpectedly observes a group of rogue vampires killing a human. Since the body, along with any forensic evidence, disappears, no one believes her. However, a powerful Breed vampire has also observed the event, including Gabrielle, and now feels he must interfere to protect her from the rogues who might come for her. Succeeding novels each focus on a different member of the Order and the Breedmate to whom he is attached.

As the series develops, a blood war develops that reveals the existence of vampires to humanity in general. Human knowledge of vampires sets up a new dynamic in which the Order's role has become the keeping of the peace that has been established between humankind and the Breed. New enemies arise from among both humans and vampires, who see value in destroying the peace.

The original *Midnight Breed* series consisted of ten novels and two novellas issued between 2007 and 2012. Picking up the story after the blood wars, the *Midnight Breed: The Next Generation* series has (by 2019) added six additional volumes, along with six additional novella. Adrian has also issued *The Midnight Breed Series Companion*, which reflects upon and provides a backstory for the first ten novels. She maintains a website at http://www.laraadrian.com.

Arthur, Keri (1967–)

Australian paranormal romance author Keri Arthur was born and raised in Melbourne. An imaginative child, she grew up in a world populated with various supernatural creatures from dragons and elves to vampires and werewolves and began writing when she was 12 years old. Prior to becoming a full-time writer, she held a variety of jobs from clerk to cook.

Arthur was attracted to paranormal romance and urban fiction as she began to turn her teenage writing projects into a more serious activity as a professional author. Content-wise, she was motivated by what she perceived was a lack of capable female leads in many action-oriented books and, based on that perception, began writing fantasy and later moved to paranormal romance.

Arthur introduced a substantive appearance of vampires into her writing at the beginning of the new century in the *Nikki and Michael* series, in which an Australian private investigator, Nikki James, and a 300-year-old vampire, Michael Kelly, join forces to battle supernatural evil. Kelly is constantly distracted by his personal battle to master his vampire cravings, a factor that looms large in their first case (*Dancing with the Devil*, 2000), in which they face off against an evil vampire. The *Nikki and Michael* series consisted of four novels released between 2001 and 2004.

Even as she wrote the successive volumes of the *Nikki and Michael* series, Arthur launched a series about the Damask Circle, a group of paranormal investigators who fight supernatural

Australian writer Keri Arthur pens paranormal romances.

based in Melbourne, Australia, created to police the spectrum of known supernatural races. Riley's major hinderance in her supernatural battles comes from her werewolf nature. As the full moon approaches, her need to mate becomes quite strong. In her initial case, detailed in *Full Moon Rising* (2006), she must find her brother, who has disappeared, but as the full moon approaches, her search leads to a confrontation with a vampire, who brings her sensual desires to a peak. Riley Jenson proved to be one of Arthur's favorite characters, and the series ran for nine volumes (2006–2009). As the Riley Jenson series concluded, Arthur continued the thrust in her next series, the *Dark Angels*, which features another guardian, Aedh Risa Jones, also a half werewolf/half vampire. The *Dark Angels* series ran for seven volumes (2011–2014).

evil. Each volume of this trilogy centers on a strong female who pairs with a male counterpart to battle the evil paranormal. In the first volume of the series, *Circle of Fire* (2001), for example, Jon Barnett joins forces with Madeline Smith to solve the case of 15 teenagers who have been taken from their homes. The bodies of 11 of the teens turn up completely drained of blood. The immediate hypothesis is that they have been victims of vampires, but as the pair goes to work, other possibilities arise.

Shortly after completing the *Nikki and Michael* series, Arthur introduced one of her major heroes, Riley Jenson. A half werewolf/half vampire, Jenson is joined by her twin brother, Rhoan, and the pair act as guardians who hunt a variety of evildoers. They are employed by the Directorate of Other Races, an organization

Through the new century to the present, Arthur has distinguished herself as a most prolific (and popular) paranormal romance writer who, in her various series, writes about a world inhabited by a spectrum of supernatural characters. Vampires are an integral part of that world and remain present in the background even when others (werewolves, witches, shapeshifters) take center stage. Her popular books have won three Australian Romance Readers Awards for Favorite Scifi, Fantasy, or Futuristic Romance, and the Romance Writers of Australia RBY Award for Speculative Fiction. In 2008, she received the *Romantic Times* Career Achievement Award for Urban Fantasy, even though her writing career was far from over. Arthur maintains a personal website at https://www.keriarthur.com.

᪣ *Ashley, Amanda (1963–)* ᪣

Amanda Ashley is the pseudonym of writer Madeline Baker. Baker was born, raised, married, and still resides in southern California. Her first books were Western historical romances written under her real name. At one point, her editor asked if she would like to try her hand at a paranormal story. She produced a short story, "Masquerade," for an anthology,

The Topaz Man Favorites, Secrets of the Heart. She found she liked vampires, so she chose a pseudonym and got to work. Having read a few vampire books, Baker came to see the potential of vampires as great heroes with an element of danger built in. In different novels, she experimented with a variety of types from the pure hero to the conflicted vampire still struggling to be human. At one point, she even played with the idea of Elvis Presley as a vampire. Their heroic quality is best seen in their willingness to give up everything, even their immortality, for the one woman who can perceive the humanity that resides hidden behind their monstrous exterior.

> Having read a few vampire books, Baker came to see the potential of vampires as great heroes with an element of built-in danger.

Ashley/Baker was among the pioneers of the contemporary vampire romance novels, though she followed a generation of romance vampire novelists such as Lori Herter, Florence Stevenson, and the prolific Daniel Ross. Of almost a dozen vampire romance titles that appeared in 1995, her book *Embrace the Night* and a title by Linda Lael Miller rose from the stack. Ashley and Miller began to redefine the field and open the way that numerous later authors have tred.

In her first novel, Ashley introduced Gabriel who, through his hundreds of years of existence, had yet to solve the problem of loving mortals who aged and died on him and the resultant loneliness. The novel begins with his love of Sara, who he meets as a child in 1881, and then moves 100 years into the future, when he meets a new Sarah to whom he is drawn. The magnetic Gabriel would become the model for a number of vampires that appeared after him.

Much to the delight of her readers, she would frequently revisit the theme of the lonely vampire searching for eternal love in the present but always haunted by his knowledge that while his life goes on, the best of love will die. Ashley's vampires began as rather traditional, especially in their need for darkness during the daylight hours, but as she wrote more and more, she varied the rules. Vincent Cordova, the vampire of *Night's Touch*, for example, will father two children (twins). They are human, even though their mother is the daughter of a vampire couple. Other vampires have become daywalkers, and some see their reflections in mirrors. Ashley has survived the ups and downs of the vampire book market, and even with more than a dozen vampire titles on the shelves, she has shown no hint of stopping, with additional new titles in the pipeline. She began her career with the Love Spell imprint of Dorchester Publishing, switching later to Zebra Books at the much-larger Kensington Publishing Corporation in 2004. Most of her vampire titles remain in print (as of 2020).

🦇 *Bangs, Nina* 🦇

Romance writer Nina Bangs is the author of several series of vampire novels. Bangs was born in San Antonio, Texas, but largely grew up in New Jersey. She attended Rutgers University and, after graduating with a degree in English, became an elementary school teacher. Only after she had spent some years teaching, and reading romance novels in her leisure time, did she try her hand at writing. She was between jobs, with time on her hands, when she penned her first book, and she had written five book-length manuscripts before selling one of them, *An Original Sin* (1999), to Dorchester Publishing at the end of the 1990s.

After producing a half dozen romance novels, Bangs turned her attention to her first vampire series, which came to be called the *Mackenzie Vampires*, the first volume appearing early in 2004. Each of the four novels pits a female protagonist against one of the Mackenzies, a Scottish vampire line whose unattached males tend to be young, handsome alpha males ready for love and adventure. The first novel finds Blythe, an employee of Ecstasy, Inc. (a company that assists clientele in obtaining happiness), dealing with the seductive Darach Mackenzie, a 500-year-old vampire. Subsequent volumes focus on other couples—human female and vampire male—but bring back characters from the earlier stories.

Just as the second volume of the *Mackenzie Vampires* saga was to appear, the first volume of the *Castle of Dark Dreams* trilogy introduced readers to three vampires: Eric, Brynn, and Conall McNair. They inhabit a castle that is also an adult theme park, where adventurous women can assume fantasy roles in which eroticism is a commanding factor. Each of the three volumes introduced one of the brothers and the woman who challenged him.

> After producing a half dozen romance novels, Bangs turned her attention to her first vampire series, which came to be called the *Mackenzie Vampires*....

After the original trilogy, the *Castle of Dark Dreams* series was extended, with the eighth volume, *Forever Wicked*, appearing in 2017.

In 2008, Bangs initiated a new *Gods of the Night* series, which did not involve vampires as major players but included vampires as part of the supernatural environment in which all the action takes place. The third volume, *Eternal Prey*, appeared in 2011, with a promised fourth volume still in production. Thus, while Bangs is not bound to vampires, the good-guy vampires she has created assumed an important and continuing role in pushing her career forward, even as she has become a member of the small cadre of romance authors best known for their vampire characters. She has most recently returned to vampires, now part of the bad guys, in her novel *Eternal Pleasure* (2018).

Bergstrom, Elaine (1946–)

Elaine Bergstrom, a science fiction/horror fiction writer who has written five vampire books, was born in 1946 in Cleveland, Ohio. She later attended Marquette University, from which she graduated with a degree in journalism. She subsequently settled in Milwaukee, where she emerged as one of the state's best-known novelists.

Bergstrom burst onto the vampire scene in 1989 with the publication of *Shattered Glass*, a novel that introduced a new vampire, Stephen Austra, and his vampire family. They were an old and powerful family who quietly existed as glass workers, specifically the special leaded glass that went into the old cathedrals of Europe and their modern imitations. *Shattered Glass* brought Austra to the United States, where he met artist Helen Wells, who he turned into a vampire like himself. She became a continuing part of his story. The initial conflict concerned Austra's renegade brother, who forced the "good" Stephen into a final showdown. Included in the novel was one of the more horrific chapters in vampire literature: Austra's brother surprised the two lovers in bed in a hotel room and proceeded to vampirize them in a slow, torturous act.

The Austra family story was resumed in the subsequent novels *Blood Alone* (1990), *Blood Rites* (1991), and *Nocturne* (2003), and Elizabeth

Elaine Bergstrom is a sci-fi/horror novelist notable for her Austra family novels, beginning with Shattered Glass.

Austra meets the supernatural-seeking reporter Carl Kolchak in a short story included in the anthology *Kolchak: The Night Stalker Chronicles* (2005). Bergstrom's fourth vampire novel, *Daughter of the Night* (1992), was based on the life of Elizabeth Báthory and was especially inspired by its treatment in Raymond T. McNally's biographical study *Dracula Was a Woman.*

Additional titles from this very productive author have included *Tapestry of Dark Souls* (1993), a novel built around the characters of TSR, Inc.'s *Ravenloft*, one of their vampire-oriented role-playing games. It introduced the first lesbian couple to the *Dungeons & Dragons*/TSR universe. She followed it with a second *Ravenloft* novel, *Baroness of Blood* (1995). After the turn of the century, she turned to *Dracula* and explored the further adventures of Mina Harker in *Mina*, a character attacked by Dracula in the original Bram Stoker novel, and its sequel, *Blood to Blood: The Dracula Story Continues* (2000), the latter winning the Lord Ruthven Award as the best vampire fiction of the year.

ᶠ *Brewer, Zac (Heather)* ᶠ *(1973–)*

Novelist Zac Brewer was born on September 21, 1973, and was known until 2015 as Heather Brewer. He is the author of the five-volume vampire series *The Chronicles of Vladimir Tod*. Brewer currently resides in southern Illinois with his husband and daughter. His older son is currently serving in the U.S. Air Force. At the time of his name change, Brewer announced that he was transgender and in the process of physically transitioning. He has also emerged as an antibullying advocate.

The Chronicles of Vladimir Tod traced the middle and high school career of the vampire Vlad Tod, the product of a vampire father and human mother, the first volume of which, *Eighth Grade Bites*, explores his awakening to his vampire powers, even as he has to fend off a determined vampire hunter. Subsequent volumes reveal his awakening realization about himself and his ingenuity at balancing the pressures of high school with the need to survive the attacks of those who would rather see him dead.

Zac Brewers books have settings in the worlds of middle and high school.

Brewer followed the very successful *The Chronicles of Vladimir Tod* with a two-volume series focusing on Vlad's high school friend, Josh McMillan. After seeing his sister's murder by a vampire, Josh discovers his family's affiliation with the secretive Slayer Society, a group dedicated to ridding the world of vampires. He is recruited, trained, and sent into the world as a promising vampire slayer, possibly the youngest and strongest slayer in history.

Almost immediately, Josh is distracted by a more immediate problem: a traitor seems to be present in the society, whose identity he must discover before being killed himself. He will subsequently go on to full-time slaying as needed, first in New York and then in California. The three volumes of the *Slayer Chronicles* (*First Kill*, *Second Chance*, and *Third Strike*) appeared between 2011 and 2014.

Along with his very popular young-adult vampire series, Brewer has written multiple volumes in various genres.

Caine, Rachel (1962–2020)

Rachel Caine, a pen name of Roxanne Longstreet Conrad, was the author of the very popular young-adult vampire series the *Morganville Vampires*. She was born in 1962 at White Sand Missile Range in New Mexico and grew up in west Texas. She graduated from Texas Tech University in 1985. As she developed her career as a writer, she held various jobs in the business world and was, for a period, a professional musician. She was married to fantasy artist R. Cat Conrad.

The *Morganville Vampires* series, which initially appeared in 2006 (and continued for almost a decade) centers on Claire Danvers, who was born and raised in Morganville, a fictional town in Texas, which, unbeknownst to most residents, is being run by a group of vampires. As the story begins, Claire is 16 years old but has become an entering freshman at Texas Prairie University following her early graduation from high school.

Morganville had been originally founded by Amelie, a vampire who had been turned by Mr. Bishop, the oldest vampire in the world. She appears to be very young but is actually some 1,500 years of age. As the series develops, she manifests a particular relationship with Claire, at times treating her almost like a daughter. Bishop is an old vampire with grandiose goals. He is arrogant and considers all humans beneath him, little more than walking blood bags. At one point, Amelie joins with Myrnin, a Welsh vampire and alchemist who is seeking a cure to the disease many vampires contract as they age, and tries to kill Bishop, for which act Bishop seeks revenge.

The *Morganville Vampires* series found an audience very quickly and eventually ran for 15 volumes (2006–2013). Efforts were made to turn it into a TV series, but plans never reached fruition.

The Morganville Vampires *series was created by Rachel Caine.*

🦇 Cast, Kristin (1986–), and 🦇 P(hyllis) C(hristine) (1960–)

P. C. (Phyllis Christine) and Kristin Cast coauthored a popular young-adult vampire series called *House of Night*, which launched in 2007. P. C. Cast, Kristin's mother, was born in Watseka, Illinois. After high school, she joined the Air Force and, after her service, pursued a college degree with a literature major and a minor in secondary education. She resides in Oklahoma and, since 1993, has taught English at South Intermediate High School in Broken Arrow. Her first book, *Goddess of the Sea*, appeared in 2003. Meanwhile, in the 1980s, she married and had a daughter. Kristin grew up in Oklahoma and, after high school, attended Tulsa University. She now lives in Portland, Oregon.

In 2005, P. C.'s book agent suggested that she try to do a young-adult vampire novel. As Kristin was showing a bent for writing, it seemed natural to work together on the new venture. Their *House of Night* series introduced 16-year-old Zoey Redbird, who lives at a time when vampires are out in the open and tolerated by humans, at least most of them. As children grow up, the vampires will mark some as special, and they will be transferred from their normal situation to the House of Night school, where they will continue their education and be groomed as future "vampyres." Should their body reject the transformation, they will die.

Zoey is part white and part Native American (with a Cherokee grandmother). She is a typical, angst-filled teenager. She has been marked by no less a personage than the goddess Nyx (a reflection of the pantheon the Casts' earlier books had featured) and an indication that she has strong inherent powers. She seems to fit right in at the new school. She has friends and several boys who wish to be her special one, including the hottest of the lot. She has an antagonist, Aphrodite, who seems to be the jealous type, among her other faults, and, if Aphrodite fades, Neferet stands ready to cause trouble. The various cliques at the school set the possibilities of a host of stories. The vampires in the several books of the *House of Night* series are basically good-guy vampires, and Saint Germain (Chelsea Quinn Yarbro's main character) plus Angel and Spike from *Buffy the Vampire Slayer* inform the Casts' vampyres. However, their real distinctiveness comes from their mining the world of Western Paganism. They exist in a culture that is matriarchal. Also, their vampirism is more a biological condition than a supernatural transformation. In addition, the vampire mythos is based on biology. In some teenagers, hormones trigger a reaction in their DNA; their bodies begin a physiological process that transforms them either into a vampyre or a corpse. Their special powers are all earth-based abilities, such as controlling the element of air or having a special connection to horses. The Casts' vampires are also not immortal, just very long lived.

> The vampires in the several books of the *House of Night* series are basically good-guy vampires....

The Casts' vampires, as might be supposed from their all attending the same school, have a very communal existence. Early in one, the reader is introduced to a coven, the Dark Daughters, headed by Zoey's rival, Aphrodite. When she abuses her powers, Aphrodite loses her position as high priestess in training, and Zoey becomes the new leader.

In 2014, the mother–daughter team completed the *House of Night* series with the twelfth volume, *Redeemed*, but then extended Zoey's story with a second series called *House*

of Night: Other World, which extended through four volumes (2014–2020). Meanwhile, Kristin Cast moved out on her own and authored her own series, *The Escaped*, which explores a parallel world. Even earlier, P. C. Cast had begun to publish a new *Goddess Summoning* series, launched in 2008. Continued updates are always available from P. C. Cast at https://www.pc castauthor.com and from Kristin Cast at https:// kcastauthor.com.

Collins, Nancy A. (1959–)

Nancy Collins, an Arkansas native and the creator of the vampire character Sonja Blue, was born on September 10, 1959, and raised in Arkansas. She has traced her interest in horror to her grandfather's inviting her to join him at the local theater to watch the latest horror movies. He was a devout fan of Boris Karloff. After practicing her writing skills with short stories, Collins suddenly became a popular person in the literary world following her first novel, *Sunglasses after Dark* (1989), receiving the Bram Stoker Award. The novel introduced heiress Denise Thorne, who was raped and vampirized while in London and emerged out of the experience as the vampire Sonja Blue. Since adapting to her new existence, she had been searching for the man who attacked her. Blue's adventures would continue in three sequels: *In the Blood*, *Paint It Black*, and *A Dozen Black Roses*. The first three of the Sonja Blue novels were collected in the single volume *Midnight Blue: The Sonja Blue Collection* from White Wolf Publishing. *Sunglasses after Dark* was also adapted as a comic book by Verotik.

While best known for her vampire character, Collins has written widely in the horror field. Her short stories have appeared in various anthologies (*The Year's Best Fantasy and Horror*, *Best New Horror*, *The Definitive Best of the Horror Show*, *Splatterpunks*, and *The Best of Pulphouse*), and she is the coeditor of the erotic horror anthologies *Forbidden Acts* and *Dark Love*. Additional novels include *Walking Wolf*, *Wild Blood*, and *Tempter*, and for two years (1991–1993), she scripted DC Comics's *Swamp Thing* comic book series.

While authoring several vampire short stories, Collins returned to the vampire genre in a big way in 2008 with the first volume of a new vampire series directed at teenagers: *VAMPS*, which was about life at Báthory Academy, a private school for training the daughters of the finest vampire families. By the end of 2009, three volumes had appeared.

Collins has received the British Fantasy Society's Icarus Award and is also the founder of the International Horror Critics Guild.

Nancy Collins is the creator of the vampire character Sonja Blue.

Davidson, MaryJanice (1969–)

MaryJanice Davidson, the author of a 15-volume paranormal romance series of vampire novels, the *Undead* series, is the daughter of a U.S. Air Force officer. Like many children of those serving in the armed forces, she grew up in multiple locations, occasioned by her father's different postings. She began writing when she was 13. She later married and is the mother of two offspring.

The *Undead* series focuses upon Elizabeth Anne "Betsy" Taylor, a character introduced in an initial novel, *Undead and Unwed*, in 2004. Betsy is 30 years old and still single. Having recently joined the ranks of the unemployed, her condition is made worse when she is run over in a traffic accident and killed. She wakes up in a coffin only to discover that she is now a vampire. A former model, she is equally upset over the tacky shoes the undertaker has put on her feet for her viewing, and among her first acts after leaving her coffin, she reclaims her designer shoe collection.

Quite apart from her shoes, Betsy must come to grips with her new existence as a vampire. Even as she begins her new life, however, she is abducted by a 500-year-old vampire named Nostro, who currently rules the undead community. He targets her specifically, as he is aware that Betsy has shown a set of unique vampiric characteristics: she can walk in the sunlight without being consumed into flames; she has some control over her desires to consume blood; and she has no negative reaction to the cross and similar religious symbols. These attributes suggest that she is the prophesied Queen of the Vampires, and hence, her very existence challenges Nostro's authority. She frees herself from Nostro and aligns with a handsome vampire, Eric Sinclair, to challenge Nostro and his minions.

Undead and Unwed was an immediate success with readers of paranormal romance literature and received a *Romantic Times* Reviewers' Choice Award. Often cited as a major asset of Davidson's writing was the humor integrated throughout her novels. One manifestation of the humor was in the titles given the volumes—*Undead and Unappreciated, Undead and Unpopular, Undead and Underwater*—with the last volume being titled *Undead and Done*. Davidson was also lauded for including gay characters within Betsy's circle of close friends and supporters.

The *Undead* series ran for 15 volumes (2004–2016) and was supplemented with a number of short stories and novellas, a few issued as stand-alone publications. While few have attained the response as has the *Undead* series, Davidson has also expanded her writing and produced additional series involving different paranormal characters (werewolves, mermaids) and titles in other romance genres. She maintains a website at https://www.maryjanicedavidson.org.

Elrod, P. N. (1954–)

Patricia Nead Elrod, a popular author of vampire novels, began writing at the age of 12. She developed an interest in vampires at a young age while watching vampire movies and especially the *Dark Shadows* television series. In the 1980s, she became an active participant in role-playing games, particularly one called *Mercenaries, Spies, & Private Eyes*. In 1986, she entered a role-playing module into a *Dragon* magazine contest that eventually was bought

P. N. Elrod writes in genres ranging from mystery and sci-fi to paranormal romance and comedy. When it comes to vampires, she is known for her "Vampire Files" series.

and published in the first issue of *Dungeon Adventures*. This was her first professional publication. Meanwhile, through her role-playing, she developed a supernatural character, a vampire detective. At one point, she began to write up the game scenario, and it became the first of *The Vampire Files* novels, *Bloodlist*. She quickly followed it with *Lifeblood* and *Bloodcircle*. All three novels were published in 1990. Their success prompted the continuation of the series, and three more volumes appeared: *Art in the Blood* (1991), *Fire in the Blood* (1991), and *Blood on the Water* (1992). This series features Jack Fleming, a reporter who had been transformed into a vampire. After his transformation, he became a detective with a nonvampire partner, Charles Escott.

By this time, Elrod built her writings around what she thought of as interesting characters, some of whom just happened to be vampires who had to work out their relationship with the "normal" world. One such interesting character, Jonathan Barrett, who had appeared briefly in *Bloodcircle*, became the central figure for a second series, which recounted his life after becoming a vampire on the eve of the American Revolution. Having drunk blood from a vampire while away at college in England in an incident he merely thought of as kinky sex, Barrett became a vampire when he was killed shortly after his return to the colonies in America. His story of discovering what he had become on awakening from the dead was told in three volumes, the first of which, *Red Death*, appeared in 1993. Meanwhile, Elrod was asked by TRS, Inc., the publishers of the *Ravenloft* role-playing series, to write the autobiography of their main character, the vampire Strahd. *I, Strahd* appeared in 1993, and a sequel, *I, Strahd: The War with Azalin*, came out in 1998. Through the 1990s, Elrod became one of the most recognizable names among vampire fiction writers, and a P. N. Elrod Fan Club emerged in 1993. Through it, she kept her growing legion of fans aware of her new writing projects.

Into the new century, she has remained active in writing vampire fiction. She continued the adventures of Jack Fleming in *A Chill in the Blood* (1998), *The Dark Sleep* (1999), *Lady Crymsyn* (2001), *Cold Streets* (2003), *Song in the Dark* (2005), and *The Devil You Know* (2009), with additional titles in the pipeline. In the mid-1990s, she began a series of novels with coauthor Nigel Bennett (better known at the time as LaCroix in the *Forever Knight* television series). The first one, *Keeper of the King*, appeared in 1996. The novels were based upon the fantasy of a Sir Lancelot-like character having become a vampire. In the first novel, the knight, Richard d'Orleans, is brought into the modern age, where he meets contemporary challenges while tying up loose ends from his past. It proved popular enough to continue the adventures through sequels, *His Father's Son* (2001) and *Siege Perilous* (2004).

Feehan, Christine

Romance writer Christine Feehan is the author of the *Dark* series of novels, which is about a vampiric race called the Carpathians. Through 2019, some 34 titles have appeared, with additional volumes announced. Feehan was born Christina King in California, where she also grew to adulthood in a large family. She married Richard Feehan. Her first novel, *Dark Prince*, appeared in 1999. It was the first of her *Dark* novels, which together form about two-thirds of the novels she has written.

> The *Dark* series centers on the lives, struggles, and adventures of a people known as the Carpathians, who in the novels are an ancient race of hominids....

The *Dark* series centers on the lives, struggles, and adventures of a people known as the Carpathians, who in the novels are an ancient race of hominids that live unnoticed within the human community. Like traditional vampires, they live on human blood and have extremely long life spans. They can shape-shift and have considerable personal strength. Carpathians attempt to feed on humans in such a way as to not kill them and begin to arouse the world to their presence.

In the present, the Carpathians have a problem. In recent centuries, they have been unable to produce children who can survive their first year. It is also the case that it has been more than 500 years since a female has been born. Meanwhile, if unable to connect with a life mate, male Carpathians lose both their ability to see in color and to feel emotionally. They are only moved emotionally by the rush that comes from killing; however, the price of killing is their transformation into a soulless monster and a close resemblance to the traditional monster as an undead vampire. Vampires who are unable to find a mate often commit suicide by walking into the dawning sun. The dilemmas faced by the Carpathian males provide the majority of the material to be explored in Feehan's different novels, most of which center on the story of one particular individual. More recent novels will bring back fan-favorite characters for updating and encores.

Feehan has yet to announce any conclusion to her *Dark* series. In 2007, her novel *Dark Hunger* was adapted as a manga-style comic book. She maintains a website at http://www.christinefeehan.com. Meanwhile, her *Dark* series shows no sign of being exhausted, with volumes 34 and 35, *Dark Song* and *Dark Tarot*, appearing in 2020 and 2021, respectively.

Forrest, Bella

Bella Forest is simultaneously one of the most prolific and one of the more elusive paranormal romance authors, offering very little data on her personal history, even as she has turned out multiple titles monthly through the second decade of the new century. Beginning with a small self-publishing effort in 2012, through the remaining years of the decade, she has become widely known and read. She claims an early passion for writing that began as a child, having produced her first stories with her crayons. Through her school years, she began to practice her future craft more seriously.

Her first novel, *A Shade of Vampire*, which was published in 2012, centers on 17-

year-old Sofia Claremont. While walking on the beach, she is approached by a pale creature, who kidnaps her and takes her to The Shade, an island where the sun is eternally forbidden to shine. This enchanted place, not found on any map, is overseen by a powerful vampire. When she first awakes on the island, she finds herself as a chained captive. Amid other young women in a similar situation, she is selected to be sent to the harem of Derek Novak, the island's prince. She must now find a way to survive, and survive she does. Her story will continue through seven volumes and set the stage for additional stories of the other residents of The Shade. By the spring of 2020, 88 volumes of the *A Shade of Vampire* series had appeared, with no end in sight.

Meanwhile, even as the *A Shade of Vampire* series continued, Forrest produced multiple additional series, though none with anything approaching the number of volumes of her vampire series. In one such series, *Beautiful Monster*, for example, Liam Swift, an up-and-coming Hollywood star, quits his career and takes a job at a boarding school teaching drama. A female fan and resident at the school soon discovers the secret that led to Liam's career change: he has become a vampire.

> Beginning with a small self-publishing effort in 2012, through the remaining years of the decade, she [Bella Forrest] has become widely known and read.

Forrest's high output over eight years has led to speculation, with fans suggesting, among several possibilities, that Bella Forrest might be the name for a group of writers. Some fans have found it unbelievable that one person could have such a high output for any length of time. However, no evidence to provide credence to such speculations has, to date (2020), appeared.

Hamilton, Laurell K(aye) (1963–)

Laurell K. Hamilton is the author of an ongoing series of novels built around an alternative American history where, especially in the futuristic St. Louis, Missouri, vampires and werewolves have been integrated into the normal social order. Through the 1990s, the series steadily gained an ever-increasing readership, and Hamilton's books rose to the top of the vampire genre market.

Hamilton was born Laurell Kaye Klein on February 19, 1963, in rural Arkansas. Raised in a Christian Holiness environment, she began writing horror fiction as a youth. She then attended Marion College (now Indiana Wesleyan University), where she enrolled in a creative writing program, but she eventually left it, as her instructor was offended by her writing about vampires and other horrors. With a prediction that her writing would never amount to anything, she finished her college education in the biology department. After college, with her husband, Gary Hamilton, she moved to suburban St. Louis. In 1992, she saw her first novel, *Nightseer*, published. The first of the vampire/horror novels appeared the following year.

The key person in the new social order of alternate St. Louis in Hamilton's novels is Anita Blake, described as an animator and vampire hunter. Blake is a good example of what in comic book publishing is now termed a bad girl, a woman who is able to keep up with the best of the superheroes but is at the same time

Laurell Kaye Hamilton created an alternative history in which vampires and werewolves are integral members of society.

completely feminine and attractive to her male contemporaries. In Blake's case, both a vampire and a werewolf are after her—and not to satiate their thirst and hunger.

In the novels, Blake earns her living by reanimating the dead and facilitating the gaining of important information from them. She also operates as a vampire hunter when the situation calls for it. At all times, she is an intimate of the vampires and werewolves who live in St. Louis. Hamilton had noticed that in mystery novels, female detectives did not get to do any of the fighting that their male counterparts enjoyed, so she made sure that Anita did not lack violent encounters.

Hamilton's first novel, *Nightseer* (1992), did not bring much notice, but the first of her Anita Blake novels, *Guilty Pleasures* (1993), took off and led to six sequels over the next five years. By the end of decade, she had become one of the most noted writers in the vampire genre, and the early novels were brought out in omnibus volumes by the Science Fiction Fan Club. A Laurell K. Hamilton Fan Club flourished. Much to the delight of fans, Hamilton continued to produce new Anita Blake adventures through the second decade of the new century, with some 30 on the shelves by 2020 and no end in sight. In addition, she wrote a collection of short fiction, *Strange Candy* (2006), and a novella published, with a similar work by Charlaine Harris, are included in an anthology, *Bite* (2005).

Meanwhile, in 2006, a graphic art adaptation of the initial Anita Blake novel, *Guilty Pleasures*, was brought out as a cooperative venture by Dabel Brothers Productions and Marvel Comics. The monthly comic was drawn by Brett Booth from a script produced by Stacie M. Ritchie from Hamilton's text. The comic books were regularly gathered into graphic novels. After a brief hiatus following issue No. 6 in 2007, the monthly issues resumed from Marvel, with Ron Lim and Jess Ruffner as artist and writer. Along with *Guilty Pleasures*, Marvel also released a unique Anita Blake story, *First Death*, a prequel to *Guilty Pleasures*, which told the backstory for Blake. It was written by Jonathon Green and drawn by Wellington Alves. In 2009, Marvel released a new Anita Blake series, *The Laughing Corpse*.

As of 2020, Hamilton has, for almost two decades, remained near the top of the list of those writers best known for their vampire-related novels, though, like most of her peers, she writes other novels as well. She tries to maintain contact with her large readership through her website at http://www.laurellk hamilton.com. She is assisted in this process by the Laurell K. Hamilton Fan Club, which publishes the quarterly *News to Die for Newsletter*.

Harkness, Deborah (1965–)

Deborah Harkness, the author of the *A Discovery of Witches* series of novels, is a professor of history specializing in the history of science and medicine, with a concentration on the early modern world (1400–1700) at the University of Southern California. She earned degrees from Mount Holyoke College and Northwestern University prior to completing her doctorate at the University of California at Davis. Her scholarly output has included several books, among them *John Dee's Conversations with Angels* (1999) and *The Jewel House: Elizabethan London and the Scientific Revolution* (2007).

She attributes the addition of fictional writing to her career to a simple question she addressed to herself in 2008: "If there really are witches and vampires, what do they do for a living?" That question had been prompted by her noticing the number of books on the occult and on vampires and related creatures on display in an airport bookstore. As she continued her ruminations on that question, the first volume of her trilogy, *A Discovery of Witches* (2011), emerged.

A Discovery of Witches traces the story of Diana Bishop, a professor of the history of science (as is Harkness), who is conducting research at the famous Bodleian Library at the University of Oxford. She is also a witch, though having abandoned the family tradition as a child, she has not practiced magic/witchcraft in her adult life, stayed some distance from other witches, and allowed her powers to remain purely latent. All that changes when she discovers the existence of a lost manuscript, *Ashmole 782* (aka *The Book of Life*), within the library's collection. (The alchemist Elias Ashmole [1617–1692] was a real historical figure.) When Bishop requests it, the lost manuscript suddenly becomes available. It has an astounding result, triggering the emergence of her latent powers as soon as she touches it but also producing an unintended consequence of alerting other supernatural entities to the manuscript's reappearance.

The most important person attracted to the manuscript is Matthew Clairmont, a vampire who has been searching for it over the last century and a half. He hopes the manuscript will enlighten him and thus support his effort to stop a decline among vampires he has discerned and even turn it around. He soon arrives in Oxford ready to see the manuscript but encounters Diana Bishop instead. He subsequently develops protective feelings toward her, believing that her life may have been put in danger by her access to the manuscript. That initial relationship develops into a romantic attraction, even as Diana begins to investigate and develop the magical abilities she has inherited.

Author Deborah Harkness wrote the popular A Discovery of Witches *series.*

The story of Diana and Matthew's relationship is continued in two subsequent volumes: *Shadow of Night* (2012) and *The Book of Life* (2014). *A Discovery of Witches* had immediate success and debuted as number two on the *New York Times* best selling list. It went through seven printings in the first two months after its appearance. Film rights were sold to Warner, but that project never reached fruition. Instead, the novel was turned into a television series by Sky One in the United Kingdom. The first season ran in 2018 (eight episodes), with a second and third season ordered. The second season (ten episodes) is scheduled to appear in 2021. Meanwhile, Harkness has issued a volume exploring the historical and contemporary background of her novels, *The World of All Souls: A Complete Guide to* A Discovery of Witches, Shadow of Night *&* The Book of Life (2019).

Harris, Charlaine (1951–)

Mystery writer Charlaine Harris is the popular author of the *Southern Vampire Mysteries*, a series of vampire novels that began to appear in 2001 and were subsequently adapted as a popular television series, *True Blood*, on HBO. The series takes its name from the premise that vampires have been able to become a public segment of human society because a substitute for blood, which they needed to survive, has become commercially available. It is being bottled and distributed under the label "Tru Blood."

Charlaine Harris is the author of the popular Southern Vampire Mysteries *series.*

Harris was born and raised in Tunica, Mississippi, the daughter of a librarian mother and school principal father. She attended Southwestern (now Rhodes) College in Memphis and later settled in southern Arkansas with her husband, where she attended writing classes at the University of Missouri at St. Louis. She had begun writing in her youth but only after settling into family life did she turn to writing novels and find a publisher to accept them for publication. Her first novel appeared in 1981. She initially attained success writing mysteries built around an amateur female sleuth, Aurora Teagarden, which first appeared in 1991. That series continues to the present (2020).

She later launched a second detective series before turning to write the *Southern Vampire Mysteries* series at the end of the 1990s. The first of the vampire novels, *Dead until Dark*, appeared in 2001. At least one new novel in the series appeared annually through the decade. The series was hailed for both its captivating storytelling and a raucous sense of humor.

Dead until Dark introduced Sookie Stackhouse, a waitress in a small Louisiana community, Bon Temps, and her vampire mate, Bill Compton, a Civil War veteran who was turned into a vampire as he made his way home with the close of hostilities. Sookie is a telepath who can read people's minds, an ability setting up numerous situations when their thoughts and words diverge widely. As the reader is introduced to Sookie, vampires have entered the mainstream, taking a place in contemporary society. They are opposed by some who believe them to be an alien, evil species. They are supported by vampire-rights activists. Sookie has a live-and-let-live approach. Then, she meets Bill Compton, whose thoughts she cannot read. Around him, she can have some peace and quiet. One evening, after he had come to the restaurant where she works, she discovered him under attack from some people who wanted to rob him of his blood. Vampire blood is a hot, if illegal, substance which has a powerful effect on humans. She saved Bill, who had been immobilized under a chain of silver.

The television series follows Sookie's (Anna Paquin) career as a waitress at Merlotte's, the restaurant in Bon Temps, which is owned by Sam Merlotte (Sam Trammell), who turns out to be a shapeshifter. Bill Compton (Stephen Moyer), the handsome, 173-year-old vampire, has returned to Bon Temps to inherit the family property after his last remaining human relative has died. The main storyline of the first season concerned the murders of several women all connected to Sookie's brother, Jason (Ryan Kwanten), including his grandmother. Three young women—Maudette Pickens, Dawn Green, and Amy Burley—were all strangled shortly after having been alone with Jason. Though Detective Bellefleur had little doubt that Jason was the killer, the town sheriff did not suspect him. Jason and Sookie's grandmother was murdered shortly afterward. As the season ends, it was revealed that Arlene Fowler's fiancé, Rene Lenier, was actually a man named Drew Marshall who created a fake identity and had been killing women he considered "fang-bangers."

The vampires in Harris's books are organized into a hierarchical society with their own

own system of laws. Local areas are administered by a sheriff and larger areas by a queen or king. As a whole, the vampires are very traditional. They are bound to the night, have retractable fangs that leave marks on their victims, and have extra (if not extraordinary) strength. Many are good guys, but others are more traditionally bad. Vampires are opposed by an antivampire religious movement called the Fellowship of the Sun.

> The vampires in Harris's books are organized into a hierarchical society with their own system of laws.

Subsequent volumes (eight in all as of 2009) in the Sookie Stackhouse saga continue her misadventures as a human telepath working with the vampire community, who prize her ability to find bad guys who try to mess with them. At the same time, she develops relations with the werewolf shapeshifters, especially when she has problems with Bill. At the same time, Bill is not the only vampire who finds her attractive.

Harris's vampire books have been among the most heralded ever in the paranormal romance field. The HBO series that began in 2008 concluded after seven seasons in 2014. The last of the *Southern Vampire Mysteries*, *Dead Ever After*, was released in 2013, though a volume of short stories, *Dead But Not Forgotten: Stories from the World of Sookie Stackhouse*, was brought out in 2014.

In the wake of the Sookie Stackhouse stories, Harris launched a second vampire-related series, the *Midnight, Texas* trilogy. The stories are built around psychic/medium Manfred Barnardo, who flees to the small Texas town of Midnight to escape his problems. There, he finds a community of supernatural creatures from Fiji Cavanaugh, a witch who manages Midnight's occult shop, to the reverend (Emilio Sheehan), a minister and weretiger. Among the most important of the local residents is Lemuel "Lem" Bridger, a vampire who had come to Midnight in the 1950s. He is married to Olivia, a professional assassin. The triolgy was turned into a television series, which ran for two years (2017–2018).

Harris maintains a website at http://www .charlaineharris.com.

🦇 *Harrison, Kim (1966–)* 🦇

Kim Harrison is a pen name used by writer Dawn Cook, an author of young adult fantasy novels who in 2004 began a new series of books about Rachel Morgan, a witch and agent for a security force who keeps the supernatural creatures of Cincinnati, Ohio, in line. Cook, the only daughter among her parents' many children, became a tomboy in self-defense. She grew up near Ann Arbor, Michigan. She majored in science in college and, after graduation, married and settled down in South Carolina, where she continues to reside. She has two children. In the process, she became a devotee of romance novels, the world of fantasy and science fiction, and Clint Eastwood movies. Prior to 2009, she tried to keep the Cook and Harrison identities separate.

Kim Harrison is a young adult fantasy novelist known for her witch character, Rachel Morgan.

The Kim Harrison novels center on a fictional Cincinnati, where a science fiction/fantasy world makes romance possible. In the not-too-distant future, the Inderland has become visible. It is the realm in which vampires, witches, werewolves, and other supernatural creatures have existed on the edge of human awareness. A tomato virus that proved fatal only to humans wiped out most of the human race and ultimately brought the Inderlanders into the open. In Cincinnati, the Inderlanders reside in an area known as the Hollows.

Rachel Morgan, the heroine featured in Harrison's books, is a witch who works for Inderland Security. While the Federal Inderland Bureau (managed by humans) has ultimate charge of controlling Inderlander–human interaction, Inderland Security (run by Inderlanders) has charge of any matters that mystify the FIB. Tired of her job, Morgan found a way to sever her contract with IS and become an independent bounty hunter with a vampire named Ivy Tamwood and a pixie named Jenks as her partners. As she pursues her supernatural villains, she constantly has to be on the alert for Ivy, who really wants to bite the boss and turn her into a mere minion. She also has to contend with Kisten, her boyfriend, who is also a vampire. (Ivy got her own story in "Undead in the Garden of Good and Evil," a short story in the anthology *Dates from Hell.*) Rachel Morgan made her first appearance in *Dead Witch Walking* in 2004. By 2009, she had invited readers along on seven adventures that included tracking down a drug dealer and a serial killer, dealing with a war between vampires and werewolves, and facing off against a spectrum of demons (who smudged her aura). More adventures were waiting in the wings.

Cook's books, written as Kim Harrison, numbered 17 by 2020. One unique characteristic of the successive volumes is that their names were all variations of the names of Clint Eastwood movies: *Dead Witch Walking, Every Which Way But Dead, The Outlaw Demon Wails, The Undead Pool,* and *The Witch with No Name.*

Through her first decade as a published author, Harrison won several awards for her books from both romance and fantasy/science fiction colleagues. She maintains a website at http://www.kimharrison.net.

Holder, Nancy (1952–)

Nancy Holder is the prolific author of a set of novels and several nonfiction books related to the popular vampire television shows *Buffy the Vampire Slayer* and *Angel*. She was born Nancy Lindsay Jones in Los Altos, California, on August 29, 1953. Her father was a Navy officer, and she grew up in California and Japan. She left school at 16 to study ballet in Germany, but several years later, she returned to California and studied communications at the University of California at San Diego, graduating summa cum laude. Her daughter, Belle Claire Christine Holder, was born in 1996.

Holder published her first novel in 1983 under her family name. Then, just as the *Buffy the Vampire Slayer* series began its television run, she was invited to be one of the authors who would write the spin-off novels, both original stories and adaptations of the episodes of the series. Almost half of those novels were coauthored with friend and colleague Christopher Golden, including the *Sunnydale High Yearbook*, while several were also written with Jeff Mariotte. In one sense, novels that are part of franchises are hardly the place where a fiction writer shows their greatest creativity, as they must be developed according to strict guidelines of, in this case, the television show, and on what any given character may or may not be or do. At the same time, however, such writing demands a set of special skills to be able to write with a creative edge and in an entertaining fashion while maintaining the guidelines.

Holder has shown a special ability in this regard and, in addition to *Buffy* and *Angel*, has written for a variety of television franchises. In between these assignments, she has been able to produce additional novels on self-chosen topics.

She and Golden also cowrote the first volume of the *Buffy the Vampire Slayer: The Watcher's Guide*, the first of several semi-official books about the show. Holder joined with her colleagues Jeff Mariotte and Maryelizabeth Hart to produce volume two of the *The Watcher's Guide* plus *Angel: The Casefiles*. In the process of writing the many novels and working on the two volumes of the *The Watcher's Guide*, she

Nancy Holder pens spin-off novels based on the Buffy the Vampire Slayer *franchise.*

became somewhat of an expert on the show and was invited to contribute essays to two of the nonfiction anthologies on *Buffy* and *Angel*. She was one of the featured speakers at the Slayage scholars' conference in Nashville in 2004.

Most recently, while also producing novels in various genres, Holder worked on several projects for the 20th anniversary of the premiere of the *Buffy the Vampire Slayer* series. First, writing as fictional librarian Rupert Giles, she produced *Demons of the Hell Mouth: A Guide for Slayers* (2017), a survey of the evil (and not-so-evil) supernatural inhabitants of the *Buffy* universe. She followed it with the

Buffy the Vampire Slayer Encyclopedia (2017), possibly the best overall guide to the series. Both volumes drew on her earlier experience with producing *Buffy* guides.

Holder is a four-time winner of the Bram Stoker Award, given by the Horror Writer Association for superior achievement in horror writing, a sign of the respect for Holder among her professional colleagues. Having authored over 80 novels, she occasionally teaches courses in writing and on *Buffy the Vampire Slayer* at the University of California at San Diego. She maintains her website at http://www.nancy holder.com.

🦇 *Huff, Tanya (1957–)* 🦇

Tanya Huff, a Canadian writer and author of several science fiction/fantasy novel series and preeminently of two series of vampire novels, was born in Halifax, Nova Scotia, and attended Ryerson Polytechnical Institute, where she earned an associate degree in radio and television arts. In the mid-1980s, she opened the Bakka Phoenix, now Toronto's premier science fiction bookstore, and turned to writing during her spare time. Her first published works were children's fantasy fiction stories.

Huff endeared herself to vampire fans with a series of novels about detective Vicki Nelson, formerly a police officer who had been forced to retire due to failing eyesight. In her first adventure, *Blood Price*, she becomes involved in a case in which a serial killer is leaving bodies scattered around Toronto drained of blood. She soon encountered Henry Fitzroy, an illegitimate son of King Henry VIII and a vampire now living in Canada. Fitzroy was brought out of his private world by the killing, which he attributed to a young vampire in the throes of a feeding frenzy. Their work together to solve the case would lead to their sharing both their bedroom and a series of adventures into the supernatural.

Fitzroy is similar to traditional vampires except, since he is not evil, Huff saw no reason for religious symbols, like the cross, to harm him and, equally, could see no reason that he should defy the laws of physics by creating no reflection in the mirror. After the fourth Nel-

Tanya Huff is noted for her Blood Books *series in which a vampire works with a detective to solve crimes.*

son/Fitzroy novel in 1993, rumors flew through the sci-fi world that Huff was abandoning her characters and, for five years, nothing more was heard of her. However, in 1997, they again appeared, much to the delight of Huff's fans. Then, in 2007, the novels were adapted for two seasons on television, which aired in the spring and fall of 2007 under the title *Blood Ties*. DVDs of the series were released in 2009.

Meanwhile, Huff launched a new series of novels built around Tony Foster, Fitzroy's former donor and gay lover. In this series, he has moved to Vancouver to take a job in television—interestingly, on a show about a vampire detective. The first of the trilogy, *Smoke and Shadows*, appeared in 2004, to be followed by *Smoke and Mirrors* (2005) and *Smoke and Ashes* (2006).

🦇 *Jungman, Ann (1938–)* 🦇

Ann Jungman, a British author of juvenile literature, was born in London, the daughter of Jewish refugees from Germany. She later entered Exeter University to study law but soon shifted her focus to education in preparation for becoming a primary school teacher.

In the 1970s, Jungman emerged as an author of children's books, her first title, *Fang the Fiery Dragon*, being released in 1972. A decade later, she released her most heralded title, *Vlad the Drac* (1982). As a baby vampire, Vlad was discovered sleeping under a stone by two children, Paul and Judy Stone, who had come to Romania on a tour with their parents. Vlad reveals his secret to his new acquaintances. He is a vampire but also a vegetarian who faints at the sight of blood. They, in turn, take it upon themselves to keep his secret, hide him from their parents, and oversee his safe arrival in England. They were able to keep Vlad's secret for almost a year, during which time the two children and their new friend have multiple adventures. The secret finally comes out when Vlad confronts Judy's teacher after she dared to deny that vampires really existed. The incident forces the children to reveal Vlad's existence to their parents. After the revelation, Vlad makes plans to return to Romania, where he will eventually marry and have a family of his own.

> Ann Jungman is known for *Vlad the Drac,* which is about a baby vampire who is adopted by humans.

The success of the original *Vlad the Drac* book led to five additional books, tracing his career through the 1980s into the 1990s. The reception given to *Vlad the Drac* would also lead to Jungman developing further vampire books. In 1989, she issued the first of three books featuring Count Boris Bolescu, an evil vampire who lived in a castle in a remote corner of Transylvania whom everyone thought was dead long ago (*Count Boris Bolescu and the Black Pudding*, 1989). The Romanian Tourist Board came to the castle, hoping to turn it into a tourist site for vampire enthusiasts from other countries. Shortly after the castle is opened, a visiting group leaves one of their number, a young girl named Mandy, behind. She discovers the count and his wife, Caroline, while exploring the castle. As the evening proceeds, Mandy meets the elderly couple and shares her food, especially some blood pudding, with him. He likes it, and she promises to keep him supplied in the future. The police and Mandy's parents arrive, and over the next few years, a package faithfully arrived at the castle, which the count and his wife consumed. In subsequent volumes, the count and his wife visit England to judge a pudding contest (*Count Boris Bolescu and the Transylvania Tango*, 1991) and a tour arrives at the castle in Romania to celebrate Midsummer's Eve (*Count Boris Bolescu and the Midnight Madness*, 1994).

Still interested in presenting vampires to children, Jungman did a series of chapbooks (1989–1996), this time about Count Dracula himself. In the series, Dracula becomes the center of a monster mash as he successively meets a ghost, Frankenstein's monster, a witch, and a werewolf.

In 1999, Jungman, now nearing retirement age, founded Farm Owl Books, a publishing house specializing in publishing worthy children's books that had gone out of print. She maintains a website at http://www.ann jungman.com.

Even as she emerged as a beloved author of children's books, Jungman has also made a place for herself as an independent voice on Jewish affairs. She was particularly concerned about rights for Palestinians, a stance that separated her from many British Jews.

🦇 *Kalogridis, Jeanne (1954–)* 🦇

Jeanne Kalogridis, who also writes under the pen name J. M. Dillard, is the author of a series of novels based on Dracula. She grew up in Florida with an interest in books and language. She attributes her love of reading as a response to her less-than-ideal childhood, during which she found that fantasy provided an escape from the unpleasant present and horror a safe means of confronting fear, pain, and death. After earning a bachelor's degree in Russian, she attended graduate school at the University of South Florida, where she received a master's degree in linguistics in 1980.

Jeanne Kalogridis has written stories drawing from the Dracula character in The Diaries of the Family Dracul.

Afterward, she did postgraduate work at Georgetown University and taught English as a second language at American University. After teaching for eight years, she decided to begin writing full time. For more than a decade, she wrote quite successfully under a pseudonym and then, in the mid-1990s, decided to publish under her own name.

Kalogridis was particularly affected by reading *Dracula* and reread it several times. She also read biographies of Vlad the Impaler. When she finally went to write about the Dracula family, she modeled her Dracula after Vlad. In the Dracula trilogy through which she began to introduce herself to the reading public, she focuses on the idea of Dracula having a covenant with his human family that has been kept alive over the centuries. The first of the novels, *Covenant with the Vampire* (1994), introduces Dracula's family some 50 years prior to the events in Bram Stoker's *Dracula*. According to Kalogridis's novel, at the castle of Prince Vlad, Vlad's great-nephew Arkady has recently taken over the job of managing the thriving, busy estate. Arkady is honored to care for his beloved, though eccentric, great-uncle ... until he begins to realize what is expected of him in his new role. Dracula's family members are bound by a covenant to serve Dracula and to protect him, meaning that Arkady must provide his great-uncle with victims to satisfy his needs, or Vlad will kill those whom Arkady loves.

The covenant traps him into becoming an accessory to murder and sadistic torture. When Arkady discovers that his newborn son has been designated as Dracula's successor, Arkady decides that he must oppose Dracula and save his son. The scene is set for the battle that continues in the two sequels, *Children of the Vampire* (1995) and *Lord of the Vampires* (1996).

Since her Dracula trilogy, Kalogridis has written a number of books but has not returned to the vampire theme.

Kenyon, Sherrilyn (1965–)

Sherrilyn Kenyon, who also writes under the pen name Kinley MacGregor, is the author of the multivolume *Dark-Hunter* vampire series. She was born and raised in Columbus, Georgia. She began writing during her grammar school years, actually winning a writing contest in the third grade and another the following year. Writing provided an escape from an abusive family situation, and she was only seven when she wrote a "novel," a horror story reflecting her life at home. She was an early devotee of movies with horror and paranormal themes.

Unable to afford her first choice for college, the Savannah College of Art and Design, Kenyon attended the local state college and majored in English, hoping to be admitted into the creative writing program. Several physical problems blocked her admission to both the creative writing and the journalism programs. She wound up with an interdisciplinary degree in history, language, and classical studies. At about this time, the untimely death of her older brother took away her desire to write, which only returned several years later.

In the early 1990s, she sold her first novel, *Born of Night*, which was soon followed by several others, but she encountered a period where she was unable to sell anything and battled personal problems, which drove her to the brink of giving up on a writing career for the second time. Then, in 1998, she sold a book that appeared under the pseudonym of Kinley MacGregor. She signed up with a new agent and began circulating her first vampire book. Unfortunately, it arrived in New York just as many publishing houses had decided to shy away from vampire novels (despite the fact that the market for them had not diminished). The Dracula centennial had passed, and *Buffy the Vampire Slayer* had yet to manifest its potential. It took several years to finally sell her novel *Fantasy Lover*, which was eventually published in 2002.

Fantasy Lover was a success, and Kenyon was able to develop a series of interconnected books, which became known as the *Dark-Hunters* series. They draw directly upon her clas-

The *Dark-Hunter series is by Sherrilyn Kenyon, aka Kinley MacGregor.*

sical studies and revolve around a group of human protectors who shield people from supernatural predators sent by ancient Greek gods. The three types of protectors include Dark-Hunters, who protect the night; Dream-Hunters, who protect the subconscious and unconscious; and Were-Hunters, who protect the outer reaches of our world. Among the supernatural predators are the vampires, who in Kenyon's world are called Daimons. Daimons are unique (relative to traditional fictional vampires) in that they can only live 27 years, the result of a curse that the god Apollo placed on them. To extend its life, a Daimon must steal a human soul, but Apollo's sister, Artemis, established the Dark-Hunters, whose job is to kill the Daimons and free any human souls before they die.

Over the next seven years, Kenyon would write 19 *Dark-Hunter* novels (most but not all with vampires), including one published as an e-book. As the series took off, she also published a number of *Dark-Hunter* short stories, which appeared in various romance anthologies. Most of the novels center on a particular Dark-Hunter, the women in his life, and the particular personal problems he has to solve as he goes about slaying the evil vampires. Kenyon also coauthored *The Dark-Hunter Companion*, a nonfiction guide to the Dark-Hunter universe and its inhabitants.

In what became a complete reversal of her situation in the 1990s, in the new century, she has become a very successful, best selling, award-winning author who has generated a very different approach to vampires. She is also among the minority of authors in the romance field to portray primarily evil vampires. Kenyon continues to produce projects and future *Dark-Hunter* novels, of which 30 volumes had appeared by 2018; she also maintains an expansive website (https://www.sherrilynkenyon.com). Though primarily known for her *Dark-Hunter* vampire novels, she has written a variety of other books, including some well-received nonfiction titles.

Kikuchi, Hideyuki (1949–)

Japanese author Hideyuki Kikuchi is the creator of the character Vampire Hunter D, the main character in an expansive series of novels, comic books, and two movies, where his image has been additionally brought to life by artist Yoshitaka Amano. Kikuchi was born in Choshi, Japan; he attended Aoyama Gakuin University and then received training from Kazuo Koike (1936–2017), a famed writer of Japanese manga (comic books) who was credited as a major force in the development of Japanese popular culture in the 1970s.

Kikuchi published his first novel, *Demon City Shinjuku*, in 1982. It gave birth to six sequels and also prepared the way for the first *Vampire Hunter D* novel the following year.

Kikuchi conceived D as a *dhampir*, the offspring of a vampire father and a human hunter. In Slavic vampire lore, a *dhampir* is seen as especially talented as a vampire hunter. D lives, however, in a future postnuclear dystopian Earth. Prior to the nuclear war, the ruling vampire nobility had planned for such a possibility and buried all the necessities that would be needed to rebuild. As D's story begins, the vampires are restoring society in their image. He is one of a small group of independent hunters-for-hire dedicated to eliminating supernatural threats.

In this new world, vampires have the technology to create a blood substitute as food but prefer to feed on humans. Thus, they are creating

The 1983 debut cover of Vampire Hunter D *by Hideyuki Kikuchi; illustrated by Yoshitaka Amano.*

a civilization in which vampires and humans coexist but one that stagnates as the vampires are at their zenith of existence and appear doomed to fall at the hands of humans. The human race at this time fears the vampires but has an inability to remember vampire weaknesses, such as garlic and crucifixes. D exists as neither vampire nor human and is feared by both. He has the strength of a vampire with additional supernatural powers that make him even stronger. He periodically suffers from sunsickness, a severe type of sunstroke, but also recovers from it at a rate far more rapid than other *dhampirs*. D is also the host for a sentient symbiote in the form of a wisecracking homunculus (a miniature, fully formed human) residing in his left palm, named simply Left Hand, possessed of a spectrum of useful powers such as inducing sleep or diagnosing the medical condition of someone.

Periodically reappearing in D's life is Dracula, the legendary god-king to the vampires. Dracula has two sides, sometimes manifesting as an intelligent lawgiver and other times as a ruthless scientist breeding experiments with humans in order to perpetuate the vampire species. Dracula may be D's physical father.

D's adventures initially found release in 31 novels (some multivolume), published in Japanese. They are currently (2020) still in the process of being translated into English, with the first volume having appeared in 2005. As of 2016, 21 volumes have appeared in English. In 2011, Kikuchi launched a spin-off series, *Another Vampire Hunter: The Noble Graylancer.* This series is set some 5,000 years in the past, before *Vampire Hunter D*, and follows the story of the rise of vampire nobility, especially the exploits of Lord Graylancer.

Even prior to the translation of the novels, an English-speaking audience was introduced to Vampire Hunter D through a full-length anime movie. Released in 1985, it is deemed by many critics as one of the best vampire movies ever. A sequel, *Vampire Hunter D: Bloodlust*, appeared in 2000. Meanwhile, *Vampire Hunter D* was adapted as a video game in 1999.

In 2007, the initial volume of a *Vampire Hunter D* manga series was issued simultaneously in the United States, Japan, and Europe. It was intended to adapt all of the books into the manga format but ended after eight volumes due to an injury that sidelined the primary artist, Saiki Takaki. Additional adaptations have been announced but have yet to appear.

Kikuchi remains a prolific and popular writer in Japan, though his production on new *Vampire Hunter D* stories seems to have been abandoned for the moment. Meanwhile, artist Yoshitaka Amano has produced a set of volumes highlighting his artwork for *Vampire Hunter D*.

King, Stephen (1947–)

Since the mid-1970s, Stephen King has been America's premier horror fiction writer. He was born in Portland, Maine, the son of Nellie Ruth Pillsbury and Donald King. As a child, he began to write science fiction short stories and, at the age of 12, submitted his first stories to *Fantastic* and *The Magazine of Fantasy and Science Fiction.* King graduated from the University of Maine in 1970. His first published story, "The Glass Floor," appeared in *Startling Mystery Stories* in 1967, while he was still in college.

Unable to obtain a job as an English teacher, King started working in an industrial laundry. During this period, he wrote a number of short stories and, in 1972, began working on his first book, *Carrie,* eventually published by Doubleday & Company. King then turned his attention to a vampire tale originally called "Second Coming" but later renamed "Jerusalem's Lot." The story was published in 1975 as *Salem's Lot.* Meanwhile, King, a methodical writer, was working on his subsequent novels, *The Shining* (1977) and *The Stand* (1978).

In 1976, *Salem's Lot* was nominated for a World Fantasy Award in the best novel category. That same year, *Carrie* was released as a movie, starring Sissy Spacek. King, a very fertile storyteller, also began to publish material under a pseudonym, Richard Bachman; the first title, *Rage,* appeared in 1977. He also published a second vampire short story, "One for the Road," that year.

In the 1980s, King enjoyed immense success. In his novels, he has attempted to explore the vast world of horror and terror and, by choice, has rarely returned to a theme once treated. Thus, after one successful vampire volume, he has not returned to the topic for a book, though he published a vampire novella story, "The Night Flier," in 1988. Meanwhile, several of his novels flirted with vampirism.

The most obvious was *The Tommyknockers* (1987), which featured an alien vampire.

In 1979, *Salem's Lot* was made into a television miniseries under the direction of Tobe Hooper, and a sequel movie (not based on King's writing), *A Return to Salem's Lot,* appeared in 1987. *Salem's Lot,* this time starring Rob Lowe, was remade in 2004 under the direction of Mikael Solomon. *The Tommyknockers* was brought to the screen (for television) in 1993 and *The Night Flier* in 1997.

King has continued to write about two novels annually, his output only slowing slightly following the accident in 1999 that almost

Stephen King was a pioneer in bringing horror to modern, ordinary American towns, including with several vampire tales.

killed him. He did not return to the vampire theme in the 1990s. Vampires reappeared in his fiction, however, in 2003 in *Wolves of the Calla* in the middle of *The Dark Tower* series. Its sequel, *Song of Susannah* (2004), features psychic (or emotional) vampires. The most notable of the vampire characters is Dandelo (aka Joe Collins), who almost succeeds in killing Roland, the hero of the series.

Among King's most recent contribution to vampire literature has been his collaboration with Scott Snyder on a graphic novel, *American Vampire* (2011). This volume intertwines two stories. One story, by Snyder, follows Pearl, a young woman

in Los Angeles in the 1920s who pursues a path of vengeance against the vampires who tortured and abused her. King's story focuses on Skinner Sweet, the original American vampire, who exists as the strongest and fastest vampire ever seen and is endowed with rattlesnakelike fangs.

Since 1985, when it was it revealed that he had written the Richard Bachman books, King's name has appeared on new printings of them. As might be expected, King has received numerous awards for his writing, including eight Bram Stoker Awards and a Lifetime Achievement Award (2003) bestowed by his colleagues in the Horror Writers' Association.

🦇 *Lumley, Brian (1937–)* 🦇

Brian Lumley, author of the *Necroscope* series of vampire books, was born on December 2, 1937, in Horden, Durham, England. Trained as a lawyer, he joined the British Army in the 1950s and served in Germany and Cyprus. He was in Cyprus when he began to write seriously, and the island inspired his first professional short story, "The Cyprus Shell." It and others were collected to make his first book, *The Caller of the Black*, published by Arkham House in 1970. Arkham House specialized in books in the H. P. Lovecraft horror tradition. Lumley adopted the Lovecraft myth of Cthulhu, the idea of ancient, demonic forces that had been pushed aside by the forces of civilization but lay just beneath the surface of civilization, awaiting any opportunity to return to power. This myth stood behind his first novels *The Burrowers Beneath* (1974) and *Beneath the Moors* (1974) and most of his subsequent writings.

In 1986, *Necroscope* was published, the first book in what became one of the most popular series of vampire books ever. The series tells the story of Harry Keogh, a necroscope (someone who can speak to the dead). Scottish-born Keogh was the son of a psychic-sensitive Russian

émigré. As he grew up, he discovered that he not only had his mother's sensitivity but that his psychic talents were even more extraordinary. He was able to contact the dead in their graves.

Necroscope *series author Brian Lumley.*

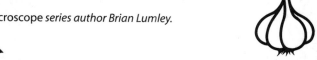

In Lumley's alternative world, the dead moved into a new state of immobility and incorporeality but retained a continued existence through conscious mental processes. Their relationship to Keogh allowed them an outlet to the world. Thus, they loved and respected him.

Keogh's talents pushed him into the world of espionage. He was pitted against Boris Dragosani, a ghoulish necromancer who dissected dead bodies with his hands to gain information by holding their various body parts. Dragosani killed the head of the psychic branch of British intelligence to gain the secrets of their work with people of psychic ability. Keogh decided he had to kill Dragosani but, at the time, was unaware of the real threat; Dragosani had developed a relationship with a powerful vampire named Thibor Frenczy. The battle with

Frenczy and Dragosani became the prelude to an ongoing battle with the vampiric world that unfolded in the subsequent volumes of the *Necroscope* series: *Vamphyri!* (1988), *The Source* (1989), *Deadspeak* (1990), and *Deadspawn* (1991). The story continued in a second series, *Vampire World*, three volumes of which appeared in the mid-1990s.

Lumley continued to work on his vampire mythos through 2001 and then took a break for several years but has continued with two volumes in 2009. In these later volumes, Harry Keogh's place has been taken by a new necroscope, Scott St. John. The entire *Necroscope* library currently consists of some 20 volumes, including the collections of related short stories, the most recent of which, *The Last of the Lost Years*, appeared in 2020.

Mead, Richelle (1976–)

Richelle Mead, an author of fantasy literature especially aimed at young adults, is best known for authoring several series of vampire fiction. Born and raised in Michigan, she attended the University of Michigan, from which she earned her bachelor's degree. She later earned master's degrees from both Western Michigan University and the University of Washington. She subsequently taught school and settled in Kirkland (suburban Seattle), Washington.

She began writing in her free time and finally sold an initial novel in 2007. *Succubus Blues* introduced Georgina Kincaid, a human who is also an immortal succubus. She holds a mundane job at a bookstore, though her real job consists of tempting men to illicit sex, a task that has the added consequence of allowing her to keep her own personal magical essence fully charged. In the initial novel, Kinkaid's situation is threatened when her favorite author's arrival in town for a book signing coincides with several of her immortal colleagues dying under mysterious cir-

Richelle Mead pens fantasy fiction for young adults, including the Vampire Academy *novels.*

cumstances. Something seems to be stalking them. The Georgina Kinkaid series would eventually include seven volumes (2007–2011).

Even as the Georgina Kinkaid novel series took off, Mead launched a second series with an initial volume, *Vampire Academy*, released some six months after *Succubus Blues*. This new series focused upon Rosemarie "Rose" Hathaway, a 17-year-old (as the series begins) *dhampir* (half human/half vampire) who is training to be a guardian who will eventually serve her best friend, Vasilisa "Lissa" Dragomir, who is a *moroi* (vampire). Her training will equip her to defeat *strigoi* (evil undead vampires).

In the initial novel of the series, an experienced guardian, Dimitri Belikov, is selected to be Lissa's immediate guardian and the person to oversee the training of her future guardian, Rose. It has been determined that Rose would make an excellent future guardian for Lissa, as the two have a rare, if one-sided, psychic bond that allows Rose to know Lissa's thoughts and emotions and, most importantly, her whereabouts. Shortly thereafter, circumstances are set up for trouble as Lissa develops a relationship with a fellow *moroi* named Christian Ozera, whose parents have become *strigoi*. Simultaneously, Rose and Dimitri develop forbidden feelings for each other.

Vampire Academy was an immediate hit and would lead to five subsequent volumes (2007–2010). Its first volume would be adapted as a movie (2014) starring Zoey Deutch (Rose Hathaway), Lucy Fry (Lissa Dragomir), and Danila Kozlovsky (Dimitri Belikov). In 2011, Mead oversaw the production of a resource guide for fans of the series.

In volume four of the *Vampire Academy* series, *Blood Promise*, Rose encounters an alchemist named Sydney Sage. Alchemists are humans who help keep the existence of vampires a secret from the larger human community. As the *Vampire Academy* series reached its culmination, Mead pulled Sage out of her relative obscurity to become the central figure in a spin-off series, *Bloodlines*, which was also the name of the first volume in the new series. Sage's fellow alchemists entrusted her to become the central figure in a complex plan to keep Lissa's little sister, Princess Jillian Dragomir, safe. Lissa, now a vampire queen, is opposed by a group of *moroi* who are conspiring to undermine her rule by assassinating her sister. The *Bloodlines* series ran for six volumes (2011–2015).

Mead's several vampire-oriented series have won a spectrum of awards, beginning with a 2010 Teen Read Award for the *Vampire Academy* series. All three series have won awards from Goodreads. Mead remains at the height of her career, and more titles are expected from her in the next decades. Mead maintains a website at https://www.richellemead.com.

Miller, Linda Lael (1949–)

Linda Lael Miller, a popular writer of romance literature, was born Linda Lael in Spokane, Washington. She married shortly after high school and worked as a clerk-typist for a number of years before becoming a writer of fiction for women. Her first book, *Fletcher's Woman*, appeared in 1983. She found a growing readership and produced more than 20 romance novels by the end of the decade. Her 1987 book *Wanton Angel* won the *Romantic Times* award for the Most Sensual Historical Romance Book of the Year.

In the wake of Anne Rice's success, which proved that books about vampires could find a readership among fans of romance novels, Miller produced her first vampire novel, *Forever and the Night*. It became one of the first books on the subject to be marketed as a romance title. A best seller, it told the story of Aidan Tremayne, a handsome, 22-year-old young man with black hair and blue eyes. In 1782, he began an affair with a woman named Lisette, who turned out to be an ancient, female vampire from Atlantis. During one of their lovemaking sessions, she bit him and then shared her blood with him. He became an undead creature, but unlike most vampires, he was tortured by the remnant of humanity that remained alive in him. He later moved to Connecticut and there, in the modern world, met Neely Wallace, a woman that a Romani predicted would be either his salvation or ultimate damnation. He

> *Forever and the Night* … became one of the first books on the subject to be marketed as a romance title.

also had a sister, Mauve, who was turned into a vampire.

Forever and the Night concentrated on the story of Tremayne and Wallace, but in the wake of its success, successive novels developed the accounts of Mauve and the other vampires with whom they were associated. While Miller's was by no means the first gothic romance novel (a tradition that dates at least as far back as author Florence Marryat in the 1890s), the response to Miller's book led to a flurry of vampire romance novels that has continued to the present. She has not returned to the vampire theme since her four novels, now known collectively as the *Black Rose Chronicles*, in the mid-1990s.

Neill, Chloe (1975–)

Chloe Neill, a writer of paranormal romance novels, is best known for her *Chicagoland Vampires* series. Born and raised in Arkansas, she pursued a law career at the University of Nebraska. Her early choice of a career was in part due to trouble with writing, and she eventually settled in Omaha as a contract lawyer. During her college career, however, she became involved in journalism, and beginning with short writing pieces, her skills and then her attraction to writing evolved. She began with writing fan fiction and subsequently moved on to writing her own stories featuring characters she created. She released her first novel, *Some Girls Bite*, in 2009. It became the initial installment of the *Chicagoland Vampires* series, which by 2017 had spawned 13 volumes.

In Neill's novels, the vampire community is organized in a somewhat feudal system around 12 houses. Soon after being turned, a new vampire will generally swear allegiance to a particular house. A variety of supernatural creatures (shapeshifters, angels, demons, etc.) are residing in the

same spaces as humans, but vampires are the only ones who have let humans know of their existence. In Chicago, the Navarre House is the oldest, having been created shortly before the Great Chicago Fire (1871). Second in age is the Cadogan House, noteworthy as the only house in Chicago whose members still consume blood from humans. Some 100 local members reside in their headquarters house in Hyde Park, a southside neighborhood adjacent to Lake Michigan. While most vampires are attached to one of the houses, some rogue vampires remain who exist independently of the houses.

The main character in Neill's books is Caroline Evelyn Merit, whose story begins while she is pursuing a graduate degree at the University of Chicago (also located in Hyde Park). She is attacked on campus and left for dead. She is then bitten by a vampire in order to save her life. Once turned, she swears fealty to the Cadogan House and develops an intense love/hate relationship with Ethan Sullivan, the master of Cadogan House and the vampire who initially bit her. He is 394 years old. Merit rises in the ranks of her community quickly and is named the sentinel of the house. Early in her vampire life as she is figuring out her place within it, she learns of the existence of an ombudsman's office within the mayor's office, which is assigned to handle matters related to the supernaturals residing in the city. As it turns out, Merit's grandfather works with that office, which is at the moment investigating a series of murders and the possible vampire connection to them.

Merit's story attracted an immediate audience and led to her starring in the subsequent 13 *Chicagoland* vampire novels, which were translated into several languages (German, Spanish, Italian). Neill has also produced a spin-off of the *Chicagoland* series, *The Heirs of Chicagoland,* built around Merit's daughter (with Ethan Sullivan), Eliza Sullivan, and her shapeshifter partner, Gabriel Keene. The first of three *Heirs* novels, *Wild Hunger,* appeared in 2018.

Neill resides in Omaha, Nebraska, and continues both her law career and her writing. Neill maintains her website at http://www.chloe neill.com.

Newman, Kim (1939–)

Kim Newman, the author of the award-winning vampire novel *Anno Dracula,* was born in London in 1959 but was brought up in Somerset. He attended the University of Sussex, where he majored in English. At the end of the 1970s, he moved to London and began his career working in the theater and cabaret circles. He finished his first play, *Another England,* in 1980 which, along with a few others over the years, were produced by the Sheep Worrying Theatre Group at the Arts Centre, Bridgewater. To bolster his income, Newman also played the kazoo in a cabaret band.

In the early 1980s, he also wrote several short stories, some of which were published, and numerous scripts for radio and television. His first book, *Ghastly Beyond Belief: The Science Fiction and Fantasy Book of Quotations,* written with Neil Gaiman, appeared in 1985. Over the next decade, he contributed widely to various literary reference books, and his broad knowledge of the horror field led to his first award-winning book, *Horror: 100 Best Books* (with Stephen Jones, 1988), which received the Bram Stoker Award as the year's Best Non-fiction Title. Additional reference titles include *Nightmare Movies: A Critical History of the Horror*

Film Since 1968 (1988) and the *BFI Companion to Horror* (1996).

Newman's first vampire novel, *Bad Dreams,* appeared in 1990, and over the next few years, he established himself in the horror field as a fic-

The winner of a Bram Stoker Award, Kim Newman is an authority on film history in addition to writing horror and alternative history novels.

tion writer of note. His talent was confirmed in 1992 with the appearance of the alternative-history volume *Anno Dracula*, which hypothesized a future for England as if the characters in Bram Stoker's novel had been real and if Dracula had won. The volume won three awards: the Children of the Night Award (the Dracula Society) for Best Novel (1992); the fiction award of the Lord Ruthven Assembly (1994); and the International Horror Critics' Guild Award for Best Novel (1994). It was followed by a sequel, *The Bloody Red Baron* (1994), which followed an alternative history through World War I.

In the meantime, under the pseudonym Jack Yeovil, Newman has written a set of novels, including several based on the *Warhammer* games. Of his Yeovil novels, three feature vampires: *Warhammer: Drachenfels* (1989), *Orgy of the Blood Parasites* (1994), and *Warhammer: Genevieve Undead* (1993).

In the late 1990s, Newman returned to the world he had created in *Anno Dracula* and produced a series of sequels, beginning with *Anno Dracula: The Bloody Red Baron* (1995) and more recently adding *Anno Dracula: Judgment of Tears* (1998), *Anno Dracula: Johnny Alucard* (2013), *Anno Dracula: One Thousand Monsters* (2017), and *Anno Dracula 1999 Daikaiju* (2019), plus a collection of short stories, *Anno Dracula 1899 and Other Stories* (2017).

 *Niles, Steve (1965–)*

Steve Niles burst upon the comic book world in 2002 with his successful comic book series *30 Days of Night*. Written by Niles with the collaboration of artist Ben Templesmith, the story opined about happenings when a small town in remote Alaska, where a month passed without sunlight, was cut off from the outside world and came under attack by vampires. Niles's story of the horrific, zombielike vampires was perfectly complemented by Templesmith's rendering of a night world where the only whiteness was the vampires' mouths of sharp teeth.

Niles was born in Jackson, New Jersey, on June 21, 1965. He grew up in suburban Washington, D.C., in an environment informed by comic books and punk rock. For a short period of time, he was in a punk rock band. He also credits Washington's television horror host, Count Gore De Vol, as influencing his interest in vampire lore.

In the late 1980s, while still in Washington, Niles formed Arcane Comix, an independent graphic arts publishing concern, through which he published several works he edited. At the beginning of the 1990s, he moved to California and began to write for different comic

Comic book author Steve Niles wrote Batman: Gotham County Line, *in addition to his vampire miniseries,* 30 Days of Night.

publishing houses, most notably Fantaco/Tundra and Eclipse Comics. Then, at the beginning of the twentieth century, he began working with IDW, a relatively new comic book publisher based in San Diego. Niles had done a four-issue adaptation of Richard Matheson's *I Am Legend* for Eclipse. His first work for IDW became a collection of the four issues to produce a black-and-white graphic novel (1991). *30 Days of Night* then became the IDW's first comic book series—a series of a mere three issues.

The series became an immediate success and heralded the birth of a new force in horror writing (while simultaneously serving as a notable start to Templesmith, who was working his first job as a comic artist). The pair moved on to work together in two further series, *Criminal Macabre* (for Dark Horse) and *Dark Days*. *Criminal Macabre* centered on the drug-addicted detective Cal McDonald, who operates in a world inhabited by ghouls and vampires. He eventually becomes a vampire himself. Niles had introduced the character in some stories that appeared in his Arcane Comix anthologies and later in the Dark Horse anthology *Dark Horse Presents*. In 2002, Niles issued two Cal McDonald novels, *Savage Membrane* and *Guns, Drugs and Monsters*. The novels set the stage for further comics, the 2003 Dark Horse series with Templesmith, a 2004 sequel, *Last Train to Deadsville* (Image), and a 2005 series, *Supernatural Freak Machine: A Cal McDonald Mystery* (IDW).

Meanwhile, the success of *30 Days of Night* led to its first sequel, *Dark Days*. By this time, Niles had become a star within the horror-writing community, and he has gone on to write a series of successful comics while the writing of additional *30 Days of Night* miniseries sequels was turned over to new writers and artists. Niles would do two *Annuals* (2004, 2005); *30 Days of Night: Return to Barrow* (2004); *30 Days of Night: Dead Space* (2006); and *30 Days of Night: Eben and Stella* (2007). Meanwhile, other writers tried their hand with *30 Days of Night: Spreading the Disease* (2006) and *30 Days of Night: Dust to Dust* (2008). Additional vampire titles among the many works Niles has written include *Aleister Arcane* (2004), *The Cryptics* (2006), and *City of Others*, a zombie story with vampires (2007).

In 2007, *30 Days of Night* finally made it to the screen as a successful horror movie. By 2009, it had emerged as the 12th-highest-grossing vampire movie in history. A sequel and a *Criminal Macabre* movie remain a possibility. That same year, *I Am Legend* was made into a movie starring Will Smith. Niles counts Richard Matheson as the single greatest influence on his writing career and jumped at the chance to participate in the promotional comic *I Am Legend: Awakening*, produced by DC Vertigo and distributed at the San Diego Comic-Con. The movie also led to a third printing of his IDW graphic novel of *I Am Legend*.

Pike, Christopher (c. 1955–)

Christopher Pike is the pseudonym of Kevin Christopher McFadden, one of the most popular writers of juvenile literature today. Few biographical details, including his exact birth date, are known about the author, but he was born in Brooklyn and held various jobs while practicing his writing skills and trying to sell his first books. He did not have much success until an editor at a

publishing company suggested that he try his hand at writing for a younger audience. The result was *Slumber Party* (1985), his first novel, which was well received and led to additional titles. By 1989, Pike had published seven books.

Pike specializes in mystery/suspense and the supernatural, not avoiding pure horror stories, aimed at adolescents making their transition to adulthood. He describes violent activity in some graphic detail. The primary characters are teenagers, and the subtext of the stories generally integrates some of the perennial concerns of teen existence. Among his best-selling books are the titles in the *Spooksville* series, featuring stories set in the mythical town of Springville, where spooky things seem to occur all the time. The continuing characters—Sally, Adam, and Watch—explore the range of the sinister supernatural.

> Pike specializes in mystery/suspense and the supernatural, not avoiding pure horror stories, aimed at adolescents making their transition to adulthood.

In the 1990s, Pike occasionally turned to the vampire theme, the first time in his book *Monster* (1992). Even adults appreciated his six-part story of Alisa Perne, the youthful vampire in *The Last Vampire* series. Alisa was an ancient vampire living as a high school student in contemporary Los Angeles. Her mate, Yaksha, who had originally forced her into the vampiric life, saved his own life by promising to kill all of the vampires he had made. Now, 5,000 years later, he had largely completed his task—only Alisa remained. Her mission became assisting the nearly invulnerable Yaksha to die while preventing him from killing her. The solution to that dilemma set the stage for the various adventures throughout the novels.

In 1994, Pike published *The Midnight Club*, which was about a group of terminally ill teens at a hospice called Rotterdam House. Five of the residents began to meet together at midnight to tell stories. Then, one night, the members of the Midnight Club created a pact that the first to die would make an attempt to contact the others from wherever he or she was in the great beyond. In 1996, some youthful readers of *The Midnight Club* founded their own Midnight Club online. The club has evolved into the Christopher Pike Fan Club, which can be accessed through the author's homepage online. Those who join the club are invited to take the name of one of Pike's characters.

In 2009, the six volumes of *The Last Vampire* series were reissued as a two-volume set called *The Thirst*. Shortly afterward, he added three new volumes, extending the original story: *The Eternal Dawn* (2010), *The Shadow of Death* (2011), and *The Sacred Veil* (2012). Additional titles in the series have been promised but have yet to appear (2020).

⚫ *Pozzessere, Heather Graham* ⚫ *(1953–)*

Heather Graham Pozzessere is the name of a popular paranormal romance writer who writes under two pen names, Heather Graham and Shannon Drake, with most of her vampire titles appearing under the latter. Pozzessere was born Heather Graham in 1953 in Miami, Florida, and attended the University of South Florida. She married and worked a variety of jobs while raising a family. After the birth of her third child, she withdrew from outside employment and stayed at home. She also began to write. She sold her first book, *When Next We Love*, in 1982. She subsequently wrote novels in the romance, science fiction, and horror genres but had her major success in romance. She was a founding member of the Florida chapter of Romance Writers of America. She began hosting the annual *Romantic Times* Vampire Ball, a charity affair, in 1999.

Because of her wide popularity, she was chosen to write the launch books for Dell's "Candlelight Ecstasy Supreme" line, Silhouette's Shadows line, and Harlequin's imprint, Mira Books. Her books have been translated into approximately 20 languages.

Very early in her career, Pozzessere authored her first vampire novel, *This Rough Magic* (1988), somewhat lost amid the many ephemeral Silhouette titles. Then, after authoring a number of books, Pozzessere wrote her first vampire novel under the pen name Shannon Drake, *Beneath a Blood Red Moon*, at the end of the 1990s. For what would become a six-volume series, Pozzessere created the vampire character Maggie Montgomery, who ran a clothing boutique in New Orleans's French Quarter. She found herself drawn to a police detective named Sean Canady, with whom she feels a deep connection, but he has come into her life while investigating a murder in the French Quarter. A blood trail from the victim ended at Maggie's shop. To solve the murder, she had to reveal her secret identity to him.

In the sequel, Maggie and Sean take second place to Lucian, the king of the vampires, who has been attracted to travel writer Jade Mac-Gregor. They had met in Scotland, where he saved her from an attack by other vampires. The vampire followed her to New Orleans, where Lucian had to risk his secret identity in order to continue assisting her. Each of the remaining four titles takes the reader to a different exciting setting, such as Venice, Italy, or Salem, Massachusetts, focusing on another couple while reintroducing the characters from the earlier novels.

Pozzessere revives the vampire world of her Shannon Drake series in the most recent novels written as Heather Graham for Mira Books. She returns to her favorite New Orleans setting and invites characters from the past to attend to the two new characters who will become the focus of each novel. In *Kiss of Darkness* (2006), for example, Maggie and Sean Canady (now married) and Lucian reappear to assist Jessica and Byron (the latter a vampire hunter just awakening to the existence of "good" vampires).

> Very early in her career, Pozzessere authored her first vampire novel, *This Rough Magic* (1988), somewhat lost amid the many ephemeral Silhouette titles.

The prolific Pozzessere had continued to turn out dozens of novels through the first two decades of the twenty-first century, including vampire novels. Prominent among these are the *Vampire Hunters* series, a three-book series in which each story focuses upon a couple who has united to fight the local bloodsuckers. Titles include *Night of the Wolves* (2009), *Night of the Vampires* (2010), and *Bride of the Night* (2012). Shortly thereafter, she republished a series of books that were issued in the 1990s with some titles as Heather Graham and some titles as Shannon Drake. The new editions were reissued as the *Alliance Vampires* series, beginning with *Beneath a Blood Red Moon* in 2013.

Sands, Lynsay

Canadian romance author Lynsay Sands was born in Leamington, Ontario, grew up in southern Ontario, and studied at the University of Windsor. She emerged as a romance author following her first book, *The Deed*, re-leased in 1997, but she did not distinguish herself from the mass of other romance writers until the middle of the next decade (2003) with the first of her vampire novels, *Single White Vampire*. This and her subsequent novels about the Argeneaus, a family of modern vampires, became known for the humor she injected into the stories.

The stories center on a nuclear vampire family: a mother, Marguerite; three sons (Lucien, Bastien, and Etienne); and a daughter (Lissianna). Later, members of the extended family are introduced, all hundreds of years old, and are now having problems facing the modern world. Cousin Vincent is an actor living in Los Angeles. The Argeneau family traces their lineage back to Alexandria and Ramses, who emerge in the sixteenth century B.C.E. and get caught in Pompeii when Vesuvius erupted in 79 C.E. Sands traces vampirism back to Atlantis and the fabled scientific advances that rival those of the twenty-first century. Atlantean scientists discovered nanos, microscopic entities that could be injected into the bloodstream, where they lived and reproduced. The nanos live off blood. Once in the body, on the good side, they help to constantly regenerate one's body by repairing organs and any damage due to accidents and aging. The body, however, cannot manufacture blood at a rate to meet the needs of the hungry nanos. Hence, the descendants of the original Atlanteans, to whom the nanos have been passed, need to regularly ingest more blood.

Apart from the scientific nature of their origin, Sands's vampires are fairly traditional:

they have great strength, have to avoid sunlight, need blood regularly, possess fangs, and even sleep in coffins.

While *Single White Vampire* was the first of the 12 volumes to be published by Sands, she now suggests that her new fans might want to read the novels as she intended them to appear, beginning with *A Quick Bite* (2005) and proceeding to *Love Bites* (2004) before *Single White Vampire* and then the fourth novel, *Tall, Dark and Hungry* (2004). Most recently, she has begun a subseries within the series built around a group of vampires commissioned by the vampire powers that be to hunt rogue vampires who have broken the laws of the vampire community. They also investigate cases of mortals learning of the existence of vampires, who exist in a secret world shielded from the knowledge of the larger human community.

Sands has also participated in several anthologies of vampire stories: *His Immortal Embrace* (2003), *Dates from Hell* (2006), and *Holidays Are Hell* (2007). Meanwhile, she has kept the *Argeneau Vampires* series alive. It now includes 31 titles, the most recent of which, *The Trouble with Vampires*, was issued in 2019. The *Argeneau Rogue Vampire* series has also continued. It now includes 30 titles, the most recent being *Vampires Like It Hot*, released in 2018.

> Sands traces vampirism back to Atlantis and the fabled scientific advances that rival those of the twenty-first century.

Shan, Darren (1972–)

Darren Shan is the pen name of Darren O'Shaughnessy, as well as the name of the main character in O'Shaughnessy's *Cirque du Freak* juvenile vampire novels, the second of which jumped to the movie screen in 2009 as *Cirque du Freak: The Vampire's Assistant.*

O'Shaughnessy was born in London on July 2, 1972, and lived there for the first six years of his life, after which his parents moved to Ireland, where he grew up and continues to reside. He returned to England to study sociology and English at the University of Roehampton in London. After

Darren Shan's The Saga of Darren Shan *sold over 30 million copies and was turned into a 2009 movie and a manga series that ran from 2006 to 2009.*

a few years of working for a cable television company, he became a full-time writer in 1995.

He started writing as a teenager and wrote several novels, none of which were published, while in college. His first published book hit the bookstores in 1999. Shortly thereafter, the first of the *Cirque du Freak* novels, *The Saga of Darren Shan*, appeared. It proved successful and was reprinted in the United States under the title *Cirque du Freak* the following year. O'Shaughnessy discovered that he liked writing for the younger crowd, and a growing body of fans seemed to enjoy probing his world of unique vampires. Beginning with *The Vampire's Assistant*, the second book in the series, he averaged three titles a year. The final volume (No. 12) appeared in 2004.

The Saga of Darren Shan begins when he visits a freak show with his friend Steve. Steve discovers that one of the show's personnel, a Mr. Crepsley, is, in fact, a vampire. Meanwhile, Darren steals a spider (because of a longtime fascination with arachnids) and a flute to train and control it. Unfortunately, at one point, Darren loses control of the spider, which fatally bites Steve. Darren appeals to Mr. Crepsley,

who has the antidote to the spider's venom that will save Steve. His price is that Darren becomes his assistant. He subsequently helps to fake Darren's death, and after Darren's funeral and burial, he digs up his future assistant. Darren is now a *dhampir*-like "half vampire," similar to Blade the Vampire Slayer, and ready to live his next years in the world of vampires.

The vampires of *Cirque du Freak* are not the undead. O'Shaughnessy wished to create what to him were more realistic vampires. They are alive and could be killed by various means. They differ from humans in that they age slowly, with life spans at least ten times that of humans. They are strong and fast. The oldest vampire character in the series, Paris Skyle, is a Dracula-like vampire who is some 800 years old. Vampires fit across the same range of personality as humans and may thus be good, bad, or somewhere in between. Vampires possess long, sharp fingernails, which they use for a variety of feats. Most importantly, the nails assist their feeding. They will cut into a human vein and suck small quantities of blood. The vampire's saliva has a healing effect and will close the cut made for feeding. The sharp nails replace the need for fangs.

Normally, O'Shaughnessy's vampires will drink only enough blood to survive for a short time, thus avoiding taking the life of their victims. Vampires are negatively affected by sunlight but can move about in the day if they stay indoors or in the shade. They may consume garlic, cast a shadow, and be seen in mirrors, but they cannot be photographed. They can survive on animal blood but prefer that of humans. On the other hand, vampire blood is poisonous to humans. They are deterred with neither crucifix nor holy water. They had dropped any religion followed in their prevampire existence and now relate to a new pantheon of deities. They have a belief in the afterlife and will be born as wolves in Paradise. They believe that the first vampire evolved from wolves. Vampires cannot transform into various animals or mist. On the other hand, they have some telepathic powers that allow them to communicate with other vampires and locate humans by following thought patterns.

As O'Shaughnessy envisions it, a vampire society is ruled hierarchically. The society values tradition, honor, and personal pride. Among their traditions is the avoidance of using weapons that work with projectiles. If they fight, it is up close and personal with weapons such as swords or the traditional Japanese weapon the *shuriken*, the small blade familiar from Japanese ninja movies. At one end of the spectrum of vampire society are the evil vampires, distinguished by their pattern of drinking all of their victim's blood (and, in the process, taking a part of their victim's spirit also). These evil vampires, called "vampaneze," are rogue vampires out to destroy their more benevolent kin. The fight against the vampaneze takes up

> As O'Shaughnessy envisions it, a vampire society is ruled hierarchically. The society values tradition, honor, and personal pride.

much of the plot of the last half of the *Cirque du Freak* novels. O'Shaughnessy's vampires carry signs of their battles. While their saliva heals, it does not do so miraculously, and scars remain. Many are thus disfigured and not the beautiful creatures that inhabit the vampire world of Stephenie Meyer or Anne Rice.

As Darren Shan, O'Shaughnessy cemented his place as one of the top writers for young people in the United Kingdom by following his very successful vampire series with *The Demonata*, a series about demons. Meanwhile, his *Cirque du Freak* series has been translated into a variety of languages, including Japanese and Chinese. His success also allowed him the leisure to write novels for an adult audience, three of which appeared in the wake of *The Demonata* series. O'Shaughnessy resides in rural Ireland. *Shanville*, O'Shaughnessy's website, is found at http://www.darrenshan.com.

Smith, L(isa) J(ane)

L. J. Smith is an author of books for children and young adults. She graduated from the University of California at Santa Barbara with a degree in experimental psychology and later received teaching credentials from San Francisco State University in elementary education and special education. She abandoned school teaching, however, to write fiction and, in 1987, saw her first book, *The Night of the Solstice*, published. She subsequently became the very successful author of *The Vampire Diaries* series, the initial four volumes of which appeared in 1991.

The first volume of *The Vampire Diaries*, *The Awakening*, introduces Elena Gilbert, a popular and intelligent high schooler in Mystic Falls, a small town in Virginia. She

is in grief from the recent loss of her father but finds an outlet in a new boy at school, Stefan Salvatore. The mysterious Salvatore turns out to be a youthful-looking vampire, who was only 17 when turned. Stefan had been a vampire since the Italian Renaissance. He has a slightly older brother, Damon, also a vampire, with whom he has a love-hate relationship. Stefan, a good-guy vampire, has found a way to survive without taking human blood, while Damon is the bad-boy vampire who acts out the role of an amoral predator. The brothers were transformed into vampires by a mutual love, Katherine, a young vampire who is now deceased. Elena's relationship with the two vampires begins over her resemblance to Katherine and eventually leads to her death at the end of volume two of Smith's books.

She awakens as a vampire herself at the beginning of volume three.

Smith's vampires generally follow the traditional myth of the literary vampire. People become vampires by drinking a vampire's blood, and they must regularly ingest blood to survive. They burn in the sunlight but uniquely wear a ring that allows them to walk about in daylight. They are very quick in moving about. They can be killed by a stake to the heart. They show a reflection in a mirror and are not affected by garlic or sacred symbols. They are able to control people's memories so that victims can be forced to forget traumatic memories, such as a vampire's attack upon them.

In 2009, in the wake of the success of *Buffy the Vampire Slayer* and Stephenie Meyer's *Twilight* series, the WB channel brought *The Vampire Diaries* to television as a prime-time series. Nina Dobrev portrayed Elena Gilbert, with Paul Wesley and Ian Somerhalder as the brothers Stefan and Damon Salvatore, respectively.

Several years after the original series of *The Vampire Diaries* was published, Smith returned to the vampire theme in a new series, *Dark Visions* (1994–1995), in which Kaitlyn, an artist with some precognitive abilities, develops a telepathic link with a brooding loner named Gabriel. Gabriel turns out to be a psychic vampire who drains the life-force out of those around him to survive. Kaitlyn must choose between the dark one, Gabriel, or the good option, a healer named Rob.

> Smith's vampires generally follow the traditional myth of the literary vampire. People become vampires by drinking a vampire's blood, and they must regularly ingest blood to survive.

Smith finished out the 1990s with a nine-volume series called *Night World*, in which she created a fantasy universe where the normal world of her main characters is enlivened by the presence of vampires, witches, and shapeshifters. The characters of *Night World* have two basic rules: do not tell humans that they exist, and do not fall in love with a human. Not all of the nine novels focus on vampires, but vampires are present in each and integral to the plot in several, such as the first one, appropriately named *Vampire Secret*. James, a vampire, has fallen for a classmate, Poppy, who has contracted a fatal illness. Having broken a basic rule of falling for a human, he must now decide whether or not to make her a vampire.

In conjunction with the new television series of *The Vampire Diaries*, Smith has issued three new volumes of what was called *The Vampire Diaries: The Return*, which included *Nightfall* (2009), *Shadow Souls* (2010), and *Midnight* (2011). In 2011, Smith submitted a draft to her publishers for what would become the first volumes of a new series, *The Vampire Diaries: The Hunters*, which occasioned an intense disagreement over the direction of the plot. The publisher, which now had control over *The Vampire Diaries*, terminated Smith from the ongoing project and hired a ghostwriter to complete the volume and, indeed, the remaining two volumes of the series. Smith publicly announced her separation from the ongoing series. Two more series were later authored by ghostwriters: *The Vampire Diaries: Stefan's Diaries* (six volumes, 2010–2012) and *The Vampire Diaries: The Salvation Trilogy* (three volumes, 2013–2014).

Even as the writing dispute occurred, *The Vampire Diaries* television shows proved quite successful, continuing for eight seasons (2009–2017). It had generated two spin-off series: *The Originals* (five seasons, 2013–2018) and *Legacies*, which premiered in 2018 and continues as this almanac goes to press. Smith maintains a website at http://www.ljanesmith.net.

⤙ *Sommer-Bodenburg, Angela* ⤚ (1948–)

Angela Sommer-Bodenburg, an author of children's fiction, created *The Little Vampire* series. Born in Reinbek, Germany, she attended the University of Hamburg and later assumed a position as the assistant master at an intermediate and secondary school (1972–1984), during which time she wrote the initial chapter of *Der kieine Vampir* (*The Little Vampire*) as part of a larger search for material that could hold the attention of her young students. The first edition of the book appeared in Germany in 1979 and found immediate success. It was translated into English, with both British (*The Little Vampire*) and American (*My Friend the Vampire*) editions issued in 1982. Additional adventures of *The Little Vampire* appeared through the decade, the first five of which were issued in both British and American editions, with the American editions notable for dropping the word "little" from the title. Sommer-Bodenburg resigned her teaching position in 1984 and has since made her living as an author and artist.

The Little Vampire series begins with nine-year-old Anton Bohnsack, a boy notable only for his fascination with vampires, his intense interest leading to his discovery and befriending of a vampire boy named Rüdiger, who had become a vampire when he was 11. Rüdiger's family, the Schlottersteins, reside in the local cemetery. Their friendship leads to Anton's also befriending Rüdiger's younger sister, Anna (nine years old), and older brother, Lumpi, but the action centers on Rüdiger taking Anton on trips around the vampire world in the evening. As their relationship develops, secrecy is important, and Anton must initially conceal his human nature from other vampires and his friendship with Rüdiger from his own parents. Anton will regularly wear a vampire cloak when roaming around with Rüdiger and Anna.

The adventures of Rüdiger and Anton (and their vampire acquaintances), which were related in 21 German language volumes of which 16 were translated into English, have Rüdiger becoming Rudolph Sackville-Bagg and Anton taking the name Tony Thompson. In the process of writing the series, Sommer-Bodenburg complained

> In the process of writing the series, Sommer-Bodenburg complained that she had come to be seen by many as simply a writer of children's vampire fiction....

that she had come to be seen by many as simply a writer of children's vampire fiction, though she also wrote numerous titles that had nothing to do with the subject. Her *Little Vampire* titles, with their translation into English and some 30 additional languages, certainly was the source of her fame. Early on, a 13-episode television series (1986) starred Joel Dacks as Rüdiger von Schlotterstein. A second television series, also produced in Canada, was released in 1993. In 2000, a movie, *The Little Vampire*, set in Scotland, starred Jonathan Lipnicki as Tony Thompson and Rollo Weeks as the little vampire, Rudolph Sackville-Bagg. Richard Grant portrayed Rudolph's father. An animated movie, *The Little Vampire 3D*, was released in 2017.

Sommer-Bodenburg moved to the United States in 1992 and now resides in New Mexico. She maintains a website at http://www.angelasommer-bodenburg.com.

Somtow, S. P. (1952–)

S. P. Somtow, the pseudonym of Thai American writer Somtow Sucharitkul, was born in Bangkok in 1952. He started writing early in life, and his first published piece, a poem entitled "Kith of Infinity," was written when he was 11 years old. It was seen by actress Shirley MacLaine in the *Bangkok Post* who, moved by its expression of alienation and under the impression that it had been written by an ancient, dead sage, reprinted it in her autobiographical book *Don't Fall Off the Mountain.* Somtow was educated in Switzerland, where his uncle, a member of the diplomatic corps for Thailand, was stationed. He subsequently attended St. Catherine's College in Cambridge, Massachusetts, from which he received both his bachelor's and master's degrees.

Before Somtow was a writer, he was a musician. He composed numerous musical selections and was the director of the Bangkok Opera Society (1977–1978). In 1978, he was the director of the Asian Composer's Conference-Festival held in Bangkok. Through the 1990s, he returned to music and wrote a ballet, *Kaki,* which premiered at a royal command performance in Bangkok.

Somtow began writing science fiction in the 1970s and, following the appearance of his novel *Starship and Haiku* (1981), published a series of novels under his given name. *Starship and Haiku* won the Locus Award for Best First Novel, and Somtow won the John W. Campbell Award as Best New Science Fiction Writer. His first vampire novel, *Vampire Junction* (1984), was heralded as one of the finer examples of the genre and appeared as the first novel under his pseudonym. Recently, it was cited by the Varma Gothic Literary Society as "an outstanding contribution to gothic literature in the twentieth century." The novel traces the career of Timmy Valentine, a young boy made a vampire just as Vesuvius erupts and destroys his hometown.

Amazingly, he has been able to survive and has reappeared throughout history with his beautiful, boyish voice. In the contemporary world, he is a charismatic rock star. *Vampire Junction* prompted the writing of two sequels, *Valentine* (1992) and *Veritas* (1995).

Somtow has roamed across genres and has written an outstanding werewolf novel, *Moondance.* He last returned to the vampire genre in the juvenile novel *The Vampire's Beautiful Daughter* (1997).

In the new century, Somtow's musical side has come to the fore. Though continuing to write fiction, he is now the director of the Siam Philharmonic Orchestra and has written operas for its associated Bangkok Opera. In 2008, he announced that *Vampire Junction* was being adapted into an opera.

S. P. Somtow is not only a popular author of horror, sci-fi, and fantasy but also a talented musical composer.

Tan, Cecilia (1967–)

Writer/editor Cecilia Tan is the founder of Circlet Press, a publishing concern based in Cambridge, Massachusetts, specializing in erotic science fiction and fantasy. She developed a love of writing as a teenager and had her first efforts accepted for publication even before entering Brown University, where she earned a B.A. degree in linguistics and cognitive science in 1989. She worked at Beacon Press for several years before entering Emerson University to pursue a master's degree in writing.

Simultaneous with her educational pursuits, she became involved in the world of science fiction and fantasy and alternative sexuality. These interests merged at moments such as the Gaylaxicon conventions, which focused interest on science fiction, fantasy, and horror with a particular focus on lesbian, gay, bisexual, and transgender (LGBT) topics. The original

Gaylaxicon convention was held in Provincetown, Massachusetts, in 1988. At the 1991 Gaylaxicon, Tan was one of a cabal of five conspirators who began hosting parties for bond age/dominance/sadism/masochism (BDSM) parties, which quickly became a standard feature of the regular convention activities. Tan emerged as a BDSM activist.

While at Emerson, Tan began building Circlet Press, its first book being *Telepaths Don't Need Safewords*, a chapbook of Tan's erotic science fiction stories. After receiving her M.A. degree in 1994, she became the full-time head of Circlet Press. While its publications range across the world of science fiction, fantasy, and horror, vampirism, with its notable sexual component, has enjoyed a particular emphasis among the press's publications, with Tan's belief that the vampire has been a perfect subject for erotic fantasy. Its first anthology of vampire stories, *Blood Kiss*, appeared in 1994.

Tan's interest in vampires has been most evident in the many vampire anthologies she has compiled and edited. She followed *Blood Kiss* with *Erotica Vampirica* (1996), *Cherished Blood: Vampire Erotica* (1997), and *A Taste of Midnight: Sensual Vampire Stories* (2000). These three volumes were later brought together in an omnibus volume as *Erotica Vampirica: Thirty-one Tales of Supernatural Powers* (2001). In the new century, Tan also compiled/edited three additional volumes of vampire short fiction that were released through other publishers as *Blood Surrender* (2005), *Women of Bite: Lesbian Vampire Erotica* (2009), and *Bites of Passion: An Anthology of Vampire Erotica* (2010).

Tan has received a spectrum of awards, especially as more sexually explicit adult material has been integrated into romance literature. Among these, in 2010, she was inducted into the Hall of Fame for LGBTQ writers, and the

In addition to being an author, Cecilia Tan founded Circlet Press.

novel *Slow Surrender* won the *RT* (*Romance Times*) Reviewers' Choice Award in the erotic romance category from *RT Book Reviews*. At the *RT* Booklover's Convention in 2015, she won both the *RT* Pioneer Award for Genre Fiction and the *RT* Career Achievement Award in Erotic Fiction. In 2008, Circlet Press began a transition to become largely an e-book publisher. Most recently, in 2014, adding to its awards, it was named the Bi Book Publisher of the Year at the Bisexual Book Awards.

Ward, J. R. (1969–)

J. R. Ward is the pen name used by Jessica Rowley Pell Bird, a successful lawyer, hospital administrator, and writer of a popular vampire romance series of novels called *The Black Dagger Brotherhood*. Ward attended Smith College, majoring in medieval history and art history. She obtained her J.D. from Albany (New York) Law School and subsequently worked for a number of years at Beth Israel Deaconness Medical Center in Boston, Massachusetts. She had been writing, primarily for her own enjoyment, for many years, but after she married in 2001, her husband encouraged her to seek publication. Her first book, *Leaping Hearts*, a romance novel written under her family name, was published in 2002.

Several years later, under the pen name J. R. Ward, she created a fantasy world populated by six warrior vampire brothers (Wrath, Rhage, Zsadist, Phury, Vishous, and Tohrment) and their allies, who live together as the Black Dagger Brotherhood. The brotherhood's task is to defend their race against the soulless humans who constitute the Lessening Society, enemies of the vampire race.

The brotherhood members look for guidance and inspiration from the Scribe Virgin, experienced as a mystical force and known to be the creator of vampires. She is venerated as a deity. In Ward's mythology, the Scribe Virgin has a brother called the Omega. Unable to create, he became jealous of his sister and targeted her creations for extinction. He is the acknowledged deity of the Lessening Society. The Omega has many powers and, like his sister, exists in a noncorporal realm.

Ward's novels about vampires tell the story of one of the brothers or one of their allies, such as Butch (aka Dhestroyer), the only human within the brotherhood. Each book highlights the protagonist's fight with the Lessers and his path to true love. The series has also become notable in its inclusion of storylines involving same-sex love affairs.

The first of *The Black Dagger Brotherhood* series appeared in 2005 under the title *Dark Lover*. Seven volumes appeared by 2009; that number grew to 22 by 2020. In addition, Ward wrote *The Black Dagger Brotherhood: An Insider's Guide*, a book with explanatory material about her mythological world. Among the several awards for her very popular series, *Romantic Times* gave Ward the Reviewer's Choice Award for *Lover Awakened*. In 2008, she received the Romance Writers of America's RITA award for *Lover Revealed*, named the best paranormal romance novel of the year. Ward maintains a website at http://www.jrward.com.

> Each book highlights the protagonist's fight with the Lessers and his path to true love. The series has also become notable in its inclusion of storylines involving same-sex love affairs.

Yarbro, Chelsea Quinn (1942–)

Chelsea Quinn Yarbro, creator of the *Saint Germain* series of vampire books, was born on September 15, 1942, in Berkeley, California, the daughter of Lillian Chatfield and Clarence Elmer Erickson. She attended San Francisco State College from 1960 to 1963, after which she worked for her father's business, C. E. Erickson and Associates, as a cartographer. In 1969, she married Donald Paul Simpson; the couple divorced in 1982. The family business failed in 1970 and, since she enjoyed writing, she explored the possibility of doing it professionally. She joined the Science Fiction Writers of America and served for two years (1970–1972) as its secretary. A firm believer in extrasensory perception and the occult, she was employed for brief periods as a tarot card reader in the early 1970s before her writing career was firmly established.

Her initial writings were short stories that appeared in mystery, fantasy, and science fiction periodicals, three areas that interested her. In 1972, three of her stories were included in anthologies. The first of her several writing awards came in 1973 from the Mystery Writers of America for her novelette "The Ghosts at Iron River." Her first novel, *Time of the Fourth Horseman*, a suspense story, was published by Doubleday in 1976. To date, she has written over 30 novels, by far the best known being the *Saint Germain* series.

Yarbro gave much thought to the vampire in post-*Dracula* writing. An occultist rather than a traditional religionist, she concluded that the tradition was wrong. If one removed the religious overlay, the vampire became an entity who shared somewhat enjoyable (if unusual) sex and bestowed a conditional immortality. She also reflected upon the problems of the vampire's extended life span. Rather than monotonous attacks on the neighbors, the vampire would cultivate a life of scholarship and culture. As early as 1971, she tried to sell a book in which the vampire was the hero but could not locate an interested publisher. She finally sold the idea to St. Martin's Press in the late 1970s.

In creating the Saint Germain myth, Yarbro combined her interest in fantasy and gothic writing with a love for history. Saint Germain was a 3,000-year-old vampire who, in each of the novels, showed up to interact with a more or less well-known historical personage or event. The character of Saint Germain was suggested by a real person, an alchemist who lived in eighteenth-century France and around whom numerous occult legends, some of which he initiated, collected. However, Yarbro took the germ of information available on the real person and created a very human, sympathetic vampire character that joined with the characters in Fred

Chelsea Quinn Yarbro is the creator of historical novels featuring the vampire Count Saint-Germain.

Saberhagen's novels in bolstering up the sensual side of the vampire's character while downplaying its image as a monster.

Saint Germain's story continued through six novels: *Hotel Transylvania* (1978); *The Palace* (1979); *Blood Games* (1980); *Path of the Eclipse* (1981); *Tempting Fate* (1982); and *The Saint Germain Chronicles* (1983). *The Palace* was nominated for a World Fantasy Award. After a break, the story was continued in the *Olivia* series, *A Flame in Byzantium* (1987) and the *Crusader's Torch* (1988). Olivia was a recurring character in the *Saint Germain* series.

> In the *Saint Germain* series, Yarbro created one of the more intriguing variations on the Dracula myth.

In the *Saint Germain* series, Yarbro created one of the more intriguing variations on the Dracula myth. Apart from his longevity and his immunity to most things that would be fatal to an ordinary person, Saint Germain was largely devoid of the supernatural powers thought to be possessed by vampires. He also was immune to many of the traditional weapons of vampire hunter: mirrors, the crucifix, and garlic. He was comforted by earth from his homeland and had specially constructed, hollow shoes with his native soil in them. He was troubled in crossing running water, a problem helped by the hollow shoes. Death, the true death, as it was called, occurred primarily if the spine was severed (decapitation) or the body burned. Saint Germain was a romantic hero and developed ongoing relationships with women, Olivia being the most important. He could make love to women but had no semen. Rather, he took their blood. He, in fact, lived largely upon willing female donors. One important limitation was put on his sexual life, however, in that the joys and benefits of the sexual sharing could only occur between a vampire and a nonvampire. These were blocked between two vampires. Thus, while the vampire lived for many years, he could not bring his lover, or lovers, with him. He could transform his lovers into vampires, but then, they ceased to be lovers.

Yarbro continues to be active as of 2020, though she essentially brought the *Saint Germain* series to a conclusion in 2014 with the novel *Sustenance*, by which time the number of his adventures reached 25 (plus two collections of *Saint Germain* short stories). The 1990 novel *Out of the House of Life* had explored the adventures of Madelaine de Montalia, initially introduced in *Hotel Transylvania*. She then got her own independent novel in 2004, *In the Face of Death*.

In the late 1970s, Yarbro became involved with a group of people in the San Francisco Bay area who were channeling (acting as a spirit medium) for a complex spiritual entity named Michael. In 1979, she wrote a nonfiction book, *Messages from Michael on the Nature of the Evolution of the Human Soul*, about Michael and the people who have assembled around "his" teachings. Subsequently, in the 1980s, she authored two more books out of the voluminous material the Michael group had channeled.

As the *Saint Germain* series developed, Yarbro's work was repeatedly noticed by her contemporaries, beginning in 1997 (at the Dracula centennial); the Transylvanian Society of Dracula bestowed a literary knighthood on Yarbro. Early in the new century, in 2003, the World Horror Association named her a grandmaster, followed in 2006 by the International Horror Guild enrolling her among their Living Legends, the first woman so honored. In 2009, the Horror Writers Association presented her with a Life Achievement Award, and five years later, the World Fantasy Convention followed suit.

DRACULA IN THE CINEMA

🦇 *Dracula on the Silver Screen* 🦇

Dracula, a popular inspiration for stage plays, has become the single literary work most frequently adapted for the cinema, with more than 40 adaptations. The most well known of the early adaptations was *Nosferatu, Eine Symphonie des Grauens*, a silent version of *Dracula* released in 1922. Considered one of the great movies of the era by contemporary students of the cinema, it was produced under questionable circumstances. The German company that was adapting the novel for the screen used a screenplay that had changed the location of the novel's setting, the names of the major characters (including Dracula), and enough of the plot to allow it to get away with not paying any royalties to Bram Stoker's widow for rights to the novel. Florence Stoker sued and won, and most copies of *Nosferatu* were destroyed. Only a generation later did the surviving copies of the film resurface; it then began to gain an audience, and its director, F. W. Murnau, and star, Max Schreck, acquired an appreciation for their artistic accomplishment.

Meanwhile, rumors surfaced that two attempts had been made to adapt *Dracula* to the screen, one in Russia and one in Hungary. No copy of any Russian adaption, or any real evidence of its production, has surfaced to date, and it remains simply a rumor. More solid evidence of the Hungarian film was produced by Hungarian Dracula scholar Jeno Frakas, who discovered a filmbook for a film entitled *Drakula halála* (or *The Death of Dracula*). This discovery would lead to other materials about the film and, finally, the discovery of a copy in a Hungarian archive. While the storyline does not follow the plot of the novel *Dracula*, this film does represent Dracula's first movie appearance. In the film, a woman visits her father in the hospital and, while there, encounters a once famous composer who has gone mad and now claims to be Dracula, the immortal one who will live forever.

Dracula finally attains cinematic fame in 1931, with Universal Pictures buying the film rights following the success of the *Dracula* play on Broadway. It would be filmed in two versions with two separate casts, one in English starring Bela Lugosi and one in Spanish starring Carlos

A Century of Dracula Movies

Year	Movie	Comments
1922	*Nosferatu, Eine Symphonie des Grauens*	
1931	*Dracula*	Bela Lugosi
	Dracula	Spanish version
1953	*Drakula Istanbula*	Turkey
1956	*Dracula*	John Carradine
1958	*Horror of Dracula*	Christopher Lee
1961	*Ahkea Kkot's The Bad Flower*	South Korea
1966	*Dracula*	
1967	*Dr. Terror's Gallery of Horrors, Zinda Laash*	Pakistan
1968	*Dracula*	Denholm Elliott
1969	*Santo and Dracula's Treasure*	Mexico
1970	*El Conde Dracula*	Christopher Lee
1973	*Dracula*	Norman Welsh
1974	*Dracula*	Jack Palance
1977	*Count Dracula*	Louis Jourdan
1978	*Dracula*	Mexico
1979	*Dracula*	Frank Langella
	Nosferatu the Vampyre	Klaus Kinski
	Dracula Sucks	James Gillis
1980	*The Passion of Dracula*	Christopher Bernau
1982	*Dracula*	Frank Langella
1984	*Dracula*	
1992	*Bram Stoker's Dracula*	directed by Francis Ford Coppola
1994	*Dracula*	Mario Salieri
1995	*Dracula: Dead and Loving It*	comedy; Leslie Nielsen
1997	*Dracula: A Chamber Musical*	
2002	*Il Bacio di Dracula*	aka *Dracula's Curse*
	Dracula: Pages from a Virgin's Diary	
2004	*Vulture's Eye*	
	Lust for Dracula	
2005	*Alucard*	
2006	*Dracula*	Marc Warren
2008	*Bram Stoker's Dracula's Guest*	
	Red Scream Nosferatu	
2009	*Dracula*	Juan R. Caraccioli
2012	*Dracula 3D*	
	Hotel Transylvania	animated
2013	*Dracula 2012*	India
	Dracula the Dark Prince	
2014	*Dracula Untold*	Gary Shore
2015	*Hotel Transylvania 2*	animated
2018	*Hotel Transylvania 3: Summer Vacation*	animated
2021	*Dracula on Holiday*	comedy; UK

RIP

In one of the comedic takes on the Dracula story, Dracula: Dead and Loving It *is a 1995 parody by Mel Brooks. In this scene, Renfield (Peter MacNicol)) has his hands full with two vampire women.*

Villarias. Between the two versions, this first talkie vampire film made Dracula famous and infamous worldwide. Even as *Dracula* would go on to become the single literary work most frequently brought to the screen, Dracula would become the single character most frequently portrayed on-screen, with the possible exception of Sherlock Holmes.

The chart on page 376 lists all of the cinematic versions of *Dracula* made over the century from 1921 through 2021. The 40-plus adaptations of the novel *Dracula* to the screen (as opposed to the many movies that merely include Dracula as a character) can be divided into three distinct types: films released as feature-length movies, stage dramas (some broadcast on television) and later released on film, and sexually explicit adult adaptations of the novel. Beginning with *Nosferatu, Eine Symphonie des Grauens* in 1922, the adaptations took considerable artistic liberty with the novel, especially when creating musical versions, not to mention the adult versions. Most drop and conflate characters, often move the action away from London, and/or bring the action from the 1890s into a more contemporary moment. Nevertheless, the overall thrust of the novel remains.

The most recent spate of Dracula moviemaking began in 2012, the centennial of Bram Stoker's death.

❧ *Actors* ❧

Carradine, John (1905–1988)

Born Richmond Reed Carradine on February 5, 1905, in New York City, John Carradine first appeared as Dracula in the 1944 movie *House of Frankenstein* and frequently recreated the part throughout the rest of his career. Carradine grew up in an educated family. His mother was a surgeon and his father a lawyer, who also worked at times as a poet, artist, and Associated Press correspondent in London. Carradine originally planned to become a sculptor and, to that end, attended the Graphic Art School in Philadelphia. However, inspired by the Shakespearean actor Robert Mitchell, he began to train for the stage.

In 1925, he set out on his own, making a living as a sketch artist. In New Orleans that year, he made his stage debut in *Camille* and then joined a touring Shakespearean company. In 1927, he moved to Hollywood and worked as an actor, in Shakespearean plays when possible. In 1930, he appeared for the first time in a movie, *Tol'able David*, using the name Peter Richmond. He appeared in his first horror movie, which was also his first motion picture for Universal Pictures, in 1933's *The Invisible Man*. In 1935, he signed a long-term contract with 20th Century Fox and changed his stage name to John Carradine. That same year, he married Ardanelle Cosner.

Through the 1930s, he appeared in a number of notable movies, including *The Prisoner of Shark Island* (1936) and *Stagecoach* (1939), but he is possibly most remembered for his portrayal of the drunk minister in *The Grapes of Wrath* (1939). In the 1940s, he appeared in the B horror movies that had become a staple of Universal Pictures's schedule. Then in 1944, he accepted the role of Dracula in *House of Frankenstein*, which he agreed to do if he could take his portrayal from Bram Stoker's

novel rather than the then more famous portrayal by Bela Lugosi. Carradine's performance somewhat saved the movie and its highly contrived plot and established him as one of the most popular interpreters of the count.

Meanwhile, Carradine had formed a drama company and laid plans for a career as a Shakespearean actor. His work was greeted with rave reviews, but his plans were blocked by his first wife (whom he had divorced in 1944), who had him thrown in jail for "alimony contempt." With his new wife, Sonia Sorel, he returned to Hollywood and accepted the offer to assume his vampiric role in *House of Dracula*. Carradine's most famous scene was Dracula's attack upon the heroine as she played "Moonlight Sonata" on the piano. About to claim his victim, he was repulsed by the crucifix hanging around her neck.

Prolific character actor John Carradine acted in over 350 films in his career, including a few vampire movies.

RIP

John Carradine starred in 1945's House of Dracula, *which also featured Lon Chaney and Martha O'Driscoll.*

Carradine returned to the Dracula role in the 1950s on the stage. He moved even farther from the Lugosi presentation of Dracula and referred directly to the text of the novel in creating his own makeup, which included white hair and a white mustache. He kept both the opera cape and the evening clothes. Memorable in his performance was a humorous line he added to the script at the end: "If I'm alive, what am I doing here? On the other hand, if I'm dead, why do I have to wee-wee?" In 1956, Carradine became possibly the first television Dracula in a program for NBC's live *Matinee Theatre*. In 1957, following a divorce two years earlier, Carradine married Doris Rich.

From the 1960s until his death in 1988, Carradine appeared in numerous B films, in-cluding a variety of vampire movies. The first of the new vampire movies was *Billy the Kid vs. Dracula*, an unfortunate marriage of the vampire and western genres. In 1969, Carradine traveled to Mexico for *Las Vampiras* (*The Vampires*), a film in which he had little creative input. The only English-speaking person on the set, he learned enough Spanish to deliver the famous line he had added to the play. He followed *Las Vampiras* with *The Blood of Dracula's Coffin* (1968), the first of several movies he made under the direction of Al Abramson. The next came almost immediately, *Dracula vs. Frankenstein* (also known as *The Blood of Frankenstein*) in 1971. Through the 1970s, he appeared in *Vampire Men of the Lost Planet* (1970), *Horror of the Blood Monsters* (1971), *House of Dracula's Daughter* (1973), *Mary, Mary,*

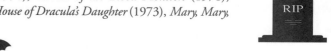

Bloody Mary (1975), *Nocturna* (1978), and *The Vampire Hookers* (1979). His final appearances in vampire movies were in *Doctor Dracula* (1980) and *The Monster Club* (1981). In most of these movies, though by no means all, Carradine played the part of the vampire.

Carradine married Emily Cisneros in 1975, four years after the death of his third wife. He continued to make movies through the 1980s and won an award at the Sitges Film Festival in 1983 as best male actor for his work in *House of the Long Shadows* (1983). He died on November 27, 1988, in Milan, Italy, after climbing the 328 steps of the Duomo, the famous cathedral. He collapsed and was taken to the hospital, where he died of heart and kidney failure.

Known for his deep, distinctive, classically trained baritone voice, Carradine appeared in an unknown number of films (some estimates go as high as 500). In spite of the negative reaction to his later portrayals of Dracula (and other vampires), he is remembered from his early films and stage work as one of the most important people to take up these roles. Except for Christopher Lee, he played Dracula more than any other actor and appeared in a starring role in more vampire movies than any actor before or since.

The Carradine name was carried on after John's death by his sons David (1936–2009) and Keith (1949–), though neither was well known for his vampire appearances. Keith made no vampire movies. David, who appeared in over 100 movies during his lengthy career, starred in three vampire movies: *The Last Sect* (2006), *Sundown: The Vampire in Retreat* (1989), and *Nosferatu: The First Vampire* (1998), none being particularly notable roles.

Jourdan, Louis (1921–2015)

Louis Jourdan, the actor starring in the role of Dracula in the made-for-television production *Count Dracula* (1977), was born in Marseilles, France. A star and experienced actor by the 1970s, he had made his first movie in 1940 in a French production, *Le Corsaire*. After World War II, he came to the United States and appeared in *The Paradine Case* (1947), which was followed by multiple appearances on the stage and screen.

In 1977, Jourdan starred in his first vampire role as Count Dracula in the BBC production of the Bram Stoker novel. The lengthy production (two and a half hours) is remembered as one of the more faithful reenactments of the original work and included the famous scene in which Jonathan Harker saw Dracula crawling down the walls of his castle. The movie was noted for its emphasis on drama and tension rather than blood and violence. A sexual element was present, but because *Count Dracula* was produced for television, it did not contain nudity. Jourdan played the role in a manner similar to Frank Langella (then starring in the Broadway revival of the play): as a suave, continental, romantic hero. Women swooned in ecstasy when he bit them. After his Dracula role, Jourdan went on to star in several other movies, including the James Bond movie *Octopussy* (1983) and *The Return of the Swamp Thing* (1989) and made numerous television appearances. His final role was in *The Year of the Comet* (1992).

He formally retired from acting in 1992 and spent his retirement years between his home in Beverly Hills and a residence in Vielle, in southern France. He died in 2015 in Beverly Hills.

Langella, Frank (1940–)

Frank Langella, star of the 1979 film version of *Dracula*, was born in Bayonne, New Jersey. His parents were Frank Langella, a businessman, and Ruth Weil, a magazine editor. He attended Syracuse University and, in 1959, was awarded the Syracuse Critics Award for

RIP

best actor. He went on to study acting, dance, and voice with private teachers and launched a career that has included both acting and theatrical management. Langella made his stage debut in 1960 in *The Pajama Game* at the Erie Playhouse. In 1963, he made his New York debut in *The Immoralist* at the Bouwerie Lane Theatre. That same year, he became one of the original members of the Lincoln Center repertory training company.

In 1967, Langella first appeared in the title role of Dracula at the Berkshire Theatre Festival. Three years later, he made his film debut in *The Twelve Chairs*, a part that would be followed by more notable roles in *Diary of a Mad Housewife* and *The Deadly Trap*. In 1977, he attained a new level of recognition as the star in the revival of the Hamilton Deane/John L. Balderston version of *Dracula*, which in 1978 received two Tony Awards. He was later chosen

Actor Frank Langella, seen here in 2012, starred in the 1979 version of Dracula.

to star in the movie version of *Dracula* directed by John Badham.

An accomplished actor, Langella brought a new depth and dimension to a part that had become rather narrowly stereotyped. Langella had reflected upon the count's character. Dracula would, he assumed, carry himself as a member of royalty who was, on one hand (in the presence of females), gracious and mannered but, on the other hand, ruled and commanded and was used to having his own way. He also understood Dracula's problem with immortality. While an extended life gave him wisdom beyond his contemporaries, it also brought a great weariness. In possibly the most important element of his performance, in large part attributable to the changing times, Langella highlighted the sensual and sexual elements of his relationship to Lucy Westenra (renamed Lucy Seward), the main character in the Deane/Balderston play. As Dracula, Langella would not only act with defensiveness when attacked, but he was also as a jealous lover. Langella clearly understood the relationship between Dracula and women. In reflecting on the role, he noted:

> ... the women have to want to make love with Count Dracula. And he must want to make love to them as a man loves a woman ... not as a vampire goes after blood. The things that go on between Dracula and his women must be the result of her needs as well as his. Something is calling her, and it's not fangs, or his wolf's eyes.

Langella created the most appealing and human Dracula since Bela Lugosi. He played the character not as a traditional monster but as a creature of a different species. Dracula was not so much cruel and evil as he was operating out of his very different nature. Langella took his place as one of the most memorable actors to assume the role of Dracula though, for the sake of his career, he was able to walk away

RIP

from the part and avoid being typecast. Thus, unlike that of Bela Lugosi and Christopher Lee, Langella's portrayal consumed only a few years of his lengthy career. He followed his success as Dracula with other movies and additional success on the stage. In 1980, he was able to return to Broadway as Salieri in the highly acclaimed *Amadeus*. Langella has continued to play a wide variety of roles onstage, with occasional movie roles.

In 1981, he assumed the title role of Dracula's contemporary in a television production of *Sherlock Holmes*. He returned to this role in 1987 in *Sherlock's Last Case* in New York and Washington, D.C. In 2007, he won a Tony Award for Best Performance by a Leading Actor in a Play for his portrayal of Richard Nixon in *Frost/Nixon*. He subsequently played the same part in the movie adaptation, for which he received an Academy Award nomination. Since portraying Nixon, he has maintained an active career with parts onstage, television, and the movies, most recently appearing in the 2020 movie *The Trial of the Chicago 7*. His autobiography was released in 2012.

Lee, Christopher (1922–2015)

Actor Christopher Lee, who, after Bela Lugosi, is most often identified with portraying the vampire Dracula, portrayed the count in a higher number of differentiated motion pictures than anyone else. He was born on May 27, 1922, in London, England, and later attended Wellington College. In 1947, as the British movie industry revived following World War II, he signed a contract with J. Arthur Rank, which led to his first film appearance in *Corridors of Blood*. Thus began one of the most active screen careers of any actor, which, by the mid-1980s, saw Lee with parts in more than 130 movies.

His career rose steadily through the 1950s to 1957, when he was brought together with three other people at Hammer Films who altered

his life dramatically. Responding to the success of several science fiction/horror movies, Hammer Films obtained the motion picture rights to some of Universal Pictures's classic monster movies and hired Terence Fisher, Jimmy Sangster, Peter Cushing, and Lee to film a new version of *Frankenstein*. Lee starred as Frankenstein's monster in the highly successful *The Curse of Frankenstein* (1957). The four were reassembled the following year to do a remake of *Dracula* (1958), best known as *Horror of Dracula*. Although *The Curse of Frankenstein*, in Lee's words, "started it all," it was *Horror of Dracula* that made Lee a star and put Hammer Films on the map as the new king of on-screen horror.

Changes in technology and public mores allowed Lee to present a much different Dracula. Most noticeably, Lee was more directly a creature of horror, dropping much of the image of the suave, continental gentleman perpetuated by Lugosi. Unlike Lugosi, Lee had fangs, which he showed to the audience, and he attacked his female victims on camera. Lacking any clear direction from the production staff, Lee devel-

Next to Bela Lugosi, Christopher Lee is probably one of the top actors who come to mind when you think of classic Dracula movies. Here he is in the 1958 version of Dracula.

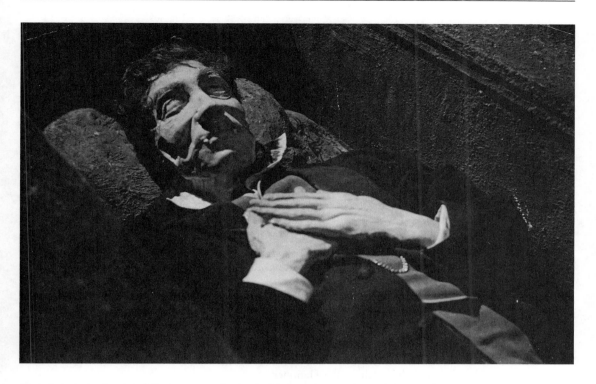

Dracula kicks back in his coffin in Horror of Dracula *(aka simply* Dracula*) in the 1958 release.*

oped Dracula as a complex human who had great positive qualities—leadership, charm, intelligence, and sensuality—coupled with a savage and ferocious streak that would lead to his eventual downfall. Dracula also had a tragic quality: his undead immortality.

Horror of Dracula was an unexpected success, but it would be some years before Lee would return to the role. Meanwhile, he went to Italy to make a comedic vampire movie, *Tempi duri per i Vampiri* (*Uncle Was a Vampire*) and, in spite of some observation of his role, Lee has insisted that the vampire he portrayed was not Dracula but Baron Rodrigo. He then returned to Hammer Films for further work on the first round of the Universal Pictures horror series as Kharis in *The Mummy* (1960). Moving back to Italy, he worked with director Mario Bava, for whom he played the vampire Lico, whom Hercules confronts in the underworld.

While Lee was working on the continent, Hammer Films had made its first movie about Carmilla, the vampire in Sheridan Le Fanu's 1872 tale of the same name. Lee was then invited to assume the part of Count Ludwig Karnstein in the 1964 Spanish version of the story, *La maldición de los Karnstein* (aka *Terror in the Crypt*). It would be another five years before Lee returned to Hammer Films where, together with Fisher and Sangster, he made his next Dracula movie, *Dracula, Prince of Darkness*, which began with the final scene from *Horror of Dracula*, in which Abraham Van Helsing killed Dracula. Dracula was then revived by pouring blood on his ashes.

For Lee, this second Dracula movie was unique in that he never spoke a line; he merely grunted and groaned. Whereas *Horror of Dracula* had made Lee a star, the series of movies made during the seven years beginning in 1966, when *Dracula, Prince of Darkness* was filmed,

RIP

forever identified him with the role. Most of these—*Dracula Has Risen from the Grave* (1968), *Taste the Blood of Dracula* (1970), *Scars of Dracula* (1970), *Dracula A.D. 1972* (1972), and *The Satanic Rites of Dracula*, aka *Count Dracula and His Vampire Bride* (1973)—were panned by the critics but found an appreciative audience among the growing legion of vampire fans.

While Lee was turning out the series of Hammer Films movies, two historians, Raymond T. McNally and Radu Florescu, were researching the historical Dracula, the Romanian ruler Vlad the Impaler. Their first report on their research appeared in 1972 as *In Search of Dracula*. In 1974, a Swedish production crew filmed a documentary based on the book, bearing the same title. Lee was selected to narrate the movie and to appear in scenes as Vlad.

Lee believed that each of the Hammer Films movies moved him further and further from the Dracula of Bram Stoker's novel. For example, *Dracula Has Risen from the Grave* contained a scene in which Lee pulled a stake out of his own heart, an action he considered at the time to be completely out of character. Thus, in 1970, he jumped at the chance to star in Jesús Franco's version of the Dracula story, *El Conde Dracula*. Unlike previous versions, Franco's *Dracula* made a place for all of the novel's main characters and, during the opening scenes, stayed relatively close to the book.

The script soon began to deviate, however, and, in the end, wandered far from the text (attributed partly to an extremely low budget). In one aspect, Lee was very happy with the film; it allowed him to portray Dracula as he was pictured in the book, although Lee lacked the hairy palms and elongated ears and fingers. Lee did bring out Dracula's progressively more youthful appearance as he drained the blood of Lucy Westenra and Mina Murray. Franco's film soon entered the ranks of the for-

gotten movies, although high marks were given to Pedro Portabella, who made a film about the making of *El Conde Dracula*. Portabella's *Vampir* was acclaimed as an artistic meditation on death. Lee starred in the final scenes, in which he described Dracula's death and read the last chapter of the novel, in which Dracula was killed.

Lee's last appearance in a vampire movie was as Dracula in the 1976 film *Dracula and Son* (a French comedy originally released as *Dracula père et fils*). Lee had played enough different roles to stave off the terror of any actor typecasting but, at this point, he

> Lee's last appearance in a vampire movie was as Dracula in the 1976 film *Dracula and Son*....

swore off vampire movies altogether. He had supporting parts in *The Private Life of Sherlock Holmes* (1970) and *Hannie Caulder* (1972) and the title role as the villain in the James Bond movie *Man with the Golden Gun* (1974).

Lee had moved to the United States in 1977, in large part to escape being typecast as an actor primarily fit for horror films. He went on to have significant character roles in a variety of films, such as *Return to Witch Mountain* (1977) and *1941* (1979). He also appeared in the film *Cyber Eden* (1994), an Italian science fiction production.

Lee's career would reach a new level at the beginning of the new century, when he was chosen to portray Saruman in *The Lord of the Rings*, a series of three films made from J. R. R. Tolkien's popular fantasy books. Saruman the White leads Istari, a set of wizards whose original goal is to challenge Sauron, the major villain in the novels. As the novel proceeds, however, he decided to take Sauron's place and take over Middle Earth. With a career now at a high point, he moved on to play Count Dooku, the main villain in two *Star Wars* films: *Star Wars: Episode II—Attack of the Clones* (2002) and *Star Wars: Episode III—Revenge of the Sith* (2005). He remained active over the next decade, his final performance coming in the independent film *Angels of Notting Hill*. Lee passed away in 2015.

Lee wrote an initial autobiography, *Tall, Dark, and Gruesome* (1977, revised edition 2009), which he revised on several occasions, a final revision being issued in 2003 as *Lord of Misrule: The Autobiography of Christopher Lee*. He also worked with both Michael Parry and Peter Haining on anthologies of horror stories. He also contributed numerous comments to Robert W. Pohle Jr. and Douglas C. Hart's study *The Films of Christopher Lee* and an afterword to Tom Johnson and Mark Miller's 2004 filmography of his films. *The Christopher Lee Film Encyclopedia* appeared in 2017.

Lugosi, Bela (1882–1956)

Bela Lugosi, the actor most identified with the image of Dracula and the vampire in the public mind, was born Bela Blasko on October 20, 1882, in Lugos, Hungary. At the time of his birth, Lugos was part of the Austro-Hungarian Empire and was located some 50 miles from Transylvania. Lugosi attended school locally.

Lugosi was still quite young when a traveling theater company came to Lugos and he gave up ideas of entering a profession in favor of a life on the stage. He began to write and stage amateur productions and, in 1893, left school for good. He also left home looking for an acting job; not finding any, he held various jobs as a laborer in the mines, a factory, and on the railroad.

When he had the opportunity to act, his first experiences were negative. His lack of education made him appear stupid. He began a self-education program and read voraciously. His first formal stage role was as Count Konigsegg in *Ocskay Brigaderos* (*Brigadier General Ocskay*) in 1902. The following year, he played Gecko, Svengali's servant, in *Trilby*, his first

part in a horror production. During this time, he tried out a number of stage names but finally settled on Lugosi, meaning "one from Lugos." In 1910, he starred in *Romeo and Juliet*, for which he received good reviews, and went on to become a featured actor on the Hungarian stage. In 1911, he moved to Budapest to work at the Hungarian Royal Theatre and, two years later, joined the National Theatre of Budapest; although his salary increased, the young actor was not given any starring roles.

Lugosi's acting career was interrupted by World War I. He returned to the theater in 1917. That same year, he risked his career by taking a job with the Star Film Company and appeared in his first film, *The Leopard*. For the film, he adopted a new stage name, Arisztid Olt. His second role was in *Az Elet Kiralya*,

Bela Lugosi looking suave and dashing in this 1912 headshot.

based on *The Picture of Dorian Gray*. He starred in a variety of films until the chaos following the end of the war forced him to leave Hungary. He settled in Germany, where he appeared in several movies, including *Sklaven Fremdes Willens* (*Slave of a Foreign Will*) and *Der Januskopf* (based on *Dr. Jekyll and Mr. Hyde*).

Producers had a tendency to cast Lugosi in the role of the villain, although his last role was that of a romantic lead in *Der Tanz auf dem Vulkan*. Banned from Hungary because of his political views, in 1920, he decided to immigrate to the United States. He barely escaped death when his identity was discovered by some Hungarian crewmembers of the ship on which he traversed the Atlantic. Although an illegal alien, he was granted political asylum and allowed to work. He organized a Hungarian repertory company, which played to the Hungarian–American community.

He got a break in 1922, when he was offered a part in *The Red Poppy*—if he could learn the part. Unable to speak English, he nevertheless memorized the part and opened to his first English-speaking audience in December 1922 at the Greenwich Village Theatre. Lugosi received far better reviews than the play, which ran for only six weeks on Broadway before closing. *The Red Poppy* led to Lugosi's first Hollywood movie part as the villain in *The Silent Command* (1923), an action spy movie.

Unable to obtain further roles in Hollywood in spite of positive reviews, Lugosi returned to New York and made several movies. He also appeared in several plays and made it back to Broadway briefly in *Arabesque*. The events that were to change his career and life forever can be traced to 1927.

That year, the Hamilton Deane version of the play *Dracula* opened in London. Pro-

ducer Horace Liveright perceived some possibilities for the play in the United States and negotiated the purchase of the American rights. He also had John L. Balderston do a thorough rewrite of the script. Director John D. Williams, familiar with Lugosi's work in other plays, cast him in the title role. He fit the part Balderston had created as if it were made for him. His face, especially his eyes, his hand movements, and his Hungarian accent contributed greatly to the success of the play, which opened on October 2, 1927, at the Fulton Theater. It played for 40 weeks on Broadway, after which several companies took it on the road.

Lugosi continued his part with the West Coast production of *Dracula*. Back in southern California, he picked up several small movie parts. In 1929, an eventful year, he made his talkie debut in *Prisoners* and worked with director Tod Browning on *The Thirteenth Chair*. In 1930, Universal Pictures purchased the motion picture rights to *Dracula*. The company used Lugosi to negotiate the agreement with Bram Stoker's widow, and he was somewhat insulted when he was not automatically given the part. Rather, Lugosi was among five men considered for the role. Browning wanted Lon Chaney, but he died soon after Universal Pictures finished its negotiations with Florence Stoker. Lugosi was finally signed on for $500 a week. His hardest job was to adapt the part he had played hundreds of times on the stage to the film medium.

Dracula opened on February 12, 1931, and became an immediate, though somewhat unexpected, hit. The film would influence all vampire films that came after it, and Lugosi's Dracula would be the standard against which all later vampires were judged. Lugosi became a star, with 97 percent of his fan mail coming from women. He responded by suggesting that generations of subjection had given women a masochistic in-

> He [Lugosi] got a break in 1922, when he was offered a part in *The Red Poppy*—if he could learn the part. Unable to speak English, he nevertheless memorized the part....

RIP

Lugosi in 1940's The Devil Bat.

up again in *Mark of the Vampire*. Lugosi played Count Mora in the remake of Browning's silent film *London after Midnight*. For the rest of the decade into the early 1940s, Lugosi played in a variety of horror movies and appeared as the villain in nonhorror flicks, mostly mysteries. Of these, his team-up with Boris Karloff and Basil Rathbone in *Son of Frankenstein* (1939) is possibly the most memorable. Publicity for *The Devil Bat* (1940), a routine mystery, made use of Lugosi's identification with the vampire in its advertising.

Through the early 1940s, Lugosi made as many as five movies a year, overwhelmingly in villain or monster roles. He played a Dracula-like role in the comedy *Spooks Run Wild* (1941) and finally portrayed Frankenstein's monster in *Frankenstein versus the Wolfman* (1943). He played his first genuine vampire role since Dracula in Columbia Pictures's *Return of the Vampire* (1944). Lugosi was cast as Armand Tesla, a vampire hardly distinguishable from Dracula, and, as might be expected, Universal Pictures filed suit against Columbia Pictures for infringement upon its rights. In 1948, Lugosi returned to Universal Pictures for his next vampire role. The horror theme having largely run its course, as many at Universal Pictures thought, the idea emerged to get the major monsters together with the studio's comic stars, Bud Abbott and Lou Costello, for a monster spoof. Lugosi re-created his Dracula role for *Abbott and Costello Meet Frankenstein*. He played the part with as much dignity as possible and must have enjoyed it somewhat, as he did it a second time for Abbott and Costello's television show in 1952.

terest, an enjoyment of suffering experienced vicariously on the screen. Lugosi moved from Dracula to portray an Eastern mystic in a Charlie Chan movie, *The Black Camel*, and then began shooting for *Frankenstein*. The monster proved to be a part not made for him, so he was replaced by Boris Karloff and instead starred in *Murders in the Rue Morgue*, where he did well as a mad scientist. He drifted from Universal Pictures in 1932 to make *White Zombies*, in which he played a sorcerer, and returned to the stage in Los Angeles in a horror play, *Murdered Alive*. By this time, he had already been hit by the actor's nemesis: typecasting. Studios continually offered him parts to bring terror to the audience.

In 1933, Lugosi returned to New York for a brief (and last) appearance on Broadway as the villain in *Murder of the Vanities*. He went from Broadway to a vaudeville touring company, in which he played Dracula. He periodically returned to the part in summer stock whenever his film work was light. In 1934, he made one of his better movies when Universal Pictures teamed him with Boris Karloff in *The Black Cat*. At the end of the year, both Lugosi and Browning moved over to MGM to team

The downturn in horror movies left Lugosi out of a job. He did some television and, in 1950, began to make personal appearances at movie theaters showing his old horror films. In 1951, he traveled to England to do a new production of *Dracula*, but the play flopped, and he found himself without enough money to get back to the States. A friend arranged for him to do his next movie, *Mother Riley Meets*

the Vampire (aka *My Son, the Vampire*), released in 1952. (Mother Riley was a character in a series of British comedies.) Lugosi's return to America was less than spectacular. His ability to get parts was very limited, and a downward slide landed him in a drug rehabilitation program in 1955. Lugosi made a few more films and then, in 1956, was hired by director Edward Wood Jr. to play a vampire for his quickie movie *Plan 9 from Outer Space*. He and Vampira were to play a pair of vampires raised from their graves by outer space aliens. A week after shooting began, however, on August 16, 1956, Lugosi died. Another actor, doing scenes with the vampire cape pulled across his face, filled in for Lugosi for the rest of the film. *Plan 9* has since become known as one of the worst films of all time and has a substantial cult following.

Lugosi's last years were years of loneliness and abandonment by the industry for which he had worked all his life. He did not live to see the acclaim of a new generation of fans who had an appreciation for the horror genre and understood his contribution to it. Only in the last generation, with the revival of the horror movie in general and the vampire movie in particular, has Lugosi's impact been understood.

🦇 *Movies* 🦇

Bram Stoker's Dracula (1992)

The most heralded of the several attempts to bring the novel *Dracula*, by Bram Stoker, to the motion picture screen appeared in 1992 from Columbia Pictures. Directed by one of Hollywood's top directors, Francis Ford Coppola, it opened on Friday, November 13 and became the largest nonsummer movie opening of all time.

Coppola had a goal of making a more accurate version of Stoker's original novel, and his version relied more closely on the storyline of the book than any previous Dracula movie. The story opened with Jonathan Harker (played by Keanu Reeves) leaving his fiancée Mina Murray (Winona Ryder) to travel to Castle Dracula in Transylvania. His first encounters with Dracula (Gary Oldman) reflected the major incidents recorded in the book, though Dracula's colorful appearance could hardly have been more different from his description in the novel. Their encounter as Harker was shaving produced one of the film's most memorable moments. Harker had cut himself, and Dracula took the razor from Harker and licked it to taste the drops of blood. Harker was attacked by the three female vampire brides, residents of the castle, and was only able to escape after Dracula left for England.

In England, the three suitors of Lucy Westenra (Sadie Frost)—Quincey P. Morris (Bill Campbell), Arthur Holmwood (Cary Elwes), and Dr. John Seward (Richard E. Grant)—rose to the occasion as Dracula launched his attack on her. Unable at first to determine the cause of her problems, Seward called in Dr. Abraham Van Helsing (Anthony Hopkins). Van Helsing organized the opposition that finally defeated Dracula after tracking him back to his castle.

While Coppola's version of *Dracula* is by far the most faithful to the book, it deviated at several important points. For example, as a prelude to the movie, Coppola briefly told the story of Vlad the Impaler, the fifteenth-century Romanian ruler who served as a historical reference for the Dracula character. This prelude indicated the influence of the books by Raymond T. McNally and Radu Florescu, creating fans for Vlad, the historical Dracula. In introducing the theme of Vlad the Impaler, Coppola borrowed an idea from the Dan Curtis/Jack Palance version of *Dracula* (1974). Curtis used Vlad's

RIP

(Left to right) Actors Bill Campbell, Cary Elwes, Anthony Hopkins, Richard E. Grant, and Sadie Frost starred in the 1992 adaptation of the original novel, Bram Stoker's Dracula.

story to provide the rationale for Dracula's attack upon the specific women he chose as targets in England. In *Dracula* (1974), Palance saw a picture of Lucy, Harker's fiancée, who was the mirror image of his lost love of the fifteenth century. He traveled to England in order to recapture the love of his prevampire life. In *Bram Stoker's Dracula*, Winona Ryder played not only Mina Murray but also Elizabeth, Dracula's original love. To continue the storyline, Coppola allowed Dracula to walk around London freely in the daytime (as Dracula seemed to be able to do in the novel), but he now used his time in the city to establish a liaison with Mina and, with his suave, continental manners, win her love. In the final scene, Mina went to the dying Dracula and, through her love, facilitated his redemption as he died.

Vlad's reaction to the death of Elizabeth (or Elisabeta), who committed suicide and hence could not go to heaven in Eastern Orthodox theology, provided Coppola with an explanation of the origin of Dracula's vampirism. Since she could not go to heaven, Dracula blasphemed God and symbolically attacked the cross with his sword. Blood flowed from the impaled cross, Dracula drank, and presumably, as a result, was transformed into a vampire.

Coppola also enlarged upon the account of R. N. Renfield, another character in the original novel who was introduced as a resident of the insane asylum managed by John Seward, with no explanation as to the reason for his being there. His mental condition was explained by Coppola as a result of having traveled to Castle Dracula; Renfield became insane because of his encounters with the residents. This earlier connection with Dracula also explained why he, but none of the other inmates of the asylum, reacted to Dracula's arrival and activities in London.

Bram Stoker's Dracula was accompanied by a massive advertising campaign, which included more than 100 separate pieces of paraphernalia and souvenir items, including a novelization of the script, a four-issue comic book series, two sets of trading cards, jewelry, T-shirts, posters, a board game, and several home computer games. The TNT cable television network sponsored a sweepstakes the week of the movie's opening that offered the winner a trip to London, "one of Dracula's favorite cities!" While it opened to mixed reviews (an occupational hazard with any horror genre film), the Coppola movie shows every sign of taking its place as one of the most memorable *Dracula* adaptations of all time. It opened in Bucharest, Romania, in July 1993, at which time a special drink, dubbed "Dracula's Spirits" and made of vodka and red fruit juice, was issued by a Romanian distillery. In spite of the mixed reviews, the movie surprised media observers by becoming the largest box office opening ever experienced by Columbia Pictures and the largest ever for a nonsummer opening. It played on almost 2,500 screens around the country and grossed more than $32 million.

Count Dracula (1977)

Count Dracula (1977) was a made-for-television coproduction of the BBC and American Public Television. It consisted of three 45-minute segments and, thus, became and remains the screen adaptation of *Dracula* with the longest running time.

Count Dracula began with Jonathan Harker (Bosco Hogan) saying goodbye to Mina Westenra (now Lucy Westenra's sister), Lucy (Susan Penhaligon), and their mother. He traveled to Castle Dracula, where he had his initial confrontation with Dracula (Louis Jourdan) and the three female vampire residents. He eventually escaped and returned to England. Lucy was engaged to Quincey P. Holmwood (Richard Barnes), now transformed from a

Texan into a staff person at the American embassy in London. Once Dracula began his attack on Lucy, Dr. John Seward (Mark Burns) called Abraham Van Helsing (John Finlay) to his assistance. Van Helsing arrived, as in the novel, as an elderly foreign expert. He taught the men that supernatural evil existed and that they must unite to fight it.

Lucy finally died, and her postdeath activity convinced the men that Van Helsing was correct. They proceeded to Lucy's tomb to finally kill her in one of the most graphic vampire death scenes to that point in time. With Harker back in England and married to Mina (Judy Bowker), Van Helsing built a united front to kill Dracula. Meanwhile, Dracula attacked Mina and forced her to drink his blood. The attack made her a full partner in the final drive to kill the vampire.

In the final scenes, Van Helsing and Mina arrived at Castle Dracula only to confront the three women (the vampire brides), who call to Mina as their new sister. Van Helsing protected her before going into the castle to kill the women. The Romani people, who brought Dracula's sleeping body back to the castle, were fought off in a Western-style gunfight. The last of the Romani got the box to the entrance of the castle,

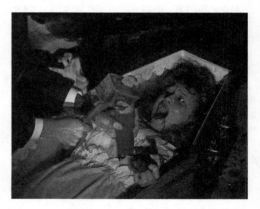

Lucy (played by Susan Penhaligon) discovers the stakes are high in the 1977 TV movie Count Dracula.

where he was stopped. In the end, it was Van Helsing, not the younger men, who pried open the lid of the box and killed Dracula with a stake.

Count Dracula, even more than *El Conde Dracula*, most faithfully reproduced the storyline of Bram Stoker's novel of all adaptations through the 1970s. Only the more recent *Bram Stoker's Dracula* (1992) would, for example, return all of the major characters in the novel to the movie storyline. *Count Dracula* also raised the level of realism in the depiction of the vampire's attack and the scenes of the vampire women attacking the baby in the early segment of the movie (a scene that would be cut from the American version). *Count Dracula* also returned the essential scene in the novel in which Dracula forced Mina to drink his blood and the subsequent events in which she was branded with a eucharistic wafer.

Louis Jourdan assumed the role of Dracula in this version. He brought to the part a suave, continental manner. He was an aristocratic lover but a man used to getting what he wanted. He seduced women and took them away from the mundane gentlemen with whom they had previously been paired. Jourdan thus laid the groundwork for the sensual Dracula so effectively portrayed by Frank Langella a few years later in *Dracula* (1979).

Dracula (1931)

In the wake of the success of the stage production of *Dracula* that had opened in New York in 1927, producer Horace Liveright (1886–1933) developed touring companies to take the play to various parts of the country. Actor Bela Lugosi, who had starred in the New York play, joined the West Coast company and eventually settled in Los Angeles, where he could resume his hoped-for film career. Then in 1930, Universal Pictures moved to purchase the film rights for *Dracula* from Florence Stoker. The original asking price, reportedly $200,000,

was far too high from the studio's perspective, so Bela Lugosi was cajoled into negotiating Stoker's widow down to a more reasonable amount. Universal Pictures eventually got the rights for $40,000 and hired director Tod Browning to take charge of the project.

Because of his role in negotiating the rights, Lugosi expected that the part of Dracula would automatically be offered to him. It was not. Rather, Universal Pictures announced that John Wray, who had just had a major part in *All Quiet on the Western Front*, would play the role. Universal Pictures also considered Conrad Veidt (who declined the honor), Ian Keith, William Courtney, Paul Muni, Chester Morris, and Joseph Schildkraut. Not until a few weeks before shooting began did Lugosi secure the part. He sold his services for a special lower fee and, as a result, was paid very little money—$3,500 for seven weeks of filming (about half of David Manners's salary). Helen Chandler was chosen to play Mina Murray (now Mina Seward), and Frances Dale took the part of Lucy Westenra (changed to Weston). David Manners assumed the now greatly diminished role of Jonathan Harker. The other major part, R. N. Renfield,

Bela Lugosi gives his iconic performance in the unforgettable, classic 1931 version of Dracula.

went to Dwight Frye. Edward Van Sloan, who had previously played Abraham Van Helsing, moved west for the movie part, and the cast was filled out by Herbert Bunston as Dr. John Seward. The movie was able to do much that the play could not. The film added the opening segment of the novel, in which Jonathan Harker traveled to Transylvania and had his initial encounter with Dracula and his three brides. This chapter included what many consider the most dramatic moments of the book. However, in the movie, Renfield, not Harker, made the trip to Castle Dracula. His experiences there accounted for his "insane" behavior following his return to England. An elaborate set was developed for the memorable scenes in the castle, but it was poorly utilized. Browning has been justly criticized for the restricted and flat manner in which he shot Dracula's encounter with his English guest, which was so ripe with possibilities. In spite of Browning's limitations, however, the scenes that began with Lugosi's opening line, "I am … Dracula," are among the most memorable, powerful, and influential ever seen in a horror film. *Dracula* also included a brief scene aboard the *Demeter*, the ship that brought Dracula to England.

From this point, the film rejoined the revised version of the Hamilton Deane/John L. Balderston play. Dracula had moved to London and targeted Mina Seward after previously disposing of Lucy. He abducted her to Carfax, now transformed into Carfax Abbey, his London home, but was tracked by Van Helsing, Dr. Seward, and Harker and finally destroyed. As in the play, the closing chapters of the book, describing the return to Transylvania, were deleted. Also, true to the play, at the end, Van Helsing stopped the credits and made the famous closing speech on the reality of vampires.

Dracula was set to open on Friday, February 12, 1931, at the Roxy Theater in Man-

hattan. New York was plastered with blood-red signs. Papers on the West Coast panned the production. The *Los Angeles Times* dubbed it a freak show—a curiosity without the possibility of wide appeal. The New York coverage was mixed. Critics did not like it, but they also had to respond to Universal Pictures's intense publicity and advertising campaign. The run at the Roxy lasted only eight days. The national release came in March. A silent version was prepared for theaters that had not yet added sound equipment. (Also, to make full use of the expensive set, a Spanish-language version with a completely new cast was filmed simultaneously with the Lugosi English-language version.) The movie opened in Los Angeles with no fanfare because Universal Pictures was in the midst of a budget crunch. In spite of its slow start, *Dracula* (the first of what would become a lineage of horror talkies) caught the imagination of the public and became the largest grossing film for Universal Pictures that year. For the first time since the Depression had started, the studio, threatened with closing, actually turned a profit.

Today, two generations after its release, some assessment of Universal Pictures's *Dracula* is possible. Certainly, it is the most influential vampire film of all time. All subsequent performances of the vampire have been either based upon it or a direct reaction to it. However, its original success did not lead, at least immediately, to a second vampire movie; rather, it was followed by the production of a very different horror movie, *Frankenstein*, and a string of horror movies covering a variety of nonvampire horror themes. Additionally, its continued success through the years did not lead at first to the production of many additional vampire movies, which appeared only sporadically until the 1960s. In the 1960s, however, the vampire genre was discovered as a unique creation, not just another variation on the horror genre.

> Today, two generations after its release, some assessment of Universal Pictures's *Dracula* is possible. Certainly, it is the most influential vampire film of all time.

RIP

Beginning with *Horror of Dracula* (1958), Hammer Films's remake of *Dracula* starring Christopher Lee, the novel *Dracula* has now been adapted to the screen more than 40 times, the character Dracula has appeared in literally hundreds of films, and characters largely based on Dracula have been featured in several hundred more. The more important remakes of the *Dracula* novel after the first Lee version included *El Conde Dracula* (1970), also with Lee; *Dracula* (1974) with Jack Palance; *Count Dracula* (1977) with Louis Jourdan; *Dracula* (1979), starring Frank Langella; *Nosferatu the Vampyre* (1979); and director Francis Ford Coppola's *Bram Stoker's Dracula* (1992). Ranking with each of these was the delightful satire/comedy *Love at First Bite* (1979), starring George Hamilton. Non-English versions of *Dracula* were produced in Turkey (*Drakula Istanbula*, 1953), Korea (*The Bad Flower*, 1961), Pakistan (*Zinda Laash*, 1967), Spain (*El Conde Dracula*, 1970), Japan (*Lake of Dracula*, 1971), Italy (*Dracula's Curse*, 2002), and India *Dracula 2012 3D* (2013).

Dracula (Spanish, 1931)

At the same time that Universal Pictures produced its famous version of *Dracula* starring Bela Lugosi, it produced a second version in Spanish. The Spanish version grew out of the studio's decision to respond to the changes brought about by the addition of sound to movies. Universal Pictures received a high percentage of its revenue from the foreign distribution of silent films, but talkies in English could threaten revenue because the techniques of dubbing had yet to be perfected. Universal Pictures's Czechoslovakian-born executive Paul Kohner suggested a solution to the studio's head, Carl Laemmle Jr.: shoot foreign-language versions of motion pictures simultaneously with the English versions, thus cutting costs by using the sets more than once. Kohner also argued that salaries for foreign actors and actresses were far less than those of Americans. Laemmle appointed Kohner as head of foreign productions. The first result was a Spanish version of *The Cat Creeps*, a talkie remake of *The Cat and the Canary*, which Universal Pictures had originally done as a silent film. Released in 1930 as *La Voluntad del Muerto*, it was an overwhelming success in Mexico and made actress Lupita Tovar a star. Kohner decided to make a Spanish version of *Dracula* and moved quickly to secure the youthful Tovar for the lead before she could return to Mexico. He chose Carlos Villarias (or Villar) for the role of Dracula and secured a capable supporting cast with Barry Norton (Jonathan "Juan" Harker), Eduardo Arozamena (Abraham Van Helsing), and Pablo Alvarez Rubio (R. N. Renfield).

Though it continued to be shown in Latin American countries into the 1950s, the Spanish version of *Dracula* became a largely forgotten entity in the United States. Universal Pictures failed to register its copyright of the film and did not make extra copies to preserve it. Donald F. Glut's 1975 work *The Dracula Book* mentioned it only in passing. In 1977, the American Film Institute attempted to make an archival print, but the only copy available (at the Library of Congress) had a decomposed third reel. In 1989, author/researcher David J. Skal followed up a rumor that a copy had survived in Cuba. Having located the copy, he was able to facilitate the preparation of a complete print of the film, which was presented in the United States for the first time since the 1930s. The initial public viewing took place on Halloween of 1992 at the University of California at Los Angeles. It was later released on video.

> Though it continued to be shown in Latin American countries into the 1950s, the Spanish version of *Dracula* became a largely forgotten entity in the United States.

The Spanish version followed a Spanish translation of the same script as the Lugosi version. However, as Skal noted, it was very different in that the more mobile camera movement employed by director George Melford and his shooting team gave it a much livelier quality. Both mood and action were enhanced. It stands as "an almost shot-by-shot scathing critique of the Browning (Lugosi) version," said Skal.

The original film opened in Mexico City and New York in April 1931 and in Los Angeles in May. It was one of the last Spanish-language films made in Hollywood—such productions being discontinued in the post-Depression business atmosphere. While possibly the superior movie of the two, it is very unlikely, given the development of the vampire film, that more than a few film historians and vampire buffs will ever see it. In spite of its being released for home video (later on DVD) and becoming somewhat of a best seller in that media, the film has become a historical curiosity rather than an important and influential film.

Dracula (1974)

In 1973, producer-director Dan Curtis, who had great success with vampire Barnabas Collins in the daytime television series *Dark Shadows*, teamed with screenwriter Richard Matheson (best known for his science fiction vampire novel *I Am Legend*) to produce a new version of *Dracula* for television, which was released in 1974. The pair attempted to bypass both the play by Hamilton Deane and John L. Balderston (the basis for the version of *Dracula* [1931] with Bela Lugosi) as well as *Horror of Dracula* and the other Hammer Films productions with Christopher Lee. At the same time, they were strongly influenced by the work of Raymond T. McNally and Radu Florescu, who published *In Search of Dracula: A True History of Dracula and Vampire Legends* (1972).

> Curtis's *Dracula* was preeminently the fifteenth-century Wallachian ruler and military hero as still alive in the nineteenth century.

This was the first book to highlight the exploits of Vlad the Impaler, the historical person who stands, in part, behind the lead character in Bram Stoker's novel. Curtis's *Dracula* was preeminently the fifteenth-century Wallachian ruler and military hero as still alive in the nineteenth century. The painting of him, astride his horse, dominated a room of Castle Dracula and, in several scenes, stole the attention of the camera. In the corner of the painting, a young woman was pictured. This woman was Dracula's true love (or true passion) from the fifteenth century, who had not survived with him into the nineteenth century.

Very early in the movie, Dracula saw a picture of Jonathan Harker, Mina Murray, Arthur Holmwood, and Lucy Westenra. Lucy looked nearly identical to the woman in the painting, so Dracula immediately decided that he must possess her. His quest for Lucy dominated the action in the first part of the film, while revenge for her death (the second time his love had been taken from him) occupied the remainder of the show. Curtis chose veteran character actor Jack Palance as Dracula. The story began with Jonathan Harker (Murray Brown) traveling to Transylvania. There, he moved through forbidden portions of the castle and discovered Dracula's secret.

As Dracula departed for England, Harker was left behind to be bitten by Dracula's brides. In England, the action centered on the two women, Lucy (Fiona Lewis) and Mina (Penelope Horner), Lucy's fiancé Arthur Holmwood (Simon Ward), and, most importantly, Abraham Van Helsing (Nigel Davenport). The novel's subplot concerning Dr. John Seward and the insane R. N. Renfield were pushed aside.

Van Helsing came to the fore after Lucy was bitten by Dracula. It was his task (Holmwood was unable to face his duty) to drive the

RIP

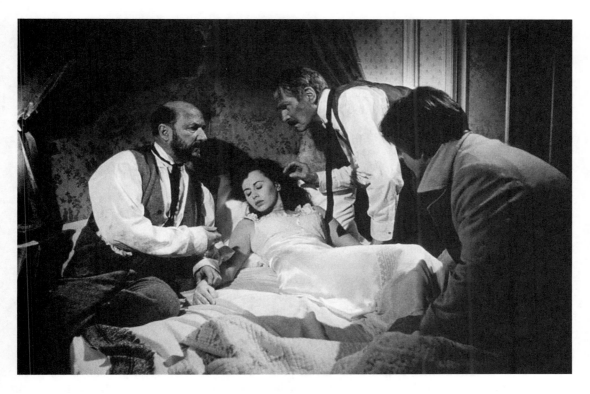

(Left to right) Donald Pleasence (as John Seward), Kate Nelligan (as Lucy), Laurence Olivier (as Van Helsing), and Trevor Eve (as Jonathan Harker) in the 1979 Dracula *that starred Frank Langella in the title role.*

stake into her heart. With his true love dead again, Dracula turned on Mina. Eventually, Van Helsing and Holmwood acted together. They drove Dracula back to Transylvania and followed him to Castle Dracula. One by one, they faced and defeated the three vampire brides, Jonathan Harker (who had become a vampire and had to be killed), and, finally, Dracula himself. Dracula was first weakened by letting in the sunlight (as he was killed in *Horror of Dracula*). Then, Van Helsing grabbed a spike from a suit of armor and impaled him. Dracula thus suffered the same fate that he was said to have inflicted on so many others.

The Jack Palance/Dan Curtis *Dracula* was viewed by a national television audience and has been cited as a more than competent version of the familiar tale. However, it never gained the following of the Hammer Films ver-

sion and was subsequently eclipsed by the Frank Langella/John Badham *Dracula* (1979) and *Bram Stoker's Dracula* (1992).

Dracula (1979)

In 1979, Universal Pictures replayed a scenario that first occurred a half century before, when it again filmed a version of the Hamilton Deane/John L. Balderston production of *Dracula: The Vampire Play in Three Acts*. In the original case, Universal Pictures purchased the film rights to the play following its successful run on Broadway and in touring companies around the country. In 1978, it reacted to the award-winning Broadway revival of the play starring Frank Langella. Universal Pictures had stayed away from the wave of quickie vampire movies, the production of which reached a new high in

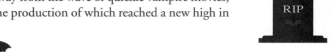

the 1970s, and it turned the new *Dracula* into a lavish production.

The film opened with the wreck of the *Demeter*, the ship that transported Dracula to the English town of Whitby. These scenes, merely alluded to in the play, were filmed on the coast of Cornwall. Safely on land, Dracula then proceeded to invade the household of Dr. John Seward (Donald Pleasence), whom Balderston had turned from a young suitor into the middle-aged father of Lucy Westenra (now Lucy Seward). When Mina Murray (now Mina Van Helsing) died under mysterious circumstances, Seward called Mina's father, Dr. Abraham Van Helsing (played by the equally eminent Laurence Olivier), to assist him in handling the problem of Dracula.

The distinctive difference of the Langella version was its underlying understanding of the relationship between sexuality and horror. Dracula was the object of horror—the undead. Yet, as he entered the Seward household, he did not accomplish his goals by brute force. He fell in love, first with Mina and then with Lucy. He won them over when his sensuality attracted their attention, and he then completely seduced them. Dracula's triumph occurred when he invaded Lucy's bedroom and shared his blood with her in as sensual a scene as could be found in any vampire movie. Subsequently, Lucy, completely captivated by Dracula's magnetism, rushed off to Carfax to join him.

This version of *Dracula* offered a new twist to Dracula's eventual destruction. He attempted to escape England, accompanied by a very willing Lucy, but Van Helsing and the other men were in pursuit. They finally caught up with Dracula on the ship, where he emerged from his coffin to battle the forces of good. In the end, he was impaled on a hook and hoisted high into the air to be burned to death in the sunlight. The film got mixed reviews. Some applauded its sensual quality, while others saw it as an empty parody of the vampire movie. Interestingly enough, it appeared in the same year as the best and most successful of the several *Dracula* spoofs, *Love at First Bite*. In spite of its mixed reception, the Langella film took its place as one of the better and more interesting of the *Dracula* remakes.

> In spite of its mixed reception, the Langella film took its place as one of the better and more interesting of the *Dracula* remakes.

Dracula 3D (2012)

Generally referred to as Argento's *Dracula*, *Dracula 3D* was directed by Italian Dario Argento, who developed a reputation for his attention to horror, and starred his daughter, Asia Argento. As the story begins, Count Dracula (Thomas Kretschmann) has been mourning the loss of his wife, Countess Dolingen de Gratz, for 400 years. She is a character from Bram Stoker's deleted chapter of *Dracula*, which was later published by his wife as a short story, "Dracula's Guest." Jonathan Harker, on his way to Transylvania, passes through Munich and visits the countess's tomb. While there, the tomb is destroyed by a lightning strike, and Harker encounters a wolf.

None of this background is known as Argento's *Dracula* opens, however, and Jonathan Harker (Unax Ugalde) arrives at Passo Borgo, a village near Dracula's castle. Before proceeding to the castle to take up duties as the count's librarian, he visits with a local acquaintance, Lucy Kisslinger (Asia Argento), his wife, Mina's best friend, and the daughter of the local mayor. Mina (Marta Gastini) will be following him to Passo Borgo in a few days.

Harker proceeds to the castle, where he has an encounter with Tanya, a young village woman recently bitten by the count and on her way to become one of his vampire brides. The count has a large library, including a book connecting Count Dracula with the legendary

RIP

Vlad Dracula. Before he can get far with his librarian's work, however, Tanya tries to bite him only to be interrupted by Dracula, who claims Harker for himself. Meanwhile, Dracula discovers a picture of Mina and comes to see that she is the image of his lost, beloved wife.

After a visit with Lucy, Mina goes to the castle looking for Jonathan, unaware that he is now a vampire. Thinking that he is away on a business trip, she entertains Dracula's advances on her. Dracula's plan to seduce Lucy and turn her into his replacement wife are interrupted by the arrival of Abraham Van Helsing (Rutger Hauer), who proceeds to dispatch both Harker and Tanya. He then heads for the tomb of the countess, where Dracula has taken Mina and where the audience learns the backstory of what drives Dracula and guides his actions. The confrontation with Dracula does not go well. Dracula knocks both Van Helsing's stake and gun aside and begins to beat him severely. Mina, however, saves the day by picking up the gun and shooting him. Dracula dissolves away into dust. Mina and Van Helsing leave the site.

In a final shot, Dracula's ashes fly up into the air and take shape as a large wolf that leaps at the screen.

Even with the 3D effects, the film was not received well either by critics or fans. It compressed the story from the novel while including odd bits from older *Dracula* remakes, especially the Dan Curtis version starring Jack Palance.

Dracula 2012 3D (India, 2013)

Dracula 2012 3D (aka *Saint Dracula 3D*) is a 2012 adaptation of *Dracula* by Indian director/actor T. G. Vinayakumar (1957–), best known by his stage name Vinayan. His version begins with Roy Thomas (Sudheer Sukumaran) and his wife, Lucy, arriving in Romania for their honeymoon. One site they will visit will be Bran Castle, a site with no connection to the historical Dracula but which has been tied to the fictional Dracula by modern Romanian tourist officials. Roy dabbles in magic and, while staying near Bran Castle, absents himself to conduct a ritual. He is surprised when the spirit of Dracula appears to him and takes possession of his body. Roy's wife, Lucy, becomes his first victim.

In Roy's body, Dracula returns to Kerala motivated by a single-minded search of his long-lost love, who had sacrificed herself for Dracula centuries earlier in Romania. He encounters a string of beautiful women, from whom he consumed the blood he needed to survive, until he finally meets Princess Meena (Monal Gajjar), who bears a remarkable resemblance to the much-sought-after former lover.

Dracula's relationship with Meena catalyzes opposition in the form of a psychologist-slash-ghost hunter, a Van Helsing figure (portrayed by Sudheer) who offered an infection theory of vampirism, and a sorcerer (Nassar), who assemble a cadre of men to bring Dracula down.

Made in 2012, *Dracula 2012 3D* was actually released early in 2013. It was filmed in Malayalam and later dubbed into Telugu, Tamil, and English. Largely panned by critics, it enjoyed some acclaim from horror fans in India.

Horror of Dracula (1958)

Second only to the Bela Lugosi version of *Dracula* (1931) in setting the image of Dracula in contemporary popular culture was the first of the Hammer Films Dracula movies, starring Christopher Lee. Originally released as *Dracula* (1958), it subsequently was released in the United States as *Horror of Dracula*, the title commonly used to distinguish it not only from the other Dracula movies but also from the host of Christopher Lee Dracula/vampire films. The movement of Hammer Films into the horror market has become one of the most famous stories in motion picture history. *Horror of Dracula* came on the heels of the company's success with a new version of *Frankenstein* and utilized the following team: Christopher Lee as Dracula; Peter Cushing as Abraham Van Helsing; and Terence Fisher and Jimmy Sangster as director and screenwriter, respectively.

While having the 1931 Universal Pictures production as a persistent reference point, *Horror of Dracula* attempted to reinterpret the story and return to the Bram Stoker novel for inspiration (though it deviated from both the novel and the previous movie in important ways). The story opened with Jonathan Harker (John Van Eyssen) coming to Castle Dracula not as a real estate agent but as Dracula's new librarian. Here, prior to Dracula's appearance, he encountered a young woman dressed in nightclothes. It soon was revealed that he was an undercover agent and had, in fact, come to Castle Dracula as Van Helsing's assistant in order to kill Dracula. Harker was attacked and bitten by the woman (Valerie Gaunt), whom he, in turn, killed, but, in the process, he became a vampire himself. (*Horror of Dracula* popularized the assumption that a single bite by a vampire was all that was necessary for one to become a vampire—an opinion not proposed in Stoker's novel.) In this movie, Dracula escaped before Van Helsing arrived at Castle Dracula to check on his coconspirator. Discovering that Harker had been compromised, Van Helsing was forced to stake him, and he returned to England to begin a one-on-one confrontation with Dracula, which was the true subject of the film.

Dracula beat Van Helsing to England, where a new configuration of Stoker's familiar characters had been created. Gone were Dr. John Seward, R. N. Renfield, and Quincey P. Morris.

Arthur Holmwood (Michael Gough) emerged as the dominant male. Rather than a suitor of Lucy Westenra (Carol Marsh), however, he was married to Mina Murray (Melissa Stribling), and Lucy was recast as his sister (and Harker's fiancée). Lucy also was the primary object of Dracula's interest, having taken her picture from Harker before leaving the castle. Van Helsing discovered that Lucy already had been bitten and was vampirizing others, so he took the lead in killing her. An angry Dracula then attacked Mina.

In the final scene, Holmwood and Van Helsing chased Dracula back to his home. Dracula had discarded Mina in an open grave and was burying her when the hunters arrived. Arthur went to his wife's side while Van Helsing chased Dracula into his castle. Dracula had all but defeated Van Helsing but, as so many villains before him, he paused to experience a very human moment of satisfaction. In that moment, Van Helsing recovered and, pushing the vampire aside, he rushed across the room and pulled the draperies from the window, allowing sunlight to stream into the room. The sunlight, which was fatal to vampires, caught Dracula's foot and quickly burned it. Grabbing a crucifix, Van Helsing pushed Dracula farther into the light, which then completely consumed him. Dracula's ashes blew away in the wind, leaving only his large ring. (The ring and ashes would become important in future Hammer Films *Dracula* sequels, though it's unlikely that Fisher had a sequel in mind when completing *Horror of Dracula*.) By the same sunlight that killed Dracula, Mina was cured of her vampirism, and she and her husband were happily reunited.

Two elements contributed to the success of *Horror of Dracula*. First, the movie presented a new openness toward sexuality. It is likely that the interpretation of the psychological perspectives on vampire mythology, such as that offered

> Second only to the Bela Lugosi version of *Dracula* (1931) in setting the image of Dracula in contemporary popular culture was the first of the Hammer Films Dracula movies....

RIP

by Ernest Jones's now classic study *On the Night-mare* (1931), underlay the movie's presentation. That sexual element began with Harker's encounter with one of Dracula's brides. While Harker drew her to what he thought was a protective embrace, she gleefully took full advantage of the situation and bit him, a scene that has been the object of various psychological interpretations relative to teenage sexual awakening. That interpretation was reinforced by his subsequent attack on the woman with his stake. Harker's naïve actions, of course, prove fatal.

Dracula was just as sexual as his vampire bride. He seduced the women he bit with kisses and gained their loving attention before he sank his teeth into their necks. As David J. Hogan, in *Dark Romance: Sexuality in the Horror Film*, notes, "When he (Lee) bites a young lovely's throat he is not merely feeding but experiencing (and inducing) a moment of orgasmic ecstasy." Lee would go on from *Horror of Dracula* to become an international star and, like Lugosi, develop a large and loyal female following.

The second element of success of *Horror of Dracula* can be attributed to its being the first Dracula movie to be made in Technicolor. It made full use of red liquids from the still little-understood blood dripping on a crypt during the opening credits to its more appropriate reappearances throughout the picture. Color added a new dimension to the horror movie and secured its revival in the 1960s. Color also cooperated with the heightened level of freedom concerning what could be pictured on the screen. In 1931, Dracula never showed his fangs or bit anyone on camera. However, Lee regularly showed his teeth and had no problem offering the women his vampire kiss.

Nosferatu, Eine Symphonie des Grauens (1922)

The earliest surviving film based on *Dracula* (1897) is *Nosferatu, Eine Symphonie des Grauens* (*Nosferatu, a Symphony of Horrors*), an unauthorized 1922 adaptation of Bram Stoker's novel by Prana Film, a German company founded in 1921. The movie was the only finished product of the company. One of the company's codirectors, Albin Grau, was a spiritualist and familiar with *Dracula*. He saw the book's possibilities for presentation as a powerful motion picture. Grau hired Friedrich Wilhelm Murnau (1888–1931) as director and Henrik Galeen as screenwriter.

Murnau and Galeen proceeded to make a very loose adaptation of the novel. The title was changed to *Nosferatu*, a term derived from an Old Slavic word, *nosufur-atu*, a word borrowed from the Greek and tied to the concept of carrying a plague. The location for the latter part of the story was changed to Bremen, Germany, and set in 1838, the year of an actual outbreak of the plague in that city. The Dracula character's appearance was altered to appear rodentlike and his persona tied to the rats who would gather in great numbers in Bremen when he arrived.

In the screenplay, Murnau made a variety of additional changes, including the names of all of the leading characters. Dracula was transformed into Graf Orlock, played by Max Schreck. Orlock was developed into a monstrous figure with exaggerated features, including a bald head and long, clawlike fingernails. His pair of vampire fangs, rather than being elongated canines, protruded from the very front of his mouth, like a rat's teeth. He walked with a slow, labored gait and wore a long coat. He was closer to the vampire of Eastern European folklore than Stoker's Dracula, but his distinct appearance radically limited his ability to easily move among normal society in the manner of Dracula. Thus, Orlock became, to some extent, a very different character.

In *Nosferatu*, Jonathan Harker (renamed Waldemar Hutter and played by Gustav von Wangenheim) left his wife, Mina Murray (re-

Director F. W. Murnau's silent film Nosferatu, a Symphony of Horrors *(1922), starring Max Schreck (above), was an unauthorized version of the Stoker novel. The title character is much more monstrous in appearance than the vampire in* Dracula.

named Ellen Hutter and played by Greta Schroeder-Matray), to travel to Transylvania in order to conduct the sale of a house next door to their home in Germany. Hutter was taken to a bridge and left there. Upon crossing the bridge, it was as if he had entered a new world. A coach with a mysterious driver met him to take him to Orlock's castle. In his bedroom at Orlock's castle, Hutter was bitten by Orlock, while back in Bremen, Ellen simultaneously cried out Hutter's name. The next day, Hutter discovered Orlock's coffin, but it was too late; the vampire was already on his way to Germany.

While Orlock traveled to Germany, the major characters (soon to assemble in Bremen) were shown acting independently of each other. First, Hutter escaped but was hospitalized. Hutter's boss, R. N. Renfield (renamed Knock, played by Alexander Granach), went mad and was confined to an asylum. Professor Abraham Van Helsing (renamed Bulwar, played by John Gottow) experimented in his laboratory with a meat-eating plant, a "vampire of the vegetable kingdom." Orlock killed the crew on the ship that was carrying him to Bremen.

Upon the count's arrival in Bremen, a plague broke out in the city, which was caused by the rats Orlock controlled. Hutter arrived with a book he had taken from the castle. It suggested that the way to defeat a vampire was through the sacrifice of a virtuous woman who allowed the vampire to remain with her until dawn. In the end, Orlock attached himself to Ellen's neck and stayed until the sunlight destroyed him. Ellen died from the sacrifice, and immediately, the plague abated.

Later Controversy: *Nosferatu, Eine Symphonie des Grauens* premiered in the Marble Gardens of the Berlin Zoological Gardens in March

RIP

1922. The movie received good reviews initially. However, Prana Film was financially unstable, and unpaid creditors soon asserted themselves. Several weeks later, Florence Stoker, the widow of Bram Stoker, received a copy of the announcement of the film's premiere. She immediately joined the British Incorporated Society of Authors and turned to it for assistance. Because Prana Film had neglected either to ask permission to use her late husband's book or to pay her for using it, the society represented her. It presented the matter to its German lawyer. By June, the company was in receivership, and it was clear that no money would result from pursuing the case. However, the society continued to press the matter because of its implications for later cases.

The case with the receivers, Deutsch-Amerikansch Film Union, dragged on for several years. Florence Stoker asked for the destruction of all copies of the film. The matter was finally settled in July 1925, when all copies owned by the German receivers were destroyed. However, in October of that year, she was contacted by a new organization in England. The Film Society solicited her support for its private screenings of "classic" movies. On its first list was *Nosferatu* by Murnau. She now engaged in a dispute with the society, which initially refused to cancel its showing or tell her where they had obtained a copy of the film.

In 1928, Universal Pictures purchased the film rights to *Dracula*. As owners of the film rights, they then granted the Film Society the privilege of showing *Nosferatu*. Florence Stoker protested, and in 1929, the Film Society turned over its copy to her for destruction. Later that year, copies appeared in the United States in New York and Detroit under the title *Nosferatu the Vampyre*. In 1930, these copies were turned over to Universal Pictures to also be destroyed.

> *Nosferatu, Eine Symphonie des Grauens* premiered in the Marble Gardens of the Berlin Zoological Gardens in March 1922. The movie received good reviews initially.

After Florence Stoker's death in 1937, various versions of the film reappeared and became available, though demand for it was scarce. In the 1960s, a condensed version was aired on television as part of *Silents Please*, a show based on old silent movies. In this version, the characters' names were changed back to those in the Stoker novel and the name of the movie was changed to *Dracula*. This version was then released by Entertainment Films under the title *Terror of Dracula*. In 1972, Blackhawk Films released the original film to the collectors' market under the title *Nosferatu the Vampyre* and the *Silents Please* version as *Dracula*. In spite of the destruction of most of the copies of the original *Nosferatu*, one copy did survive, and a restored version of the film was finally screened in 1984 at the Berlin Film Festival and has since become commonly available.

A sound remake of *Nosferatu, Die Zwolfte Stunde: Eine Nacht des Grauens,* appeared in 1930 by Deutsche Film and was probably made without Murnau's knowledge. The film gives a reference to "artistic adaptation" by a Dr. Waldemar Roger, who apparently re-edited the original film with some of Murnau's discarded footage and then added a dance scene and a death mass. The censors later cut the death mass due to religious objections but, unlike the original, the film ended on a happy note.

In 1979, a remake of *Nosferatu* was produced. *Nosferatu the Vampyre* featured Klaus Kinski in the title role. The new movie was written, produced, and directed by Werner Herzog. Although it kept the distinctive aspects of the original storyline, it more clearly acknowledged its being an adaptation of *Dracula,* in part by using the names of the characters in Stoker's novel.

Nosferatu the Vampyre was one of three important vampire movies released in 1979. The

Klaus Kinski starred in the 1979 remake of Nosferatu.

other two were *Love at First Bite*, the Dracula spoof with George Hamilton, and the Frank Langella version of *Dracula* (1979). The movie inspired a novel based on the screenplay, and a phonographic recording of the movie soundtrack was issued.

In 2000, director E. Elias Merhige's *Shadow of the Vampire* told the saga of the making of Murnau's 1922 original *Nosferatu* with one crucial change: Max Schreck was an actual vampire. According to Merhige's version, Murnau (John Malkovich) secretly hired Schreck (Willem Dafoe), a sniveling, rodentlike demon in a long coat who occasionally lunches on the film's cast and crew. One of the movie's producers was Nicolas Cage.

RIP

OTHER CINEMATIC VAMPIRES

African American Vampire Films

Vampires have made only infrequent appearances in African American folklore and, similarly, African Americans have been largely absent from vampire movies and novels through the twentieth century. The few Black vampire movies emerged in the era of blaxploitation movies in the early and mid-1970s. Only one African American vampire character, Prince Mamuwalde (better known as Blacula), attained any fame beyond the fans of vampire movies. The prince, portrayed by Shakespearean actor William Marshall, appeared in two movies, *Blacula* (1972) and *Scream Blacula Scream* (1973). Released the same year as *Blacula* was *Alabama's Ghost* (1972), a blaxploitation movie in which a vampire rock group battles a ghost.

Another lesser-known African American vampire movie is the 1973 *Ganja and Hess* (released on video under a variety of names, including *Blood Couple*, *Double Possession*, *Black Evil*, and *Black Vampire*). Like *Blacula*, the movie was set in New York. It concerned Dr.

Hess Green (played by Duane Jones), who becomes a vampire after being stabbed with an ancient African dagger by his assistant. The vampire never became a prominent role for Black actors, however, and with a few notable instances—Teresa Graves in *Old Dracula* (also known as *Vampira*), Grace Jones in *Vamp*, Aaliyah as Queen Akasha in *The Queen of the Damned*, and Eddie Murphy in *Vampire in Brooklyn*—few have appeared in leading roles.

One recent exception amid the recent dearth of African American vampire films is *Da Sweet Blood of Jesus* (2014), director Spike Lee's remake of the 1973 *Ganja and Hess*. It stars Stephen Tyrone Williams as Dr. Hess Green, the wealthy African American anthropologist who acquires an ancient Ashanti dagger. A visiting colleague, Lafayette Hightower (Elvis Nolasco), visits Green's mansion. Hightower becomes drunk and later stabs Green with the knife, thus turning him into a vampire. Several days later, Hightower's estranged ex-wife, Ganja (Zarah Abrahams), comes looking for her missing husband. When she learns what has happened, the pair's love affair turns to love, and they marry.

Meanwhile, in the 1970s, Marv Wolfman, who created the very successful vampire comic series *The Tomb of Dracula*, included the African American character Blade the Vampire Slayer among the major protagonists. Through several attempts to revive the series, Blade emerged as the single most popular of Wolfman's characters and eventually, in the mid-1990s, got his own Marvel comic book series. As Blade pushed to the front of Marvel's vampire universe, his appearance was altered to more closely conform to the image of the superhero for which Marvel was best known and his half-vampire nature emphasized. Beginning in 1997, this new Blade became the subject of three very successful movies starring Wesley Snipes. In the wake of Blade's success, as the DVD market and independent movie industry

Actor Wesley Snipes played the part of the vampire Blade in a series of popular films.

expanded, a set of new African American vampire movies, most going straight to DVD, appeared. These latter include *Cryptz* (2002), *Vegas Vampires* (2004), *Vampiyaz* (2004), *Vampz* (2004), *Vampire Assassin* (2005), *Bloodz Vs. Wolvez* (2006), *Dead Heist* (2007), *Brotherhood of Blood* (2008), and *The Transfiguration* (2017).

Through the first two decades of the twenty-first century, numerous African Americans have portrayed vampires and vampire hunters in supporting roles in the movies and especially in television. Laurent (portrayed by Kenyan-born actor Edi Gathegi), for example, emerges as the main African American vampire to appear in the several movies of *Twilight*, which is primarily concerned with Native Americans but references characters from a variety of the world's races and cultures. Laurent is a member of James's coven in the first movie.

On television, the popular *Buffy the Vampire Slayer* (1997–2003) show introduced major African American characters as vampire Slayers, initially through Kendra (portrayed by Bianca Lawson), a Jamaican woman who appears in season three, and later by Charles Gunn (portrayed by J. August Richards), who assisted the vampire Angel in the *Buffy* spin-off series *Angel* (1999–2004). The series was, however, later criticized for its relative lack of Black characters. Harper, a soldier killed during the American Civil War, was the first African American vampire to show up in *The Vampire Diaries* (2009–2017) series, which also included an African American witch among its major continuing characters. He would then be followed by Marcel Gerard (Charles Michael Davis), who emerged as a major character in the spin-off series *The Originals* (2013–2018). *True Blood* (2008–2014) included the stories of the Thornton family, most notably Tara Thornton (played by Rutina Wesley), one of the show's stars. In the latter seasons, Tara is made a vampire in order to save her life. A variety of Black vampires appear in the last seasons as a vampire war breaks out.

Like the recent vampire movies and television seasons, some vampire novels were included among the growing number of books written especially for an African American audience. Only a few of these, most notably Jewelle Gomez's *The Gilda Stories* (1991), gained a larger audience. Then in 2003, Leslie E. Banks, writing under her pseudonym L. A. Banks, issued *Minion*, the first of what became her *Vampire Huntress* books. The series, built around a young African American vampire hunter named Damali, found an audience among readers of romance novels and, by 2009, a dozen titles had appeared. Banks emerged as the most successful African American vampire author to date.

Bara, Theda (1889–1955)

Theda Bara is best known as the silent movie star who brought the character of the vamp—the woman who used her allure to attach herself to a man and then seduce and destroy him—to the silver screen. Bara was born Theodosia Goodman in Cincinnati, Ohio. Her father was an immigrant from Eastern Europe and her mother a wigmaker of French/German descent. She grew up in a prosperous Jewish community in the Avondale section of the city. She was drawn to acting at an early age and was a member of the drama club in high school. After two years at the University of Cincinnati, she dropped out, moved to New York, and became a stage actress.

In 1914, with her career stagnant, she met movie director Frank Powell. Through him, she obtained her first part as an extra in a now lost film, *The Stain*, but by the end of the year, she had been cast as the villainess in the Fox Film Corporation's new film *A Fool There Was*. It was shot at the Fox Studio in Fort Lee, New Jersey, while Theda lived in New York. The play from which the film had been adapted was inspired by a Rudyard Kipling poem, "The Vampire," and was written by Porter Emerson Browne. It opened in New York in 1909 to critical and popular acclaim. The film version made Goodman, reborn as Theda Bara, a star. She played the vampire who destroyed the life of an American diplomat. William Fox may have decided to bank his future on the film because of the success of another recent film with a similar theme, *The Vampire*, released by the Kalem Film Company.

The uniqueness of *A Fool There Was* rested not so much with its originality as with the publicity program created by Fox. To sell a film with an unknown star, a fictional biography of Theda Bara was created and presented at a press conference in January 1915. She was described as an Arabian actress and came before

Theda Bara was one of Hollywood's first sex symbols, cast as a femme fatale and known as "the Vamp," which was short for vampire.

the reporters in a fur-bedecked coat. After the press conference, movie columnist Louella Parsons was granted a few minutes with Bara, who confessed to the charade. Parsons sucked up the exclusive, a leak planned all along by Fox's publicity men. The day after the newspapers published the press account, Parsons released her exclusive, and the planned leak turned Bara into one of the most talked-about women in the country. The movie had not yet opened.

> By 1919 …, from the heights of stardom, her career began to wane. Bara was assigned to a series of bad films, and her drawing power dropped seriously.

A Fool There Was became one of the highest-grossing films of 1915. It was introduced by a live actor, who read Kipling's poem. The critics praised Bara as a great actress and commended the film for not giving in to demands for a happy ending. Fox searched for other films for his new star and assigned Bara to a role in her second movie, *The Kreutzer Sonata*. She again played a wicked woman who stole the husband of another woman. She did not get away with it this time, however, and the wife eventually killed her. Her third film, *The Clemenceau Case*, could also be classified as a vamp movie and was enormously successful. Bara was being praised by critics, drawing large audiences, and becoming the target of moral critics who were calling for the banning of her films.

During the filming of Bara's fourth movie, *The Devil's Daughter*, the nickname she had picked up around the set, "Vamp," was mentioned to a reporter. He used it, and it became the common way to describe Bara and the roles in which she was being cast. As she played the part to reporters at press conferences, the publicity scripts became more involved and eventually suggested that she was a reincarnation of some famous wicked ladies such as Lucretia Borgia or Elizabeth Báthory.

While Bara received good reviews for her next film, *The Two Orphans*, in which she

played a heroine, it was a flop at the box office due in large part to Fox pulling the publicity budget. Fox wanted her to return to vamping.

The next film was a gangster movie with the made-for-Bara title *Sin*. The Fox publicity camp went to work calling the nation to "sin with Theda Bara." *Sin* was a great success in spite of being banned in several states.

Over the next several years, Bara starred in a host of films (without dialogue to worry about, the production time on films was relatively short), and while she played a variety of roles, she continually returned to the vamp role her audiences yearned for. Her star status earned her leads in more impressive films such as *Carmen*, *Camille*, and *Cleopatra*. Bara's vamp image permeated popular culture and inspired a number of songs (mostly comedies) such as "The Vamp," "I'm a Jazz Vampire," "Since Sarah Saw Theda Bara," and "Sally Green, the Village Vamp," as well as a new dance, the Vampire Walk. By 1919, however, from the heights of stardom, her career began to wane. Bara was assigned to a series of bad films, and her drawing power dropped seriously. In attempting to change her image, she starred as an Irish lass in *Kathleen Mavourneen*, which received good reviews but turned into a disaster. It was rejected by the Irish because it portrayed poverty in the old country and because Bara, a Jew, starred as an Irish girl. Angry theater patrons set off stink bombs and riots.

Bara left Fox in 1920 and found herself at age 35 a largely unmarketable commodity. While she made several movies in the 1920s, her career was obviously over, and after *Madame Mystery* in 1926, she never returned to the movies (although she did appear on the stage occasionally). She lived a long life in her Beverly Hills home, remembered to her death as the original vamp. She died in Hollywood in 1955.

Blacula (1972)

In the late 1960s, the movie industry began to generate a series of movies specifically directed toward the African American community. While the vampire was essentially a European folk character and only a few references have been made to vampires in Africa or in African American lore, it was inevitable that blaxploitation producers would consider the possibilities of a Black vampire motion picture. In 1972, the first of the two most important African American vampire movies, *Blacula,* starring William Marshall, appeared.

In 1972, the first of the two most important African American vampire movies, *Blacula,* starring William Marshall, appeared.

Blacula told the story of Prince Mamuwalde, an African leader in 1780 who was trying to find a way to stop the slave trade that haunted Africa's west coast. He sought out Count Dracula (Charles Macaulay) to obtain his assistance in the endeavor. Dracula merely laughed at the prince who, with his wife, Luva, started to leave. Before they could get away, however, they were attacked by Dracula and his vampire cohorts. Mamuwalde was vampirized and sealed in a tomb. Luva was left to die of starvation, unable to help her husband as Dracula cursed Mamuwalde to become Blacula, his African counterpart.

The story then switches to 1965, when some Americans purchase the furnishings of Castle Dracula and ship them to Los Angeles, unaware that the ornate coffin they have obtained houses Blacula's body. Blacula is awakened and discovers a new love, Tina, the exact image of his Luva. As the plot progresses, she falls victim to a shooting incident, and he turns her into a vampire to save her, but then, she is staked to death and, in his grief, Blacula commits suicide by walking into the sunlight.

Blacula was revived by the magic of voodoo a year later in a sequel, *Scream Blacula Scream.* In collusion with the voodoo priestess Lisa, he searches for a way to rid himself of his vampirism but is thwarted by the police. In a novel, but entirely appropriate, twist of the storyline, he is killed by a pin stuck through the heart of a voodoo doll.

Because of the large audience of vampire movie enthusiasts, the *Blacula* movies have had a heightened popularity and joined the list of those few blaxploitation films that found a broad audience beyond the African American community. *Blacula* was awarded the Ann Radcliffe Award by the Count Dracula Society.

Buffy the Vampire Slayer (movie, 1992)

The popularity attained by the *Buffy the Vampire Slayer* television series often obscures the modestly successful 1992 movie that began the whole phenomenon and essentially launched the career of Joss Whedon. Although the *Buffy the Vampire Slayer* movie was based

on his original screenplay, Whedon has complained that the end product bore but faint resemblance to his original work.

The storyline of the movie centers upon Buffy Summers (Kristy Swanson), a cheerleader

Actress Kristy Swanson (pictured) starred as Buffy in the 1992 film, but for the TV series the role went to Sarah Michelle Geller.

at Hemery High School in Los Angeles in the early 1990s. As she went about her vapid existence in which the next trip to the mall or the school dance were her only concerns, she met a strange man named Merrick (Donald Sutherland), who informed her that she was the Chosen One. Once each generation, a Chosen One will stand alone against the vampires and the forces and entities of the evil supernatural world. That person is called the Slayer. As can be imagined, this news was, to say the least, most disturbing to the young teenager.

Buffy initially rejected the idea, but the naturally athletic cheerleader also found herself drawn to Merrick, the man destined to be her trainer. She had had strange dreams in which she faced enigmatic creatures in historical settings. Merrick claimed that her dreams were, in fact, her memories of real events from pre-

vious lives. He also claimed that he was also present when they occurred.

Once he secured Buffy's attention, Merrick elaborated on her role as one of the Order of Slayers. Each woman who was a Slayer had a birthmark on her left shoulder. Each would be reincarnated over and over again and spend each new lifetime stopping the spread of vampirism. History aside, Buffy had a more immediate crisis. Lothos (Rutger Hauer), a 1,200-year-old vampire king, had come to Los Angeles, and Merrick took Buffy to the local cemetery to observe the emergence of some of Lothos's first victims from their graves. Her encounter with the new vampires convinced Buffy of the truth of everything that Merrick had told her.

While trying to lead an outwardly normal life, Buffy spent her afternoons perfecting her fighting skills, which she demonstrated each evening by dispatching Lothos's minions with a stake. Her activity soon caught the attention of Lothos who, in his anger, killed Merrick. He also concluded that Buffy was the new Slayer. Because she stood between him and his destiny, she had to be slain. He gathered his group of new followers for an attack upon the upcoming school dance in the gym. At the dance, Buffy squared off against Lothos, although it took all of her martial arts skills. During the fight, she made a stake from a broken chair and drove it home with a well-placed kick. Lothos died with one now immortal word: "Oops!" With Lothos out of the way, it appeared that Buffy could finish high school and resume her vampire slaying as an adult, but such was not to be the case. As would be made known in 1997 in the new *Buffy the Vampire Slayer* television series, she had burned down the very gym in which Lothos had died in order to destroy more of his minions. She was then transferred to a suburban high school in the community of Sunnydale.

The *Buffy* movie was released to mixed reviews and a largely negative reaction from vampire fans. It clicked neither as a horror movie nor as a comedy. However, it did reasonably well at the box office, emerging over the years as one of the 25 highest-grossing vampire movies, ahead of such honored classics as *The Hunger* and *Near Dark*, and a soundtrack CD followed.

In 1999, the movie would be adapted as a comic book/graphic novel, *Buffy the Vampire Slayer: The Origin*, with the storyline slightly altered to allow it more closely to fit into the plot of the first season of the television series, with several discrepancies between the movie version of the story and the television version. In the movie, Buffy comes from a well-to-do family and is a stereotypically shallow valley girl. Buffy is a senior in the movie but will begin the television series as a sophomore. The movie vampires do not turn to dust when staked, nor do they show the facial change so notable of the series vampires. Both Slayers and their Watchers are repeatedly reincarnated, the former identified by a mole on one shoulder.

Also see the *Buffy the Vampire Slayer* (television series, 1997).

Chaney, Leonidas "Lon" Frank (1883–1930)

Leonidas "Lon" Chaney, the actor known for his numerous extraordinary characterizations in over 100 silent movies in the first decades of the twentieth century, was the first actor to play a vampire in an American feature-length movie. He was born on April 1, 1883. Both of Chaney's parents were deaf, and during most of his early life, his mother was bedridden. Chaney developed his skill as a silent movie actor by communicating to his mother through mimicry and gesture every day. He was still a boy when, in 1901, he began his acting career on the stage. He played a variety of roles and became fascinated with makeup and its interaction with characterization.

Chaney's first film role was in 1913 in *Poor Jake's Demise*. Then, Universal Pictures signed him to an exclusive contract (for $5.00 a day) and, through the rest of the decade, he assumed roles in over 100 films. He was first promoted as a star in 1919, when he played a fake cripple in *The Miracle Man*. He went on to his greatest successes as Quasimoto in *The*

Lon Chaney Sr. (pictured) was a renowned character actor and makeup artist. His son, Lon Chaney Jr., followed in his father's footsteps.

Hunchback of Notre Dame (1923) and in the title role of *The Phantom of the Opera* (1925).

Chaney worked, on occasion, with director Tod Browning. Their first collaboration was in 1921 in *Outside the Law*. Browning's alcoholism prevented their steady association. It

was Chaney's second encounter with alcoholism; earlier, he had divorced his wife and taken custody of their son because of her addiction to the bottle. In 1925, Chaney signed a long-term contract with MGM. Soon afterward, he again teamed with Browning to do *The Unholy Three*. He would return to Universal Pictures only once, for *The Hunchback of Notre Dame*.

In 1927, Browning and Chaney teamed for the last time in *London after Midnight*. Chaney played a double part as a vampire and a police inspector from Scotland Yard. As the police sleuth, Chaney initiated a scheme to uncover a murder. He assumed the role of a vampire in order to force the real murderer to reveal himself. Once that occurred, Chaney took off the elaborate makeup and revealed himself as the inspector.

Although *London after Midnight* turned out to be his only vampire role, this was almost not the case. In 1930, he made the transition to sound in a new version of *The Unholy Three*, directed by Jack Conway. Meanwhile, Browning had moved back to Universal Pictures, which had finally attained the film rights to *Dracula*. The studio announced the reunion of Browning and Chaney for the film. Unfortunately, Chaney had developed cancer, and before he could even be signed for the part, he died on August 26, 1930. In 1957, his life was brought to the screen in *Man of a Thousand Faces*, with James Cagney in the title role.

Cushing, Peter (1913–1994)

Peter Cushing, a British movie actor known for his portrayal of Abraham Van Helsing, Dracula's main protagonist, was born in 1913 in Kenley, Surrey. His formal stage debut was in *The Middle Watch* in 1935 in a performance at Worthing, though he had done minor roles onstage previously. Cushing worked in 1936 as an assistant stage manager

of the New Connaugh Theatre in Worthing and moved on in 1937 to work as a stage actor in a repertory theater in Southampton. He made his film debut in 1939 in *The Man in the Iron Mask*, directed by James Whale. In 1941, he made *Vigil in the Night* and also made a number of short films in the 1940s as part of the war effort.

Peter Cushing drives home his point in The Brides of Dracula.

Following the war, Cushing moved between stage, movie, and television roles, the most noteworthy acclaim coming in the 1954 British television production of *1984*. He was, at the time, regarded as a major British TV star, being featured in productions like *Pride and Prejudice*, where he played Darcy.

In 1957, he starred as monster-maker Victor Frankenstein in the first of Hammer Films's famous horror series. After the success of *The Curse of Frankenstein*, Cushing teamed again with director Terence Fisher and opposite Christopher Lee in Hammer Films's 1958 production of *Dracula* (better known under its American title as *Horror of Dracula*). As Van Helsing, Cushing assumed the image of a cultured intellectual who had chosen to confront absolute evil in the persona of a vampire. He returned to the role of Van Helsing in one subsequent Hammer Films Dracula movie—*The Brides of Dracula* (1960)—and as a vampire-hunting descendant of Van Helsing in *Dracula A.D. 1972* (1972) and *The Satanic Rites of Dracula*, released in the United States as *Count Dracula and His Vampire Bride* (1973). He also played a Van Helsing relative in the Hammer/Shaw coproduction of *The Legend of the Seven Golden Vampires* (also known as *The Seven Brothers Meet Dracula*), which mixed horror and martial arts themes. As the only person to play Van Helsing so many times, Cushing has become the best-known actor associated with the role.

While Cushing became well known for his portrayal of Van Helsing, he was able to play a number of other parts, sometimes appearing in three or four movies a year, and had some success not only in vampire movies but also in a variety of others. He returned to his portrayal of Dr. Frankenstein in several Hammer Films productions with the same theme. (Cushing ultimately played Frankenstein six times.) He also played a Van Helsing–like role of an intellectual and/or scientist in horror movies that, when considered alongside his famous Van Helsing roles, reveal Cushing as having continually portrayed a symbol of a stable, normal world that turned back the challenges of the chaotic forces of evil. This role was seen in its extreme form in *Twins of Evil* (Hammer Films, 1971), in which he played a fanatical witch hunter who actually encountered the supernatural.

Above and beyond his Van Helsing roles, Cushing appeared in several other vampire films, including *The Blood Beast Terror* (1968), *The Vampire Lovers* (Hammer Films, 1970), *Incense for the Damned* (1970), and *Tender Dracula* (1974). He also teamed with Christopher Lee in several nonvampire movies such as *The Creeping Flesh* (1973) and *House of the Long Shadows* (1983), in which Lee, Cushing, and Vincent Price joined in a tribute to the gothic "old dark house" film. Possibly his most notable nonvampire appearance was as a villain, Grand Moff Tarkin, in *Star Wars*, though not to be forgotten was his highly successful role as Sherlock Holmes, the first appearance of Holmes in color. Cushing passed away on August 11, 1994.

Note: I am grateful to Uwe Sommerlad, a German movie expert and personal friend of Cushing, who read and commented on an earlier version of this entry.

Dark Shadows (movie, 2012)

In the twenty-first century, faithful *Dark Shadows* fans nurtured hopes that their favorite television series would find new life either on television or in the movies. Then in 2010, filmmaker Tim Burton, who had previously done movies such as *The Nightmare before Christmas*, *Ed Wood*, and *Sleepy Hollow*, announced his own plans to do a new *Dark Shadows* movie. It would reunite him with Johnny Depp, who, it appears, had been a fan of *Dark Shadows* since his childhood and had a role in motivating Burton to consider the project. Depp had starred in Burton's early movie *Edward Scissorhands* (1990).

The movie is set in 1972 but had a backstory from the eighteenth century. In the 1760s, Barnabas Collins (Johnny Depp) led his family to Maine, where they established the town of Collinsport and built a mansion, Collinwood. In the mid-1770s, a servant named Angélique (Eva Green) made advances on Barnabas, but he rejected her. Being a witch, Angélique cursed Barnabas, one result being that his fiancée, Josette (Bella Heathcote), died from a fall off a nearby cliff. Barnabas was cursed to become a vampire. Angélique subsequently united the town against him, and he was buried alive.

Meanwhile, in 1972, a young Maggie Evans (who looks just like Josette) arrived at Collinwood to become the Collins family governess and, for this position, adopted the name Victoria Winters. On her first evening after taking the job, she was visited by Josette's ghost.

Simultaneously, a construction crew ran into Barnabas's tomb, which occasioned his being released from two centuries of imprisonment. Showing up at the mansion after feeding on those who had freed him, he met the caretaker, Willie, whom he hypnotized into his minion. He subsequently met Elizabeth Collins Stoddard (Michelle Pfeiffer), the current family matriarch, and ingratiated himself to her by

claiming to be a long-lost relative and showing her some of the secrets of the mansion, about which she was unaware. He then announced plans to revive the family and its fortune.

Barnabas was successful in restoring the family business, the Collins Canning Company, and refurbishing the mansion, which was in need of some restoration. Along the way, he found himself attracted to Victoria. However, his nemesis, Angélique, was still alive and still in love with Barnabas. She owned Angel Bay Seafood, the rival of Barnabas's canning company. After allowing Angélique back into his life, he again rejected her.

As his company is revived, Barnabas hosted an event at Collinwood and invited the entire town. He hired rock star Alice Cooper to entertain the guests. Among the attendees as townpeople, the original stars of *Dark Shadows*—Jonathan Frid, Kathryn Leigh Scott, Lara Parker, and David Selby—make cameo appearances.

The adept Johnny Depp took on the role of Barnabas Collins for the 2012 movie adaptation of Dark Shadows.

As events sped up, Barnabas and Angélique had a new confrontation. During their meeting, Angélique led him into confessing murders he committed in the past. When he again rejected her love, he was again confined to a coffin. Using a recording of Barnabas's confession, she organized the two against the Collins family. Angélique destroyed the Collins family's cannery and, with a recording of Barnabas's confession, rallied the town against the family. However, young David Collins (Gully McGrath) freed Barnabas from his coffin, and they then confronted Angélique. In that encounter, Angélique revealed that she was responsible for the death of David's mother. The ghost of David's mother (Josephine Butler) incapacitated Angélique, and she died.

Barnabas then had to find Victoria before she again died at the cliff. She loved him but was unwilling to live with him as just a mortal. He was unwilling to transform her into a vampire. She jumped from the cliff and he jumped after her, biting her on the way to the ground. She awoke in his arms as a vampire.

> **Dark Shadows** received a mixed critical review and underperformed in the United States, though it made up for that performance by its popularity overseas.

The movie was notable for a number of cameo appearances, among them Christopher Lee, who plays Silas Clarney, a fisherman who is a regular at Collinsport's local pub, The Blue Whale.

Dark Shadows received a mixed critical review and underperformed in the United States, though it made up for that performance by its popularity overseas. A conversation on possible sequels failed to reach a positive result.

Also see the *Dark Shadows* (television series, 1966–1971, 1991).

Dreyer, Carl Theodor (1889–1968)

Carl Theodor Dreyer, thought by many to be Denmark's greatest film director, was born on February 3, 1889, in Copenhagen. He began his working career in 1909 as a journalist, and in 1911, he married Ebba Larsen. On the side, he began writing scripts for a motion picture company, Scandinavisk-Russiske Handelshus, and in 1913, Dreyer quit his job to work for Nordisk Films Kompagni.

Six years later, he was given the opportunity to direct his first film, *Praesidenten* (*The President*), for which he also wrote the screenplay. Dreyer made several movies in Denmark and Germany but gained prominence with *Du Skal Aere Din Hustru* (*The Master of the House*) in 1925. He was invited to France to work, and there, he made his notable *La Passion de Jeanne d'Arc* in 1928. Soon after the appearance of *La Passion de Jeanne d'Arc*, the film industry began its transition to sound, and it was not until 1932 that Dreyer directed again. His first sound movie remains the one for which he is best remembered.

In 1932, he directed *Vampyr* (released to English-speaking audiences as *The Dream of David Gray*), lauded by some critics as the greatest vampire film of all time. Others have complained about the slow pace of the film, suggesting that it failed as entertainment. Loosely inspired by Sheridan Le Fanu's female vampire

Danish film director Carl Theodor Dreyer was famous for his 1928 film The Passion of Joan of Arc. *He also directed* Vampyr *in 1932.*

shadow cast on the wall behind him. Suddenly, the shadow started to operate separately from the policeman and walked away. Later, Gray dreamed of his own funeral. He could see out of the casket, which had a small window just above his face. As he awoke and gazed through the opening, the vampire's face appeared, looking back at him. Dreyer produced part of the atmosphere of *Vampyr* by shooting much of the film at dawn and at twilight. He also discovered a flour mill where the white dust in the air and white walls added an eerie quality to the scenes photographed there. Dreyer chose amateur actors whose overall appearances, especially their faces, communicated aspects of personality he wished to explore. He brought out their inherent features by the frequent use of close-up shots and little makeup. He sought to create a feeling of uneasiness in his audience, a feeling that would remain even after the conflict of the story had been resolved.

Following the completion of *Vampyr*, Dreyer left filmmaking and resumed his journalism career. He did not make another film until 1942, when he produced a documentary during World War II. He made a number of films through the 1940s and early 1950s. In 1952, he was given the management of a film theater by the Danish government. His 1955 film, *Ordet*, received the Golden Lion Award. *Vampyr* was his only treatment of the vampire theme.

Dreyer died in Copenhagen on March 20, 1968. He spent his last years on a project to make a movie about the life of Christ, but the film was never produced.

story "Carmilla," *Vampyr* implied the horror that surrounded the action on the screen and invited viewers to participate with their imagination.

The story concerned an older, female vampire who was preying on the daughter of the owner of the local manor. David Gray, a visitor in the town, discerned the true nature of her malevolence and took the lead in destroying her.

Two memorable scenes stood out in Dreyer's communication of horror. In one, early in the picture, a policeman was sitting with his

From Dusk till Dawn (1996)

From Dusk till Dawn was an American vampire film notable for its alternative vampire mythology. The screenplay for the original film was written by Quentin Tarantino and directed by Robert Rodriguez.

As the movie opens, brothers Seth (George Clooney) and Richie Gecko (Quentin Tarantino) are headed to Mexico after having held up a bank and taken a hostage. As they head south, they stop at a convenience store in

Texas and, while there, they kill the clerk and a Texas Ranger. Later, holding up a motel, Richie kills the hostage, and the brothers kidnap a minister, Jacob Fuller (Harvey Keitel), his son, Scott (Ernest Lui), and his daughter, Kate (Juliette Lewis). Using Fuller's vacation van, they make their way across the border and arrive at the Titty Twister, to all appearances a strip club for truckers in the Mexican desert, where they hope to make contact with a person who can hide them for a period of time.

While waiting inside the club and watching the show, which features an exotic dancer known as Santanico Pandemonium (Selma Hynek), a fight breaks out. Most of the people working in the club show themselves to be vampires, and most of the club's patrons are bitten and either killed or turned into a vampire. In the end, only Seth and Kate survive. As the movie ends and Seth and Kate go their separate ways, a panoramic view of the club shows it to be the top of a largely buried, ancient pyramid.

When Santanico Pandemonium makes her appearance, she is holding a two-headed snake. Then, as the vampires began to turn and reveal their vampiric nature, their vampiric appearance is decidedly snakelike, their faces dominated by scalelike skin and fangs resembling those of vipers. While suggestive, the unique aspects of the vampires' appearance was not disclosed in the film.

From Dusk till Dawn enjoyed some degree of success and received awards primarily from fans of the genre. The success led Robert Rodriguez to create two spin-off movies, described as prequels.

From Dusk till Dawn 2: Texas Blood Money (1999) was written and directed by Scott Spiegel. After escaping from prison, bank robber Luther Heggs (Duane Whitaker) is the subject of a manhunt by the Texas Rangers. Meanwhile, Luther contacts his reluctant former accomplice Buck Bowers (Robert Patrick) and instructs him

to reassemble their old gang, a project upon which Buck begins to work. They arrange a rendezvous at a motel. Meanwhile, as Luther heads for the rendezvous point, he hits a bat with his car. The car breaks down, and Luther goes for help on foot. Upon arriving at a bar called the Titty Twister (but not the same bar from the previous movie), he locates a ride to the hotel from one Razor Charlie (Danny Trejo). As they head for the motel, Luther relates what has happened to him. Razor changes course and drives to the broken-down car, where he attacks Luther and transforms him into a vampire. Luther now heads to the rendezvous but as a vampire.

Once reunited with his gang, Luther leads a robbery of the local bank. As the bank robbery proceeds, the police and one Texas Ranger named Otis Lawson (Bo Hopkins) arrive. Buck has a falling-out with Luther and escapes the bank. Outside, he teams up with Otis, even as a fight to the finish is about to begin between the cops and the robbers (now all vampires). The lengthy fight leaves only Buck and Otis alive, and the movie ends with the two going their separate ways.

Actress Juliette Lewis plays Kate, the daughter of a minister, in 1996's From Dusk Till Dawn.

This second installation in the *From Dusk till Dawn* series does little to tie its storyline back into the first movie above a few superficial attributes and completely abandoned the snake-related vampire myth. The third feature in the series, *From Dusk till Dawn 3: The Hangman's Daughter* (1999), directed by P. J. Pesce, serves as a true prequel to the first movie. It is set at the beginning of the twentieth century, with the pilgrimage into Mexico of American writer Ambrose Bierce to join the revolution led by Pancho Villa. Once in Mexico, Bierce disappears, and his fate is still unknown.

> Both *From Dusk till Dawn 2* and *3* were direct-to-video releases and, thus, did not receive the acclaim to the original movie.

Early in the movie, Johnny Madrid (Marco Leonardi), a local outlaw, escapes as he is about to be hung and, in the process, kidnaps his hangman's 19-year-old daughter, Esmeralda (Ara Celi). He also is assisted by another woman named Reece (Jordana Spiro), who wants Madrid to teach her the skills of an outlaw. On Reece's advice, Madrid robs the stagecoach upon which Bierce (Michael Parks) is traveling, but finding nothing of value, he abandons Reece and heads for the local full-service inn named the Titty Twister. Here, the outlaw Esmeralda and the passengers of the stagecoach will assemble only to be later joined by the posse searching for Madrid.

The Titty Twister is, of course, run by the vampires encountered in the first movie. They appear when a fight begins in the bar. As the patrons fall one by one, Madrid, Bierce, Reece, Esmeralda, her father the hangman (Temuera Morrison), and a few others escape and try to find a way out. They leave the inn only to be captured by an older, female vampire named Quixtla (Sonia Braga) and her vampire cohorts. At this point, it is revealed that Esmeralda is, in fact, a half-human/half-vampire princess named Santanico Pandemonium (who, of course, stars in the first movie). She is the daughter of Quixtla and the hangman, who had wanted to raise her apart from the vampires.

The vampires hang Madrid, Bierce, Reece, and the hangman upside down for later feeding while Quixtla completes the transformation of Esmeralda into the vampire princess. This act gives Madrid time to escape his bonds and free his fellow prisoners, but only he and Bierce ultimately escape. As they leave the Titty Twister, the camera makes a panoramic sweep of the inn to reveal that it is the buried pyramid. Esmeralda is left behind very much against her will to continue her life, now among the vampires.

Both *From Dusk till Dawn 2* and *3* were direct-to-video releases and, thus, did not receive the acclaim to the original movie. However, the entire *From Dusk till Dawn* series received new life after 2013, when Robert Rodriguez founded a new television network, the El Rey Network, as a joint venture between Univision and Cox communications. Among the first project for the new network, which targeted Hispanic Americans, Rodriguez developed the original movie into a three-season television series.

The first season of the series essentially covered the storyline of the movie, adding detail, characters, and a backstory to the account of the Gecko brothers (D. J. Cotrona and Zane Holtz), whose further adventures became the major thrust of the second and third seasons. Along the way, Kate Fuller's (Madison Davenport) and Santanico Pandemonium's (Elza Gonzalez) stories are more fully explored.

New characters include Texas Ranger Freddie Gonzales (Jesse Garcia), who reacts to the death of the original Texas Ranger killed by the Gecko brothers with a vow to bring them in. Two minor characters in the original movie,

the Sex Machine (Jake Busey) and the Regulator (Danny Trejo), are lifted from obscurity and given a continuing role through the series. Trejo is the only person who had a part in each of the three movies and the television series.

The television series lays out the story of the unique snake-related vampires, a myth that begins with the conquistadors entering Mexico and encountering the native Mexicans. The vampires arise as native mythology encounters the brutality of the conquistadors and is devel-oped slowly through the series. Carlos Man-drigal (Wilmer Valderrama), who came with the Spanish conquerors as an officer, emerges as the major vampire heading the vampire com-munity.

From Dusk till Dawn ran for three seasons (2014–2016) on the El Rey Network. Also, when the original *From Dusk till Dawn* movies were released on video, a documentary on the making of the original movie, *Full Tilt Boogie*, was also included.

Hammer Films

Hammer Films, the film studio whose horror movies in the 1960s brought a new di-mension to the vampire myth, was founded in 1948 by Will Hammer and Sir John Carreras. Largely based upon public response to its horror movies, Hammer Films became the most suc-cessful British film company in the generation after World War II. Hammer Films burst upon the scene after the film industry had neglected the horror genre for several decades, partly out of censorship considerations and partly from its own conservative nature. Hammer Films's openness to the horror film was due in large part to Carreras's understanding of the com-pany's credo: motion pictures should first and foremost simply entertain and tell a good story. Beginning as a small, relatively poor company with limited capital, Hammer Films turned out low-budget B movies following patterns set in Hollywood. A television series, however, became the catalyst for major changes for the company.

In the 1950s, British television produced the successful science fiction series *The Qua-termass Experiment*, built around the character of Bernard Quatermass. He was a scientist who sent a rocket into space only to have it return with a new form of alien life, which took over the body of the surviving astronaut. Hammer Films brought Quatermass to the screen in 1955 in *The Quatermass Xperiment*. This was quickly followed by *X the Unknown* (1956) and *Quatermass II* (1957). The success of these science fiction "monster" movies suggested that new films with classical horror themes might be equally successful. Universal Pictures, which owned the motion picture rights to both *Frank-enstein* and *Dracula* at that time, was essentially separating itself from producing horror movies. The owners worked out a deal by which the company sold the rights to *Dracula* and *Frank-enstein* to Hammer Films.

In creating the new horror features, Hammer Films drew upon a French and British stage tradition originally developed at the Théâ-tre du Grand Guignol in Paris. Grand Guignol emphasized the shock value of presenting grue-some and terrifying scenes to the audience re-alistically. Vampires were a standard fare of these stage productions. Hammer Films horrors were in full color. Blood flowed freely, and monstrous acts were fully portrayed on-screen—not merely implied for the audience to imagine. Hammer Films then assembled one of the more famous teams ever to work on what would become a series of horror pictures: director Terence Fisher, screenwriter Jimmy Sangster, and actors Chris-topher Lee and Peter Cushing. Their first pic-ture was *The Curse of Frankenstein*, a new ver-

Bray Film Studios in Berkshire, England, was the headquarters of Hammer films from 1951 to 1966.

sion in Technicolor of Mary Shelley's original *Frankenstein*. It differed markedly from the older Universal Pictures version in its graphic depiction of Frankenstein's monster's violence, now in full color.

The same team plunged immediately into a second classic horror volume, *Dracula*, better known under its American title, *Horror of Dracula* (1958). Sangster and Fisher decided not to use the play upon which Universal Pictures's *Dracula* (1931) was based; they also deviated rather freely from Bram Stoker's story, which was transformed into the final battle of a long-standing war between Abraham Van Helsing (goodness) and Dracula (evil). The first victim of this war, at least in the segment seen by the audience, was Jonathan Harker, who arrived at Castle Dracula as a secret Van Helsing operative. After he was turned into a vampire, Van Helsing was forced to kill him. The next victim was

Lucy Westenra (now called Lucy Holmwood). Before Van Helsing finally defeated Dracula, the war almost claimed the life of Mina Murray (now known as Mina Holmwood).

Horror of Dracula was even more influenced by Grand Guignol than was *The Curse of Frankenstein*. Its graphic presentation of gore began with memorable opening frames of dripping, red blood and was highlighted by Christopher Lee showing his fangs to the audience just before bending over a yielding Mina, whom he held tightly in his arms. Vampiric sexuality also was more overt, with biting as a metaphor for the sex act. Dracula unleashed all of the chaotic life forces, most powerfully symbolized by sex, that society tried to suppress and science attempted to understand and control.

Like *The Curse of Frankenstein*, *Horror of Dracula* was an immense success. It made Christopher Lee an international star in ways his portrayal of Frankenstein's monster had not and, as would be true of other Draculas, Lee's fans tended to be women, a high percentage of them teenagers. Hammer Films moved quickly to capitalize on both of its successes, but in the long run, Dracula proved to be the more lucrative theme. As Hammer Films moved ahead with its next vampire (and other horror) movies, it began to encounter problems from censors. It had purchased the rights to *I Am Legend*, a classic vampire book, and hired its author, Richard Matheson, to work on the screenplay. However, the censor's office let it be known that the movie would be banned in England, and Hammer Films stopped filming. The subsequent banning of Mario Bava's Italian-made *Black Sunday* served to inform Hammer Films of strict limits to what could, for the moment, be put on the screen; thus, for a brief period, the company postponed new considerations of the vampire motif. In its second Dracula movie, *The Brides of Dracula* (1960), Dracula did not actually appear, though David Peel was present as the Dracula-like Baron Meinster. Meinster succeeded where Dracula failed in his biting of Van Helsing (Cushing), but Van Helsing cauterized the wound, thus preventing the vampire's affliction from infecting him. Before the successful team from *Horror of Dracula* was reassembled, however, Hammer Films produced the first of its movies with a female vampire, *Kiss of the Vampire* (1962), starring Clifford Evans, Edward de Souza, Isobel Black, and Noel Williams as the vampire.

Lee made his return as Dracula in *Dracula, Prince of Darkness* (1966). To establish continuity, director Terence Fisher began the new film with footage from the end of *Horror of Dracula*. The film also developed one of a series of creative ways to resurrect the dead count. In this case, Dracula's servant killed a man whose blood was allowed to drip on Dracula's ashes. This sequel was memorable both for Lee's impressive performance (though he had few lines) and for the graphic staking of Barbara Shelley

by a group of monks, made possible by some easing of the standards of censorship through the decade.

In *Dracula Has Risen from the Grave* (1968), Dracula was resurrected by a priest who allowed his blood to drip on the count's frozen body. (Dracula had died by drowning in an icy pond in *Dracula, Prince of Darkness*.) Meanwhile, Fisher had moved on to other projects and did not direct this film, which marked the beginning of the downward trend that would characterize future vampire movies, which Hammer Films assigned to less experienced directors. The most memorable scene was Dracula pulling the stake from his own body (a scene that Christopher Lee protested at the time). Sexual themes were also becoming increasingly explicit. In *Dracula, Prince of Darkness*, Dracula embraced the passive Mina as he bit her, but in *Dracula Has Risen from the Grave*, the vampire's female victims/lovers began to react to the count, signaling their participation in the event and experiencing a sexual thrill from it. The sexual give and take of the vampire's bite became even more graphic in *Taste the Blood of Dracula*

Christopher Lee in the title role from Dracula Has Risen from the Grave.

(1970), which brought the count back to Victorian England. In the film, a member of the British royalty witnessed Count Dracula's demise, as depicted in *Dracula Has Risen from the Grave*, and collected some of his blood and several personal possessions. In a magic ceremony, he attempted to revive Dracula by drinking his blood. Dracula arose but at the cost of his benefactor's life. Meanwhile, several men who had been privy to the process of resurrecting Dracula stole his ring and cloak. Dracula proceeded to attack the men by way of their two female children. The interaction of Dracula and his female victims suggested a conscious use of vampirism as a symbol responding to new attitudes about sexuality that developed in the late 1960s.

Immediately after *Taste the Blood of Dracula*, Lee began filming *Scars of Dracula* (1970) under the direction of Roy Ward Baker. The story was set in Castle Dracula, where a young man, his girlfriend, and several others were exploring. Dracula began to kill them one by one until only the young man stood as a barrier to the woman, the real object of the vampire's quest. The story of Dracula and the woman, however, became a subplot set in the parentheses of Dracula's encounter with a more transcendental force: nature. At the beginning of the movie, Dracula was awakened by a bolt of lightning that struck his coffin. In the end, he was killed by a similar bolt, which struck a metal spike that he had intended to use on the remaining live male.

Hammer Films's most intense attention to vampirism came in the years from 1970 to 1972. The studio produced six films, which necessitated going beyond mere variations on the *Dracula* story. The first choice for a new thrust was Sheridan Le Fanu's story "Carmilla." *The Vampire Lovers* (1970), possibly the most faithful adaptation of "Carmilla,"

opened with the awakening of the vampire Carmilla Karnstein (who assumed an anagram of her name, Mircalla). She had returned to Karnstein Castle in the present, where she was introduced to the social world. She first attracted and then vampirized Laura, the subject of the original story, and then Emma, an acquaintance. Before she was able to kill Emma, however, her work was discovered, and a group of male vampire hunters tracked her down in the chapel and killed her. *The Vampire Lovers* reached a new level of sexual explicitness and visual gore. The amply endowed Ingrid Pitt played Mircalla, who seduced Laura (Pippa Steele) and Emma (Madeleine Smith) in scenes with lesbian overtones. Following the trend set in the Dracula movies, the film continued the depiction of blood and violence, especially in the opening and closing scenes, during which the vampire was killed.

The Carmilla character inspired a second film, *Lust for a Vampire* (1971), a film that gave Jimmy Sangster the opportunity to move from his screenwriting role to directing. The movie, with its standard emphasis on graphic violence, opened with one of the more memorable horror scenes. Mircalla/Carmilla (now played by Yutte Stengaard), Count Karnstein (Mike Raven), and his wife were all awakened by the blood of a sacrificial victim killed over their graves. The revived Mircalla then turned to several males as her victims (rather than her usual female ones), but as the deaths mounted, the villagers discovered her vampirism and killed her and the Karnstein family in a fire. Ingrid Pitt returned to the screen for her second vampire role in 1971 as Elizabeth Báthory in *Countess Dracula*. The film centered on Báthory's last years, when she attempted to vampirize teenagers (both male and female) of their youth so that her own beauty and youthful appearance would remain intact. The voluptuous

> Hammer Films's most intense attention to vampirism came in the years from 1970 to 1972. The studio produced six films, which necessitated going beyond mere variations on the *Dracula* story.

Blood and mayhem splatter across the screen in Vampire Circus, *the tale of a troop of thirsty circus performers invading a town during a plague.*

Pitt, transforming back and forth from the aging countess to the rejuvenated vampire, made the film work.

The trend toward violence seemed to peak in the 1972 vampire release, *Vampire Circus*. Set in Serbia in 1810, Count Mitterhouse (Robert Tayman), a vampire, was revived and set out to seek revenge on the town he held responsible for his death a century before. The instruments of his revenge were circus performers who had set up their tents to entertain the townspeople. However, the performers soon joined the count in murdering the town's leading citizens. The bloody murders set the stage for a closing battle scene, with aroused villagers attacking the circus. The film ended with Mitterhouse being staked and decapitated.

On the heels of its 1971 successes, Hammer Films exploited the Dracula theme again with *Dracula A.D. 1972*, which attempted to bring Dracula into the contemporary world. The film did not deal with the role that Dracula

might assume in the complex, modern world; rather, it moved a Victorian plot into a contemporary setting. The story concerned Dracula's emergence among a group of young people in the early 1970s. Constantly encountering hostile, unfamiliar structures that left him ineffective in the present-day world, Dracula vampirized several of the youngsters and used them as his instruments. Peter Cushing returned in his Van Helsing role of the vampire hunter—a dedicated descendant of the original—to track Dracula to his death.

The second 1972 offering to vampire fans was *Captain Kronos, Vampire Hunter*, the story of a young hero who traveled the country searching out and disposing of vampires. Based in part on American cowboy heroes, Kronos arrived complete with an assistant for some comic relief. The film's failure at the box office not only canceled Hammer Films's plans for a new series based on Kronos but, in fact, highlighted a significant aspect of the vampire myth. The myth was about vampires and all that they symbolize, not necessarily the destruction of evil.

The 1971 *Twins of Evil* returned to the story of Carmilla for inspiration. Hammer Films selected twins Mary and Madeline Collinson to play Mary and Frieda Gelhorn. The two were unleashed by Count Karnstein on the local village to avenge the death of the Karnstein family. The spread of the vampire epidemic attracted the Van Helsing-like Gustav Weil (played by Peter Cushing) to mount a crusade to destroy all the vampires. As the plot unfolded, the movie pictured two opposing and ambiguous forces: the vampire and the overly zealous, puritanical vampire hunter, who was himself tainted with evil. The conflict resulted in the death of Count Karnstein and the vampires, along with Weil and some of his cohorts. The twins were relatively innocent bystanders, and one escaped (the other was killed).

Lee's final appearance in the Hammer Films Dracula movies occurred in *The Satanic*

Rites of Dracula (1973), also known as *Count Dracula and His Vampire Bride*. Again, the scene was contemporary London, where an aging Van Helsing was consulted by Scotland Yard on a black magic group that had come to their attention. His investigation led him, however, to Dracula, who had emerged as a real estate dealer and was surrounded by a group of corrupt (but not vampirized) businessmen. Because of his partners, Dracula escaped Van Helsing's first attack, which utilized—for some inexplicable reason—a silver bullet (a werewolf remedy). With the aid of his granddaughter, Van Helsing continued the attack. This movie revived an old folk remedy for conquering vampires, as Dracula was led into a hawthorn bush. The vampire world created by Hammer Films was finally exhausted with a cooperative project between the studio and Shaw Brothers, a massive movie production company in Hong Kong.

Directed by Roy Ward Baker, *The Legend of the Seven Golden Vampires* (1974) (also known as *The Seven Brothers Meet Dracula*) had Abraham Van Helsing (again portrayed by Peter Cushing) traveling to China to find the elusive Dracula. Early in the film, Van Helsing met Hsu Tien-an, the local vampire hunter. In China, both vampires and vampire hunters naturally knew martial arts, and the film emerged as a feeble attempt to merge the two genres. Needless to say, the film was a commercial failure.

By 1974, at the time it authorized the filming of *The Legend of the Seven Golden Vampires*, Hammer Films was in financial trouble. It had hoped that its exploitation of the martial arts theme, added to its tried-and-true vampire theme, would be a great success. Instead, the combination had quite the opposite effect. Warner Bros., which had distributed many of Hammer Films's productions in America, refused to release this one and, in the end, the Chinese vampires merely speeded Hammer

Films's swift move into bankruptcy in 1975. An era of vampire movies was over. The studio had explored the vampire theme for a generation. Its movies inspired a worldwide boom in vampire (and horror) movies in the 1960s as many directors attempted to copy the Hammer Films successes but, hampered by low budgets and even lower production values, they rarely reached Hammer Films's proficiency.

Hammer Films was then moved into receivership. In 1975, it was purchased by Ray Skeggs, who set about restructuring the business. The main product of this period was two 1980s television series. *Hammer House of Horror* aired 13 episodes in 1980, and its followup, *Hammer House of Mystery and Suspense*, aired 13 episodes from 1984 to 1986. After the series, the company seemed moribund. Occasionally, announcements of projects that never appeared or rumors of productions circulated, but nothing made it to the screen.

Then in 2007, Dutch producer John de Mol purchased the Hammer Films rights, which bought him ownership of some 300 Hammer Films productions. De Mol's company set plans to restart the studio and produce two to three movies (horror or thrillers) each year. The first film under the new Hammer Films banner was made in 2008. The vampire film *Beyond the Rave* premiered free online exclusively on MySpace in April 2008. It came out as a 20-part serial, with each episode lasting four minutes. Since its original run, the episodes have been available on YouTube. The story concerned a soldier on his last night before shipping out to war. Ed goes searching for his former girlfriend Jen at a rave party led by the mysterious Melech, who turns out to be the leader of a growing vampire community. To get through the evening, he must deal with both some mean drug dealers and some seductive vampires, neither of whom have his well-being in mind.

> By 1974, at the time it authorized the filming of *The Legend of the Seven Golden Vampires*, Hammer Films was in financial trouble.

In the new century, several attempts have been made to revive Hammer Films but have shown only marginal success. Meanwhile, since the mid-1970s, the memory of Hammer Films has been kept alive by its fans.

Hammer Films Fandom: The devoted fans of Hammer Films have organized and created a world of fanzines and collectibles, which in the 1990s was given focus by the Hammer Horror Collector's Network based in Campbell, California, and supported by the continuing Hammer Films. Since the mid-1970s, a series of Hammer Films–related periodicals have appeared, including *The House of Hammer, Hammer Horror* (which ran for seven issues in 1995), *Little Shoppe of Horrors, The House That Hammer Built, Dark Terrors,* and *Behind the Screams.* These have been superseded by Hammer Films's significant presence online, sites easily located with any search engine.

The most valued items by collectors are the various movie posters and theater cards, including the ones produced for the non-English releases and the various novelizations of the later movies that appeared in the 1970s. Among the vampire titles with accompanying novels are *The Vampire Lovers, Countess Dracula, Scars of Dracula, Lust for a Vampire,* and *Kronos* (aka *Captain Kronos, Vampire Hunter*). However, over the years, a wide variety of products have been produced just for the continuing legion of fans. Topping the list are trading cards, a set of which appeared each in 1975 and 1976 from Topps called Shock Theater. These were not widely distributed and are among the most valued items for collectors. Two sets were produced— Hammer Horror I and Hammer Horror II— which included posters, art, and stills from different movies, more than half from the vampire titles. A set of playing cards with stills from the Hammer Films movies was also produced. Since 1997, when a 40th-anniversary set of trading cards appeared, at least three additional sets have manifested the continued fan interest.

A variety of histories of Hammer Films have been written, and several stars, most notably Christopher Lee and Peter Cushing, have produced autobiographies. Musical fans can track down *Dracula: Classical Scores from Hammer Horror,* released by Silva on vinyl in 1989 and on CD in 1993.

Hotel Transylvania (animated; 2012)

Hotel Transylvania emerged as one of the most successful vampire-related movie projects of the twenty-first century. An animated feature, it focuses upon a contemporary Count Dracula, who has survived and recovered from the attacks in Bram Stoker's novel and now owns and manages Hotel Transylvania as a place where vampires and the world's other monsters, famous and not so famous, can have a time of rest and relaxation from the mundane world, where they are often harassed by humans. As the movie opens, Dracula (voiced by Adam Sandler) is a widower, his wife having been killed in 1895, and he has become the overprotective parent of a daughter, Mavis (Selena Gomez). They reside in a massive, five-star hotel, which gives the movie its name.

The movie opens as a celebration for the teenagelike Mavis's 118th birthday. Among those arriving for the party are Frankenstein (Kevin James) and his wife (Fran Drescher), Wayne and Wanda Werewolf (Steve Buscemi and Molly Shannon), the Invisible Man (David Spade), and the Murray Mummy (CeeLo Green). Also arriving uninvited is a 21-year-

Dracula runs a hotel staffed by monsters in the goofy, animated film Hotel Transylvania. *(2012).*

old human, Jonathan "Johnny" Loughran (Andy Samberg). The stage is now set for Mavis to gain a boyfriend and for Dracula to learn how much the world has changed since he originally built the hotel.

Hotel Transylvania proved a hit with its young target audience and found the widespread approval of parents in spite of its vampire/monster theme and mixed reviews from critics. Genndy Tartakovsky had been eventually selected as the director, and he brought a dynamic quality to the production. He drew his inspiration from the classic monster mash *Abbott and Costello Meet Frankenstein*. Among its many awards, it won the Golden Globe award for Best Animated Film, and Tartakovsky did a book highlighting the art used in the film. A number of books, also aimed at the children's market, were published in the wake of the film's release.

Sony Pictures soon put a sequel into production. It brought together the original cast while adding Mel Brooks as Dracula's father, and Tartakovsky remained in place as the director. *Hotel Transylvania 2* was released in

2015. The movie is set some seven years after the first film. Mavis and Johnny have married and are now parents to five-year-old Dennis. Dracula finally approved their marriage. Also, the world is different, having become aware of the existence of monsters and seemingly being no longer afraid of them.

The plot of the movie is driven by the newborn, but as he approaches his fifth birthday, he has yet to show any fangs. Dracula is afraid that his grandson may never manifest any vampiric powers. Even as Dracula attempts to enlist the aid of his monster friends to assist Dennis in the development of his vampiric side, Mavis is planning a visit to California, where her husband's parents live. Possibly, she and her husband and child should move there. Dracula opposes any such move.

Hotel Transylvania 2 became Sony Pictures Animation's highest-grossing film to date and, like its predecessor, won multiple awards, led by the People's Choice award. Soon after its appearance, Sony Pictures announced that a second sequel was already on the schedule.

Again, the original cast was largely reassembled, and Tartakovsky returned to direct.

Hotel Transylvania 3: Summer Vacation begins with Dracula, his daughter Mavis, and her husband Johnny running Hotel Transylvania and living out their as-normal-as-possible, mundane lives. The fly in the ointment is Dracula, who is depressed that he has been unable to find a new mate in the more than a century since the death of his wife. Mavis responds to Dracula's depressed state by suggesting a cruise, and thus, Dracula, Johnny, and Mavis; their son, Dennis; and a host of their regular hotel guests board the good ship *Legacy* for a trip. As they board, Dracula is immediately attracted to Ericka, the female captain of the cruise ship.

Shortly after the cruise begins, Ericka goes below deck, where she has a private meeting with her great-grandfather, who turns out to be no less a personage than Abraham Van Helsing. They discuss the aged vampire hunter's plan to eliminate Dracula and the other monsters onboard. That plan would be carried out when they arrived at the lost city of Atlantis, toward which the ship is secretly headed. On the way there, Ericka makes several attempts to kill Dracula, but each attempt is foiled. Meanwhile, Dracula begins to approach Ericka out of his attraction to her.

Hotel Transylvania 3 would replace *Hotel Transylvania 2* as the largest-grossing film of Sony Pictures Amination. Following its success, not only would a fourth film in the series be announced but a television series would begin development as a joint project of Sony Pictures Animation, Nelvana Limited, and the Disney Channel. It premiered on the Disney Channel in June 2017. The storyline focuses on the years prior to the first movie and Mavis as a teenager growing up in the hotel. It is a continuing series as of 2020.

> *Hotel Transylvania 2* became Sony Pictures Animation's highest-grossing film to date and … won multiple awards, led by the People's Choice award.

London after Midnight (1927)

Frequently cited in histories of the horror movie as the first American vampire motion picture, *London after Midnight* (1927) remains important as a pioneering force in future American treatments of the vampire theme. *London after Midnight* came during the fruitful period of collaboration between director Tod Browning and character actor Lon Chaney, who had first worked together in 1919 on *The Wicked Darling Law*, again in 1921 for *Outside the Law*, and in 1925 on *The Unholy Three*. In 1925, Chaney returned to Universal Pictures for one of his most memorable roles, *The Phantom of the Opera*. Chaney and Browning were united for the last time at MGM in 1927 for *London after Midnight*, based upon a short story by Browning called "The Hypnotist," the title under which *London after Midnight* was released in England in response to British sensitivity.

The movie's storyline began approximately five years after a death had occurred in a haunted house. Inspector Burke of Scotland Yard had become convinced that the death was a murder, not an accident or suicide. He had two suspects, one a friend and the other a nephew of the deceased. He suggested to them that the murder was done by a vampire. The inspector, played by Chaney, then assumed the role of a vampire, for which he had prepared his own elaborate makeup. His actions as the vampire forced the guilty party to reveal his guilt, at which time Chaney revealed his double identity. Although all the major elements of the vampire legend

Marceline Day and Lon Chaney Sr. starred in 1927's London after Midnight. *All copies of the film were destroyed in a 1965 fire at MGM Studios.*

part was divided between Bela Lugosi (the vampire) and Lionel Atwill (the inspector).

A fire at one of MGM's vaults in 1965 appears to have destroyed the last surviving print of *London after Midnight*, and as vampire fandom grew beginning in the 1970s, the film assumed a somewhat mythical status as a classic Chaney picture. *Mark of the Vampire* had made Universal Pictures a considerable amount of money. Stills from the picture indicated that Chaney did his usual fine job of weird and grotesque makeup, with thin wires that made his eyes bulge. Chaney's animal-like teeth, shown on the poster for the movie, made speech impossible.

It has been impossible to appraise Browning's directorial skills on the movie, but in 2002, TMC commissioned Rick Schmidlin to restore the movie using the original script and a set of still photographs assembled from the collections at the Academy of Motion Picture Arts and Sciences, the Fairbanks Center for Motion Picture Studies, the Margaret Herrick Library, and the University of Southern California Cinema-Television Library. An original musical score was added by Robert Israel. This new version was subsequently released on DVD as part of the Lon Chaney Collection. One leading gothic rock band paid homage to the movie by adopting it as the name of their band. London after Midnight was founded by Sean Brennan in 1987.

were incorporated into the film, in the end, of course, the vampire was explained away as a masquerade. The movie mixed the horror and mystery genres but, in the end, was a mystery movie. It was one of Chaney's last movies and one of the last silent horror films before the major studios moved to sound. Chaney had died by the time Browning made a sound version of *London after Midnight* in 1935 under the title *Mark of the Vampire*. In the later version, the Chaney

Mexican and Latin American Films

Today, Mexico's prolific movie industry has become well known, and vampire enthusiasts have made note of the large number of vampire movies from Mexico, many of them featuring U.S. actors. The Mexican vampire image was strongly influenced by Universal Pictures's Spanish-language rendition of *Dracula* (Spanish, 1931), starring Carlos Villarias and

Lupita Tovar. This American-made version circulated freely in Mexico in the years prior to World War II and directly influenced the image of the vampire in the emerging urban culture.

The vampire arrived in force in 1957, when German Robles starred as the vampire Count Lavud in three vampire movies: *El Vam-*

piro (*The Vampire*), *El Ataud del Vampiro* (*The Vampire's Coffin*), and a comedy inspired by the earlier movies, *El Castillo de los Monstruos* (*Castle of the Monsters*). Count Lavud, obviously influenced by Bela Lugosi, was pictured as a suave, Hungarian nobleman. In the first movie, he was killed with a stake that subsequently was removed to allow him further life in the second.

Robles secured his claim as Mexico's first vampire star in 1959 by starring in a 12-part serial as a bearded descendant of the prophet Nostradamus, who had become a vampire. Subsequently, the serial was recut into four feature-length movies: *La Maldición de Nostradamus* (*The Curse of Nostradamus*), *Nostradamus y el Destructor de Monstruos* (*The Monster Demolisher*), *Nostradamus, El Genii de las Tinieblas* (*The Genie of Darkness*), and *La Sangre de Nostradamus* (*The Blood of Nostradamus*). (To avoid certain Mexican government film regulations, films were often made as serials and then quickly recut into feature films.) These features were released in the United States by Roger Corman's American International Pictures. Robles also played a vampire in the Argentine film *El Vampiro Aechecha* (*The Lurching Vampire*, 1962). His final appearance was in *Los Vampiros de Coyoacan* (1973), in which he played the hero instead of a vampire.

Robles's success quickly led to an exploitation of the market. Alfonso Corona Blake made his first vampire movie, *El Mundo de los Vampiros* (*World of the Vampires*) in 1960. Two years later, Blake was one of the directors called upon to work on the movies of the masked wrestler-turned-actor Santo. He directed Santo's first vampire movie, *Santo Contra las Mujeres Vampiro* (*Samson vs. the Vampire Women*). Santo emerged as one of Mexico's favorite movie characters and, over two decades, fought a variety of supernatural villains. In 1967, he battled Dracula in *Santo en el Tesoro de Dracula*, which was also made into an adult version as *El Vampiro y el Sexo*. The vampire women returned in 1969 in *Santo en la Venganza de las Mujeres Vampiros*.

Frederico Curiel, the director of *Santo en la Venganza de las Mujeres Vampiros*, had emerged in 1959 as the director of the Nostradamus films. In 1967, he directed *El Imperio de Dracula* (*The Empire of Dracula*) and, two years later, *Las Vampiras*, one of actor John Carradine's last films. He was joined as an important director of vampire titles by Miguel Morayta, who was responsible for *El Vampiro Sangriento* (*The Bloody Vampire*, 1961) and *La Invasion de los Vampiros* (*The Invasion of the Vampires*, 1962).

The vampire as a theme in Mexican cinema peaked in the 1960s. In the early 1970s, the last of the Santo vampire movies, *Santo y Blue Demon Contra Dracula y el Hombre Lobo*, appeared. René Cardona, who had directed *Santo en el Tesoro del Dracula*, continued his work in *Santo Contra Cazadores de Cabezas* (1970), *La Invasion de los Muertos* (1972), and the two comedies *Capulina Contra Los Vampiros*

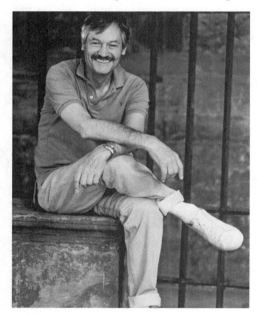

Director Roger Corman was a prolific moviemaker and a trailblazer in independent films. Among his many films as producer and director was a slew of vampire movies.

(1972) and *Capulina Contra Los Monstruos* (1972). He was followed by Juan Lopez, who directed *Mary, Mary, Bloody Mary* (1975) and *Alucarda* (*Sisters of Satan*, 1975). Few new vampire films appeared through the remainder of the decade. From being a center of the vampire cinema in the 1960s, Mexico seems to have largely abandoned the genre through the 1980s and into the 1990s, though a number of Mexican masked wrestlers adopted a vampire persona. The vampire theme reemerged briefly at the end of the 1990s, when Mexican moviemakers jumped on the chupacabra bandwagon with movies such as *Ataca el Chupacabras* (1996) and *Chupacabras* (2000).

> *Quem tem Medo de Lobishomem* has been commonly reported in vampire filmographies because of the misunderstanding that the *lobisomen* was a vampire rather than a werewolf.

South America: The vampire made periodic appearances in the movies of South America, primarily in Argentina and Brazil. The first South American vampire movie was *El Vampiro Negro* (1953), directed by Roman Vinoly. It was based upon the true case of Peter Kürten, the vampire of Düsseldorf. It was almost a decade before a second film, *El Vampiro Aechecha* (1962), a joint Argentine–Mexican picture, was produced. This movie was notable for its inclusion of German Robles in the cast.

Brazil produced its first vampire film in 1969–1970. The movie was *Um Sonho de Vampiros* (*A Vampire's Dream*), a comedy about a doctor who had to choose between death or vampirism. Others released through the decade include *O Macabro Dr. Scivano* (1971), *Quem tem Medo de Lobishomem* (1974), and *A Deusa de Marmore Escrava do Diabo* (1978).

Quem tem Medo de Lobishomem has been commonly reported in vampire filmographies because of the misunderstanding that the *lobisomen* was a vampire rather than a werewolf. Over the last quarter century, only a very few vampire movies have been made in South America, most notably *As Sete Vampiros* (*The Seven Vampires*, 1986), *J-ok-el Sangre eternal* (*Eternal Blood*, 2002), *Tremendo Amanecer* (*Tremendous Dawn*, 2004), *Mala Carne* (*Carnal*, 2004), *La Llorona: The Wailer* (2006), *Jo-k'el* (*Curse of the Weeping Woman*, 2007), *La Levenda de la Llorona* (2014), and *The Curse of la Llorona* (2019).

Rollin, Jean (1938–2010)

Jean Rollin, a French horror movie director, is best known for his production of a number of adult erotic vampire films, beginning with *La Reine des Vampires* (*Queen of the Vampires*) in 1967. Rollin entered the film industry as a teenager in 1955 as an assistant director working on animated films. A short time later, he produced his first film, a short entitled *Le Amours Jaunes*. In 1965, he met American producer Sam Selsky. Selsky asked him to put together a half-hour short to run with one of his already produced films. The resulting *La Reine des Vampires* proved superior to the feature with which it ran and led Selsky to support Rollin's first feature film, *Le Voil du Vampire* (*The Rape of the Vampire*), which met with relative commercial success. In this film, into which most of *La Reine des Vampires* was edited, he established what was to be the hallmark of his subsequent work: a preference for visual effects that carry the film's message and dominate the often weak storylines. His first feature, in fact, has a rather flimsy plot about the attempt to free two women from a vampire's curse. It enjoyed success, in large part, because of the sexual scenes; the audiences reacted to a decade of

rather strict censorship during the reign of Charles de Gaulle.

Rollin followed the success of his first work with his first color feature in 1969, *La Nue Vampire* (released in English as *The Nude Vampire* or *The Naked Vampire*), and in 1970 one of his more heralded productions, *Le Frisson des Vampires* (released in English as *Sex and the Vampires* or *Vampire Thrills*). *Le Frisson des Vampires* concerned a young couple who encounter the vampire Isolde, who makes her first appearance in a suit of chain mail and thigh-high, leather boots. Again, the visual imagery overshadowed the plot, and Rollin saturated the audience with his portrayal of vampirism as a perverse form of sexuality.

By the time of his third film, he had assembled a group of specialists who assisted him through the 1970s in a series of low-budget productions. He regularly returned to the vampire theme, feeling that vampirism provided an effective vehicle for portraying erotic themes. In 1971, he directed *Le Cult de Vampire*, followed in 1972 by *Requiem pour un Vampire* (also released as *Vierges et Vampires* and *Caged Virgins*).

Rollin also directed a number of horror and adult features. In 1974, he produced *Lèvres de Sang* (*Lips of Blood*) and followed it in 1979 with *Fascination* and in 1982 with *La Morte-Vivante*. *Fascination* featured a cult of vampire women (a theme Rollin had used in earlier films) that conducted ritual sacrifices of men in a remote castle home. His last vampire movie concerned a dead woman revived as the result of a chemical waste spillage. She began attacking people to drink their blood, an appetite that grew stronger as the film progressed. In his spare time, Rollin authored several horror–fantasy novels.

He continued to make movies through the 1980s and into the 1990s and currently lives in Paris. In the 1990s, he returned to the vampire theme with *Les Deux Orphelines Vampires (Two Orphan Vampires)* (1996), which told the story of two girls who were blind orphans by day but turned into bloodthirsty vampires by night. He also released an oversized volume of essays on his vampire movies illustrated with numerous stills. His most recent encounter with vampires, *La fiancée de Dracula* (2002), has a vampire hunter tracking down Dracula's vampire descendants in the contemporary world.

Schreck, Max (1879–1936)

Max Schreck was a German character actor chosen to play Count Orlock, the Dracula figure in F. W. Murnau's classic silent film *Nosferatu: Eine Symphonie des Grauens* (1922). His last name, Schreck, which means "terror" in German, was his actual name and not a stage pseudonym. He became an actor for Max Reinhardt, a prominent theatrical producer in pre–World War I Germany, where he most likely had come to the attention of director and screenwriter Henrik Galeen. While he played many parts, none are as memorable as his single performance in *Nosferatu*.

In the film, Schreck portrayed Dracula as a repulsive, rodentlike creature. Dracula's fangs became two teeth in the center of his mouth. All of his facial features, from his nose to his ears, were exaggerated. His head was bald. His hypnotic eyes were surrounded by dark makeup. His fingers were not simply long but elongated. He walked in a stiff, halting manner. The grotesque characterization was also further distorted by the use of Schreck's shadow, which (in spite of the fact that vampires as nocturnal, soulless creatures are not supposed to have shadows) emphasized the

German actor Max Schreck is remembered by many for his role as Count Orlock in Nosferatu.

horrific features. However, he did have a reflection in the mirror.

The idea of Dracula as rodent was carried through by associating Count Orlock with rats and an outbreak of the plague that had occurred in Bremen, Germany, in the 1830s. As an in-terpretation, it was most effective but essentially a dead end as far as the vampire character was concerned, relating it to a traditional, inhuman monster rather than a suave and very human seducer and sexual predator, which would come to the fore in the British stage and American film versions.

Schreck's interpretation of Dracula would be revived in the 1970s by Klaus Kinski for the remake, *Nosferatu the Vampyre* (1979), and its Italian sequel, *Vampire in Venice* (1988). Writer Stephen King also adopted a Schreck-like vampire for his villain in *Salem's Lot*, and it inspired the character of Radu, the evil vampire in the *Subspecies* video series.

E. Elias Merhige's movie *Shadow of the Vampire* (2000) cast Willem Dafoe as Max Schreck, who portrayed an actual vampire hired to star in Murnau's original version of *Nosferatu*.

Schreck would go on to play a variety of parts in close to 30 films in the remaining 14 years of his life, but none was as noteworthy as his single performance in the one film that was suppressed during his lifetime and would bring him fame only a generation after his death. In 2008, German author Stefan Eickhoff wrote the first biography of Schreck, *Max Schreck— Gespenstertheater*, published in Munich.

⚡ *Twenty-first Century Films* ⚡

Since the production of vampire movies hit a low in the 1980s, the number of productions increased annually through the 1990s and have remained at an unprecedented high through the first two decades of the twenty-first century. Of more than 2,500 feature-length vampire films produced in the century between 1920 and 2020, more than 1,000 (between 40 and 50 percent) have been released since the beginning of the new century. These films cover the major types of vampire films through the decades, including horror, action, comedy, juvenile (both animated and live action), and adult. The one area that a noticeable decline has been seen is in films out of Hong Kong, the last notable entry being the 2003 film *The Twins Effect*, though other East Asian countries, especially Japan, remain fertile ground for imaginative vampire films.

The best of the vampire movies found success in terms of the revenue they brought in to their makers and the large audiences who viewed them both in North America and around the world, and the very best of the movies turned into franchises that led to sequels, jumped to television, and produced a spectrum of fan merchandise. As the new century began, several 1990s movies were in the process of making the transformation into a successful franchise, most notably *Blade*, the first installment of which had appeared in 1998 with Wesley Snipes in the title role as a *dhampir* (half-vampire/half-human) vampire slayer. *Blade II* would appear in 2002 and *Blade: Trinity* in 2004. It would jump to television with the *Blade* series in 2006, though the series failed to find an audience and lasted only one season.

The first of the new series to appear in the new century was *Underworld*, built around a world in which vampires and werewolves are at war with each other. In the first installment, Selene (Kate Beckinsale) is a Death Dealer, a vampire specializing in killing Lycans (i.e., the werewolves). She is motivated by her belief that the werewolves targeted and killed her family. However, as she goes about her job, she meets and falls in love with a werewolf. Selene is the primary character appearing at the center of each *Underworld* installment, and as each appeared, time and plot was allotted to unpacking the backstory to the original movie detailing the story of the origins of the two communities, why they are at war, and how the conflict can possibly be resolved. Fans followed the action through four subsequent movies: *Underworld: Evolution* (2006); *Underworld: Rise of the Lycans* (2009); *Underworld: Awakening* (2012), in which humans discovered that they share space with vampire and werewolf clans; and *Underworld: Blood Wars* (2016). An animated film, *Underworld: Endless War*, appeared in 2011. A television production was announced but was never brought to fruition.

Two years after *Underworld* appeared, another film built around a female lead was issued: *BloodRayne*. Rayne, the primary protagonist, was, like Blade, a *dhampir*. As her story unfolds, she learns that her father is a vampire named Kagan, who would later kill her human mother. She sets out on a mission to kill Kagan. *BloodRayne* had a unique origin, having begun as a video game. The original movie went straight to video but built on an initial audience from the gaming world. Video sales justified two sequels: *BloodRayne: Deliverance* (2007) and *BloodRayne: Third Reich* (2011).

In 2008, *Twilight*, the most successful vampire movie series to date, was launched. It was based on the very successful, four-volume book series written by Stephenie Meyer, which was aimed at a young teen audience. Rivaling the *Harry Potter* series, *Twilight* was able to match, and even top it movie by movie, as it told the story of Bella Swan (Kristen Stewart) and her love life with vampire Edward Cullen (Robert Pattinson) and the unsuccessful attempt of Jacob Black (Taylor Lautner), a werewolf, to woo her away from the bloodsucker. As each movie outgrossed the last one in revenue, the movies not only became the largest-grossing vampire movies ever made but, for a brief few years, were the largest-grossing films ever made.

The four volumes of Meyers's *Twilight* series were turned into five movies: *Twilight* (2008); *The Twilight Saga: New Moon* (2009); *The Twilight Saga: Eclipse* (2010); *The Twilight Saga: Breaking Dawn, Part 1* (2011); and *The Twilight Saga: Breaking Dawn, Part 2* (2012).

An unexpected entrance into the world of outstanding vampire movies arrived in 2012 just as *Twilight* was reaching its climax, an animated film targeting a children's audience, *Hotel Transylvania* (2012). It told the tale of a contemporary Count Dracula, now managing an upscale hotel catering to the world's monsters who needed a retreat from the world's hostility

Twenty-first Century Vampire Movies

Year	Movie	Year	Movie
2000	Shadow of the Vampire	2012	Dark Shadows
	The Little Vampire (juvenile)		Kiss of the Damned
	Vampire Hunter D: Bloodlust (animated)		Abraham Lincoln: Vampire Hunter
2001	The Forsaken		Dracula Reborn
	The Breed	2013	Only Lovers Left Alive
2003	The League of Extraordinary Gentlemen	2014	Afflicted
			Da Sweet Blood of Jesus
2004	Van Helsing		Dracula Untold
	Night Watch		A Girl Walks Home Alone
	Salem's Lot		What We Do in the Shadows
	Vampire Effect		Vampire Academy (juvenile)
2006	Day Watch	2015	Bloodsucking Bastards
	Frostbite		He Never Died
	The Hamiltons		Yakuza Apocalypse
2007	I Am Legend	2017	The Little Vampire 3D (animated)
	Rise: Vampire Hunter		
	30 Days of Night		Eat Local
2009	Let the Right One In	2018	Dracula in Love
	Cirque du Freak: The Vampire's Assistant (juvenile)	2019	Dracula
			Bad Girl Dracula
2010	Let Me In		Rabid
	Stake Land	2020	Dracula Sir (India)
	Suck		Ten Minutes to Midnight
	We Are the Night		A Place among the Dead
	Vampires Suck	2021	The Dracula Cult
2011	Midnight Son		Dracula on Holiday
	Priest		Bram Stoker Is Van Helsing
	The Moth Diaries	2022	Morbius
2012	Byzantium		

toward them. Dracula was an overprotective father with a daughter coming of age, who was finding a desire to know more about the outside world of humans and maybe even finding a boyfriend. Meeting mixed reviews as it arrived in the theaters, the movie proved a favorite of its youthful audience and their parents alike and immediately prompted two sequels—*Hotel Transylvania 2* (2015) and *Hotel Transylvania 3: Summer Vacation* (2018)—with additional films being planned. It also led to an equally successful television series, still continuing as this almanac goes to press. As *Twilight* began by adapting a very successful book series, the *Hotel Transylvania* movies are producing a wealth of children's story activity books.

Above and beyond the blockbuster films that led to multiple sequels amid the hundreds of vampire movies that have appeared through the first two decades of the twenty-first century, some have risen above the herd as most note-

worthy, some for their plot or unique twist on the vampire myth, some for their drama and acting, some for the special effects and atmosphere, and a few for their presentation of the vampire world to a youthful audience. Space does not allow a review or even a comment on each; hence, a bare list is offered (though some are discussed in more detail elsewhere in this almanac).

Underworld (2003)

Underworld, a 2003 film pitting vampires against werewolves, introduced an original epic story concerning the origin and history of vampires and their relation to werewolves and humanity in general. The story begins at an indefinite point in the early Middle Ages and subsequently passed through two decisive events in 1210 and 1409 C.E. that brought it to the present. The events of the original movie continued in its sequel, *Underworld: Evolution* (2006), while a third movie, a prequel, *Underworld: Rise of the Lycans* (2009), filled out the medieval background. *Underworld* originated with a story by Kevin Grevioux and Len Wiseman and a screenplay written by Danny McBride.

At some point in the early Middle Ages, Alexander Corvinus survived a plague as a result of his body mutating the plague virus, thus allowing him to emerge as the first Immortal. He subsequently fathered three sons—Markus, William, and a third unnamed son. Markus was bitten by a bat and became the first vampire. He would, in turn, create several other vampires, including Viktor and Amelia, who would constitute a triad of Elders that ruled the emerging vampire community. The three worked out an arrangement by which each ruled for a century while the other two slept. Meanwhile, William Corvinus was bitten by a wolf and became a werewolf. Unfortunately, the first generation of werewolves, as created by William, was hampered by the fact that the individual wolves could not turn back into their human form. Then in the thirteenth century, a second generation of werewolves appeared in the persona of Lucian, who could move back and forth from human to wolf form. The third son continued as human but unknowingly passed the Corvinus blood to his descendants. That blood had the potential of creating a hybrid that possessed the strengths of both werewolves and vampires.

In the thirteenth century, the vampire community was focused on a European castle/fortress from which Viktor, the vampire elder, operated as a feudal lord. He ruled over the local human population, whom he agreed to protect from the wild wolves in the surrounding forests. The wolves residing in the castle provided the manual labor necessary to maintain the castle and protected the vampire residents during the daylight hours. Along the way, Viktor discovered that the young Lucian killed his mother, took him to the castle, and raised the unique, young werewolf as a privileged leader of the castle's werewolf community. Lucian had hopes beyond his station, however, and fell in love with Sonja, Viktor's daughter.

In 1202, Lucian led a revolution by organizing the wolves throughout the land and overran Viktor's castle. Only Viktor, the hastily awakened Markus and Amelia, and their assistant Andreas Tanis escaped what became a slaughter. Two hundred years later, in 1409, a group of vampire warriors, called Death Dealers, attacked Viktor's former castle. They underestimated the number of werewolves and were all killed, save one, a cowardly vampire named Kraven. Capturing Kraven, Lucian offered him a deal in return for his life (and some future rewards). Kraven agreed to tell of a limited victory, in which Lucian died along with

An endless war wages between vampires and werewolves in the Underworld *movie franchise that ran from 2003 to 2016.*

all of Kraven's cohorts. As Kraven fled back to the vampires, Lucian burned the castle and escaped into the night, and everyone believed him dead.

Lucian was, in fact, the first of a new race of werewolves, the Lycans, distinguished by their ability to morph between human and wolf form. Over the next centuries, the vampires and Lycans would fight a continuing war that in the nineteenth and twentieth centuries would become technologically sophisticated. Vampires would be armed with bullets that contained silver nitrate and the Lycans with bullets that projected ultraviolet rays (that had the effect of killing the vampires with sunlight). A crisis would develop in the contemporary world as Amelia, the present waking elder, was about to transfer power to Markus and begin her century of sleep.

In the modern world, Selene, a Death Dealer, fought the Lycans as she believed that they killed her family back in the thirteenth century. She also believed that the Death Dealers were essentially wiping out a remnant community that had survived the 1409 debacle. Her world began to unravel after she rescued a human, Michael Corvinus, from the Lycans but not before he was bitten and began the

transformation into a werewolf. She also became attracted to him. Simultaneously, she came to distrust Kraven. Step by step, she uncovered two main lies. First, she discovered that Viktor, with whom she had a father–daughter relationship, had executed his daughter Sonja because of her affair with Lucian and subsequently executed Selene's family for their knowledge of his actions against his brother, William Corvinus. He had spared Selene and raised her because she reminded him of Sonja. Second, she discovered Kraven's lie about the events of 1409, most notably his report of Lucian's death.

As these secrets undergirded the continuous war between the vampires and the Lycans, Selene was now questioning her whole existence in light of her falling in love with Michael. She ended up killing Viktor because of his lies and because he was trying to kill Michael. Eventually, they would uncover further secrets held by Markus, the surviving vampire elder, and Alexander Corvinus, the still-living first Immortal.

The vampires of *Underworld* are rather traditional in that blood is the major issue of their existence. They are nocturnal creatures and are killed by sunlight. They are also contemporary in that they live together in a community that has adapted some modern technology and is ruled by a vampire moral code. They keep their identity (and the location of their centers) from the larger human world and secure from their werewolf enemies. They appear as normal humans and do not shift into animal forms.

Amid mixed critical reviews, each of the three *Underworld* movies would, by 2009, appear on the list of the ten highest-grossing vampire movies of all time, with *Evolution* slightly ahead of the other two. Of the cast, actress Kate Beckinsale (1973–) would attain the most acclaim for her portrayal of Selene. In the midst of the making of the *Underworld* movies, she also appeared in *Van Helsing*, also a popular vampire movie. Other important *Underworld* roles were filled by Scott Speedman (Michael Corvinus), Tony Curran (Markus Corvinus), Derek Jacobi (Alexander Corvinus), Bill Nighy (Viktor), Shane Brolly (Kraven), Michael Sheen (Lucian), and Zita Görög (Amelia).

IDW, a San Diego-based comic book publisher, issued comic adaptations of the movies, and Greg Cox produced novelizations of them.

After *Underworld* appeared, White Wolf Inc., which publishes the *Vampire: The Masquerade* game (and the associated *Werewolf: The Apocalypse* game), joined with author Nancy Collins in filing a lawsuit against Sony Entertainment, which claimed that the movie infringed upon their copyrights and plagiarized from a short story written by Collins that focused upon a Romeo-and-Juliet-type relationship between a vampire and a werewolf. In their major brief, they claimed that the first *Underworld* movie copied the plot of Collins's story and borrowed some 70 characteristics of White Wolf's World of Darkness universe, shared by

British actress Kate Beckinsale has received a positive reception for her portrayal of Selene in the Underworld *movie series.*

its two games. Sony countered by noting that neither the plot of the Collins story nor the overwhelming majority of the cited characteristics shared by the movie and the World of Darkness were original to the World of Darkness. Rather, claimed Sony, almost all of the characteristics had appeared in the previous 50 years of vampire movies and literature, most on multiple occasions. A story very similar to Collins's story had, for example, appeared in a 1950s horror comic book. The court case was settled prior to its scheduled court date, with both sides agreeing not to discuss the elements of the settlement.

🦇 *Universal Pictures* 🦇

With its production of *Dracula* (1931), Universal Pictures became the first studio to bring the vampire theme to the talking motion picture and initiated a wave of interest in horror movies. The studio was founded by Carl Laemmle, who entered the industry in 1906. Universal Pictures initially opened two studios in Los Angeles, then in 1915, it shifted its headquarters to Universal City, on the site of the former Taylor Ranch in the San Fernando Valley (it is now the oldest continuously operated studio in America). After many years of making silent movies, Universal Pictures made its first sound movie in 1930, *The King of Jazz*. That same year, the studio obtained the rights to the Hamilton Deane/John L. Balderston play *Dracula*, which was then making successful appearances around the country after completing a lengthy run on Broadway. The star of the West Coast production, Bela Lugosi, worked with the studio to secure the motion picture rights from Florence Stoker, the widow of Bram Stoker. Tod Browning was chosen to direct the picture.

> As people became aware of Universal Picturess plans for *Dracula*, Paul Kohner ... suggested that *Dracula* would be an excellent candidate for a Spanish version.

As people became aware of Universal Pictures's plans for *Dracula*, Paul Kohner, the executive in charge of foreign-language productions, suggested that *Dracula* would be an excellent candidate for a Spanish version. He already had in mind Lupita Tovar (Kohner's future wife) as the female lead. Thus, as the English-language version of *Dracula* was filmed, the Spanish-language version, using the same stage settings but a different cast, was simultaneously produced.

Dracula (Spanish, 1931) was a success in what was then a relatively small market. However, the English version, starring Bela Lugosi—after a slow start—became Universal Pictures's top-grossing film of the year and was credited with keeping the studio from closing after two years of losing money. The success led to a series of horror films: *Frankenstein* (1931), *The Mummy* (1932), *The Invisible Man* (1933), *The Black Cat* (1934), and *The Bride of Frankenstein* (1935). For nearly two decades, Universal Pictures became known for its horror movies, but interestingly enough, it was not until 1936 with the production of *Dracula's Daughter* that a second vampire film was produced. Vampire fans waited until 1943 for a third film, titled *Son of Dracula*.

In 1936, Laemmle lost control of Universal Pictures to Charles Rogers and J. Cheever Cowdin. Over the next decade, the company produced a large number of low-budget films, including many horror features and several vampire movies. In 1948, it merged with International Pictures. Except for the comedy *Abbott and Costello Meet Frankenstein*, Universal-International did not produce any other movies with major vampire themes—part of a general trend away from horror films at the time.

After many years, Universal Pictures produced a new vampire film, *Blood of Dracula*, in 1957. The movie was aimed at a youthful audience, and the inclusion of a female vampire made the movie more interesting. The success of the movie was responsible for several other vampire movies over the next few years but, after the 1959 production of *Curse of the Undead*, the studio dropped vampire movies from its schedule for more than a decade. Its reluctance to return to releasing vampire movies and, thereby, placing too much emphasis on the horror genre was amply demonstrated in

Poor Bela Lugosi continued being stuck in the role of Dracula in increasingly subpar B films, as seen here in 1948's Abbott and Costello Meet Frankenstein.

the summer of 1958, when Universal Pictures announced that it had worked out a deal with British upstart Hammer Films. Hammer Films acquired all of the copyrights that Universal Pictures owned on its classic horror titles, including *Dracula*. Universal Pictures largely abandoned the horror movie business for an entire generation.

In 1978, Universal Pictures bought the cinema rights to the remake of the Hamilton Deane/John L. Balderston play, which had enjoyed a revival on Broadway and brought its star, Frank Langella, to Hollywood for the screen version. Langella's *Dracula* (1979) proved to be one of the most effective presentations of the sexual/sensual element that coexists with the terror theme in the Dracula/vampire myth. Since the 1979 *Dracula*, Universal Pictures had largely stayed away from the vampire theme altogether. In the early twenty-first century, announcements were made that Universal Pictures was considering several new vampire-oriented projects, including the screen adaptation of Darren Shan's *Cirque du Freak* series of children's books and a new version of Anne Rice's *Interview with the Vampire*, but these never came to fruition. Universal Pictures will, of course, always be remembered for its launching of *Dracula* into the consciousness of a nation.

Vampyr (1932)

Made the same year as the film *Dracula* (1931), *Vampyr*, having been forgotten by all but the most devoted students of the horror genre, has nevertheless been regarded by some critics of classical horror films as the best such motion picture ever made. *Vampyr* was produced and directed by Carl Theodor Dreyer, who also, with the assistance of Christen Jul, wrote the script. The film was purportedly modeled on Sheridan Le Fanu's "Carmilla," but the only similarity seems to be Dreyer's use of a female vampire.

The film opens with David Gray (played by Julian West) arriving in a European village only to discover that a room had already been booked for him at the local inn. That evening, he was visited by an old man (Maurice Schultz), who gave him a package to be opened in case of his death. After the man mysteriously disappeared, Gray wondered if it was all a dream, although he still possessed the package. Unable to sleep, he went for a walk. He followed a disconnected shadow that led him to the local manor house. There, he met the man, who turned out to be the owner of the mansion and one of his daughters, Gisele (Rena Mandel). While Gray visited with Schultz, the latter was shot and killed. Gray then learned that Schultz's other daughter, Leone (Sybille Schmitz), was manifesting some strange symptoms. Upon opening the package after Schultz was shot, Gray found a book on vampires. Leone, who had been wandering about in her sleep, was discovered out on the grounds with an old woman, Margueritte Chopin (Henriette Gerard), hovering over her. Because Leone had lost a lot of blood, Gray offered her a transfusion of his own blood. While giving the transfusion, Gray had a hallucination in which he was being buried alive. Through a window in the coffin, he saw the old woman's face staring at him. He realized that she was a vampire and that a doctor he had met earlier was her assistant. After the halluci-

nation, he awakened in the local cemetery. Accompanied by a servant from the manor house, he found the old woman's grave, and together, they killed her by staking her with an iron pole. The spirits of those whom she had killed then arose to attack and kill the vampire's human cohorts, including the doctor.

Carl Dreyer (the film's producer and director) was known for his artistic attention to a mood of terror rather than any graphic presentation of horrific action. In *Vampyr*, he slowly developed an environment that was supernatural and disjointed and in which the vampire's presence was strongly felt but rarely seen. The terror was suggested early, especially as Gray followed the shadow, which led him to a place where more disconnected shadows dance to some loud music. The old woman appeared and, as she raised her arms and demanded quiet, the music suddenly stopped.

To add even more to the atmosphere of total terror, Dreyer also had the picture filmed with some light leaking into the camera, thus producing a foggy quality on the finished film. To enhance the exact quality he wanted in the characters, Dreyer recruited nonactors to play the various roles. Only Sybille Schmitz and Maurice Schultz were professionals. Dreyer allowed the film's plot to develop slowly, thus inviting viewers to participate in the film through their imagination. In the face of competing horror epics, however, the effect was to leave most audiences bored and to deny the film commercial success. Dreyer's artistic accomplishment was understood and appreciated by very few. In the United States, a condensed version of the film, with a voice-over narration, was issued as the *Castle of Doom*, but it, too, failed to attract a significant audience.

A DVD copy of *Vampyr* was issued in 2008 in the Criterion Collection, a series of

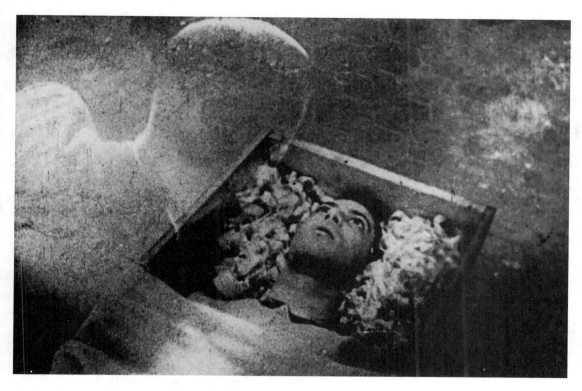

David Gray (Julian West) hallucinates he is being buried alive in the 1932 horror classic, Vampyr.

classic and contemporary films, which were published using the best technical advancements along with original supplements. In this case, the two-disc set included a 1958 radio broadcast of Dreyer reading an essay about filmmaking, a documentary by Jörgen Roos on Dreyer's career, an essay by Casper Tybjerg about influences on Dreyer's *Vampyr*, and a supplemental book of essays on the film.

~ *What We Do in the Shadows* ~ (2014)

What We Do in the Shadows is a vampire comedy that pretends to be a documentary in which a film crew is invited into a home in Wellington, New Zealand, to make a movie about the life of the vampires who reside there. They are rather traditional vampires, who are active only after sundown, possess fangs, and regularly venture into the city to obtain blood. They have various special powers, such as flying and transforming into animals. They are loosely associated with a larger vampire community and are assisted by human familiars.

The subjects of the documentary include the 862-year-old Vladislav; the 379-year-old Viago (Taika Waititi), who had come to New Zealand early in the twentieth century in search of his true love; and the relatively young, 183-

year-old Deacon (Jonathan Brugh). Deacon has a female familiar named Jackie (Jackie van Beek), who cleans up any messes left by the vampire's feeding and hopes to be turned into a vampire himself someday. A fourth vampire, Petyr (Ben Fransham), also resides at the house. He is thousands of years old and resembles Count Orlock, the vampire in the original Dracula film *Nosferatu.*

Early in the movie, Deacon requests for Jackie to bring two virgins to the home, and she entices a woman who arrives with her boyfriend, Nick (Cori Gonzalez-Macuer). Their visit results in the woman being killed and Nick being turned into a vampire. Nick is later accepted into the home, and Nick's friend Stu (Stu Rutherford) introduces the vampires to various modern inventions, such as the internet. Unfortunately, Nick reveals his new life to some outsiders, which leads a vampire hunter to the house, who kills Petyr. For his role in the affair, Nick is banished from the house.

The latter half of the movie begins when the vampires receive an invitation to the annual Unholy Masquerade, an event attended

Taika Waititi plays a 379-year-old vampire named Viago in the 2014 comedy What We Do in the Shadows.

by the local vampires, zombies, and witches. When they arrive, the vampires discover that Nick and his friend Stu are present as well as their former familiar Jackie, who has been made a vampire by Nick. The event turns into a brawl and ends with the vampires encountering a group of werewolves. One of the camera crew is killed, and Stu is mauled and believed dead. Weeks later, Nick returns to the vampires' home and brings Stu with him. Their reunion leads to the vampires and werewolves getting to know each other. The movie ends with Deacon focusing on those watching the film and commanding them to forget what they have just seen.

The film was well received by horror movie fans and met critical acclaim. A sequel was proposed but never made it into production; however, television found the series a fruitful source. New Zealand took two police officers, who had a minor role in the film, as characters around which to build a new series, *Wellington Paranormal.* In America, the FX channel developed a televised version of the movie, now set on Staten Island in New York, which began airing in 2019.

In the American *What We Do in the Shadows* television series (2019–), the vampire home is shared by four vampires. Nandor the Relentless (Keyvan Novak), formerly a ruler of a kingdom in medieval Iran, has a faithful familiar, Guillermo (Harvey Guillén), who hopes to be made into a vampire. Nadja (Natasia Demetriou) is of Romani heritage. She turned Lazlo Cravensworth (Matt Berry), a nobleman in England, and the two are now married. As with the others, Lazlo is subject to a certain grandiosity. He has dreams of his own sexual prowess and, in the midst of his lengthy vampire existence, spent a period of time as a porn actor. Colin Robinson (Mark Proksch) is an energy vampire who lives in the basement. He is very different from the other three vampires. He can walk around in the daylight and has a daytime office job. He lives off the energy he drains from both humans and vampires, an ability he manifests merely by boring or frustrating his victims.

The television series has featured the documentary film crew following the vampires in their adventures as they confront the modern world, interact with other supernatural beings, and deal with members of the larger vampire community with conflicting goals and plans. As this almanac goes to press, two seasons have aired, with a third in production.

⤙ *Yorga, Count* ⤚

Among the several new vampire characters to appear in the 1970s was Count Yorga, the subject of two films released by American International Pictures. The idea for Count Yorga grew out of the collaboration in the late 1960s between director Bob Kelljan and independent producer Michael Macready. The two had made some money on a joint low-budget, soft-core pornographic film, and Kelljan had the idea of doing a second porno film with a vampire theme. At this point, actor Robert Quarry (1925–2009), a friend of Kelljan, got involved. Quarry suggested that they produce a straight horror movie and offered to play the lead role.

Quarry had entered the world of film at the age of 14, when he got a job as a bellhop on Alfred Hitchcock's *Shadow of a Doubt*, which was shot in Santa Rosa, California. Hitchcock took a liking to him and gave him several lines in the movie, though they were cut from the finished product. He went on to play a variety of bit parts in the movies and appeared on radio and television. As his career proceeded, he became typecast as a "heavy." *The Loves of Count Yorga*, as the first of the Yorga films was originally named, became his debut role.

Quarry's vampire drew upon both the suave Dracula of Bela Lugosi and the more dynamic and vicious portrayal by Christopher Lee. The story was set in Los Angeles in the late 1960s. Yorga moved into an old mansion and emerged as a spiritualist medium. His first victim was Erica, a young woman who had attended the first séance and was vampirized as she tried to leave the mansion. Her car had become stuck in the mud. A friend, Dr. Hayes, though ignorant of vampires, researched the subject after Erica was discovered sucking the blood from a cat. After a second young woman was attacked, he concluded that a vampire was operating in Los Angeles. Hayes and Michael, Erica's boyfriend, went to the mansion after Yorga and eventually dispatched the vampire by means of a broomstick through his heart. The first film was an enormous success. Made for $64,000, it grossed several millions, the most successful American International Pictures film to that time. Quarry became a horror film star. A sequel called *The Return of Count Yorga* was quickly planned and just as quickly made. In the sequel, a revived Yorga attended a masquerade party, where he met and fell in love with Cynthia (played by Mariette Hartley).

He decided to possess her in spite of her engaged status. In a scene reminiscent of the Charles Manson slayings, Yorga sent a group of female vampires he had created to gorge themselves on the members of Cynthia's household. Yorga confessed his love to Cynthia and invited her into his vampiric life. She rebuffed him. Meanwhile, her fiancé convinced the police to go to Yorga's home. They were met by his vampire harem and, while a fight ensued, the fiancé went in search of Yorga. Yorga died from a knife in the heart, but in a twist ending, the fiancé had, by this time, become a vampire himself. The film ended as he turned and bit into the neck of his beloved Cynthia.

Count Yorga holds an audience for his vampire brides in The Loves of Count Yorga *(aka* Count Yorga, Vampire*) from 1970.*

American International Pictures planned to do a third Yorga film but eventually dropped the idea, in part because it was engaged in promoting its blaxploitation *Blacula* films. Quarry continued his acting career in various nonvampire roles.

VAMPIRE BOOK-TO-FILM ADAPTATIONS

The Vampire Chronicles by Anne Rice

Rice, Anne (1941–)

Among the people who have most contributed to the significant increase of interest in the vampire in the last generation, few rank with writer Anne Rice. Her major vampire character, Lestat de Lioncourt, who was introduced in her 1976 book *Interview with the Vampire*, has taken his place beside Bram Stoker's Dracula and *Dark Shadows*'s Barnabas Collins as one of the three major literary figures molding the image of the contemporary vampire.

Rice was born Howard Allen Frances O'Brien in the Irish community in New Orleans, Louisiana, and changed her name to Anne shortly after starting school. During her late teens, she grew increasingly skeptical of the teachings of the Roman Catholic Church in which she had been raised. She not only rejected the unique place of the Roman Church among other religious bodies, but she also pronounced her disbelief in its major affirmations of the di-

vine work of Jesus Christ and the existence of God. She replaced her childhood religious teachings with a rational ethical system, an integral element in her reworking of the vampire tradition. Both Rice and her poet husband, Stan Rice, began writing professionally in the early 1960s, but he was the first to receive recognition. In 1970, he won the Joseph Henry Jackson Award for poetry. Rice sold her first story, "October 4, 1948," in 1965, but it was not until 1973 that she felt ready to quit her job in order to write full-time.

The Vampire Chronicles: As early as 1969, Rice had written a short story that she called "Interview with the Vampire." In 1973, she turned it into a novel and attempted to sell it. Following several rejections, Alfred A. Knopf bought it, and it was published in 1976. The book became an unexpected success and has remained in print both in hardback and paperback. Her second novel, *The Feast of All Saints*, was published by Simon & Schuster three years later, and a third, *Cry to Heaven*, appeared in 1982.

Meanwhile, another side of Rice emerged in a series of novels published under a pseudonym, A. N. Roquelaure. *The Claiming of Sleeping Beauty* (1983), *Beauty's Punishment* (1984), and *Beauty's Release: The Continued Erotic Adventures of Sleeping Beauty* (1985) were adult erotic fantasy novels. The sadomasochistic theme in the Roquelaure novels carried over into the more conventional novels published under a second pseudonym, Anne Rampling. In the midst of the release of these novels, her important vampire short story appeared in *Redbook* in 1984, "The Master of Rampling Gate." Rice returned to the vampire theme in 1985 with *The Vampire Lestat*, the most heralded of what was to become *The Vampire Chronicles* series. This volume further developed the character of Lestat introduced in her earlier work.

Novelist Anne Rice is best known for her Vampire Chronicles *series, featuring the vampire Lestat.*

He emerged as a strong, secular individualist who took to the vampire's life quite naturally. Born into the lesser aristocracy, he defied the vampire establishment in Paris and decided to make his own way in the world. A man of action who rarely rested in indecision, he was also deeply affected by poetry and music and freely showed his emotions. Rice described him as both an androgynous ideal and an expression of the man she would be if she were male. Like Rice, Lestat rejected his Catholic past and had no aversion to the religious weapons traditionally used against his kind. Seeking moral justification for his need to feed on fresh blood, he began to develop a vampire ethic, selecting those who had done some great wrong as his victims.

The success of *The Vampire Lestat* led to demands for more, and Rice responded with *The Queen of the Damned* (1988). Like the previous volumes, it became a best seller and soon found its way into a paperback edition. Previously, *Interview with the Vampire* had also appeared in an audiocassette version (1986), and the publishers moved quickly to license audio versions of *The Queen of the Damned* (1988) and *The Vampire Lestat* (1989).

Rice was now a recognized author, and her writing was regularly the subject of serious literary critics. She continued to produce at a steady rate and successively completed *The Mummy* (1989), *The Witching Hour* (1990), and *Lasher* (1993). In the meantime, further adventures of Lestat appeared in the fourth volume of *The Vampire Chronicles*, *The Tale of the Body Thief* (1992), which was released on audiocassette simultaneously with its hardback edition. In 1991, Katherine Ramsland finished her biography of Rice, entitled *Prism of the Night*, and moved on to compile a comprehensive reference volume, *The Vampire Companion: The Official Guide to Anne Rice's The Vampire Chronicles* (1993).

No sooner did Ramsland's volume appear than a fifth volume of *The Vampire Chronicles*,

Stuart Townsend played Lestat de Lioncourt in the 2002 film The Queen of the Damned, *based on the third installment of Anne Rice's novel series.*

Memnoch the Devil, took Lestat into the supernatural realms of heaven and hell (after which Ramsland issued a revised edition). *Memnoch* was not as well received as the previous volumes, as its story tended to subordinate plot to philosophical musings on theological issues. After the publication of *Memnoch*, Rice announced that Lestat had left her and, to the disappointment of his fans, that no more Lestat novels would be published. However, she soon returned to the vampire theme with *Pandora* (immediately available on cassette and CD), the first of several volumes following the other characters in *The Vampire Chronicles*.

Lestat's Vampire Culture: Rice's novels have permeated the culture like no other recent vampire writings. Lestat was honored by a gothic rock band that took his name as their own, and the androgynous ideal has been adopted by the gothic subculture. In 1988, a group of women in New Orleans founded an Anne Rice fan club. Rice approved the effort but suggested that a reference to Lestat be added to the club's name. It emerged as Anne Rice's Vampire Lestat Fan Club. Two years later, Innovation Publishing picked up the comic book rights to *The Vampire Lestat*, which it issued as a 12-part series. A similar release of *Interview with the Vampire* and *The Queen of the Damned* followed in 1991 (though Innovation unfortunately folded before the final issue of *The Queen of the Damned* could be released). Her short story "The Master of Rampling Gate"

was also issued in 1991. Innovation brought together one of the finest teams in comic book art to produce the three. Innovation also released three issues of *The Vampire Companion*, a fanzine in comic book format, which included stories about Rice's vampire books, Innovation's artists, and the process of producing the comic adaptations.

In 1976, Paramount bought the rights to *Interview with the Vampire*. The rights had a ten-year option, which expired in 1986. The rights reverted to Rice and she, in turn, sold them to Lorimar along with the rights to *The Vampire Lestat* and *The Queen of the Damned*. Lorimar sold its rights to *Interview with the Vampire* to Warner Bros., which then passed them on to Geffen Pictures. In 1993, Geffen announced that it would begin the filming under Neil Jordan's direction. The studio signed Tom Cruise to play Lestat and Brad Pitt to play Louis, the vampire who is interviewed in the story. Rice, who had earlier envisioned Rutger Hauer as the perfect Lestat, reacted emotionally to the choice of Cruise, whom she saw as devoid of the androgyny so definitive of her favorite vampire character. However, when she finally previewed the film in 1994, she retracted all she had said and praised Cruise for his success in bringing Lestat to the screen. *Interview with the Vampire* went on to be one of the largest-grossing films of the decade.

Everyone believed that, in spite of Rice's ending the Lestat stories, he and his fellow vampires would remain a popular reference point for the vampire community for many years to come. *Interview with the Vampire* has remained in print and went on to become one of the best-selling vampire books of all time (second only to *Dracula*) and was translated into a number of foreign languages. A second period of intense attention on her vampire universe

> Everyone believed that, in spite of Rice's ending the Lestat stories, he and his fellow vampires would remain a popular reference point for the vampire community for many years to come.

began to manifest in 1998, when two new novels, *The Vampire Armand* and *Pandora* appeared. They were quickly followed by *Vittorio the Vampire* (1999), *Merrick* (2000), *Blood and Gold* (2001), *Blackwood Farm* (2002), and *Blood Canticle* (2003). The last two novels brought both *The Vampire Chronicles* series and the *Lives of the Mayfair Witches* series to a culmination.

Even as she was finishing what would appear to be the novels bringing the vampire storing to a fitting endpoint, Rice was undergoing a period of intense religious ferment, which included a renewed faith in Christ and active membership in the Roman Catholic Church (beginning in 1998). In 2000, she quietly saw to the disbanding of Anne Rice's Vampire Lestat Fan Club and the discontinuance of its annual Halloween parties. In 2004, she announced her return to the Catholic faith to her fans and the general public, followed the next year by a new novel, *Christ the Lord, Out of Egypt*, the first of a trilogy on the life of Christ. Several years later, she discussed her religious pilgrimage in the autobiographical *Called Out of Darkness: A Spiritual Confession* (2008).

Even as Rice refocused her attention on religious themes, her singular role in the vampire community at the beginning of the new century was challenged by a new author, Stephenie Meyer, who produced a set of best selling books aimed at a younger audience—*Twilight* (2005), *New Moon* (2006), *Eclipse* (2007), and *Breaking Dawn* (2008)—each of which was soon translated into multiple languages. The novels were immediately followed by a set of top-grossing movies.

Meanwhile, Rice also made a very public move away from New Orleans, where she had been a very active participant in the city's political and economic life, in 2004. She sold the last of her property holding prior to the disaster of Hurricane Katrina. She quickly emerged as an advocate of relief to those hurt by the flooding and assistance for rebuilding. As part of her effort, she gave her blessing to some of the leaders in the former fan club to reopen it and again begin holding the annual Halloween event. She stayed away from any return to the vampire world she had created for more than a decade, but finally in 2014, she again made public her reconnection with her main character, Lestat, with the release of the first of three novels that would continue *The Vampire Chronicles*: *Prince Lestat* (2014). It would be followed with *Prince Lestat and the Realms of Atlantis* (2016) and *Blood Communion: A Tale of Prince Lestat* (2018).

For some 12 years (2005–2017), Rice employed an assistant, Becket Ghioto. In 2014, Ghioto issued a self-published set of novels, *The Blood Vivicanti* series. The Blood Vivicanti, who reside in the quiet mountain village of Idyllville, are a new breed of blood drinkers who eat memories. Rice is listed as the cocreator of the series. After leaving Rice's employment, Ghioto also issued *Anne Rice's Vampire Chronicles: An Alphabettery* (2018), an encyclopedic work focused upon the characters, locations, and subjects covered by *The Vampire Chronicles*. It supersedes the earlier reference work by Katherine Ramsland.

Rice's vampire writings include *The Vampire Chronicles* series (in order of appearance)

- *Interview with the Vampire* (1976)
- "Interlude with the Undead" *Playboy* (January 1979)
- *The Vampire Lestat* (1985)
- *The Queen of the Damned* (1988)
- *The Tale of the Body Thief* (1992)
- *Memnoch the Devil* (1995)
- *The Vampire Armand* (1998)
- *Merrick* (2000)
- *Blood and Gold* (2001)
- *Blackwood Farm* (2002)

- *Blood Canticle* (2003)
- *Interview with the Vampire: Claudia's Story* (graphic novel, 2012)
- *Prince Lestat* (2014)
- *Prince Lestat and the Realms of Atlantis* (2016)
- *Blood Communion: A Tale of Prince Lestat* (2018)
- *New Tales of the Vampires* series:
- *Pandora* (1998)
- *Vittorio the Vampire* (1999)

Other vampire books by Rice:

- "The Master of Rampling Gate." *Redbook* (February 1984)

By Becket Ghioto:

- *The Blood Vivicanti: Part 1. Mary Paige* (2013)
- *The Blood Vivicanti: Part 2. Wyn* (2013)
- *The Blood Vivicanti: Part 3. Theo* (2013)
- *The Blood Vivicanti: Part 4. The Origin Blood* (2014)
- *The Blood Vivicanti: Part 5. Lowen the Dark Man* (2014)
- *The Blood Vivicanti: Part 6. The Locomotive Deadyards* (2014)

Interview with the Vampire

Interview with the Vampire, the first vampire novel by Anne Rice, appeared in 1976. As sequels were produced in the late 1980s, it became known as the first volume of a saga, *The Vampire Chronicles*. In 1994, a movie based upon it starring Tom Cruise, Brad Pitt, Kirsten Dunst, and Antonio Banderas became one of the largest-grossing films of that year. The book introduced one of the most important contemporary vampire characters, Lestat de Lioncourt, and went on to become the second-best selling vampire novel of all time, second only to Bram Stoker's *Dracula*. The novel is presented as a story within a story. Louis (Pitt), a 200-year-old vampire, met with a journalist to tell his story and try to prove the truth of his tale. Louis's story began when he became a vampire

(Left to right) Sara Stockbridge, Kirsten Dunst, Brad Pitt, and Antonio Banderas in 1994's Interview with the Vampire, based on the first Anne Rice book in the "Vampire Chronicles" series.

in colonial Louisiana. In the midst of a period of despair, he was found by Lestat (Cruise), a vampire who had come to Louisiana from France. Once changed, the two lived at Louis's plantation outside New Orleans until the slaves figured out that their master had become a creature of the night and drove them away. They then established themselves in the city, where Lestat indulged himself and Louis worried about killing humans in order to survive.

A short time later, the pair was joined by Claudia (Dunst), a five-year-old orphan child whom Louis made into a vampire. Seven years afterward, resentful that she had been trapped in the body of a child, Claudia attempted to kill Lestat, and she and Louis left for Europe. In Paris, they encountered a group of vampires who operated out of a theater, using the facilities as their home and the draw from the shows as income. Louis was very

much impressed with one of their number, Armand (Banderas). Afraid of being abandoned, Claudia demanded that Louis create a vampire out of a childless woman, Madeleine, to act as Claudia's surrogate mother.

All was fine until the group at the Theatre of the Vampires discovered that Claudia had attempted and nearly succeeded in killing their benefactor Lestat, who had provided them with the theater. They kidnapped Louis, Claudia, and Madeleine and locked the two females in a room, where they were consumed in the morning sun. Louis was confined to a coffin but released by Armand. In retaliation, he set fire to the theater and killed most of the vampires. He then left with Armand and had a meeting with Lestat in New Orleans.

Interview with the Vampire explores numerous themes relevant to the vampire myth:

sexuality in general and homosexuality in particular, the role of community in vampiric existence, the nature of vampirism in a secular age, and the morality of murder. All of the strong characters in the book are male, with the exception of the child, Claudia. The vampires, however, live in a communal setting quite distinct from most previous vampires, who were overwhelmingly loners. Rice's vampires have no problem with religious symbols and know nothing of God or a sacred space. Lestat, who emerges from the novel as the most appealing character, has little thought of taking life if that is the way he will survive. Again, with the exception of Claudia, the main characters in *Interview with the Vampire* would reappear multiple times in the succeeding novels.

The novel has been translated into a number of languages, including most of the European languages, Chinese, and Japanese. It has been reproduced on cassette tape and CD and in a number of deluxe and souvenir editions. Fans of the book and its sequels gathered annually through the 1990s in New Orleans for a Halloween party put on by Anne Rice's Vampire Lestat Fan Club.

The Queen of the Damned

The Queen of the Damned is the title of the third volume in Anne Rice's *The Vampire Chronicles* series and the designation of Akasha, the original vampire who ruled as a queen in ancient Egypt more than six millennia ago. Although Akasha first appears in *The Vampire Lestat* (1985), she became the subject of *The Queen of the Damned* (1988), which recounts the story of the origin of Rice's vampires and the return of the queen in 1985 with a grandiose scheme to take over the world.

Akasha ruled beside her weaker husband, Enkil, and became known for her lack of tolerance of those who thought differently than she did. While she showed some enlightened

rulings, she also had a dark side, expressed in her desire to experience the supernatural. In that endeavor, she had two young, female witches brought to her court to demonstrate their contact with the spirit world. The antics of the spirit Amel caused the pair to receive some severe punishments.

Mad at Akasha, Amel attacked Khayman, the court's chief steward, and the priests were unable to exorcise his dwelling. Meanwhile, those opposed to Akasha and Enkil assassinated the pair. As she lay bleeding, Akasha's soul escaped but was seized by Amel. Binding himself to her soul, Amel then entered her body, with which he fused, thus creating a new entity and the first vampire. Akasha's body healed almost immediately, and she shared her blood (and, as it turned out, the presence of Amel) with Enkil. He also healed miraculously.

They sought a cure to their vampiric condition, but the witches informed them that the only way they could end the possession by Amel was to kill themselves. They discovered that Amel

Rhythm and blues singer Aaliyah plays Akasha in the 2002 film The Queen of the Damned.

had a tremendous thirst. They killed many and, in the process, created additional vampires. Then, they noticed that as the number of vampires increased, their hunger decreased, and eventually, they had no need for blood at all. Once they reached that state, they remained together but as living statues. In this condition, they gained legendary status in the vampire community as "those who must be kept." They were preserved and protected by vampire guardians, who were aware that somehow, their existence was dependent upon the two.

> Then, in 1985, Akasha was awakened by Lestat's music. She sucked the life out of Enkil and initiated her plan of world domination.

The tie between Akasha and Enkil and all other vampires was made abundantly clear when suddenly, several millennia ago, vampires everywhere were severely burned, many fatally. When one new vampire, Marius, was sent to Egypt, he discovered that the person whose responsibility it was to guard the pair had grown tired of his job and placed them in the sun. Akasha begged Marius to take her to Europe. He then became the new guardian, and she became the impersonal observer of the world, projecting her consciousness from her body and utilizing the eyes of others, both vampires and mortals.

Over the years, she was visited by only a few outsiders. Marius had allowed his new love, Pandora, to drink from Akasha. At another time, while visiting Marius, Lestat made his way to the underground shrine room where the two were located. He awakened Akasha, and they embraced and exchanged blood. Suddenly, Enkil awoke and separated them. Only Marius's appearance saved Lestat from being killed.

Then, in 1985, Akasha was awakened by Lestat's music. She sucked the life out of Enkil and initiated her plan of world domination. She set out to destroy most of the males (both mortal and vampire) and to establish an Eden in which the women, but especially Akasha herself, would reign. Along the way, she invited

Lestat to join her and took him on one of her killing sprees. However, she targeted the two witches who had been the instrument leading to her vampirism. Maharet and Mekare were present at a gathering of vampires in Sonoma, California, strategizing about the deaths Akasha had caused. When Akasha appeared but before she could act, Mekare pushed her through a glass wall. She was decapitated, and Maharet moved immediately to isolate the heart and brain of the fallen queen. Both were passed to Mekare, who quickly devoured them. In the eating of Akasha's organs, the essence of Amel passed to Mekare, and she became the nexus of the life force flowing through the vampire community. With Akasha destroyed, undead life could return to some degree of normalcy.

The Queen of the Damned was brought to the screen in 2002 in a production with Stuart Townsend as Lestat and Akasha played by rhythm and blues singer Aaliyah. Already possessed of a strong following as a singer, this movie was seen as a major step in turning her into a major movie star. Unfortunately, she died in a plane crash before the movie was released. Though far behind *Interview with the Vampire* in appeal, the movie went on to become one of the top 20 vampire films in gross receipts.

Armand

Armand is a 400-year-old, teenaged-looking vampire and a major character in *The Vampire Chronicles* series of Anne Rice. He is introduced in *Interview with the Vampire* where in the years immediately prior to the French Revolution, he headed a group of vampires who performed at the Theatre of the Vampires in Paris. He first appeared on the streets of Paris after learning of the presence of fellow vampires Louis and Claudia in the city. He broke up a fight between Louis and one of the other vampires, whom he had sent to present the two with an invitation to the theater. After the performance the following evening, he and Louis, who were strongly attracted to each other, had a conversation concerning God and the meaning of existence, during which Louis was forced to confront the meaninglessness of life.

Louis also had to deal with Claudia's jealousy over his obvious infatuation with Armand and her own dilemma of being trapped in the body of a child. His acknowledgment of his feelings for Armand freed him to create a companion for Claudia in the older woman Madeleine, a dollmaker. Armand's feelings for him saved Louis's life when he, Madeleine, and Claudia were taken captive by the Parisian vampires who executed Claudia and Madeleine. The vampires had confined Louis in a coffin, but Armand released him. In return for the favor, an angry Louis warned Armand that he was about to vent his anger. Thus, Armand escaped when Louis burned the theater down, killing the vampires caught in its confines.

In the second volume of the *Chronicles* series, *The Vampire Lestat*, Armand's background is laid out. He was born in southern Russia, but as a child, his family was taken prisoner by Tartars and sold into slavery in Constantinople. He was bought by a vampire named Marius and taken to Venice. Marius used him as a model for a painting, *The Temptation of Amedeo*. Armand was only 17 years old when Marius made him a vampire. Through the centuries, he retained his youthful appearance with auburn hair, brown eyes, and a beautiful face. When Marius's home was invaded by a group of Satanists, Armand was inducted into their coven and went on to become an accomplished Satanist leader. He moved out across Europe, gathering potential Satanists into new covens. Eventually, he settled in Paris as the head of a coven. Over the years, he had fed regularly and perfected a technique of drawing people with a death wish to him but kept several matters to himself. He never made another

vampire. He also had lost (or never possessed) any belief in God or Satan.

He had been in Paris for a century when Lestat arrived and, as a new vampire, encountered Armand and his coven. Attempts to bring Lestat into the coven resulted in its being destroyed and most of their number being killed. Eventually, Lestat bought and gave them the theater; hence, when they discovered that Claudia had attempted to kill Lestat, they were particularly incensed.

After Louis burned the theater down, he and Armand traveled the world together. They lived together in New York City for many years, only returning to New Orleans in the mid-1970s. A short time later, they went their separate ways.

After Louis gave the interview that became the book *Interview with the Vampire*, Dan-

Antonio Banderas played Armand, a 400-year-old vampire, in Interview with the Vampire.

iel Molloy, the interviewer, came to New Orleans looking for Lestat but found Armand instead. He developed a relationship with Armand but was frustrated, as Armand would come and go at will, leaving Daniel begging Armand to give him the Dark Gift (transformation into a vampire). Through Daniel, Armand learned about the twentieth century and finally decided to leave his old ways behind. He became obsessed with new technological gadgets from food blenders to television. He quickly made a fortune and built a fantasy shopping entertainment complex near Miami called the Night Island.

> In 1985, a crisis occurred in the vampire community. Around the world, vampires were being killed. It was the work of Akasha, the awakened primal vampire....

While he refused to make Daniel a vampire, Armand did give Daniel an amulet that contained a vial of his blood. If he was ever in danger from other vampires, he was to break the vial and drink it. They would feel Armand's power and stay away from him. However, Armand's continued refusal to make him a vampire was a constant source of conflict. Daniel left and allowed his life to degenerate. Finally, in 1985, Armand reconnected with his disparate, young lover.

In 1985, a crisis occurred in the vampire community. Around the world, vampires were being killed. It was the work of Akasha, the awakened primal vampire, but Armand was not yet aware of her activity. Through his clairvoyance, Daniel perceived Akasha as the name of the new evil. In the face of the threatening situation, Armand broke down and made Daniel a vampire, the only time he had ever transformed anyone.

After the final confrontation with Akasha, the surviving vampires gathered at Night Island to recoup, but then, they went their separate ways. Several years later, Armand went to New Orleans to meet Lestat, about whom he had developed some concern. He met his old friend

as Lestat was about to embark on his adventure into heaven and hell. He was still around when Lestat returned. Lestat again destroyed Armand's worldview with his story of the great beyond. The religious feelings that welled up inside him led him to commit suicide by exposure to the sun. Several other vampires imitated his action.

In the vampire world, dying is often not the end, and such was the case with Armand. In Rice's later book *The Vampire Armand*, we learn that his suicide attempt was a failure, though he was badly burned in the process. He is eventually rescued by two children, Benji and Sybelle, whom he came to love and with whom he resided. To his chagrin, Marius turned the pair into vampires, blunting Armand's hope that they have a full, normal life.

de Lioncourt, Lestat

Lestat de Lioncourt was the central character in *The Vampire Chronicles* series, several novels by Anne Rice that became key works in the revival of interest in vampires in the 1990s. In the first two novels treating Lestat, Rice gave a detailed description of his two centuries of existence, other than the several decades of childhood and youth before he became a vampire. His physical appearance was summarized in the opening paragraphs of her second vampire book, *The Vampire Lestat* (1985). He was six feet tall with thick, blond hair. His eyes were gray (not red) and easily picked up blue or violet from the environment. He had a very expressive face capable of conveying his wide range of strong, even exaggerated, emotions, with a mouth that seemed to be a little too big for his face. His skin was white and had a slightly reflective quality. It changed noticeably while he was feeding. When he was hungry, his skin was tight, with his veins protruding.

After feeding, it appeared more normal, and Lestat had little trouble passing among "normal" humans. The most striking aspect of his physical appearance was his fingernails, which looked like glass.

Elsewhere, Rice revealed that Lestat, like all vampires, experienced a significant increase in strength from his human form. He developed a pair of caninelike fangs. He had some unusual abilities, both telepathic force and hypnotic power, but could not change into animal forms (a bat or wolf, for instance). He could still see himself in a mirror but lost the ability to engage in normal human sex and, hence, could not procreate. He normally slept in a coffin. An atheist before his transformation, Lestat had no problem with holy symbols or being in consecrated places. Traditionally, sunlight and fire hurt vampires, but Lestat communicated his doubts that they could ultimately kill him. He even believed that a stake in the heart had little effect.

> Elsewhere, Rice revealed that Lestat, like all vampires, experienced a significant increase in strength from his human form. He developed a pair of caninelike fangs.

Lestat's Life: When Lestat first appeared in *Interview with the Vampire* (1976), he was in New Orleans. However, his story really began (in *The Vampire Lestat*) in France around 1760 during the reign of Louis XVI and Marie Antoinette. Lestat was about 20 years old, the youngest son in a royal family whose estate was in the Auvergne, in rural France. The family was relatively poor and had no money for their sons to attain proper vocational training. Lestat wanted to escape this life and go to Paris. Shortly after finally realizing his dream, he was kidnapped from his sleeping quarters by a vampire named Magnus. Magnus turned Lestat into a vampire and then forced him to oversee the elder vampire's apparent death. In return, Lestat inherited Magnus's fortune.

The first phase of Lestat's vampiric existence centered in Paris. It included a visit by his dying mother, Gabrielle, whom he turned into a vampire. She took to the nocturnal life well, and together, they challenged the vampire community of Paris, which had trouble accepting their new way of integrating into human life. After this intense encounter, they traveled around Europe as Lestat sought a senior vampire named Marius. Meanwhile, France was rising in revolt (1789). Lestat's family estate was mobbed and his brothers killed. His father escaped to New Orleans. He and his mother parted, and he buried himself in the ground to rest.

A short time later, Marius found and revived him and related the account of the beginnings of their lineage of vampirism. Marius's account took Lestat back into ancient Egypt, long before the first pyramid. Egypt was ruled by a couple, Akasha and Enkil. For the good of their people, they were forced to encounter a demon and became vampires. Marius had brought them out of Egypt to save them from total destruction. They were alive but sat motionless. Lestat had a private encounter with the pair, including sharing blood with Akasha, who moved for the first time in several centuries.

Lestat then left Marius and sailed to Louisiana in 1789. In New Orleans, he met Louis, whom he turned into a vampire; he wanted Louis's plantation as a home for his father. Lestat also found Claudia, a child whom he turned into a vampire. She could grow mentally but not physically, and her situation became the focus of intense conflict. After several decades of adventures and fighting, Louis and Claudia attempted to kill Lestat.

Lestat was hurt but not killed. He could not get help from the old vampire community in Paris and lived out the nineteenth century in seclusion. In 1929, he buried himself again and had no motivation to awaken until 1984, when he was attracted by the sounds of a rock band, Satan's Night Out. He arose and introduced himself to the group. They handed him a copy of *Interview with a Vampire*, Louis's story of their life together. He reacted by writing his own autobiography, published as *The Vampire Lestat*, the same name adopted by the band. Concurrently, he found success as a rock idol. As a rock performer, he could appear in public as a vampire; people accepted it as part of his public persona.

The sound of Lestat the rocker soon drifted into the frozen northland, where Marius had eventually taken Akasha and Enkil. In 1985, Akasha awoke in response to the music. She killed Enkil and left the sanctuary to dominate the world and create a new Eden, inhabited primarily by a select group of females. She intended to kill off most of the males, though Lestat was a favored individual. She initiated the killing almost immediately, but as Halloween approached, her activity increased.

Lestat had a concert set for San Francisco. Many of the living vampires headed for the concert. After the concert, Akasha forced Lestat to accompany her on one of her massacres. They then journeyed to Sonoma County, California, for what became a final confrontation. Akasha was killed, and her threat ended. The surviving vampires, including Lestat, went to Miami for some rest and relaxation.

Akasha was killed, and her threat ended. The surviving vampires, including Lestat, went to Miami for some rest and relaxation.

In the meantime, Lestat had learned of one David Talbot, the aging leader of the occult research group the Talamasca. His organization had taken an interest in vampires and had sent a researcher to New Orleans to research the truth of the story recounted by Louis in *Interview with the Vampire*. Lestat traveled to London to meet Talbot, and the unusual pair became friends, though Talbot refused Lestat's offer to become a vampire. While developing his relationship with Talbot, Lestat received an offer from an unusual individual, Raglan James, who wanted to swap bodies with Lestat. Talbot advised against it, but Lestat was intrigued with James and agreed to a temporary exchange. Too late, he learned that James planned to assume his identity and life.

Lestat enlisted Talbot's assistance to track James, and once they found him, they devised a scheme to force a new transfer. In the process, Lestat got his body back, and Talbot found himself in James's body. In his new, relatively young body, Talbot reconsidered Lestat's offer of a vampire's life. The widely traveled Lestat's next adventure took him into the supernatural realms of heaven and hell. Guided by the devil, he found himself confronting the nature of evil, the significance of Christ's life, death, and resurrection, and the often bloody history of the church. He traveled backward in time to watch Christ's passion and crucifixion, including the legendary moment when a young woman, Veronica, wiped the sweat from Christ's face and his visage miraculously appeared on her veil. Lestat responded by drinking Christ's blood, stealing the veil, and fleeing back to Earth. Memnoch, the devil, tried to prevent him and, in their struggle, Lestat lost his left eye.

Lestat returned to Earth where, in Manhattan, he met up with several of his old acquaintances. Talbot listened to him recount the story of his adventure. Dora, the daughter of one of his victims who happened to be a televangelist, took the veil and showed it to her audience as a miraculous sign. Lestat eventually found his way back to New Orleans, where he encountered one of the ancient vampires who returned the eye he had lost. He knew that his adventure had been real, but he could not explain the meaning of it all.

As Lestat's story continued in Rice's *The Vampire Chronicles* series, the books themselves became part of the vampire mythology. The first book, *Interview with the Vampire*, was published as Louis's memoirs of Lestat. Lestat then countered with his version of the story in *The Vampire Lestat*, his "autobiography." In the third volume, *The Queen of the Damned* (1988), the modern Lestat had to deal with the situation of becoming a public figure when his story became known. *The Tale of the Body Thief* (1992) recounted the story of his adventure with Raglan James and *Memnoch the Devil* of his adventures in the supernatural realms. After *Memnoch*, Rice announced that he had left her and that she would not, at least in the near future, be writing about him again.

As a character, Lestat caught the imagination of a new generation of vampire enthusiasts in the 1990s. He successfully combined the popular image of the vampire derived from books and movies (e.g., Lord Ruthven and Dracula) and his own distinct personality. Rice described that uniqueness in terms of androgyny, implying the movement away from culture-bound gender designations and the development of a whole personality that combines strong elements of female and male traits regardless of physiology. In practice, given the intense gender assignments common in Western culture, androgyny is often expressed by a person adopting obvious attributes or expressions of the other sex. Thus, women may adopt male hairstyles, and men may wear feminine dress and makeup. More significantly, androgyny may lead people to develop aspects of their personality that have generally been assigned by the culture to the other sex. Thus, women may develop their assertiveness and men their ability to express their feelings. The current gothic subculture has taken the lead in living out an androgynous lifestyle, which is largely owed to Lestat.

Although emphasizing Lestat's androgynous nature, Lestat fans have also emphasized their attraction to his embodiment of typically male attributes. He is a man of strong will and action. He lifted himself up by his own bootstraps; given only a minimal knowledge by his vampiric creator, he taught himself to be a vampire. His discoveries left him with little need of traditions, and he made his own way in the world according to his own rules. "My strength, my refusal to give up, those are the only components of my heart and soul which I can truly identify," he definitively states in *The Tale of the Body Thief*. He faced the problem of his vampiric situation, a condition for which he did not ask and which imposed a bloodthirst upon him. He had to kill to survive, which was evil by human standards. His evolved ethic, though infused with self-interest, led to the choice to feed on the worst of humankind and thus find some moral justification in the necessary search for food.

> As Lestat's story continued in Rices *The Vampire Chronicles* series, the books themselves became part of the vampire mythology.

Lestat in the 1990s: Lestat's central role in the 1990s revival of interest in vampires is illustrated by the numerous places he can be found. He inspired the creation of a gothic rock band, Lestat; a role-playing game, *Vampire: The Masquerade*; and Anne Rice's Vampire Lestat Fan Club. His story has appeared on audiotape and in comic books, has been translated into a number of languages (from Romanian to Japanese), and was finally brought to the motion picture screen in 1994.

Lestat in the Twenty-first Century: After *Memnoch*, Rice turned her attention to developing the story of other vampires such as Armand, Pandora, and Vittorio. While Lestat was never far from the storyline, he returned to the center of attention in *Blood Canticle* (2003). This book also integrated his story with that of the Mayfairs, a family of witches about which Rice had written several books. In the story, Mona Mayfair is in love with Lestat's close friend, the vampire Tarquin "Quinn" Black-

Tom Cruise is the vampire Lestat in Interview with the Vampire.

wood. She is, however, dying of a wasting disease. In what she believes is her last hour, she visits her lover's home, where Lestat turns her into a vampire. He also falls in love with the already married Rowan Mayfair.

As a vampire, Mona has great strength and manifests anger over the child she bore that had caused her illness. The child is a Taltos, a member of a supernatural race that once inhabited parts of the Scottish Highlands. The child has disappeared, and Lestat promises to find it if it is still alive. It is finally found on a remote island, where the Taltos now reside. As the story concludes, the remaining Taltos move to New Orleans, where Rowan's husband runs a large medical center and they can survive in a relatively happy family situation. Mona and Quinn are able to resume their relationship. In the end, Rowan asks Lestat to turn her, but he refuses.

Blood Canticle was the last of the vampire novels written by Rice, but Lestat lived on in the cinema (with *The Queen of the Damned* appearing in 2002) and through musician Elton John, who wrote the music for the 2006 Broad-

way production of *Lestat the Musical.* Then, after a break from writing about Lestat, Rice gave him new life in the three volumes of *The Vampire Chronicles* series that starred Prince Lestat.

Lestat, Prince

More than a decade after leaving New Orleans and its vampires behind, Anne Rice once again turned her attention to the sanguinarian world she had created and to its most recognized character, the vampire Lestat. Eleven years after the last novel of *The Vampire Chronicles* series was released, she released *Prince Lestat* (2014), which picked up the storyline most clearly from *The Queen of the Damned* (1988) and reintroduced many of the characters from the series.

As the vampires are re-encountered, their world is facing some degree of chaos. The number of vampires has radically increased, and in response, older vampires turning on their younger cohorts and massacres have become the order of the day. These widespread events seem to originate with a single source, a voice commanding the indiscriminate killings. Some voices of sanity, including characters introduced in the older novels, appear: Louis de Pointe du Lac; Armand, Mekare, and Maharet, Pandora, and Flavius; David Talbot; and Marius. Together, they launch a search for the nature of the voice that pushes their actions and attempt to designate a leader who can unite them and bring an end to the present destructive course of action.

Their search for the voice leads to a powerful spirit entity named Amel (who first, however briefly, appeared in the novel *The Vampire Lestat* [1985]). He is seen as the very essence of vampirism, the real source of a vampire's power. Briefly fused with Lestat, he separated and moved into a body especially created for him. Amel now resides in the body of Mekare, and as he begins calling out to the other vampires, he especially instructs the vampire Roshamandes to destroy Maharet and Mekare and become the new bearer of the sacred core of vampirism. While holding Mekare captive, Roshamandes loses his confrontation with the newly formed vampire government, led by its designated leader, Prince Lestat. Mekare emerges from this confrontation as the new sacred core.

> The number of vampires has radically increased, and in response, older vampires turning on their younger cohorts and massacres have become the order of the day.

The story continues in *Prince Lestat and the Realms of Atlantis* (2016), in which Lestat is having visions of a ruined city. He and the vampire spirit entity Amel search for the meaning of the visions. That search leads them to outer space, to a distinct star named Brevena, and to an extraterrestrial race, the Replinoids. The Replinoids are a created race. Amel, it appears, was once a human but was turned Replinoid by the Brevenans and sent back to Earth, where he established and ruled over the city of Atlantis. The revelation of the existence of the Replinoids and their history will lead to a new alignment between Lestat, the vampire community, and the extraterrestrials.

In the final volume of the most recent of *The Vampire Chronicles, Blood Communion* (2018), Prince Lestat recounts his story of the confrontations with the vampire Roshamandes, his relative success in ruling the emerging vampire community, and the task of uniting them into something resembling a family tribe. Telling the story is an act of self-exploration for Lestat, and he brings to the foreground his own personal goals both as an individual and in his new princely role.

~ *Twilight by Stephenie Meyer* ~

Cullen, Edward

Edward Cullen, whose full name is Edward Anthony Masen Cullen, is Stephenie Meyer's vampire hero throughout her book series *Twilight*. Edward is described as lanky; six feet, two inches in height; and boyish looking, with bronze, untidy hair and green eyes that turn gold/black when he becomes a vampire. Meyer describes Edward as a "beautiful boy" with a "dazzling face," "flawless lips," and "perfectly ultra white teeth" and compares him to the mythical Greek god Adonis. On Meyer's website, she said that Charlotte Brontë's Edward Rochester (*Jane Eyre*) and Jane Austen's Edward Ferrars (*Sense and Sensibility*) were the characters that led her to the name Edward.

Before he became a vampire, Edward was the biological son of Elizabeth and Edward Masen, a successful lawyer. Edward was born on June 20, 1901, and grew up in a moderately wealthy family in Chicago; by 1918, his fairly happy life vanished when the influenza epidemic claimed the lives of both his parents. Edward became stricken as well, but his attending physician, Dr. Carlisle Cullen, saved his life by changing him into a vampire. Edward subsequently became the "adopted son" of Carlisle and Esme Cullen and the brother to Alice and Emmett Cullen as well as to Rosalie and Jasper Hale. Edward has been to medical school twice (though he never practiced medicine), and he collects cars as a hobby and enjoys a wide range of music.

Edward is often described as very charming and polite. In fact, he retains some of the same mannerisms and outdated speech from his previous life in the early twentieth century.

Robert Pattinson played Edward Cullen in the Twilight Saga *vampire movies based on the books by Stephenie Meyer.*

As a vampire, he possesses superhuman speed, agility, and strength and is not able to sleep. His skin, according to Meyer, is "satin smooth, cool as stone" and sparkles like small diamonds when exposed to sunlight. Edward's vampire family renounces human blood on moral grounds and instead feeds off animals. Edward initially rebelled against this lifestyle, so from 1927 to 1931, he left Carlisle and Esme and limited his hunting of humans to those who were truly evil. His special ability to read other people's minds helped him to avoid killing innocent people for food, but after awhile, the taking of human lives—whether evil or innocent—weighed heavily upon Edward's conscience, and he returned to Esme and Carlisle and resumed their lifestyle.

Edward and his family first moved to Forks, Washington, in 1936. They traveled around frequently until they returned to Forks in 2003, and two years, later Edward met Isabella "Bella" Swan, a human female only 17 years old. Emotionally, Edward was stagnant or fossilized until Bella came into his life. He fell in love for the first time and was both attracted to Bella yet wanted to kill her. He fought this impulse every moment he was with Bella and became obsessed with her. Yet, Edward was very protective of Bella and put her safety and welfare before anything else. Although their vampire–human relationship had many obstacles, he married Bella on August 12, 2006, and fathered a half-human, half-vampire daughter through her.

As Edward's character develops through the *Twilight* series, he experiences many new emotions around Bella. He breaks off the relationship with her because he fears she is not safe around his vampire family and goes through a very dark, reclusive period. He even contemplates suicide. Once Edward and Bella reunite, he asks her to marry him. As his relationship with Bella deepens, he learns to control his thirst for her blood and is able (although somewhat reluctantly) to make love to her on their honeymoon. He also forms an uneasy alliance with Jacob Black, a Quileute Indian who has the ability to transform into a werewolf and whose ancestors were once enemies of the Cullens and other vampire families. In the movie *Twilight* and its sequels, Edward Cullen is played by British actor Robert Pattinson.

Meyer, Stephenie (1973–)

Stephenie Meyer is the author of the *Twilight* series, five novels about a teenage girl's romance with a vampire. The novels were published by Little, Brown and Company beginning with *Twilight* (2005) and followed by *New Moon* (2006), *Eclipse* (2007), and *Breaking Dawn* (2008). A fifth manuscript, *Midnight Sun*, was delayed for more than a decade, but it was finally completed and released in 2020. During this decade, she completed a novella about one of the *Twilight* series' lesser characters, *The Short Second Life of Bree Tanner*, and in celebration of the tenth anniversary of *Twilight* (2015), she issued an imaginative retelling of the story with the two main characters swapping their genders. The story revolves around 17-year-old Beaufort Swan moving to Forks, Washington, where he meets Edythe Cullen, seemingly just another high school student.

In 2011, Meyer also issued *The Twilight Saga: The Official Illustrated Guide*, which, as the name implies, was a reference book to the series, a valuable but now somewhat outdated volume in light of the publication of the more recent texts.

Stephenie Meyer was born on Christmas Eve 1973 in Hartford, Connecticut, although

Great success came to author Stephenie Meyer, whose Twilight *books have sold over 100 million copies and have been translated into nearly 40 languages around the world.*

her family moved to Phoenix, Arizona, when she was four years old. She was one of six children and was raised as a member of the Church of Jesus Christ of Latter-day Saints (commonly known as Mormons). She attended Brigham Young University as an English literature major and graduated in 1997. Meyer and her husband, Christian Patrick Meyer, were married in 1994; she was a homemaker and mother to three sons before she embarked upon her first book.

Meyer has said that she received her inspiration for *Twilight* on June 6, 2003, when she had a "very vivid dream" of an average girl and a young, attractive, male vampire having an intense conversation in the woods. That dream eventually became chapter 13, "Confessions," in *Twilight*. Meyer has stated that she had no interest in vampire literature prior to writing *Twilight* and hadn't even read Bram Stoker's *Dracula*. She has viewed only parts of the movies *Interview with the Vampire* and *The Lost Boys* since she generally avoids R-rated films as a follower of the Mormon faith.

Although Meyer doesn't write overtly Mormon literature, she has said that her religious upbringing has filtered into her stories. She avoids any type of sexual explicitness in her writing; in fact, her books' appeal lies in "their fine moral hygiene," according to *Time* magazine. "What makes Meyer's books so distinctive is that they're about the erotics of abstinence," the magazine explained. The theme of free agency or individual choice throughout her books also draws from Mormon doctrine.

Her science fiction novel *The Host* (2008) follows *Twilight's* themes of love and choice and also includes nonhuman creatures. *The Host* is set in the near future on Earth, which is inhabited by parasitic aliens who take over the bodies of humans and annihilate their hosts' personalities. After some years away from the *Twilight* storyline, she returned to it in 2020 and completed a new book, which she had been contemplating for over a decade, *Midnight Sun*, which retells the story of the Bella Swan–Edward Cullen romance from his perspective.

Swan, Isabella Marie "Bella"

Isabella Marie Swan, also known as Bella or Bells, is Stephenie Meyer's heroine and main narrator throughout *The Twilight Saga* series. Bella is described as slender; five feet, four inches in height; and fair skinned, with long, straight, dark brown hair, brown eyes, and a thin nose. On her website (www.StephenieMeyer.com), Meyer said that she named her female heroine Isabella because she loved the character "like a daughter" and always wanted to give that name to a daughter of her own.

Bella was born on September 13, 1987, and is the only child of Renee and Charlie Swan. She was born in Forks, Washington, and her parents divorced when she was six months old. Bella and her mother moved to Phoenix,

Bella Swan was brought to life on the screen by actress Kristen Stewart.

Arizona, and when Renee remarried Phil Dwyer, Bella moved back to Forks to be with her father.

Meyer describes Bella as extremely accident prone and clumsy. Bella avoids sports and dancing; she occasionally bites her fingernails and feels as if she doesn't "fit in" with any social group, although she easily makes friends with a few people in Forks. Meyer describes Bella as having a "quiet strength"; she is a bookworm who likes to cook and draw as well as take care of her parents by housekeeping and shopping. Like her vampire boyfriend, Edward Cullen, Bella is a loner and says she finds her "true place" only when she is transformed into a vampire and, thus, becomes a bona fide member of the Cullens and their extended family.

Bella's strongest quality is that her mind is closed to Edward's abilities to read her thoughts. This unusual skill—Bella is apparently the only human whose mind is beyond Edward's powers—later serves as a "shield" that she can extend to protect her child and others around her. She also has a penchant for danger and habitually stumbles into situations that put her own life at risk. When Edward breaks off the relationship with Bella in *New Moon*, she decides to deliberately place herself in danger just so she can "hear" his voice. Ironically, these risky situations bring Edward and Bella closer as he repeatedly saves her life and vows to protect her.

Bella's character experiences several changes as the *Twilight* series progresses. She graduates from high school, begins to assert her newfound adulthood, and gradually grows more confident about herself and her relationship with Edward. When she turns into a vampire in *Breaking Dawn*, she is no longer clumsy and discovers her own physical agility. Meyer has explained that although Bella is physically weaker than others, she eventually develops into one of the most powerful characters in *The Twilight Saga* series. In the movie *Twilight* and its sequels, Bella is played by actress Kristen Stewart.

Twilight Book Series

The *Twilight* series consists of six novels by Stephenie Meyer about a teenage romance between a human girl and her vampire boyfriend. The books were published by Little, Brown and Company beginning with the first, *Twilight*, in 2005, followed by *New Moon* (2006), *Eclipse* (2007), and *Breaking Dawn* (2008). A fifth manuscript, *Midnight Sun* (2008), was the expected companion novel to *Twilight* retelling the events from the perspective of the vampire Edward Cullen rather than that of Isabella Swan. Meyer completed only the first 12 chapters of *Midnight Sun* before it was illegally leaked online. The incomplete and unfinished manuscript was subsequently posted on Meyer's website, www.StephenieMeyer.com. After putting the completion of *Midnight Sun* on hold for more than a decade, Meyer announced in May 2020 that she had finally completed the book and that it would be released on August 4, 2020.

In 2012, Meyer released *The Short Second Life of Bree Tanner: An Eclipse Novella*, a short volume that detailed the life of a marginal character that had been briefly introduced in *Eclipse*. She is a member of the army of newborn vampires created by the vampire Victoria, which she designed to attack the Cullen family. When the Volturi arrive on the scene, Jane, a member of the elite Volturi guard, orders her death.

In an interview, Meyer has said that *Twilight* is loosely tied to Jane Austen's *Pride and Prejudice*, while *New Moon* was influenced by Shakespeare's *Romeo and Juliet*.

The *Twilight* series quickly rose to international fame and made record-breaking sales. *Publishers Weekly* reported book sales of $27.5 million from the four vampire novels in March 2009, which prompted the publication to crown Meyer as the "new queen" in children's literature, succeeding J. K. Rowling and her *Harry Potter* series. The first four books from *The Twilight Saga* have been translated into more than 20 languages and published in over 40 countries with over 42 million copies sold worldwide. The movie *Twilight* (2008) earned $69.6 million in its opening weekend in North America and over $191 million for its total domestic gross. The *Twilight* DVD sold over three million copies in its first day of release. Meyer's novels have also spawned close to 350 fan sites and inspired *Twilight*-related merchandise sales online.

Much of *Twilight* departs radically from nineteenth-century vampire literature. Meyer has explained that "almost all of the superstitions about vampire limitations are entirely false" in her novels. Her vampires are instead immune to the harmful effects of crosses, wooden stakes, holy water, garlic, and sunlight (which, rather than burning them up, makes their skin glitter like diamonds). *Twilight*'s vampires do have mirror reflections but also do not have fangs. Their pale skin is cold and icy to the touch, and they don't need sleep. They have extremely quick reflexes and can run fast and leap high, but they don't shapeshift into bats or fly. While Bram Stoker's Dracula has bad breath, Edward's is sweet. However, Meyer's vampires are sustained by blood alone, which lightens their eyes and flushes their skin slightly. They are immensely strong (especially during the first year of their vampire life), and their transformation makes them physically stunning and beautiful.

On the other hand, Meyer's vampires owe much of their characteristics to juvenile literature and good-guy vampires. In the *Twilight* series, the Cullens and their extended

> **Meyer has said that *Twilight* is loosely tied to Jane Austen's *Pride and Prejudice*, while *New Moon* was influenced by Shakespeare's *Romeo and Juliet*.**

family call themselves "vegetarians" in that they obtain blood from animals as opposed to killing humans. Meyer instead has placed the Cullens—especially Edward—in a situation where they continually fight against their vampirism yet retain the ability to make ethical choices. Like the vampire hero Saint Germain of Chelsea Quinn Yarbro's novels, Edward Cullen is a romantic hero immune to the traditional weapons of vampire hunters and prefers to cultivate a life of scholarship and culture and, like television's Angel, Edward was once a vicious killer before he chose to become a "vegetarian," who refrains from human blood. Edward also develops a romantic attachment to a woman, but in a sharp departure from vampire literary tradition, he seriously raises the issue of marriage and abstains from all sexual relations until marriage. The backstory of each of the Cullens was ultimately explored as the successive novels appeared.

> Meyer's vampires owe much of their characteristics to juvenile literature and good-guy vampires.

The subject of werewolves and vampires resurfaces in the *Twilight* books as well as the movie series. Initially, Meyer refers to the transformation of Quileute tribal members as werewolves, although at the end of *Breaking Dawn*, Edward reveals that the werewolves are actually shapeshifters who take the form of wolves. The vampires of the *Twilight* series outnumber the werewolves because werewolves can't change people by biting them but instead can transform only through a genetic link. They do not age as long as they regularly transform into wolves. Although vampires and werewolves are traditional enemies in Meyer's novels, they eventually agree to coexist peacefully.

Twilight, the first book in the series, introduces 17-year-old Isabella Swan (Bella), who is moving from Phoenix, Arizona, to be with her father in Forks, Washington. At Forks High School, Bella meets the handsome Edward Cullen and soon learns that he is a member of a vampire family that drinks animal rather than human blood. Edward and Bella fall in love, but the sadistic vampire tracker James tries to confront her and kill her. Bella is seriously wounded, but the Cullens rescue her and return her to Forks.

New Moon, the second book, begins when a minor incident at Bella's 18th birthday party convinces Edward that he and his family are endangering Bella's life. Edward leaves Bella, and the Cullens move out of Forks. Bella slips into a depression until she befriends Jacob Black, a Quileute Indian who has the ability to transform into a werewolf. Bella discovers that when she places herself in danger, she subconsciously hears Edward's voice. Meanwhile, James's mate Victoria returns to Forks to avenge his death, prompting Jacob and his wolf pack to protect Bella, but a misunderstanding occurs when Edward's sister Alice sees Bella dead in a vision. Edward is heartbroken and decides to commit suicide among the Volturi, a powerful vampire coven in Italy. Alice and Bella fly to Italy to stop Edward, and the couple is reunited. The Cullens move back to Forks and agree to turn Bella into a vampire in the near future.

Eclipse opens with a mysterious string of murders in Seattle. The vampire Victoria has created an army of "newborn" vampires to battle the Cullens and kill Bella. Meanwhile, Bella must choose between her love for Edward and her friendship with Jacob. She pressures Edward to have sex, and he refuses until they are married. Edward proposes to Bella and promises that he will turn her into a vampire when she marries him. Edward, the Cullens, and the wolf pack all join forces to fight the newborn vampires and protect Bella. Jacob is furious about Bella's decision to become a vampire, so he leaves Forks, and Bella agrees to marry Edward.

Breaking Dawn, the fourth book in the *Twilight* series, is divided into three books, two from Bella's perspective and one from Jacob's. Bella and Edward are now married, and he takes her to a remote island off the coast of Brazil for their honeymoon. However, Bella discovers that she is pregnant, and the child is growing rapidly. The couple rush home to the Cullens, and Bella nearly dies giving birth to her half-vampire, half-human daughter, Renesmee. Jacob rushes back to Forks and is angry when Edward transforms Bella into a vampire. Jacob involuntarily "imprints" on Renesmee, causing the child to be bonded to him for life. A vampire from another coven sees Renesmee and mistakes her for an "immortal child" (which violates vampire law), so the Volturi set out with an army of vampires to destroy her. The Cullens summon their extended family and friends of various vampire covens and, together with Jacob's wolf pack, they gather for the final showdown with the Volturi.

> Bella must choose between her love for Edward and her friendship with Jacob. She pressures Edward to have sex, and he refuses until they are married.

The final volume of the series, *Midnight Sun*, retells the story of the budding romance between Bella and Edward from the first volume in the series from Edward's point of view. In exploring Edward's reaction to the arrival of Bella in Forks, his complex emotional reaction is exposed and his backstory detailed. Of particular concern is the possibility that in pursuing his fascination with Bella, he might also do great harm to her.

Like *Buffy the Vampire Slayer*, the *Twilight* series began to gather scholarly comment as the movies made their impact on popular culture. By the end of the first decade of the twenty-first century, a number of books had appeared probing *Twilight*, but unlike *Buffy*, the interest in *Twilight* waned rather quickly and had largely disappeared by the middle of the following decade.

Twilight Movie Series

Several years after the completion of the four basic novels (2005–2008) defining and describing the vampiric *Twilight* world of author Stephenie Meyer, the novels were turned into five movies (2008–2012), the last novel *Breaking Dawn* being brought to the screen as two movies. The first novel had originally been in production by Paramount, but eventually, Summit Entertainment acquired the filming rights. The release of *Twilight* in 2008 and the income from its first day in the theaters (some $35 million) led immediately to Summit's launching production of *The Twilight Saga: New Moon* and acquiring the rights to the other books, *Eclipse* and *Breaking Dawn*. The movie series followed the success of the books and grossed over $3 billion from its global distribution.

Summit hired Catherine Hardwicke, then an up-and-coming director, to direct *Twilight*, and they simultaneously assured Meyer that it wanted to make an adaptation that remained faithful to the book's plot and characters and would allow her to have a role in the film's production. Much of the movie's success has been attributed to Hardwicke developing a relationship with Meyer and deciding that part of her role was to bring the book to life on the screen.

Chosen to star in *Twilight* and continuing through its four sequels were Kristen Stewart as Bella Swan, Robert Pattinson as the vampire Edward Cullen, and Taylor Lautner as the Native American werewolf Jacob Black. The storyline initially posits a human world unaware of the supernatural world that impinges upon them: the vampires, represented by the Cullen family, and the werewolves, which are an integral part of the local Native American people, the Quileute Nation. Both the werewolves and vampires emerge as good, even though they are natural enemies. In the larger vampire world, evil individuals also emerge as direct threats, and a ruling vampire authority, the Volturi, because of the authoritarian and arrogant manner of exercising their power, can become evil given the right context. Ideally, vampires should integrate into human society without revealing their true nature to their human associates. The storyline of *Twilight*, which begins with a vampire revealing himself to a human and then a Native American werewolf doing the same, is driven by personal intervampire conflicts, the antagonism between vampires and werewolves, the problems created by rogue vampires, and the impinging of the vampire authority on individuals—all of which provide the context for the love relationship to mature.

The *Twilight* series, both as novels and movies, met with mixed critical reviews. As a series aimed at teenagers, it was dismissed by many critics as juvenile and unworthy of adult attention. Meanwhile, vampire fans, however tolerant of authors deviating at points from the traditional description of the vampire set in the image of Dracula, often panned Stephenie Meyer's reworking of the vampire myth as inap-

Director, production designer, and screenwriter Catherine Hardwicke was selected to direct the first Twilight *movie.*

propriate and an abandonment of the horror realm. Simultaneously, supporters saw the novels as well written and most appropriate for the target audience. The movies were praised for their close adherence to the novel's storyline and character development.

The movies proved a box office success, by far the top-grossing vampire movies of all time and ranking with the top movies of all time. They provided ample competition for other top movies directed at a young adult audience, including those developed from comic book superheroes: Spiderman, the Avengers, Wonder Woman, and the like. While eclipsed in subsequent years, each of the *Twilight* movies broke income records as they appeared.

The Twilight Saga: Eclipse, for example, set a new record for biggest midnight opening in the domestic box office, surpassing the previous holder of the record, *The Twilight Saga: New Moon*. *The Twilight Saga: Eclipse* also set a record for the number of theaters in which it was released: 4,416. *The Twilight Saga: New Moon* had previously set records for advance ticket sales. Prior to the *Twilight* movies, the biggest midnight-opening records were held by *Harry Potter and the Half-Blood Prince*.

When released on DVD, all of the *Twilight* movies ranked in the top five in the number of sales in their first year on the market, with the first *Twilight* movie and *The Twilight Saga: Breaking Dawn, Part II* being the number-one DVD.

Twilight

The movie *Twilight* was based upon the first novel of the same name in the four- (now five-) book *Twilight* series by author Stephenie Meyer. The novel was adapted for the screen by Melissa Rosenberg (co-executive producer and writer on TV's *The O.C.* and *Dexter*) and directed by Catherine Hardwicke (*Lords of Dog-*

town and *The Nativity Story*). The movie stars Kristen Stewart as 17-year-old Isabella "Bella" Swan and Robert Pattinson as Bella's vampire boyfriend, Edward Cullen. The movie cost an estimated $37 million and was released in U.S. theaters by Summit Entertainment on November 21, 2008.

The movie *Twilight*, which follows the novel's basic storyline and essential themes, begins when teenager Bella Swan leaves Phoenix, Arizona, to move to the small town of Forks, Washington, to live with her father, Charlie. At Forks High School, she finds herself drawn to a mysterious classmate, Edward Cullen, who is a 108-year-old vampire but is physically only 17 years old. Although Edward discourages the romance at first, he soon falls in love with Bella and allows himself to be with her, knowing he can't live without her. Edward and his family are "vegetarian vampires" who feed off animal rather than human blood, but the arrival of three nomadic vampires, James, Victoria, and Laurent, puts Bella's life in danger because they feed off humans. Edward and his family—Alice, Carlisle, Esme, Jasper, Emmett, and Rosalie—attempt to save Bella by fighting to keep the lethal tracker James from killing her.

Meyer's novel was first optioned by Paramount Pictures's MTV Films in April 2004. According to director Hardwicke, Paramount's screenplay was substantially different from the original novel, with Bella introduced as a star athlete. When Paramount's rights to the project were about to expire, Summit Entertainment pursued it. Screenwriter Rosenberg attempted to stay as close to the book as possible but had to condense the dialogue and combine some of the characters. As Hardwicke explained, "So we kept to the [novel's] spirit. But there are changes." Meyer worked closely with Summit during the script's development. She drew up a list of rules for her vampire world that could not be changed and made her own suggestions on the script.

Producer and screenwriter Melissa Rosenberg adapted the Twilight Saga *books for the screen. She is also notable for her work on such programs as* The O.C. *and* Dexter.

In an MTV interview, Rosenberg explained that *Brokeback Mountain* (2005), the story of two gay cowboys who fall in love, actually provided her with a great model of poignancy and forbidden love between Bella and Edward. Rosenberg remained true to *Twilight*'s emotions and spirit but did change a number of the novel's key passages. The villainous vampires (Victoria, James, and Laurent) were introduced much earlier in the film than in the book. The movie's scenes of dinner at the Cullen house and Bella and Edward jumping out to the treetops were not in the book. Likewise, the novel's scene in the biology room where the students do blood typing and Bella faints is not in the movie. In the book, Bella reveals that she knows he is a vampire while in Edward's car driving back from Port Angeles, but the movie instead provides a more visually dynamic setting of a lush forest and meadow.

Principal photography for *Twilight* took 44 days. Portland and Vernonia, Oregon, served as locations for the Forks, Washington, setting of the novel, and St. Helens, Oregon, stood in for the small town of Port Angeles. A year after its initial release, the film grossed $191 million in North America and more than $384 million in worldwide box offices. In addition, more than nine million DVDs of *Twilight* have been sold. *Twilight* won five MTV Movie Awards as well as ten Teen Choice Awards. A graphic novel form of the movie is scheduled to be published by Yen Press, with Korean artist Young Kim creating the art and Meyer herself closely involved with the project.

> Portland and Vernonia, Oregon, served as locations for the Forks, Washington, setting of the novel, and St. Helens, Oregon, stood in for the small town of Port Angeles.

Twilight's first movie sequel, *The Twilight Saga: New Moon*, was released in U.S. theaters on November 20, 2009, and *The Twilight Saga: Eclipse* was released in the summer of 2010. *Breaking Dawn*, the fourth novel in the *Twilight* series, was adapted into a two-part movie, with releases in 2011 and 2012.

The Twilight Saga: New Moon

The movie *The Twilight Saga: New Moon* (2009) was based upon the second novel *New Moon* in Stephenie Meyer's four- (now five-) book the *Twilight* series. The novel was adapted for the screen by Melissa Rosenberg (co-executive producer and writer on TV's *The O.C.* and *Dexter*) and directed by Chris Weitz (*The Golden Compass*, *About a Boy*, and *American Pie*). Continuing their roles from the first *Twilight* movie, *The Twilight Saga: New Moon* stars Kristen Stewart as Isabella "Bella" Swan and Robert Pattinson as Bella's vampire boyfriend, Edward Cullen. It also features Taylor Lautner as Bella's Native American friend Jacob, Ashley

Greene as Edward's sister Alice, and Michael Sheen as Aro, the leader of the powerful Volturi, the overall authority in the international vampire community.

The movie begins when a minor incident at Bella's 18th birthday party convinces Edward that he is endangering her life. He leaves Bella, and she slips into a depression. However, Bella discovers that when she puts herself in danger, she can summon Edward's image. With the help of her childhood friend Jacob Black, a member of the Quileute tribe, Bella refurbishes a motorcycle for some risky adventures. Bella's budding relationship with Jacob helps her through her breakup with Edward, although she soon learns that Jacob has a supernatural secret of his own. When Bella wanders alone into a meadow, she confronts a deadly attacker. The intervention of a pack of large wolves saves her from a grisly fate. She later faces a potential deadly reunion with Edward, who has decided to commit suicide among the Volturi at their headquarters in Italy.

Summit Entertainment announced the production of *The Twilight Saga: New Moon* one day after *Twilight* opened in theaters on November 21, 2008. The movie closely followed Meyer's novel, with a few exceptions. The scenes leading to Edward's breakup with Bella were omitted as well as the couple's plane trip returning to Forks, Washington, after their encounter with the Volturi in Italy. Throughout much of the novel, Bella hears Edward's voice in her head when she is in danger, but in the movie, Edward is manifested as a visual presence or an "apparition." Screenwriter Rosenberg added motorcycles to a scene in which Bella decides to become reckless and approaches young men in Port Angeles, prompting Edward's first apparition to appear. For the overall visual "look" of the film, director Weitz moved away from the blue tones of *Twilight* and in-

Hey! Vampires can be nice, too! In Twilight, *a kindly family of vampires that only drinks animal—not human—blood tries to live in peace in human society.*

stead created a warm color palette of golden tones for *The Twilight Saga: New Moon.*

The Twilight Saga: New Moon's promotional material included tie-ins with Burger King Corp. and a line of jewelry and apparel through Nordstrom Stores. Burger King Corp. developed a multifaceted promotion surrounding *The Twilight Saga: New Moon* by offering aluminum water bottles featuring "Team Edward" and "Team Jacob" designs along with *The Twilight Saga: New Moon* paper crowns. Nordstrom Stores offered an exclusive fashion collection of T-shirts, hoodies, tanks, and jackets as well as gold-plated jewelry and keychains all

inspired by *The Twilight Saga: New Moon.* The larger effort of promoting *The Twilight Saga: New Moon* collectibles, from trading cards to clothing accessories and toys, was handled by the NECA (National Entertainment Collectibles Association), which set up a special page on Amazon to market its products.

The producers of *The Twilight Saga: New Moon* pursued an aggressive production schedule to meet the film's November 20, 2009, release. *The Twilight Saga: New Moon's* estimated budget was $50 million, and filming took place in Vancouver, British Columbia, Canada, and Montepulciano, Italy, from March 23 to May 30,

2009. *The Twilight Saga: New Moon* was released in U.S. theaters on November 20, 2009, and presold more online tickets through Fandango than any other movie title in its history. *The Twilight Saga: New Moon* grossed $142.8 million in North America during its opening weekend, far surpassing *Twilight*'s initial opening of $69.6 million. The movie's foreign box office grosses reached $124.1 million by the opening weekend. The website *Box Office Mojo* reported that within a week of its release, *The Twilight Saga: New Moon* had become the all-time top-grossing vampire movie in North America.

The Twilight Saga: Eclipse

Eclipse, the third novel in Stephenie Meyer's *Twilight* series, was issued in 2007 and immediately took its place on the best seller list. It was soon adapted as a movie, which was released in June 2010.

The story begins away from Forks, the small town in western Washington State where most of the series action is based. Bella Swan, the teenage girl around whom the plot focuses, is in Seattle, where a series of murders have come to her attention. Her beau, Edward Cullen, a vampire, hypothesized that the victims have been killed by a newborn vampire. Newborns have a strong thirst for blood, which they find next to impossible to control.

Attention to the deaths is interrupted by Bella's desire to leave Seattle for a visit with her friend Jacob Black. He is a member of the Quileute people, who reside on a reservation close to Forks and, like many of his people, can shape-shift into a wolf. His people have an abhorrence that feeds an anger at vampires. Before leaving, Bella quells Edward's fear that the wolves might harm her. Jacob is in love with Bella, but she is already committed to Edward and, while considering him a close friend, will let him know that they will never be mates.

As Bella is visiting with Jacob, the vampire Victoria returns to Forks. She seeks to kill Bella for her role in the death of her mate, James (which occurs in *Twilight*). While Victoria develops her plot, Bella retreats to the home of Edward's family, where she bonds with his sister, Rosalie. She had been raped by her boyfriend and left for dead, an event that was integral to her becoming a vampire. Bella has envisioned becoming a vampire as an outgrowth of her love for Edward. She overcomes her distaste for marriage and accepts Edward's proposal, but she wants to experience sex with him at least once before taking the decisive step into the vampire life.

After Edward returns to Forks, the full extent of Victoria's plan becomes visible. She is creating an army of newborn vampires with the idea of focusing their insatible appetite on Bella and, by extension, her vampire allies. The Cullens enlist the Quileute wolves in the battle. While the Cullens and the wolves prepare to take the army head-on, Bella, Edward, and Jacob retreat to a separate location. Victoria tracks Bella via Edward's scent. Edward and Victoria fight it out, with Edward emerging victorious.

Meanwhile, Bella realizes that her love for Jacob is stronger than she had earlier realized but not enough to override her feeling for Edward. She intends to marry Edward and, fortunately, Edward's family thoroughly defeats the vampire army. Unfortunately, Jacob is distraught and leaves the scene in a suicidal mood. The resolution of the Bella–Edward–Jacob triangle waits until much later.

The Twilight Saga: Breaking Dawn

The fourth novel, which will conclude the story of Bella Swan and her two suitors, the vampire Edward Cullen and the shape-shifting wolf Jacob Black, *Breaking Dawn*, was published in 2008. It would later be made into two movies, with part one appearing in 2011 and part two appearing in 2012.

The story opens with Bella making plans for her wedding to Edward, the next event being a reception. Jacob Black, who is dealing with Bella's having chosen Edward over him, shows up, and he and Bella share a moment apart from the other attendees. She tells him of her plans to have one sexual encounter with Edward before being turned into a vampire. Knowing that such an event could kill her, Jacob's rage emerges, and only the actions of his fellow tribe members prevent his turning into a wolf then and there.

After the wedding, the couple spends their honeymoon on Isle Esme, and they make love for the first time. The next morning, Edward realizes that Bella has numerous bruises and is upset at himself for hurting her, though Bella insists that she enjoyed the experience. Edward vows not to make love to her again until she becomes a vampire. Two weeks after the wedding, Bella vomits after waking and notices that her period is late. Alice and Carlisle call Bella, asking if she is all right. She states that she is not completely sure and realizes that she is pregnant. As she is not yet a vampire, Edward believes that the pregnancy will be fatal and advises her to allow his physician father's advice to surgically remove the baby. Bella refuses and recruits Rosalie, Edward's sister, as an ally.

When they return home to Forks, Washington, everyone realizes that the baby is growing exceedingly fast; this is not a normal pregnancy.

Jacob again emerges and becomes upset over what he perceives to be Bella's physical decline. He aligns with Edward's thinking that Carlisle should step in and terminate the pregnancy. Her decline is finally thwarted when she begins to consume blood to meet her vampire child's immediate need. The pregnancy reaches a new crisis when Bella's backbone unexpec-

tantly breaks and she collapses. Carlisle is absent, so Rosalie and Edward perform a cesarean birth. The baby arrives successfully, but Bella is dying. Edward moves quickly and turns her into a vampire then and there.

In the midst of the situation, Jacob, believing that Bella may die, decides to kill the baby, but instead, as he looks into its eyes, he decides to imprint the baby, a female who is named Renesmee. Imprinting is an act that an individual wolf does that ties them unconditionally to a human of the opposite sex, a concept that Jacob had introduced to Bella in the previous novel/movie, *New Moon*. As Jacob is acting, a group of wolves attack the house attempting to kill the baby, whom they feel might be too great of a threat to them. Jacob is able to stop the fight by letting them know what he has done with his imprinting. The wolves depart. Bella is revived, her body heals, and as the movie ends, her eyes open to reveal their new, blood-red color.

The story from the book continues in the movie *The Twilight Saga: Breaking Dawn, Part II.* As Bella fully recovers from the traumatic birth and near-death experiences, she begins her relationship with her new child and deals with her anger at Jacob for imprinting her. Jacob reconciles with Bella by explaining the nature of the imprinting relationship.

The Cullens bring Bella's father up to date on what has happened. He comes to grips with being a grandfather and having a daughter who is a vampire. The Cullens are relieved at his attitude, thinking that had he reacted negatively, they might have to abandon their home.

Once outside the womb, Renesmee continues to grow and age at a rapid speed. Another vampire, upon seeing her out playing, believes that she is a child who has been turned. Children who are turned show no restraint and have been known to be most destructive. She reported her observations to the Volturi, an unofficial but powerful governing force within the international vampire community. Having received the accusation that Renesmee is an immortal child who has been illegally turned, they demand the Cullens to gather any evidence to the contrary or face potential execution of all concerned.

The Volturi gather near the Cullen residence, prepared for battle. Their witnesses give their evidence and Aro, who leads the Volturi forces, meets Renesmee and is convinced that she is what the Cullens have said she was. However, a second consideration has emerged. Aro suggests that the child is a future threat to the vampire community; hence, she needs to be killed. As the battle is about to proceed, a

final witness appears in the form of Nahuel who is, like Renesmee, a half-mortal, half-vampire being who has grown to adulthood. His presence demonstrates that as he has not been a threat, it is unlikely that Renesmee will be one, either. The Volturi retreat back to their home in Italy. The battle is avoided.

The novel and movie end with Alice, another of Edward's sisters, sharing a prophecy of a happy future for Edward and Bella and of an adult Renesmee with Jacob. With the intense events of their immediate past behind them, Bella is able to share an intimate moment with Edward, in which both again swear their everlasting love for each other.

THE VAMPIRE ON TV

It was in the late 1940s that regularly scheduled television programs emerged in the United States, and early programming was based on well-established radio shows of the day. *Texaco Star Theater* on NBC featured comedian Milton Berle, and it was on this variety series that the vampire was first introduced to American households. A live broadcast on September 27, 1949, featured Bela Lugosi as one of the guest stars, and although not called Dracula by name, he appeared in one sketch dressed as the iconic vampire. Lugosi fared well in unfamiliar comedic territory, but after he flubbed a punchline, Berle ad-libbed, "You kill people on the screen and you also kill jokes!" In 1953, Lugosi again appeared as Dracula on the audience-driven show *You Asked for It*, where he performed a "weird vampire bat illusion." Lugosi rose from a coffin, hypnotized a girl, and then, after placing her within a magic cabinet of sorts, transformed her into a bat. Afterward, he promoted the 3D film *The Phantom Ghoul* and a television series called *Dr. Acula*, neither of which ended up being produced.

Dracula on Television: Following the initial TV appearances by Lugosi, Dracula,

the novel and the character, periodically reappeared in both new productions and unrelated series. The first adaptation of the novel aired live on NBC in 1956 as part of the series *Matinee Theatre*. This version was based on the 1931 film and starred John Carradine, who had previously played the count onstage as well as in the films *House of Frankenstein* (1944) and *House of Dracula* (1945). British actor Denholm Elliott starred in a 1968 UK adaptation of *Dracula* that aired as part of the series *Mystery and Imagination*. Although this version began its story in Whitby with only a flashback to the happenings in Transylvania, it did include several scenes from the novel that had been left out by previous adaptations. The same year, in what was quite possibly the first televised foreign-language adaptation of the novel, Gianni Lunadei starred as Dracula in the Argentina-produced miniseries *Hay que matar a Drácula*.

The Canadian series *Purple Playhouse* aired its version of *Dracula* on CBC in 1973. It starred Norman Welsh as the count and, like many early adaptations, this version had the look of a televised stage play. It was also in this year that *Dark Shadows* creator Dan Curtis helmed a televised movie written by Richard Matheson that starred Jack Palance. This was the first adaptation to be influenced by the historical work on the fifteenth-century Romanian ruler Vlad the Impaler by Raymond T. McNally and Radu Florescu. It also was the first to incorporate the search for lost love as a motivation for Dracula returning to England. A few years later in 1977, Louis Jourdan starred in a full-length BBC production entitled *Count Dracula*, written by Gerald Savory, who also adapted his screenplay into a tie-in novel. It aired in the United States as part of the *Great Performances* series on PBS, and this lengthy, two-and-a-half-hour production was the first to closely follow the original novel.

Subsequently, *Dracula* continued to be adapted in new and interesting ways, although in some cases, only the character names remained while the stories themselves strayed far from the source material. In 1979, *The Curse of Dracula* aired in weekly, 20-minute installments as part of *Cliffhangers*, an hourly series based on the format of early movie serials. In this story, Dracula lived in modern-day San Francisco covertly as a college professor of Eastern European history. After the series was cancelled, all ten chapters were edited together as a two-hour TV movie entitled *The World of Dracula*.

Also in 1979, the kid-friendly and Emmy Award–winning telefilm *The Halloween That Almost Wasn't* aired on ABC. It featured Judd Hirsch as Count Dracula who, in an attempt to save Halloween, seeks the help of his monster friends the Mummy, Warren the Werewolf, Zabaar the Zombie, and Frankenstein's monster. In 1980, Marvel Comics commissioned a TV movie based on its popular *The Tomb of Dracula* comic book series, which briefly aired under the title *Dracula: Sovereign of the Damned*. Also in that year, Showtime aired *The Passion of*

> *Dracula* continued to be adapted in new and interesting ways, although in some cases, only the character names remained....

Dracula, adapted from the tongue-in-cheek off-Broadway play from the late 1970s.

In 1980, ABC took a similar comedic approach with *Mr. and Mrs. Dracula*, which had the count and his family trying to adjust to life in America after being ousted from their castle in Transylvania. Viewer response to the pilot episode was tepid, and although a partially recast version aired again in 1981, the sitcom wasn't picked up by the network. A more traditional adaptation aired in 1982 on HBO Live! and starred Frank Langella, who reprised his role from the *Dracula* stage play. In Japan, the short-lived 1982 anime series *Don Dracula* aired on TV Tokyo and had the titular character moving to Japan along with his daughter, Chocola, and their servant, Igor. A total of eight episodes were produced, only half of which went to air, as it was quickly cancelled after the sponsoring company went bankrupt.

Dracula appeared often as a guest villain in television shows such as *Get Smart* (1968), *The Monkees* (1968), *Night Gallery* (1971), and *Happy Days* (1981). He also appeared in animated series such as *The Beatles* (1965), *The All-New Popeye Hour* (1978), *Challenge of the Super Friends* (1978), *The Fonz and the Happy Days Gang* (1980), *The New Scooby-Doo Mysteries* (1984), and *Ghostbusters* (1986). The 1970 series *Sabrina and the Groovie Goolies*, which ran for 16 episodes on CBS, featured Sabrina the Teenage Witch and her cousins, the Groovie Goolies. They all resided at Horrible Hall, a haunted boardinghouse run by Count Dracula. The show also featured the vampiress Bella La Ghostly, a telephone switchboard operator, and Batso and Ratso, young vampire twins who liked to cause all sorts of trouble. In 1971, Sabrina was spun off into her own series, as were her cousins, who reappeared in the *Groovie Goolies* show, which ran for an additional season.

Dracula and a cast of monsters, including a werewolf, Frankenstein's monster, a mummy, and others, were featured in the 1970s cartoon Groovie Goolies.

The count was often cast alongside other classic movie monsters such as in the 1979 cartoon series *Spider-Woman*. In the episode "Dracula's Revenge," villagers in Grumania find the crypt of Count Dracula, who rises from the grave and soon adds both the Wolfman and Frankenstein's monster to his entourage. Inexplicably, the count creates other vampires by shooting a laser from his fingertips, while the Wolfman shoots lasers from his eyes to create other lycans. Frankenstein's Monster, not to be outdone, uses the bolts on his neck to shoot lasers to create more like him. The three also appeared in *Spider-Man and His Amazing Friends* (1983), but this time, Dracula is aided by Frankenstein (a robot) and the Wolf Thing. As in all other cases, the gruesome threesome is foiled in the end. Dracula also appeared in the short-lived animated series *Drak Pack* (1980–1982) and in *The Comic Strip* (1987).

Another children's television series, the Canadian-produced *The Hilarious House of*

Frightenstein (1971), featured the adventures of the mad scientist Count Frightenstein, the 13th son of Count Dracula, and his green-skinned assistant, Igor. This sketch-based series showcased the talents of Billy Van, who played several characters aside from the count, including Grizelda (the ghastly gourmet cook), Bwana Clyde Batty (a nineteenth-century British explorer) and the Wolfman, most likely based on the famous DJ Wolfman Jack. Vincent Price also appeared in each episode, where he introduced sketches and occasionally recited intentionally bad (but often funny) poetry. Following its initial run, the series aired in syndication across Canada and in some parts of the United States, and eventually, a few episodes became available on DVD.

Another long-forgotten series now available on DVD is *Monster Squad*, which aired for 13 episodes on NBC beginning in 1976. It featured Dracula, the Wolfman, and Frankenstein's monster, three wax statues inadvertently

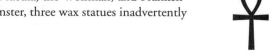

The early '80s cartoon show Drak Pack *was about the nephew of Dracula forming a team of monster superheroes to battle the evil Dr. Dred.*

brought to life by Walt, a criminology student working as a night watchman at a wax museum. The monsters, in order to atone for their past misdeeds, decide to become crime fighters. In 1988, a British cartoon series was launched, built around a leading character that was a mixture of Donald Duck and Dracula. Count Duckula became a popular children's comedic character as a vegetarian vampire, and *Count Duckula* would run for 65 episodes. The series came to the United States and was aired on several cable channels.

The count continued his reign in 1990 as Alexander Lucard in the short-lived TV series *Dracula: The Series.* Here again, Dracula is in the modern world, this time as a billionaire businessman whose real identity was discovered by three teenagers and their vampire-hunting uncle. In 1991, the Fox Kids channel's animated adventure *Little Dracula* featured a younger protagonist in his quest to become a great vampire just like his dad. In that same year, the animated adventure *Draculito, mon saigneur* aired on French television for 26 episodes.

In 2000, CBC aired *Dracula: A Chamber Musical,* a Shakespeare Festival production with no bats or blood but a lot of singing. In another updated version of the novel, produced in Italy in 2002, Count Vladislav Tepes relocated to

modern-day Budapest in an attempt to leave the superstitious world of Transylvania behind him. In 2006, a German adaptation with Marc Warren as Dracula certainly had a unique take on the story. Arthur Holmwood, soon to be married to Lucy Westenra, desperately seeks a cure for his syphilis infection. He summons Dracula to London, having heard that the Romanian count possesses extraordinary powers, but, of course, Dracula has his own agenda and soon begins to wreak havoc on the local population. In that same year, the British series *Young Dracula* aired on CBBC (the BBC's channel for kids) and lasted two seasons. The story, loosely based on the children's book by Michael Lawrence, followed the Dracula family as they relocated to a small town in Britain.

More recently, the British series *Demons* (2009) followed the last descendant of the Van Helsing line, Luke Rutherford, as he fights against the dark forces of the world with the assistance of one Mina Harker, a blind concert pianist well versed on demons, zombies, werewolves, and vampires.

Vampire Television Series: It was in the 1960s that vampires first became featured in a continued leading role, with two of the most famous and successful series having been launched in 1964. ABC brought Charles Addams's *New Yorker* cartoon series to television as *The Addams Family,* which featured Carolyn Jones as the vamp Morticia Addams. CBS also created a new oddball family, *The Munsters,* with characters based on the classic monsters from early Universal Pictures horror films. This series featured two vampires, Yvonne de Carlo as Lily Munster and Al Lewis as Grandpa (who, over the course of the series, was revealed to be, in fact, Count Dracula). Both series were similar in tone, with each family believing they were typical suburbanites, not quite understanding why everyone around them found their habits so peculiar. Both ran for only two seasons yet proved popular enough to spawn several progeny.

In the comedy TV series The Munsters, *the character of Grandpa, played by Al Lewis, is slowly revealed over the course of the show to be Count Dracula.*

In 1973, NBC took an animated version of *The Addams Family* on the road in a haunted RV, a series that ran for two seasons, although the second simply re-aired the original 16 episodes. *The Munsters Today*, essentially a 1988 sequel to the original series, updated the cast and the time period, with the characters remaining the same. The premise: Back in the 1960s, one of Grandpa's experiments with a sleep machine went horribly wrong, and the entire family ended up in suspended animation.

Twenty years later, a developer looking to turn the site of their house into a parking lot accidentally awakens the family, who now find themselves in similar comedic situations in a new era. After the success of the 1991 *Addams Family* feature film, ABC brought the family back to television in 1992 for a new animated series that ran for three seasons. Both this and the earlier animated *Addams Family* series were geared toward a more youthful demographic, with much of the macabre nature toned down for a Saturday-morning audience. In 1998, the clan returned to a live-action format in *The New Addams Family*, a Canadian-produced series that updated the original story into current times. It ran for a successful two seasons, and two episodes featured John Astin, the original Gomez Addams, as Grandpapa Addams.

Audiences in the year 1966 said goodbye to the Addams and Munster families and hello to the Collins clan in a show that was to become a television enigma. Producer Dan Curtis sold ABC on a gothic daytime soap opera that he called *Dark Shadows*. The original show did not do well, so in an attempt to boost ratings and avoid cancellation, Curtis introduced a supernatural element, and ghosts soon began to inhabit the Collinwood mansion. With the introduction of vampire Barnabas Collins nine months into the show's run, *Dark Shadows* finally became a huge success. It ran for more than 1,200 episodes and found among its many viewers teenagers who rushed home from school to watch it in its late-afternoon time slot. The series ended its network run in 1971, and during that time, the Collins family also faced werewolves, witches, and warlocks, with stories taking place in parallel dimensions and even different time periods. Truly a groundbreaking series, the popularity of the original *Dark Shadows* has since been kept alive to the present through fan clubs, fanzines, and annual conventions.

Although the immortal Count Dracula made several appearances on television in the decades following *Dark Shadows*, it wasn't until the early 1990s that other vampires would once again be featured in a continued leading role. Fitting, then, that the decade that saw the beginning of a resurgence of vampires on television was initiated by the same creature that popularized them 25 years earlier. In 1991, *Dark Shadows* reappeared on network television in a new lavish, prime-time series that starred Ben Cross as Barnabas Collins. While hailed by vampire enthusiasts, especially the still-active *Dark Shadows* fans, it failed to find a sufficient audience and was cancelled after only one season.

In 1992, the Canadian–German–American television series *Forever Knight* made its debut and told the story of 800-year-old vampire Nick

Knight (played by Geraint Wyn Davies), a Toronto police detective trying to hide his vampiric nature while seeking redemption for his past misdeeds. It was an early example of the vampire-as-romantic-hero, seen so often in the twenty-first century. The series originated as a 1989 made-for-television movie that starred Rick Springfield as a vampire cop in Los Angeles, and although meant to be a pilot for a television series, it was never optioned at the time. However, the show was recast and the story was relocated to Toronto, and it found a home at CBS as part of its new "Crimetime after Primetime" lineup, which aired each evening as an alternative to NBC's popular *The Tonight Show*. The series, although popular with fans, had trouble staying on the air during its three-season run and ultimately ended in 1996. In that same year, the popularity of White Wolf Game Studio's *Vampire: The Masquerade* role-playing game led to a loosely based television series called *Kindred: The Embraced*. Produced by Aaron Spelling, some called this Fox series a cross between *The Godfather* and *Melrose Place* but, failing to find an audience, it was cancelled after eight episodes.

The daytime soap opera *Port Charles*, a spin-off of the long-running series *General Hospital*, debuted in the summer of 1997. Initially focused on doctors and interns at a medical school, it ultimately took a page from *Dark Shadows* and began to include some gothic and supernatural elements such as vampires and life after death. About halfway into its run, it abandoned the standard open-ended writing style of most soaps and adopted 13-week story arcs, much like those found in Spanish telenovelas. Ultimately, these changes weren't enough to pull in high ratings, and it was cancelled in 2003, unintentionally ending the series with a cliffhanger episode.

Buffy the Vampire Slayer, by far the most successful vampire-oriented television series to date, aired on the WB and UPN networks from 1997 to 2003. Developed from the 1992 movie that had met with decidedly mixed reviews, the series featured Sarah Michelle Gellar as a high

school cheerleader selected as the chosen Slayer for her generation, fighting supernatural creatures with the help of several classmates and her librarian "Watcher." Airing for 145 episodes over seven seasons, *Buffy* has since become a cultural phenomenon; it spawned the spin-off TV series *Angel*, inspired hundreds of novels, magazines, and comic books, and has even graced the halls of academia, becoming a hot topic of discussion among scholars of popular culture. Development began in 2001 for an animated series based on the live-action show; however, no network was interested at the time. Yet, Fox still tried shopping it around even as late as 2004, when a pilot was produced that included the voices of most of the original cast members. Buffy's love interest, Angel (David Boreanaz), the vampire with a soul, was a regular on *Buffy the Vampire Slayer* until the end of season three. In 1999, the spin-off series *Angel* premiered, where the titular vampire relocated to Los Angeles in search of redemption, vowing to "help the helpless." Darker in tone than its precursor, *Angel* had a successful run over five seasons but was unexpectedly cancelled in 2004.

The cast of the TV version of Buffy, the Vampire Slayer.

Bill Compton (played by Stephen Moyer) is shown here with his vampire daughter, Jessica (played by Deborah Ann Woll) in the HBO series True Blood.

The Buffyverse proved so popular that in 2007, four years after the show completed its original network run, Dark Horse Comics began publishing *Buffy the Vampire Slayer Season Eight*, a canonical continuation of the original television series in comic book form, which itself has also spawned several limited-series spin-offs. Much like the Buffyverse, the Angel universe also proved quite popular and inspired a number of books, comics, and other merchandise. Like the *Buffy* comic, Angel also found renewed life in a canonical comic book series *Angel: After the Fall* from IDW Publishing, which continued his story in 44 issues over four years (2007–2011).

Thanks to the popularity of *Buffy* and *Angel*, networks soon expanded their lineup of vampire television series, but most haven't gar-

nered the same critical praise as their predecessors, with many lasting only one season. In 2006, a short-lived spin-off of the *Blade* movie trilogy featured Kirk "Sticky Fingaz" Jones in the role made popular by Wesley Snipes. *Blade: The Series* had the vampire hunter teaming up with a veteran of the Iraq War as she investigated her brother's mysterious death. The year 2007 would be a banner year for new vampire television series, including the animated *Blood+* as well as the gay-themed *Dante's Cove* and *The Lair*. Also in that year, two new series featured a mixture of vampires and crime drama, two genres seeming perfectly suited for one another as shown by the previous success of both *Forever Knight* and *Angel*.

The series *Blood Ties*, based on the novels by Tanya Huff, had private investigator Vicki

Nelson teamed up with vampire Henry Fitzroy as she investigated supernatural events in Toronto. The equally popular *Moonlight* starred Alex O'Loughlin as Nick St. John, a vampire and private investigator in Los Angeles who falls in love with a mortal woman. However, as with many vampire series, these were both cancelled, even though they had quickly established an avid fan base, many of whom are still crying for more from their beloved bloodsuckers.

HBO's *True Blood*, loosely based on *The Southern Vampire Mysteries* series of novels by Charlaine Harris, has quickly rivaled *Buffy* in terms of popularity and cultural impact. The premise is that after the creation of synthetic blood, vampires are now "out of the coffin" and live freely and openly among humans. One such vampire, the 173-year-old Bill Compton (Stephen Moyer), soon finds himself in the company of telepathic barmaid Sookie Stackhouse (Anna Paquin), and they become romantically involved as the series progresses. The show was a runaway hit for HBO and continued for seven seasons (2008–2014). Hot on its tail and aimed toward a younger audience, *The Vampire Diaries*, based on the series of books by L. J. Smith, made its debut in the fall of 2009. The series premiere was the most-watched launch ever on the CW network to date, with an estimated 4.8 million viewers in the United States. The storyline centered on two vampire brothers, Stefan and Damon Salvatore (portrayed by Paul Wesley and Ian Sommerhalder) and their love interest, Elena Gilbert (played by Nina Dobrev). It continued for eight seasons and produced two successful spin-off shows, *The Originals* (2013–2018) and *Legacies*, a continuing series that began its run in 2018.

The resurgence in the popularity of vampires on television that manifested in the 1990s has not been limited to North America. In 1991, the Brazilian soap opera *Vamp* began its run, telling the story of the invasion of vampires into a pacific town called the Bay of Angels. In late 1992, the serial opera *The Vampyr—A Soap Opera* aired for five episodes on the BBC, an updated version of *Der Vampyr* (1828), a German Romantic opera that itself was based on "The Vampyre" (1819) by John William Polidori. Other series included the German production *Der Kleine Vampir* (1993); the Cantonese series *Vampire Expert* (1995); the British series *Ultraviolet* (1998); the Japanese series *My Date with a Vampire* (1998); the Brazilian production *O Beijo do Vampiro* (2002); and the Korean series *Hello Franceska* (2005). In 2008, the British series *Being Human* followed a vampire, a ghost, and a werewolf as they shared a flat in modern-day Bristol. Having achieved strong ratings in its first season, it would continue for five seasons (2008–2013) and produce a North American version that ran for three seasons (2011–2014). The past of the vampire John Mitchell was portrayed by Aidan Turner in the original series and, renamed Aidan Waite, the vampire was portrayed by Sam Witwer in the North American series.

Through the first decade of the new century, the Japanese television market has seen a major increase in vampire-themed series. Although some have been live action, most are anime series based on manga publications, the most popular of which have also been translated into English and aired in North America. These include *Vampire Princess Miyu* (1997), *Descendants of Darkness* (2000), *Hellsing* (2003), *Lunar Legend Tsukihime* (2003), *Tsukuyomi: Moon Phase* (2004), and *Karin* (2005). A more adult-themed manga publication, *Negima! Magister Negi Magi*, has inspired the anime series *Negima!* (2005), an alternate retelling called *Negima!?* (2006), and the live-action series *Negima!!* (2007). Other titles available on DVD that have not yet been televised in North America include *Rosario + Vampire* (2008) and *Vampire Knight* (2008). The series *Trinity Blood* (2005) and *Black Blood Brothers* (2006) were both based on novellas that also inspired popular manga adaptations. Other anime series not directly based on manga include *Nightwalker: The Midnight Detective* (1998), *Vampiyan Kids* (2001), and *Legend of Duo* (2004).

Animated series have continued to appear on Japanese television through the second decade of the new century. Included among the titles are *Nyanpire: The Animation* (2011); *Diabolik Lovers* (2013); *Blood Lad* (2013); and *Seraph of the East* (2015). Meanwhile, *Castlevania*, a *Dracula*-based storyline that originated in a popular 1980s video game, continues to make appearances internationally, its most recent incarnation being an American animated series released in 2017.

Made-for-Television Movies: In the last decades of the twentieth century and continuing into the new century, feature-length movies produced specifically for a television audience, rather than being released to theaters, became a growing portion of all movies produced. Among the first of such movies was *The Night Stalker*, produced by Dan Curtis in 1972. Much like his *Dark Shadows* series, it became the highest-rated television show aired to that date. The story followed reporter Carl Kolchak (Darren McGavin) as he investigated a series of gruesome murders, ultimately discovering and then killing a vampire. The success of the movie led to a second telefilm, *The Night Strangler* (1973),

Carl Kolchak, played by Darren McGavin, is an intrepid reporter investigating the supernatural in the 1970s TV drama The Night Stalker.

followed by the *Kolchak: The Night Stalker* series in 1974; it pitted the intrepid reporter against a variety of supernatural elements. One of the first episodes had Kolchak following the trail of a vampire in Las Vegas, herself a victim of Janos Skorzeny, the vampire from *The Night Stalker* telefilm. The series lasted for one season and was "reimagined" in a short-lived 2005 series that unfortunately bore little resemblance to the original storyline.

Dan Curtis worked with writer Richard Matheson on the script for both Kolchak movies as well as his version of *Dracula* (1974). In 1977, the two teamed up once again for *Dead of Night*, which dramatized three of Matheson's stories. One of them, "No Such Thing as a Vampire," told the story of Professor Gheria, who tried to kill his wife by creating the impression that she was wasting away due to a vampire's attack. This story was first adapted in the United Kingdom as part of the *Late Night Horror* BBC television series in 1968.

Even before *The Night Stalker*, the popular series *The Munsters* led to the production of a made-for-television movie in 1966. *Munster, Go Home!* was made on the heels of the cancellation of the original series and was intended as a pilot for a new series featuring the family in England. Ultimately, the networks were not interested, so instead, it was released theatrically as a stand-alone film. A second television movie, *The Munsters' Revenge*, reunited most of the original cast members and aired on NBC in 1981. Similarly, NBC had earlier attempted to revive *The Addams Family* franchise in 1977 with *Halloween with the New Addams Family*, again reuniting most of the original cast members, but it also failed to recapture the magic of the original series.

The 1970s ended with a handful of noteworthy movies, some of which were pilots for series that were never picked up by the networks. One of these was *The Norliss Tapes*, produced for NBC and directed by Dan Curtis in

A charming New England town is invaded by vampires in 1979's TV miniseries Salem's Lot, *based on the Stephen King novel.*

1973. It told the story of David Norliss (Roy Thinnes), an author researching a book aimed to debunk supernatural occurrences, whose quest leads him to ultimately cross paths with a group of modern-day vampires. A second pilot, *Vampire*, aired on ABC in 1979 and starred Richard Lynch as the vampire Prince Anton Voytek. Not so much a blood-and-fangs story as it was a tale of revenge, the movie concluded with an open ending but was never picked up as a series. In that same year, Tobe Hooper directed the dramatic version of Stephen King's early vampire novel *Salem's Lot* for CBS, where vampires invade a small town in New England. An unrelated sequel, *A Return to Salem's Lot*, was briefly released theatrically in 1987, while an updated version of the original story was produced for television in 2004.

Additional made-for-television vampire movies include *Desire, the Vampire* (1982), *The Midnight Hour* (1985), *Nightlife* (1989), *Daughters of Darkness* (1990), *Shadow Zone: The Undead Express* (1996), *Dracula 3000* (2004), *Bloodsuckers* (2005), and *The Librarian: The Curse of the Judas Chalice* (2008). One of the most unique telefilms to date was *London after Midnight*, a 2002 reconstruction of the lost 1927 Tod Browning film. Director Rick Schmidlin utilized some 200 still photographs to recreate the movie and based the intertitles on the original shooting script.

Other Vampire Productions: In addition to the vampire-oriented series and made-for-TV movies, the undead proved popular enough to be written into nonvampire series. Many early appearances played for humor and usually had the supernatural element explained away, as found in such popular 1960s series as *Get Smart* (1965), *Gilligan's Island* (1966), and *F Troop* (1967). Among the more notable shows that treated vampires a little more seriously were those that were part of *Adventure Inc.*, *Blue Murder*, *CSI: Crime Scene Investigation*, *Diagnosis: Murder*, *The Dresden Files*, *Doctor Who*, *The Man from U.N.C.L.E.*, *Nash Bridges*, *Nip/Tuck*, *Quantum Leap*, *St. Elsewhere*, *Starsky & Hutch*, *Superboy*, *Supernatural*, and *The X-Files*.

As comic books expanded into the television medium, so, too, did their vampire characters. Marvel's fourth animated *Spider-Man* series (1994–1998) had several episodes featuring Morbius, the living vampire. However, due to restrictions in place by Fox, no traditional vampires were to be part of the series, so the creators had to include a modified Morbius character, one who subsisted on plasma rather than blood and drained his victims through the suckers on his hands. This is reminiscent of the pseudovampire episode "Man Trap" from the original *Star Trek* series, where a creature uses suckers on its hands to drain the salt from the bodies of its victims. Other vampires eventually appeared on *Spider-Man* in name only; none were ever shown biting their victims on the neck. The HBO series *Spawn: The Animated Series* (1997–1999) featured a vampire during the third season, while on the WB network, *Batman: The Animated Series* (2004–2008) showcased the DC character Man-Bat on several occasions. In 2009, Marvel's psychic vampire Selene, a sorceress and mutant, appeared in the season one finale of *Wolverine and the X-Men*, which aired on the Nicktoons network.

Television anthology series, which ran a new story each week, also had a tendency to air episodes that featured vampires. These series included *Alfred Hitchcock Presents, Are You Afraid of the Dark?, Friday the 13th: The Series, The Hunger, Mystery and Imagination, Night Gallery, The Ray Bradbury Theater, Tales from the Crypt, Tales from the Darkside*, and *The Twilight Zone*. The most well-known female vampire in literature, Carmilla, has also made rare appearances on television. The British series *Mystery and Imagination* first dramatized the story in 1966, and in 1989, "Carmilla" was updated and presented in the Showtime series *Nightmare Classics*. The late 1980s also saw television movie adaptations in both Spain and France.

Prior to *Buffy the Vampire Slayer*, with few exceptions, the vampire tended to remain just on the edge of television culture, not having the strength to hold a continuing spot on prime-time television, but that has all changed. In the first 20 years of the new century, vampires have experienced a population explosion like none other. From the horrific to the romantic, the undead are now firmly entrenched within our television airwaves, much to the delight of their avid fans.

The Internet: Over the past decade, broadcasters have increasingly used the internet to create awareness for new vampire series, leading up to the official television launch. A rising trend has been to produce webisodes that feature new content created solely for the internet. These video clips, usually two to four minutes

in length, often feature character backstories, prequel scenes, and other tales falling within the canon of the show.

The most successful viral marketing campaign to date was for the HBO series *True Blood*. Several hilarious videos released online were often fake news segments pertaining to the premise of the series, where vampires are "out of the coffin" and living freely among human beings. Leading up to the launch of *The Vampire Diaries*, the CW network produced a four-part webisode series entitled *A Darker Truth*, where vampire hunter Jason Harris followed the trail of Stefan Salvatore, whom he believed was responsible for his sister's death. The MTV show *Valemont* began as a short series of webisodes that aired on both MTV and *MTV.com,* while the Canadian series *Sanctuary* started out as eight webisodes in 2007 and was subsequently picked up as a traditional television series by the Syfy channel.

Hammer Films also used this medium to attempt a return to feature film production, releasing *Beyond the Rave* in 2008 as a series of short video installments. Two short films based in the *30 Days of Night* universe, *Blood Trails* and *Dust to Dust*, were released as a series of webisodes through *FEARnet*. Unfortunately, Hammer Films was never able to return to its glory days of the 1960s. Emerging filmmakers, as well as everyday fans of the genre, are also using the internet to broadcast their vampire stories. Early web series included *Vampire Trucker* and *Too Shy to Be a Vampire*, and more recent series include *Bleed, 3 Vampires, Vampire Killers, Bleeder*, and *Transylvania Television*.

Vampire Series on Television

Series	Years Broadcast
The Munsters	1964–1966
Dark Shadows[1]	1967–1971
Wacky Races	1968–1970
Groovie Goolies	1970–1971
The Hilarious House of Frightenstein	1971–1997
Sesame Street[2]	1972–
Monster Squad	1976
Quacula	1979–1980
Drak Pack	1980
The Little Vampire	1986
Ernest Le Vampire	1988–1989
Count Duckula	1988–1993
Dracula: The Series	1990
Gravedale High	1990–1991
Little Dracula	1991
Forever Knight	1992–1995
Darkstalkers	1995
Vampire Expert	1995–1996
Kindred: The Embraced	1996
Van-Pires	1997
Buffy the Vampire Slayer	1997–2003
Master of Mosquiton the Vampire	1997–1998
The Hunger: Vampires	1997
The Vampire Princess Miyu (Japan)	1997–1998
Ultraviolet	1998
My Date with a Vampire	1998
Nightwalker: The Midnight Detective (Japan)	1998
Angel	1999–2004
Little Dracula	rerun, 1999
Mona the Vampire	1999–2003
Monster Mash	2000
The Baskervilles	2000–2001
Vampire High	2001–2002
My Date with a Vampire II	2001
Descendants of Darkness (Japan)	2001
Greg the Bunny	2002
Vampire Syndrome: Hatu	2002
Hellsing (U.S.)	2002
Vampiyan Kids (Japan)	2002–2003
My Date with a Vampire III	2003
Lunar Legend Tsukihime	2003
Petit Vampire (France)	2004

Vampire Series on Television (contd.)

Series	Years Broadcast
Vampire Host (*The Vampire Gigolo*) (Japan)	2004
Tsukuyomi: Moon Phase (Japan)	2004–2005
Karin (Japan)	2005
Trinity Blood (Japan)	2005
Blood+	2005–2006
Blade: The Series (US)	2006
Young Dracula	2006
Negima!? (Japan)	2006–2007
Black Blood Brothers (Japan)	2006–2008
Blood Ties	2007
The Lair	2007–2009
Moonlight	2007–2008
The Last Van Helsing (UK)	2008
True Blood	2008–2014
Rosario + Vampire (Japan)	2008
Sanctuary	2008–2011
Vampire Knight (Japan)	2008
Being Human (UK)	2008–2013
The Vampire Diaries	2009–
Valemont	2009
The Gates	2010
Dance in the Vampire Bund	2010
Lost Girl	2010–2015
Being Human (North America)	2011–2014
Blood-C	2011
Death Valley	2011
Blade (Japan)	2011
The Originals	2013–2018
Dracula (US)	2013
Vampire Heaven	2013
Hemlock Grove	2013–2015
Higanjima (Japan)	2013
From Dusk till Dawn	2014–2016
Penny Dreadful	2014–2016
The Strain	2014–2017
Preacher	2016–2019
Bunnicula	2016–2018
Van Helsing	2016–
Vampirina	2017–
Castlevania	2017–2018
Hotel Transylvania	2017–
Midnight, Texas	2017–2018

Vampire Series on Television (contd.)

Series	Years Broadcast
Legacies	2018–
The Passage	2019–
Dracula (UK)	2019
What We Do in the Shadows	2019–
NOS4A2	2019–
Dracula	2020

[1] *Dark Shadows* began airing in 1966 but did not add Barnabas Collins, its initial and main vampire character, until 1967.

[2] *Sesame Street* began airing in 1969 but did not add its famous vampire character, Count von Count, until the 1972–1973 season.

🦇 *Being Human* 🦇

Being Human was a television series introduced by the BBC in the United Kingdom in 2008. It was created by screenwriter Toby Whithouse who, as a writer for the *Doctor Who* series, is credited with writing "The Vampires of Venice" episode (2010). The storyline for *Being Human* posited three supernatural characters (a vampire, a werewolf, and a ghost) who try to live together while simultaneously trying to blend into human society. In the *Being Human* universe, werewolves and vampires are natural enemies, and these differences fuel the personal relations of the main characters, even as they must periodically choose between their personal friendship and loyalty to their kind. At the same time, as supernatural beings, they can see, hear, and communicate with ghosts and, thus, assist their new housemate with her problems with afterlife existence, even as she observes and advises them on their unique chosen path.

The story begins with Annie Sawyer (portrayed by Lenora Crichlow) being murdered and, thus, turned into a housebound ghost. George Sands (a werewolf portrayed by Russell Tovey) and John Mitchell (a vampire portrayed by Aidan Turner) rent the home in which Annie has died. They will be joined through the second season by Nina Pickering (portrayed by Sinead Keenan), a female werewolf and George's love interest. The series ran for five seasons, but in season four, a new set of principal characters were introduced and, by the last season, had emerged with their own storylines—the vampire Hal Yorke (Damien Molony), the werewolf Tom McNair (Michael Socha), the ghost Alex Miller (Kate Brackett), and Dominic Rook, a human who is part of a government bureau

Russell Tovey (left) is a werewolf and Aidan Turner is a vampire trying to get along in Being Human, *which ran on BBC TV from 2009 to 2013.*

In the Canadian version of Being Human, *the cast featured (left to right) Sam Huntington, Meaghan Rath, Sam Witwer, and Kristen Hager.*

that quietly deals with supernatural entities when necessary.

The show opened to mixed reviews, but it quickly gained an audience and became a cult favorite. In 2010, it won the Writer's Guild of Great Britain Award as the Best Television Drama Series. It was successful enough to inspire a reimagining of the series in a North American remake. The new series is set in Boston and features the vampire Aidan Waite (Sam Witwer), the werewolf Josh Levison (Sam Huntington), and the ghost Sally Malik (Meaghan Rath). In the second season, the werewolf Nora Sergeant (Kristen Hager) is introduced as Josh's love interest. The show follows the story of the British series as it begins but soon varies sharply from the original.

In the North American series, the vampire Aidan Waite is given a detailed backstory of life as a farmer at the time of the Revolutionary War. Turned while away from home fighting, upon his return to his prewar life the local minister, having heard that Aidan had been killed in the war, believes that his wife is a witch and that he has been resurrected to perform a devilish act. His actions lead to Aidan's wife's death, which, in response, drives Aidan to kill the minister and his local associates.

Filmed in Canada, the North American version of *Being Human* ran for four seasons (2011–2014) on the Syfy channel.

Buffy the Vampire Slayer Television Series

The original *Buffy the Vampire Slayer* movie appeared in 1992 to mixed reviews. Its creator, Joss Whedon (born Joseph Hill Whedon), considered it a significantly altered representation of his original screenplay but also a stage of development of the Buffy character he wanted. He has noted that he traces his interest in the character of Buffy as an attempt to reimagine a horror stereotype, the image of a naïve but beautiful, young woman wandering into a dark alley only to be dispatched by some monster. He looked for a movie in which the girl goes into the alley and turns the tables on the monster using her own remarkable strength and powers.

In the years following the movie, Whedon expanded his knowledge of the vampire genre as it had appeared on both television and in the movies and thought more about the nature of horror. The darker world inhabited by the television Buffy manifested from the very first episode, in which Whedon now set his characters in a world reminiscent of the Cthulhu mythos of H. P. Lovecraft. Whedon concentrates on the immediate battle between good and evil—between the Powers That Be and the forces of supernatural evil that once overran planet Earth. These forces have been pushed back into the nether reaches but are constantly trying to return through the Hellmouth, which Whedon locates in Sunnydale, a small California city that bears a remarkable resemblance to Santa Barbara. (An original Hellmouth is found in the sleepy town of Caicais, Portugal, so designated because of an unusual rock formation that an angry sea had carved out of the rocky shoreline.) Whedon's world is inhabited by a spectrum of demonic characters, most importantly the vampires. To keep the vampires in check, the cosmos regularly spits up a Slayer, a young female with some extraordinary abilities.

Traditionally, only a single Slayer exists at any given moment, but should a Slayer be killed, a new one is waiting in the wings and immediately arises to take the deceased Slayer's place. Several Slayers are in training at any time. At the end of season one, Buffy dies for a few minutes only to be revived. Her death, however, calls up the next Slayer, first Kendra Young (Bianca Lawson) and then Faith Lehane (Eliza Dushku), and for the remainder of the series, two Slayers exist simultaneously. On the final season of the series, a large cadre of Slayers are being trained and commissioned, symbolic of the empowerment of females in general as the twenty-first century begins.

Actress Sarah Michelle Gellar took over the role of Buffy in the TV version of Buffy the Vampire Slayer.

Whedon conceived of vampires as deceased humans reanimated by invading, demonic spirits. When killed, they immediately disintegrate into dust (very much as had Dracula in Hammer Films's *Horror of Dracula*), a convenient revision of the vampire myth that keeps the authorities uninvolved since the Slayer does not leave a pile of corpses behind, no matter how many vampires she eliminates. Vampires have the memory of the person whose body they inhabit but no soul and, hence, no conscience. Most vampires in *Buffy*, lacking a soul, are evil and fit only for quick dispatch, and most episodes began with the Slayer doing just that. Angel, the vampire who falls in love with Buffy, is cursed with a soul/conscience that continually wars with his vampiric urges, thus creating his special hell.

In creating Angel, Whedon adapted his unique idea of the vampire to the new conflicted vampire explored by Dan Curtis in *Dark Shadows*, Anne Rice in her novels, and the good-guy vampire developed in the comic book *Vampirella* and the novels of Chelsea Quinn Yarbro and Fred Saberhagen. Just as the original *Buffy* movie was released, a good-guy vampire appeared on television in the persona of Nick Knight, the vampire detective in *Forever Knight*. When emotionally upset or about to feed, the vampires of *Forever Knight* show their fangs and put on what became known as a "game face," a horrific appearance not unlike that of a Klingon on *Star Trek*. Finally, from the Hong Kong vampire movies, Whedon introduced the martial arts as a major weapon in the Slayer's arsenal.

In spite of Whedon's maturing vision, the television series attempted to provide some continuity with the movie. After the events at her Los Angeles high school, Buffy Summers and her mother hoped to finally resume a normal life, but through the show's early episodes, Buffy comes to understand that normality and peace were not central to her existence.

She was bothered by dreams and, more importantly, has the burden of understanding the significance of the wave of deaths and disappearances among her new classmates. One body had even dropped out of a locker in the gym. The librarian, Rupert Giles (Anthony Stewart Head), offered her a book on vampires.

Very early in her career at Sunnydale, Buffy found a support group among a small collective of students who come to believe in the existence of vampires and appreciate Buffy's distinctive position in life. Willow Rosenberg (Alyson Hannigan) is a shy computer nerd; she is pretty but rather inept socially. Xander Harris (Nicholas Brendon) is a young teen who is too unhip to be popular. Cordelia Chase (Charisma Carpenter), one of the most popular (and shallow) girls in school, was rewarded for her attempts to introduce Buffy into the circle of the school's elite by being drawn into the Slayer's supernatural world. The group was held together by the wise Giles, Buffy's Watcher, whose library also became their headquarters. Giles relied on Willow to extend his knowledge through her abilities, like surfing the internet.

> Only reluctantly did Buffy reconcile herself to her chosenness. Her immediate task was to handle the Master, a powerful, ancient vampire king....

Only reluctantly did Buffy reconcile herself to her chosenness. Her immediate task was to handle the Master, a powerful, ancient vampire king who had planned to re-enter the world of humans from which he had been banished. Each century, an evening, called the Harvest, he has the opportunity to select another vampire, a vessel, and send him out into the world. On the evening in question, his vessel, Luke, took over The Bronze, a teen club, and began to feed. The Master felt the strength received from each feeding, as if he had been feeding himself. Unfortunately for the Master, before he could gain the strength to break free, Buffy arrived at The Bronze and killed Luke.

The key person in her last-minute rescue of her classmates was a young man who warned her about the Harvest. Although he appeared to be a young man only a few years older than Buffy, he turned out to be a 240-year-old vampire named Angel (David Boreanaz). Once a vicious killer, he encountered some Romani people, who punished him by restoring his soul, or conscience, with a magical curse. With his soul restored, Angel found that he could no longer kill.

Although Buffy stopped the Master, it was only temporary. He would be back, and it would be Angel who again would intervene and tell of a prophecy indicating that on the following evening, Buffy would have to fight the Master, and she would lose. The next evening, at the school dance, Buffy and the Master did fight, and Buffy did lose. However, she was rescued and revived by her friends and ended the initial season by destroying the Master permanently.

Seasons two and three saw Buffy and her colleagues through the last two years of high school, during which time they slew countless vampires and a few supernatural baddies of a nonvampiric nature, mostly demons of one sort or the other. Buffy's love life with her vampire boyfriend, Angel, blossomed but had a disastrous ending when, during their intimate time together, Angel had a moment of joy and reverted to his former vampire nature, in which state he was known as Angelus. Buffy had to impale him with a sword.

As the series continues, Buffy has her first encounters with the vampire Spike (James Marsters) and his slightly crazy girlfriend, Drusilla (Juliet Landau), in what would become a rocky relationship. Her friend Willow, who likes Xander, has her heart broken when he became involved with someone, but she would

recover with the help of Oz (Seth Green), a lovable werewolf. Buffy's rivalry with the other Slayer, Faith, would lead Faith into an alliance with Sunnydale's mayor, who turned out to be a demon, and would culminate at Buffy and her friends' high school graduation. When the vampires were able to come out in the daytime momentarily, Buffy and her friends had to organize the student body to fight for their future. The mayor would be killed when he chases Buffy into the school, which had been loaded with explosives. Recalling the fire at her first high school in Los Angeles, Buffy ended her high school career by destroying Sunnydale High.

Angel, who has returned from the hell Buffy had sent him to, recovered to join the graduation battle but, immediately afterward, left for Los Angeles, and his new series was built around his quest for redemption. Cordelia would soon also find her way to Angel's door, leaving Giles, Willow, and Xander to carry on in Sunnydale. Willow and Buffy would attend college at the University of California at Sunnydale, while Xander tried his hand at a construction job. With the school library destroyed, their new headquarters would become a local magic shop, now run by Giles. Buffy got a new love life in the persona of Riley Finn (Marc Blucas), a soldier with a unit called

Buffy's death sets the scene for Willow to emerge as a witch whose magic is real and powerful.

the Initiative, which specializes in fighting supernatural invaders with the latest technology. Among their victims is Spike, who has a chip placed in him to prevent him from doing any harm to humans. Eventually, Oz would leave to try to find a cure for his lycanthropy, and Willow would discover that she is a lesbian. Unlike Riley, whom the fans generally disliked, they fell in love with Willow's girlfriend, Tara Maclay (Amber Benson). Xander would eventually fall for Anya (Emma Caulfield), a demon who gave up her powers to be with him.

Buffy's family would be enlarged at the beginning of season five with the addition of a sister, Dawn (Michelle Trachtenberg), who arrives out of nowhere, complete with a set of memories involving the main characters, who weave her into the action as if she had always been present. Buffy eventually discovers that Dawn is a mystical object known as the Key, transformed into human form and sent to the Slayer for protection. When the villainous Glory (Clare Kramer) uses Dawn to break down the barriers separating the dimensions, Buffy sacrifices her own life to save the world as we know it.

Buffy the Vampire Slayer remained on the air for seven seasons (1997–2003), while the spin-off, *Angel*, ran for five (1999–2004).

Buffy's death sets the scene for Willow to emerge as a witch whose magic is real and powerful. It is powerful enough to bring Buffy back from the grave and send her on a quest for power that becomes addictive and almost costs her the relationship with Tara. In her attempt to readjust from being pulled back from her brief visit to a heavenlike realm, Buffy begins an intense relationship with the vampire Spike, who falls for Buffy only to find her still in love with Angel.

Willow is recovering from her addiction to magic only to have Tara taken from her by a stray bullet intended for Buffy. In her grief, she tracks down Warren Mears, who fired the bullets, and she uses her magic powers to skin him alive. She then transforms into her opposite, popularly called Dark Willow, but recovers to engage in the final battle that pits Buffy against the First Evil, a being that has manifested from all the evil in existence. The First makes itself known through its agent sidekick Caleb, a serial killer who appears as a priest. The First is an incorporeal entity who is able to come to Earth because of the instability introduced into the cosmos when Buffy is raised from the dead. He sets about to destroy the Slayers-in-waiting and the Watchers' Council that oversees them. The surviving Slayers come to Sunnydale, where a final battle is in the making at the Hellmouth.

In the final episode, Buffy, Spike, the rehabilitated Faith, and all the would-be Slayers fight against the horde of vampires who are storming into the human realm. In the battle, Anya dies, and Spike shows his love for Buffy by sacrificing himself. The amulet he wears, which channels the sun's light, turns the tide of the battle. Sunnydale is destroyed, but humanity is saved.

Whedon used the last episode to punctuate the feminist message he had been projecting through the series: Every woman is a potential Slayer; they just have to step forward and claim their status. In the final episode, Willow uses her magic powers to turn all of the potential Slayers into actual Slayers. Henceforth, more than one Slayer will exist at the same time.

Buffy's Impact on Television: The first episode of *Buffy the Vampire Slayer* aired on March 10, 1997, on the WB network and is credited with saving the young network and setting it on a firm footing with its youthful audience. The first five seasons remained on the WB, but the last two were run on the UPN network. The show then ran in syndication on the FX cable network. In England, the show ran on Sky1 and BBC2. On both networks, it was run in two versions. In the afternoon, presumably when a younger audience was watching, it was run in a more sanitized version, with the violence reduced and sex deleted. The original version was run in the evenings during prime time. The series was also translated for viewing in France, Germany, Italy, Russia, and other countries.

Buffy Aftermath: *Buffy the Vampire Slayer* remained on the air for seven seasons (1997–2003), while the spin-off, *Angel,* ran for five

(1999–2004). *Angel* became the first storyline developed from the original series. Besides Cordelia, several *Buffy* characters found their way to Los Angeles to become regulars on the show, including Faith and the vampires Harmony Kendall (Mercedes McNab), Darla (Julie Benz), and, after the last battle in Sunnydale, Spike.

In 2007, season eight of *Buffy* would appear in a most unusual format: a comic book. An original *Buffy the Vampire Slayer* comic series had appeared from Dark Horse Comics, with 63 issues being published between 1990 and 2003. A variety of miniseries were subsequently published. In 2007, however, Dark Horse began a second series that was partially written by Joss Whedon and sanctioned as an official continuation of the story after the end of the television series. It is popularly termed "the eighth season." A set of 40 issues ran from 2007 through 2011. Immediately after the end of season eight, season nine began and ran for two years (2011–2013) with 25 issues. Each series has several associated one-off issues and/or miniseries published concurrently that explored particular substories in more depth. Meanwhile, the *Angel* storyline was continued in *Angel: After the Fall,* a comic series from IDW. A concurrent *Spike* comic connected the continuing Angel and Buffy character stories. As most of the major characters go their separate way, with each producing a separate story, the overall storylines in the comics become much more complicated.

As the eighth season unfolded, Buffy robbed a Swiss bank to obtain the funds to set up a technologically sophisticated central command for those Slayers aligned to her (about 500 of the 1,800 in existence). Also, at Buffy's command is a large number of psychics and witches. To help protect the famous Slayer, two decoy Slayers have been deployed. From their headquarters in a Scottish castle, Buffy and Xander have organized the Slayers into ten squads. Giles heads one in England, while Robin, the principal of Sunnydale High School at the time when the town was destroyed, leads one in Cleveland, Ohio. Two other Slayers, Vi and Rona, who appeared in the seventh season, are operating squads in New York and Chicago.

The U.S. government, already aware of the existence of a variety of demonic beings, did not ignore the destruction of Sunnydale. They now look upon Buffy and her allies as a dangerous "terrorist" group that must be handled in the same manner as vampires and demons. They have recruited Amy Madison (a witch from the original series) and the still-skinless Warren Mears, and in case the government's coming after her is not enough, Buffy must stave off the ambitions of a British socialite-turned-Slayer named Lady Genevieve Savidge, who wishes to take Buffy's place at the head of the Slayer organization. Among the vampires, a savvy group from Japan are working on a way to reverse Willow's global activation of the potential Slayers. Behind all these forces targeting Buffy is an enigmatic character named Twilight. He heads a secret organization not unlike the original Initiative that views Buffy and the Slayers as the enemy of humanity as harmful as the vampires and demons. Twilight aims to end the age of magic, both good and evil.

***Buffy* Culture:** *Buffy the Vampire Slayer* became a "cult" phenomenon that spun off numerous items beginning with a series of books, some novelized versions of the different episodes and others as entirely new stories. Comic books, action figures, and more than 20 sets of trading cards followed. Pictures of the primary cast members and the show's logo could be found on items from watches to lunch boxes, with T-shirts being among the most popular items.

The show grew with the expansion of the internet, and fan activity made full use of it. Internet networks led to organization of the first fan gatherings in the late 1990s, and many of the cast members showed up for an annual

The cast of Buffy the Vampire Slayer *attends a panel at the 2017 German Comic Con in Dortmund. Even after the show ended, Buffy culture continues to be popular around the world.*

gathering in Los Angeles. Fan fiction also became quite popular until suppressed for a host of copyright and trademark considerations.

A most fascinating phenomenon was found within the scholarly community, where an appreciation of Buffy, then Angel, and then the work of Joss Whedon evolved. Interest developed initially among professors of cinema and television but soon spread to scholars of literature, sociology, philosophy, and religious studies. An initial conference was held at the University of East Anglia in Norwich, England, in October 2002 under the title Blood, Text and Fears: Reading around *Buffy the Vampire Slayer*. The conference brought together 100 scholars from across Europe and North America and as far away as Australia. Recognizing the emerging field of Buffyology, two American scholars, Rhonda Wilcox and David Lavery, put together *Slayage*,

an online scholarly journal, a network of scholars, and, beginning in 2004, biennial conferences. Almost 400 scholars showed up for the 2004 conference in Nashville, Tennessee.

The scholarly attention to Buffy and Angel evolved into a focus on Whedon's additional post-*Buffy* work that has included additional movies and television series, now termed the Whedonverses. The scholarly attention to Whedon and his work has had a dramatic effect on the production of academic work on vampires. As of 2020, almost half of all the published scholarly articles and books on vampires have had *Buffy the Vampire Slayer* and/or *Angel* as their subject. The biennial Slayage conferences also present a set of Mr. Pointy awards for the best writing on the Whedonverses, the award being named for the stake that the Slayer Kendra gave to Buffy in season two.

Also see the *Buffy the Vampire Slayer* (movie, 1992) entry, p. 407.

Angel

The successful 1997 television series *Buffy the Vampire Slayer* introduced several new vampire characters as objects of the Slayer's deadly intentions. However, one of the vampires proved distinctive: Angel or Angelus (David Boreanaz). He was young and handsome. He appeared to be only a few years older than vampire Slayer Buffy Summers (Sarah Michelle Gellar) but, in fact, was some 240 years old. After an intense but doomed attempt to have a relationship with Buffy, he left for Los Angeles and, for five years, was head of Angel Investigations, his own detective agency, searching for redemption.

Angel was born as Liam in 1727 in Galway, Ireland, the son of a cloth merchant. Living a life in the taverns, he eventually met a woman named Darla (Julie Benz), who turned out to be a vampire. She sired him and, as a vampire, he took the name Angelus, a reference to his reputation as a vicious monster with an angelic face. He spent the first decades as a vampire in Europe. He killed freely, like other vampires, lacking any conscience. Early victims included his own family and neighbors. His search for further victims eventually led him to Eastern Europe. In 1898, Angelus slew the favorite daughter of a tribe of Romani people. In retaliation, the Kalderash clan cursed him by restoring his human soul, thus afflicting him with a conscience and condemning him to an eternity of remorse for the many people he had killed as Angelus. From that time forward, in spite of the bloodlust, he found himself unable to feed on a human being. He changed his name from Angelus to Angel and, shortly thereafter, he moved to America (1902). He lived alone and shunned the company of other vampires.

Angel found his way to the California town of Sunnydale in 1996, where he renewed his acquaintance with some old friends, Darla and the Master. He refused the offer of the Master to return to the fold. In the meantime, Angel took a liking to Buffy and made himself her self-appointed guardian, warning and protecting her. One evening, as three vampires sent by the Master attacked Buffy, Angel helped defeat them. His intervention warned her of the Master's initial attempt to establish himself in Sunnydale, taking advantage of a particular moment each century, the Harvest. Later, he again came to her aid and was injured. Buffy found herself falling in love with him as she cared for his wounds.

Angel soon had to confront two new vampires who arrived in Sunnydale to fill the vacuum caused by the death of the Master: Drusilla, whom he had driven mad and sired; and Spike (James Marsters), whom Drusilla (Juliet Landau) had sired.

While Buffy was concentrating on Spike and Drusilla, Angel placed his ability to feel human emotion in jeopardy when he and Buffy shared an intimate moment. The result was disastrous; Angel lost his soul (conscience) and reverted to his previous persona of Angelus. As the second season ended, Buffy now realized that she had to destroy the evil vampire with whom she had fallen in love, stabbed him with a sword, and sent him to the hell realms.

He returned the next season after what had for him been a century in hell-time and spent much of the season readjusting to life as Angel again. He recovered and won everyone's trust in time to fight the last battle on Buffy's graduation day but, knowing that his relation-

> From that time forward, in spite of the bloodlust, he found himself unable to feed on a human being.

ship with Buffy was doomed, he withdrew from Sunnydale (and the *Buffy the Vampire Slayer* show) and moved to Los Angeles.

Angel's further adventures would continue on his own show, called simply *Angel*, which finds him in Los Angeles fighting evil, including his fellow vampires, but trying to find some means of ridding himself of his load of guilt, balancing the ledger of his life that now weighed against him with the many people he had killed and looking for some possible future redemption. Meanwhile, as he moves through the city, he runs into Cordelia Chase (Charisma Carpenter), one of Buffy's classmates who had joined her circle of vampire fighters but who was in Los Angeles unsuccessfully pursuing an acting/modeling career and broke. She talked her way into a job by convincing Angel to form a detective agency in order to give a businesslike structure to his activities as well as provide an income for himself.

They were initially joined at Angel Investigations by Doyle, a half demon with the ability to have visions of people in distress and in need of their services. Doyle also supplied a connection to the Powers That Be, ancient beings who operate from a different dimension and who, as far as they have the ability (which is strictly limited), guide humanity in goodness. When Doyle is killed, he passes his powers to Cordelia. Angel Investigations is subsequently joined by former Watcher Wesley Wyndam-Pryce (Alexis Denisof), now describing himself as a "rogue demon hunter," and the streetwise African American demon fighter Charles Gunn (J. August Richards). They are also assisted by demon and karaoke bar owner Lorne (Andy Hallett), whose major ability is sensing the futures of people when they sing for him.

Emerging as the major enemy opposing Angel Investigations is the large law firm of Wolfram & Hart, a powerful international law firm that is a front organization for a demonic cabal known as the Wolf, Ram, and Hart, who now appear as the firm's senior partners. Among the first actions against Angel is sending the rogue vampire Slayer over whom Wesley had watched, Faith (Eliza Dushku), to kill Angel. She is defeated and, under Angel's influence, begins her own redemptive process. Along the way, the team enters into another dimension, where they encounter the psychically wounded Fred (i.e., Winifred "Fred" Burkle, portrayed by Amy Acker), who eventually joins their team, adding her genius-level intellect.

Angel's life takes a new direction when Darla resurfaces, pregnant with what proves to be their son Connor (Vincent Kartheiser). Soon after his birth, however, Connor is stolen by Angel's old enemy, the vampire Slayer Holtz (Keith Szarabajka), who takes Connor into the hell dimension, where he is raised to think that Angel is completely evil. When they return, with Connor now a young man, Holtz com-

David Boreanaz portrayed Angel, a conflicted vampire who wants to be a good guy.

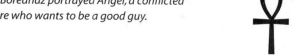

mits suicide in such a way that it appears that Angel has murdered him. Angel now has to attempt a reconciliation with his estranged son; deal with a possessed Cordelia, who has lost her memory; and tame a powerful beast creature, who seems beyond him and his team. In order to kill the latter, he has to relinquish his soul for a period of time and revert to his Angelus persona.

To deal with Connor, he makes a deal with Wolfram & Hart to take over their offices in Los Angeles. In return, Connor's memories are erased, and he is placed with a normal family. Cordelia was finally freed from the evil entity Jasmine who had possessed her, but immediately, she fell into a coma. She revived only for a short time before dying, though she later reappeared as a spirit entity. After the final battle in Sunnydale that left only a crater where the city had once existed, Spike survived as a spirit, who popped up at Wolfram & Hart to join the fight against evil. He finally gets his body back. Once he and Angel resolve their jealousies over Buffy, they become staunch allies.

In the end, Angel comes to see that he cannot stop the forces of evil represented by Wolfram & Hart, but he can have a temporary victory by severing the senior partners' hold on Earth. He and his remaining team assassinate the members of the Circle of the Black Thorn, the group through which the senior partners work on Earth. In the process, Wesley is killed and Gunn is wounded but manages to make it to the spot behind the Hyperion Hotel in Los Angeles. He joins Angel, Spike, and Illyria (a demon who has taken over Fred's body) for the final battle with the forces the senior partners have aligned for their destruction. As the final episode ends, they move forward with the words, "Let's go to work."

Angel, the Comic Book: In 1999, Dark Horse Comics, which had the license for the *Buffy the Vampire Slayer* comics, began publishing an *Angel* comic book. Two series appeared before it was discontinued in 2002. Then in 2005, IDW picked up the license and began issuing *Angel* comics as a set of successive miniseries. Finally, in 2007, creator Joss Whedon authorized an official continuation of the story from the *Angel* television show. The story was developed by writer Brian Lynch, working with Whedon.

In *Angel: After the Fall*, the battle with the senior partners launched in season five has resulted in the movement of the city of Los Angeles into a hell dimension. In an attempt to deprive him of his strength and immortality when he needed it most, the senior partners have also turned Angel into a human, forcing Angel and his ally, Wesley, to rely on mystical enchantments to provide Angel with at least a measure of his old abilities. He begins to reassemble his team, including Illyria. Lorne helps recruit new friends. In the process, Connor is killed. They defeat the demons that infest Los Angeles, but the city is still the target of the senior partners. Angel finally devises a scheme. Knowing that they need him alive, he allows Gunn to kill him. Time began again, and they are returned to the spot behind the hotel ready to fight and defeat the forces sent by Wolfram & Hart. Everyone, including Connor, retains their memory of what has occurred, and Angel became a hero.

Angel as Cult Phenomenon: Though never as popular as *Buffy the Vampire Slayer*, *Angel* and its characters attained a following of their own, especially in the year after the end of the *Buffy* episodes, when *Angel* continued. Among the most important items indicative of the show's permeation of popular culture, along

> In the end, Angel comes to see that he cannot stop the forces of evil represented by Wolfram & Hart, but he can have a temporary victory by severing the senior partners' hold on Earth.

with the comic books, were a set of young adult novels, some of which, like the *Buffy* novels, were translated into several languages, including German and French. A number of action figures and trading card sets were also produced. Along with *Buffy*, *Angel* attracted the attention of the scholarly community as part of the larger Whedonverses. Consideration of the show manifested in a number of academic papers delivered at the various Whedonverses conferences and at least two books. Spike, who came to rival Angel as the most popular vampire character, bolstered the crossover attention between the two television series. Most of the comic books featuring Spike have been part of the *Angel* comics from IDW.

Angel was portrayed by David Boreanaz. The part was his first big break, though earlier, he had a bit part in one vampire movie, *Macabre Pair of Shorts* (1996). He followed eight years of work on first *Buffy the Vampire Slayer* and then *Angel* with several movies before starring in the very successful ongoing series *Bones* beginning in 2005. He has been the subject of an annual wall calendar since 1999.

Chase, Cordelia

Cordelia Chase (Charisma Carpenter) was a companion of Buffy Summers and later of the vampire Angel on the *Buffy the Vampire Slayer* television series and then on its spin-off, *Angel*. A character created by Joss Whedon, she initially appeared in the first season of *Buffy the Vampire Slayer*, with the plot featuring her initially in the 11th episode, "Out of Mind, Out of Sight," when she is running in the Sunnydale High School May Queen contest. By this time, she has been introduced as the beautiful daughter of well-to-do parents and the head of a group of the most popular girls on campus, informally called the Cordettes. Needless to say, she represents the glamorous, high-status females who have no trouble attracting multiple dating partners.

Cordelia was initially interested in recruiting the attractive Buffy into her clique of cool people but began to avoid her after seeing her association with "losers" such as Willow Rosenberg and Xander Harris. Buffy, attacking Cordelia with a stake (while searching for a vampire behind the local teen hangout spot, The Bronze), did little to cement an initial positive relationship.

Cordelia's relationship with Buffy changed when she and the Cordettes find themselves under attack from an invisible entity. She came to Buffy and asked for help. Buffy was able to track the problem to Marcie Ross, who had been treated as if she were invisible during her high school years and, as a result, became literally invisible. Buffy's stopping Marcie begins a new relationship with Cordelia, which is really reoriented when a short time later, she sees Buffy kill the vampire known as the Master. Cordelia is now fully aware of the supernatural realities invading the high school from the Hellmouth below.

Charisma Carpenter played Cordelia Chase on both the Buffy *and* Angel *TV series.*

In the second season, Cordelia hangs out increasingly with Buffy and her vampire/demon-fighting group. About halfway through the season, she finds herself arguing vehemently with Xander, whom she has previously held in contempt, only to end the argument in his arms kissing him passionately. Though seeming to have little in common, they begin dating. Publicly dating Xander further changes her, leads to a split with the Cordettes, and revises her opinion of uncool boys. She dates Xander into season three but eventually breaks up with him. Shortly thereafter, her status is deflated when tax problems cause her family to lose everything. Though they are no longer dating, Xander quietly pays for a dress so Cordelia can attend the senior prom.

Cordelia helps Buffy fight the mayor at the graduation ceremony but then leaves for Los Angeles, where she hopes to have a career in acting. She works at Angel Investigations, the vampire Angel's private detective agency, while awaiting a break that would never come. Actually, she is the one who convinces Angel, Buffy's former vampire boyfriend, to found the agency as a vehicle for his efforts to do good. When Angel's associate Doyle dies, he passes to Cordelia his ability to have visions of people in need of Angel's help. Though painful when they occur, she comes to see the visions as her reason to be alive. After a particularly painful vision on her 21st birthday, she accepts an offer to become a half demon, which allows her to have the visions without pain and deterioration of her brain.

Her new status allows Cordelia to be deceived, and after three months, she is fed half truths about Angel that lead to their alienation. She also takes up with Connor, Angel's alienated son, and becomes possessed by the entity Jasmine, during which time she has sex with Connor and becomes pregnant. Connor and Cordelia finally perform a ritual to force Jasmine out, but as a result, Cordelia falls into a coma.

Cordelia awakens to find Angel in charge of the Los Angeles office of Wolfram & Hart, the legal firm that both represents and controls the dark forces against which Buffy, Angel, and their cohorts fight. She believes that Angel is making a bad decision but finally informs him that her return is only temporary, and she kisses him goodbye. Angel then receives word that Cordelia died in the hospital. After her final death, Cordelia reappears in spirit form on several occasions, once in the final episode of the *Angel* series and later in the *Angel* and *Buffy the Vampire Slayer* comic books.

Noting the significant transformation of the Cordelia Chase character, film and literature scholar Jes Battis observed that Cordelia began as a "self-centered, acerbic, and popularity-obsessed teenager" but ends as an elevated being, whose last favor to Angel is to remind him that he is quite capable of doing his work without "the nefarious resources of Wolfram and Hart." She reminded those around Angel that they were family, and she pushes them beyond their alleged limitations.

Cordelia Chase was portrayed by Charisma Carpenter (1970–). She had appeared in several television series prior to becoming part of the *Buffy* cast and has continued her television and movie career since *Angel* concluded, including appearing in several episodes of *CSI*.

Giles, Rupert

Rupert Giles, a major character on the TV series *Buffy the Vampire Slayer*, was the Watcher who in 1997 was assigned to Buffy Summers, the new Slayer who had just arrived at Sunnydale High School. His cover was to pose as the school librarian, which was very convenient, as it allowed him to accumulate, store, and have immediately available a spectrum of ancient and obscure texts that Buffy and her vampire and demon-hunting associates would need. It was also the perfect place to hold strategy sessions with the students who had gathered around the Slayer. Giles's cool, unflappable, and thoroughly British style contrasted with Buffy's often impulsive and bottom-line approach to her work. Over time, however, they developed a close relationship, and she credits him with her maturity.

Giles came from a line of Watchers, which included his father and grandmother. He was a reluctant recruit to the Watcher's ranks, but after a period of time dabbling in the occult and working in a museum—both of which would provide a useful background for his task—he accepted the assignment with Buffy. As her Watcher, he provided information, guided the emergence of her own powers and talents, trained her in various fighting skills, and offered magical and other backup as needed. At times, he operated as a substitute for Buffy's largely absent father.

It is Giles who laid out the mythical world in which the Slayer operates in the first two episodes of *Buffy*, and he was usually the one who brought forth the texts that were relevant to the current situation. As the series progresses and Buffy's friend Willow Rosenberg masters the computer, she begins to rival Giles in knowledge, albeit from a different source.

Once in Sunnydale, he began dating and fell in love with Jenny Calendar, a teacher at the high school. He later learned that she was from the Romani tribe that cursed Angel by giving him back his soul and that it was her job to keep an eye on him. When Angel reverted to his evil Angelus-self in season two, Jenny worked to reinstitute his soul, but Angel killed her before she could finish the spell. A short time later, Giles was kidnapped by Angel and tortured. He never really trusted Angel after that incident.

Following the destruction of Sunnydale High School at the end of season three, Giles spent a year unemployed but then purchased an occult shop that became the new headquarters of the Slayer and her friends. He is especially helped by Anya, the former demon who became Xander Harris's girlfriend. Naïve in the ways of the world, she was fascinated with the idea of sales and moneymaking. At one point, Giles ate some enchanted candy supplied by an old acquaintance named Ethan Rayne (Robin Sachs). As a result, he reverted to his teen consciousness, committed some acts of vandalism and thievery, and had a brief sexual encounter with Buffy's mother, Joyce (Kristine Sutherland).

As Buffy matured, she became more independent and developed a significant distrust of the Watcher's Council. She eventually cut her ties with the council but asked Giles to remain her Watcher. He did so for a little while, during which time Buffy's new sister, Dawn, appeared and Buffy's mother died.

In the midst of the final season, Giles returned to Sunnydale for the last time, bringing with him all the potential Slayers for the final battle set up by the First Evil.

With the death of Joyce, Buffy was left without an income and slowly developed a mountain of debt. Meanwhile, she sacrificed herself to save Dawn and the world. Giles decided it was time for him to withdraw, and he returned to England just as Willow, now an accomplished witch, organized Buffy's friends in a great, magical action that brought her back from the dead. Upon learning that Buffy had come back, Giles returned to Sunnydale. Though happy to see Buffy again, he denounced Willow's action as the work of an amateur. Having surmised that his presence was blocking Buffy's further growth and independence, he now readied himself to return to England, but before leaving, he gave Buffy a substantial check, enough to pay off her debt and carry her until she could reestablish herself financially.

The Watcher Rupert Giles was played by actor Anthony Head, who is not only a successful actor but also a singer and musician.

After Giles left for England, Willow went on a magical rampage after her lover, Tara, was killed. Hearing of her destructive activity, Giles returned and allowed her to drain him almost to the point of death. His act infused Willow with some positive magical energy and set the stage for Xander to reason her back to her senses, after which Giles took Willow to England for a time of recovery.

In the midst of the final season, Giles returned to Sunnydale for the last time, bringing with him all the potential Slayers for the final battle set up by the First Evil. In the final episode, he was present for the battle at the Hellmouth and was one of the survivors.

Giles played a role, though never seen, in the last season of *Angel:* he was in Europe training a host of new Slayers and working with former Sunnydale resident (and comic relief) Andrew Wells, who is in training to be a Watcher. Angel contacted Giles in an attempt to find Buffy.

In the comic book season eight of *Buffy,* Giles headed Buffy's international slaying operations in England. At one point, he recruited the Slayer Faith to assist him in killing a rogue Slayer named Gigi and her colleague Roden, both headed on a highly destructive course. As a result of their actions, Buffy broke relations with Giles, but he and Faith continued their antivampire activities. Meanwhile, Angel came under the veil influence of the entity known as Twilight. While under Twilight's influence, Angel killed Giles. Angel later joined with Faith and partially undid his act by resurrecting Giles except that Giles returned as a 12-year-old boy. He continued to act under his new persona.

Although one of the most popular characters in the show, Giles was among the least featured in the paraphernalia spun off from the show. He appeared on a variety of trading cards, most notably the "Men of Sunnydale" set from Inkworks (2005), and in several action figures. Meanwhile, librarians appreciated the identification of Giles's occupation and wisdom with his many skills in martial arts and magic, leading some to argue that he had done more to improve the image of the profession than anyone in recent years.

Harris, Xander

Xander Harris (Nicholas Brendon), short for Alexander LaVelle Harris, a main character in the *Buffy the Vampire Slayer* TV series, grew up in Sunnydale, California, the town in which the show was set. He was a childhood friend of Willow Rosenberg, and both were sophomores at Sunnydale High School when Buffy Summers transferred from Los Angeles. He learned of Buffy's calling to the fight against vampires soon after her transfer and, along with Willow (Alyson Hannigan), insisted on joining the crusade. He had no particular skills or intelligence to offer but became Buffy's faithful friend and supporter.

Xander had a variety of relationships with women, most disastrous. His longest high school relationship was with Cordelia Chase (Charisma Carpenter), their attraction being an enigma among Cordelia's former friends, the more wealthy and trendy girls. He eventually built a reputation for falling for women who turned out to be demons. In season three, he encountered Anyanka, a vengeance demon, who had dedicated the last thousand years to granting wishes of revenge to women who had been wronged by their man. She showed up in Sunnydale after Xander cheated on Cordelia with Willow. In the process of granting a wish to Cordelia, she was transformed into the human Anya (Emma Caulfield). She eventually started dating Xander, and they remained a twosome, off and on, for the rest of the series.

Xander helped Buffy defeat Sunnydale's demonic mayor at the end of season three. Afterward, he did not attempt to enter college but spent a year trying to find himself. He lived with his parents and worked at a series of jobs. Anya left before the final battle at the school but later returned, and she and Xander began an affair that led to his asking her to marry him. By this time, he had gotten a more permanent job in construction.

At the beginning of season five, Dracula briefly visited Sunnydale and Xander became one of his first victims, spending most of the episode as his servant. His real crisis came later, however, as the reality of his marriage to Anya approached. In the end, he got cold feet and left her at the altar. In her humiliation and anger, she once again became a vengeance demon, though after only a short time, she sought to become human again. His own maturity was shown when he argued Willow out of destroying the world in her anger over her girlfriend Tara's death.

Xander remained loyal to Buffy until the end and, in the last season, it cost him his eye. Buffy appreciated the fact that even though Xander never developed any special talents or powers, he was always there to assist and never left her for even a short time. He faced the last battle over the Hellmouth with an eye patch. He survived the final battle, but Anya did not. In the final season of *Angel*, Xander was mentioned as being in Africa working with recently activated Slayers.

Xander's attachment to and faithfulness toward Buffy would be again demonstrated when he joined her in Scotland at the international headquarters of the vampire-fighting organization she created in the comic book season eight.

Xander was overshadowed in popularity throughout the series by Angel and Spike, though he remained a constant presence. As *Buffy* paraphernalia began to appear, he was a ubiquitous presence in the trading cards and the subject of a set of action figures.

After a successful run on Buffy *playing Xander Harris, actor Nicholas Brendon portrayed Kevin Lynch on* Criminal Minds *from 2007 to 2014.*

Lehane, Faith

Faith (Eliza Dushku), whose family name is revealed to be Lehane, was a new vampire

Slayer introduced in the third season of the popular *Buffy the Vampire Slayer* television show. She arrived in Sunnydale, California, as a response to the death of her predecessor, Kendra. Buffy died briefly at the end of season one only to be revived. Her brief death had, however, called forth her successor somewhat prematurely, thus creating a situation in which two Slayers would exist simultaneously at any given moment until the end of season seven, during which a multitude of Slayers were created. After Faith's appearance, she would alternate between being Buffy's companion, rival, and enemy.

Faith arrived in Sunnydale with an old vampire, Kakistos, chasing her. He had killed her overseer (her Watcher) but was dispatched by Buffy. As their relationship developed, Buffy and Faith worked together while demonstrating two very different personalities and approaches to fighting vampires. They worked together until Faith accidentally killed a human who was mistaken for a vampire in the heat of battle. She went rogue and aligned with the demonic Mayor Wilkens. She subsequently

Like some other cast members, Eliza Dushku continued her role as Faith in Angel.

fought Buffy to a draw but wound up in a coma. Upon her recovery, she swapped bodies with Buffy for a period of time but eventually fled to Los Angeles rather than face a felony warrant for her arrest.

In Los Angeles as a cast member of *Angel*, Faith found redemption under Angel's care, a process that led her to confess to the murder back in Sunnydale, which resulted in spending time in prison. She escaped her imprisonment to deal with Angel when he reverted to his evil self as Angelus, but in the end, she returned to Sunnydale to help train the cadre of new Slayers and take up the final battle with the First Evil (portrayed by Nathan Fillion) that ended season seven.

As the storyline from the *Buffy the Vampire Slayer* and *Angel* shows continued in the comic books, Faith initially aligned with Robin Wood, the former principal of Sunnydale High School, and with Giles. Giles sent her to assassinate a rogue Slayer, and they subsequently formed a working team. She was present when Angel, under the influence of an evil demonic entity named Twilight, killed Giles. She refused to kill Angel because of his earlier effort to assist her at her low point. She also inherited Giles's estate, where she led a group of new Slayers on a variety of adventures, including some to clean up the mess that Twilight created. Her story continues as the series continues (2020).

Rosenberg, Willow

A primary member of the Scooby Gang, a small group surrounding Buffy the Vampire Slayer for support, Willow Rosenberg (Alyson Hannigan), a lifelong resident of Sunnydale, met the Slayer when she moved from Los Angeles to begin her sophomore year at Sunnydale High School. Willow soon became Buffy's best friend. She is smart and has a mastery of the internet, which proved valuable in diagnosing the demonic forces that Buffy must defeat.

As the *Buffy* story began, Willow was sweet on Xander (Nicholas Brendon) but later developed a relationship with Oz (Seth Green), a werewolf. Willow also began to explore magic and the occult. Her search for occult knowledge and power led her to a Wicca group. Though largely incapable of accessing any real magic, she met Tara Maclay (Amber Benson), who led her into some magical prowess, and the two developed a primary personal relationship. Meanwhile, Willow's magical abilities became a key element in defeating many of the demonic enemies with whom the Slayer encountered.

Willow's magical accomplishments reached a peak following Buffy's sacrificial death at the end of season five. She organized a magical ritual early in season six that brought Buffy back to earthly life. After becoming possibly the most

Alyson Hannigan, who portrayed Willow Rosenberg, has had a robust acting career after Buffy, *including on the successful comedy series* How I Met Your Mother *and in the* American Pie *movies.*

powerful practitioner of magic on the planet, Willow also realized that she was addicted to magic and backed away from its practice for a period of time. That distance from magic ended with Tara's death and the overwhelming desire to wreak violence on those responsible for her death. As she carried out her vengeance, she briefly allowed a darker side to come to the fore, and her appearance changed dramatically into what was termed "Dark Willow."

Xander became instrumental in talking Willow back from the dark side, and she thereafter worked to keep that side of her suppressed. During season seven, she was able to both assist Angel in recovering his soul and bring him back from his latest stint as the soulless Angelus, empowering the cadre of new Slayers to face the final battle with the First Evil.

In season eight, which continued the story in comic book form, Willow joined Buffy's international vampire-slaying organization, though she did not move to Scotland to work side by side with her. Buffy, however, destroyed what is termed the seed of wonder, which has the effect of driving all magic from Earth. Devastated by her action, Willow worked to bring magic back to Earth by producing a new seed. Willow thus continued her magical career through season nine.

Also in season eight, Willow stepped away from her duties with Buffy's Slayer organization in order to develop her magical powers under the guidance of a half woman, half snake demon named Aluwyn. The story of her timeout was the subject of a one-shot comic book called *Willow: Goddesses and Monsters* (2009).

Spike

Spike, also known as William the Bloody, was a vampire character from the *Buffy the Vampire Slayer* television series, portrayed by James Marsters. He made his initial appearance in season two, arriving in town as one episode closed. Later, however, he became—along with his female cohort, Drusilla—one of the show's more popular villains. He hung around long after his initial storyline was exhausted and emerged as one of the leading ongoing characters on the show. After the *Buffy* series ended, a place was found for him on the *Buffy* spin-off show *Angel.*

Spike's life before his arrival in Sunnydale, California (Buffy's hometown) was revealed in various episodes of *Buffy.* He emerged as a young poet in London, England, at some point in the late nineteenth century. He got his nickname, William the Bloody, from friends who thought his poetry was "bloody awful" but was saved from a life of bad reviews by Drusilla (Juliet Landau), the slightly deranged vampire who turned him. He then met the evil Angel (before he was cursed with the return of his soul) and was thus trained in the vampire life by the one known as Angelus. Angel aside, however, while developing his close relationship with Drusilla, Spike turned on those who complained that they would rather have a railroad spike driven through their head than listen to his poetry. From his acts of revenge, he adopted the name by which he became known. He seemed to enjoy killing people.

Spike often bragged about killing two Slayers (one in China in 1900 and another, named Nikki Wood, in 1977 in New York) and came to Sunnydale to kill number three. He wore a black jacket, which he took from the second Slayer. He had at least one encounter with Dracula, who tossed Spike's autographed copy of Bram Stoker's novel into a fire. Spike claimed that Dracula owed him £11 for the lost book. He also came to Sunnydale (the site of the Hellmouth, the entrance to the hell realms) in an attempt to find healing for Drusilla, who had been hurt while under attack from a mob.

By the time Spike and Drusilla arrived in Sunnydale, Spike had taken on the persona

of a punk rocker. His love of killing was immediately manifested when he attacked a group of people at Sunnydale High School and almost got to Buffy. He then aligned with Angel but broke off their friendship when Angel (now reverted to his evil side) attempted to make Drusilla his lover. The ups and downs of his relationship with Drusilla became a sub-plot of season three and eventually took him from the city.

Spike returned to Sunnydale in a quest to find the Gem of Amarra, a ring with the power to make any vampire immune to sunlight. His effort was thwarted, however, and he was eventually taken captive by the Initiative, a secret government agency that was tracking and fighting the various kinds of creatures that Buffy opposed. It planted a microchip in Spike that prevented him from biting (or otherwise hurting) any human. Once freed of their control, he turned to Buffy for assistance. Over the next year, he assisted Buffy's friends but also betrayed

James Marsters, who played Spike in Buffy *and* Angel *has made a career of being in sci-fi and fantasy TV and movies; he also has an interest in comic books and even authors one.*

them on occasion, constantly searching for a way to get the chip removed. He also fell in love with Buffy only to have her constantly reject him. She was horrified to discover that he had a robot double of her upon which to exercise his fantasies.

A significant change in Buffy and Spike's relationship began when he refused to disclose the identity of Buffy's sister Dawn as the Key the demon goddess glory was seeking. He then aligned with Buffy's friends to continue the fight against vampires in the period after Buffy's death at the end of season five and prior to her resurrection in season six. His unusual status as a member of the close circle around Buffy allowed him to become Buffy's confidant. It is to Spike that Buffy revealed that she had been in a heavenly state while dead and was unhappy with her friends for bringing her back. While still grieving her situation, Buffy began a sexual relationship with Spike, notable for its violence. Buffy finally ended the relationship, considering it unsatisfying. Unwilling to accept being cut off, Spike attempted to rape Buffy. Finally, realizing that in his present condition he could never have the relationship he wanted with her, he departed Sunnydale for a remote location, where he found a shaman who was capable of giving him his soul (the major component being a conscience).

As the only vampire other than Angel with a soul, Spike returned to Sunnydale ready to make things right with Buffy and to assist her against the ultimate opponent, the First Evil. Meanwhile, even as he attempted to establish some trust, his new conscience forced him to deal with guilt over his past actions. Buffy finally took him in and oversaw his recovery. She also facilitated the removal of his chip. He then had to withstand the attention of the son of the Slayer Nikki Wood, whom he had killed, and who, as the new principal of Sunnydale High, had aligned with Buffy.

While not renewing their sexual relationship, Spike and Buffy became close emotionally.

In the final battle with the horde of vampires emerging from the Hellmouth, Buffy trusted Spike with the key action. He wore a magical amulet and, in an act of self-sacrifice, allowed its energy to radiate from him to destroy the horde and close the Hellmouth. In the process, Spike was consumed along with all of Sunnydale. Just before Spike died, Buffy professed her love for him.

As had been demonstrated throughout the *Buffy* and *Angel* series, it was difficult to kill a vampire with any finality. Thus, it was not surprising that, given Spike's popularity, he reappeared on the continuing *Angel* series. He was resurrected by another amulet but initially manifested as a ghostlike being. He haunted the law firm Wolfram & Hart, whose Los Angeles office had been taken over by Angel and his new group of colleagues. After some time, he was finally reembodied. His rivalry with Angel gave him an ambiguous role, and he truly aligned with Angel only after one of his team, a woman called Fred (short for Winifred), was killed by the demon Illyria, who took over Fred's body. In the final episode, Spike joined Angel in the battle to sever, at least temporarily, the senior partners of Wolfram & Hart's positioning on Earth by destroying the Circle of the Black Thorn, their major point of access.

The fact that Spike ended his television appearances on *Angel* has had serious implications for the continuation of the character in the post-television comic books. While both Spike and Angel had cameo appearances in the season eight series of *Buffy the Vampire Slayer* comics from Dark Horse Comics, Spike's major adventures have been in the *Angel* comics from IDW Publishing. In *Angel: After the Fall*, the official comic book that continued the television storyline, we learned that both Spike and Angel survived the battle that was just beginning as the television series ended but that the city of Los Angeles now existed in a hell dimension. As Angel regrouped, Spike took up residence in Beverly Hills, where he and Illyria were living outwardly as demon lords while assisting humans to escape life in Los Angeles and joining Angel's efforts to bring down his fellow demon lords. Spike also continued to protect Illyria because she possessed the essence of Fred and, hence, the possibility of her resurrection.

As Spike's character increased in popularity, he began to appear on all of the paraphernalia that developed out of the television series. He was pictured on numerous trading cards, had his own action figures, and eventually, as noted above, was featured in his own comic books (from IDW). Spike has also prompted significant comments from scholars studying Buffy and Angel.

Summers, Buffy

Buffy Summers was the vampire Slayer who was the main protagonist of the *Buffy the Vampire Slayer* movie (1992) and television series, which lasted for seven seasons, five on the WB network (1997–2001) and two on the UPN network (2001–2003). She has subsequently appeared in seasons eight and nine, which continued the story of her post-television years in comic book form.

Buffy was born Buffy Anne Summers in California on (according to her tombstone) January 19, 1981, the daughter of Hank and Joyce Summers (Kristine Sutherland). Little is known of her life prior to her entering Hemery High School in Los Angeles, where she became a cheerleader and was eventually named both Prom Princess and Fiesta Queen.

During her first year at Hemery, Buffy (Kristy Swanson) was approached by a man named Merrick (Donald Sutherland), who informed her that she was the "chosen one," the new Slayer of vampires; he was sent to be her

> As Spike's character increased in popularity, he began to appear on all of the paraphernalia that developed out of the television series.

Watcher and train her. She reluctantly began to accept her role. Eventually, she was forced to square off against Lothos (Rutger Hauer), the main vampire in town. She was able to kill him, but their confrontation led to a fire that consumed the high school gym. In the wake of the fire, Buffy was expelled, and her parents separated. Buffy moved with her mother, a dealer in exotic art, to Sunnydale, California, where she tried to begin a new life as a sophomore at the local high school.

The television series took up the story with Buffy (now portrayed by Sarah Michelle Gellar) beginning her sophomore year at Sunnydale High School. She soon became aware of people dying in ways that she recognized. She also met Rupert Giles (Anthony Stewart Head), the school's librarian, whose job provided cover for his real role as Buffy's Watcher. Over the next few years, he trained and mentored her. She made two new friends, Willow Rosenberg (Alyson Hannigan) and Xander Harris (Nicholas Brendon), neither of whom was in the "in" crowd. Willow would become Buffy's best friend and later use her computer skills and magical talents to assist Buffy in her slaying activities. Buffy was invited into the circle of beautiful people led by Cordelia Chase (Charisma Carpenter) but chose to keep her friendships with Willow and Xander. Cordelia soon learned the truth about vampires and demons firsthand and was brought into the inner circle somewhat against her wishes.

The kids from the high school gathered at The Bronze, the local nightclub for teens. An encounter with vampires outside the club occasioned Buffy meeting Angel (David Boreanaz), a good-guy vampire with whom she fell in love. In the second season, she lost her virginity to him. He, however, existed under a curse. Vampires are normally soulless revenants, but Angel had been given his soul and, with it, a conscience. The curse is that should he experience a moment of true happiness, as what occurred when making love to Buffy, he would lose his soul. He transformed into his vicious former self, Angelus, and Buffy was forced to send him to hell. By this time, Buffy had already experienced death, if only for a few minutes, and her death triggered the emergence of her successor, Kendra (Bianca Lawson). Kendra's relatively brief career as a Slayer led to the appearance of a new Slayer, Faith (Eliza Dushku).

Buffy fought a series of vampires and demons, the first major one being the Master, who killed her at the end of season one. Gradually, a set of continuing vampire antagonists would emerge, most notably Darla (Julie Benz), Spike (James Marsters), and Drusilla (Juliet Landau).

Buffy's high school years would culminate in a monumental battle at Sunnydale High School in which the forces of evil organized around Sunnydale's mayor (Harry Groener), who had allied with Faith, who had, by this time, become a rogue Slayer. The battle ended with the mayor's death and the high school being blown up. After the victory, Angel departed to Los Angeles to begin a new life away from Buffy. Cordelia followed him and assisted him in forming his new supernatural detective agency.

Buffy and her Sunnydale cohorts, affectionately called the Scooby Gang (a reference to the group of cartoon-character teenagers who solve crimes with their dog, Scooby Doo), continued to fight the evil that seemed to be focused on Sunnydale, which unfortunately rested upon the Hellmouth, the entranceway to the hell realm. In the absence of Angel, Buffy developed a relationship with Riley Finn (Marc Blucas), a soldier who worked with the Initiative, a secret government project that was attempting to respond to the presence of vampires and demons. She cooperated with the Initiative for a short time but learned that it had created a dangerous, experimental, Frankenstein-like entity, Adam (George Hertzberg), who was a bigger threat than anything the Initiative was opposing. Using Willow's developing magical powers, Buffy united her resources to take him down.

Buffy began season five with an encounter with Dracula, with whom she exchanges blood before destroying him in the typically tongue-in-cheek style that had come to characterize her. The next morning, Buffy awakened to find that she had a sister, Dawn (Michelle Trachtenberg), and that all of her friends had been given the memories of her life as if she had been in the Summers home all along. Much of season five was spent battling Glory (Clare Kramer), a deity from the hell dimension who was searching for the Key, a mystical artifact that would break down the barriers separating the different dimensions and allow her to return and reign in her own dimension, though at a significant cost to the earthly dimension. Buffy finally figured out that Dawn was the Key. Her attempt to understand the nature of Dawn and protect her led her to embrace the fact that "death is her gift." At the end of season five, Buffy sacrificed herself to save Dawn (and the world) from Glory's attempt to destroy the separate dimensions.

Early in season six, Buffy was brought back to life by her friend Willow, who uses her witchy powers and works a resurrection spell. Because of their knowledge of Angel's visit to hell, Willow and Xander mistakenly believe that Buffy was in the hell dimension, but she was actually in a heavenly place, which she did not want to leave. In the despair and alienation following her resurrection, she began to develop a relationship with Spike. The evil vampire had been tamed by the Initiative, who placed a chip in his head that prevented him from harming any human. The intense sexual relationship that developed between Buffy and Spike, often violent, was fueled by Spike's attempt to replace Angel in Buffy's heart. When his love was rebuffed, he attempted to rape her. Their relationship destroyed, he left town to do what was necessary to make himself acceptable to her.

Meanwhile, Willow, who realized that she was a lesbian and developed a relationship with Tara (Amber Benson), went through a period of fighting her addiction to magic, but as Willow's magical prowess had increased, Tara was killed during an unsuccessful attempt to kill Buffy. Willow's grief sent her into a dark period, which culminated in her threatening to destroy the world with her powers. Ultimately, Xander brought Willow back from the brink.

Buffy began season seven with a new, more positive outlook for Dawn's sake. Buffy now had to face her greatest enemy yet: the First Evil. The fight, in the end, focused on the Hellmouth, with a horde of vampires attempting to move through the opening to return to control the Earth dimension. In this final battle, Buffy was joined by Faith, who had found some redemption through Angel's efforts, and Spike, who had regained his soul and returned to win Buffy's trust and love. Of the old gang, only Giles was missing, as he had returned to his native England. Most importantly, she was joined by a number of potential Slayers-in-training, whom she nurtured and with whom she shared her powers.

In the final episode, like the Spartans at Thermopylae, she led the small Scooby Gang, now bolstered with the new cadre of Slayers, against a massive wave of vampires who rose up through the Hellmouth. They won the battle but at the cost of the town of Sunnydale (i.e., Santa Barbara, California). The key to their success was Spike, who wore a magical amulet and incinerated himself in a process that destroyed the attacking vampires and closed the Hellmouth. Before he died, Buffy professed her love for him. He knew he did not have her love but had won her respect.

After the end of the television show, Spike reemerged as a spirit creature on the spin-off television show *Angel.* After he recovered a body, the two searched for Buffy and, at one point, saw her from a distance in Rome.

Buffy's chief nemesis is The Master, played by Mark Metcalf, who manages to kill our heroine.

Throughout the run of the television show, Dark Horse Comics had published a comic book that included both adaptations of storylines from the series and completely new stories. That series went on to become the second longest-running English-language vampire comic book (surpassed only by *Vampirella*), but the comic only survived for a short time after the discontinuation of the television show. Then in 2007, Dark Horse, in cooperation with Joss Whedon, the show's creator, began issuing a new comic book that officially constituted season eight of *Buffy the Vampire Slayer.* In this new comic book series (2007–2011), Buffy emerged as the head of a command center in Scotland that was the nexus of an international antivampire and antidemon organization. Of her former close associates, she had close contact with Xander, who was in Scotland with her, and Giles, who was in England. Willow continued to emerge as an ever-more powerful magical force, and the Slayers who survived the battle in Sunnydale scattered around Europe and North America.

The destruction of Sunnydale did not go unnoticed, and government authorities then branded Buffy and her associates as a terrorist organization. Buffy's real enemy, however, was Twilight, a person who wanted to destroy Buffy and the new legion of Slayers, as they were seen to be a threat to humanity. Those loyal to Twilight include the witch Amy Madison (a former classmate of Buffy's from Sunnydale, portrayed by Elizabeth Anne Allen) and her former boyfriend, Riley Finn.

Buffy became one of the most popular and influential characters in the popular culture community that focused on vampires and has inspired a number of vampire Slayer characters in more recent books, movies, and television shows. Joss Whedon indicated that he created Buffy in reaction to the popular stereotype of the dim-witted female victim in teen-oriented horror movies. Buffy emerged as both attractive and believable. As the show became successful, Sarah Michelle Gellar's image graced the covers of numerous fan magazines and appeared on a spectrum of paraphernalia from lunch boxes to cell phone covers, clothing, and jewelry. Meanwhile, the character became the subject of intense scholarly scrutiny.

Bunnicula

Bunnicula, the vegetarian vampire rabbit, originated as a character in a book of the same name by James (1946–) and Deborah (1946–1978) Howe. Rather than attacking humans, Bunnicula sinks his fangs into vegetables, from which he sucks out the juice, leaving his victims as a white husk. Bunnicula resides in the household of the Monroe family, where he shares space with two respectable pets—the dog, Harold, and the cat, Chester—and a later addition, the dachshund puppy, Howie. Bunnicula came to reside with the Monroes after being found in a theater during a showing of the film *Dracula*. Bunnicula made his initial appearance in a children's book published in 1979. The original story became immensely popular, was reprinted numerous times, was made into an episode of the *ABC Weekend Special* television series (1982), and spawned more than a dozen additional titles (half being new stories written by Howe).

Then in 2016, the Cartoon Network brought a very new series to the screen, one very loosely adapted from the children's book series, entitled *Bunnicula*. In this animated series, a teenager named Mina (inspired by the character from the novel *Dracula*) lives with her pets Chester (a cat) and Harold (a dog) and inherits her recently deceased aunt's apartment in New Orleans. Once settled in, they encounter Bunnicula, the vegetarian vampire rabbit, who now possesses supernatural connections (different powers manifesting after drinking different vegetables) and a mischief-oriented personality. That premise sets the stage for numerous Saturday-morning adventures over its three-year run (2016–2018).

In the television series, Bunnicula is presented as having once been the pet of Dracula (as far back as the 1470s) and with whom he travels to New Orleans in 1833. At some point, he was locked in a chest, where he remained for almost two centuries until Mina Monroe sets him free. Mina remains wistfully unaware of Bunnicula's vampire existence, though Harold and Chester quickly discover it. They subsequently become his major companions in his many adventures.

Also see the *Bunnicula* book, p. 271.

︶ *Count von Count* ︶

Count von Count is a beloved character on the children's television show *Sesame Street*. He is a vampire modeled on Bela Lugosi, with fangs, a cape, and a widow's peak. Though he has fangs, he has not been seen using them on anyone. Biographical details are sparse, but he is rumored to be a distant relative of Count Dracula and was born on October 9 some 1,832,652 years ago. Like his relative, he lives in a castle with a pet cat and a number of bats, enough so he will never lack for enough to count. Count has had two girlfriends, Countess von Backwards, known for counting backward, and, more recently, Countess Dahling von Dahling. At different times, his mother, brother, and grandparents have appeared on the show.

Others suggest that he was the product of the fertile imagination of writer Norman Stiles and brought to life by puppeteer Jerry

The Sesame Street *character Count von Count is shown here during a Halloween parade.*

Nelson (1934–2012). On the versions of *Sesame Street* shown internationally, his appearances are facilitated by a number of different puppeteers. He originally appeared in 1972 in the show's fourth American season.

Prior to the appearance of Count, very few vampire characters in any medium were directed toward children and none toward preschoolers. The justification for including the vampire puppet was as a tool to teach children about basic numbers and counting. Count has a love of counting and demonstrates that love by counting anything he sees. A penchant for counting to this extreme would in the real world be considered a mental disease called arithmomania, but on the show, this activity is perfectly normal and functional.

After working through some elements of the original character that were, upon examination, deemed possibly too scary for young children (such as the use of thunder and lightning after he finished a counting session), Count settled in as a standard character of the show.

Count has been a ubiquitous character in *Sesame Street* videos and books. He has been the primary character in three videos (now on DVD): *Learning about Numbers* (1986); *Count It Higher* (1988); and *Rock & Roll!* (1990). He has appeared in dozens of *Sesame Street* books and has been the featured character on titles such as *The Count's Counting Book* (1980); *Count All the Way to Sesame Street* (1985); *Learn about Counting with the Count* (2006); *The Count's Hanukkah Countdown* (2012); *Numbers with the Count* (2017); *The Count* (2020); and *I See 1, 2, 3: Count Your Community with Sesame Street* (2020).

Dark Shadows

Dark Shadows (television series, 1966–1971, 1991)

Dark Shadows began in 1966 as a daytime soap opera on ABC television. With low ratings threatening cancellation, the show added supernatural elements to the plot and then in April 1967 introduced a vampire. This vampire—Barnabas Collins—has joined Dracula and Lestat de Lioncourt as one of the most easily recognizable vampires ever.

Once Collins was introduced to the show, the ratings turned around, and the show became a hit. While the show went off the air in 1971, fans have kept its memory alive to the present day through fan clubs, publications, and conventions.

The Origin of *Dark Shadows*: *Dark Shadows* began as an idea of producer Dan Curtis. The beginning of a story had come to him, according to one account, from a dream in which he saw a young woman with long, dark hair. The woman was traveling by train to New England, where she had been offered a job as a governess. After she got off the train, she went to a large "forbidding" house. Curtis approached ABC with the idea of taking his opening and creating a gothic-flavored daytime show. He collaborated with Art Wallace in developing the idea and assembled a production crew that included Robert Costello, Lela Swift, John Sedwick, Sy Tomashoff, and Robert Cobert.

As the story developed, it first centered on Victoria Winters (Alexandra Isles, née Moltke), the young woman of Curtis's dream. She was an orphan who had been found with a note: "Her name is Victoria. I can no longer care for her." The rest of her name was added because she was found in the wintertime. As she grew up, the orphanage received donations for Victoria's care from Bangor, Maine. On her twentieth birthday, Victoria received an offer from a Mrs. Elizabeth Collins Stoddard (Joan Bennett) of Collinsport, Maine, who wished to hire Victoria as a governess for her nephew. This gave her not only employment but the possibility of an opportunity to learn about her past.

Collinsport was a small fishing town on the Maine coast. Collinwood, the Collins family home, was a 40-room mansion built in the 1700s. The family resided in its central structure and had closed both wings of the house. Also on the property was an older house, which was built in the 1600s and now abandoned.

At Collinwood, the family estate where she was employed, Victoria interacted with the residents. Mrs. Stoddard, the family matriarch, had become a recluse after her husband disappeared 18 years before. David Collins (David

Though she was only on the show from 1966 to 1968, Victoria Winters (played by Alexandra Isles, pictured) was a key figure in the storyline.

Henesy), her nephew, was nine years old and somewhat of a problem. He had driven off previous governesses by his undisciplined behavior, especially his nasty pranks at their expense. David's father, Roger Collins (Louis Edmonds), had a drinking problem and was generally neglectful of his son. Carolyn Stoddard (Nancy Barrett), Elizabeth's daughter, was a girl enjoying her youthful years and running through a series of loves. The mansion also was home to Matthew Morgan (Thayer David), the caretaker.

> The supernatural element first entered into the *Dark Shadows* story when Malloy's ghost appeared to Victoria and told her that he had been murdered.

The cast was rounded out with several townspeople: Maggie Evans (Kathryn Leigh Scott), a waitress in the local diner who lived with her father, Sam (David Ford), an alcoholic artist; Joe Haskell (Joel Crothers), who was employed by the Collins Fishing Fleet and involved with Carolyn Stoddard; and Burke Devlin (Mitchell Ryan), a businessman that Victoria met on the train ride to Collinsport.

Devlin became Winters's first friend and confidant. He was also the focus of the initial storyline, which was built around his reasons for returning to Collinsport after an absence of ten years. He was certain that Roger Collins had lied in court and that Burke had been sent to prison as a result. He wanted revenge. In the tension resulting from his return, Bill Malloy (Frank Schofield), a local man who tried to mediate the situation, was killed. The supernatural element first entered into the *Dark Shadows* story when Malloy's ghost appeared to Victoria and told her that he had been murdered.

Taping for *Dark Shadows* began on June 13, 1966, and the first episode aired with little fanfare two weeks later. In the first year of *Dark Shadows*, an additional character appeared, one that would become of long-term importance to the emerging story. As the supernatural element was increasing, a painting over the fire-

place in the Old House came alive. The new character turned out to be the ghost of Josette DuPrés Collins (also played by Kathryn Leigh Scott). After a brief appearance in episode 40, she appeared again in episode 126 to protect Victoria from Matthew Morgan, the murderer of Malloy, who had kidnapped her. Morgan died from fright upon seeing Josette, thus resolving that subplot. Afterward, Josette became intricately integrated into the storyline.

The *Dark Shadows* audience was introduced to new supernatural subplots almost weekly. Around the two-hundredth episode, a transition began. First, the original Burke–Devlin situation was resolved when Roger Collins confessed to manslaughter and perjury. Then, a new character, Willie Loomis, took up residence at Collinwood. Almost immediately, Loomis called attention to a portrait in the foyer of the mansion. It was one of the family ancestors, Barnabas Collins.

The Emergence of Barnabas Collins: Though the addition of supernatural elements improved the show's ratings, ABC executives indicated early in 1967 that *Dark Shadows* was still in danger of being cancelled. Curtis, who had always wanted to do a vampire picture, gambled and decided to add a vampire to the show. Canadian Shakespearean actor Jonathan Frid was finally hired for the part. The original idea was to have the vampire jazz up the show, improve its ratings, and then quietly fade away. That plan would soon be discarded.

Barnabas Collins made his first appearance in episode 210 in April 1967. Willie Loomis discovered a secret room with a chained coffin in the family mausoleum. He undid the chains, and Barnabas came out of his resting place. In the next episode, he appeared at the front door of Collinwood and confronted the family as their

Sagging ratings for Dark Shadows *motivated producer Dan Curtis to explore a paranormal angle by introducing the vampire Barnabas Collins (Jonathan Frid, pictured) to the plot.*

long-lost cousin from England. He moved into the abandoned, old house on the estate, and soon, the community was plagued by a mysterious illness. The symptoms included fatigue, bite marks, and the loss of blood.

As the story unfolded, the audience discovered that Barnabas was a vampire who had lived two centuries earlier. (He actually was the person in the portrait in the mansion.) In his human life at the end of the eighteenth century, he had loved and lost Josette DuPrés, and he still longed for her in his new life at Collinwood. Having noticed Maggie Evans's resemblance to Josette, he tried to turn her into another Josette. When she refused his advances, he nearly killed her.

By this point in the story, which was being broadcast in the summer of 1967, the ratings had jumped in a spectacular manner: the show became a hit. In a matter of weeks, Jonathan Frid became a star, and the quantity of his fan mail soared. Overwhelmingly, the mail was from young women, even teenagers.

Crowds regularly gathered at the entrances to the ABC studio where the show was taped. The first *Dark Shadows* paraphernalia appeared. Meanwhile, as the story continued, another new character was introduced: Dr. Julia Hoffman (played by Grayson Hall). Called on to treat Maggie Evans, Hoffman became intrigued with Barnabas, discovered his vampiric nature, and offered to help him overcome it. Initially, he accepted her ministrations, but he eventually turned on her. He was about to kill the doctor when the ghost of his beloved sister Sarah appeared to save her.

The Origin of Barnabas Collins: With Sarah making her ghostly presence known to a number of people, the decision was made to hold a séance. During the séance, Victoria went into a trance, and the lights went out. When the lights returned, she had disappeared, and her place had been taken by Phyllis Wick. Victoria woke up in Collinsport in 1795. The scene was now set to relate the story of Barnabas's origin. The son of a prominent local landowner, Barnabas traveled to the DuPrés plantation on the island of Martinique. There, he began an affair with Angélique Bouchard (played by Lara Parker), a beautiful servant girl who, it was later revealed, knew witchcraft. Then, he met and fell in love with the plantation owner's daughter, Josette, and they made plans to wed. Barnabas broke off the affair with Angélique.

Meanwhile, back in Collinsport, Victoria had found work in the Collins home as governess to Barnabas's young sister, Sarah. The members and acquaintances of the family from the 1960s reappeared as their counterparts in the 1790s storyline. Barnabas returned from the West Indies to prepare for his marriage but did not anticipate that Angélique would use her powers of witchcraft to disrupt the plans. She caused Josette to fall in love with Jeremiah, Barnabas's brother. She then claimed Barnabas for herself. Barnabas, in turn, killed his brother in a duel and turned on Angélique. She cursed him and sent a bat to attack him, and Barnabas emerged from the encounter as a vampire.

After considering various options, he decided to make Josette his vampire bride. Before he could follow through on his plans, Angélique interfered again and caused Josette to commit suicide. Barnabas told his father of his condition and asked to be killed. His father could not kill him but did chain Barnabas into a coffin (which Willie Loomis eventually discovered).

She cursed him and sent a bat to attack him, and Barnabas emerged from the encounter as a vampire.

While Barnabas fought Angélique, Victoria had been condemned as a witch. As she was about to be killed, she suddenly reappeared in 1967. Only a few minutes of the séance had passed while she was lost for some months in the 1790s. Barnabas realized that Victoria now knew his identity and decided to court her, but he was immediately distracted by the arrival of Angélique as Cassandra, the new wife of Roger Collins.

New Storylines: With five half-hour shows to write each week—the equivalent of more than a feature-length movie—story ideas were exhausted at a rapid rate. In 1968, the writers turned to classic, nineteenth-century gothic novels for ideas and, in the last three years of the show, merged subplots from a variety of horror themes into the ongoing story. The major confrontation between Barnabas and Cassandra, for example, was based around a subplot derived from *Frankenstein*. Late in 1968, Henry James's *The Turn of the Screw* inspired a plot that led to the introduction of the second most popular member of the cast, Quentin Collins (played by David Selby).

The storyline again sent Victoria into the past—this time for good. Thus, Elizabeth Stoddard needed another governess for her nephew, David. Meanwhile, David and Amy (a young girl visiting at Collinwood) went exploring in one of the unoccupied wings of the house, where they discovered a disconnected telephone. While the children played with the phone, a ghostly voice called them to a room, where a gramophone mysteriously played music. The ghost of Quentin (his name derived from James's text) appeared. He attempted to take control of both children, but a female spirit intervened. She blocked Quentin's effect on Amy but was of little help to David. Eventually, Barnabas was drawn in to protect David. In his attempt to contact Quentin, Barnabas was thrown back to 1897 (the year Bram Stoker's novel *Dracula* was published), the time when Quentin actually lived. Barnabas found himself chained into his tomb. One of his ancestors, however, hired Romani people, who discovered the mausoleum and freed Barnabas. Again, he arrived at the door as a long-lost cousin from England.

Quentin and Barnabas started as rivals. However, as the story developed, Quentin and his male descendants were cursed; because of this, they would become werewolves. In the face of this new reality, Barnabas and Quentin came to some understanding of each other. Each, in turn, was transported back to the present, and the story continued.

While based on *Dracula*, from which it drew its understanding of the vampire and the vampire's powers, *Dark Shadows* created the most elaborate and complex alternative to the *Dracula* story in modern mythology. It played to an ever-growing audience from the time Barnabas Collins was added to the storyline until the spring of 1967 and became the most popular soap opera on ABC, pushing the network past CBS and putting it in a position to challenge NBC for the daytime audience. It was estimated that 20 million people were regular viewers. Frid received several thousand letters every week and David Selby only slightly less. Additional thousands of letters were directed to the rest of the cast. The show lasted for two more years before its ratings began to sag, and it was finally cancelled. The final show (the 1,245th segment) was aired on April 2, 1971. Many believe that it was not so much a dip in the ratings but the exhaustion of the story that led to its cancellation.

Additional *Dark Shadows* Vampires: While Barnabas Collins was the dominant vampire of the *Dark Shadows* series, other characters also had a brush with vampirism. The most prominent was Angélique. Following the return of the story to the 1960s from the 1790s, Angélique reappeared in the persona of Cassandra Collins, the new wife of Roger Collins. Shortly thereafter, one Nicholas Blair, a warlock claiming to be Cassandra's brother arrived at Collinwood. When Cassandra got in his way, he used his strong magical powers to turn her into a vampire. Through the ministrations of Dr. Hoffman, Barnabas was temporarily cured of his vampirism. However, Angélique/Cassandra, wanting Barnabas to be with her in her new form, attacked him and turned him back into a vampire. Angélique's plans were foiled, however, when she was set on fire by Barnabas. She died screaming as the flames enveloped her.

The vampiress Angélique (played by Lara Parker) served as a nemesis for Barnabas, whom she wanted for herself.

During Angélique's career as a vampire, she attacked handyman Tom Jennings, who had discovered the location of her coffin. He survived as a vampire for only a few episodes before being staked. The continuing storyline took the cast back to the nineteenth century, where a prevampirized Angélique reappeared. After being attacked by Barnabas, a servant, Dirk, was made into a vampire. He was soon staked by Edward Collins.

Later, the storyline led Barnabas and the Collins family into an encounter with the Leviathans, old demonic forces in the tradition of H. P. Lovecraft. The Leviathans were responsible for turning him back into a vampire. Among the Leviathans was Audrey, a vampire who made a brief appearance in a single episode. The most notable fact of Audrey's otherwise inconsequential appearance was that she was played by a young Marsha Mason, later to go on to stardom in the movies. Another female vampire at this time was Megan Todd (Marie Wallace), a victim of Barnabas. She eventually was staked by Willie Loomis.

Finally, toward the end of the show, Roxanne Drew appeared as a young woman involved in a bizarre experiment to transfer her life force to Angélique. At this point in the story, the major characters were moving between parallel times with the same people but different histories. In real time, Barnabas met Roxanne again as the girlfriend of an astrologer, Sebastian Shaw. She was a vampire and, before being discovered, bit Maggie Evans. Meanwhile, the story shifted to 1840. There, Barnabas also met Roxanne, and they fell in love.

However, the ever-present and vengeful Angélique killed her. Roxanne then rose as a vampire and was soon cornered in her coffin. She disintegrated in her crypt when a crucifix was placed on top of her.

***Dark Shadows* Books and Paraphernalia:** The show had a far-reaching effect on popular culture. Under the pseudonym of Marilyn Ross, from 1966 to 1972 Daniel Ross authored 33 paperback novels developed from the show. Despite the Comics Code, which banned vampires from comic books from 1954 to 1971, Gold Key produced the *Dark Shadows* comic books, the first vampire-oriented comics in almost two decades. In 1968–1969, *Dark Shadows* paraphernalia began to appear, including the *Dark Shadows Game*, View-Master stereo pictures, model kits, jigsaw puzzles, and trading cards, to name just a few. A *Dark Shadows* original soundtrack album (1969) was one of four record albums of *Dark Shadows* music. "Quentin's Theme," the most popular piece of *Dark Shadows* music, appeared on the first album and was also released as a single. Initially heard on the gramophone in the room where Quentin first appeared, the theme was recorded more than 20 times by various artists.

> Despite the Comics Code, which banned vampires from comic books from 1954 to 1971, Gold Key produced the *Dark Shadows* comic books, the first vampire-oriented comics in almost two decades.

***Dark Shadows* in the 1990s:** In 1990, NBC announced that it had asked Dan Curtis, the creator of *Dark Shadows*, to put together a new cast for a prime-time version of the old soap opera. Ben Cross was chosen to play the vampire Barnabas Collins. His role was strongly reminiscent of Jonathan Frid, the original Barnabas Collins. In spite of his moments of genuine anger and vicious attacks on individuals, Cross's Barnabas was a sensitive, reluctant vampire who allowed hematologist Julia Hoffman to try to cure his vampiric condition. Even though *Dark Shadows* fans gave the new series strong support, it was cancelled after only 12 episodes (13 hours of programming) in the second half of the 1990–1991 season.

More *Dark Shadows*: The most substantial spin-offs of the television series were two full-length feature movies, *House of Dark Shadows* (1970) and *Night of Dark Shadows* (1971). These were later made available on video. A short time after its cancellation, the show went into syndicated reruns on independent stations and PBS—the first time that had happened to a daytime soap opera. It was later picked up by the new Syfy cable channel. All 1,245 segments were released on VHS video and have now been transferred to DVD by MPI Home Video. Additionally, a variety of specialized videos have been developed from the series, including *Dark Shadows: Behind the Scenes*, *Dark Shadows Bloopers*, *Dark Shadows 35th Anniversary Reunion*, and *Dark Shadows: Vampires and Ghosts*.

Dark Shadows fandom has remained active through the first decades of the twenty-first century. Over 1,000 people showed up for Jonathan Frid's appearance at the 2008 annual convention. In response to the continued interest in the series, new books, CDs, and DVDs continue to appear, and actors who had had even a small role on the original series are still invited to make appearances at fan gatherings. The fans have also created a continuing market for *Dark Shadows* collectibles, and several businesses have arisen to cater to the demand.

Also see the *Dark Shadows* (movie, 2012) entry.

Dark Shadows Fandom

After *Dark Shadows* (1966–1971), the popular daytime television soap opera, went off the air, interest in the series stayed alive primarily in the imaginations of teenagers who had rushed home from school to watch it. Several years after ABC's cancellation of the show, fans continued to manifest a high level of devotion to the series. *The World of Dark Shadows* fanzine appeared in 1975, and two years later, the first Shadowcon fan convention was organized in San Diego as part of Starcon, a science fiction convention. In 1979, Shadowcon emerged as an independent gathering in Los Angeles, where it continued annually until 1986. Within a few years, the nature of the Shadowcon conventions began to expand and diversify by including all aspects of science fiction, fantasy, and horror. Thus, in 1983, a new organization that had an exclusive focus on *Dark Shadows*, the Dark Shadows Festival, was created by the combined efforts of *The World of Dark Shadows, Shadow-Gram*, and *Inside the Old House*, published by Old House Publishing.

The annual Dark Shadows Festival convention led to the growth of existing *Dark Shadows* fan publications (most prominently *ShadowGram*, edited by Marcy Robin), the founding of new fanzines, and the opening of fan clubs that kept interest alive. Their work came to unexpected fruition in 1991, when a new version of *Dark Shadows* aired in prime time on NBC. Unfortunately, the new show was canceled after only one season, but it was not before it led to the creation of a whole new set of *Dark Shadows* books, collectibles, and souvenirs.

Dark Shadows fans find that the most effective way to enter the fold is through the Official Dark Shadows Fan Club, which provides contacts for local fan clubs and information on obtaining *Dark Shadows* books, videos, and paraphernalia. The club was founded in 1982 as the World Federation of Dark Shadows Clubs. It was a coalition of clubs in three countries that publish newsletters and magazines (now all discontinued), dedicated to preserving the memory of the two television series of *Dark Shadows*. The present name was adopted in 1992. The club keeps members informed of the continuing careers of the stars of the two shows and maintains an active biographical archive, a library of fan club publications, and an archive of *Dark Shadows* paraphernalia. The

> **For a number of years, *ShadowGram*, published by Marcy Robin, and *The World of Dark Shadows*, published by Kathleen Resch ..., served as official periodicals for the club.**

club may be contacted through its website, http://www.darkshadowsfestival.com. In the 1990s, the club maintained an active list of over 30,000 fans.

For a number of years, *ShadowGram*, published by Marcy Robin, and *The World of Dark Shadows*, published by Kathleen Resch (both of Temple City, California), served as official periodicals for the club. *ShadowGram* was founded in 1979. The first issue was a two-page sheet reporting on what the major actors from the original *Dark Shadows* series were doing eight years after the series was canceled. The newsletter went online in 2001 and then became a social media group with updates available at https://groups.io/g/shadowgram. *The World of Dark Shadows* is now published only rarely, but *ShadowGram* appears quarterly and has emerged as the major *Dark Shadows* news periodical.

The fanzine specializes in reports on the current activities of the cast of both the original and the 1991 television series, information on new *Dark Shadows* paraphernalia, and announcements of fan activities. It also reports on the 2004 *Dark Shadows* pilot for the WB network and on the Tim Burton/Johnny Depp *Dark Shadows* feature film, which was released in 2012.

Marcy Robin has been active in *Dark Shadows* fandom since the mid-1970s. She participated in the Shadowcon conventions of the 1970s and, in 1983, was among the founders of the Dark Shadows Festival, the group that currently organizes the annual national gatherings of *Dark Shadows* fans. With Kathleen Resch, she has coauthored two books: a novel, *Beginnings: The Island of Ghosts*, and a volume on the series, *Dark Shadows in the Afternoon*.

She has written a number of short stories around the *Dark Shadows* themes, some of which have been gathered into an anthology titled *From the Shadows*. She was one of the main contributors to *The Dark Shadows Companion*, a volume celebrating the 25th anniversary of *Dark Shadows*, which was assembled by one of its stars, Kathryn Leigh Scott.

In the 1990s, *The World of Dark Shadows* was the oldest existing fanzine serving the fans of *Dark Shadows*. Its first issue was circulated to 30 people in 1975 by its founder/editor Kathleen Resch; by the early 1990s, the subscriber count was over 2,000.

> The Dark Shadows Festival, founded in 1983, superseded the original Shadowcon gatherings.

Resch has been among the most active leaders in *Dark Shadows* fandom. In the 1970s and 1980s, she published a series of fanzines under the collective title *Dark Shadows Concordance*. Each concordance summarized a particular set of the original episodes. By 1992, concordances were available for episodes 365–700 and 981–1,245. When completed, the concordances covered all of the 1,225 episodes. *Shadows in the 90's* was a concordance of the 1991 prime-time *Dark Shadows* series.

The World of Dark Shadows has also included several anthologies of *Dark Shadows* short stories and novels. Resch contributed a short story, "Edges," to the website *Decades*. Additional anthologies from *The World of Dark Shadows* included two volumes under the name *From the Shadows*, one with stories by Marcy Robin and the other by Virginia Waldron; and *Echoes*, a collection edited by Resch. Additional novels from *The World of Dark Shadows* include *Shadowed Beginnings* by Carol Maschke, *Rebirth of the Undead* by Elwood Beaty and D. L. Crabtree, and Lori Paige's two books *Dark Changeling* and *The Year the Fire Came*. Resch also edited a second *Dark Shadows* fanzine, *Echoes … from the Past*.

Conventions: The Dark Shadows Festival, founded in 1983, superseded the original Shadowcon gatherings. The first "fests" were held in San Jose, California, and Newark, New Jersey, in 1983. The latter included a trip to Lyndhurst, the mansion in Tarrytown, New York, that was used as Collinwood in the feature movies *House of Dark Shadows* (1970) and *Night of Dark Shadows* (1971). The two films were then screened for those in attendance. The festival also featured a costume contest, now a regular feature of the annual program coordinated by Marcy Robin. The initial fests were followed by additional meetings in San Jose and Dallas, Texas, after which they alternated between the Los Angeles and New York City areas (plus a convention in Las Vegas in 1998). The tenth festival was held in New York and included a tour of the New England locations used in the *Dark Shadows* series and films. It featured an appearance by Jonathan Frid (the original Barnabas Collins), who attended 13 of the 16 fests held through 1993.

The festivals were designed to be fun events for fans to meet and talk to each other, to meet members of the cast, and to have the opportunity to purchase the wide variety of *Dark Shadows* souvenirs and paraphernalia.

Each of the festivals has featured many of the original stars, and the gatherings in the 1990s also included stars from the 1991 revival series. Since the mid-1980s, Jim Pierson has been the chairman of every Dark Shadows Festival. Pierson, who has authored and coauthored several *Dark Shadows* books, also works for Dan Curtis Productions and MPI Home Video.

Dark Shadows Festival Publications printed *The Introduction of Barnabas*, a book summarizing the 1967 *Dark Shadows* episodes featuring the vampire Barnabas Collins and also includes a variety of documents about the show. It also publishes an annual *Dark Shadows* calendar.

Regional Fan Organizations: Among the many *Dark Shadows* fan activities is a variety of clubs, small publishers, and journals that cooperate with the Official Dark Shadows Fan Club. One of the oldest fan structures is Old House Publishing, founded in 1978 by Dale Clark. That same year, Clark started *Inside the Old House*, a *Dark Shadows* fanzine. Each issue includes fan fiction, poetry, artwork, biographies of *Dark Shadows* characters, discussions of controversies within the *Dark Shadows* community, a fan letter column, and classified ads selling *Dark Shadows* paraphernalia. Clark, a longtime *Dark Shadows* fan, is also the author of eight volumes of *The Dark Shadows Book of Questions and Answers* and a series of seven *Dark Shadows* novels: *Reunion, Retribution, Revelations, Destiny, Disaster, Damnation,* and *Ritual.* Clark was also one of the cofounders of the Dark Shadows Festival.

Through the 1990s, numerous fan clubs and small press publishing endeavors thrived in the *Dark Shadows* fan world. Dark Shadows over Oklahoma was a *Dark Shadows* fan club founded by Brett Hargrove and later led by Letha Roberts. The group gathered monthly, and Roberts edited *The Graveyard Gazette,* the club's newsletter.

Harmony Road Press was a small publishing company founded in 1992 that specialized in *Dark Shadows* books and periodicals. It was headed by Connie Jonas. Among its publications were *Christmas in Collinsport,* a seasonal anthology of pictures, poetry, and prose; Anna Shock's collection of short stories, *Shadowed Reflections;* and the novels *Masks and Facades* and *A Matter of Trust,* both by Jonas. Jonas also edited *The Music Box,* a *Dark Shadows* fanzine named for the music box owned by *Dark Shadows* character Josette. *The Music Box* featured fiction, art, poetry, and fan news. In 1992, the press announced the publication of a single-issue fanzine edited by Travis McKnight called *The Lara Zine,* which was built around the *Dark Shadows* actress Lara Parker, who played the witch Angélique. Connie Jonas is a member of the Collinsport Players, a fan-founded dramatic group that presents skits at the annual Dark Shadows Festival. In 1993, Harmony Road Press published an anthology of scripts of the group's original productions, *The Collinsport Players Companion,* edited by Jeff Thompson and Jonas.

Lone Gull Press was founded in Massachusetts in 1984 by author Lori Paige and artist Jane Lach to publish materials for *Dark Shadows* fans. Their first product was *The Secret of the Chalice,* a fanzine that appeared that same year. They followed it with a series of fanzines, including *Tales of Hoffman,* a one-shot publication built around the *Dark Shadows* character Julia Hoffman, and *Cauldron,* of which six issues appeared in 1987 and 1988. In 1988, Paige wrote *Balm in Gilead. The Gates of Hell* is the name of a full-length novel that provided the substance for the fanzine of the same name. In addition, Lone Gull Press published Sharon Wisdom's *Love's Pale Shadow* (1992).

The Long Island Dark Shadows Society was a *Dark Shadows* fan club founded in 1988 by Steven C. Schumacher and Cindy Avitabile Conroy. While active, the club held five meetings each year, which included screenings of *Dark Shadows* videos and discussions of various *Dark Shadows* topics. In 1993, the society reported approximately 25 members. The New England Dark Shadows Society was founded in the early 1990s by Ron Janick. The society held monthly meetings, at which *Dark Shadows* videos were screened followed by discussions related to *Dark Shadows.* Also among its activities was an annual visit to Seaview Terrace in Newport, Rhode Island, the house used for exterior shots of Collinwood, the Collins family home, in the 1966–1971 television series. The society published a fanzine titled *Widow's Hill Quarterly.*

Seaview Terrace (now known as Carey Mansion) in Newport, Rhode Island, was used as "Collinwood Mansion" in Dark Shadows.

The Oregon Dark Shadows Society was founded in 1991 by Connie Jonas, a longtime and active *Dark Shadows* fan, who also edited *The Music Box*, an independent fanzine published by her company, Harmony Road Press. In 1993, the club reported about a dozen members. It gathered monthly to screen video releases of *Dark Shadows* episodes, share fandom gossip, engage in dramatic readings, hold trivia contests, and plan for upcoming *Dark Shadows* events, such as the annual Dark Shadows Festival. The group joined the effort that brought the Syfy channel to the Portland area cable system in 1992. The club also published a monthly newsletter, *News & Notes*. Many of the members of the earlier *Dark Shadows* club in Seattle later affiliated with the Oregon society.

The Pittsburgh Dark Shadows Fan Club was founded in 1987 for fans of *Dark Shadows* in southwestern Pennsylvania and nearby counties in Ohio and West Virginia. Although *Shadows of the Night* was used as the name of two different vampire fanzines, founder Dan Silvio edited the one that has served as the official publication of the Pittsburgh Dark Shadows Fan Club. Silvio began *Shadows of the*

Night in 1987, and it has continued to the present both as a printed fanzine and as an e-newsletter. *Shadows of the Night* may be contacted at sotnight@aol.com.

The Wyndcliffe Dark Shadows Society was founded in 1988 by May Sutherland. It began as an effort to publish a newsletter, *Wyndcliffe Watch*, for *Dark Shadows* fans. However, with the help of Sutherland's friends Jane Lach and Lori Paige, founders of Lone Gull Press, the newsletter grew into a full-sized fanzine with the first issue, which appeared in October 1988. The society soon followed. Medallion Press is the society's publishing arm. Sutherland was also the president of the Seattle/Tacoma Dark Shadows Fan Club, a position she held from March 1989 to May 1992. The club met monthly and lobbied the local public television station to pick up the syndicated *Dark Shadows* reruns. After KTPS (now KBTC) began carrying the show, the club held fundraisers to support the station. Meanwhile, Sutherland also became head of the West Washington chapter of the Sci-Fi Channel Fan Club. In 1992, the local club stopped meeting. However, the continuing society and its associated fanzine grew to approximately 250 members/subscribers and includes people from across North America, plus members in Turkey and Japan. May Sutherland authored one novel, *Sins of the Fathers*, a *Dark Shadows* story that has the vampire Barnabas Collins under attack from another vampire running loose at his Collinwood estate.

Like all fan communities, clubs and periodicals come and go, and among the defunct fan organizations are *Alternate Shadows*, a *Dark Shadows* fan club headquartered in Ithaca, New York. It was founded and led by Patrick Garrison and his wife, Josette, who also edited a fanzine called *The Parallel Times*. In 1983, 1984, and 1985, the group sponsored the Manhattan Shadows convention, which included a blood donation contest. The prize was a dinner in New York City with Jonathan Frid, the actor who played the vampire Barnabas Collins in the original *Dark Shadows* TV series. The club disbanded in 1988, and the fanzine was discontinued soon afterward.

The Friends of Dark Shadows club began in 1983 under the leadership of Sharida Rizzuto as the New Orleans branch of the International Dark Shadows Society. Rizzuto, who had broad experience in fanzine publishing, published four issues of *Inside Dark Shadows*. Rizzuto and the New Orleans group then separated from the International Dark Shadows Society and reorganized as the Friends of Dark Shadows. She issued a new fanzine, *The Collinwood Record* (seven issues), and a newsletter, *The Collinwood Journal* (three issues). She was assisted by associate editor Sidney J. Dragon, the group's vice president. The Friends of Dark Shadows and its periodicals were discontinued in 1987. Rizzuto, however, continued to publish *Dark Shadows* news in another publication, *The Vampire Journal,* now a publication for the Realm of the Vampire organization.

The Dark Shadows Society of Milwaukee was a short-lived *Dark Shadows* fan club founded in 1986 by Lynn L. Gerdes and others in southeastern Wisconsin. The club met for discussions and screenings of *Dark Shadows* episodes. It disbanded in 1989. The Houston Dark Shadows Society was a *Dark Shadows* fan club founded in 1986 by Parker Riggs. It served primarily *Dark Shadows* fans in the greater Houston, Texas, area, although its membership grew to include fans around the country. The society published *Lone Star Shadows*, a quarterly newsletter edited by Riggs featuring news of *Dark Shadows* fandom. It ran for 20 issues. Both the club and the magazine were discontinued in 1991.

The Dark Shadows Society of Milwaukee was a short-lived *Dark Shadows* fan club founded in 1986 by Lynn L. Gerdes and others in southeastern Wisconsin.

***Dark Shadows* Fandom in the Twenty-first Century:** *Dark Shadows* fandom is currently represented by the Central Florida Dark Shadows Fan Club (https://www.facebook.com/CentralFlaDarkShadows*);* the late longtime fan Craig Hamrick's *Dark Shadows* website (http://www.darkshadowsonline.com); the Dark Shadows DVD Club (https://www.mpihomevideo.com/collections/dark-shadows-collection); and, most importantly, the Official Dark Shadows Fan Club, which sponsors the annual Dark Shadows Festival (pansyfaye@darkshadowsfestival.com). The festival has been held annually since 1983 and remains a major *Dark Shadows* fan event. It generally alternates meeting sites between New York City and Los Angeles. Fans may join the club and subscribe to its online periodical, *ShadowGram: The Official Dark Shadows Newsletter*, published by Marcy Robin, for no cost. Marcy also heads the World Federation of Dark Shadows Clubs. The Dark Shadows Festival site (http://www.darkshadowsfestival.com) provides data on the annual convention and distributes official *Dark Shadows* memorabilia. The convention has featured reunions of cast members and, in more recent years, memorial remembrances of those who have passed away.

Collins, Barnabas

Barnabas Collins was a vampire character introduced into the storyline of the daytime television soap opera *Dark Shadows*. He went on to become the show's central character and saved it from early cancellation. *Dark Shadows*, the gothic tale of the Collins family, had begun in 1966 on ABC's afternoon schedule; however, by early 1967, the show was facing cancellation. Threatened with that fate, producer Dan Curtis began to experiment successfully with supernatural elements. Finally, he decided to add a vampire.

Barnabas, played by actor Jonathan Frid, made his first appearance in episode 210. Willie Loomis, looking for a hidden treasure, discovered a secret room in the nearby mausoleum that contained a coffin secured shut with a chain. Not knowing what he was doing, he released Barnabas from his prison of many decades. In the next episode, Barnabas presented himself at the door of Collinwood, the family estate, as the family's long-lost English cousin. He received permission to take up residence in the Old House, the former family manor. In his search for blood, Barnabas discovered Maggie Evans (Kathryn Leigh Scott), the image of his long-lost love whom Barnabas vampirized in an attempt to bring her into his world. Barnabas's attacks upon Maggie led to the introduction of Dr. Julia Hoffman (Grayson Hall), a blood specialist. Brought in to deal with Maggie's illness, she discovered Barnabas's nature, but rather than destroying him, she fell in love. In her infatuation, she initiated a process to cure him.

At this point, Barnabas Collins and *Dark Shadows* had become a phenomenon of daytime television. As the audience grew, the decision was made to give Barnabas a history. Through the instrument of a séance, the cast of *Dark Shadows* was thrust into the 1790s to assume the roles of their ancestors or eighteenth-century counterparts. The new storyline began with

episode 366. In 1795, Barnabas was the son of family patriarch Joshua Collins. As the story developed, the family became host to Andre du Prés and his daughter, Josette du Prés Collins (Kathryn Leigh Scott), Barnabas's fiancée, who arrived from their plantation in Martinique for the wedding. Josette was accompanied by her maid, Angélique Bouchard (played by Lara Parker, a new addition to the cast), who was a witch. Angélique, in her desire for everything her employers possessed, moved on Barnabas but was repelled. She then turned on Josette and, through her witchcraft, caused Josette to marry Barnabas's uncle, Jeremiah Collins, instead. Barnabas killed Jeremiah in a duel.

Eventually, Barnabas was tricked into marrying Angélique, but when he discovered her occult actions, he shot her. Believing that she was dying, Angélique cursed Barnabas with the words that set the pattern of his character for the future: "I set a curse on you, Barnabas Collins. You will never rest. And you will never be able to love. Whoever loves you will die.

Actress Kathryn Leigh Scott not only played the role of Barnabas' love interest Maggie Evans but also took on the parts of Lady Kitty Hampshire, Rachel Drummond, and Josette du Prés.

That is my curse, and you will live with it through all eternity." As the words died out, a vampire bat flew into the room and headed straight for Barnabas's throat. He died from the attack only to arise as a vampire. He decided that Josette should join him in his vampiric existence and began to drain her of her blood. Before he could finish the transformation, however, Angélique's spirit lured Josette to a cliff, where she fell to her death. Jeremiah Collins, having learned of his son's condition, locked him in the mausoleum and chained him up to stop the plague of his vampiric attacks.

In 1990, Barnabas's story was revived when NBC began a prime-time version of *Dark Shadows*.

With episode 461, the storyline returned to the present. Barnabas had been given a history and a complex personality. Besides his bloodthirst, he had a moral sensitivity, the ability to show great passion and love, and was the victim of great suffering. In Angélique, he had an enemy who returned in various guises to thwart his plans for happiness. His adventures would continue for almost 800 more *Dark Shadows* episodes. In 1970, *Dark Shadows* creator/producer Curtis borrowed the cast for a feature movie, *House of Dark Shadows*, at the close of which Barnabas was killed. Thus, he did not appear in the 1971 follow-up, *Night of Dark Shadows*. In 1991, Barnabas's story was revived when NBC began a prime-time version of *Dark Shadows*. It covered the basic storyline of the emergence of Barnabas Collins (portrayed by Ben Cross) in the present and his origin in the 1790s prior to its cancellation after only one season.

In 1966, Marilyn Ross (a pseudonym of Daniel Ross) began what would become 33 *Dark Shadows* novels based upon the television series. Barnabas appeared first in the sixth volume, and his name and image dominated it for the remaining titles. The first issue of the comic book *Dark Shadows* (from Gold Key), which included a picture of Barnabas on the cover of most issues, appeared in March 1969.

The series continued through 1976. In 1992, a new *Dark Shadows* comic based on the NBC series was initiated by Innovation Publishing. In spite of the television series being canceled, Innovation's comic book continued beyond the television story with a fresh storyline until Innovation's demise in 1994.

By 1968, Barnabas's image began to appear on a wide variety of products, among the first being the *Dark Shadows Game* from gum card producer Whitman and a Halloween costume. Through 1969, the variety of paraphernalia included another set of trading cards, two jigsaw puzzles, pillows, a poster, and several model kits. Other items appeared over the years, and a new set of memorabilia was generated in response to the 1991 television series.

Collins was only the second vampire in modern history to gain a wide public following. In spite of occasional rumors to the contrary, it is unlikely that a third *Dark Shadows* series will come to television; however, the continuation of *Dark Shadows* conventions and the numerous new *Dark Shadows* writings ensure that Barnabas will have high visibility at least as long as those people who watched the original series on television survive.

In early 2010, director Tim Burton confirmed that he was directing a *Dark Shadows* movie, starring Johnny Depp as Barnabas. That movie was released in 2012.

Collinsport Players

The Collinsport Players are a fan-led *Dark Shadows* dramatic group that was founded at the Dark Shadows Festival in Newark, New Jersey, in 1984 by Jeff Thompson and Dr. Laura Brodian, hosts of the festival. Both were already in costume and decided to enliven their hosting chores with a set of improvisational sketches.

The positive reaction of the audience led to a formalizing of their activities as the Collinsport Players (named for the town in which the Collins family resided in the television show). Improvisation dominated the 1985 performance of a skit entitled "Julia's Trump." From that point, scripts were written, and the cast size increased. "Spelling Bee," presented in 1985, involved five actors. In 1986, the 20th anniversary of the premiere of *Dark Shadows*, the group performed "The More Things Change: The Official Twentieth Anniversary Skit," a major step forward into a full one-act play, with some two dozen actors participating.

The Collinsport Players have regularly performed at every annual national Dark Shadows Festival since their initial performance in 1984. They draw their cast from fans around the country. The new scripts each year are sent to the players six weeks ahead of time. They memorize their parts and gather upon their arrival at the festival site for two rehearsals before their performances. The plays have been comedies full of inside jokes. Many have spoofed actual episodes of the television series, while others have moved in more speculative directions, taking the characters into hypothesized situations. Among the Collinsport Players's most successful comedies, complete with costumes, sound effects, and music, have been "Quiet on the Set," "The Times They Change," "The Loco-Motion," "Double Play," and "A Julia Carol." In 1993, the first of two volumes of the Players's skits was published by Harmony Road Press. Connie Jonas, the press's founder, is a member of the group.

Jeff Thompson, cofounder of the Collinsport Players and their current producer–director, has been a *Dark Shadows* fan for many years and has written widely for several of the fanzines. He wrote most of the plays for the Collinsport Players, one fan-press book on *Dark Shadows* comic books, and in 1990 completed his master's degree program with a thesis on the historical novels of Daniel Ross, who wrote 33 *Dark Shadows* novels under the pseudonym Marilyn

Ross. Thompson completed his thesis at Tennessee State University, where he teaches English.

The Collinsport Players were among the performers at Dracula '97: A Centennial Celebration in Los Angeles. They performed their 25th annual performance at the Dark Shadows Festival held in Elizabeth, New Jersey, in 2009.

Curtis, Dan (1927–2006)

Dan Curtis, the producer–director who developed the *Dark Shadows* television series, was born in 1928 in Connecticut. His first work in television was as a salesman for MCA. A sports buff, he sold CBS on doing a show called *CBS Golf Classic*, which is best remembered for the live microphones that Curtis had the golfers wear; the show won an Emmy Award in 1965. The success of the show helped Curtis become an independent producer. He decided that soap operas were a good field and began to think about developing a daytime show.

Richard Matheson had a long list of credits before working with Curtis, including episodes of The Twilight Zone, *Edgar Allan Poe adaptations with Roger Corman, and his script for* I Am Legend.

The initial idea for *Dark Shadows* began to take shape after a vivid dream that Curtis had. It concerned a young woman traveling by train to a new job as a governess at an old place in New England. The dream concluded with the girl standing at a railroad station. Curtis described his dream to officials at ABC, and they risked a small budget to begin development. He gathered a team to put together what would become a daytime serial with a gothic flavor. Over several years, *Dark Shadows* evolved from the original idea. As the storyline matured, it centered on the Collins family of a mythical fishing village called Collinsport, Maine. The young woman from Curtis's dream became Victoria Winters, an orphan in search of her past, which she believed lay in New England. An early storyline concerned a man she met on the train as she headed for her new job. He accused one member of the Collins family of lying at a trial in which he was convicted and sent to prison. The show went on the air on June 27, 1966. At the time, no mention of vampirism or any thought of a vampire character was made. It was only later, when the show was threatened by low ratings, that supernatural elements in the form of ghosts were added. They helped to raise the ratings but not enough. In the winter of 1966–1967, with little hope that the show would survive, Curtis made a radical decision. He had the writers create a vampire character. If the show failed after that, he reasoned, at least he would have had fun. The vampire, Barnabas Collins, made his first appearance in April 1967. The response was enormous and, by the summer, both Curtis and ABC realized they had a hit. As the show steadily rose in the ratings, Curtis borrowed the cast and created the first of two movies with MGM based on the show, *House of Dark Shadows* (1970). The following year, a second feature, *Night of Dark Shadows*, was produced.

Due to low ratings, the original *Dark Shadows* daytime series ended in 1971, though it went into syndication several years later. Meanwhile, Curtis allowed his interest in vampires to influence his future projects. At the same time, he began a fruitful relationship with horror writer Richard Matheson, who would write the scripts for a number of Curtis's productions through the decade. In 1972, he worked with ABC to produce *The Night Stalker*, a Matheson script concerning a reporter (Carl Kolchak, played by Darren McGavin) who discovered a vampire operating in Seattle. The show became the most-watched made-for-television movie to that date. ABC then had Curtis produce and direct the sequel, *The Night Strangler*, based on Jack the Ripper themes. The two movies led to a television series based on the Kolchak character. Curtis and his company, Dan Curtis Productions, went on to produce other television horror movies, including *The Norliss Tapes* (1973) and *Scream of the Wolf* (1974).

Curtis still had an interest in vampires, however, and, in 1973, decided to produce a new version of *Dracula*, which was brought to the screen in 1974. He chose veteran actor Jack Palance as its villain star and Matheson as his writer. He also wanted to bypass the stage play that had been the basis for both the Bela Lugosi

Jack Palance played the role of the most famous vampire of all in the 1974 adaptation.

movie in 1931 and the more recent *Horror of Dracula* from Hammer Films. The script drew on fresh research on Vlad the Impaler, the fifteenth-century Wallachian prince thought of as the original Dracula. In the end, Curtis's *Dracula* was driven to reclaim his long-lost love, whom he saw reborn in the persona of Jonathan Harker's fiancée. This need took him to England. At the same time, he was under attack from vampire hunter Abraham Van Helsing (played by Nigel Davenport), and their personal battle formed the second dynamic of the script.

In 1975, Curtis brought to television a movie, *Trilogy of Terror*, composed of three of Matheson's short stories. It was followed two years later with a similar horror collection, *Dead of Night*, which included Matheson's story "No Such Thing as a Vampire." A successful producer who had found his niche in developing made-for-television movies, Curtis reached a new high in the next decade with the production of two very successful TV miniseries. *The Winds of War* (1983) and its sequel, *War and Remembrance* (1988–1989), were based on the books of Herman Wouk. Curtis's productions were thus diversified, only occasionally returning to the horror genre. However, the continuing popularity of *Dark Shadows* in syndication suggested the possibility of its revival. In 1990, Curtis sold the idea of a prime time *Dark Shadows* series to NBC. With a new set and a new cast, a pilot show was filmed. Based on the old series, it began with the awakening of Barnabas Collins and his entrance into the Collins household. From there—while keeping the basic framework of the old series—the storyline developed in novel directions. The series aired in early 1991 but, seemingly due to the outbreak of the Gulf War, did not make the ratings cut and was cancelled after only 12 episodes. In the meantime, Innovation Publishing began production of a comic book based on the new series. The comic was a success, and the new storyline and characters continued into 1994 when Innovation ceased operations.

Curtis continued as a celebrity among the very loyal fans of *Dark Shadows* but was himself upset that he was remembered more for the series than for some of his other work. He died on March 27, 2006, at the age of 78.

Frid, Jonathan (1924–2012)

Jonathan Frid, the actor who portrayed vampire Barnabas Collins on *Dark Shadows*, the original ABC daytime series, was born in Hamilton, Ontario, Canada. Frid made his stage debut during his teen years in a school production of Sheridan's *The Rivals*. However, it was not until his years in the Canadian Navy during World War II that he made the decision to pursue an acting career. After the war, Frid moved to London to attend the Royal Academy of Dramatic Arts. While in England, he appeared in his first film, *The Third Man*. In 1950, Frid moved back to Canada to attend the Toronto Academy of Arts and continue his acting career. He graduated from Yale in 1957 with a master's degree in fine arts with a major in directing. Frid then settled in New York where, for the next decade, he played in several stage productions and was known for his portrayal of a variety of Shakespearean characters. He appeared with Ray Milland in a 1967 touring company production of *Hostile Witness*. After the tour concluded and he returned to New York, Frid made plans to move to California. His career in New York was at a standstill, and he decided to seek a position on the West Coast as a teacher.

Before he had a chance to leave for California, however, he received a call to join the cast of *Dark Shadows*. He interviewed for the part because it was to be only a few weeks' work and would provide him with some money to start over in his new home. At that point, the show's ratings dropped, and ABC threatened cancellation. To boost ratings, the show's producer, Dan Curtis, decided to experiment with adding supernatural elements to the storyline. He had successfully introduced ghosts and de-

Though he had a long acting career that continued until the year he died in 2012 at age 87, Jonathan Frid will forever be remember as Barnabas Collins.

cided to add a vampire. Frid, as vampire Barnabas Collins, began to appear in April 1967. The audience responded, especially women and teenagers (the show was on at 4:00 P.M.), and ratings steadily climbed. By the summer, everyone recognized that the show was a hit, and numerous spin-off products for fans began to appear.

Frid played the part of Barnabas Collins for the next four years until the show was finally canceled in 1971. He also starred in the first of two movies based on the show, *House of Dark Shadows* (1970). At the end of the movie, Barnabas Collins was killed. No vampires appeared in the second movie, *Night of Dark Shadows* (1971), which featured other characters from the *Dark Shadows* cast. Although Frid gained star status, he also experienced some degree of typecasting that limited his choice of parts once the show ended.

After he joined the show, Frid's character became the trademark image of *Dark Shadows*.

His likeness dominated the publicity materials for the show, including the first *Dark Shadows* movie. More than 30 paperback books were written based on the show by Harlequin author Daniel Ross, and nearly all featured Frid's picture on the cover. His representation also graced the covers of most issues of the *Dark Shadows* comic book (the first vampire comic to appear after the lifting of the ban on vampires in 1954). Soon after he joined the show, a Barnabas the Vampire Model Kit was issued, complete with a glow-in-the-dark walking stick.

Following the cancellation of the show, Frid kept a low profile. He tried to distance himself from *Dark Shadows* and the role of Barnabas Collins. He did not want to find himself in a position similar to that of Bela Lugosi—trapped in the Dracula persona. He took a part onstage in *Murder at the Cathedral* and in two movies: *The Devil's Daughter* (1972), an ABC made-for-television movie, and *Seizure* (1974), director Oliver Stone's first film. Most of Frid's time, however, was devoted to the development of three one-man shows: *Jonathan Frid's Fools & Fiends*, *Shakespearean Odyssey*, and *Fridiculousness*. He toured the country with the shows, performing readings from Shakespeare, humor, and classic horror pieces by authors such as Edgar Allan Poe. In 1986, he joined an all-star cast in a Broadway revival of *Arsenic and Old Lace* and toured with the company the following year.

Frid's association with the show did not go away. *Dark Shadows* went into syndication, and a new audience became delighted with Barnabas Collins. In the 1980s, somewhat surprised (as have been many observers) at the persistence of fan interest in *Dark Shadows*, the Dark Shadows Festival (fan conventions) began to be held in 1983. Frid made his first appearance in 1983 and at every festival from then through 1993. Then, for many years, he did not appear, though he remained the fans' most popular character. His long hiatus ended in 2007, when he starred at the convention, and he made back-to-back appearances in 2008 and 2009.

Frid's last appearance was a brief cameo in the 2012 *Dark Shadows* movie starring Johnny Depp in the part he previously portrayed on television. He died just before the movie was released in the theater.

Forever Knight

During the 1992–1993 television season, *Forever Knight* emerged as one of the more popular late-night alternatives to talk shows. The story was built around Nick Knight, an 800-year-old vampire whose current role was that of a policeman on the Toronto police force. *Forever Knight* first appeared as a two-hour made-for-television movie and pilot for a possible series. Titled *Nick Knight*, it aired on August 20, 1989. In the movie, Nick Knight (Rick Springfield) was a 400-year-old Los Angeles detective assigned to investigate a series of murders in which the victims were drained of blood. One of the murders occurred in a museum, where a goblet that was used to drink blood in an ancient ceremony had been stolen.

Knight was determined to recover his mortal nature. In the meantime, he survived on bottled blood. He recognized the murders as possibly having been committed by his old enemy Lucien LaCroix, who regularly reappeared as Nick's major obstacle. In the process of investigating the museum murder, Knight met Alyce Hunter, an archaeologist who became his human confidante. She discovered that the goblet was used in a ceremony to cure vampirism. In the end, Knight's investigation led him not to LaCroix but to Jack Fenner, a bloodmobile attendant and not a vampire, who had been committing the murders because he held a grudge against transients. LaCroix had actually committed only one murder—the one that occurred in the museum with the stolen cup. In their initial encounter, LaCroix destroyed the cup. At the end, LaCroix drained Hunter's blood, which set the stage for Knight to destroy LaCroix.

When finally produced as a television series in the 1990s, several changes had occurred, including a new name: *Forever Knight*. The action shifted from Los Angeles to Toronto, and Knight had aged four centuries; his birth date as a vampire was set in 1228. His real name was changed from Jean-Pierre (mentioned in passing in the earlier movie) to Nicolas de Brabant. As the series proceeded, the story of his past was gradually revealed through flashbacks. In the opening episode, Nicolas (Geraint Wyn Davies), a knight, awakened to find himself turned into a vampire by Lucien LaCroix (Nigel Bennett), who would appear in the flashback scenes throughout the series. He had previously been seduced by Jeannette (Deborah Duchene), a female vampire, and the three had

The Welsh-born actor Geraint Wyn Davies is best known for playing Nick Knight in the 1990s TV series Forever Knight.

lived together for many years until Nick renounced their vampiric evil and began a search to become mortal again. In the series, Knight worked as a Toronto policeman on the graveyard shift. His sole confidante was Dr. Natalie Lambert (Catherine Disher), a forensic pathologist who was working on a means to transform Knight. The opening episode picked up the storyline from the movie concerning the theft of the sacrificial cup at the museum. The story was completed in the second episode, in which Fenner was discovered to be the murderer and both LaCroix and Alyce Hunter were killed.

CBS added *Forever Knight* as a weekly entry in its late-night crime series, "Crimetime after Primetime," which was aired against NBC's popular *The Tonight Show*. It garnered a high rating and a loyal audience of vampire fans. However, it disappeared along with all of the Crimetime series after CBS signed comedian David Letterman to do his talk show opposite *The Tonight Show* in August 1993. In the meantime, two fan clubs (the Forever Knight Fan Club and the Official Geraint Wyn Davies Fan Club) and a variety of fanzines began to work on pushing for a revival of the show. Their campaign resulted in the show being picked up by TriStar and finding new life in syndication.

At the beginning of the second season, *Forever Knight* found a home on the USA cable network. However, fans were disappointed to learn that neither John Kepelos nor Deborah Duchene would be returning. Instead, the series introduced several new characters; not too long afterward, it was announced that actors Blue Mankuma, Lisa Ryder, and Ben Bass would assume the roles, respectively, of Captain Reese (the new precinct commandant), Tracey Vetter (Nick's new partner), and Javier Vachon (a new vampire character). Unfortunately, in spite of a well-organized campaign by the Friends of Forever Knight, the series was permanently cancelled at the end of the third season.

Although no signs appeared of the show being renewed, *Forever Knight* fandom (including an active publishing effort) remained active through the 1990s: reruns of the show appeared on the Syfy cable channel, and in 1997, a new set of books based on the *Forever Knight* series began to appear. The television series was notable for its introduction of the game face, the changed facial appearance of a vampire when s/he is angered or about to feed. This aspect of the vampire was picked up as a central aspect of vampire existence in *Buffy the Vampire Slayer*.

ᓚ *Lost Girl* ᕼ

Lost Girl was a Canadian television series that centered upon a succubus, a vampire-like creature from folklore that comes to men in their dreams and, after having sexual intercourse, leaves the men drained of energy. Acting as a psychic vampire, her repeated visits can leave her male victims lethargic and, in extreme cases, cause death. In the series, Bo Dennis (portrayed by Anna Silk) appears as a beautiful woman who is initially unaware of what she is and seeks to gain some self-knowledge as to why whenever she has sex, it culminates in the

death of her mate. As she learns to take control of her nature and the abilities that go with it, she drains energy from people by kissing them and allowing the energy to flow. She also has the ability to control and manipulate humans by touching them.

As the series unfolds, Bo encounters the world of the Fae, supernatural beings who live incognito among humans, and learns that she is one of them. The Fae are basically divided into two groups, the Light Fae and the Dark Fae, but

Anna Silk (right) plays Bo Dennis is a succubus, and Kris Holden-Ried plays Dyson, a cop who is also a werewolf in Lost Girl.

she refuses to identify with either one. The Fae also come in a number of varieties, including succubi, werewolves, vampires, and an additional rage of creatures, which Bo meets and learns about episode by episode as the series progresses.

As her search continues to understand herself and track her personal origin, Bo is aided by several people, beginning with a human, a young woman named Kenzi (Ksenia Solo), a street person who assists Bo in creating a business as a private investigator and ombudsman, and she quickly emerges as the succubus's best friend and confidante. Dyson (Kris Holden-Ried), a policeman and werewolf, assists Bo with his vast knowledge of the Fae world and politics. As their relationship develops, they often have each other's back. Hale (K. C. Collins), Dyson's partner on the police force, is a

siren, a Fae who can whistle and thus can, as the situation dictates, control, heal, or debilitate humans. Dr. Lauren Lewis (Zole Palmer) is a human physician who works for the Fae and is considered to be the personal property of the Ash (Clé Bennett), the head of the Light Fae community. Bo develops sexual attachments to both Dyson and Lauren.

Trick (Rick Howland) is the owner of the Dal Riata, the Fae's bar and major meeting place. The bar is considered neutral ground and is one of the few places where both Light and Dark Fae can mingle. Trick is also a knowledgeable elder in the community and hence a frequent source of ancient wisdom. As new kinds of Fae appear, it is often Trick who identifies them and provides information on how to successfully deal with them.

Lost Girl was originally developed in Canada and initially appeared on Showcase, a Canadian television channel, in 2010. It ran for five seasons, with the last season, originally scheduled for 13 episodes, being extended to 16 episodes. The series ran in United States on the Syfy channel beginning in 2012. *Lost Girl* became the highest-rated Canadian scripted series to premiere on Showcase. It found an immediate audience and was especially popular within the LGBT community.

Midnight, Texas

Midnight, Texas was a three-book series written by Charlaine Harris, already well known for *The Southern Vampire Mysteries*, a series of novels featuring Louisiana waitress Sookie Stackhouse and her vampire boyfriend Bill Compton. *The Southern Vampire Mysteries* were transformed into the popular television series *True Blood* (2008–2014). The three *Midnight, Texas* novels were released in 2015–2016 and, in the wake of the completion of the very successful *True Blood* series, they became candidates for adaptation for television.

Midnight, Texas followed the story of a young psychic/medium named Manfred Bernardo (played by François Arnaud), who flees to Midnight to hopefully escape a troublesome past that still threatens him. As the story begins, his major confidante is his deceased grandmother, who appears as a ghost and offers him advice. The small town of Midnight turns out to be home to a spectrum of "supernatural" beings, including a witch, a fallen angel, and a minister, who turns into a were-tiger each month. Notable among the town's residents is Lemuel "Lem" Bridger (portrayed by Peter Mensah), a vampire who brought a very dark past to town in the 1960s and has settled there along with his wife, a deadly professional assassin.

As the larger story of the town unfolds, Lemuel's vampire sire arrives in Midnight, accompanied by a cadre of fellow vampires. The vampires incapacitate Lemuel and unleash a plan to kill all the town's residents. As this plot was being put into place, Lemuel revealed his backstory along with his special relationship to one of the town's residents, who had taught him to feed on human energy. During the climatic fight between the vampires and the town's inhabitants, the vampires are finally destroyed, but in the process, Lemuel is wounded and saved from being killed by Olivia dragging him to safety outside of the sunlight.

The *Midnight, Texas* adaptation premiered on July 24, 2017, on NBC at prime time. The second and final season premiered on October 26, 2018, with the final episode airing on December 28, 2018.

The Munsters

The Munsters emerged in 1964 as one of two new situation comedies in the fall television season featuring a cast of "monstrous" characters attempting to live as an otherwise normal family. Included in the Munster family were two vampires, Lily (played by Yvonne De Carlo) and Grandpa (Al Lewis), who in the course of the series was revealed to be none other than Count Dracula. The family was completed by the Frankenstein-ish Herman (Fred Gwynne) and the children, the wolfish Eddie (Butch Patrick) and the very "normal" Marilyn (Beverly Owen, and later

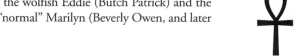

François Arnaud stars as Manfred Bernardo in the short-lived Midnight, Texas, *the story of a young psychic who tries unsuccessfully to flee his paranormal life.*

Pat Priest). Herman worked in a mortuary that was owned by classic horror actor John Carradine. *The Munsters* ran for two seasons. It gave birth to a comic book from Gold Key that ran for 16 issues from January 1965 to January 1968. The original cast joined in a movie, *Munster, Go Home!,* released in 1966, in which John Carradine assumed a different role as the family's butler.

A second movie—*The Munsters' Revenge*—was made for television and aired on February 27, 1981. It included the major stars: Fred Gwynne, Yvonne De Carlo, and Al Lewis. The series was revived for the 1988 season as *The Munsters Today,* starring John Schuck (Herman), Lee Meriweather (Lily), and Howard Morton (Grandpa). In spite of bad reviews by fans of the original series, its 72 episodes carried it into 1991.

Possibly the most vampiric of all *The Munsters* shows was the animated sequel *The Mini-Munsters,* which aired in 1973 for *The*

ABC Saturday Superstar Movie on ABC. The story concerned a Dracula-like relative sending two teenagers, Igor (a Frankenstein-like monster) and Lucretia (a vampire), to stay with the Munster family.

Originally, *The Munsters* ran opposite the ABC series *The Addams Family.* Both were popular in their original format and both have had numerous spin-offs in the forms of movies, comic books, and various paraphernalia. *The Munsters* and *The Addams Family* tended to appeal to the same set of fans, and in the 1990s, some fans of the two shows banded together to form The Munsters and the Addams Family Fan Club.

The mid-1990s saw a new wave of *Munsters* nostalgia. A trading card series, *The Munsters Collection,* was issued by Kayro-Vue Productions in 1996, and the following year at the annual Comic-Con International in San Diego, a new *Munsters* comic book was launched. Ad-

One of the most favorite, nostalgic cars from the world of TV is the Munster Koach from The Munsters. *It was modified by combining three Ford Model Ts into an 18-foot-long body that took 500 hours to build.*

ditionally, as a result of this new wave of interest, two new *Munsters* movies were made: *Here Come the Munsters* (1995) and *The Munsters' Scary Little Christmas* (1996). A documentary on the show entitled *The Munsters—America's*

First Family of Fright ran on national television in 2003. Even though *The Munsters* still has a fan base, this documentary would prove to be the last major production featuring the original characters.

NOS4A2

NOS4A2 was a 2013 novel by author Joe Hill (pseudonym of Joseph Hillström King). Its main character was Victoria "Vic" McQueen, a young artist who is set against the seemingly immortal Charlie Manx, a vampire who feeds on the souls of children, then

stashes what's left of his victims in Christmasland, a Christmas village where every day is Christmas Day and unhappiness is against the law. Christmasland is purely a product of Manx's own imagination. After learning of her ability to track the allusive Manx,

McQueen sets upon herself the task of defeating the psychic vampire and rescuing his victims. In carrying out her task, she is threatened with losing her own mind or even becoming his next victim.

In 2019, *NOS4A2* was launched as a new television series on the AMC channel and ran for two seasons. In the series, McQueen was portrayed by Ashleigh Cummings and Manx by Zachary Quinto.

Penny Dreadful

Penny Dreadful was a horror series created by John Logan and produced by the Showtime and Sky Atlantic premium television networks in the United States and the United Kingdom. It ran for three seasons (2014–2016). Penny dreadfuls, from which the series derived its name, were cheap serials that were sold weekly for a penny a copy in Victorian England. Some of the serials would later be collected and published as a novel, such being the case, for example, for *Varney the Vampire*, which originated as a penny dreadful publication release in the years 1845–1847.

Penny Dreadful centered on Sir Malcolm Murray (Timothy Dalton), who had a career as an African explorer but then sought to reverse the damage of the actions that have been most destructive relative to his family. His initial quest was to locate his daughter, Mina Murray, who had disappeared (and whom the audience knows as a character from the novel *Dracula*). To facilitate his search, Sir Malcolm enlisted the aid of Vanessa Ives (Eva Green), a talented medium and a childhood friend of Mina's. The two further gained additional assistance from Ethan Chandler (Josh Harnett), an American cowboy, and Victor Frankenstein (Harry Treadaway), the creator of the monster in the novel *Frankenstein*. Their quest brought them into contact not only with the creature (Roy Kinnear) brought to life by Dr. Frankenstein but other characters from the era, including Dorian Gray (Reeve Carney), Dr. Henry Jekyll (Shazad Latif), and Dracula (Christian Camargo). Along the way, Vanessa also sought the help of Dr.

Seward (another character from *Dracula*, portrayed by Patti LuPone), now pictured as a female and an alienist (psychotherapist).

Dracula made his initial appearances in season one. He assumed the role of a hospital orderly but was originally a fallen angel, the brother of Lucifer, who had been banished from heaven to earth, even as his brother had been banished to hell. He was the progenitor of all vampires. His immediate aim was to make Vanessa his vampire bride, a step toward his larger plan to world domination. Dracula's first attempt to reach Vanessa was blocked, so he seduced Mina Murray and brought her under his control. To keep Mina from biting Vanessa, Sir Malcolm had to shoot Mina.

Dracula later approached Vanessa as Dr. Alexander Sweet. She was initially impressed by the collection at the London Natural History Museum. She eventually uncovered his true nature, but he convinced her that he had fallen in love with her. Swayed by his presentation, Vanessa allowed Dracula to bite her and feed off of her blood and then had to extricate herself from his intent.

Penny Dreadful ended after three seasons, but in 2020, a spin-off show, *Penny Dreadful: City of Angels*, appeared for a first season on Showtime. It attempted to re-create the atmosphere of the original series but in a new time and place: Los Angeles in 1938. Vampires were not a significant part of the supernatural world of the new series.

Rory Kinnear is The Creature in the TV series Penny Dreadful *in which Dr. Frankenstein teams up with a medium, a gunslinger, and an explorer to battle supernatural beings.*

The Strain

The Strain originated as a proposal by Mexican filmmaker Guillermo del Toro for a television series for Fox. Despite del Toro's status as one of the most outstanding directors of this generation, he was unable to get his idea accepted. He subsequently teamed with American novelist Chuck Hogan, and the pair turned the idea into three novels, published as *The Strain* (2009), *The Fall* (2010), and *The Night Eternal* (2011). By this time, del Toro had a long history with vampires that went back to his writing and directing *Cronos*, a low-budget but unique 1985 vampire film, his directing the second *Blade* (2002) film, and his writing and directing *Hellboy: The Golden Army* (2008).

The Strain focused upon an epidemic that hit New York City. It began with a plane landing at John F. Kennedy Airport. The passengers and crew all appeared dead except for four. After being removed from the plane, however, the dead arose and began the spread of the disease by returning to their families' homes. Meanwhile, the Centers for Disease Control and Prevention was brought into the situation through the persona of Dr. Ephraim Goodweather, who heads a rapid-response team. As the epidemic spread, he teamed up with Abraham Setrakian, a Holocaust survivor, and they created a small cadre of vampire hunters to try to warn the public

(Right to left) Corey Stoll is Ephraim Goodweather, David Bradley is Abraham Setrakian, and Ruta Gedmintas is Dutch Velders in The Strain, *another version of the premise in which a virus causes vampirism—this time, in modern New York City.*

and the government of the situation, even as they acted directly against an emerging vampire horde. They were opposed by an ancient vampire Master; Thomas Eichorst, a former Nazi death camp officer; and Eldritch Palmer, a well-connected New York billionaire who seeks immortality. Through Palmer, the vampires were able initially to block any effective government response to their plans for domination.

The novels were subsequently turned into a television series that ran for four seasons on FX (2014–2017). The series stared Corey Stoll as Dr. Ephraim Goodweather, David Bradley as Abraham Setrakian, Richard Sammel as Thomas Eichorst, and Jonathan Hyde as Eldritch Palmer. Several people, such as Robin Atkins Downes and Jack Kesy, portrayed the Master, who moved from one body to another during the battle for control of the city.

🦇 *True Blood* 🦇

True Blood was a popular vampire-oriented television series that aired for seven seasons (2008–2014) on HBO. The show took

its name from the storyline premise that vampires were real and had recently gone public in the wake of an artificial blood substitute, dis-

Anna Paquin (left) and Stephen Moyer as Sookie Stackhouse and Bill Compton in True Blood, *a popular TV series based on the books by Charlaine Harris.*

tributed as "Tru Blood," which they could consume, hence no longer needing to attack humans and consume their blood. The series posited the existence of a vampire society governed by authorities at the local (sheriffs) and state (kings) levels, operating under an international Vampire Authority. While the majority of vampires and humans approved the new rapprochement between the two communities, some vampires did not like "Tru Blood" and wished to return to the earlier state of affairs, and some humans, including members of the Fellowship of the Sun, an antivampire church, opposed all things vampirish.

True Blood was based upon *The Southern Vampire Mysteries,* a book series written by mystery author Charlaine Harris. The story began in rural Louisiana and focused on waitress Sookie Stackhouse (portrayed by Anna Paquin). Partially of fairy blood, she had the ability to hear customers' thoughts, an ability she had trouble shutting off. Then, she met Bill Compton (Stephen Moyer), a 173-year-old vampire who had recently taken up residence in his former home, all of his human relatives having died out. Sookie was immediately drawn to him because she could not hear his thoughts. As the series developed, besides Compton and his vampire cohorts, the characters included a variety of additional "supernatural" entities, including shapeshifters and were-animals.

The first three seasons of *True Blood* roughly followed the plot of the first three books of *The Southern Vampire Mysteries* series: *Dead until Dark, Living Dead in Dallas,* and *Club Dead.* They introduced the primary set of characters, including Jason Stackhouse, Sookie's brother (Ryan Kwanten); Sam Merlotte, the owner of the cafe where Sookie was employed (Sam Trammell); Tara Thornton, Sookie's best friend (Rutina Wesley); Eric Northman, a vampire who serves as the vampire community's local sheriff (Alexander Skarsgard); and Lafayette Reynolds, a gay African American who also works in Merlotte's cafe (Nelsan Ellis). In the later seasons, some deviation from the series storyline occurred.

Werewolves began to gain a prominent place in the *True Blood* storyline in season three with the introduction of Alcide Herveaux (Joe Manganiello), a local pack leader who would become a major love interest of Sookie's during times that she was alienated from Bill Compton. Sam Merlotte was also a were-animal, though he normally turned into a border collie.

Much of the success of *True Blood* was attributed to director/producer Alan Ball. He discovered the books of *The Southern Vampire Mysteries* somewhat by accident and shared honors with author Charlaine Harris for the series. Among the many awards that Harris received were the Lord Ruthven Award, given annually by the Lord Ruthven Assembly, a group of academic scholars specializing in vampire literature. She became one of the few authors to receive the award twice (2003 for *Living Dead in Dallas* and 2018 for *The Complete Sookie Stackhouse Stories*). Meanwhile, her first book, *Dead until Dark,* received the Anthony Award for Best Paperback Mystery in 2001. Meanwhile, for his work on *True Blood,* Ball received the 2009 Writers Guild of America Award for Best New Series and the 2010 Producers Guild of America Award for Best Dramatic Series.

The show received critical acknowledgment for its seeming discussion of a variety of social issues, most notably homosexuality, with vampires serving as a metaphor for gay and lesbian people. The show also highlighted issues of religion, discrimination against various minorities, civil rights, and the current state of the family.

🦇 *Vampira* 🦇

Vampira is the stage persona of actress Maila Nurmi (1921–2008). The character was created in 1954 when Nurmi was a horror show hostess at KABC in Los Angeles. After a two-year run, she moved to KHJ. Nurmi's enduring fame came from her joining Bela Lugosi in the classic cult movie *Plan 9 from Outer Space* (1959). They played the initial two vampires/zombies that the space invaders hoped to create in their plan to take over Earth. After the run of her television show, she also appeared in several other movies, including two vampire films, *The Magic Sword* (1964) and *Orgy of the Night* (1966), the latter put together by *Plan 9*'s director Edward Wood Jr. Nurmi also appeared in several other nonvampire movies and, for a while, she operated a boutique in Hollywood. In the 1980s, Nurmi sued Cassandra Peterson for stealing her Vampira persona to create the persona Elvira; however, the suit came to nought. In 2006, Kevin Sean Michaels put out a DVD documentary of Nurmi's life, *Vampira the Movie*.

Actress Maila Nurmi made her career playing the alter ego Vampira, who hosted horror shows on KABC in Los Angeles.

Several volumes celebrating Vampira's career have appeared in the years since her death, the most recent being *Glamour Ghoul: The Passion and Pain of the Real Vampire, Maila Nurmi* (2021), a biographical volume compiled by her niece, Sandra Nurmi, from Vampira's diaries, photos, and other documents she left behind, with added insights supplied by her family members.

🦇 *The Vampire Diaries / The Originals / Legacies* 🦇

The Vampire Diaries brought the very successful young-adult novels of L. J. (Lisa Jane) Smith to the television screen for eight seasons (2009–2017). The show further demonstrated its popularity through its two spin-off series, *The Originals* and *Legacies*. Prior to writing *The Vampire Diaries*, Smith had written another young-adult series featuring vampires, *The*

Night World, nine volumes of which were published over three years (1996–1998). Each story in the series featured a young woman searching for true love somewhere close to the boundary where the normal human world and what Smith envisioned as the Night World overlapped. The Night World included vampires, witches, werewolves, and various shapeshifters. Inhabitants of the Night World were charged with never allowing humans to come to know of its existence and were mandated never to fall in love with a human.

The action in *The Night World* series is supplied by the need for the young woman featured in each story to discover her love object, or soul mate. In the first novel, for example, a teenage girl was dying of cancer. Her soul mate was actually a vampire and, in order to save her, he turned her into a vampire, not a decision he should have made on his own. After the turning, the young girl was kidnapped and taken to Las Vegas to face her fate, since she was an illegitimate new member of the Night World scene.

Smith followed the reasonably successful *Night World* series with *The Vampire Diaries*. The basic story focused on a young Elena Gilbert, who encountered two brothers who happened to be vampires, Stefan and Damon Salvatore. Attracted to both, she had to choose between them. As the series began, Elena was nearing the end of her high school career in Mystic Falls, Virginia. Her parents had recently died. While appearing to be Elena's contemporary, the Salvatore brothers were more than 170 years old, having come of age during the Civil War. Of the two, Stefan is the younger, "good-guy" vampire, while his older brother, Damon, is the "bad boy." As teenagers in the nineteenth century, they both vied for the love of one Katherine (or Katarina) Gilbert, who bore an uncanny resemblance to Elena Gilbert.

> Inhabitants of the Night World were charged with never allowing humans to come to know of its existence and were mandated never to fall in love with a human.

The Elena–Stefan–Damon love triangle would energize the storyline through the four volumes of the original series (*The Awakening, The Struggle, The Fury,* and *Dark Reunion*), published in 1991 and 1992. Besides the three focal people of the series, it also introduced several additional key characters to Elena's social circle, most notably Caroline Forbes, Bonnie McCullough, and Matt Honeycutt. The operation of the triangle led to Elena's becoming a vampire in the third volume.

More than a decade after the publication of *The Vampire Diaries*, the recently established CW network targeted the books for adaptation as a television show. Kevin Williamson and Julie Plec took the lead in developing the series. Chosen to assume the lead roles were Nina Dobrev (as Elena Gilbert), Paul Wesley (as Stefan Salvatore), and Ian Somerhalder (as Damon Salvatore). Additional key characters included Jeremy Gilbert (portrayed by Steven R. McQueen), Elena's brother; Jenna Sommers (Sara Cramer), Elena's aunt and guardian in the absence of her parents; Bonnie Bennett (Kat Graham), Elena's friend and a powerful witch; Caroline Forbes (Candice King), Elena's friend, who became a vampire in the second season; and Matt Donovan (Zach Roerig), a former boyfriend of Elena's, who became increasingly intolerant of any supernatural elements in his world.

The Vampire Diaries would run for 171 episodes over eight seasons (2009–2017). While beginning with storylines largely derived from the book series, as the show proceeded, it deviated from and moved beyond the books. Even as the television series was being launched, L. J. Smith, who had given little consideration to the characters she had created in the early 1990s, began to turn out a new series of books, picking up the storyline she had abandoned in 1992 and including characters such as Elena's

Paul Wesley plays vampire Stefan Salvatore, and Nina Dobrev is Elena Gilbert in the long-running TV series The Vampire Diaries *(2009–2017).*

friend Meredith, who was absent from the television series. Termed *The Return Trilogy*, the new volumes included *Nightfall* (2009), *Shadow Souls* (2010), and *Midnight* (2011).

Then, as Smith prepared to begin writing an additional trilogy of *The Vampire Diaries* novels, she had a falling-out with her publisher (who owned the copyright to the series) and was cut off from further work on the project. A ghostwriter was hired to do the two subsequent series, *The Hunters Trilogy*, which included *Phantom* (2011), *Moonsong* (2012), and *Destiny Rising* (2012); and *The Salvation Trilogy*, which included *Unseen* (2013), *Unspoken* (2013), and *Unmasked*

(2014). The latter trilogy was written by Aubrey Clark. As these latter volumes appeared, Smith renounced any connection with or responsibility for them.

Among the characters introduced by *The Vampire Diaries* was that of Klaus (or Niklaus) Mikaelson. He emerged as the main villain in *Dark Reunion*, the last of the original 1990s novels, and was revealed to be one of the "old ones," a very old vampire who cannot be killed, though he suffered a monumental defeat as the novel ended. He was introduced into the second season of the television series, where he was called an "original" vampire. Part of the driving force in his actions concerned the fact that he was also part werewolf, making him a vampire–werewolf hybrid. He wished to break a curse that had been placed upon him in order to liberate his werewolf side, an event that would allow him to create a new superspecies of werewolf–vampire hybrids.

Klaus Mikaelson's appearances in *The Vampire Diaries* received enough fan support to create the first spin-off of the show in the form of *The Originals*. *The Originals* followed the life of Klaus (portrayed by Joseph Morgan) and family, particularly his brother Elijah (Daniel Gillies) and half sister Rebekah (Claire Holt), but also his parents, other siblings and half siblings, and, eventually, a daughter named Hope (portrayed by several people as she grew to be a teenager, Danielle Rose Russell). The Mikaelsons were the first vampires, having originated in medieval Norway over 1,000 years ago. Their modern history began with their arrival in New Orleans in colonial times. Klaus, Elijah, and Rebekah were responsible for building the French Quarter, and Klaus exerted considerable authority, especially over the "supernatural" community of witches, werewolves, and vampires, until 1919, when they left the city. In their absence, a former slave whom they had taken under their care, Marcel (Charles Michael Davis), took over. Klaus wanted to retake control from Marcel, who proved reluctant to relinquish his new status. Once back in New Orleans, Klaus also developed a relationship with Hayley Marshall, a werewolf, and fathers a child named Hope with her.

The five seasons of *The Originals* (2013–2018) covered some 15 years of the battles of the Mikaelsons with the various supernatural communities based there and other supernatural forces that entered the city; their attempt to reestablish themselves in New Orleans while keeping the family united; and increasingly to raise and protect Klaus's daughter Hope from harm. As the series drew to a close, Hope emerged as a powerful entity on her own and, as such, was enrolled in the Salvatore Boarding School for the Young and Gifted. The school, located back in Mystic Falls, Virginia, was where the story of *The Vampire Diaries* had begun and provided a haven where students with supernatural powers could learn to control and utilize their abilities.

Hope Mikaelson's career at the Salvatore school became the subject of the second spin-off of *The Vampire Diaries*. The initial episode aired in 2018 on the CW network and continues as this almanac goes to press. A character from *The Vampire Diaries*, Alaric Saltzman (Matt Davis), emerged as the headmaster of the school.

🦇 *Vampirina* 🦇

Vampirina, an animated vampire-oriented children's television series, adapted its major character and plotline from two *Vampirina Ballerina* books authored by Anne Marie Pace: *Vampirina Ballerina* (2012) and *Vampirina Ballerina Hosts a Sleepover* (2013). Both were illustrated by LeUyen Pham. They were originally published by Disney-Hyperion, and the character of Vampirina was brought to television by Disney Junior, one of several Disney cable channels. The first episode was aired in 2017, and it remains a continuing series as this almanac goes to press. Since the television series began, Pace has published additional storybooks, and Disney has issued a variety of children's activity books featuring Vampirina.

As the series began, Vampirina "Vee" Hauntley is an eight-year-old child who was born in Transylvania but recently moved to

Vampires don't get any cuter than in the children's cartoon series Vampirina, *which debuted on the Disney Channel in 2017.*

Pennsylvania with her parents and grandparents. They operate the Scare B&B, designed to host any visiting ghouls and goblins, even as the family engages in a learning trajectory of the way of their new home. They keep their own unusual origins secret so as not to scare their new American neighbors.

In the television series, Vampirina (voiced by Isabella Cvetti) is also the member of a band, The Ghoul Girls, for which she serves as the lead singer and plays a ukulele-like "spookylele." Her sidekick friend, Gregoria (voiced by comedian Wanda Sykes) is a 473-year-old gargoyle. A ghost named Demi (voiced by Mitchell Whitfield) also lives with the Huntley family. Poppy Peepleson (voiced by Jordan Alexa Davis), Vee's best friend, was the first human to learn of her vampire identity but promised not to reveal the secret to anyone.

A very successful series, *Vampirina* has received multiple Emmy nominations, has been translated into 15 languages, and is currently (2020) seen in some 115 countries.

Young Dracula

Young Dracula was a popular children's television series that aired on CBBC from 2006 through 2014. Seasons one and two aired in 2006–2008 and, following a gap, seasons three through five aired in 2011–2014. The series followed the contemporary life of Count Dracula (portrayed by Keith Lee Castle) and his children, a son, Vlad (Gerran Howell), and a daughter, Ingrid (Clare Thomas). They originally lived in Transylvania, but after some encounters with angry peasants, they left their homeland and settled in the United Kingdom, specifically in Wales.

Young Dracula was inspired, if not directly based, on a children's book of the same name by Michael Lawrence. It has Dracula's male heir as the main focus. Vlad has to mix his loyalty to his family, from whom he has inherited a spectrum of characteristics and powers, with his own desire to integrate into his new home. In season three, Vlad moved from childhood into his teen years. He has powers but must develop and gain control of them. Meanwhile, Count Dracula wishes to have his son and heir confirmed as the Chosen One. As the series continues, Vlad finds love with a human (a "breather," as vampires refer to humans), much to his father's consternation. He must also contend with the growth of a Slayer community, with whom he seeks reconciliation. He looks forward to a time in which vampires will not bite and Slayers will not kill but finds that the vampires are deeply attached to their old ways.

In 2007, *Young Dracula* was named the Best Children's Drama by both the Royal Television Society and the Welsh branch of the British Academy of Film and Television Arts.

VAMPIRES IN POP CULTURE

In the decades since World War II, popular culture has come into its own again. It has claimed its space in society against "high" culture, the culture generally considered the best that any given nation could produce and which was generally generated and owned by its elite. High culture included such things as the buildings produced by the best architects; the songs sung in the best theaters, which could be attended only by the few who could afford the tickets; the academic establishment, and the paintings accepted for display in museums. In contrast, pop culture refers to cultural products welcomed and consumed by the majority of a society's population. It includes music and dance, art and architecture, clothing and fashion, film and television, and practiced religion and sports.

As the population has grown, various distinctive and often contradictory popular cultures exist side by side. Large segments of the public can coexist as fans of horror, mysteries, science fiction, or romance simultaneously.

Large numbers can listen to one form of music (country or folk), while an equally enthusiastic community can be largely unaware of its artists and listen to another (hip-hop or jazz). Some can follow sports, while others denounce football or basketball as a waste of time. Many can love vampires, while others find them silly, disgusting, or even as the embodiment of evil.

Popular culture, especially in the modern context, includes those objects created by manufacturers for mass consumption. As the vampire has permeated the modern world, primarily through literature and the cinema, it has established itself as a bulwark in popular culture beginning with the books, short stories, motion pictures, and stage dramas that were discussed in previous chapters. However, the vampire has reached even further than that, being the subject of comic books, games and toys, humor, and organizations of fans, to name a few. In this chapter, we highlight just a few select areas in which the vampire has entered our lives as it quietly emerges in almost every social arena we have created.

> As the vampire has permeated the modern world, primarily through literature and the cinema, it has established itself as a bulwark in popular culture….

Atlanta Vampire Alliance

The Atlanta Vampire Alliance is a vampire organization founded in 2005 in Atlanta, Georgia. It describes itself as an alliance of like-minded individuals, including both sanguinarian (those who drink blood) and psychic (or energy) vampires, who work for the progress and education of both the greater and local vampire community. It offers self-identified vampires a respectful environment and promotes serious dialog and continuing education. The organization consults with a wide range of interested outsiders, including members of the media, law enforcement, clergy, and the academic world.

Members of the organization have tried to correct stereotypical images of self-identified vampires and, in 2006 in conjunction with their research company, Suscitatio Enterprises, LLC, launched a massive, two-part survey of the vampire community. This 988-question survey, known as the Vampirism and Energy Work Research Study, was distributed worldwide to people who have identified themselves as vampires both online and offline. Between 2006 and 2009, more than 950 vampires from over 40 countries completed the surveys. The results detailed the reality of vampire existence and what appeared to be a rather mundane community of people who otherwise blended into their larger environment, society, and culture. However, the unusual characteristics revealed by the study include individual vampire activities, higher-than-normal prevalence rates of certain medical conditions, and a diversity of religious beliefs and practices. The research study results are posted at http://www.suscitatio.com.

The organization contends that vampirism itself is neither a religion nor a faith-based collective. Members represent a variety of diverse spiritual beliefs or paths across the religious spectrum (although a high percentage follow paths representative of Western esotericism). The organization also hosts frequent gatherings in the Atlanta area and cosponsors larger conferences of vampires that include such well-known speakers as Michelle Belanger, Pam Keesey, and members of the law-enforcement community. The Alliance also participates in the Voices of the Vampire Community.

Baron Blood

The vampire Baron Blood was one of a host of supervillains created by Marvel Comics as worthy adversaries of its very successful superheroes. He first appeared in *The Invaders* (No. 7) in 1976, a time when Marvel was well into its creation of what came to be known as the alternative Marvel Universe (a world where all of their comic superheroes could exist and interact). Baron Blood was born late in the nineteenth century as John Falsworth, the younger son of Lord William Falsworth, a British nobleman. Shortly after the turn of the century, when his brother inherited control of the family fortune, the younger Falsworth went to Romania to search for Dracula. He planned to gain control of Dracula and become a powerful person, but he underestimated the count's powers and was instead turned into a vampire. Falsworth returned to England as Dracula's servant and agent to create havoc in England. He became Dracula's instrument of revenge for the defeat described in Bram Stoker's novel.

Falsworth became a German agent during World War I, which is when he first assumed his identity as Baron Blood. After the war, he disappeared until he reemerged as a Hitler supporter in World War II. He returned to England, posing as his own grandson, and took up residence at Falsworth Manor. He attacked his own family but was defeated by the Invaders, the superteam that had been assembled to defeat the Third Reich. He was killed by a stalactite threaded through with silver. He was then entombed in a chapel with a stake in his heart and his casket surrounded by garlic.

Baron Blood did not reappear until 1981, when Captain America, one of the original Invaders, was summoned to England. The now aged Lord Falsworth believed that Baron Blood was the cause of a rash of what had been defined as slasher murders. Captain America then discovered that Baron Blood was not in his tomb. He had been resurrected some years before by a Dr. Charles Cromwell, who had been sent to Baron Blood's tomb by Dracula. After awakening, Baron Blood killed Cromwell and assumed his identity. He lived quietly for many years, taking blood from his patients. Captain America tracked him down, killed him, and then decapitated him and burned his body.

Captain America had finally disposed of Baron Blood, but he was too worthy a villain to leave in the ashes. He initially reappeared in the form of Victor Strange, brother of Marvel's sorcerer hero, Dr. Stephen Strange. Victor had died and was frozen cryogenically. When Dr. Strange tried to revive him with magical spells, one of the spells worked but turned Victor into a vampire. Therefore, when the cryogenic machine was turned off in 1989, Victor awoke as a vampire. He donned a costume similar to Baron Blood's and was named Baron Blood by Marie Laveau, the Voodoo priestess

> **The now aged Lord Falsworth believed that Baron Blood was the cause of a rash of what had been defined as slasher murders.**

whom Strange was fighting at the time of Victor's resurrection. Baron Blood settled in Greenwich Village and, like the vampire Morbius (another Marvel vampire), satisfied his craving for blood by attacking criminals. He reappeared occasionally in Dr. Strange's adventures until August 1993, when he committed suicide by plunging a knife into his midsection. Dr. Strange buried the baron, but it was unlikely that Baron Blood had finally been destroyed.

Baron Blood had a second reincarnation in 1999 in the persona of Kenneth Creichton, a relative of the original Baron Blood. Suffering from anemia, he is approached by Baroness Blood and finally accepts her offer to be changed into a vampire. Thus, he becomes the new Baron Blood. Meanwhile, the baroness discovers the Holy Grail. The baron is present at Glastonbury when, in the presence of the group of vampires, she drinks from the grail, thus attaining the power to walk about in the daylight. She refuses to share the power with the others and destroys the grail. As the sun rises, Baron Blood is among those who disintegrate in its rays.

In 2007, Baron Blood was resurrected yet again in the storyline of the third series of comics devoted to Blade the Vampire Slayer, in which Blade's father becomes a vampire in order to survive a terminal disease. He has lost his soul and, in the process of seeking its restoration, encounters a prophecy. This prophecy, when fulfilled—as it is at the end of the series (No. 12)—causes the reemergence of a number of vampires. All of these vampires, including the infamous Baron Blood, remained alive to walk the earth.

Batman

Like Superman, Batman, one of the most popular twentieth-century superheroes, remains so in the twenty-first century. Batman (a DC Comics character) created a popularized image of the bat, the development of which, to some extent, must be credited to *Dracula*, the 1897 book by Bram Stoker, especially in its translation through the 1920s and 1930s to the stage and motion picture screen. However, Batman was not a vampire; he was a human hero with human resources, and his enemies, while often very strange, were usually human as well.

Batman first appeared in *Detective Comics* No. 27 in 1939. Dr. Thomas Wayne and his wife were killed in a mugging. In his grief, their son, Bruce Wayne, grew up with the idea of becoming a policeman. He studied criminology and developed his body to an amazing degree. As a young adult, he changed his plans and decided to become a vigilante. He settled on the Batman costume after two events: first, a bat flew in the window as he was trying to find a uniform to put fear into the hearts of his criminal enemies. Later, the independently wealthy Wayne fell through the floor of his mansion and discovered a bat-infested cave—the perfect headquarters for Batman.

The clear association of Batman with Dracula must have been in the mind of his creators because a scant four months after his initial appearance, he encountered a vampire in a two-part story in issues No. 31 and No. 32 of *Detective Comics* in September and October 1939. A vampire tried to take control of Bruce Wayne's girlfriend, unaware that Wayne was Batman. Batman tracked the Monk, as the vampire was known, to his home in Hungary, which was also the home of his allies, the werewolves. Batman eventually found the vampire and his vampire bride asleep and killed them with a silver bullet fired into the coffins.

The full development of Batman as a definitive comic book hero in the years after World War II occurred as the debate over the effect of comic books on children proceeded. After DC Comics subscribed to the Comics Code in 1954, little opportunity (or reason) existed for Batman and his new sidekick, Robin the Boy Wonder, to encounter vampires and the supernatural. However, as Batman's popularity—and, subsequently, the number of comic books carrying his stories—increased, new villains were continually generated. Thus, it was inevitable, after the lifting of the ban on vampires by the revised Comics Code in 1971, that Batman would come face to face with additional bloodthirsty enemies.

Batman's next encounter with a vampire, Gustav Decobra, occurred in the January 1976

Batman debuted as a character in the May 1939 issue of Detective Comics.

Detective Comics (No. 455). Stranded by car trouble, Bruce Wayne and his butler, Alfred, entered a seemingly deserted house only to find a coffin in the center of the living room. As they searched the house, a vampire emerged from the coffin. After Wayne saw the vampire, he changed into Batman. In the ensuing fight, Batman rammed a stake into the vampire's chest. However, this did no good because Decobra had cleverly hidden his heart elsewhere. Batman then retreated from this first battle. By the time of their next confrontation, he figured out that Decobra had hidden his heart in a grandfather clock at the house. When Batman impaled the heart with an arrow, Decobra died.

After DC Comics subscribed to the Comics Code in 1954, little opportunity (or reason) existed for Batman and his new sidekick, Robin the Boy Wonder, to encounter vampires and the supernatural.

Several years prior to this encounter with Decobra, Batman had begun an ongoing relationship with Kirk Langstrom. Langstrom developed a serum to turn himself into Man-Bat. Though not originally a vampire bat, Man-Bat would eventually encounter vampires and bring Batman into the realm with him. Both Man-Bat and Batman's encounters with vampires were orchestrated by writer Gerry Conway, the first writer for Marvel's *The Tomb of Dracula*, and artist Gene Colan, who had worked through the 1970s on *The Tomb of Dracula*. Both were working for DC in the early 1980s.

In 1982, immediately after the conclusion of the first episode with Man-Bat, where he was cured of the condition that had turned him into a bat, Batman (now in the hands of writer Conway and artist Colan) squared off against vampires again. An unsuspecting Robin was captured by his girlfriend, Dala, who turned out to be a vampire. He attempted to escape, but in the process, he was confronted by Dala's colleague, the resurrected Monk. Robin was bitten and then allowed to escape. Because the only way to save Robin was with a serum made from the vampire's blood, Batman went after the vampires. Unsuccessful in his first encounter, Batman was bitten and also became a vampire. He then set up a second confrontation that was successful, and he was able to obtain the necessary ingredients to return himself and Robin to normalcy.

Except for his ongoing relationship with Man-Bat, Batman did not confront a vampire again until 1991. The new story was published as a stand-alone graphic novel rather than as part of either of the *Batman* comic book serials. It concerned Batman's adventures in what was described in the introduction as an "alternative future" and a Batman who was "an altogether different Batman than we're used to." In *Batman & Dracula: Red Rain*, Gotham City was under attack by a group of vampires led by Dracula. Batman (without Robin) was drawn into the fray. In his effort to find what was believed to be a serial killer, he met Tanya, a "good" vampire who had previously organized an opposition to Dracula. She had developed a methadonelike artificial substitute that quenched the vampire's need for blood. After they united to fight Dracula, Batman was wounded in battle and became a vampire. In his closing lines, he repeated Tanya's phrase, "Vampires are real ... but not all of them are evil." In the sequel, *Batman: Bloodstorm*, Batman finally defeated Dracula and the vampires and, in his closing report to Commissioner Gordon, indicated the means for disposing of the last vampire, Batman himself. Commissioner Gordon and Alfred, Bruce Wayne's faithful butler, killed Batman by staking him.

The fact that Batman was staked but not decapitated allowed him to return in the third volume of the *Batman & Dracula* series, *Crimson Mist* (1998). Alfred removed the stake, hoping that Batman would revive to handle a crime wave striking Gotham. He succeeded in killing and drinking from a number of his old enemies, but finally, two of them, Killer Croc and Two-Face, made common cause with Commissioner Gordon and Alfred. They agreed that the human Batman would not handle the situation in the same manner as the vampire Batman. They also agreed to lure Batman to the Batcave, where they planned to set off explosions that would collapse the roof and expose Batman to the sun. Once the five were in the Batcave, a fight ensued. Alfred, Killer Croc, and Two-Face were killed and, subsequently, Commissioner Gordon sprung the trap. Gordon was killed as the roof collapsed on him and, as the story ended, Batman walked into the sunlight, presumably to die the final death.

In 2007, DC released the *Batman & Dracula* trilogy in a collected edition under the title *Tales of the Multiverse: Batman–Vampire*. The storyline appears to have had some in-fluence on the 2005 feature film *Batman vs. Dracula: The Animated Movie*. Meanwhile, the unvampirized Batman has continued his adventures in *Batman* and *Detective Comics* to the present and a variety of spin-off titles, where he occasionally confronted a vampire. In the vast literature on the Batman character, very few additional appearances of a vampirized Batman have occurred.

In 2015, Len Wein worked with Kelly Jones to produce *Convergence*, a sequel to the *Batman & Dracula* trilogy in which the Swamp Thing, a popular DC character, teams up with the vampirized Batman to fight the remaining vampires plaguing Gotham. They succeed in turning all the vampires back into humans except Batman, who ends the storyline by committing suicide by watching a sunrise.

Belanger, Michelle (1973–)

Through the first decade of the twenty-first century, Michelle Belanger emerged as a prominent spokesperson for the self-identified real vampire community. She was born and raised in Ohio. According to her own account, she was born with a heart defect that, while significantly repaired with some early surgery, left her low in vital energy. She learned before she knew what she was doing to take energy from those she came into contact with and, thus, markedly improved her own vitality. As a teenager, she learned to take such energy while she gave people back rubs. She experienced a watershed event when her grandmother cut her off from her friends. She stopped giving many back rubs and grew ill. Over her early adult years, as her condition failed to respond to medical care, she finally figured out her vampire nature.

Belanger welcomed the emergence of the vampire community in the 1980s. While mostly built by people interested in vampire novels and movies, a variety of people showed a more

Recognized as an expert on the occult and paranormal who is a prolific author and consultant on these topics, Michelle Belanger is also a spokesperson for the vampire community.

serious interest, and she became aware that several groups had appeared that provided an initial home for real vampires. In the 1980s, she also began her study of various systems based on psychic energy, such as reiki and qigong.

In the early 1990s, she attended John Carroll University in Cleveland, Ohio. While there, she founded a magazine, *Shadowdance*. She also became involved in the role-playing game *Vampire: The Masquerade* and began to write the early version of what became her 2004 publication on working with magical and psychical energies, *The Psychic Vampire Codex*. *Shadowdance* provided a point of contact for people to write to her about their vampire experiences. By 1994, she saw a need to provide a forum for this small group of people and founded the International Vampire Society. In September 1995, she began publishing the society's magazine, *The Midnight Sun*.

> By 1994, she saw a need to provide a forum for this small group of people and founded the International Vampire Society.

Belanger's public role facilitated her contact with Father Sebastiaan, who had developed similar interests and begun to organize vampires in the New York City area. The two came into contact in 1998. He encouraged her to make her presence felt online. She saw the first edition of his vampire ethics code, *Black Veils*, which he had adapted from *Vampire: The Masquerade*. The two worked together for several years; in 2000, she rewrote *Black Veils* into a more acceptable version, which she expanded from seven to 13 codes of ethics. Her version now circulates as *13 Rules of Community*. She also allowed Sebastiaan to publish a version of the codex. During the years in contact with Father Sebastiaan, the International Vampire Society evolved into the House Kheperu. The occult-oriented group began to explore past lives and came to feel that they were once together in ancient Egypt. The group associated for a while in the 1990s with the Sanguinarium, a network of vampires and groups founded by Father Sebastiaan.

In more recent years, Belanger and Sebastiaan have gone in separate directions. Through the first decade of the twentieth century, Belanger became well known as a self-identified vampire willing to speak to the media. She published a series of books and numerous articles. Among her more important texts, *Vampires in Their Own Words: An Anthology of Vampire Voices* (2007) assembled a spectrum of self-identified vampires to speak about their lives. Most of Belanger's recent writings have been on nonvampire subjects, though in 2014, she brought out a new, 20th-anniversary edition of her seminal work, *The Psychic Vampire Codex*, a guidebook for real vampires.

Belanger continues to reside in her home state.

ᨆ *Blade the Vampire Slayer* ᨆ

In April 1971, following a change in the Comics Code that allowed vampires to return to comic books, Marvel Comics introduced a new vampire comic book, *The Tomb of Dracula*. It brought the story of Dracula into the 1970s and brought together descendants of the characters in Bram Stoker's novel to fight the revived vampire. Over the course of the long-running series, Marvel also introduced several new characters. Among the most enduring was Blade the Vampire Slayer. Blade, an African American, further reflected the social changes in post–World War II America. These changes had also been noted by readers in the appearance of a woman, Rachel Van Helsing, as a strong, weapon-carrying vampire slayer who assumed the role once held by her grandfather, Abraham Van Helsing.

Blade was a warrior equipped with a set of teak wood knives. He initially appeared in the July 1973 (No. 10) issue of *The Tomb of Dracula* on the London docks, where he proceeds to kill several vampire members of Dracula's Legion. Their deaths led to Blade meeting Quincy Harker and Rachel Van Helsing. After introductions, the action takes Blade to the ship *Michelle*, over which Dracula has assumed control. Their initial confrontation ends in a draw, but Dracula escapes, and the ship is destroyed by an explosion. Blade returned two issues later to help Harker and Frank Drake (a modern descendant of Dracula) find Harker's daughter, Edith, who had been kidnapped by Dracula.

The story of Blade's early involvement with vampires was finally told in the October 1973 (No. 13) issue. At the time of his birth, his mother was visited by a physician, Deacon Frost, who turned out to be a vampire. Frost killed his mother, and Blade dedicated his life to looking for him. That search grew into an enmity against all vampires and led him to the recently revived Dracula. He had worked primarily in America and, thus, had never met Harker, Van Helsing, or Drake but had heard about their activities.

Blade frequently reappeared through the 70 issues of *The Tomb of Dracula*. He also made a guest appearance in the Fall 1976 issue (No. 8) of *Marvel Preview*. The battle between Blade and Dracula seems to reach a conclusion when Blade sticks one of his knives into Dracula, who apparently dies. However, others steal the body, the knife is removed, and Dracula is revived. Later, Dracula seems to win when he bites Blade, but it turns out that because of the unusual circumstances involving the vampire who was present at the time of Blade's birth, Blade is immune to the vampire state.

Wesley Snipes (left) takes on the role of a kick-ass vampire slayer who is himself a vampire in the movie Blade, *which is based on the Marvel comic book character.*

In the June 1976 issue (No. 48), Blade teams with another new character introduced into *The Tomb of Dracula*, Hannibal King. He, too, had an encounter with Deacon Frost, the vampire that killed Blade's mother. In the February 1977 issue (No. 53), the two finally track Frost down and destroy him.

Vampires were banished from Marvel Comics in 1983, and very few characters from *The Tomb of Dracula* appeared during the next six years. Blade practically disappeared but quickly made his presence felt after the reintroduction of vampires into the Marvel Universe in issues 10 and 14 of *Dr. Strange: Sorcerer Supreme* (November 1989 and February 1990). Blade next appeared in the revival by Epic Comics (a subsidiary of Marvel) of *The Tomb of Dracula* (1991–1992), which resumed the story from the end of the first series without reference to the banishment of vampires and the destruction of Dracula in 1983.

In 1992, Marvel united its older, occult-oriented characters and introduced some new ones when it created a new realm on the edge of the Marvel Universe that would be the arena of the *Midnight Sons*. In this new storyline, vampires had been banished from the world in 1983 by a magical formula of Marvel's master of the occult arts, Dr. Strange. His magical operation created the Montesi Formula. That effect was being weakened and allowed a new assault upon the world by the forces of supernatural evil. These forces were led by Lilith (the ancient Hebrew demoness, not Dracula's daughter).

> In this new storyline, vampires had been banished from the world in 1983 by a magical formula of Marvel's master of the occult arts, Dr. Strange.

The new evil forced the return of the old vampire fighters, including Blade, who received a new image more akin to Marvel's other superheroes and had his weapons system upgraded. The fresh storyline was created simultaneously in five different comic book titles under the collective heading *Midnight Sons*. Blade and his old acquaintances, Frank Drake and Hannibal King, unite as a private investigation organization, the Nightstalkers. The adventures of the Nightstalkers lasted until early in 1994, when both Drake and King were killed in the war with the supernatural forces of evil. Blade survived to continue the fight in his own new comic book series *Blade the Vampire Hunter*, which ran for ten additional issues (1994–1995).

For several years, Blade was not heard from, and then, in 1997, a new *Blade* series was launched, with a preview issue (reprinting a story from *The Tomb of Dracula*) being released in anticipation of the series, which began in March 1998, and the movie, *Blade*, with Wesley Snipes in the title role, which appeared later in the year. The movie, in which Blade emerged as a day-walking, half-vampire superhero, gave the evolving character an audience unavailable to the average comic book character, and the initial movie became one of the top five all-time-grossing vampire movies. The initial story pitted Blade against his old nemesis, Deacon Frost, and a global vampire community whose clans (called houses) are organized under a council. It prompted two sequels, in the first of which Blade fights a breed of new supervampires and, in the second, a revived Dracula. An underlying theme throughout the series is the vampire's search for Blade's ability to move about in the daylight without disintegrating into ash.

The success of the *Blade* movies led to a television series that began airing in 2006 on Spike TV. *Blade: The Series* starred Kirk "Sticky Fingaz" Jones as Blade and was based in Blade's birthplace, Detroit. He found himself up against Marcus Van Sciver (Neil Jackson), a powerful vampire with the House of Chthon. Unfortunately, it failed to find an audience and was cancelled before the first season was aired.

Chapman, Erin (1977–)

Through the second decade of the twenty-first century, Canadian writer Erin Chapman has provided a vital service to the larger vampire-interest community and is best known for her investigative journalistic contributions to the general-interest vampire site *Vamped* (https://vamped.org), which she founded in 2014 and uses as a platform to cover such topics as vampire pop culture, sanguinarians and blood drinking, recent trends in vampire scholarship, the continuing Highgate Vampire saga, holiday listicles, travel pieces, movie reviews, and interviews. To

Canadian Erin Chapman is the founder of the website Vamped.

cover vampire events for *Vamped*, Erin has traveled across North America and to the United Kingdom and Ireland.

From her base in the Vancouver metropolitan area, Chapman has done primary research into blood drinking and sanguinarism, which motivated her to create her own online survey project, The Sanguinarian Survey 2019. This unique survey explores new ground. In total, she heard from some 73 respondents, each of whom responded to 151 questions on a spectrum of issues, including drinking blood for health reasons, medical issues, lifestyle and habits, diet, and digestion. The survey was conducted from September 9 to October 28, 2019, and the final 112-page report of her findings has been made available on her personal website (https://erinchapman.ca).

In 2018, Chapman expanded her own dedication to things vampiric and her expanding interest in the morbid and macabre by branching out into her own blog in 2018 called *Morbid Planet* (https://morbidplanet.com). "*Morbid Planet* is a blog that explores the horror genre and showcases the extraordinary and mysterious world of dark tourism. We also highlight unique people and macabre things, review films and cover current events and news," she says.

Erin holds a volunteer position as the operations coordinator for the Vampire Studies Association (https://vampirestudies.org). The mission of the organization is to "establish vampire studies as a multidisciplinary field by promoting, disseminating and publishing contributions to vampire scholarship." She is also the administrator for 26 vampire-themed Facebook groups and pages.

 ## *Comic Books*

Comic books emerged as a distinct form of popular literature in the 1930s, arising from the comic strips that had become a standard item in newspapers. The first vampire in a comic seems to have appeared in an early comic book title, *More Fun*, each issue of which carried the continuing stories of Dr. Occult, a ghost detective who fought various supernatural villains. In issue No. 7, Dr. Occult's first major case pitted him against a creature called the "Vampire Master." The story ran for three issues, each installment being one large page. It concluded with the vampire being killed when a knife was plunged into his heart. Before the end of the decade, in the fall of 1939, Batman would encounter a Transylvanian vampire, the Monk, in issues 31 and 32 of *Detective Comics*. As more horror stories appeared in the adventure and crime comics of the 1940s, the response suggested that an audience for an all-horror comic book could be found.

In 1948, the American Comics Group issued the first, and one of the most successful, horror comics, *Adventures into the Unknown*. Very quickly, vampires found their way onto its pages, and through the early 1950s, each issue commonly had at least one vampire story. *Adventures into the Unknown* soon spawned imitators. In 1950, writer William Grimes and artist Al Feldman of EC Comics began *Crypt of Terror* (later *Tales from the Crypt*), which was quickly joined by the *Vault of Horror* and *Haunt of Fear*. Over the next four years, over 100 horror comic book titles joined the pioneering efforts. Among the horror comics of the 1950s were a variety of titles by Atlas Comics (later Marvel Comics) such as *Suspense Comics* (1950–1953), *Mystic* (1951–1957), and *Journey into the Unknown* (1951–1957), each of which carried vampire stories. Avon's *Eerie* No. 8 (August 1953) became the first of many to adapt Bram Stoker's novel *Dracula* (1897) to comic book format.

Vampires under Attack: The boom in horror comics did not go unnoticed by the larger society, and attacks upon them began to mount. Psychology spokespersons such as Frederic Wertham (1895–1981) decried the violence and sex he found in some comic books as a direct source of the growing phenomenon of juvenile delinquency and began to demand their suppression. Feeling the intensity of the attack, a number of comic book publishing firms found it in their best interest to create the Comic Magazine Association of America (CMAA). The CMAA quickly concluded that some form of self-regulation was necessary in order to prevent government intervention in its business. In 1954, the CMAA issued a Comics Code, which went into effect in October of that year. The code dealt with some broad issues such as glamorizing crime and the graphic portrayal of death and responded to the criticisms of horror comics directly.

At the same time that controversy raged in America, a similar controversy developed in England. In 1955, the Children and Young Persons (Harmful Publications) Act was passed, which led to the disappearance of horror comics from stores. The bill was renewed in 1965 and is still on the books, which is one reason that so few horror/vampire comics have originated in the United Kingdom.

> Psychology spokespersons such as Frederic Wertham (1895–1981) decried the violence and sex he found in some comic books....

The Comics Code called for the elimination of the words "horror" or "terror" in the titles of comic books and forbade the picturing of, among other things, scenes of depravity, sadism, or excessive gruesomeness. One paragraph dealt forcefully with the major characters associated with the horror story.

Thus, in October 1954, Dracula and his kin were banished from the pages of the comic book. The only major appearance of a vampire following the implementation of the code was by Dell Comics, a company that did not formally subscribe to the code though, in large part, tried to adhere to it. A single October/December issue of a new title, *Dracula*, appeared in 1962. The story, set in the present time, centered upon an encounter between several Americans and Count Dracula in Transylvania. However promising the first issue might have been, though, a second issue did not appear to be forthcoming.

Meanwhile, Dracula and his cohorts were discovering a new format by which they could sneak back into the comic book world. In 1958, four years after the implementation of the Comics Code, a new type of magazine, the horror movie fan magazine, arrived on the newsstands. The first, *Famous Monsters of Filmland*, was developed by James Warren and Forrest J. Ackerman and published by the Warren Publishing Company. Projected as a movie fanzine, it was not subject to the regulations of the Comics Code, even though it began to include black-and-white horror comics interspersed with movie stills and feature stories. In 1964, Warren risked the publication of a black-and-white horror comic, featuring the very characters and scenes specifically banned by the

Comics Code, in a new, full-size (8 1/2" X 11") magazine format.

Technically, *Creepy* was not a comic book, but it reached the same youthful audience. It was so successful that in 1965, it was joined by *Eerie*, which followed a similar format. That same year, vampires crept back into comic books (full color in a standard comic format) through *The Munsters*, a comic book based upon the popular television series that featured two vampires, Lily and Grandpa (really Count Dracula), in a comedy format with no visible bloodsucking.

Finally, in 1966, Dell decided to release a second issue of *Dracula*. While continuing the numbering from the original issue of 1962, the new issue carried a completely new storyline and an entirely new "Dracula" recast in the image of a superhero. The new Dracula character, a descendant of the original count, had been experimenting with a serum made from the brains of bats. After he accidentally consumed some of the potion, he discovered that he had the ability to transform into a bat. In two subsequent issues, he moved to the United States, donned a superhero costume, and launched a war on the forces of evil.

In 1969, with rising pressure to revamp the Comics Code and provide some liberalization in its enforcement, Gold Key issued the first new comic books to feature a vampire as the leading figure. Like *The Munsters*, also by Gold Key, *Dark Shadows* was based on a popular television series. It featured the adventures of vampire Barnabas Collins. *Dark Shadows* was joined in September by Warren Publishing Company's *Vampirella*. The latter, featuring a sexy, female vampire from outer space in stories combining humor, horror, and romance, became the most popular and long-lived vampire comic book ever issued in North America.

> In 1969, with rising pressure to revamp the Comics Code and provide some liberalization in its enforcement, Gold Key issued the first new comic books to feature a vampire as the leading figure.

The Vampire's Return: Finally, bowing to the needs of companies eager to compete with black-and-white comic books, CMAA formally revised the Comics Code, effective January 1, 1971. The change also reflected both an awareness of changing times and the inability of the critics of comic book art to produce the evidence needed to back up the charges leveled at them in the 1950s. The code still discouraged the portrayal of situations that involved, for example, excessive gore, torture, or sadism. However, the important sentence concerning vampires was rewritten to read:

> Vampires, ghouls, and werewolves shall be permitted to be used when handled in the classic tradition such as Frankenstein, Dracula, and other high-caliber literary works written by Edgar Allan Poe, Saki (H. H. Munro), Conan Doyle, and other respected authors whose works are read in schools throughout the world.

Marvel Comics responded immediately to the new situation. It launched a line of new horror titles and, in 1972, led in the return of the vampire. Joining Warren's *Vampirella* was *The Tomb of Dracula*, which provided a new set of imaginative adventures for Dracula in the modern world. It lasted for 70 issues, had two revivals, and influenced the 1990s adventures of the *Midnight Sons*, who united a variety of forces to fight malevolent occultism. That same year, Marvel introduced a new vampire, Morbius. After several appearances as a guest villain in other Marvel magazines, Morbius became part of the regular cast appearing in *Vampire Tales* (beginning in 1973), was the leading figure in *Fear* (beginning in February 1974), and in the 1990s was an integral part of the *Midnight Sons*, a short-lived venture by Marvel into the creation of a horror universe similar to its superhero universe.

The rapidly rising sales in horror comics in the early 1970s slowly leveled off and, in the latter part of the decade, began to decline. While *Vampirella* survived the decade, few others did. The enthusiasm for horror comics had been overwhelmed by the proliferating number of superheroes. As interest for horror comics in general slumped, vampire comics all but died. *The Tomb of Dracula* was discontinued in 1979 to be followed by six issues of a black-and-white, full-sized comic magazine, which died in 1980. *Vampirella* was issued for the last time in 1981. With two exceptions, no comic book in which a vampire was the leading character was issued through the early and mid-1980s.

In 1981, DC Comics, by no means a major voice in the horror comics field, introduced a new vampire character, Andrew Bennett, in its long-standing horror comic book *The House of Mystery*. His life and adventures were told in a series of episodes under the title "I ... Vampire." Bennett was, according to the story, 400 years old. Four centuries ago, he bit his fiancée, Mary, who, of course, also became a vampire. She resented what had happened to her and, as a result, spent the rest of her existence trying to get even with Bennett and the world. "I ... Vampire" dominated most (but not all) issues of *The House of Mystery* from March 1981 (No. 290) through August 1983 (No. 319). DC had also introduced another vampire-like character, Man-Bat, who appeared periodically throughout the decade, usually in association with Batman. In 1975 and 1976, DC tried to establish Man-Bat in a comic book of his own, but it lasted for only two issues. A second Man-Bat comic, a one-shot, was issued in December 1984.

Following the demise of *The Tomb of Dracula* in 1979 and its sequel in 1980, Dracula made a number of appearances as a guest villain in various Marvel comics. A definitive encounter occurred in *Doctor Strange* (No. 62, December 1983). In a faceoff with Dracula, the occultist Dr. Stephen Strange performed a magical ritual, the Montesi Formula, which demolished Dracula and supposedly killed all of the vampires in the world. By this single act, Marvel banished the vampire from the Marvel Universe.

The Vampire Revival: After this low point of interest in vampires following Marvel's banishment in 1983, the vampire slowly made a comeback. The situation in the comic book world was paralleled in the movie world. The production of vampire movies hit bottom in 1984, when only one, *The Keep*, was released. At the same time, the number of new vampire novels dropped to nine in 1983, half the number of 1977.

Meanwhile, radical changes were occurring in the world of comic books. First, and most noticeably, the technology of producing comic books measurably improved. A higher-

Man-Bat was the result of Dr. Kirk Langstroms experimental serum going bad, transforming him into a monster that battled Batman. Whos up for a Batman–Man-Bat fight?

quality paper allowed for a more brilliant, eye-catching color. Then, as comic book illustrations were being recognized as an art form, artists demanded and got more freedom, most obvious in the disappearance of the box into which cartoon art had traditionally fit. At the same time, the comic book market was shifting in order to accommodate a new adult readership. No longer were comic books just for children and youth; numerous new titles were developed exclusively for the ever-expanding adult audience that had grown up with comics. Third, the X-rated comic had emerged as part of a new specialty line for the adult reader. Fourth, a significant portion of the new adult-oriented comics were not open-ended series but rather miniseries designed to last for a predetermined number of issues, most frequently four. Fifth, to accommodate the new market, a host of new companies, collectively called independents, came into existence.

Thus, when the vampire comic began to make its comeback in the 1990s, it did so in a radically new context. The initial issue of *Blood of the Innocent*, the first of the new vampire comics, was released at the beginning of 1986 by Warp Comics. It ran for four issues and was followed by *Blood of Dracula* from Apple Comics. Rick Shanklin was the writer of both projects. Marvel, the giant of the comic book industry, entered the picture with its very unconventional vampire title *Blood* (four issues, 1987–1988), a good example of the new artistic and technological advances that were setting the standards of the industry. In 1989, Eternity Comics (an imprint of Malibu Graphics) released the first of two four-issue titles, *Dracula* and *Scarlet in Gaslight*. Then, in 1990, Innovation (another of the new companies) launched a 12-issue adaptation of Anne Rice's best selling novel *The Vampire Lestat*. These six titles heralded the spectacular expansion of vampire comic book publishing, which became evident in the early 1990s. The ten new vampire titles

that appeared in 1990 became 23 titles in 1991. In 1992, no fewer than 34 new titles were published, followed by a similar number in 1993.

In 1983, Marvel had killed off all of the vampires and, for six years, none had appeared. At the end of 1989, Morbius reappeared in issue No. 10 (November 1989) of *Dr. Strange: Sorcerer Supreme*. It seemed that he had survived when the other vampires had been killed. He had been returned to his human state before Dr. Strange worked his magic and, for a number of years, lived a somewhat normal life. On a vacation in New Orleans at the end of the decade, however, he encountered the witch Marie Laveau, who changed him back into a vampire. The cover of *Dr. Strange: Sorcerer Supreme* No. 14 (February 1990) announced the return of vampires to the Marvel Universe. Morbius, after several appearances with Dr. Strange, got his own comic in September 1992.

Innovation's *The Vampire Lestat* featured some of the best artwork in the field, and its success justified the equally well-done series adapting Rice's other vampire novels—*Interview with the Vampire* and *The Queen of the Damned*. Following Innovation's lead were *Big Bad Blood of Dracula* (Apple), *Blood Junkies on Capitol Hill* (Eternity), the adult adaptation of *Carmilla* (Aircel), *Death Dreams of Dracula* (Apple), *Dracula the Impaler* (Comax), *Dracula's Daughter* (Eros), *Ghosts of Dracula* (Eternity), Richard Matheson's *I Am Legend* (Eclipse), *Night's Children* (Fanta Co), *Nosferatu* (Tome), and *The Tomb of Dracula* (Epic). In 1991, Harris Comics acquired the rights to *Vampirella* and revived it with a new storyline that picked up the title character ten years after the last episode in the original series. The response led to a new, full-color *Vampirella* comic and a set of reprints from the original series.

An equally expansive year for vampire comics, 1992 had a 50 percent growth in new titles from the previous year. Innovation continued its leadership with its adaptation of the briefly revived television series *Dark Shadows*. Its artwork was rivaled by the equally spectacular Topps Comics production of *Bram Stoker's Dracula*, based on the Francis Ford Coppola movie. Other new titles included *Blood Is the Harvest* (Eclipse), *Children of the Night* (Night Wynd Enterprises), *Cristian Dark* (Darque Studios), *Dracula in Hell* (Apple), *Dracula, The Suicide Club* (Adventure), *Little Dracula* (Harvey), and *Vampire's Kiss* (Friendly).

By 1992, Marvel Comics was fully involved in the vampire revival. It issued several reprints of its 1970s success, *The Tomb of Dracula*, under new titles: *Requiem for Dracula*, *The Savage Return of Dracula*, and *The Wedding of Dracula*. More importantly, it began several entirely new comics that featured vampires. *Team Titans*, a spin-off of the superhero comic *The New Titans*, included the vampire Nightrider. *The Nightstalkers* was built around vampire hunters Blade the Vampire Slayer, Frank Drake, and Hannibal King, all characters from *The Tomb of Dracula*, which had disappeared in 1983. Morbius finally got his own series.

These titles were then integrated through crossover stories with several other nonvampiric horror series, including *Ghost Rider*, *Darkhold*, and *Spirits of Vengeance*. The response was significant enough for Marvel to begin talking about a separate area of the Marvel Universe which dealt with occult issues. In late 1993, Marvel announced its new Universe structure by briefly setting apart these five titles, plus a new title, *Midnight Sons Unlimited*, and the older *Dr. Strange: Sorcerer Supreme* under a distinct Marvel imprint, *Midnight Sons*, which appeared in the October, November, and December 1993 issues of its several occult titles.

The vampire revival at Marvel proved to be short-lived. As part of a general reorganization of Marvel titles, all of the *Midnight Sons* series were discontinued in the spring of 1994.

The only vampire-related character to survive was Blade, who got his own series, but even it was discontinued the following year after only ten issues, caught in the continued rethinking of Marvel's overall direction as a comic book company. Marvel again largely abandoned the world of horror and vampires, though its characters from *The Tomb of Dracula* would make occasional appearances. Blade's comic series was revived in anticipation of *Blade*, the movie starring Wesley Snipes (released in 1998).

A major event in comic book publishing occurred in 1994 with the emergence of the Bad Girls—the female superheroes who were both feminine and deadly. Brian Pulido at Chaos! Comics is generally given the credit for producing the first successful Bad Girl, Lady Death, but she was soon joined by Shi and the revamped Vampirella, who were introduced in the Harris series *Vengeance of Vampirella* (1994–1996), written by Thomas Sniegoski and utilizing a variety of artists. Chaos! Comics soon expanded into the vampire field with its characters Purgatori and Chastity. Collectively, the bad-girl titles from Chaos! and the various *Vam-*

Comic book writer Brian Pulido is credited with creating Lady Death, the first in a line of Bad Girl superheroines.

pirella titles (Harris having featured her in a number of miniseries) were notable for their consistency in appearing at the top of comic sales lists. The bad-girl phenomenon also opened a market for a variety of new titles with a lead female character, a number of whom were vampires. Other notable vampires included Luxura in *Vamperotica* from Brainstorm Comics; Bethany the Vampfire in *Bethany the Vampfire* from Brainstorm; Donna Mia, the succubus introduced in the horror anthology series *Dark Fantasies: Lady Vampré* from Blackout; Sonja Blue in *Sunglasses after Dark* from Verotik; and Taboo in *Backlash* from Image.

Quite apart from the bad-girl titles, the number of new vampire titles continued to multiply through the 1990s. Most notable of the new series was *Preacher* by Garth Ennis and Steve Dillon from DC's dark adult *Vertigo* series, which included the vampire Cassidy as a continuing character. *Wetworks* from Image set a group of modern commandos against the supernatural

Garth Ennis (pictured) is well known for creating the series Preacher *with Steve Dillon.*

world of the Balkans, which included werewolves and the Blood Queen's Vampire Nation. Vigil, the female vampire detective created by Arvin Laudermilk who was first introduced in 1992, continued her adventures in a number of one-shots and miniseries through the 1990s, though having to change publishers on several occasions.

At the end of the 1990s, some predicted the vampire's demise as a topic of comic books, but the vampire theme continued unabated. Leading the way was *Buffy the Vampire Slayer*. Dark Horse began to issue a comic title, which included both new stories and comic versions of selected episodes, in September 1998. The series would continue into 2003 (63 issues), becoming the third-longest vampire comic book series in the English-speaking world. It was also reprinted in several languages in Europe. In 1999, Dark Horse also began the companion *Angel* comic book, but it was discontinued in 2001.

Some expected that following the demise of the *Buffy* and *Angel* television shows, fan interest would dissolve away. Though diminishing somewhat, it continued, and eventually, IDW picked up the *Angel* franchise. *Buffy*/*Angel* creator Joss Whedon decided to continue the storyline in the two shows through comic books and, in 2007, picked up the story from the last episode of *Angel* with a new series of comics from IDW, *Angel: After the Fall*, while the *Buffy* storyline was continued in the *Buffy the Vampire Slayer* series from Dark Horse, which ended with season 12 in 2018.

Succeeding Anne Rice as the most popular vampire novel author was Laurell K. Hamilton. After producing more than a dozen novels featuring her monster enforcer character Anita Blake, Hamilton's first vampire novel, *Guilty Pleasures* from the *Anita Blake: Vampire Hunter* series, was brought to comics in 2006 by Marvel. Hamilton's popularity as a novelist did not displace the most popular writer of vampire comics in the new century, Steve Niles. His *30 Days of Night*, a miniseries from IDW, became an instant hit and led to a number of sequels as well as additional Niles horror titles, including several series featuring his vampire detective, Cal McDonald. *Vampirella* remained a popular commodity in the new century. In 2001, Harris Comics began a new *Vampirella* monthly series, each issue coming with multiple variant and enhanced covers. The series was discontinued after 23 issues but, after a brief hiatus, since 2010, the Vampirella character has continued to manifest in a variety of new miniseries and one-shots in series issued by Dynamite Entertainment. In 2019, for example, for the character's 50th anniversary, Dynamite revived the series *Vengeance of Vampirella* (originally published by Harris Comics) and asked the original author, Thomas Sniegoski, to continue the storyline.

The comic book has proved to be a natural venue for vampires and seems to have settled in as the second main type of character (next to the superhero) in comics. Literally hundreds of new titles featuring vampires appeared in the decade after the Dracula centennial in 1997. Dracula remained a popular sourcebook and, over the years, more than three dozen adaptations of the novel have appeared as well as recent new editions of the novel with illustrations by prominent graphic artists such as Jae Lee and Ben Templesmith (the original artist used to bring Steve Niles's works to life).

Note: A complete listing of the more than 10,000 comic book issues containing vampires published in the twentieth century, compiled by Massimo Introvigne, J. Gordon Melton, and Robert Eighteen-Bisang, has been posted at http://www.cesnur.org/2008/vampire _comics.htm.

Dracula (Marvel Comics character)

Immediately after the Comics Code was revised in 1972 (lifting the ban on vampires that had been in effect since 1954), Marvel Comics moved to issue several horror titles that fell within the new guidelines. One of these was a series based on Count Dracula. *The Tomb of Dracula* devised a completely new set of adventures for the count and became one of the most successful vampire-oriented comic books of the century. The central hero was Frank Drake, a descendant of the count, whose family had abandoned the family estate and anglicized their name. Drake had inherited the family fortune but quickly squandered it. Destitute, his only asset was Castle Dracula. As the story opened, Drake traveled to Transylvania to see the castle with the idea of either selling it or turning it into a tourist attraction. Accompanying him were his girlfriend, Jeanie, and another friend, Clifton Graves, who had originally suggested the possible value of the castle.

As they explored the castle, Graves discovered the crypt containing the remains of

A page from Issue #40 of The Tomb of Dracula (January 1976) has Dracula trying to turn Rachel Van Helsing into a vampire.

Dracula complete with the stake in his heart. Graves pulled out the stake, thus awakening the count. Dracula confronted Drake and Jeanie but was driven off by her silver compact. While the pair considered the implication of the encounter, Dracula fled to the nearby town to find fresh blood. After the townspeople found the body of Dracula's first victim, they marched on the castle and set fire to it.

Drake, Jeanie, and Graves went back to London, and the count followed. Drake sold the Transylvania property, but his more immediate problem was that Jeanie had been bitten by Dracula and was now a vampire. During Drake's next confrontation with the count, Jeanie was killed. Distraught, Drake attempted suicide. He was stopped by Rachel Van Helsing, granddaughter of Abraham Van Helsing, who also had dedicated her life to being a vampire hunter. Taj, a mute Asian Indian, accompanied her. Rachel Van Helsing carried a crossbow whose wooden arrows amounted to wooden stakes. Together, the three set out to kill Dracula.

They were soon joined by two more vampire fighters, Quincy—not the same Quincey as in the novel—Harker (the son of Jonathan Harker and Mina Murray, who was mentioned in the last paragraphs of the novel), and Blade the Vampire Slayer, an African American whose mother had been killed by a vampire. A generation older than either Drake or Van Helsing, Harker used a wheelchair equipped with devices such as a weighted net and a cannon that fired poisoned wooden darts. Blade's major weapon was a set of wooden knives. Later in the series, Hannibal King, a detective who had been turned into a vampire, allied himself with the team. He and Blade had their initial encounter not with Dracula but with Deacon Frost, another vampire from Blade's past.

> The Marvel Dracula was strongly affected by the Hammer Films Dracula movies in one respect: those bitten by Dracula died and immediately became vampires.

The team fought Dracula for a decade through 70 issues of *The Tomb of Dracula*. Dracula was portrayed very much as he was in popular lore. He was evil but with some traits of human feeling, pining over love betrayed and the capture of his son by the forces of good. Drake, Van Helsing, Harker, and Blade fought him with wooden stakes (their most consistently effective tool), the crucifix, silver, fire, and daylight. While partial victories occurred on both sides, each defeated character recovered to carry the series to its conclusion. For example, very early in the series, Dracula was killed, but he was brought back to life. Later in the series, he lost his vampiric powers for a time. As was common in Marvel Comics, Dracula made appearances in other Marvel titles (*Dr. Strange, Frankenstein, Thor*), and several of the Marvel characters (Silver Surfer, Werewolf by Night) appeared in *The Tomb of Dracula* to offer their services to defeat him.

The Marvel Dracula was strongly affected by the Hammer Films Dracula movies in one respect: those bitten by Dracula died and immediately became vampires. In the novel, they were merely weakened by their first encounter. *The Tomb of Dracula* concluded in issue 70 with what appeared to be Dracula's definitive death. He was killed in a confrontation with Quincy Harker, who impaled him with a silver spoke from his wheelchair. Harker also cut off Dracula's head, stuffed his mouth with garlic, and buried both himself and Dracula under stones dislodged from Castle Dracula in an explosion.

However, the count was quickly revived in a new series of *The Tomb of Dracula* issued by Marvel in a black-and-white magazine format (not covered by the revised Comics Code). When his body was discovered and the silver spoke removed, Dracula was freed for further adventures. He starred in the revived series of *The Tomb of*

Dracula, which lasted for six issues. Over the next few years, he also made guest appearances as the villain in several Marvel Comics. For example, in 1983, he had a confrontation with Dr. Strange, the superhero with magical powers. Dr. Strange invoked what was termed the Montesi Formula, a magical incantation designed to destroy all the vampires in the world. Dracula disintegrated in the process. Hannibal King, who had never ingested human blood, was turned back into a normal man by the same process.

By the beginning of the 1990s, the Montesi Formula had weakened, and vampires began to reappear in the Marvel Universe. While most of the vampires killed in 1983 remained dead, the old and powerful vampire Dracula was resurrected and made his first appearance in issue No. 10 of *Dr. Strange: Sorcerer Supreme* in November 1989. Then, in 1991, *The Tomb of Dracula* was revived a third time by writer Marv Wolfman and artist Gene Colan for four issues published by Epic Comics, a Marvel subsidiary. The story picked up the lives of Drake and Blade ten years after the death of Dracula at the hands of Quincy Harker. Drake had continued to suffer psychological upset as he tried to deal with his own ancestry, his problems with females, and his immediate need to deal with the return of Dracula to his life. They put Dracula away again, but the never-dead-for-long vampire would return in 1994 to bedevil Drake and Blade again in their further adventures as the Nightstalkers. Since then, Dracula has been a visiting villain in various Marvel comics.

The Dracula Society (UK)

The Dracula Society, the primary organization in the United Kingdom keeping the study of Dracula alive, was founded in October 1973 by Bernard Davies and Bruce Wightman (1925–2009) as a vampire interest group to help facilitate travel to Romania. At the time, standard tours were just beginning to respond to tourists who wished to visit sites associated with Dracula. Closer to its home base in London, the society sponsors lectures, films, auctions, and parties; its regular meetings are occasions for members to celebrate Dracula and his literary and cinematic cousins. It also arranges visits to nearby locales associated with gothic literature, especially the northern England town of Whitby where, in the novel, Dracula landed. The society focuses on Dracula and Bram Stoker but also reaches out to literary vampires in general, associated monsters such as The Werewolf and The Mummy, and folklore.

The society maintains an archive to preserve materials related to Dracula and the gothic theme in literature, the stage, and the cinema. The archives house the complete papers of Hamilton Deane, who brought Dracula to the stage. It also contains the cloak worn by Christopher Lee in his screen portrayals of Dracula. Annually, the society makes two awards: the Hamilton Deane Award for the most outstanding contribution to the gothic genre in the performing arts and the Children of the Night Award for the most outstanding contribution to the gothic genre in the literary field.

The society adopted the shield of the Voivodes of Wallachia (Dracula's family) as its crest, adding a ribbon with a Latin quote from the third-century Christian theologian Tertullian: "I believe because it is impossible." The society is open to anyone over the age of 18; in 1993, it reported approximately 150 members. It may be contacted through its website at http://www.thedraculasociety.org.uk. Members receive *Voices from the Vaults*, the society's quarterly newsletter, and an invitation to the annual Bram Stoker Birthday Dinner. The first chairman was cofounder Bernard Davies

The British cartoon character Count Duckula, voiced by David Jason, is rather like Bunnicula in that he is also a vegetarian vampire.

(1924–2010). In 2012, the society inaugurated the Bernard Davies Award, presented for achievement in scholarship.

🦇 *Duckula, Count* 🦇

Count Duckula, a cartoon character introduced in the United Kingdom in the 1980s, is a cross between Dracula and Donald Duck who resides in modern-day Transylvania at Castle Duckula with his servants, Igor and Nanny. While coming from a long line of vampire ducks and feared by the local villagers, Count Duckula is actually a vegetarian who prefers vegetable juice to blood. He wears the requisite evening dress and opera cape but possesses no fangs. He sleeps in a magical coffin that could transport him, and even his entire castle, to various parts of the world for his adventures. He has an archenemy in Dr. Von Goosewing, the vampire hunter. The unfortunate count had fallen in love with the doctor's niece, Vanna Von Goosewing.

Count Duckula was brought to television as an animated cartoon series in the United Kingdom in 1988, a series later shown in America. Also in 1988, Marvel Comics introduced a *Count Duckula* comic that appeared bimonthly for 15 issues.

Frost, Deacon

Deacon Frost, a vampire and antagonist of Blade the Vampire Slayer, was introduced in the pioneering comic series *The Tomb of Dracula* (Marvel, 1972–1980), one of the many characters created by writer Marv Wolfman. The first reference to Deacon Frost occurred in issue No. 13, in which he killed Blade's mother as she was going into labor with him. Frost's bite tainted the blood remaining in her, and Blade was thus born as a *dhampir*, a half vampire, his mother's blood having passed to him several extramundane abilities, including the *dhampir's* traditional sensitivity to the presence of vampires. Blade also cannot be transformed into a real vampire. Deacon Frost had been high on his list of hoped-for targets when he met the cadre of vampire hunters headed by the wheelchair-bound Quincy Harker (in issue No. 10).

Frost, as originally conceived, was a white-haired but vigorous senior citizen, with a full beard and mustache. He tended to dress in nineteenth-century European garb.

In later appearances in *The Tomb of Dracula*, we learn that his vampire career dates to the 1860s when, as a scientist in search of immortality, he injected himself with vampire blood, which resulted in his transformation into a vampire (No. 53). He turned Hannibal King into a vampire and a vampire hunter. Through the issues of *The Tomb of Dracula* in the 1970s, he periodically reappeared and broadcasted his grandiose idea of replacing Dracula as the Lord of the Vampires. He was endowed with the ability to produce vampire doppelgangers (clones). They were automatically generated after he bit someone. With a vampire army of doppelgangers, he attacked Blade and King. They ultimately defeated and killed him. Later, one of his doppelgangers showed up and had to be dispatched.

In 1998, Blade emerged again as the star of his own movie, in which he again faced off against Deacon Frost (portrayed by Stephen Dorff). The movie began with Blade's unusual birth. The action moved immediately to a nightclub, where the now adult Blade (portrayed by Wesley Snipes) confronted a room full of vampires, whom we later discover were minions of Frost, who appeared as a much-younger, completely clean-shaven man.

Frost maintained his grandiose plans that focused on ruling the various vampire "houses" or clans and becoming a vampire god, La Magra, which he initially accomplished through performing a magical ritual that included the slaying of the heads of the 12 vampire houses. With his new status and the powers it conferred, he and Blade were set up for their final confrontation. In relatively quick fashion, Blade seemed to have finally killed the vampire by first cutting off his arm and then cutting him

Stephen Dorff played Blade's nemesis Deacon Frost in the 1998 film.

into two pieces. Frost, however, was not done. He reassembled the two halves and regenerated a new arm. In the end, he was seemingly killed from darts filled with pure sunlight.

Since no vampire seems to ever be killed for good, it was not surprising when Frost and his clones reappeared. In a *Blade* one-shot comic, *Blade: Cresent City Blues* (1998), Frost again manifested, affirmed that the previous reappearance was in fact one of his clones, and then proceeded to build a power base in New Orleans. Blade again thwarted Frost's plans, but the vampire ultimately escaped. He reappeared again in *Blade: Vampire Hunter* (1999–2000), where he journeyed to the desert to meet Dracula, who was about to engage in a Rite of Ascension that would greatly expand his powers. Blade arrived in the nick of time and, after a lengthy battle, again killed Deacon Frost, this time with a stake to the heart. This story was cut short in 2000 and only completed in a new *The Tomb of Dracula* series in 2004.

Games

In the late 1960s, vampires moved from being of interest to only a few horror fans to capturing the popular imagination. Games built around vampirism are one sign that vampires have become an entrenched element into popular culture.

Board Games: The first set of vampire games were board games; possbily the very first vampire-oriented board game was the *Dracula Mystery Game*, which was issued in 1963 as part of a *Universal Monster Mystery Games* set from Hasbro. Based on the Universal Pictures monsters of the 1930s, the series included games focusing on *The Creature from the Black Lagoon, Frankenstein, The Mummy, The Phantom of the Opera, The Wolf Man,* and, of course, *Dracula.* Each game was similar: a spin-and-move game with cards and player pieces that resembled the famous monsters.

Two years later, the first game based on a popular television series, *The Munsters Masquerade Party Game,* appeared, which was also from Hasbro. Players spun a wheel and drew good and bad outcome cards to reach home with pawns based on the show's main char-acters. As they progressed on the board, cards instructed them to sing or perform imitations. *The Munsters Masquerade Party Game* was actually one of four based on the show during its brief, two-year run.

Toward the end of the decade, a board game appeared as a spin-off from the *Dark Shadows* daytime television show. The *Dark Shadows Game* was distributed by Whitman in 1968. In the game, up to four players raced each other through a maze.

The following year, Milton Bradley released the *Barnabas Collins Dark Shadows Game,* which was developed in response to the popular introduction of the vampire Barnabas Collins to the cast. Quite distinct from the Whitman game, it required that players assemble a skeleton on a scaffold. The winner got to wear Barnabas's fangs.

In the mid-1970s, British horror and vampire fan Stephen Hand, disappointed at the lack of horror-oriented games, created his first board game, *Barnabas's.* The game featured a set of vampire hunters searching

> The first set of vampire games were board games; possibly the very first vampire-oriented board game was the *Dracula Mystery Game*....

Castle Dracula for Dracula to kill him with a stake. In the 1980s, Hand revised the game and introduced ideas for a military game based on Vlad the Impaler's wars.

A few years later, it was followed by *The Undead* (1981), which was designed by Steve Jackson. Based on Bram Stoker's *Dracula*, the game matched one player, who assumed the role of the count and was unleashed upon London (a map of the city formed the game board), against one or more other players, the vampire hunters. The game could be played as a straight board game or expanded to be a role-playing game. The next vampire board game to hit the market was released in 1987 as *The Fury of Dracula*. As with *The Undead*, the players assumed the roles of vampire hunters pitted against one player, who acted as Dracula. The vampire hunters had to find Dracula and kill him before he was able to establish vampire accomplices in the cities of Europe. The game gave a slight advantage to Dracula—an advantage that was overcome only if the hunters worked together. *The Fury of Dracula*, now in its fourth edition, has remained one of the more popular horror board games.

Among the more unique vampire-related games was *Dracula's Bite on the Side*, a dinner-table mystery game in the *Murder à la Carte* game series. The game was designed as part of an entire evening that included a dinner held to celebrate the 1893 betrothal of Count Dracula's ward, Bella Kashiasu, to Ivan Evenstich. Each of the eight dinner guests became a murder suspect, and the evening was spent trying to determine who the murderer might be. As the game proceeded, guests interrogated each other and revealed what they had discovered. At the end of the game, each player guessed the murderer's identity.

Most recently, a board game was released in connection with Francis Ford Coppola's movie *Bram Stoker's Dracula* (1992) by Leading Edge Games. The players in this game assumed the role of one of the vampire hunters from *Dracula*: Abraham Van Helsing, Jonathan Harker, Quincey P. Morris, etc. Their goal was to overcome a set of Dracula's servants, such as his vampire brides or Lucy Westenra as a vampire. Then, the players had to defeat the various forms of Dracula to rescue Mina Murray, who was trapped in Dracula's clutches.

> Among the more unique vampire-related games was *Dracula's Bite on the Side*, a dinner-table mystery game in the *Murder à la Carte* game series.

For many years, board games were the only vampire games, but in the 1990s, they were joined by a variety of what have been termed role-playing games.

Role-playing Games: In the last generation, the most popular vampire-oriented games have been role-playing games. Fantasy role-playing games center on an alternative fantasy world that the players enter through their imaginations. They are games of make-believe, in which the players enter into the story they simultaneously tell. Telling and playing give an experience that goes beyond simply listening to someone tell a story.

Some games are led by the "gamemaster," or storyteller, who sets the starting point and guides the course of the game. Prior to the game, each character is assigned a unique combination of helpful attributes (strength, dexterity, stamina, intelligence) and talents. For the purpose of the game, the character's traits are quantified on a descriptive character sheet that assigns numerical values to each attribute. Thus, each character starts the game with a unique set of attributes, a variety of weapons, and other appropriate abilities. As the game begins, the characters are placed in situations they get out of through a combination of their own choices and sheer chance (represented by a throw of the dice). The gamemaster describes what has happened after each player's action choice and decides how well the players have either succeeded and prospered or failed and suffered in the quest of their goal.

Each role-playing game has created its own myth that defines the imaginative world in which the game operates. As might be expected, vampires appeared in *Dungeons & Dragons* (*D&D*), a role-playing game that deals in the widest possible world of fantasy and magic. As early as 1982, a module of *D&D* located in Ravenloft that featured a vampire, Count Strahd von Zarovich, was written for *D&D* by Tracy and Laura Hickman. By 1990, this module had grown into an "advanced" variant game with a primary vampire theme based upon the *D&D* worldview. The new *Ravenloft* game was designed and written by Bruce Nesmith and Andria Hayday.

Ravenloft is a fictional island continent containing a number of kingdoms. Near its middle is the kingdom of Barovia, the land where Ravenloft Castle is located. Barovia is ruled by Count Strahd. In the past, the count loved a young woman, Tatyana, but she did not return his love and, instead, planned to marry his brother, Sergei. Rejected and angry, the count killed Sergei which, in turn, led to Tatyana's suicide. Through an unclear transaction, the count made a pact with "death" and became a vampire. Count Strahd's castle and land were drawn out of the physical world into the etheric plane. Ravenloft, like most *D&D* landscapes, is a magical land. The various domains that surround Barovia are inhabited by a variety of werewolves, ghouls, and supernatural creatures, and the various games of *Ravenloft* are built on their interaction. The popularity of the game has led to the publication of a number of spin-off novels based on Ravenloft and its inhabitants by authors such as Elaine Bergstrom and P. N. Elrod. Shortly after vampires invaded *Dungeons & Dragons*, Pacesetter also introduced a horror role-playing game in which vampires play a key role.

Chill was built around the myth of the Societas Argenti Viae Eternitata (SAVE), the

Eternal Society of the Silver Way. According to the *Chill* story, SAVE was founded in 1844 in Dublin, Ireland, by a group of scientists led by Dr. Charles O'Boylan. O'Boylan posited the existence of little-understood natural laws used by two separate, opposing sets of entities who exist in the noncorporeal world. Most importantly, he believed that a highly disciplined source of evil intruded into the human realm and threatens our safety. Afraid that they could not convince the public of the existence of the evil unknown, the decision was made to turn SAVE into a secret organization to fight the evil. SAVE kept an archive of its activities in Dublin.

The early research of SAVE led to its confrontation with vampires in the Pirin Mountains of Bulgaria (1868) and Lucerne, Switzerland (1975). Fighting vampires was a central aspect of SAVE's work. In the 1985 book *Vampires* by Gali Sanchez and Michael Williams, the *Chill* mythology was continued in a summary of the major cases investigated over the

A young woman dressed as a D&D *vampire priestess for the Comic and Entertainment Expo Parade in Calgary, Alberta.*

years, in which the goal was the destruction of vampires and vampire-like creatures. The vampires were found in Eastern Europe, the Orient, and Mexico. Gamers are invited to assume the persona of one of the ten typical vampire types.

The most popular vampire-oriented role-playing game has been *Vampire: The Masquerade*, which evolved into *Vampire: The Eternal Struggle* and, more recently, *Vampire: The Requiem*. The game was created by Mark Rein-Hagen and initially appeared in 1991 in an edition by White Wolf Game Studio. Its basic myth was called the Masquerade, a secret realm that began with Cain (the biblical character who, in Genesis 4, killed his brother and was afflicted with an undesignated curse). According to the Masquerade, the curse was eternal life and a craving for blood. After wandering in the wilderness for many years, Cain once again lived among mortals and created a city and progeny—a small number of vampires who carried Cain's curse. The city was destroyed, but later generations periodically appeared as a secret force in history. The bulk of existing vampires constitute the sixth generation and their children, and they face pressure to stop creating vampires because it is believed that vampiric powers diminish as each generation from Cain is created.

The Masquerade myth stated that beginning in 1435, the Inquisition was able to arrest and kill many of Cain's progeny, the Kindred. The Inquisition stamped out whole bloodlines by burning them. This period of attack drove the vampire community, which had lived somewhat openly on the edge of human society completely underground. In 1486 at a global convocation, a secret worldwide network was established. It promulgated the law of the Masquerade, an attempt to convince the world that either all vampires were dead or, better still, they never existed. The Masquerade demanded that all vampires make a reasonable effort at secrecy.

The accumulated wisdom of the nearly immortal vampires was given to intelligent mor-

American game designer Mark Rein-Hagen is behind the hugely popular RPG Vampire: The Masquerade *and its later iterations.*

tals who then turned their attention to the development of science and the suppression of superstition. As a result, the early belief in vampires was crushed. The Masquerade, however, was threatened by the mysticism that arose from a combination of forces: the mysticism of psychedelic drugs, new music, and the establishment of the vampire image in popular culture. In the myth, those affected by the new mysticism are ready to believe in the existence of vampires. Also, a generation gap exists between those vampires who created the Masquerade and understand its necessity and those vampires created in the last century whose brashness, the elder vampires felt, drew unwelcomed attention to the vampire community.

According to the myth of the game, the elder vampires had more powers than the younger vampires. Although the stake was hurtful for both old and young, it was not, by itself, fatal. Sunlight and fire were the vampires' greatest dangers. Holy objects had no effect, nor did running water. The vampires had sharpened senses that aided them in hunting—including the power to impose their will on mortals. The elder vampires could even change their forms.

Vampire: The Masquerade explained that new vampires could be created by having their blood drained and receiving some of the vampire's blood. The new vampires had slightly less power than the vampires who created them. Vampires no longer breathed but could fake respiration. Their hearts did not beat. The blood they consumed spread through their bodies by osmosis rather than through arteries or veins. It also carried the necessary oxygen. The vampires' wounds healed quickly; however, the stake produced a form of paralysis. The vampire in the game moved in the world of mortals very much like historic nobleman hunters moved among beasts in the forest. The worldwide vampire society thus existed as a parallel society beside that of mortals. The vampires were organized into territorial clans ruled by princes. Every major city of the mortal world supported a vampire community, and vampires who entered a new city had to present themselves to the powers established there. As *Dungeons & Dragons* spun off a card game, *Magic: The Gathering*, so *Vampire: The Masquerade* led to a card game variation originally published as *Jyhad* and then revised and reissued in 1995 as *Vampire: The Eternal Struggle*. The Camarilla, the international vampire organization, ruled the city's controlling clan and enforced the Masquerade.

Players of *Vampire: The Masquerade* create a character in the imaginary vampire community and gather with others to enact the almost infinite number of possible situations created by the gamemaster/storyteller. The success of *Vampire: The Masquerade* allowed its evolution. In 1993,

a live-action version of the game appeared. This version freed the game from the delays caused by the use of dice, which has been replaced with a series of hand signals. The new form of the game allows players to remain in character during virtually all of the game and expands the number of players who can play at one time.

Other Vampire-oriented Role-playing Games: Although the *Vampire* game series emerged in the early 1990s as the most popular vampire-oriented role-playing game, it was not the only one. Among its competitors was *Vampire Kingdoms* (1991) (created by Kevin Siembieda), a game within the larger fantasy role-playing world of Rifts, published by Palladium Books. *Vampire* centers on life and conflicts within the vampire community, while *Vampire Kingdoms* draws its adventures from the conflicts between vampires and nonvampires, especially Doc Reid and his vampire hunters.

According to *Vampire Kingdoms*, the undead come in three varieties: master vampires, secondary vampires, and wild vampires, which, together, form a hierarchy of vampiric life. At the top are the master vampires, which appear most like humans. Secondary vampires are somewhat more savage, with pale skin, corpselike bodies, and strange eyes. They are, however, still able to move in human society on a limited basis. The wild vampires are far more ghoulish in appearance and, with their strange appearance, terrible stench, and obvious wildness, instantly communicate their distinctive threat.

In this game, all vampires operate under a superpower, the Vampire Intelligence, making them the true Lords of the Undead, described as monstrous, elemental beings.

In *Vampire Kingdoms*, since the devastation of the Earth (termed the time of the Rifts), vampires have risen to dominate sections of Mexico, Central America, and South America. Old Mexico City is Vampire Central. The area is organized into a set of vampire kingdoms, tribal groupings, and city-states.

The Mexico Empire is composed of one Vampire Intelligence, one master vampire, 1,700 secondary vampires, and some 65,000 humans (the food source). The master vampire runs the kingdom from Mexico City, while the local Vampire Intelligence lives in Tula, some 70 miles north. Several other vampire kingdoms are also located in the former Mexico.

Human civilization in *Vampire Kingdoms* is centered in the Midwest. Most of the Southwest is wilderness, with a handful of scattered settlements located on the sites of the former cities of El Paso, Houston, or San Antonio. Kenneth Reid and his vampire-hunting rangers are headquartered at Fort Reid, in what is now northern Mexico. Reid is a human who has undergone bionic reconstruction. He hates vampires and is committed to destroying them. Because of his bionic component, he is immune to being transformed into a vampire. He is helped by a set of superhero assistants, both humanoid and otherwise. One, Carlotta the White, is a dragon who usually appears in the form of a beautiful woman.

Another game highlighting vampires was *Nightlife* (1990), designed by L. Lee Cerney and Bradley K. McDevitt and published by Stellar Games. *Nightlife* delves into the world of what is termed "splatterpunk," a reality created by combining the ghoulish terror of *Night of the Living Dead* and the rudeness of punk rock. David Scrow, who first defined splatterpunk reality, saw previous attempts at horror as being too polite, so splatterpunk attempted to confront the reader or viewer with the gore and re-

volting nature of the horror world. At the same time that the splatterpunk world was emerging, a modern vampire, usually spelled with a "y" as "vampyre," emerged. This new vampire is sensual, urbane, and the object of sympathy. This type of vampyre appeared in the writings of Chelsea Quinn Yarbro and Anne Rice and had appeared in such movies as Frank Langella's *Dracula* (1979) and *The Lost Boys* (1987).

> At the same time that the splatterpunk world was emerging, a modern vampire … emerged. This new vampire is sensual, urbane, and the object of sympathy.

Nightlife fantasizes about characters who live secretly in New York City in the not-too-distant future. They include vampyres, werewolves, ghosts, and demons. These "extra-natural" creatures together make up the Kin. Their term for humanity is the Herd. In addition to the vampyres who suck human blood, several varieties of the Kin might be termed psychic vampires. The Wyghts and the Animates live on human life energy. Each form of the Kin has special abilities, which they term their "edges." Vampyres can, for example, transform into such various shapes as a bat or a cloud of mist. Edges are countered by "flaws," such as the vampyre's problem with sunlight.

In *Nightlife*, vampyres are just one character among several others. They form the transition to a number of role-playing games in which a vampire character was one of many from which a player might choose. Typical of these games was *Shadowrun* (1989), a game that fantasized about the year 2050, a time when technology and human flesh have mixed. Humans interface with computers, and bionic people were common. In this world, an awakening of the mystical occurred, and magic had returned as a potent force in human life. A variety of creatures, such as elves and trolls, who survived by assuming human form, had reverted to their more natural appearance. Within this world of human, part-human, and other-than-human life, vampires appeared as one of a number of "critters." The vampires were described as diseased humans who have been infected with the Human-Metahuman Vampiric Virus. Vampires consumed both the blood and life energy of their victims.

One role-playing game, *Bram Stoker's Dracula*, capitalized on the popularity of the 1992 movie. The game assumed that following Dracula's death, he left behind a brood of newly created vampires that must be tracked down and defeated. Players chose a character and generated that character's attributes by a throw of the dice. In the game, the vampires had special powers (especially the older ones), but the modern hunter characters had the benefit of high-powered modern weapons—including automatic assault rifles.

Most of the role-playing vampire games of the 1990s have faded into oblivion, but *Vampire: The Eternal Struggle* in its several mutations, most notably *Vampire: The Requiem*, has maintained a continuing playing audience.

Computer Games: In the 1980s, games that could be played on a personal computer, especially the several systems that could be connected to a television screen (Nintendo being the most popular), made sizable inroads into the toy market. By the 1990s, retail stores specializing exclusively in computer games were common in urban areas. The first vampire-oriented computer game appears to have been *Elvira: Mistress of the Dark* (produced by Accolade). It appeared in 1990 and won the Game of the Year Award from *Computer Gaming World* the following year. The game's success led to a sequel, *Elvira II: The Jaws of Cerberus* (1992).

In 1993, the world of computer games discovered vampires. Early that year, three new vampire games appeared: *Dracula Unleashed* (Viacom), *Vampire: Master of Darkness* (Game Gear), and *Veil of Darkness* (Strategic Simulations). More significantly, however, Psygnosis Ltd., a British company, released a game based on *Bram Stoker's Dracula* after

nearly two years of development. The game was developed to fit the Mega CD-ROM system developed by Sega. The system allowed for a significant expansion of memory and permitted the inclusion of clips and sound from the film in the game. Versions of the finished game have been released in several formats for various game systems.

As vampire games have developed through the 1990s, they have provided an alternative avenue for speculation about the meaning of being vampiric. The rules of the games, which in the case of the role-playing games constitute book-length publications, have become a forum where ideas about vampiric existence are tested and bartered. The appearance of the number of games based on the vampire myth symbolizes the renewed enthusiastic level of interest in vampires.

Among electronic games, *Castlevania* stands out. *Castlevania* initially appeared in Japan in the mid-1980s. More than two dozen new versions of and sequels to the original game have appeared through the intervening decades, each incorporating the latest advances in electronic gaming and then being adapted to different gaming systems. The storyline of the game concerns an ongoing war between the Belmont family of vampire hunters and Dracula. Dracula seems to reappear every century, and it is the charge of the Belmonts to block

A screenshot from the first-ever video game about vampires, the award-winning Elvira: Mistress of the Dark, *which was released in 1990.*

his plans to dominate the world. BradyGames has published a series of strategy guides to the different *Castlevania* games.

Twenty-first Century: In the new century, White Wolf emerged as a dominating force in the world of live-action role-playing (LARP) games. Its *Vampire: The Requiem* has been an ongoing presence as other vampire role-playing games have come and gone. By the middle of the first decade, it was virtually the only vampire-themed LARP still on the market. The associated card game had also been able to re-create itself continually with expansion decks that offered ever-new variations on the basic game.

> In the new century, White Wolf emerged as a dominating force in the world of live-action role-playing (LARP) games.

The two most popular vampire phenomena of the decade—*Buffy the Vampire Slayer* and the *Twilight* books and movies—both spawned a host of cult paraphernalia, including games. Both *Buffy* and its spin-off *Angel* led to the production of jigsaw puzzles, board games, a chess set, and electronic computer games. A short-lived LARP game never really took off, but an associated role-playing card game produced three large sets of trading cards complete with enhanced variant cards, which are now valued by collectors.

As the *Twilight* book series was adapted into movies, a similar variety of games appeared: jigsaw puzzles and board games, including a *Twilight* version of the trivia game *Scene It*. Also, in 2009, several decks of playing cards were issued, with a *Twilight* illustration and pictures of the stars on the back of each card. There have been a couple of video games based on *Twilight*—*Lego Twilight: The Video Game* was released in 2011, followed in the next year by *Lego Twilight 2: Breaking Dawn*. Meanwhile, action-oriented movies such as *Van Helsing*, the *Underworld* series, *Blood: The Last Vampire*, *Vampire Hunter D*, *Blade*, and *BloodRayne* spawned new electronic games.

Glut, Donald Frank (1944–)

Donald Frank Glut, author and editor of vampire books, was born in Pecos, Texas, the son of Julia and Frank C. Glut. He attended DePaul University for two years (1962–1964) and completed his bachelor's degree (1967) at the University of Southern California. Following his graduation, Glut launched a career as a writer and, during the intervening quarter century, has produced numerous horror titles, especially around the *Frankenstein* and *Dracula* themes. Throughout the early 1970s, he authored a series of *Frankenstein* books, including *Frankenstein Lives Again* (Spanish ed. 1971; English ed. 1977); *Terror of Frankenstein* (Spanish ed. 1971; English ed. 1977); and *The Frankenstein Legend: A Tribute to Mary Shelley and Boris Karloff* (1972).

In 1972, Glut produced his first vampire book, *True Vampires of History*. It proved to be a landmark volume: the first to bring together the accounts of all real (as opposed to legendary) vampires in what was a historical narrative. He followed it in 1975 with *The Dracula Book*, a monumental bibliographical work on the character of Dracula as he appeared in the different media, such as books, comic books, stage, and film. It was awarded the Montague Summers Award by the Count Dracula Society and became the foundation of all future vampire bibliographical and movie research. In 1977, Glut brought together his two primary loves in a novel, *Frankenstein Meets Dracula* (German edition, 1980).

In the 1970s, Glut contributed articles to numerous comic books, including *Eerie*, *Ghost Rider*, *The Occult Files of Dr. Spektor*, and *Vampirella*. He created the vampire character Baron Tibor, who appeared in several stories in *The Occult Files of Dr. Spektor*. His novelization of *The Empire Strikes Back* earned him the Galaxy Award in 1980.

Glut continued his interest in Frankenstein and produced *The Frankenstein Catalog* (1984), an updated edition of his prior bibliographical work. He also pursued an interest in dinosaurs and has authored a number of titles on that topic, beginning with *The Dinosaur Dictionary* (1972). In the early 1990s, he began compiling a comprehensive work on dinosaurs. His completed work, *Dinosaurs: The Encyclopedia* published in 1997, was named as an outstanding reference source by the American Library Association.

In his youthful years, Glut produced a set of short amateur films about vampires, which became well known among those interested in vampires, though many people had not actually seen the films. Over the years, Glut improved his moviemaking skills and, after making a variety of movies over the years, turned to vampires once again and produced a feature film trilogy—*The Erotic Rites of Countess Dracula* (2003), *Countess Dracula's Orgy of Blood* (2004), and *Blood Scarab* (2008)—which present the contemporary story of Elizabeth Báthory's search for a way to live and move about in the daylight. In the series, she is presented as Count Dracula's widow. At about the same time, Glut assembled all of his early amateur movies into an anthology collection published on DVD as *I Was a Teenage Moviemaker: Don Glut's Amateur Movies* (2006).

Hogg, Anthony John (1981–)

Australian writer and editor Anthony John Hogg, an independent scholar in vampire studies, was born in 1981 in East Melbourne, Victoria, Australia. He attended Victoria University, where he completed diplomas in professional writing and editing (2012) and in library and information services (2012). An early interest in vampires manifested in a blog discussing the infamous Highgate Vampire affair, *Did a Wampyr Walk in Highgate?* (https://dawwih.blogspot.com), which was launched in 2008 as a spin-off from his online forum of the same name.

He also created *Diary of an Amateur Vampirologist* (https://doaav.blogspot.com), which ran from 2008 to 2011, followed by *The Vampirologist* (http://thevampirologist.blogspot.com) (2011–2013) and *The Vampirologist* (https://thevampirologist.wordpress.com) (2013–). However, his

Scholar Anthony Hogg has established several important vampirology websites.

most notable vampire site may be *Vamped* (https://vamped.org), an expansive website that reports on all things vampire-related, of which he remains the editor-in-chief, working closely with his Canadian colleague, Erin Chapman. In 2017, *Vamped* was recognized with the Lord Ruthven Award for Media/Popular Culture.

As he immersed himself in Dracula and vampire studies, he collaborated with academic librarian and vampire historian Dax Stokes to help organize the There Are Such Things! Vampire Studies Symposium 2015, a scholarly conference held at North Central Texas College in Corinth, Texas. This event culminated in him founding the Vampire Studies Association, a research and networking organization, based in Melbourne but with an international membership, in 2018. He serves as the association's first president and, through it, he has launched the *Journal of Vampire Studies*, which he edits. The first issue appeared in 2020.

✦ *The Hollywood Vampires* ✦

The Hollywood Vampires was originally a drinking club founded by rock musician Alice Cooper, which held its gatherings at the Rainbow Bar and Grill in West Hollywood, California. Soon after the restaurant's founding, it became a hangout for musicans. Formed in the mid-1970s, the club included Keith Moon (the Who), Ringo Starr (the Beatles), Micky Dolenz (the Monkees), and singer–songwriter Harry Nilsson as its core members and dubbed occasional visitors John Lennon (the Beatles) and Keith Emerson (Emerson, Lake & Palmer) as honorary members.

To honor and remember the music produced by a spectrum of rock stars who had died from their excessive behavior in the 1970s, Cooper formed a supergroup, which he named for the former drinking club. The group included three core members—Cooper, movie star Johnny Depp, and Joe Perry (Aerosmith)—plus a number of additional star musicians such as Duff McKagan and Matt Sorum (Guns N'

A plaque from the Hollywood Vampires drinking club displays some of the regular stars who used to hang out there.

Roses) and, at times, such outstanding personalities as movie star Christopher Lee, who was an accomplished musician in his own right. The band has released two albums: *Hollywood Vampires* (2015) and *Rise* (2019). Information on the Hollywood Vampires club is found in Cooper's biographical video *Prime Cuts* (1991).

✦ *Humor* ✦

To some, the stage vampire was essentially humorous, and the thought of being lampooned in the press was partially responsible for keeping Hamilton Deane from bringing his original *Dracula* play, which had been quite successful in rural England, to London. In fact, a comedic version of the Deane play, *Dracula, the Comedy of the Vampire*, appeared in various locations around Europe in the 1930s. With his knowledge of the theater, Deane could have expected some amount of fun to be had at his play's expense. A century earlier, Charles Nodier brought the vampire to the stage in Paris. Within a few months, several other vampire plays, all farces of his play, opened in competing Parisian theaters. The fact that vampire humor first appeared onstage was an indication of its future. Vampires as objects of humor made their primary appearance on the stage and, more recently, in motion pictures rather than in novels. Vampire books usually have been horror stories, with only very rare hints of humor. Meanwhile, a stereotypical vampire was gradually created in the successive productions of *Dracula*, Hamilton Deane's original play in England (1924), and the portrayals of Bela Lugosi in the American play in 1927 and Universal Pictures's movie version in 1931. The creation of the vampire's image on the stage and screen provided the context for future opportunities to lampoon that image. To a much lesser extent, vampire fiction was not tied to the Lugosi vampire, while even the most variant vampire movie had to use the stereotypical Dracula as its starting point.

The spread of popular vampire humor awaited the creation of the widely recognized stereotypical cinematic vampire by Bela Lugosi in the 1930s. The first major attempt to exploit the humorous possibilities of Lugosi's Dracula occurred in the 1948 film *Abbott and Costello Meet Frankenstein*. The plot of the movie revolved around Dracula's attempt to steal comedian Lou Costello's brain and place it in the head of Frankenstein's monster. Lugosi returned to his Dracula role for the spoof, which in retrospect received high marks as one of Abbott and Costello's best movies. It was said to be far superior to *Abbott and Costello Meet Dr. Jekyll and Mr. Hyde* (1953), in which an unnamed actor made a cameo appearance as Dracula.

The 1950s: Mainstream vampire humor in the 1950s was limited to two movies and a play. Early in the decade, Lugosi traveled to England to portray another vampire, Count Von Housen, in one of a series of Old Mother Riley comedies. *Mother Riley Meets the Vampire* (aka *My Son, the Vampire* and *Vampire Over London*, 1952) was one of his less-remembered roles. Lugosi's stereotyping as a horror actor drastically limited the roles offered to him as he aged and led him to construct a 1954 Las Vegas stage production, *The Bela Lugosi Review*, in which he was forced to play a spoof of the part he had made famous. In the second 1950s comedic vampire movie, *The Bowery Boys Meet the Monsters*, the vampire was secondary to the plot, which featured one of the Bowery Boys (Huntz Hall) being turned into a werewolf. More important than both of these movies was the first new vampire play in several decades. *I Was a Teen-Age Dracula*, a three-act mystery by Gene Donovan, heralded some 40 subsequent plays featuring Dracula for high school and other amateur productions, the great majority of which were comedies.

The 1960s: The 1960s saw the production of one of the best comic vampire movies ever made, Roman Polanski's *The Fearless Vampire Killers, or Pardon Me, But Your Teeth Are in My Neck* (1967). Polanski's film (originally called *Dance of the Vampires*) concerned the antics of two vampire hunters, Professor Ambronsius and his assistant (played by Polanski), as they tracked down the villainous Count Von Krolock (Ferdy Mayne). Among the more memorable scenes was a bizarre dance sequence, from which the movie took its name.

However, the comic vampire really found a home on two television series, *The Addams Family* and *The Munsters*. Both shows attempted to place the classical "monsters," including several vampire-like characters, in an ordinary, "normal," middle-class, American setting, and both ran through the 1964–1965 and 1965–1966 seasons. Both shows inspired early comic books that introduced the comic vampire to that medium. *The Munsters*, which featured a thinly disguised Count Dracula, spawned sev-

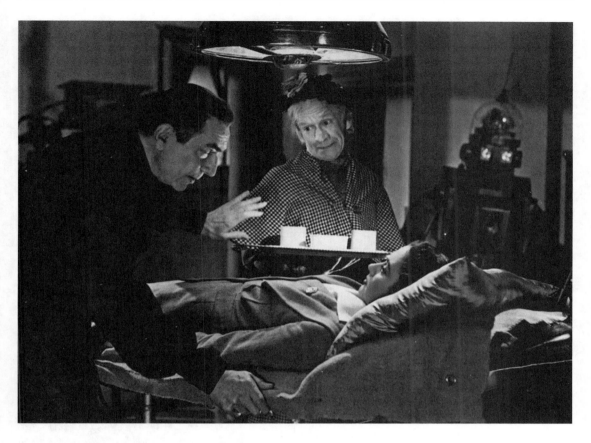

Bela Lugosi (left) with Arthur Lucan as Mother Riley and Maria Mercedes in the campy vampire movie Mother Riley Meets the Vampire *(1952).*

eral movies, *Munster, Go Home!* (1966), *The Munsters' Revenge* (1981), and *The Munsters' Scary Little Christmas* (1996). The gothic soap opera *Dark Shadows* became a hit daytime show on NBC in the last years of the decade. Among the items created as a result of the show was possibly the first vampire joke book, *Barnabas Collins in a Funny Vein*, published in 1969. A second *Dark Shadows* joke book appeared in 1981, *Die Laughing*, compiled by Barbara Fister-Liltz and Kathy Resch. A comedy drama featuring the Transylvanian count included two plays simply entitled *Dracula* that originally were staged in 1965 and 1966, respectively.

The 1970s: The 1970s opened with a new vampire play, *I'm Sorry the Bridge Is Out, You'll Have to Spend the Night*, a musical comedy featuring the songs of Sheldon Allman and Bob Pickett. Allman had made a record titled *Sing Along with Drac*, which included such memorable titles as "Children's Day at the Morgue" and "Fangs for the Memory." Pickett had been the Dracula voice on the 1962 album *The Original Monster Mash*, which included not only the title song but "Blood Bank Blues" and "Transylvania Twist." The spoof opened in Los Angeles on April 28, 1970, at the Coronet Theatre. It featured several of the classic Universal Pictures monsters and included the insect-eating R. N. Renfield from *Dracula*, who had his solo moment with a song called "Flies."

Several other vampire plays made their initial appearance in the 1970s. Both *Count*

Dracula; or, A Musical Mania for Transylvania and *Monster Soup: Or That Thing in My Neck Is a Tooth* were staged in 1974. They were joined by *The Vampire's Bride: Or, The Perils of Cinderella* (1979) later in the decade. The decade closed with what generally has been considered the best of the many comedy vampire movies, *Love at First Bite* (1979). George Hamilton played a modern Dracula in prerevolutionary Romania. As the movie opened, Dracula played the piano. The howls of the wolves grew louder and louder and, in a slightly altered version of one of Bela Lugosi's famous lines, he shouted out, "Children of the night, shut up!" Forced out of his castle by the Communist government, he took the opportunity to search out a New York fashion model (Susan Saint James), with whose picture he had fallen in love. There, he met Saint James's psychiatrist, a descendant of Abraham Van Helsing (Richard Benjamin). The movie was a delightful mixture of hilarious one-liners and humorous situations, such as Dracula waking up in the midst of a funeral service in an African American church.

Possibly second in popularity only to *Love at First Bite* as a humorous treatment of the vampire theme was *Andy Warhol's Dracula* (aka *Blood for Dracula*), an Italian production in which Dracula traveled to Italy looking for the blood of "wirgins." The humor centers upon his comment on modern society and inability to find a virtuous (sexually pure) young woman—a fact graphically displayed by his regurgitating every time he got blood from an apparently virginal female. In 1977, the first family of television comic horror, the Addams family, returned with a full-length movie, *Halloween with the New Addams Family*, but the response was disappointing. Meanwhile, an adult sexually oriented comedy, *Dracula Blows His Cool* (1979), as produced in West Germany and dubbed into English for an American audience, received an equally lackluster response.

In 1974, Phil Hirsch and Paul Laikin compiled a new collection of vampire humor in *Vampire Jokes and Cartoons*. The 1970s also marked the appearance of juvenile vampire literature, specifically designed for children and teens. Overwhelmingly, the approach to the vampire in children's books was very light (using vampires to teach tolerance for children who were different) to comedic. One of the more comic and delightful vampire characters for kids was *Bunnicula* (1979), a vegetarian vampire rabbit who slept during the day and attacked vegetables to suck out the juice at night. The rabbit presaged *Count Duckula* of the late 1980s.

The 1980s and 1990s: Vampire humor prospered in the 1980s with movies leading the way. By far, the best of the comic films (harking back to Andy Warhol's movie) was *Once Bitten*, in which a female vampire (Lauren Hutton) went in search of a male virgin in Hollywood. Unlike the Warhol vampire, Hutton quickly found the inexperienced Mark Kendall (Jim Carrey) and began to vampirize him. His attempts to discover what was happening to him and then extract himself from the vampire's clutches pro-

George Hamilton (right) is Dracula and Arte Johnson (left) is his faithful servant Renfield in the 1979 parody Love at First Bite.

Geena Davis plays the vampiress Odette (here, about to chomp Ed Begley Jr.) in the 1985 vampire spoof Transylvania 6-5000.

vided the setting for hilarity. Other comic vampire movies of the decade included *I Married a Vampire* (1984), *Who Is Afraid of Dracula?* (1985), *Transylvania 6-5000* (1985), and *Transylvania Twist* (1989). In the 1980s, Elvira, the vampiric television horror show hostess, burst onto the national scene as a comic personality who combined features of the vamp with a Marilyn Monroe-type dumbness. Elvira attracted a devoted following and had her own fan club. She also developed a line of cosmetics and inspired a Halloween look-alike costume and a comic book. In 1988, she starred in her first feature-length movie, *Elvira: Mistress of the Dark.*

Developing in the 1980s and coming into their own in the 1990s were vampire Halloween greeting cards. As Halloween emerged as one of urban America's most celebrated holidays, it dropped much of its earlier role as a harvest festival and became a time for fun for youngsters. Vampires and bats have been perennial Halloween characters. In response, the greeting card industry produced hundreds of cards featuring the vampire, most built around vampire-oriented one-liners, to send to friends at Halloween. Accompanying the cards were many cartoon vampire party products. These Halloween products illustrated most clearly the severe stereotyping of the vampire image. Vampires could be quickly recognized (and distinguished from witches, ghosts, or other monsters) by their fangs, cape, widow's peak, and accompanying bats.

The 1980s also saw the flowering of vampire literature for children and youth. A large percentage of the more than 50 titles were humorous, though serious horror stories for teenagers were also produced. Typical of comedic literature were the many titles of Victor G. Ambrus. Written for younger children, Ambrus developed a comical Dracula (complete with cartoon illustrations) who, in his initial appearance in *Count, Dracula* (1980), was content to teach children to count. *Dracula's Bedtime Storybook* (1981) had Dracula romping through British literature with Frankenstein's monster, Dr. Jekyll and Mr. Hyde, and Sherlock Holmes. A series of new titles continued into the 1990s. For older children, in addition to the further adventures of Bunnicula, such titles came out as Judi Miller's *A Vampire Named Murray*, the story of a vampire cousin from Vulgaria who came to live with the Kaufmans. Murray was allergic to human blood but loved V-8 juice (and could warm up to vegetable soup). Murray did stand-up comedy for the kids and they loved him, but the neighbors thought he was too different, and they wanted him to leave town.

The 1980s ended and the 1990s began as interest in vampires reached an all-time high. From 1980 through 1993, the number of vampire novels doubled, and the number of vampire short stories and comic books multiplied several times. Thus, it was fitting that the period should be capped with a doubling of the number of vampire joke books. In 1986, Charles Keller finished his compilation of *Count Draculations: Monster Riddles*, followed in 1991 by Gordon Hill's *The Vampire Joke Book*, 64 pages of riddles. "Why did Dracula become a vegetarian? Because he couldn't bear stakes" was typical fare for Keller and Hill. The next year, Jeanne Youngson, president of the Count Dracula Fan Club (now the Vampire Empire), compiled *The World's Best Vampire Jokes*. Jokes, for example, included "Why do vampires have such a tough time? Some people never give a sucker an even break" and "What do you get when you cross a woolen scarf with a vampire? A very warm pain in the neck." James Howe followed Hill and Youngson in 1993 with the *Bunnicula Fun Book* (1993), combining jokes with fun activities for children.

Vampire humor continued but at a decreased level into the new century. While a few vampire movies and television shows had their funny moments, as a whole, comedy was not a significant part of either world, even in those movies and shows made for youth and children. Vampire humor primarily survived in new collections of vampire jokes and Halloween greeting cards.

🦇 *Jacula* 🦇

An Italian adult comic book of the 1970s, and possibly the most successful vampire comic book of all time, *Jacula* ran for 327 issues from 1968 to 1982, plus an additional 129 reprint issues from 1982 to 1984. The comic took its name from the female vampire whose adventures were featured in its pages. According to the storyline, Jacula became a vampire after being bitten by another vampire in 1835 in Transylvania. She eventually became so proficient (learning, for example, to live unscathed in sunlight) that she was elected as the vampire queen. According to the mythology of the stories, vampires are in a league with the devil (Satan), who uses them in pursuit of his long-term goal: to discover Jesus Christ's grave and thus prove to the world that his resurrection is a myth. Quite apart from Satan's plan, however, Jacula had a number of remarkable adventures, often with the assistance of her mortal lover, Carlo Verdier, including encounters with Frankenstein's monster, Jack the Ripper, and the Marquis de Sade.

Jacula was created by a group of comic artists who operated collectively as Studio Giolitti and was published by Erregi (later Edipe-riodici). The publisher was continually harassed because of, by 1960s standards, the slightly pornographic nature of the publication (whose lead character was frequently pictured sans clothing). Public protest eventually brought the series to an end. The title character inspired the naming of an Italian experimental progressive rock band, also founded in 1968 in Milan. The band included Antonio Bartoccetti, Doris Norton (also known as Fiamma Dello Spirito), Charles Tiring, and Franz Porthenzy.

Morbius

Morbius, a Marvel Comics vampire character introduced in 1971, was the first original vampire introduced after revision of the Comics Code allowed vampires once again to appear in comic books, from which they had been banished in 1954. Michael Morbius, according to the story, was an outstanding biologist whose work had won him the Nobel Prize. He was engaged to be married. However, he contracted a rare blood disease. As his condition worsened, he began to work on a cure. He developed a serum from vampire bat blood and treated himself with electric shock. His efforts finally stopped the effects of the disease, but he experienced unwanted side effects: he grew fangs and developed an intense thirst for blood, which led to him vampirizing his best friend. He also developed some superpowers, including the standard heightened strength and flying ability because his bones became hollow.

Morbius was introduced in issue No. 101 of *Amazing Spider-Man* (1971), and his encounter with Spider-Man launched a series of battles with various Marvel superheroes. He was able to survive battles against the Bestial Lizard and the Human Torch and then took on the X-Team in the pages of *Marvel Team-Up* (No. 3 and No. 4). In *Marvel Team-Up*, after defeating Iceman and the Avenging Angel, he was bested by Cyclops. In the X-Men laboratory, he was treated by X-Team scientist Professor X, but the experimental enzyme merely confirmed Morbius's status as a living vampire.

Morbius quickly escaped to begin his many adventures, in most of which he fought villains more evil than himself while searching for ways to meet his need for blood without killing the innocent. Periodically, he turned his attention to finding a cure for his condition.

In 1973, Morbius was established in the new Marvel magazine-size *Vampire Tales*, the first issue of which appeared in the fall. Then,

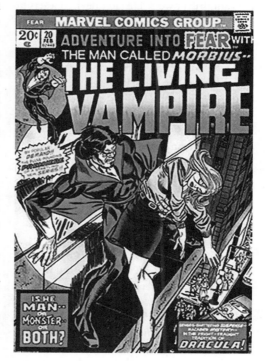

Morbius's first starring role in a comic book came in 1974 with issue #20 of Adventure into Fear.

in February 1974 in issue No. 19, Morbius became the featured character of *Fear* and, for the next few years, the Morbius stories appeared simultaneously in the two comics. *Vampire Tales* lasted for 11 issues through June 1975, and *Fear* concluded its Morbius story in issue No. 31 in December 1975 with Morbius flying off to possible future adventures.

In 1976, his adventures resumed. He appeared in issue No. 15 of *Marvel Two-in-One* to fight The Thing. He squared off against Blade the Vampire Slayer in issue No. 8 of *Marvel Preview*. In 1980, in issue No. 38 of the *Spectacular Spider-Man*, Morbius was finally cured. He had drunk some of Spider-Man's radioactive blood and was then struck by lightning, which drained him of his vampiric powers. He later devised a serum that returned him to a normal human life. He was brought to trial for his multiple murders but acquitted when judged insane. It seemed to be the end of the story, and Morbius faded into oblivion in the 1980s, especially after Marvel killed off all of its vampires in December 1983.

After many years' absence, Morbius made a dramatic reappearance in November 1989 in issue No. 10 of *Dr. Strange: Sorcerer Supreme.* Issue No. 14 in February 1990 revealed the events of Morbius's missing years. After living normally for several years, he had gone on a vacation to New Orleans.

One evening, he met a beautiful woman named Marie and went home with her. He discovered that she was actually Marie Laveau, who had kept herself young with the blood of vampires. Since no more true vampires existed, she was aging again. She treated him with an intense but less-than-fatal electric shock, causing him to again become a vampire. He went on to battle Dr. Strange, who had accidentally become the instrument allowing vampires to return to the real world.

In September 1992, with vampires returning and supernatural evil on the rise, those characters most capable of interacting with the supernatural were brought together in a new realm of the Marvel Universe. Those who were to oppose the supernatural were designated the Midnight Sons. They included old Marvel heroes such as Ghost Rider and Blade the Vampire Slayer. Morbius joined the Midnight Sons with the first issue of his own comic book, *Morbius, the Living Vampire.* The initial adventure of Morbius and the other Midnight Sons set them against a union of evil entities led by Lilith, Queen of Evil and Mother of Demons. Their conflicts late in 1993 led to the demise of Darkhold and the Nightstalkers, but Morbius continued his life on the edge of the world of good and evil, a reluctant vampire with a conscience and a bloodthirst. In his most recent adventures, he has fought a new round in his continuing struggle with Spider-Man (1997).

In the new century, Morbius has made relatively few appearances in Marvel Comics, engaging in a time of wandering in search of a cure for his condition. To this end, at one point, he sought out a scientist, Dr. Andrea Jansen, only to discover that she had joined the international conspiratorial organization known as Hydra and aligned with the villainous Crown. Morbius was taken prisoner and experimented upon. Later freed by Blade and Spider-Man, in his bloodlust, he bit Blade before fleeing.

A very different re-imagined version of Morbius appeared in *Ultimate Spider-Man* No. 95 (2006). The new Morbius was a real vampire whose origins reached back to the brother of Dracula. Struggling against his vampire nature, the Ultimate Morbius became a vampire slayer, though because he is also a vampire, his motives

After many years' absence, Morbius made a dramatic reappearance in November 1989 in issue No. 10 of *Dr. Strange: Sorcerer Supreme.*

are immediately called into question whenever he appears. Such is the case with his first meeting with Spider-Man in the Ultimate Universe. Vampires are attacking a young man, and it is not clear on whose side Morbius is fighting.

A movie adaptation of *Morbius* is, as of this writing, scheduled to be released in 2022. Part of the Marvel comics pantheon, it stars Jared Leto in the title role.

New Orleans

Since it has been introduced as a home for vampires, New Orleans has emerged as the true American vampire city. While many different American cities, especially New York and Los Angeles, have provided locations for vampire stories, none has become so identified with the nocturnal creatures as has the Crescent City. The association is not from a history of vampire incidents in the city's folklore. A vampire figure, the *fifollet* in the folklore of the African Americans of Louisiana, exists, as well as the *loogaroo*, a variation on the West African vampire found among the Haitian slaves who came into the city in the early nineteenth century, but only two vampire stories can actually be traced to the city. One of those involved two serial killers in the 1930s who drank blood from their victims before killing them. The city's reputation for vampires has purely modern roots—in the writings of Anne Rice—especially *Interview with the Vampire*, one of the most popular vampire books of all time, which sets much of the action in New Orleans. Throughout the 1990s, a number of other authors have also enjoyed success with New Orleans vampires.

New Orleans is a unique place on the American landscape and an appropriate setting for vampires. It was the center of Voodoo, a religion practiced in secret during the night by slaves who built a different culture in order to survive away from their homeland. New Orleans also stands as a foreign enclave within a country dominated by English-speaking British influence. In the French Quarter, New Orleans is also a land separated from the present by its unique architecture and heritage. The recognition of the old European setting as providing an appropriately "gothic" setting was heralded in the 1943 Universal Pictures film *Son of Dracula*, set in rural Louisiana near New Orleans.

Interview with the Vampire tells the story of Louis, an eighteenth-century New Orleans vampire raised on a plantation near the city, who is brought into the nightlife by the vampire Lestat. They try living on the plantation for a time, but the slaves soon figure out what is occurring in the mansion house and force the pair into the anonymity of the city. By the 1790s, when Louis is made into a vampire, New Orleans had spread far beyond the old French Quarter and provided ample food for the thirsty pair. Its bawdy nightlife also provided a cover for their nefarious activities. It is here that they find the little girl Claudia and make her into a vampire.

Claudia and Louis left New Orleans in 1862 after trying to kill Lestat. However, after Claudia's death in Paris later that year, he and his new companion, Armand, finally settled in New Orleans after living in New York for a number of years. While there, Louis again met with Lestat before moving on, leaving Armand behind. In 1929, Lestat went underground in New Orleans, where he would remain in a vampiric sleep for many decades. Armand remained in New Orleans through the twentieth century and is the one found by Daniel Molloy when he comes looking for Louis. Louis had given his now famous interview to Molloy,

With its above-ground tombs, colonial mansions, and old French Quarter, New Orleans sets the mood that makes it the perfect home for vampires in the United States.

who had published it under the pseudonym Anne Rice.

While Armand and Daniel were busy with their relationship, Lestat was awakened by the rock music of a band rehearsing not far from the cemetery in which he lay asleep. Awakened by the music, he made his way to the band's room and soon began his new career as a rock star. The publication of his autobiography, *The Vampire Lestat*, brought Jesse, an employee of the occult studies organization the Talamasca, to New Orleans, where she found the home where Louis and Claudia had lived and the several items that Claudia had hidden and left behind.

Once Lestat left New Orleans in 1985, the city was less essential to *The Vampire Chronicles*, the action shifting to California, Miami,

New York, and the world beyond. However, after Lestat's visit to heaven and hell, he returned to New Orleans and resided in St. Elizabeth's, the former orphanage on Napoleon Street (an actual building once owned by Rice).

Rice, of course, is not the only vampire fiction writer to place her novels in New Orleans. In 1982, George R. R. Martin brought Josiah Yorke to the Crescent City on his 1850s riverboat, the *Fevre Dream*. There, he found the vampire community for which he had been searching. Damon Julian had led a group of vampires from Portugal in the 1750s. Using the city as their headquarters, they moved along the river among the slaves, whom they treated as their personal food supply. Yorke presented his blood substitute, which would allow vampires to stop killing and integrate into human society. Julian rejected his plan, and their con-

The character Nothing in Lost Souls *is born in the French Quarter, a location that influences his life even after he is raised in Maryland.*

flict would provide the action for the rest of the novel.

Nancy Collins, author of the highly acclaimed series of novels featuring the vampire Sonja Blue and a resident of New Orleans, finally brought her character to New Orleans in the second volume of the series, *In the Blood*. Sonja had been made into a vampire in a most brutal manner by a vampire named Morgan and set out to find and kill him. Upon her return to the United States, she settled in New Orleans. Pangloss, the old vampire who had made Morgan, wanted to find Sonja. Palmer, the private detective Pangloss hired to track her, caught up with her in the French Quarter, where Pangloss happened to keep an apartment. While soaking up the atmosphere, they would come to know each other, and from there, they would launch the next phase of Sonja's search for Morgan.

Nothing, the central character in Poppy Z. Brite's *Lost Souls* (1992), was born in New Orleans in a room over a bar in the French Quarter, the result of the union between his mother Jessy, a teenager infatuated with vampires, and Zillah, a 100-year-old vampire who gave her more than she bargained for. From their one-night stand in the mid-1970s and Jessy's subsequent death giving birth, Nothing was taken to live with a "normal" couple in Maryland, far from New Orleans, but his origin was stronger than the loving environment of his youth. As a teenager, he ran away from home and began the pilgrimage that would lead him to his father and then to his birthplace, where his history would suddenly catch up with him.

In the early 1990s, Carnifax was a vampire who integrated himself into New Orleans society and became a viable candidate for governor. Only a werewolf, Desiree Cupio, the lead character in Daniel Presedo's comic book series *Dream Wolves*, recognized him for what he was. Many years before, he fell in love with Desiree's mother, sired a child, and also killed the one he loved. When they finally met, they were infatuated with each other and only slowly recognized their prior connections. Their adventures led them around the French Quarter until they converged on Desiree's aunt's house, where the truth was revealed.

In 1993, Blade the Vampire Slayer squared off against his reappearing nemesis, Deacon Frost, in New Orleans where, with the assistance of Hannibal King and Brother Voodoo, he blocked Frost's attempt to take over a local industry, though the good guys were unable to finish off the evil vampire.

In 1994, the story of New Orleans vampires was re-created for followers of the role-playing game *Vampire: The Masquerade*. The story begins with Doran, a Frenchman turned into a vampire in 1471. He settled in what was to become New Orleans in 1705 and, as the vampire community of the city grew, fought for his place in the moonlight, his main competitor over the centuries being Spanish vampire Simon de Cosa. He led the city's Kindred until after World War II, when he announced his grandiose plan for a new time in which vampires and mortals could live side by side. Some did not like his idea and, in 1955, he was assassinated. Today, the city is led by a new prince, Marcel.

As Anne Rice's books gained in popularity following the release of *The Vampire Lestat* in 1988 and then the *Interview with the Vampire* movie in 1994, New Orleans became a popular site for vampire fans, who flocked to the city and joined in the

various tours of the locations featured in the novels and movie or took the midnight tour exploring the French Quarter's vampiric heritage. The most dedicated came at the end of October for the annual Halloween Coven Party, sponsored by Anne Rice's Vampire Lestat Fan Club, which was started in 1988 by a fan, Sue Quiroz, who met Rice at a book signing and subsequently received permission to start the club. Through the 1990s, the club sponsored a popular annual vampire ball in New Orleans (the name of which changed as new books appeared and as Rice herself changed), with each attracting thousands of fans to the city. In 1995, the annual gathering was rechristened as the Memnoch Ball.

Anne Rice's Vampire Lestat Fan Club dissolved in 2000. In 2004, following the death of her husband, Rice announced that she was leaving New Orleans and put the last property she owned in the Garden District up for sale. She had, by this time, written what was believed to be the last of her vampire novels, *Blood Canticle* (2003), and moved on to other themes.

In 2006 in the wake of Hurricane Katrina, some former members of Anne Rice's Vampire Lestat Fan Club approached Rice about restarting the club, in part as an effort to assist the city in its recovery. The first of the new gatherings occurred in 2007 and, in successive years, broadened their appeal. The 2009 event was announced as the True Blood and Gold Ball. She began to actively support the events in the middle of the second decade of the century as she began to again write books in *The Vampire Chronicles* series, and in 2014, the ball featured a coronation ceremony for the new prince Lestat. In 2015, it was termed the Vampire Ball.

Adding to the role of New Orleans for vampires … the real vampire community emerged in the city and Father Sebastiaan created the Endless Night Vampire Ball….

Adding to the role of New Orleans for vampires, even as the Anne Rice event was revived, the real vampire community emerged in the city and Father Sebastiaan created the Endless Night Vampire Ball, which began to rival the Anne Rice event in popularity every Halloween. Rice withdrew her support from these events in the middle of the first decade of the new century after she renounced her vampire associations and made a highly publicized return to Catholicism.

New Orleans was changed significantly by Hurricane Katrina, which struck the city in August 2005. Much of the city was flooded, though the French Quarter remained above water and the Garden District was less affected than other parts of the city. As the city rebounded, the vampire aspect of life slowly began to reappear, beginning with the nightly vampire tours that focused on the French Quarter and the Garden District. Tours to Oak Alley, the plantation outside the city that was used as a location in the *Interview with the Vampire* movie (1994), also returned. In 2008–2009, the movie version of Darren Shan's *Cirque du Freak: The Vampire's Assistant* was shot in New Orleans, though the novel does not specify it as the story's setting.

Through and since the disaster of Katrina, though, New Orleans has remained a favorite location for fiction writers to set their novels. Just before Katrina struck, Andrew Fox had set his two novels, *Fat White Vampire Blues* (2003) and *Bride of the Fat White Vampire* (2004), in the city. His work has been joined by various titles of Shannon Drake (Heather Graham) such as *Beneath a Blood Red Moon* (1999) and *Kiss of Darkness* (2006); Lynn Viehl's *When Angels Burn* (2005); Denise Wilkinson's *Isabella St. Clair: Vamp of New Orleans, the Vieux Carre* (2007); and Adrian Phoenix's *A Rush of Wings* (2009), to mention a few. Pete Callahan's self-published novel *Vampire in New Orleans* carries the storyline through the Katrina event. In her seventh vampire novel, *All Together*

Dead, Charlaine Harris features a new character, Sophie-Anne Leclerq, the vampire queen of Louisiana, who resides in post-Katrina New Orleans. The early L. A. Banks novels, while basically operating out of Philadelphia, frequently mentioned New Orleans as a place the characters have either come from or visited, while later novels, such as *The Wicked* (2007) and *The Shadows* (2008), reflected on Katrina.

Through the second decade of the twenty-first century, a variety of novelists, primarily writing in the tradition of the paranormal romance, authored fiction series focusing on the vampire of New Orleans. These include Kym Grosso's *The Immortals of New Orleans* series, which began in 2012 and continues as of 2020; Julie Morgan's *Covenant of New Orleans* series; Pagan Knight's *New Orleans Vampires* series; Erin Bedford's *New Orleans after Dark* series; and Carrie Pulkinen's *New Orleans Nocturnes* series, which was initiated in 2020.

Through the second decade of the century, the single most notable story of New Orleans vampires was undoubtably *The Originals*, a television series that ran from 2013 to 2018. A spin-off of *The Vampire Diaries*, a series set in Mystic Falls, Virginia, *The Originals* tells the story of the Mikaelson family, the core of whose members constitute the original vampires created some 1,000 years ago. The three main vampire siblings—Klaus, Elijah, and Rebekah—were among the founders of the city. Arriving in 1722, they find a city that has become a lawless haven for vampires, witches, and werewolves, who exist at each other's throats unwilling to share power. After much effort, they emerge as the power holding the supernatural underworld together, at least until they abandon the city in 1919. In the present, they return hoping to reestablish their rule. The series ran for five seasons on the CW network.

🦇 *Preacher* 🦇

Through the 1990s, DC Comics nurtured its *Vertigo* series, comics written for an adult audience that featured a variety of horror titles. Among the series' top entries was *Preacher*, which was written and drawn by the team of Garth Ennis and Steve Dillon. The series was named after Jesse Custer, a preacher who had become possessed by Genesis, a new entity created by the mating of an angel and a demon. Genesis had great strength but lacked willpower. In his possessed state, Jesse had the power to speak the Word and bend people to his desires. Jesse was driven into a number of situations by his knowledge that God retired from running the universe. He sought God to call him to account for this patent neglect of creation.

Jesse was accompanied by two friends/colleagues: Tulip, his girlfriend, and Proinsas Cassidy, a vampire from Ireland. Born in 1900, as a young man, Cassidy was an Irish vampire. Cassidy joined the Irish Volunteers and took part in the Easter Rising in 1916, though his brother, William (Billy), also joined to keep watch over him. Billy eventually forced Cassidy to desert the army because of its impending failure, and Cassidy was soon bitten by a hag, who seemingly left fatal injuries. His body fell into the water, and he soon learned that he was not succumbing to the injuries and that the sun burned his skin. He began to wear sunglasses to hide his eyes, which had turned blood red as part of his transformation into a vampire. He decided to travel to the United States so his family and other soldiers would believe that he was dead. He lived in the United States, picking up alcohol and drug problems, even going as far as prostituting himself for drugs.

Preacher by Garth Ennis and Steve Dillon (art by Glenn Fabry) is about a preacher who is possessed by a half angel/half demon named Genesis. It ran from 1995 to 2000.

All of the preceding information was revealed to Jesse atop the Empire State Building in New York City. What he left out was that his addictions made him parasitical and irresponsible (in a way, making him a figurative vampire as well as a literal one), causing harm and death to those around him when he abandoned them to circumstances that he set in motion. Repeatedly showing a remarkable lack of forethought, many women he hooked up with and lived off of over the years ended up critically injured, hopelessly addicted to drugs, or dead. After he got the girlfriend of a friend of his killed during the "Dixie Fried" story arc, Xavier, who is a Voodoo priest, says, "I honestly don't believe he's an evil man. Just careless. And thoughtless. And terribly, terribly weak."

He eventually met Tulip O'Hare and Jesse Custer. Cassidy formed a strong friendship with Jesse and eventually fell in love with Tulip, though she did not reciprocate the feelings. He constantly struggled with his addictions and his feelings for Tulip, though after believing Jesse to be dead, both he and Tulip took up heavy drugs and alcohol and started a sexual relationship. After reuniting with Jesse, he was told that Jesse no longer wanted anything to do with him after finding out about his history, though the two agreed to meet one more time. They engaged in a fistfight that Jesse's skill easily allowed him to dominate while constantly berating Cassidy. When Cassidy finally accepted his failures and began, as Jesse put it, "acting like a man," Jesse took Cassidy's hand in forgiveness. Cassidy proved that he was worth the gesture by walking into the sunrise to atone for all he had done, burning up in the process.

Once Jesse was gunned down by the Grail, it was revealed that Cassidy had made a deal with God hours before his confrontation with Jesse: he would beat Jesse to the point of surrender and allow Genesis to be destroyed. In return, God would allow both Jesse and Cassidy to live. Despite events not quite going according to plan, God kept His word. Jesse was revived and went looking for Tulip while Cassidy watched his first sunset in years as a human being, then drove off with a pledge to act like a man.

Cassidy had superhuman strength and speed that could easily rip regular humans apart, though he had no formal training, allowing Jesse to easily beat him without taking any injuries (except for a broken breastbone, which occurred when Cassidy offered his hand in friendship and then sucker-punched Jesse). Cassidy could survive any physical wound, although he felt the full pain associated with the injury. He could heal superhumanly fast, and drinking blood allowed him to accelerate the process. The only thing that could kill him was being directly in the sunlight for a period of time, though he could stand indirect exposure with discomfort. Although Cassidy needed blood to sustain himself, he did not need human or even fresh blood, preferring instead the taste of beer or whiskey. He generally drank blood from live humans only if they threatened him.

As a comic book, *Preacher* ran for 66 issues and was quickly reprinted in trade paperback editions. Five related one-shot special issues were published as well as a spin-off series, *Saint of Killers*, which was void of vampires. Several attempts were made at turning the series into a movie, but none were put into production. It was finally picked up by AMC and ran as a television series for four seasons. It premiered on May 22, 2016, and concluded on September 29, 2019. In the AMC *Preacher* television series, Cassidy was portrayed by Joseph Gilgun. Unlike in the comics, he usually appeared without his trademark sunglasses.

Ravenloft

Ravenloft, a role-playing game, began in the 1980s as an optional adventure module of the popular *Dungeons & Dragons* role-playing game. Within the game, Ravenloft is a fictional place, a demiplane that exists in an alternate time and place. As conceived, the *Dungeons & Dragons* Demiplane of Dread consists of several domains that have been assembled as a mysterious force known as the Dark Powers. Each domain of the Demiplane of Dread is ruled by a being called a Darklord, a person who has committed an act so vile as to attract the attention of the Dark Powers and who is now trapped by the mists that surround his/her domain. Ravenloft was introduced to the world in 1983 in the advanced *Dungeons & Dragons* module 16, which focused on the vampire Strahd von Zarovich, the Darklord of his own personal domain of Barovia. Count von Zarovich's backstory would become the subject of an early *Ravenloft* novel, *I, Strahd: The Memoirs of a Vampire* by P. N. Elrod. Much of the early material released for players of the game centered on Strahd and Barovia, giving the whole series a vampiric element, even though additional *Ravenloft* domains and Darklords were eventually added in various products beginning with the second edition of the game. Among the added Darklords was Kas the Bloody-Handed, also a vampire.

> Ravenloft was introduced to the world in 1983 in the advanced *Dungeons & Dragons* module 16, which focused on the vampire Strahd von Zarovich....

From its beginning as advanced *Dungeons & Dragons* module 16 in 1983, *Ravenloft* materials were published by TSR, Inc., a gaming company based in Lake Geneva, Wisconsin. Unfortunately, by the end of the 1990s, TSR began to fail and, in 2000, sold its assets to Wizards of the Coast. Wizards of the Coast, in turn, licensed White Wolf, Inc., then riding high with its *Vampire: The Masquerade* role-playing game. In 2001, White Wolf began to release materials through its Sword & Sorcery

Studios under its Arthaus imprint, which had been created to publish products that White Wolf owned but did not originally develop. White Wolf's license ended in 2005, and *Ravenloft* reverted back to Wizards of the Coast.

Strahd von Zarovich, the Darklord of Barovia and the main vampire in the *Ravenloft* game, was originally a nobleman and a warrior and leader of armies. By middle age, however, he was in despair, believing that he had squandered his life away. He had established himself as the lord of Barovia, a region he had recently conquered. He resided in Ravenloft Castle. He subsequently fell in love with Tatyana, a young, Barovian woman. Tatyana rejected him in favor of the affections of Strahd's younger brother, Sergei. In his disappointment, he turned to magic and sought to regain his youth. His efforts included making "a pact with death." The pact was sealed when, on the day of their wedding, he killed Sergei, Tatyana threw herself off of the walls of Ravenloft Castle, and the castle guard shot Strahd with multiple arrows. Strahd did not die but now ruled Barovia as a vampire.

🦇 *Riccardo, Martin V. (1952–)* 🦇

Martin V. Riccardo, a writer, researcher, hypnotist, and lecturer on vampires, is the founder of Vampire Studies. He grew up in the Chicago metropolitan area and graduated with a bachelor of science degree from the University of Illinois in 1974. Originally created as the Vampire Studies Society in Chicago, Illinois, in 1977, Vampire Studies ("Society" was dropped from the name in 1990) was designed as a means for vampire enthusiasts to share information on the subject. It was the first vampire-oriented fan club to use the word "vampire" in its title. Riccardo had initially developed an

interest in the subject several years earlier, when he had heard a lecture by Leonard Wolf, author of *A Dream of Dracula*. After some extensive research on the subject, he began lecturing on vampires in 1976.

In 1977, Vampire Studies began publishing the *Journal of Vampirism*, one of the first periodicals devoted to vampires in folklore, fiction, film, and fact. The journal published nonfiction articles, book and movie reviews, news reports, fiction, humor, cartoons, and poetry. A primary interest of the journal was reports of vampires and vampire attacks. The journal folded in 1979 after six issues. While being the center of vampire fandom in Chicago, Riccardo built a large correspondence network and was himself an active member in many of the vampire-oriented fan clubs. He also built a large collection of vampire books, magazines, and comic books. Among the members, contributors, and correspondents to Vampire Studies were Dorothy Nixon and Eric Held, who later founded the Vampire Information Exchange. Jan L. Perkowski, a Slavic studies scholar from the University of Virginia and an authority on the Slavic vampire, was also a contributor to the *Journal of Vampirism*, as was Dr. Jeanne Youngson, founder of the Count Dracula Fan Club, now known as the Vampire Empire.

> While being the center of vampire fandom in Chicago, Riccardo built a large correspondence network and was himself an active member in many of the vampire-oriented fan clubs.

In 1983, Riccardo saw the publication of two vampire books: *Vampires Unearthed*, the first comprehensive bibliography of vampire literature and filmography, which has become the basis of all vampire bibliographic work since; and *The Lure of the Vampire*, a collection of Riccardo's essays. Through the 1980s and 1990s, Riccardo has also written a number of articles on vampires for various vampire and occult periodicals. He coined the term "astral vampirism" to refer to a form of psychic vampirism in which the astral body or ghost form leaves the physical body for the purpose of draining blood or vital energy. In the early 1990s, he concentrated his research on vampire dreams and fantasies. Riccardo does not believe that Dracula-like creatures exist but does believe in the process of psychic vampirism in the sense that people can suck the energy or life force from others.

After the *Journal of Vampirism* folded, Riccardo continued to stay in contact with the subscribers and others interested in the varied issues related to vampires. Over the years, he received thousands of letters from individuals interested in vampires and reporting their experiences with them. Letters he had received through his correspondence network first suggested a line of research he pursued through the mid-1990s on dream experiences. The work resulted in his book *Liquid Dreams of Vampires* (1996). Riccardo is a hypnotist by profession. From 1984 to 1985, he edited *Hypno-News of Chicagoland*. He also has an interest in the larger occult world and, in 1981, founded the Ghost Research Society. For six years in the 1980s, he hosted the Midwest Ghost Expo, a yearly convention for ghost researchers and enthusiasts. He also has coordinated programs on a variety of occult topics from reincarnation to ancient Egypt.

In the 1990s, Riccardo hosted the Vampire Forum, gatherings of fans and personalities in the vampire world for lectures, discussions, and fun. He is a popular lecturer on vampires and the occult in the greater Chicago area. He received the Count's Award for Meritorious Service at Dracula '97: A Centennial Celebration for his many years of work in building vampire fandom.

Sebastiaan, Father (1975–)

Emerging in the 1990s, Father Sebastiaan initially manifested as a leader within and spokesperson to the outside world of the real vampire community, those persons who self-described as actual vampires or expressed a hope to become vampires. Born Sebastiaan van Houten in San Diego to a military family, he grew up in various locations depending upon

Beginning his career as a dental assistant, Father Sebastiaan became a "fangsmith," making custom fangs for his vampire friends, and founded the Sabretooth Clan.

his parents' stationing. As a teenager, he discovered the goth and vampire subcultures, was attracted to the books of Anne Rice, and began to join in the role-playing game *Vampire: The Masquerade*. In his early years, he also worked as a dental assistant.

In the 1990s, he became active in the vampire club scene in New York City. He also became active in writing and (with Michelle Belanger) revising *Black Veils*, a code of conduct he offered for guiding those choosing to act as a vampire in the modern world. At the beginning of the new century, he began to issue a set of books designed to inform real vampires of the ins and outs of the vampire community and provide outsiders with factual knowledge of what had become a most controversial movement to the larger community.

Along the way, Sebastiaan became an event organizer for the vampire community beginning with the creation of the New York Vampire Ball in 1996 and the Endless Night Vampire Ball in New Orleans in 1998, the latter becoming one of the largest vampire gatherings ever held. From that beginning work, he has emerged as the impresario of the Endless Night Vampire Ball, held each Halloween in New Orleans, and of associated events throughout the year for the vampire community around the United States.

Sebastiaan has also taken advantage of his dental training to create the Sabretooth Clan, a networking community of vampires that includes a service providing personalized, custom-made fangs for people who wish to wear them. Sebastiaan describes himself as a fangsmith.

Father Sebastiaan maintains offices in Los Angeles and New York and may be contacted through his website: http://www.fathersebastiaan.com.

The Tomb of Dracula

The Tomb of Dracula is second only to *Vampirella* as the most successful English-language vampire-oriented comic book series. Vampires had been banned from comic books in 1954 by the Comics Code, but the revised code promulgated in 1971 allowed vampires if they were presented in a manner similar to the vampires of classic gothic literature. Marvel Comics responded to the change immediately by resurrecting Dracula and setting his new adventures in the 1970s. A familiar cast, composed of the descendants of the characters of Bram

Stoker's 1897 novel, were assembled to fight him. Reflecting the changing times, a major female character, Rachel Van Helsing, was an active vampire fighter armed with a crossbow. Blade the Vampire Slayer, an African American, also joined the team.

The Tomb of Dracula characters were soon integrated into the Marvel Comics alternate world. Dracula, Blade, and Hannibal King, another original character introduced in the series, began to appear in various Marvel titles (Dr. Strange, Marvel Premiere, Frankenstein, and Thor), and characters from other titles (Werewolf by Night, Silver Surfer) appeared in The Tomb of Dracula. The Tomb of Dracula was developed under the guidance of writer Marv Wolfman, who created the new characters, and artist Gene Colan. It would be reprinted in England under the title Dracula Lives! (in black and white); be translated into German, French, Swedish, Spanish, Italian, and other languages; and inspire a Japanese feature-length, animated video.

It was finally cancelled after 70 issues, though it found a brief continuance for six issues in a black-and-white magazine format. One story in each issue continued the Dracula saga. However, Wolfman and Colan moved on to other projects and, through the 1980s, Marvel lost interest in horror fiction. Only in the 1990s was a new attempt to integrate horror into the Marvel Universe attempted. In the early 1990s, Wolfman and Colan revived the storyline from their successful series in a four-part set, The Tomb of Dracula (1991–1992), from Marvel subsidiary Epic Comics. The story picked up the life of Frank Drake and Blade the Vampire Slayer a decade after the killing of Dracula at the end of the original series (and the demise of all Marvel vampires in 1983). Dracula had made his initial return several years previously in Dr. Strange: Sorcerer Supreme (No. 10) and now wished to take revenge on Drake and his loved ones.

Subsequently, in 1992, as vampires were enjoying what proved to be a temporary return to the Marvel Universe, various individual issues of the original series were reprinted as one-shots under the titles Requiem for Dracula, The Savage Return of Dracula, and The Wedding of Dracula. The Tomb of Dracula one-shots heralded the return of several characters from The Tomb of Dracula, including Blade, Hannibal King, and Frank Drake, who were given new life as partners in a present-day Boston detective agency. They were known as the Nightstalkers, an antivampire/antidemonic force team. Their adventures appeared in 17 issues, in which they worked with other like-minded crusaders collectively called the Midnight Sons. At the end of The Nightstalkers issue No. 17, Drake and King were killed. Blade survived in a new series for several years, has made subsequent appearances in other Marvel titles, and was featured in the three Blade movies starring Wesley

The Tomb of Dracula comic book series from Marvel had a successful run from 1972 to 1979.

Snipes. In 1998, Hannibal King was brought back from the dead for some additional interaction with Dracula, including an appearance in the third of the *Blade* movies.

From 2003 to 2005, Marvel Comics reprinted all *The Tomb of Dracula* stories in black and white in four large volumes as part of its *Essential* reprint series, *The Essential Tomb of Dracula.*

Vamp

The vamp, a popular stereotypical figure of the silent film, developed from an extension of the vampire myth into an analogy of male/female relationships. Both psychological and feminist interpretations of the myth emphasized the maleness of the vampire legend. It was a projection of male fears, goals, and attitudes toward the world. The role of the vamp was established in large part by "The Vampire," a short poem by Rudyard Kipling:

> A fool there was and he made his
>   prayer
> (Even as you and I)
> To a rag and a bone and a hank
>   of hair
> (We call her the woman who did
>   not care)
> But the fool he called her his lady
>   fair—
> (Even as you or I!)
> Oh, the years we waste and the
>   tears we waste
> And the work of our head and
>   hand
> Belong to the woman who did
>   not know
> (And now we know that she
>   never could know)
> And did not understand!
> A fool there was and his goods
>   he spent
> (Even as you and I)
> Honour and faith and a sure in-
>   tent
> (And it wasn't the least what the
>   lady meant)

> But a fool must follow his natural
>   bent
> (Even as you and I!)

The poem, inspired by a famous painting by Philip Burne-Jones, in turn inspired a play by Porter Emerson Browne, *A Fool There Was,* which in turn was made into a movie (1915) by the Fox Film Corporation. The story involved a triangle composed of a husband (portrayed by Edward José), his wife (Nabel Frenyear), and a vampire (Theda Bara). The husband, John Schulyer, was a lawyer who had been sent on a diplomatic mission for the president of the United States. Off in a scenic land, he encountered a vampiress, who injected herself into his life. His wife reasserted herself at various points, first with a letter, which the vampiress tore up. Later, Schulyer tried to cable his wife but was blocked. So tight did the vampiress's hold become that, upon Schulyer's return to the States, he provided a townhouse for her. Meanwhile, he was degenerating into a hopeless alcoholic. The wife made one last attempt to reclaim her husband, but as she was leading him away, the vampiress appeared, and the man lost all desire to leave. Because he had abandoned his wife for the temptress, his will had left him, and he was destroyed.

A Fool There Was became an important film in many respects. It was the film through which Fox, then a small company, successfully fought the monopoly of General Film. It also introduced Theda Bara to the screen as the vamp. Theda Bara would become the embodi-

Theda Bara is a vampire preying on Edward José in 1915's A Fool There Was.

ment of the vamp in a series of pictures for Fox. She provided a powerful image for the public to place beside that of the virtuous woman under attack by evil cultural forces that had been so powerfully cultivated by D. W. Griffith (1875–1948) at General.

The vamp was the dark shadow of the Victorian virtuous woman. She was immoral, tainted with powerful, dark sexuality. Her power derived from her ability to release in males similar strong but latent sexual energies, strictly contained by modern cultural restrictions. She attached herself to men and sapped their vitality. Her image was carefully constructed. She wore tight, revealing, black clothes, sometimes decorated with either spiders or snakes. Her nails were long and cut to a point. In a day when women rarely used tobacco in public, she frequently smoked cigarettes from a long holder. Her demeanor sug-

gested that she was foreign, either from continental Europe or the Middle East.

Theda Bara (1885–1955), born Theodosia Goodman in Cincinnati, Ohio, initially defined the vamp for the American public. In cooperation with Fox, through the second decade of this century, she carefully created a public persona. Fox's role marked the first attempt by a studio to manufacture a star's image in such depth. The name Theda Bara was an anagram for Arab Death. Various stories were circulated about her suggesting a mysterious origin in the Middle East, the product of an affair between exotic mates. Supposedly, she had been weaned on snake's blood, and tribesmen had fought over her. Studio publicity compared her to Elizabeth Báthory, the seventeenth-century blood countess. When Theda Bara appeared in public, she often pretended not to speak English and traveled with her African footmen in a white limousine. Once developed, the vamp persona proved a continuing interest. Theda Bara's image passed to the likes of Nita Naldi (1899–1961), who starred in the 1922 Rudolph Valentino film *Blood and Sand*, and Greta Garbo (1905–1990), who became a star with her 1927 film *Flesh and the Devil*. Garbo's vampish role was spelled out for those in the audience who could not pick it up otherwise by a minister who told the hero that the devil created

> Garbo was credited with humanizing the vamps role and thus contributing to the destruction of the image, at least as it had previously existed.

women with beautiful bodies so that they could tempt men in a fleshly manner when they failed to reach them through more spiritual means. Garbo was credited with humanizing the vamp's role and thus contributing to the destruction of the image, at least as it had previously existed. The vamp evolved into the femme fatale, the temptress who still appears in a wide variety of settings in motion pictures.

~ *Vampire Fandom* ~

Through the last quarter of the twentieth century, the growing interest in vampires in the English-speaking world led to the formation of a broad spectrum on vampire-oriented fan organizations. In the United Kingdom, fandom has been anchored by the Dracula Society (founded in 1973), which has combined a lively celebration of Dracula and the vampire in the arts with the serious consideration of issues in Dracula and vampire studies. However, in the wake of the renewed interest in vampires that began in the late 1980s, a number of new and varied organizations emerged.

Among the more impressive of the 1990s groups was the Vampire Guild of Dorset, England, which grew out of the childhood fascination with vampires of founder Phill M. White. White had collected vampire materials during his teen years and officially founded the guild in August 1990 as a vampire interest group. Its primary goal was to bring people together who shared the founder's interest in vampires and wished to meet and correspond with others of like mind. As the membership expanded, the concerns of the guild broadened.

One of White's purposes in founding the guild was to explore some of the lesser-known aspects of vampirism; the guild investigated obscure cases of vampirism such as those of William Doggett, the Tarrant Valley Vampire, and the Black Lady of Durweston, both from Dorset. The research files of these cases sit in the guild's vampire archive. Access to archive information was available to members of the guild and any serious researchers. The guild also published a quarterly journal, *Crimson*, which emerged in the 1990s as one of the best vampire fanzines in the entire world of vampire fandom. The Vampire Guild developed an international membership but has not been visible in the new century and does not appear to have survived.

The Whitby Dracula Society (originally the Dracula Experience Society), centered in the resort community in northern England where Dracula reportedly first landed on British soil, emerged in stages in the mid-1990s. It became known for its sponsorship of the annual Vamps and Tramps event, the first of which was held in 1995. The society began a quality periodical, *The Demeter*, and over the weekend of June 13–15, 1997, cosponsored Dracula:

The Centenary Celebration 1897–1997 with the Vampire Guild.

The Whitby Dracula Society currently sponsors a monthly gathering and an annual Grand Masked Ball and may be contacted through its website: http://www.whitbydrac ulasociety.org. Members receive copies of its periodical, *Harker's Journal.* Since the mid-1990s, Whitby has also been home to a large gathering of goths, who arrive for the Halloween weekend.

Throughout the 1990s, two groups operated in Great Britain with the name the Vampyre Society. One was founded in 1987 by Allen J. Gittens. Several months before establishing the society, he had written an article on vampires for a British rock fanzine. People contacted him asking questions about vampires, resulting in the formation of a correspondence circle of about a dozen people. Rather than write back to each one individually, Gittens decided to produce an information leaflet and organized the correspondence circle into the Vampyre Society, taking its name from a novella by John Polidori. Within a year, the free information leaflet had become a newsletter offered for subscription through the society. A short time later, Gittens had a falling-out with one of the society's leaders, who then left and established a rival organization with the same name. Both organizations claimed to be the continuation of the original society.

The Vampyre Society is primarily a correspondence club for its members, who share a common interest in the vampire in all of its aspects. The society held no meetings and eschewed any association with either adherents of the occult or with blood drinking. New members were asked to fill out a brief questionnaire concerning their interest in vampires. The society's newsletter grew into a quarterly journal, *For the Blood Is the Life,* which featured occasional special issues devoted to poetry and fiction written by the members. The society was based in Chippenham, Wiltshire.

The Vampyre Society that was headed by Carole Bohanan was also founded in 1987. Bohanan was originally associated with Allen J. Gittens, but soon after the founding of the original Vampyre Society, they parted company. The society led by Bohanan went on to become one of the largest vampire interest groups in England, with local groups across the country. It published a high-quality journal, *The Velvet Vampyre,* which carried articles, short stories, and book and movie reviews. As the Dracula centennial approached, the society was split with dissension that led to its disruption as a national organization and the discontinuance of the *Velvet Vampyre.* A number of local groups, most prominently one in London, survived briefly but were soon superseded by the presently existing Vampire Connexion. The Vampire Connexion published a journal, *Dark Nights.*

Not really part of vampire fandom are the two rival organizations headed by people who believe in the reality of vampires, the Vampire Research Society led by Sean Manchester and the Highgate Vampire Society founded by David Farrant. Manchester in particular sees the activities of vampire enthusiasts as dangerous, and all agree that vampire fans and the Vampire Research Society are pursuing very different goals.

Meanwhile, the growth of interest in vampires also spawned a host of fan clubs, small publishing enterprises, and fanzines in the United States beginning in the 1960s. Of these, the first is the Count Dracula Fan Club (now known as the Vampire Empire), founded in 1965 by Jeanne Youngson. A short time later,

> Throughout the 1990s, two groups operated in Great Britain with the name the Vampyre Society.

the Vampire Studies Society was founded by Martin V. Riccardo, which placed Dracula and vampire studies in a more scholarly vein. This society led to the founding of the Lord Ruthven Assembly and to the spread to America of the international Transylvanian Society of Dracula.

Anchoring vampire fandom on the West Coast was the Count Dracula Society, founded in 1962 by Dr. Donald A. Reed (1935–2001), a law librarian who served as its president. It was devoted to the serious study of horror films and gothic literature. Its members gathered periodically for screenings of new vampire and horror films, highlighted for many years by the annual awards gathering at which the winner of the Ann Radcliffe Award was announced.

> Among the most active of fan organizations on the national level through the 1990s was the Vampire Information Exchange (VIE), founded by Eric Held and Dorothy Nixon in 1978....

In the 1980s, the Count Dracula Society was superseded by the Academy of Science Fiction, Fantasy and Horror Films, dedicated to honoring films and filmmakers in the several horror genres. The academy continues to host regular screenings of films (approximately 100 annually) and sponsors an annual awards ceremony, at which the Saturn Trophy is presented to winners in a variety of categories, including the best film in each of the three areas of prime concern (science fiction, fantasy, and horror) and an annual lifetime achievement award. The *Count Dracula Society Quarterly* (also known at various times as the *Castle Dracula Quarterly* and the *Gothick Gateway*), published by the society, was discontinued by the academy.

Among the most active of fan organizations on the national level through the 1990s was the Vampire Information Exchange (VIE), founded by Eric Held and Dorothy Nixon in 1978 as a correspondence network for people interested in vampirism. Nixon had been interested in vampires since her high school days,

when she was shown a copy of Donald Glut's *True Vampires of History*. She became interested in the question of the existence of real vampires and began a search that led her into association with Stephen Kaplan of the Vampire Research Center. Held was brought into the world of vampire fandom after listening to a radio interview of Kaplan in October 1978. The next day, he called Kaplan, who put him in touch with Nixon. During that phone conversation, they discovered their mutual interests. They began to correspond, and by October 1979, they had been joined by six others. At that point, Held and Nixon began an irregular newsletter to simplify the circulation of general information, thus initiating the Vampire Information Exchange. Among the early correspondents were Jeanne Youngson of the Count Dracula Fan Club (now the Vampire Empire); Gordon R. Guy, editor of the *Castle Dracula Quarterly*; and Martin V. Riccardo, then president of the Vampire Studies Society.

The now defunct *VIE Newsletter* was a bimonthly, informative journal for active members. It carried reviews of recent books and movies, news about vampire publications, and bibliographies of various kinds of vampire literature. For a time, Held also put out an annual calendar of vampire events and published *The Bibliography of Vampire Literature*.

Launched in 1991, *Vampire Junction* was a high-quality vampire fanzine devoted to the promotion of vampire fiction, poetry, and art. The editor, Candy M. Cosner, had been interested in vampires since her teen years, and her fascination with the subject resulted in a fanzine that was interesting and affordable. Cosner was also one of the first vampire aficionados to go online and, through the 1990s, devoted more and more of her time to communicating with people electronically. In the process, she began to build an expansive vampire information site online. She discontinued *Vampire Junction* as a fanzine, but her website may still be accessed at http://www.afn.org/~vampires.

The Dynamite Fan Club was a vampire horror fan club founded in 1991 by Mark Weber and Garry Paul, who served as president and vice president respectively. The primary activity of the club was the issuance of a quarterly *Horror Newsletter* that included a number of regular columns (including "From the Coffin" by Count Vamp), book and movie reviews, and a section of classified ads placed by club members who wanted to either sell something or meet other members who resided in their hometown. *Good Guys Wear Fangs* was a short-lived annual vampire fanzine dedicated to what founder/editor Mary Ann B. McKinnon termed good-guy vampires. In the mid-1970s, McKinnon, never a horror fan, discovered the novels of Chelsea Quinn Yarbro, whose vampire character, Saint Germain, was a romantic hero. McKinnon considered Yarbro as an isolated author and enjoyed most of her novels as they continued to appear through the 1980s. It was not until 1989, when she saw the made-for-television movie *Nick Knight* and, later, the two *To Die For* movies that McKinnon developed some hope that other good-guy vampire fiction existed. She decided to announce the development of a fanzine based on the theme of the vampire as a hero. The response to her announcement showed the vast interest and supporting material for her approach to vampirism.

The first copy of the 300-page *Good Guys Wear Fangs* appeared in 1992. It featured original short stories and poetry in which the vampire was the hero. By this time, *Forever Knight*, the television series that grew out of the *Nick Knight* television movie, was airing on CBS late-night television. The Nick Knight character

> The Dynamite Fan Club was a vampire horror fan club founded in 1991 by Mark Weber and Garry Paul, who served as president and vice president respectively.

was featured in *Good Guys Wear Fangs*. In 1993, McKinnon added a related periodical, the *Good Guy Vampire Letterzine*, a newsletter for good-guy vampire fans. The *Letterzine* kept fans aware of newly discovered good-guy vampire fiction and movies and carried an ongoing discussion on the nature of good-guy vampirism.

McKinnon has encouraged not only completely original fiction but new stories that feature popular characters from television and the movies. By far, the most popular character who appeared in *Good Guys Wear Fangs* was *Nick Knight*, but other stories have featured characters from *Starsky & Hutch*, *Columbo*, and *Dark Shadows*. Through the 1990s, McKinnon also produced a line of fanzines that included storylines built around the popular fictional characters Zorro, the Highlander, and Robin of Sherwood.

Gothica, whose first issue appeared in 1992, was a fanzine based upon the ideal of what is termed the Anne Rice vampire nature. It was founded by Susan M. Jensen, who became friends with a group of vampire horror movie fans in college in the late 1980s. The group, called the Drac Pac, gathered regularly to watch horror movies and, through them, explore the uncommon and the sublime. Although the group scattered after graduation, Jensen decided to begin a small magazine based on the ideas the Drac Pac had discussed. The first issue, in March 1992, produced only 16 copies. It increased to 35 copies in August 1993 and to several hundred by the end of the first year, but it was soon discontinued.

Loyalists of the Vampire Realm International Vampire Association is an international club founded in 1984 in Berlin, Germany, by a woman named Lucinda (the club's name being derived from her initials). It is solely dedicated to the "preservation and re-creation of all vampire styled art forms." It publishes a quarterly newsletter, *Jugular Vein*, that features the poetry, fiction, and graphic art of the club's members and thus provides them with an outlet for their own viewpoints on the vampire as opposed to those of an editor or paid staff. The Vampire Realm also offers a very limited pen pal service known as the Vampire Correspondence Network. New members are invited to fill out a lengthy questionnaire concerning their interests. The realm may be reached at https://www.facebook.com/LoyalistsOf-TheVampireRealm.

> Loyalists of the Vampire Realm International Vampire Association is an international club founded in 1984 in Berlin, Germany, by a woman named Lucinda....

Closely related to the Loyalists of the Vampire Realm was Vampires, Werewolves, Ghosts, and Other Such Things That Go Bump in the Night, an informal group of scholars and researchers who investigated vampires and related paranormal phenomena. The organization was founded in the early 1980s and worked quietly through the 1990s gathering and documenting accounts of individuals' encounters with vampires, werewolves, spirits of the dead, and demonic beings.

Midnight to Midnight, the Vampire Writers' Circle was founded in 1990 by Karen E. Dove, the High Priestess. Dove had a desire to create a more human vampire figure somewhat removed from the image of a bloodsucking monster or a fantastic superhuman creature. She also became aware of a type of organization operated by fantasy genre writers in which a shared fantasy world was created and each writer collaborated with the others and shared characters. She constructed an initial Midnight to Midnight universe of characters and circulated them to potential members of the circle.

As it evolved, Midnight to Midnight averaged fewer than ten members. Members had one basic rule: that they write and contribute to the circle at least once every two months. It was Dove's expectation that as writers come and go, the most serious ones would persevere and the circle would have been a means of their growth; in any case, all would have had an enjoyable experience.

The vampires of Midnight to Midnight shared a world very similar to those in the fanzine *Good Guys Wear Fangs*. They could not change shape or fly. They were not affected by holy objects such as the crucifix or by running water. Their night vision was not enhanced. However, they did cast a reflection in a mirror; they could live forever but were vulnerable to various dangers; they were nocturnal creatures but were not confined to the dark; sunlight burned them. Three kinds of vampire beings populated the Midnight to Midnight world. "Born" vampires are children of two vampires. They grow normally until their early twenties, when they cease to age. "Made" vampires are vampires created after a period of mortal life. They remain at the age they were when created. "Half vampires" are people born to one vampire and one mortal parent. They can live for many generations but eventually die of old age after several centuries.

The P. N. Elrod Fan Club, devoted to the writer of vampire fiction, was founded in 1993 by Jackie Black for Elrod's many fans. Elrod had burst onto the scene in 1990, when three novels under the collective title *The Vampire Files* were published by Ace Books. *Bloodlist*, *Lifeblood*, and *Bloodcircle* related the continuing story of reporter Jack Fleming, who had been turned into a vampire and then became a detective. The trilogy was well received, and three more volumes appeared in 1991 and 1992. Suddenly, Elrod joined that small circle of writers who identified with the vampire community. The club's newsletter grew into a substantial periodical, but in the new century, fan activity moved online.

The Vampirism Research Institute was a nonmembership research organization founded by Liriel McMahon, a musician and college student majoring in sociology. For several years, McMahon published the *Journal of Modern Vampirism*, and in 1993, the institute began a series of new publications and a program of sociological research. In 1992, inspired by Rosemary Guiley's *Vampires among Us* and with the cooperation of the Count Dracula Fan Club (now the Vampire Empire) and the Vampire Information Exchange, McMahon conducted a survey of vampire fans in which she asked about such matters as their belief in the existence of vampires and their opinions about people who claim to be vampires. Results of the survey were released in the summer of 1993. The institute also published a monograph entitled *Dysfunctional Vampire: A Theory from Personal History* and a compilation, *Best of the Journal of Modern Vampirism*. The Vampirism Research Institute continued into the new century but has more recently been discontinued.

The Munsters and the Addams Family Fan Club was founded in 1988 by Louis Wendruck for fans of *The Munsters* and *The Addams Family*, two popular television families of homey vampires and other friendly monsters. The club provided information about the television series, their movie spin-offs, and the stars who played the family members. The club distributed various items related to the shows and helped members locate and obtain the many other pieces of paraphernalia that have been produced featuring the Addams family and the Munsters. For a time, the club had an annual convention and published a quarterly newsletter, *The Munsters and the Addams Family Reunion*. Wendruck also presided over an unofficial Dark Shadows Fan Club and edited the *Dark Shadows Announcement*. The Dark Shadows Fan Club was independent of the larger scene of *Dark Shadows* fandom.

Vampire fandom, of the kind that produced fan clubs, peaked in the 1990s. Through that decade, numerous small clubs made a brief appearance under names such as Cheeky Devil Vampire Research, Club Vampyre, Dracula and Company, The Miss Lucy Westenra Society of the Undead, and the Secret Order of the Undead (SOUND). Even more numerous were a large number of short-lived fanzines and newsletters, including *Nefarious, Nightlore, Nox, Onyx: The "Literary" Vampire Magazine, Vampire Archives, Báthory Palace, Bloodlines: The Vampire Magazine*, and the *Realm of the Vampire*.

Beginning in the late 1990s, the more traditional format for fan clubs with their informally produced fanzines was abandoned as the internet became a more pervasive instrument for contacting and chatting with like-minded fans. Those fan clubs that did survive from the twentieth century into the twenty-first morphed into online-based (or, in a few cases, email-based) fan collectives. Very few fanzines continued to be published, and the larger fan conglomerates were taken up in both the marketing world and legal realm of large corporations.

The new world of fandom was amply illustrated by the emergence of *Buffy the Vampire Slayer*, the television show that came to dominate the scene at the end of the 1990s. A fan club arose, fan paraphernalia began to appear, and fans began to write fan fiction using the characters from the show. (Some limited concern was expressed by copyright and license holders of the infringement on their rights by fan fiction, especially the so-called slash fiction, which placed the characters in homoerotic situations.) As the show grew in popularity, a variety of licenses were issued for the production of everything from trading cards and T-shirts to cell phone covers and jewelry. An official fan club with a slick, professionally produced magazine (whose format followed one developed for a spectrum of other television shows) was organized, with its activities largely consisting of selling items to the fans. As the *Angel* fan club developed in parallel to the *Buffy* fan club, the same development and management of fandom occurred. As the fan scene began to decline and was no longer a viable marketing collective, the company managing the fan clubs first merged the *Buffy* and *Angel* clubs and then merged continuing fan interest into a collective of fans of the several television shows for which it had produced magazines.

Behind the more visible world of the official *Buffy* and *Angel* fan clubs, a more dedicated group of fans had emerged in the Los Angeles area that was able to attain access to the sets where the show was filmed and hold annual gatherings at which the stars frequently appeared. Fans were also able to meet with the stars of the show at various fan conventions that were held irregularly in North America and Europe.

By 2007, the fan scene around the *Twilight* books of Stephenie Meyer was clearly on the upswing, and by 2009, after the first movie had appeared, more than 250 fan sites (in English) had appeared online, with additional sites in French, Italian, German, and Spanish. All appeared to consist of a few friends of the person creating the site and an internet collective. The sites contained pictures of the book covers and of the stars of the movies and pictures of the fans but were largely limited to supplying space for the fans (overwhelmingly teenage females) to express their feelings about the show. News was at a minimum, as was information on fan paraphernalia, both being readily available elsewhere online. Information about the movies was concentrated on the official movie site hosted by Summit Entertainment. Information on fan paraphernalia (clothing, posters, toys, room accessories, candy) was concentrated at the site of NECA, which produced it. Both the movie sites and the NECA site had links to Amazon's retail site. Borders Books maintained a space for *Twilight* items (books, posters, trading cards, and related paraphernalia) at all its stores, held gatherings for *Twilight* fans, and published special exclusive editions of *Twilight* books and movies. Fan conventions and the appearances of *Twilight* stars were under the direction of Creation Entertainment, which had, for example, scheduled *Twilight* conventions through 2010 in cities across the United States where fans could, for a price, briefly meet the stars and obtain autographs.

Similar websites were developed by the producers of recent popular television series *True Blood* (HBO), developed from the writings of Charlaine Harris, and *The Vampire Diaries*, developed from the books of Lisa Jane Smith. The official site for the show included a fan site and a merchandising page.

Among the most active creator of vampire-oriented fan sites online was John T. Folden, who also operated as the JTF Network. He created sites devoted to a spectrum of television shows, including *True Blood, Moonlighting, Dark Shadows, Being Human*, and *The Vampire Diaries* (as well as a number of non-vampire shows). Each site was informative, contained a number of pictures, and emphasized the purchasing of fan paraphernalia.

> Among the most active creator of vampire-oriented fan sites online was John T. Folden, who also operated as the JTF Network.

Meanwhile, a new generation of vampire fan clubs and interest groups have also appeared online. They present a massive and bewildering array of interests within the ever-growing vampire realm and grade into the new organizations that serve the so-called real or self-identified vampires.

Some sites are quite general and provide information and news on the vampire fan scene, some are devoted to one or more of the older movie or television series (from the Hammer Films movies to *Forever Knight* to *Vampire Hunter D*), and some are limited to Dracula, vampire movies, or the writings of Anne Rice. Rice's main fan club, which was disbanded when her religious life was revived, was re-opened after the Katrina hurricane devastated New Orleans as a means of helping the city rebuild economically.

⚜ *Vampire: The Eternal Struggle* ⚜

The success of White Wolf's *Vampire: The Masquerade*, the popular role-playing game created by Mark Rein-Hagen in 1991, suggested to Richard Garfield of Wizards of the Coast the possibility of its adaptation as a card game. As the role-playing game *Dungeons & Dragons* had been a great success in the 1980s, the card game *Magic: The Gathering* (also from Wizards of the Coast) had become the new phenomenon of the early 1990s. On the heels of completing *Magic*, Garfield met with Rein-Hagen, who was a player of *Magic*, and opened discussions of creating a vampire-based card game version. Garfield's staff began designing cards and adapting the concept to the new format.

Originally released as *Jyhad* in 1994, a reference to the battles going on inside the vampire community, the new card game pitted several older vampires, called Methuselahs, against each other. These hidden figures, who never show themselves, manipulate the more public vampires of the contemporary vampire community in order to accomplish their goals, including the destruction of other Methuselahs. In the game, usually played at midnight, the Methuselahs seek the control of vampire society, which means using the minion that the player controls to destroy the influence of the other Methuselahs over their minions. Working through Machiavellian political action and using cunning in the face of various conspiracies, the successful player gains influence in the form of blood counters while others lose theirs. When a player runs out of influence (blood counters), he or she must leave the game.

Jyhad was slow to take off, in part due to its adult theme and in part due to some level of confusion in the original version. As with *Vampire: The Masquerade*, *Jyhad* required the new player to master the rather detailed world of the vampire, including its vampire clans and their varying attributes and the nature of vampiric power. Thus, Wizards of the Coast redesigned the game, streamlining the rules for beginners, and reissued it as *Vampire: The Eternal Struggle*, with a 437-card deck. The deck included cards for vampires, the Methuselah's primary minions; equipment cards to be given to the minions to increase their effectiveness; reaction cards to block another's action; and political action cards, concerning the political ploys tried by a Methuselah. The cards used in play are also designed as artistic works, much as modern trading cards are, and hence also function as tradable and collectible items. As with *Magic*, individual cards are designated as common, uncommon, and rare, and those more difficult to obtain assume an enhanced value.

As *Vampire: The Eternal Struggle* took off, Wizards of the Coast quickly issued three expansion sets: *Dark Sovereigns* (1995), *Ancient Hearts* (1995), and *The Sabbat* (1996). New expansion sets have subsequently been issued regularly. Lists of cards and info on new expansion sets can be found at White Wolf's website, https://www.worldofdarkness.com.

The popular fantasy card game Magic: The Gathering *helped inspire the vampire role playing game* Vampire: The Masquerade, *which later became the foundation for a new card game* Vampire: The Eternal Struggle.

🦇 *Vampire: The Masquerade* 🦇

Vampire: The Masquerade is a popular role-playing game introduced in 1991 by creator Mark Rein-Hagen of White Wolf Game Studio. It quickly challenged the popularity of *Dungeons & Dragons*, the original role-playing game, and itself became the basis of several other horror role-playing games based on the *Werewolf* and *Wraith* games and a role-playing card game, *Vampire: The Eternal Struggle* (originally named *Jyhad*). From the beginning, the game presented a completely alternate worldview, the fantasy into which the player enters, a world in which vampires and other creatures of horror such as ghouls and werewolves populate the landscape. The popularity of the game, however, has allowed for its expansion and the development of different aspects of the fantasy world in great detail.

Role-playing games are built around a storyteller, who begins a story in which all of the players are characters. As the story unfolds, the players become active participants and their actions have consequences for winning and losing. Players of *Vampire: The Masquerade* enter the fantasy world by creating a character (numerous suggestions are given in the literature published to support the game), a vampire or, possibly, a werewolf or ghoul minion, and, during the game, they assume and act as that character along with all of the other characters who inhabit the local vampire community. In the world of this role-playing game, a community of vampires exists incognito within the space otherwise inhabited by humans. Since they closely resemble humans and thus have little problem passing as such, they can come out at night and comingle, especially when they are in search of food. However, mostly they move among themselves. An organized vampire society exists whose power is held by older vampires, the majority of whom have withdrawn into their solitude. The more visible society is highly politicized, and power is the valued commodity. Thus, most stories concern the jockeying for power among the players.

> *Vampire: The Masquerade* began as the table game *Vampire*, in which a small group of players gathered to listen to a storyteller and periodically stopped action to interact....

Vampire: The Masquerade began as the table game *Vampire*, in which a small group of players gathered to listen to a storyteller and periodically stopped action to interact, the consequences of the player's acts being determined by a throw of the dice. Players had a supply of blood, and when their acts led to a complete loss of blood, they lost. However, the game continued to evolve, and in 1993, Rein-Hagen introduced the live-action version of the game, *The Masquerade*. This version freed the game from delays caused by the use of dice, which were replaced with a series of hand signals. The new form of the game, termed LARP or live-action role-playing, allowed players to remain in character during virtually all of the game and vastly expanded the number of people who can play at one time. As currently played as *Vampire: The Masquerade*, as many as 20 or more players can for several hours each enter a new persona and act out a situation presented to him or her or carry over play from the last session. A local playing group will usually gather to play at midnight on a predetermined day once or twice a month.

At present, the typical game is set in the local community, and the players assume a position in the local vampire society. A prince serves as the nominal head of the community, and the vampires identify with one of several clans, each clan having its own particular characteristics and local leaders. Overall, the members of the community must keep up the Masquerade, that is, perpetuate the idea among humans that vampires are a thing of the past, a myth best sold as the scientific conclusion that vampires never really existed. Breaching the rules of secrecy brings the wrath of the community down upon a vampire. It is also the assumption of the game that the Masquerade is currently threatened by the current youth culture. Mind-altering drugs, rock music, and the popularity of the vampire image in Western culture have opened large segments of the public to the possibility that the vampire exists, and many people even view vampiric existence as a desirable life they would assume if only it were possible. A second threat is posed by the new generation gap between the older vampires, who originally conceived the Masquerade and have enforced its existence, and a brash younger generation of new vampires, who are seen as acting in such a way as to call human attention to vampire society.

As a sophisticated role-playing game, *Vampire: The Masquerade* assumes the following vampire myth: Succinctly stated, vampire society originated with Cain (the cursed brother introduced in the Bible in the fourth chapter of Genesis). According to the game, the curse was that he was made into a vampire. After wandering in the wilderness for many years, he settled down and created a city. He also created other vampires, the second generation, who in turn created a third generation. They built a city. The city was destroyed by a flood, and the survivors of the third generation scattered around the world. Whether or not Cain or any of the second generation survived is unknown. Various individuals of the third generation would become the originating vampire of the bloodlines that would later become the clans. The vampires of the fourth and fifth generations have largely withdrawn from any involvement in the larger vampire community.

The bulk of the presently existing vampires constitute the sixth generation, and they face pressure to create no more vampires, as it is believed that the blood thins (the vampiric powers diminish) as each generation from Cain is created. The vampire clans originated from the banding together of the children (new generations) of the third generation, who found in their physical relationship shared characteristics of the one who originated the bloodline. Enlightened self-interest became a reason to organize more or less loosely and create a clan ethos. Seven major clans exist: the Brujah, the youthful rebels; the Gangrel, the wanderers; the somewhat insane Malkavian; the rodentlike Nosferatu; the Toreador, often described as hedonists; the Tremere, the best organized of the vampires; and the Ventrue, the most human of the vampires. Also, other clans exist who are not members of the Camarilla, such as the Assamite and the Giovanni, plus the Caitiff, or clanless, vampires. The latter are usually the result of having been abandoned by those who made them vampires. The clans are at the heart of the political intrigues of the vampire community.

In the middle of the fifteenth century, the Inquisition wreaked havoc on the Kindred, and whole bloodlines were stamped out (put to the true death in fire). At about the same time, some of the youthful vampires, who were being used as a barrier between the elders and the Inquisition, rose in revolt. The revolt of the Anarchs spread. This period of attack drove the survivors completely underground. In 1486 at a global convocation, a secret worldwide network, the Camarilla, was established. It established a rule of law for the community of vampires. Within the community are some powerful individual vampires called Justicars, who have been granted the power to punish lawbreakers. Vampires are largely urban dwellers, and currently, each major city supports a vampire community. It is headed by a prince,

and any vampire changing locations is expected to present him- or herself to the prince of their new city (or alternate authority where no prince has been designated, as in Los Angeles).

According to the game's myth, the elder vampires have more powers than newer ones. For both old and young, the stake is hurtful, producing a form of paralysis, but, by itself, is not fatal. Sunlight and fire are the main dangers. Holy objects have no effect nor does running water. The vampire has sharpened senses that aid them in hunting, including the power to impose their will on mortals. The elder vampires can change shapes, but most of the newer ones cannot. New vampires can be created by first having their blood drained and then receiving some of the vampire's blood, although the new vampire has slightly less power than that of the vampire who created him or her. Vampires no longer breathe, although they can fake respiration. The heart no longer beats, the blood consumed spreads through the body by osmosis rather than through the old artery/vein system. It carries the necessary oxygen. The vampire heals quickly from most wounds.

Vampire: The Masquerade has continued to evolve. In 2004, it was basically superseded by a new version of the game, *Vampire: The Requiem*, which kept the basic myth and playing structure but offers a variety of modifications, such as revamping the clan structure. It emphasized five clans—the Daeva, the Gangrel, the Mekhet, Nosferatu, and the Ventrue—as well as a set of new, nonclan groups. All add new storylines and variety to the play. *Vampire: The Requiem* was immediately incorporated into World of Darkness, by which the various fictional storylines of the several White Wolf horror-based games are related. A new World of Darkness text was issued simultaneously with the initial *Vampire: The Requiem* text in 2004. *Vampire: The Requiem* was also

> Unwittingly, *Vampire: The Masquerade* became the environment for the emergence of the new real vampire community.

an integral part of the *Mind's Eye Theatre*, the name given to the live-action role-playing (or LARP) version of White Wolf's various games.

Unwittingly, *Vampire: The Masquerade* became the environment for the emergence of the new real vampire community. In the 1990s, hundreds of people who self-identified as real vampires (among the thousands who simply played the game) found their way to the Camarilla, the game's fan club, and emerged as leaders. Possibly the most notable, Michelle Belanger in Ohio and Father Sebastiaan in New York City, were active for several years in the gaming world, which provided a context to meet other real vampires and out of which some of the early real vampire organizations emerged in the mid-1990s. The Camarilla has transformed over the years and suffered greatly in the middle of the first decade of the new century when, for a period, White Wolf viewed it primarily as a tool for marketing new products. Meanwhile, as the World of Darkness has expanded, a vast literature has emerged to support the game. Literally hundreds of books exist with suggestive new plots for the game's storytellers and a host of novels derived from White Wolf's vampire universe.

In 1996, Rod Ferrell, who had played the game in Kentucky, came to see himself as a real vampire and put together a small group of people who more or less believed him. The group was responsible for the murder of the parents of Ferrell's girlfriend in Florida. They became the subject of a highly publicized trial that became a watershed moment for both White Wolf and the emerging real vampire community. White Wolf moved to distance itself from any real vampire-like contact and emphasized its entertainment focus. The new rules enforced in the wake of the Ferrell case worked for the new community of self-identified vampires, who discovered that they no longer needed the LARP world. Enough real vampires had surfaced that they could operate on their own quite apart from the vampire gaming world (or other vampire interest groups).

🦇 *Vampire Weekend (rock band)* 🦇

Vampire Weekend is a rock band based in New York City that was assembled by students from Columbia University. It grew out of an initial collaboration between Ezra Koenig and Chris Tomson and took its name from a film project upon which Koenig worked the summer following his freshman year. He had viewed *The Lost Boys* (a 1987 vampire film that is set in a California town on the Pacific Ocean) and decided that he wanted to make a similar film based in the northeast United States. He envisioned a story set on Cape Cod in which the hero, Walcott, makes his way to the seaside community to warn the mayor of a vampire infestation. Koenig never brought the short-lived project to fruition.

While inspired by a vampire film, Vampire Weekend has made its reputation from its mixture of punk rock and a variety of world musical sounds. It received critical acclaim from the time of its first album, *Vampire Weekend* (2008), and has gone on to win Grammy Awards in 2013 for *Modern Vampires of the City* and in 2019 for *Father of the Bride*.

(Left to right) Edgar (Corey Feldman), Sam Emerson (Corey Haim), and Alan (Jamison Newlander) devise a plan to sneak into the vampire hideout and kill the ghouls in their sleep.

🦇 *Vampirella* 🦇

Warren Publications pioneered the black-and-white comic book magazine format in the 1960s as a means of, among other goals, skirting the restrictions of the Comics Code, which had been adopted by the industry in 1954. The code was very harsh on horror comics and specifically banned vampires, werewolves, ghouls, and zombies. Following the format established in *Famous Monsters of Filmland,* Warren successfully introduced two new horror comics, *Creepy* and *Eerie,* in 1964 and 1965, respectively. Both were successful, and both carried vampire stories. They set the stage for the introduction in 1969 of *Vampirella,* a new vampire-oriented comic, and *Dark Shadows,* issued by Gold Key, the first two

vampire comics since the adoption of the Comics Code in 1954.

Vampirella, a character developed by Forrest J. Ackerman, was somewhat different. She was, first of all, a woman, and female vampires had been rare in comic books, especially in starring roles. Second, she was not of the undead; rather, she was from outer space. According to the storyline, she was a native of the planet Drakulon, a dying planet where blood had replaced water as the life-sustaining liquid. Vampirella had come to Earth, where she could get a steady supply of blood to survive. She was pictured as a beautiful, dark-haired, young woman (late teens to early twenties), with a scanty costume that hid little of her voluptuous body. Barbarella, a character developed by French artist Jean-Claude Forest and the subject of a motion picture by Roger Vadim, was the direct inspiration for Vampirella, whose red costume had a gold bat insignia just below her navel. When she smiled, her two extended canine teeth were prominently displayed. She also had the ability to change into a bat. Vampirella was impish as well as sexy. She engaged in a constant search for blood (or its equivalent), but she was the heroine and, hence, did not take life without reason. She was always mournful about the choices that her own survival often pressed upon her.

Through the years of her existence on Earth, the story of Vampirella's origin has been retold on several occasions and left her with several very distinct accounts of her origin. In the early stories, her origin was described very

Vampirella creator Forrest J. Ackerman was actually won of the founders of the science fiction fandom alongside such great names as Isaac Asimov and A. E. Van Vogt.

superficially. She was from a planet in which blood was like water on Earth. It was present abundantly in rivers and streams. However, the blood source was being threatened by the double suns around which Drakulon whirled. Vampirella had grown up on Drakulon and was engaged to a young man, Tristan. Like other vampires, she exhaled carbon monoxide. Over the centuries, the carbon monoxide in the atmosphere had broken down the protective layer, made of creatone, which protected the residents of the surface from the most harmful rays coming from their suns. The planet was now dying. Vampirella had an opportunity to escape when a spaceship from Earth arrived. She discovered that the veins of the crew's bodies provided the life-giving fluid she needed. She killed to survive and then took the spaceship to Earth.

Vampirella was a superheroine vampire who first appeared in Vampirella *#1 in September 1969.*

In the 1974 story "The Vampire of the Nile," Vampirella's pre-Drakulon career was explored and traced to ancient Egypt. As Cleopatra, she had been summoned to the temple of her husband (and brother) Ptolemy to consummate their marriage. As soon as she entered his temple, she was grabbed and shackled to a large column. Out of a crypt in front of the column, the vampire-king arose and bit Cleopatra. She became the enchantress of popular history, a tragic career broken only by a brief affair with her true love, Mark Antony After Anthony died, she again entered the vampire temple and staked Ptolemy. Suddenly, the god Amun-Ra appeared. He could not remove her vampiric condition but rewarded her by promising her reincarnation on Drakulon. Thus, she quickly moved to commit suicide with the poisonous snake.

Vampirella on Earth: Vampirella arrived on Earth in 1969. She needed blood daily and became a huntress for the blood within humans. However, soon after her arrival, she was involved in an airplane crash, after which she was taken to a rural clinic for the wealthy. The doctor who rescued her also fell in love with her. More importantly, he created a synthesized blood substitute, which freed Vampirella from her need to attack humans. Unfortunately, the doctor's nurse was a disciple of Chaos, the evil force that continually infringes upon the orderly universe and became jealous of the doctor's feelings for Vampirella. She carried *The Crimson Chronicles*, the bible of the believers of Chaos, and below the clinic was a temple where Chaos's worshippers gathered. Here, Vampirella would have her first encounter with Chaos and be taken prisoner by his followers.

Meanwhile, two experts in the ways of evil supernaturalism, Conrad Van Helsing and his son Adam, were investigating the plane crash in which Vampirella was involved. Conrad's brother was also on the plane, and his body was found drained of blood. With pictures of four people on the flight whose bodies were not found, the somewhat psychic Conrad spotted Vampirella as the odd entity and con-

cluded that she had killed his brother. The pair tracked down Vampirella, who was being held prisoner by the leader of the Chaos followers, who wanted Vampirella to make him a vampire. After the Van Helsings arrived, he also took them as prisoners. While Conrad lay unconscious, Vampirella told her story to Adam, who became convinced that she was not guilty of his uncle's death. Vampirella finally broke free of her chains and, having been starved, was about to feed from Adam as Conrad awoke. What he saw merely confirmed his opinion of Vampirella. They escaped and went their separate ways. Vampirella fed off her willing captor, but he did not become a vampire, as her bite could not transmit vampirism.

Vampirella found a job as the assistant to an aging magician and alcoholic, Pendragon. Their first tour took them to the Caribbean. Shipwrecked on an island, they encountered a man attempting to find a serum to cure his wife of werewolfism. He took Vampirella pris-

Underground comix artist Trina Robbins drew the voluptuous Vampirella.

oner to use her as a guinea pig. Meanwhile, Adam showed up, and together, they extricated themselves from the situation.

Conrad had also come to the island to look for Adam and was taken prisoner on Cote de Soleil by the followers of Chaos. Pendragon, Adam, and Vampirella conspired to free him. Once they escaped, Conrad's opinion of Vampirella began to change, but it was not revised until together they tracked the real killers of Conrad's brother to a group of Chaos's followers in New Orleans. Once their relationship was established, the four would have numerous adventures through the 1970s. The emergence of the Van Helsings, tied as they were to Bram Stoker's *Dracula* (1897), signaled the eventual return of its main character as well, one of the most interesting revisions of the Dracula myth. Awakened in the contemporary world, a cosmic being known as the Conjuress sent Dracula back to the 1890s to undo some of the damage he had done and reverse the process that made him a vampire. Vampirella joined him through the device of a magic mirror. In their initial conversation, Dracula revealed that he too was from Drakulon. He began to use magic to solve the planet's problems but contacted Chaos instead of accomplishing his task. Chaos had originally forced him to Earth. Vampirella agreed to help him redeem himself.

As Dracula and Vampirella met all of the principal characters from *Dracula*, the novel, Dracula's basic problem was to find some way to stave off his bloodthirst. After Lucy Westenra was resurrected when the stake was pulled from her heart (her decapitation being ignored), Dracula remembered his love for her. He was able to keep from biting Lucy but could not restrain himself when it came to Mina Murray. Lucy saw him attack Mina and dropped dead. In spite of Vampirella's help, the Conjuress pro-

nounced Dracula a failure, and he was taken out of the storyline for the moment. The first issue of *Vampirella* appeared in September 1969. Forrest Ackerman was the first writer, and the soon-to-be-famous Frank Franzetta was the original artist. The original team was filled out by Trina Robbins and Tom Sutton. Ackerman was followed by Archie Godwin and a host of different writers over the years, most notably John Cochran, T. Casey Brennan, and Steve Englehart (under the pseudonym Chad Archer). Franzetta and Sutton were later succeeded by José Gonzales, with whom the image of Vampirella became most identified.

> *Vampirella* became (and, as of 2020, remains) the longest-running English-language vampire comic book of all time, its last issue (No. 112) appearing in February 1983.

Vampirella became (and, as of 2020, remains) the longest-running English-language vampire comic book of all time, its last issue (No. 112) appearing in February 1983. Meanwhile, in the mid-1970s, Ron Goulart had produced a series of six *Vampirella* novels adapted from the comic book storyline. In the late 1980s in the atmosphere of reviving interest in vampires, Harris Comics acquired *Vampirella* and, in 1988, issued a single issue (No. 113) following the old Warren Comics format. Three years later, Harris Comics launched its new *Vampirella* program with reissues of the old Vampirella stories in a new format and the creation of new Vampirella stories, the first of which appeared in a four-part series written by Kurt Busiek. Busiek picked up the story of Vampirella after her disappearance in the final Warren issue. Busiek also wrote the first of the Harris stories to appear in color the following year. In the 1990s, under Harris's guidance, a number of writers have taken up the challenge of writing Vampirella; however, Thomas Sniegoski is usually given the credit of remolding her as a 1990s bad girl, a totally feminine creature who can nevertheless function as a superhero for the youthful readership. In the process of producing the 25-issue series *Vengeance of Vampirella*, he

also re-created the myth underlying Vampirella's existence. In a storyline called "The Mystery Walk," Vampirella's extraterrestrial origin was put aside for a mythological one. Lilith, the first wife of Adam in Hebrew folklore, sought to earn forgiveness from the God of Order. After her creation, she rejected Adam. She was expelled from Eden. In her rage, she hated God, and her hatred took on form as the *lilin* who, in turn, spread evil in the world God created. She finally decided to return to the light and forced herself back into Eden, a place neglected since Adam and Eve had been expelled.

As the twenty-first century gains steam, Vampirella remains one of the most influential vampire characters in the literary realm.

In Eden, Lilith initiated her plan for her own redemption that began with caring for the garden. She then created the twins Magdelene and Madek and sent them into the world to undo the evil that had resulted from Lilith's hatred. The plan backfired, and the twins merely created more evil. Vampirella was created to defeat the twins and then pick up the mission of opposing the world's evil. Before going into the world, she was trained to master the dark side that resided within her, which was inherited from Lilith. The Sniegoski reworking of *Vampirella* has launched a new career for Vampirella and kept her comic books regularly among the best selling in the industry.

The *Vampirella* Movie (1996): Through the years, plans were announced and rumors circulated about a *Vampirella* movie. Model/actress Barbara Leigh was designated as the future star of a movie to be produced in the 1970s, and her picture appeared on the cover of a number of *Vampirella* comic books. However, it was not until the mid-1990s that a movie actually was shot. In the made-for-television movie, directed by Jim Wynorski, Vampirella's origin took a more sinister science fiction turn. In ancient time, people of Drakulon would attack and drain the blood from each other. They had arisen to a point where such behavior was

no longer acceptable. Then, approximately 3,000 years ago, a new cult led by Vlad (Roger Daltrey) and a small cadre of people arose on Drakulon. They plotted revolution. Vlad was arrested and was to be tried. During his audience before Drakulon's council, an escape team arrived, and they and Vlad killed all of the members of the council. Vlad himself drank from Vampirella's father. Determined to bring her father's killers to justice, Vampirella (Talisa Soto) followed them to Earth on a returning Mars probe. The journey took 3,000 years. Once on Earth, she made common cause with Adam van Helsing, the head of a vampire eradication agency, and together, they tracked down Vlad and his minions.

In 2009, Vampirella celebrated her 40th anniversary at the Vampire-Con in Los Angeles, at which a new Vampirella model was selected. As the twenty-first century gains steam, Vampirella remains one of the most influential vampire characters in the literary realm. She had been the subject of multiple trading card sets, six novels (by Ron Goulart), over 300 comic book issues, several model statues, and one movie. The comics have been translated into more than a dozen languages, including most of the European languages and several in Asia. Harris continued to employ a spectrum of top comic writers and artists that attracted new fans and revived interest in the older fans. In the wake of the revived interest in Vampirella in the 1990s, Harris Comics organized a fan club, the Vampirella Scarlet Legion, which provides an avenue for fans to share their enthusiasm and through which Harris offered a number of Vampirella premiums and limited editions not otherwise available to the public. After 40 years, Vampirella was more popular than ever.

Having first appeared in 1969, Vampirella is now seen as the original "good-guy vampire," whose lineage would be traced forward from the comic to the novels of Chelsea Quinn Yarbro and Fred Saberhagen to the hundreds of romance and young-adult novels of the present to the very successful television characters such as Nick Knight, Angel, Henry Fitzroy (created by Tanya Huff), and the principal characters of the *Twilight* novels and movies of Stephenie Meyer.

In 2019, Vampirella celebrated her 50th anniversary. This occasion was marked with a new volume delineating the vampire's pilgrimage over the past decade, *From the Stars … A Vampiress* by Steven Roman; a Vampirella 50th-anniversary art book; and new reprint editions of the classic *Vampirella* comics from the Warren era.

Vampires Everywhere! (rock band)

Vampires Everywhere! was an early twenty-first-century horror punk/gothic rock band (2009 to 2016). Like another rock band, Vampire Weekend, its name was inspired by the movie *The Lost Boys* (1987). The band was founded in 2009 in Los Angeles by singer Michael Orlando, who assumed the stage name Michael Vampire. He took the band's name from a comic book that appears in the movie. The comic book lists the rules that vampires must follow and explains how to kill them.

Unlike the other recent bands that indicated a relationship to vampires in their name, Vampires Everywhere! has manifested an interest in vampire lore in its music. Their first album (2010) was called *Lost in the Shadows* and included songs such as "Immortal Love" and "Undead Heat." Their next albums were entitled *Kiss the Sun Goodbye* (2011) and *The Hellbound and Heartless* (2012). The band disbanded in 2013 and reorganized as The Killing Lights only to again take the name Vampires Everywhere! in 2015. Vampires Everywhere! permanently disbanded. Subsequently, in 2016, Michael Vampire started a new band, which took the name Dead Girls Academy.

Michael Vampire was quoted in a 2013 interview as saying, "We didn't get inspired by *Twilight* or *True Blood* at all. I love *True Blood* and own season 1, but all of our influences come from the classics. By classics, I mean *The Lost Boys*, *Nosferatu*, Bram Stoker's *Dracula*, Bela Lugosi, *Fright Night*, and more."

Wolfman, Marv (1946–)

Marv Wolfman, the writer for Marvel Comics's *The Tomb of Dracula*, was the comic book world's most prolific writer of vampire stories in the last decades of the twentieth century. He grew up in Brooklyn and Flushing, New York, and, while in high school, he became interested in comic books. He was intrigued by a fanzine called *Alter Ego*, produced by future cartoonist Roy Thomas (who would go on to produce the graphic art version of *Bram Stoker's Dracula*), and subsequently produced several of his own. He attended Queens College in the 1960s as an art major, during which time he wrote and sold his first stories for comic books.

Following graduation, he taught school on Long Island for a year and landed a job with a comic book house as an assistant editor. One of the earliest stories he wrote was for Skywald Publishers's *Psycho*, a black-and-white comic magazine. At the beginning of 1973—a year and a half and one job later—Wolfman moved to Marvel (where Roy Thomas was an editor) and was assigned the task of writing for *The Tomb of Dracula*, already in its sixth issue.

Working with artist Gene Colan, Wolfman turned it into one of the longest-running vampire series in American comic book history. At the time he took over the series, he had little background or interest in vampires or Dracula and got started by a first reading of Bram Stoker's novel. While doing the series, he created the characters Blade the Vampire Slayer, Frank Drake, Rachel Van Helsing, Quincy Harker, and Hannibal King, most of whom, especially Blade, continue to this day in Marvel Comics. At the same time, he assumed duties for Marvel's black-and-white magazine *Dracula Lives!*, he was the primary writer for *Werewolf by Night*, and he wrote additional stories for other black and whites *Marvel Preview* and *Vampire Tales*. Wolfman left Marvel in 1979, and *The Tomb of Dracula*, which had become a black-and-white magazine, was soon discontinued. He became a senior editor at DC Comics in 1980, where he worked on a variety of projects throughout the 1980s. Most notably, he created the second series for which he has become best known, *Team Titans*, the story of a group of teenage superheroes, including Nightrider, a vampire. The series won a number of awards and became one of DC's top sellers until the series was turned over to others, in whose hands it languished.

Since leaving DC as an editor in 1987, Wolfman has worked on a variety of projects for different companies. In 1990, he wrote the four-part vampire-oriented *R.I.P. Comics Module* for TSR, Inc., which was then developing its vampire role-playing game *Ravenloft*. A year later, he teamed with his old colleague Gene Colan to produce a four-part sequel to *The Tomb of Dracula* (Marvel was just beginning its brief vampire revival), which brought the characters (Dracula,

Frank Drake, and Blade) up to the 1990s. Frequently overlooked among Wolfman's credits is the spoof on his Marvel series, which he did in the final issue of the *Goofy* comic book, *The Tomb of Goofula*, one of the very few vampire stories ever to appear in a Walt Disney production in North America. (Wolfman served as an editor at Disney for four years, from 1990 to 1994.) In the 1990s, with fellow TV writer Craig Miller, Wolfman formed Wolfmill Entertainment, a company dedicated to creating quality children's television programming. The company's first production, *Pocket Dragon Adventures*, an animation series for the Bohbot Kids Network, premiered in 1996 and ran for 52 episodes.

In the later 1990s, Marvel worked to bring Wolfman's character, Blade the Vampire Slayer, to the screen in a film starring Wesley Snipes. It was successful enough to lead to two sequels. In 1999, Wolfman sued Marvel Characters, Inc., and its licensing partners, attempting to gain ownership of the characters he created while an employee at the company. Marvel, like most other companies at the time,

Award-winning writer Marv Wolfman was behind The Tomb of Dracula *comic books, creating the character of Blade as well. He has also been acclaimed for* The New Teen Titans.

considered itself the owner of such characters. In the trial, which was held November 15–17, 1999, Wolfman attempted to argue that since he owned the characters, Marvel could not license characters such as Blade to motion picture companies. Unfortunately for Wolfman, the court ruled in Marvel's favor.

Through the first decades of the twenty-first century, Wolfman has remained active but has rarely returned to the vampire themes in his work. He maintains a website at http://www.marvwolfman.com/marv/frontpage.html.

Youngson, Jeanne Keyes (1924–)

Dr. Jeanne Keyes Youngson, founder of the Vampire Empire (originally the Count Dracula Fan Club), was born in Syracuse, New York, the daughter of Margaret E. Gardiner and Dr. Kenneth W. Keyes. She received her education at Franklin Junior College (Lugano, Switzerland), Maryville College (Tennessee), the Sorbonne (Paris), and New York University (New York City). She later taught extension courses in literature for USC at both Oxford and Cambridge in England.

In 1960, she married Robert G. Youngson, a renowned movie producer and historian, and that same year, she launched a career as an independent filmmaker, winning numerous prizes as an animator. She also produced medical documentaries, including *My Name Is Debbie*, about the life of a postoperative male-to-female transsexual. The film is still being shown at gender identity conferences in tandem with a Canadian documentary featuring the actual operation.

The idea for a Dracula club came to Youngson in 1965 while on a trip to Romania.

Club headquarters were set up in London, England, and New York City upon her return, and by the beginning of the 1970s, the club had become a growing concern. In the meantime, she found it necessary to give up filmmaking in order to devote her energies to the Dracula and Bram Stoker genres.

For the next 45 years, she oversaw the development of the Count Dracula Fan Club (renamed the Vampire Empire), which became a large, international organization with 15 active divisions that she mainly initiated. She also acted, for ten years, as curator for the society's Dracula Museum, which is now located in Vienna, Austria. As of 2020, the Vampire Empire cut back its programming and currently serves only as a research facility.

Prior to her retirement, Youngson wrote over 40 books, pamphlets, and brochures, both fact and fiction, on horror and fantasy themes and, in 2009, reorganized the extensive club research library, which is available to registered club members under contract to a publisher.

FURTHER READING

Abbott, G. F. *Macedonian Folklore*. Chicago: Argonaut, Inc., Publishers, 1986.

Abbott, Stacey, ed. *Reading Angel: The TV Spin-off with a Soul*. London: I. B. Tauris, 2005.

"About the Romance Genre." Romance Writers of America. http://www.rwanational.org/cs/the_romance_genre. Accessed April 11, 2010.

Adams, Michael. *Slayer Slang: A Buffy the Vampire Slayer Lexicon*. Oxford: Oxford University Press, 2003.

Adrian, Lara. *The Midnight Breed Series Companion*. Lara Adrian LLC, 2013.

Amano, Yoshitaka. *The Art of Vampire Hunter D: Bloodlust*. Screenplay by Yoshiaki Kawajiri. San Diego: IDW Publishing, July 2006.

———. *Coffin: The Art of Vampire Hunter D*. Milwaukie, OR: DH Press, 2007.

———. *The Collected Art of Vampire Hunter D*. Milwaukie. OR: Dark Horde Books, 2007.

Ambrogio, Anthony. *Peter Cushing*. Austin, TX: Luminary Press, 2009.

Ambrose, Kate. *Spirits of New Orleans: Voodoo Curses, Vampire Legends and Cities of the Dead*. Covington, KY: Clerisy Press, 2012.

Amy-Chin, Dee. and Milly Williamson, eds. "The Vampire Spike in Text and Fandom: Unsettling Oppositions in Buffy the Vampire Slayer." *European Journal of Cultural Studies* 8, 3 (August 2005).

Anatol, Giselle Liza. *Bringing Light to Twilight: Perspectives on a Pop Culture Phenomenon*. New York: Palgrave Macmillan, 2011.

Anglo, Michael. *Penny Dreadfuls and Other Victorian Horrors*. London: Jupiter, 1977.

Anne Rice: A Reader's Checklist and Reference Guide. Middletown, CT: CheckerBee. 1999.

Anyiwo, U. Melissa, ed. *Race in the Vampire Narrative*. Rotterdam: Sense, 2015.

———, and Amanda Hobson, eds. *Gender Warriors: Reading Contemporary Urban Fantasy*. Rotterdam: Sense, 2018.

———, and Amanda Hobson. *Queering the Vampire Narrative*. Leiden: Brill Publishers. 2021.

Arata, Stephen D. "The Occidental Tourist: Dracula and the Anxiety of Reverse Colonization." *Victorian Studies* 33, 4 (Summer 1990): 621–645.

Armitt Lucie. "Vampires and the Unconscious: Marge Piercy, Margaret Atwood, Toni Morrison and Bessie Head." In *Contemporary Women's Fiction and the Fantastic*. London: Palgrave Macmillan, 2000.

Artenie, Cristina. *Dracula: A Study of Editorial Practices*. Montreal, PQ: Universitas Press, 2016.

———. *Dracula Invades England: The Text, the Context, and the Readers*. Montreal, PQ: Universitas Press, 2015.

Ashbury, Roy. *Nosferatu*. London: York Press, 2001.

Ashcraft, Donna M. *Deconstructing Twilight: Psychological and Feminist Perspectives on the Series*. New York: Peter Lang Publishing, 2012.

Ashley, Mike. *Who's Who in Horror and Fantasy Fiction*. London: Elm Tree Books, 1977.

Aubrey, James, ed. *Vampire Films around the World: Essays on the Cinematic Undead of Sixteen Cultures*. Jefferson, NC: McFarland Press, 2020.

"Author Interview: Rachel Caine on Glass Houses." *Cynsations* (October 9, 2006). Posted at http://cynthialeitichsmith.blogspot.com/2006/10/author-interview-rachel-caine-on-glass.html. Accessed September 1, 2020.

Aylesworth, Thomas G. *The Story of Vampires*. Middletown, CT: Weekly Reader Books, 1977. Rept. Middletown CT: Xerox Education Publications, 1977.

Bacon, Simon. *Dracula as Absolute Other: The Troubling and Distracting Specter of Stoker's Vampire on Screen*. Jefferson, NC: McFarland & Company, 2019.

———. *Eco-Vampires: The Undead and the Environment*. Jefferson, NC: McFarland & Company, 2020.

———, and Katarzyna Bronk, eds. *Growing Up with Vampires: Essays on the Undead in Children's Media*. Jefferson, NC: McFarland & Company, 2018.

———, and Katarzyna Bronk, eds. *Undead Memory: Vampires and Human Memory in Popular Culture*. Oxford: Peter Lang International Academic Publishers, 2014.

Bacon-Smith, Camile. *Enterprising Women: Television Fandom and the Creation of Popular Myth*. Philadelphia: University of Pennsylvania Press, 1991.

Baldick, Chris. *In Frankenstein's Shadow*. Oxford: Clarendon Press, 1987.

Barber, Paul. *Vampires, Burial, and Death: Folklore and Reality*. New Haven, CT: Yale University Press, 1988.

Baring-Gould, Sabine. *The Book of Werewolves*. London: Smith, Elder, 1865. Rept. New York: Causeway Books, 1973.

Barker, Martin. *A Haunt of Fears: The Strange History of the British Horror Comics Campaign*. London: Pluto Press, 1984.

Barnett, Pamela E. "Figurations of Rape and the Supernatural in Beloved." *PMLA* 112, 3 (May 1997): 418–427.

Baroja, Julio Caro. *The World of the Witches*. Chicago: University of Chicago Press, 1965.

Bathory, Gia. *The Trouble with the Pears: An Intimate Portrait of Erzsebet Bathory*. Bloomington, IN: AuthorHouse, 2006.

Battis, Jes. *Blood Relations: Chosen Families in Buffy the Vampire Slayer and Angel*. Jeffersonville, NC: McFarland & Company, 2005.

Beahm, George, ed. *The Anne Rice Companion*. Williamsburg, VA: GB Ink, 1995.

———. *Bedazzled: Stephenie Meyer and the Twilight Phenomenon*. Nevada City, CA: Underwood Books, 2009.

Beatrice, Allyson. *Will the Vampire People Please Leave the Lobby? True Adventures in Cult Fandom*. Naperville, IL: Sourcebooks, Inc., 2007.

Beck, Calvin Thomas. *Scream Queens: Heroines of the Horrors.* New York: Collier Books, 1978.

Beckett. *Anne Rice's Vampire Chronicles an Alphabettery.* New York: Anchor Books, 2018.

Begbie, P. J. *The Malayan Peninsula.* Vepery Mission Press, 1834. Rept. Kuala Lumpur: Oxford University Press, 1967.

Begnal, Michael H. *Joseph Sheridan Le Fanu.* Lewisburg, PA: Bucknell University Press, 1971.

Belanger, Michelle A. *Psychic Vampire Codex: Manual of Magick & Energy Work.* York Beach, ME: Weiser Books, 2004.

———. *Sacred Hunger.* Lulu.com, 2005.

———. *The Vampire Ritual Book.* CreateSpace, 2007.

———. *Vampires in Their Own Words: An Anthology of Vampire Voices.* York Beach, ME: Weiser Books, 2007.

———. *Walking the Twilight Path: A Gothic Book of the Dead.* St. Paul. MN: Llewellyn Publications, October 1, 2008.

Belford, Barbara. *Bram Stoker: A Biography of the Author of Dracula.* New York: Alfred A. Knopf, 1996.

Bell, Michael E. *Food for the Dead: On the Trail of New England's Vampires.* New York: Carroll & Graf, 2001.

"Bella Forrest Books in Order." *Book Series in Order* (2020). Posted at https://www.bookseriesinorder.com/bella-forrest/. Accessed September 1, 2020.

Benefiel, Candace R. *Reading Laurell K. Hamilton.* Santa Barbara, CA: Libraries Unlimited, 2011.

Bentley, C. F. "The Monster in the Bedroom: Sexual Symbolism in Bram Stoker's Dracula." *Literature and Psychology* 22, 1 (1972): 27–34.

Benton, Mike. *Horror Comics: The Illustrated History.* Dallas, TX: Taylor Publishing, 1991.

Billson, Anne. *Let the Right One In.* Leighton Buzzard, UK: Auteur, 2011.

Biondi, Ray, and Walt Hecox. *The Dracula Killer.* New York: Pocket Books, 1992.

Blake, Michael F. *The Films of Lon Chaney.* Lanham, MD: Madison Books, 2001.

———. *A Thousand Faces: Lon Chaney's Unique Artistry in Motion Pictures.* Lanham, MD: Vestal Press, 1995.

Bleiler, E. F. "A Note on Authorship" In *Varney the Vampire.* New York: Dover Publications, 1932.

Blum, Jonathan, and Kate Orman. *Doctor Who: Vampire Science.* London: BBC Books, 1997.

Blum, Richard, and Eva Blum. *The Dangerous Hour: The Lore of Crisis and Mystery in Rural Greece.* London: Chatto & Windus, 1970.

Bojarski, Richard. *The Films of Bela Lugosi.* Secaucus, NJ: Citadel Press, 1980.

Bone, Drummond. *The Cambridge Companion to Byron.* Cambridge, UK: Cambridge University Press, 2005.

Bordwell, Carl. *The Films of Carl-Theodor Dreyer.* Berkeley: University of California Press, 1981.

Borzellieri, Frank. *The Physics of Dark Shadows: Time Travel, ESP, and the Laboratory.* New York: Cultural Studies Press, 2008.

Bostaph, Melissa. "Interview with Steve Niles." Dread Central.com. Posted at http://www.dreadcentral.com/interviews/niles-steve-30-days-night. Accessed April 10, 2010.

Brandon, Elizabeth. "Superstitions in Vermillion Parish." In Mody C. Boatright, Wilson M. Hudson, and Allen Maxwell, eds. *The Golden Log.* Dallas: Southern Methodist University, 1962, 108–118.

Brautigam, Rob. "Asema: The Vampires of Surinam." *International Vampire* 1, 1 (1990): 16–17.

———. "Some Blood Drinkers." *For the Blood Is the Life* 2, 9 (Summer 1991): 12–14.

———. "Vampires in Bulgaria." *International Vampire* 1, 2 (Winter 91): 16–17.

Briggs, Katherine. *A Dictionary of Fairies.* London: Penguin Books, 1976. Reprinted as *An Encyclopedia of Fairies, Hobgoblins, Brownies, Bogies, and Other Supernatural Creatures.* New York: Pantheon Books, 1976.

Browne, James J. *Blood Lust in Whitby and Highgate.: An Introduction to English Vampire Lore and History.* Whitby, UK: privately printed, 2014.

Browne, Nelson. *Sheridan Le Fanu.* London: Arthur Barker, 1951.

Browning, John Edgar. *Bram Stoker's Dracula, The Critical Feast: An Annotated Reference of Early Interviews and Reactions, 1897–1913.* Berkeley, CA: Apocryphile Press, 2011.

———. *The Forgotten Writings of Bram Stoker.* Basingstoke, UK: Palgrave Macmillan, 2012.

———, and Caroline Koan (Kay) Picart. *Dracula in Visual Media: Film, Television, Comic Book and Electronic Game Appearances, 1921–2010.* Jefferson, NC: McFarland & Company, 2010.

———. *Draculas, Vampires, and Other Undead Forms: Essays on Gender, Race, and Culture.* Methuen, NJ: Scarecrow Press, 2009.

Brunas, Michael John, and Tom Weaver. *Universal Horrors: The Studios Classic Films, 1931–1946.* Jefferson, NC: McFarland & Company, 1990.

Buber, Martin, ed. *Chinese Tales: Zhuangzi, Sayings and Parables and Chinese Ghost and Love Stories.* Atlantic Highland, NJ: Humanities Press International, 1991.

Bucciferro, Claudia. *The Twilight Saga: Exploring the Global Phenomenon.* Lanham, MD: Scarecrow Press, 2013.

Burton, Richard, trans. *Vikram and the Vampire; or, Tales of Hindu Devilry.* 1870, 1893. Rpt.: New York: Dover Publications, 1969.

Byrne, Lora. "Chelsea Quinn Yarbro: An Alternative Reality." *The Tomb of Dracula* 6 (August 1980): 56–59.

Calhoun, Crissey. *Love You to Death: The Unofficial Companion to the Vampire Diaries.* Vols 1–4. Toronto: ecw press, 2010–2013.

———, and Heather Vee. *Love You to Death: The Unofficial Companion to The Vampire Diaries, Season 5:.* Toronto: ecw press, 2014.

Calmet, Augustin. *Dissertations sur les Apparitions des Anges des Démons et des Esprits, et sur les revenants, et Vampires de Hungrie, de Boheme, de Moravie, et de Silésie.* Paris: 1746. Reprinted as *The Phantom World.* 2 vols. London: R. Bentley, 1850.

Capp, Edwin R. "La Belle Dame as Vampire." *Philological Quarterly* 27, 4 (October 1948): 89–92.

Carney, Raymond. *Speaking the Language of Desire: The Films of Carl Dreyer.* Cambridge: Cambridge University Press, 1989.

Carradine, John. "Introduction." *House of Dracula (The Original Shooting Script).* Edited by Philip Riley. Absecon, NJ: MagicImage Filmbooks, 1993.

Carter, Margaret L., ed. *Daymares from the Crypt: Macabre Verse.* San Diego, CA: The Author, 1981.

———. *Different Blood: The Vampire as Alien.* Amber Quill Press, 2004.

———. *Dracula: The Vampire and the Critics.* Ann Arbor, MI: UMI Research Press, 1988.

———. *Specter or Delusion? The Supernatural in Gothic Fiction.* Ann Arbor, MI: UMI Research Press, 1987.

———. *The Vampire in Literature: A Critical Bibliography.* Ann Arbor, MI: UMI Research Press, 1989.

———. "What Is a Good Guy Vampire?" *Good Guys Wear Fangs* 1 (May 1992): vi–ix.

Cast, P. C., with Kim Doner. *The Fledgling Handbook 101.* New York: St. Martin's Griffin, 2010.

Cast, P. C., with Leah Wilson. *Nyx in the House of Night: Mythology, Folklore and Religion in the P. C. and Kristin Cast Vampyres Series.* Dallas, TX: Benbella Books, 2011.

Centorcelli, Kristin. "Interview: MaryJanice Davidson, Author of 'Undead and Underwater'." *SF Signal* (March 21, 2013) Posted at http://www.sfsignal.com/archives/2013/03/interview-mary janice-davidson-author-of-undead-and-un derwater/. Accessed September 1, 2020.

Chaplin, Susan. *The Postmillennial Vampire: Power, Sacrifice and Simulation in True Blood, Twilight and Other Contemporary Narratives.* Cham, Switzerland: Palgrave Pivot/Springer Na ture, 2017.

Chapman, Paul M. *Birth of a Legend: Count Dracula, Bram Stoker, and Whitby.* York, UK: G H Smith, 2007.

"Charlaine Harris: Putting the Bite on Cozy Mysteries." Crescent Blues (2001). Posted at http://www.crescentblues.com/4_4issue/int_charlaine_harris.shtml. Accessed April 8, 2010.

Cherry, Brigid, ed. *True Blood: Investigating Vampires and Southern Gothic.* London: I. B. Tauris, 2013.

Clarens, Carlos. *Horror Movies: An Illustrated Survey.* London: Secker & Warburg, 1968.

Clebert, Jean-Paul. *The Gypsies.* Harmondsworth, Middlesex, U.K.: Penguin Books, 1963.

Coker, Cait, ed. *The Global Vampire: Essays on the Undead in Popular Culture around the World.* Jefferson, NC: McFarland Press, 2020.

Coolidge-Rust, Marie. *London After Midnight.* New York: Grosset & Dunlap, 1928.

Copner, Mike, and Buddy Barnett. "Bela Lugosi Then and Now!" Special issue of *Videosonic Arts* 1 (1990).

Coppola, Francis Ford, and James V. Hart. *Bram Stoker's Dracula: The Film and the Legend.* New York: Newmarket Press, 1992. 172 pp. Rept. London: Pan Books, 1992.

Coppola, Francis Ford, and Eiko Ishioka. *Coppola and Eiko on Bram Stoker's Dracula.* San Francisco: Collins Publishers, 1992.

Cotter, Robert Michael "Bobb." *Vampira and Her Daughters: Women Horror Movie Hosts from the 1950s into the Internet Era.* Jefferson, NC: McFarland & Company, 2016.

Cox, Greg. *The Transylvanian Library: A Consumer's Guide to Vampire Fiction.* San Bernardino, CA: Borgo Press, 1993.

Cox, Stephen. *The Munsters: A Trip Down Mockingbird Lane.* Back Stage Books, 2006.

———. *The Munsters: Television's First Family of Fright.* Chicago: Contemporary Books, 1989.

Coxwell, C. Fillingham. *Siberian and Other Folk-Tales.* London: C. W. Daniel Company, 1925. 1,056 pp. Rept. New York: AMS Press, 1983.

Crisan, Marius. *The Birth of the Dracula Myth: Bram Stoker's Transylvania.* Bucuresti: Editura Pro Universitaria 2013.

———, ed. *Dracula: An International Perspective.* N.p.: Palgrave Macmillan, Springer, Nature 2017.

Cullen, John. "Rupert Giles, the Professional-Image Slayer." *American Libraries* 31, 5 (2000): 42.

Craigie, William A. *Scandinavian Folklore: Illustrations of the Traditional Beliefs of the Northern Peoples.* Detroit, MI: Singing Tree Press, 1970.

Crandle, Marita Woywod. *New Orleans Vampires: History and Legend.* Charleston, SC: Haunted America/History Press Library Editions, 2017.

Crawford, Gary William. *J. Sheridan Le Fanu: A Bio-Bibliography.* Westport, CT: Greenwood Press, 1995. The author maintains a Web page on Le Fanu at http://www.jslefanu.com/.

Cremer, Robert. *Lugosi: The Man Behind the Cape.* Chicago: Henry Regnery Company, 1976.

Crooke, William. *Religion and Folklore of Northern India.* Humphrey Milford: Oxford University Press, 1926.

Curtin, Jeremiah. *Tales of the Fairies and of the Ghost World Collected from the Oral Tradition in South-West Munster.* 1882. Rept. New York: Lemma Publishing Corporation, 1970.

Cushing, Peter. *An Autobiography and Past Forgetting.* Baltimore, MD: Midnight Marquee Press, 1999.

Dalby, Richard, ed. *Dracula's Brood.* Wellingborough, Northamptonshire, UK: Crucible, 1987.

———. *Vampire Stories.* London, Michael O'Mara Books, 1992.

———, and Brian J. Frost. *Dracula's Brethren.* London: HarperCollins, 2017.

Dalton, Margaret. *A. K. Tolstoy.* New York: Twayne Publishers, 1972.

Dangerfield, Elma. *Byron and the Romantics in Switzerland, 1816.* London: Ascent Books, 1978.

Danielou, Alain. *Hindu Polytheism.* New York: Bollingen Foundation, 1964.

d'Arch Smith, Timothy. *Montague Summers: A Bibliography.* Wellingborough, Northamptonshire, UK: Aquarian Press, 1983.

D'Assier, Adolphe. *Posthumous Humanity: A Study of Phantoms.* San Diego, CA: Wizards Bookshelf, 1981.

Davidson, Carol Margaret, ed. Bram Stoker's *Dracula: Sucking through the Century, 1897–1997.* Toronto: Durndun Press, 1997.

Davies, Bernard. *Whitby Dracula Trail.* Scarborough, North Yorkshire, UK: Department of Tourism and Amenities, Scarborough Borough Council, n.d.

Davis, Michael. *Street Gang: The Complete History of Sesame Street.* New York: Viking, 2008.

de Aragon, John. *The Legend of La Llorona.* Las Vegas, NV: Pan American Pub. Co., 1980.

de Groot, J. J. M. *The Religious System of China.* 5 vols. Leyden, The Netherlands: E. J. Brill, 1892–1910.

De Roos, Hans Corneel. On "*Dracula's* Lost Icelandic Sister Text: How a Supposed Translation Proved to Be Much More." *Literary Hub* (February 6, 2017). Posted at: https://lithub.com/on-drac ulas-lost-icelandic-sister-text/. Accessed September 1, 2020.

De Visser, M. W. *The Dragon in China and Japan.* Wiesbaden, Germany: Dr. Martin Sändig, 1913, 1969.

de Wit, Augusta. *Java: Facts and Fancies.* The Hague: W. P. van Stockum, 1912. Rept. Singapore: Oxford University Press, 1984.

Deane, Hamilton, and John L. Balderston. *Dracula: The Vampire Play in Three Acts.* New York: Samuel French, 1927.

DeCandido, GraceAnne A. "Bibliographic Good vs. Evil in Buffy the Vampire Slayer." *American Libraries* 30, 8 (1999): 44–47.

del Toro, Guillermo, and Chuck Hogan. *The Fall.* "The Strain Trilogy," Book 2. New York: William Morrow/HarperCollins, 2010.

———. *The Night Eternal.* "The Strain Trilogy," Book 3. New York: William Morrow/HarperCollins, 2011.

———. *The Strain.* "The Strain Trilogy," Book 1. New York: William Morrow/HarperCollins, 2009.

Del Vecchio, Deborah, and Tom Johnson. *Peter Cushing: The Gentle Man of Horror and His 91 Films.* Jefferson, NC: McFarland & Company, 1992.

Dickinson, Joy [Joy Dickinson Tipping]. *Haunted City: An Unauthorized Guide to the Magical, Magnificent New Orleans of Anne Rice.* New York: Citadel Publishing/Kensington Publishing Corp, 2004.

Dömötör, Tekla. *Hungarian Folk Beliefs.* Bloomington, IN: Indiana University Press, 1982.

Donovan, Gene. *I Was a Teen-Age Dracula.* Chicago: Dramatic Publishing Company, 1968.

Dorff, Stephen. *Blade.* New York: HarperPaperbacks, 1998.

Dorson, Richard M. *Folk Legends of Japan.* Rutland, VT: Charles E. Tuttle Company, 1962.

Dove, Karen E. *Midnight to Midnight Guidelines*. Mt. Clemens, MI: privately printed, 1994.

Dracula (The Original 1931 Shooting Script). Atlantic City, NJ: Magic Image Filmbooks, 1990.

Dresser, Norine. *American Vampires: Fans, Victims, Practitioners*. New York: W. W. Norton & Company, 1989.

Dreyer, Carl Theodor. *Four Screen Plays*. Trans. by Oliver Stallybrass. Bloomington, IN: Indiana University Press, 1970.

Du Camp, Maxime, and Andrew Lang. *Théophile Gautier*. Honolulu, HI: University Press of the Pacific, 2004.

Dumas, Alexandre. *The Memoirs, Being Extracts from the First Five Volumes*. London: W. H. Allen & Co., 1891. The condensed English edition of the *Memoirs*, published under the title *The Road to Monte Cristo*, eliminated all references to *The Vampyre*.

———, and Frank N. Morlock. *The Return of Lord Ruthven the Vampire*. Encino, CA: Hollywood Comics, 2004.

Durand, Kevin K., ed. *Buffy Meets the Academy: Essays on the Episodes and Scripts as Texts*. Jeffersonville, NC: McFarland & Company, 2009.

Durham, M. Edith. "Of Magic, Witches and Vampires in the Balkans." *Man* 121 (December 1923): 189–192.

Dvornik, Francis. *The Slavs: Their Early History and Civilization*. Boston: American Academy of Arts and Sciences, 1956.

"Early New Englanders Ritually 'Killed' Corpses, Experts Say." *New York Times* (October 31, 1993): 1.

Edwards, Anne. *Haunted Summer*. New York: Coward, McCann & Geoghegan, 1973.

Eighteen-Bisang, Robert, and Elizabeth Miller. *Bram Stoker's Notes for Dracula: A Facsimile Edition*. Jeffersonville, NC: McFarland & Company, 2008. Rev. ed. as: *Drafts of Dracula*. N.p.: Tellwell Talent, 2019.

Eighteen-Bisang, Robert, and J. Gordon Melton. *Dracula: A Century of Editions, Adaptations and Translations*. Santa Barbara, CA: Transylvanian Society of Dracula, 1998.

———. "Dracula by Arthur Conan Doyle." *The Sherlock Holmes Journal* 29, 3 (December 2009): 94–98.

———. "Dracula in Print: A Checklist." In John Edgar Browning & Caroline Joan (Kay) Picart. *Dracula in Visual Media*. Jefferson, NC: McFarland, 2011.

———, and Martin H. Greenberg, eds. *Vampire Stories*. New York: Skyhorse Publishing, 2009.

Eisler, Benita. *Byron: Child of Passion, Fool of Fame*. New York: Vintage, 2000.

Elden, Gro. *The Buffyverse and Its Inhabitants: A Study of Fans of Buffy the Vampire Slayer*. (Master's thesis). Amsterdam, Netherlands: International School for Humanities and Social Sciences, Universiteit van Amsterdam, 2002.

Eliade, Micea. *Domnisoara Christina Bucharest, 1935*. French edition published as *Mademoiselle Christiana*. Paris: Editions de l'Herne, 1978. Italian edition as published as *Signorina Christiana*. Milan: Jaca Book, 1984.

Enthoven, R. E. *The Folklore of Bombay*. Oxford: Clarendon Press, 1924.

Everson, William K. *Classics of the Horror Film*. New York: Citadel Press, 1974.

Eyles, Allen. *Sherlock Holmes: A Centenary Celebration*. London: John Murray, 1986.

———, Robert Adkinson, and Nicolas Fry, eds. *The House of Horror: The Story of Hammer Films*. London: Lorrimer Publishing Ltd., 1973.

Farrant, David. *Beyond the Highgate Vampire*. London: British Psychic and Occult Society, 1991. Third revised ed. London: British Psychic and Occult Society, 2002.

———. *The Vampire Syndrome: The Truth Behind the Highgate Vampire Legend*. London: Mutiny! Press, 2000.

Fary, Lisa. "Interview: LA Banks." Pinkraygun .com. Posted at http://www.pinkraygun.com/2009/02/18/interview-la-banks/. Accessed on July 1, 2009.

Ferry, David. *Gilgamesh: A New Rendering in English Verse*. New York: Farrar, Straus, & Giroux, 1992.

Finné, Jacques. *Bibliographie de Dracula*. Lausanne, Switz.: L'Age d'Homme, 1986.

Fitzgerald, Gil. "History as Horror: Chelsea Quinn Yarbro." In Darnell Schweitzer, ed. *Discovering Modern Horror Fiction, II*. Mercer Island, WA: Starmont House, 1988, pp. 128–34.

Florescu, Radu, and Raymond T. McNally. *The Complete Dracula*. Boston: Copley Publishing Group, 1992. (A combined publication of *In Search of Dracula* and *Dracula; A Biography of Vlad the Impaler*.)

———. *Dracula: A Biography of Vlad the Impaler, 1413–1476*. New York: Hawthorn Books, 1973. 239 pp.

———. *Dracula: Prince of Many Faces: His Life and Times*. Boston: Little, Brown, 1989. 261 pp.

Flynn, John L. *Cinematic Vampires*. Jefferson, NC: McFarland & Company, 1992.

Fontenrose, Joseph. *Python: A Study of Delphic Myth and Its Origins*. Berkeley, CA: University of California Press, 1959.

Forbes, Duncan, ed. *The Baital-Pachisi; or, The Twenty-five Tales of a Demon*. London: Crosby, Lockwood, 1857.

Forde, Daryll. *Yako Studies*. London: Oxford University Press, 1964.

Fortune, Dion. *Psychic Self-Defense*. London: Aquarian Press, 1952.

Frank, Frederick S. *Montague Summers: A Bibliographical Portriat*. Metuchen, NJ: The Scarecrow Press, 1988.

Frayling, Christopher. *Vampyres: From Lord Byron to Count Dracula*. London: Faber and Faber, 1991.

———. *Vampyres: Genesis and Resurrection from Count Dracula to Vampirella*. London: Thames & Hudson, 2016.

Frazer, James G. *The Golden Bough*. Vol. 10. *Balder the Beautiful: The Fire-Festivals of Europe and the Doctrine of the External Soul*. London: Macmillan and Co., 1930.

Frid, Jonathan. *Barnabas Collins: A Personal Picture Album*. New York: Paperback Library, 1969.

Fry, Carol L. "Fictional Conventions and Sexuality in Dracula." *The Victorian Newsletter* 42 (1972): 20–22.

Gallop, Rodney. *Portugal: A Book of Folk-Ways*. Cambridge: Cambridge University Press, 1936.

Garza, Thomas, comp. and ed. *Slavic Blood: The Vampire in Russian and East European Cultures*. Course Reader. San Diego: Cognella Publishers, 2018.

———. *The Vampire in Slavic Cultures*. San Diego, CA: Cognella, 2009. Rev. and exp. ed. San Diego: Cognella Academic Publishing, 2010.

Genini, Ronald. *Theda Bara: A Biography of the Silent Screen Vamp, with a Filmography*. Jeffersonville, NC: McFarland & Company, 2001.

Gentle, Dee. "Interview with Nina Bangs." Posted at http://paranormalromance.org/Nina Bangs07.htm. Accessed June 15, 2009.

George, Andrew R., *The Babylonian Gilgamesh Epic*. Introduction, Critical Edition and Cuneiform Texts. 2 vols. Oxford: Oxford University Press, 2003.

George, Samantha, and William Hughes, eds. *Open Graves, Open Minds: Representations of Vampires and the Undead from the Enlightenment to the Present Day*. Manchester, UK: Manchester University Press, 2013.

Georgieva, Ivanichka. *Bulgarian Mythology*. Sofia: Svyet, 1985.

Gerard, Emily. *The Land Beyond the Forest.* 2 vols. London: Will Blackwood & Sons, 1888.

Gifford, Denis. *A Pictorial History of Horror Movies.* London: Hamlyn, 1973.

Giles, Rupert (pseudonym of Nancy Holder). *Demons of the Hell Mouth: A Guide for Slayers.* London: Titan Books, 2017.

Giurescu, Constantin C. *The Life and Deeds of Vlad the Impaler: Dracula.* New York: Romanian Library, 1969.

Glut, Donald F. *The Dracula Book.* Metuchen, NJ: Scarecrow Press, 1975.

———. *True Vampires of History.* New York: HC Publishers, 1971.

Goldberg, Benjamin. *The Mirror and Man.* Charlottesville, VA: University Press of Virginia, 1985.

Goldberg, Enid, and Norman Itzkowitz. *Vlad the Impaler: The Real Count Dracula.* Franklin Watts: New York, 2007. 128 pp.

Golden, Christopher, and Nancy Holder. *Buffy the Vampire Slayer: The Watcher's Guide.* New York: Pocket Books, 1998.

———, Stephen R. Bissette, and Thomas E. Sniegoski. *Buffy the Vampire Slayer: The Monster Book.* New York: Pocket Books, 2000.

Golden, Eva. *Vamp: The Rise and Fall of Theda Bara.* Vestal, NY: Emprise Publishing, 1996.

Goudie, Robert, Ben Peal, and Ben Swainbank. *Vampire: The Eternal Struggle Players Guide.* Stone Mountain, GA: White Wolf Publishing, 2005.

Goulart, Ron. *The Encyclopedia of American Comics.* New York: Facts on File, 1990.

Greenberg, Andrew, et al. *The Eternal Struggle: A Players Guide to the Jyhad.* Stone Mountain, GAL White Wolf Game Studio, 1994.

Greenberg, Martin H. *Vampire Detectives.* New York: DAW Books, 1995.

Gresh, Lois H. *The Twilight Companion: The Unauthorized Guide to the Series.* St. Martin's Griffin: New York, 2008.

Gross, Edward. "Robert Quarry: Count Yorga Rises Again." In *The Vampire Interview Book* by Edward Gross and Marc Shapiro. East Meadow, NY: Image Publishing, 1991.

———, and Marc Shapiro. *The Vampire Interview Book: Conversations with the Undead.* East Meadow, NY: Image Publishing, 1991.

Grossman, Gael Elyse. *The Evolution of the Vampire in Adolescent Literature.* (Ph.D. dissertation). East Lansing, MI: Michigan State University, 2001.

Guiley, Rosemary Ellen. *Vampires Among Us.* New York: Pocket Books, 1991.

Guinn, Jeff, with Andy Grieser. *Something in the Blood: The Underground World of Today's Vampires.* Arlington, TX: The Summit Publishing Group, 1996.

Gullo, Christopher. *In All Sincerity ... Peter Cushing.* Princeton, NJ: Xlibris, 2004.

Guran, Paula. "Interview: Nancy Holder: Staying on Target." Dark Echo Horror (1998). Posted at http://www.darkecho.com/dark echo/archives/holder.html. Accessed April 8, 2010.

Haines, Jeff. "Strange Things in the Night." *Inquest* 1, 1 (May 1995): 16–20.

Hall, Robert L. "Cozies with Teeth!: An Interview with Charlaine Harris." Southern Scribe (2004). Posted at http://www.southernscribe .com/zine/authors/Harris_Charlaine.htm. Accessed April 8, 2010.

Haller, William. *The Early Life of Robert Southey, 1774–1803.* New York: Columbia University Press, 1917.

Hamilton, Laurell K., ed. *Ardeur: 14 Writers on the Anita Blake Vampire Hunter Series.* Dallas: BenBella Books, 2010.

Hamrick, Craig. *Barnabas & Company: The Cast of the TV Classic Dark Shadows.* Lincoln, NB: iUniverse, Inc., 2003.

Hanke, Ken. *A Critical Guide to Horror Film Series.* New York: Garland Publishing, 1991.

Hanson, Robert R. *A Profile of John Polidori with a New Edition of The Vampyre.* (Ph.D. dissertation). Columbus, OH: Ohio State University, 1966.

Harding, Elizabeth A. Kali: *The Black Goddess of Dakshineswar.* Lake Worth, FL: Nicolas-Hays, 1993.

Hardwicke, Catherine. *Twilight: Director's Notebook: The Story of How We Made the Movie Based on the Novel by Stephenie Meyer.* New York: Little, Brown Young Readers, 2009.

Harkness, Deborah. *The World of All Souls: A Complete Guide to A Discovery of Witches, Shadow of Night & the Book of Life.* London: Headline Publishing, 2019.

Harrell, Megan. "Interview with Tanya Huff." Foxfire News. Posted at http://firefox.org/news/articles/258/1/Interview-with-Tanya-Huff/Page1.html. Accessed April 8, 2010.

Harris, Charlaine, ed. *The Sookie Stackhouse Companion.* New York: Ace Hardcover, 2011.

Harrison, Kim. *The Hallows Insider. New Fiction, Facts, Maps, Murders, and More in the World of Rachel Morgan.* New York: Harper Voyager, 2011.

Hartnup, Karen. *On the Beliefs of the Greeks: Leo Allatios and Popular Orthodoxy.* Leiden: Brill, 2004.

Hawkins, Colin, and Jacqui Hawkins. *Vampires Joke Book.* London: Picture Lions, 2001.

Held, Eric, ed. *The 1992 Vampire Bibliography of Fiction and Non-Fiction.* Brooklyn, NY: Vampire Information Exchange, 1992.

———. *1993 Calendar of Vampire Events.* Brooklyn, NY: Vampire Information Exchange, 1993.

Hellekson, Karen, and Kristina Busse. *Fan Fiction and Fan Communities in the Age of the Internet: New Essays.* Jeffersonville, NC: McFarland & Company, 2006.

Henningsen, Gustav. *The Witches' Advocate: Basque Witchcraft and the Spanish Inquisition (1910–1614).* Reno, NV: University of Nevada Press, 1980.

Higashi, Sumiko. *Virgins, Vamps, and Flappers: The American Silent Movie Heroine.* Montreal: Eden Press Women's Publications, 1978.

Hill, Gordon. *The Vampire Joke Book.* London: Foulsham, 1991.

Hill, Joe. *NOS4A2.* New York: William Morrow, 2013.

Hobson, Amanda, and U. Melissa Anyiwo, eds. *Gender in the Vampire Narrative.* Rotterdam: Sense, 2016.

Hodne, Ornulf. *The Type of the Norwegian Folktale.* Oslo, Norway: Universitetforlaget, 1984.

Hogan, David J. *Dark Romance: Sexuality in the Horror Film.* Jefferson, NC: McFarland & Company, 1986.

Holder, Nancy, with Jeff Mariotte and Maryelizabeth Hart. *Angel: The Casefiles.* Vol. 1. New York: Simon Pulse, 2002.

———. *Buffy the Vampire Slayer: The Watcher's Guide.* Volume 2. New York: Pocket Books, 2000.

Holder, Nancy, and Lisa Clancy. *Buffy the Vampire Slayer Encyclopedia: The Ultimate Guide to the Buffyverse.* New York: Harper Design, 2017.

Holte, James Craig. *Dracula in the Dark: The Dracula Film Adaptations.* Westport, CT: Greenwood Press, 1997.

Hopkins, Ellen, ed. *A New Dawn: Your Favorite Authors on Stephenie Meyer's Twilight Saga: Completely Unauthorized.* Benbella Books, 2009.

Hoppenstand, Gary, and Ray B. Browne, eds. *The Gothic World of Anne Rice.* Bowling Green, OH: Bowling Green University Popular Press, 1996.

———. *The Gothic World of Stephen King: Landscape of Nightmares.* Bowling Green, OH: Bowling Green State University Popular Press, 1987.

Horn, Maurice, ed. *The World Encyclopedia of Comics.* New York: Chelsea House Publishers, 1976.

Hort, Barbara E. *Unholy Hungers: Encountering the Psychic Vampire in Ourselves & Others.* Boston: Shambhala, 1996.

Horton, George B. *Home of Nymphs and Vampires: The Isles of Greece.* Indianapolis: The Bobb-Merrill Company, 1929.

Hotchner, Stephen. *Dracula.* Denver, CO: Pioneer Drama Service, 1978.

Housel, Rebecca, and J. Jeremy Wisnewski, eds. *Twilight and Philosophy: Vampires, Vegetarians, and the Pursuit of Immortality.* New York: John Wiley & Sons, 2009.

Howard, Malia. *Jonathan Frid: An Actor's Curious Journey (A Career Biography).* Privately printed, 2001.

Howe, Deborah, and James Howe. *Bunnicula.* New York: Atheneum Publishers, 1979. Rept. New York: Avon, 1980.

Howell, Signe. *Society and Cosmos: Chewong of Peninsular Malaysia.* Singapore: Oxford University Press, 1984.

Hrbkova, Sárka B. *Czechoslovak Stories.* Freeport, NY: Books for Libraries Press, 1970.

Hughes, William. *Beyond Dracula: Bram Stoker's Fiction and Its Cultural Context.* London: Macmillan Press, 2000.

———. *Bram Stoker: A Bibliography.* Brisbane, Australia: University of Queensland Press, 1997.

———. *Bram Stoker: Dracula.* New York: Palgrave Macmillan, 2009.

———. *Bram Stoker's Dracula: A Reader's Guide.* Series: Readers' Guides to Essential Criticism. London: Continuum International Publishing Group, 2009.

———, and Andrew Smith. *Bram Stoker: History, Psychoanalysis, and the Gothic.* Basinstoke, UK: Macmillan, 1998.

Hunter, Jack. *Eyes of Blood: The Hammer Films.* London: Glitter Books, 2012.

Hurwood, Bernhardt J. *Passport to the Supernatural: An Occult Compendium from All Ages and Many Lands.* New York: Taplinger Publishing Company, 1972.

Hutchings, Peter. *Hammer and Beyond: The British Horror Film.* Manchester: Manchester University Press, 1993.

In Highgate Cemetery. London: Friends of Highgate Cemetery, 1992.

The International Dictionary of Films and Filmmakers, Volume II, *Actors and Actresses.* Edited by James Vinson. Chicago: St. James Press, 1985.

"Interview—Lynsay Sands." *Darque Review.* http://darquereviews.blogspot.com/2007/11/interview-lynsay-sands.html. Accessed September 15, 2009.

"An Interview with Novelist L. J. Smith." *Forbidden Tales.* 1996. Posted at http://www.nightworld.net/witchlight/forbiddentales.htm. Accessed October 15, 2009.

The Introduction of Barnabas. Maplewood, NJ: Dark Shadows Festival, 1988.

Introvigne, Massimo. *La stirpe di Dracula: Indagine sul vampirismo dall'antichita ai nostri giorni.* Milan: Arnoldo Mondadori Editore, 1997.

Irwin, Megan. "Stephenie Meyer's Vampire Romance Novels Made a Mormon Mom an International Sensation." *Phoenix New Times* (July 12, 2007).

James, Louis. *Fiction for the Working Man, 1830–1850.* London: Oxford University Press, 1963.

Jerome, Joseph. *Montague Summers: A Memoir.* London: Cecil and Amelia Woolf, 1965.

Jewel, John. *Lips of Blood: An Illustrated Guide to Hammer's Dracula Movies Starring Christopher Lee.* London: Glitter Books, 2002.

Johannsen, Albert. *The House of Beadle and Adams and Its Dime and Nickel Novels.* 3 vols. Norman, OK: University of Oklahoma Press, 1950.

Jones, Aphrodite. *The Embrace.* New York: Pocket Books, 1999.

Jones, Ernest. *On the Nightmare.* 1931. Rept. New York: Liveright, 1971.

Jones, Stephen. *The Illustrated Vampire Movie Guide.* London: Titan Books, 1993.

Jowett, Lorna. *Sex and the Slayer: A Gender Studies Primer for the Buffy Fan.* Middletown, CT: Wesleyan University Press, 2005.

Kabdebo, Thomas. *Hungary.* Santa Barbara, CA: Clio Press, 1980.

Kaffenberger, William M., and Gary D. Rhodes. *Bela Lugosi in Person.* Albany, GA: BearManor Media, 2015.

Kaplan, Stephen. *Pursuit of Premature Gods and Contemporary Vampires.* Port Jefferson Station, NY: Charles A. Moreno, 1976.

———. *Vampires Are.* Palm Springs, CA: ETC Publications, 1984.

Kaveney, Roz, ed. *Reading the Vampire Slayer.* London: Tauris Parke Publishing, 2001.

Kawajiri, Yoshiaki. *The Art of Vampire Hunter D Bloodlust.* Vol. 2. Idea & Design Works, 2007.

Keesey, Pam. *Dark Angels: Lesbian Vampire Stories.* Pittsburgh/San Francisco: Cleis Press, 1995.

———. *Daughter of Darkness: Lesbian Vampire Stories.* Pittsburgh/San Francisco: Cleis Press, 1993.

———. *Vamps: An Illustrated History of the Femme Fatale.* San Francisco: Cleis Press, 1997.

Kelly, Sean, ed. *Irish Folk and Fairy Tales.* New York: Gallery Press, 1982.

Kelly, Tim. *Young Dracula; or, The Singing Bat.* Denver: Pioneer Drama Service, 1975.

Kennedy, Raymond. *The Ageless Indies.* New York: John Day Company, 1942.

Kenyon, Sherrilyn, and Alethea Kontin. *The Dark-Hunter Companion.* New York: St. Martin's Griffin, 2007.

Kingsley, David. *Hindu Goddesses: Visions of the Divine Feminine in the Hindu Religious Tradition.* Berkeley, CA: University of California Press, 1986.

Kinsey, Wayne. *Hammer Films—A Life in Pictures: The Visual Story of Hammer Films.* Sheffield, UK: Tomahawk Press, 2009.

———. *Hammer Films: The Bray Studio Years.* Richmond, UK: Reynolds & Hearn, 2002.

———. *Hammer Films: The Unsung Heroes.* Sheffield, UK: Tomahawk Press, 2010.

Kikuchi, Hideyuki, and Yoshitaka Amano. *Vampire Hunter D: Reader's Guide.* Trans. by Kevin Leahy. Milwaukie, OR: Dark Horse Books, 2010.

"Kim Harrison: Secret Identity." Locus Online. Posted at http://www.locusmag.com/Perspectives/2009/05/kim-harrison-secret-identity.html. Accessed April 8, 2010.

Kirby-Diaz, Mary., ed. *Buffy and Angel Conquer the Internet: Essays on Online Fandom.* Jeffersonville, NC: McFarland & Company, 2009.

Klaniczay, Gabor, "The Decline of Witches and Rise of Vampires in the Eighteenth-Century Habsburg Monarchy." *Ethnologia Europaea* 17 (1987): 165–180.

Klonsky, E. David, and Alexis Black, eds. *The Psychology of Twilight.* Dallas, TX: Smart Pop/Benbella Books, 2011.

Koontz, K. Dale. *Faith and Choice in the Works of Joss Whedon.* Jeffersonville, NC: McFarland & Company, 2008.

Kraul, Edward Garcia, and Judith Beatty. *Weeping Woman: Encounters with La Llorona.* Santa Fe, NM: Word Process, 1988.

Kreider, Jodie A., and Meghan K. Winchell. *Buffy in the Classroom: Essays on Teaching with the Vampire Slayer.* Jefferson, NC: McFarland & Company, 2010.

Kreuter, Peter Mario. *Der Vampirglaube in Südosteuropa: Studien zur Genese, Bedeutung und Funktion. Rumänien und der Balkanraum.* Berlin: Weidler, 2001.

Kuhn, Annette, with Susannah Radstone, eds. *The Women's Companion to International Film.* London: Virago, 1990. Reprinted as *Women in Film: An International Guide.* New York: Fawcett Columbine, 1991.

Kvideland, Reimond, and Henning K. Sehmsdorf, eds. *Scandinavian Folk Belief and Legend.* Minneapolis, MN: University of Minnesota Press, 1986.

Langella, Frank. *Dropped Names: Famous Men and Women as I Knew Them.* New York: Harper, 2012.

Lansdale, Edward Geary. *In the Midst of Wars.* New York: Harper & Row, 1972.

"Lara Adrian Bibliography and Interview." *Love Vampires.* Posted at http://www.lovevampires.com/ladrian.html. Accessed September 1, 2020.

Lavergne, Remi. *A Phonetic Transcription of the Creole Negro's Medical Treatments, Superstitions, and Folklore in the Parish of Pointe Coupée.* (Master's thesis). New Orleans, LA: Louisiana State University, 1930.

LaVey, Anton Szandor. *The Satanic Bible.* New York: Avon, 1969.

Lawson, John Cuthbert. *Modern Greek Folklore and Ancient Greek Religion.* 1910. Rept. New Hyde Park, NY: University Books, 1964.

Laycock, Joseph. *Vampires Today: The Truth about Modern Vampirism.* Westport. CT: Praeger, 2009.

Leadbeater, Charles W. *The Astral Plane: Its Scenery Inhabitants, and Phenomena.* London: Theosophical Publishing House, 1915.

Leake, William Martin. *Travels in Northern Greece.* 4 vols. 1835. Rept. Amsterdam: Adolf M. Hakkert, 1967.

Leavenworth, Maria Lindgren. *Fanged Fan Fiction: Variations on Twilight, True Blood, and The Vampire Diaries.* Jefferson, NC: McFarland & Company, 2013.

Lee, Christopher. *Tall, Dark and Gruesome: An Autobiography.* London: W. H. Allen, 1977. Rev. ed.: *Lord of Misrule: The Autobiography of Christopher Lee.* London: Orion Publishing, 2003.

Lehrer, Ernst, and Johanna Lehner. *Folklore and Odysseys of Food and Medicinal Plants.* New York: Tutor Publishing Company, 1962.

Leland, G. G. *Gypsy Sorcery.* New York Tower Books, n.d.

Lennig, Arthur. *The Count: The Life and Films of Bela "Dracula" Lugosi.* New York: G. P. Putnam's Sons, 1974. Revised ed. *The Immortal Count: The Life and Films of Bela Lugosi.* Lexington, KY: University Press of Kentucky, 2003.

León, Luis D. *La Llorona's Children: Religion, Life, and Death on the U.S.-Mexican Borderlands.* Berkeley: University of California Press, 2004.

Leonard, Arthur Glyn. *The Lower Niger and Its Tribes.* London: Macmillan and Co., 1906.

Leonard, William Tolbert. *Theatre: Stage to Screen to Television.* Vol. 1. Metuchen, NJ: Scarecrow Press, 1981.

Levine, Elana, and Lisa Parks, eds. *Undead TV: Essays on Buffy the Vampire Slayer.* Durham, NC: Duke University Press, 2007.

Lewis, Budd, and Jose Gonzalez. "The Origin of Vampirella." *Vampirella* (Warren) 46 (October 1975): Reprinted in *Vampirella Annual* 1972. Reprinted in *Vampirella* 100 (October 1981): 29–43.

Liming, Wei. *Chinese Festivals: Traditions, Customs, and Rituals.* Hong Kong: China International Press, 2005.

Linedecker, Clifford L. *The Vampire Killers.* New York: St. Martin's Paperback, 1998.

London, Sondra. *True Vampires: Blood-Sucking Killers Past and Present.* Feral House, 2003.

Loew, Flaxman, and Jose Ortiz. "The Vampire of the Nile." *Vampirella* (Harris) 113 (1988): 17–28.

London After Midnight. New York: Cornwall Books, 1985.

Lopez, Mellie Leandicho. *A Handbook of Philippine Folklore.* Diliman, Quezon City: The University of the Philippines Press 2006.

Luckhurst, Roger. *The Cambridge Companion to Dracula.* Ser.: Cambridge Companions to Literature. Cambridge, UK: Cambridge University Press, 2017.

Lumley, Brian, and Stanley Wiater, eds. *The Brian Lumley Companion.* New York: TOR, 2002.

Lynch, Jack, ed. *Dracula.* Ser. Critical Insights. Ipswich, MA: Salem Press, 2009.

MacCulloch, J. A. *The Celtic and Scandinavian Religions.* London: Hutchinson's University Library, 1948.

Macdonald, D. L. *Poor Polidori: A Critical Biography of the Author of "The Vampire."* Toronto: University of Toronto Press, 1991.

MacDonell, A. A. *Vedic Mythology.* Strassburg, Germany: Verlag von Karl J. Trübner, 1897.

Mackenzie, Andrew. *Dracula Country.* London: Arthur Barker, 1977.

MacKenzie, Donald A. *Myths of China and Japan.* London: Gresham Publishing Company, 1923.

Macnaughtan, Don. *The Buffyverse Catalog: A Complete Guide to Buffy the Vampire Slayer and Angel in Print, Film, Television, Comics, Games and Other Media, 1992–2010.* Jefferson, NC: McFarland & Company, 2011.

Madison, Bob, ed. *Dracula: The First Hundred Years.* Baltimore, MD: Midnight Marquee Press, 1997.

Magill, Frank N. *Survey of Modern Fantasy Literature.* Vol. 3. Englewood Cliffs, NJ: Salem Press, 1983.

"Maila 'Vampira' Nurmi on Wood, Dean and 'Bunny.'" *Hollywood Book and Poser News* 11 (October 1992): 3–4.

Mallory, Michael, and Andrea Robinson. *The Vampire Diaries: Unlocking the Secrets of Mystic Falls.* Insight Editions, 2017.

Manchester, Sean. *The Highgate Vampire: The Infernal World of the Undead Unearthed at London's Highgate Cemetery and Environs.* London: Gnostic Press, 1985. Revised ed. London: The Gothic Press, 1991.

———. *The Vampire Hunter's Handbook.* London: Gothic Press, 1997.

Marrero, Robert. *Horrors of Hammer.* Florida: RGM Publications, 1984.

Martin, Timothy P. "Joyce and Wagner's Pale Vampire." *James Joyce Quarterly* 24, 4 (Summer 1986): 491–496.

Martone, Eric. *Alexandre Dumas's the Vampire: A Novel Based on the Drame Fantastique.* Lincoln, NB: iUniverse. 2003.

"Marv Wolfman Trial." *The Comics Journal.* Part 1: 236 (August 2001): 22–84. Posted at http://www.tcj.com/236/wolfman1 .html. Accessed September 15, 2009.

Masters, Anthony. *The Natural History of the Vampire.* New York: G. P. Putnam's Sons, 1972. Rept. Berkley Publishing Corporation, 1976.

Matheson, Richard, and Mark Dawidziak. *Bloodlines: Richard Matheson's Dracula, I Am Legend and Other Vampire Stories.* Colorado, CO: Gauntlet Press, 2006.

Maxford, Howard. *Hammer, House of Horror: Behind the Screams.* London: B. T. Batsford, 1996.

McCabe, Joseph. *What War and Militarism Cost: A Realistic Survey of the Vampire of the Human Race and the Supreme Enemy of Human Progress.* Girard, KS: Haldeman-Julius, 1938.

McCarty, John. *Hammer Films. Pocket Essentials.* Harpenden, Herts., UK: Pocket Essentials, 2002.

McCormack, W. J. *Sheridan Le Fanu and Victorian Ireland.* Oxford: Clarendon Press, 1980.

McCubbin, Chris W. *Vampire: The Masquerade Companion.* Steve Jackson Games, 1994.

McMahon, Liriel, ed. *Best of the Journal of Modern Vampirism.* Seattle, WA: Vampirism Research Institute, 1993.

———. *Dysfunctional Vampire: A Theory from Personal History.* Seattle, WA: Vampirism Research Institute, 1993.

———. *Results Report: Vampire Fan Survey No. 9221.* Seattle, WA: Vampirism Research Institute, 1993.

McNally, Raymond T. *A Clutch of Vampires: These Being among the Best from History and Literature.* New York: Bell Publishing Company, 1974.

———. *Dracula Was a Woman: In Search of the Blood Countess of Transylvania.* New York: McGraw-Hill, 1983. 254 pp. Rept. London: Hamlyn Paperback, 1983.

———. "An Historical Appraisal of the Image of Vlad Tepes in Contemporary Romanian Folklore." In *Dracula: Essays on the Life and Times of Vlad Tepes.* New York: Columbia University Press, 1991.

———, and Radu Florescu. *In Search of Dracula.* New York: Greenwich, 1972. Rev. ed. as: *In Search of Dracula: Twenty Years Later.* Boston: Houghton, Mifflin, 1994.

———, eds. *The Essential "Dracula": A Completely Illustrated and Annotated Edition of Bram Stoker's Classic Novel.* New York: Mayflower Books, 1979.

Meikle, Denis. *A History of Hammer: The Rise and Fall of the House of Hammer, 1949–1979.* Lanham, MD: Scarecrow Press, 2008.

Melton, J. Gordon. *Chronicling the Vampire: A Collector's Guide to the Vampire Writings of Anne Rice.* Santa Barbara, CA: Transylvanian Society of Dracula, 1998.

———. "Introduction." In S. P. Somtow. *Vampire Junction.* Lakewood, CO: Vampire Junction. Centipede Press, 2019, pp. 7–14.

———. "Vampire." *Garemag* 1, 5 (October/November/December 1993): 8–15.

———. *Vampirella: A Collector's Checklist.* Santa Barbara, CA: Transylvanian Society of Dracula, 1998.

———. *The Vampire in the Comic Book.* New York: Count Dracula Fan Club, 1993.

Meyer, Stephenie. *Breaking Dawn.* Boston: Little, Brown Young Readers, 2008.

———. *Eclipse.* Boston: Little, Brown Young Readers, 2007.

———. *New Moon.* Boston: Little, Brown Young Readers, 2006.

———. *The Short Life of Bree Tanner.* Boston: Little, Brown Young Readers, 2006.

———. *Twilight.* Boston: Little, Brown Young Readers, 2005. Special Tenth Anniversary Edition. New York: Megan Tingley Books, 2015. Double bound with *Life and Death: Twilight Reimangined.*

———. *The Twilight Saga: The Official Illustrated Guide.* Boston, MA: Little, Brown Books for Young Readers, 2013.

Middleton, Brad. *Un-Dead TV: The Ultimate Guide to Vampire Television.* Pepperell, MA: By Light Unseen Media, 2012.

Middleton, J. A. *Another Grey Ghost Book.* London: E. Nash, 1914.

Miller, David. *The Peter Cushing Companion.* London: Reynolds & Hearn, 2000.

Miller, Elizabeth. *Bram Stoker's Dracula: A Documentary Volume.* Volume 304: *Dictionary of Literary Biography.* Detroit: Thomson Gale, 2005.

———. *Dracula.* New York: Parkstone Press, 2001.

———. *A Dracula Handbook.* Philadelphia: ExLibris, 2004.

———. *Dracula: Sense & Nonsense.* Southend-on-Sea, UK: Desert Island Books, 2000. Rev. ed., 2006.

———, ed. *Dracula: The Shade and the Shadow.* Westcliff-on-Sea: UK: Desert Island Books, 1998. 256 pp.

———. *Reflections on Dracula: Ten Essays.* White Rock, BC: Transylvania Press, 1997.

———, and Margaret L. Carter. "Has Dracula Lost His Fangs." In Elizabeth Miller. *Reflections on Dracula: Ten Essays.* White Rock, BC: Transylvania Press, 1997, pp. 25–46.

Miller, Mark A. *Christopher Lee and Peter Cushing and Horror Cinema: A Filmography of Their 22 Collaborations.* Jefferson, NC: McFarland and Company, 1995.

Miller-Zarneke, Tracey. *The Art and Making of Hotel Transylvania.* London: Titan Books, 2012.

Monaco, Richard, with Bill Burt. *The Dracula Syndrome.* New York: Avon, 1993.

Moore, James A., and Kevin Murphy. *House of Secrets.* Clarkston, GA: White Wolf Game Studio, 1995.

Mordeaux, A. *Bathory: Memoir of a Countess.* Charleston, SC: Book Surge, 2000.

Morrow, Felix. "The Quest for Montague Summers." In Montague Summers, *The Vampire: His Kith and Kin.* New Hyde Park, NY: University Books, 1960: xiii–xx.

Morrow, Robert W. *Sesame Street and the Reform of Children's Television.* Baltimore, MD: Johns Hopkins University Press, 2006.

Muir, John Kenneth. *Terror Television.* Jefferson, NC: McFarland, 2001.

Murgoci, Agnes. "The Vampire in Romania." *Folk-Lore* 27, 5 (1926): 320–349.

Murphy, Michael. *Fear Dat New Orleans: A Guide to the Voodoo, Vampires, Graveyards & Ghosts of the Crescent City.* Foreword by Anne Rice. New York: Countryman Press, 2015.

———. *The Celluloid Vampires: A History and Filmography, 1897–1779.* Ann Arbor, MI: Pierian Press, 1979.

Nakazono, Barry. *Bram Stoker's Dracula Role-Playing Game.* Pasadena, CA: Leading Edge Games, 1993.

Nelson, Hilda. *Charles Nodier.* New York: Twayne Publishers, 1972.

Nethercot, Arthur H. *The Road to Tryermaine: A Study of the History, Background, and Purposes of Coleridge's "Christabel."* Chicago: University of Chicago Press, 1939. Rept. New York: Russell & Russell, 1962.

Nevárez, Lisa, ed. *The Vampire Goes to College: Essays on Teaching with the Undead.* Jefferson, NC: McFarland Press, 2014.

Newman, Kim, ed. *BFI Companion to Horror.* UK: Cassell Academic, 1996.

———. *Nightmare Movies: A Critical History of the Horror Film since 1968.* London: Bloomsbury, 1988.

Nicoloff, Assen. *Bulgarian Folklore.* Cleveland, OH: The Author, 1975.

Niemi, Sandra. *Glamour Ghoul: The Passions and Pain of the Real Vampira, Maila Nurmi.* Feral House, 2020.

Nocturnum, Corvis. *Allure of the Vampire: Our Sexual Attraction to the Undead.* Dark Moon Press, 2009.

Nodier, Charles. *Le Vampire.* Edition critique by Ginette Picat-Guinoiseau. Geneva: Librairie Droz S. A., 1990.

Nutini, Hugo G., and John M. Roberts. *Bloodsucking Witchcraft: An Epistemological Study of Anthropomorphic Supernaturalism in Rural Tlaxcala.* Tucson: University of Arizona Press, 1993.

Odell, Colin, and Michelle LeBlanc. *Vampire Films.* Halpenden, Hertsfordshire, UK: Pocket Essentials, 2008.

Ohmart, Ben. *Tim Kelly: Master of Stage Fright: The Life and Times of America's Most Prolific Playwright.* Albany, NY: BearManor Media, 2009.

Oinas, Felix J. "Heretics as Vampires and Demons in Russia." *Slavic and East European Journal* 22, 4 (Winter 1978): 433–441.

Olcott, H. S. *The Vampire*. Adyar, Madras, India: Theosophical Publishing House, 1920.

Oliver, A. Richard. *Charles Nodier: Pilot of Romanticism*. Syracuse, NY: Syracuse University Press, 1964.

Owen, Dean, and Philip J. Riley *The Brides of Dracula*. Duncan, OK: BearManor Media, 2011.

"P. C. Cast & Kristin Cast Interview & Bibliography." Love Vampires. Posted at http://www.lovevampires.com/pccast.html. Accessed April 5, 2010.

Page, Carol. *Bloodlust: Conversations with Real Vampires*. New York: HarperCollins, 1991. Rept. New York: Dell, 1992.

Parker, Lara. *Dark Shadows: The Salem Branch*. New York: Tor Books, 2006.

Pateman, Matthew. *The Aesthetics of Culture in Buffy the Vampire Slayer*. Jeffersonville, NC: McFarland & Company, 2006.

Peel, John. *The Addams Family and Munsters Program Guide*. Virgin: London, 1996.

Pender, Patricia. *I'm Buffy and You're History: Buffy the Vampire Slayer and Contemporary Feminism*. London/New York: I. B. Tauris, 2016.

Penrose, Valentine. *Erzsebet Bathory, La Comtesse Sanglante*. Paris: Mercure du Paris, 1962. English translation as: *The Bloody Countess*. London: Calder & Boyars, 1970. Rept.: London: Creation Books, 1996. 157 pp.

Perkowski, Jan L., ed. *The Darkling: A Treatise on Slavic Vampirism*. Columbus, OH: Slavica Publishers, 1989.

———. *Vampire Lore: From Writings of Jan Louis Perkowski*. Bloomington, Indiana: Slavica 2006.

———. *Vampires of the Slavs*. Cambridge, MA: Slavica Publishers, 1976.

Petrovitch, Woislav M. *Hero Tales and Legends of the Serbians*. London: George G. Harrap, 1914. 393 pp. Rept. New York: Kraus Reprint Co., 1972.

Philostratus. *The Life of Apollonius of Tyana*. Translation by F. C. Conybeare. London: William Heineman, 1912.

Pierson, Jim. *Dark Shadows Resurrected*. Los Angeles: Pomegrante Press, 1992.

Pike, Christopher. *The Last Vampire*. New York: Archway/Pocket Book, 1994.

Pirie, David. *The Complete Vampire Cinema*. London: Gallery Books, 1984.

———. *The Vampire Cinema*. London: Hamlyn, 1977.

Pohle, Robert W., Jr., and Douglas C. Hart. *The Films of Christopher Lee*. Metuchen, NJ: Scarecrow Press, 1983.

——— and Rita Pohle Baldwin. *The Christopher Lee Film Encyclopedia*. Lanham, MD: Rowman & Littlefield Publishers, 2017.

Powell, Arthur E. *The Etheric Double and Allied Phenomena*. Wheaton, IL: Theosophical Publishing House, 1925, 1969.

———. *The Astral Body and Other Astral Phenomena*. Wheaton, IL: Theosophical Publishing House, 1927, 1973.

Pratt, Lynda. *Robert Southey and the Contexts of English Romanticism*. Farnham, Surrey, UK: Ashgate Publishing, 2006.

Prawer, S. S. *Nosferatu: Phantom der Nacht*. Ser.: BFI Film Classics. British Film Institute, 2004.

Praz, Mario. *The Romantic Agony*. London: Oxford University Press, 1970.

Puckett, Newbell Niles. *Folk Beliefs of the Southern Negro*. Chapel Hill, NC: University of North Carolina Press, 1926. Rept. New York: Negro Universities Press, 1968.

Ralston, William Ralston Shedden. *The Songs of the Russian People*. 1872. Rept. New York: Haskell House, 1970.

———. *Russian Folk-Tales*. London: Smith, Elder, 1873. Rept. New York: Arno Press, 1977.

Ramos, Maximo D. *Creatures of Philippine Lower Mythology*. Manila: University of the Philippines Press, 1971.

Ramsland, Katherine. *Piercing the Darkness*. New York: HarperPrism, 1998.

———. *Prism in the Night: A Biography of Anne Rice*. New York: Dutton, 1991.

———. *The Science of Vampires*. New York: Berkley Boulevard Books, 2002.

———. *The Vampire Companion: The Official Guide to Anne Rice's The Vampire Chronicles*. New York: Ballantine Books, 1993. Revised. 1995.

———. *The Witches Companion: The Official Guide to Anne Rice's "Lives of the Mayfair Witches."* New York: Ballantine Books, 1994.

Rattray, R. Sutherland. *Ashanti Proverbs*. Oxford: Claredon Press, 1916.

Ravensdale, Tom, and James Morgan. *The Psychology of Witchcraft*. New York: Arco Publishing Company, 1974.

Rector, Brett. *The Art of Hotel Transylvania 2*. Petaluma, CA: Cameron Books, 2015.

Reed, Donald. *The Vampire on the Screen*. Inglewood, CA: Wagon & Star Publishers, 1965.

Reid, Jane Davidson. *The Oxford Guide to Classical Mythology in the Arts, 1300–1990s*. New York: Oxford University Press, 1993.

Reines, Kathryn. *The Kiss*. New York: Avon Books, 1996.

Reino, Joseph. *Stephen King: The First Decade, Carrie to Pet Sematary*. Boston, MA: Twayne Publishers, 1988.

Resch, Kathleen, ed. *Decades*. Santa Clara, CA: Pentagram Press, 1982.

———, and Marcy Robin. *Beginnings: The Island of Ghosts*. Temple City, CA: The World of Dark Shadows, 1982.

———. *The Dark Shadows Concordance 1840*. Temple City, CA: Pentagram Press, 1987.

———. *The Dark Shadows Concordance 1970 Parallel Time*. Temple City, CA: The World of Dark Shadows, 1988.

———. *The Dark Shadows Concordance 1795*. Temple City, CA: The World of Dark Shadows, 1989.

———. *The Dark Shadows Concordance 1968*. 2 vols. Temple City, CA: The World of Dark Shadows, 1989.

———. *Dark Shadows in the Afternoon*. East Meadow, NY: Image Publishing, 1991.

Rhodes, Gary D. *Tod Browning's Dracula*. Sheffield, UK: Tomahawk Press, 2015.

———, and Richard Sheffield. *Bela Lugosi-Dreams and Nightmares*. Collectables Press, 2007.

Ricardo, Martin V. *Liquid Dreams of Vampires*. St. Paul, MN: Llewellyn Publications, 1996.

———. *The Lure of the Vampire*. Chicago: Adams Press, 1983.

———. *Mystical Consciousness*. Chicago: MVR Books, 1977.

———. *Vampires Unearthed*. New York: Garland Publishing, 1983.

Richardson, Beverly. "Vampire City: A Visit to New Orleans." *The Borgo Post* (Transylvanian Society of Dracula-Canadian Chapter) 3, 5 (June 1998): 2.

Riffaterre, Hermine. "Love-in-Death: Gautier's 'morte amoureuse.'" In *The Occult in Language and Literature*. New York: New York Literary Forum, 1980, pp. 65–74.

Rigby, Jonathan. *Christopher Lee: The Authorised Screen History*. Reynolds & Hearn, 2007.

Riley, Michael. *Conversations with Anne Rice*. New York: Ballantine Books, 1996.

Riley, Philip J., ed. *MagicImage Filmbooks Presents Dracula (The Original 1931 Shooting Script)*. Atlantic City, NJ: MagicImage Filmbooks, 1990.

Roberts, Bette B. *Anne Rice*. New York: Twayne Publishers, 1994.

Robin, Marcy. *From the Shadows... Marcy Robin*. Ed. by Kathleen Resch. Temple City, CA: Pentagram Press, 1986.

Rollin, Jean. *Virgins & Vampires*. Edited by Peter Blumenstock. Schwenningen, Germany: Crippled Dick Hot Wax, 1997. 153 pp.

Roman, Steven A. *From the Stars ... a Vampiress: An Unauthorized Guide to Vampirella's Classic Horror Adventures*. New York: Starwarp Concepts, 2020.

Ronay, Gabriel. *The Truth about Dracula*. London: Gallancz, 1972. Rept. New York: Stein and Day, 1972.

Rondina, Christopher. *The Vampire Hunter's Guide to New England: True Tales of the Yankee Undead*. North Attleborough, MA: Covered Bridge Press, 2000.

———. *Vampire Legends of Rhode Island*. North Attleborough, MA: Covered Bridge Press, 1997.

———. *Vampires of New England*. N.p.: On Cape Publications, 2008.

Roth, Phyllis. *Bram Stoker*. Boston: Twayne, 1982.

———. "Suddenly Sexual Women in Bram Stoker's Dracula." *Literature and Psychology* 27, 3 (1977): 113–121.

Rovin, Jeff. *The Encyclopedia of Super Villains*. New York: Facts on File, 1987.

Rowe, Beverly. "An Interview with Darren Shan." Posted at http://www.myshelf.com/babetoteen/01/shan.htm. Accessed October 15, 2009.

Rowen, Michelle, with Richelle Mead. *Vampire Academy: The Ultimate Guide*. New York: Razorbill, 2011.

Ruditis, Paul. *Buffy the Vampire Slayer: The Watcher's Guide*. Volume 3. New York: Simon Spotlight, 2004.

Rudkin, David. *Vampyr*. London: British Film Institute, 2008.

Russell, Sharon A. "The Construction of the Vampire in Yarbro's *Hotel Transylvania*." In James Craig Holte, ed. *The Fantastic Vampire: Studies in the Children of the Night: Selected Essays from the Eighteenth International Conference on the Fantastic in the Arts*. Vol. 19. Westport, CT: Greenwood Publishing Group, 2002, pp. 129–134.

———. "Introducing Count Saint-Germain: Chelsea Quinn Yarbro's Heroic Vampire." In Leonard Heldreth and Mary Pharr, eds. *The Blood Is the Life: Vampires in Literature*. Bowling Green, KY: Bowling Green State University Press, 1999, pp. 141–153.

Saberhagen, Fred, and James V. Hart. Bram Stoker's Dracula. New York: New American Library, 1992.

Schierup, Carl-Ulrik. "Why Are Vampires Still Alive?: Wallachian Immigrants in Scandinavia." *Ethnos* 51, 3–4 (1986): 173–198.

Schürmann, Thomas. *Der Nachzehrerglauben in Mitteleuropa*. Marburg, Germany: N. G. Elwert, 1990. The definitive book on vampires, ghouls, and ogres in cemtral Europe.

Scott, Kathryn Leigh, ed. *The Dark Shadows Companion: 25th Anniversary Collection*. Los Angeles: Pomegranate Press, 1990.

———. *My Scrapbook Memories of Dark Shadows*. Los Angeles: Pomegranate Press, 1986.

———, and Jim Pierson. *Dark Shadows Almanac: Thirtieth Anniversary Tribute*. Los Angeles: Pomegranate Press, 1995.

———, Jim Pierson, and David Selby. *The Dark Shadows Almanac: Millennium Edition*. Los Angeles: Pomegranate Press, 2000.

———, and Lara Parker. *35th Anniversary Dark Shadows Memories*. Los Angeles: Pomegranate Press, 2001.

Sebastiaan, Father [pseudonym of Sebastiaan Van Houten]. *Black Veil: The Vampire Lexicon*. Sabretooth, 2018.

———. *The Sabretooth Clan Book*. Sabretooth Press, n.d.

———. *Vampire Sanguinomicon: The Lexicon of the Living Vampire*. San Francisco: Red Wheel/ Weiser, 2010.

———. *Vampyre Virtues: The Red Veils*. Sabretooth Press, 2011.

Senf, Carol A., ed. *Critical Response to Bram Stoker*. Westport, CT: Greenwood Press, 1993.

———. *Daughter of Lilith: An Analysis of the Vampire Motif in Nineteenth-Century English Literature*. (Ph.D. dissertation). Buffalo, NY: State University of New York at Buffalo, 1978.

———. *Dracula: Between Tradition and Modernism*. New York: Twayne Publishers, 1998.

———. "Polidori's The Vampyre: Combining the Gothic with Realism." *North Dakota Quarterly* 56, 1 (Winter 1988): 197–208.

———. *Science and Social Science in Bram Stoker's Fiction*. Westport, CT: Greenwood Press, 2002.

———. *The Vampire in Nineteenth-Century English Literature*. Bowling Green, OH: Bowling Green State University Popular Press, 1988.

Senn, Harry A. *Were-Wolf and Vampire in Romania*. New York: Columbia University Pres, 1982.

Shapiro, Marc. *Stephenie Meyer: The Unauthorized Biography of the Creator of the Twilight Saga*. New York: St. Martin's Griffin, 2009.

Shepherd, Mike. *When Brave Men Shudder: The Scottish Origins of Dracula*. Wild Wolf Publishing, 2018.

Sherida, Barbara. "Interview with Amanda Ashley." Posted at http://paranormalromance.org/AmandaAshley.htm. Accessed April 10, 2010.

Somtow, S. P. "Reinventing Oneself as a Southeast Asian Writer." *The Nation* (October 16, 2006).

Shuter, Michael. "Sex among the Coffins; or, Lust at First Bite with William Margold." *Draculina* 17 (December 1993): 32–34.

Shuttle, Penelope, and Peter Redgrove. *The Wise Wound*. New York: Richard Marek, 1978.

Sienkiewicz, Bill. "Dracula." *The Official Handbook of the Marvel Universe* 2, 17 (August 1987): 10–13.

Silver, Alain, and James Ursini. *The Vampire Film: From Nosferatu to True Blood*. Milwaukee, WI: Hal Leonard Corporation, 2011.

Skal, David. *Dark Carnival: The Secret World of Tod Browning, Hollywood's Master of the Macabre*. New York: Doubleday and Company, 1995.

———. *Hollywood Gothic: The Tangled Web of Dracula from Novel to Stage to Screen*. New York: W. W. Norton & Company, 1990.

———. *The Monster Show: A Cultural History of Horror*. New York: W. W. Norton & Co., 1993.

———. *Romancing the Vampire: From Past to Present*. Atlanta, GA: Whitman Publishing, 2009.

———. *Something in the Blood: The Untold Story of Bram Stoker: The Man Who Wrote Dracula*. New York: Liveright Publishing, 2016.

———. *V Is for Vampire: The A–Z Guide to Everything Undead*. New York: Plume/Penguin, 1996.

———. *Vampires: Encounters with the Undead*. New York: Black Dog & Leventhal Publishers, 2006.

Skeat, Walter William. *Malay Magic: An Introduction to the Folklore and Popular Religion of the Malay Peninsula*. London: Macmillan and Co., 1900. Rept. New York: Barnes & Noble, 1966.

———, and Charles Otto Blagden. *Pagan Races of the Malay Peninsula*. 2 vols. New York: Macmillan and Company, 1906. Rept. New York: Barnes & Noble, 1966.

Slate, Joe H. *Psychic Vampires*. St. Paul, MN: Llewellyn Publications, 2002.

Smith, Curtis C., ed. *Twentieth-Century Science-Fiction Writers*. Chicago: St. James Press, 1986.

Smith, Jennifer. *Anne Rice: A Critical Companion*. Westport, CT: Greenwood Press, 1996.

Smith, Kalila Katherine. *Journey into Darkness ... Ghosts & Vampires of New Orleans.* New Orleans: DeSimeon, 2004.

Smith, Timothy d'Arch. *A Bibliography of the Works of Montague Summers.* New Hyde Park, NY: University Books, 1964.

Smith, W. Ramsey. *Myths and Legends of the Australian Aboriginals.* New York: Farrar & Rinehart, 2003.

Snead, John. *Buffy the Vampire Slayer Role-Playing Game: The Magic Box.* Loudenville, NY: Eden Studios, 2003.

South, James, ed. *Buffy the Vampire Slayer and Philosophy.* LaSalle, IL: Open Court, 2003.

Speck, W. A. *Robert Southey: Entire Man of Letters.* New Haven, CT: Yale University Press, 2006.

Spence, Lewis. *Myths and Legends of Babylonia and Assyria.* London: G. G. Harrap, 1928.

St. Clair, Stanislas Graham Bower, and Charles A. Brophy. *Twelve Years Study of the Eastern Question in Bulgaria.* London: Chapman & Hall, 1877.

Stafford, Nikki. *Bite Me! The Unofficial Guide to Buffy the Vampire Slayer.* Toronto: ECW Press, 2007.

Stamp, Cordelia. *Whitby: A Brief History.* Whitby, UK: Caedmon of Whitby, 2007.

Steiger, Brad. *Real Vampires, Night Stalkers, and Creatures from the Darkside.* Visible Ink Press, 2009.

Stephens, Christopher P. *A Checklist of Anne Rice.* Hastings-On-Hudson, NY: Ultramarine, 1991.

Stetson, George R. "The Animistic Vampire in New England." The *American Anthropologist* 9, 1 (January 1896): 1–13.

Stevenson, Gregory. *Televised Morality: The Case of Buffy the Vampire Slayer.* Lanham, MD: Hamilton Books, 2004.

Stevenson, John Allen. "A Vampire in the Mirror: The Sexuality of Dracula." *PMLA: Publications of the Modern Language Association of America* 103, 2 (March 1988): 139–149.

Stockel, Shirley, and Victoria Weidner. *A Guide to Collecting "Dark Shadows" Memorabilia.* Florissant, MO: Collinwood Chronicle, 1992.

Stoker, Bram. *Bram Stoker's Notes for Dracula: A Facsimile Edition.* Edited by Robert Eighteen-Bisang and Elizabeth Miller. Jefferson, NC: McFarland & Co., 2008. Rev. and exp. ed. as: *Drafts of Dracula.* Victoria, BC: Tellwell Talent, 2019.

———. *Dracula.* Westminster, London: A. Constable & Co., 1897.

———. *Dracula: or The Undead.* Edited by Sylvia Starshine. Nottingham, UK: Pumpkin Books, 1997.

———. *Dracula's Guest and Other Weird Stories.* London: George Routledge & Sons, 1914. Rpt. as: *Dracula's Guest.* New York: Zebra Books, 1978.

———. *The Forgotten Writings of Bram Stoker.* Ed. by John Edgar Browning Basingstoke, UK: Palgrave Macmillan, 2012.

Stoker, Dacre, and Elizabeth Miller, eds. *The Lost Journal of Bram Stoker: The Dublin Years.* London: The Robson Press/Biteback Publishing, 2013.

Straub, Peter. "Meeting Stevie." In *Fear Itself: The Horror Fiction of Stephen King.* San Francisco: Underwood-Miller, 1982.

Stuart, Bonnye E. *Haunted New Orleans: Southern Spirits, Garden District Ghosts, and Vampire Venues.* Guildford, CT: Globe Pequot Press, 2012.

Stuart, Roxana. *Stage Blood: Vampires of the Nineteenth-Century Stage.* Bowling Green, OH: Bowling Green University Popular Press, 1994. 377 pp.

Stuller, Jennifer Kate, ed. *Fan Phenomena: Buffy the Vampire Slayer.* Chicago: Intellect, 2013.

Summers, Montague. *The Vampire: His Kith and Kin.* London: Routledge, Kegan Paul, Trench, Trübner, & Co., 1928. Rpt. as: *The Vampire, His Kith and Kin: A Critical Edition.* Ed. by John Browning. Berkeley, CA: Apocryphile Press, 2011.

———. *The Vampire in Europe.* London: Routledge, Kegan Paul, Trench, Trübner, & Co., 1929. Rpt as.: *The Vampire in Europe: A Critical Edition.* Ed. by John Browning. Berkeley, CA: Apocryphile Press, 2014.

Sutherland, Gail Hinich. *The Disguises of the Demon: The Development of the Yaksa in Hinduism and Buddhism.* Albany, NY: State University of New York Press, 1991.

Svehla, Gary J., and Susan Svehla, eds. *Bela Lugosi.* Baltimore, MD: Midnight Marquee Press, 1995.

———, eds. *Memories of Hammer.* Baltimore: Luminary Press, 2002.

Switzer, Richard. "Lord Ruthwen and the Vampires." *The French Review* 19, 2 (December 1955): 107–12.

Talbot, P. Amaury. *In the Shadow of the Bush.* London: William Heinemann, 1912.

Tarantino, Quentin. *From Dusk to Dawn.* New York: Miramax Books/Hyperion, 1995.

Terrace, Vincent. *Encyclopedia of Television.* 3 vols. New York: New York Zoetrope, 1985.

Thomas, Nicolas. *International Dictionary of Films and Filmmakers.* Volume II: *Directors.* Chicago: St. James Press, 1991.

Thompson, E. Campbell. *The Devils and Evil Spirits of Babylonia.* 2 vols. London: Luzac, 1903, 1904.

———. *Semitic Magic: Its Origin and Development.* London: Luzac, 1908.

Thompson, Jeff. *The Dark Shadows Comic Books.* Los Angeles: Joseph Collins Publications, 1984. Revised ed. 1988.

———. *The Effective Use of Actual Persons and Events in the Historical Novels of Dan Ross.* (Master's thesis). Nashville: Tennessee State University, 1991.

———. *The Television Horrors of Dan Curtis: Dark Shadows, The Night Stalker, and Other Productions, 1966–2006.* Jeffersonville, NC: McFarland & Company, 2009.

———, and Connie Jonas, eds. *The Collinsport Players Companion.* 2 vols. Portland, OR: HarmonyRoad Press, 1993–94.

Thorne, Tony. *Countess Dracula: The Life and Times of Elisabeth Bathory, the Blood Countess.* London: Bloomsbury, 1997. 274 pp.

Thurston, Edgar. *Omens and Superstitions of Southern India.* New York: McBride, Nast & Company, 1912.

Topping, Keith. *The Complete Slayer: An Unofficial and Unauthorised Guide to Every Episode of Buffy the Vampire Slayer.* London: Virgin, 2004.

———. *Hollywood Vampire: A Revised and Updated Unofficial and Unauthorized Guide to Angel.* London: Virgin, 2001.

Treptow, Kurt W., ed. *Dracula: Essays on the Life and Times of Vlad Tepes.* New York: Columbia University Press, 1991. 336 pp.

Trigg, E. B. *Gypsy Demons & Divinities: The Magical and Supernatural Practices of the Gypsies.* London: Sheldon Press, 1973.

Trow, M. J. *Vlad the Impaler: In Search of Dracula.* Thrupp, Shroud, Gloucestershire, UK: Sutton Publishing, 2003. 280 pp.

Tuczay, Christa, and Julia Bertschik, ed. *Poetische Wiedergänger. Deutschsprachige Vampirismus-Diskurse vom Mittelalter bis zur Gegenwart.* Tübingen, Germany: Francke, 2005. The most important collection of studies on vampires in Germany.

Turan, Kenneth. "The Missing 'Dracula.'" *Los Angeles Times* (October 31, 1992).

Twitchell, James B. *The Living Dead: A Study of the Vampire in Romantic Literature.* Durham, NC: Duke University Press, 1981.

Ursini, James, and Alain Silver. *The Vampire Film: From Nosferatu to True Blood.* Milwaukee, WI: Hal Leonard Corporation, 2011.

"Vampires in Hungary." *International Vampire* 1, 4 (Summer 1991).

Vampiri: Miti, legende, letteratura, cinema, fumetti, multimedialità. Milan, Italy: Casa Editrice Nord, 1998.

Van Etten, Gerard. *The Vampire Cat: A Play in One Act from the Japanese Legend of the Nebeshima Cat.* Chicago: Dramatic Publishing Company, 1918.

Vania, Count Trans L. *The Vampire Joke Books.* New York: Pinnacle Books, 1995.

Vaz, Mark Cotta. *Twilight: The Complete Illustrated Movie Companion.* Boston/New York: Little, Brown, 2008.

Vellutini, John L. "The African Origins of Vampirism," *Journal of Vampirology* 5, 2 (1988): 2–16.

———. "The Myth of the New England Vampire." *Journal of Vampirology* 7, 1 (1990): 2–21.

———. "The Vampire in Africa," *Journal of Vampirology* 5, 3 (1988): 2–14.

———. "The Vampire in China." *Journal of Vampirology* 6, 1 (1989): 1–10.

Vespertilio, Lono Fructus. *The Psychic Vampires Guide: To Subtle Body Language and Psionics.* Fort Wayne, IN: Dark Moon Press, 2011.

Volk, Stephen. *Gothic.* London: Grafton, 1987. Novelization of Ken Russell film.

Volta, Ornella. *The Vampire.* New York: Award Books, 1962.

Voltaire. *Philosophical Dictionary.* 1764. Rept. New York: Alfred A. Knopf, 1924.

Von Haxthausen, August. *Transcaucasia.* London: Chapman & Hall, 1854.

Vukanovic, T. P. "The Vampire." In *Vampires of the Slavs.* Jan L. Perkowski, ed. Cambridge, MA: Slavica Publishers, 1976, pp. 201–234.

Walker, Benjamin. *The Hindu World: An Encyclopedia Survey of Hinduism.* New York: Frederick A. Praeger, 1986.

Waller, Gregory A. *The Living and the Undead: From Stoker's Dracula to Romero's Dawn of the Dead.* Urbana, IL: University of Illinois Press, 1986.

———. *The Living and the Undead: Slaying Vampires, Exterminating Zombies.* Urbana, IL: University of Illinois Press, 2010.

Waltje, Jörg. *Blood Obsession: Vampires, Serial Murder, and the Popular Imagination.* New York: Peter Lang, 2005.

Ward, J. R. *The Black Dagger Brotherhood: An Insider's Guide.* New York: New American Library, 2008.

Wax, Rosalie H. *Magic, Fate and History: The Changing Ethos of the Vikings.* Lawrence, KS: Coronado Press, 1969.

Weaver, Tom. *John Carradine: The Films.* Jeffersonville, NC: McFarland & Company, 2008.

Weinstock, Jeffrey. *The Vampire Film: Undead Cinema.* New York: Wallflower Press, 2012.

Weiss, Andrea. *Vampires and Violets: Lesbianism in the Cinema.* London: Pandora Press, 1991.

Weller, Lea Cassandra. *The Evolution of the Vampire in Film and Television: From Beast to Beauty.* Derby, UK: privately printed, 2013.

White, Luise. *Speaking with Vampires: Rumor and History in Colonial Africa.* Berkeley, CA: University of California Press, 2000.

"White Wolf Games." *Game Shop News* 16 (April 28, 1993): 4–6.

Whitehead, Gwendolyn. "The Vampire in Nineteenth-Century Literature." *The University of Mississippi Studies in English* 8 (1990): 243–248.

Whitelaw, Nancy. *Bram Stoker: Author of Dracula.* Greensboro, NC: Morgan Reynolds, 1998.

Wiater, Stanley, Christopher Golden, and Hank Wagner. *The Complete Stephen King Universe: A Guide to the Worlds of Stephen King.* New York: St. Martin's Griffin, 2006.

Wiater, Stanley, Matthew Bradley, and Paul Stuve. *The Twilight and Other Zones: The Dark Worlds of Richard Matheson.* New York: Citadel Press, 2009.

Wieger, Leo. *A History of the Religious Beliefs and Philosophical Opinions in China.* 1927. Rept. New York: Paragon Book Reprint Corp., 1969.

Wilcox, Rhonda V. *Why Buffy Matters: The Art of Buffy the Vampire Slayer.* I. B. Tauris & Company, 2005.

———, and David Lavery, eds. *Fighting the Forces: What's at Stake in Buffy the Vampire Slayer.* Lanham, MD: Rowman & Littlefield Publishers, 2002.

Wilgus, Neal. "Saberhagen's New Dracula: The Vampire as Hero." In *Discovering Modern Horror Fiction.* Darrel Schweitzer, ed. San Bernardino, CA: Borgo Press, 1987: 92–8.

Williamson, Millie. *The Lure of the Vampire: Gender, Fiction and Fandom from Bram Stoker to Buffy the Vampire Slayer.* London: Wallflower Press, 2005.

Willoughby-Meade, G. *Chinese Ghouls and Goblins.* New York: Frederick A. Stokes Co., 1926.

Wilson, Katherine M. "The History of the Word 'Vampire.'" *Journal of the History of Ideas* 44, 4 (October–December 1985): 577–83.

Winstedt, Richard. *The Malay Magician Being Shaman, Saiva, and Sufi.* London: Routledge and Kegan Paul, 1961.

Winter, Douglas E. *Stephen King: The Art of Darkness.* New York: New American Library, 1984.

Wolf, Leonard, ed. *Blood Thirst: 100 Years of Vampire Fiction.* New York: Oxford University Press, 1997. 380 pp.

———. *A Dream of Dracula: In Search of the Living Dead.* Boston: Little Brown, 1972. Rept. New York: Popular Library, 1977.

Wolfman, Marv. "Yes, Marv Wolfman Is His Real Name!" *Dracula Lives!* 4 (January 1994): 49.

Woo, Diane. *Werewolf, Ghost, and Vampire Jokes You Can Sink Your Teeth Into.* New York: Tor Classics, 2009.

Workman, Christopher, and Tony Howarth. *Tome of Terror: Horror Films of the Silent Era.* Midnight Marquee Press, 2016.

The World Almanac Book of Buffs, Masters, Mavens and Uncommon Experts. New York: World Almanac Publications, 1980.

Wright, Dudley. *Vampires and Vampirism.* 1914, Rev. ed. 1924. Rept. *The Book of Vampires.* New York: Causeway Books, 1973.

Wynne, Catherine, ed. *Bram Stoker and the Gothic.* Houndmills, Basingstoke, Hampshire, UK/New York, NY: Palgrave Macmillan, 2016.

———. *Bram Stoker, Dracula and the Victorian Gothic Stage.* Houndmills, Basingstoke, Hampshire, UK/New York, NY: Palgrave Macmillan, 2013.

Yarbro, Chelsea Quinn. *Hotel Transylvania.* New York: St. Martin's Press, 1978.

Yeffeth, Glenn, ed. *Five Seasons of Angel: Science Fiction and Fantasy Writers Discuss Their Favorite Vampire.* Dallas, TX: Benbella Books, 2004.

———. *Seven Seasons of Buffy: Science Fiction and Fantasy Writers Discuss Their Favorite Television Show.* Dallas, TX: Benbella Books, 2003.

Youngson, Jeanne, ed. *Private Files of a Vampirologist: Case Histories & Letters.* Chicago: Adams Press, 1997.

———. *The World's Best Vampire Jokes.* New York: Dracula Press, 1992.

———, and Shelley Leigh-Hunt, eds. *Do Vampires Exist? A Special Report from Dracula World Enterprises.* New York: Dracula World Enterprises, 1993.

Zimmerman, Bonnie. "Daughters of Darkness: The Lesbian Vampire on Film." In Barry Keith Grant, ed., *Planks of Reason.* Metuchen, NJ: Scarecrow Press, 1984: 153–63.

INDEX

Note: (ill.) indicates photos and illustrations

D

E

L

O

Q

Z